**Foreign Relations of the
United States, 1961–1963**

Volume XIII

West Europe
and Canada

Editors   Charles S. Sampson
                  James E. Miller

General Editor Glenn W. LaFantasie

United States Government Printing Office
Washington
1994

DEPARTMENT OF STATE PUBLICATION 10087

Office of the Historian

Bureau of Public Affairs

For sale by the U.S. Government Printing Office
Superintendent of Documents, Mail Stop: SSOP, Washington, DC 20402-9328
ISBN 0-16-041810-0

Preface

The *Foreign Relations of the United States* series presents the official documentary historical record of major foreign policy decisions and significant diplomatic activity of the United States Government. The series documents the facts and events that contributed to the formulation of policies and includes evidence of supporting and alternative views to the policy positions ultimately adopted.

The Historian of the Department of State is charged with the responsibility for the preparation of the *Foreign Relations* series. The staff of the Office of the Historian, Bureau of Public Affairs, plans, researches, compiles, and edits the volumes in the series. This documentary editing proceeds in full accord with the generally accepted standards of historical scholarship. Official regulations codifying specific standards for the selection and editing of documents for the series were first promulgated by Secretary of State Frank B. Kellogg on March 26, 1925. These regulations, with minor modifications, guided the series through 1991.

A new statutory charter for the preparation of the series was established by Public Law 102–138, the Foreign Relations Authorization Act, Fiscal Years 1992 and 1993, which was signed by President George Bush on October 28, 1991. Section 198 of P.L. 102–138 added a new Title IV to the Department of State's Basic Authorities Act of 1956 (22 USC 4351, *et seq.*).

The statute requires that the *Foreign Relations* series be a thorough, accurate, and reliable record of major United States foreign policy decisions and significant United States diplomatic activity. The volumes of the series should include all records needed to provide comprehensive documentation of major foreign policy decisions and actions of the United States Government, including facts that contributed to the formulation of policies and records that provided supporting and alternative views to the policy positions ultimately adopted.

The statute confirms the editing principles established by Secretary Kellogg: the *Foreign Relations* series is guided by the principles of historical objectivity and accuracy; records should not be altered or deletions made without indicating in the published text that a deletion has been made; the published record should omit no facts that were of major importance in reaching a decision; and nothing should be omitted for the purposes of concealing a defect in policy. The statute also requires that the *Foreign Relations* series be published not more than 30 years after the events recorded.

The editors of this volume, which was compiled in 1989 and 1990, are convinced that it meets all regulatory, statutory, and scholarly standards of selection and editing. Although this volume records policies and events of more than 30 years ago, the statute of October 28, 1991, allows the Department until 1996 to reach the 30-year line in the publication of the series.

Structure and Scope of the Foreign Relations Series

This volume is part of a triennial subseries of volumes of the *Foreign Relations* series. This subseries documents the most important issues in the foreign policy of the 3 years (1961–1963) of the administration of John F. Kennedy. In planning and preparing the 1961–1963 triennium, the editors chose to present the official record of U.S. foreign affairs with respect to Europe, the Soviet Union, and Canada in six print volumes and one microfiche supplement.

Volume V, Soviet Union, includes documentation on U.S.-Soviet bilateral relations. Volume VI, Kennedy–Khrushchev Correspondence, includes the comprehensive record of correspondence between President Kennedy and Soviet Chairman Khrushchev. Volume XIII, Western Europe and Canada (presented here), documents U.S. policy regarding European economic and political integration, U.S. participation in NATO, and U.S. bilateral relations with Canada, France, Italy, Portugal, Spain, and the United Kingdom. Volume XIV, Berlin Crisis, 1961–1962, and Volume XV, Berlin Crisis, 1962–1963, document U.S. involvement in the continuing Four-Power negotiations over divided Germany and the status of the Western-occupied sectors of Berlin. A combined microfiche supplement to volumes XIII, XIV, and XV will be published separately. Volume XVI, Eastern Europe, presents the basic record of U.S. relations with Austria, Finland, Poland, Yugoslavia, Greece, and Turkey, as well as documentation on general U.S. policy toward the Eastern European region and U.S. efforts to resolve the Cyprus problem.

The statute of October 28, 1991, requires that the published record in the *Foreign Relations* series include all records needed to provide comprehensive documentation on all the major foreign policy decisions and actions of the U.S. Government. It further requires that government agencies, departments, and other entities of the U.S. Government cooperate with the Department of State Historian by providing full and complete access to records pertinent to foreign policy decisions and actions and by providing copies of selected records. The editors judge that this volume was prepared in complete accordance with the standards and mandates of this statute.

Sources for the Foreign Relations Series

In planning and preparing this volume and the other five documenting U.S. foreign policy regarding Europe during the Kennedy administration, the editors concluded that the records of the Department of State would constitute the central core of the published record. In preparing this volume, Department of State historians have enjoyed complete and unconditional access to all records and papers of the Department of State: the central files of the Department; the special decentralized (lot) files of the policymaking levels; the files of the Department of State's Executive Secretariat, which comprehend the official papers created by or submitted to the Secretary of State; the files of all overseas Foreign Service posts and U.S. special missions; and the official correspondence with foreign governments and with other Federal agencies. Any failure to include a complete Department of State record in the *Foreign Relations* series cannot be attributed to constraints or limitations placed upon the Department historians in their access to Department records, information security regulations and practices notwithstanding.

The editors of this volume fully researched the papers of President Kennedy and other White House foreign policy records. These Presidential papers have become a major part of the official record published in the *Foreign Relations* series. Presidential papers maintained and preserved at the Presidential libraries include some of the most significant foreign affairs-related documentation from other Federal agencies including the National Security Council, the Central Intelligence Agency, the Department of Defense, and the Joint Chiefs of Staff. All of this documentation has been made available for use in the *Foreign Relations* series thanks to the consent of these agencies and the cooperation and support of the National Archives and Records Administration. Particular thanks are due to officials at the John F. Kennedy Presidential Library for their assistance in preparing this volume.

These Presidential files were supplemented by White House documents in Department of State files. The Department of State files were particularly valuable for documenting the implementation of the White House policy presented in this volume.

The editors also had complete access to the papers of General Maxwell Taylor at the National Defense University, which proved to be a valuable source for the formulation of policy under President Kennedy. In addition, the editors reviewed the body of declassified JCS files at the National Archives and Records Administration. Copies of individual classified JCS materials were obtained from the Joint Staff on a request basis.

Completion of the declassification of this volume and the final steps of its preparation for publication coincided with the development since early 1991 by the Central Intelligence Agency, in cooperation with the Department of State, of access by Department historians to high-level intelligence documents from among those records still in the custody of that Agency. The Department of State historians have been provided selective access to particular special files of the Agency. The Department has used this access, as arranged by the CIA's History Staff, in the compilation of this volume.

The List of Sources, pages XIII–XV, identifies the particular files and collections used in the preparation of this volume.

Principles of Selection for Foreign Relations, 1961–1963, Volume XIII

In selecting documents for inclusion in volume XIII, the editors recognized the predominant role of the Department of State in formulating policy with respect to Western Europe and Canada. This volume focuses on the many meetings of the Secretary of State with his advisers and with representatives of the White House and other agencies, as well as the written advice to the Secretary of State from these advisers. The editors have included internal U.S. Government policy recommendations and decision papers relating to Western Europe and Canada. They have also included the advice and recommendations on foreign policy issues from top-level military commanders and advisers with regard to NATO.

In focusing on the major lines of policy development toward Western Europe and Canada, the editors have also presented a record of the U.S. reaction and response to the major political events within France, Italy, Portugal, Spain, the United Kingdom, and Canada insofar as they figured directly in ongoing high-level political negotiations.

Editorial Methodology

The documents are presented chronologically according to Washington time or, in the case of conferences, in the order of individual meetings. Incoming telegrams from U.S. Missions are placed according to time of receipt in the Department of State or other receiving agency, rather than the time of transmission; memoranda of conversation are placed according to the time and date of the conversation, rather than the date the memorandum was drafted.

Editorial treatment of the documents published in the *Foreign Relations* series follows Office style guidelines, supplemented by guidance from the General Editor and the chief technical editor. The source text is reproduced as exactly as possible, including marginalia or other notations, which are described in the footnotes. Texts are transcribed and printed according to accepted conventions for the publication of historical documents in the limitations of modern typography. A heading has been supplied by the editors for each document included in the volume. Spelling, capitalization, and punctuation are retained as found in the source text, except that obvious typographical errors are silently corrected. Other mistakes and omissions in the source text are corrected by bracketed insertions: a correction is set in italic type; an addition in roman type. Words or phrases underlined in the source text are printed in italics. Abbreviations and contractions are preserved as found in the source text, and a list of abbreviations is included in the front matter of each volume.

Bracketed insertions are also used to indicate omitted text that deals with an unrelated subject (in roman type) or that remains classified after declassification review (in italic type). The amount of material not declassified has been noted by indicating the number of lines or pages of source text that were omitted. Entire documents withheld for declassification purposes have been accounted for and are listed by headings, source notes, and number of pages not declassified in their chronological place. The amount of material omitted from this print volume and from the microfiche supplement because it was unrelated to the subject of the volume, however, has not been delineated. All ellipses and brackets that appear in the source text are so identified by footnotes.

The unnumbered first footnote to each document indicates the document's source, original classification, distribution, and drafting information. The source footnote also provides the background of important documents and policies and indicates if the President or his major policy advisers read the document. Every effort has been made to determine if a document has been previously published, and this information has been included in the source footnote.

Editorial notes and additional annotation summarize pertinent material not printed in the volume, indicate the location of additional documentary sources, provide references to important related documents printed in other volumes, describe key events, and provide summaries of and citations to public statements that supplement and elucidate the printed documents. Information derived from memoirs and other first-hand accounts have been used when appropriate to supplement or explicate the official record.

Advisory Committee on Historical Diplomatic Documentation

The Advisory Committee on Historical Diplomatic Documentation, established under Title IV of the Department of State's Basic Authorities Act, amended on October 28, 1991, reviews records, advises, and makes recommendations concerning the *Foreign Relations* series. The Advisory Committee monitors the overall compilation and editorial process of the series and assists with any access and/or clearance problems that arise. Time constraints prevent the Advisory Committee from reviewing all volumes in the series.

This volume has not been reviewed by the Advisory Committee.

Declassification Review

The declassification review of this volume, which was completed in 1993, resulted in the decision to withhold 2.2 percent of the documentation originally selected. The remaining documentation provides a full account of the major foreign policy issues confronting, and the policies undertaken by, the Kennedy administration with respect to Western Europe and Canada.

The Division of Historical Documents Review of the Office of Freedom of Information, Privacy, and Classification Review, Bureau of Administration, Department of State, conducted the declassification review of the documents published in this volume. The review was conducted in accordance with the standards set forth in Executive Order 12356 on National Security Information and applicable laws.

Under Executive Order 12356, information that concerns one or more of the following categories, and the disclosure of which reasonably could be expected to cause damage to the national security, requires classification:

    1) military plans, weapons, or operations;
    2) the vulnerabilities or capabilities of systems, installations, projects, or plans relating to the national security;
    3) foreign government information;
    4) intelligence activities (including special activities), or intelligence sources or methods;
    5) foreign relations or foreign activities of the United States;
    6) scientific, technological, or economic matters relating to national security;
    7) U.S. Government programs for safeguarding nuclear materials or facilities;
    8) cryptology; or
    9) a confidential source.

The principle guiding declassification review is to release all information, subject only to the current requirements of national security and law. Declassification decisions entailed concurrence of the appropriate geographic and functional bureaus in the Department of State, other concerned agencies of the U.S. Government, and the appropriate foreign governments regarding specific documents of those governments.

Acknowledgements

The editors wish to acknowledge the assistance of officials at the John F. Kennedy Library, in particular Suzanne Forbes, who assisted in the collection of documents for this volume.

Under the supervision of former Editor in Chief John P. Glennon, Charles S. Sampson collected, selected, and edited all the material presented in this volume except for that on Italy which was done by James E. Miller. General Editor Glenn W. LaFantasie supervised the final steps in the editorial and publication process. Vicki E. Futscher and Rita M. Baker did the copy and technical editing and Barbara-Ann Bacon of the

Publishing Services Division (Natalie H. Lee, Chief) oversaw the production of the volume. Thomas J. Hoffman prepared the index.

William Z. Slany
The Historian
Bureau of Public Affairs

June 1994

Contents

List of Sources

Department of State

Decimal and Subject-Numeric Indexed Central Files: One of the principal sources of documentation for this volume was the indexed central files of the Department of State. Many of the documents were selected from the following files:

375: NATO
375.800: West European regional questions
396.1: International conferences
611.41: U.S.-U.K. relations
611.42: U.S.-Canadian relations
611.51: U.S.-French relations
611.53: U.S.-Portuguese relations
611.65: U.S.-Italian relations

In February 1963 the Department of State changed to a subject-numeric system. Under this system, the most significant files for West Europe and Canada are:

DEF (MLF): U.S. policy toward the Multilateral Force
DEF NATO: U.S. policy toward NATO
ECIN EEC: U.S. policy toward the Common Market
NATO: NATO meetings and organizational questions
POL 7 US/Merchant: trips of Ambassador Merchant
POL W EUR: Political developments in Western Europe

Lot Files: Documents from the centralized files have been supplemented by materials from decentralized office files, the lot files of the Department of State. A list of the major lot files used or consulted for this volume follows:

Conference Files: Lot 65 D 366

Collection of documentation on official visitis by heads of government and foreign ministers to the United States and on major international conferences by the Secretary of State and Under Secretary of State for 1961 maintained by the Executive Secretariat.

Conference Files: Lot 66 D 110

Collection of documentation on official visitis by heads of government and foreign ministers to the United States and on major international conferences by the Secretary of State and Under Secretary of State for 1961–1964 maintained by the Executive Secretariat. This lot includes records of the President's trips to Europe in 1961 and 1963.

G/PM Files: Lot 69 D 258

Papers and documents of the Office of Political-Military Affairs for 1961–1963.

Italian Desk Files: Lot 68 D 436

Papers and documents of the Italian Desk of the Bureau of European Affairs for 1961–1963.

PPS Files: Lot 67 D 548

Subject files, country files, chronological files, documents, drafts, and related correspondence of the Policy Planning Staff for 1957–1961.

PPS Files: Lot 69 D 121

Subject files, country files, chronological files, documents, drafts, and related correspondence of the Policy Planning Staff for 1962.

Presidential Correspondence: Lot 66 D 204

Exchanges of correspondence between the President and the Secretary of State with the heads of government and foreign ministers of the United Kingdom, France, Germany, the Soviet Union, and certain other countries for 1953–1964, maintained by the Executive Secretariat.

Presidential Correspondence: Lot 66 D 476

Correspondence of the Presidents with various heads of state for 1961–1966.

Presidential Correspondence: Lot 77 D 163

Correspondence of the Presidents with the Chairman of the Soviet Union and other high officials of the two countries for 1961–1969.

Presidential Memoranda of Conversations: Lot 66 D 149

Memoranda of the President's conversations for 1956–1964.

Rusk Files: Lot 72 D 192

Files of Secretary of State Dean Rusk including texts of speeches and public statements, miscellaneous correspondence, White House correspondence, chronological files, and memoranda of telephone conversation for 1961–1969.

Secretary's Memoranda of Conversation: Lot 65 D 330

Memoranda of the Secretary's and Under Secretary of State's conversations for 1961–1964.

S/S–NSC Files: Lot 70 D 265

Master set of papers pertaining to National Security Council meetings including policy papers, position papers, and administrative documents, but not the minutes of the meetings themselves, for 1961–1966, maintained by the Executive Secretariat.

S/S–NSC Files: Lot 72 D 316

Master files of National Security Action Memoranda (NSAMs) for 1961–1968.

S/S–S Files: Lot 66 D 219

Miscellaneous records of the Executive Secretariat of the Department of State for 1961–1963.

Washington National Records Center, Suitland, Maryland

Record Group 330, Records of the Office of the Secretary of Defense

McNamara Files: FRC 71 A 3470

Files of Secretary of Defense Robert McNamara for 1961–1968.

National Defense University, Fort McNair, Washington, D.C.

Lemnitzer Papers

Papers of General Lyman L. Lemnitzer, Chief of Staff of the Army, 1959–1960; and Chairman of the Joint Chiefs of Staff, 1960–1962.

Taylor Papers

> Papers of General Maxwell D. Taylor, Military Adviser to the President, 1961–1962; and Chairman of the Joint Chiefs of Staff, 1962–1964.

John F. Kennedy Library, Boston, Massachusetts

National Security Files

President's Office Files

Lyndon B. Johnson Library, Austin, Texas

National Security File

Rusk Appointment Books

Vice Presidential Security File

Yale University, New Haven, Connecticut

Bowles papers

List of Abbreviations

ABC, atomic, biological, chemical
ACE, Allied Command Europe
AEC, Atomic Energy Commission
AF, Bureau of African Affairs, Department of State
AFL–CIO, American Federation of Labor–Congress of Industrial Organizations
AFMED, Air Force, Mediterranean
AID, Agency for International Development
APAG, Atlantic Policy Advisory Group
ARA, Bureau of Latin American Affairs, Department of State
APC, armored personnel carriers
ASAF, Asian/African
ASCS, Agricultural Stabilization and Conservation Service
ASW, anti-submarine warfare
B, Office of the Under Secretary of State for Economic Affairs
BAOR, British Army in the Rhine
Benelux, Belgium, Netherlands, Luxembourg
Bercon/Marcon, Berlin contingency; Maritime contigency
BNA, Office of British Commonwealth and Northern European Affairs, Department of State
BOP, balance of payments
Busec, series indicator for telegrams to the U.S. Mission to European Regional Organizations
CAP, common agricultural policy
CD, Christian Democrat, Christian Democratic Party
CENTO, Central Treaty Organization
ChiCom, Chinese Communist
ChiNat, Chinese Nationalist
CINCHAN, Commander in Chief, Channel
CINCLANT, Commander in Chief, Atlantic
CINCMED, Commander in Chief, Mediterranean
CLC, Canadian Labour Confederation
CMU, Canadian Maritime Union
COCOM, Coordinating Committee of the Consultative Group, based in

Paris, consisiting of nations seeking to control the export of strategic goods to Communist countries
CONUS, Continental United States
cxt, common external tariff
DAG, Development Assistance Group
DC, Democrazia Cristiana (Christian Democratic Party)
DCI, Director for Central Intelligence
DDG, guided missile destroyer
DefSec, Defense Secretary
Deptel, Department of State telegram
Deptcirtel, Department of State circular telegram
DOD, Department of Defense
E/OT(F), Office of External Trade and Finance, Bureau of Economic Affairs, Department of State
Ecbus, series indicator for telegrams from the U.S. Mission to European Regional Organizations
ECSC, European Coal and Steel Community
EEC, European Economic Community
EFTA, European Free Trade Area
EMA, European Monetary Agreement
Embtel, Embassy telegram
ENI, Ente Nazionale degli Idrocarburi (Italian National Hydrocarbon Trust)
EPC, European Political Community
EUR/RA, Office of European Regional Affairs, Bureau of European Affairs, Department of State
EUR/WE, Office of Western European Affairs, Bureau of European Affairs, Department of State
Euratom, European Atomic Energy Community
EX-IM, Export-Import Bank
FBI, Federal Bureau of Investigation
FedRep, Federal Republic
Fed Govt, Federal Government
FLN, Front de Libération Nationale (National Liberation Front)
FonMin, Foreign Minister
FonOff, Foreign Office
FRG, Federal Republic of Germany
fyi, for your information

G, Office of the Deputy Under Secretary of State for Political Affairs

G/PM, Deputy Assistant Secretary of State for Political-Military Affairs

GA, United Nations General Assembly

GATT, General Agreement on Tariffs and Trade

GER, Office of German Affairs, Bureau of European Affairs, Department of State

GFR, German Federal Republic

GOB, Government of Belgium

GOC, Government of Canada

GOF, Government of France

GOI, Government of India

GOP, Government of Portugal

GOS, Government of Spain

HMG, Her Majesty's Government

IANF, interallied nuclear forces

IBRD, International Bank for Reconstruction and Development

ICBM, intercontinental ballistic missile

ICC, International Control Commission

IDA, International Development Association

ILO, International Labor Organization

IMF, International Monetary Fund

INR, Bureau of Intelligence and Research, Department of State

IO, Bureau of International Organization Affairs, Department of State

IRBM, intermediate-range ballistic missile

IRI, Instituto per la Ricostruzione Industriale

IS, International Staff

JCAE, Joint Committee on Atomic Energy

JCS, Joint Chiefs of Staff

JSSC, Joint Strategic Survey Committee

LANTCOM, Atlantic Command

LDC, less developed country

LS, Division of Language Services, Department of State

M, Office of the Under Secretary of State for Political Affairs

MAAG, Military Assistance Advisory Group

MAP, military assistance program

MATS/TAC, Military Air Transport Service/Tactical Air Command

MC, military committee, memorandum of conversation

memcon, memorandum of conversation

MFN, most favored nation

MLF, multilateral force

MOD, Minister of Defense

MPLA, Movimento Popular de Libertacao de Angola (Angola Popular Liberation Movement)

MRBM, medium-range ballistic missile

MRP, Mouvement Republicain Populaire (Popular Republican Movement)

NAC, North Atlantic Council

NADGE, NATO air defense ground environment

NATO, North Atlantic Treaty Organization

NDP, New Democratic Party

NEA, Bureau of Near Eastern and South Asian Affairs, Department of State

NFP, NATO Force Planning

niact, night action, communications indicator requiring attention by the recipient at any hour of the day or night

NNF, NATO nuclear forces

noforn, no foreign dissemination

NORAD, North Atlantic Air Defense Command

NSC, National Security Council

OAS, Organization of American States; L'Organisation de l'Armee Secrete

OECO, Organization for Economic Cooperation and Development

OEEC, Organization for European Economic Cooperation

OSD, Office of the Secretary of Defense

OTF, Office of International Trade and Finance, Bureau of Economic Affairs, Department of State

P, Bureau of Public Affairs, Department of State

PCI, Partito Communista Italiano (Italian Communist Party)

perm rep, permanent representative

PJDB, Permanent Joint Defense Board

PM, Prime Minister

POLAD, political advisor

Polto, series indicator for telegrams from the U.S. Mission to the North Atlantic Treaty Organization

PRI, Partito Republicano Italiano (Italian Republican Party)

PriMin, Prime Minister
PSDI, Partito Socialista Democratico Italiano (Italian Democratic Socialist Party)
PSI, Partito Socialista Democratico Italiano (Italian Socialist Party)
QR, quantitative restrictions
R and D, research and development
RA, Office of Regional Affairs, Bureau of European Affairs, Department of State
RCAF, Royal Canadian Air Force
RPE, Office of Atlantic Political-Economic Affairs, Bureau of European Affairs, Department of State
S, Office of the Secretary of State
S/AE, Special Assistant to the Secretary of State for Atomic Energy and Outer Space
S/MF, Special Assistant to the Secretary of State for NATO Multilateral Force Negotiations
S/P, Policy Planning Staff, Policy Planning Council, Department of State
S/S, Executive Secretariat, Department of State
S/S–RO, Reports and Operations Staff of the Executive Secretariat, Department of State
SAC, Strategic Air Command
SACEUR, Supreme Allied Commander, Europe
SACLANT, Supreme Allied Commander, Atlantic
SAM, surface to air missile
SC, United Nations Security Council
SEATO, Southeast Asia Treaty Organization
Secto, series indicator for telegrams from the Secretary of State or his delegation at international conferences
SETAF, Southern European Task Force
SET/MC, Secretary's European trip/memorandum of conversation
SHAPE, Supreme Headquarters, Allied Powers, Europe

SSB(N), SSN(B), ballistic missile submarine, nuclear powered
STR, Office of the Special Representative for Trade Negotiations
STRAAC, Strategic Air Command
SYG, Secretary-General
TAC, U.S. Air Force Tactical Air Command
TAGG, series indicator for telegrams from the U.S. GATT delegation at Geneva
TEA, Trade Expansion Act
Topol, series indicator for telegrams to the U.S. Mission to the North Atlantic Treaty Organization
Tosec, series indicator for telegrams to the Secretary of State or his delegation at international conferences
U, Office of the Under Secretary of State
UAM, Union Africaine et Malagache (African and Malagasy Union)
UKG, United Kingdom Government
UNGA, United Nations General Assembly
USA, United States Army
USAF, United States Air Force
USEC, United States Mission to the European Communities
USG, United States Government
USIA, United States Information Agency
USIS, United States Information Service
USN, United States Navy
USREP, United States Representative
USRO, United States Mission to the North Atlantic Treaty Organization and European Regional Organizations
WE, Office of Western European Affairs, Bureau of European Affairs, Department of State
WEU, Western European Union
WHO, World Health Organization
WNG, Western New Guinea

List of Persons

Acheson, Dean, former Secretary of State and Chairman of the President's Advisory Committee on NATO

Adenauer, Konrad, Chancellor of the Federal Republic of Germany until October 1963

Alphand, Hervé, French Ambassador to the United States

Armstrong, Willis C., Minister in Canada until August 1966; thereafter Director of the Office of British Commonwealth and Northern European Affairs, Bureau of European Affairs, Department of State

Beaudry, Robert M., International Relations Officer, Office of Western European Affairs, Bureau of European Affairs, Department of State

Beigel, Edgar J., International Relations Officer, Office of Western European Affairs, Bureau of European Affairs, Department of State

Blue, William L., Deputy Director of the Office of Western European Affairs, Bureau of European Affairs, Department of State, until July 1961; Director until January 1962

Blumenthal, W. Michael, Deputy Special Representative for Trade Negotiations from December 1962

Bohlen, Charles E., Ambassador to France from September 1962

Bowie, Robert, Director of the Center for International Studies

Bowles, Chester B., Under Secretary of State until December 1961

Brasseur, Maurice P., Belgian Minister of Trade

Brentano, Heinrich von, Foreign Minister of the Federal Republic of Germany until October 1961; thereafter Chairman of the CDU faction in the Bundestag

Brosio, Manlio, Italian Ambassador to the United States until May 1961

Bruce, David K.E., Ambassaor to the United Kingdom from March 1961

Bundy, McGeorge, Special Assistant to the President for National Security Affairs

Burdett, William C., Director of the Office of British Commonwealth and Northern European Affairs, Bureau of European Affairs, Department of State, until September 1962; Deputy Assistant Secretary of State for European Affairs thereafter

Butterworth, W. Walton, Representative to the European Communities until October 1962; Ambassador to Canada thereafter

Caccia, Sir Harold, British Ambassador to the United States until October 1961

Carlson, Delmar R., Officer in Charge of Canadian Affairs, Office of British Commonwealth and Northern European Affairs, Bureau of European Affairs, Department of State, until September 1963

Castiella y Maiz, Fernando Maria, Spanish Foreign Minister

Chayes, Abram, Legal Advisor, Department of State, from February 1961

Cleveland, Harlan, Assistant Secretary of State for International Organization Affairs, from February 1961

Cleveland, Stanley M., Director of the Office of Atlantic Political-Economic Affairs, Bureau of European Affairs, Department of State, from August 1962

Couve de Murville, Maurice, French Foreign Minister

Debré, Michel, Prime Minister of France until April 1962

de Gaulle, Charles, President of France

de Staercke, Andre, Belgian Permanent Representative to NATO

Diefenbaker, John G., Prime Minister of Canada until April 1963

Dillon, C. Douglas, Secretary of the Treasury

Dowling, Walter C., Ambassador to Germany until April 1963

Elbrick, C. Burke, Ambassador to Portugal until August 1963
Erhard, Ludwig, Vice Chancellor and Minister for Economic Affairs of the Federal Republic of Germany until October 1963; Chancellor thereafter

Fanfani, Amintore, Prime Minister of Italy until April 1963
Feldman, Myer, Deputy Special Counsel to the President
Fenoaltea, Sergio, Italian Ambassador to the United States from May 1961
Fernandes, Luis E., Portuguese Ambassador to the United States until June 1961
Fessenden, Russell, Director of the Office of European Regional Affairs, Bureau of European Affairs, Department of State, until August 1962; Minister at Brussels thereafter
Finletter, Thomas K., Permanent Representative to the North Atlantic Council from March 1961
Franco y Bahamonde, General Francisco, Chief of the Spanish State
Freeman, Orville L., Secretary of Agriculture
Furnas, Howard E., Executive Director of the MLF Negotiating Team

Gaitskell, Hugh T.M., Leader of the British Labour Party
Galbraith, J. Kenneth, Ambassador to India, April 1961–July 1963
Gammon, Samuel, Officer in Charge of Italian Affairs from July 1962
Garrigues, Antonio, Spanish Ambassador to the United States from June 1962
Gavin, James M., Ambassador to France, March 1961–September 1962
Gorbach, Alfons, Chancellor of Austria
Green, Howard C., Canadian Secretary of State for External Affairs until April 1963
Grewe, Wilhelm, German Ambassador to the United States until September 1962
Gronchi, Giovanni, President of the Italian Republic until May 1962

Hallstein, Walter, President of the Commission of the European Economic Community
Hare, Raymond A., Ambassador to Turkey from March 1961
Harriman, W. Averell, Ambassador at Large, February–November 1961; Assistant Secretary of State for Far Eastern Affairs, November 1961–March 1963; Under Secretary of State for Political Affairs from April 1963
Heath, Edward, British Lord Privy Seal
Heeney, Arnold D.P., Canadian Ambassador to the United States until April 1962
Heller, Walter W., Chairman of the President's Council of Economic Advisors
Herter, Christian A., Special Representative for Trade Negotiations from December 1962
Hillenbrand, Martin J., Director of the Office of German Affairs, Bureau of European Affairs, Department of State
Hodges, Luther H., Secretary of Commerce
Home, Alexander Frederick Douglas, British Secretary of State for Foreign Affairs until October 1963; Prime Minister thereafter
Horsey, Outerbridge, Deputy Chief of Mission to Italy until November 1961

Imhof, Johannes V., International Relations Officer, Office of Western European Affairs, Bureau of European Affairs, Department of State

Johnson, Lyndon B., President of the United States from November 22, 1963
Johnson, U. Alexis, Deputy Under Secretary of State for Political Affairs from May 1961

Kaysen, Karl, member of the National Security Council Staff
Kennedy, John F., President of the United States, January 21, 1961–November 22, 1963
King, James E., senior analyst, Institute for Defense Analysis, 1961
Kitchen, Jeffrey C., Deputy Assistant Secretary of State for Political-Military Affairs from May 1961 and from December 1962, Chairman of the Steering Group on Implementation of the Nassau Decisions

Knappstein, K. Heinrich, German Ambassador to the United States from October 1962

Knight, William E., II, Office of Western European Affairs, Bureau of European Affairs, Department of State

Kohler, Foy D., Assistant Secretary of State for European Affairs until August 1962; Ambassador in the Soviet Union thereafter

Komer, Robert, member of the National Security Council Staff

Kranich, Robert H., International Relations Officer, Office of European Regional Affairs, Bureau of European Affairs, Department of State

Kreisky, Bruno, Austrian Foreign Minister

Lee, Rear Admiral John M., member of the MLF Negotiating Team, 1963

Leone, Giovanni, Prime Minister of Italy, July–December 1963

Lilienfeld, Georg von, German Minister to the United States

Luns, Joseph, Netherlands Foreign Minister

MacArthur, Douglas, II, Ambassador to Belgium from February 1961

Macmillan, Harold, Prime Minister of the United Kingdom and First Lord of the Treasury until October 1963

Magill, Robert N., Deputy Director of the Office of European Regional Affairs, Bureau of European Affairs, Department of State, until February 1962

Mansholt, Sicco L., Vice President of the Commission of the European Economic Community

Marjolin, Robert E., Vice President of the Commission of the European Economic Community

Martin, Paul, Liberal Party member of Parliament and from April 1963 Canadian Minister of External Affairs

Mattei, Enrico, Chairman of the Italian State Oil Corporation (ENI), until 1962

Matthews, H. Freeman, Jr., Second Secretary in the Embassy to Spain from September 1963

McBride, Robert H., Director of the Office of Western European Affairs, Bureau of European Affairs, Department of State, until June 1961; Deputy Chief of Mission to Spain thereafter

McCone, John A., Director of Central Intelligence from November 1961

McGhee, George C., Under Secretary of State for Political Affairs from December 1961; Ambassador to Germany from May 1963

McNamara, Robert S., Secretary of Defense

McNaughton, John, General Counsel in the Department of Defense

Meloy, Francis E., Jr., Director of the Office of Western European Affairs, Bureau of European Affairs, Department of State, from June 1962

Merchant, Livingston T., Ambassador to Canada, March1961–May 1962; Head of the MLF Negotiating Team, 1963

Messmer, Pierre A., French Minister of Defense

More Otera, José Antonio, Secretary General of the Organization of American States

Moro, Aldo, Secretary of Italian Christian Democratic Party, 1961–1963; Prime Minister of Italy from December 1963

Nenni, Pietro, Secretary of Italian Socialist Party, 1961–1963; Vice President of Council of Ministers from December 1963

Nitze, Paul, Assistant Secretary of Defense for International Security Affairs

Nogueira, Alberto Franco, Portuguese Foreign Minister

Nolting, Frederick E., Jr., Deputy Chief of the Mission to the European Communities

Norstad, Lieutenant General Lauris, Supreme Allied Commander, Europe, until December 1962

Ormsby Gore, Sir William David, British Ambassador to the United States from October 1961

Owen, Henry D., Deputy Chairman of the Policy Planning Council from November 1962

Pearson, Lester B., Leader of the Canadian Liberal Party and from April 1963, Prime Minister of Canada

Pereira, Pedro Theotonio, Portuguese Ambassador to the United States from August 1961

Piccioni, Attilio, Italian Foreign Minister May 1962–December 1963

Pisani, Edgard, French Minister of Agriculture

Pitblado, David D., Economic Minister in the British Embassy in the United States

Platzer, Wilfried, Austrian Ambassador to the United States

Pompidou, Georges J.R., Prime Minister of France from May 1962

Popper, David H., Director of the Office of Atlantic Political-Military Affairs, Bureau of European Affairs, Department of State, from September 1962

Ramsbotham, Peter E., Counselor in the British Foreign Office

Reinhardt, G. Frederick, Ambassador to Italy from May 1961

Rey, Jean, European Economic Community Commissioner for External Relations

Ricketts, Admiral Claude, Vice Chief of Naval Operations

Ritchie, Charles, Canadian Ambassador to the United States from May 1962

Roijen, J.H. van, Netherlands Ambassador to the United States

Rostow, Walt W., Deputy Special Assistant to the President for National Security Affairs until December 1961; thereafter Counselor of the Department of State and Chairman of the Policy Planning Council

Rusk, Dean, Secretary of State

Salazar, Antonio de Oliveira, President of the Council of Ministers of Portugal

Saragat, Giuseppe, Secretary of Italian Social Democratic Party until December 1963; Italian Foreign Minister from December 1963

Schaetzel, J. Robert, Special Assistant to the Under Secretary of State for Economic Affairs until September 1962; Deputy Assistant Secretary of State for Atlantic Affairs thereafter

Scheyven, Louis, Belgian Ambassador to the United States

Schlesinger, Arthur M., Jr., Special Assistant to the President

Schroeder, Gerhard, Foreign Minister of the Federal Republic of Germany from November 1961

Seaborg, Glenn T., Chairman of the Atomic Energy Commission

Segni, Antonio, Italian Foreign Minister until May 1962; President of the Italian Republic thereafter

Smith, Bromley, Acting Executive Secretary of the National Security Council until August 1961; Executive Secretary thereafter

Smith, Gerard C., Consultant to the Policy Planning Council, Department of State and, in 1963, member of the MLF Negotiating Team

Spaak, Paul-Henri, Secretary General of NATO until February 1961; Belgian Foreign Minister thereafter

Spiers, Ronald I., Director of the Office of Atlantic Political-Military Affairs, Bureau of European Affairs, Department of State, from November 1962

Stikker, Dirk U., Secretary General of NATO from April 1961

Stoessel, Walter J. Jr., Political Adviser to the Supreme Allied Commander, Europe, April 1961–July 1963

Strauss, Franz Joseph, Minister of Defense of the Federal Republic of Germany until October 1961

Sweeney, Joseph, Officer in Charge of United Kingdom-Ireland Affairs, Office of British Commonwealth and Northern European Affairs, Bureau of European Affairs, Department of State, July 1961–August 1962

Taylor, General Maxwell D., President's Military Representative, July 1961–July 1962; Chairman of the Joint Chiefs of Staff thereafter

Thompson, Llewelyn E., Ambassador to the Soviet Union until July 1962; Ambassador at Large thereafter

Thorneycroft, George Edward Peter, British Minister of Defense from 1962

Trezise, Philip H., Acting Deputy Assistant Secretary of State for Economic Affairs from October 1961

Tuthill, John W., Representative to the European Communities from October 1962

Tyler, William R., Deputy Assistant Secretary of State for European Affairs until August 1962; Assistant Secretary of State for European Affairs thereafter

Van Hollen, Christopher, International Relations Officer, Office of Atlantic Political-Military Affairs, Bureau of European Affairs, Department of State

Vine, Richard D., International Relations Officer, Office of European Regional Affairs, Bureau of European Affairs, Department of State, until July 1963

Von Hassel, Kai-Uwe, Minister of Defense of the Federal Republic of Germany from June 1962

Weiss, Leonard, Director of the Office of International Trade, Bureau of Economic Affairs, Department of State, September 1961–February 1963

Weiss, Seymour, Special Assistant to the Secretary of State from November 1961

Williams, G. Mennen, Assistant Secretary of State for African Affairs

Wormser, Olivier B., Director General of Economic Affairs, French Foreign Ministry

Economic and Political Integration

1. Memorandum of Conversation

Washington, February 6, 1961.

SUBJECT

European Community of "Six"

PARTICIPANTS

Manlio Brosio, Italian Ambassador
Mr. Carlo Perrone-Capano, Italian Minister
The Under Secretary
WE—Mr. Knight

At the conclusion of a conversation on another subject Ambassador Brosio raised without notice a question which he said was of deep concern to him. He said that in the course of a recent conversation with a prominent (though unnamed) official of the new Administration the official had expressed the opinion that if in the course of their forthcoming meeting in Paris the Heads of Government of the Six were to work out a common position on matters pertaining to political and economic cooperation for presentation in NATO councils, this might jeopardize NATO itself. In view of the gravity of this question for Italy the Ambassador wished to comment on it promptly and to ask the Under Secretary's views.

The Ambassador said that in his opinion the question of objective was all important. If the aim of the consultation were to move the Six towards a separate Third Force-type position for Europe (which he said Italy would never accept) concern on the part of the US Government would be completely understandable. Actually, however, the objective of the Six was the strengthening of NATO. This being the case, even if the Six were to speak in NATO with one voice the US should feel no concern. He emphasized that if Italy should ever be forced to choose between the Atlantic Alliance and the Community of Six, the Alliance would come first.

Source: Department of State, Secretary's Memoranda of Conversation: Lot 65 D 330. Confidential. Drafted by Knight. A summary of this conversation was transmitted in telegram 3221 to Paris, February 6. (Ibid., Central Files, 375.800/2–661)

1

The Under Secretary commented that to its credit the American people, as well as the Government, had approved the Common Market concept from the first in view of its long-term political implications, even though it had been apparent that it might in the short term be to the United States' economic disadvantage. He went on to say that we must realize the enormous strength of the countries of North America and Western Europe, with their advanced state of development and their high population (double that of the Soviet Bloc, excluding China). He said that in his opinion the West had nothing to fear if it could succeed in rapidly developing its resources and its effective instruments for common action. Many in the U.S. would accept forms of multilateral cooperation with Western Europe going far beyond those now existing. This should be our goal. The new relationships should go beyond purely military bonds to encompass political and economic matters, since the military relationship was based purely on fear which could prove to be a transitory phenomenon. The Under Secretary said that the Korean War had been a particular tragedy because it had diverted American thinking away from consideration of new forms of political and economic integration of the free world, and imposed an absolute priority on purely military relationships.

Ambassador Brosio agreed with the substance of the Under Secretary's remarks and concluded by saying that Italy viewed the Community of Six as a step towards a larger grouping, and not towards division of the NATO grouping already in existence.

---

2.   Circular Telegram From the Department of State to Certain Missions in Europe

Washington, March 24, 1961, 4:01 p.m.

1459. Ref: The Hague's G–364 and 1205.[1] Following is Dept's assessment of results of Six Heads of Govt meeting and related problems

---

Source: Department of State, Central Files, 375.800/3–2461. Official Use Only. Sent to 15 missions in Europe. Drafted by Vine on March 21; cleared with Fessenden, McBride, and Hillenbrand; and approved by Kohler.

[1] Dated February 28 and March 23 respectively, they reported on conversations with Netherlands officials concerning EEC political consultations. (Ibid., 756.00/2–2861 and 375.800/3–2361) In the concluding paragraph of telegram 1205 the Embassy suggested that the Netherlands would agree to political consultations only after extracting the maximum concessions in areas of its concern.

which addresses may draw upon for background information and guidance.

Analyses:

1) Meeting clearly mended fences between Adenauer and de Gaulle and restored Franco-German solidarity on broad aspects European problems. This appears be based largely de Gaulle–Adenauer understanding on maintenance of Community institutions, on importance of NATO, and necessity for equal status among the Six.

2) By same token, it was degree and suddenness of Franco-German agreement on major problems which disturbed Dutch, who now appear as much concerned with protecting position of small powers against Franco-German domination as they were previously suspicious of de Gaulle's motives in advancing proposals for further cooperation among Six.

3) Establishment of intergovernmental study group to submit concrete proposals to next meeting represents achievement of limited objective of meeting as Dept understood it. It seems good device for assuring that proposals which have significance and are divorced from thorny question of de Gaulle's motives can be arrived at.

4) While no agreement reached on principle of periodic meeting of Six Heads of Govt date of next meeting (May 19) appears de facto establish this.

5) Statements in communiqué particularly reference to "laying foundations of a union which could develop progressively" and entire penultimate para are indicative of extent by which proposals have been modified since first stated by de Gaulle. Assurance re existing Communities and deferral of Defense Committee proposal seem further evidence of this. Conciliatory attitude of French appears in large measure due their desire achieve some measure of success their European policy.

6) Dutch opposition position in Paris has created a position of strength during deliberations of intergovernmental committee which can be helpful if constructively utilized and not used for obstructionist ends.

7) Underlying motive for Dutch position, as described para 2 above, appears to be desire to slow down further moves among Six which would make more difficult accommodation with British and establishment of wider trading area, for Dutch have always considered Six as a start toward a wider integration of European Nations and ultimately an Atlantic Community. Negative UK reaction in WEU Council meeting to use of that forum for political consultation may weaken Dutch position; Heath statement in WEU also evidence that UK not yet prepared at this time go as far as necessary to make Dutch holding action tenable.

Conclusions:

1) Dept in accord with Hallstein assessment given to European Parliamentary Assembly (Strasbourg's 110)[2] which sees Feb 10 communiqué as important expression of political will of member govts which completes economic objectives of Communities.

2) Dept supports in principle any further cooperation among Six in political or other fields which will strengthen and bolster NATO. Overriding importance which five other countries have in unity of NATO alliance, and assurances which French appear to have given them in this regard, lead Dept to conclusion that positive recommendations of intergovernmental study group by May 19 meeting could be important forward step in increasing institutional unity of Six. We would certainly wish examine carefully these recommendations before committing ourselves, but fail to see how French can use political consultation for "Domination of Six," when other five have every means to insist upon appropriate safeguards in study group.

3) In brief, Dept believes that evolution of de Gaulle's proposals for political consultation has been healthy and that other five countries, through their vigorous reaction to possible less desirable features, have been able to divert essentials into constructive channels. This development is one which should be judged intrinsically and independently of de Gaulle's possible motives as to role France might play, since other five can clearly be relied upon in their own interest to achieve relative balance among the Six.

Bowles

---

[2] Dated March 11. (Ibid., 375.800/3–1161)

---

3.   **Circular Telegram From the Department of State to Certain Missions in Europe**

Washington, April 12, 1961, 9:52 p.m.

1566. 1. Following are developments on Six-Seven problems arising out of Macmillan conversations with President[1] and Ball conversa-

---

Source: Department of State, Central Files, 375.800/4–1261. Secret. Sent to 14 missions in Europe. Drafted by Vine on April 11; cleared by Ball, Kohler, Fessenden, and Burdett; and approved by Schaetzel.

[1] Macmillan visited the British West Indies, Canada, and the United States March 24–April 12, staying in Washington April 4–9; see Document 381.

tion with Heath in London. Full text of memcon of Ball–Heath talks sent as separate instruction.[2]

2. British presented "classic outline of problems which confront UK and EFTA countries by virtue development of EEC and need for an accommodation. In response we indicated if UK worked out association with Six involving merely a commercial arrangement, this would continue present serious problems for us, since it would create additional commercial discrimination while at same time weakening Six. When pressed by British to indicate what solution would not present US with similar difficulty we stated if UK were to join Six and wholeheartedly accept political and institutional obligations of EEC, we could give such an arrangement our support, provided no substantial derogations from Rome Treaty principles.

3. In discussion this point, we did not address ourselves to problems of other EFTA countries. British recognized problem posed by neutrality of some members of Seven, and Macmillan at one point stated he had general view that UK and NATO members of Seven might join Six but that some special arrangement might be made for the neutral members of the Seven.

4. Embs in EEC countries and USEC may draw upon above in discreet and confidential conversations with host govts. Such conversations should be in low key with comments along following lines:

a) US position on Six-Seven accommodation has not changed.
b) We have however for first time stated to British in affirmative fashion that if they should make decision to take part in the dynamic process of European integration and fully accept political and institutional obligations of Rome Treaties, we would support them.
c) This is a decision which UK alone must make. We are not urging UK to take this step for it is momentous decision involving profound commitment to Europe. Our view is that if British make this commitment, it deserves our support. FYI Only, in talks here, Macmillan indicated that Britain is now seriously prepared consider this step. End FYI.
d) Our position on Six-Seven commercial arrangement or accommodation remains as stated Dept's CA–7908.[3] We count heavily, now as before, on vigilance of Six countries in avoiding half-way measures or solutions which are primarily commercial in nature.
e) Our position should not be construed as measure of support for any expressed British position to date nor should it be viewed as pressure on Six govts for an accommodation, either with the UK or the EFTA. It is applicable only to a possible future British position which

---

[2] Not found, but on April 11 Ball sent President Kennedy a memorandum summarizing the talk with Heath on March 30. He also stressed that the United States should not directly urge the British to join the Common Market, but assure them that assumption of the obligations of the Treaty of Rome would be welcomed by the United States. (Department of State, Central Files, 611.41/4–161)

[3] Not found.

must satisfy the Six and us that it involves a UK commitment to a movement toward European integration which involves not only static treaty obligations but a long-term evolutionary political process.

5. EFTA capitals except London should for time being remain silent on substance of Macmillan talks since we expect that UK will wish brief fully EFTA partners. If unavoidable, you may state that you understand Macmillan was informed our traditional position on preferential bridge or commercial accommodation (draw here upon CA–7908) and was further informed that UK could not count upon our support for a British association with Six unless it were to adhere wholeheartedly to political and institutional objectives of Rome Treaties.

Press and public affairs guidance follows.

Rusk

---

4.   **Memorandum of Conversation**

Washington, April 13, 1961, 10:30 a.m.

SUBJECT

European Integration and the Six and Seven Problem

PARTICIPANTS

(See attached list)

The President said that the United States appreciated German efforts to unite Western Europe. We had informed Prime Minister Macmillan that we hoped the United Kingdom would play a leading role in the economic and political integration of Europe and that the British would join the European Economic Community. However, that was a decision which the Six and England would have to make for themselves. The United States did not want to see other countries taken into EEC at the expense of the Rome Treaties. It is best for the Atlantic Community if the United Kingdom joined the EEC on an unconditional basis.

Source: Department of State, Conference Files: Lot 65 D 366, CF 1835. Confidential. Drafted by Freshman, and approved by S on April 25, U on April 24, and the White House on May 11. The meeting was held at the White House. Chancellor Adenauer visited Washington, April 12–13.

The President added that the more closely integrated Western Europe becomes, the more likelihood that economic problems will be created for the United States. In the interest of a stronger Atlantic Community, however, we are prepared to meet these problems. We would nevertheless be reluctant to face these economic problems and adjustments both as regards the US and Latin America, unless definite political benefit results therefrom. Therefore the US is hopeful that before the year's end, the UK and possibly other EFTA countries will have joined the EEC with full acceptance of the Rome Treaties.

The Chancellor stated that he had recently discussed this matter with Hallstein, who saw no insurmountable problem to the entry of the UK into the Common Market. Hallstein felt that the question is whether the UK is ready to negotiate seriously on joining; up to the present time, however, he saw no indication that they were. The Chancellor said he will consult once again with Hallstein. The Common Market countries are ready for the UK today, and not tomorrow.

The President responded that it was his impression from his talks with the British that they seriously desired to join the EEC, but the British have the impression that not all of the Six welcome their entry. This would be in our common interest, and we should use our influence—the Federal Republic within the EEC and the United States on the outside—to induce the UK to associate with the EEC.

Foreign Minister von Brentano said that it was most interesting to have the President's views on this matter. The Federal Republic will do its utmost to strengthen the EEC and not to let it be weakened. Germany would welcome the UK as a member of the EEC and the Foreign Minister was happy that the US had now modified its position. Up to now this had been a difficult situation. He went on to state that the former Administration had opposed expansion of the Six on grounds that it would hurt the United States. This position of the US had been used to good advantage by countries opposed to expansion of the EEC and to European integration. Foreign Minister von Brentano stated that he was glad that the present Administration supports the German view. The Federal Republic could see that problems did exist for the US economy in this European movement. When the Chancellor and Prime Minister Macmillan had last met,[1] the Chancellor had suggested bilateral talks in which the EEC countries could make known the conditions which the British would have to meet in order to join. This proved to be a useful suggestion, and subsequent discussions were held between Paris and London and between Rome and London, which indicated that, as the President had so frankly stated, not everyone is ready to let the UK join the EEC. The French in particular are doubtful. The Federal Republic

---

[1] Macmillan visited Bonn, August 10–11, 1960.

will do everything possible to assist in a solution to this problem, if the UK really wishes to come in, and would appreciate any US assistance with London and Paris.

Foreign Minister von Brentano pointed out that the existence of EFTA had not made matters easier for the EEC to find a solution, since the purposes are so different. The EEC has political character and motivation. EFTA has neutral member-countries who may have difficulty in associating themselves with the Common Market. The United Kingdom would like to join the EEC on a basis which excluded the agricultural sector and enabled them to maintain their Commonwealth association. The Six cannot accept this arrangement, but the Foreign Minister said that Germany will do its utmost to find a way for the United Kingdom to join.

Minister von Brentano added the view that once the UK comes in, the Common Market could be broadened by the inclusion of Norway, Portugal, Denmark and other NATO countries—possibly not on a full membership basis—although he felt that something could be worked out. A rapprochement could be brought about in conformity with GATT. He was happy at news of the UK interest.

Under Secretary Ball emphasized that there had been no change in the United States position between the former Administration and the present Administration concerning the expansion of the EEC. Actually, the problem had not previously been formulated as the British have now done, but rather in the thought that a loose association between the EEC and EFTA might weaken the political institutions of the Six and result in economic discrimination against the United States. However, if Macmillan had asked point blank whether we favored their joining the Six within the Rome Treaties, the former Administration would have said yes. If this new question did present itself as an actuality, Mr. Ball believed that the US would find a formula for cooperation.

Mr. Ball had the following impressions on this subject, as a result of his discussions recently with UK officials, including the Prime Minister:

a) Many elements in the British Government wanted major steps taken in this direction, although this will present difficulties within the UK;

b) EFTA is not a serious bar to a solution, and it should be possible for NATO members to join; special arrangements for Portugal and the neutral countries would be needed;

c) The institutional consequences of the Rome Treaties do not constitute a problem and the UK could live with them. Nor are the non-commercial obligations an obstacle;

d) The UK saw two problems—Commonwealth preferences (which could be worked out) and Agriculture, which is the most serious hindrance to association with the Six. The French do not agree to special arrangements accommodating the British agricultural sector.

Mr. Ball concluded by stressing that the Six will be weakened if a common agricultural policy is not developed. This is a most serious problem for the Federal Republic which should enlist the highest possible support to induce the UK to find a solution. It may be necessary for the German Government to take the longest step within the Six in overcoming present domestic difficulties impending a common agricultural policy.

Foreign Minister von Brentano noted that Italy and Holland have the same difficulties on agriculture.

[Here follows a list of participants.]

---

5.   Memorandum of Conversation

Washington, May 2, 1961.

SUBJECT

U.S. Position on European Economic and Political Integration

PARTICIPANTS

Mr. George Ball, Under Secretary for Economic Affairs
Sir Harold Caccia, British Ambassador
Mr. David Pitblado, Economic Minister, British Embassy
Mr. G. Lewis Jones, Minister-Counsellor Designate, American Embassy, London, England
Mr. J. Robert Schaetzel, Special Assistant to the Under Secretary for Economic Affairs
Mr. Richard D. Vine, Bureau of European Affairs, RA

The British Ambassador came in at Mr. Ball's request to discuss the U.S. position on European economic and political integration.

Mr. Ball began by referring to the position that had emerged out of his conversations with Heath and the President's conversation with Macmillan. He noted that it was very important indeed that the UK and all other countries involved have a clear and exact understanding of our policies in this regard. He gave Sir Harold an aide-mémoire which

---

Source: Department of State, Central Files, 375.800/5–261. Confidential. Drafted by Vine and approved in B on May 11.

spelled out ours in some detail (see Circular 1722).[1] He stated that he wished particularly to emphasize three points:

1) That this was something we were not urging.[2]

Before Mr. Ball could go any further Caccia interjected to inquire what that something was. Prime Minister Macmillan understood it to mean the organization of the whole industrial world, but while waiting for this longer-term result Europe should organize itself more closely as an interim step. The question is, therefore, is the UK to go into Europe as a step in a process, or does the United States envisage the organization of Europe as a separate thing and an end in itself.

Ball stated that we saw the problem as political. Both Germany and France have strong potential which would tend over the long run to make the EEC an inward-looking organization. Britain is a force that can bring cohesion to this movement, but he wanted to stress that he meant Britain and not the Seven as a whole. He also wanted to make clear that this was not a position which we advanced. Ball noted that in his conversation with Heath he was asked what we had in mind as pertained to the UK and he replied.

In terms of the future of European integration, Ball said, Britain is a major pole of attraction for several countries in the Community and tends to be a disruptive force in the pattern of European integration so long as it remains outside the framework. Moreover, we had a great respect for British political genius. If it were brought to bear on the organization of Europe, we would go forward with more assurance with an Atlantic arrangement.

As far as the Seven were concerned, Prime Minister Macmillan indicated to us that the NATO members of the Seven would not have much difficulty on the principle of joining, although there would be difficulties of detail.

Sir Harold showed Mr. Ball an account of the most recent German-British bilaterals in which the clear point emerged that the Germans thought it would be a pity if the British were not steadfast on a derogation for agriculture. Moreover, it seemed clear that the Germans were prepared to see the British in on very liberal terms.

Mr. Pitblado said that the UK was tied to a contractual relationship, however, which was more than a trade relationship. Sir Harold further stated that the UK could not say "go jump" to its EFTA partners. This would be damaging to UK prestige. It would not, moreover, be designed for increased unity, but "designed for slaughter."

---

[1] Not found. A copy of the aide-mémoire, which stressed U.S. support for the principles of economic and political integration laid out by the Treaty of Rome, was transmitted to London in circular instruction CW 788, July 27. (Ibid., 375.800/7–2761)

[2] The other two points were never enumerated in the memorandum.

Mr. Ball stated that this would clearly make for difficulty in the negotiations. He thought the question of EFTA depended largely upon how it was handled, and that we saw no difficulty in talks in two stages.

Sir Harold specifically addressed himself to that part (paragraph eight) of the aide-mémoire dealing with our position on a Six-Seven accommodation and making a distinction between this and the accession of those countries who could assume the obligations of the Rome Treaty. To put it crudely, he said, if the UK were to stand honorably on its commitments to the Seven, the United States would not lend it its support.

Pitblado then stated that the Swiss and Swedes would have real difficulty in meeting the obligations of the Rome Treaty.

Ball said that in his view, if the British, Norwegians and Danes were to join then after the dust had settled, some commercial arrangements might be worked out for the Swiss and the Swedes. Otherwise, he said, it would be very difficult for us to do anything. If the negotiations were carried out in one package, he said, it would be on the basis of the lowest common denominator, which would badly weaken the final result. He believed it would be a mistake to clutter up the negotiations at the beginning. It would probably not be negotiable as a total package; it should be taken in steps and probably then could be negotiated. We could assume that there would also be later special arrangements for Finland, Austria, and Portugal.

Sir Harold said that this was a prescription for the destruction of Europe. This formula was quite different from what the Prime Minister had understood, and was not designed for the increase of unity in Europe but its destruction. Taken at its face, our position was fairly absolute and was aimed at the "bustup" of EFTA. Did he really mean that?

Mr. Ball said that as regards a Six-Seven accommodation we were firm in our view, but that the difficulty was not in this, but rather in negotiating technique, which we believed should be staggered. The Swiss and Swedes and others must accept as we have done the fact of the EEC and learn to make adjustments if they are not prepared to accept the obligations and responsibilities of the Rome Treaties. We would have great difficulty in accepting the principle of derogations to take account of the special problems of any country.

Mr. Schaetzel pointed out that this was a straightforward continuation of our policy which was based on the idea that the age of preferences was dead. Pitblado said that Britain was engaged in solemn political obligations.

Sir Harold wished to recapitulate to make certain that he had understood our position correctly. First, there was to be a "bustup" of EFTA. Secondly, the UK would negotiate. Finally, the others would be picked up at a later time. This was unthinkable, he said. He turned to the statement of our views on EFTA. It is more than a commercial arrangement, he said, and cited the Finnish case. If this was our position, he said, a great many questions would be raised in London, for it implies that the UK has to "rat" on its obligations and simply put its signature on the Treaty of Rome.

Mr. Schaetzel pointed out that this had been raised before in London in a thorough discussion of the problem and had not seemed to raise any serious obstacle.

Breaking up the EFTA, if it were discussed in London, was something Sir Harold said he had not been informed about. It must have been incorrectly assumed that the UK would "rat on its partners." The UK has made clear from the beginning that a settlement would have to include the problems of obligations to EFTA and the Commonwealth and the agricultural problem. Mr. Ball pointed out that this was an overstatement, since the British public statements on this subject had indicated only that these problems would have to be taken into consideration. If this was the British viewpoint, this was a new understanding as far as we were concerned, since our thinking has been of the negotiations proceeding in two phases.

Sir Harold inquired whether the US seriously thought that the UK would simply take a blank check and disregard its other commitments. It was not the greater unity of Europe which we appeared to have in mind, but a far smaller thing. Mr. Schaetzel pointed out that if the UK were to join the EEC this would provide a much greater unity and that one could not compare moves of Switzerland or Sweden with moves the UK might make. They were not at all of the same order.

Mr. Ball stated that clarity of view was absolutely essential to our relations. He wished to make it clearly understood that he was representing ideas which were approved by the President. (Sir Harold quickly asked whether the President has seen and approved this aide-mémoire. Mr. Ball said he had not although the ideas represented therein had been thoroughly discussed with him and approved by him.) Mr. Ball agreed that there might have been a possibility that the views could have been interpreted two ways and during the meeting between Macmillan and the President there was insufficient time to go into them thoroughly. It is possible that Mr. Macmillan did not understand our view on the phasing. Sir Harold agreed and welcomed this exchange of views in the interest of greater understanding.

There was a short discussion of the French views on the whole problem. Sir Harold believed there was considerable doubt that the French would have the UK on any terms. Mr. Ball stated that we believed it was a question of the scope of a settlement and the extent of derogations, and if satisfaction could be gotten on these, the French would probably not be an obstacle.

6.   Memorandum of Conversation

Washington, May 13, 1961.

SUBJECT

Preliminary Discussion for Dr. Hallstein's Meeting with the President

PARTICIPANTS

Dr. Walter Hallstein, President of the Commission of the European Economic Community

Mr. George W. Ball, Under Secretary for Economic Affairs

Mr. Richard D. Vine, Office of European Regional Affairs

Mr. Ball had invited President Hallstein to come in informally to discuss what Hallstein might usefully talk about with the President.

Mr. Ball said that the British appeared anxious to go ahead toward a solution with the Common Market. EFTA seemed to be the all important problem now and the UK seems to insist upon a simultaneous arrangement for the neutrals. We thought that this would be difficult and would probably jeopardize the success of any talks. It would cause us a real problem since it was essentially a six-seven merger. On agriculture, the British seemed to have made substantial progress and now appeared to be ready to work for a solution in the framework of a common agricultural policy after entering the Common Market. It is not a condition of membership. The Commonwealth problem seems to be soluble if transitional measures can be found.

President Hallstein inquired whether we had seen Mr. Macmillan's comments of two days ago, in which he replied to a question in the House from Wyatt in the sense that there was no thought of the UK's joining the Rome Treaty as it is although it might be prepared to "associate with membership" based on the three conditions of EFTA, Commonwealth and agriculture.

Mr. Ball said that he expected some move before the House rises.

Mr. Ball also stressed that we did not wish to play the role of honest broker. Dr. Hallstein said that this was just as well since he did not particularly like the atmosphere in Paris these days.

In regard to the UK in the Common Market, Dr. Hallstein said that his first concern was the change in voting power. The British will be entering with clients whom they can rely on. On the other hand, even if this

Source: Department of State, Central Files, 375.800/5–1361. Official Use Only. Drafted by Vine on May 19 and approved in B on May 22. During his visit to Washington, Hallstein discussed the relationship between the EEC and the Organization of African States on August 16 with President Kennedy and the relationship between the EEC and the OECD with the Chairman of the Council of Economic Advisors the same day. Memoranda of their conversations are ibid., 375.800/5–1661. A memorandum of Hallstein's conversation with Secretary of Agriculture Freeman is printed as Document 7.

brought about a change, the British would be welcomed if the final results or objectives of the Rome Treaty would remain the same.

He was also concerned that the traditions of the British civil servant working in the Commission would lead to its evolution into a compromise-making machine by making it more an administrative or consultative mechanism.

Dr. Hallstein was inclined to wait for majority rule so that the British could not veto any of the major trends now in process. He cited the example of the evolution of the Council of Europe. The British stopped this. It could have been a confederation, looser than the EEC, but still very good. In the Consultative Assembly, for example, one sees the British parliamentarians always in line with the Government. In the EEC countries, on the other hand, strength on behalf of Community institutions could always be counted on in the Parliament. This was one of the reasons why he was not worried about de Gaulle, for in France the Parliament undoubtedly still retained an influence. It would be just the opposite in the UK where Parliament remained hostile to the European concept.

Hallstein wished to stress that he meant none of this in any moralizing sense. It is just in the British tradition. The British have not accepted European unity as an ideal; they have accepted it as a fact. For them the idea means the reversal of 400 years of policy toward the Continent and they must have time to digest and adjust to these new concepts. There is no great hurry.

Another factor, said Hallstein, is Europe's 11 years of experience with the integration process which the British have missed. His inclination was to add conditions, not to take them away, in order to take account of the British state of mind which had not kept up with the European evolution on this problem. To do otherwise, would amount to retrogression.

He welcomed the way we have laid out our position with the British. He thought that firmness and clarity was the only position we could continue to take.

Dr. Hallstein believed that the old policy of national states in Europe no longer has legitimacy. Psychologically the people of Continental Europe are prepared to accept European unification. They have learned the real lesson of the disaster of two world wars. The British on the other hand, are not yet so prepared. Forward progress must be maintained, and Hallstein would not wish to see a lower common denominator achieved by bringing in new states before they are psychologically prepared.

Mr. Ball stated that he thought it would be helpful if President Hallstein could tell the President this when he saw him, that it would be a great contribution if the British came in in the right spirit, but there was no great hurry.

There followed a brief discussion of the recent history of British antagonism to the Six in Europe and efforts on the one hand to stay out of Europe, while on the other to slow down Europe's own efforts to unite. Hallstein thought there were two clear aspects of importance. The first was a French tendency represented by Debre to use a British move to back out of the integration structure to bolster their own preference for a looser union. The other, was the British view, represented by Macmillan, that the EEC is only a trade agreement and that once the French are convinced of this the rest will fall in line. Both these views represent great dangers to further progress and must be combatted.

---

7.   Memorandum of Conversation

Washington, May 17, 1961.

SUBJECT

Common Agricultural Policy of the EEC

PARTICIPANTS

Dr. Walter Hallstein, President of the Commission of the European Economic Community
Dr. Berndt von Staden, Executive Assistant to Dr. Hallstein
The Honorable Orville Freeman, Secretary of Agriculture
Ambassador W. Walton Butterworth, U.S. Representative to the European Communities
Mr. John P. Duncan, Jr., Assistant Secretary of Agriculture
Mr. Gerald E. Tichenor, Deputy Administrator, Agriculture, FAS
Mr. Gustave Burmeister, Assistant Administrator, Agriculture, FAS
Mr. Raymond Ioanes, Deputy Administrator, Agriculture, FAS
Mr. Richard D. Vine, Department of State, EUR/RA

President Hallstein, after an exchange of amenities, began by noting that he was not an expert on the problems of agriculture and would not be able to talk in detail on its various aspects. He did wish to make some general comments, however.

He noted that the greatest problem he had encountered thus far in the execution of the treaty was agriculture. The treaty rules for industry were different than for agriculture and he and his Commission were charged with working out these rules. The basic rules have in fact already been laid down by the Commission. He explained that the Commission was independent of the national governments and was

---

Source: Department of State, Central Files, 375.800/5–1761. Official Use Only. Drafted by Vine on June 29.

responsible only to the Council of Ministers. Both must agree before specific measures are taken; the Commission must propose a course of action to the Council of Ministers which must agree or dissent.

The President indicated that they were slowly making progress. Progress was slow largely because of the recurring problem of national elections.

The Commission, he said, recognized the need to take into account the interests of the trading partners of the Six in its proposals. There were problems, however. He noted that there were two times as many farms in the EEC countries as in the United States, but those in the United States covered ten times as much area. Moreover, there was the problem of merging the national policies of six countries, which meant in effect, undoing all the mistakes of the past one hundred years.

The goals of a common agricultural policy, he continued, were to assure farmers in the six countries income relatively as favorable as other members of their societies, while rationalizing production and avoiding the creation of surpluses. The secret to achieving these objectives was price policy, but there were many problems in lowering existing price levels. It had to be done moreover, in a framework which was as little protectionist as possible.

Variable levies were the instrument which the Commission had selected to carry out its policies. While there has been a great deal of dispute over the merits of variable levies, there is nothing intrinsically good or bad in them. Whether they are good or bad depends upon the price level which is established to make them operative—these levels may be good in one case and bad in another. Wheat is a case in point. The French have unused land which can be devoted to increased wheat production and want protection. The Commission, on the other hand, has worked up figures indicating the extent to which U.S. imports must be maintained and knows what the U.S. problem is.

The Commission, moreover, has obtained the services of some of the best experts available to solve the problem. Mansholt, the Commissioner charged with the responsibility for agriculture, has had 12 years experience in the Netherlands and is not narrow-minded or protectionist. He makes a great effort to reconcile the legitimate needs of farmers with the larger interest. He is interested in maintaining a greater flow of agricultural imports to balance the exporting interests of certain of the larger countries in the Community.

Secretary Freeman said that he had followed the negotiations carefully. He said that our primary interest is in the future of new trade agreements legislation which the administration had said has first priority. The Secretary said that he hoped we could go forward with this but that in order to do so we would need to have balanced concessions to demonstrate to the Congress and American people the efficacy of our efforts.

President Hallstein said he realized that there is a great need to find solutions. Both sides must recognize this need to find a solution and work toward that end. President Hallstein said that, as regards industry both the Six Governments and the Commission recognize the problems of third countries. Agricultural problems, however, the GATT mechanism has not solved. The GATT technique is commercial and agricultural problems cannot be solved on commercial policy grounds.

The GATT rules, he continued, are not effectively applied to agriculture. His analysis of the problem is some source of encouragement since progress is being made. He warned that they are coming to the place where countries were producing more than they are consuming and efficiency was taking a secondary place. An understanding of this fact is of primary importance since food consumption cannot be increased. There is some flexibility on this in the EEC but not much.

Secretary Freeman in this respect commented on the poultry problem which was geared to the pattern of increasing consumption in Europe. President Hallstein compared this with the problem of increasing imports of textiles from low-wage areas.

President Hallstein said that the Commission was interested that protectionism be avoided to permit order in the whole of world trade. No longer could one make a distinction between internal or external affairs since sovereignty was no longer so important in modern international relations. The answer is not to escape the problem but to attack it.

Secretary Freeman said he was most encouraged by this outlook. President Hallstein continued that one-quarter of the population was working in agriculture in the EEC countries as against one-tenth here and still its surpluses are seeking markets. Secretary Freeman said that one farmer is now feeding about 25 people in the United States whereas 20 years ago one farmer fed only 11. This is an alarming but wonderful development. President Hallstein said that the problem in Europe was somewhat different since agriculture is not so much a branch of production but a way of life. The trick consequently has been to encourage the movement of industry into economic areas. This is the reason for the emphasis in the EEC on regional development which enables less-developed areas to solve the problems less painfully.

Secretary Freeman said that he could see the problem. We are coming to the point where famine can be prevented, and resources must be guided to other areas. To a certain extent the same rule applies to industry. One sees this in the GATT negotiations. In the long run the goal is to produce efficiently; in the short run the goal is to avoid protection. This is the same point that the EEC has in mind.

8.   Telegram From the Embassy in the United Kingdom to the Department of State

London, May 18, 1961, 8 p.m.

4726. Paris for Embassy and USRO. Brussels for Embassy and USEC. Pass McGeorge Bundy. From Ball. Following summary of conversation with Heath and Barclay May 18 re UK-EEC relations:[1]

1. Heath described his speech in Commons May 17 as "opening gun in grand debate." It represented beginning of campaign to educate Conservative Party and country generally about issues involved in UK moving into Common Market. This is necessary first step to reaching point where government can make decision; Heath felt good progress was being made in this direction. Re position of Labor Party, Heath agreed that they would not oppose outright UK entry into Common Market and in any event were not united or strong enough to prevent government from moving ahead.

2. Heath welcomed reiteration of US position that basic decision was one for Britain to make and US does not want to appear to be pushing UK. He said that from public presentation point of view it could not appear that HMG was doing anything under pressure rather than on merits of issues.

3. Heath described aide-mémoire we had given to Caccia[2] as very useful. Also expressed appreciation for clarification of US position re other EFTA countries more bargaining power with Six and therefore they are very sensitive to any reports that Britain would join without them. [sic] At recent EFTA meeting in Geneva UK attempted to get down to details with other EFTA countries. However, Barclay reported that most of them had not yet clarified their thoughts on how they want negotiations with Six to proceed. While other EFTA countries still emphasizing importance of UK not moving alone, Barclay said idea of separate arrangement for other EFTA countries "seemed to have gotten through." He confirmed that Denmark and probably Norway would also go into Common Market. Position of Sweden and Switzerland still not clear, but opinion seems to be moving toward close association. Austrians have particular difficulty with idea of common commercial

---

Source: Department of State, Central Files, 375.800/5–1961. Confidential. Repeated to Bonn, Brussels, Bern, Lisbon, Copenhagen, Oslo, The Hague, Stockholm, Luxembourg, Vienna, and Rome. Ball was in Europe to discuss textiles in preparation for GATT and OECD meetings.

[1] A memorandum of this conversation is ibid., Conference Files: Lot 65 D 366, CF 1874A. Sir Roderick Barclay was Adviser on European Trade Questions in the Foreign Office.

[2] See Document 5.

policy which might mean application of quotas against USSR. Generally agreed at EFTA meeting that all EFTA countries would have to be in wider market in some way—some accepting Treaty of Rome and others being associated in Customs Union. Barclay reported that matter will be discussed further at EFTA Ministerial Meeting in London next month. Re technique of carrying out negotiations between Six and other EFTA countries, Heath said UK officials working out paper on this and will keep in touch with US.

4. Heath did not react to Ball's observation that we tended to feel there was nothing much US could usefully do at this time with the Six in view of the danger that any intervention might be considered "Anglo-Saxon conspiracy". On US position re other EFTA countries. Heath said would be useful if we talked further with neutrals—in particular Swedes who are still thinking in terms of plans to bring Six and Seven together as groups. Heath seemed to accept US position that arrangements for neutrals would have to be looked at individually on merits and approval could not be given in advance. Heath also appeared to agree would be useful to think in terms of some EFTA countries joining EEC and others working out special arrangements later.

5. Heath did not give direct answer to question re timing of Britain's decision. He said further discussions with French scheduled for next month. In these talks there would be discussion of non-trade aspects of Rome Treaty. Further work would also have to be done on Commonwealth trade problem. Usefully, EFTA Ministerial Meeting in June would clarify EFTA problem. There was also question of attitude of Six. In light of developments on these problems and movement of public opinion as result of parliamentary discussion, HMG hoped to be getting closer to time when they could make up their mind.

6. Re attitude of EEC Commission, British have impression that Mansholt, Rey and Marjolin are more flexible and that Commission position on UK joining Common Market now being formulated. Agreed that Hallstein is somewhat more concerned about British entry from point of view of possible setback in progress which has been made toward cooperation among the Six and acceptance of role of EEC Commission. Recognized that attitude UK adopted in entering Common Market would be important factor in quieting Commission's fears.

7. Impression from discussion with Heath and other UK officials is that UK Government has made tentative decision to go into Common Market assuming that the several elements (UK parliamentary and public opinion, particularly agricultural interests EFTA and Commonwealth) bearing on this decision can be satisfactorily cleared up. When the big decision will be taken depends on progress in these fields.

Bruce

9.   Telegram From the Department of State to the Embassy in the United Kingdom

Washington, May 23, 1961, 3:55 p.m.

5456. London eyes only Ambassador Bruce. Geneva eyes only Under Secretary Ball. Following is text President's letter to Macmillan transmitted through British Embassy May 22:

"Dear Mr. Prime Minister:

"I have been slow in responding to that part of your letter of April 28th which deals with the possible relation of the United Kingdom to the Common Market,[1] but I am sure you will understand that this is not because of any lack of interest in the problem. We have been thinking hard here about it, and about your important comments.

"George Ball, on our side, has been in good close touch with your people, both here and in London, and I think he has presented our views so clearly in an aide-mémoire and in conversations that it would not be useful for me to go into repetitive detail. We quite understand that the great decision to join the Common Market will necessarily carry with it a concern for your special obligations in three fields—agriculture, the Commonwealth, and your relations with EFTA. If we also hope and trust that ways can be found to deal with these matters, it is of course because of our own conviction that the West will be greatly strengthened if the United Kingdom can become a full member of the Rome Treaty.

"Our central interest here, as I am sure you know, is political. We believe that only with growing political coherence in Western Europe can we look to a stable solution of the place of Germany. Although the success of the Six has been striking, we doubt if the weights and balances will be right without your great influence at the center.

"It is because of this political conviction that we have been willing to face the prospect of significant—although we hope temporary—economic disadvantages to the United States in the spread of the Common Market. A customs union alone would be a source of economic difficulty for us, without compensating political advantages, and we should be most reluctant to see such a result.

"For similar reasons we have hoped that perhaps the problem of your relation to EFTA might be handled in stages, always of course with

---

Source: Department of State, Presidential Correspondence: Lot 66 D 204. Secret. Also sent to Geneva.

[1] Macmillan's letter discussed European unity and attached a memorandum with two annexes that he thought the President might find useful in a meeting with de Gaulle. (Ibid.)

full responsibility to your partners in EFTA, so that the accession of the United Kingdom to the Rome Treaty might be possible without await-ing complete arrangements for everyone else. We cannot help thinking that if you are once safely and strongly in the Common Market, you will be in a very good position to protect all of the interests which so legiti-mately give you concern at present.

"I remain at your service to raise this question with General de Gaulle in any way that you think may be constructive. It would certainly be easy for me to say to him, quite informally, the sort of thing you sug-gest in your letter, though of course I would want to stay clear of any appearance of judging just what special arrangements may turn out to be right. I am sure the General would dislike any appearance of pressure from me. Perhaps it may be best for me to see how our talks go. But I would like to do whatever you think wise. Will you let me know your view?

"I am looking forward more and more to our meeting in London. There will certainly be much to talk about then. Sincerely,"

Rusk

---

10.   **Telegram From the Mission at Geneva to the Department of State**

Geneva, May 24, 1961, 10 p.m.

1423. London eyes only for Ambassador Bruce. Bonn eyes only for Ambassador Dowling. From Ball. Department telegram 2036[1]. In com-pany with Ambassador Dowling I had twenty-minute conference with Chancellor Adenauer yesterday.

I mentioned that we were watching with keen interest evolution Brit opinion toward possible adherence European Common Market. I said I had seen Heath in London and gained impression from him and others that Brit Govt was in process of making decision. Chancellor then asked when did I expect Brit Govt to make up its mind. I replied that

---

Source: Department of State, Central Files, 375.800/5–2461. Secret; Limited Distribu-tion; Eyes Only. Repeated to London and Bonn.
[1] Printed as telegram 5456, Document 9.

presumably they would have to educate Brit opinion first and that Heath had said in reference to his speech in the House of Commons, "This is the beginning of the great debate". I further said that Heath had indicated that this represented a major decision for Britain since it meant reversal of several hundred years of policy toward the continent.

The Chancellor responded vigorously, pointing his finger at me and saying, "Mr. Ball, don't you know that that is just what Churchill and Eden both told me. They also said they were reversing hundreds of years of policy toward Europe. Then they set up the Western European Union which has been in a state of rigor mortis ever since". The Chancellor continued, "No, Macmillan will never join in any serious move toward European unity. Heath might wish to and several of the other Ministers. Selwyn Lloyd I believe has been converted. But the Macmillan govt will never make the necessary decision". He said that he had just discussed this matter with de Gaulle and that he and de Gaulle fully agreed on this view. That was why they had decided to move quickly to extend the political character of Community. They had decided to have political consultation by the heads of state of the Six four times a year and were going to move toward political unity as fast as possible.

Chancellor said that he and de Gaulle were convinced that some day Britain would join Europe but not while the Macmillan govt was in power. Macmillan would never make the necessary decision and he and de Gaulle had decided that they could not wait for the British.

I told him that we had felt that the best contribution the United States could make to the furtherance of unity was not to try to exert any pressure on the Brit but simply to insist from the point of view of American policy that while we would favor full Brit membership we could not accept with equanimity any proposals that would weaken the economic and political unity achieved by the Six.

The Chancellor replied, "That is the position for you to take".

The vehemence with which the Chancellor indicated his and de Gaulle's extreme skepticism regarding Macmillan's intentions clearly suggest that de Gaulle is not likely to view a Brit proposal to join Common Market with hospitality. This impression was reinforced by statement volunteered by Carstens, State Secretary FRG FonOff, that he had been told by French that they had not yet made up their minds whether to agree to a Brit move at this time. Also other senior German officials present Saturday afternoon session with Chancellor and de Gaulle confirmed impression that neither de Gaulle nor Adenauer believe Macmillan is prepared to join Europe. They feel therefore they must go ahead and solve the major problems impeding movement toward political unity before conditions are ripe that will compel some later Brit Govt to take full decision.

Under these circumstances I would urge that President exercise caution in any attempt to interpret Brit position to de Gaulle and that he avoid raising subject altogether unless Macmillan insists further. Otherwise danger President may find himself placed in middle of involved European dispute.

Martin

---

11.   Memorandum of Conversation

US/MC/8   Paris, June 2, 1961, 3:45 p.m.

PRESIDENT'S VISIT
Paris, May 31–June 2, 1961

SUBJECT

Friday Afternoon Talks

PARTICIPANTS

United States	*France*
President Kennedy	General de Gaulle
Mr. Glenn (Interpreter)	Mr. Andronikoff (Interpreter)

[Here follows discussion of tripartite consultations.]

Common Market

The President said that he would be in England for the christening of the young Princess Radziwill; at that occasion, he would lunch with Prime Minister Macmillan and might be asked something by the latter about the Common Market question. He would therefore like to have the General's opinion on the matter.

General de Gaulle said that it was his wish and his intent to work towards the establishment of an organization for close European coop-

---

Source: Department of State, Conference Files: Lot 66 D 110, CF 1891. Secret. Drafted by Glenn. The meeting was held at the Elysée Palace. President Kennedy visited Paris on his way to Vienna to meet with Soviet Premier Khrushchev. For documentation on the discussions with de Gaulle, see Documents 107 and 230.

eration, in particular between France, Germany, and Italy, and also (although these countries do not have a great importance) with Belgium and the Netherlands, but particularly between France and Germany. The six European countries which have established the Common Market consider this as only the beginning and they intend to develop their cooperation. Contacts between them will take place in December and it is hoped that at that moment the customs duties between the Six will be reduced by 20 percent as compared with the 10 percent by which they had been reduced to the present moment. This would mean de facto an elimination of internal customs duties in Europe. There still are some difficulties in the area of agriculture but it is hoped that in December all these difficulties will be overcome. The six nations feel that if they are to be linked in a common economy, they must also establish a regime of close political cooperation. Some people even think that there should be a political integration of Europe. The French feel, however, that this would be premature and oppose such integration in favor of an organized cooperation of states. This is what they want and proposals have been made to that effect which may well be accepted in December. Therefore, what may emerge from the December meeting is a genuine common economy and a likewise genuine political cooperation. Now what is the position of the United Kingdom? At first the U.K. said that it would never participate in such an enterprise. Three years ago the British said that this entire enterprise was directed against them, to which the General had answered that such an opinion, as well as the British fears, were greatly exaggerated.

Now the position of the United Kingdom is different but it still has considerable difficulties to join the Community. There are some difficulties of an economic nature, both internal to the United Kingdom and deriving from the Commonwealth Preference System. The British may have the Commonwealth Preference System or a membership in the Common Market but they cannot have both. Up to this moment, they still have not chosen between the two possibilities. As for political cooperation, they are very leery of it for reasons which derive from their history. True enough, there is a movement for joining the Common Market without, however, joining it fully. This would be a somewhat hollow pretense which would make Britain appear a part of Europe without it being a part of the European reality. This is not acceptable to the Europeans who would be glad to accept Britain if Britain were to join without reservations of either an economic or a political nature, but not otherwise.

The President said that he fully realized that such questions were primarily the responsibility of the Europeans and not of the U.S. He nevertheless wished to describe American thinking on the question. The Common Market has some adverse effects on American economy. At the same time, however, it greatly strengthens Europe both economically and politically. The United States feels that the advantages by far outweigh the drawbacks in regard to the United States and in consequence the United States has taken a strong position in favor of the Community. There is also another reason why we favor the Community. It is because it contributes to tie West Germany to Europe. It is not clear what will happen in Germany after Adenauer and, therefore, every tie which links Germany to Europe should be welcome.

Britain is moving closer to the Common Market, it has, however, some difficulties both with its own and with the New Zealand agriculture. There is a tendency on the part of the British to seek a limited association with the Community on the basis of a trade association without any of the political obligations provided by the Rome Treaty. The U.S. position in this respect is that such a limited association of the U.K. with the Community would add somewhat to the economic difficulties of the U.S. without having any favorable political results. Therefore, the U.S. does not favor such a limited association, although it does favor a full membership in the manner in which the General also favors it; this the more so that such a membership would have a strong effect on West Germany. The President hopes the British will end up by seeing it that way.

General de Gaulle said that he was taking note of the President's statement and position. The desire to tie Germany to the West is the most profound reason for his own backing of the European Community. A limited accession by the U.K. would have only drawbacks and be an appearance without a reality. Full membership would be viewed with favor. The General doubts, however, whether the U.K. will seek such membership. The Community, in any case, will keep the door open. British reluctance stems from their very nature and tradition which is that they always try to play the part of a broker within any group within which they participate—even at times between the U.S. and the French.

The President added that even at times between the U.S. and the Soviets.

General de Gaulle said that he did not mean this in any disparaging way but, in any case, that his position towards British membership is either/or, either full, or none.

[Here follows discussion of NATO.]

12.   Memorandum of Conversation

Washington, June 12, 1961, 5 p.m.

SUBJECT

Common Market

PARTICIPANTS

US Side
The President
The Secretary of State
Mr. Nitze, Assistant Secretary of Defense
Ambassador Reinhardt
Mr. Tyler, Deputy Assistant Secretary
Mr. Schlesinger, Special Assistant to the President

Italian Side
Prime Minister Fanfani
Foreign Minister Segni
Ambassador Fenoaltea, Italian Ambassador
Mr. Fornari, Director General of Political Affairs
Mr. d'Archirafi, Diplomatic Adviser to the Prime Minister

The President said he had talked with Prime Minister Macmillan[1] on this subject. It seems that British opinion is moving toward joining the Common Market, in spite of the problems this poses for the UK. He asked the Prime Minister what he thought the opinion of the Common Market countries is on possible UK membership. While this is primarily a European matter, he added, it is of interest to the United States in various ways, including the bearing it has on the future of Germany.

Fanfani said that he had conveyed Italy's position to Macmillan during his visit in Rome at the end of last year. Italy welcomes the idea of the UK joining the Common Market, since it is particularly concerned lest the cleavage between the Sixes and the Sevens might grow deeper, and thereby result not only in economic but also in political frontiers between the two groups. This is why Italy wants to facilitate UK access to the EEC. She recognizes that the UK has problems, such as with regard to the Common Market, though these may possibly have been exaggerated. For example, Macmillan said that New Zealand was worried about selling her butter. Italy has no problem: she is prepared to stop buying butter from the Yugoslavs and Hungary and to buy it instead from New Zealand. Also the southern Commonwealth countries feared

---

Source: Department of State, Presidential Memoranda of Conversation: Lot 66 D 149. Secret. Drafted by Tyler, approved in S on August 4, and by the White House on August 11. The meeting was held at the White House. Fanfani visited Washington June 12–13.

[1] See Document 3.

for their food and vegetable market in the UK. But this was merely a matter of watching the seasons and staggering the supply. A committee of experts on the subject had already met three times and had found no great problems in the way of a solution. As for South African wines, the problem has been taken care of by South Africa breaking away from the Commonwealth.

Fanfani went on to say that the problem of membership in the EEC is not so much economic as political, because of the instinctive reluctance of the British to join a supra-national organization. He said that it was important to recognize this and to do everything possible to bring the British in. Macmillan had said to Fanfani that he was not a die-hard conservative and that he was open to new ideas. The President commented that in spite of certain commercial disadvantages to the United States inherent in the organization of a large single European market, the benefit to us of a stronger alliance induced us to favor progress toward European unity.

Fanfani said he was sure that Foreign Minister Segni, who signed the Rome Treaty, was very pleased to hear the President's last remark. He wished to assure the President that Italy would do everything possible to take US interests into consideration, and he had told Macmillan this. The President said he thought it would be advantageous for Italy, and for other countries such as Germany, to facilitate the UK's admission to the Common Market. The Prime Minister said the President could rest assured that Italy would continue to work in this direction.

The President mentioned the problem posed by possible economic disadvantages to Latin America as a result of the EEC. The Prime Minister said that this problem had frequently been raised by people in Latin America during President Gronchi's recent trip there. Fanfani had raised it himself with de Gaulle in Paris. This problem, he felt, must be solved but should be approached cautiously in order not to disappoint expectations. In seeking to protect Latin American interests by means of association, it would be necessary to consider carefully the problem of commodity surpluses, which has a bearing on prices and wages and on the stability of the economy. The Latin American problem was essentially threefold: 1) the need for training leaders, 2) the development of appropriate institutions and organizations, 3) the stabilization of prices and the disposal of surpluses.

In this respect EEC might first turn its attention to the third item, as a preliminary step on the road toward association.

The President said he had asked de Gaulle if the EEC could send an observer to the Montevideo conference in July. He had in mind a man of stature who could influence the trend of discussions constructively and smooth the approach to mutual advantage. Fanfani concurred with this idea. The President suggested that Italy consider how she might play an increased role in Latin America particularly in countries such as Argentina where she already has particular assets and good-will. Fanfani said he would look into the matter and see what Italy could do to be helpful, both bilaterally and multilaterally. Commenting on the sensitivities of the Latin Americans he would permit himself to say that he had occasionally been surprised by actions of US citizens in Latin America, but he thought that this had been doubtless due to the strain of competition. The President reiterated his view that it would be useful if Europe were to play a larger role in Latin America, since there were limits to what the United States could undertake. Fanfani said he was worried by the Communist offensive in Latin America. He thought that this might well be the next big battle-field which Khrushchev would choose, rather than Africa, in order to challenge and to seek to undermine the prestige and the position of the West. He thought that developments in Latin America should be carefully studied in the light of the assumption. Italy stood ready to play whatever useful role she could. She did not want the United States to add difficulties in Latin America to those we already had on our hands elsewhere. The President commented that he shared this view.

---

13.   Letter From Secretary of State Rusk to Foreign Minister Kreisky

Washington, July 1, 1961.

DEAR MISTER MINISTER: It was indeed a pleasure to receive your letter of June 7[1] and to recall our interesting, but brief, discussion on the very important subject of European economic integration, which I know is of vital concern to you and your colleagues in the Austrian Federal Government.[2]

I have also recently had discussions in the same sense with Mr. Wahlen and Mr. Petitpierre in Switzerland.[3] Upon my return, conse-

---

Source: Department of State, Central Files, 375.800/6–761. No classification marking. Drafted by Vine and Sulser (WE) and concurred in by Ball, Tyler, Beaudry, and Brandin (EUR).

[1] Not printed. (Ibid.) In it Kreisky stressed the importance of British entry into the Common Market and the need for countries such as Austria, Sweden, and Switzerland to find special relationships with the EEC.

[2] No record of this discussion has been found.

[3] A memorandum of Rusk's conversation with President Wahlen and Federal Councillor Petitpierre on May 18 is in Department of State, Central Files, 110.11–RU/5–1961.

quently, I was able to give Under Secretary Ball a detailed account of developments elsewhere. Your timely letter setting forth your views was thus of great assistance to us.

It is a source of encouragement to us that your analysis of the problem of European integration is so similar to ours in most important respects. The forces set in motion by the establishment of the European Economic Community are an important element in a Franco-German rapprochement and provide a constructive channel for German energies and dynamism. These aspects are too important for the future of the Atlantic Community to be lost, as well they might should the European Economic Community be diluted or "watered down". Moreover, it is just these political elements which have been the basis for our support of integration in Europe.

It was with these considerations in mind that the President responded to Prime Minister Macmillan's query as to how we would view the United Kingdom's accession to the Rome Treaty. The President indicated to Mr. Macmillan that if the United Kingdom were wholeheartedly to accept the political and institutional obligations and objectives of the Rome Treaty we would welcome the United Kingdom's membership. We thus seem to be entirely in accord with you that the United Kingdom's adherence on this basis would be in the interest of all European countries and the Atlantic Community as a whole.

I would like in this connection to emphasize that we are not urging the United Kingdom to join the EEC. The United Kingdom must itself decide what it must do, taking into account the balance of its own political and economic interests and commitments. If the United Kingdom should decide to accede to the EEC it is clear that there are a number of problems which will have to be worked out with the EEC countries.

There will certainly be problems for countries such as your own, which, for a number of valid reasons, are unable to accept the political and institutional obligations of the Rome Treaty. We recognize this and understand it. There will also be problems for the Commonwealth and, indeed, for us—for all those outside the enlarged European Community.

You will appreciate, I think our desire to assure that any solutions proposed to European commercial problems do not unduly affect our own trade interest or similar interests of other countries. For this reason, we would continue to oppose a generalized commercial solution. The administration is keenly aware that trade and commercial developments in Europe, particularly if they are preferential and discriminatory, can greatly influence the outcome of the trade agreements legislation we will seek next year. We would urge, consequently, that proposed solutions contribute to the greatest extent possible to the objectives of European integration while reducing the impact of this process on the trade and commerce of all third countries. If either of these objectives is lost sight of, our problems are greatly increased. On the other hand, we understand Austria's special status and special problems. We could not prejudge any arrangements in advance, but we are quite willing to view on a pragmatic basis, any relationship that might meet the needs of the EEC and Austria's special needs. We would thus not take a firm position until specific proposals have been made and can be examined.

I do not share your view that a multilateral solution will solve the problems created by enlargement of the European Economic Community. I welcome, however, your reference to the OECD as a possible vehicle for their solution. We have consistently envisaged the OECD as an instrument of far-reaching and close cooperation among the members of the Atlantic Community. We are determined to make it an effective mechanism for the coordination of economic policies and the resolution of economic problems among its members. In our view, it should be the principal instrument for solving the economic problems arising out of a decision by the United Kingdom to adhere to the Treaty of Rome.

I think we must assume that the OECD will fulfill the hopes we have for it. If it does, then the possibility of an economic or political division ever developing in the heart of the Atlantic Community is remote.

Under Secretary Ball will be in Vienna in September for the IMF meetings, and would welcome the opportunity to discuss our views on European integration with you. If you find this agreeable, a mutually convenient time and date can be arranged at a later date. In the meantime, you may be sure that I and other interested officials of the United States Government will follow Ambassador Matthews' reports of your thinking and problems with the greatest interest.

I share your regret that our visit to Vienna was too short and the schedule of activities too crowded to enable us to become better acquainted. I have the utmost respect for Austria's achievements and her position in the Community of free nations, and I would have been delighted to have seen more of the country and to have had a better chance to know her leaders. I trust that we will have the opportunity to get together again during the United Nations General Assembly later this year.

Sincerely yours,

Dean Rusk[4]

---

[4] Printed from a copy that bears this stamped signature.

14.   Message From Prime Minister Macmillan to President Kennedy

London, July 28, 1961.

DEAR MR. PRESIDENT, The exploratory talks with E.E.C. Governments, in which we have been engaged in recent months, have been taken as far as they can. It has now become clear that, if we are to discover whether membership of the European Economic Community is really open to the United Kingdom, it will be necessary to undertake formal negotiations. We have recently concluded consultations with other Commonwealth governments and have consulted the other members of the European Free Trade Association. Many and great difficulties remain to be resolved. Nevertheless, after long and earnest consideration Her Majesty's Government have come to the conclusion that it would be right for Britain to apply to join the E.E.C. preparatory to negotiations with a view to securing satisfactory arrangements to meet the special needs of the United Kingdom of the Commonwealth and of E.F.T.A. I shall be making a statement to this effect in the House of Commons on July 31.

2.   This is not the end of the road. Indeed it may well be only the beginning of what can still prove to be a most difficult and dangerous period for the future unity of Europe. When you wrote to me on May 22,[1] you spoke of your conviction that the West would be greatly strengthened if the United Kingdom could become a full member of the E.E.C. These considerations have been very much in our minds in reaching the decision which we have now taken. But, as you will know, several Commonwealth governments—old and new—have expressed anxiety about the possible consequences which may result from negotiations between Britain and the Six. These anxieties, and our obligations to our partners in the European Free Trade Association impose clear limits on the freedom of action with which we can negotiate. I need hardly tell you how much I would value your encouragement and support in this great enterprise. We for our part will spare no efforts to bring the negotiations to a successful conclusion. Meanwhile, I hope that you will feel free to let me have your views at any time on these issues which are so vital for us all.[2]

With warm regard,

Harold Macmillan[3]

Source: Department of State, Presidential Correspondence: Lot 66 D 204. Top Secret.

[1] See Document 9.

[2] President Kennedy replied the same day stressing the good will and firm support that the United States had for the British decision, and concluding that in ways which the United States could be useful, the British could count on the United States "absolutely." (Department of State, Presidential Correspondence: Lot 66 D 204)

[3] Printed from a copy that bears this typed signature.

15.   National Security Action Memorandum No. 76

Washington, August 21, 1961.

MEMORANDUM FOR
    Under Secretary of State George Ball

I am concerned about what will be the economic effect upon the United States if England joins the common market. I believe we should have a realistic detailed study made by State. Treasury and the Council of Economic Advisers. I have been informed that the effect will be extremely serious. Could you consider the matter and talk to me about it and suggest what action we should properly take. We have been in the position, of course, of encouraging the expansion of the common market for political reasons. If it should have an extremely adverse effect upon us a good deal of responsibility would be laid upon our doorstep.

JFK

Source: Department of State, NSAMs: Lot 72 D 316. No classification marking. Another copy bears the date August 20. (Ibid.)

---

16.   Memorandum From the Under Secretary of State for Economic Affairs (Ball) to President Kennedy

Washington, August 23, 1961.

SUBJECT
    U.K. Adherence to the European Common Market

I have received your memorandum of August 21, 1961,[1] inquiring as to what steps we should take to protect United States interests in connection with the proposed move by England to join the Common Market.

Source: Department of State, NSAMs: Lot 72 D 316. Confidential.
[1] Document 15.

I should welcome the opportunity to discuss this question with you in some depth. Meanwhile, you can be assured that the situation is well in hand.

In the following few pages I shall outline the substantive situation, as we see it, together with the measures we are taking on a government-wide basis to protect American trading interests.

I. Economic Effect on the United States of
Great Britain's Joining the Common Market

Britain is already a member of the Free Trade Association, along with Norway, Sweden, Denmark, Switzerland, Austria and Portugal. If Britain does not join the Common Market, the full development of the Free Trade Association and the Common Market will result in two large areas within each of which trade will move without restriction. Whether or not Britain joins the Common Market, the full coming into being of these trade arrangements will have an impact on United States exports.

It is clear belief that even though these arrangements are by their nature discriminatory, the net impact on our trade will tend to be more favorable than unfavorable—although admittedly it will result in the need for some adjustments. It is our further belief that the adherence of Britain to the Common Market, while resulting in some additional discrimination, will also, on balance, be favorable for our exports.

A.   *A detailed State Department study has shown that the net effect of European economic integration will be to expand rather than diminish United States industrial exports.*

These conclusions are borne out by a State Department study completed about six months ago. This study was directed at determining what effect the full achievement of the Common Market and the Free Trade Association would have on United States exports of industrial products.

This study showed that the coming into being of these two trading areas might be expected to have two separate and opposite effects on United States trade—an effect of *trade diversion* and an effect of *trade creation*.

1. Trade Diversion

Some trade diversion would be expected to result from changes in relative tariff levels. Our study estimated that the trade diversion resulting from the Common Market (the EEC) would have a *gross* effect on United States exports of about $390 million annually and that the trade diversion resulting from the Free Trade Association (EFTA) would have a *gross* effect of about $285 million annually. The effect of such diversion would not be fully felt until the complete free movement of goods within each area was finally achieved (1970 or sooner).

2. Trade Creation

The *gross* effect of trade diversion is, however, only part of the story. Our study showed that an increase in the incremental growth rate of as little as 1/4 of 1% in the Common Market or the EFTA would enlarge the demand for our industrial goods so as to more than compensate for the diversionary effects resulting from the establishment of these two trading areas. We have every reason to believe that economic integration may be expected to increase the rate of economic growth considerably in excess of 1/4 of 1%. Certainly this has been the case so far in the Common Market.

3. The Net Effect of British Adherence to the Common Market

The foregoing analysis would suggest that the *net* effect of British adherence to the Common Market should be favorable to our industrial trade. The British growth rate at the moment is well below that of the Common Market countries. There is every reason to believe that Britain's joining the EEC would have a stimulating effect in Britain as it so dramatically did in France. (This is, of course, the compelling motive for Macmillan's decision to apply for membership.)

Under these circumstances, I think we are justified in believing that the anticipated higher growth rate will more than compensate for whatever additional discrimination may result from Britain's joining the EEC.

B.   Agriculture poses essentially different problems.

The effect of the Common Market on agricultural exports is not as clear as on industrial products; in fact, it cannot yet be determined with any certainty. The problems for agriculture are essentially different than for industry. The Free Trade Association arrangements do not include agricultural products. While agricultural products are included under the Common Market Treaty, the level of protection accorded them will be effectively determined not by the common external tariff but by measures taken in pursuance of a common agricultural policy. This policy is just now being developed.

Until such a policy is finally established we shall not be able to assess the degree of discrimination against United States agricultural exports. We have however, been insisting that the Common Market authorities and governments assure reasonable access for our farm products. The Department of Agriculture has been fully cooperating with us in this effort. Secretary Freeman will be in Europe next month and will be further pressing the United States' point of view.

The problem of assuring fair access to the Common Market for our agricultural goods would, of course, exist even if Britain did not succeed in joining. In fact, British adherence should tend to reduce the level of protection—and hence of discrimination—since Britain is committed to low food prices for its consumers. Thus, the effect on our own agricultural exports of Britain's joining the Common Market is quite likely to be beneficial rather than harmful.

However, this is a problem which bears most careful watching.

C. *United States Trade would be harmed if British Commonwealth preferences were extended to the Common Market.*

The principal danger to United States trading interests involved in the British move to adhere to the Common Market lies in the possible extension of Commonwealth preferences to the Common Market countries.

In my memorandum to you of August 7, 1961, (Tab A)[2] I pointed out that if Britain attempted to work out a relationship with the Common Market that would result in extending Commonwealth preferences to the Common Market countries, United States trade would be adversely affected in two ways:

(1) To permit the Commonwealth to have either free or preferential access to the Common Market would be highly prejudicial to our own temperate agriculture as well as to both the tropical and temperate agriculture of Latin America; and
(2) To permit the Common Market countries to have free or preferential access to the markets of the Commonwealth would be highly prejudicial to our industry.

For this reason, the United States Government has consistently made clear both to the Common Market countries and to the United Kingdom that we cannot accept any arrangement which contemplates the extension of Commonwealth preferences to the EEC. I have explained this on repeated occasions to the British and to EEC Governments. When I am in Europe next month for the International Bank and Fund meeting, I plan to re-emphasize this to Heath and Thorneycroft, as well as to the French Government and the Common Market Commission.

Meanwhile, we are preparing an aide-mémoire for the United Kingdom and the Six countries of the Common Market. In this aide-mémoire we are setting forth the basic requirements of American policy, including our opposition to any extension of Commonwealth preferences to the Common Market countries.

But, while taking a firm position against the extension of Commonwealth preferences we must recognize that we cannot reasonably expect the existing preferential system to be terminated over night. The long-

---

[2] Tab A was not attached to the source text; however, a copy of Ball's August 7 memorandum is in Department of State, Central Files, 375.800/8–761.

term solution of this problem must rest, as I suggested in my earlier memorandum (Tab A), on a phasing out of present arrangements over a reasonable transition period.

We must be firm on this objective. At the same time—although I would not propose it as an initial negotiating position—we may realistically have to face the possibility that the ultimate agreement between the United Kingdom and the Common Market will require some special cushioning arrangements for individual members of the Commonwealth. I have in mind particularly New Zealand which is heavily dependent upon the United Kingdom market for the sale of dairy products.

II. Administrative Arrangements for
Protecting United States Interests

A. We have established an interdepartmental group to follow the negotiations.

The negotiations between the United Kingdom and the Common Market will inevitably be complicated. In the course of these negotiations there will be substantial pressures to work out compromise solutions. We plan to follow those negotiations with the greatest care in order to prevent any compromises that might be prejudicial to United States commercial interests. At the same time, we must be prepared to play a constructive role. If necessary, we may have to put forward concrete proposals to insure that our interests are safeguarded and the objectives to which we are committed are attained.

In order that the United States Government may be fully prepared to deal with these problems, and to assure that we shall all speak with one voice, we have established an Interdepartmental Ad Hoc group under the chairmanship of the Department of State. This group includes representatives of the Departments of Commerce, Treasury, Labor, Agriculture, Interior and the Council of Economic Advisers.

In addition, the major policy questions raised by the negotiations as they develop will be under constant review by the Department of State with the assistance of the interdepartmental committee of Under Secretaries which has recently been created.

B. Comprehensive studies are in progress.

We have under way departmental and interdepartmental studies covering all phases of the problem. These studies will include elaborate statistical analyses of the trade implications of various alternative solutions that may be considered in the course of these negotiations.

III. Conclusion

The whole process of economic and political integration involves change and the construction of new patterns of relationship. The negotiations between the United Kingdom and the EEC will, if successful, inevitably bring about alterations, not only in Europe's own economic order, but also in Europe's traditional political and economic ties with the rest of the world. The anticipated benefits of European integration cannot be achieved without such a revolution.

Such a profound process of change will necessarily involve fundamental problems of adaptation and reorientation. In the course of these negotiations, we can anticipate, in addition to individual domestic relations, protests and importunings from the African, Commonwealth and Latin American nations whose relationships will be affected by the outcome. We must be prepared for this, and with imagination, perception, and resolution, do what is necessary to cushion the impact on ourselves and on our friends.

On the commercial plane, I think it clear that if the United States successfully resists efforts to extend Commonwealth preferences to an enlarged Common Market, we can be reasonably confident that the overall net effect of British adherence will be beneficial to our trading interests. At the same time, we must recognize that the whole process of the economic realignment of Europe is a step of major consequence which will result in inevitable shifts in trading patterns and commercial and other economic effects world-wide in scope.

These shifts in trade patterns will not affect all sectors of American production alike. Some American products will be benefited; others may suffer dislocations. Such a complex process cannot be completed without evoking cries of alarm as the negotiations progress and the implications become apparent to individual affected interests.

From the long-range point of view there is only one appropriate course for the United States to follow—that is to work toward bringing about a progressive reduction in the level of the common external tariff of the Common Market. But in this connection I should like to inject a cautionary note. During the course of the Common Market negotiations there will undoubtedly be proposals that this be brought about by the United States' joining in a bilateral preferential arrangement with the Common Market and abandoning our traditional policy of most-favored-nation treatment.

Such proposals may have a certain seductive plausibility but I can think of nothing more corrosive to the maintenance of our world-wide responsibilities. We cannot be in a position of forming a cabal of the industrialized countries against the rest of the world or of attempting to negotiate a single preferential trading area which would include ourselves and our European friends but exclude not only the underdeveloped world but such powerful and growing nations as Japan.

The proper road to the defense—and, indeed, the advancement—of our trading interests is to pursue liberal trade policies ourselves and to insist that the Common Market do likewise. This means that we must be in a position to reduce our own tariffs on a reciprocal basis. This in turn will require that Congress adopt the most effective possible trade legislation next Spring.

George W. Ball[3]

---

[3] Printed from a copy that bears this stamped signature.

---

17.   Circular Telegram From the Department of State to Certain Missions in Europe

Washington, September 5, 1961, 8:26 p.m.

395. Dept contemplating sending aide-mémoire along following lines to UK and EEC Govts by end of this week. Your comments and suggestions on following preliminary draft text should be available in Washington by Thursday A.M.

Begin Text.

1. The Govt of the United States of America has noted the application of the Govt of the United Kingdom to the President of the Council of Ministers of the European Economic Community for membership in the European Economic Community under Article 237 of the Treaty of Rome and the reply of the President of the Council of Ministers welcoming this step.

2. The successful outcome of these negotiations is bound to lead to profound changes in the existing order of political and economic relationships throughout the world. These negotiations presage a Europe

---

Source: Department of State, Central Files, 375.800/9–561. Secret; Limit Distribution (No Distribution Outside Department). Drafted by Vine; cleared with Tyler, B, and E; and approved by Fessenden. Sent to London, Brussels, Paris, Rome, Luxembourg, The Hague, and Bonn.

united to achieve increased economic well-being for all its citizens and the democratic ideals which are our common heritage. With these goals in mind, the Govt of the United States of America can only express its profound hope for a successful outcome.

3. The Govt of the United States of America is particularly anxious that the changes which might be wrought by these negotiations serve to strengthen the structure of the Free World and provide a basis for the further development of an Atlantic Community devoted to the same objectives.

4. Recognizing that the Govts of the United Kingdom and of the countries members of the European Economic Community share with it the importance of an increasingly liberal trade policy, the Govt of the United States of America, in assessing the outcome of these negotiations, would be particularly concerned that:

a) the present system of preferences obtaining between the United Kingdom and the countries of the Commonwealth not be carried over into any new arrangements;
b) the system of special trade relations with less developed countries now associated with the European Economic Community not be expanded to include additional countries and that this system be reexamined with a view toward eliminating discrimination between regional sources of supply, e. g., by the introduction of orderly marketing arrangements on a global basis;
c) the common external tariff which might result from any new arrangements be set at a level sufficiently low to offset any additional discrimination which third countries not parties to the arrangements might be required to accept;
d) any new arrangements not impair the reasonable access to the market of the manufactures and produce of third countries.

5. If these criteria are met, the Govt of the United States of America would consider that the new arrangements will make a major contribution to the creation of an Atlantic Community and to the strength and unity of the Free World.[1]

Rusk

---

[1] On September 6 and 7, the missions replied that such an aide-mémoire would produce "sharp" or "lively" reactions. The Embassy in London appreciated the reasons for making U.S. views known, but believed it "would be highly undesirable to send aide-mémoire," stressing that it was premature to inject the United States directly into the negotiations. (Telegram 985 from London; ibid., 375.800/9–661; the other responses are ibid., 375.800/9–661 and 375.800/9–761) On September 7 Ball cabled the Embassy in London that the United States would delay sending the aide-mémoire at least until he had talked with Bruce and Heath. (Telegram 1230 to London; ibid., 375.800/9–661)

18.   Telegram From the Mission to the European Communities to the Department of State

Brussels, September 21, 1961, midnight.

Ecbus 177. Luxembourg also for Embassy, Paris also for USRO. From Schaetzel.[1] Under Secretary Ball, Ambassador Bruce met with Lord Privy Seal Heath and Ambassador Pierson Dixon on September 14 for extensive discussion of imminent negotiations between British and Six.[2]

Re organization of negotiations, Heath referred to his recent conversations with Couve de Murville which led to agreement on roundtable approach beginning, hopefully, second week in October. Ministerial level discussions, in which Ambassador Dixon would be British representative, would cover month or six weeks, agreeing and disposing of such matters as possible and remanding other issues for study at expert level. Heath would remain Minister in London primarily responsible for negotiations but would not become directly involved in aforementioned Ministerial activities which would be Dixon's job. Locus of negotiations not yet determined. In answer Heath's question who would be concerned with these matters in Europe for US Government, Ball replied would look to Ambassador Butterworth and USEC as our primary point of contact.

Regarding enigmatic attitude of French and particularly De Gaulle Dixon recited again mildly optimistic impression drawn from his recent discussion with General, noted that De Gaulle had affirmed importance of France and Britain consolidating their historic association. General alluded to convenience of community in providing effective means for post-war relations between France and Germany which would otherwise have been very awkward if handled on bilateral basis.

Ball set forth in detail US attitude toward negotiations against backdrop of US economy today—our balance of payments problem, high level of unemployment aggravated by continuing pressures on labor force due automation and war babies now of age to seek jobs. Country therefore increasingly restless in face of prospective discrimination and fearful of consequences on US interests of expanding and possibly

---

Source: Department of State, Central Files, 375.800/9–2161. Confidential. Repeated to Canberra, Wellington, Ottawa, and 13 posts in Europe.

[1] Ball and Schaetzel visited Europe in mid-September for talks relating to the British application for membership in the Common Market.

[2] A memorandum of this conversation is in Department of State, Central Files, 375.800/9–1561.

autarchic economy. Ball warned that while strong underlying support of US for European integration remained, confluence of American economic difficulties and prospective UK adherence brought to surface latent US fears about effects on our own exports. Of these fears agricultural exports to Europe loomed most important. Europe is America's largest market and agricultural interests remain significant and vocal element in US Congress. Support of this segment of US economic and political society vital to general program of administration and particularly to acceptance of President's 1962 commercial policy program.

Ball repeated central US thesis, namely that US had always accepted inevitability degree of discrimination implicit in European common market but acceptance of this discrimination remained conditional on maintenance and vigor of political content of community and on community adopting liberal policies. In principle, US could not accept continuance or extension of Commonwealth preferences under expanded EEC arrangement.

In response Heath called attention to dependence of such countries as New Zealand on UK market. Said major Commonwealth problems were centered in Canada, Australia and New Zealand. He reiterated that Britain would honor obligations she had undertaken to Commonwealth not to join common market if terms of agreement unacceptable to Commonwealth. He referred specifically to insistence of Parliament that Commonwealth be satisfied.

Heath noted once more obligations British had undertaken to EFTA partners and said that Britain would not enter community on basis unacceptable to Seven. Heath speculated that of course Danes would seek full membership but was less certain of early Norwegian action in view of their recent election. He thought that Portugal might seek membership rather than association. Austria, Switzerland and Sweden would presumably be candidates for association under Article 238.

Ball expressed concern over certain implications of picture Heath painted. While not prejudging arrangements yet to be devised, Ball warned that outcome could be nothing more than European free trade area by another name. Heath recognized that US could not give any advance assurances and accepted fact US would examine proposed arrangements on their merits. Dixon and Heath discoursed at length problems of neutrals and argued value Swiss-type neutralism to Western world.

In response inquiry Heath said British had not overlooked and were studying administrative dangers inherent in expanded community coupled with concentric circles of associate members. Organization of such complexity might be unable conduct effective business.

Heath and Ball agreed on value of maintaining close but informal contacts during developing negotiations with patterns of contact differing according to subject. For instance British welcomed close US collaboration on discussion of tropical products and manner in which Commonwealth African states should be associated with expanded community. Heath also saw value of working out critical and difficult agricultural problems within framework larger than that of UK-Six negotiations.

Butterworth

---

19.   Telegram From the Department of State to the Embassy in the United Kingdom

Washington, October 17, 1961, 12:03 p.m.

2031. For Ambassador Bruce from Ball. I have been seriously disturbed by the impression I have received over the past few weeks that the British do not appear to take seriously our views on the need for ultimate elimination of preferential arrangements as an objective of the UK-EEC negotiations. Heath's statement in Paris reinforces this concern. I shall shortly be sending a personal letter to Ted Heath[1] regarding some of our views.

I hope that in the meantime, however, you would do what you can to impress upon the top levels of the UK Govt the importance we attach to arrangements coming out of these negotiations which protect the interests of all third countries whether Commonwealth or non-Commonwealth and on a non-preferential basis.

I will send letter through you to give you an opportunity to comment.

Rusk

Source: Department of State, Central Files, 375.800/10–1761. Limited Official Use; Limit Distribution. Drafted by Vine on October 16, cleared with Burdett and Fessenden (B), and approved by Ball. Repeated to Brussels for Butterworth.

[1] Not found.

20.   Circular Telegram From the Department of State to Certain
       Missions in Europe

Washington, October 27, 1961, 11:06 p.m.

793. Department is studying intricate problem of possible association of countries with EEC posed by entry of UK and Denmark. This
message sets forth current thinking.

Our political objective with respect an enlarged EEC (i.e., Six plus
UK plus Denmark) is to have tightly knit core group of major European
powers united on common basic principles within economic union and
dedicated to same political objectives. Our position on negotiations between EEC and EFTA as a group was designed to give UK leeway to
disengage and negotiate separately to achieve end of enlarged, but
strong and cohesive European Community.

Department recognizes that element of leeway only temporary. UK
has undertaken important commitment to other EFTA partners to see
that their interests are safeguarded and has made clear that successful
conclusion UK-EEC negotiations depend upon satisfactory resolution
this problem. Issue is bound to come to a head prior to the end of UK-
EEC negotiations.

At the same time we recognize that there are some interests that
must be met of EFTA countries, and in strict justice, of all Western European and affected third countries who will not be included in enlarged
EEC. These interests are largely economic and in this respect do not differ in kind from problems the U.S. has, although they differ in degree.

Way most commonly discussed of meeting economic problems of
countries outside EEC is association under terms of Article 238 of Treaty
of Rome. While Department has not precluded this possibility and has
said too early to opine on eventual solutions, in our view this procedure
not only has little to recommend it, but could produce results contrary to
our major political objectives in Europe. It would do this by creating
patchwork quilt of association agreements which have only one feature
in common, i.e., preferential trade arrangements. This moreover, is
process which has no clear end, since number of potential associates is
legion. Without defining maximum size for workable economic-politi-
cal union, it is evident that increasing number of states associated with it
could so burden Community as to destroy its effectiveness and its ability to move ahead in both economic and political fields. By same token,
while argumentation is often used that U.S. can afford discrimination of

Source: Department of State, Central Files, 375.800/10–2761. Confidential; Noforn.
Drafted by Vine and Schaetzel; cleared with Fessenden, Burdett, and S/S. Sent to 19 missions in Europe.

one or two small additional countries occasioned by new association agreements, we would in fact be faced over long term by a growing number of associated countries united in single Europe-wide preferential trade grouping. Clearly this would not be in our best interest and would encounter strong resistance on part of U.S. business community.

Presently posed alternative of membership of these countries in enlarged EEC appears equally undesirable in foreseeable future since strongly conservative and neutral tendencies of number of them would inevitably slow down moves toward political integration. Reservations they have privately advanced demonstrate extent unwillingness to join in political process to which Heath's statement[1] commits U.K.

Finally, solutions of varying degrees of association tend to ignore the fact economic problem involved is not purely European, but one in which other members of Atlantic Community, particularly United States and Canada, have stake as well.

In Dept's view, one promising approach which could avoid or minimize difficulties outlined above and permits achievement of our political objective of a tightly knit and united group of European states is effective utilization of OECD. As we have suggested to several European countries in response to probing on association (Rusk–Kreisky exchange and Kekkonen–Rusk recent conversation)[2] we conceive OECD as umbrella under which problems arising out of developing regionalism can be discussed and solutions examined.

We are not thinking of Trade Committee of 21, which has not proved useful.

U.S. is prepared to utilize OECD for thorough examination of the problems arising for members and third countries arising out of an enlarged EEC. (See separate cable this subject.)[3] We prepared examine what solutions might be appropriate which would take account of economic and political interests of all members and at same time be sensitive to posture of OECD countries toward less developed countries of world. We believe premature to suggest when this examination should begin on kinds of solutions possible. Should also be clear, however, that whatever steps may ultimately be required need not necessarily be taken in OECD framework.

---

[1] On October 10 at a meeting with Common Market officials, Heath had presented the British proposal concerning its entry into the European Economic Community. An analysis of his statement was transmitted in Ecbus 249 from Brussels, October 17. (Ibid., 375.800/10–1761)

[2] A memorandum of Rusk's conversation with Kekkonen on October 17 is ibid., Conference Files: Lot 65 D 366, CF 1972.

[3] Not further identified.

Within procedural framework outlined above we can visualize discussions leading to recommendations for common policies for OECD members regarding tariffs designed to eliminate dangerous economic split growing up within Atlantic Community and to avoid increased discrimination against U.S. exports. We are already exploring kinds of U.S. legislation best suited permit us work with enlarged EEC to achieve lowest possible level industrial duties.

With applications for association from EFTA neutrals likely in December and possibility that Norway may apply even sooner, a constructive OECD approach will facilitate channeling these pressures along constructive line. Thus way can be kept open for a generalized solution rather than one which involves association or membership in EEC for what are essentially commercial reasons.

Department would appreciate soonest comment from posts most directly affected by these suggestions along with assessment of difficulties and opposition which U.S. likely to encounter along way.

Posts will recognize from this analysis importance of avoiding in any presentations to foreign officials of arguments inconsistent with this analysis.

On this problem, as well as others which will be raised in process of UK-EEC negotiations, it is likely that there will be increasing number of general comments from U.S. public and private sources, which may in some regards not accord with our position. Department wishes again stress para 2 Department's circular 271[4] and note that if posts have any question on use of material not in accord with outstanding instructions or guidances, specific guidance should be requested from Department.

Rusk

---

[4] Dated August 16, it asked recipient posts to report "on current basis" developments that bore on the UK-EEC negotiations. (Department of State, Central Files, 375.800/8–1661)

21.   Telegram From the Department of State to the Embassy in the United Kingdom

Washington, October 30, 1961, 8:39 p.m.

2347. London for the Ambassador. Busec for the Ambassador. From Ball. This week we must come to grips with both the kind and timing of the commercial policy program the Administration will put before the Congress. Several courses of action are being considered.

First, to seek improvements in the present Trade Agreements Act which would permit the United States to negotiate linear cuts with the EEC, but maintaining in diluted form the present peril point and escape clause provisos.

Second, to defer any action until 1963, allowing the Trade Agreements Act to lapse on the ground that the shape of the new trading world is not yet clear. In the interim new legislation would be designed which would take into account the results of the UK-Six negotiations.

Third, to present in 1962 an entirely new commercial policy program the major title of which would expressly and specifically authorize the President to negotiate with an enlarged European Community with the objective of reducing specified categories of industrial tariffs to zero in rhythm with the reductions in internal tariff of Community. The MFN principle would be retained. (We may well try to take temperate and tropical agriculture out of this context no matter the decision reached on the foregoing alternatives.)

This is the most sketchy reference to three of the principal alternatives, but sufficient for the question I wish to pose to you.

There is obviously no easy answer to what the Administration should do. The President's decision must balance out a number of major considerations, one of which is the effect of the Administration's action (or inaction) on the course of the U.K.-Six negotiation. This includes the interest of third countries in U.S. commercial policy, particularly EFTA and the Commonwealth. If we were to go ahead with alternative three the following are several of the pro and con considerations:

A. *Pro*

1. It would avoid the adverse psychological effect on Europe of a postponement or the presentation of a program which might well be construed as little more than the traditional Trade Agreements Act with revisions.

2. Presidential determination to seek a major new program designed to enable the United States to negotiate down the external barrier

---

Source: Department of State, Central Files, 375.800/10–3061. Confidential; Priority; Limit Distribution; No Distribution Outside Department. Drafted by Schaetzel, cleared with Vine and S/S, and approved by Ball. Also sent to Brussels.

of the enlarged community could be of crucial help with the third country problem and thus minimize demands for special arrangements with the Common Market.

3. Determination on the part of the United States to adopt a new commercial program oriented towards the free movement of industrial goods could be used to orient the Common Market towards an outward looking policy at the critical stage in the Community's development.

B. *Con:*

1. The potentiality for talk at cross purposes would be high; viz, the Administration would necessarily be preoccupied with defense of its legislative requests and would be tempted to employ arguments to this end without particular reference to their impact abroad. Contrariwise, the Europeans and the British would be in the most acute stage of negotiations with extreme positions advanced for bargaining purposes, but with the prospect that the positions would be seized upon in the United States as weapons to be used in our own Congressional battle. Considerable opportunity would exist for misunderstanding and political damage on both sides.

2. A disclosure of what authority the Administration intended to seek would deny the U.S. the advantage of keeping the Europeans in the dark. We would not be able to use the veiled threat to act against them if their negotiations seemed to be leading in the direction of a closed European market, surrounded by concentric preferential circles.

3. If the United States were not involved in a full fledged battle with the Congress in 1962, the Executive Branch could concentrate its full force on influencing the European negotiations.

I trust that this illustrative résumé of considerations is sufficient for you to give me your considered judgment on the crucial question, namely the effect of a U.S. commercial policy debate in 1962 on the basis of the third alternative on the successful outcome of the U.K.-Six negotiations. By "successful" outcome I mean of course U.K. adherence to the Common Market on a basis that assures the political and economic integrity of the enlarged community.

Schaetzel will telephone you for your preliminary reactions Tuesday October 31.[1]

Bowles

---

[1] No record of these telephone conversations has been found, but in Ecbus 291, October 31, Butterworth reiterated what he had said in his conversation, emphasizing his assumption that repercussions from any debate in Congress would not mean the success or failure of the UK-EEC negotiations. (Ibid., 375.800/10–3161) Ambassador Bruce, however, reported that, in his judgment, "debate would be very likely to affect the outcome adversely and could hardly be expected to affect it favorably." (Telegram 1833 from London, November 3; ibid., 375.800/11–361)

22.   Circular Telegram From the Department of State to Certain Missions

Washington, November 3, 1961, 9:23 p.m.

848. Dept has noted with interest recent reports that European Community countries are considering further steps toward integration in political and defense fields. Discussions have centered around French draft treaty submitted October 19 to "Fouchet" Committee, which was charged last July by Six Heads of Government to prepare European statute by their next meeting. French draft as described to US officials clearly provides loose "confederal" ties in political and defense fields, falling short of real integration. However a significant feature of French draft is stipulation that present steps are only first stage in a process, subject to complete review after three years.

Reportedly all other members of Six except Dutch are favorably disposed toward French initiative, although there may be efforts to strengthen form of association beyond apparently very loose structure envisaged in French draft. De Gaulle has personally approved French draft and Adenauer reportedly is very enthusiastic. Italians also very favorable and pressing for early progress. Given this combination of circumstances we consider it quite possible that there may be major initiative by Six in political field in relatively near future, possibly at forthcoming Heads of Government meeting which will probably be held beginning next year. This can have significant impact, especially coinciding in time with major step forward in economic field which will result if Six enter EEC "Second Stage" next January.

While UK attitude on these developments not known, should be recalled that Heath in basic statement to EEC on October 11 [10] said: "We desire to become full, whole-hearted and active members of the European Community in its widest sense and to go forward with you in the building of a new Europe." and "One of our main purposes today is to discover afresh the inspiration and the stimulus of working together in a new effort of political and economic construction." In light these forthcoming statements, can be assumed that UK basically accepts fact that Community will develop in political field and is prepared to accept implication of this.

Dept is preparing full analysis which will be transmitted when prepared along with guidance. Following is interim guidance for use by

---

Source: Department of State, Central Files, 375.800/11–361. Confidential; Verbatim Text. Drafted by Fessenden; cleared with Schaetzel, Beigel, and BNA; and approved by Burdett. Sent to Ottawa and 20 missions in Europe.

posts when occasion appropriate for US comment. (US reps should not take initiative at this time):

1. Although we do not believe it appropriate for us to comment on specifics of French proposal, US continues to feel that any moves which maintain momentum toward integration are desirable and what we know of proposed French draft appears to us to be useful to this end.
2. US does not believe it should take position on whether Six should associate UK with discussions. U.S. officials should not comment degree with which UK should now be associated with discussions.

FYI. We assume French and British will discuss this subject on occasion de Gaulle–Macmillan talks this month. End FYI.

3. US does not in principle oppose efforts by Six to develop common policies and closer ties in defense field. We see no more inherent inconsistency between Six role in defense field and NATO than there is between Six role in economic field and OECD.

Bowles

---

23. **Memorandum of Conversation**

Washington, November 6, 1961.

SUBJECT

EEC and EFTA

PARTICIPANTS

Mr. Frank Figgures, Secretary General, European Free Trade Association
Mr. Anders Burass, EFTA Washington Information Office
Under Secretary Ball
J. Robert Schaetzel, B
William C. Harrop, EUR/RA

As substantive conversation began, Mr. Ball and Mr. Figgures agreed that the Heath October 10 presentation to the EEC Foreign Ministers had been excellent. Ball commented that the French now seem to

Source: Department of State, Central Files, 375.800/11–661. Confidential. Drafted by Harrop on November 7 and approved in B on November 14. A memorandum of a similar conversation between Figgures and Tyler on November 7 is ibid., 375.800/11–761.

regard British membership as inevitable and the problem is how it will be accomplished. Ball asked how great a complicating influence the de Gaulle political union initiative might prove to be in Figgures' opinion.

Figgures had not seen the text, but felt it would provide no complications at all. The proposals seemed to contemplate an absolute minimum of real integration—a requirement of unanimous vote on foreign policy decisions meant little and would scarcely trouble the British. To give substance to political union a binding majority vote was essential. The Dutch take it seriously because they resist any commitments before the UK is a member. In reply to a comment from Mr. Schaetzel, Figgures said he thought the Dutch would accept from the British proposals they would resist if made by the French.

Schaetzel asked about Norway, and Figgures said that in the end the Norwegians would apply for full membership. Norway had been independent for only 50 years, and emotional resistance to integration was greater for them than for any other country. Except for the neutrality concept, even the Swedes would have less difficulty with supra-national aspects of EEC. The German invasion of Norway had turned that country from neutrality. Norway traditionally feels closer to the UK, North Sea, and the U.S. than to Europe. Another reason for the present heated debate in Norway was that the EEC issue had by agreement been ignored in the recent election campaign and now was discussed with greater fervor. Norway was sincerely troubled by the possible split in Scandinavian unity, and was interested in seeing Sweden become associated with the EEC.

In reply to Ball's question as to whether the EFTA neutrals were now taking their problems more calmly, Figgures said that this was partly the case and that it was in the power of the United States to assist. The problem was to balance neutrality and commercial interest. It must somehow become clear to all which issues were not negotiable because of neutrality. For example, the neutrals would have to retain their option over the amount of domestic agricultural production they would sustain. They must preserve the right to withdraw at any time from their associate status. By the first of the year the neutrals will be ready to negotiate with the EEC.

Mr. Ball commented that the U.S. had been of service in enabling the British to disengage from an impossible negotiating position—that of all seven EFTA members confronting the EEC at once, or of the UK speaking for all. The UK is not off the hook, Figgures said. Britain remained firm that all EFTA countries must be satisfied.

Ball asked about Portugal's position. Portugal, said Figgures, will have to move for association leading to later membership, on the Greek pattern. The favorable timetable Portugal had obtained from EFTA could be repeated by EEC. The real difficulty was Angola. The Portuguese planned for all practical purposes to merge with Angola as a single country—what would Angola's relationship to EEC be? Portugal would have to obtain concessions for Angola similar to those the UK could obtain for the Commonwealth. Of course if the Portuguese were meanwhile thrown out of Angola this problem would not arise.

Ball said that U.S. policy was absolutely clear in opposition to any piling up of preferential areas. We would object most strenuously to proposals of this nature, and were seeking solutions in other directions. The U.S. was opposed to any extension of Commonwealth preferences to the EEC or even to their continuation over an extended period. We were actively exploring commodity agreements on certain tropical products. Some sort of world commodity system would probably be required also for such items as wheat, butter and perhaps some others. Figgures commented that retention of Commonwealth preferences in the UK market was not the prime objective of UK negotiators. What they sought was protection for those Commonwealth export industries which were centered on the UK market. The answer need not be through preferences.

Ball said that the U.S. has spoken frankly with Australia, New Zealand, and Canada about our opposition to preferences. We will have to sit down before long with all interested countries to seek global solutions to many of these trade problems. Figgures felt that with sufficient leverage from the U.S. an acceptable tropical products solution could be found. He went on to say that it was important that the EEC-UK negotiations be completed, at least in substance, before the next British election campaign, which could come in the summer of 1962.

---

24.   **Telegram From the Embassy in Belgium to the Department of State**

Brussels, November 29, 1961, 6 p.m.

954. Paris For USRO. Geneva for Under Secretary Ball. European Integration. Spaak discussed European integration confidentially with me last night, expressing very serious reservations about developing trend to downgrade importance of political integration, particularly in connection with: (A) French draft treaty of political Union, and B) asso-

Source: Department of State, Central Files, 375.700/11–2961. Confidential. Repeated to Paris, London, Bonn, The Hague, Luxembourg, and Geneva.

ciation of neutral and other countries with European Community. He said he knew US had given full support to European integration only on basis that integration would be political as well as economic, for if there were only economic integration US would ultimately find itself in competition with a European trade bloc which might have discriminatory tendencies without any of long term benefits of a politically unified Europe. In other words, US is willing to accept a measure of economic difficulty insofar as common market is concerned only if political integration envisioned in Rome Treaty is not sacrificed.

Spaak fears decision of Britain, Denmark and other countries to adhere to common market and of neutrals to seek association, coupled with French draft treaty for union of states will, unless there is great vigilance, result in European Common Market being expanded, but price will be death knell of political unification.

Spaak says French treaty of union is not step toward political unification, but is actually retrogressive. He explained Rome Treaty is at present "the bible" insofar as political unification is concerned. If De Gaulle's draft treaty, which does not provide for real political unification, is stampeded through it will then become "bible" on political unification and efforts to use commitment under Rome Treaty for political unification can be countered by argument that French treaty has modified Rome Treaty. (Baron Snoy strongly shares this view.)

This situation, Spaak believes, coupled with fact that some countries desire join European Community only for economic and commercial advantage, presents considerable danger to continued progress in field of political unification. Basically speaking, Spaak does not believe it permissible for a European country to join European Community and benefit from trade and commercial advantages without accepting political aspects. Insofar as European neutrals concerned, Spaak feels that should they be allowed to obtain all commercial benefits of common market through association without accepting political philosophy of Rome Treaty there will be no reason or way to deny equal commercial benefits to Commonwealth countries. One can make strong case, he said, for "association" of country like Greece which shares both political and economic objectives of Rome Treaty but is economically not yet able to assume full membership. However, he is extremely dubious about membership or association of any country that is opposed or does not accept objective of political unification.

In light of foregoing situation Spaak feels US has major stake in present discussions for if European integration movement takes wrong turn we may not only lose large part of political advantages we had counted on but will also suffer serious damage to our trade and commercial interests. He is totally opposed to letting French stampede De Gaulle's draft treaty through in December, for he believes it will play into hands of those European nations which desire to benefit from common market but do not really support European political unification. He said it was with foregoing in mind that he requested postponement of Fouchet Committee meeting of November 29 (Ecbus 347)[1] and asked that Foreign Ministers of Six meet in Paris December 10. Purpose of this meeting insofar as Spaak concerned is to get down to what he calls "brass tacks". Before there is any further consideration of French treaty he wants certain fundamental matters thrashed out, such as: 1) whether European states can participate in economic benefits of European community without accepting ultimate goal of political unification; 2) whether is desirable and feasible to have the so-called neutral states be associated with the common market and what this will mean in terms of Commonwealth problems; 3) whether provisions of "treaty of union" as proposed by De Gaulle will not emasculate or replace commitment of Rome Treaty for political unification and result in real regression and death knell of movement toward politically unified Europe, et cetera.

Spaak said he had talked confidentially but with great frankness, as he recognizes we have just as vital and overriding interests in how European integration movement develops as do Europeans themselves.

MacArthur

---

[1] Dated November 27, not printed. (Ibid., 375.800/12–2761)

---

25.   Telegram From the Department of State to the Embassy in Sweden

Washington, December 20, 1961, 3:57 p.m.

336. Brussels pass USEC; Paris pass USRO. Re Stockholm's 416.[1] Apparent from reftel Department's thinking re complicated question of association with EEC not fully understood. Our position this question falls naturally into two categories: first, an appraisal of the developing

---

Source: Department of State, Central Files, 375.800/12–1661. Confidential. Drafted by Schaetzel on December 19; cleared in draft with Tyler, Vine, Bruce, and S/S; and approved by Ball. Repeated to Ottawa and 14 posts in Europe.

[1] Dated December 16, this 5-page telegram stressed that antipathy to neutral association with the EEC seemed to be playing into Soviet hands and that the short-term disadvantages of association would be balanced by a long-term liberal commercial policy and the strengthening of Western political ties. (Ibid., 375.42/12–1661)

European Community, the directions in which we wish to see it develop taking into account our ability to influence these developments; second, American tactics in immediate future.

Stockholm's 416 contains a major misinterpretation of Department's reservation regarding extension use of association under Article 238 Treaty of Rome. In addition to our natural concern about widening circles of discrimination against U.S., other third countries exports and effect of such discrimination on the Administration's 1962 trade program, Department has been consistently and deeply concerned about possible erosive effects of association on political content of European Community. Scrutiny of Greek association enforces this worry.

Phrase "European integration" to encompass variety forms European cooperation reflects conceptual ambiguity and leads to same semantic confusion which occurred in debate over free trade area and EFTA, in which non-Six insisted development of European Community was breaking up "unity" of Europe. This permitted them to turn over coin and argue that any move which associated Western European countries was ipso facto unifying. Department construes "integration," as it always has, as pragmatic economic and political movement among six European nations leading toward economic fusion on a broad front. Out of this process we have anticipated that political integration would emerge, as Bonn declaration seems to demonstrate. Association of states willing merely to accept limited commercial arrangements with European Community does not fall within Department's concept "European integration."

There has been tendency to construe our reservations regarding association as springing from antipathy for political or military neutrality. U.S. of course prefers and has worked for commitment of Western nations to common defense against a common enemy within the NATO framework. Therefore it is impossible to ignore the fact that we are at policy odds with European neutrals on this central point. However, this disagreement is not at the root of our differences with EFTA over association. Here we are concerned about their insistence on "economic neutrality" with their assumption that it is possible to become a part of one limited aspect of European integration process as conceived by Six. Neutrals have made abundantly clear that they must reserve their full rights for independent action field of economic policy, in short, insistence on sovereign powers in support of policy of economic neutrality.

Reftel suggests that our coolness towards association aimed at neutrals. Quite the contrary—these reservations strike at association in general and rest on concern about the dilution and compromise of the Community which might well flow from overly broad interpretation of Article 238. For instance, British continue reiterate determination obtain association or equivalent for both EFTA partners and Commonwealth.

After July 31 Macmillan speech British Government hard pressed to explain its tendency to give greater importance to accommodating EFTA than to Commonwealth. Backtracking of British in face this Commonwealth attack makes certain that achievement association for neutrals would unquestionably create a major political problem for London. Two unpleasant alternatives would then be on British back: one, U.K. Government would be accused of getting better deal for neutrals than they able to get for Commonwealth or, two, an all-out drive for similar association for Commonwealth which would mean nothing more than creation new far flung preferential area.

Department keenly sensitive to increasing awareness of Soviets to mounting strength and purpose of European Economic Community. Evident that USSR has been slow in assessing this development and extent to which EEC can contribute to frustration of broad Soviet objectives. We expect step-up of Soviet political and propaganda moves aimed at the Community. We are not, however, persuaded that only way to counter these moves to extent they are directed at the neutrals is to promote association of these countries with Community. For sake of argument, if association should be negotiated for Sweden, Switzerland and Austria this could increase rather than decrease Finnish isolation and that of other European non-Six. Alternative case can be made that concerted action by enlarged European Community and U.S. towards substantial MFN lowering of duties only effective way of dealing with problems of non-members. This could meet real needs of countries unprepared to accept full economic and political commitment to the European Community while at the same time exposing non-member countries to market and economic dynamism of EEC.

Thrust of trade legislation to be submitted Congress early 1962 is to empower U.S. Executive with authority to create foregoing situation. The goal would be to establish through negotiation with enlarged European Community a tariff regime so liberal that it would not be significant factor in distorting or diverting trade between Community and non-members. Already signs that this alternative is attractive to important elements in neutral and other third countries.

Department remains of view that on balance broadest U.S. interests not served by extensive use Article 238. All missions should take position when asked that U.S. feels must be continued effort made by all parties to examine actual and specific economic and commercial problems arising out of prospective U.K. adherence to Common Market. In course coming weeks we should join in objective analysis of best means of dealing with these problems. We do not exclude association as one possible answer. We do object to insistence at this juncture that it is only answer.

(See Circular instruction CW 4872, December 13.)[2] While U.S. cannot get in front of Six and assume posture greater opposition to association than EEC, on other hand we cannot afford to act in such a way as to prejudge negotiations between U.K. and Six, a process which has just begun. Department not therefore prepared to endorse Stockholm's suggestion that we should take association as inevitable and garner whatever good-will might fall to us from embracing their ambitions.

Ball

---

[2] Not found.

---

26.   Memorandum of Conversation

Washington, January 8, 1962.

SUBJECT

Meeting at the White House Between President Kennedy and Professor Erhard, German Minister for Economic Affairs

PARTICIPANTS

The President
Professor Erhard
Mr. Lilienfeld
Mr. George W. Ball
Mr. Foy D. Kohler
Professor Heller
Mrs. Lejins, Miss Boure (Interpreters)

Professor Erhard indicated that he considered it a great honor to be able to meet with the President. He conveyed the greetings of Chancellor Adenauer who, like Professor Erhard, was hopeful that the United States would become more determined and clear in assuming world leadership. Professor Erhard stated that in his earlier meetings in the Department today, he had indicated that this was a historical moment.

Source: Department of State, Conference Files: Lot 65 D 533, CF 2029. Secret. Drafted by Kohler, approved in U on January 23 and in the White House on January 29.

Over and above the many things the West was at present doing for the defense and security of the free world, for economic development and industrial production, Professor Erhard had come to realize more and more that, in order to withstand the onslaught of communism and totalitarian mentality, the spiritual strength and values of the West would have to be bolstered. The West needed to develop an ideology in order to survive.

Professor Erhard continued by saying that he had felt a real need to meet President Kennedy. He felt that here was a political force that had freed itself from the conservative past. Here was a man who saw life as a whole and not divided into many different compartments. Unless we can succeed in convincing the people of the world that our present problems must be viewed as part of one indivisible whole, Professor Erhard feels that we shall get lost in a multitude of technical and technological details. Judging by the President's recent talks, Professor Erhard feels that the President has the courage to do what is needed. The Minister had told Mr. Ball[1] that, just as the value of the Marshall Plan had been less of material rather than spiritual or ideological nature, having brought about in Europe a consciousness of the oneness of Europe, what was needed at this moment was a spiritual inspiration which would lift the world above material considerations. Professor Erhard feels that we have reached the crucial hour. The old ideas of a century ago will no longer do. At the same time Professor Erhard wishes to assure the President that in political life it is easier to put across big, broad sweeping ideas rather than small, technical details. The President's ideas on international trade, Professor Erhard continued, are well designed to cope with the dangers of discriminatory actions such as threaten to grow out of, for instance, UK membership in the Common Market. The ills of the world can be healed only by following the type of ideas put forth by the President in this respect, and Professor Erhard promised to do everything in his power to push this approach.

The President indicated appreciation for the Minister's statements. He agreed that discussions concerning the Common Market should not over-emphasize techniques, reserve lists and dollar balances, but deal with the broader aspects to a greater extent. Nevertheless, the President stated, there were a number of matters in this respect which were of concern to the United States. The US had given its support to the Common Market in spite of the degree of economic disadvantage which this would entail for the United States, because of the distinct political advantages which this type of arrangement meant for Western Europe.

---

[1] No record of a conversation between Erhard and Ball prior to this one with the President has been found, but a memorandum of Erhard's discussion with Ball on January 11 on tariffs and trade legislation is ibid., Secretary's Memoranda of Conversation: Lot 65 D 330.

The matters which concerned the President were, more particularly, first, that France had been withdrawing more and more from world concerns since 1945, and the United Kingdom was doing the same, both countries concentrating more and more on Europe. For this reason the United States was left not only with an excessively heavy burden of military commitments in Europe, but also the burden of aid to under-developed countries all over the globe. In other words, the United States was now trying to do to an even greater extent what England and France had attempted at an earlier period. The President was concerned that the United States have the power to carry on the negotiations with the Common Market in such a manner that they would not lead to friction between the United States and Europe, but rather result in the establishment of closer ties. Secondly, the President was concerned about the effect which the Common Market, which meant so much to Europe, would have on countries outside the Atlantic Community, especially the countries of Latin America and Japan, for instance. It was necessary to keep in mind at all times our obligations toward the rest of the world, and the President was hopeful, therefore, that the Common Market would concern itself with the development of these countries and with their security. Latin America was in an especially vulnerable situation, and every effort must be made not to cause any damage to these countries. The countries of Africa were in a somewhat better situation because of their former or present ties with France and England; but real damage could be done in Latin America.

The President then asked Professor Erhard's opinion on what might be done to revitalize the spirit of the Atlantic Community. He enumerated the international organizations such as DAG, OECD and others through which the United States is attempting to work, but he felt sure that additional measures are possible to improve the existing ties so that no country of the free world be excluded from the possible advantages.

Professor Erhard stated that he had always been a strong supporter of the Common Market, but he had also always feared that the stressing of certain economic and political aspects would lead to a kind of European inbreeding. For this reason he had always tried to do whatever he could to keep the Common Market open for the admission of additional countries, since he felt that the larger the area involved, the more liberal it would have to be in the policies it applied. He then turned to the concept of the Atlantic Community, a term which he had been using for about two years. Professor Erhard envisaged the Atlantic Community as a spiritual force rather than an organizational or formalized entity. He stated that he agreed with Mr. Bundy, who had put things in the proper perspective in his recent speech.[2] It was clear to Professor Erhard that there can be no tariff union which does not create different conditions inside and out. Thus, during the next seven to eight years during which the Common Market will be coming fully into effect, there will be constant bickerings with third nations who feel discriminated against, and the European Community will have to spend a great deal of time to listen to these complaints, to make adjustments, make gifts, heal wounds, make compromises and appease. The only way to improve this type of situation, as Professor Erhard sees it, is to follow the lead indicated by President Kennedy by adopting an extremely liberal policy which would place the entire non-Communist world on one and the same footing. This would result in real strength. The Minister stressed that he knows whereof he speaks. He himself lowered German tariffs, unilaterally, at a time when it took real courage to do so, and therefore he feels that he can appreciate the President's situation, and can permit himself to speak of these matters. The West is in a bad situation. Although Professor Erhard knows US military power, and Germany is extremely thankful to the United States for the support given in the Berlin question and to West Germany as such, Khrushchev can come up at any time with a statement that Western "capitalism" is decaying, dying, and devoid of spiritual force, and that the future belongs to Communism. What can the West reply to all this? We can hardly counter this type of statement by citing automobile statistics or other production figures. We must have an ideology. We must have the faith that the West is and will remain united. We must not always be beset by Khrushchev's idea that we are existing within an obsolete capitalistic system. We must awaken the realization that this is a new era, with new ideas and with new content; but we have not yet accomplished this. Professor Erhard shares Chancellor Adenauer's view that Europe, which is not a political unit and in which there is a great deal of diversity, cannot assume spiritual leadership. Therefore Chancellor Adenauer and Professor Erhard would be happy to see President Kennedy consolidate his Administration and assume world leadership with determination. Unless the free world can show unity to the outside, it cannot hope to maintain itself vis-à-vis communism.

The President stated that he is of the conviction that we ought to emphasize to the outside world that the basis premise of the communist interpretation of the world situation is wrong. The Communists are constantly speaking of the decay of the Western World, while our efforts to draw closer to the Common Market are an actual reversal of Communist

---

[2] For text of Bundy's address to the Economic Club of Chicago, December 6, 1961, see Department of State *Bulletin*, March 12, 1962, pp. 419–425.

prophesy. It is the West that is drawing closer together, while the Communist world is falling apart.

Another problem which is of concern to the President with regard to the relations between the Atlantic Community and the rest of the world is that it would be most unwise to give the impression of our creating a rich white man's club. The Common Market is not enough for the solution of the world's problems. For this reason the President is appreciative of the intentions expressed by Professor Erhard with regard to Latin America and the Asian and African countries, all of whom are so very much dependent on us and who will judge or determine their future conduct by what we now do. Thus, if the Common Market is to become more than an economic exchange, it must concern itself with the needs of the under-developed countries. Both Germany and the United States will be called upon to do their utmost in this respect. France did a great deal in the past, but concerned itself primarily with its colonial territories. The United Kingdom had done a good deal but now finds itself in difficult straits. Italy has not done very much and probably never will. That leaves Germany and the United States to carry the brunt of the burden. The United States, this coming Thursday, will recommend the largest aid program in its history, with three to four billion dollars of aid planned for this hemisphere, including one billion dollars for the year. The President expressed hope—he had discussed this matter with the Chancellor in the spring—that Germany would be prepared to play an ever greater role in the aid program. If Germany will not go along in this, the efforts of the Western world will fail, because the United States does not have sufficient resources to do it alone.

Professor Erhard stated that he had been fighting in Germany since 1953 to awaken the realization there that once the needs of the German population were taken care of, Germany should fulfill its obligation vis-à-vis the rest of the world. Professor Erhard was happy to see that Germany has been assuming this responsibility increasingly, especially since 1959 and 1960, and that the understanding of this problem has been achieved to a gratifying extent. He indicated that in the period 1960–1961 Germany committed itself—although this has not been paid out in cash—to foreign aid payments in the amount of 1-1/2 billion dollars or six billion marks. He is convinced that the needs in this respect will grow rather than decline. At the present moment, Professor Erhard stated, it is not known what obligations Germany might have to assume in connection with the special arrangements which might become necessary as the result of the association of the African countries with the Common Market. He pointed out that the German situation with respect to foreign aid differs somewhat from the situation of the United States. For instance, it is extremely difficult to raise the necessary budgetary means in Germany, and it should not be forgotten that Germany's gross national product amounts to only 80 billion dollars as compared to the 550 billion dollars of the United States. At the same time, Germany is in a more favorable position than the United States with regard to trade balances and payments surpluses and the resulting absence of transfer problems. Professor Erhard feels that Germany has done justice to its international obligations by making the necessary debt prepayments and by making its defense purchases overseas. That too, he feels, contributes toward an improvement of the free world financial situation. Nevertheless, Professor Erhard is prepared to work for increased aid efforts, since he views this matter not so much as an economic, but as a moral question. President Kennedy indicated that he fully recognized what Professor Erhard had said but that he was eager to stress that without German help the United States could not hope to accomplish the necessary aid assistance on a global scale. While the agreement reached in the fall by Mr. Gilpatric was a definite help, there was no denying that the United States was carrying an extremely heavy burden as the result of its troop commitments in Western Europe, the aid programs in the Far East and Latin America and the military commitments with reference to the Congo, to mention but a few. The fact that the United States has lost 5-1/2 billion dollars in gold during the last four years showed that the well was not bottomless. For this reason it was important that a certain ratio be established between a country's gross national product and the amount it was prepared to put into foreign aid. France had been contributing somewhat over one percent, but most of this had been directed to its colonial territories. The President hoped that the Common Market would not assume France's obligations in this respect but would devote itself to other and additional programs instead. Moreover, the kind of aid being given was of considerable consequence. If very high interest rates were demanded, the loans thus extended did not prove really helpful in the economic development of the under-developed countries. At the same time the donor-countries should also consider accepting re-payment in local currencies. The President pointed out that the matter of foreign aid was always a very difficult one to justify before the US Congress. Matters would be much easier, however, if we could go before the Congress and show that a country which once upon a time was the recipient of such aid itself is now our full-fledged partner in our endeavors to help the world. The loss of US gold has been a very serious matter and has had its effects. Only if Germany is prepared to assume its full share of the responsibility can we hope to convince our Congress of the merits of our aid plans.

Professor Erhard indicated his conviction that the stability of the dollar is a very vital concern to the entire world. Germany feels that this is Germany's problem too, and he so told Professor Heller. Professor Erhard pointed out, however, that he himself is more confident in this respect than US opinion appears to be.

Then Professor Erhard stated that he would feel better if he were absolutely convinced that the aid that is being given is really the correct thing. Unfortunately, he is not entirely convinced that these very generous gifts are the best kind of aid. He fully realizes that one cannot expect to apply the usual type of commercial terms to matters of this kind, but he fears that too great generosity may not necessarily be the best thing. At the same time, he pointed out that Germany was on the way to adapting itself to the apparent needs of the aid program and might be willing to consider eventually accepting local currency. It was very important, however, to discuss these matters thoroughly, particularly the best kind of aid, and he was sure that DAG would take these matters up. Professor Erhard pointed out that something appeared to be wrong if one considered the truly remarkable contribution made by the United States in the foreign aid field, and the results thereof, and then looked at how little the Soviet Union had done and the reaction of the world thereto. Professor Erhard felt prompted to ask whether it had been the right investment. Perhaps it could be done better. Professor Erhard continued to say that he was afraid that the six member countries of the Common Market would take over the French aid obligations instead of devoting themselves to additional programs. He could not say so finally, but this is how it appeared to him. Perhaps Germany could assert influence and leadership in this respect.

The President indicated that the Soviet Union had a much easier problem with regard to foreign aid than the United States. The Soviet Union could achieve a great deal of effect by concentrating its efforts on a few selected spots, for instance, United Arab Republic, Indonesia, or Guinea, or, in Latin America, Ecuador, Bolivia, and Brazil, while the United States had the entire non-communist world or an entire hemisphere to deal with.

Professor Erhard voiced the opinion that perhaps we are not doing the right selling job from a spiritual or an ideological viewpoint. We must be able to awaken the under-developed countries to the fact that by association with us they can save their lives and improve their lot in freedom. This, however, is the area of our weakness, and Professor Erhard has not found the answer.

The President came back to the question of the French contribution and that it would not be desirable if this amount were now spread over the six countries of the Common Market. Much more was needed with reference to Africa alone and Mr. Kennedy was hopeful that France might be persuaded to continue to carry the load with reference to the former French colonies and that the other Common Market countries could therefore be spared for other aid programs.

Professor Erhard indicated that a few millions one way or another don't matter so much. Of greater importance was that in the equatorial area of Africa a preference zone might be created which might discriminate against another equatorial territory, namely Latin America. This would result in a very bad situation.

The President fully agreed and expressed the hope that what with British and French interests in their former possessions, the Common Market would not concentrate its efforts in the same area. Latin America and its development was of concern to the entire free world. If Germany, for instance, would stop buying its coffee and bananas in Latin America and shift to Africa instead, this would lead to disaster.

Mr. Ball interjected at this point that the problems created as a result of the African situation were under discussion with the Common Market and that it was hoped a preference system might be avoided and a free flow of trade be attained by attacking the problem on a commodity basis.

Professor Erhard stated that with reference to this problem Germany had already proposed that if a preference system were established for Africa, then the tropical or subtropical products of all countries were to be accorded a 50 percent cut in tariff and that within a six years' period, when the Common Market will become finalized, the tariff on such products the world over should be brought to zero.

The President stated that he had accorded so much time and emphasis to this matter because the situation of Latin America was an extremely precarious one and like a razor's edge, since the countries there depended on three or four commodities, a small shift with reference to these could result in complete collapse. He mentioned Brazil in this connection.

Professor Erhard replied that he would certainly take home one thing from his present visit to the United States and this would undoubtedly have a political effect. He promised to try seriously to do away with the high consumer taxes still levied on coffee, tea, and similar products, which were no longer justified. If the President indicated that such procedure would help improve the situation in Latin America and was in line with American policy, Professor Erhard was prepared to make every effort in this direction.

The President indicated that this would be a great help. Professor Heller added at this point that he could remember the days when joint efforts were made in Germany some years ago to increase the taxes on such matters since it was considered wise for Germany to keep such products out. But times had changed.

Professor Erhard stated that the whole world had changed unexpectedly in many ways. Thinking back of the Marshall Plan, he recalled that Europe thought in those days that the dollar gap would be with us eternally; now it no longer existed. This showed what could be accomplished with political will and determination. Professor Erhard was convinced that the present currency problems would likewise be solved in time.

In closing, the President indicated that his brother would visit Berlin and Bonn in February.

---

27.   Circular Telegram From the Department of State to Certain Missions

Washington, January 12, 1962, 4:01 p.m.

1247. Ball–Heath talks provided most useful exchange of views on our trade legislation and direction our foreign economic policy and on progress of UK-EEC negotiations.

On Commonwealth issues, discussion was confined to questions of principle. We indicated that medium term essentially transitional solutions were matter for UK to examine with Six, and that longer term arrangements had to be compatible with a sensible global structure and that medium and long term should dovetail. Agreed that we must busy ourselves to create long-term framework consonant our mutual objectives. We made strong point that our trade legislation would contribute to solution many problems of Commonwealth.

Major portion of discussion focused on EFTA neutrals. Ball restressed position spelled out in Schaetzel–Lee talks (see CW 4872)[1] that other feasible alternatives should be examined. He noted that we had serious reservations on association as a principle, although clearly recognized trading problems of neutrals with which we sympathetic. We stated that neutrals appeared to be essentially preoccupied with trading problem and that it should be resolved as such. We stated further that we were strongly of belief that our trade legislation would create a situation in which the reasonable trade requirements of the neutrals could be worked out.

Source: Department of State, Central Files, 375.800/1–1262. Confidential. Drafted by Vine and cleared in draft with Ball and Schaetzel. Sent to Ottawa, Canberra, Wellington, and 14 missions in Europe.

[1] Not found.

UK position was that it had made a pledge, a political commitment to other EFTA partners and was not prepared to place this commitment in doubt. They asked whether US would still take this position if UK later on had to make choice whether enter EEC or not on basis of EFTA association. Under Secretary replied that he hoped it would not come to that.

Under Secretary noted that our position, as has consistently been the case, is that we are prepared examine any proposed arrangements, including association. If association were to be alternative proposed we would test against GATT.

When British asked if we would make this position clear to the Six, we said that we have taken this position both with Six and with neutrals themselves.

Detailed Memcon is being sent by pouch.[2]

Comment: Talks were on the whole useful. Dept did not anticipate that UK could do more than elaborate position it has taken on which it must stand until negotiations are further along. We wished make certain that our viewpoint clearly understood, and believe this objective attained.

Rusk

---

[2] Memoranda of the conversations with Heath on January 6 are in Department of State, Secretary's Memoranda of Conversation: Lot 65 D 330.

---

28.   Telegram From the Department of State to the Embassy in Belgium

Washington, February 23, 1962, 9:59 p.m.

2200. During visit February 20 Spaak and Under Secretary discussed European Integration.[1] Ball opened meeting by asking Spaak for

---

Source: Department of State, Central Files, 611.55/2–2362. Secret. Drafted by Beaudry, cleared with Cleveland and Vine, and approved by Tyler. Also sent to London, Bonn, Paris, Rome, and Luxembourg.

[1] Memoranda of these conversations are ibid., Secretary's Memoranda of Conversation: Lot 65 D 330.

his impressions of recent de Gaulle–Adenauer conversations.[2] Spaak replied that he had very little information. He had seen a vague document on subject from German sources, which gave impression that all areas of confusion remained. In Spaak's views de Gaulle wants nothing serious in direction of political Europe. He noted that in December it was decided to make tie between political and economic integration by requiring any country wishing join economic community should also join political work growing out of Bonn Declaration.[3] Spaak expressed opinion there was no real chance for revival of the integration movement on political side while General de Gaulle in power, but Spaak maintained his hopes for the future, as de Gaulle's policy was not that of France and as five other countries have made it clear that they are opposing the French Government on this issue.

Under Secretary asked Spaak for his impressions British negotiations. Spaak replied that they had not yet really begun. Thus far negotiations limited laying out positions and certain amount of sparring. Spaak concerned that organization of conferences was wrong as there is nobody responsible for providing the political push which is necessary to make the negotiations work. Under these circumstances they will inevitably bog down in detailed discussions. Spaak suggested it would be possible change structure of negotiations. Indeed, he thought that time would come very shortly when new proposals should be made in these sessions. Reception these proposals by French would be test of real will succeed. (De Bassompierre of the Belgian Embassy subsequently passed on message from Spaak that he wanted make clear his view that discussion change organization of conferences was imminent necessity, and if it did not take place within next two months or so there was a real danger that conference would not succeed.)

Mr. Spaak gave his opinion that on balance de Gaulle did not want British in, as it might threaten France's leading role in community; he pointed to de Gaulle's letter to Khrushchev[4] which made clear that France desires speak in Four-Power councils on behalf of Europe, which Spaak said Europe would not accept. In answer to question from Ball whether de Gaulle might be easier deal with after Algerian settlement reached, Spaak said at first he thought there would be no change, but as he thought about it more, he concluded that General would be if anything more difficult afterwards. Concerning British position Spaak's opinion it was important from their viewpoint that negotiations not last

---

[2] February 15.

[3] A reference to the communiqué of the Heads of Government meeting of the Common Market, July 18, 1961, which instructed a committee to draft proposals for political union.

[4] For text of this letter on disarmament, see *The New York Times*, February 20, 1962.

too long—say no more than three to five months longer. Under Secretary noted apparent deterioration of the domestic climate in United Kingdom and need for movement in negotiations to keep up momentum. Ball had received the same impression after talks with Mr. Gaitskell.[5] Spaak agreed that as the negotiations stagnated, there was on the whole a tendency for the opposition to become stronger in the UK.

With respect association problem Spaak said countries asking for association were in fact asking for permission pick and choose things they liked in Treaty and reject others. This proposition was unacceptable as such arrangements could seriously hold back both economic and political development Europe.

In summing up, he believed the American position on association was entirely correct and hoped we would hold to it. Spaak said he believed Italians generally shared his viewpoint and that the Germans would probably go along with it, while others were considerably less sure. When Under Secretary asked Spaak why he thought British had been so strong on this subject, Spaak replied that the British had led the neutrals on in matter of EFTA and now felt they could not afford abandon them.

Rusk

---

[5] A memorandum of Ball's conversation with Gaitskell on February 19 is in Department of State, Central Files, 375.800/2–1962. A memorandum of a second Ball–Gaitskell conversation on February 24 is ibid., 375.800/2–2462.

---

29.   Telegram From the Embassy in Belgium to the Department of State

Brussels, March 20, 1962, 4 p.m.

1749. Paris for USRO. Embassy telegram 1744.[1] When Ambassador saw Spaak last evening latter had received news from Minister of

---

Source: Department of State, Central Files, 411.004/3–2062. Official Use Only. Repeated to Geneva, Paris, Bonn, Rome, The Hague, Luxembourg, and London.

[1] Dated March 19, telegram 1744 reported that the Belgian Ministry of Foreign Commerce had been informed that morning about U.S. tariff increases on carpets and glass. The immediate Belgian reaction was that the increase was "unfortunate" and would not only damage U.S.-Belgian trade relations, but also have repercussions on the other EEC members. (Ibid., 411.004/3–1962) A memorandum of the conversation during which Trezise informed representatives of the Belgian, British, French, Italian, German, and Japanese Embassies for the tariff increases is ibid.

Foreign Trade Brasseur re tariff increases on carpets and glass. Spaak was restrained, saying GOB "shocked and Brasseur wild" by our action. While he would not wish to make a further official comment until he had received full report, he wanted Ambassador to know frankly and on personal basis that general impression within GOB was that he had engaged in very sharp if not unethical practice. He did not understand how we could take such action when we had just completed long and difficult tariff negotiations under GATT in which there had been give and take and where European nations had made very considerably greater concession to United States than they had received from us. Our action gave rise to unfortunate impression that we had deliberately extracted all possible concessions from Europeans while apparently knowing all along that we were going to take action against glass and carpets after we had gotten maximum in GATT negotiations. Spaak said our action came at unfortunate time and fears there will be great hue and cry in Belgium and among other members of Six which may have adverse affect on President's new trade legislation.

He particularly regrets that some may use our action to question American good faith at a time, he said, when Europe needs to have full faith in American leadership if NATO and free world unity and strength are to be maintained.

Ambassador explained to him great difficulties of this problem for us and reasons for our action along lines of action Secretary Ball's message (Department telegram 2512)[2] which Ambassador also conveyed to Spaak. Ambassador expressed strong hope this matter would be kept in perspective and not unduly inflated.

Spaak said this was serious matter which he would wish reflect on and would be in touch with Ambassador after his return from Luxembourg which he is visiting today in connection with European integration matters.

Spaak's whole attitude was one of sorrow rather than anger.

MacArthur

---

[2] Dated March 17, the message to Spaak reads:

"I am aware of the seriousness with which the Belgian Government views the proposal of the US Tariff Commission to increase duties on certain types of carpet and glass which are of particular importance to Belgian trade with the United States. It is for this reason that I wish to inform you personally that the President has considered all aspects of this problem carefully over a period of time, and he feels that he must accept the Tariff Commission's recommendation to raise duties on these items. The decision was taken in the context of the presently existing legislation in the United States. I realize that you will be disappointed at this decision and I regret that in this instance this action was necessary. As you, we are trying to devise other ways to deal with problems of this kind." (Ibid., 411.004/3–1762)

30.   Telegram From the Department of State to the Embassy in Belgium

Washington, March 21, 1962, 6:07 p.m.

2545. Re: Embtel 1749.[1] Belgian Ambassador called on Dept officer (Trezise) March 21 under instructions to express shock Belgian Government at US decision accept Tariff Commission recommendations increase duties on carpets and glass.[2] Amb Scheyven emphasized that Belgians not convinced that difficulties US Wilton carpet industry caused by imports but rather are due competition domestically-produced tufted carpets. Regarding glass Scheyven expressed Belgian view that evolution US economy contradicts thesis that US glass industry suffering from foreign competition. He commented that new duties on glass would damage Western European suppliers but would not injure Communist countries engaged this trade.

Reviewing strain on US/Belgian relations resulting from US support UN Congo operations, Ambassador expressed serious concern that US decision this instance would cause further difficulties between US and Belgium. Scheyven said it would be difficult convince Belgian public that Belgium had not been singled out by US for discriminatory treatment since only two items on which tariffs raised were those of major interest to Belgium. Ambassador suggested that further Belgian reaction would soon be forthcoming and indicated that US action on carpets and glass might have adverse effect on Belgian attitude toward Textile Agreement. Ambassador assured Trezise that new tariff rates on carpets would effectively eliminate all such exports which account for one-half total Belgian foreign sales this item.

Scheyven also noted that new tariff rates would become effective within thirty days of announcement and suggested that this was extraordinary speed considering the long delay in making the announcement in these cases.

Ambassador emphasized U.S. action inconsistent with project reduce tariff barriers recently concluded Geneva. He noted U.S. action not taken until after Geneva tariff agreement concluded. He indicated against background Geneva negotiations Belgians and rest of EEC as well would find it difficult understand both timing and substance our

Source: Department of State, Central Files, 411.004/3–2062. Confidential. Drafted by Beaudry, cleared by Weiss, and approved by Trezise (E). Repeated to Paris, Tokyo, Geneva, London, Bonn, Rome, The Hague, and Luxembourg.

[1] Document 29.

[2] A memorandum of Trezise's conversation with Scheyven is in Department of State, Central Files, 411.004/3–1962; similar memoranda of conversations with the Netherlands and Luxembourg Ambassadors on March 23 and 28 are ibid., 411.004/3–2362 and 3–2862.

action. Belgian Commercial Minister, who accompanied Ambassador, suggested U.S. action taken with view obtain domestic support for new U.S. trade legislation and said Belgians and others are finding price of such legislation costly.

Trezise said that Department understands seriousness this matter for Belgium and assured Ambassador that Department had brought to White House attention Belgian views this matter which had been so fully presented by Belgian Embassy. While thus aware these considerations, the President felt obliged take this action in view requirements of Trade Agreements Act and report of Tariff Commission. Trezise strongly emphasized that there was never any attempt to single out Belgium on this matter.

Department Officer (Weiss) pointed out that thirty day period for application tariff increases normal practice and stated that long delay announcing decision was due thorough consideration all aspects, including foreign policy problems which Department had presented to White House in detail. Weiss explained that through proposed trade legislation US seeking other means handle vexatious problems of this nature. Trezise expressed hope that increase in duties as finally applied would not injure trade as seriously as Belgians feared.

Ball

---

31.   Telegram From the Embassy in Belgium to the Department of State

Brussels, March 22, 1962, 11 p.m.

1774. Paris for USRO. Spaak and Foreign Commerce Minister Brasseur convoked Ambassador last evening and handed him formal note (translation in following cable)[1] protesting strongly against our tariff increase on carpets and glass. They said our action was not only a major economic blow against Belgium but would have most serious social and political consequences in Belgium. It had created such a crisis that Brasseur had been obliged to cancel his long scheduled official trip to London with Prince Albert this week.

Source: Department of State, Central Files, 411.004/3–2262. Confidential; Priority; Limited Distribution. Repeated to Geneva, Paris, London, Rome, Luxembourg, The Hague, and Bonn.

[1] Telegram 1776, March 22, not printed. (Ibid.)

Speaking with great heat and bitterness Brasseur then reminded Ambassador of support he had given Acting Secretary Ball in connection with GATT, OECD, cotton textile and other matters. He recalled it was Belgium, acting on our urgent request (Embassy telegram 497)[2] that had first initialed cotton textile accord, thus preparing way for rest of Six to do so. Belgium, he said, had mistakenly believed that US regarded her as a friend and partner. Now it was clear US Government does not regard cooperation as two-way street and has no understanding of Belgium's problems. US obviously views Belgium as small insignificant country that can be disregarded since it has no retaliatory power. He remarked how differently we behaved when large, important country such as Japan was involved, and noted that whereas all four items President had considered (carpets, glass, ceramic tiles and baseball gloves) are important to Japan, we had balanced our action with respect to Japan by only acting unfavorably on two whereas we had shown no consideration for Belgium. Furthermore, since Japanese carpet industry wages were much lower than in Belgium, net effect of our action on carpets would be to exclude Belgian carpets totally from US and permit Japan to fill this import gap. He thought we would soon find a universal belief in CM countries that we had acted in bad faith.

Brasseur said he assumed we knew our action would oblige Belgium to retaliate. He deeply regretted this, because inevitably it would weaken NATO solidarity and create serious problems between US and Europe. Europe was no longer a weak non-entity and had ability to retaliate. In fairness he wanted us to know that insofar as he is concerned Belgium will not sign and implement Geneva cotton textile agreement where we apparently are going to act in similar fashion as in carpet and glass matter and place additional 8-1/2 cent per pound compensatory tariff on imports of cotton textiles. Belgium is also already in touch with other five members of Six urging them also to refuse sign and implement cotton textile agreement. Furthermore, Belgium has also requested Six to make urgent and immediate study of recently concluded GATT negotiation commodity list with view to have CM countries take supplementary retaliatory action against items in recently concluded GATT negotiations, which are of particular importance to US.

Brasseur concluded by stating our action in raising duties on carpets virtually 100 percent and on certain types of glass almost 150 percent would wall these products totally out of American market. Belgian Government fully understood US Government under some pressure from carpet and glass manufacturers just as Belgian Government is under pressure from some of its industries to raise tariffs against certain American and other foreign products. If we had felt it essential to take

---

[2] Dated September 19, 1961. (Ibid., 394.41/9–1961)

some action we could have granted partial increases in tariffs on both carpets and glass, which would have given some relief without taking action to exclude all Belgian carpets and glass from American market since these industries totally dependent on US market. Our action would result in the loss of jobs of some 4,500 to 5,000 Belgian workers, and a reduction in Belgian exports to US of 14 to 16 million dollars worth of carpets and about 8 million dollars worth of glass. While we might derive satisfaction from these results he thought in long term we would pay an infinitely greater price in terms of NATO solidarity and trade and commercial relations between US and Europe.

Ambassador defended our action making reference to Acting Secretary Ball's message to Spaak (Department telegram 2512).[3] However, Brasseur brushed explanations off, saying material which Belgian Embassy had submitted to Department clearly refuted basis on which we alleged our action was necessary, and that for us to invoke "urgency" on a matter which had been under consideration for months with not undue damage to American industry was "inadmissible."

Spaak then spoke briefly with restraint but deep concern repeating comments he made to Ambassador March 19 (Embassy telegram 1749),[4] saying our action had created deplorable impression re lack of good faith and would place great stresses and strains on unity and cooperation of West. At a time when wounds to US-Belgian relations from Congo were healing it particularly deplorable. He would be sending a personal message to Acting Secretary Ball very soon in response to latter's message.

Comment: We have reported violence of Belgian reaction in detail as there is no useful purpose in trying to minimize it in this restricted message. Our action has, as Spaak says, opened up old wounds in Belgian-American relations stemming from Congo, and there is mounting protest and bitterness. We do not know if anything can be done to soften blow but we urge any possibilities be considered as much more serious than reopening Congo wounds is potential adverse effect on Atlantic unity and future economic and trade cooperation. We do not know whether Belgium will be successful in dissuading other Common Market countries from implementing cotton textile agreement, but suspect that if we add eight and one-half cents per pound compensatory tax on cotton textiles, the six may refuse to implement it as a mark of solidarity with Belgium.

MacArthur

---

[3] See footnote 2, Document 29.
[4] Document 29.

32.   **Telegram From the Department of State to the Embassy In Belgium**

Washington, March 31, 1962, 3:59 p.m.

2689. Bonn Hanainy for Ball. Belgian Ambassador visited Trezise March 31 at our request. Trezise stated he wished express Dept's serious concern over potentially unfortunate consequences which might result if pattern of recriminations and threats of retaliation continues in Europe against decision increase carpet and glass duties. He emphasized that the European reaction could not fail cause hardening views within United States. Trezise stated we wished to express our concern to Belgian Government before the situation gets out of hand.[1]

It was pointed out that there are a number of groups in the United States aggrieved over trade restrictions in Europe, for example, farmers and coal producers, and their spokesmen would be happy have opportunity stress such grievances. Inevitably, talk of retaliation in Europe will excite suggestions of counter-retaliation here, in U.S. press and in Congress. Exchange of mutual recrimination cannot help anyone, certainly not U.S.-Belgium or U.S.-EEC relationships.

Recognizing that Belgians do not agree with escape clause findings, they should remember that existing Trade Agreements Act requires President take account of Tariff Commission findings, declining employment or production or profits or relatively increasing share of imports in total consumption. President has asked for new Act that would enable us handle injury cases in different fashion but for now we bound by terms existing legislation. Kind of situation that appears to be developing, however, will not help us get new and more flexible authority deal with import adjustment problems.

As Ambassador knew, GATT Article XIX provided procedures under which Belgium and EEC could seek recourse. We prepared consult promptly under Article XIX and indeed were drafting instructions our Geneva mission at this very time. In response Ambassador's question meaning of "promptly" we replied we ready consult whenever Belgium or EEC ready. We suggested site consultation might best be Geneva or Washington where expert personnel available, in order expedite talks.

Finally, Trezise observed that if Belgian comments on lack of merit of escape clause findings had validity, this fact would become evident

---

Source: Department of State, Central Files, 411.004/3–3162. Secret. Drafted by Beaudry and Trezise, cleared with Weiss. Also sent to Bonn, Paris, The Hague, Rome, Luxembourg, and Geneva GATT.

[1] On March 31 the Department of State sent circular telegram 1654 to 20 posts in Europe stressing that the Belgian campaign against the tariff increases went to unreasonable lengths and asking the posts to use every opportunity to counter it. (Ibid.)

after reasonable period experience with new duties. Existing Executive Order requires review of case within two years and permits earlier review on initiative of Tariff Commission or on request of President. Only after experience with new tariff has been developed could any judgment about possibility reconsideration be reached. However, Dept would propose watch developments carefully and would be ready recommend review if warranted by events. Ambassador should understand, at the same time, that acrimonious row that appeared building up would obviously make more difficult any future reconsideration this matter. Finally we emphasized strongly that any public discussion possibility of review escape clause findings prior expiration two years would be highly prejudicial.

Rusk

---

33.   Memorandum of Conversation

Washington, April 9, 1962, 4 p.m.

SUBJECT

The Common Market

PARTICIPANTS

Mr. Hallstein, President of The European Economic Community (EEC)
Mr. von Staden, Chef du Cabinet EEC
The Secretary
The Under Secretary
Ambassador Butterworth
J. Robert Schaetzel

President Hallstein began by expressing his gratitude for the help which the United States had given the Community over the years and indicated that the integration process would not have reached its present maturity without this assistance. The Secretary affirmed the deep commitment of the United States to the European Community, and while it was not for us to say how the process should develop in all of its details nonetheless he could reiterate the broad political commitment.

The Secretary said that he had several questions he would like to put to President Hallstein, the first of which related to the timing of our

---

Source: Department of State, Secretary's Memoranda of Conversation: Lot 65 D 330. Confidential. Drafted by Schaetzel and approved in U on April 19 and in S on April 20. Memoranda of Hallstein's conversations with Butterworth, Freeman, Hodges, and the Attorney General during his visit to Washington are ibid., Central Files, 375.800/4–962 through 4–1262.

trade legislation debate on the U.K.-Six negotiations. He noted that when we were considering our legislative program Washington had worried about whether this might introduce a new complication into European affairs.

President Hallstein replied that there had been no sign of any difficulties nor had their negotiations been in any way adversely affected. He noted that in fact the United States legislative strategy presupposes that the U.K. will join the Community.

Mr. Ball injected that the legislation had been carefully drafted in such a way as to do just this.

The Secretary indicated his surprise and pleasure at the exceedingly favorable United States reaction to the trade program; the most satisfactory progress in the hearings, the widely favorable editorial comment—all this against his somewhat more pessimistic anticipations and indeed his expectations that there would be more bloodletting.

President Hallstein added that as far as other countries were concerned, particularly the Swedes and the Swiss, he felt that the President's Trade Expansion Program might very well contribute to the solution of their problems. On the other hand, Austria was on the outside and in a special status and in a confused domestic political environment, not clear just what to do.

Mr. Ball observed that the problem of the neutrals was one that would have to be left for a near final stage of the negotiations at which point a solution would be found.

The Secretary referred to the deep anxiety of the countries on other continents about the effect of the enlarged Community on their interests. While he was aware that no one can deal with any precision with these anxieties until the negotiations are finished, he suggested that it might be possible for the EEC to keep in close touch. The Secretary mentioned in this connection the worries of Brazil. President Hallstein said that unfortunately they had not been in too close communication with third countries although he said he would be seeing Mr. Mora in the course of his visit here in Washington. President Hallstein suggested that in his view the problem of third countries was more psychological than substantial. It was difficult because the Community wished third countries to be more specific but at the same time recognized that it was quite impossible for them to be so at this particular moment.

Ambassador Butterworth injected a personal observation that one of the problems was the fact that the Latin Americans, for instance, merely accredited their diplomatic representatives to Belgium to the Community. By and large these diplomats were not known for either their expertise or their ardor and much benefit would derive from improving the competence of these officials. President Hallstein said he had no reason to disagree with Ambassador Butterworth's observation.

In responding to a question from Mr. Ball, President Hallstein said that some headway had been made on the extension of the European agreement and on the lowering of preferences, but not as much as he had hoped for. Earlier it had looked as though the French would be prepared to compromise but at the most recent Council of Ministers meeting their position had hardened. Nonetheless, he was convinced that by December 31 when the present European agreement expired a solution would be found, recalling the observation of Pisani at the time of the agricultural debate, "We are condemned to agreement."

Secretary Rusk asked what effect the new association arrangements would have. President Hallstein surmised that it would probably not be possible to cut the level of preferences by 50% without compensation and yet it was difficult to determine what compensation was acceptable to all the parties. He also noted that the main point of the present system was the assured markets in France. President Hallstein speculated that it might be possible to find some inelegant but tolerable arrangement whereby the African states could be assured access to the French market.

Mr. Ball emphasized the impact of European arrangements on Latin American and other third countries and the sensitivities of these countries to the resulting arrangements. In this connection President Hallstein noted the psychological ramifications of the problem. The present generation of Africans is very pro-European, anxious to replace the old colonial ties with a relationship with the new Europe. Therefore a special association, which would have both political and economic advantages (which it might not be possible to develop with the next African generation), should be established in the near future.

The Secretary hoped that the Community would move in the direction of closer economic and political relations with Latin America over the next few years and stressed that the time had passed for special relationships between the United States and Latin America. President Hallstein indicated his understanding of this point and was in agreement with it.

In answer to an inquiry as to what President Hallstein would like to see the United States do at this moment of European affairs, President Hallstein asked for understanding; that while the new Europe might be moving too slowly on some points, nonetheless they are trying to do the best they can in the circumstances. President Hallstein agreed with Mr. Ball that United States pressure on the Community was most useful and that we should keep it up, not only with respect to the broad problem of tropical products but in other areas as well.

In this general connection the Secretary said he wished to deny categorically one canard that he heard from time to time, namely that the United States was interested in taking over the old colonial areas. He could not deny this too categorically and noted that our plate was already quite full enough.

Returning to an earlier topic the Secretary suggested to President Hallstein that the latter might very well speak to Mr. Mora about the desirability of raising the level of competence of Latin American ambassadors stationed in Brussels. Mr. Ball noted that a representative of the Organization of American States was apparently to be assigned to the OECD and it was suggested that this individual might also be assigned to Brussels. The Secretary suggested that thought might be given to assigning two or three among the Latin American wisemen to the Community.

The Secretary then inquired about the pace of the U.K. negotiations. President Hallstein felt the stage had been reached where each side must agree to be more specific about the concessions necessary for agreement, as the real negotiations are about to begin. He agreed with Mr. Ball that it looked as though the British objective would be agreement in principle with the Community by the end of July leading to a general debate in the Commons prior to the summer recess, but with a definitive debate at the end of the year following the Prime Ministers' conference in September and the Conservative Party conference in October. The Secretary inquired as to whether the Conservative government was in touch with the Labor Party and seeking their support. Mr. Ball said there appeared to be a somewhat different strategy on the part of the British Government, namely that if the Conservatives hold firm Labor would not exploit the situation, but if there should be evidence of division among the Tories then there would be a great temptation to seize upon the U.K. move towards Europe as a major political issue. Ambassador Butterworth noted the Conservatives seemed to be taking considerable satisfaction in the disunity of the Labor Party on this question. President Hallstein expressed his view that the Conservative Party wanted to get the matter settled between now and the end of the year so that it would be forgotten when the elections in Britain were held, presumably in the spring of 1964.

Returning to the initiative in the political field, President Hallstein noted the constructive compromise formula which had emerged from the recent meeting of Fanfani and de Gaulle.[1] Fanfani had stood firm on the critical issue as to whether the heads of government would have authority in the economic field and had been successful as well in estab-

---

[1] April 4.

lishing the point that nothing in the new political field would be done which would undercut the Treaties of Rome and Paris. President Hallstein said he still was uneasy about the suggestion that the heads of government could discuss economic matters which were within the competence of the European Community. It would be possible for the heads of government in conference to restrict the Council of Ministers which operated under special rules, voting and otherwise, as provided for in the Treaty. An erosive action of this nature could hinder the great progress which had been made in a body of ministers supporting the Community rather than merely representing the national states. In this connection President Hallstein said he felt there had been two issues which could create a real crisis in the integration process. The first was in the field of agriculture, and here Chancellor Adenauer had been indispensable. The second was still unsettled, and that was whether the proposed political community would undermine rather than contribute to the integrating process.

Mr. Ball inquired whether there had been any sign that the French intended to inject the nuclear issue into the negotiations when the chips were down. President Hallstein said he had nothing more than a suspicion and felt this matter might very well have been a part of the periodic U.K.-French bilateral discussions. He admitted that he had not been able to confirm this suspicion, however.

---

34.   Telegram From the Embassy in Belgium to the Department of State

Brussels, April 18, 1962, 5 p.m.

1959. As agreed with Myer Feldman and Trezise in White House meeting April 11,[1] I met alone with Foreign Commerce Minister Brasseur April 17 to cool him off on carpets and glass and try to deter him from unhelpful statements and retaliatory action against US during vitally important period of congressional consideration of President's trade expansion legislation. I took helpful line suggested by Feldman, emphasizing that while decision on increased duties on carpets and

---

Source: Department of State, Central Files, 411.004/4–1862. Confidential; Priority; Limit Distribution.

[1] No other record of this meeting has been found.

glass is final, President is personally interested in arriving at mutually satisfactory solution and we prepared make meaningful concessions during Geneva Article 19 negotiations to compensate for trade lost as result of tariff increases. In confidence discussed reasons why Belgians should be patient in Article 19 negotiations which, because of their complexity, probably could not successfully be concluded for three months or so. Also indicated that while negots will be carried on in Geneva Belgians may always bring their views to President's attention through Mr. Feldman if they feel situation so warrants.

I then pointed out that existing executive order requires review of escape clause action within 2 years and permits earlier review in certain circumstances. In strictest confidence I indicated personal view that we would be willing consider review of escape clause action after it had been given reasonable trial for period of year. However, there could be no commitment as to outcome of such a review and this possibility was for private and confidential information of Spaak and Brasseur only.

Concluded by stressing to Brasseur great importance of our working closely and intimately together on this difficult problem in spirit of mutual understanding and give and take. Emphasized that if our tariff increase action on carpets and glass resulted in threats and retaliations by Belgium and CM countries it would harden views within US and in long run do great damage to European cause of Atlantic solidarity. Therefore, while knowing what disappointment increase in tariffs on glass and carpets were to our Belgian friends I trusted we could work to avoid situation developing unfavorably for all concerned.

Brasseur replied with some feeling that while he had always been and continued to be friend of US and strongly believed in cause of Atlantic unity, our action had not in judgment of GOB been justified, our timing had given impression of bad faith and Belgium had no recourse but to defend itself. Furthermore, members of Common Market and other countries such as Japan "were incensed" by our action and were urging Belgium, which had been most injured, to lead retaliatory struggle against US. Insofar as compensation under Article 19 was concerned, GOB did not see how we would be able to give meaningful compensation in light of position we had taken in Dillon round discussions and in any event whatever compensation was forthcoming would not help those Belgian industries destroyed by our action.

I went over situation again at great length with Brasseur explaining cogent reasons which required US in long term interest of both Europe and US to increase tariffs. If Belgium wished to begin an all out trade war we could not prevent them, but frankly believed in long term Belgium and Europe would pay unacceptable price. Any such dispute would be tragedy for all and I urged him to think positively rather than negatively, assuring him again of our sincere desire to cooperate in finding concessions with which Belgium could live. In conclusion pointed out that in light of our increases in glass prices, I understood Belgian glass industry might not be as badly damaged as Belgians had first anticipated, and that it was most important that GOB not react hastily and that it give time to assess real effect of our action on both carpets and glass and compensation we proposed to offer before thinking of any retaliatory action.

Brasseur simmered down and said he believed in our sincerity and appreciated very much my frankness. He would of course be willing not push Geneva Article 19 negotiations too fast and appreciated reasons why they might take about 3 months. While he understood difficult problem President had faced, we must recognize that GOB also faced with explosive political problem. He wished to describe situation with complete frankness as follows:

Despite views of Belgian glass industry, in Brasseur's own judgment this industry, while hurt, would not suffer mortal damage as result of our action, particularly if tariff increases could be reviewed after reasonable period such as a year with possibility of some amelioration. On other hand, carpet industry was "mortally wounded" and unless something is done numerous factories which for years had produced largely for American market would go under. There was no possibility of converting these plants to other production and end result would be widespread unemployment in certain key carpet producing areas with ensuing economic distress and great political hue and cry. Even if we reviewed carpet situation after a year and reduced tariffs damage would be done since affected industries could not convert and operate during one whole year and would lose their markets to other suppliers such as Japan which because of lower labor costs could still enter our market. It was essential from Belgian viewpoint to find some way to ameliorate carpet problem and if we could do so he promised not to press us on glass and also to use his influence with other members of Common Market to handle entire problem of glass and carpets with temperance and in way designed to avoid retaliation and recriminatory statements. He therefore hoped President would find some means to defer tariff increase on carpets or reduce amount of tariff increase so that affected carpet industry would not go under.

I reiterated to Brasseur that President's action on tariffs was final and it would only be possible to consider modifying tariffs after reasonable time had elapsed and if facts and circumstances then so warranted. Brasseur replied that with imagination there must be something we could do to ameliorate carpet problem in such way as to permit him to "unfuse political bomb" that our action had created in Belgium. If we could do nothing on carpets except give him secret personal assurance we would look at matter again after lapse of a year, it would be totally impossible politically for Belgian Government to keep situation in manageable bounds and to sign textile agreements since Belgian textile industry was also affected by action against carpets and would not tolerate GOB signing. If GOB did not sign other EEC countries would also refrain. He was not saying this as a threat, but simply stating political fact. He fully agreed that Belgium should not take retaliation against us and should try to work out some solution within framework of Article 19 of GATT. For his part he was willing to do so and also to do everything possible to avoid stirring up trouble. For example, an American news agency and Belgian radio and television had yesterday asked him to appear at press conference to lay out Belgium's position with respect to carpets and glass. As result our talk he would put them off, as he feared that what he would be obliged to say because of Belgian internal political considerations would inflame situation further.

At same time, he wished specifically request me to let White House know in confidence of our talk and that Belgium could live with glass situation, but some amelioration of carpet problem seemed essential. He did not know what could be done, but with imagination and good will he hoped White House and our experts could find some proposition which would give partial satisfaction to Belgians and at same time meet President Kennedy's own difficult domestic political problems relating to trade expansion legislation which he fully appreciated. At all costs he wished to avoid Washington having any impression that he was trying to engage in blackmail or threats. He was only asking for tool that could enable him and Spaak to meet a most critical domestic political problem caused by carpets and glass which had serious implications in terms of future US-Belgian and US-European relations. He concluded by reiterating it was essential to do something about carpet problem and that only Spaak would know of our talk. [3 *lines of source text not declassified*] I said I would of course report what he had told me, and would be in touch with him in due course when I heard from Washington.

Comment: I was encouraged by Brasseur's general attitude, his obviously sincere desire to avoid recriminations and retaliatory steps against us, and his confidential statement that GOB could live with glass problem on basis of appropriate compensation under GATT Article 19. On other hand, I was disappointed that I could not shake him on the carpet problem which obviously has difficult and emotionally charged political implications. I personally am inclined to doubt somewhat his statement that if Belgium does not sign textile agreement other EEC countries will necessarily refuse to sign unless Belgium makes a major issue of it in terms of Common Market solidarity. I gave him no encouragement whatsoever that President could modify tariff action on carpets. I do not know enough about technical, political and other elements involved to know whether there is anything we can do. If something can be done we will, as Brasseur puts it, be able to "unfuse bomb" and should be out of woods on carpets and glass insofar as both Belgium and Common Market are concerned. If there is nothing further we can do or say, then we will have to try to ride out storm and run the risks of re-criminations and retaliatory steps against us, which I will do my best to reduce to minimum. Would appreciate reaction to foregoing as soon as feasible.[2]

MacArthur

---

[2] On April 27 MacArthur was informed that after further discussion with Feldman it was not practicable for the United States to go beyond the position which he had taken with Brasseur. MacArthur should inform Brasseur that the White House and the State Department understood the seriousness of his domestic problem, but that failure to ratify the cotton agreement or other retaliation would help no one. (Telegram 2965 to Brussels; ibid.) On April 30 MacArthur met again with Brasseur who was "crestfallen" that the United States could do nothing on the carpet problem. Brasseur stated that the tariff issue would now become a Common Market question, and unless some satisfaction were given, retaliation would follow. MacArthur was convinced that Brasseur was the key to the issue and suggested that the problem of compensation be discussed under GATT to gain time to come to an agreeable solution. (Telegram 2053 from Brussels, April 30; ibid., 411.004/4–3062)

---

35.   Circular Telegram From the Department of State to Certain Missions in Europe

Washington, April 27, 1962, 6:35 p.m.

1844. In handling questions related to European political and de-fense treaty and particularly aftermath of Foreign Ministers' Conference on April 17, following is position recommended to Secretary for NATO Ministerial in Athens:

1) Because of the sharp differences of view among the Six, and the crucial role of the British in this issue, we should refuse to be drawn into any discussion of the pros and cons of this issue. Any indication that the U.S. was taking sides in the matter would complicate still further an extremely complex issue. We should make explicitly clear that we are keeping out of this.

2) We can handle this issue by stating that we have three desiderata:

Source: Department of State, Central Files, 396.1–AT/4–2762. Confidential. Drafted by Vine, cleared with Schaetzel and WE, and approved by Cleveland and Kohler. Sent to Bonn, Brussels, London, Luxembourg, Paris, and The Hague.

(a) a successful conclusion to the U.K.-EEC negotiations;
(b) a great interest in seeing progress toward political and defense cohesion among the Six which would strengthen NATO and the Atlantic Alliance;
(c) the desire to see the most tightly knit organization formed consistent with political realities and the temper of the times.

3) We should be careful then explicitly to point out that an appropriate balance among these factors is a matter for the Six countries and the U.K. to negotiate among themselves and any expression of views by the United States in the matter would probably be unhelpful.

Posts should follow this line for present. FYI. Dept's analysis of recent developments this subject is as follows:

Spaak appears to have seized on Heath's statement in WEU to serve both of his somewhat paradoxical aims. Spaak wants the U.K. in Common Market; "Europe" without Britain will be incomplete and low countries, without British counterpoise, will be forced to follow line of Paris-Bonn axis. He further convinced that de Gaulle may block British entry into EEC and consequently into political union.

Spaak also bothered by desire of French and de Gaulle to create confederal Europe based on sovereign states, which he considers the antithesis of the supranational Europe centered around the Brussels institutions. Although he is advocate of British entry, he is interested in a Treaty which makes revision necessary after given period of years in order examine question of majority voting. He wants British to have to accept this principle before they enter Common Market rather than have them join de Gaulle in solidifying conception of separate sovereign states operating on unanimity principle.

He thus wants to assure British entry into EEC without French interposing obstacles and achieve a commitment from both British and French that political institutions may become more supranational in time.

The Athens meeting will see furious negotiation in the corridors among the principals to put this back on the track. Heath will try to restore atmosphere of UK-EEC negotiations by pointing out that Spaak has gone further than British position and that Heath's statement misunderstood.

Spaak, however, is kingpin. He will wait till others come to him. He may try to assure British that he will keep open final ratification of political treaty as a hostage to assure that French do not try block U.K. entry. In return for this commitment, Spaak would presumably ask U.K. to agree revision clause at some future date which involved possibility of majority voting.

With French, he will ask for agreement on acceptable revision clause as price for his agreement to treaty at this time, although he will make his final agreement on signature and/or ratification contingent upon no major French obstacles to U.K. entry.

Spaak's objectives, both with the British and the French, are those we share but any overt intervention by the U.S. at this time would only lead to further recriminations. Spaak has apparently sufficient leverage to make progress on his own. End FYI.

Rusk

---

36.   Summary of Discussion

Washington, April 28, 1962.

SUBJECT

U.K. EEC Negotiations

The Prime Minister opened the discussion by saying he would like to tell the President about the status of the U.K.-EEC negotiations. Much of the spade work had been done, and by the end of July a general pattern should have been established on major issues. The British Government would then have to make up its mind. On September 10 the Commonwealth Prime Ministers would meet. The Government would then decide whether to put a proposal to proceed before Parliament. The Prime Minister could not honestly tell now what the answer would be. Obviously, Britain had to take care of Commonwealth interests and those of its friends in EFTA. There would have to be some continuation of the advantages Commonwealth members now enjoy, as no British Government could stand which tried to put forward an agreement regarded as abandoning them. Furthermore, it would be wrong to abandon Britain's EFTA friends, and reasonable arrangements would have to be made for them. With one half of Europe at least temporarily lost, it would be a tragedy if the remainder was divided into two blocs. He wanted the European Community to be not an inward-looking grouping but an outward-looking and developing organization. The Prime Minister hoped that we would not take a too-unfavorable view of the neutrals; they were part of European civilization and tradition. Some,

---

Source: Department of State, Central Files, 840.00/4–2862. Secret. No drafting information appears on the source text. Macmillan visited Washington April 27–29.

such as Finland, had neutrality imposed on them by their geographic situation; Austria was neutral, but he had observed himself the Austrian delight at the Soviets' departure.

The Prime Minister expressed his appreciation for the help we had so far given in the British application; he would describe our attitude as benevolent neutrality. The Prime Minister thought he could carry the U.K. with him into the Common Market; it was an exciting and dramatic moment. The British people thought that joining the Common Market was historically right and sound economically and politically but the task would be impossible if it were portrayed as a betrayal of the Commonwealth, and especially the old Commonwealth countries. If Britain succeeded, it would play a great part in Europe and bring Europe closer to America; if it failed, Britain's whole policy would have to be reconsidered. This would involve an agonizing reappraisal. If the views of some countries which wished to keep Britain out prevailed, it would mean that Europe was pursuing an inward-looking policy reverting to the days of Charlemagne.

The Prime Minister remarked that two major problems confronted him; the Brussels negotiations and, secondly, persuading the British population that joining was in accord with their traditions and interests. It was the biggest decision by the U.K. since Britain lost its last foothold on the Continent. Leadership had fallen to him, but he would not predict how things would work out; the whole project could easily be overthrown, even at the last moment, by an appeal to emotion. The Prime Minister said it was his responsibility to lead the country away from its traditional approach, and there were indications that the new larger concept was growing. Nonetheless, there was still strong, even violent, opposition to joining by important segments of British opinion.

The President noted that this administration, as had the previous one, supported the Common Market for political, not economic reasons. Ambassador Bruce had pointed out that the Common Market was not in U.S. economic interests. The President commented that Britain's joining Europe could be the biggest action since the Marshall Plan. He recognized the Commonwealth problem, and realized that the Labor Party had not committed itself. We had to balance our economic interests and the political advantages we foresaw from the Common Market; if after Britain joined and if her dependencies also went in, this would leave the U.S. and Latin America outside. Obviously, the political consequences of the economic effects of such a situation would be very serious. Britain could not take care of everyone in its wake as it joined. Our balance of payments problem would be accentuated, and possibly cause us to withdraw our forces overseas, now costing us $3 billion annually, from around the world. While we realize that certain built-in preferences must be temporarily continued, we think there should be commodity negotiations on a world-wide basis, with preferences terminated by a fixed date.

As to the neutrals, the President remarked that we had every sympathy for Austria, and wanted to proceed carefully; we were less sympathetic toward Sweden and Switzerland which wanted the best of both worlds. The President noted that Mr. Heath and Mr. Ball had had a good talk,[1] and there was understanding of, if not agreement on, our respective positions. We recognized that the decision was up to Britain, and we might not be able to influence it. We were prepared to make many sacrifices but could not go all the way.

Mr. Ball explained in some detail the U.S. position with respect to Commonwealth preferences and the EFTA neutrals. Temperate zone agricultural products posed the most serious problem as far as Commonwealth preferences were concerned. In the recent Geneva GATT negotiations we had tried unsuccessfully to obtain assurances that our position would be protected; if Canada, Australia, and New Zealand were to be granted an assured market for wheat, this would cause difficulties here. As to products now receiving preferences in the U.K. market, we advocated global solutions for the great export crops. We could not, Mr. Ball said, accept continuation of preferences, without a termination date, until an agreement was worked out. As to industrial preferences, Mr. Ball said we saw little justification for the continuation with respect to high-cost products from the older Commonwealth countries; and have told the Canadians as much. We supported the British effort to put industrial raw materials on the free list. Mr. Ball paid tribute to the British attitude and actions toward low-cost manufactures, and encouraged the U.K. to disinvoke Article 35 at the conclusion of the current negotiations with Japan, as we understood they were planning to do.

Mr. Ball explained our concern about preferences for African tropical agricultural products, stemming from our conviction that these would cause acute disturbances in Latin America. We recognized the U.K.'s situation with respect to the African Commonwealth countries, that the U.K. could hardly do less for them than had been done for the former French African territories. Our approach was on a commodity basis, and we hoped agreement could be reached by the end of five years. Reverting to the problem of the EFTA neutrals, Mr. Ball emphasized that had we viewed the Common Market only as a customs union we would have had grave doubts about giving it our blessing. We were convinced that our new trade legislation would greatly ease the problem for non-member countries by achieving further liberalization of

---

[1] A 14-page memorandum of Ball's conversation with Heath on April 4 is ibid., 375.800/4–462.

trade, including the Community's. Special attention was required for hardship cases, but they should be approached as trading problems.

In summing up, the Prime Minister said he hoped Britain could enter the Common Market. All its influence would be used for liberalization, as liberal trade is part of an old tradition for the U.K. He agreed with Mr. Ball about raw materials. He thought that if Britain were rebuffed it would try to build up more preferences and fight to live as it had in the past. He said he must warn the President that pressures against entry, compounded of tradition, a continuation of national sentiments, instinct, and a dislike for things abroad, were very strong. He was convinced he could teach new attitudes, but the U.S. must help occasionally. The Commonwealth countries asked what would happen to them after the transitional period; Britain replied they must adjust. But, they inquired, how? Some of the smaller things caused the greatest trouble; the Prime Minister cited the example of old soldiers settled in New Zealand and taught to grow pineapples. They could do nothing else. Were whole communities to be allowed to suffer? Time was required to permit adjustments.

Present at the meeting in addition to the President and the Prime Minister were:

U.S.

Under Secretary Ball
Ambassador Bruce
Mr. McGeorge Bundy, White House
Mr. Pierre Salinger, White House
Mr. William R. Tyler, Acting Assistant Secretary of State
Mr. William C. Burdett, Acting Deputy Assistant Secretary of State
Mr. Joseph Sweeney, BNA

British

Sir Norman Brook, Secretary to the Cabinet
Ambassador Ormsby Gore
Sir Evelyn Shuckburgh, Deputy Under Secretary of State, Foreign Office
Mr. Harold Evans, Public Relations Adviser
Mr. M.A.M. Robb, Information Minister, British Embassy
Mr. John Thompson, First Secretary, British Embassy
Mr. Philip de Zulueta, Private Secretary to the Prime Minister

37.   Circular Telegram From the Department of State to Certain Missions in Europe

Washington, May 4, 1962, 9:32 p.m.

1895. Following is preliminary summary based on uncleared memcons of discussions with Gorbach and Kreisky re Austrian relations with EEC on which posts may draw for guidance:[1]

1. Austrians presented moderate and measured statement their traditional position on relations with the EEC stressing:

a. Dependence on trade with Community;

b. Urgency of need for solution in view expected rapid impact discrimination on Austrian economy;

c. Willingness to accept a degree of economic integration with Community. Described what they were seeking as an "arrangement" rather than using word "association."

2. President and Acting Secretary explained Austrians were told we wished be helpful in finding solution Austrian problem. We did not consider "association" with Community desirable and hoped pragmatic approach would produce practical solutions which would meet four principal objectives which we believed we shared with Austrians:

a. Keep Austria tied to West;

b. Not interfere with development of process Western European political and economic integration based on European Communities;

c. Meet Austria's economic problems; and

d. Not create grounds for Soviet protest or violation Austrian neutrality.

3. Acting Secretary reiterated our feeling that association Austria with Community under Article 238 Rome Treaty objectionable on political grounds because:

a. Could lead to Soviet charges breach neutrality in view fact "association" involved political tie to Community, and Community was organization with political and possibly defense implications. Acting Secretary stressed that we could not see Community playing kind of role we expected of it without somehow becoming involved in Western defense.

b. Association of neutrals with Community could create situation where every new step forward towards closer political union among members Communities would be delayed or frustrated by question whether this created new problems for neutral associates.

4. US pointed out that Austria's economic position in terms dependence trade with Community similar to that of number of other

---

Source: Department of State, Central Files, 375.800/5–462. Confidential; Priority. Drafted by Cleveland, cleared with WE and U, and approved by Tyler. Sent to 12 missions in Europe.

[1] Memoranda of the conversations with President Kennedy and Acting Secretary of State Ball on May 3 are ibid., Conference Files: Lot 65 D 533, CF 2086.

countries in Europe and outside. It was primarily to deal with these problems of third countries (including US) that President had proposed trade expansion program, and we believed action under that program would deal with substantial part of trade problems Austria and other third countries. However, we recognized that Austria as involuntary neutral was in special position and we therefore particularly anxious be helpful finding solutions to its problems. This reason, we would favor possible special arrangements between Austria and Community to deal with especially difficult residual problems not covered under negotiations pursuant Trade Expansion Act.

5. Acting Secretary added that as concerns Austrian desire align its economic policies more closely with Community, this would seem possible through bilateral arrangements and in OECD. In any case, stressed our belief that more active Austrian role OECD desirable in order create closer ties with West in a forum to which Soviets could not object.

6. Replying to Acting Secretary, Austrian FonMin Kreisky stressed four points:

a. His view that Austria must remain in step with Sweden and Switzerland, as failure do so could lead to Soviet charge Austria being granted special concessions in order encourage Anschluss. For this reason, he (Kreisky) and "half of Government" feel Austria must keep in step with other two neutrals.

b. Austria as prewar political football recognized importance political unity Western Europe and did not wish do anything interfere with it.

c. Austria strongly supported OECD because of US membership. However, not certain yet whether OECD would be able to play necessary role; was essential it pass from research to action. If OECD could be made into real instrument for economic coordination, this might help solve Austria's problems with regard coordination and integration economic policies.

d. Austria supported pragmatic and flexible approach to solutions its problems. Envisaged "exploratory discussions" between three neutrals and Community, in course of which could decide what next steps should be. Next steps he mentioned explicitly included possibility separate rather than joint negotiations with EEC.

7. *Comment:* Austrian position appeared considerably less rigid in these talks than in previous discussions. We are particularly encouraged by Kreisky's emphasis on pragmatic approach and desire not interfere with political progress European union. We have impression Austrians went away with a clearer and more sympathetic picture of US position, including an understanding of our sympathy for Austria's special role, and an inclination to make serious effort to find pragmatic solutions.

Ball

38.   Telegram From the Department of State to the Embassy in Belgium

Washington, May 18, 1962, 6:33 p.m.

3242. Brussels for Embassy and USEC. Paris for Embassy and USRO. Brussels 2182, 2184, Ecbus 899; Geneva TAGG 617 and 619; Rome 3063.[1] Council preparations for retaliatory step of withdrawing recently granted concessions and public announcement thereof not well received here. Open threat of retaliation which now posed by EEC may create serious difficulties for us and if pursued to conclusion especially on tobacco will inevitably result in general hardening of attitudes. In past US has consistently agreed to consider compensation instead of resorting to retaliation in comparable cases involving Article XXVII tariff increases or impairment of concessions and has consistently sought amicable solution of problems in GATT. Same consideration due to US in carpet and glass case.

US had made clear from beginning it prepared to discharge fully its obligations under Article XIX this case and intended to negotiate restoration of balance of concessions. To date however EEC has refused to even entertain possibility of compensation and on contrary has devoted energies and publicity to preparations for retaliation. US intends to table meaningful compensation package in Geneva next week as initial down payment on amount owed and will be prepared thereafter to explore with EEC additional steps which could be taken once Congress grants President additional authority. Possibility working out solution along these lines only realizable, however, if EEC willing meet US halfway and tones down talk of retaliation. If EEC begins retaliation as procedure for GATT instead of compensation, implications should be apparent, not only for economic but also political relations.

1. Butterworth requested convey foregoing to Hallstein and Rey and indicate concern that EEC may be pushing issue close to point of no return for both parties.

2. MacArthur requested inform Brasseur that despite Council action we proceeding as promised to table best compensation offer possi-

---

Source: Department of State, Central Files, 411.004/5–1762. Confidential; Niact. Drafted by Coster (OTF) and cleared with Trezise, Tyler, Beaudry, Vine, and Feldman. Repeated to Geneva, Rome, Bonn, Paris, and The Hague.

[1] TAGG 619 and telegram 3063 from Rome are dated May 17; the remaining telegrams, May 16. (Ibid., 411.004/5–1662 and 5–1762) On May 15 the EEC Council of Ministers took the position that if the United States did not modify its decision to increase the tariffs on carpets and glass, the EEC would retaliate by withdrawing its previous tariff concessions on American products. The cables under reference reported this decision and early reactions to it.

ble at this time which will be of substantial proportions. We cannot complete our package by weekend because of need for formal inter- agency and White House approval but will cable you soonest summary containing significant items of interest to Belgium. This will represent maximum possible under present legislation but we will be ready con- sider further steps once President has new authority. (FYI. Delay in completing preparation compensation offer due to fact that almost all items available peril pointed and some especially sensitive at this time; interagency agreement has therefore been difficult obtain. End FYI)

3.   All addressees should note US tactic is to avoid appearing flus- tered by threats of EEC and member countries and make clear its inten- tion submit compensation package on assumption EEC will consider seriously. Addressees should avoid sharp reactions if this subject raised in conversations but stress dangers of retaliation and potential implica- tions for our relations. Dept's assessment is that Six are presently serious in carrying out line to which they now appear committed. Six would ap- pear have no qualms about increasing tobacco duty in view past history this commodity. If this assessment correct, implications are extremely disturbing. Without directly approaching host governments, Dept would appreciate assessment by addressee posts of likelihood EEC withdrawal recently negotiated concession on tobacco.

Rusk

---

39.   Memorandum of Conversation

Paris, May 21, 1962, 10:30 a.m.

PARTICIPANTS

> Minister of Foreign Affairs, Maurice Couve de Murville
> Under Secretary of State George W. Ball[1]
> Ambassador James M. Gavin

I had a one-hour conversation with the Foreign Minister Monday, May 21, with only the Ambassador present. The discussion was con- fined very largely to the problems and implications of the entry of the United Kingdom into the European Community.

I began the discussion by recalling the consistent American support for the Community and for the development of a United Europe. This support had been motivated primarily by political considerations. We

---

Source: Department of State, Conference Files: Lot 65 D 533, CF 2111. Confidential. Drafted by Ball on May 29. The meeting was held at the Quai d'Orsay.

[1] Ball visited Europe May 17–23 for discussions on various economic questions.

had seen in the development of a United Europe, a means of containing Western Germany and tying it irretrievably to the Western World. Because of our emphasis on political unity we had discouraged British efforts either to build a European Free Trade Area or to merge the Free Trade Association with Europe, since we had regarded these efforts as a step toward diluting the political content of Europe. However, we were persuaded that the British were now on the verge of a major national decision. While no British politician would dare to admit it, we were persuaded that the British were preparing to reverse four hundred years of policy toward the Continent. More and more thoughtful Englishmen recognized that their destiny no longer lay in being the center of a world system—a posture they could no longer afford—and that their historic role should now be played out within a European framework. We were therefore of the view that if the United Kingdom became a full member of the European Community, the British would work toward progressively greater unity and would not drag their feet.

I reminded Couve that when this matter had been originally discussed with the British we had made clear that we would welcome their decision to seek membership in the Community only if they were, on their side, ready to accept the full commitments expressed and implied of the Rome Treaty and were willing to regard the Treaty not as a static document but as a living process.

They were now, we felt, prepared to play a full role in Europe. What remained was the working out of technical problems. This required good faith and pragmatism on both sides. Obviously not only the United Kingdom but the Six had to show flexibility. Some accommodation would have to be made for the special problems of Britain just as major accommodation had been made for the special problems of France at the time the Treaty was negotiated originally.

We felt it necessary to emphasize that while we did not think it useful for Britain to seek a relationship with Europe that would compromise the political character of the Community, we had always felt that the Community would be incomplete without British participation. So long as Great Britain remained outside the Community, it would operate as a lodestone drawing with unequal degrees of force on different parts of the body of the Community. Thus Britain, outside the Community, would remain an element of disintegration but, inside the Community, Britain would ensure European cohesion.

The Foreign Minister replied to this long statement by the assertion that he agreed with most of what I had said. However, he was inclined to disagree somewhat on our appraisal of British intentions. This was of course a matter of judgment in which we might be right or the French Government might be right.

The French concept of the Community of the Six had been based fundamentally on a political relationship. The French Government felt that, if not expanded beyond its present membership of Six, the Community would probably move toward a progressively higher degree of economic—and ultimately—political integration. It might well become a kind of Federal system; in fact, he would not exclude the possibility that it might become a true United States of Europe. He stated emphatically that this view was shared by General de Gaulle. *The General did not exclude the possibility that the Community in its present form could evolve into a true United States of Europe.*

As now constituted the Community was relatively homogeneous. It consisted of Continental powers except for one nation that was not so much a European as a maritime nation. The Netherlands was an island in the same sense that the United Kingdom was an island. The Dutch had never really been interested in Europe; they had always been looking out over the waters at other areas of the world. As a consequence they had resisted the development of Europe at almost every point. The Dutch were, of course, in many ways the best of the partners in the Community since they were the most honest and the most steady. But they were not Europeans—at least they were not Continental Europeans—as were the French and Germans.

This was a point that bothered the French very much in considering the problem of the adhesion of the United Kingdom. What British adhesion meant was not merely United Kingdom membership in the Common Market; it meant also that the United Kingdom would bring with it Denmark and Norway. These were not true European nations. Denmark was a small country concerned primarily with butter and eggs and bacon. Norway was preoccupied with fishing and shipping. Neither cared much about Europe.

If British accession were to mean also the accession of the Scandinavian countries and Ireland, then, after the Community had passed into the next Treaty phase in which decisions would be made not by unanimity but by some form of qualified majority, Germany and France might be outvoted by countries that were not really European but maritime in character.

As a result of these considerations, he and General de Gaulle had become persuaded that if the United Kingdom should become a part of the European Community, the nature of the Community would be transformed. One could no longer expect progress towards a United States of Europe; the Community would assume the character of an economic or commercial arrangement, which was something very different. It would be more like NATO or the EEC. France had had long experience with Great Britain in European enterprises and his conclusions reflected that experience.

Nevertheless he and General de Gaulle felt that if Great Britain was, in fact, prepared to accept the Rome Treaty, the British were entitled to join and the same would be true of their Scandinavian colleagues.

I told the Foreign Minister that I thought our difference of view lay to considerable extent in the different appraisal we made of British intentions. We would not be very enthusiastic about British membership if we thought that it would involve a weakening of the Community, an influence that would transform the Community into a mere commercial arrangement.

I reminded the Foreign Minister that the Britain of today was very different from the Britain they had known in the past. A new class was coming into power which had not been oriented to the concept of Empire. It would readily adjust, in my view, to a major role within the European framework. It was a mistake to assume that Britain's adhesion to the Rome Treaty would mean a watering down of political progress. So far as the United States was concerned we had always been interested in the idea of Europe as a full partner with us in our endeavors. We wanted very much, therefore, for Europe to move toward as much political integration as possible.

We were not very much concerned about the problems of a third force since we were persuaded that all of us were committed to the same general objectives. On our side we were prepared to develop the Atlantic institutions as rapidly as possible to make it practicable for Europe speaking with one voice and America to work in the closest of harmony and the closest of cooperation toward the achievement of common goals.

I then turned the conversation to the question of a political treaty asking the Foreign Minister how he envisaged the development of the negotiations for such a treaty.

The Foreign Minister replied that he thought that the process had now been stopped until such time as it became clear whether or not the British were going to join. After the last meeting it was made clear that the Six were not in full agreement to go forward without British participation. Mr. Spaak had been quite emphatic about it and as far as the French were concerned they were now prepared to wait until it was clear whether or not Great Britain would come in. He was not impressed with the Italian idea that they could negotiate a political arrangement, that there would then be a meeting with the British who would agree on it and that then there would be a signature of the Treaty prior to British participation but nothing coming into effect until after British adhesion.

This, he said, seemed to them to be a device which added very little and they were prepared to wait now until after the British came in.

The discussion then turned to the economic problems involved in British accession to the EEC. I said that I did not believe that any of these problems was insuperable. The position of the temperate agricultural products of the Commonwealth presented, of course, the most difficulty. The Foreign Minister stated that he agreed this was the principal problem. British domestic agriculture also faced difficult problems but he thought these could be worked out. Temperate agriculture of the Commonwealth remained, however, hard to resolve.

I then stated that so far as we were concerned we saw the possible key to a solution in proposals along the general line of the French initiative for some kind of global solutions. We were prepared to work toward such global solutions with the understanding, of course, that there would have to be some transitional arrangements in the meantime. He agreed that this seemed to be the proper course. He recognized that there would have to be some transitional arrangements but felt that they should be short. He volunteered one specific comment regarding the British insistence on a review of Commonwealth preferential arrangements at the end of the transition period. He felt that such a preferential provision was undesirable. The whole matter should be settled immutably during the course of the present negotiations just as it had been settled at the Treaty of Rome itself.

He then said that I had not noted two problems which were of importance. One was the question of tropical products on which he thought that France and the United States were farthest apart. The second was the problem of the neutrals. I said that I did not regard either one of these problems as constituting a breaking point. Our views on tropical products were motivated by two considerations; one was our sense of responsibility for Latin America and the second was our concept of what the trading world of the future should be like. Nevertheless we would be content if we felt that there was progress being made in the right direction. If, as I understood, arrangements were being completed for a new treaty of association to last for the next five years but at a lower level of preference we would want to work with the Community during this five years to try to bring about some commodity-by-commodity solutions that would make possible free access to Northern Hemisphere markets on a nondiscriminatory basis for all tropical products. The same principle might well be applied to the products of the African states and territories of the Commonwealth. At this point the Foreign Minister raised the question as to what kind of commodity arrangements we envisaged. He suggested that we might do better to approach the problem by trying to ensure income rather than price stability for these products. I told him that income stability and price stability were both within the range of our consideration.

He then turned to the question of the neutrals. I told him here again that we were not adopting a doctrinaire position. However, we saw nothing but disadvantage to the United States in the neutrals having exclusive trading arrangements with the Community if that was what "association" involved. So far as I was concerned I had never been able to find out what the neutrals meant by "association", and I didn't think that anybody knew.

The Foreign Minister agreed, saying that he appreciated that the association of the neutrals, if that meant a mutual trading arrangement, would be disadvantageous to us and that he could understand our position. He also did not know what was meant by association but thought that what concerned the neutrals principally was their trading problems. I told him that I did not believe that the question of the neutrals would ever be a breaking point and he agreed.

We then turned to a discussion of the time schedule of the UK-EEC negotiations. I asked him if he thought it possible that the British time schedule might be met; that is, did he think it likely that the outline of a solution might be seen by the latter part of July so that the British would have something reasonably concrete to present to the Commonwealth Conference in September. *He said that he thought this was not impossible; in fact he said he thought it was quite possible that such a time schedule might be kept.*

We then spoke briefly of both Laos and the Congo. So far as Laos was concerned he had taken a strong line with Souvanna and thought that Souvanna realized that he had better get back to Laos before his position was eroded. He said he felt confident that there was only one course for us to pursue and that was for us to try to bring about a neutral government under Souvanna with Soviet agreement and support.

So far as the Congo was concerned, I reported on recent efforts to get Adoula and Tshombe to compare their differences. He said that he was persuaded that this again was the only course to follow. The two must be brought together if there were to be a peaceful solution to the Congo.

In conclusion I expressed the hope that we could work toward improving Franco-American communications. He replied he hoped to have some systematic talks with the Secretary before too long. He understood that this could probably not be arranged until Congress adjourned. I did not reply directly other than to say that we had many matters before Congress this year that were of particular interest to the Department and that required the Secretary's personal attention. He then asked me when Congress might adjourn. I told him that I hoped it might be not later than the middle of August or Labor Day at the latest. He then commented that in his experience Congress always adjourned later than anyone predicted.

While I did not raise the question of any discussions with General de Gaulle, Couve himself volunteered the comment that in his view no purpose would be served by any direct contact between the heads of our two states at the moment. Such a meeting, he said, would be necessary at some point but certainly should not occur before the end of summer.

---

40.   Letter From President Kennedy to the Chairman of the House Ways and Means Committee (Mills)

Washington, May 23, 1962.

DEAR MR. CHAIRMAN: I have your letter of April 27[1] concerning United States agricultural exports to the European Economic Community. I very much appreciate your writing to me about this highly important question.

I am fully conscious of the necessity of protecting and improving access for American agricultural products into the European Common Market. A great deal of attention has been given this problem and I shall see that it remains high on the list of priorities.

There is no doubt that the European market for the produce of American agriculture is undergoing evolutionary changes. Some of these changes result directly from the formation of the European Economic Community (the Common Market). Others are a consequence of the vaulting improvement in farm productivity made possible by agricultural technology.

The problem is by no means a simple one. Indeed I suspect its complexity has to some extent obscured the efforts already made to develop adequate solutions.

Our efforts have extended over a considerable period of time. Even at an early stage in the tariff negotiations recently concluded in Geneva,

---

Source: Department of State, Central Files, 440.119/5–2362. No classification marking. No drafting information appears on the source text, but a memorandum for the White House, dated May 17, states that it was drafted in the Department of State after consultations with the Departments of Agriculture and Commerce. (Ibid., 440.119/5–1762)

[1] Not printed. (Ibid., 440.119/4–2761)

representatives of the State and Agriculture Departments discussed the problem at length with the Commission of the European Economic Community as well as with the Governments of the Six member countries during a series of bilateral consultations.

The negotiations at Geneva resulted in adequate arrangements with respect to 70 per cent of our agricultural exports to the European Economic Community. We obtained valuable concessions, as well as compensation, for the tariff changes implicit in the formation of the European Economic Community with regard to cotton, soybeans, tobacco, citrus fruits and many other products. This does not mean, however, that I am satisfied to leave it at this. I am determined that we shall obtain further concessions once I have the negotiating authority that will be provided by the legislation now under consideration by your Committee. In fact, with respect to tobacco we already have an understanding with the European Economic Community that further negotiations will be held after the new trade bill has been approved.

The major difficulties in the Geneva negotiations narrowed down to a range of commodities representing less than 30 per cent of our agricultural exports to the EEC, or about 10 per cent of our total exports to that area. The problem arose in connection with grains and livestock products for which the EEC proposed to include variable import levies in their community-wide Common Agricultural Policy. The specific commodities of major interest to U.S. producers and exporters include wheat, feed grains, rice and poultry. During the Geneva negotiations, the EEC countries had not reached agreement on the provisions of the Common Agricultural Policy, or on the common price levels to be achieved. The EEC still has reached no agreement on common price levels. The EEC was not, therefore, prepared to include these commodities in negotiations under GATT Article XXIV (6) as they had not been able to work out their community-wide trade problems in these commodities with each other; and, therefore, they could not negotiate with outside countries.

Originally, the EEC had intended to withdraw concessions previously made to us on these commodities and to balance the bargain by offering concessions on other products. Had this happened, we would have had absolutely no legal protection with respect to our future trade in these important farm commodities.

We, therefore, successfully pressed our EEC friends not to insist on immediate withdrawals and instead sought to obtain the best possible interim assurances for these products, and to impress the Six and the Commission with the importance the United States attached to longer term market access. Despite our limited bargaining authority under existing trade agreements legislation, I directed that the conclusion of the negotiations be deterred until we had secured the most advantageous commitments then obtainable on these agricultural commodities.

The Secretary of Agriculture and the Under Secretaries of State and Agriculture on a number of occasions negotiated with the Commission and with Governments on these items. My Special Assistant, Mr. Howard Petersen, later went to Brussels for the final stages of these negotiations. These key men continue to give this matter their personal attention.

For quality wheat, we obtained a commitment to protect our trade interests from any possible adverse effects of the Common Agricultural Policy while a longer term trade arrangement is negotiated. This commitment, in fact, covers the great bulk of our wheat exports to the EEC. For soft wheat, corn, sorghums, poultry, and rice, however, we obtained a commitment to negotiate trade arrangements at an early future date. This is a significant step, because we preserved all our legal rights on these commodities for use in negotiations. If withdrawals had been made as the EEC first proposed, we doubt that we would have been able to keep the door open for future negotiations on these commodities. Furthermore, this maintenance of our legal rights serves to inhibit the adoption by the EEC of excessive levies for bargaining purposes because under the GATT, this would only increase their obligations for compensatory adjustments.

The EEC and the member countries are currently developing detailed regulations for implementation of their Common Agricultural Policy for wheat, feed grains, and poultry, among other commodities. These regulations will involve the use of variable import levies during the transitive period. These interim arrangements, including the variable levies for these commodities, will become effective on July 1, 1962. For many other commodities of key importance to the U.S.—such as fruits, cotton, tobacco and soy beans—the EEC proposes to use techniques other than variable import levies.

We are keeping a close watch on these regulations as they are evolved to make sure that they develop in a manner as favorable as possible to our interests. We have sought, and will continue to seek modification of the regulations on a pragmatic basis to protect our export interests. On poultry, for example, we have undertaken to work closely with the Commission and with the Six to assure that access for our poultry is continued through import arrangements which will not substantially change our competitive position in the EEC market. Representations are now being made at the highest level to cushion the impact of the proposed new poultry system, scheduled to go into effect this July 1, pending the conclusion of further negotiations. At the same time we have made it clear that we would demand compensation if access to our poultry exports were restricted in any of the six countries.

I am satisfied that everything possible has been done to impress officials of the Six and the Commission with the critical importance that we attach to the maintenance of our agricultural exports. I stressed this point to President Hallstein on his recent visit. We are sending a technical mission to Europe next week to discuss further our problems on those commodities.

We shall do everything within our power to ensure that our agricultural products receive a fair break in the markets of the world. If we are to succeed, however, we must have bargaining leverage such as that provided in the Trade Expansion Act.

Your leadership in connection with that legislation has been of vital importance to the attainment of the objective we both seek.

Sincerely,

John Kennedy[2]

---

[2] Printed from a copy that indicates the original was signed by President Kennedy.

---

41.   Telegram From the Department of State to the Embassy in Belgium

Washington, May 31, 1962, 9:18 p.m.

3382. Brussels USEC for info. Personal for Ambassador from the Secretary. Please deliver following as personal message from me to Spaak.

Begin text.

Dear Mr. Minister:

I know that the carpets and glass problem has been a serious preoccupation of the Belgian Government and that the matter has been widely discussed in the councils of the European Community. Since returning from Athens I have personally reviewed the situation. Because I

Source: Department of State, Central Files, 411.004/5–3162. Confidential. Drafted by Ball and Vine, cleared by Trezise and Cleveland, and initialed by Rusk. Repeated to Bonn, Luxembourg, Paris, Rome, and The Hague.

am persuaded that events may get out of hand and seriously damage the whole fabric of our Atlantic relationships, I feel that I must write to you personally.

As you know the President decided only after long consideration that he must invoke the escape clause with respect to these two products. Under existing legislation this was the only mechanism available to him for dealing with a critical domestic problem.

I must tell you frankly that there is no possibility, under present circumstances, that this action can be reversed. However, it was always the President's intention to take the necessary measures to provide adequate compensation. We have already made some initial proposals in this direction. These represent the most that can be offered under existing legislation. But the President has definitely in mind that when the new trade legislation becomes effective we can work out with you a mutually satisfactory arrangement.

Compensation is, of course, the traditional method by which such matters are arranged between friends under the provisions of the GATT. I am concerned, therefore, that the member nations of the European Community may elect not to pursue this normal course but instead to take retaliatory action against American exports.

I cannot over-emphasize the lamentable effects of such a decision for Atlantic relations. It would be deeply disturbing to America. It could unleash formidable pressures here to continue the process. At the very least, it would almost certainly lead to the imposition of legislative rigidities in our policy and foreclose any possibility of an amicable readjustment at a later date.

For the Community to insist on retaliation as almost its first exercise of a common commercial policy would be regarded here as presaging a future of strained commercial relations just at a time when we are attempting, through the development of far-reaching trade legislation, to enter a new age of commercial cooperation that can mark a long forward step toward an effective Atlantic Partnership.

Because of the grave consequences of the situation that I fear may be developing I am appealing to you as a friend and statesman—as the man who almost more than anyone else has provided the inspiration and drive for a united Europe and a strong Atlantic Partnership. I want you to know I fully understand the difficulties this problem created for you, and I will do my best to work for an eventual solution which would be mutually agreeable. I ask you to do everything possible to avoid an action that could mark a serious setback for the great common enterprise we are undertaking together. *End text.*

Rusk

42. Circular Telegram From the Department of State to Certain Missions

Washington, June 7, 1962, 8:17 p.m.

2978. Brussels for Embassy and USEC. Paris for Embassy and USRO. Geneva for GATT.

1. Following for your background information connection EEC decision re carpets and glass:[1]

For reasons indicated previous messages we consider EEC Council decision to resort to tariff increases for U.S. escape clause actions carpets and glass most unfortunate and unwise. We had prepared compensate EEC in form new tariff concessions and our representative Geneva had been consulting EEC representative to this end. We believe this would have been appropriate manner to deal with situation.

In view EEC decision, however, there is no further point proceeding with consultations with EEC Geneva. We have accordingly instructed our representative to terminate EEC consultations. We intend however to proceed with consultations Geneva with UK and Japan (as well as Sweden and Canada) in order provide compensation for our action. (British have reportedly decided withdraw concessions on kraft paper; we are taking steps to dissuade British from such action and instead to negotiate for new compensatory concessions.)

Our major concern now is to prevent EEC action from being blown up unduly in U.S. with possible prejudice to trade bill. We are thus taking public posture to effect that given our escape clause action, it was up to us to provide compensation; because of limitations authority under existing trade legislation, we were not able provide full compensation to EEC; lacking compensation on our part, EEC countries were acting within their rights under GATT to make compensatory withdrawals to restore balance under the agreement. We believe public statements should refer EEC action as "compensatory withdrawals" rather than retaliation.

In discussions with officials other countries, however, we wish make clear our keen disappointment that EEC had resorted to tariff increases rather than seeking work out modus vivendi in accordance usual GATT manner of new concessions. We intend (a) stress that retaliation is shortsighted way dealing with this sort of situation and has tra-

---

Source: Department of State, Central Files, 411.004/6–762. Limited Official Use. Drafted by Vine, Weiss, and Coster (OTF) and cleared with RPE and E. Sent to Tokyo and Ottawa, and 19 missions in Europe.

[1] Despite U.S. efforts to prevent it, on June 4 the EEC decided to retaliate against the U.S. tariff increases on carpets and glass.

ditionally been avoided by U.S. and other GATT countries and (b) make clear EEC decision precludes possibility early U.S. review of escape clause action. In making these points we intend avoid becoming engaged in exchange of polemics and do not intend press EEC withdraw or modify their present decision. We wish close whole matter with air of finality so far as EEC concerned.

2. Dept proposes take following line with Spaak over weekend[2] and other posts should draw upon this line and conform closely with it in their discussions this subject:

(a) U.S. disappointed that EEC elected follow path compensatory withdrawals rather than compensation negotiations.
(b) EEC decision follow retributive path when, as we repeatedly stressed, U.S. had no other alternative, noted here with regret.
(c) In face this attitude, U.S. considers that EEC Council decision has closed matter and no point in further consultations. This will of course preclude possibility early U.S. review of escape clause action. U.S. has consequently terminated the consultations with EEC in Geneva.

3. Posts should also emphasize in any discussion this subject (a) that U.S. made a significant partial compensation offer in Geneva which held major benefits for Belgium and was fully prepared complete settlement when President received additional authority; and (b) that there is no possibility further postponing June 17 date for tariff increase.

4. Bonn should express U.S. appreciation German efforts prevent EEC retaliation and fact agricultural items were omitted.

5. Dept agrees substance last para Ecbus 988[3] and is considering possibility of instructions this effect. Dept believes, however, that there should be no linkage EEC Council action to representations on QRs for short period of time in order to allow passions cool. Linkage will only tend perpetuate spiral of retaliation which U.S. considers undesirable. Instruction CW 9557[4] should therefore be made for time being completely on own merit without reference to EEC Council action.

Rusk

---

[2] A memorandum of Spaak's conversation with Rusk at 10:30 a.m. on June 9 along these lines is scheduled for publication in volume IX. A memorandum of his conversations with Rusk at 11:40 a.m. and 3 p.m. on European integration and NATO is in Department of State, Secretary's Memoranda of Conversation: Lot 65 D 330. A brief memorandum of his conversation with the President at lunch at the White House, in which Kennedy asked Spaak's view on the best way to deal with the British application for membership in the Common Market, is ibid., Presidential Memoranda of Conversation: Lot 66 D 149.

[3] Dated June 6 Ecbus 988 recommended that the United States step up the pressure on both the EEC Council and its individual members to remove the restrictions they maintained on U.S. exports. (Ibid., Central Files, 375.800/6–662)

[4] Dated May 29 it instructed the Mission to the Economic Communities at Brussels to discuss with the appropriate EEC officials the need to avoid establishing procedures on fruits and vegetables that ran counter to previous assurances given to the United States. (Ibid., 375.800/5–2962)

43.   Telegram From the Department of State to the Embassy in Germany

Washington, June 8, 1962, 9:35 p.m.

3343. Please deliver following message from President to Chancellor:

"Dear Mr. Chancellor:

Ambassador Dowling and Under Secretary Ball have reported to me fully on their recent discussions with you.[1] I am gratified with the measure of understanding that has been reached in these conversations and pleased that the Secretary of State will have the chance to have further discussions with you and your Ministers in the near future.[2]

Meanwhile I want to tell you of my particular concern over the poultry import regulations which the Federal Republic of Germany and the other countries of the European Economic Community have indicated they may place in effect on July 1. I appreciate your assurance to Secretary Ball that you will look into this matter.

These regulations, particularly those relating to gate prices and equalization fees, will affect drastically the trade in poultry products between the Federal Republic of Germany and the United States. Since poultry is produced in every part of the United States any substantial reduction in our export market will affect adversely domestic production and prices and the contemplated measures will have a severe effect on this segment of our economy. Poultry producers regard the proposed regulations as unfair and inconsistent with efforts to liberalize trade under the principles of the GATT. This feeling could, in turn, be an important adverse factor in the consideration of the Trade Bill now before Congress and injure our common attempts to build lasting trade partnerships with the members of the Common Market.

Within the past few days Senator Fulbright, Chairman of the Senate Foreign Relations Committee, has addressed the Senate in criticism of the proposals. The governors or their representatives of 11 states personally called upon me to point out the harmful effect of increased du-

---

Source: Department of State, Central Files, 611.62A/6–862. Confidential. Drafted by the White House and cleared with Tyler.

[1] On May 23, during a general European trip, Ball discussed European integration, nuclear questions, and U.S. policy toward China with the Chancellor. At the end of the conversation Ball pointed out U.S. concern over the apparent EEC protectionist agricultural policy especially in relation to U.S. poultry exports. When the impact of this policy on German domestic policy was pointed out, the Chancellor indicated he would look into the matter. (Telegram 2858 from Bonn, May 23; ibid., 110.12–Ball/5–2362)

[2] Rusk was scheduled to visit Europe June 18–28.

ties. If the competitive position of poultry products is undermined through the establishment of new and increased import restrictions, it would be more difficult to maintain support for liberalized trade policies for goods coming into the United States.

I recognize that this problem is not an easy one for you but I am asking your help on this problem because I am convinced that it bears directly upon my own ability to mobilize support here for policies which are vital to both sides of the Atlantic and to our common aims for the future of the Atlantic Community.

I hope you will consider favorably taking such action as may be necessary to prevent the unilateral application of increased duties upon our poultry products and that the determination of trade policy with respect to these products will be deferred until we can enter into appropriate negotiations following the enactment of the pending Trade Bill.

I know that you share our desire to strengthen our economic relationships and am confident that I can count on your understanding cooperation.

Sincerely, John F. Kennedy"

White House desires text this message not become public. Signed original follows in pouch.

Rusk

---

44.   Scope Paper Prepared in the Department of State

SET–D–1/1   Washington, June 11, 1962.

SECRETARY'S EUROPEAN TRIP
June 18–29, 1962

SCOPE PAPER

General

In the four principal capitals the Secretary will be visiting, the central preoccupations will be the same: Berlin; the UK-EEC negotiations

---

Source: Department of State, Conference Files: Lot 65 D 533, CF 2126. Secret. No drafting information appears on the source text, but other papers in the SET series were drafted in the Department of State. Briefing papers, telegrams to and from Rusk, and memoranda of his conversation during his visit to Europe are ibid., CFs 2121–2127.

on British membership in the Common Market and their political implications; and the problems of national, European and NATO nuclear capabilities.

The leaders in Paris, Bonn, Rome and London will be listening not only to what we say to them directly, but also to the reports they receive on what we say in the other capitals. Our proposed presentation in the countries visited therefore must be viewed as parts of a coherent whole, in the following context.

1. American interests in the present complex are essentially those we have been pursuing over more than a decade: to hold the line against Soviet expansion and insure the continued freedom and viability of West Berlin; to build Western Europe into an effective entity; to promote British membership in this entity; and to insure that a united Western Europe works with us ever more closely in the framework of an Atlantic alliance for ensuring our common security and a close partnership for carrying out our common responsibilities in Asia, Africa, and Latin America.

2. The great mass of public opinion and political leadership in Western Europe shares a deep commitment to these same objectives—European unity, NATO and partnership with the United States.

3. The principal current obstacle to our objectives lies in General De Gaulle's policies:

a. De Gaulle has a different concept of the future shape of Europe, based on a loose cooperation of states guarding their sovereignty jealously, a conception which is designed in particular to insure French hegemony, at least on the continent.

b. In De Gaulle's view the main thrust of the policy of such a Europe should be independence of action from the United States, and the capacity to act together separately from the United States. This is particularly important to him in matters of defense, and most important of all in the key nuclear field.

c. De Gaulle's views on British entry into the Common Market—and hence into a political Europe—are resolutely obscure. His doubts appear based on the fear of British challenge to French hegemony and on a sense that Britain would be a permanent spokesman for American interests within the European complex.

4. De Gaulle's power to inhibit progress towards our objectives depends on his ability to seduce Chancellor Adenauer into support of his policy line. Without this support he is isolated in Europe. Experience has shown that De Gaulle will bend his policies away from his real objectives to the extent necessary to prevent such isolation which would threaten his claim to continental leadership. Therefore Chancellor Adenauer is the key to the situation.

5. Adenauer's fundamental purposes and convictions are the same as ours. The two equally important cornerstones of his foreign pol-

icy have been (a) the preservation of the U.S. political and military com
mitment to Europe; and (b) Franco-German rapprochement and the
integration of Germany into the West on a basis of equality. He tends to
favor British entry into a united Europe as consistent with these objectives. So far he has felt that Franco-German reconciliation, European
unity and the American Alliance were mutually consistent objectives,
and he has tried to manage things in such a way as to avoid having to
face a situation where he might have to choose among them.

6. De Gaulle's basic tactic in order to get Adenauer's support has
required him to undermine the Chancellor's confidence in the United
States over the problem of Berlin and relations with the Soviet Union. In
pursuing this tactic, he has been able to take advantage of the Chancellor's basically suspicious temperament, of German concerns arising
from their exposed position, of their fear of being discriminated against,
and of the Chancellor's deep distrust of British policy on the German
problem.

The result of the Chancellor's suspicions and De Gaulle's play on
them has been manifested in a periodic mistrust of American policy,
which seems to us unjustified, and in a continual demand for reassurance which seems to us unnecessary. Needless to say we cannot afford
to yield to the natural tendency to be irritated by these manifestations of
insecurity. Rather we must be prepared to reiterate to the Chancellor as
often as necessary our assurance that the United States is firmly on his
side on the problem of Berlin and Germany and to encourage him not to
desert his own deep convictions on the future shape of Europe and the
Atlantic Alliance, convictions which we fully share.

7. At the same time our objective in the rest of Europe should be not
publicly to attack and isolate De Gaulle, but to let him draw for himself
the conclusion that he cannot bring the Germans along with him on his
conception of the shape of Europe. Experience indicates that if he recognizes that his present tactic will not work, De Gaulle will adjust to the
situation by moving in the direction of policies more nearly consistent
with our own.

8. As a part of this same strategy, it is important to avoid the impression in Paris and Bonn that we are the principal sponsors of British
membership in the Common Market, or that our objectives are identical
with those of Britain on Berlin and East-West policies. We must also
avoid anything which extends or calls undue attention to the special US-
UK relationship in the nuclear field. Such actions can only play into De
Gaulle's hands by strengthening the image of an "Anglo-Saxon" bloc in
opposition to continental interests.

9. In summary the following basic objectives are recommended
for the four principal capitals visited:

a. In Paris, to create a general impression of good will (especially in connection with our wholehearted support of De Gaulle's Algerian policy), while adhering firmly but politely to our policies which involve differences of opinion with De Gaulle on assistance to national nuclear weapons capabilities in Europe, on the collective defense concept, and on the future shape of Europe.

b. In Bonn, to reassure the Chancellor in the strongest terms of our determination to preserve the freedom of Berlin and Allied rights there; to recall to the Chancellor our wholehearted support of his own basic convictions on the creation of a strong united Europe (including the UK) in close and continuing partnership with the United States within a strong Atlantic Alliance; and to emphasize the close inter-relation of our nuclear policies to these goals.

c. In Rome to stress our common dedication to European unity and Atlantic partnership, and to try to secure Italian support of nuclear policies which are consistent with this purpose.

d. In London, to reiterate our support for British membership in the Common Market and in a united Europe on terms which will safeguard the interests of non-member countries as a group; to suggest to the UK our view that the nuclear future of Europe lies via the multilateral, not the national, route; and at the same time to avoid saying anything which would strengthen the image of an "Anglo-Saxon" bloc on the problem of Germany and East-West relations.

---

45. Telegram From Secretary of State Rusk to the Department of State

Paris, June 20, 1962, 11 p.m.

Secto 16. Brussels also for Embassy. Following based on uncleared Memorandum of Conversation.[1]

In meeting with FonMin Couve de Murville this afternoon, Secretary raised question of UK–EEC negotiations and future shape of Europe. He asked if UK–Common Market negotiations succeed how much effect French believed this would have on other problems we were discussing. Couve's reply covered four points:

1) Will Britain join? In FonMin view only one real difficulty but this is formidable one—problem of Commonwealth. The Six say Britain

---

Source: Department of State, Conference Files: Lot 65 D 533, CF 2122. Confidential; Priority. Drafted by Cleveland. Repeated to London, Bonn, The Hague, Rome, and Brussels.

[1] Not printed. (Ibid., CF 2123)

must enter Common Market fully with appropriate transitional arrangements for Commonwealth but at end of given period Britain must be subject to same regime as partners. This meant Commonwealth preferences, as well as "habits" which had governed UK-Commonwealth trade in agricultural field, would have to disappear. British say ready sacrifice a lot in this area, but cannot abandon Commonwealth and need important exceptions. On balance, Couve said he believed Britain would go very far in direction of Six, and "probably we will come to an agreement", though this was not certain. (At several other points during meeting when UK-EEC negotiations mentioned tangentially Couve carefully used in every case the same formula—Britain might join or might not join Common Market, but would probably join.)

2) Whether or not Britain joins Common Market, political development of Community would continue. If Britain joins, however, political arrangements would necessarily be looser. In Couve's view, mere size of Community of nine or ten would make close political integration difficult. In this event, he foresaw development towards "loosely united confederation" tied together by strong economic ties and less solid political ones. Nature military arrangements in this case not clear. Couve referred in this connection to "idea which is being mentioned" of some nuclear role for Community, but did not express any opinion thereon.

3) If Britain does not join and Common Market survives resultant crisis (which FonMin believes it would if British were clearly responsible for breakdown), then Community might be expected develop closer unity in political and military field. In defense, smaller group countries would make task unification both easier and harder—easier because fewer countries involved, but considerably harder because of nuclear problem. Couve pointed out that would be much easier deal with nuclear problem on British-French-German basis than on French-German basis alone.

4) As to implications developing political unity for NATO, Couve believed this development did not change basis of alliance, but might affect its operation. If Europe more closely united, would modify "method of discussion" as well as organization of NATO. This process would, however, take a long time. Nevertheless, Couve referred to development already taking place of greater sense of solidarity among European countries, which he referred to as "growing European national feeling", rather than "European nationalism".

Rusk

46.   Telegram From Secretary of State Rusk to the Department of State

London, June 24, 1962, midnight.

Secto 66. Paris for Embassy and USRO; Brussels for Embassy and BUSEC. Following based uncleared Mencon is summary report Secretary's conversation with German For Min Schroeder on European integration.[1]

1. *Schroeder's basic stress* was on importance political aspect European integration movement. Common Market (even with British in) not itself unified Europe. Needed to develop "common bonds" as U.S. had in its federal institutions. This only way to solve major problems we face (possibly, though not explicitly, referring nuclear problem).

2. *UK-EEC Negotiations.*

Schroeder optimistic on outcome negotiations. Only real problem is find solution in spirit of Treaty which will leave open opportunities for Commonwealth exports (especially temperate agricultural products) after 1970; possible to deal with this through world-wide arrangements. Such solution feasible. Also stressed British need to wrap up negotiations by summer.

3. *Political Union.*

Schroeder referred difficulties caused by French withdrawal their own proposal on political integration, and later by Benelux insistence await outcome UK-EEC negotiations before agreeing Political Union Treaty. German position was that Six should proceed rapidly work out political arrangements among themselves in consultation with U.K. and on understanding U.K. would join Political Union as soon as Common Market issues settled. German Government favors speed: if political integration allowed to sleep, would push economic arrangements into front row and increase obstacles to further progress. Immediate task, therefore, was ask British persuade Benelux withdraw objections to immediate forward movement on political front.

4. *Role of other Applicants.*

Schroeder opened discussion entire subject with statement Rome Treaty contains offer of membership all European states prepared accept objectives and obligations of Treaty. Britain, Norway, Denmark, Ireland and Cyprus (*sic*) have applied membership, many others want

---

Source: Department of State, Conference Files: Lot 65 D 533, CF 2122. Confidential. Drafted by Cleveland. Repeated to Bonn, Rome, Brussels, The Hague, Paris, and Luxembourg.
[1] A memorandum of this June 22 conversation is ibid., CF 2123.

association. In German view Common Market countries must be prepared discuss problem with all applicants and stand by offer once made in Treaty. Later in conversation Schroeder said rapid adoption political statute acceptable to British would make political problem soluble, "irrespective of exact arrangements which are made for other countries."

Secretary replied we are not raising European integration problem in any detail on his trip as position well known and we feel our help at this stage intrusion. (Schroeder had earlier said he was glad we had avoided "excessive interest," which might indeed create difficulties). Nevertheless, we hope U.K.-EEC negotiations would succeed and had good impression this subject in Paris. Despite potential economic difficulties resulting Common Market extension we recognize political gains potentially very large.

As country made up of immigrants from all over Western Europe, Secretary said, we inclined to be less skeptical than some of our friends on Continent about how fundamental differences among European countries really are. We also feel Britain has been becoming more and more European since war. Finally, Secretary commented we see current developments as major chapter in developing broader solidarity in Atlantic Community. This means unified Europe and U.S. should move together in concert with no hegemony or domination.

Rusk

---

47.   Circular Telegram From the Department of State to Certain Missions

Washington, July 3, 1962, 3:21 p.m.

8. Following is summary appraisal Secretary's trip to Europe which addresses may use as appropriate in discussions with host country officials. Dept is using this material here in response to numerous requests.

General: Secretary's discussions in all capitals visited were very full and frank and led to harmonization or better mutual understanding US

Source: Department of State, Central Files, 110.11–RU/7–362. Secret. Drafted by Fessenden on July 2, cleared by Hillenbrand and Kohler, and initialed by Rusk. Sent to New Delhi, Ottawa, Tokyo, and 18 missions in Europe.

and European views on key questions of day. Dept feels trip created better atmosphere in all countries visited, impression which appears be borne out by European press reaction.

1. *European Integration:* Predominant subject in Europe at present is US negotiation with EEC. One highlight of trip was evidence that, although there may be climactic crises before completion, ultimate success these negotiations is generally expected. Fact of UK membership seems accepted everywhere, including France. British have apparently succeeded in fully persuading French of seriousness their intentions in joining Common Market. Interest in political integration remains strong, this being particularly emphasized in Germany and Italy. Secretary took special pains make clear we were not seeking drive wedge between France and Germany; on contrary, encouragement of Franco-German rapprochement remains one of fundamental bases our support for European integration.

2. *Nuclear Issues:* Second highlight of trip was frankness with which nuclear issues were discussed in capitals visited and with NATO Council, resulting in advancement of thinking by all concerned. US made plain its continuing opposition to proliferation of independent national nuclear deterrents, stressing essential indivisibility of nuclear warfare. US also made plain its willingness consider multilateral solution, if Allies so desire. US pointed out we not pressing this issue and not submitting "made in America" plan. Trip revealed growing European interest in multilateral solution, although at same time there was general tendency not to meet nuclear issues "head on" at present moment, since UK entry into Common Market generally considered to be first priority step. Discussions with French on nuclear issue resulted in no change in US or French position, although frankness of discussion was such as to be mutually beneficial. Discussions with Germans revealed strong German interest in finding multilateral solution to nuclear question.

3. *Berlin and Germany:* US carefully laid out rationale of its approach to Berlin problem in all capitals visited and in NATO Council. US posture of maintaining contact with Soviets while refusing yield in any way on vital interests received widespread support from nearly all NATO members. French acknowledged talks had not led to concessions or to unsettling results in FRG they had anticipated, but feared indefinite continuance would induce European mood of leaving all problems to "big two." Discussions in Bonn especially beneficial in creating full German understanding of US posture.

4. *NATO:* US expressed agreement with generally held sentiment that any steps to reorganize NATO not timely at moment in view UK-EEC negotiations. US stressed importance improving political consultation in NATO, encouraged particularly countries visited to take more

initiatives, citing US record on consultation. US also stressed importance strong conventional forces and forward strategy.

5. *Khrushchev Offensive against Common Market:* US raised with
countries visited and in NATO Council dangers of Khrushchev offensive against Common Market and importance of EEC and Common
Market countries preventing Soviets from exploiting concerns of LDC's
and non-aligned countries. There was generally sympathetic reaction to
this on part countries with which raised.

6. *Economic Problems:* Secretary raised various specific economic
problems in countries visited, including actions looking toward liberalization of trade and increase in aid to LDC's by Western Europe. Secretary stressed need these liberal international economic policies as aid to
balance of payments problem.

7. *Portugal:* Secretary had discussions with Salazar and Nogueira[1]
on basic US-Portuguese problems, including full exploration on situation in Africa with Nogueira. Secretary stressed that US desires find
common solution and is not seeking replace Portugal in Africa. Discussions with Portuguese did not result in concrete accomplishments but at
least produced some improvement in mutual comprehension.

Rusk

---

[1] Regarding Rusk's conversations with Salazar and Nogueira, see Document 343
and footnote 1 thereto.

---

48.   Telegram From the Department of State to the Mission to the European Communities

Washington, July 31, 1962, 8:10 p.m.

Busec 54. From Ball for Ambassador Butterworth.

1. On the basis of field comments and an assessment of the pros
and cons of putting our views forward in written form at this time, the

---

Source: Department of State, Central Files, 375.800/7–3162. Secret; Eyes Only; Limit
Distribution; No Distribution Outside Department. Drafted by Vine, cleared by Schaetzel
and the White House, and initialed by Ball.

White House believes that our interests have been sufficiently represented and that our injecting ourselves into the negotiations at this time would do more harm than good. We are therefore not proposing to send an aide-mémoire at this time, nor do we propose to make an oral presentation.[1]

2. French Ambassador Alphand came in this morning however, asking for suggestions, and I was able to use a large part of the substance of the aide-mémoire in response to his request. A separate telegram will report the discussion with Alphand.[2] I thought it nevertheless indispensable for you to have the basic document from which we have been working.

3. I am sending the text of the document which we have decided not to send for your information. I would appreciate it if you would hold it very closely.

Begin text.

1) We are not party to negotiations now being conducted between EEC countries and UK, and have no wish to impose our views as to form or content of any agreement that may result from those negotiations. At same time, as non-member country, US has important trading interests that can be significantly affected by manner in which certain outstanding problems are resolved in course of negotiations.

2) Bearing in mind that EEC will play central role in world trade, it essential that trade problems arising out of UK accession be resolved in such a manner as to maximize access and trading opportunities for third countries. United States would have great difficulty with solutions that have effect of making the United States, as against other third party countries, residual supplier to an expanded EEC with respect to commodities and products in which it has a significant export interest.

3) US expects that solutions to problems involving temperate zone agricultural commodities and products will not include interim preferential arrangements where there are today no preferences accorded. It recognizes that, for certain commodities interim arrangements to assure maintenance of trade may be required. Such arrangements should provide comparable treatment for trade from all third countries.

---

[1] On July 25 the Department of State asked Ambassadors Gavin, Bruce, and Butterworth about the wisdom of submitting to the United Kingdom and Common Market a written communication setting forth U.S. requirements in connection with the outcome of their negotiations. (Telegram 41 to Brussels; ibid., 375.800/7–2562) Bruce and Butterworth both counseled against a written communication. (Telegrams 375 from London, July 27, and Ecbus 119 from Brussels, July 26; ibid., 375.800/7–2662) No response from Gavin has been found.

[2] Telegram 191 to Brussels, July 31. (Ibid., 375.800/7–3162)

Should there be exceptional treatment for Commonwealth trade involving certain commodities, we would expect this to be limited to cases where other third party interests are not of major importance.

US is fully prepared to play its part in carrying forward negotiations for more permanent arrangements aimed at maintaining international trade in agricultural products at satisfactory levels. On products not involving fixed tariffs in an enlarged EEC, US stands ready to negotiate special arrangements, including international commodity agreements, beginning with grains as the most important agricultural commodity. In US judgment, a conference to negotiate special arrangements for the maintenance of trade in grain should be convened immediately after the conclusion of an agreement between the UK and the EEC. As an interim measure pending the conclusion of these special arrangements, US believes that the Govts of the member states of the EEC should undertake not to raise their respective producer prices on grains.

US also wishes to state its willingness to negotiate in the World Grains Agreement Conference concerning its domestic price support level.

For commodities or processed foodstuffs subject to fixed tariffs, US anticipates that non-discriminatory solutions will be found, such as a reduction in the common external tariff.

US notes that it has existing rights and obligations in the agricultural field with respect to EEC. Some of these rights and obligations arise, or have been reserved, in connection with earlier negotiations and are not directly involved in UK-EEC negotiations. US looks forward to further discussions and negotiations with regard to these rights and obligations, and in that context, is prepared to discuss its own agricultural restrictions.

By same token, US expects that EEC will show a continuous awareness of its obligations to third country suppliers by pursuing reasonable price, production and trade policies.

4) With respect to association under terms and conditions of Part IV of Rome Treaty, US expects that this would continue to be confined to less developed countries having predominantly tropical economies.

5) In respect of industrial raw materials, US favors adoption of zero or low duties for these items wherever possible.

6) US wishes to make plain that, in any future tariff negotiations, it is prepared to accord an enlarged EEC appropriate credit on certain critical items in which the United States has a substantial export interest, such as industrial raw materials or processed foodstuffs, should a reduction in, or elimination of, the common external tariff for these items result in an unrequited benefit.

US has already informed certain of the Commonwealth countries that it is prepared to recognize that the trade benefits resulting from the elimination of margins of preference, which those countries presently accord imports from UK, would represent a valuable consideration to their credit in future tariff negotiations. *End text.*

Rusk

49.   Memorandum of Conversation

Washington, September 14, 1962, 3 p.m.

SUBJECT

Meeting with Vice Chancellor Erhard September 14, 1962

PARTICIPANTS

Germans
Vice Chancellor Erhard
Ambassador Knappstein
Dr. Langer, Ministerialdirektor, Economic Policy Division, Ministry of
    Economics
Dr. Ernecke, Economic Counselor, Germany Embassy
Mr. Dittmann, Second Secretary, German Embassy
Mr. Jirka, Second Secretary, German Embassy

United States
The Secretary (toward end of meeting)
The Under Secretary
Mr. Freshman, German Affairs

The Under Secretary stated that the Trade Expansion Act had today been approved by the Senate Finance Committee. He anticipated that it would be passed by the Senate sometime next week and go to the White House for signature. This legislation would enable the President to take great initiatives looking to trade liberalization. The Vice Chancellor

Source: Department of State, Central Files, 611.62A/9–1762. Secret. Drafted by Freshman on September 17 and approved in U on September 18 and S on September 19. Erhard was in Washington to attend a meeting of the International Monetary Fund. A memorandum of his conversation with the President earlier in the day is ibid., Presidential Memoranda of Conversation: Lot 66 D 149.

commented that this was a fine development. He was confident that the law would be implemented along the lines of the President's ideas. As soon as practicable after passage of the Act, the US and EEC should enter into detailed discussions.

Turning to the UK accession issue, Professor Erhard stressed that notwithstanding some public misinterpretation of the de Gaulle visit,[1] the German Government had not changed its attitude. It is convinced that the UK should join the EEC.

Mr. Ball doubted that intensive US/EEC discussions would commence much before 1964. He would be interested in Erhard's views regarding the degree of likely European receptivity. He noted French views that the EEC could not manage general reductions in trade barriers without concerting with the US. In principle we favor the concerting of policy; we are convinced of the interdependence of the economies of free world countries. Where in Europe would policies have to be so concerted?

Professor Erhard agreed with the French view. Agriculture is the main problem in Europe, although we must also contend with nationalistic tendencies in some countries and industries. He noted the amazing economic recovery of France and its strong balance of payments position. Political factors will determine the next step there. The UK problems are greater. While industry accommodations are readily foreseeable, agriculture will have problems. This is also true in the Federal Republic. Domestic policies in this regard are not entirely virtuous but some allowances are necessary for obvious reasons. A world-wide conference is needed for product-by-product examination so as not to interfere with trade currents. Politically, however, a new line of argument has arisen. In the last three months the idea has arisen for a political union which would require that everyone joining the economic community also became part of the political community. This was the French view. The question in the German mind is whether the UK would join a political community. He assumed that the Under Secretary would be discussing this question with Foreign Minister Schroeder next month. Erhard felt that countries joining the EEC would be entitled to political association. The neutrals had to be taken into account, however. The German position is still reserved. They will be talking with Heath about this toward the end of September.

The Under Secretary commented that European political unity would be enormously facilitated by UK accession. We had taken for granted the fact of full UK accession. (At this point Erhard interjected "I too".) We hope accession means full rights for the members. Separate

---

[1] De Gaulle paid a State visit to Bonn September 4–9.

commercial or political arrangements would be divisive and self-defeating. Mr. Ball believed that Couve de Murville saw the problem as not one of UK assimilation per se but of other nations coming along which would transform the nature of the EEC. Couve had in mind two kinds of nations, commercial and maritime. He felt that such countries as the Scandinavian group and Ireland would dilute the character of the Community. Mr. Ball said that the US, of course, is not a party to this, but would—if asked—say that UK exclusion would be very unfortunate. Other countries are another matter. Their political interests are possibly different from their commercial interests. There should be full participation, however, for the UK.

The Vice Chancellor agreed about the UK. Regarding the other countries, their participation could contribute to the strengthening of Europe. However, they couldn't come in politically and not economically; this would be inconsistent with the historical facts. It might be possible to recast the EEC in a new political form. De Gaulle might feel that other arrangements were possible. The UK should not appear to be rejected by German public opinion. De Gaulle was made to understand in Germany the need for UK accession.

The Under Secretary asked whether de Gaulle's visit was essentially to symbolize France/German rapprochement. Professor Erhard said that the visit had a somewhat deeper purpose. De Gaulle wanted to convince the German people that a new chapter had begun. He spelled out the reconciliation and indicated areas where forward movement was possible. He learned that the Germans had achieved an entirely new sense of national consciousness. Professor Erhard said that he had told de Gaulle that it was not possible to exclude Great Britain; that while a key aspect of European policy was French/German understanding, he didn't mean this in the sense of an axis or clique. The UK/German relationship, however, was not the same as that of France and Germany. Erhard said the French accepted this view.

The Under Secretary expressed the view that if the UK joins, they will work with great will to identify with and become a part of Europe. He had told the Chancellor[2] that a great social revolution was taking place in the UK. They no longer thought of themselves as a world system but as a nation leaning closer than ever to Europe. We are optimistic about the future of EEC if the UK joins. Mr. Ball hoped the London discussions will see approval for UK action. The US present planning on trade liberalization and more systematic reallocation are predicted on UK accession. We see more clearly how Europe and the US can share the

---

[2] Regarding Ball's May 23 conversation with Adenauer, see footnote 1, Document 43.

common burden, thus enabling the US to divest itself of the lonely and onerous role of carrying the load. This is something about which we must eventually have serious discussion.

The Vice Chancellor felt that UK accession was not the only problem. The Iberian Peninsula (Spain and Portugal) also wanted in.

Mr. Ball noted signs of awakening in Spain which, with European help, should be encouraged. This is likewise true of Portugal. In this regard, Europe can do more than the US. There are great resources in the Iberian Peninsula which may well be added to Free World resources.

The Vice Chancellor then asked about Turkey. Mr. Ball noted that economic progress is better than before but their financial problems are still acute. He was more hopeful than before about the situation. Europe and Germany can do a real job here. At this point Erhard said "Yes, with a great deal of money." He offered to exchange the Turkish/German bilateral arrangements for the US/Greece bilateral arrangements. Mr. Ball felt this would require some discussion.

The Vice Chancellor and the Under Secretary agreed that communism is a considerably greater danger in Latin America than in Africa. Mr. Ball noted that an enormous effort is needed in Latin America. The dangers of expanding communist influence are considerable, as an outgrowth of the long delays in social changes. In response to Erhard's question on this point, Mr. Ball felt that very few social changes had in fact taken place, to judge from a recent Alliance for Progress study. Some of those countries exist on a very rigid structure and the problem is therefore difficult. No stability is likely without social change, and there are very considerable elements of instability today in such key countries as Brazil, Argentina, Chile and Venezuela.

Cuba, like Berlin, is a problem for the western world. We should consider the development of common policies toward Cuba. What happens there is related to the entire free world. It is a particular source of Latin America infection. The US hoped this problem could be resolved by a common effort.

The Vice Chancellor then asked whether Khrushchev wanted to get rid of the Berlin issue. Mr. Ball replied that no move was expected before November or December, at which point the problem would sharpen. It might take the form of a peace treaty or other tests of wills. We are prepared for this test of will, which we anticipate as a real possibility. The Russians seem to be putting themselves in a position of less flexibility. The recent reference to US elections might be a ploy. The outlook for the fall or winter does not bode for an easy situation.

Erhard then turned to US policies in regard to its balance of payments situation. Under US procurement policies for its armed forces, American firms will get the business even though their bids exceed German bids by as much as fifty percent. Some relaxation is necessary so that "several million dollars" of this business could be picked up by German companies. This would help in Germany and forestall counter-arrangements in self protection.

Mr. Ball stressed his own belief in liberal trading policies. The US problem is its burdensome global commitments. Defense alone costs us $3 billion in foreign exchange annually. Our gold loss has an effect on the strength of the dollar, which we are obliged to maintain. Pressures to maintain equilibrium are very great. To achieve this, the US can (a) reduce its global obligations; (b) reduce its foreign exchange outlay; or (c) impose restrictive measures on goods and capital. We will not take the third step, however. We want to balance at a high level rather than through restrictions at a low level. The US is firmly resolved not to devalue the dollar by raising the gold price or by other measures. This would be the least desirable of a whole process of measures.

The Vice Chancellor stressed the importance of maximizing trade. This would help the US. German cost increases over the past three years have been considerable, what with a 30 percent increase in wages and other pressures on profits. US costs have stayed relatively level during the same period and it is now more competitive. The German people must practice moderation.

In response to Mr. Ball's question about the state of the German economy, Professor Erhard said that the problem of excessive budgets has been brought under control, although it is still DM 5.2 billion short of balancing. He has pressed industry and labor to show more responsibility in the situation, but the Government must also practice restraint and thus set the right climate to make demands on the public. The budget cannot be raised beyond the real increase in GNP. Notwithstanding our belief in US principles, we can't turn the country over to capital and labor. There must be harmony in collective agreements in which the public interest is dominant. The Government can't continue to spend beyond its income and meet its costs in Berlin and on defense. He had so informed the trade unions.

Mr. Ball commented that the wage/price spiral also gave us problems. He pointed to the President's intervention with the steel industry, comparing it with Professor Erhard's action with Volkswagen. Erhard commented that this comparison is often made.

At this point the Secretary entered the meeting.

The Secretary stated that while he had to leave to testify before a congressional committee on Cuba, he wanted to take the time to comment briefly on Berlin. We see a serious situation between now and the end of December. This will require maximum strength, unity and firmness. The President is deeply concerned that we meet the situation with whatever means may be necessary. If Moscow knows that this is the Alliance position we may avoid war. If Moscow doubts this, then we may have war.

The Vice Chancellor expressed his gratitude for the unmistakable determination of the US to defend freedom. This, he said, strengthens the German intention to do everything in their power.

At this point Ambassador Knappstein reported a message from Foreign Minister Schroeder which noted that the German defense budget for 1963 would actually increase by DM 2 billion over last year to a total of DM 17 billion. This represented a reduction in the Defense Ministry request, but was nonetheless an increase in the budget.

Secretary Rusk then reverted to the Russian threat on Berlin. If we can do anything in other capitals between now and November 1 to stimulate preparations we should do so. The US and the Federal Republic have met their obligations but others have not. Perhaps the Federal Republic could address itself to this in Paris and London.

Noting that the Secretary would be testifying on Cuba, Ambassador Knappstein stated that the Federal Republic would support any US initiative in the North Atlantic Council regarding vessel charters for transporting cargo to Cuba. No German vessel is carrying arms to Cuba, under penalty of law. Legislation would be needed to prevent German shipping from delivering anything else to Cuba; notwithstanding which the Federal Republic would support a US embargo on shipping.

The Secretary stated that the American people are concerned regarding Cuba. We also face a severe crisis in Berlin. We must follow the best course in both places. He greatly appreciated the German statement of support on Cuba.

The Secretary then recalled to Professor Erhard that at their last meeting he had spoken of poultry. He thanked the Vice Chancellor for the outcome of this matter.

Vice Chancellor Erhard said that Foreign Minister Schroeder will come to the US next month. He and Schroeder agreed fully on foreign policy, European integration and UK accession. The US should encourage Schroeder on UK accession. This vital subject must be cleared up as soon as possible.

The Secretary noted Moscow's obvious concern about the EEC prospects. He also informed the Vice Chancellor that the Soviets had acquiesced today in the Allied ban on the use of Soviet APCs in West Berlin.

50.   Letter From the Ambassador to the United Kingdom (Bruce) to the Deputy Assistant Secretary of State for Atlantic Affairs (Schaetzel)

London, November 1, 1962.

DEAR BOB: It seemed better to write than telegraph you. I had a long talk with Ted Heath today. He was thoroughly frank and forthcoming.

It was obvious that, although not defeatist, he is worried over the slow, and, in some respects, unsatisfactory progress of Common Market negotiations. The French, especially Wormser, remain obstructive.

1. The difficulties over agriculture are great; what has been demanded of Britain in that field cannot possibly be reconciled with UK domestic political pressures.

2. No acceptable arrangement to take care of New Zealand's particular needs has been suggested by the French, nor have they indicated a willingness to be accommodating.

3. India and Pakistan are somewhat unreasonable in their demands, but the deal, that may be somewhat improved, worked out for them is reasonable.

4. He thinks any serious consideration of world-wide commodity agreements should be postponed until after UK has been admitted to Rome Treaty organization.

5. Re Trade Expansion Act, he favors US intention of conducting bilateral soundings, and finds March or April 1963 suitable times.

6. Euratom membership does not present insuperable problem, but must be tactfully negotiated.

7. UK will not neglect interests of EFTA friends, but little serious on this subject can be negotiated until after UK's own position has been clarified.

8. He hopes treaty might be signed in March or April, with enabling legislation passed later in year after much debate. Does not, however, believe general election will be precipitated on issue.

9. He thinks US Government should continue to refrain from intervention in situation. He suggested, however, if I could use any personal influence discreetly with Hallstein and Marjolin I do so, and also see Monnet to tell him outlook far from rosy.

10. I do not wish to intrude on duties or in territory our representative in Brussels. If, however, you wish me to see Hallstein, once a great friend, I shall do so, as well as talk informally with Marjolin and Monnet

---

Source: Department of State, Central Files, 375.800/11–162. Confidential.

separately. I do not believe I should see Marjolin without prior consent Monnet.

In summary, Heath is not certain the cat can be put back in the bag. The continued insistence of French on agricultural provisions, including financial arrangements, gravely troubles him. Moreover, if acceded to, British agricultural constituencies would largely desert Conservatives.

Smallest practicable distribution should be given to these comments.

Best regards.

Sincerely yours,

David

P.S. I have just had word from Ted that Marjolin, commencing at once, will be away from Brussels a month, campaigning for election to the French Parliament.

---

51.   Memorandum From the Under Secretary of State (Ball) to President Kennedy

Washington, November 15, 1962.

Foreign Minister Schroeder told me privately last night that he is deeply concerned because Chancellor Adenauer has developed a considerable ambivalence regarding British entry into the European Common Market.[1] Schroeder says that he and most of his colleagues are keen to see the negotiations concluded, and that he would personally intervene and try to help out the British if he could get any word from the Chancellor.

The Chancellor, said Schroeder, could be influenced only by you. If the United States felt as I had indicated to Schroeder—that we would regard it as a major defeat for the solidity of the Western world if the UK-EEC negotiations broke down—then he devoutly hoped that you would make this clear to the Chancellor when you meet with him this afternoon.

Source: Kennedy Library, President's Office File, Germany/Security. Secret.

[1] Schroeder accompanied Chancellor Adenauer on his official visit to Washington November 13–16. For documentation on the visit, see vol. XV, pp. 427–443.

Our own reports from London and the European capitals are alarming. All of the captiousness of the French and the monarchical intolerance of de Gaulle are being brought to bear on the other Europeans to render the British position intolerable. A strong lead from the German side is needed if there is not to be a complete *impasse.*

The consequences of a breakdown would be serious. It would mean a deepening bitterness between the British and the Continent. It would encourage the most parochial elements in the Six—a growing protectionism, and a considerable erosion of the Alliance. It would almost certainly mean a Conservative defeat in Britain with all the implications that a Labor Government would have for Anglo-American relations.

I do not think I am overstating the case. I feel it very important that you underline to Adenauer this afternoon that lamentable results would follow from letting the UK-EEC negotiations break down over commercial trivia. If Adenauer wants to be a statesman, now is an opportunity.

Secretary Rusk made this general point to the Chancellor this morning, but it will take strong reinforcing from you if it is to have decisive effect.

Geroge W. Ball

---

52.   Memorandum of Conversation

Washington, November 15, 1962, 4 p.m.

SUBJECT

Discussion between the President and Chancellor Adenauer

PARTICIPANTS

The President
Mrs. Lejins, LS, Department of State
Chancellor Adenauer
Mr. Weber, Interpreter

After an exchange of gifts the President and the Chancellor exchanged a few preliminary remarks about the Chancellor's appearance

---

Source: Department of State, Conference Files: Lot 65 D 533, CF 2181. Secret. Drafted by Lejins on November 29 and approved in the White House the same day.

at the Press Club, and in that connection briefly discussed the merits and demerits of correspondents in general and women correspondents in particular, the latter comments, in a joking vein, not being too flattering.

The President then indicated that there was one question which he was very anxious to discuss with the Chancellor at this time. This was the question of UK accession to the EEC, a matter which the President felt to be highly critical at the present time. In his opinion, and he was saying this confidentially, if UK were not to join the EEC, the Labor Party is bound to win in the coming elections. While Mr. Gaitskell is a good person, the Chancellor is fully aware of the fact, no doubt, that there are a very large left-wing faction and many neutralists in the Labor Party. While Macmillan gave the US full support in the Cuban crisis, the Labor Party was much less inclined to do so; moreover, the Labor Party did not have any position on Berlin, nor did the Liberals. Non-accession to EEC on the part of UK would lead to political deterioration in Great Britain in the President's opinion. This was a very dangerous situation for all concerned. No one could foresee what the future would bring as regards France five or ten years hence. This made it all the more important for Great Britain to be firmly allied with the other Western European nations and the Common Market in particular, because this would be a greatly stabilizing influence for all of Europe. To be sure the Common Market as such would continue to prosper even without the UK as a member, but the situation, politically speaking, would be much less promising for an Atlantic partnership. However, the President emphasized, the decision concerning UK accession was purely a European matter and therefore up to the Chancellor. Nevertheless, the President feels that it is extremely important to keep the US, Canada and Great Britain closely allied with the EEC. Actually, the President pointed out, UK accession to EEC will create many more economic difficulties for the US, which is the case as regards EEC in general. In this connection the President expressed his appreciation for the cooperation shown by the Federal Republic in the poultry matter. In spite of the difficulties created for the US by UK accession the President felt it was extremely vital for Europe that the UK become a member of the Common Market, since Europe would be much stabler as a result thereof. He reiterated repeatedly that UK accession was not in the narrow interests of the US.

The Chancellor expressed full support for UK accession to the EEC, agreeing with everything the President had said. He indicated, however, that England should handle herself a bit more skillfully and more wisely in the negotiations. While he did not want to go into any details, he thought he should tell the President that the British were acting in such a manner that one of the French representatives had felt obliged to tell them: "After all, you are the ones who are seeking something from EEC, and not we who want something from you."

The Chancellor then indicated that he would like to take the time to tell the President something he had told the Secretary this morning and which would explain some of the Chancellor's misgivings with reference to EEC in general. He was greatly concerned by the tremendous bureaucracy growing up in the name of EEC. The thing had gone to the head of the EEC Directorate. The latest was that the EEC was asking all member states to prepare two budgets, one political and one economic budget. The economic budget was then to be sent to Brussels, to be worked over and combined into one joint budget. At the same time, when the member nations had signed the Rome Treaty they had not anticipated any such development. Actually, they had believed that they would obtain a European Parliament before very long. Instead, they now had a tremendous bureaucratic apparatus without any parliamentary controls whatsoever. He, the Chancellor, had qualms about continuing to go along with this kind of arrangement. He felt sure that the American Congress would be reluctant to relinquish any of its rights to a bureaucratic machine of this type. All these were misgivings which the Chancellor had with reference to EEC quite aside from the matter of UK accession. He felt that there might need to be a complete reorganization of EEC.

The President agreed that these things might present a problem, but he felt the matter of UK accession was of greater importance since everything possible needed to be done to avoid a set-back to the Conservative Party. If the UK were to be refused admission to EEC there would be a strong reaction within England which would have a harmful effect on the relations between the UK and the rest of Western Europe. In the final analysis, this would prove harmful to Germany, a fact which should be of grave concern to the Chancellor. Moreover, there would be bitterness between France and England which would be harmful to the prospects for the Atlantic Community. The President was under the impression that General de Gaulle was reluctant to dilute the area of the Common Market by the inclusion of the UK. Perhaps this was based primarily on historical reasons . . . [1] perhaps even some political considerations of the present. But for political considerations in the future it was absolutely essential for Britain to become a member of the EEC. At the present time, the President said, there are three massive power blocs in the Atlantic area, the US, the Six, and then Britain and the Commonwealth. It was absolutely necessary to join these three blocs more closely together into one Atlantic Community.

The Chancellor indicated that he fully subscribes to the President's views. He feels that this is the right approach, but he is not at all sure that

---

[1] Ellipsis in the source text.

it will be successful. As for de Gaulle, the Chancellor is of the opinion that de Gaulle is actually little concerned with the matter of British accession. The Chancellor has discussed the matter with de Gaulle on occasion. Both felt that UK accession was a matter for very serious examination and consideration. As a matter of fact de Gaulle had stated that an application like that of Great Britain was not a thing that could be simply rejected. On the other hand, Great Britain was handling herself most unwisely in this affair and was asking much too much, for instance as regards agricultural products. The UK argued that four percent of its population is dependent on agriculture. The Chancellor wished to point out that twelve percent of the German population are engaged in agriculture, and what is more, they and their families give their support to the CDU. Therefore, the agricultural population of Germany was an element to be seriously considered by the Federal Government. As for the Labor Party, the Chancellor indicated that George Brown was the most intelligent of them all, and that he had a more positive attitude toward EEC than Gaitskell, for example. The Chancellor then stated that he would do everything in his power to help along the matter of UK accession. He said, however, that he would be lying if he were to say that he was sure of the success of this matter.

The President emphasized once more that the main thing to keep in mind was the effect on the Atlantic Community of any possible failure of the Conservative Party in England. Actually, he was not very optimistic about their remaining in power in any event. As for the Labor Party, Gaitskell was on the way down, he felt, and Wilson was going up. He was fearful of the very leftist elements in the Labor Party, the Communists and pacifists. These were against the concept of a firm stand in Europe, and a firm stand was in the direct interests of the US and the Federal Republic. Any disharmony within the Atlantic Community in these matters would have bad effects for Germany as well as for the US.

The Chancellor reiterated that he would do everything in his power to help this matter along.

The President referred to the talks between General Heusinger and General Taylor during the Chancellor's visit. In this connection he handed the Chancellor the memorandum on the Strauss–Gilpatric arrangement which he had promised him earlier. In conclusion the President then told the Chancellor how happy he was that the Chancellor had accepted his invitation to come to Washington.

The Chancellor stated that he was particularly happy about the timing of his visit, because he felt that this showed solidarity among partners and he felt that this was of utmost importance in a decisive situation of this sort.

The President reminded him that the Cuban situation had still not reached a satisfactory conclusion, in view of the bomber situation, but, he indicated, this was typical of negotiations with the Soviets. He promised to keep the Chancellor informed of developments, indicating that the further actions with reference to Berlin would be carried out in accordance with the discussions of the past few days, depending on the outcome of the Cuban situation.

---

53.   Memorandum From Secretary of Agriculture Freeman to President Kennedy

Washington, November 26, 1962.

SUBJECT

> European Trip—Brussels, Common Market Conference—OECD Agriculture Ministers, Paris[1]

I.   Conclusions.

A. It is the consensus accepted almost matter of factly by European statesmen and also Americans in Europe that the basic issue of U.K. entry into the Common Market has been determined. I found nowhere any doubt of this although the details have not been settled, and the period before final settlement remains uncertain.

This fact, I think, is important for the gentleness and reserve with which we have urged upon the Community and associated nations our own interests in light of the overwhelming political fact of furthering the community and accomplishing the U.K. entrance need no longer inhibit our action.

B. The European Nations will not accord any trade opportunities to American agriculture unless vigorous coordinated consistent pressure is brought to bear. Without attempting to evaluate each nation's posture, it is clear that in both Germany and France prominent and effective political leadership is very responsive to what is felt to be national interest and as such not concerned with the rights or interests of the United States. They will respond, I submit, only to a coordinated evidence of firm intention of our Government to be treated fairly or to re-

---

Source: Kennedy Library, National Security Files, Belgian Country Series. No classification marking. No drafting information appears on the source text.

[1] November 16–21.

sort to reprisals if we are not accorded fair treatment. The fact that we have contributed enormously to their present strong economic position and also to the furtherance of the Community as a practical matter has almost no influence. It makes nice drawing room conversation, but it is of little practical use at the bargaining table.

II.   *Basic factors to consider.*

A. The French are intractable. The French Agricultural Minister is the strongest personality of the Agricultural Ministers and as such will exert, even if French agriculture was not generally speaking dominant, great influence. Add to this that the gentleman in question has strong political ambitions and will be motivated almost exclusively by political factors, primarily domestic, and we have a very sharp customer to deal with. It would be my evaluation that he will respond to only one thing and that is power rather than persuasion. There are strong political forces in agriculture in all the countries of the Six, but so far as I can determine in most of the countries the political leaders in agriculture are much more vociferous than their followers, and those who hold public office, including the Ministers, are following rather than shaping what they feel to be public opinion.

The following by way of background should be noted in connection with Mr. Pisani. I am informed that until very recently he was not an outspoken DeGaullist. DeGaulle's recent successes, according to some members of the Agriculture Ministry, have changed this and he now is a strong supporter of the General.

When I discussed Article 23 of GATT where we had gotten certain directives issued calling on the French to comply with concessions they had withheld contrary to GATT, Pisani all but said that he would not do as GATT had directed regardless of the decision rendered. He included in this statement a charge that the United States had been dumping wheat in Africa to the detriment of French markets. I countered this almost intractable attitude by responding that I would personally review the wheat question in Africa and if French markets had been adversely affected we would act accordingly, and in that spirit I called on him to personally review the items which the French had been mandated to act upon under GATT Article 23. To this he grudgingly agreed. He did state that we were in agreement on attempting to keep grain prices low and that he hoped that they would be very close to the French grain price rather than the German although he acknowledged that something would have to be given. This was encouraging and we did agree to work together on this, which of course is the single most critical decision which will be made in connection with the Common agricultural policy. As it now stands, it is scheduled for determination next April.

Pisani's activities are quite erratic. I have not yet had the opportunity to review the transcript of the discussions at the closed session of the Agricultural Ministers although parts of it were leaked to the press. His response to my sharp but friendly statement of American policy where agricultural trade in the Community is concerned was not to dispute it on the merits but rather to counterattack obliquely by contending that this was an effort to undermine the Common Market. He spoke, I thought, rather sharply although the translation from French was clumsy and I couldn't be sure. After having spoken positively and strongly the day before I responded to him relatively mildly, rather than getting into any direct confrontation either Nation-wise or personality-wise, but made certain that I reiterated repeatedly in subsequent discussion on resolutions and statement of policy what the policy of our country was.

Subsequent discussions resulting in the passage of resolutions and a statement of policy which was released to the press found Pisani as presiding officer reasonably cooperative and we succeeded in getting the Ministers to adopt both a resolution and a statement of policy acknowledging the importance of International Trade and that such trade must not be jeopardized by internal policies. His press conference also was moderate, particularly when his previous statements would have led us to expect a very sharp public statement. All in all, his actions and statements of policy were most erratic, showing on the one hand inconsistency and lack of resolution, and on the other a determination to touch every political base and to not give an inch if it involved any political hazard.

B. The key decision to be made by the Community will be to set the target price on grain which will, according to present plans, be done early next year, probably in April. If the Community grain price is close to the French, we believe that uneconomic production will not be substantially stimulated. The German price, on the other hand, will result in bringing millions of acres into production, which together with modern technology will seriously threaten our markets in Western Europe not only for grain but also of poultry and related items where the variable fee will be set, based on the differential between Community support prices and American prices, much lower.

C. I was very pleased and consider it significant that the Council of Agricultural Ministers did adopt a resolution on International Trade and issue a statement incorporating that resolution. It will be of critical importance that the State Department, and particularly Under Secretary Ball, follow up firmly in support of our position. Otherwise there will be doubt if the Departments of State, Agriculture, and the American Government are really insistent that we receive fair treatment.

I believe it fair to say that my policy statement was well received but there is some skepticism that we might not really mean it which makes the position subsequently taken by the State Department crucial.

III. Miscellaneous.

Certain background information is important.

A. Minister Mansholt of the Community told me himself confidentially that although Adenauer and the German Cabinet recommended to the Community that the poultry fee be lowered, that Schwartz, the German Minister of Agriculture, strongly and vigorously opposed and that the fact the Commissioners cut the recommendation of the German Cabinet in half resulted from the insistence of Minister Schwartz. Therefore, it is clear the Germans are playing both sides of the street on this one.

B. Poultry—The doubling up of the gate price on poultry has been rectified. This was a matter of administration that we were able to correct by vigorously bringing it to the attention of the authorities who acted as a result of our strong representations including our statement of the President's personal interest in this matter. It is our contention, of course, that the use of gate prices to set a levy is contrary to GATT, as well as an abuse of the whole gate price concept which is to prevent dumping, not to set fees. As a practical matter I do not believe they will eliminate the gate price any more than we were able to get them to eliminate variable fees. However, Mansholt did agree to review again the level of the gate price and it is possible that it will be lowered. We found out that the Commissioners had set it lower and the Council of Ministers had raised it to its present level of 33.43.

Mansholt indicated the Commission would welcome a German request to lower the fees on poultry beyond the end of 1962 when the present reduction (not yet actually passed on by the Bundestag and therefore not in effect) runs out. We should push the Germans very strongly on this. If we can get the German Cabinet to act again we will be very alert to try and prevent the Community from cutting it as they did last time. (The Council rather than the Commissioners cut the German Cabinet request from 4-1/4 cents to 2 cents.) He was also receptive to our request for adjustment on chicken backs and necks now totally shut out because they increased the evaluation ration to whole birds from 35 percent to 125 percent and then to 75 percent equally prohibitive.

C. The Council of Ministers showed some understanding that food for economic assistance purposes has very real possibilities, but that it requires good administration and has practical limitations. I was concerned that the idealistic goal of using food and fiber to reach hungry people might be a rationale to encourage over-production everywhere. Should this be the case and surpluses mount, the practical problems utilizing them could be critical resulting in dumping, international trade conflict and general international trade chaos. Some of Pisani's speeches had led me to believe that he might follow this route, but during the conference he had little to say about it. Most nations seemed, if anything, conservative rather than liberal in connection with food aid.

On balance, it would appear to me that they would need stimulation rather than any effort to hold them back. In this connection Jean Monnet is strongly emotionally involved, as is incidentally Pisani's wife, a very intelligent woman who recently wrote a book on French history during the Colonial period and I would estimate has very real influence on the French Minister of Agriculture.

There are certain semantics involved in the question of international agricultural trade and historic practice that need to be kept in mind. I found that the statement "historic markets" results in immediate emotional response. One of the rationales for the Common Market is to look forward, not back, and reference to the concept "historic market" stimulates an immediate adverse response.

IV. Key facts about American agriculture to keep in mind.

A. That American policy as a major importer and exporter of agricultural commodities is the most liberal in the world. We admit great quantities of agricultural items duty free; for example, over $300 million worth of beef killed and on the hoof each year. It will be impossible for us to maintain low tariffs in the United States and face high levies and restrictions on the same commodities in Western Europe. Where we use export subsidies they have been used with discretion so that we have not disturbed historic markets, disrupted international trade or stimulated price fluctuations. Rather than do so, we have ourselves accumulated substantial surpluses at heavy costs. Thus, our own responsible conduct in agricultural international trade merits considerate attention on their part.

B. This Administration has been highly responsible in its agricultural policy. We have sought to bring surpluses into balance and to cut back production in excess of our needs, rather than to dump on the world market—witness the Farm Act of 1962, particularly the Wheat Bill which includes both acreage and bushelage controls, and the Feed Grain program. By the end of 1963 we expect to have the feed grain surplus down to essential security and stabilization reserve. By 1966 we expect wheat surpluses to reach that same position. Our programs have been sufficiently successful to reduce grain surpluses over 700 million bushels while at the same time they have increased net farm income over $1 billion $100 million a year—something which it was said was impossible. Thus the United States has been under the Kennedy Administration both responsible and successful in its agricultural policies.

In this connection it is to be noted that Finland, Sweden and some other countries among the North Atlantic Nations have acted to do something along the supply management line, but it has been primarily to get land out of production by curtailing its sale or use rather than by having supply management applied to commodities. I found no willingness on the part of European agricultural leaders at this time to take on the difficult task of applying supply management in terms of acreage, bushel, bale, or pound limitations.

Pisani was particularly outspoken in his opposition to any such program, stating that French farmers with income down and resistance to price increases everywhere evident could only look towards increased acreage to improve their income position, completely ignoring of course the whole factor of improving productivity.

V.

On balance I believe it is fair to say that my trip was successful. The statement of policy in connection with agricultural markets received very wide attention. It will now provide a rallying point for other countries which had previously been lacking as the political dominated the economic.

I expect some domestic objections to our offer to bargain where our own restrictions are concerned, but the flat statement that we did not expect other countries to do what we were unwilling to do was and will be, I predict, very important.

Now we need to move vigorously ahead, missing no opportunity to bargain effectively and to represent at all levels privately and publicly that we mean business. I look forward to talking with Mr. Herter, as you suggested, immediately upon his return from Paris. I believe it essential that one of his assistants be thoroughly versed in agricultural trade matters.

We will continue to give this strong, vigorous attention here in the Department and in cooperation with the balance of the Government. I am confident that we can protect our markets so that we won't be apologizing come 1964 for losing hundreds of millions of dollars of Common Market agricultural markets when the Trade Expansion Act has led to high expectations of progress rather than losses.

VI.

Attached herewith is a more detailed and technical report of my trip,[2] including some specific action recommendations.

---

[2] Not printed.

VII. *Domestic.*

A. Consultations continue with commodity groups concerning our legislative program. At the same time detailed staff work is going forward on all commodities. There is little new to report. The various elements of the cotton world are not getting together on a program acceptable to us as quickly as I had hoped.

B. Reaction to the reorganization of ASCS has been generally good both by the public and within the Department.

---

54.   Memorandum of Conversation

Washington, November 27, 1962, 10:30 a.m.

SUBJECT

European Economic Problems

PARTICIPANTS

United States	*Belgium*
The Secretary	Foreign Minister Paul Henri Spaak[1]
Ambassador Douglas MacArthur	
Mr. Edmund S. Glenn (LS)	

The Secretary said that there were some questions other than that of the Congo which he wished to discuss with the Foreign Minister. The first one of these affects the future of the Atlantic Community and the Common Market since it involves the whole question of future trade between the European Economic Community and the United States. Secondly, the momentum gained through the partial resolution of the Cuban crisis has undoubtedly provided the Atlantic Community with many opportunities; if such opportunities are not exploited there will result a malaise which will please only Moscow.

Source: Department of State, Secretary's Memoranda of Conversation: Lot 65 D 330. Secret. Drafted by Glenn and approved in S on December 5. A shorter memorandum of Spaak's conversation with the President on this topic at 4 p.m. is ibid., Presidential Memoranda of Conversation: Lot 66 D 149.

[1] Spaak was in the United States to attend discussions on the Congo at the United Nations.

The Secretary would also be interested in the Foreign Minister's interpretation of such questions as the recent French elections, from the point of view of their influence on the Common Market and of the future of trade relations between Europe and the United States. The Secretary is somewhat concerned with these questions and would like to know if there is anything that the Foreign Minister could suggest for US action. The United States has tried to avoid any direct participation in the negotiations between its friends in Europe, since European economic and political integration is primarily a matter for the Europeans themselves and intervention on our part could be misunderstood. Nevertheless, such questions as the entry of the United Kingdom into the Common Market and the question of Common Market agricultural policy, which is protectionist [and] could lead to a possible future trade war between the United States and Europe, are of utmost importance and require attention if serious differences of policy within the Atlantic Community are not to occur.

The Foreign Minister said that he had not yet had an opportunity to congratulate the Secretary on the outcome of the Cuban crisis, where the United States has had a spectacular success. Our policy of acting with firmness but restraint had greatly strengthened the Free World. The Secretary replied we had tried to handle Cuba in a way to avoid having "a wounded bear" on our hands because wounded bears could be very dangerous.

The Foreign Minister is also concerned about the influence of the French elections on the European idea. In regard to future developments he is afraid that, if the UK joins the Common Market, General de Gaulle will no longer be truly interested in the development of the political unification of Europe and furthermore will do nothing to bring life and vigor to the various economic communities. The negotiations on the question of UK participation have reached a crucial point. Recently the questions faced by the negotiators were primarily at the level of technicalities and not those of basic principle. Now, however, a genuine question of principle is being raised in regard to agricultural policy. The Foreign Minister finds it difficult to see how the UK could agree to the proposals put forward by the Six regarding agriculture. He believes that the UK position is right and what the Six ask for is not reasonable. We will see this coming week what the position of France will be. France is, however, in a strong tactical position because she can say that she is merely asking for the implementation of decisions already agreed to by the Six last January. It was in order to achieve such a state of affairs that France has insisted that the agricultural question be resolved before serious negotiations began with the UK. At present the French can say that an agreement on agriculture was reached only a year earlier and that it is impossible to have exceptions for the UK. If the French insist on this approach, the British government will be faced with an exceedingly difficult position, because what the Six are forced to ask is not wise.

The UK has an agricultural system different from that of the Community, and the Community is saying now that the British system must be abrogated to be replaced for the next four years by a different, but still provisional system, which would then be adapted step by step to the practices of the Community. The British answer is that it is absurd that they should replace their present system by another one which would be only temporary; they ask instead to be given four or five years to align their system with that of the Community. This is reasonable, but it is doubtful whether the French would accept it. All the French seek is to obtain immediately all the immediate advantages which can accrue to them from the Common Market in the field of agriculture.

As a matter of fact, it is doubtful whether the very policy which they seek is a wise one from the point of view of agricultural management.

The Secretary remarked that the policy in question is likely to result in the repetition on the part of the Community of all the mistakes which had been made earlier by the United States in its agriculture with overexpansion of uneconomic production.

The Foreign Minister said that the situation is different in the negotiations with the UK from what it was at the time of the negotiation of the Rome Treaty. At that time the Six had the will to succeed. At the present moment it is not certain whether the French really want the negotiations with the UK to succeed. In this light, even the United States policy might have to be reconsidered. U.S. policy has always been that the United States is willing to accept certain economic drawbacks resulting from European integration because of the advantages that flow from the political integration of Europe. At the present moment there exists a distinct possibility of seeing an economic community in which the British, the Danes, the Norwegians and the Irish would participate without any degree of political integration.

The Secretary said that it is quite true that the United States was and is ready to accept certain economic discomforts for the sake of the accrued strength which would be gained by the free world through European political integration. However, the United States is not willing to accept deep economic injury, such as might result from a loss of several hundreds of millions of dollars a year of agricultural sales to Europe. Such a loss would have very serious consequences unless it were overcome first of all by a successful European integration, and then by successful trade negotiations between the United States and Europe. If the hopes of such economic solutions were to be dashed, the result would be not simply a return to an earlier state of affairs but rather a deep injury to the entire Atlantic Community.

The Foreign Minister said that he is also concerned by the possibility of such developments. It was a great mistake to place the negotiations on agricultural policy in the hands of agricultural experts without subordinating it to an integrated overall policy of the European community at world level. The experts arrived at the solution which is always put forward by agricultural experts, that is to say a protectionist system. The Six let them do it because they were so full of admiration for the fact that they had been able to agree on a coordinated agricultural policy, and they did not think sufficiently about the consequences. At present it is necessary for the Six to reconsider their position and to see where they stand not only in regard to the admission of the UK but also in regard to their entire policy. Unfortunately there are deep divergencies of opinion among the Six.

The Secretary asked whether the United States itself should not be doing more to influence the outcome. So far, the United States has always tried to refrain from trying to exercise a direct influence on affairs in which its European friends are more directly concerned than itself. The United States does not wish to be presumptuous by trying to exercise leadership in questions of a more direct concern to Europe. We have sensed a certain reassertion of Europe, which basically we favor; nevertheless we will be prepared to exercise more leadership unless we thought that this might be counter-productive. So far, whenever we tried to exercise such leadership in questions in which we were very directly concerned, such as that of armaments, of Berlin, or of disarmament, we were very conscious of an empty chair, that of France. What, under such circumstances, should be our attitude?

The Foreign Minister said that to conclude the agricultural question he wanted to add that he and Ambassador MacArthur had discussed this on a number of occasions recently. He had requested Ambassador MacArthur to write him a letter on the United States' preoccupations with regard to this question. [2] He had received this letter on the eve of his departure for New York and has circulated copies among his colleagues. There were possibilities of action in this area and he would take this matter up with the other members of the Common Market. However, we should make approaches in other European capitals similar to that which Ambassador MacArthur had made to him.

---

[2] MacArthur transmitted a copy of this letter in telegram 743 from Brussels, November 24. (Ibid., Central Files, 785.820/11–2462)

55.   Memorandum From the Under Secretary of State (Ball) to President Kennedy

Washington, December 10, 1962.

SUBJECT

United Kingdom-Common Market Negotiations

With the failing domestic strength of the Macmillan Government, the negotiations in Brussels with the European Economic Community have seriously slowed down and are nearly on dead-center. This partly reflects the distaste of de Gaulle and Adenauer for British entry into Europe; it also reflects the negative reaction of the "good European" members of the Commission of the Common Market to a British tendency to treat the negotiations as a commercial haggle rather than a major political undertaking.

During the OECD Ministerial Meeting in Paris ten days ago, I met with Bohlen, Bruce, Dowling, Reinhardt, Tuthill and Rice, to discuss how we might breathe some new life into these negotiations and insure against their failure. They recommended that I discuss certain aspects of this question with the Prime Minister at Nassau and try to see Heath some time early next year with a view to proposing to the British lines of attack that might improve their posture.

In the meantime, Heath, on his own motion, approached Bruce with the request that I see Hallstein, who was coming to the United States to make a speech. Heath hoped that I might soften Hallstein up to play a more constructive role. Subsequently, Heath also sent word that he himself would like to have a completely confidential meeting with me in Paris the middle of January, prior to the resumption of the negotiations in Brussels.

In response to Heath's request and in order to give the British side a helpful push, I arranged to have Hallstein fly to Washington Saturday, where he and I had a long and frank lunch. A report of the conversation is contained in the attached memorandum.[1] It is too long to read, but its

---

Source: Kennedy Library, National Security Files, United Kingdom. Secret. No drafting information appears on the source text.

[1] Not printed. In this 24-page memorandum of conversation Hallstein and Ball explored the attitudes of each of the Common Market countries toward British membership with Hallstein stressing that he was optimistic about the United Kingdom being successful. Ball stated the U.S. belief that the free world was moving into a "climactic" period when its total strength needed to be consolidated. British membership was vitally important as a first step to this strengthening, and Ball asked Hallstein whether, and how, the United States could be helpful.

essence is that Hallstein welcomed the idea that we might serve as a channel of communication between the Commission and the British, and he has made one or two suggestions that I can pass back to Heath as a starter.

I think Hallstein was impressed with the seriousness that we attached to a quick conclusion of these negotiations and I feel we have paved the way for some work backstage that can give the negotiations a helpful shove. Meanwhile, you will be in position to advise the Prime Minister at Nassau that we have struck a blow on his side.

George W. Ball

---

56.   Telegram From the Mission to the European Communities to the Department of State

Brussels, December 16, 1962, 10 p.m.

Ecbus 591. Eyes only for Secretary and Under Secretary from Tuthill. Subject: Relation of Polaris Decision to UK-Six Negotiations.

While in Paris during NATO meeting,[1] I discussed Skybolt-Polaris problem with Ambassador Finletter and was present Monnet meeting[2] during which this matter raised. Inasmuch as ultimate decision may have crucial effect on UK-Six negotiations, felt I should submit my reactions.

Today, both Six and UK have insisted publicly that current negotiations are not related to nuclear issues including whole range of special US-UK relations, French force de frappe and prospects for a multilateral instead of independent nuclear forces. It has seemed to me that, up until now, this public posture was entirely desirable as it offered the possibility that issue would not be decisively joined until after UK entry into Common Market had been decided. Then NATO and European multilateral force possibilities (within NATO context) could be examined on their merits.

Source: Department of State, Central Files, 375.800/12–1662. Secret; Niact.
[1] December 13–15.
[2] No other record of the meeting with Monnet has been found.

I am deeply concerned however that this truce on nuclear issues will burst wide open if the US should decide to offer aid to the UK for an independent Polaris deterrent to replace Skybolt. Major shock of change would come from fact that Polaris represents an indefinite deterrent while Skybolt has been generally assumed by Europeans to have a limited period of effectiveness—general impression being that it would rapidly become obsolete after 1970—the very year the Common Market would enter into full force. Thus, I have had impression that Europeans—and especially the French—were prepared to live with a special UK-US arrangement that in effect had a terminal date. French I believe are aware of fact that before original Skybolt agreement was reached with British, UK had been interested in obtaining Polaris submarines for purely independent force but had been turned down by US because of our unwillingness to prejudice multilateral force prospects and unduly prolong independent UK deterrent. I believe French would have serious doubts re UK membership in Community if UK has a special relation of indefinite validity in the nuclear weapons field.

Longer-term effects on Germans would also be grave. In line with their support of European integration, they have hitherto favored principle of a multilateral approach to nuclear problem and tacitly approved our policy of not aiding independent national nuclear efforts. US aid to British independent deterrent through Polaris could well alter this German position and cause Germans to look with more favor on French efforts to foster France-German collaboration as well as surfacing of latent German pressures for own independent national program.

Certainly Monnet was deeply shocked by newspaper reports that US might offer Polarises to UK apparently without insisting upon firm multilateral conditions. Having in mind timing aspects mentioned above, he felt such a decision would run directly counter to well established US opposition to proliferation of independent nuclear forces. It would strengthen De Gaulle's insistence upon his force de frappe and would reduce or perhaps eliminate possibility of achieving a genuine multilateral nuclear force. Quite clearly it would cause De Gaulle to reconsider UK entry into the Common Market as it would build in an indefinite structural preferential arrangement for the British in the most sensitive field of national security and prestige.

Personally I believe odds are still favorable that UK-Six negotiations will succeed in early months of 1963. However, this assumes no political changes such as a US offer of Polaris to UK without an effective multilateral framework. Effects of such a development would of course depend considerably on conditions attached and on how matter handled. However two grave (alternative) results appear possible in field of European unity. First would be that French might simply decide oppose British entry into Common Market. Second, French might resign themselves to British, Danish, Norwegian and Irish membership plus association or preference trading arrangements with other Europeans including neutrals in a big flabby trading arrangement with little political content. French acceptance of this would probably be based upon plan to change political content to bilateral France/German relationship for which they have already made quite extensive preliminary plans. This of course would result in a travesty of the united Europe that we have been seeking both economically and politically.

Tuthill

---

57.   Telegram From the Embassy in France to the Department of State

Paris, January 15, 1963, 7 p.m.

2804. Brussels for Embassy and USEC. The views of General De Gaulle on the subjects treated in his press conference[1] were on the whole fairly well known and have been previously reported. The only surprise at the press conference was that he should have stated these publicly with such frankness and brutality.

1.   In describing the reasons why Great Britain was not suitable to be included in the Common Market of the Six, De Gaulle did not dwell on any of the particular points at issue in the negotiations but went behind these matters to emphasize certain fundamental factors in the British picture which it should be noted are not questions which are susceptible of correction in short order, indeed if ever by any British Government. De Gaulle therefore made it plain that in his view (which certainly means that of France in the present circumstances) there were profound and unchangeable considerations which would prevent this development. In addition he pointed out that the entry of England

---

Source: Department of State, Central Files, 375.800/1–1563. Secret; Limit Distribution. Repeated to London, Bonn, Rome, and Brussels.

[1] For a transcript of de Gaulle's press conference on January 14, see *Major Addresses, Statements and Press Conferences of General Charles De Gaulle, May 19, 1958–January 31, 1964* (New York, undated), pp. 208–222; see also *American Foreign Policy: Current Documents, 1963*, pp. 441–443.

would probably mean the adherence of other countries which would transform the Common Market into a free trade area and lead to the creation of a "colossal Atlantic Community dependent on and directed by the Americans". This, he said, did not at all coincide with what the French wanted—an entity essentially European. He did however hold out as bait the possibility that there could be between the Common Market and Great Britain an "agreement of association", a nature to safeguard exchanges. (This tentative hint has already been rejected by Great Britain).

In short insofar as France is concerned De Gaulle slammed and locked the door to an immediate British entry into the Common Market. It remains to be seen whether the attitude of the other five members of the Market will be able to persuade France to modify these views and exactly what will be the British tactic in relation to this publicly declared position.

2.   In his remarks on the Nassau agreements[2] De Gaulle went considerably farther in the direction of complete rejection than had been anticipated. According to information that I had from various French ministers it was not expected that he would be so negative but would in effect leave the door open for future discussions. In addition to restating the well-known reasons why France desires to have its own independent nuclear deterrent, De Gaulle in this section also confused the elements of the American offer by speaking disdainfully only of a multilateral force. He either had not absorbed or deliberately disregarded the explanations which Ball gave to NAC on Friday.[3] It is of course possible to read into his remarks a hint that a more extended offer from the United States in regard to submarine construction and warhead secrets might be acceptable, but I think that this is too slender a possibility for us to base any action or policy upon.

It also will be noted that he referred to "technical" and "strategic" cooperation if desired by France's allies.

His interpretation of the meaning, from the point of view of Europe, of the Cuban crisis was of course completely inaccurate and lacking in elementary logic. It will be recalled that he advanced this interpretation to me during our meeting on January 4[4] and was apparently not affected in any way by my reply. This view appears to have become a French dogma.

---

[2] For text of the Statement on Nuclear Defense Systems issued by President Kennedy and Prime Minister Macmillan at Nassau, December 21, 1962, see ibid., *1962*, pp. 635–637.

[3] See Document 164.

[4] See Document 263.

3.   On the subject of Franco-German relations he seemed to be emphasizing the "special relationship" which has developed in the last year or so between France and Germany, but in reply to a question his statement that it is entirely up to Germany what she wished to do in the nuclear field disregarded completely the effect of the WEU treaties.

A Foreign Office clarification subsequently stated that these remarks did not indicate any change in French policy on the subject. His flat rejection of any integrated multilateral force was in ironic contrast with the German acceptance on the same day of this concept and I imagine that this will be an active subject of consideration at his meeting next week with Adenauer.

The conference was indeed the "conference de choc" that one French paper predicted several days [ago] as it involved in effect French rejection of two major American objectives, 1) on the question of Great Britain's joining the Common Market, and 2) the NATO nuclear force. In the face of these two rejections I strongly believe it would be most unwise and indeed dangerous for us to attempt any further move towards France in the unwarranted hope that the sweetening of the Nassau offer might produce some fundamental change in French thinking. I should point out in this connection that the views expressed by De Gaulle, although more sharply put than in the past, represent little more than continuance of certain basic ideas which De Gaulle has consistently held since his return to power in 1958.

I believe in the present circumstances we should press forward on Polaris agreement with Great Britain and also with other NATO powers on multilateral force. In regard to France I would undertake no new initiative but merely stand pat on our present positions and await the course of events and avoid insofar as possible at this juncture US official reaction.

Bohlen

58.   Memorandum of Conversation

Washington, January 16, 1963, 3 p.m.

SUBJECT

European Integration

PARTICIPANTS

Italy
Amintore Fanfani, Prime Minister of the Italian Republic
Sergio Fenoaltea, Ambassador of Italy
Edoardo Martino, Director General of Political Affairs
Giovanni Fornari, Director General of Political Affairs
Carlo Marchiori, Foreign Policy Advisor to the Prime Minister
Umberto La Rocca, Chief of Secretariat to the Under Secretary
Giuseppe Bartolomei, Chief of Secretariat to the Prime Minister
Gian Luigi Milesi Ferretti, Italian Minister

United States
The Secretary
Under Secretary Ball
Under Secretary McGhee
Mr. Bell, Administrator, AID
Ambassador Reinhardt
Assistant Secretary Tyler
Mr. Francis E. Meloy, Jr., Director, WE
Mr. Samuel R. Gammon, WE, Italian Desk

The Secretary stated that he did not wish to detail the U.S.'s distress at de Gaulle's press conference. However, on the topic of European unity, he wished to state that the current troubles within the Soviet bloc give us a chance to write a new chapter in developing the strength and unity of the West. We had supposed the UK application to enter the EEC was a great chance to enlarge this unity and to build toward a new Atlantic partnership as described by President Kennedy in his speech last July 4.[1] On the other hand, if the West splits into factions, it gives the Kremlin great comfort and all of us serious discouragement. The Secretary expressed his worry at the effect on American public opinion if the West appears to falter, stumble, or pull back.

Asking for Prime Minister Fanfani's comments, the Secretary stated that he presumed to say that Italy had now a chance to play an historic role at a time when others are faltering—a chance to find ways and

---

Source: Department of State, Central Files, 375.700/1–1663. Secret. Drafted by Gammon and approved in U on January 23 and in S on January 24. The meeting was held in the Under Secretary's Conference Room.

[1] For text of this speech, see *Public Papers of the Presidents of the United States: John F. Kennedy, 1962*, pp. 537–539.

means to keep up the momentum of the West's progress toward strength and unity despite a temporary setback. The Secretary said that the U.S. feels deeply that these developments affect the quality of the Atlantic relationship. We refuse categorically to accept the false suggestion of some that it is we and not the Soviets who somehow threaten Western Europe or are trying to swallow it. The U.S. wants partners. Our one million men in uniform in every continent want to return home. The Secretary asked Prime Minister Fanfani whether at this crossroads the rest of us might move ahead without one or two members or whether the present situation was a genuine crisis in which we could not move ahead without the participation of all countries.

Prime Minister Fanfani stated frankly that de Gaulle's speech had exceeded his worst expectations and had surprised many people. He had feared such an attitude by de Gaulle and on the previous Saturday, through the French Ambassador, had passed on to de Gaulle Italy's concern and modest advice toward moderation. The result had not been very encouraging, even though Italy's opinion had been sought. Nevertheless, it might have been worse without this advice. Even before de Gaulle's press conference, the Prime Minister had told Italy's Ministers at Brussels, Messrs. Colombo and Rumor, by telephone to press on to find a solution which would result in the UK's admission to the EEC. Prime Minister Fanfani asserted that he would not let himself become discouraged over external acts. Minister Colombo had also been authorized to pass on Italy's views to Belgian Foreign Minister Spaak who had solicited them. These views appeared to be shared by representatives of all five countries at Brussels. It was feared that French Foreign Minister Couve might be bringing a veto to Brussels that very day, but the Prime Minister, though concerned, did not think this likely. He hoped that a solution to individual technical problems might bring a joint EEC agricultural solution acceptable to the UK and within the EEC principles which would allow gradual conversion of the UK system and would also protect Prime Minister Macmillan at the polls.

Concerning financial problems, German Foreign Minister Schroeder had told the Italian Foreign Minister that in the UK-EEC negotiations Germany favored a solution which would satisfy France. Italy counted on, and hoped that we would assist, the UK in making some practical concessions on this topic to create a new situation which would permit de Gaulle to accept it and escape from the impasse created by his press conference.

Replying to the Secretary's question, Prime Minister Fanfani asserted that the UK must show a new attempt to evolve in this direction. If the UK really wanted it, if Macmillan could act in this way before elections, and if it would not alarm British labor, Britain could perhaps take a less critical attitude. In that case—perhaps not now but in February—it might be possible to find an acceptable solution. In the meantime, if de Gaulle can see that his fears of American hegemony in the UK and in Europe are exaggerated, well and good.

Under Secretary Martino then took up the question of UK-EEC negotiations. He pointed out that the European group in the European Parliament at Strasbourg was unanimously in favor of UK entry, favoring particularly its effect on the political balance in Europe. Italy also accepts this viewpoint at face value. Foreign Minister Piccioni, he said, was now endeavoring in Brussels to obtain a successful outcome in the negotiations. Mr. Martino added that Italy strongly favored UK entry into Europe and also welcomed President Kennedy's concept of Atlantic partnership. These two developments would lead to even greater political stability and would guarantee peace in the world. If accomplished quickly, they would be deeply positive factors for peace. Even the Soviets now see that the EEC is not a threat to the peace but rather an element of balance in the world.

The intention of the six in developing the EEC was to build a tool for harmony and peace and a better world. Without the UK in it, the EEC would become a weakening or divisive factor. This is why Italy favored British participation in a greater Europe.

The Prime Minister concluded by suggesting that the discussion be continued at dinner.[2]

---

[2] No record of any further discussion has been found.

---

59.   Circular Telegram From the Department of State to Certain Missions

Washington, January 19, 1963, 8:57 p.m.

1277. Paris for Embassy and USRO. Brussels and Luxembourg for Embassy and USEC. US foreign policy towards Europe rests on two premises. One, the inexorable move toward closer European unity and

---

Source: Department of State, Central Files, 611.40/1–1963. Limited Official Use. Drafted by Cleveland and Freedman (EUR); cleared with Schaetzel, Ball, P, RPM, WE, and the White House; and approved by Tyler. Sent to Ottawa and 18 missions in Europe.

integration and, two, increasingly close, cooperative relations between this Europe and the United States. In this movement toward the growing unity of the West, there may well be temporary diversions which challenge both our patience and ingenuity. We are, however, firmly convinced of the inevitability of a more closely knit Atlantic partnership. Man's achievements in science and technology, which can be used for constructive as well as destructive purposes, give the contradiction to the presumed ability of the leading nations of the West to act for their own narrow self-interest.

We believe Europe will not be turned away from the progress and prosperity these relationships make possible, but will move closer together and join with us in a common approach to common problems.

In view of the current situation in Europe resulting from de Gaulle's public reaffirmation of views long known to be held and the difficulties which now confront the negotiations for British membership in the EEC, the Department believes it important to reiterate the above views in official and non-official contacts.

In addition to the general policy background outlined above specific points listed below should be used.

1. US foreign policy is guided by judgment that in fundamental sense security and progress of Western Europe and US are indivisible. Specifically, defense of Western Europe is the defense of the US, and in our view, the reverse is equally true for Europe. Neither area can go it alone without imperiling survival and progress of both. This applies to security, economic and political action. We see the course of history in the Atlantic area moving irresistibly toward closer integration.

2. In our constant and unswerving post-war support for European integration we have always envisaged full British participation as essential to the process of unity. Further the UK can perform a uniquely constructive role in the developing Atlantic Partnership.

3. Our policies are based on the hard realities of geography, history and common interests. It is in recognition of these realities that the US provided Europe tremendous and critical support under the Marshall Plan; gave full support from the beginning to the movement for closer economic and political integration in Europe, including the Common Market; continues to maintain in Europe 400,000 troops and has committed its full military power in support of the defense of Europe. US policy will continue as it has for 17 years and not be deflected by short-term developments or attitudes.

4. Nassau and post-Nassau proposals for a NATO multilateral force are also direct results of long-term US policy and explicit recognition that nuclear defense of North Atlantic area is indivisible. Proposals at Nassau designed to begin the process of increasing European partici-

pation in nuclear defense. By building upon the letter and spirit of these proposals, the Alliance can avoid the ineffective and dangerous consequences which would flow from the creation of small national nuclear forces. To imply that Nassau constitutes a turn away from Europe is a gross distortion of the intent of the agreement.

5. The crisis arising out of the UK-Six negotiations may raise questions about the continued effectiveness of the Common Market, ECSC and Euratom as viable European institutions. We do not hold this view. For reasons stated above we believe the historical imperatives that led to the creation of European integration remain: The US for its part will continue to work to the maximum feasible extent with these institutions. FYI. There will of course be speculation whether French intransigence will carry over to calculated use of the Community institutions for narrow, national French purposes. We see no merit at this juncture in anticipating this as an inevitable development or in fact in discussing now the kinds of actions that might be taken should this situation develop. End FYI.

In summary, there is no change in broad direction of US policy. Nor do we believe there will be a long term change in European moves toward integration. Immediate events, regardless of how serious they are in fact or appearance, cannot long delay this trend. The immediate next steps in Europe are a matter for the Europeans themselves. It is their economic growth and defensive capability which are at stake. They should understand that the US as in the past, stands ready to assist and work with them in maintaining their security and prosperity.

FYI. It would be counterproductive to US policy to enter into a public dispute with de Gaulle and therefore any comments on the French action should be limited to the above. End FYI.

Rusk

---

60.   **Telegram From the Department of State to the Embassy in Germany**

Washington, January 23, 1963, 8:11 p.m.

1698. Following based on uncleared memcon:

Source: Department of State, Central Files, 651.62A/1–2363. Secret; Priority; Eyes Only. Drafted by Creel (GER) and cleared with EUR and in substance with Bundy.

Ambassador Knappstein called on Secretary this afternoon to transmit copy of letter from Chancellor to President (text in immediately following telegram) which he had delivered to President few hours earlier.[1]

Knappstein commented that while he had felt he was delivering good news to President, latter had expressed disappointment over Chancellor's letter and had in fact been quite outspoken to point of suggesting he considered Franco-German Treaty signed in Paris Jan 22 "an unfriendly act" on FedRep's part. According Knappstein, President had said he was disappointed that only a week after de Gaulle press conference FedRep should embrace de Gaulle. Knappstein said he had pointed out that principles of treaty had been agreed to long ago and that date of signing merely coincidental.(Secretary interjected that date might not have been coincidence from French point of view at least insofar as timing of de Gaulle press conference was concerned.)

According Knappstein, President had stressed to him that US had consistently fought off de Gaulle's idea of tripartite directorate because of our desire to protect interests of FedRep and had gone on to express disappointment that latter had now concluded a directorate with France. Knappstein said he had taken line that no directorate was involved but only principle of mutual consultation in which FedRep would retain complete liberty of independent decision. Furthermore it was now necessary under terms of treaty for France to consult with FedRep before taking major decisions; this would give FedRep opportunity to present its own viewpoint, which in fact coincided with those of US on all issues of importance including Nassau accords and UK accession to Common Market.

Knappstein commented to Secretary that based on preliminary reports he had received first beneficial effect of treaty was already being felt since it appeared de Gaulle had acceded to Chancellor's request in Paris that UK accession issue be kept alive by procedure of commission study of points of agreement and disagreement.

Knappstein also said President had impliedly charged FedRep with taking sides with France against US and had made several references this connection to *New York Times* article of Jan 21. Knappstein told

---

[1] Knappstein met with the President from 11:30 a.m. to 12:10 p.m. (Kennedy Library, President's Appointment Books) and with Rusk for 30 minutes at 2 p.m. (Johnson Library, Rusk Appointment Book), but no other record of these conversations has been found. In the letter Adenauer informed the President that he had signed the Franco-German treaty, which he believed would promote the unification of Europe and strengthen the whole free world, and that he would continue to support "vigorously" the British application for membership in the Common Market. (Telegram 1701 to Bonn, January 24; Department of State, Central Files, 651.62A/1–2463) For text of the Treaty, see *American Foreign Policy: Current Documents, 1963*, pp. 486–488.

Secretary he wished to stress most emphatically that FedRep had made no choice between France and US because they believed "the two things went together". Chancellor and all Germans after centuries of conflict regarded reconciliation with France as of vital importance but it would be suicide for Germans to take sides with France against US.

Secretary said he agreed it was fundamental to bring about Franco-German reconciliation and this was in fact a great historical achievement. As concerned Chancellor's letter, he found it encouraging on the specific points commented therein on. Issue which really concerned us at this time (and this was not just a matter affecting the US) was where center of gravity of policy was going to be in this relationship. Over last 3–4 years de Gaulle had been pursuing broad role of abstention from affairs of Western community (for example French engaged in minimum participation in NATO, their participation in UN proceedings was at a minimum, they were not filling their chair in current disarmament discussions, they had been a minority of one out of fifteen in NATO on the Berlin issue, they had threatened to resign their commitments to SEATO). If center of gravity of policy making in new Franco-German relationship were to shift to Paris, there would be serious problems ahead. Over past years our friends in Bonn had repeatedly asked us for reassurances. Now in fact things had shifted somewhat to point where we might wish reassurance from the Germans. We needed to understand where we were going.

Knappstein commented that FedRep's vital interests were closer to those of US than to France, and opportunity was presented here for FedRep to help get de Gaulle out of his current isolationism. Secretary replied that if things worked out that way we would welcome it but this had unfortunately not been our experience of how consultation with de Gaulle worked. We had for example learned more about his thinking from his press conference than from months of diplomatic discussions. However to extent that German policy could be sustained vis-à-vis French he agreed this would have important influence on situation.

Knappstein reiterated that first effect of such influence had already been felt in de Gaulle's reported agreement not to close door on discussions on UK accession to Common Market. Franco-German treaty did in fact afford Germans excellent opportunity to work on de Gaulle. He would be very happy if President could see this possibility.

Secretary said he thought it would be wise to adopt position of wait-and-see as to how things worked out under the treaty. We could evaluate the situation better when we saw more clearly where center of gravity of policymaking would rest. Meanwhile there was absolutely no argument over point re beneficial effect of French-German reconciliation.

In conclusion Secretary asked Ambassador to seek clarification from Foreign Office regarding clause in Franco-German treaty making it applicable to Berlin. We would have to study this matter within context our reserved powers in Berlin. We were not sure that as one of the powers involved we would like to have Berlin Senat ratify this treaty, since it was questionable whether we could accept this kind of special bilateral interest in Berlin.

FYI. Contrary to Knappstein report to Secretary the President did not refer to *New York Times* Reston article of January 21. However, President did express concern over meaning of reference to "private consultation" outside NATO by France and Germany bilaterally on NATO matters. End FYI.

Rusk

---

61. **Telegram From the Department of State to the Embassy in Germany**

Washington, January 24, 1963, 9:10 p.m.

1712. Brussels also for Embassy. Paris inform USRO. Next crucial phase of UK-Six affair is January 28 Foreign Ministers meeting at which decision will be taken on future of negotiations. This decision, though technically procedural, will probably be determining. We must therefore concentrate on insuring decision which will bring negotiations to rapid conclusion; this is probably last crisis in negotiations, and if it passes without conclusion, negotiations liable to peter out with no clear assignment of responsibility.

We understand Germans will probably propose at Monday meeting procedure whereby EEC Commission would be asked take stock of issues in negotiations. In our view success requires that two elements be added to proposal, and that "five" insist on adoption of entire proposal with no dilution. Two additional elements are (1) on basis assessment of situation Commission be charged with job of bringing forward specific proposals on basis of which agreement can be rapidly concluded; and (2) that charge by the Ministers to the Commission contain early deadline for concluding the study and recommendations.

Source: Department of State, Central Files, 375.42/1–2463. Confidential. Drafted by Cleveland, cleared in substance with Schaetzel, and approved by Ball. Also sent to Rome, Brussels Busec, The Hague, London, and Luxembourg, and repeated to Paris.

Seems clear that in Paris meetings de Gaulle agreed with Chancellor to avoid spectacular breakdown negotiations. Seems equally clear from Embassy Paris reporting that French will do everything they can to prevent decision on above lines which would vitiate their ability to draw out negotiations while avoiding responsibility for breakdown. Presumably French efforts will be addressed to limiting Commission to report on issues or even on "feasibility" of a seven-nation community, with no deadlines and with later resumption of negotiations subject to French veto.

However, our judgment is that if other five hold firm to proposal along lines second paragraph above, and Germans make absolutely clear they will accept nothing else, de Gaulle may be induced to yield. Firmness of German position at all levels is therefore key to situation, but others must also play their role.

Action:

For Bonn: Separate instruction in preparation for possible further approach to Chancellor.[1] In meantime, however, you should approach Erhard and Schroeder and make clear we consider they hold key to situation and everything depends on their taking the initiative in Brussels on above line, and holding absolutely firm. Our intervention should be explained on ground our serious concern over effect recent events on Western unity and consequences of appearance Western disarray on Soviet calculations re Berlin and other danger points, and our conviction that only rapid successful conclusion UK-EEC negotiations can restore that unity.

For Embassy Brussels: You should explain our view situation to Spaak, and urgently request him to give full support to proposed formula. Whatever his reservations about French motives (which we share), a common position of five on a practical proposal is key to success on Monday, and we hope he will play usual constructive role in achieving it and in persuading Germans to take the lead. You may also say we are convinced that if given this mandate Commission will use it constructively to move negotiations towards a successful conclusion.

For London: You should approach Heath, explain our thinking as above, and express our judgment that (1) British should accept suggested procedure without quibbling on details; and (2) they should be prepared to help Commission by putting forward to it their last concessions. This is moment of truth and we believe Heath aware of fact.

For Rome, Hague, Luxembourg: You should take whatever action you feel appropriate to help bring about common front on proposed procedure and to persuade your clients to stiffen German position along these

---

[1] No instruction along these lines has been found.

lines. Last opportunity may be bilateral talks with German delegation in Brussels on Sunday.

For USEC: You should see Hallstein and impress on him importance we attach to rapid success conclusion negotiations using line of argument suggested in instructions for Bonn above. You should urge him insure that Commission stand solidly with "five" in favor broad terms of reference and deadline, and be prepared act promptly if mandate received. We have been disturbed by rumor Commission might take as long as two months to make report; in our view this much delay could be disastrous to success negotiations and we count on Hallstein and his colleagues be prepared move much faster than this.

Rusk

---

62. Telegram From the Department of State to the Mission to the European Communities

Washington, January 28, 1963, 9:53 p.m.

Busec 312. Eyes only Ambassador from Secretary. Brussels for Ambassador Tuthill. Please deliver following personal message from Secretary to Foreign Minister Schroeder prior to meeting tomorrow morning:

"We have been giving the most careful and anxious consideration to the underlying causes of the present crisis in Europe. We cannot escape the conclusion that one government is proposing to deny British entry into Common Market because of a historic relation between the United Kingdom and the US and as a part of a calculated policy to eliminate the American presence in Europe and the intimacy of trans-Atlantic relations. This runs directly counter to the most elementary notions underlying the NATO Alliance, namely, that the defense of Western Europe and of North America is indivisible and that the vitality of the Alliance depends upon mutual confidence on both sides of the Atlantic.

We have regarded the problems between the UK and the European Community as matters to be resolved by the participants. We have from

---

Source: Department of State, Central Files, 375.42/1–2863. Secret; Niact. Drafted and initialed by Rusk and cleared with Ball, Tyler, and the President. Repeated to Bonn.

the beginning recognized the possibility that these negotiations might fail through an inability to agree on a wide range of economic and technical problems which affect the daily lives of the citizens of the countries involved. It is obvious, however, that such negotiations have not failed. Instead, in the very prospect of success, one government is seeking to halt them on grounds which seem to us to be a part of a campaign to break up the North Atlantic Alliance. These present decisions are essentially for Europe to make, and particularly concern the Federal Republic, but if this negotiation should fail on the grounds mentioned above, there would result a most serious injury to Western cohesion in cooperation across the Atlantic. I would be strongly opposed to any developments which would set in motion events which could separate the two sides of the Atlantic and lead to the exposure of Europe to pressures from the East which it cannot possibly withstand alone.

I am sending you this message because I know that you understand what present decisions mean for Europe as a whole and that you do not wish to see the very heart of the free world weakened by decisions now to be taken. We fully appreciate the difficulty of your position in facing a possible choice between two great objectives of German policy, namely, European and Atlantic unity and cordial and closer relations with France. I send you this message to express my full personal appreciation for your own attitude in these difficult days. I am fully aware of the complexities you face but I wanted you to know that we have a deep appreciation for the transcendent issues which are of the deepest concern to all of us."[1]

Rusk

---

[1] On January 29 Tuthill reported that he had met with Schroeder shortly before the 9 a.m. meeting with his Common Market colleagues. Schroeder read the message from Rusk and said: "I agree with every word." The Foreign Minister also told Tuthill that he was not optimistic about the negotiations with the United Kingdom, but would do everything he could to keep the French from obscuring the reasons or responsibilities for their failure. (Ibid., 375.42/1–2963)

63.   **Telegram From the Department of State to the Embassy in Italy**

Washington, January 30, 1963, 8:41 p.m.

1440. Ref: Rome 1509.[1] From Under Secretary for Ambassador Reinhardt. I would appreciate it if you would seek appointment with Fanfani prior Macmillan visit and convey to him our warmest appreciation of steadfast Italian position in Brussels yesterday and the show of solidarity on the question of UK entry and implicitly Atlantic Partnership. FYI. We shall be communicating similar views to Adenauer for the steadfast German position. We are hopeful that solidarity between UK and Germans will develop into closer and more fruitful relationship and we wish to encourage similar Italian-UK understanding. The Multilateral Force represents a specific and important way for UK to seek closer ties with Germans and Italians among alliance members seeking interdependence. End FYI.

I would like you to emphasize to Fanfani the line that France's veto of British entry is the first time since the establishment of the Communities that one nation has taken it upon itself to slow down the drive toward true European unity. This is to be regretted, particularly since this defection is based upon a reversion to the divisive and dangerous furtherance of nationalist ambitions by techniques that history teaches us have failed.

For our part, we shall be moving ahead as rapidly as possible with negotiations for a NATO Multilateral Nuclear Force and we are gratified by the wholehearted Italian willingness to participate in this project. Might be useful for you to mention to Fanfani favorable evolution of recent UK thinking on Multilateral Force. UK apparently sees as we do how it can contribute materially to cohesion in NATO of EEC members. UK itself now considering participation in MLF. Would be helpful if Fanfani could indicate Italian readiness to work together with interested NATO members to strengthen Atlantic partnership at this critical moment, through MLF exercise and in other ways. We believe this would strike responsive chord.

We shall also be moving ahead as rapidly as possible with negotiations under the Trade Expansion Act and Governor Herter's initial contacts with the Commission will soon be followed up by more concrete

Source: Department of State, Central Files, 033.4165/1-2963. Secret; Priority. Drafted by Vine and Popper; cleared by Schaetzel, Spiers, and Meloy; and approved by Ball. Repeated to Bonn, Brussels, and London.

[1] Telegram 1509, January 29, asked if the Department of State had any issues it wanted to raise with Fanfani prior to Macmillan's visit to Italy February 2-4. (Ibid.)

action. Progress along this line will tend to minimize the damage that the French veto will cause for all of us.

In the meantime, we would welcome any indications of Italian Government view on what positive steps can be taken to maintain the momentum for European unity and Atlantic Partnership in the face of French recalcitrance.

Rusk

---

64.   **Summary Record of NSC Executive Committee Meeting No. 39**

Washington, January 31, 1963, 6 p.m.

The President said today's meeting was preliminary to numerous ones which he thought should be held during the next two weeks on the subject of our European policy. He said the meetings would be most confidential and should not be known to any one. He hoped that it would be possible for us to conduct the reappraisal of our policy without it becoming known because, following a reappraisal, we may decide to make no major change in our existing policy. He said the purpose of the current exercise was to try to see where we are going in Europe without the public surmising that we would be studying proposals for drastic changes in our relation with Europe. The President read the following questions which he said we should seek to answer in the near future.

1. U.S. trade negotiations with the Common Market

We need to decide what our tactics should be and which questions we should negotiate about first.

2. Spaak's political future

Can Spaak survive in Belgium if he continues to advance his anti-de Gaulle position? He is under attack because of his standing with us on the Congo as well as for the position he has taken following France's rejection of UK membership in the Common Market.

Source: Kennedy Library, National Security Files, Executive Committee Meetings. Top Secret; Sensitive.

3. *Will the African countries now apply for admission to the Common Market?*

Do you think the Belgians and the Dutch would hold up their admission as a means of applying pressure on the French? Would this action come before we know what effect the Common Market tariffs will have on Latin American economies?

4. *What is the future of the NATO multilateral force?*

Should we go ahead along this line? Will the French seek to include nuclear arrangements in their new Franco/German treaty? Should Mr. Merchant push forward negotiations for the establishment of the NATO multilateral force or should he wait until we know better what we want to do?

5. *Should we wait for the German Defense Minister to come here or should we send Mr. Merchant to talk to him in Bonn about a U.S./German bilateral arrangement?*

6. *How can we get our view to American reporters in Europe so that their stories do not reflect the French point of view?*

7. *Can we improve liaison with Washington correspondents of foreign newspapers to ensure that our view is presented and the French press line is countered?*

8. *How can we improve our techniques of being certain that U.S. reporters understand our policy and the reasons behind our actions?*

9. *What kind of a deal can de Gaulle make with the Russians which would be acceptable to the Germans?*

10. *What are the prospects for a tripartite deal with de Gaulle?*

Does he still want this? Should we try now to go for a tripartite directorate?

11. *Balance of payments problem*

How do we defend ourselves if the French decide to create problems for us in connection with the one billion dollar balances which they now control?

12. *What are the prospects for a French nuclear force?*

When will it be a deterrent, even in a limited sense? Would even a few weapons in fact be a deterrent to the Russians?

13. *What should we propose at the NATO meeting in May?*

Should we reduce the number of our divisions in Europe and bring them home? Should we close U.S. installations in France?

The President interjected an additional question following point number 9. He wondered if the Soviet position was hardening in view of the fact that the Russians had broken off the current test ban discussions. He asked whether the French had been talking to the Russians and whether Soviet decision to end the test ban talks now had anything to do with the division existing among the NATO allies.

The President said we should concentrate our intelligence resources on finding out everything we can about discussions and negotiations between the French and the Russians. The President concluded his remarks by saying that we can go in four different directions but that, following our study, perhaps our decision would be to make no changes and await further developments in Europe. It was important, however, to deal with the multilateral nuclear force proposal in such a way as not to commit us before we knew exactly which direction we wished to take.

In response to a suggestion by Secretary Rusk, Assistant Secretary Tyler said he had heard from an allied diplomatic source that when the Soviet Ambassador in Paris talked to de Gaulle he presented a fourteen page letter attacking the Franco/German treaty, especially the defense arrangements included in it. Secretary Rusk said de Gaulle's January 14 press conference had caught everyone by surprise, including close friends and intimates of de Gaulle. Even de Gaulle may have failed to anticipate the worldwide reaction to his press conference.

Secretary Rusk said our relations with the French were proceeding along several tracks, none of them dependent on UK admission to the Common Market. He recalled that we knew there was a possibility that the UK might not be taken into the Common Market, but even so, we had proceeded in NATO to discuss the buildup of conventional forces and ways to improve consultation among the allies. In addition, in the OECD we had seen French support for our efforts to improve economic cooperation among the allies. He urged that we avoid fighting the French in those areas where they are cooperating with us, i.e. in Africa, except in the Congo; in financial matters; and to an extent, in Southeast Asia. He expressed his view that we should not start a vindictive chain of reaction, that we not block every line of policy we are now following toward France.

The President replied that while we did realize that the UK might not get into the Common Market, we did not expect the rejection to be accomplished in the way de Gaulle had done it. In addition, he said the Franco/German treaty had created a new situation. He felt that de Gaulle, certain of our willingness to go to the defense of Europe, was attempting to exploit us. He wondered whether de Gaulle's next move would be a treaty with Italy. Conceivably, de Gaulle might try to organize the Six and create a nuclear force responsible to this grouping. He said we might not get into an across-the-board battle with de Gaulle but he wanted to be certain that if de Gaulle did continue to harass us, we would be in a position to defend ourselves. The U.S. military position is good but our financial position is vulnerable. Our influence in Latin

America has been decreased by the French actions. He hoped for the best but said we must look at all aspects of the current situation. Perhaps the NATO multilateral nuclear force idea is finished. De Gaulle may appeal to Italy and Belgium and the others on the Continent and possibly win them to his European idea.

Secretary Dillon said he agreed that we were weak in the financial area but strong in the political and military fields. He felt that if the French did attack our financial stability we should consider ways of responding by actions in the military and political areas. He noted that the British economic position, as reflected in the market, had already been weakened by de Gaulle's action. One British reaction might be to withdraw their forces in Germany in order to defend the British balance of payments position. Whether this was a good or bad move, we should be prepared to make our position known.

The President thought that the British, in an attempt to gain the support of Germany, might decide to keep British troops in Germany.

Secretary Ball suggested that we ought to look at our assets as well as the French assets in viewing the future of Europe. De Gaulle is a European and the head of a metropolitan country. In addition, he has the advantage of being able to act irresponsibly. The U.S., on the other hand, is a world power while France is not. The U.S. now has nuclear strength but the French only hope to have a nuclear force later. Since the war, the U.S. has filled the vacuum created by a weak Europe. We have been leading the Europeans back into a wider world. The Europeans need a sense of participating in world problems. Failing to have this sense, they become psychotic.

Secretary Ball said that we turned down de Gaulle's proposal for a tripartite directorate in 1958 because (a) there was no place in the scheme for the Germans, (b) de Gaulle was presuming to speak for all of Europe, and (c) the scheme was limited to planning military strategy. Mr. Ball said we should now envisage some mechanism which would make possible systematic political cooperation with competent European states. His proposal would mean that Europe would take over from us some of the burdens we have been carrying worldwide and at the same time they would be participating in military planning and control of a nuclear force. He said one way would be to take the proposed Executive Committee which was devised to provide political control of a NATO nuclear force and add to it responsibility for political consultation. The Executive Committee, holding regular meetings, would be available for consultation in crisis situations, such as Cuba and the Congo, and, in addition, could work out a new allocation of responsibility of the European powers for countries in which we are now carrying the entire burden. He envisaged a planning board of directors for world problems.

Mr. Ball said de Gaulle cannot offer the Europeans this kind of participation because France is not a world power. Such an offer by us to the Europeans would have great appeal to the Europeans because it would be a meaningful partnership. Mr. Ball admitted that during the past fifteen years we have gotten into some bad habits and have been carrying all the burden. We would now ask the Europeans to take real responsibility by turning over to them certain countries or allies and telling them we would help the European states on the assumption that they would be in charge of the operation. We would be in the position not of asking them to help us run an area but of offering to help them if they would take on the responsibility of running the area. We would thus be able to exploit the resource of our world power position.

The President replied that apparently de Gaulle does not want to associate with us. Some European states may be prepared to follow de Gaulle while others may not want to get out from under our shelter. We face the decision as to whether we should go around de Gaulle or whether we should wait and then propose to him establishment of the three-power directorate. However, we must avoid an appearance of trying to enter the back door when the front door is closed. We must also recognize that anything we propose may arouse the full force of de Gaulle's opposition.

Mr. Nitze felt that Secretary Ball's proposal to expand the terms of reference of a NATO executive committee would cause great confusion. He did not think that political consultation should take place in the Executive Committee because it would mix up the handling of the NATO multilateral nuclear force. He suggested instead that the North Atlantic Council was the proper forum to use for political consultation.

The President said it was mandatory that we get foreign states to help share free world burdens. He said Congress might well conclude that we should not help Europe if de Gaulle continues to act as he has been. He felt that we must get the Europeans to share in the free world programs in Latin America, Africa and Asia.

Secretary Rusk said we must plan for the worst case but we should not adopt a policy based on an assumption that de Gaulle has declared war on us across the board.

The President said what we must figure out is what does de Gaulle want during the next two years, recognizing that he would proceed to achieve it step by step. No one, including intimates, knew what de Gaulle was going to say in his January 14 press conference. The President recalled that a sizeable part of the Nassau arrangements was designed to please the French. We did not know how the French would react and we must do better in trying to find out how de Gaulle will act in the future.

Secretary Rusk pointed out that we are in Europe not because the Europeans want us there but because we believe our presence there is essential to the defense of the U.S. He said we cannot permit de Gaulle to force us out of Europe without the greatest effort to resist such a move.

The President said NSC Executive Committee should look at all aspects of the European problem. He thought we ought to have an estimate of the political effect on each European country of de Gaulle's current policy.

Secretary Dillon asked that we examine the question of how many forces the U.S. must have in Europe. In view of the $750 million cost of our military effort in Europe and the impact of these expenditures on our balance of payments, he wondered whether withdrawal of U.S. forces would be the disaster some say it would or whether Europe could now, by itself and without the U.S. troops on the ground, hold back the USSR.

Mr. Bundy noted that Secretary Rusk was planning to hold a press conference the following morning.[1]

The President felt that the timing of the press conference was not good and he wondered whether the conference would be useful.

Secretary Rusk said that to call off the conference would create a great deal of speculation. He felt that the conference would be useful in order not to heat up the Common Market problem. He said he did not intend to strike at de Gaulle or aim barbs at the British for the remarks which Macmillan made about national control of UK nuclear forces to be included in the NATO force.

The President said he thought that the Secretary should not give the impression that nothing has been changed in the past few days. He added that if de Gaulle got very rough we would be required to deal with him. He said he believed that after the Skybolt development de Gaulle thought that the British would offer the French a deal or accept de Gaulle's offer of Franco-British nuclear cooperation but Macmillan had not done so. The Nassau agreement followed and de Gaulle must have decided to act at once. The President said that we had narrowly averted a disaster which would have occurred if the British had decided to join with de Gaulle in a nuclear arrangement. He believed that Macmillan had not understood that de Gaulle was offering the British a French/British nuclear arrangement. He added that Macmillan must now be kicking himself for not having realized that de Gaulle was offer-

---

[1] For a transcript of Rusk's press conference on February 1, see Department of State *Bulletin*, February 18, 1963, pp. 235–243.

ing him this arrangement. The President concluded that we had dealt with Skybolt as a weapons problem and that the reaction had surprised all of us.

Secretary Ball said there was one problem which needed prompt attention, i.e. should we try to get the Germans to amend the Franco-German treaty in such a way as to link the Franco-German arrangement to NATO? Secretary Rusk said the Dutch wanted us to try to persuade the Germans to postpone ratification of the treaty or amend it.

The President said we cannot let the Germans think we are telling them what to do, but on the other hand, we cannot let them think nothing has changed. He referred again to "the Mansfield effect," i.e. the U.S. has done much to help Europe and now the Europeans are acting in this way toward us.

Secretary Dillon said he had been asked by a Congressional Committee about the effect of de Gaulle's actions on our new trade act and on economic relations in general. He said he told the Committee to look to the State Department for an answer.

The President thought that we should exert pressure on Germany by means of trade proposals instead of asking them to postpone or revise the treaty.

The President said that his list of questions should be revised in the light of the discussion and circulated to the Executive Committee members.

Secretary Ball said that as a result of the breakdown of the Brussels negotiations certain advantages would accrue to us. The Common Agricultural Policy would probably not now go into effect. The agricultural problems, which were Secretary Freeman's worries, would now be greatly eased. In addition, the Latin American aspect of the problem would not become serious because the Dutch, if they chose, could block the association of African countries with the Common Market.

The President expressed reservations about using Dutch Foreign Minister Luns and preferred to work closely with the British.

Secretary Rusk noted that under no circumstances would the British break their ties with us in order to join the French.

The President responded that the British might have joined the French on the condition that the two of them then come to us jointly. At Nassau they could have proposed establishment of the directorate.

The President said again that the Franco-German treaty is aimed at us, particularly the clause which calls for German/French consultation on NATO matters. He said he realized that others disagreed with him and he hoped they were right.

Secretary Ball handed the President a draft letter to Adenauer.[2] The President, upon reading it, commented that it was too nice and that he preferred to hold it over night, revising it in the morning. He thought that we ought to suggest to Adenauer some of the dangers which Europe would face if we were separated from it. He cited (a) the opportunity to the Russians to fish in troubled waters, (b) reaction in the U.S. which might result in a public demand to get out of Europe, harking back to the major fight which it took to persuade the American people to enter Europe, and (c) the difficulty of exploiting the Sino-Soviet split. The President said de Gaulle can't move without Adenauer's agreement, but if we tell Adenauer that he has done fine, he may well think that he can continue to support de Gaulle. The President thought we must tell the Germans that they can't have it both ways.

The President said we should draw up precise assignments for the studies he requested, review them with the Secretary of State, and circulate them to the Executive Committee members. On Monday or Tuesday the Committee should meet again to see where we are going. On Saturday he would have a chance to talk with Ambassador Bruce. Mr. Bundy said the problems could not be handled in separate compartments but that part of the work could be done by the State group, which is already working.

The President summed up by saying that the basic theme is, given the existing balance of power, a division between the U.S. and Europe can only help the Russians. Our problem is to find out how we can continue to work with the Europeans. If the Europeans do not wish to continue with us, then, indeed, a turning point is here.

As the meeting broke up, the President looked at recent aerial reconnaissance photographs of Cuba and agreed, in the light of Senator Keating's statement that afternoon, to release some of them to the press. Director McCone was authorized to confront Senator Keating with all our current reconnaissance intelligence in the hope that the Senator would correct his statements of yesterday with respect to the continued existence of missile bases in Cuba.

Bromley Smith[3]

---

[2] The draft has not been found; the final text is printed as Document 65.

[3] Printed from a copy that bears this typed signature.

65.   Letter From President Kennedy to Chancellor Adenauer

Washington, February 1, 1963.

DEAR MR. CHANCELLOR: The weeks and months immediately ahead seem certain to call for hard and crucial decisions affecting the future of the Atlantic Alliance; and the preservation and strengthening of that Alliance, to which both our nations are committed and to which you have devoted so much of your life, require the most frank and intimate communications between ourselves and our two governments. I want very much to receive your views as to specific ways that you and I can work together to help restore the prospects for broader European community and Atlantic partnership.

At a time when the communist world is beset by internal political and economic disarray, it would be a tragic mistake for the West to dissipate the momentum it gained in the Caribbean and elsewhere by reversing its drive toward greater unity. Already there are signs that Soviet confidence and intransigence have been bolstered by the evidence of Western dissension. I need not tell you that a prime ambition of Soviet foreign policy for the last 17 years has been to split the Western alliance, to separate the United States from Europe and thereby to emasculate our common defensive posture. Surely it is inconceivable that their ambitions are now to be realized without apparent effort on their part.

I would also be less than frank if I did not convey to you my grave concern over the mounting suspicion in the American Congress and public that this Nation's presence and views are no longer welcome in Europe. Those who feel that $45 billion and 16 years of continuous economic and military assistance have earned us nothing but the hostility of certain European leaders and newspapers are likely to take out their resentment by pressing for a return to restrictive, isolationist concepts that would end Western unity and, according to our best military judgment, seriously weaken the security of Western Europe as well as the United States. I intend to do everything in my power to prevent this trend for, as this Nation made clear in rejecting the proposed "3 power directorate" as well as in supporting the United Kingdom's application to the EEC, Western unity and security cannot be assured if any major power is denied its proper role. I am hopeful, however, that I will be aided in these efforts by a visibly constructive response in Europe to our continued explorations on trade, on a multilateral nuclear force and on other cooperative undertakings, including the possibility of an Executive Committee in the Alliance such as Mr. Ball discussed with you.

Source: Department of State, Presidential Correspondence: Lot 66 D 204. Secret. No drafting information appears on the source text.

I am hopeful, in short, that your government will make clear its view that the action at Brussels must not end the effort for wider European unity, rooted in the search for a consensus and a recognition that the present balance of forces requires increasing Western solidarity. I believe your government shares my view, that, once Western Europe and the United States begin to deal with the Soviet Union on the basis of separate demands and conflicting approaches, thereby enabling Mr. Khrushchev to play one off against the other in his ambition to seize Europe and isolate the United States, the certain disintegration of our security and all our hopes for the future will have irreversibly begun.

I am hopeful, therefore, that our two nations share a common determination to find a way by which the West can soon present to Mr. Khrushchev once again the kind of strong and united front he has heretofore faced in Berlin, in the Caribbean, and elsewhere around the world. If the successful demonstration of that united strength has recently caused him to pause momentarily in his movements against us—and that is far from clear—that is surely no reason for us to abandon our own movement toward unity.

Because the decisions of your government will be particularly crucial in determining which path we are to follow, I repeat my strong hope that you and I can work together on a close and confidential basis, and that you will give me your full and candid views as to how the Alliance can now regain its former forward thrust.[1]

Sincerely,

John F. Kennedy[2]

---

[1] On February 2 the Department of State informed Dowling that rather than presenting this letter from the President, he should ask the Chancellor for his views on the ideas expressed in it. (Telegram 1782 to Bonn; ibid., Central Files, Pol 15–1 W Ger) On February 4 Dowling reported that the Chancellor had told him that after 10 years the United States surely needed no assurances of his support of U.S. policy. When Dowling tried to explain the U.S. concern, the Chancellor was unreceptive except to repeat variations of his belief that de Gaulle was a staunch friend of the United States. Dowling concluded that he had made no impression at all. (Telegram 2002 from Bonn; ibid.)

[2] Printed from a copy that indicates the original was signed by President Kennedy.

66. Telegram From the Department of State to the Embassy in Germany

Washington, February 1, 1963, 3:58 p.m.

1773. Paris pass USRO. Brussels also for Busec. In course meeting requested with Asst Secy Tyler January 31, German Minister von Lilienfeld expressed concern over fact that interpretation of Franco-German Treaty prevailing in US, arising from coincidence in timing de Gaulle press conference and treaty signing, seems to be that treaty foreshadows basic change in FRG policy vis-à-vis US. Minister stated this completely out of question; even if were contemplated by FedGovt (which not case), German people would not accept this. In view heightened concern German leaders following Brussels collapse, Minister said much thought being given to ways in which can be made clear again and again that signature Franco-German Treaty does not denote FRG endorsement de Gaulle policies, especially with respect UK-EEC accession and implementation Nassau Agreement.

In Tyler response, emphasis placed on our determination to press forward main lines our basic policy elaborated over period of years and concerted within Atlantic Alliance. We will in particular not be deflected from policy based on concept of Nassau, namely indivisibility of threat and of means required to meet threat. Tyler further emphasized need to avoid creating impression in US public and Congressional mind that Europe has turned its back on US or that FedRep has opted for alternative to close relations with US. Resulting disenchantment would make it difficult to pursue policy based on Atlantic concepts shared by FRG and US.

According to Minister, as result increasing awareness US attitude on part of German public, press, cabinet and parliament (particularly after Brussels), feeling is growing that FedGovt will be obliged make clear statement to effect 1) FedRep not turning back on US, and 2) Franco-German Treaty does not signify German identification with de Gaulle policies on EEC and Nassau. In response Tyler question re what Germans might have in mind this connection, Minister noted press statements along these lines already issued had not been strong enough. Minister said thought being given to "unusual gesture" such as Carstens' visit to Washington, in return Under Secretary Ball's recent visit Bonn, during which Carstens could explain German position "with certain amount of authority."

Source: Department of State, Central Files, Pol 4 Fr-WGer. Secret. Drafted by Stalder (GER) and approved by Tyler. Also sent to London, Brussels, and Paris.

Tyler expressed view present moment grave and noted that conjunction in which recent events had taken place has given rise to type of speculation about future of Atlantic Alliance which could have far-reaching consequences in US. He emphasized in particular enormous responsibility FedRep bears in post-Brussels shock period to make its position clear.

Memcon follows.[1]

FYI. Re Lilienfeld suggestion of Carstens' visit to Washington, Dept has subsequently informed German Embassy here it would welcome such a visit and feels it might prove very useful. End FYI.

Rusk

---

[1] A copy of the 4-page memorandum of conversation is ibid., 611.62A/1–3163.

---

67.   Telegram From the Mission to the European Communities to the Department of State

Brussels, February 2, 1963, 11 p.m.

Ecbus 844. Luxembourg for USEC and Embassy. Paris for Embassy and USRO. Purpose this message is to suggest considerations relevant to posture US in period immediately ahead.

1.   Fact of capital importance on January 29 was solidarity of other five in standing up to De Gaulle. First and immediate task is to do everything possible to encourage maintenance this solidarity. We should let the other five and the UK take the lead, giving our support to any appropriate proposals they develop designed to keep open British movement toward Europe.

2.   The pivotal element in this picture is Germany. The decision to make their stand against the French has undoubtedly been a very difficult and even agonizing one for them. Since they have nevertheless made the right decision it behooves us to be sensitive and as forthcom-

---

Source: Department of State, Central Files, ECIN 3 EEC. Confidential, Priority. Repeated to Bonn, The Hague, Luxembourg, Paris, Rome, London, Oslo, Copenhagen, Ottawa, Stockholm, Vienna, and Geneva.

ing as possible with respect to their other major preoccupations. The British should be encouraged to adopt a similar posture and work seriously for rapprochement at national level.

3. Although we should coordinate closely in all moves with the British, we should avoid taking steps that will give the appearance that the special relationship is being strengthened. This would be fully exploited by De Gaulle on the continent to serve his ends. In this connections, do not favor joint US-UK Ministerial meetings proposed London's 2890 to Department.[1]

4. We must fully accept the fact that De Gaulle is carrying out calculated policy to terminate the American presence in Europe and to destroy the entire concept of an Atlantic partnership. We must not be hesitant in accepting his challenge and combatting it. Publicly, however, we should assume a calm posture, avoiding the appearance of open split. But privately, through diplomacy, we should do everything we can to support those opposing De Gaulle. Essential make clear however that US support for European integration including EEC remains.

5. There are now various lines of action open to us:

(A) We should continue to restate often the kind of Atlantic partnership we stand for, with special emphasis on Europe as a unified, strong and equal partner.

(B) In particular, we must continue to make clear that there is no intention on our part to reduce or remove US forces in Europe.

Doing otherwise would seem to confirm in the minds of the Germans De Gaulle's claims on an issue on which the Germans are extremely sensitive.

(C) However, such reaffirmations, although very necessary, are not nearly enough in the present situation. Of greatest importance is moving ahead on solid programs with those allies prepared to do so.

(D) Most important of these is the NATO multilateral force. De Gaulle is extremely vulnerable in this area. It will be particularly important if we can demonstrate concrete progress at the earliest possible moment and if we can bring into being a force which will be effective sooner and be technically better than the force de frappe. It would be useful if we could discreetly make these points publicly now. The appointment of Merchant for this program is an excellent omen and should be widely talked up by USReps. (We need some convincing answer to charge that even MLF will deny Europe access to advanced industrial techniques.)

(E) On the negative side we should of course remain absolutely firm in our refusal to assist De Gaulle in any way in developing his inde-

---

[1] Document 412.

pendent nuclear weapons and delivery capability. (Such gestures as we have made in the past, as for example, the sale of KC 135 tankers, have clearly had no beneficial effects—in fact every gesture that has been made by us has been interpreted by French spokesmen as proof of wisdom De Gaulle's tactics re US).

(F) Fullest possible British participation in the multilateral force is essential, including the multinationally manned force. We should press the British hard in this direction. British should at all costs avoid threats about withdrawal of BAOR from Germany, just as we should assure that there is no question about US withdrawals.

(G) It may well prove necessary to consider steps going beyond the multilateral force (see Ecbus 730).[2]

(H) Other constructive programs, such as the Trade Expansion Act, should also be moved steadily ahead, although guarding carefully against French campaign to present our position as attempt dilute EEC. For reasons explained in Ecbus 834[3] separate message, we have reservations about practicality and value of speeding up implementation TEA via earlier GATT Ministerial meeting.

(I) We must be especially careful now to avoid US actions (e.g., woolen textiles and public over-emphasis on our concerns re agricultural policies of the Six) which will be distorted by the French in their present ruthless campaign to sow distrust of the US and to portray us as attempting to destroy the Common Market.

(J) On the counter propaganda side, we must be prepared to enter the lists and, through discreet means, counteract the vicious campaign being waged against us. As examples of the kind of points we should get across are the following:

(1) It is De Gaulle, not the US, who is forcing Western Europe to make a choice between himself and the US.

(2) De Gaulle is fundamentally antagonistic to European integration. De Gaulle's policies will lead to the opposite of what he intends, i.e., he will create a weak and divided Europe and will lessen, not increase, European influence elsewhere.

(3) Perhaps most pretentious of all De Gaulle's claims—that he alone stands firm on Berlin, Cuba and other East-West issues—is a position which he is able to take only under the umbrella of the US deterrent in which he professes to have no confidence. For the benefit of the Germans we need stress continuously that it is US not France which is lead-

---

[2] Ecbus 730, January 22, suggested a variety of steps that might be taken relating to British accession to the Common Market in the face of de Gaulle's statement on January 14. (Department of State, Central Files, 375.42/1–2263)

[3] Not printed. (Ibid., ECIN 3 EEC)

ing proponent of forward strategy and gives that strategy effect by actual deployment of forces.

(4) Most telling of all would be to encourage thought re meaning of "from Atlantic to the Urals". Stress on this theme should be especially telling for its effect on the Germans, with their concerns on Berlin.

[*1 paragraph (9-1/2 lines of source text) not declassified*]

In conclusion, we suggest the following program of action procedurally:

1. Primary emphasis should be given to ensuring continuing strong ties between the UK and other five. The other five are showing a disposition to do this (Ecbus 835),[4] and Brussels is the logical point of contact. British should be encouraged to strengthen their staff here for this purpose by assigning two or three top quality people.

2. NATO becomes the forum of primary importance for pushing ahead with those programs (especially multilateral force) in which French cannot exercise veto and in which we can demonstrate our readiness move ahead.

3. In monetary field, best procedure might be to use OECD WP-Three meeting as an opportunity for US-UK-Five-Canada to caucus in order assure British on sterling (second numbered paragraph three in London's 2890 to Department). Believe this preferable to bilateral US-UK arrangements for obvious reasons.

4. As for TEA, believe we should move steadily ahead as planned, not calling for earlier meeting of GATT.

Tuthill

---

[4] Ecbus 835, February 1, reported that talk of continued negotiations between the five EC countries and the British was dead, but that they were exploring other ideas. (Ibid., ECIN 6 EEC)

68.   Telegram From the Embassy in France to the Department of State

Paris, February 3, 1963, 3 p.m.

3098. Brussels also for Busec. Ref: London 2858 to Department.[1] In absence Ambassador, Embassy submits following comment re US posture in face de Gaulle tactics.

De Gaulle's recent actions create special problem for US and NATO allies in sense that failure react may create impression he can continue to impose his will on other countries by unilateral action. However, since there is apparently no course of action which can immediately efface reversal suffered by UK and US at Brussels, US objective would seem on one hand to be to avoid measures likely further reduce considerable progress already achieved toward European integration and Atlantic interdependence and on other hand to pursue our own announced policies in manner which re-enforce considerable doubt which exists in Europe and even in France as to wisdom de Gaulle's policies.

Success de Gaulle's effort develop a "European" Europe under French leadership capable of functioning as third great concentration of international political force may depend to certain extent on his ability arouse potential anti-American forces which are becoming apparent in France and which are latent in various degrees elsewhere in Western Europe. Obviously punitive measures against France (likely for most part to be injurious to wider US interests) and especially measures resulting from clear US initiatives would undoubtedly play into hands of those who allege we are seeking dominate Europe economically, militarily and politically. Some of us are concerned that themes such as needed for "independence" of Europe, for independent European defense capability (including nuclear), and protection from economic exploitation by behemoth of American capitalism have considerable political potential in hands of de Gaulle and perhaps other European leaders who are convinced that nineteenth century nationalism is motor force of international affairs. Effective manipulation of these nationalistic forces could result in serious erosion of American position.

Source: Department of State, Central Files, Pol Fr-US. Confidential. Repeated to London, Brussels, Rome, The Hague, Luxembourg, and Bonn.

[1] Telegram 2858, January 30, stated that in view of the rejection of the British application, the United States should reexamine the situation and perhaps "give General de Gaulle a discreet touch of the whip." The telegram suggested that without an "open display of feverish diplomatic activity," the United States should secure the opposition of the other five governments in the community and concurrently examine how it could contribute to alternatives to British entry. (Ibid., 375.42/1–3063)

Consequently, we should move steadily ahead, with those allies who are prepared to cooperate on projects which will contribute to our goal of an Atlantic Community such as NATO nuclear force and reduction of trade barriers. France should be offered continuing opportunity participate in those projects to which she is prepared respond.

Best way exploit French fears of being isolated is to offer our friends programs which they will find more in their long-term interests than French proposals.

In our dealings with France we must not forget that harsh or discourteous attitude would quickly alienate sensitive nationalistic feelings in important segments of population and government cadres who may entertain basic sympathy for US and our objectives and who constitute vital long term US asset.

Attempting to whip up opposition by other five to France within framework of EEC seems to us to be dangerous course and would also cast us in role for which France being severely criticized. While de Gaulle's arbitrary action in ending negotiations with UK will undoubtedly seriously affect working relations within community, community should and will survive. Therefore we must bend our efforts to seeing that, as far as it lies within our power to influence events, it develops an outward-looking community.

We would question desirability of our encouraging other EEC countries to reject trade arrangements which were incorporated in recently negotiated convention with African-associated countries. While trade arrangements in this convention are not in many ways satisfactory to US, they represent improvement over present arrangements and a move in right direction. Moreover, they are integal part of agreements which also provide financial assistance. Refusal to carry out these arrangements or otherwise obstruct EEC assistance to Africa might embarrass French, but real injury would be not to France but to African countries. We believe that we should direct our energies toward improving trade aspect of these arrangements in forthcoming GATT negotiations and commodity agreements. We do not think they should be used as a means of attempting to exert pressure on de Gaulle.

While it undoubtedly lies in our power to complicate the situation for the French in Africa and elsewhere in a number of ways, this could lead to attitudes here which would destroy what up to now still remains a reasonably satisfactory collaboration in this area and one of great interest to the US, especially re Algeria. We might find that in the end we would do untold damage to the fragile structures of the new states and end up by advancing the Soviet capacity for mischief as well as increasing the expense both political and financial to the US.

As regards agriculture, French effort to expand agricultural exports in Common Market area is directed partly at expense of overseas countries and partly at expense of less-efficient production with community, e.g. Germany. Our policy is already directed at defense of our own efforts. To the extent that French efforts, for example to get prices fixed around French level within community, are adverse to Germans' interests, they coincide with ours. It seems to us that agricultural problem is something of a double-edged sword and it is not clear to what extent it could usefully be employed as political instrument. It seems to us difficult enough to protect our interests as it is without introducing additional political element.

In longer term, some of us believe effective Atlantic Community will depend upon our ability create political superstructure which will accommodate sensibilities of both large and small members and serve as practical alternative to other solutions (such as de Gaulle's which would tend disperse and fragment resources of West).

Bohlen

69.   Summary Record of NSC Executive Committee Meeting No. 40

Washington, February 5, 1963, 4:30 p.m.

Second Portion: U.S. Policy Toward Europe

The President opened the discussion of U.S. policy toward Europe by commenting on the attached draft instructions from him to Ambassador Bruce with respect to the subjects which would be discussed in the immediate future as we proceed with our reappraisal.[1] His first question concerned our plans for a multilateral mixed manned seaborne Polaris force. He suggested that Ambassador Merchant not proceed too

---

Source: Kennedy Library, National Security Files, Executive Committee Meetings. Top Secret; Sensitive. In the first portion of the meeting, the Executive Committee discussed Cuba.

[1] The draft has not been found; the final text of Bruce's instructions is printed as Document 70.

rapidly with his discussions with the Europeans about this force. He thought that de Gaulle would probably oppose it, that it might turn out that the proposal was not very attractive to other Europeans because it did not have enough in it to interest them.

A second question involved the relationship of our foreign economic policy to our political objectives in Europe. The President asked Secretary Acheson to look at our balance of payments problem, consulting with Treasury, Defense, State, and Governor Herter.

Parenthetically, the President asked for a recommendation as to whether we should take an initiative now, wait to see how things developed, or go on as we now plan. He asked Secretary Acheson to concern himself with this problem as well.

The President said he did not want us to appear as if we were approaching the Europeans hat in hand. Possibly it would be best for the U.S. to negotiate alone, but he also wanted the views of those present as to whether it would be best to go forward with a group consisting of the British and other Europeans except France.

Governor Herter said de Gaulle's position was not yet clear and would not be in the immediate future. The situation in Europe had not yet jelled and the views of European powers other than France were changing rapidly. He said that the European powers might take reprisals against the French, but we did not yet know whether they would do so or, after a short time, calm down. The Dutch were now blocking discussions with the French, but the Italians appeared to be going one way, while the Belgians were going another way. If we decide to go with the Six, that would be one thing, but if we decide to support some kind of a trade association between the U.K., the EFTA countries, and the Common Market, a different way of proceeding would be necessary.

Secretary Rusk said we did not know which way the Five would go. One way they could move in the political area would be to use the Western European Union structure, and economically, some association with the Common Market. (Earlier the President had stated that if the U.K. in some way joins in an economic association with Europe, but is not a part of the political structure of Europe, the U.S. would get the worst of both worlds.)

The President's next question concerned our stance in negotiations with the Russians. He noted that Gromyko had made a specific approach to Ambassador Kohler, and that we must shortly give instructions to our Ambassador. The President said the Germans appeared to be relaxed on this issue because the Russians were not now exerting pressure on Berlin. He asked whether we were consulting our allies on the proposal made by the Russians. He asked what we would do if the Germans and the French agree to proceed with negotiation with the

Russians only on the condition that the talks do not involve discussion of the removal of allied forces from Berlin.

Secretary Rusk said that if the French and the Germans made this pre-condition, we were back where we were before the last negotiations with the Russians. He said we should go ahead and talk to the Russians as we had done before, but give the French and the Germans a chance to accept or to turn down participation in such talks.

The President expressed his view that we should ask the allies whether they wished to join with us in these discussions, but not tell them now what we would do if they decide not to participate.

Assistant Secretary Tyler explained that he would make known to the French and the British Ambassadors here the proposal which Gromyko had made. (The Germans have already been informed.) The Ambassadors would seek instructions from their governments as to whether they wished to make the negotiations tripartite. A variant of this suggestion would be for a quadripartite group to approve positions which we would take as the sole negotiator with the Russians.

The President's next question concerned our relations with Germany. He felt that unless we make clear our opposition to the Franco-German treaty we would not be able to make clear to the Germans that they faced a choice between working with the French or working with us. If the Franco-German treaty is approved, the Germans would be able to tell us that nothing really had changed as a result of the treaty when, in fact, the Germans would be accepting de Gaulle's policy.

Parenthetically, the President asked Secretary Dillon why the Spanish were buying gold. Secretary Dillon replied that they were doing so primarily for psychological reasons, i.e. they had always hoped to regain the amount of gold they had prior to their civil war.

The President did not specifically discuss questions five and six on the attached list[2] covering our relations with the U.K. and our relations with France. He did raise the question of nuclear weapons for Europe and touched on the tripartite U.S./U.K./France concept. He said that Ambassador Bruce and Secretary Acheson would be looking at these questions for the next two weeks. They would be free to do this outside of the day-to-day routine other officials were obliged to follow. The objective would be to agree on a plan covering our relations with Europe during the next five or six months.

Ambassador Dowling, who had just arrived from Bonn, expressed his view that the Germans would not lead the Five in opposition to de Gaulle unless we keep them nervous about our relations with them. He felt that the Germans would not stick their necks out in opposition to de

---

[2] Questions five and six in Bruce's instructions.

Gaulle unless they were uncertain as to how we would react if they did not so act. He felt we should discreetly encourage Erhard to insist that the Germans would ratify the treaty with France only with two reservations; (a) it would be understood that Germany would work for a resolution of the Common Market and U.K. problem, and (b) it would be understood that no provision of the Franco-German treaty would override existing NATO treaty provisions. He felt that we should not try to prevent ratification of the treaty because we could not be successful in so doing. However, he thought we should send German State Secretary Carstens back to Bonn with full knowledge of our concern in the hope that he would urge the German Government to proceed carefully.[3]

The President asked Ambassador Dowling whether we should ask the Germans for something specific. The Ambassador responded that we could not become specific until we had answered some of the questions raised by the President.

Secretary Dillon said an item of interest as to existing European attitudes had arisen in connection with our efforts to increase European subscriptions to IDA. In the past, the French had been willing to try to persuade the Germans to subscribe larger amounts. The Germans had been resisting larger subscriptions. The French were still putting pressure on the Germans to add to their IDA subscription.

Ambassador Bruce said that some of the questions the President had raised required immediate answers, i.e. our attitude toward the Franco-German treaty and our stance toward the USSR. Other questions were not so immediate. He said he wanted to feel free to deal with the short term questions promptly and take more time to provide replies to other questions.

The President asked how the WEU would solve any problems which arose following the veto of British membership in the Common Market. Ambassador Bruce replied that the British could get a political tie to the Continent via WEU. If the French refused to go along with such a political tie, the other members of the WEU could go forward with the British. He cautioned that no European government had yet chosen its course of action.

The President said the British were seeking any kind of a substitute for the Common Market. Any deal which they could make would hurt us economically.

Ambassador Dowling reported that the Germans might support some economic association of the British with the Continental states in addition to emphasis on the WEU. He urged that we decide promptly

---

[3] For a memorandum of Rusk's conversation with Carstens at 6 p.m., see Document 71.

whether we want them to follow this line. If we do not soon inform them of our view, they may adopt this policy in the belief that this is what we would want them to do.

The President pointed out that we cannot be in the position of keeping the British from joining some economic association with the other European powers. He asked for an estimate of the economic effect on the U.S. if the British did accept some form of association with the Common Market. If it turned out that the economic effect on us would be bad, then we would be in a most difficult position, i.e. opposing British *association* with the Common Market, having supported British *membership* in the Common Market.

Governor Herter reported that the British had flatly rejected association with the Common Market, but added that the EFTA powers favored an association and were anxious to work out economic arrangements with the Common Market.

Secretary Acheson and Carstens had told him something he did not fully understand, namely, that the Germans were thinking of suggesting that they join with the British and with us and the Five countries in promptly negotiating lower tariffs now. If de Gaulle refused to join this effort, the Germans could threaten to use the Common Market voting rules which become applicable in 1966 to cause de Gaulle real difficulties. After 1966 the Common Market provisions do not give a veto to France.

Ambassador Bruce felt that despite what the British had said so far, they would consider some type of association with the Common Market and that the EFTA countries would exert strong pressure on them to do so.

Governor Herter pointed out to the President that a year from this April is the earliest time when we can begin the Kennedy round of trade negotiations. He said we were in a very difficult box and could not proceed promptly. The EEC is now studying our tariff simplification proposals and we cannot move until they have completed this study. They will then ask for recompense as a result of our tariff simplifications. Following that, we must hold public hearings, make our proposals, and then table them in Congress sixty days prior to negotiations.

Following an exchange between the President and Mr. Bundy, it was agreed that we should not let the Germans make a proposal in the mistaken belief that it would please us. In effect, we must try to see that no state makes any proposal which we are not aware of in advance.

General Taylor gave a brief report of his discussions with Lord Mountbatten:

a. The British are highly skeptical that a multilateral second phase force will ever become a reality. Hence, they wish to emphasize a first phase NATO force to which they would like to ask others to contribute, i.e. the Germans to offer to include their tactical bombers.

b. The cost to the British for Polaris is apparently going to be higher than that for Skybolt. Hence, the British feel they must cut the cost of their NATO contribution, reduce their military commitments worldwide, or undertake to persuade the government to increase the total defense budget, a highly doubtful task.

c. The British are convinced that the French are serious about building their own submarine missile force.

Secretary Acheson referred back to the Bruce instructions and said he did not think we would get answers to these questions and that the effort to do so would bog down in futile discussions involving national sovereignty questions and other unrealistic issues. He asked whether the memorandum he had written on the January debacle had been read by those present.[4] He urged that a decision be taken now to give the Germans and Italians something which, if they did not follow our leadership, we could take away from them. He urged that we initiate training of foreign officers for the NATO nuclear force now while we are discussing the longer range proposal of a multilateral force.

Ambassador Dowling noted that the multilateral force has appeal for the Germans, even if we keep the veto, as long as we set up something like the NATO Executive Committee in which they would have a role.

General Taylor asked that we talk to the German military leaders as we are now doing with the British.

Ambassador Dowling said the Germans do want to participate in the manning of the multilateral force, they want a voice in the Executive Committee, and they are quite prepared to contribute to the cost of the multilateral force.

The President said that before we undertake any discussions with the Germans we should firm up our multilateral proposal. He thought that Ambassador Merchant should work on this proposal, consult with Ambassador Bruce, and then we could discuss the proposal again. The President pointed out that Secretary Acheson had recommended that we tell everyone we will not remove our troops from Europe for at least eighteen months. He said the threat of withdrawing our troops was about the only sanction we had, and, therefore, if we made such a statement, we would give away our bargaining power.

Secretary Acheson said he had not recommended that we guarantee we would not withdraw our troops from Europe, but merely that we would let the Europeans know that we would not fiddle with this force for eighteen months for peripheral reasons, i.e. budgetary or balance of

---

[4] Not found.

payments. Any action looking to troop withdrawal would rock the boat and convey to the Europeans uncertainty as to our intentions. At the end of eighteen months, we could examine the situation, and, if, during this period, the Europeans had not come around to supporting us fully, then we could consider withdrawal. He opposed conveying to the Germans the thought that unless they acted in a certain way they could not be sure of our continued support.

The President asked then how we could put any pressure on the Germans.

Ambassador Dowling said that those Germans who are our friends say we will not pull out of Europe. If by our actions we caused the Germans to doubt that we would remain in Europe, de Gaulle could take great advantage of the uncertainty created.

The President asked what we want the Germans to do.

Secretary Acheson replied that we want them to add reservations with respect to NATO provisions when they ratify the Franco-German treaty. He said he had made clear to Carstens that the Germans must take action to clear up the doubt about their intentions which they created by accepting the Franco-German treaty. He said he had suggested that the Germans must make clear that they are for France *and* for NATO.

Secretary Rusk pointed out that if the Germans insisted on making clear the continued existence of their pledge to NATO, de Gaulle would be influenced.

Ambassador Dowling emphasized that the Germans looked at the Franco-German treaty as the way to acquire equal partnership for Germany. At the same time, he acknowledged that the German association with the U.S. is very meaningful to them.

Secretary Acheson gave additional details of his conversation with Carstens.[5] He said he bluntly told Carstens that Adenauer's agreeing to the Franco-German treaty and statements to the effect that this action made no real difference meant that the Germans either thought the Americans were stupid or that the Germans were admitting they were duplicitous.

Bromley Smith[6]

---

[5] No other record of Acheson's conversation with Carstens has been found.

[6] Printed from a copy that bears this typed signature.

70.   Instructions From President Kennedy to the Ambassador to the United Kingdom (Bruce)

Washington, February 5, 1963.

After discussion with Secretary Rusk, and on his recommendation, I request that you make a review of certain of our leading policies toward Europe and make recommendations for action in the coming months. In this review you should feel free to request reports or studies or other assistance from any Department, and you should act directly for me and for Secretary Rusk. When your recommendations are in preliminary form I shall plan to meet with you to determine what further study they may require before decisions are taken.

The following list sets forth some of the topics which seem important to me and in which I hope for your specific comment. But you should not feel limited by this list, if other elements of the problem seem of equal importance to you. You should understand that I am asking other officers to review the broad problems of our military posture in Europe and our monetary relations in that area. Progress of these other studies will be reported to you through Mr. Bundy's office.

Questions for your consideration:

1.   I would like you to review our plans for a NATO Nuclear Force, and in particular the plans for a multilateral, mixed-manned seaborne Polaris force. I would like your judgment of this plan not only in terms of its immediate political attraction, but also in terms of its durable value as an instrument for strengthening the alliance. I want your judgment on the preferred means of command and control—and in particular your opinion of the value of this force if it is organized with—and without—a U.S. vote. I also wish your judgment of the proposal that this force, in whole or in part, might be organized under *European* multilateral arrangements, integrated with ours much as we now expect British forces to be integrated—possibly under the auspices of WEU. In the light of Soviet complaints about the Franco-German treaty and its possible relation to a German nuclear capability, I should also like your judgment of the relation between our effort for a multilateral force and a possible Soviet reaction. Finally, I should like to have your judgment on the best way of using this and other instruments to produce a shared sense of understanding, responsibility, and confidence with respect to the nuclear defense of the alliance.

Source: Johnson Library, Vice Presidential Security Files, NSC I. Secret. No drafting information appears on the source text, but the instructions were discussed and approved at the NSC Executive Committee meeting on February 5; see Document 69.

2. What plan is recommended for coordinating our foreign economic policy with our political objectives in Europe? This question includes such matters as our own negotiating requirements, our views of a possible UK economic association with the Five or the Six, the varied relations between commercial and political issues, and important problems of domestic political pressure. Mr. Herter has leading responsibilities here, and I would like to have recommendations, co-ordinated with him, which connect these matters firmly to our European policy as a whole.

3. What should be our stance in negotiations with the Russians? This problem is one of substance, on such questions as Berlin, testing, and German reunification. It is also one of tactics, including such questions as the use of the Ambassadorial Group, and the degree of British, French and German participation in such discussions.

4. What combination of actions will be most effective in our relations with Germany? What should be our position toward the Franco-German Treaty? How far can we ensure German cooperation in other fields, like finance, as a price for our own steadfast presence?

5. What policy should we follow with respect to the UK, on economic, political and military problems? I assume that our negotiations on Polaris will proceed on the lines already approved, but it is clear that we need decisions also on economic relations and on processes of political cooperation.

6. I do not wish to lose sight of the continuing problem of our relations with France. I should like to have your recommendations for ways and means of sustaining such cooperation as may be possible with France, while at the same time limiting the damage that may be done to our policy and to the alliance by General de Gaulle's commitment to purposes which are not readily aligned with ours. What is your judgment of the eventual prospects for a new relation with General de Gaulle, in political consultation or nuclear cooperation, which might be to our interest, and what preparations would you recommend for such a possibility?

71.   Memorandum of Conversation

Washington, February 5, 1963, 6 p.m.

SUBJECT

> Franco-German Treaty

PARTICIPANTS

> State Secretary Carstens   Secretary Rusk
> Ambassador Knappstein   Asst. Secretary Tyler
> Counselor Schnippenkoetter   Mr. Brandin, GER

Dr. Carstens opened the subject by referring to de Gaulle's January 14 press conference which raised the question of whether the Germans should go to Paris. The Government and political leaders decided they should. Here was the cause of the misunderstanding now between the US and Germany. Germans were as shocked as the US, the UK and the others by de Gaulle's press conference. Germany favored UK accession to the Common Market then and does now. The German delegation did its best at Brussels with Vice Chancellor Erhard and Foreign Minister Schroeder participating personally.

Dr. Carstens explained that it was originally planned to make an executive agreement with France, not requiring ratification, but lawyers had asserted such an agreement would not be valid and could be successfully challenged in the Constitutional Court. Hence it was decided at the last minute to make it a treaty. He conceded that later political party leaders wanted the chance to ratify the agreement, but insisted it was originally a legal question.

Dr. Carstens said there was a general feeling in Germany that the Treaty constituted an important step in Franco-German relations because of the strong desire to create harmony and end the historical struggles between the two countries. In addition to this sentimental reason there were strong political reasons, which is why all political parties in Germany favored putting Franco-German relations on a new, solid basis. Another reason was Germany's desire to be informed about any move de Gaulle might make affecting Germany or the Western Alliance. For example, Germany was not informed in advance about what de Gaulle intended to say at his press conference. Rumors that Ambassador Blankenhorn in Paris was so informed were untrue.

The Secretary asked whether it was the German understanding at Paris that a study by the EEC Commission would be agreed.

Dr. Carstens said there was partial agreement on a report, but no agreement on submitting proposals for a solution, on setting a time limit

---

Source: Department of State, Central Files, Pol WGer-Fr. Secret. Drafted by Brandin and approved in S on February 7. A memorandum of Carstens' conversation with Tyler at 11:30 a.m. along these lines is ibid., ECIN 6 EEC.

for negotiations, on submitting the report to the Six or Seven, or on whether the Seven should meet again in a few weeks to discuss the report.

Dr. Carstens went on to say there were many discussions in Paris at all levels. It was apparent that the French did not want to commit themselves to further negotiations with the British. The Germans had thought a compromise would be possible—e.g., sending the Commission report to Fayat for his disposition—but in the end the French were unyielding.

Dr. Carstens digressed to mention that he had seen Mr. Acheson earlier in the day. The Secretary said that if Mr. Acheson expressed concern it was important because he was a close friend of Germany and a strong supporter of the Chancellor.

Dr. Carstens said there seemed to be a great misunderstanding in the US. There were fundamental differences between Germany and France on UK accession to the EEC, on whether the EEC should pursue a liberal or restrictive economic policy and on defense matters, such as the forward strategy and the Nassau Agreement. The Franco-German Treaty would not affect the substance of Germany's position on any of these matters. Yet the impression in the US seemed to be that Germany had changed its attitude.

The Secretary then outlined the elements of US concern. Germany might find us sharp about de Gaulle on certain points but we wanted to work with him as much as possible. But de Gaulle was not President of the US and could not veto US policy. We read his press conference under a microscope from a different viewpoint than the German one, noting particularly the undertones about the US. We were deeply concerned that in rejecting UK entry into the Common Market, the reason given by de Gaulle was not that the UK was not ripe, which would be up to the UK and certainly could be settled by discussion, but rather that the UK was too close to the US. Because de Gaulle resented US presence in Europe he took this drastic action. De Gaulle's strong attitude toward US-European cooperation against the background of current US efforts to strengthen that cooperation—e.g., in the nuclear field—came as shock if not a surprise. The notions that the US was trying to smother Europe or use the UK as a stalking horse were deeply resented.

The Secretary said there was deep sympathy in the US for Franco-German reconciliation, but it was noted that Germany agreed to consult with France to reach a common viewpoint on questions in NATO, although there was no reaffirmation of NATO as such in the Treaty. We knew de Gaulle's attitude toward NATO. He told Mr. Macmillan at Rambouillet that "France was going to be less and less in NATO".[1] At

---

[1] Macmillan visited Paris December 15–16, 1962.

the time of the meeting with President Kennedy, de Gaulle objected to a reaffirmation of NATO in the communiqué. Apparently de Gaulle equated NATO with the US. The French army was being reduced from 750,000 to 500,000, which does not favor the forward strategy. France was disinclined to assign its forces to NATO, Couve de Murville maintaining that there must be three French (not NATO) divisions in France to defend France. This combination gave us concern. If the commitment to NATO had been reaffirmed in the Treaty we might not have been so concerned.

The Secretary said another point, as he had mentioned to Ambassador Knappstein, was where the weight of influence would be in the Franco-German Alliance. Even if Germany continued to hold its present views, we could be forgiven a certain skepticism about Germany's ability to influence de Gaulle, having barked our own shins on that tree.

The Secretary emphasized he was not trying to sow seeds of distrust, but merely explaining US concerns. France sees itself as the senior partner on the Continent. We have encountered this attitude in our efforts to bring Germany fully into the picture. At Geneva and Paris the French proposed tripartite meetings before the quadripartite meetings. We resisted at some expense to our relations with France. (Ambassador Knappstein added that the French also proposed a tripartite directoire in NATO.) The question of where the balance of weight would lie might be more serious than Germany realized.

Dr. Carstens said he thought the US overestimated de Gaulle's intentions. He would not defend de Gaulle's views. In fact he thought de Gaulle was all wrong on the atomic weapons issue. But de Gaulle was reacting to the Nassau Agreement, not to the US position in Europe; he would not go so far as to suggest US withdrawal from Europe. De Gaulle thought Macmillan was not frank with him at Rambouillet, and at Nassau had chosen in favor of the US instead of Europe (i.e., France). De Gaulle was never enthusiastic about the UK's entry into the Common Market, but the Germans thought (mistakenly) that he would not go against the other Five. Still, Germany did not conclude from this that de Gaulle wanted the US to withdraw from Europe.

The Secretary said he would concede Dr. Carsten's last point, but in another direction. De Gaulle was utterly confident the US would not withdraw from Europe and was acting on that assumption.

Dr. Carstens agreed that de Gaulle was maneuvering in a small area for purely national purposes.

The Secretary said we understood de Gaulle's passionate desire to rebuild the structure and morals of France.

Dr. Carstens replied that this was an element of strength for Germany. De Gaulle had built up France politically and economically. On balance France was better now than five years ago when there was chronic political instability.

Dr. Carstens then turned to the question of NATO's inclusion in the Treaty. The Germans had asked for consultation on NATO matters because they felt it their duty to confront and influence France with their views.

The Secretary asked whether de Gaulle would have signed the Treaty if it had contained a strong reaffirmation of NATO.

Dr. Carstens doubted it, but pointed out the Treaty was procedural and did not contain any substance. The US could trust Germany, especially on NATO matters. For eight years Germany had favored strengthening NATO on every issue. Germany was convinced NATO was the only effective basis for defending itself. Support of NATO was taken for granted in Germany.

The Secretary asked whether this position would not be diluted by the commitment to reach a common view.

Dr. Carstens agreed it would be hard to move de Gaulle, but perhaps not impossible.

The Secretary recalled that the US was always expected to pledge its allegiance to NATO. Perhaps a general "pledging session" was needed. We ought to know the French commitment to NATO.

Dr. Carstens said he could not speak for France, but he could speak for Germany. Germany was absolutely firm on NATO. The US might think Germany would move toward the French position on NATO, but he could vouch that it would not. Would the US have preferred no reference to NATO in the Treaty?

The Secretary observed that the Treaty called for a maximum effort to reach agreement on political, defense and other matters, including those in NATO.

Dr. Carstens acknowledged it would be difficult to get a strong reaffirmation of NATO from de Gaulle, but said it was easy to get one from Germany. Perhaps Germany could move France. For example, there was a current press report that France had agreed to move a division from Trier to Bavaria. If true, it represented a success for German efforts.

Dr. Carstens then addressed the question of the center of gravity in Franco-German relations. It was an important matter. But Germany was not inclined to give up on vital points to meet France. It had not done so at Brussels, which the UK had recognized.

The Secretary apologized for pressing the point, but asked whether there really would be any agreement if the Germans were to say what they meant and de Gaulle were to say what he meant about the Treaty.

Dr. Carstens repeated that the Treaty was a procedural document. Germany and France agreed on some points—e.g., European security— but not on others.

The Secretary then mentioned the inclusion of the Berlin clause in the Treaty, saying we would have to reserve our position on applying a treaty of this nature to Berlin. We would like to discuss the question because we considered ourselves a partner in Berlin. Moreover we had always taken the position with the USSR in negotiations about Berlin that the USSR could not confer rights on East Germany that it did not have itself. Had the Berlin clause been a problem in the Paris negotiations?

Dr. Carstens replied that it was not a problem in Paris. He pointed out that the defense clause specifically excluded Berlin. The clause was included in the Treaty because the USSR contested the Federal Government's right to represent Berlin, which was granted by the Allies. Since 1956 the Federal Government had worked this clause into every agreement, except one with the USSR, to avoid setting any precedent the USSR could use to influence neutral countries. But Allied rights in Berlin would not be affected. It should be easy to find a formula to clarify this matter—perhaps a joint letter to the US and UK. In any event, the question would be submitted to the Allied Kommandatura in Berlin.

Dr. Carstens turned to the ratification of the Treaty, saying it should be ratified. Germany could not refuse to ratify after it had signed. The Treaty should be ratified in due time, without haste, probably before the Bundestag recessed around July 1. First the Treaty would go to the Bundesrat for three weeks, then to the Bundestag committees, then back to the Bundesrat for two weeks.

Dr. Carstens said his personal idea was to ask the Bundestag to pass a resolution reaffirming Germany's commitment to the Western Alliance, which would be published with the ratification.

Ambassador Knappstein said the reaffirmation of NATO could be inserted in the resolution.

The Secretary asked whether the connection to ratification would be close enough to be effective.

Dr. Carstens replied that since the Treaty was procedural there could be no conflicts on points of substance like Germany's ties to the Atlantic Alliance and its Western allies.

The Secretary said it would be hard to persuade the American public that the Treaty was procedural.

Mr. Tyler added that the public impression in the US was that Germany had jumped on the de Gaulle bandwagon.

The Secretary stressed his concern that a fuse might be lit in Europe that would cause a public explosion in the US. If the American people got the impression Europe did not want them over there anymore, they would say "the hell with it". Most Americans still preferred to stay home and leave the rest of the world alone. It was a fantastic misunderstanding to think the US wanted to smother Europe.

Dr. Carstens said no German wanted the US to leave Berlin or Germany. What was so upsetting about the US reaction was that Germans thought the US understood how they felt. It was a fascinating experience in diplomacy to see how friends could misjudge each other.

The Secretary said some Germans seemed to have got the idea that the US should give assurance without realizing the US might want assurances too. They took the US for granted.

Dr. Carstens said Germans took it for granted the US favored Franco-German reconciliation. The coincidence of dates, involving de Gaulle's press conference, the signing of the Treaty and the Brussels negotiations, gave a false impression. He hoped the impending Bundestag debate on domestic and foreign policy would clarify matters.

The Secretary asked about French and German motives in signing the Treaty.

Dr. Carstens said Germany wanted to keep close to de Gaulle so that together with others Germany could influence de Gaulle to keep in line with common policies. The Treaty could be a useful instrument for this purpose. Erhard, Schroeder or anyone else succeeding Adenauer would be 100% in favor of the Western Alliance.

The Secretary said there was no distrust in the US because of the Treaty. We were concerned about what Germany might have to pay to give reality to it. We had confidence in German views but with two streams of policy (Bonn and Paris) moving in different directions, we wondered what reconciliation would mean.

Dr. Carstens said there would be agreement on some points, but not on others.

The Secretary observed that the US was in the same position vis-à-vis France. We wanted to cooperate in Africa, the Near East and on nuclear weapons. We had hoped de Gaulle would follow his first inclination to study the Nassau Agreement carefully. Instead he rejected it without full knowledge or study, thereby missing a great opportunity. Unfortunately, because of press leaks, there had to be a great deal of last-minute improvisation at Nassau.

The Secretary ended the hour-long meeting by inviting Dr. Carstens to resume the discussion at breakfast the next morning.[2]

---

[2] Brief memoranda of Carstens' conversation with Rusk at 8:45 a.m. on February 6 on the Franco-German treaty and European integration and a more extensive memorandum of his conversation with Ball at 10 a.m. are in Department of State, Secretary's Memoranda of Conversation: Lot 65 D 330.

72.   Editorial Note

On February 9 Ambassador Bruce completed his report to the President. The 10-page report consisted of sections on U.S. objectives, obstacles that recent events had posed to the attainment of these objectives, U.S. strategies to overcome the obstacles, and some specific steps that should be taken to carry out U.S. strategies. Bruce proposed two objectives: (1) to deny Europe to Communist control and (2) to mobilize U.S. and European resources to serve the free world. After examining the question of European unity, Bruce concluded that it was still in the U.S. interest and went even further to state that European integration was an imperative of modern history. The prospect of a close connection between Europe and the United States was equally important.

Having reached these conclusions Bruce wrote that de Gaulle had created three obstacles to these objectives: (1) excluding the United Kingdom from the Common Market, (2) blocking the Common Market as a road to European political unity, and (3) presenting intra-European and Atlantic relationships contrary to U.S. interests and conceptions. To overcome these obstacles Bruce stated that the United States must make more clear its willingness to treat a united Europe as an equal partner and break the present European dependence and U.S. predominance in the relationship. The two critical areas available to do this were the multilateral mixed manned force and political consultations with the Europeans.

With regard to specific actions, Bruce suggested that for Germany the President should write Adenauer stressing U.S. willingness to maintain forces in Germany, a strong endorsement of the multilateral force, and a reiteration of U.S. support for bringing the United Kingdom fully into Europe. On the negative side Bruce stated that the United States should make no attempt to prevent ratification of the Franco-German treaty. With regard to the United Kingdom Bruce stressed the need for close but unobtrusive consultations, without doing anything publicly to reinforce the appearance of special ties. The British should also be encouraged to exploit whatever opportunities existed for closer ties with the continent and in particular to make adjustments in their economy to bring it into closer conformity with developments in the Common Market.

Bruce concluded his report with a short paragraph on France, stating that no immediate action was necessary. He believed:

"Our tactic with France must be to provide a counter attraction, not aimed at France, but at the legitimate ambitions of Europe. The opportunity for France to join in these efforts must always remain open. In the meantime, we should have well-informed contingency plans against a de Gaulle assault on NATO, our trade negotiations, or our balance of payments." (Department of State, S/S–NSC Files: Lot 70 D 265)

73.   Telegram From the Department of State to the Mission to the European Communities

Washington, March 6, 1963, 8:18 p.m.

Busec 377. From Under Secretary. Hallstein saw President with only Under Secretary accompanying.[1] Ball and Hallstein both agreed most useful, candid and cordial discussion.

Principal preoccupation of meeting was trade negotiations and prospects for effective EEC participation. President impressed upon Hallstein that we looked to him to see that negotiations succeed. Hallstein expressed impatience with Italian deferral of action on African Association saying that inevitably they will fall in line. Added caustic observation on their general ineffectiveness and speculated that after elections Italians will fall in line with the French.

Hallstein preoccupied with misfortunes of timing. In particular fact that trade negotiations cannot take place in 1966 when Community operating on less than unanimity role.

Hallstein concerned about one aspect Franco-German Treaty, namely provision for consultation regarding Community affairs. Is concerned that France has in mind developing extra-Community procedure whereby Franco-German action could negate work of Community and particularly such a bilateral arrangement could make the 1966 procedures ineffective. Hallstein felt essential that Bundestag resolution deal with this problem. At same time he expressed confidence that Germans would not be trapped by French attempts to exploit Franco-German Treaty in this way. He remains convinced that French will not take action to prevent 1966 procedures to come into play.

President and Ball stressed once again high importance to U.S. of agriculture issue in both economic and political terms and specific problem poultry imports into Community.

Comment:

While atmosphere Hallstein's visit cordial and he displayed usual optimism, I believe he went away convinced of the importance President attaches to trade negotiations. You should make use of Hallstein's conversations here to bear down heavily on the role that Commission

Source: Department of State, Central Files, ECIN 7 EEC. Confidential. Drafted by Schaetzel, cleared with the White House, and approved by Ball. Repeated to Bonn, The Hague, London, Luxembourg, Paris, and Rome.

[1] The meeting with the President took place from 10:03 to 11 a.m. on March 4 (Kennedy Library, President's Appointment Book), but no other record of it has been found.

and particularly Hallstein must play. In this connection we suggested to Hallstein the fact that Five should strive to work out an arrangement whereby they would strive for a "deal" with France whereby concessions of Five to French with regard to African Association, Algeria, agriculture and the financial regulation be made in return for French commitment in specific terms with regard to trade negotiations.

Rusk

---

74.   Memorandum of Conversation

Washington, March 22, 1963, 2:30 p.m.

SUBJECT

Western Unity; Franco-German Treaty; de Gaulle; Common Market; TEA

PARTICIPANTS

Germans
Dr. Heinrich von Brentano, Chairman, CDU Bundestag Faction and former
   German Foreign Minister
Ambassador Heinrich Knappstein, German Embassy
Mr. Hermann Kusterer, Interpreter, German Embassy

Americans
The Secretary
Under Secretary George W. Ball
Mr. Robert M. Brandin, EUR/GER

Western Unity

Dr. von Brentano referred to the unfortunate coincidence in the dates of de Gaulle's press conference, the Franco-German Treaty, and Brussels meeting. He assured the Secretary there would be no change in German policy after ratification of the Treaty and that Germany's position on NATO and European matters would remain the same. Germany wanted the UK in the EEC. No one in Germany dreamed of a Franco-German bloc in Europe or NATO. Only a fool would think of sacrificing anything on the altar of Franco-German reconciliation. All German political parties realized Europe's freedom depends on close cooperation with the US in all fields. German decisions in recent weeks confirmed this view—e.g., support of the MLF and maintenance of the pipe embargo.

The Secretary agreed that the coincidence of dates in January was unfortunate and had raised questions better left unasked. In 1948–49,

---

Source: Department of State, Central Files, Def W Eur. Secret. Drafted by Brandin and approved in S on March 26. Brief memoranda of Brentano's conversations with Ball on March 21 and the President at 10:30 a.m. on March 22 along similar lines are ibid., Pol 4 Fr-W Ger and Pol 1 Eur. The meeting was held in the Under Secretary's Conference Room.

the US people made an utterly fundamental decision of historic importance; viz., that US and European security could not be separated. Consequently, we regarded ourselves committed to European security like our own security. The danger of de Gaulle's press conference was that it raised the possibility that American people would get the feeling that the American connection was not wanted in Europe. If this happened, it would be impossible for any American Government to keep US troops there. For this reason, the attitude of the Five at Brussels was most important in demonstrating to the American people that the rest of Europe did not agree with de Gaulle on this point.

Later in the conversation, the Secretary said that what Moscow thought about Western unity was important. Moscow might think the West was divided but there was no real indication that the USSR would be tempted to try to take any advantage of the West on a matter of security. The Soviet reaction to the Franco-German Treaty and the Soviet refusal to negotiate on nuclear testing indicated that the USSR understood there was no weakening in Western unity where essential security was concerned. The USSR knew that de Gaulle and the rest of the Alliance had backed the US even at the risk of war.

Franco-German Treaty

The Secretary expressed the hope that the Bundstag and the Federal Government would be able to make it clear that the Franco-German Treaty would not mean a change in German policies.

Dr. von Brentano replied that all three parties were resolved to make a clear statement on this point. There were two possible procedures. First, a paragraph might be inserted in the ratification law. Dr. von Brentano did not know whether this would be possible under international law. The second possibility was the passage of a resolution. Such a resolution would not be simply a resolution of the Bundestag; it would be an authentic interpretation of the Treaty which the Federal Government would have to accept before final ratification. Dr. von Brentano said this was the position of himself, his party, and of the opposition parties. This procedure might lead to irritation in Paris but Dr. von Brentano said he was prepared to accept this because Germany did not want and could not afford any ambiguity with its friends or its opponents.

The Secretary said it would be very helpful for the future if no government in Paris or Bonn could read any other interpretation into the Treaty. There should be a clear legislative record of intent.

De Gaulle

The Secretary went on to say that for the past four years we had felt an absence of exchange of views with de Gaulle. Since our rejection of his proposals for reorganizing the three, there had been no contact with the mind and personality of de Gaulle. Such contact with national leaders was necessary to NATO. The personal isolation of de Gaulle seemed to exist within his own Government as well as toward foreign governments. It was difficult to see how to move toward greater cooperation. In this situation things were all right when conclusions coincided, but when they did not, there was a pulling away.

The Secretary hoped a way could be found to talk things out with de Gaulle. It was not possible through normal diplomatic channels or Foreign Ministers. For example, we had found de Gaulle's press conference very informative. Apparently, we were not the only ones in this position.

The Secretary said we felt we should be prepared to cooperate with France on whatever points were possible. Perhaps there was no fundamental change in de Gaulle's views, but we were puzzled about what he had in mind and the relationship between his long-range ideas and current problems. The concept of a Europe from the Atlantic to the Urals might be something for fifty years hence, but Foreign Ministers had to live from day to day.

Dr. von Brentano acknowledged that what the Secretary had said also applied to Germany. It was a strange contact. De Gaulle said "no" to everything, especially in the NATO field. We should not fear letting de Gaulle feel he was isolating himself. He had isolated himself from the US, the UK, Italy and Benelux countries. He must be made to fear that he would isolate himself from Germany too. This was a task for Germany. It was questionable whether de Gaulle could be influenced, but Germany would make it clear that it would not go the wrong way with him.

Later Dr. von Brentano returned to the subject of de Gaulle and said that while he was an awkward partner, he was still a very intelligent man.

The Secretary said we fully understood a man who had lived through his experiences, was patriotic and wanted to bolster his country's morale. It was a question of method however. If France had thrown itself wholeheartedly into the EEC, French prestige would have come. In isolation it might be possible to build French prestige.

Dr. von Brentano said one must be aware that de Gaulle thought in nationalistic terms. Nevertheless, he had showed courage in solving the Algerian problem and in opposing his earlier supporters. France suffered greatly during and after World War II and de Gaulle felt the need for national prestige in order to rebuild France's confidence. Such prestige was also a means of meeting the accusations of treason regarding Algeria. Germany recognized these things, but that did not mean Germany would follow de Gaulle or make his mistakes. But it was necessary to understand de Gaulle, because this was the only means of persuading him.

Common Market and TEA

The Secretary then raised the question of where we all go after the breakdown of the Brussels talks. Europe was unanimous that the US should stay out of the UK-EEC negotiations. Part of the present problem of US-European relations, however, was how to share leadership. In the late 40s and early 50s, special circumstances existed: Europe was recovering and rebuilding. This situation was at an end and we realized the importance of Europe's having a new role. This was relevant to the question of who would take the initiative after Brussels. We were reluctant to inject ourselves into the matters largely of a European character—i.e., the shape and arrangements of the future Europe. The Secretary invited Dr. von Brentano's comments on this problem.

Dr. von Brentano replied that first of all efforts should be continued in the Six to fulfill the Rome Treaties. France must not be let out of its responsibilities in that connection, but permanent close contact would also have to be maintained with the UK. Therefore, the positions in Britain and under the Rome Treaty should be developed along parallel lines even if France did not participate. The objective should be to achieve the same decisions in London and Brussels and to avoid decisions that would make more difficult the UK entry into the EEC.

Dr. von Brentano said that in the second place, the talks with Mr. Herter should be continued. Dr. von Brentano said he had just learned that the Foreign Trade Commission of the European Parliament had formed a subcommittee to contact the US in implementing the TEA and preparing for Atlantic partnership. This initiative of the European Parliament was welcome.

The Secretary observed that the timing of the TEA itself was based on the expectation that the UK would join the EEC. It was hoped that this year would see each side working out its internal problems so that trade negotiations could begin next year. It was unfortunate that things could not move as fast as the Act permitted.

The Secretary asked whether there was any support in Europe for de Gaulle's views on economic autarchy.

Dr. von Brentano said even if it wanted to, Germany could not pursue fatal ideas. Germany would wither away in such a system because it was more dependent than others on foreign trade. It had to import raw materials and to export the products of its labor. Autarchy would be fatal for foreign trade. Germany favored liberal trade as laid down in Vice Chancellor Erhard's policies. It would not permit the European Community to develop an inward looking policy.

Dr. von Brentano said he did not want to see one wrong nationalism replaced by a worse nationalism; he personally opposed German, French and European nationalism. Friendship with the US was essential. Balance-of-trade problems and balance-of-payments problems should be solved through cooperation. Any serious balance-of-payments deficit of one country was harmful to others.

The Secretary said we would try to avoid unwise actions in meeting the balance-of-payments problem, but that the problem would have to be met in the next two years or three years. It could be settled if the Alliance looked at it together. We wanted to avoid bad trade policies and would continue to keep in close touch with our Allies.

Later, the Secretary asked whether it could be anticipated that the Common Market would function in a normal way despite the problems created at Brussels.

Dr. von Brentano said that the Common Market should be developed within the framework of the Rome Treaty. A standstill would be a setback. Developments should be in close contact with the UK. No one could prevent concerted action with the UK and decisions should be avoided which might prejudice the UK's entry into the EEC. Permanent contact with the UK would show that the breakdown at Brussels was an interruption in and not the end of developments.

---

75.   Memorandum of Conversation

Washington, April 9, 1963, 10 a.m.

PARTICIPANTS

United States	*EEC*
The President	Mr. Sicco L. Mansholt, Vice
Secretary Freeman	President of the European
Under Secretary Ball	Economic Commission
Mr. Carl Kaysen	Mr. Mozer, Chef de Cabinet
Ambassador John W. Tuthill	

Source: Department of State, Central Files, ECIN 3 EEC. Confidential. Drafted by Tuthill on April 10 and approved by the White House on April 24. The meeting was held at the White House. A 9-page memorandum of Mansholt's conversation with Freeman on April 8 concerning poultry, grains, and rice is ibid., INCO Poultry US.

SUBJECT

Trade; Common Market; European Unity

The following informal memorandum is not based upon notes taken during the meeting but is, I believe, a summary of the essential points covered during the 50-minute conversation.

The President opened the conversation by welcoming Mr. Mansholt and asking what in his view should be done in the light of the European situation "over the next 18 months."

In reply Mr. Mansholt stated that Europe and the Atlantic area are in a crisis caused by de Gaulle. The question was how far one could let de Gaulle proceed. While de Gaulle is not a positive force, he is a negative force and unity is required in opposing him. Because of de Gaulle the U.K. negotiations have failed and if now the Trade Expansion Act negotiations fail it will be the end of the Common Market. While Mansholt stated he was not an expert in the nuclear field, he understood that de Gaulle was in technical trouble. Mansholt fully supported the U.S. project for a multilateral nuclear force and warned about French participation in a NATO national nuclear force. In that case the French would be free to withdraw whenever they wished. He felt that it was too soon to know whether a European nuclear force was the answer.

Mansholt also set forth his conviction that we are faced with a basic conflict of political concepts. De Gaulle wishes a "Europe des patries" under French leadership. He stated further that de Gaulle's concept was of a Continental Europe which would be inward looking. Thus there was no place in this Europe for the United Kingdom and the U.K. application for accession had to be vetoed.

In opposition to this concept there is that of a unified Europe based on common democratic institutions and oriented outward. In Mr. Mansholt's view this concept is supported by the other Five members of the Common Market, by many Frenchmen, and is fully consistent with the policies of the United States.

Mr. Mansholt felt that de Gaulle's concept must be resisted vigorously by the supporters of the democratic concept. He believed that while de Gaulle's views would not change that de Gaulle would adjust himself to a Europe and an Atlantic area which insisted upon a unified, democratic and outward-looking orientation.

Mr. Mansholt stressed that the major element in our relationship with de Gaulle is the nuclear weapons problem. He felt that if de Gaulle achieved his objective of national nuclear forces that it would be catastrophic because it would lead to fourth, fifth, and sixth, etc. nuclear powers. He stressed that de Gaulle was attempting to obtain concessions from the United States in the nuclear weapons field.

Mr. Mansholt stressed that the next test for the Common Market is the Kennedy Round negotiation. The Benelux, Germany, and Italy all wish these negotiations to succeed not only because this would mean a general lowering of tariff barriers but also because this has become the next—and vital—test of the relationship of the Common Market to outside countries. Furthermore, if the negotiations are successful this would greatly facilitate the subsequent adherence of the U.K. and certain other European countries to the Common Market. Mr. Mansholt warned, however, that there is no assurance that de Gaulle will not veto the negotiations under the Trade Expansion Act at some future date. In Mr. Mansholt's view, de Gaulle does not want successful negotiations but might allow them to run on looking for the right moment to attempt to achieve a deal in the nuclear weapons field.

In view of Mansholt's emphasis on the importance of nuclear matters in determining de Gaulle's position, the President asked Mansholt whether he felt that the United States should have made nuclear concessions to de Gaulle in 1961 or 1962 in order to avoid the collapse of the U.K. negotiations. Mansholt vigorously rejected this idea and furthermore, looking to the future, stated emphatically he felt under no circumstances should de Gaulle be offered aid for his national nuclear force as a bargain in order to obtain his agreement on economic considerations. The President agreed.

The President asked Mansholt about U.S. agricultural policies toward the Common Market pointing out that if the United States lost a substantial portion of such exports that it would adversely affect the U.S. balance of payments and reduce our ability to support our foreign policy. Mr. Mansholt pointed out that U.S. agricultural exports to the Common Market had increased from the start of the Common Market in 1958 until the year 1962. He did not expect that there would be any substantial decline from the present high level of U.S. agricultural exports within the next few years unless of course the Common Market followed high price policies especially in grains. He pointed out to the President that he favored a common agricultural policy which would offer continued reasonable access for the United States and other traditional agricultural exporters. Mr. Mansholt stressed that the common agriculture policy was "merely machinery" which could be used for liberal or protective purposes. In his view the negotiations under the Trade Expansion Act must be used to turn the machinery in a liberal direction. He therefore welcomed the U.S. proposal to include agriculture in the negotiations under the Trade Expansion Act. He pointed out, however, that he was very doubtful about the effectiveness of the GATT especially in the field of agriculture. He stated that Agriculture Ministers could always find ways to avoid GATT commitments. However, he was prepared to negotiate on tariffs for those items where tariffs represent the major trade obstacles. For other items such as grain and meat he favored international commodity agreements. He emphasized however, that the key to the U.S. and the world's interest, in terms of the Common Market, is the internal price of wheat. If this price is kept near the current French level there will not be such an expansion of European production as seriously to jeopardize access for foreign exporters. If, however, the price of grain goes to a high price, then U.S. exports in grains would be eliminated in the next five years.

At this point the President pointed out that high grain prices would be in the interest of some of the members of the Common Market and asked how one could avoid the increase in price. In reply Mr. Mansholt stated that it was essential that internal prices be kept low and stressed that U.S. policies designed to reduce U.S. surplus, plus bargaining under the TEA would help to achieve this.

Mansholt recognized that poultry was a special case. He recognized that U.S. exports had been almost eliminated because of the current obstacles. Having this in mind, he had proposed to the European Economic Commission a reduction in the gate price which would have the effect of reducing the charges against imports by 1.8 cents a pound. However, poultry was a hot political issue not only in the U.S. but in Europe as well. While Europe is now moving towards mass production on the American style, there remain many small poultry farmers. Nevertheless his proposal had been agreed to by the Commission and has now been referred to the Council of Ministers. He expected opposition to this proposal by Germany and France and he hinted broadly that American representations, at least to these two countries, would be appropriate.

Secretary Freeman stated that he felt the U.S. was entitled to average poultry exports of 50,000 to 70,000 tons per year. In order to achieve this he suggested a reduction of price from 13 cents to 8 cents and a quota arrangement of up to 50,000 to 70,000 tons. Mr. Mansholt did not respond directly to this proposal.

The President stated that he was very much concerned at the inability of the Atlantic countries to coordinate policies on the inter-related problems of agriculture, defense spending, interest rates, capital movements, tourism, and all the other items which go into the balance of payments. He felt that these issues were being dealt with by technical experts but that no one is bringing all of the related factors into one coherent whole. Thus there was lacking a coherent overall policy which would influence decisions on the individual technical issues. He asked Mr. Mansholt whether he had any idea as to how to achieve this high level coordination.

In the discussion which followed Mansholt did not provide any real response to the President on this issue. However, Mr. Mansholt did stress that agricultural problems consisted of much more than simply trade. He felt that if satisfactory answers were to be reached that they would have to include basic agricultural policies. For example, he stated that if the United States could enter the negotiations under the Trade Expansion Act in the agricultural field on the basis of an internal program which would gradually reduce U.S. domestic surpluses that it would put the United States negotiators in a very strong position to insist that their European partners also follow policies designed to avoid surpluses which would create international difficulties. In terms of the Common Market, the important point he stressed was the internal price for wheat. Secretary Freeman pointed out that in his presentation of the current Administration proposals to the American farmer on "supply management" that he stressed that if the U.S. was going to demand reasonable policies on the part of other countries in the agriculture field, that it must have internal policies which take better into account international repercussions. Mr. Mansholt was thoroughly in agreement with this position.

At the close of the conversation, Mr. Mansholt stated that he wished to comment on the President's plan for a trip to Germany.[1] Mr. Mansholt stated that he knew all good Europeans were delighted at the prospect of this trip and especially welcomed the President's plan to visit Berlin. He hoped the President could cover as much of West Germany as possible and especially recommended he visit Hamburg. He stated that if the President visited Hamburg 100,000 people would line the streets to greet him. Mr. Mozer corrected the figure to "300,000."

The President pointed out that there are, of course, some limitations as to what he, as President of the United States, can say in Europe and asked for Mr. Mansholt's reactions. Mr. Mansholt stated that, of course the President must not seem to be telling Europeans the type of Europe that they should want, but that the major theme which was fully consistent with U.S. policies over the past 15 years was one supporting a unified, democratic Europe which could operate as a full and equal partner of the United States. Mr. Mansholt felt that the partnership theme stressed the importance of an Atlantic Alliance and the fact that Europe, in order to play the proper role, must develop democratically and in a manner which takes fully into account the needs of other nations of the Free World. Without attacking de Gaulle specifically, the President could point out that only this type of Europe could play its full and effective role.

---

[1] Scheduled for June 1963.

76.   Memorandum of Conversation

Bonn, May 20, 1963.

PARTICIPANTS

Chancellor Adenauer   Ambassador McGhee
Ambassador von Holleben
Dr. Osterheld (Interpreter)

SUBJECT

Franco-German Treaty

The Chancellor said that he wished to discuss with me the Franco-German Treaty. He said that he had before him a communiqué from the Agence-France Press which took the general line that there was a natural affinity between the Soviets and French and that they should get together. They could provide a link between the East and West. He said that he wanted us to understand that the primary objective he had in negotiating this treaty was to prevent just such an alliance. There had, of course, been many historical precedents dating back from the time of the Czars. In 1944 de Gaulle himself had gone to Russia to reaffirm the Franco-Russian alliance made prior to the war. It was necessary that this not happen again.

I pointed out to the Chancellor that a Franco-German rapprochement was, as he knew, something which we desired as much as he. In fact, had he not arranged one we would probably be urging him to do so. The only thing that caused concern for some, and this appeared to have been taken care of by the preamble which was a part of the enabling legislation of the treaty, was that it would become a basis for agreement between the two nations which would then be presented as a fait accompli in bilateral relations with us and in the multilateral councils such as NATO and the EEC. It was our hope that matters affecting Europe as a whole could be worked out jointly in the multilateral context.

The Chancellor came back very sharply on this point. Had we, for example, discussed with Germany and France the matters which were agreed to in Nassau? It was the fact that Macmillan, after his visit with de Gaulle in which he had not mentioned that he was going to seek Polaris weapons from the United States or help to create a multilateral force, had made an agreement with President Kennedy on these points, that had precipitated the de Gaulle press statement.

Source: Department of State, Central Files, Pol 7 US Kennedy. Confidential. The source text was transmitted as enclosure 2 to airgram 2465, May 22. The meeting was held in the Chancellor's office at Palais Schaumburg. McGhee presented his credentials on May 18; this was his first meeting with the Chancellor.

I responded that I understood the inferences that might have been derived from the Nassau meeting and communiqué.[1] However, it should be pointed out that this meeting was basically to solve a bilateral US-UK problem, i.e., our inability to supply weapons which we had agreed we would supply to the British if they became available. The solution to this problem, which involved our offer to furnish the Polaris without nuclear warheads was in a sense a bilateral problem. The proposal for a multilateral force was made at this time largely as a result of circumstances, however, it might be considered as a gesture to compensate the other members of NATO for the Polaris offer.

In any event, it was clearly a proposal which had no validity unless it was acceptable to other NATO members, including the Germans. We had immediately discussed it with the Germans before finalizing any of its details. Perhaps it would have been better if we had been able to engage in talks with all concerned before making the proposal public, however, it is not always possible to control the precise timing under which questions like this arise. Our concept of the way allies should deal with each other is to discuss a new matter quietly with all concerned, and then to seek decisions within a multilateral framework in a give-and-take manner, with everyone sitting around the table. It was General de Gaulle alone who appeared to inject the nationalistic element into the growing consensus in favor of the "European idea."

The Chancellor rose rather sharply to the defense of General de Gaulle. In the first place, he said, it was necessary that General de Gaulle revive confidence in France before anything could be accomplished. He had first to revive the pride of the French army and then to solve the problem of Algeria. These were very great achievements.

I agreed and stated that we gave full marks to General de Gaulle on these counts. I pointed out that other European nations, however, had made very considerable progress without injecting a nationalistic element into their relations with other European nations. Germany itself was the best example of this. Chancellor Adenauer had rebuilt the German army and German prosperity while still favoring European integration.

The Chancellor replied that this was easier for Germany. Germany had a great problem to overcome after the war. They did not want to incur reactions. It was better for Germany to keep quiet about its army and its economic progress, and to merge into the European context.

---

[1] For text of the Nassau Communiqué and Attached Statement on Nuclear Defense Systems, December 21, 1962, see *American Foreign Policy: Current Documents, 1962*, pp. 633–637.

I pointed out that other countries who did not face this problem—Belgium and Holland in particular, but also Italy, and now, I thought, Britain—had also accepted the "European idea".

The Chancellor then complained that it was not de Gaulle but in fact the other European nations, particularly Belgium and Holland, who had in 1961 rejected the results of his efforts for a European political union, which de Gaulle had accepted. He admitted that de Gaulle had changed it somewhat by including the existing Community institutions in it, but he still insisted it was their fault.

The Chancellor insisted that it was not de Gaulle's fault that Europe had not made progress toward union. He said that he himself had told General de Gaulle during his stay in Paris after the Press announcement, when the treaty was concluded, that he was in favor of the multilateral force and Britain's entry in the Common Market. De Gaulle assured him that he also favored Britain's (I assume ultimate) entry into the Common Market. He said that de Gaulle was not nationalistic, as he understood the distinction, but national.

---

77. Telegram From the Department of State to the Mission to the European Communities

Washington, June 12, 1963, 2:09 p.m.

Busec 544. From Herter to Tuthill. To set the proper atmosphere for the poultry negotiations, I believe it would be useful if you could make clear to Mansholt (and probably also to Rey) that our primary objective in negotiations opening Geneva June 20 is to obtain reasonable access for US poultry exports to the EEC. If this is not possible, public pressure and the obligations of my office would leave me no alternative but to proceed with the necessary steps to redress the loss we have suffered as a result of the Community actions on poultry. The restoration of the US position in poultry trade is clearly still the best solution but recent developments have left little confidence here in the good-will of the Community as a whole. I appreciate, however, the Commission's recent efforts to establish a more equitable situation and hope it will continue to play a

Source: Department of State, Central Files, INCO Poultry EEC. Limited Official Use. Drafted in E/OT and RPE and cleared with Vine, E, and STR.

constructive role, seeking to use its negotiating powers to achieve with our negotiators a mutually acceptable solution. It is obvious that a satisfactory poultry solution would go a long way toward improving relations between the US and EEC.

Any information which you or your staff can secure regarding the likely attitude of the Community in the poultry negotiations would, of course, be most welcome. For our part, in pursuing our objective of access for US poultry, we would be prepared to consider any reasonable proposals which may be suggested.

You should also convey my view that if progress is to be made at Geneva, it is essential that the Commission representatives have adequate mandate ad referendum to Council to negotiate seriously. In this connection, Blumenthal will also be prepared elaborate on our thinking to Commissioners in Brussels June 20. Accordingly, it would be desirable for Commission negotiators in Geneva to have flexibility to move ahead rapidly thereafter.[1]

Rusk

---

[1] On June 13 Tuthill reported that he had carried out these instructions and that Rey was sympathetic to the U.S. position, but the Agriculture Committee of the Common Market was not entirely sympathetic. (Ecbus 1451 from Brussels; ibid.)

---

78.   Circular Telegram From the Department of State to Certain Missions in Europe

Washington, June 14, 1963, 9:11 p.m.

2153. Ref: Bonn's 3349.[1] There have been recurring rumors since mid-February of possible French initiative in field of European political integration. Some have concentrated on motion along lines suggested

---

Source: Department of State, Central Files, Pol 3 W Eur. Secret. Drafted by Vine; cleared with RPE, BNA, WE, GER, and EUR; and approved by Tyler. Sent to Bonn, Brussels, London, Luxembourg, Paris, Rome, and The Hague.

[1] Telegram 3349, June 8, reported that de Gaulle might make an initiative on European political union during his visit to Bonn in July and suggested that this would further ossify the division between the United Kingdom and the Common Market. (Ibid.)

reftel, namely that French might resurface political union proposals by proposing extension of Franco-German Treaty to others of Six who wish to accept.

There have also been suggestions that fusion of existing executives of three Communities might be another aim of French proposals, along with some proposals on role of European Parliament.

Dept now believes there is real possibility that de Gaulle will use occasion of his visit to Germany in early July to lay out a set of European initiatives. Reasons for this belief are: (a) French themselves will wish to set stage for relations with post-Adenauer Germany; (b) to counter widespread notion that French are no longer interested in objective of unified Europe; and (c) to identify France and de Gaulle with Europe in contrast to transatlantic emphasis of President's trip.

As for the substance of the proposals, it is possible that they will be comprehensive and include not only a proposal to extend the Franco-German Treaty to the other members of the Six if they so desire, but possibly also a comprehensive plan for the reorganization of existing Communities. There may well be some innovations.

The Fouchet discussions on political union and the discussions in Brussels on the reorganization of the executives have given us a clear idea of what likely positions of the Six are. The Fouchet political union proposals shattered on three points: (a) the revision clause; (b) inclusion of the British; and finally (c) links with existing Communities. Points of view on these points have not greatly changed, so that if French were to make "new" proposals, any innovations would probably be related to these points in some way in order to make them palatable.

When Couve de Murville talked with Under Secretary[2] he mentioned possibility of a "European Council of Governments," which might ultimately be chaired by a President, who might, according to Couve, be elected by the Council, or alternatively, voted on directly by a European Parliament. This is the only reference we have seen to French thinking on this subject, but it is quite possible, in view of the stress which Couve appeared to lay on it, that any new French initiative might incorporate such an idea, or be designed ultimately to lay the groundwork for it.

While it obviously fruitless to speculate in detail on any proposal, and a fortiori to give guidance on such basis, following comments may help addressees in interim.

We would have open mind on proposals if they aimed at true European unification. Questions of links with Community and revision

---

[2] A memorandum of Couve de Murville's conversation with Ball on May 25, covering trade, monetary policy, and nuclear matters, is ibid., Pol Fr-US.

clause are matters that Europeans themselves will have to work out on basis of what is politically feasible and palatable.

From U.S. viewpoint, there are three major desiderata to which posts may address themselves on ad hoc basis:

1) Whatever form of any political arrangements, they must be based solidly on NATO framework and contribute to its functioning and strengthening;
2) Effect of proposals should not undermine progress which has been made and can be made in three existing Communities; and
3) Provision should be made for present or later inclusion such major European powers as UK.

The issue of a strengthened UK-EEC institutional link will be major subject of discussion during de Gaulle visit in Germany in order to find a Franco-German compromise for July 11 EEC Council meeting. Possible that French will therefore suggest to Germans "gesture" permit development compromise position to which they have several times recently alluded. Effect of this gesture could well be vitiated by other proposals in political field, however. On this matter, Dept believes that other Five will have difficult choice between close ties with British and forward progress of "Europe" in view of obvious inability of Britain to move closer to Europe in next eighteen months or two years. On other hand, this is not matter in which U.S. can or should take initiative. Believe defense of this point should be left to others of Six and UK itself.

Rusk

---

79.   Memorandum From the Under Secretary of State (Ball) to President Kennedy

Washington, June 20, 1963.

SUBJECT

The Mess in Europe and the Meaning of Your Trip [1]

This paper is not written in the spirit of alarmism. Nor do I believe that pessimism is a useful working hypothesis. But if your European

---

Source: Department of State, Central Files, Pol 7 US/Kennedy. Secret. Drafted by Ball.

[1] President Kennedy visited Italy, West Germany and Berlin, the United Kingdom, and Ireland during his European trip, June 23–July 2. Regarding his stop in Rome, see Documents 318 and 319; regarding the stops at Bonn and Berlin, see vol. XV, pages 528–530 and 535–537.

trip is to pay off fully, we must make a hard-boiled appraisal of what is going on in Europe today.

Unquestionably, Europe is in a mess, and it is not going to get out of that mess quickly. Never, at any time since the war, have European voices been so discordant, European opinions so confused, European Governments so lacking in direction.

Never, at any time since the war—and this is the main point—has Europe been in graver danger of back-sliding into the old destructive habits—the old fragmentation and national rivalries that have twice brought the world to disaster in the past.

Your trip must be planned in cold-blooded recognition of these lamentable facts.

THE NATURE OF THE MESS

I do not propose in this memorandum to undertake a full diagnosis of why Europe has gotten sick so fast. The problem is necessarily complex and only the simple-minded would offer a pat answer. As the past few months have shown, political developments can be influenced by events as disparate as a Papal Encyclical and the occupational triumphs of a Christine Keeler. [2]

But the over-riding change in the condition of Europe—and the change that has given other influences special force and meaning—has been the halting, and at least momentary reversal, of the drive toward unity in Europe. This has come about, as the whole world knows, from the abrupt reassertion of old-style competitive nationalism expressed in a new-style rhetoric.

Some interruption in the progress toward unity was to be expected—was perhaps overdue. Progress toward unity had come about from the fortunate convergence of a number of forces. Except for the defeat of the EDC in 1954, it had proceeded with deceptive speed and smoothness. The coincidence of accelerating economic growth with the progress of the Common Market had tended to create an impression of a wider and more solid political integration than in fact existed.

It was to be expected that this apparently smooth and rapid evolution toward European unity would at some point be challenged by a counter-revolution of nationalism. We hoped, of course, that the movement had obtained such momentum that once Europe had survived the parturition of British membership, the ultimate achievement of unity would be secure. We were betting that the addition of a third major pil-

---

[2] On June 4 John Profumo, British Secretary of State for War, admitted that Christine Keeler had been his mistress, a fact that he had previously denied; see Document 415.

lar in the European edifice would render it structurally stable and proof against the erosion of any one pillar.

This was the postulate of American policy during the first two years of your Administration. It was a sound postulate, and over the long pull, still is, since the European structure it envisaged would satisfy the requirements of scale demanded by the modern age.

Unfortunately, the nationalist counter-attack came at a particularly bad time. Not only did it frustrate—or at least seriously postpone—British adherence, but it demoralized Europe just at the time when it was undergoing other major adjustments.

THE CONSEQUENCES

The mess that resulted is real enough. What are the dangers that it offers?

The Concealed Time Bomb of French Instability

Many of the Frenchmen who worked most ardently for European unity were moved by a deep conviction that France could never solve her own political problems within a national context. France concealed within her body politic deep divisive forces. Only by diluting those forces within the larger caldron of Europe could Frenchmen achieve lasting political stability. This conviction was widely and firmly held, and I have no doubt that the promise and prospect of a European solution was a powerful element in keeping the ramshackle Fourth Republic from falling apart.

But—and this is one of its most dangerous consequences—de Gaulle's revival of nationalism has pushed French problems back into a narrowly French setting. In the process, it threatens to restore the disastrous cycle that has marked modern French history.

Preeminently a country with an unassimilated revolution, France for two centuries has tended to oscillate between governments kept deliberately weak and vulnerable on the left and strong-man governments afflicted with a progressive absolutism. The pendulum has swung with monotonous regularity from an impotent Directory to Napoleon I; from Louis Philippe to the Second Empire to the French Commune; from Leon Blum and the *Front Populaire* to Marshal Petain.

Each week de Gaulle's France grows perceptibly more absolutist, while the French people have packed off on a political holiday—an Indian Summer of political irresponsibility. By destroying the whole structure of parties except the Communist Party, the General has eliminated the institutional means for resisting Communism. Today the CP offers opponents of Gaullism the only visible center of effectively organized strength. As a result, the French Communists—demoralized only a short time ago—have been given a new lease on life. And the way once more lies open for a *Front Populaire*. This threat is vividly described in a *Reporter* article by Ed Taylor attached as Tab A.[3]

We must never forget, therefore, that in spite of its material prosperity and the lack of visible political agitation, France conceals a profound political malaise. De Gaulle will not last forever and the hazards involved in France's ultimate return to constitutional government is an omnipresence that hangs heavily over Europe.

The Dangers of Germany Adrift

The second major motivation of the French "Europeans"—and the prime motivation of their German colleagues—was an anxiety to tie a truncated Germany firmly to the West within the framework of a united Europe.

This involved, as an essential element, a Franco-German understanding, yet it was recognized from the beginning that a permanent understanding could never be achieved on a bilateral basis. Rivalry between France and Germany was too long-standing, history too bloody, for any resolution of their deeply-felt mistrust except in the cushioning presence of other nations that were prepared to subordinate individual national concerns to the common interest of a larger unity.

This view has been borne out by the events of the past six months. *These events have provided persuasive evidence that Germany cannot be bound securely to the West by a bilateral agreement with a France determined to use that agreement to establish and maintain French hegemony.*

Such an effort is more likely to repel Germany than attract it.

It was worth noting, for example, that the French officials who accompanied Couve to Washington[4] took an almost anti-German tone, frankly expressing their annoyance at the lack of tangible benefits from the Franco-German Treaty. And it was conspicuous during the GATT negotiations at Geneva that, while the Six felt a strong desire to hold together because of their Rome Treaty commitments, it was the Germans who led the drive to dislodge the French from their obdurate position.

Unfortunately for the West, de Gaulle has chosen the worst possible moment for reviving nationalism—just the moment when Chancellor Adenauer is relinquishing the reins in Germany. As a result, we face dangerous weather with the Federal Republic.

There are several reasons for this.

While nationalism is contagious, it is not a constructive element in the relations between nations. On the contrary, the assertion of a strong

---

[3] Not printed.
[4] See Document 271.

nationalism by one nation tends to produce an equal and opposite reaction in its neighbors.

This has dangerous implications for the future of Germany.

Nationalism in the past has led the Germans and the world into deep trouble. And the confluence of forces—the assault on the structure of European unity, the removal of the political direction of the Chancellor, and the contagious infection of resurgent nationalism—must be a cause for serious concern.

I am not overstating the dangers. No one can speak with assurance of the pressures and counter-pressures that may shape the future of a post-Adenauer Germany. We have simply had no experience of a Federal Republic freed from the Old Fox's iron discipline. [2 lines of source text not declassified] we could make a tragic error if we took it for granted that events would go on as usual.

Here are some of the reasons for concern:

Erhard as Chancellor

Professor Erhard is a man of good-will. In many ways, we should find him easy to work with. He shares our interest in liberal trade (except in agriculture, where he has been content to say that "all nations are sinners") and he has always recognized the economic advantages of an enlarged European community. In fact, he fought for British admission to the Common Market with energy and courage.

[1 paragraph (7-1/2 lines of source text) not declassified]

The French are reported to be preparing a campaign to win him over, but by temperament and intellect he is at the opposite pole from General de Gaulle. There will not be an easy working relation between a Gaullist France and a Federal Republic under Erhard.

[2-1/2 lines of source text not declassified] The most likely result is a Germany adrift—at least during Erhard's tenure as Chancellor—while an internecine power battle goes on in Bonn for the succession.

The Impact of the Force de Frappe

In an atmosphere of resurgent nationalism, the emergence of France as a nuclear power can have serious repercussions in Germany on two counts. It can stir competitive ambitions and revive a sense of resentment against discrimination.

It is no good saying that Germans do not want atomic weapons. Even if that were true today—and the evidence is confusing—what Germans will come to demand in a competitive Europe is power and equal treatment. Nothing is more dangerous than the bland assumption—detectable in both parties in Britain, as well as in France—that if the other Western allies gang up on Germany they can successfully hold the Federal Republic to her self-denying ordinances regarding atomic weapons. *If the world learned anything from the experience between the wars, it should certainly have learned that. We cannot afford to make the same mistake twice.*

I am attaching at Tab B[5] a brief memorandum relating to the history of German rearmament following the First World War. It teaches two clear lessons.

The first is that Germany cannot over an extended period be kept in a position of discrimination. Not only will the effort fail, but it will lead to a festering resentment out of all proportion to the importance of the objective.

The second lesson is that a Germany not tied institutionally to the West is dangerous—and no one has offered an effective means of tying Germany to the West except through a unified Europe within an Atlantic Partnership.

The Danger of New Soviet Tactics

Up to this point, the Germans have been tractable largely because of their fear of the Soviet Union and the knowledge that we alone can provide an effective defense. But a process of shifts and changes is under way on both sides of the Iron Curtain, and the possibility of some Soviet overture to a post-Adenauer Germany must not be overlooked.

There is no imminent danger of any German diplomatic adventure with Moscow. The realities of nuclear dependence are too well known for that. But we must think in a longer time span. The geometry of power relationships is rapidly changing, and events set in train today can shape the conditions of tomorrow.

In those changed conditions a Germany not tied closely and institutionally to the West can be a source of great hazard. Embittered by a deepening sense of discrimination and bedeviled by irredentism, a Germany at large can be like a cannon on shipboard in a high sea.

POLICY BACKGROUND FOR YOUR TRIP

These are the background facts. The policies that flow from the implications of these facts can be easily stated:

1. The main thrust of our policy must be to provide the people of Europe—and particularly the people of Germany—with the opportunity to realize their aspirations on a basis of self-respect and no discrimination, but without the need to resort to a competitive drive for domination. This means the strengthening and further development of European unity, the construction of an effective Atlantic Partnership,

---

[5] Not printed.

and—through the instrument of that partnership—the elimination of discrimination.

2. In the carrying out of that policy, we can expect little immediate help from the major European Governments. French policy is opposed to our objectives. The Macmillan Government is at bay, and even if Labour comes to power it is unlikely for some time that the UK will play a significant European role, not only because of the French veto, but because a Labour Government will tend to place prior emphasis on domestic affairs. Italy must first find a new alignment of political forces before an Italian Government can act with effectiveness.

3. Germany alone is capable of immediate constructive action—and Germany is just emerging from a long adolescence under stern parental guidance.

4. In this environment of impuissance and nonfusion, de Gaulle's interjection of competitive nationalism—even though stated in purloined terminology—is a mischief and a danger. In facing this danger, we must never forget—or let others forget—that the General's brand of nationalism can work in only one direction. It can push Europe back towards its old fragmentation, can reinstate old rivalries, revive old grievances. But it is a destructive force. It cannot build anything, since nationalism motivated by a desire for dominance or hegemony, no matter how deceptively decked out, is the negation of internationalism and supranationalism.

5. The last five months have proved the force of these assertions. De Gaulle has been able to veto and to confuse but he has wholly failed to launch any solid international arrangements. On the contrary, his attempts to coalesce European strength around France in order to advance parochial French interests have resulted only in his progressive isolation. The limited successes won for French policy have been achieved not through the agency of any new unity or allegiance, but rather through the fear that a frustrated French Government might wreck the structure of unity already created. Even this threat is a wasting asset, for the Europeans have recognized that, while de Gaulle has borrowed the vocabulary of European unification, he is peddling the same old pre-war merchandise.

6. Yet, while recognizing Gaullist policies for what they are and what they imply, we should not shape our own course in reaction to de Gaulle. Nothing could do us greater harm than to lead or join an anti-Gaullist cabal.

7. On the contrary, we must state clearly what we believe is good and right—state it repeatedly and with conviction and authority, and make it clear to all the world that we do not intend to waver or deviate

from the directions we have so long taken with such great benefit to the world.

8. At the same time, we must be on guard that our actions are at all times consistent with the policies we profess. Our ability to lead Europe and the Western Alliance depends upon our demonstrating *by our actions* that we know what is good for the Free World and will act accordingly.

9. Thus, while we should eschew any anti-de Gaulle campaign—or any appearance of such a campaign—we should, at the same time rigorously avoid any action that might give aid and comfort to the destructive policy of competitive nationalism which the General is seeking to impose.

10. This means in more specific terms that we must not yield in our insistence that further nuclear development in Europe take place in a multilateral context. We must do nothing that might facilitate—or even appear to facilitate—the creation of a *force de frappe* on a national basis. We must not, by any casual act such as the thinning out of forces, give strength to those who would undermine the credibility of our intentions.

THE APPLICATION OF THESE POLICIES
TO YOUR EUROPEAN TRIP

In your speeches and private conversations, I would suggest that the following considerations should control:

A. We should never forget that the United States is the leader of the Atlantic world and that the great mass of Europeans look to America—and specifically to you, as President—for guidance and direction. This is for them a conditioned reflex and we should not be misled by brave talk to the contrary.

B. United States influence will depend upon your being able to make it clear that we know what we want and that we are prepared to affirm our convictions with clarity and precision.

C. In principle, you should address your remarks to Europeans generally, rather than to Germans. But at the same time, there is a special effort to be made with the German people. There are several reasons for this:

1. The Federal Republic is the only major Government amenable to American ideas that is presently capable of effective action.

2. Over the next few years, Germany will be making her choice. Either she will elect to channel her energies within the framework of a unified Europe within an Atlantic Partnership, or she will choose the old way of competitive nationalism. The choice of the first course is vital to the safety of the world.

3. Finally, we still have great influence with the Germans. They are closest to the firing line. Berlin is a Soviet hostage, and the German peo-

ple know that their only defense is the American strength and commitment.

D. But, while speaking with the German problem in mind, you should speak to Europe as a whole about European unity and the Atlantic Partnership. In doing so, you should make it clear that we Americans need have no reluctance to state our views on the issues of unity with force and conviction. In expressing our opinions on this matter, we are not acting—and you should make it clear that we are not acting—merely as a disinterested friend. We have a stake in the shape of Europe and we should not hesitate to assert it. We have a vital self-interest in preventing retrogression toward a fragmented Europe which, on two occasions, has required the New World to redress the balance of the Old.

E. To the Germans specifically you should make it clear that, within a European framework and an Atlantic partnership, Germany will be able to achieve her aspirations for full nondiscriminatory treatment without the need to dominate.

F. The elimination of discrimination means that Germany must play some part in nuclear defense. I feel that those who would deny this need are merely sticking their heads in the sand. At the same time you should indicate that the illusion that nuclear participation can be achieved within an exclusively European framework has no current relevance—although we should not foreclose the possibility for the future. The hard fact is that Europe is far less able today to organize the management of a nuclear deterrent than it appeared to be six months ago.

G. This leads inevitably to the MLF. It is—and remains—the one constructive idea anyone has put forward for assuring German participation in a nuclear deterrent without proliferation. This, I think, you should say clearly and firmly. America recommends the MLF *because it is the best way to achieve a common goal.* We believe Europeans should support it. We are asking no nation to participate in it to please us, but we are convinced it is a sound enterprise.

H. In quiet conversations with Adenauer and Erhard you should make it clear that we share their belief that a MLF in a bilateral German-American setting is not good. Quite likely, neither Britain nor Italy will be in position to make a prompt decision with regard to membership, but the idea must be kept alive and forward progress must be made. You should propose to have arrangements for collective drafting go forward toward this end. At the same time, you should express confidence that within a reasonable period other European countries should be able to make a decision to join.

I. Finally, you should strongly urge the significance of the equal partnership which America is offering. This is the unique contribution that only we can make to Europe. It is a concept founded not on domination or hegemony, but on an equal sharing of the benefits and responsibilities between the "competent" halves of the Free World. Partnership and an organized Europe are not only compatible with, but essential to, one another, since neither Germany nor America wants to see a closed, autarkic, incestuous "continental" system.

George W. Ball[6]

---

[6] Printed from a copy that bears this typed signature.

---

60.   Circular Telegram From the Department of State to Certain Missions

Washington, August 3, 1963, 5:28 p.m.

220. Joint State–USIA. Also pass US Mission Geneva. US exports frozen poultry (broilers, stewers, turkeys, and parts) to countries EEC have been substantially reduced as result increases in EEC poultry charges and duties. Continuing efforts to arrive at an equitable solution have been unsuccessful. Instead of decreasing duties, duties have progressively increased. Cause and fact of damage to US trade not in question. Import charges into Germany, the principal importer of US poultry, have been tripled since institution EEC common agricultural policy. US exports of poultry to Germany have dropped from a monthly average of 4,500 tons in 1961 and 6,000 tons in 1962 to about 2,000 tons in the first four months of 1963. Denmark has also been affected by the EEC regulation and has suffered a serious drop in its poultry exports to Germany. While German production has increased, the high cost of production in Germany has left unfulfilled considerable consumer demand.

For more than a year the US has made every effort to arrive at arrangements which would provide satisfactory access for US poultry to the EEC. In a final attempt to reach a solution, US in latter part of June

---

Source: Department of State, Central Files, Inco-Poultry US. Limited Official Use; Priority. Drafted by Freedman (EUR), cleared with RPE and USIA, and approved by Blumenthal. Sent to all missions except Sofia, Moscow, Budapest, and Bucharest.

called for negotiations under what is known as the Standstill Agreement on poultry concluded between US and EEC in March 1962, following inconclusive discussions under GATT Article XXIV:6. The Standstill Agreement required the EEC to undertake negotiations on poultry. Unfortunately, these negotiations failed to arrive at a satisfactory arrangement on poultry, nor did EEC offer equivalent compensation to offset damage to US poultry exports. This situation provides legal basis under GATT for US to unilaterally withdraw concessions previously granted EEC upon 30 days' notice to GATT Contracting Parties.

As first step US announcing August 6 that public hearings will be held on items being considered for withdrawal of concessions. If by Sept 16 there still no solution US will reluctantly resort to its legal rights as principal supplier under Article XXVIII of GATT and formally notify GATT that after 30 days US will withdraw concessions negotiated with EEC of value substantially equivalent to that of injured US poultry trade with EEC.

US has determined that value of US poultry trade affected is $46 million. $46 million is estimate of what US exports to Germany would have been if Germans had not had discriminatory quantitative restrictions on poultry in calendar year 1960. This calculation is consistent with Article XXVIII of GATT which provides that a country may qualify as a principal supplier, if in absence of discriminatory quantitative restrictions, it would have had a larger share of importer market.

Article XXVIII also provides that a compensatory increase in duties must be applied on a most-favored nation basis on those items on which tariff concessions were initially negotiated with EEC or individual EEC states. Therefore, duty increases on items eventually selected will in certain instances unfortunately fall to slight degree on some non-EEC countries as well. US will, however, provide appropriate concessions for any losses suffered by third countries.

Proposed schedule for withdrawing concessions follows:

1) August 6—announcement of scheduling public hearings on items being considered for withdrawal of concessions and publication of list of items to total trade value of $110 million from which we would eventually choose items valued at approximately $46 million.

2) September 4—Public hearings to end on or before Sept 10.

3) September 16—Presidential proclamation, effective in 30 days, withdrawing concessions on items totalling $46 million of US imports from EEC. Formal notification to Contracting Parties of US intention of making compensatory withdrawals.

4) October 16—Withdrawals to go into effect.

It is clear from above schedule that any time prior final US action, EEC could prevent withdrawal concessions by agreeing to satisfactory arrangements on poultry.

Treatment

1. US action being taken most reluctantly and only following repeated efforts to arrive at mutually satisfactory arrangements. General theme should be one of regret, not of recrimination.

2. Announcement on August 6 only first step in compliance domestic practice to hold hearings. Final action still several months off and could be avoided by prompt EEC action. Output should avoid any implication, however, that present US action merely a negotiating move.

3. Note that while damage real to US producers, major loss is to European consumer due to higher retail prices.

4. Protectionist agricultural policy not in best interest of Europe or free world. Would be most unfortunate if poultry action indicative of future EEC agricultural policy. US willing to make every effort work out problems on basis equitable for all concerned.

5. While US disappointed with EEC poultry policy this has not lessened US plans to move ahead on trade negotiations.

6. US acting under legal rights and in conformity with GATT. Assert but do not argue legal rights.

7. While German imports crucial on poultry action, emphasis should be on EEC acting as a unit. We can give EEC Commission credit for valiantly trying to find compromise.

8. Note that under MFN few other countries may be affected slightly but US abiding by GATT and will compensate for any trade damage to third countries. US recognizes its responsibility. Do not speculate when or how this will be done.

9. Emphasize theme that fundamental question is whether there is to be sheltered markets with resulting high costs to consumers or low cost production of mutual benefit to all countries.

10. US action should be described as compensatory withdrawals, not as retaliation.

11. Do not speculate on final items on US list.

12. Since Europeans can be expected to argue they cannot act under US pressure to remedy the poultry situation, we should point out that for over a year we have been more patient in efforts find solution but matters have been getting progressively worse.

13. Press backgrounder on Tuesday will provide further guidance. However, do not pick up statements which directed in first instance to domestic audience.

Ball

81.   Telegram From the Department of State to the Mission to the European Communities

Washington, August 30, 1963, 4:10 p.m.

Busec 82. Brussels also for Embassy. Ref: Ecbus 197.[1]

1. After high-level interagency consideration Commission proposal, we fail to find it substantially more attractive than German overture reported Deptel Brussels 257.[2] Temporary eleven pfennig reduction to give time for negotiation of permanent solution begs question of what EEC considers negotiable. In our June discussions with Commission, EEC made no proposals that might have offered basis negotiation, merely rejected out of hand two US proposals for settlement.

2. We think it is now up to EEC Council either to come forward with specific counterproposals for permanent solution or to grant Commission sufficiently broad powers to negotiate with US. Under latter alternative we would want negotiations to be concluded by October 1 with agreement reached ad referendum on specific proposals to be submitted to Council and US for approval. Without any such specifics as to what basis might exist for negotiation or without mandate to Commission to negotiate, we feel the suggestion that negotiations be continued is quite empty and holds no reasonable hope for eventual settlement.

3. You may state that while 11 pfennig not enough for postponement, need to schedule US hearings through September 12 (about week longer than originally anticipated) will make it impossible anyway for us to proclaim withdrawals until late September.

4. You should state US prepared to respond positively to any meaningful proposals from Council and continues to hope that negotiated settlement is possible. In conjunction with alternatives indicated above US would welcome Council approval of 11 pfennig reduction as an earnest of good intentions.

Rusk

Source: Department of State, Central Files, INCO Poultry US. Limited Official Use; Operational Immediate. Drafted in STR and cleared by the Departments of State and Agriculture. Repeated to Paris, Rome, Bonn, The Hague, Luxembourg, and Geneva.

[1] Ecbus 197, August 26, reported that the EEC Commission had requested the U.S. reaction to a temporary 11-pfennig reduction pending final solution of the problem. (Ibid.)

[2] Telegram 257, August 21, reported that representatives from the German Embassy, on instructions from Bonn, had inquired whether an 11-pfennig reduction would be sufficient to cause the United States to suspend action on poultry. (Ibid.) After interagency consultation at the highest level, the German representatives were informed on August 21 that such a small reduction would not have a sufficiently meaningful effect on trade.

82.   Telegram From the Department of State to the Mission to the European Communities

Washington, September 20, 1963, 2:11 p.m.

Busec 131. Ref: TAGG 1416, Ecbus 310.[1] For Tuthill from Herter. Interagency agreement reached on following alternatives for dealing with poultry problem and avoiding collision with EEC. These alternatives should be presented during your Monday meeting with Hallstein.

1.   EEC Council at its September 23 meeting to provide Commission with meaningful negotiating mandate so that US and EEC can seek immediately to negotiate satisfactory settlement of poultry issue. We would not insist this be accompanied by 11-pfennig reduction in levies but US would welcome this reduction as token of EEC's good intentions.

We would interpret as meaningful a mandate from Council to Commission to seek agreement with US, on ad referendum basis, on reductions in poultry levies that gave reasonable assurance of restoring US poultry trade. We would not expect Council to specify amount required or to endorse either of specific proposals advanced by US in its aide-mémoire. Obviously those proposals were also negotiable. We would want formal indication however that Council was prepared to give serious consideration to any arrangement Commission worked out with US.

2.   US to defer action on compensatory withdrawals while bilateral negotiations carried out. Definite time limit for such negotiations would have to be set. From every point of view it is essential this matter be brought to prompt conclusion. We think 30 days should allow ample time. At latest negotiations would have to be terminated successfully by October 31, 1963, and Council would have to approve results promptly if US not to make compensatory withdrawals.

3.   If Council does not provide meaningful mandate to negotiate, or, if, following such mandate, US and EEC cannot reach accord on satisfactory reductions in levies within time limits indicated in (2) above, US

Source: Department of State, Central Files, INCO Poultry US. Limited Official Use; Operational Immediate. Drafted by Hedges and Rehm (STR) and cleared in draft with Herter, Ball, Freeman, and Hodges.

[1] Both dated September 19. In TAGG 1416 Blumenthal reported that the EEC would not accept the U.S. figure of $46 million and would make counter withdrawals if concessions totaling that figure were withdrawn. Blumenthal suggested that continuing along this line would not benefit the United States and proposed further negotiations and perhaps submitting to GATT the question of the amount of compensation. (Ibid.) Ecbus 310 reported that a meeting had been previously arranged with Hallstein for September 23 at which the poultry question could be discussed if Washington agreed. (Ibid.)

will have no alternative but to make compensatory withdrawals. However before making such withdrawals we would be prepared to have trade coverage issue adjudicated by GATT panel in order avoid further litigation. As reported in ECBUS 277[2] EEC is prepared to challenge $46 million figure and launch counter-move if US proceeds with withdrawals. We have sufficient confidence in our case to go to adjudication. FYI. In our view GATT panel should determine not whether specific $46 million is proper but what is proper trade exchange figure under Article XXVIII principles. Framing issue in this manner would leave US free to argue before GATT panel that figure higher than $46 million is valid. EEC should presumably not object to so framing issue if they are as confident as they seem to be that proper figure is far below $46 million. If appropriate you may indicate US may plead higher figure since we consider $46 million conservative estimate. End FYI. We would leave for later discussion whether determination of GATT panel should be approved by GATT Contracting Parties.

Adjudication would be limited solely to trade coverage figure and US and EEC would be bound by GATT panel decision. FYI. US acceptance adjudication of trade coverage not intended to waive US right to proceed under Article XXIII concerning any aspects poultry CAP inconsistent with provisions or objectives GATT. Proposed US withdrawals compensate only for EEC withdrawal of poultry binding. Neither EEC withdrawal nor payment exacted by US for withdrawal entitle EEC to adopt measures inconsistent with GATT. You should avoid suggesting contrary and may state US understanding this point if appropriate. End FYI.

If EEC bound by GATT panel decision it would necessarily follow that EEC would accept justification of US case under Article XXVIII and would forego any subsequent counter-moves such as Article XXIII action against our withdrawals. We assume from Rey's statement reported in ECBUS 227 this would create no difficulties for Commission. Pending adjudication US would of course defer issuing withdrawal proclamation.[3]

Rusk

---

[2] Dated September 3. (Ibid.)

[3] On October 16 the United States and the EEC asked the GATT Council of Representatives to render an opinion on the poultry question. (Ecbus 483 to Brussels, October 16; ibid.) In November the GATT panel issued a finding on behalf of the United States but only for $26 million. On December 3 the United States informed representatives of 16 embassies which tariff concession the United States would suspend to compensate for this loss. (Memorandum of telephone conversations, December 3; ibid.)

83. Memorandum of Conversation

Washington, October 4, 1963, 11:30 a.m.

SUBJECT

Europe and the Problem of France

PARTICIPANTS

United States	Belgium
The President	Foreign Minister Spaak
Acting Secretary Ball	Ambassador Scheyven, Belgian
Mr. William R. Tyler, EUR	Embassy
Mr. Francis E. Meloy, Jr., WE	Mr. Robert Rothschild, Chef de
	Cabinet

The President welcomed Mr. Spaak and asked for his views with regard to the current disarray in Europe. Mr. Spaak replied that Europe fundamentally is in good condition. The only trouble is caused by the policy of France and France is causing more and more difficulties.

The President said that there are those who say that if the United States had offered atomic cooperation to France things would have been different. What did the Foreign Minister think?

Mr. Spaak said he believed this was so. After all, possession of a nuclear capability is regarded by France as having the greatest importance. When he had been Secretary General of NATO he had taken the position that the United States should assist the French in obtaining a nuclear capability. The President rejoined that he has the impression now that the French want to develop their own nuclear capability on their own—that this has become a matter of national pride. Mr. Spaak agreed that it was too late now to offer cooperation to the French. He has concluded that de Gaulle is more and more determined to go his own way and to go it alone. Mr. Spaak said that de Gaulle's position is increasingly one of saying that he is for the Alliance but against NATO. De Gaulle is opposed to the organization of the Western Alliance. He wants no political organization, no military organization and no coordination. The only countries with whom de Gaulle would consult would be the U.S. and the U.K. He believes the other members of the NATO Alliance do not count. Mr. Spaak said that the experiences of two World Wars show conclusively that it is very dangerous from a military viewpoint to leave military organization to the last moment.

Source: Department of State, Presidential Memoranda of Conversation: Lot 66 D 149. Secret. Drafted by Meloy and approved in U on October 10 and in the White House on October 24. A memorandum of a similar conversation between Ball and Spaak on October 5 is ibid., Central Files, Pol Eur-Fr.

With regard to consultation in the Alliance, Mr. Spaak said that he had been present at the NATO Council Meeting when Harlan Cleveland had recently spoken there. The French representative said that he had nothing to say, the French position had been expressed elsewhere. This was illustrative of the French attitude toward consultation in the Alliance.

France was being more and more difficult with regard to the Common Market.

While agreeing that it is of the greatest importance that a Franco-German rapprochement be established, Mr. Spaak said that it was ironic that the result of de Gaulle's policy is leading to making Germany the first country of Europe. The President noted that Germany can go from France to the U.S. and back again and benefit from the situation.

Mr. Spaak repeated that it is odd indeed to think that the de Gaulle policy is leading to making Germany the primary power in Europe. After de Gaulle's Lyon speech[1] both Raymond Aron and Hubert Beuve-Mery, Director of Le Monde, had written critical articles. Spaak considered it very significant that the most important journalists in France think de Gaulle wrong.

The President said it may be that if we had helped de Gaulle develop a French national nuclear capability we might have avoided our difficulties with France. On the other hand, cooperation in the nuclear field might merely have increased de Gaulle's power and he would have gone his own way anyway. Mr. Spaak said this was probably correct but cooperation with France might have gained time—perhaps two [?] years—before de Gaulle became intransigent again.

The President asked if Mr. Spaak believed de Gaulle would run for office again. In 1965? Mr. Spaak said he was sure de Gaulle would run again and that he would run in 1964 rather than 1965. He expects him to be re-elected.

Mr. Spaak said he felt de Gaulle had been very wrong not to sign the Nuclear Test Ban Agreement.[2] The President noted that Mr. Spaak had been one of the architects of this agreement.

The President said he believed we are in a good de facto position in Europe. He did not believe we were going to get very far in our negotiations with the Soviets, however, and it was entirely possible we would not be able to reach agreement on a Non-Aggression Pact. The President

---

[1] For text of de Gaulle's speech at Lyon, September 28, see Charles de Gaulle, *Discours et Messages, Pour L'Effort, 1962–1965*, pp. 134–138.

[2] Signed by the United States, the United Kingdom, and the Soviet Union on August 5, 1963; entered into force, October 10, 1963 (TIAS 5433; 14 UST 1313).

said that Cuba is very important to the Soviets. He believed that we have means of dissuading the Soviets. Should they take measures against Berlin we could retaliate against Cuba.

Mr. Spaak said that when he talked to Khrushchev[3] about Berlin, Khrushchev had said he could twist the tail of the West or step on the West's corns at Berlin but he has hastily said to Spaak "but don't worry—I won't go too far". The President said again that we can exercise a great deal of pressure on the Soviets with regard to Cuba. The President went on to say that he was going to see Gromyko next week but did not expect a great deal of progress from the meeting.

The President said that in his view the big danger to Europe is the Communist strength in Italy and the possibility of a Popular Front in France. Mr. Spaak said that important changes were going on in the Communist ranks in Europe. The Soviet-Chinese Communist split is having an important effect. The Soviets are being much more moderate.

Mr. Ball asked the Foreign Minister if he believed that a Popular Front was a possibility in France. Mr. Spaak replied that Guy Mollet is going to Moscow but it would seem too much to have both a Popular Front and the making of Germany into the first power in Europe as the results of de Gaulle's policy. If there were a regular parliamentary system of government in France, de Gaulle would have been overthrown many times since January 14 as there is much opposition to his policies.

The President asked Mr. Spaak how he saw our position vis-à-vis the Soviets as compared to three or four years ago. Mr. Spaak said he thought the position of the Alliance was much better now. It would be perfect if it were not for troubles being caused by the French. He could not imagine de Gaulle trying to separate Europe from the United States. The idea that France could be involved in a war alone was a false one. The President wondered if French policies were not based on de Gaulle's overriding desire to make France a great world power. Mr. Spaak said this is dangerous to all of us.

The President referred to de Gaulle's statement concerning a neutral Viet-Nam.[4] He thought U.S. correspondents in Paris had been bemused by this statement. If there were ever a country that could not survive as a neutral nation it was Viet-Nam. De Gaulle made his statement to annoy the United States but no one submits these grand proposals to careful scrutiny in the light of reality. There would be no hope for either Europe or the United States in a divided world.

---

[3] Spaak visited the Soviet Union in July.

[4] For text of de Gaulle's statement on Vietnam, August 29, 1963, see *American Foreign Policy: Current Documents, 1963*, p. 869.

Mr. Spaak said the test of de Gaulle's ambitions for France is the fact that Khrushchev clearly prefers to deal with the United States, not with France.

The President said the idea of creating a Europe which could arbitrate between the "Anglo-Saxons" and the Soviets was an unreal one. What would keep the United States from arbitrating between Europe and the Soviets in such a situation?

Mr. Spaak said he thought things were going well for the Alliance. The United States has showed its strength in the Cuban crisis. The Soviets have troubles, economically, politically and with the Chinese Communists. If it were only not for de Gaulle, the West would be in a good position.

Mr. Ball asked if there were a Socialist Government in the U.K. next year would Mr. Spaak see possibilities for greater cooperation with the Socialist governments in Europe. Mr. Spaak said if the Socialists win in the U.K. we will have to wait at least six months before we can do anything about the Common Market. The same thing is true with regard to the German Socialists in the field of foreign affairs. Harold Wilson's views are well known. Mr. Spaak did not know if he would change once he were responsible for government policy.

The President noted recent statements by French officials and wondered if a U.K. Labor government might be tempted to join Europe against the United States. Mr. Spaak said a U.K. Labor government would be a good ally of the U.S. The U.S. should not be concerned.

Mr. Spaak said if de Gaulle died suddenly the situation in France would be very dangerous. The people around de Gaulle did not wish to lose power and they would not change the direction of French policy.

The President said it may be too late to cooperate with the French in the atomic field but we should make it unnecessary for de Gaulle to test in the atmosphere. There is no need for France to do this. All the information which France needs for the type of weapon the French are now developing could be obtained from underground testing. It is true that the French did not sign the Nuclear Test Ban Agreement but it would nonetheless be a breach of the agreement if France tested in the atmosphere. The President said if there were going to be a breach of the nuclear test ban he would prefer this be done by the Chinese Communists rather than by a close ally. If de Gaulle carries out atmospheric tests in spite of the fact that he does not need to do this, it will be a deliberate decision on his part. Mr. Spaak said that is exactly what he is afraid of— de Gaulle's emphasis upon defying the world. This is not politics, it is psychology.

The President asked what we should do. Mr. Spaak replied that the only person in a position to talk to de Gaulle is the President of the United States but the question is what to say. The President said he believed we could reach agreement with the French if we agreed to a directorate. This directorate might be a three part directorate at the outset but doubtless would soon become a two part directorate and thereafter there would be only one left and de Gaulle does not intend that that one should be the United States. The President referred to the Roman experience with directorates at the time of Caesar. De Gaulle does not wish the United States to be Caesar. Mr. Spaak said he is against a directorate. Mr. Ball said the de Gaulle thesis is based upon the assumption that France would speak for Europe. Mr. Spaak said no one wants France to speak for them. An attempt to establish a directorate could lead to a neutralist trend in Europe. It would be a completely false policy. We must, however, try to reach an agreement with the French for it is difficult to make policy without France. Frankly, however, he did not know what to do.

The President said de Gaulle is going to find an atomic arsenal is not of much use. To be a great power de Gaulle will find that France must also have large conventional forces. The bomb is useful only as an adjunct to conventional forces. This is evident in the situation in Viet-Nam. U.S. nuclear power is a deterrent but would not keep the Communists out without conventional forces. In Malaya the British had found their nuclear capability useless. The French cannot be a great power without making both efforts. Mr. Spaak said the French cannot make both.

The President said there can be no justification for the French effort to develop a national nuclear capability unless they really believe the U.S. is completely mad and is going to leave Europe. This is impossible. The U.S. security is too closely linked to Europe. Perhaps the French effort makes sense in internal political and psychological terms but it is difficult to understand otherwise.

84.   Memorandum of Conversation

Washington, October 4, 1963, 6:10 p.m.

SUBJECT

The United States and Europe

PARTICIPANTS

Italy	United States
Emilio Colombo, Minister of Treasury[1]	The President
Sergio Fenoaltea, Ambassador, Italian Embassy	Neil Seidenman—Interpreter
Gian Luigi Milesi Ferretti, Minister, Italian Embassy	

Minister Colombo spoke at length on the importance of consistently promoting the process of European integration. This process should be guided so as to guarantee the preservation of what has already been built up within the framework of a European community: the Coal and Steel Community, the Common Market, and EURATOM. European unity must work against frictions from within that could have disintegrating effects. The solidity of the Atlantic Alliance can only be assured through European integration and an Atlantic partnership, such as President Kennedy spoke of in his Philadelphia speech,[2] and not through special, bilateral relationships.

The President affirmed that there is no problem between Europe and the United States, but rather to what extent the differences posed by France and de Gaulle will bring confusion into United States-European ties, particularly regarding the future of NATO and economic cooperation. The latter will probably be the more important point, since there are now fewer doubts about European military security. The United States supports European unity in the hope that Europe will be able increasingly to strengthen its own security, both internally and externally, and that Europe and the United States will be able to work closer and closer together. The tide of history and necessity will undoubtedly bring about European unity, but there will be difficult times ahead as long as de Gaulle rejects partnership. United States policy before this Admin-

---

Source: Department of State, Central Files, ECIN 6 EEC. Confidential. Drafted by Seidenman on October 7 and approved in the White House on October 14. The meeting was held at the White House.

[1] Colombo was in Washington for meetings of the International Monetary Fund. A memorandum of his conversation with Ball on October 3 along similar lines is ibid.

[2] For text of the President's address at Philadelphia, July 4, 1962, see *Public Papers of the Presidents of the United States: John F. Kennedy, 1962*, pp. 537–539.

istration and surely after it, has favored and will continue to favor European unity. Therefore, we have nothing against concentric circles with Europe as a unified power within the Atlantic whole. But the present difficulty in opposition to this is de Gaulle's vision of Europe as an independent power, balancing East and West.

Minister Colombo mentioned the Franco-German Pact, and said that while France had thought to gain influence by the Pact, in reality it is Germany that has derived greater strength, since Germany has also maintained its chosen commitment to the West.

The President agreed and pointed out that if this were not the case, Germany could become a lever for the USSR to use to its advantage as arbiter whenever our countries sought agreement with the East. Any approach to the Soviet Union must be unified, in the economic sphere as well, and the unity of Europe should result in a stronger West. De Gaulle goes along with the idea of European integration, but under the political leadership of France. Hence there is the need for us to work hard together in the trade negotiations—with Italy's influence in favor of stronger partnership—so as to prevent France from playing off one country's economic interests against another's and ultimately to limit the possibilities of broader trade.

Minister Colombo agreed and expressed his support and confidence in the "Kennedy Round."

The President emphasized the role of Italy, a country free from many of the concerns that beset Germany, a divided country, and from other special problems. Italy, with its interest in European integration and Atlantic unity, can exploit its position with strength and make a large contribution toward the common cause. He expressed satisfaction with the views of the Minister, as consistent with the interests of both our countries, which in turn extend to the interests of more than a single nation, and look toward the basic goal of integrating the efforts of all our nations in their economic, military, and foreign-policy objectives. Each country has its valid and legitimate individual interests, but we are living in a time when our nations cannot afford the luxury of division and conflict. The past year has been a relatively good year for the West vis-à-vis the Communist world, but it could have been a *very* good year without the troubles that came up suddenly in January and barred Britain's entry into the Common Market, which seemed to demonstrate discord within the Atlantic Alliance. But with the Communist world in disarray, the West should be able to have an even better year in 1964.

Minister Colombo agreed that January did bring serious difficulties, but he thought it fortunate that the problem involving Britain's admission to the Common Market is now being taken up again within the framework of the Western European Union. Nothing outstanding has yet developed here, but the wound, he said, is beginning to heal.

The President referred to what he suspected could pose another danger to Europe: namely, the effect in the European countries of the Moscow–Peking rift upon the internal political unity of the democratic forces in their position against the Communist parties. In Italy, for example, the Communist Party has seemingly taken an appearance of moderation. What will be the attitude of the electorate toward the Communists in the immediate future: in Italy, in Greece, in France after de Gaulle, in Spain after Franco, in Portugal after Salazar? Hence again the importance of a genuine Atlantic unity, because the stronger NATO becomes in its influence on matters beyond defense, the less will be the domestic political pressures against the structure of Western unity. Thus, for example, Nenni, in order to participate in the government, would have to accept NATO because of his support for the concept of European unification. This would be of great political value in Italy's situation, in which important issues are subject to pressures and bargaining in the absence of an agreed-upon international orientation.

85.   Memorandum of Conversation

Washington, October 8, 1963, 10:30 a.m.

SUBJECT

European Unity and Trade Problems

PARTICIPANTS

U.S.	France
Mr. Ball	Couve de Murville[1]
Ambassador Bohlen	Ambassador Alphand
Mr. Tyler	Mr. Lucet, Director, Political Affairs,
Mr. Schaetzel	French Fon Off
Mr. Beigel	Mr. Pelen, French Embassy

Mr. Ball said he would like to speak about European unity. We had an intimation from Rome it was believed in Europe that the U.S. may have become disenchanted with the EEC. He said there should be no

Source: Department of State, Central Files, ECIN 6 EEC. Secret. Drafted and initialed by Beigel and approved in U on October 16. The meeting was held in Ball's office.

[1] Couve de Murville was in the United States to attend the U.N. General Assembly.

ambiguity on this point, and he wished to reaffirm that we see progress toward European unity through Brussels or in other forms as being an important step toward unity of the Western world. While it is a European matter as to how this unity is to be organized, we see our own interests served by progress in this direction.

Mr. Ball said that he also wished to make clear that the U.S. believes effective unity within the EEC means that there must be a common agricultural policy, and it should be understood that the U.S. is not in opposition to a CAP. We realize that it will create problems of adjustment for us as well as for the participants. Nor do we minimize the difficulties in forming a CAP, in view of the senseless bases for agricultural policies in every country.

The Foreign Minister interjected that even the Russians would agree on this last point. The Foreign Minister went on to express his appreciation for the above statements. He said that no one knows how the European concept will end, that it will be a long and painful process. There is hope of development in other fields, and there is the parallel question of whether others will join the Six, which is an open question at present. He said that the Six had only begun to do something effective, and that this process is not a matter for a few years but for one or two generations. In the process there are two aspects to note: there are differences among the partners, and there are problems with outside countries, in Europe and elsewhere, beginning with the U.S. He said that they recognized that the U.S. could not remain indifferent to developments within the Six.

The Foreign Minister recalled that the January crisis had been a topic of discussion after dinner at the Department the previous evening and said he had nothing to add to this.[2] He repeated that opinions differ as to what was at stake and the methods used, that France considers matters were not ripe in January and that the question remains open.

The Foreign Minister agreed with Mr. Ball that the immediate problem is further progress in the EEC. He said that two fields are open: the CAP and the merging or reorganization and systematization of the three communities, especially the ECSC and EEC. He said that France would like to pursue the question of the merging. He said that the partners of France are very vocal about direct election of the Assembly because they know the French oppose this step now. This would be the ultimate solution if the political situation develops the way France hopes. It is a question of method, whether the executive or the assembly should be

---

[2] No record of this conversation has been found. For a memorandum of Couve de Murville's conversation with the President on October 7, see Document 275.

developed first. He said France favors the formation of the executive before having an elected assembly.

With regard to the CAP the Foreign Minister said that France will
seek a regime before the end of 1963 for the main products, and that the
Six will have to deal with the problem of prices. Establishment of cereal
prices for the 1964 and 1965 seasons is the only thing that has been
agreed upon, and the matter of general price policy remains open.
France had discussed this only with the Germans so far, in view of the
opposite positions of France and Germany on this question. The Six
should have at least an idea of what price policy will be if they are to
discuss agriculture at the GATT negotiations next spring.

The Foreign Minister said that the CAP will have an impact on Denmark and on the important outside producers such as the U.S., Canada,
Australia, New Zealand and Argentina. He put aside tropical products
as another matter. He went on to say that if there is an EEC there must be
a CAP, and the CAP is bound to change something. On the other hand,
we are faced with problems of disruption of present arrangements. He
said that the question may be less difficult if we consider the realities of
European agriculture and European import requirements. The future of
European agriculture in which a CAP can develop relates principally to
meats and to fruits and vegetables, and less so to cereals. He dismissed
dairy products as a special, local problem. He said that fruits and vegetables are normally handled on a regional basis and the same could be
said for meat. The French people are eating more fresh meat, and increased meat output is the important future for the agriculture of France
and Denmark. He noted that Italy is importing more meat from Europe
and less from the Argentine, its traditional supplier.

The Foreign Minister said that the big problem is with cereals, since
Europe cannot produce all the types they need, and there will always be
a place for Manitoba wheat and for corn. The problem here is prices. He
said that this will, of course, be discussed internationally over the next
two years, whether in the Kennedy round or otherwise. For several
years, France has favored discussions on a world basis with the idea that
discussions would begin with respect to price policy especially for cereals. He said that when this is discussed with the U.S. they would expect
to run into problems similar to those they found in the British negotiations, over the question of comparable outlets as sought by the Commonwealth cereal producers. He said that quotas do not seem to be the
solution. If the Six can complete regulations for meat and rice this year
they can then explore how to discuss agricultural questions with outsid-
ers, either in connection with the Kennedy round or by some other procedure. He said that perhaps the EEC Commission should proceed to
have informal talks with the U.S. What is necessary is to find some com-

pensation for the German and Italian peasants, something that might be artificial but would be necessary.

Mr. Ball said that we see these problems along the same lines as the Foreign Minister, that we all have domestic problems especially in the agricultural sector.

The Foreign Minister said that another problem is what to do with farm surpluses after an export price is set. It is expensive for governments to give away surpluses to the LDC's and is self-defeating to feed LDC's whose task should be to develop their own agriculture. The problem becomes intractable if a world system is established to provide farm surpluses to the LDC's

Mr. Ball replied that we are aware of the dilemma of feeding the LDC's too well and running the danger of inhibiting local agriculture. We try to move along both lines. He said that it would be a fine thing if some general agreement could be reached with regard to surpluses.

The Foreign Minister referred to the FAO fund of $100 million and said that management of the surplus question under international supervision would be undesirable, and would risk becoming a permanent international system. He saw no difficulties with U.S. disposals.

Mr. Schaetzel said that we have been anxious to discuss this general question and noted that Secretary Freeman is willing to discuss U.S. price levels, a new departure for the U.S. He said that we would like to discuss the subject with the major countries. The Foreign Minister said that we might discuss this at Geneva in a preliminary way, with special discussions to follow sometime later.

Mr. Ball turned to poultry and said that we are very anxious to settle and dispose of this issue. We realize agreement is not likely and we therefore wish to dispose of the issue of the amount of trade damage by mutual agreement. We have suggested adjudication by a GATT panel. The Foreign Minister said that he thought the panel method was acceptable, adding that France could of course not speak for the Six. He understood the only question was whether the panel would decide or advise. Mr. Schaetzel said that both sides have agreed to the panel, to be composed of the Secretary General of GATT and two others, with non-binding conclusions. The point of contention now is over the rights that the U.S. might continue to enjoy with regard to previous negotiations with the EEC. The Foreign Minister noted that we now have lawyers in Brussels discussing the legal technicalities of this situation with the Commission. He wondered what the practical significance of these discussions might be, and noted that when they accepted the panel procedure the Six in effect renounced any rights to take counter-measures.

Mr. Ball referred to the UN trade conference next spring and said that this must be handled very carefully. He said that Kristensen[3] had suggested when he was here that the November ministerial meeting of OECD should endeavor to agree on the general position the advanced nations can take in the UN conference, not to form a solid front but to discuss among ourselves the questions involved and understand each other's position. The Foreign Minister said that there will be a question of preferences for the LDC's which is a problem for the Six in Africa as well as for the Commonwealth. Mr. Schaetzel noted that Mr. Ball would head the U.S. delegation and said that we do not want to formulate any bloc position. The Foreign Minister agreed and said that we must also avoid a quarrel between the Africans and the Latin Americans at the conference.

---

[3] Thorkil Kristensen, Secretary-General of the OECD.

---

86.   Telegram From the Department of State to the Embassy in the United Kingdom

Washington, November 9, 1963.

2994. Please deliver following message from Secretary to Foreign Minister Butler.

Begin verbatim text.

I am most grateful for your personal message of October 28.[1] I personally much regretted that the timing was not right for a brief visit with you in London, but I hope that we can find time at the NATO meeting for full talks.

Your reflections on the WEU meeting were most valuable to us. We felt encouraged by the general atmosphere of UK-EEC cooperation reflected both in the press and by comments made by the participants.

Source: Department of State, Presidential Correspondence: Lot 66 D 204. Secret. Drafted by Rusk and cleared by Bundy.

[1] Not printed. In it Butler gave his impressions of the WEU meeting at The Hague and summarized his conversations with Schroeder and Couve de Murville. (Ibid.)

I found similar encouragement in my visit to Bonn,[2] although the necessity for still another "reassurance" about the United States commitment to the defense of Europe was a bit tedious. However, it did pay a more important dividend than I expected when I left Washington. I would suggest that you look at the two speeches made by Chancellor Erhard and me at Frankfurt as somewhat related to each other. He and I did not review each other's speeches in advance but I have reason to believe that my statement helped to provide both encouragement and freedom of action to the Chancellor for what was a most important statement of German policy. I also have reason to believe that after I had indicated to him the general line that I expected to take, his own statement was strengthened in relation to European unity and Atlantic partnership. I found Chancellor Erhard confident and in good spirit and not inclined to look over his shoulder unduly at either Chancellor Adenauer or President DeGaulle. Both he and Schroeder seemed to have a clear view that the interests of Germany itself lie in the larger framework of Europe and the Atlantic in political, defense and economic fields.

In private talks with German leaders and with a few of the press people, I was quite frank about the growing sensitivities in the United States about double standards within the alliance. A certain bluntness on my part may have stirred the dovecotes a bit, but it is necessary that they understand that we, too, have some problems.

I send you this message while the Soviet motivations in the most recent convoy incident[3] are still unclear. This occurrance reminds me, however, that the most important problem that we have in the alliance is not so much our own Western housekeeping affairs but the need for a common, penetrating and sophisticated examination as to how we and the West look upon events within the communist world and what these might mean for East-West relations. Nothing is more urgent, in my view, than to find the right line between naivete and illusion, on the one side, and a certain blindness to the possibilities of major changes which could benefit the free world and contribute significantly toward peace. An example of what I have in mind is the need for a common Western position on credits to the Soviet bloc.

At the moment I must confess that I am not too optimistic about early additional agreements in the multilateral field. The Soviets have been unwilling, to come clean, for example, on the relation between their non-aggression pact proposal and the situation in Berlin. Static ob-

---

[2] Rusk visited Germany at the end of October for the dedication of a memorial to George C. Marshall. For text of his address at Frankfurt on October 22, see Department of State *Bulletin*, November 11, 1963, pp. 726–731.

[3] On November 4 Soviet military authorities had prevented a U.S. convoy from proceeding to Berlin along the autobahn.

servation posts are linked to a nuclear free zone in Central Europe and to a mutual reduction of forces in Germany. The non-dissemination agreement is temporarily stalled and not just because of the multilateral force. The prospects for significant moves ahead at Geneva are not very good. We are ready to continue our explorations on these matters but I see real difficulty.

On the bilateral Washington–Moscow line, we may be able to make a certain headway. We have had some difficulty in adjusting ourselves to the sudden interest of the Soviet Union in buying wheat, but we are doing our best on that. A possible consular convention is under discussion in Moscow. We can proceed with technical talks to clear the way for an exchange of one or two civilian air flights each week between New York and Moscow. We are also taking a look at broader trade problems despite obvious legislative and economic limitations on our side. We will do what we can to find additional points of agreement both with Moscow and other Eastern European countries.

I might conclude by saying that we are most anxious to find ways and means of bringing France back into the common discussion of the serious matters in front of us. This will not be easy because of very far-reaching differences between President DeGaulle and his own immediate neighbors on the content. But this is something which you and we should talk about; it is regrettable that we in the West should be in some disarray about our own arrangements just at the time when the communist world is faced with many difficult problems.

My warm best wishes to you as you take up your heavy responsibilities.

Cordially yours, Dean Rusk. *End verbatim text.*

[Here follows the remainder of the telegram.]

Rusk

87.   Memorandum of Conversation

Washington, November 26, 1963, 2:30 p.m.

SUBJECT

European Economic and Political Developments

PARTICIPANTS

Americans	*Germans*
The Under Secretary	The Chancellor[1]
Mr. William R. Tyler, Assistant Secretary, EUR	The Foreign Minister
	Mr. Georg von Lilienfeld, Minister, German Embassy
Mr. J. Robert Schaetzel, Deputy Assistant Secretary, EUR	Baron Herbert von Stackelberg, Minister, German Embassy
Mr. George S. Springsteen, Jr., Special Assistant, U	Mr. Dankmar Seibt, Personal Aide to the Chancellor
Mr. Richard B. Finn, Deputy Director, GER	Mr. Heinz Weber, Interpreter
Mr. Joseph E. O'Mahony, Economic Advisor, GER	
Mr. Arnold Lissance, Interpreter	

EEC and Trade Negotiations

The Under Secretary referred to the Chancellor's earlier conversation with President Johnson[2] during which the Chancellor indicated that he had had an interesting conversation with de Gaulle before coming to Washington. The Chancellor was asked about the impressions he derived from this exchange with the French President.

The Chancellor replied that de Gaulle had placed his main emphasis on the need for reaching agreement on the agricultural regulations before the end of this year. For de Gaulle, this appears to be just about the most urgent item of business facing the European states.

The Chancellor stated that he has no objection to moving forward on this matter as long as assurances can be obtained covering third country trade. Germany wants to avoid any discrimination against outside trading partners; it considers it important to maintain an unimpaired flow of trade with all countries. The present regulations as written and proposed are in the Chancellor's opinion not very good—they leave much room for improvement, but we can start with them. At the moment, the Six need to settle on a common grains price level.

Source: Department of State, Central Files, Pol Eur. Secret, Eyes Only. Drafted by O'Mahony and approved in U on November 29. The meeting was held in the Under Secretary's Conference Room.

[1] Chancellor Erhard was in Washington for President Kennedy's funeral.

[2] A memorandum of this conversation is in vol. XV, pp. 634–639. President Kennedy was assassinated in Dallas on November 22.

Europe, the Chancellor went on, must not seek self-sufficiency in agriculture. De Gaulle apparently does not agree with him on this point. French policy is definitely much more protectively inclined than is Germany's. This is true for industry as well as for agriculture.

Germany, for example, favors full 50 percent cuts in tariffs on a linear basis. The French care more about solving the disparities issue. The Chancellor said he hopes that item-by-item negotiations can be kept to a minimum—he certainly does not want to discuss 1,200 tariff items one at a time.

The Under Secretary remarked that since he had talked with the Chancellor in Germany, we have had an opportunity to analyze the Mansholt proposal more carefully, both from the standpoint of price and procedure. It is, of course, difficult to predict exactly what effect price changes would have on production, but it is our estimate that the Mansholt-proposed price level for grains would induce a sufficient increase in European grain production to cause a substantial decrease in the volume of EEC imports of grain.

This conclusion, the Under Secretary continued, leads to two questions: (1) can some form of assurance be included in the agreement on grains covering the trade of third countries, and (2) would it not be better to move toward the common grains price level over a period of time, rather than taking a single jump.

The Chancellor spoke about the delicate problems involved in the grains price issue. He said that in Paris he and de Gaulle agreed they could probably see their way toward the adoption of regulations governing dairy products and other items, but he was not sure the same could be said about the grains problem.

The Chancellor acknowledged that the Federal Republic is "not in a good position when it comes to settling this price question." He referred to the difficult internal political problems that are involved in Germany, but maintained that in his opinion the German farmers are gradually coming to realize that the Federal Republic cannot remain immobile on this issue.

Unfortunately, the Chancellor stated, he would be less than honest if he did not say that he cannot give any indication of how long it will take for the German Government to come to a decision on grain prices. As for himself, the sooner he could dispose of the problem the better he would like it. He does not want to tell the German people during the election campaign of 1965 that he doesn't know what he is going to do about this matter.

As for phasing the movement toward a common grains price, he again cannot give an answer now. His initial thinking however, is that it would be preferable to make the transition by means of a one-step opcration. Perhaps the step should be accompanied by a world-wide commodity agreement.

The Chancellor said that he had told de Gaulle that if they could somehow guarantee the US its share of the European market for agricultural commodities, the grains price issue would no longer be so important for the United States. The Chancellor then indicated that demand for grains will increase steadily in Europe and so there should not be too much difficulty in giving the US the assurances it wants. De Gaulle, the Chancellor concluded, is not entirely negative regarding commodity agreements, though he does do his best to avoid the issue whenever he can.

The Under Secretary said that while matters such as the Common Market wheat price must be solved by the EEC members, third countries will be affected in an important way by whatever decisions are reached. It is our hope, therefore, that before any decisions are reached, we will have further opportunities to discuss the subject with the appropriate European officials.

The Chancellor then asked the Under Secretary whether he expects continued increases in grain acreage and yields in the United States. The Under Secretary referred to the rejection of wheat production controls by the American farmers, but said he would expect that we will continue our efforts to put limitations on production. He, therefore, does not anticipate an expansion of acreage.

Productivity, the Under Secretary pointed out, is more difficult to make predictions about. Grain yields have been increasing at a regular pace here, but there are some indications that a point of diminishing returns may have been reached. There has been a progressive reduction of the number of persons engaged in agriculture in the United States, and as this takes place larger production units come into existence and productivity tends to increase.

The Chancellor said that this describes the situation in the Federal Republic exactly, except that the dimension is different. The same process has been going on in Germany during the past twelve years. If only he had another decade in which to deal with the grains situation, these trends would solve the problem by themselves.

The Under Secretary then indicated that the price of feed grains was even a greater problem than the wheat price. They are a major component of US exports to the EEC. As more and more grains are consumed as meat, the relative importance of feed grains increases. Under the Mansholt proposal the disparity between wheat and feed grains prices would be increased to the great disadvantage of US producers.

The Chancellor said that meat production is becoming increasingly important in Germany, and for that reason he had an interest in seeing that feed grains prices are kept low. A rational approach to problems is not always possible, though, because of the political factors involved.

The Under Secretary then listed the wide range of problems that have to be dealt with in this field—the CAP, global solutions, disparities, tariff reductions, etc. A major question is how do all these matters tie together. It is apparent that we need to discuss the subject more fully, especially at the technical level. The Chancellor agreed. Such talks, he said, would presumably be with the Ministries of Economics and Agriculture.

European Political Integration

The Chancellor said that the Under Secretary is, of course, fully aware of de Gaulle's objections to political integration at this time. The Chancellor can only add that while he would not say that de Gaulle is determined to block political integration, his (de Gaulle's) thinking on the subject is different from ours.

The Chancellor said that he told de Gaulle that it is disturbing to him that so many sovereign rights are being transferred by the European countries to non-political institutions. The EEC Commission is not an elected body, but the European states are giving it wide-ranging powers. Elected representatives are losing control over matters of great importance to the people. It is necessary that progress be made more rapidly in the political integration field. The Six should make a start along this line, but should plan to bring others in when possible.

The Franco-German Treaty, the Chancellor said he reminded de Gaulle, has been a source of worry to the US and to the other European states. One major reason why the other European countries have ceased participating in the drive for integration is their fear of Franco-German supremacy.

The Italians, however, appear to be ready to "come back into things", the Chancellor added. He therefore intends to make an early visit to Italy. De Gaulle indicated to him that he might also go to Italy in the near future.

The Under Secretary then inquired about the possibility of moving ahead in the establishment of an Assembly selected through direct elections. He pointed out that this would give the Commission the kind of legitimacy of power he was concerned about. The Chancellor said, however, that the chances of moving ahead will remain very slight for a long time to come.

The problem, the Chancellor said, is that while he recognizes that government cannot be fragmentized—the economic sector cannot be integrated by itself—how can a political body be formed that would exercise authority in Germany when we do not know where countries like Italy are headed?

The only thing the Chancellor can suggest for now is that we do what we can to strengthen tendencies toward political integration, but we should not expect rapid progress.

Atlantic Policy

De Gaulle's attitude with regard to Atlantic policy is much different from ours, the Chancellor stated. De Gaulle thinks in nationalistic terms first.

When de Gaulle speaks of Europe, he has in mind a power bloc that would be independent of the United States. His order of priorities is (1) a strong France, (2) a solid French-German relationship, (3) a powerful Europe, and lastly (4) trans-Atlantic ties. De Gaulle does not reject Atlantic partnership, but he wants it to be "a partnership of equals."

Mr. Tyler said that he has been struck by what de Gaulle says are elements of an Atlantic relationship. To de Gaulle, the Anglo-Saxon presence in Europe poses a threat to the development of Europe and to an independent European identity. It seems that de Gaulle looks upon the new world as something immature, highly active, powerful, wealthy, and too unsophisticated to understand the soul of Europe.

We need to understand what de Gaulle means, Mr. Tyler added, besides what he says. Was de Gaulle at all specific with the Chancellor regarding the interrelationship of the United States and Europe in either the commercial or strategic spheres?

Basically, said the Chancellor, de Gaulle does not want Europe to be dependent in any way on the United States. De Gaulle looks upon the Kennedy Round, American investments, etc., as elements of an attempt by the United States to increase its involvement in Europe. In de Gaulle's opinion, Europe runs the risk of becoming a satellite of the United States.

At present, the Chancellor believes, de Gaulle considers Europe to be too weak to resist the US. Europe must reduce the gap in this power relationship as far as de Gaulle is concerned. Minister von Lilienfeld quipped that in all this de Gaulle sees the UK as the American Trojan Horse.

Defense

De Gaulle, said the Chancellor, took his most negative position during their recent talk when the subject of NATO was discussed. De Gaulle stoutly maintains that he is a loyal ally, a fact he claims to have proved during the Cuban and Berlin crises. But the French President argues that the organizational structure of NATO must be changed.

France, de Gaulle also made clear, will not be argued out of its nuclear weapons. There are, in de Gaulle's view, two big military powers: the US and the USSR. They have the means to destroy themselves. Can the United States be counted on to risk its own destruction if the USSR seeks a purely European objective?

The Chancellor said he told de Gaulle that he is certain the US can be counted on to make full use of its military potential in order to live up to its European commitments. De Gaulle replied, "But can you be absolutely certain of this?" The Chancellor said, "Yes, we must, it is our only hope."

The Chancellor said he then pointed out to de Gaulle that the United States came to France's aid in two world wars. The United States, he said, is not going to degrade itself and become a second-rate power by avoiding the use of its military force. The Seventh Army, what is more, is evidence of US intentions. The French President is said to have told the Chancellor that he can understand why Germany feels it must depend on the United States, but France cannot do so. France must have its own deterrent.

Mr. Tyler said he thought there had been some inconsistency in General de Gaulle's ideas on defense matters over the past 18 months. The General at one time talked of the necessity for a defense in depth of Western Europe, but more recently he seems to be talking about a nuclear trigger, which would mean the very early use of nuclear weapons in the event of attack. Mr. Tyler asked whether the Chancellor had any comment on this apparent inconsistency.

The Chancellor replied that de Gaulle had told him that France would use nuclear weapons immediately for the defense of Germany. The Chancellor said he answered that the Soviets would immediately retaliate with nuclear weapons and in this kind of situation the Germans and the French would only be choosing which way they died.

The Chancellor went on to say that he had told de Gaulle that the best method of defense would be to use the full 23 divisions available to NATO at the German eastern frontier. He also told de Gaulle that he could not understand why the battle for Germany necessarily would be lost with 23 divisions, and yet, as the French seem to argue, the battle of France could be won with a smaller number of the remaining forces. De Gaulle replied, according to the Chancellor, that he had been misunderstood; that France agreed that the line of defense should be at Germany's eastern frontier.

The Chancellor added that he had stressed to de Gaulle the need for integration of military forces in NATO. This part of the conversation, however, had not been conclusive, the Chancellor indicated, but he thought the discussion had been useful. De Gaulle, the Chancellor offered, had found a partner who put questions to him requiring careful answers.

Erhard Visit

The Under Secretary said he had talked briefly with the President after the Chancellor's meeting at the White House that morning about possible dates for an official visit to Washington by the Chancellor. The Under Secretary mentioned January 10 and 11, explaining that this would place the visit just after the President's State of the Union Message. The Under Secretary said he could not be definite about any dates but agreed to determine whether January 10 and 11 would be suitable dates for the President, and said he would try to let the Chancellor know about this before the Chancellor left for Germany on the evening of November 26. The Chancellor emphasized that he would like, if possible, to come to Washington before his visit to London on January 15 and 16.

---

88.   Memorandum of Conversation

US/MC/3   Paris, December 14, 1963, 11 a.m.

PARTICIPANTS

United States	*Netherlands*
The Secretary of State[1]	Foreign Minister Luns
Mr. Tyler	Ambassador Boon
Mr. Meloy	Chargé Jonkheer Quarles van Ufford

SUBJECT

Common Market and European Integration Matters

The Secretary asked how much of a crisis is building up in Europe. What will happen by December 31? Will an agreement be reached on a common agricultural policy and if not what will happen? Foreign Minister Luns said that depends on the French President. He cannot read General de Gaulle's mind. It was agreed in May that the Common Market countries would reach agreement on agricultural matters by December 31 but it was also agreed that progress would be made on industrial

---

Source: Department of State, Conference Files: Lot 66 D 110, CF 2354. Confidential. Drafted by Meloy and approved in S on December 19.

[1] Secretary of State Rusk was in Paris for the 32d North Atlantic Council Ministerial meeting, December 16–17.

matters as well. There are now more than 1200 "peak" or high points on the tariff chart, many of which are not negotiable. The Dutch want a more flexible formula than has thus far been proposed. The European Commission is not very unified. This is particularly due to the position of Marjolin who opposed de Gaulle in the last French election. Marjolin's position is very weak and the Commission is therefore hesitant. The French have not shown much flexibility with regard to industrial tariffs. The Dutch are fearful that if agreement is reached on agriculture, the French will thereafter do very little on industry.

Foreign Minister Luns continued that the agricultural matters discussed May 9 were different from those now under discussion. It was agreed in May that a common price would be worked out for cereals for 1964 and 1965 by the end of December. That is what was agreed on. Mansholt has confronted the Commission with more far-reaching proposals. Mansholt says he will not accept another mandate and the Commission is being pressed to reach agreement on broad agricultural matters upon which they had not expected to reach agreement until 1970. The Dutch have two major problems: (1) they are fearful that Dutch prices will go up and there will be a resultant rise in the cost of living; and (2) they are hesitant to put large sums of money into Hallstein's hands with no Parliamentary control whatsoever.

The Dutch believe the U.S. wants to export its agricultural products. The Dutch agree. They also wish to export and must therefore envisage a situation which permits the possibility of imports. Production therefore must not exceed consumption.

It is difficult to refute Mansholt's arguments but the Dutch feel that instruments must be laid down now to control the situation automatically if production increases. This is the heart of the problem and it is important also for the U.S.

The Secretary asked the Foreign Minister if he had assessed the chances of a French withdrawal from the Common Market. Would he say they were 1 in 10? The Foreign Minister replied: "1 in 20." He thought the French were playing a war of nerves and engaging in brinkmanship. It is always possible that the French might withdraw, but he did not think it likely. Mr. Luns said he thought most countries, especially Germany and the Netherlands, will insist that the effective date of the Mansholt proposals will be such as to allow time to see how progress goes forward on industrial matters.

The Secretary asked what proportion of Dutch exports goes to countries outside the Common Market. Mr. Luns said approximately 30% of Dutch export trade is with Common Market countries. About two-thirds is with countries outside the Common Market. The Secretary noted that the Dutch and the Germans are thus in roughly the same position. Both have important trade interests outside the Common Market which must be considered.

The Secretary emphasized that political, as well as technical considerations, must be taken into account.

The Foreign Minister said that it would become evident that the Common Market discussions are linked with political matters. The Dutch are not prepared to accept political integration of Europe at this time. Just before Mr. Luns had left a previous meeting that morning, Mr. Pflimlin had asked if there were any chances in the air for anything like the Fouchet plan. Mr. Lun's parting remark, as he walked out of the meeting, was that there was no chance whatsoever. The Foreign Minister was concerned nevertheless. Mr. Spaak has been giving signs of having ideas and Italy, although weak, may want to take a political initiative.

The Secretary said he was glad that the Dutch have been able to announce they will participate in the MLF discussions. Mr. Luns said that he also was pleased but it was necessary to avoid internal political complications in the Dutch domestic scene.

Mr. Luns said he hoped the U.S. would not be resigned to seeing the creation of a tightly organized political unity of the six Common Market countries. This would mean that the U.K. would definitely be out of Europe. Such a tightly knit inward looking political organization would be a divisive element in Europe and would make an agreement with EFTA impossible. The Secretary said he was not quite sure what the Foreign Minister meant. He would like this point clarified. Mr. Luns said he hoped the U.S. will not support or passively accept the political organization of Europe on the French plan which would result in a closed Europe. The Secretary replied that the Foreign Minister need not have any concern on this point. He continued however that many of these problems are European problems for Europeans themselves to decide.

Mr. Luns said the French have been very prudent in their approaches on the political side. They realize they are suspect. In the Erhard–de Gaulle conversation, it was Erhard himself who raised the matter. When others take the initiative, the French will pursue the discussion, but they quickly drop the matter when they encounter opposition. Nevertheless, the Dutch are concerned about the dangers of a revival of interest in European political integration which under present circumstances would be likely to be on the French model.

89.   Memorandum of Conversation

LBJ Ranch, Texas, December 28, 1963, 3:15 p.m.

SUBJECT

Brussels Negotiations—Kennedy Round

[Here follows a list of participants including President Johnson, Secretary of State Rusk, Under Secretary Ball, and 9 other U.S. officials, and Chancellor Erhard, Foreign Minister Schroeder, Ambassador Knappstein, and 11 other German officials.]

The meeting opened at 3:15 p.m. At the President's request, Secretary Rusk started the discussion by asking the Chancellor[1] and Foreign Minister Schroeder for their evaluation of the recent EEC talks at Brussels.[2]

Foreign Minister Schroeder described the situation that existed at the time of the Brussels meeting. It had been agreed on May 9 that there would be a synchronized program of negotiations. For the Federal Republic that meant that there would be not only internal development within the Common Market, especially agriculture, but also outward development looking toward the Kennedy Round. This situation culminated in the Brussels negotiations.

Mr. Schroeder went on to say that difficulties existed at Brussels because the interest of France and some other participants related more to agriculture than to the Kennedy Round, and also because it was obviously impossible to lay down specific positions regarding the Kennedy Round at this early point. There was therefore a danger that the negotiations could fall apart before any decisions were reached.

The French had come to recognize, however, that the Federal Republic was serious about the importance of the Kennedy Round. As a result, the French position has become somewhat better. Reasonable compromises were achieved, Mr. Schroeder felt, both in agriculture and in the Kennedy Round position.

The change in the French viewpoint, the Foreign Minister continued, was illustrated by the latest meeting between General de Gaulle and the German Ambassador in Paris. De Gaulle said to the Ambassa-

---

Source: Department of State, Central Files, ECIN 6 EEC. Confidential. Drafted by Finn, approved in S and U on January 1, 1964, and in the White House on January 8.

[1] Chancellor Erhard visited the United States December 28–29. Memoranda of his conversations with Secretary Rusk at 12:40 p.m. on December 28 and of a brief conversation with President Johnson later in the day on European political unity are ibid.

[2] The meeting at Brussels, primarily devoted to drafting a common agricultural policy, had concluded on December 23.

dor that the Kennedy Round was an Anglo-Saxon matter but because of the German attitude France would take a different view than before.

Secretary Rusk asked when that conversation had taken place. The Foreign Minister said that it had occurred a few days before the recent Brussels talks.

The Foreign Minister continued that the Rome treaty and its implementing regulations provide not only for internal development within the Common Market but also for consideration of its external aspects. World trade and external conditions must also be considered by the Common Market nations.

Disparities had been the most difficult question to resolve at Brussels, Mr. Schroeder said. The Germans were able to bring about agreement on a new two-to-one formula. This would mean, according to German experts, a reduction in the number of disparities: previously the number would have been twelve hundred US items and a few for the Europeans, whereas now the ratio would be about four-to-one—eight hundred US to two hundred European. This is the conclusion of German experts.

The Foreign Minister emphasized that there are a number of details which are not yet clear. The EEC Commission directive is not yet available. When this is available more detailed discussion can be useful. Nevertheless, German experts believe that sufficient agreement was reached at Brussels to enable the Commission to formulate a position for the Kennedy Round. The French position is definitely more favorable than before.

The Foreign Minister repeated that Chancellor Erhard had succeeded in convincing de Gaulle in November that the Kennedy Round was as important or more important to Germany than the agricultural regulations. The French now clearly recognize this, as illustrated by recent statements by Pompidou and Giscard.

In summary the Foreign Minister expressed the belief that the Brussels compromise had been fairly good in balancing Community and Kennedy Round interests.

Foreign Minister Schroeder said he would like to add one thought. No decision was taken on cereal prices. This is to be done in April 1964. The Mansholt Plan will be the basis of consideration but it will not be accepted without change in the establishment of Common Market cereal prices. Mr. Schroeder noted that the French and other Community members object to some portions of the Mansholt Plan. Mr. Schroeder also said that the Germans had got a clause inserted in the agreement on this subject which would make agricultural policy more negotiable; this had not been easy to do in view of the Common Market agricultural regulations on the one hand and the preparations for the Kennedy Round on the other.

Governor Herter said that the US had followed the Brussels negotiations closely, had realized the difficulties faced by the Federal Republic both in its own agricultural problems and in the French position, and was most appreciative of the efforts made by the Federal Republic at Brussels to insure consideration of the position of third parties. Governor Herter noted that the US is handicapped by not having the text of the arrangements agreed to at Brussels.

Governor Herter went on to say that what was most satisfying in Foreign Minister Schroeder's comments was the point that agricultural matters would be subject to negotiation. It would have been most difficult for the US had it been presented with a fait accompli.

As regards disparities the initial analysis by the US indicates that the new formula presents many complications. The new formula would by this analysis add 250 items to the US list of disparities and nearly 500 to the European list; this complicates rather than simplifies the problem. Governor Herter expressed the view that US experts should meet with Common Market experts and attempt to reach agreement on the facts. The problem of disparities could then be worked out. Governor Herter stressed the difficulty of this problem for the United States and said that it would be difficult to say that the US is pleased by the new formula.

Under Secretary Ball agreed that it is highly desirable for experts on both sides to get together and agree on the facts. A common understanding could thereafter be developed. Mr. Ball added that if the German analysis is correct, the Brussels agreements represent a step forward.

Foreign Minister Schroeder said it is unfortunate Mr. Lahr, one of the senior experts of the Foreign Office, was not present for these discussions. The Foreign Minister said he could only sum up the results as he understood them but he could not of course prove his points.

Governor Herter noted that the EFTA countries consider the Brussels formula unacceptable. Their reasons are not clear but they obviously feel that there are very many complexities to be worked out.

Chancellor Erhard said that he has a great interest in this problem. Governor Herter and he in a sense had baptized the child at the GATT conference earlier this year. The Chancellor added that he wants the Kennedy Round to be a success. The Chancellor went on to say that the Federal Republic had relatively little interest in the Common Market regulations but was highly interested in expanding trade as much as possible. Nevertheless it must take its partners into consideration. The Federal Republic feels that it has succeeded in getting adequate agreement in preparation for the Kennedy Round. It has also succeeded in getting the interests of EFTA, Commonwealth nations and other third parties taken into account in the agricultural regulations. The Chancellor noted that less developed countries are also concerned by the EEC agricultural regulations. The Chancellor commented that the GATT negotiations will bring forth some solid opposition to the EEC regulations. The Chancellor said that he is not afraid of this opposition and that he believes positive results can be achieved.

Chancellor Erhard went on to say that it is possible to get lost in details. Foodstuffs which affect the entire world raise larger and more general problems; worldwide agreements are called for. This however is contrary to the thinking of the EEC. Nevertheless this is a worldwide problem and the EEC is not the only factor.

Regarding disparities the Chancellor said that the point is not their number. Again there is a danger of being lost in detail, especially at the GATT conference. The Federal Republic will pursue this problem in Brussels and with the United States, on the basis of factual criteria. Then there will be a sound basis for proceeding.

The Chancellor commented that there is not only the matter of the number of items involved but also a difference of trade value. Dr. Westrick noted that economic criteria had also been discussed at Brussels; complete information on the criteria adopted at Brussels is not available and this information may explain the difference in the number of disparities mentioned earlier in the conversation.

Chancellor Erhard said that the Kennedy Round will raise questions going to the future of the Common Market. The Common Market could even drift apart. The Chancellor said that he is concerned by other difficulties which may create genuine disturbances in the European economic structure. Although price stability is desirable, the Germans alone cannot maintain discipline. If price difficulties continue to develop all over the world, we will have drastic changes. For example, prices in France and Italy are rising; tariffs will not correct the situation. These price rises will cause trouble.

Mr. Ball said that he would like to make several observations. Momentum toward European integration has recently been slowed down if not reversed. The danger is growing of a divided Europe. Failure at Brussels would have been unfortunate. On the other hand, agreements at Brussels to the detriment of third countries would not have been a good thing. The US has the impression that a new counter-force showed itself at Brussels. This has restored some balance to the Common Market and some momentum to the European idea. This is to the good.

Mr. Ball said that US support of the Rome treaty and the Common Market always recognized that there would be economic problems for the US. The US, however, expected two things to happen: first, economic expansion in Europe would expand world trade; since the trade-creating effects would be greater than the trade-diverting effects. Second, it was expected that the Common Market would build upon the principle of liberal trade embodied in the Rome treaty. As regards the first point, the trend has been toward expansion of trade in Europe. It can be argued whether or not this expansion is due to the Common Market. Nevertheless, US trade with the Common Market has gone up markedly in certain areas. On the second point, the Trade Expansion Act was intended to assist liberal elements in the Common Market to move toward greater liberalism. It was thought that the TEA would contribute not only to the prosperity of the US but to that of all nations involved.

Mr. Ball continued that as the US looks at the Brussels negotiations, however, it is concerned particularly by the problem of disparities and agriculture. US exports of agricultural items are particularly important in two categories: the US is anxious to preserve its level of export of those items subject to variable levies; those items where the binding has been fixed at a zero duty, as for example cotton, the US hopes will not be disturbed. There are also other items subject to a low duty where the US would like to see quantitative restrictions eliminated. US exports of oil seeds to the Common Market has been a large and expanding item; a European tax on oleomargarine, which would subsidize European producers, would have an adverse effect on these US exports. The Common Market tax here is a threat. Another problem is presented by rice: a basing price fixed on North Germany would be harmful to US rice exports. The fixing of a cereal price is a key matter to US wheat and grain exports to Europe. The US therefore hopes to keep the problem of grain pricing in clear focus.

Quantitative restrictions, Mr. Ball continued, may be against the theology of the Common Market, as the Chancellor just said. But, theologically speaking, we may all be sinners in agriculture. In any event the US is appreciative of the strong and helpful line taken by the German representatives in agricultural matters at Brussels. Because of the worldwide effects of Common Market agricultural decisions, the US would like to have a feeling of participation in the decisions being taken. If a liberal trading world is to be created, the US should participate.

Mr. Ball summarized by saying that the developments in Brussels seem to represent an advance from a political point of view. From a trading point of view, the US must reserve judgment until it sees the results. But the US is grateful for the position taken by the German representatives.

Chancellor Erhard said that the Federal Republic must of course act within the framework of the Six Common Market nations. Nevertheless, there will be an extension of the Common Market. The Federal Republic has not given up the idea of UK entry into the Common Market. If the UK had become a member, this would have changed the picture. There is no one to talk to in the UK now, but this will change after the UK elec tions in 1964. The Chancellor also noted that Norway has applied for admission into the Common Market. The stage may be thus reached again when the entry of new members into the EEC may be considered.

The Chancellor said that when he had seen de Gaulle in November he had said that the Europeans are giving away their sovereignty to an administrative body, not to a parliamentary European organization. The Chancellor said that he questions whether it is possible to continue European integration exclusively in the economic field; this would mean union of economic interests but no unifying political ideas. A political concept is also needed. The Chancellor said that he believes de Gaulle is now favorable to such a political approach. Nevertheless, the Federal Republic feels it is difficult to make progress so long as the UK is not a member, and it is not possible to have positive negotiations at this time with the UK.

Chancellor Erhard continued by saying that the Federal Republic is pleased that internal Common Market trade is increasing, as Mr. Ball indicated. Nevertheless, the Federal Republic is only half-glad; its trade with EFTA is not so favorable. There are distortions in the trade pattern. The Common Market should not be considered as the end of a process where there will automatically be produced a political solution like a ripe fruit dropping off a tree. What is needed is a basic political will. Once that is achieved, the Common Market will no longer be thought of as narrow and discriminatory. If political and economic aspects are combined the total picture will be better. Chancellor Erhard said that his personal desire is to see the problem of the German cereal price resolved along this line of thinking. Likewise, world trade arrangements must be looked at in terms of political as well as economic aspects.

The Chancellor went on to say that in his opinion the Common Market will always require cereal imports, in a volume from 10 to 13 million tons per year. Feed grains will be required as meat production increases. If the Common Market could give a quantitative guarantee to cereal-exporting nations, this would go a long way toward solution of the problem.

The Chancellor said that if he tried to look at Europe through American eyes, he would want to see a large political community created. A large European economic community would be interested in large American investment. This in turn would be beneficial to the US balance of payments problem. Therefore it would be desirable for Europe to be unified as rapidly and on as wide a scale as possible. The larger the economic area, the more open it must be. If Europe remains small, it will be compartmentalized. The Chancellor added that he was not sure that all Europeans see the problem in the same way as he does.

Secretary Rusk said that there are clearly many problems remaining for solution. Americans and Europeans have very large reciprocal economic interests, and both have large worldwide economic interests. The immediate question is where we now find ourselves. The Secretary asked how soon it would be before the Federal Republic would have a clear statement of the results at Brussels so that there can be consultation in detail with the US. And then what would be the next step?

Governor Herter commented that the EEC Commission will have to put together the necessary documents and these will then have to be interpreted. The French and other members may have differing interpretations. Governor Herter said that the paper which Mr. Lahr of the German Foreign Office is developing would be helpful. Foreign Minister Schroeder said that the German paper should be completed by mid-January at the latest.

90.   Circular Telegram From the Department of State to Certain Missions in Europe

Washington, December 31, 1963, 5:14 p.m.

1163. Brussels also for USEC, Paris also for USRO.

Interim Political Assessment of EEC Year-End Decisions

1. EEC Council of Ministers year-end decisions on Kennedy Round and CAP, although clearly imperfect package not fully responsive either to European or third-county interests, represent on balance a positive European effort to regain momentum and move forward along path hitherto almost completely blocked in 1963.

2. As we see results with many details still lacking, Germans and French both made important concessions in showdown precipitated by French. Germans have acknowledged in principle, at least, need for progress in CAP while accepting less liberal Kennedy Round position than they had favored. French have apparently agreed to delayed implementation CAP and to more liberal Kennedy Round stance. Despite

Source: Department of State, Central Files, ECIN 3 EEC. Confidential. Drafted by Kaplan (RPE); cleared by STR, E, and EUR; and approved by Tyler. Sent to Bonn, Rome, Brussels, London, Luxembourg, Paris, The Hague, and Geneva.

fundamental conflicts, others came into line after pledging significant sacrifices national economic interests.

3. Next results appear boil down to following:

a. *European integration movement,* which we support as vital element Atlantic relationship and natural fulfillment European desires, has weathered serious storm. Differences among EEC members will doubtless recur but will probably be of degree rather than basic intent.

b. *EEC Commission* has asserted itself as key element in Community. As originator essentially "European" compromises, Commission came out of year-end session with new respect and probably enhanced role in future.

c. Several key features of package, notably *disparities formula* and *agricultural tariff negotiating plan, will create serious problems for us in 1964.*

d. *Commitment to 50 percent linear cut* as "working hypothesis", although less clear than we would have wished, is nevertheless definite plus factor in package.

e. *Respect for third-country concerns,* which Chancellor Erhard reiterated in Texas talks, not readily evident from what is known of CAP decisions and Kennedy Round plan. Such respect, which we hope is in fact built into package, is key element from U.S. viewpoint and will need constant strong reiteration.

For present, Department and STR playing package in low key with decisions directly affecting U.S.—and these are majority of decisions—requiring far more study and additional details. In contacts with appropriate officials addressees may draw on pertinent sections this message if U.S. views requested. Should emphasize, however, that full information lacking and that these are only preliminary reactions.

Rusk

North Atlantic Treaty Organization

91. Memorandum of Conversation

Washington, January 31, 1961.

SUBJECT

Dutch Request for US Statement on NATO

PARTICIPANTS

The Secretary

Ambassador J.H. van Roijen, Netherlands Embassy
Mr. E.L.C. Schiff, Minister, Netherlands Embassy

Mr. Robert H. McBride, WE

Ambassador van Roijen opened the conversation by indicating that Prime Minister Luns would be very happy to come to Washington to see the Secretary as soon as possible. The Dutch Ambassador indicated he realized it would probably be better to wait for a while. The Secretary agreed. Ambassador van Roijen said that Prime Minister Luns would, of course, like to come as soon as convenient.

Ambassador van Roijen then discussed the Spaak resignation briefly and said it would be unfortunate if this were due to any feeling of frustration with regard to progress in NATO. The Secretary said he thought we must conclude that the Belgian internal question was dominant in Spaak's decision. He noted that Spaak had been planning to come here very soon and that if our frustration with NATO were the reason for his departure he probably would have waited to make his decision until after his visit here. However, we were not entirely certain as to what all Spaak's motives might be.

Ambassador van Roijen then passed to the Dutch view that it would be important for the United States to make a forthright declaration of support for NATO prior to the meeting of the six Heads of Government in Paris at which time the Dutch believe that the French will try to formalize political consultation of the Six. The Dutch believe that this would lead to a split in NATO and that organized political consultation

---

Source: Department of State, Central Files, 375/1–3161. Confidential. Drafted by McBride and approved in S on February 12.

among the Six would cause difficulties and would lead to an inner grouping within NATO. Ambassador van Roijen said his Government believed that Chancellor Adenauer particularly was awaiting some such statement from us. Ambassador van Roijen said that there would inevitably be difficulties if the Six developed along these lines. He said that there were certain uncertainties with regard to US attitudes toward NATO now. He thought this would lead de Gaulle to take the position that the Six should not wait for a clarification of US attitudes but should proceed to organize the Six more closely. Under present circumstances the Dutch feared that Chancellor Adenauer would accept the French view. Ambassador van Roijen continued saying the Dutch believe that de Gaulle would take the line that one cannot count on the United States and that US departure from the continent was inevitable; therefore, the Six should band together. The Dutch believe that a statement by the US would be particularly helpful with the Germans.

Ambassador van Roijen said that the Netherlands Government had always favored integration but that French leadership has given it a different coloration. De Gaulle still has in mind an old-fashioned coalition type of arrangement. In this context political consultation has developed differently from the original concept.

The Secretary wondered if we gave a forthright and pervasive statement of support for NATO, how this would be interpreted in various capitals. Ambassador van Roijen said that in Bonn he believed it would be interpreted as meaning that German fears regarding redeployment of US forces were unjustified. The Dutch Ambassador said he realized we were somewhat hesitant since we expect that Europe should undertake a greater share of the defense burden. He said he sympathized with this view but said that nevertheless US leadership was eagerly awaited in Europe.

The Secretary thanked the Dutch Ambassador for his timely and useful suggestions. Ambassador van Roijen said that US statements regarding NATO by the new administration had so far been phrased more in the negative than in the positive sense and that the Dutch would hope for a vigorous and positive statement. The Secretary said that the State of the Union message[1] was primarily addressed to US internal opinion. The Secretary then wondered if a public statement along the lines suggested by the Dutch were required or if our thoughts could be communicated by diplomatic channels to the key individuals. He thought that a public statement would set off questions and speculation regarding specific steps and actions which we were not yet ready to contemplate. Am-

---

[1] For text of the State of the Union address, January 30, see *Public Papers of the Presidents of the United States: John F. Kennedy, 1961*, pp. 19–28.

bassador van Roijen said that he personally thought a public statement would be better but that a private communication would be satisfactory if the Six Heads of Government could point to it during their forthcoming session. Mr. Schiff mentioned the possibility of conveying the US views through a statement to the North Atlantic Council. Ambassador van Roijen thought that a personal message might have greater weight and said that on thinking it over he did not believe a public statement was really required.

The Secretary said that he was interested in the Dutch presentation because he had not heretofore thought that the meeting of the Six Heads of Government would lead into such concrete developments. Ambassador van Roijen said the Dutch view was that the die would be cast at this meeting. The Secretary asked if the Dutch were worried that closer political integration of the Six might lead to divided loyalty within NATO. Ambassador van Roijen replied in the affirmative and said that one of the problems was that the Germans did not at this time wish to take a position contrary to that of the French. The Secretary inquired if he thought that a political consultation among the Six along the lines envisaged by de Gaulle would give a strong focus of policy for the Six to Paris. Ambassador van Roijen replied in the affirmative and said that de Gaulle's idea clearly was that France should speak for the Six and develop common policies in advance of NATO meetings, which would then be communicated to NATO. Ambassador van Roijen concluded saying that the Dutch felt that closer integration among the Six in the political field would be satisfactory if it were based on the principles which govern the economic communities but if it developed along the lines envisaged by the French it would be unfortunate.

The Secretary said we would consider this whole matter urgently and added that he was having a meeting on NATO later in the day.

92.   Memorandum of Conversation

Washington, February 1, 1961.

SUBJECT

NATO Problems

PARTICIPANTS

The Secretary of State
General Lauris Norstad, SACEUR
Mr. Raymond A. Hare, Deputy Under Secretary for Political Affairs
Mr. Foy D. Kohler, Assistant Secretary for European Affairs
Mr. Paul Nitze, Assistant Secretary of Defense for International Security Affairs
Mr. Frederick E. Nolting, Jr., Deputy Chief of Mission, USRO
Mr. Raymond L. Thurston, SHAPE/L
Mr. Russell Fessenden, Director, Office of European Regional Affairs

The Secretary opened the meeting by emphasizing that NATO is "more than fundamental" to the policies of the new Administration. The Secretary then raised the question of lifting the threshold for the use of nuclear weapons by NATO forces so that nuclear weapons will not have to be used at the outset. He asked whether the Europeans were prepared to take an initiative to increase conventional capabilities of their NATO forces in order to raise the threshold.

General Norstad said that he doubted that they were. He referred to the case of the U.K. The decision on ending conscription appears to be an irreversible one and seems politically impossible to change. [5 *lines of source text not declassified*]

[1 *paragraph (2-1/2 lines of source text) not declassified*]

The Secretary asked whether, if we take the lead, the Europeans would then follow by increasing the capabilities of their conventional forces. General Norstad agreed that the situation is one that calls for U.S. leadership.

The Secretary asked whether differences with the Europeans on extra-NATO area problems caused difficulties for General Norstad in carrying out his responsibilities. General Norstad replied that, on the whole, these problems did not cause him serious difficulties in his responsibilities as SACEUR.

Source: Department of State, Secretary's Memoranda of Conversation: Lot 65 D 330. Secret. Drafted by Fessenden and approved in S on February 25. According to Rusk's Appointment Book, the conversation took place at 3:04 p.m. (Johnson Library)

General Norstad then raised the question of the U.K. paper on NATO strategy, [1] which will be coming up for NATO Council discussion soon. General Norstad warned that it was inadvisable to undermine the existing agreed NATO Political Directive [2] and related strategy paper before we have something to take their places. It is therefore very important to handle the questions raised in the U.K. paper so as not to tear down the agreed structure before we have some idea of what will take its place. General Norstad said that he had warned British Defense Minister Watkinson on this point on January 28th and that Watkinson appeared to take due account of it.

General Norstad then turned to the importance which he attaches to light, mobile land-based "third-generation" MRBMs. General Norstad said that such an MRBM system lends itself to very close central control. The crew itself does not know where the missile is targeted. [5 lines of source text not declassified] General Norstad spoke very negatively about mixed manning of submarines as a solution to the problem of European participation, saying that every military man he knows regarded it as completely unworkable and undesirable. He therefore concluded that it was better to have no European contribution to the Polaris program. The Europeans should concentrate entirely on the "third-generation" MRBM system.

Mr. Kohler said that, if there were no mixed manning, it is hard to conceive how there could be a program. The concept of a truly multilateral force was developed partly to deal with the German problem. Furthermore, the U.S. suggestion was not intended primarily for European submarine deployment, but for small ships. The cost factor would be a great deal less for small ships. Mr. Kohler went on to point out that the U.S. concept presented to the NATO Council in December had deliberately left the question of third-generation missiles open.

General Norstad replied that the best approach to the MRBM problem in his view would be:

1.   The U.S. would be the sole contributor to the Polaris side of the program, contributing 150 to 180 Polaris missiles deployed on submarines.
2.   The Europeans, for their part, would take over the responsibility for the deployment of the light, mobile land-based MRBMs to be developed as the "third-generation" missile. This missile system, because of its mobility and tight control system, is more acceptable politically than any sea-borne program. The third-generation missiles will be

---

[1] A copy of this paper was handed to Merchant by Ambassador Caccia on January 23 and is attached to a January 24 memorandum from Kohler to Rusk. (Department of State, Central Files, 740.5611/1–2361)

[2] Regarding the Political Directive of December 14, 1956, see Polto 1422, December 14, 1956, Foreign Relations, 1955–1957, vol. IV, pp. 149–156.

available, it is understood, by 1964–1965. The U.S. would continue to provide atomic warheads under this proposal.

Mr. Nitze said that he nevertheless believed there would be difficult political problems in any land-based missile system. General Norstad replied that there might very well be political problems, as there are with any weapons—nuclear or otherwise. This is not the real question. The fact is that modern armaments are necessary and the majority of the countries involved realize this. [2-1/2 *lines of source text not declassified*]

Mr. Nolting suggested that it might be best to let the countries themselves make the choice between participating in a sea-borne Polaris system and a land-based "third-generation" missile system.

Mr. Kohler stressed that there is widespread feeling in Europe that something needs to be done to give NATO a greater role in nuclear defense and that a fundamental purpose of the U.S. proposals was to meet this without leading to the proliferation of nuclear weapons.

Turning again to the U.K. paper on strategy, General Norstad said he felt that, on the whole, the kind of basic discussion which the British paper proposed would be a healthy thing. Although we have in NATO an agreed political directive, strategic guidance and agreed force goals, these were approved four years ago and it is probably necessary and desirable that they be looked at again. There has been a growing spirit of questioning in NATO, which was partly touched off by the U.S. proposals in December 1959 for long-range planning[3] and by the extensive press publicity on the Bowie Report.[4] This basic questioning of NATO concepts has now reached the point where it is in fact time for people to say whether or not they do continue to believe in the political directive and related documents. General Norstad doubted very much that it will be possible to shape up views within the Alliance on these basic questions by the time of the Oslo NATO Ministerial meeting in May.

Turning to the general state of the Alliance, General Norstad said that its military strength has steadily increased every single year since its founding until today it is indeed an impressive military force. On the political side, there have been truly remarkable achievements over the past four years. In fact, the major accomplishment of NATO in recent years has been the development of political consultation.

(At this point, the Secretary was called by the President and had to leave the meeting. The discussion continued without the Secretary.)

[4 *paragraphs (1/2 page of source text) not declassified*]

---

[3] Regarding these proposals, see ibid., 1958–1960, vol. VII, Part 1, p. 540, footnote 6.
[4] A summary of the report is ibid., pp. 622–627.

In response to a question as to what steps were most needed to improve NATO, General Norstad cited the following: (1) NATO military forces should be increased in effectiveness. This does not mean necessarily increasing the numbers; modernization of conventional equipment and better training to improve combat effectiveness are of great importance. (2) Political consultation in NATO is of the utmost importance. The remarkable progress made over the last three or four years should be continued and expanded. (3) The economic side of the Atlantic Community should be developed. The OECD is of course a major step in this direction. The role of NATO in the economic field should also be kept fully in mind, however. (4) Steps must be taken to give NATO an increased role in nuclear defense. The NATO Council is now about to consider this matter.

In response to further questions about raising the "threshold" for the use of nuclear weapons, General Norstad said that we should seek to avoid making our forces dependent on nuclear weapons too far down the line. It would be much better to organize our forces so that we will be in the situation to make a conscious decision to use nuclear weapons and will not be forced to use them automatically and from the outset. In response to a question as to whether there is a U.S. interest in seeing NATO have a major nuclear capability (i.e., MRBMs), General Norstad replied that there emphatically was a U.S. interest. He pointed out that there are advantages of MRBMs over ICBMs. They are less expensive and are more accurate because of their shorter range.

---

93.   Memorandum of Conversation

Washington, February 1, 1961.

SUBJECT

NATO

PARTICIPANTS

German Ambassador Wilhelm Grewe
Mr. Franz Krapf, Minister, German Embassy
The Secretary
Mr. Martin J. Hillenbrand

Ambassador Grewe said that the German Government was particularly concerned about recent developments in NATO, symbolized

---

Source: Department of State, Central Files, 375/2–161. Confidential. Drafted by Hillenbrand and approved in S on February 20. According to Rusk's Appointment Book the conversation took place at 4:30 p.m. (Johnson Library) Rusk had also discussed NATO with Brosio at 1:47 p.m., and the Italian Ambassador stated that although Italy had no objection to Stikker as a replacement for Spaak, it wanted to put up its own candidate. (Memorandum of conversation; Department of State, Central Files, 375/2–161)

by the resignation of Secretary General Spaak. He noted that the references to NATO by the President in his recent speeches had received a good reception in Germany, both among the people and in Government circles. Maintaining the strength of NATO was a matter of grave concern to Chancellor Adenauer, the Ambassador continued. He had instructed Defense Minister Strauss, prior to his recent visit to New York, to take every opportunity to urge a resumption of active United States leadership in NATO.

The Secretary said he wanted to ask a question intended purely as such and not to indicate a point of view. We have the feeling that a number of our friends in Europe are looking for fresh United States leadership. If we assume that we are prepared to do what we can but also consider how Europe has changed since 1948, if we lead, will there be followers? Ambassador Grewe responded that, as far as the Federal Republic was concerned, the answer would be in the affirmative. The Secretary observed that, in view of the changed situation in Europe, perhaps what was called for, rather than unilateral public leadership on our part, was the intensification of consultation within NATO so that the organization would move ahead concertedly without worrying about who was leading. Ambassador Grewe said he believed the situation was such that something overt in the way of leadership from the United States was necessary. A number of developments, particularly recent actions by President de Gaulle, had made the situation ripe for such open and strong leadership. His government felt that the question of a suitable successor for Spaak as Secretary General was crucial. The Secretary said we assumed that the North Atlantic Council would discuss this question. We have had some preliminary views, not actual nominations. The Council appeared to be the most natural forum in which to discuss this question so that the whole organization could move ahead unanimously behind the man eventually selected. The Secretary General was an international civil servant. It was perhaps better, therefore, that he be a representative of a small country like Stikker or Lange, who could more easily be detached to fill the position. This was a matter, however, to be discussed. Ambassador Grewe observed that, on a purely personal basis, he would like to suggest that consideration be given to the appointment of Dean Acheson to succeed Spaak. He could think of no better symbol of NATO rejuvenation. The Secretary commented that there was no more devoted friend of NATO than Dean Acheson, but he did not suppose that he would be available for a full-time post, though he could not speak for him, since it was the first time, in his knowledge, that the suggestion had been made. He supposed that an American should not be the Secretary General, especially with General Norstad continuing as SACEUR, although the qualifications of Mr. Acheson were, of course, superb. Ambassador Grewe noted that there had been difficulties originally with Spaak's appointment, but these had been overcome.

After observing that Spaak was always an interesting man, the Secretary went on to say that we had been expecting a visit from him during February. We gathered that the lure of the Belgian political situation had proved decisive. Ambassador Grewe said that he had the impression that Spaak had been gravely disappointed by the December NATO Ministerial Meeting, particularly with the rejection of his views as to NATO's appropriate role in the economic field. The Secretary observed that it was good that the Secretary General have a lively ambition for his organization.

---

94.   Telegram From the Department of State to the Embassy in Germany

Washington, February 7, 1961, 10:13 p.m.

1360. Deliver to Ambassador 9 a.m. 2/8/61. You should seek appointment Adenauer prior his departure for Paris to convey orally message drawing on text quoted below.[1] In presenting to Adenauer, you should explain that these are President's views on certain basic matters which he wished conveyed to Adenauer at earliest opportunity in view President's knowledge of Adenauer's deep interest in these matters. President also wished to have expressed his deep appreciation of Adenauer's unfailing efforts to promote the goals of NATO solidarity and European unity. You should explain also that we plan make statement in NAC shortly explaining our basic position on NATO along lines indicated in statement below.[2]

Begin Text: The Atlantic Community stands today as the principal cornerstone of human freedom in our world. The nations of Europe and North America which make up the Atlantic Community were among the first to give effect to the ideals and practices of political democracy. At great effort and sacrifice, they have maintained freedom for their

---

Source: Department of State, Central Files, 375/2–761. Secret; Priority; Eyes Only. Drafted by Fessenden, cleared with Rusk and the White House, and approved by Kohler. Repeated to Paris.

[1] Drafts of the message to Adenauer and the statement referred to in footnote 2 below were transmitted to the President on February 4 as attachments to a memorandum from Rusk. (Ibid., Presidential Correspondence: Lot 66 D 204)

[2] For text of the statement to the North Atlantic Council, February 15, see Department of State *Bulletin*, March 6, 1961, pp. 333–334.

own peoples and have helped guide to freedom and economic better-ment hundreds of millions of peoples in more than thirty new nations.

The Atlantic Community is also the central source of strength for the entire free world. Its members possess most of the free world's ca-pacity for military defense, most of its industrial production, most of its commerce, most of its general economic power and most of its scientific and technological potential. These advantages permit us to secure im-portant benefits for our peoples. But more than this, they enable us to lead the way to freedom and economic betterment for peoples every-where. We have a great responsibility to mankind as a whole.

The keystone of the Atlantic Community is NATO. Through it, we seek to safeguard the freedom, common heritage and civilization of our peoples and to achieve a basic harmony of purpose in our international relations. The military function of NATO, the preservation of our com-mon security, is as important as ever. The United States intends to con-tinue its full participation in the common defense. I am convinced that the maintenance of U.S. military strength in Europe is essential to the security of the Atlantic Community and the free world as a whole. We also expect that our friends will want to contribute their full share to the mutual defense effort.

The non-military functions of NATO are equally important. We must expand and improve the processes of consultation in order to achieve that unity of purpose and action which is indispensable in a per-ilous age. We must also use NATO as a framework for cooperation in other programs and projects aimed at advancing the cause of human freedom everywhere.

The United States is convinced that the OECD can also become an effective instrument for cooperation toward our common goals, and I have requested the Congress to give its approval to the Convention. Our own Atlantic economies will obviously benefit from closer cooperation among ourselves. But today our economic challenges are world-wide. Of greatest importance is coordination of our efforts to promote sound economic expansion in the lesser developed countries. It is a sacred trust of the Atlantic Community to build the road to peace and freedom with the paving blocks of economic and technical development. The United States intends to do its part. Here, too, I am sure our partners will want to contribute their full share.

We also continue to encourage and support the movement toward European integration. This movement is a powerful and unifying force which can multiply free Europe's strength and prestige, can furnish in-creased economic and security benefits to the European peoples and can contribute greatly toward achieving the goals of the broader Atlantic Community.

We are all aware that the Atlantic Community, in recent years, has been hampered by differences of attitude and interest among its members. Differences will always exist, of course, among free nations. I believe it is essential, however, that we work hard to compose our differences on secondary issues in the interest of our paramount concern for peace, security and freedom. It is the firm intention of the United States to move vigorously to sustain and improve the unity, safety and well-being of the Atlantic Community, making full use of all available instruments. The United States Government looks forward to considering with our partners, in the context of long-range planning, the means for accomplishing these goals. *End text.*[3]

Rusk

---

[3] On February 8 Dowling reported that Adenauer, after interrupting a Cabinet meeting to see him, expressed his appreciation for the message and stressed that without vigorous American leadership all else would fail, "no matter how well conceived or carried out." (Telegram 1214 from Bonn; Department of State, Central Files, 375/2–861)

---

95.   Memorandum of Conversation

Washington, February 21, 1961.

SUBJECT

    NATO

PARTICIPANTS

US	*NATO*
The President	Paul-Henri Spaak, Secretary General
The Secretary of State	of NATO
Dean Acheson, Chairman of the Advisory Committee on NATO	
Paul Nitze, Assistant Secretary of Defense	
Foy D. Kohler, Assistant Secretary of State	
W. Randolph Burgess, US Ambassador to NATO	
Thomas K. Finletter, US Amb-Designate to NATO	
Edmund S. Glenn, Interpreter	

The President greeted Mr. Spaak and said that the U.S. is sorry to see him leave NATO.

Source: Department of State, Presidential Memoranda of Conversation: Lot 66 D 149. Secret; Limit Distribution. Drafted by Kohler and approved in S on March 2 and by the White House on March 3. The meeting was held at the White House. A memorandum of Spaak's conversation with Secretary of Defense MacNamara on February 20 along similar lines is ibid., Central Files, 375/2–2061.

Mr. Spaak said that he had apparently caught the Potomac fever.

The President asked Mr. Spaak what he thought about the present problems and situation of NATO.

Mr. Spaak said that NATO has changed greatly since 1949. First of all from the military point of view; in 1949 the U.S. had the monopoly of nuclear weapons. Since then the fact that the Soviets had acquired an important nuclear capability has changed the military situation in Europe and has resulted in a tendency to increase the reliance of the armed forces in Europe on nuclear armaments. In 1954 the NATO Military Command stated that if a Soviet attack were launched on NATO exclusively by conventional forces, NATO would have to use tactical nuclear weapons in its defense. The policy of doing so was approved by all the nations concerned. This date marks the beginning of an evolution of the military forces in Europe towards an ever-increasing reliance on atomic forces, first of a tactical and then of a strategic nature. The latter came with the decision to place launching sites for ballistic missiles on the soil of the European members of NATO. [2-1/2 *lines of source text not declassified*] France has taken a very independent attitude since the coming into power of General de Gaulle and seeks a nuclear capability of its own. In addition, the proposals coming from the U.S. and tending towards providing NATO with a nuclear capability have been far from clear and were in fact somewhat divergent among themselves. Secretary Herter suggested that NATO might be given five Polaris submarines if the European nations were to purchase one hundred Polaris missiles; military authorities, however, put forward nuclear armament plans which were much more ambitious, calling for hundreds of land-based missiles by 1956.

The question arises first of all whether the present Administration approves of this tendency towards increasing the role of nuclear armaments in Europe. If the answer to this question is affirmative then it is very important that proposals to that effect be put forward very clearly, taking into account two existing difficulties: first the question of financing such armaments, and second the question of political and command responsibility: who would have the authority to order the use of nuclear weapons? At this moment there is no answer to this question in NATO, and therefore what needs to be done in the military field is to obtain the necessary clarification.

As for the political problems, the foremost is that of consultations within NATO. Consultations within NATO proceed reasonably well when the questions dealt with are those of the European continent, such as Germany and Berlin. Consultations are however much less effective in regard to problems of geographical areas not covered by the treaty. There is a need for increasing the amount of consultations and of coordination of policies in regard to such problems, as for example the Congo.

A number of difficulties may be expected in Africa which would affect countries such as Portugal and Belgium, not to speak of the Algerian problem. If no harmonization of the policies of NATO countries outside of the treaty area is obtained, the cohesion among the member states will be weakened even in regard to dangers which might arise within Europe. Therefore it is imperative that the problem of increased consultations in regard to problems outside of geographical areas covered by the treaty be resolved. There are, of course, members of the organization who do not wish to depend on consultations within the organization. Since the coming into power of General de Gaulle, the attitude of France within the organization has been one of silence and abstention; in most of the recent meetings the French delegate remained silent. This attitude is likely to change only if the U.S. demonstrates its willingness to proceed with a policy of consultations within NATO. The example of the U.S. would undoubtedly be followed by other countries such as the United Kingdom, Germany and the smaller powers, [1-1/2 lines of source text not declassified].

Another area of change is that of the economic problems which have become much more important for the organization than they were in 1949. There are some common problems raised by the policies of the communist bloc, particularly in such areas as petroleum and credits. These questions would have to be carefully studied. Another area for consideration is that of the position towards the lesser developed countries. A common policy should be developed to provide help to such countries. This question will assume an extremely great importance in the future. The coordination of Western policies in this respect is not easy because there are some divergencies of interest and because many of the member states have taken individual positions. What is necessary is a will to arrive at a joint policy.

These, concluded Mr. Spaak, are the main problems of NATO—they are many and difficult.

The President asked whether Mr. Spaak thought that the U.S. proposals in regard to nuclear capability of NATO, if made clearer but based on the same principles as those that had been put forward, would change the attitude of France.

Mr. Spaak replied that such proposals were of interest to France. General de Gaulle complains that France does not participate in strategic planning. It is for this reason that he pursues a policy of seeking an independent nuclear capability for France. General de Gaulle feels that when France has such a capability the U.S. will be forced to let France participate in strategic nuclear planning. A proposal such as that put forward by Secretary Herter might provide an indirect way for France to participate in the planning of nuclear strategy. It is quite clear that the five submarines which were mentioned in it would not operate independently but rather as a part of a total force, and that, therefore, their presence would provide the possibility for the European members of NATO to participate in strategic nuclear planning for such a total force. It was, however, impossible to develop the consequences of this idea because almost at the same time when the proposal was made the NATO military commands (SACEUR and SACLANT) come up with a different plan in which not five but twenty Polaris submarines were mentioned, and in addition to the Polaris submarine-mounted missiles, there were to be hundreds of missiles emplaced on the European continent. This divergency between proposals created confusion not only on the part of the civilian but also of the military organs of NATO. It would be necessary, in Mr. Spaak's opinion, to obtain a clear proposal which would draw France into cooperation. At the present moment General de Gaulle has a policy, from which he will not deviate, of seeking a French nuclear capability; once he has some such capability a compromise may be obtained by placing the French nuclear force within NATO in the same way in which American and British nuclear forces are placed there. It is necessary to take into account the fact that as long as General de Gaulle remains in power, a drive to obtain a nuclear capability will remain the main objective of French policy, with a priority higher even than that of the Algerian problem.

The President requested the Secretary General to review again the development of NATO military policy. In response, Mr. Spaak reiterated that 1954 marked a turning point in the military policy of NATO. It was at that date that the NATO High Command stated that if the Soviets were to attack NATO using exclusively conventional weapons, NATO would be forced to use tactical nuclear weapons in order to avoid defeat. It was that moment that started a tendency toward the "nuclearization" of Europe. In 1957 this tendency was strengthened when the Heads of Government took the decision to complete the defense of Europe by placing on the continent intermediate range nuclear ballistic missiles. This decision was implemented only partially; Italy has accepted IRBM bases on her territory. Thus from tactical nuclear weapons Europe passed to strategic ones.

When the President asked Mr. Spaak's opinion as to what the United States should now do in the military field, Mr. Spaak said that the first thing which must be made clear is whether the new Administration intends to continue the policy of increasing the reliance of NATO on nuclear weapons, both tactical and strategic. This is a decision of principle which needs to be taken. If an affirmative decision is taken, then the U.S. will have to put forward clear proposals which would take into account the problem of financing such armaments and also the problem of the political responsibility as to who would be entitled to order the use of such weapons. [5-1/2 lines of source text not declassified] Thus if the U.S.

intends to continue with the policy of nuclearization it should not expect any action from its European partners until the time when it is ready to present proposals which would clearly show a method of financing and which would at the very least present a clear idea for the solution of the political problem or command. Nothing should be said or can be said before the U.S. has taken a clear position.

Secretary Rusk asked what would be the situation if the U.S. did not wish to pursue a policy of giving NATO a nuclear capability.

Mr. Spaak replied that in such a case NATO would have to reconsider its entire strategic concept, since this would mark a change from a direction which had been pursued for several years already. It would become necessary to develop and to make clear a new strategy. Since 1954 NATO had got used to the idea of a defense relying on the nuclear deterrent, in regard to which there are no difficulties of principle. If it is said now that a tendency to rely on this deterrent is not a good one, the entire problem has to be rethought and clear explanations must be found as to how Europe will be defended in the face of the Soviet superiority in conventional armaments. There is a certain body of opinion in Europe, which is relatively unimportant at this moment but which nevertheless exists, which believes that there is a danger that the U.S. might not use its nuclear capability to defend Europe since the use of the American nuclear forces might bring about a Soviet counter-strike against the U.S. General de Gaulle, for example, holds such an opinion. Although this body of opinion is still small it might gain in strength, in case of reversal of direction in U.S. policy towards NATO. The superiority of Soviet conventional forces over those of Europe is such as to make a defeat highly probable, if it were not for the American nuclear capability on which Europe now depends.

The President asked if Mr. Spaak thought that a reconsideration on the part of the U.S. of the offer to provide a nuclear capability for NATO would lead to a tendency on the part of various European countries to seek nuclear capabilities of their own.

Mr. Spaak replied that this does not appear probable at the present moment. At the present moment only France seeks an independent nuclear capability. The other countries are not now thinking of one for themselves. At the same time a proposal to give NATO a nuclear capability would also have the advantage of solving the German problem. Although there is no "German problem" at the present moment, such a problem might well appear in the future. It would be necessary also to provide the European countries with some assurance that the American nuclear capability would come into place in case of need. To reverse a direction which has been followed for seven years is rather delicate. In 1949 Europeans were certain that they could rely on the American nuclear deterrent, since at that time the U.S. had a monopoly of nuclear weapons. However, since the development of the Soviet capabilities, some Europeans wonder if they can still rely on the American deterrent because of a possible fear on the part of the U.S. of a Soviet counter-retaliation.

The President thanked Mr. Spaak for presenting his views on the military problems of the Alliance and asked him about his views as to what should be done on other matters.

Mr. Spaak said that the main political problem was that of closer consultations, and that this problem could be solved if a good example were given by the U.S.

Secretary Rusk asked if policy consultations would have to proceed within the machinery of NATO or whether such consultations could proceed through the usual diplomatic channels.

Mr. Spaak said that for the sake of the future of NATO it is very important that consultations take place within the organization. This does not mean that ordinary diplomatic channels should be neglected, but rather that they should be used in order to prepare decisions which would then be taken within the organized bodies of the Alliance, in which all of the member states would have a chance to present their interests and to voice their fears. Such a course is necessary, particularly because the smaller countries within NATO are highly sensitive and do not want to be faced with faits accomplis. They consider the possibility of political consultations as the counterpart of the military efforts they are asked to make. Mr. Spaak said that he had opposed the directorate idea put forward by General de Gaulle precisely for the reason that it could strengthen the tendency towards neutralism which is traditional in the smaller countries of Europe.

The President asked whether Mr. Spaak saw General de Gaulle and how he found the General's attitude toward NATO.

Mr. Spaak replied that he talked with General de Gaulle occasionally, and stated flatly the General does not like NATO. He does not believe that NATO provides the solution to the nuclear problem. He is also against integrated armed forces, this in spite of the fact that it is absurd today for smaller countries to have a complete range of armed forces of their own, and that therefore such small countries must seek an integrated force. General de Gaulle is not, however, of this opinion. Moreover, General de Gaulle does not see in NATO a solution to the political problems. He might be willing to consult with the U.S. and the United Kingdom but not with countries such as Luxembourg and Iceland and he does not hide his ideas on the subject. In the recent consultations which took place in regard to Laos, the U.S. and the United Kingdom representatives spoke at length but the delegate of France remained silent. There had also been exchanges of opinion in NATO in regard to

Africa and the Congo; although these exchanges were useful, the French delegate had again remained silent. General de Gaulle had told Chancellor Adenauer that he did not wish to destroy NATO, but this is as far as he went. His main preoccupation is the problem of obtaining a nuclear capability, which alone, in his opinion, can maintain for France the status of a great power. General de Gaulle even told Mr. Spaak that the latter was right to go back to Belgium, as there was nothing for him to do in NATO. General de Gaulle is a man of very strong opinions and it would take at the very least the President of the United States to make him change his mind.

The President thanked Mr. Spaak. He also thanked Ambassador Burgess, Mr. Finletter, and Mr. Acheson, and said that the presence of such men is a proof of the continued great interest of the U.S. in NATO.

Mr. Spaak said that in his opinion the fate of NATO is in the President's hands; all of the European members of NATO will follow the lead of the President. Given the leadership of the U.S., the problem of consultations which appears difficult at first glance would become easy because there exists a great reservoir of good will on the part of the smaller countries, members of NATO, which only ask not to be put before faits accomplis in the domain of political decisions. A solution for the problem of France within the organization would still have to be found. There is hope nevertheless that NATO will continue to play its great part in the defense of the free world.

---

96.   Memorandum of Conversation

Washington, March 15, 1961.

SUBJECT

NATO and Nuclear Forces

PARTICIPANTS

The Secretary of State	The French Ambassador
Mr. McGhee, S/P	M. Lebel
Mr. Kohler, EUR	M. Winckler
Mr. Beigel, WE	M. Pelen

The Ambassador said that France considers NATO to be our most important alliance but that it must be adapted to new circumstances,

---

Source: Department of State, Central Files, 375/3–1561. Secret. Drafted by Beigel, cleared in draft by Kohler on March 17, and approved by S on April 4.

taking account of the Soviet worldwide tactics, the end of the Western atomic monopoly, and the fact that Europe can contribute immensely more than it could ten years ago. He said that the smaller powers are reluctant to give NATO global responsibilities to meet with the global Soviet threat, and that France does not propose any changes in the treaty in this respect. Rather, France has proposed the tripartite arrangements to deal with this global problem. Nevertheless France believes that important changes can be made within the framework of the treaty. He said that more responsibilities might be proposed for certain countries on the command side but this matter is not urgent and there will be time to consider it. He said that France hopes for the continued presence of US forces in Europe, that France has agreed to the integration of air defense in the forward zone, the training of French forces in Germany to draw upon the atomic stockpile there, and has accepted the presence of German forces in France.

The Ambassador went on to say that the question of nuclear weapons on French soil remains unsettled, and is linked to general agreement regarding strategic planning and the use of nuclear weapons throughout the world. He said that France would like to have US views on the future of NATO and the role of NATO as a nuclear power. He reiterated that the main interest of France is to have general tripartite military planning on a worldwide scale.

With regard to nuclear forces, the Ambassador said that France decided to produce atomic weapons before the advent of de Gaulle. He said that France had never asked for US help in this respect, and that it remains for the US to decide whether France has made "substantial progress" in this field in the terms of the US legislation. He said that France regrets that secrets the Soviets already have are not available to France, and noted that French missions coming here in the atomic and missile fields have not been able to get information even when it has not been classified as secret. He said he has no special instructions to request anything in this field now.

The Secretary said that we agree there is no need to revise the North Atlantic Treaty or for organic change to give the organization worldwide responsibilities. He said that Mr. Acheson is informally helping us to formulate views on questions facing NATO but no formal report is expected from this study group. We expect to be prepared in the strategic, political and economic fields in time for the May meeting of the Council. He said that we will advocate a strengthening of conventional forces, and that we are concerned about the command channels and controls for handling nuclear weapons. We will wish to know what the European members think about these subjects. He said that there is no question about keeping US forces in Europe, backing them with nuclear weapons, and considering NATO as a fundamental tenet of our foreign policy.

The Secretary went on to say that he did not believe the NATO Council was the best place to discuss non-European questions when some members did not wish to do so, adding that we do not feel we can give first priority to NATO discussions unless other members feel the same way. On a matter such as Portuguese Africa, he said, we would find it difficult to support Portugal simply because of the NATO alliance. He added that our general orientation nevertheless will be to maintain as much unity as possible in our political consultations with other NATO members. He did not feel that any new consultative machinery was needed but awaited the views of the Acheson study group on this. He said that OECD consultations on economic questions, with a view to coordinating national policies, will better enable us to meet our needs as well as assist underdeveloped countries, including such NATO countries as Greece, Turkey and Portugal.

The Secretary said that we are deeply concerned about the extension of national nuclear capabilities, and we regret that our original postwar proposals in this field were not accepted by the Soviets. Now we are reluctant to do anything ourselves to increase the spread of national nuclear forces, and we hope that a nuclear test ban treaty will restrict any more widespread developments. He said that in this circumstance it is difficult to focus on the question of assisting France in this field, since we must consider this subject within the framework of our NATO study.

Mr. Kohler said that the purpose of the original Herter proposals will remain, as a means of solving the nuclear problem through NATO in a manner that will enable France to end its compulsion toward a national nuclear force. He said that we would be receptive to any French ideas along this line.

The Ambassador went on to say that France does not favor the nuclear test ban negotiation since this does not represent real disarmament, and the result would establish a monopoly of three powers in the nuclear field, which is not acceptable to France. He said that France agrees there should be no proliferation of nuclear powers, but that the line should be drawn after France becomes the fourth power.

With regard to a NATO nuclear force, the Ambassador said that France awaits further indication of US thinking on this. He said that he could not himself imagine how the President could give to another organization the power of decision and veto with regard to use of US nuclear weapons, but that France would study any US proposals in this field.

The Secretary said that on this subject there are two questions, with regard to US commitments to others and whether the others could accept responsibility. He said that the second question would be one for the European members of NATO to consider.

---

97.   Telegram From the Embassy in Germany to the Department of State

Bonn, April 10, 1961, 1 p.m.

1632. For the President and Secretary of State from Dean Acheson. Also pass to Ambassador Dowling.

"You have lifted a stone from my heart" said Chancellor Adenauer at the end of our talk on Sunday.

Chancellor came to meet me at the airport and drove me to his own house. I was alone with him and his interpreter from 11:30 until 5:00 pm. We talked together for an hour before lunch and continued with some business and some gossip during lunch. After lunch we talked for about two hours more.

Before lunch he asked me to let him make a considerable statement to indicate his principal concerns. In course of this statement several odd observations turned up. His view of the world situation was that Khrushchev was able and tough, primarily a Russian successor of the Czars and no ideologist. Although he used communism, his chief concern was to consolidate what Lenin had started and what Stalin had so greatly expanded. He wanted to gain his ends primarily by maneuver, though he would use force, if he could do so without substantial risk. One of Khrushchev's principal objects was to break up NATO, which Adenauer thought had weakened considerably in the last 8 years due to absence of US leadership, and as a result of dissension among allies. He said that when he was in Moscow in 1955, Khrushchev asked him to help him against the Americans and the Chinese. He felt Khrushchev was very much worried about the Chinese, and that any American attempt to come closer to Chinese might produce violent Russian reaction. I asked him if he had seen any indication of such a tendency, and he said

---

Source: Department of State, Central Files, 611.62A/4–1061. Secret; Priority; Limited Distribution. Acheson visited Bonn at the personal invitation of the Chancellor.

no. The US, he said, must reassert its leadership and its interest in NATO and strengthen it politically and militarily, or it would fall apart. Some of the allies believe that we are more concerned with the under-developed countries than with our allies. He felt that there was a lack of political consultation and, from military point of view, that Allied troops in Europe did not know whether there were nuclear arms available to them in Europe. He added he had been told this by Strauss as late as previous day. (Later on, I told him that he had either misunderstood Strauss or that latter was misinformed, because all Allied commanders were thoroughly familiar with nuclear weapons available to them and where these located, as General Norstad would readily confirm. I heard no more about this complaint.) He spoke of the necessity of "NATO becoming the fourth nuclear power". Said he knew General Norstad had made recommendations to this end, but that no one knew that had happened to them. He spoke of his belief that both Dulles and Eisenhower had written NATO off, and of his anxieties as to policies of new administration. He had heard good reports of Finletter and of his statements to the Council.

To sum up his opening remarks: they were rather the expression of his deep worry, than a rational exposition of facts.

I started by explaining that the President and Secretary of State had instituted a review of the NATO situation by the officers primarily responsible for developing policies with me as chairman of this group, for the purpose of strengthening the Alliance in every way possible. Conclusions had been reached unanimously, and had been substantially approved by the Cabinet members concerned and by the President. These were essentially an American position and in no sense an attempt to dictate to our Allies. The first point was to exercise American leadership in using the NATO Council, both formally and informally, for broad consultations to bring about Allied understanding of emerging problems well in advance and, if possible, agree on courses to be pursued. On such matters as relations with former colonial peoples, we hoped to enlist Allied support for practical steps toward improving conditions, and to minimize ideological differences. In Europe the US Gov would continue to support the policy of integration, and would believe it wise and helpful should the British find it possible to join the Six. USGov would not be in favor of helping national nuclear developments. In the economic field, the policy would be for continued and close consultation within the OECD, and the coordination of national policies on financial, trade, and capital export policies. All of this the Chancellor received with mounting enthusiasm.

We then turned to NATO military matters. I said that the new administration wished to correct some harmful impressions created toward the end of the old one. In his own way and time, the President would make clear to our Allies that American troops were not to be withdrawn from Europe, nor would there be any threat to do so. He would also make clear that nuclear weapons would not be withdrawn except as better ones were substituted. The President fully understood the need for medium-range missiles, and believed that both for military and financial reasons, this had better be done by water-borne than by land-based missiles. He was prepared to take steps to this end. He also appreciated the proper desire of our Allies to play their part in the governmental decision when and how to use nuclear weapons. Several methods had been suggested. The President was willing to explore all of them, and in these discussions would advocate swift and clear methods of decision in event of sudden attacks. We believed with General Norstad, that NATO must have the capability of raising the threshold over which nuclear weapons would be used, and of stopping an attack by forces readily available for a long enough period to permit a deliberate appraisal of the situation, and a decision to move into nuclear warfare. However if the other side initiated nuclear warfare, no doubt existed as to necessity for reply in kind. Foregoing required strengthening of existing forces, better equipment and mobility, and the attainment as soon as possible of MC–70 goals. This would require priority for non-nuclear forces over the next say five years. It would be most unwise and dangerous to continue in our present non-nuclear situation, while such possibilities as trouble over Berlin lay ahead of us. The administration did not regard this as a change of policy but as a readjustment of emphasis, which had become one-sided. Several times I reiterated the point that in stressing importance of bringing conventional forces up to the goals mentioned, the administration had no intention of attempting to fight World War II over again. The sole purpose was to preserve the possibility of stopping military flare-up, without the certainty of quick escalation into nuclear war. The Chancellor received this statement with complete satisfaction.

Chancellor mentioned Berlin, asking whether the administration was giving thought to this issue. I replied that it most assuredly was, and that I had been asked to interest myself in the problem. I added that while the matter was still under study, those concerned were under strong impression that the seriousness of the situation had not been reflected in any adequate preparations, and that both consultation with some of our Allies and energetic preparation seemed urgently needed. With this he emphatically agreed.

At the end of our talk the Chancellor spoke most movingly of his gratitude for my visit, and of the great sense of relief which my report of the attitude of the new administration had brought him. He was looking forward, he said, eagerly to meeting the President and discussing these matters with him. We then adjourned our talk to play a game of bowls, at which he beat me.

May I end, with the concurrence of the Embassy, by again recommending that the attendance at the meetings with the Chancellor be limited, since he speaks much more freely in a small group and thus will disclose his preoccupations and have them removed."

Suggest Department make any further distribution foregoing message as desired.

Dowling

98.   Memorandum of Conversation

Washington, April 12, 1961, 10 a.m.

SUBJECT

NATO and East-West Relations

PARTICIPANTS

United States	*German*
The President	Chancellor Adenauer
Secretary Rusk	Foreign Minister von Brentano
Ambassador Dowling	Ambassador Grewe
Assistant Secretary Kohler	Mr. Kusterer (Interpreter)
Mrs. Lejins (Interpreter)	Dr. Karl Carstens

The President greeted the Chancellor, indicating how happy he was to have this occasion to discuss mutual problems. He indicated the great respect in which he himself, as well as previous occupants of the White House and all the citizens of the United States, held the Chancellor and his country. President Kennedy stated that, as the new President of the United States, he was anxious to hear the Chancellor's suggestions for the strengthening of United States relations with Germany, Western Europe and the security of the countries involved, including his suggestions on matters pertaining to Berlin and over-all German problems.

Source: Department of State, Conference Files; Lot 65 D 366, CF 1835. Secret. Drafted by Lejins and approved in S on April 22 and in the White House on May 11. The meeting was held at the White House. For the Chancellor's detailed account of this conversation, see *Erinnerungen, 1959–1963, Fragmente* (Stuttgart, 1968), pp. 91–98. Adenauer visited Washington April 12–13. For the German Ambassador's account of this meeting and the entire visit, see *Rückblenden, 1951–1976* (Frankfurt, 1979), pp. 461–470.

The Chancellor expressed his gratification at the President's kind words. He stated that Germany owes its spectacular recovery after the war in large measure to United States assistance and therefore feels very closely tied to this country. He expressed his thanks for this assistance by the United States and stated that he was happy to be able to make the President's acquaintance. He felt confident that in the ensuing talks many matters of great importance could be profitably discussed. The Chancellor stated that he had been watching world developments very closely these past 12 years. He had looked at them largely from the standpoint of Europe, but had also familiarized himself with the viewpoint of the United States concerning these matters. He hoped that the President would have the time to discuss some of these things with him during the next few days.

As a beginning the President stated that he understood the Chancellor had talked with former Secretary of State Dean Acheson last Saturday in Bonn.[1] He expressed hope that Mr. Acheson had given the Chancellor a clear idea of American thinking during the past two months with regard to the problems of NATO. The President hoped that Mr. Acheson had given the Chancellor assurances of American determination to strengthen NATO, to maintain American forces in Western Germany and to strengthen these forces rather than to diminish them. These were the considerations which had been discussed in Washington during the past months, since American concern was directed toward strengthening NATO and, by the guaranties connected therewith, to increase the protection of Germany and Western Europe. If Mr. Acheson had failed to make this completely clear and any questions were left in the Chancellor's mind, the President wished to reassure the Chancellor that the United States was prepared and determined to stand by its commitments.

The Chancellor replied that he and Mr. Acheson had talked for several hours. He stated that Mr. Acheson had been the first Secretary of State to visit Bonn after the war and that he and Mr. Acheson had remained friends ever since. The Chancellor and Mr. Acheson had talked very freely. The Chancellor described Mr. Acheson as a person who thinks very clearly and is able to put his thoughts into clear language. He stated that the discussions with Mr. Acheson had made him very happy.

The President indicated that in Mr. Acheson's discussions here in Washington the emphasis had been placed on increasing the capability of the conventional forces and on raising the threshhold for the use of atomic weapons. The President realized that these considerations had created a certain concern in Germany, where it was feared that these

---

[1] See Document 97.

plans might lessen the prospects for the use of atomic weapons in the defense of Western Germany, and that the relegation of the use of atomic weapons further to the background might encourage the Soviet Union to launch an attack with conventional weapons. The President stated that he hoped he made it clear that the United States was as much committed as before to the use of atomic weapons, if necessary, for the defense of Western Germany and of NATO interests. He stated that United States efforts were directed toward achieving better command and better control and to make sure that the use of nuclear weapons could not come about accidentally but would be the result of a definite decision.

The Chancellor stated that Mr. Acheson had been emphatic in insisting that MC 70[2] would have to be fulfilled, and the Chancellor agreed that Mr. Acheson was right. The Chancellor stated that he often felt that Europe must present a very sad and discouraging picture to the United States with reference to the fulfillment of its commitments. Actually the disintegration of NATO was the result of this. However, the Chancellor felt he ought to state one more thing. The United States had been standing by, tolerating this condition, for too long without making use of the moral leadership right to which it is entitled for the benefit of the free nations. The Chancellor was happy to learn from his talks with Mr. Acheson that all this seemed to be changing now. The Chancellor said that one sentence of Mr. Acheson's made him especially happy. Mr. Acheson had said that the fate of the United States is the fate of Western Europe, and the fate of Western Europe is the same as the fate of the United States. The Chancellor had told Mr. Acheson that he had never heard this truth stated as clearly by anyone from the United States before. That sentence had indicated to the Chancellor the firmness of the conviction of the new Administration and had lifted a heavy burden which the Chancellor had been carrying, not only since the entry into office of the new Administration, but for the past several years.

The President then inquired into the nature of the burden mentioned by the Chancellor. He asked what exactly was the cause of the latter's dissatisfaction and in what way NATO had failed. The Chancellor replied that he might as well speak frankly. There was no doubt about the fact that NATO had been on the decline and had actually been dying for a number of years, with member nations failing to fulfill their commitments. Moreover, there had been almost no consultation to speak of, and leadership on the part of the United States, which the Chancellor valued very highly and which he considered the only possi-

---

[2] Regarding MC–70, Minimum Essential Force Requirements, 1958–1963, see *Foreign Relations*, 1958–1960, vol. VII, Part 1, pp. 314–315.

bility, had been reticent and on the decline. This had been true even during the time of Secretary Dulles, and the Chancellor had called this fact to Mr. Dulles' attention time and again. Mr. Dulles had told him to take a look at Europe itself—at France, where no de Gaulle was in evidence at that time, at Italy and the United Kingdom. Mr. Dulles had said that the United States would remain in Europe only as long as Germany fulfilled her commitments. Thus this disease from which NATO was suffering was one of long standing. Consequently, Mr. Acheson's explanations had been most welcome, especially since, as the Chancellor understood, they expressed the will and determination of the President. The Chancellor had not heard such talk in years. He added that his concern was not confined to any very specific details but dealt rather with the general trend of things. The fact remained that there was no strength in NATO and that he was most happy to hear that the United States was undertaking to change all this.

The President asked the Chancellor whether he was talking about military commitments on the part of member nations of NATO or about other phases of the NATO program. Chancellor Adenauer replied that it was no longer possible to differentiate between military and political matters. He stated that he could not go into any great detail on any of these matters because specific instances would constitute a very long list. In essence, however, he wished to say that NATO was devoid of life. There was no longer any real activity in it. He hoped the President could succeed in reactivating NATO. This would constitute a historic achievement and a tremendous task. The Chancellor indicated that if the President were successful in achieving the reactivation of NATO it would really be the first time that the United States would emerge from an atmosphere of isolation and enter the political arena in the West. That is why Chancellor Adenauer had been greatly heartened by his talks with Mr. Acheson. He wished the President great strength and stamina, since he was faced with tremendous tasks.

In continuing the same topic, the President suggested that now that he and the Chancellor had discussed the continued intention of the United States to maintain and even increase its forces, and the United States intention to ask other nations to do the same, he would like to hear the Chancellor's suggestions on how the United States could be more effective in increasing the security and safety of Western Europe.

The Chancellor replied that the question of consultation was a decisive and determining one for NATO. The Chancellor understood that the President was very much interested in this question. Once the member nations learned that the United States was ready to consult them not only in questions that directly affected their interests and security, but also in questions which had only an indirect effect on their security, the entire atmosphere with regard to NATO would change. Thus the first step was to institute active consultation.

Next, of course, there was the economic situation, which was tied up with everything. Mr. Acheson had told the Chancellor that the President was very much interested in European integration and felt that it was very important. The Chancellor fully shared this view and had been of this conviction for many years. Chancellor Adenauer felt that the United Kingdom was on the verge of entering the European Economic Community even though Mr. Macmillan had not yet quite been able to bring himself to take this step. The younger British cabinet members, however, were in favor of giving serious consideration to joining this body. The Chancellor felt that this was a very important and an essential step, and he was happy to hear that the President felt similarly and also wanted the United Kingdom to give serious consideration to joining the European Economic Community. The Chancellor continued by stating that the economic conditions played a very important role, of course, in the relations between Western Europe and the United States and that they exerted a very direct influence on all political matters. Many difficult tasks lay ahead. Once the discussion of these economic matters is brought before NATO, the question will arise whether the national representatives to NATO are actually qualified and high-level enough to handle such matters. This in itself will lead to a re-examination of the caliber of NATO representatives and will help to raise the over-all level of NATO. Certain procedures might also have to be changed in the process. The Chancellor indicated that it was slightly ironical that the original purpose of NATO had actually been anti-German. The nations involved had gotten together at Brussels because they felt that Germany, which was on the verge of recovery, might want revenge, and therefore they wanted to protect themselves against Germany. Finally, however, largely with the intervention of the United States, Germany had been approached to join NATO and was glad to accept.

The Chancellor continued by saying that the attacks by the Soviet Union on the freedom of the world take place everywhere, of course. Europe, however, is of particular importance in this struggle. In this connection the Chancellor recalled his visit to Moscow in 1955, and six days of talks with Mr. Khrushchev, in which Foreign Minister von Brentano participated. The Germans had been treated extremely well, although, of course, they had their disagreements, which had to be expected. On one of the last days Mr. Khrushchev had come out of his inner sanctum and told Chancellor Adenauer—and there were only four persons present at that time (Bulganin and von Brentano in addition to the two principals)—that the Soviet Union had two chief enemies, the United States and Red China. Of the two, Red China was by far the greater enemy. Mr. Khrushchev had said to the Chancellor: Imagine what the future will bring, with 600 million Red Chinese increasing by about 12 million each year and living on a hand-full of rice, and Mr. Khrushchev had made a significant gesture with his hand as though he were holding just one hand of rice. The prospects, Mr. Khrushchev said, were appalling, and he had turned to Mr. Adenauer to say: "help us." In other words he wanted help against the United States and Red China, but again Chancellor Adenauer wished to be emphatic in stating that Mr. Khrushchev's real concern was primarily with regard to Red China. That was a situation which the Soviet Union really feared, not perhaps in the immediate future, but 10 or perhaps 20 years from now. Mr. Khrushchev is a person who thinks far ahead and he thinks very clearly. He may be brutal at times, but he is smart. He thinks things out, and this was one time when he abandoned some of his darker thoughts and, as it were, let his hair down and expressed his fears of Red China. The Chancellor stated that he had recounted this incident in some detail because he felt that it was important for United States policy vis-à-vis Red China. He was pleased to hear that the United States was *not* intending to follow the United Kingdom's example with regard to Red China. This was most fortunate.

The President inquired whether the Chancellor had reference to the admission of Red China to the United Nations. The Chancellor nodded. The President then continued by saying that, as the Chancellor knew, there would be great difficulty this year in trying to keep Red China out of the United Nations, since the United Kingdom, Brazil and several other countries had expressed the opinion that Red China should be admitted. Therefore it would be difficult to keep Red China out.

The Chancellor stated that he knew what these difficulties would be, but he said that this is a problem of partnership. In the Chancellor's opinion it should not be possible for two nations who are partners in such a matter of life and death as NATO to have and follow different policies in the UN. Such action would be completely unthinkable among the Communist powers. Therefore the Communist bloc has been so successful in the past years, while the Free World permits itself all sorts of divergent opinions on vital matters. This type of procedure raises hope in the Soviet Union that the free nations of the world might just naturally fall apart. All these things go together. How could the United Kingdom take a different action with reference to such vital problems? The President will certainly receive some surprises from General de Gaulle, too, and will learn that de Gaulle will go off on his own in many instances. That is the weakness and the disease affecting the West, and will break open in many places. Reactivation of the solidarity of the free nations as exemplified by NATO is a historic task but it is the only salvation for the Free World.

Secretary Rusk at this point noted that the Chancellor had spoken of the need for United States leadership in NATO. He said that the President had taken this very seriously and had asked the various branches of this government to examine very carefully what the United States could do to put new life and strength into NATO. Some other nations of Europe had also indicated that they wanted the United States to take more decisive steps in this respect. The Secretary wanted to ask the Chancellor: "Did he think that the member nations of NATO were ready to accept United States leadership? It was one thing to be ready to lead and to lead alone. It was another thing to lead and be followed. Did the Chancellor think that Europe was actually ready to be led by the United States?"

Chancellor Adenauer said that he would like to say one thing. It was very important that the country exerting leadership treat the small nations well. If the small countries feel that they are not being treated in a friendly manner, there is the danger that they will offer resistance even when things that are beneficial for them are proposed. It was wise to treat the small nations well; it would not cost much, but it bore good fruit. Leadership is not a matter of commanding, it is a matter of convincing and persuading, but above all the nation exercising leadership must show that it has a will and determination. That is essential. As for the Secretary's question whether Europe would go along with the United States, the Chancellor definitely felt it would. As regards the United Kingdom, the change of the United Kingdom from a non-European power to a European power was well underway. Chancellor Adenauer had seen these developments shape up very clearly and indicated that the young people in the United Kingdom recognized that they belonged to Europe and that the old political maxim that the continental European powers should be kept divided so that the UK could rule is passe. Italy was a slightly difficult case. Economically the country had recovered very much. Chancellor Adenauer does not expect that the Nenni socialists will be accepted into the Government and thus strengthen the Communist coalition. Moreover, the Chancellor feels that Italy is extremely responsive to good treatment. He knows that the President will see Mr. Fanfani shortly. Mr. Fanfani is very human and a few kind words addressed to him may do a great deal of good. As for the United Kingdom, the Chancellor has previously expressed his views. As regards Germany, the Chancellor stated that Germany is convinced that she can keep her freedom and peace only if the United States leads the Free World. Otherwise there is no hope of saving either freedom or peace. The small countries, the Chancellor feels, will follow the leadership of the United States if they are treated with consideration.

The Chancellor continued, stating that France is a somewhat difficult case. He stated that he himself is on good terms with de Gaulle. He did not know him prior to September 1958, but they have gotten along very well and de Gaulle is very frank with him. De Gaulle feels, however, that the United States' attitude in the UN helped bring about the setback for France in its relations with Algeria, and he cannot forget this. However, he is an intelligent man. He is the kind of General—and the Chancellor did not wish to cast aspersions on any other Generals—who thinks far ahead. The Chancellor realizes that the President will soon meet with General de Gaulle and thinks it would be a fine thing if the President were able to establish rather close contact with him. However, he is rather difficult. His chief interest is the fate of France. The Chancellor does not feel that he is motivated by personal ambitions but that he is really extremely interested in the fate of France. The task therefore will be to convince him that France will fare best in an alliance like NATO. At the present time he is not convinced of this and he can hardly be blamed, since NATO really has been rather ineffective so far. The Chancellor again expressed hope that the President may be able to convince General de Gaulle of the importance of NATO. In addition to this, it is necessary that other countries too revive their confidence in NATO, and even within the United States it would be necessary to find persons who would understand the importance of NATO for the United States. If the President succeeds in reestablishing this confidence and of convincing General de Gaulle, he will have achieved very much. The Chancellor is convinced that this can and must be done.

President Kennedy asked the Chancellor whether, in his statement concerning the United States stand in the UN, he had reference to recent events. The Chancellor indicated that he had reference to events several years ago. He elaborated that General de Gaulle felt that the rebels in Algeria would have been ready to sign a peace pact with France about two years ago if they had not been supported by the United States stand in the UN. On the occasion of President Eisenhower's visit to Bonn the Chancellor had raised the French-Algerian problem.[3] President Eisenhower had not wanted to discuss this matter, stating that the United States had been a colonial people once too and therefore could not leave Algeria in the lurch. The Chancellor had told him that he could not understand this reasoning and could not go along with it. Finally President Eisenhower had said that when the Algerian question came to a vote in the UN, the United States would *not* vote against France. The Chancellor had thereupon asked him whether he would permit him to call General de Gaulle in his presence and tell him this. President Eisenhower had indicated that he could. Consequently Chancellor Adenauer had called General de Gaulle and told him the outcome of his discussions. The up-

---

[3] For a memorandum of Adenauer's conversation with Eisenhower, August 27, 1959, see ibid., vol. IX, pp. 19–25.

shot of the matter was that later, when the matter was brought to a vote in the United Nations, the United States did vote against France anyway and General de Gaulle had never forgotten this.

The President replied that there were many factors which had a bearing on United States relations with member nations of NATO. There was, for instance, the matter of Angola and Portugal; the Congo and Belgium; Algeria and France; the differences with the United Kingdom concerning Red China, and others. All these had a direct effect on relations within NATO. The countries with whom it was relatively simple to maintain good relations were such countries as Germany, Italy, Greece and Turkey who had no such far-flung commitments, interests and involvements overseas which then had their repercussions on relationships within NATO. For instance, the President had recently talked with the Foreign Minister of the Netherlands. The Netherlands wanted the United States to take very direct action with reference to certain matters in New Guinea, in other words in the involvement of the Netherlands with Indonesia, and the Netherlands regarded the United States attitude in this matter as a test of NATO. Other nations see other problems as a test of the solidarity of NATO.

The Chancellor stated that this was correct. He pointed out, however, that President Kennedy had inherited a great bulk of difficulties which had grown up during the past years because the United States had allowed them to grow up. Now it was the President's historic task to tackle these problems and to create again a true partnership atmosphere. The Chancellor knew that this was difficult, but he felt it was possible. However it required a great deal of patience. The Chancellor was aware of the fact that the American Administration is interested in talks with the USSR, and he feels that this is correct. He feels that the United States must try to see whether any success can be achieved with the Soviet Union as regards disarmament. However, as long as NATO is weak, the Chancellor predicts that there will be no success vis-à-vis the USSR. Success can be achieved only when the USSR sees that NATO, the Alliance of the free countries of the Western world, is strong and stands as one. He strongly feels that if President Kennedy accomplishes the task of rebuilding confidence in NATO, he will at the same time have achieved a step ahead in the direction of controlled disarmament.

The President indicated that he had hoped that the present Geneva talks might give some indication whether there were any favorable prospects for talks with the USSR on the topic of controlled disarmament. The last three weeks, however, had shown that there did not seem to be much hope on reaching any agreement on nuclear tests or talks this summer. If it was impossible to achieve any agreement on nuclear tests, which after all were rather easy to control and inspect, there was not too much point in hoping for any results in the field of general controlled disarmament.

At this point the Chancellor stated that as a new President Mr. Kennedy was testing the Russians to see whether there might be any give in them. Likewise the Russians were at present testing the President to see how hard he was or how firm be would stand. This was a matter that would take some time and require great patience.

The President stated that he was prepared to be patient but that it was impossible for the United States to agree on the Soviet Union's present conditions. Unless the Soviet Union gave some indication of changing its attitude by May, perhaps by the end of May, the United States would have to see how else to proceed and it might be necessary to discontinue the talks.

Chancellor Adenauer agreed that he also saw no need for keeping on trying indefinitely, but he felt that the present Russian attitude in Geneva was no proof at all that Russia did not want controlled disarmament. Chancellor Adenauer is convinced that the Russians are first of all Russian nationalists and only secondly Communists. He emphasized the nationalistic quality of the present Russian regime repeatedly. He pointed out that the Russians had fought more wars than any other single country over the years. The Chancellor indicated that he had brought along for the President a German book called *The Russian Perpetuum Mobile*. He hoped that someone would be able to translate for the President some of the more important passages of this very excellent book. It is a very interesting book which shows the real nature of the Russians, and again the Chancellor reiterated that the Russians are Russian nationalists first of all and this explains why Mr. Khrushchev does not want to come under Red Chinese domination. Only in second place is Mr. Khrushchev a Communist, and he is convinced that the capitalist nations are doomed anyway. But Khrushchev wants communism to rule under Russian leadership. However, he also knows that an all-out war will do no one any good, neither the victor nor the vanquished, and therefore he hopes that the Free World will just fall apart. As far as he is concerned the present conditions in NATO are proof that this will come about. If President Kennedy succeeds in changing the atmosphere around NATO he will have won an important step ahead vis-à-vis the Soviet Union.

The President came back to the previously discussed question of the strengthening of NATO and how external interests of the various member states affect the relations within NATO. Perhaps something could be done to achieve a more solid stand on all the previously mentioned problems such as Angola–Portugal, Congo–Belgium, United Kingdom–Red China, etc. The President was not so sure that even if such a more consolidated stand were achieved as regards the NATO member states Mr. Khrushchev would not find something to be pleased about anyhow.

Mr. Rusk at this point interjected the remark that the President has reference to Soviet efforts in the Far East to outflank the effectiveness of NATO by intensified programs of and to underdeveloped countries.

The Chancellor replied that this was, of course, another matter which could be discussed, but as far as he was concerned, he knew that a great many of the Soviet statistics concerning their aid to underdeveloped countries were sheer lies.

As regards NATO, perhaps it was best to let by-gones be by-gones, he said, but it was important to talk of the future and the leadership which the United States would assume to instill a new spirit into NATO. He felt that, as Mr. Acheson had informed him, the President's desire to see full consultation established was a very important step in the right direction. It was the first time that this intention had been so clearly stated. Never before had this been the case. The Chancellor felt that all NATO partners would welcome this step and that it would serve to increase and reestablish confidence in NATO.

The President stated that he felt very definitely that the North Atlantic Council should be strengthened. The appointment of Mr. Finletter to the Council was evidence of the American determination to strengthen this body. Mr. Finletter was a man of great experience who had held an important post in the Truman Administration. The President hoped that other nations too would choose equally qualified persons as their representatives in the North Atlantic Council, so that these would have the authority to speak on matters coming before the Council. He understood that this had not always been the case.

The Chancellor agreed that the level of the North Atlantic Council had to be raised in all respects. In closing, Secretary Rusk suggested that the afternoon meeting might perhaps be devoted to discussing the non-Western problems now facing the West and to an evaluation of how both the United States and Germany viewed Communist strategy in that area.[4]

---

[4] A memorandum of the discussion on NATO and Development Aid is in Department of State, Central Files, 033.62A11/4–1261; a memorandum of the discussion on Berlin on April 13 is in vol. XIV, pp. 45–51.

99.   Telegram From the Embassy in France to the Department of State

Paris, April 19, 1961, 7 p.m.

4494. I had lunch with Couve de Murville today after which we sat and talked for about a half hour about NATO problems. He wanted to talk about NATO because he believes this will probably be first item of interest in forthcoming Presidential talks. I found Couve's views unusually interesting, however, I am not sure at this point of extent to which they reflect view of de Gaulle. To some degree I suppose they do. First because Couve occasionally said, "and you will find this is what General de Gaulle thinks," and next there were several comments by Couve to effect that he does not have much background in nuclear-military matters, etc.

He began by saying that NATO as now conceived would have been a good organization after World War II although, in some respects, it would not have been entirely adequate then. Since then, much has changed. At first when United States was clearly ahead in nuclear weapons it could advocate strategy of nuclear retaliation if it were necessary to do this to save Europe from being overrun by Soviets. Now, however, he thinks that this strategy is entirely unrealistic. He said he believes this to be so for following reasons: If Soviets drive back our forces into Germany, let's say, and then into France, we will if necessary use tactical nuclear weapons against them. However, we will not use strategic weapons against USSR unless they use them against United States. (He defined strategic weapons as those that would be used against United States and against USSR, and tactical weapons as those used in military operations outside of either nation's land area.) He said it was entirely unrealistic to think that we would initiate use of strategic nuclear weapons merely because Germany or France were being overrun, in the first place, and now that Soviets have an abundance of large nuclear weapons it would be more unrealistic to assume that we would launch strategic nuclear weapons knowing that we were inviting nuclear retaliation. Conclusion that France has reached therefore is that warfare under NATO auspices will be fought in Western Europe and it will result in total destruction of Western Europe, and ultimately perhaps in a nuclear liberation of Western Europe with little of Western Europe left. With this prospect any nation in Western Europe is extremely reluctant to surrender responsibility for its own defense to NATO or anyone else. In first place, giving responsibility to anyone else, such as SACEUR, will cause a reaction within country that does so. He feels that they cannot

Source: Department of State, Central Files, 375/4–1961. Secret.

surrender this national responsibility without, in effect, losing their national will to defend themselves and their strength in world affairs. France therefore must consider its own responsibility to its own people in nuclear matters as well as other affairs and that without in any way detracting from high regard it has for NATO, and its willingness to support NATO, it must be ever mindful of its own national responsibilities. He discussed this view in very broad terms in an effort to arrive at an understanding of a solution that would be responsive to these conditions and satisfactory to France. This latter we were unable to do.

We then went on to talk about present tactical deployments in NATO. He said that General de Gaulle felt that they were too shallow, that they lacked realistic depth for missile age. I asked him if he felt that this implied the need for land areas of Spain and possibly North Africa. He said, absolutely, that General de Gaulle has said this and that he believes this. He said that in General de Gaulle's opinion Germany will very likely be overrun and battle of Western Europe will be decided in France. Again, we discussed possible solutions to dilemma that confronts General de Gaulle as he sees the situation and Couve could offer none. We agreed that I should talk to General de Gaulle about these problems as soon as this can be arranged. He said that he was not too concerned that nothing in way of specific solutions came out of our discussion today because he was very pleased that we were able to talk so frankly about problem, that to his knowledge it is first time it has ever been discussed by representatives of our two countries with such candor. I am not in a position to evaluate with exactness this last comment but I do think that conversation was well worthwhile and I intend to pursue it with General de Gaulle prior to the visit of President. I should add that Couve thought it would be a good idea to talk the matter over quite thoroughly with General de Gaulle and to see President if practicable, before he leaves us.

We concluded by talking a bit about skepticism currently prevalent in some of local press about forthcoming visit. There appears to be a feeling on part of some that little will be accomplished. We both agreed that it is of utmost importance that we accomplish some specific results at this meeting.

Gavin

100. Policy Directive

Washington, April 20, 1961.

NATO AND THE ATLANTIC NATIONS

I. Political

1. *Basic Political Policy:* The political nexus between North America and Western Europe—i.e., the Atlantic Community—is and must continue to be the foundation of U.S. foreign policy. The purpose of that policy is to maintain an environment in which free societies may flourish. The U.S. alone is not strong enough to maintain that environment, by holding Soviet military power in check and by making possible the development of the less developed countries within a free and open system.

NATO is the principal form which this coalition takes. It is of first importance to the U.S. to maintain its coherence and strength. To the Soviet Union first importance is given to disrupting it.

On the political side coherence is achieved through seeking a consensus among the allies on major policies. This means consulting frankly about policies which are still in a formative stage, and being willing to alter policies, if warranted, in the light of the discussion.

At the optimum a consensus should be agreement on common action in the best interests of the alliance as a whole; at the minimum it should be an understanding on how to handle a disagreement so as to cause the minimum damage to the coalition.

Source: Department of State, NSAMs: Lot 72 D 316, NSAM 40. Secret. Attached to the source text was a memorandum to the National Security Council from its Executive Secretary, dated April 24, which stated that it had been approved by the President on April 21 and transmitted for implementation by all appropriate Executive departments and agencies. The same day NSAM 40 directed that all members of the NSC having responsibilities in connection with its implementation should report their progress to the President from time to time. (Ibid.)

Following a suggestion by Merchant on January 30, Secretary of State Rusk had called former Secretary of State Dean Acheson on February 6 to ask him to chair a working group on NATO composed of Nitze, Finletter, Kohler, McGhee, and Fessenden among others. (Ibid., Rusk Files: Lot 72 D 192 and Central Files, 740.5/2–461) Acheson met with the President March 7 and 14 to discuss his thinking about the report (Memorandum of conversation; Kennedy Library, National Security Files, Staff Memoranda, Robert F. Komer) before submitting a draft of the report on March 24. (Ibid., President's Office Files, NATO General) The draft report was considered by the NSC on March 29, which recommended various changes and additions and in particular referred the draft policy directive to McGeorge Bundy for revision of nine of its paragraphs. (NSC Action No. 2405; ibid., National Security Files, NSC Meetings) Following these revisions, which affected about 10 percent of the directive, it was approved by the President.

2. *Particular Working Principles and Policies.* To a large extent, the miseries of colonial disengagement are behind us. Where colonial problems remain, however, they can become a fertile source of disagreement between the U.S. and its NATO allies. These problems usually arise publicly in the United Nations. All differences cannot be removed but their disruptive consequences can be reduced if the U.S. will:

a.   associate cooperatively with its allies in preparing remaining dependent areas politically, socially, and economically for their independence;

b.   aid any ally or its emerging dependent area in preparing for economic adjustments which may be necessary as their political relation changes;

c.   In the United Nations, the U.S. should continue to make clear that it believes in and looks forward to the independence of peoples now under colonial rule. In deciding on when and how to vote in the United Nations, a primary U.S. purpose should be to take action which will advance constructive solutions. The U.S. should seek allied agreement to the maximum extent feasible and, where such agreement cannot be obtained, at least assure that any U.S. action is preceded by full and frank consultation.

The U.S. should seek allied agreement on a sustained effort to remedy—in both dependent and newly independent areas—the deficiencies in civil and military competence, education, and economic development which are among the principal obstacles to successful independence. In pressing this effort, problems will sometimes arise out of special interests that some of our allies have in specific less developed areas. We should make a concerted effort, through consultative machinery, to reach agreements which will subordinate such special interests to the larger goal of denying these areas to chaos or Communism.

In thus leading the Atlantic nations in common action to meet the needs of the less developed world as a whole, the U.S. can help the Atlantic Community to see its task in larger terms, which will transcend differences on specific colonial issues, and which will enable its colonial or ex-colonial members to cease to regard the only alternatives as being to hang on to historic footholds to the bitter end or return to a limited European status.

One purpose of such genuine—and often abrasive—consultation in NATO should be to bring about this change in perspective and policy by our allies, by convincing them of our understanding of their problems. Other purposes are described in the Discussion of this paper, which should serve as a general guide to U.S. action in this field.

3. *European Integration and Beyond.* The U.S. should make clear its support for the movement toward European integration. The U.K. should not be encouraged to oppose or stay apart from that movement by doubts as to the U.S. attitude or by hopes of a "special" relation with

the U.S. The Six should be encouraged to welcome U.K. association with the Community and not to set the price too high for such association, providing that there is to be no weakening of essential ties among the Six.

The ultimate goal of the Atlantic nations should be to develop a genuine community, in which common institutions are increasingly developed to address common problems. Opportunities for moving in this direction may arise over time, and the Atlantic nations will be in a better position to exploit these opportunities if they are clear beforehand that this is the general direction in which they want to move. Such a Community should be capable of embracing Japan, at least in the economic sphere, at the earliest possible time. Over the long run, it might be open to other countries willing and able to share its responsibilities.

4. *Organization and Method.* The principal organ for consultation should be the North Atlantic Council. Two subordinate instruments may be helpful:

a. *NAC Committees.* The U.S. should encourage the Council to set up informal committees to address regional and functional problems. These committees' membership should be on the basis of national involvement, and their task should be to make policy recommendations—not necessarily based on unanimity—to the Council.

b. *NATO Policy Advisory Committee.* The U.S. should propose that the Council establish a Policy Advisory Committee to meet once or twice a year to seek a consensus on basic objectives and tasks, and to report that consensus and its appraisal of movement toward or away from those ends to the Council. This Committee might consist of 3–5 men of broad repute, who would not be national representatives.

II. Military

5. *A Pragmatic Doctrine.* The U.S. should urge that:

a. First priority be given, in NATO programs for the European area, to preparing for the more likely contingencies, i.e., those short of nuclear or massive non-nuclear attack.

b. NATO continue, under this pragmatic doctrine, to prepare to meet nuclear or massive non-nuclear attack in the theater—but not to a degree that would divert needed resources from non-nuclear theater programs to meet lesser threats or from programs to assure an ample and protected U.S. strategic power.

The U.S. should urge that this view be given effect by a constructive interpretation of existing doctrine, and that this doctrine only be rewritten if needed European energies and resources cannot be mobilized in any other way, and if it is clear that NATO agreement can be reached on a revision.

288 Foreign Relations, 1961–1963, Volume XIII

6. *Non-nuclear Forces.*

a. The U.S. should announce that the U.S. means to maintain its own divisions and supporting units in Europe. While these forces have as their primary objective the defense of the NATO area, certain of these forces may be required, temporarily and in exceptional cases, to meet limited military situations short of general war outside the NATO area.

b. The U.S. should propose that the objective of improving NATO's non-nuclear forces should be to create a capability for halting Soviet forces now in or rapidly deployable to Central Europe for a sufficient period to allow the Soviets to appreciate the wider risks of the course on which they are embarked. This program should emphasize raising the manning levels, modernizing the equipment, and improving the mobility of presently projected NATO non-nuclear forces. The U.S. should then press strongly for NATO execution of this program, as a matter of the highest priority. The U.S. should urge rapid progress toward building up a mobile task force to deal with threats to NATO flanks, as part of this program.

c. The U.S. should press for greater NATO research and development regarding non-nuclear weaponry, and for coordinated alliance-wide production of major military matériel. The U.S. should lead toward further coordination and integration of defense arrangements. It is particularly important to be responsive to strong German desires in this regard.

7. *Nuclear Forces.*

a. The President should state that an effective nuclear capability will be maintained in the European area and that nuclear weapons will not be withdrawn without adequate replacement. Nuclear weapons in NATO Europe may be regrouped as further studies may indicate.

b. Additional resources should be used to strengthen the nuclear capability now in Europe only where (i) ongoing programs are so far underway that they could not be changed without serious adverse political effects, or (ii) the increase will not divert needed resources from non-nuclear tasks and is clearly required to cover needs either for replacement or expansion that cannot be met from outside the theater. The 1963 MC–70 goals, as well as the proposed 1966 goals, should be reviewed by the State and Defense Departments from this standpoint.

c. The Secretary of Defense should undertake a study of the extent to which nuclear weapons in NATO Europe could be made more secure against unauthorized use. Consideration should be given, in this study, to the problem of control after initial use of nuclear weapons, as well as before. Some possible safeguards to be considered in such a study are discussed in the body of this report. These include making SACEUR headquarters and communications more secure against wartime disruption.

d. SACEUR procedures for ordering use of nuclear weapons, once he has been given political direction, should be clarified and made more explicit.

e. It is vital that the major part of U.S. nuclear power not be subject to veto. It is not essential that the part of that power deployed in Europe be veto-free. It is, however, most important to the U.S. that use of nuclear weapons by the forces of other powers in Europe should be subject to U.S. veto and control. Therefore, the concept of a veto by another than ourselves in Europe is not contrary to our interests.

f. The U.S. should suggest that the NATO Council try to work out general guidelines regarding the use of nuclear weapons or a political method for determining such use. The U.S. should undertake to observe any agreed guidelines or political method, insofar as feasible. Until some other indication of desire reaches him, the President should make entirely clear his intention to direct use of nuclear weapons if European NATO forces have been subjected to an unmistakable nuclear attack or are about to be overwhelmed by non-nuclear forces.

g. The U.S. should announce its intention to commit, say, five Polaris submarines to NATO for the life of the alliance, for use by the President in accordance with the procedures outlined above, except that the U.S. would remain free to use them in self-defense. The U.S. should commit additional sea-borne missiles deployed in the Atlantic or the Mediterranean to NATO, as they become available. The deployment and targeting of these missiles should be worked out jointly by NATO commands and the U.S., with appropriate participation by the Standing Group, so as to cover military targets in Europe in the degree that this could be done without change in projected U.S. military programs.

h. The U.S. should urge the U.K. to commit its strategic forces to NATO, in the same manner as suggested above for U.S. forces. Since the U.K. probably would be reluctant to do so unless the U.S. also committed such B–47 SAC forces as it decides to station in the U.K. to NATO, we should seriously consider the possibility of taking such action in a manner which would maintain the essential mission and U.S. control of these forces.

i. Over the long run, it would be desirable if the British decided to phase out of the nuclear deterrent business. If the development of Skybolt is not warranted for U.S. purposes alone, the U.S. should not prolong the life of the V-Bomber force by this or other means.

j. The U.S. should not assist the French to attain a nuclear weapons capability, but should seek to respond to the French interest in matters nuclear in the other ways indicated above.

k. If the European NATO countries wish to expand the NATO sea-borne missile force, *after* completion of the 1962–66 non-nuclear build-up, the U.S. should then be willing to discuss the possibility of some multilateral contribution by them. The U.S. should insist, in any such discussion, on the need to avoid (i) national ownership or control of MRBM forces; (ii) any weakening of centralized command and control over these forces; (iii) any diversion of required resources from non-nuclear programs. The U.S. should not facilitate European production of MRBMs or procurement of MRBMs for European national forces, whether or not these forces are committed to SACEUR.

8. *Procedures*. The U.S. should lay before the NAC the general guidelines that it believes should govern future NATO military programs, based on the pragmatic doctrine suggested in this report.

If allied agreement to these guidelines can be secured, the NATO military commanders should be asked by the Council to design alternative programs that would be consistent with these guidelines and with two levels of resource availabilities: one corresponding to present levels of military spending, and one projecting as significant an increase as seems realistically feasible, in order to elicit increased NATO effort. (As part of such an increased NATO effort, U.S. military aid would probably need to be increased and should include provision of advanced non-nuclear weapons—instead of emphasizing nuclear weapons as heavily as at present.) On the basis of the NATO commanders' replies, a decision could be made as to the size and nature of future NATO programs that would be designed to fulfill the strategy outlined in this report.

III. Economic

Conclusions

9. *Purpose*. The OECD should be the principal means of achieving needed coordination between the financial, aid, and trade policies of Europe and North America and, eventually, of Japan. Its object should be to achieve higher rates of growth in some Atlantic countries and a larger allocation of resources to important tasks facing the Atlantic Community. This will require that the OECD develop organs which are capable not only of serving as forums for discussion but also of developing joint decisions and, in some cases, joint programs.

10. *Fiscal and Monetary Policy*. In the fiscal field, the U.S. and other Atlantic nations should be prepared to discuss and coordinate their most sensitive internal economic policies, e.g., interest rates. Some of this coordination should be achieved within smaller groupings of the OECD. An OECD Monetary Committee might be set up for this purpose.

11. *Aid to Less Developed Areas*. The U.S. should urge the OECD to undertake specific functions to promote modernization of less developed areas through three subsidiary organs:

a. The Development Assistance Group should seek both to recommend the increased levels of aid that various donor countries should provide and to ensure that the most urgent needs of specific less developed areas are taken care of in a coordinated fashion.

b. An Atlantic program—possibly involving establishment of an Atlantic Development Center—should be mounted under OECD auspices, on a mixed public-private basis, to promote (i) assistance to less developed countries in their development planning; (ii) certain kinds of technical aid to and exchanges with less developed countries; (iii) the training and recruiting of qualified young people from other Atlantic nations (to match the U.S. Peace Corps) for service in these countries; (iv) research in both Atlantic and less developed nations on key development problems.

c. A multilateral program of aid to the less developed countries of the Atlantic Community—Greece, Turkey, Cyprus, Spain, and Portugal—be mounted under OECD auspices, either by using the European Fund of the EMA or by establishing a new OECD fund for this purpose.

12. *Trade.* The U.S. should maintain high level representation at meetings of the Trade Committee of the OECD. Without impinging on the functions of the GATT, the U.S. should encourage wide-ranging discussion within this Committee.

13. *The Common Burden.* The costs of the military programs and the economic aid discussed under II and III, above, should be shared equitably by the members of the alliance.

a. The *amount* of these shares should reflect the differing resource capacities of these members. NATO and the OECD both offer forums in which this can be discussed.

b. The *form* of these shares should reflect these countries' balance of payments positions. For example, countries with favorable balance of payments might try to buy military equipment from countries less well situated and might, where appropriate, make joint military facilities and services available to the forces of such countries on especially advantageous terms.

---

101. Telegram From the Embassy in France to the Department of State

Paris, April 20, 1961, 9 p.m.

4522. For President and Secretary from Dean Acheson. This afternoon I spent an hour to the exact minute with General de Gaulle. The Ambassador and I concluded that I should go alone. I began by expressing the pleasure and honor that had been done me by receiving me and said that just a little bit short of twenty years ago as a junior officer of the

Source: Department of State, Central Files, 611.51/4–2061. Secret; Priority.

Department of State I had among my duties drafting speeches for Secretary Hull; that I invariably put into these speeches favorable remarks about the "free French" only to have them struck out by Secretary Hull. General de Gaulle said he was quite aware of Mr. Hull's feelings and he had followed my career long enough to know that I was a friend of France. With this we started to work.

I said that President Kennedy and the Secretary had asked me to preside over a group of officers of the Departments of State, Defense and Treasury charged with making recommendations for NATO policy. This had been done, they had met and reported to the President. He had indicated that he received the report favorably and was considering it, but was keeping his mind open until he had several important talks, one which was his forthcoming talk with General de Gaulle.

First as to political policy: We had recommended that full consultation with our NATO allies should be held within NATO on questions without regard to their geographical origin. This would not in any way preclude or interfere with the regular channels of diplomacy which would perhaps be even more important as multilateral discussions encountered difficulties. We hoped to listen as well as talk and we hoped that our own views and those of our allies would be influenced by the discussions. At this point the General said, "is this possible?"

I replied that no one could tell until the attempt had been fairly made. He said that he thought this was a mistaken use of NATO which had been created for a wholly different purpose, was a purely military alliance and not a proper forum for discussions of the type I had mentioned. I replied that the General was undoubtedly right as to both history and logic but that we Americans had often found that if something worked it was desirable to use it even though it was illogical and unhistorical. He indicated some skepticism at this suggestion and spoke of the importance of the three major powers consulting with one another.

I pointed out that this was wholly possible within the recommendation we had made since that included the possibility of informal discussions in small groups before matters were introduced into the full Council, illustrating with the fact that the British, French, Dutch and ourselves all had more concern with the problem which Castro was creating than with some of our other European Allies and that in Africa for instance the British, French, Portuguese, Belgians and ourselves all had interests.

General de Gaulle said that it was most important for France, Britain and the US to discuss matters together and then together attempt to influence the course of events. For instance, in the Congo he thought if there had been tripartite consideration of the question well in advance, the three nations could have prevented the Belgians from doing many foolish things and could perhaps have restrained the Congolese when the time finally came for them to run their own affairs. The same, he said, was true of Angola. He thought the Portuguese had made and were making many mistakes and that we, by our unfortunate vote, had encouraged the demagogues in the UN to make even more trouble for the unfortunate Portuguese. I said that I would not be insincere enough to defend the American vote, which I had criticized quite freely at home, but I pointed out that what he wished to accomplish could be accomplished if we would do just what I suggested, using the mechanism of NATO where we had these allies present and where they had been accustomed to discussions not as formal as conversations in major diplomatic capitals would be.

General de Gaulle then observed that in his opinion the US had a curious tendency to wish always to act as a member of some sort of group, whereas a state must have its own policy and that the purpose of diplomacy was to bring divergent views of states into accord. I stated that this was clearly right and was a view which I had often expressed when the last US administration seemed to believe that it should go to the United Nations in order to find out what its own policy was, but I believed that by bringing to the NATO Council or to groups within it, national policies they could be more easily harmonized by men who knew one another and were accustomed to working together than by the more conventional and laborious method of discussion in four or five or six capitals. I added that if the US Govt showed a tendency to wish to act with others, it was a tendency which our Allies should not discourage. Isolationism was all too easy for us and was by no means dead yet in the United States.

I then asked the General's permission to turn to military matters. In our consideration and recommendations in this field we had been influenced by two major considerations. One was that the decisions of 1956 and 1957 to introduce tactical nuclear weapons into NATO armaments had been wise during a period when the Soviet Union did not have such weapons. But now that the weapons are possessed on both sides it left the West in a dangerous state of weakness to be able to react with nuclear weapons. This made for inaction in the event of such crises as trouble over Berlin or West German difficulties or the problem of another Hungary. The General said he was wholly in accord with this view and thought that we suffered from this weakness now.

Our other principal consideration had been expressed by General Norstad in his statement that it was desirable to raise the threshold over which nuclear weapons would be used, to bring about a last chance for a reflection and to give the opportunity for making a decision to use such weapons by high political authorities in a deliberate manner. The General again agreed with this purpose.

I said further that another purpose of our recommendation was to correct an impression given last December that the presence of American forces in Europe might depend upon our balance of payments situation. The present administration had no such idea. Therefore, one of our recommendations had already been carried out by the President when he assured the Military Committee that American forces in Europe would not be withdrawn.[1] We had also recommended that priority should be given to attaining a non-nuclear capability sufficient to stop Soviet forces now stationed in Eastern Germany plus such reserve strength as could be quickly added. We believed that the MC–70[2] forces would accomplish this provided that they were armed with modern non-nuclear weapons and given mobility. This could not be fully achieved until the General had achieved his much-to-be-hoped-for results in Algeria.

When success had been achieved in Algeria and French troops returned to French soil, the MC–70 goals would be well within sight and it would also seem evident that France must play a great part in the military forces which could defend Western Europe. (I was much interested that the General followed what I said very closely and required very little translation. Only in the most closely reasoned sentences with technical terms did he ask for help from the interpreter.)

I pointed out that there was no idea of fighting a long conventional war in Europe or of attempting to extricate the US from the defense of Europe. As he would see, the intention was quite the opposite.

We then passed on to nuclear weapons. I said that here again I believed that the President was prepared to assure our European Allies that no nuclear weapons would be withdrawn from Europe, that others would be added, and that so far as he was concerned, they would be used in the event that nuclear weapons were used against Europe [2 lines of source text not declassified]. We had given considerable thought to the problem of intermediate or medium-range missiles. It had seemed to us that for the time being this need could be met by a fulfillment of the previous administration's offer of five Polaris submarines with their weapons, and, indeed, we had recommended that others be added as they became available, should our allies wish them. The idea would be that they would be assigned to the defense of Europe, would not be removed for other purposes unless replaced, and would be used as I have already stated [less than 1 line of source text not declassified] or by some

---

[1] For text of President Kennedy's remarks to the Military Committee on April 10, see *Public Papers of the Presidents of the United States: John F. Kennedy, 1961*, pp. 254–256.

[2] See footnote 2, Document 98.

method of political decision which we were willing to work out with our Allies. Several suggestions had been made.

One, that general rules should be laid down, and would be carried out by some high political person or persons through the Supreme Commander.

Another that a small war cabinet be authorized to make these decisions.

Third, that a system of weighted voting might be used.

We had no preconceptions and were willing to discuss this fully and freely.

General de Gaulle asked where the nuclear forces in England would fit in under the general plan I had suggested. I replied that it was our recommendation and hope that both the British bomber command, the ICBM's and our own B–47's in England would all be assigned to the defense of the NATO area.

[1 paragraph (16-1/2 lines of source text) not declassified]

I ended by saying again that President Kennedy had all of these matters under consideration, would wish to discuss them with General de Gaulle and wished him to have full opportunity for full consideration before their discussions. The General said that he appreciated this courtesy very much, would give these matters his deepest thought and would look forward to discussing them with the President.

Gavin

---

102. Telegram From the Mission to the North Atlantic Treaty Organization and European Regional Organizations to the Department of State

Paris, April 22, 1961, 6 p.m.

Polto 1484. Mr. Acheson met with NAC in private session April 21. Prefaced his remarks by stating his work with Washington study group reviewing NATO policy done as private citizen in association with officers of State, Defense and Treasury, etc. Group had no idea of revising policy but recognized importance of looking at situation to see what had changed and of ensuring all Departments followed same policy line.

Source: Department of State, Central Files, 375/4–2261. Secret. Repeated to all NATO capitals.

Not his place to discuss proposals of US Government as this was task of Ambassador Finletter. He proposed, therefore, to talk about considerations and thinking underlying recommendations of study group.

Group thought first of all in terms bringing NATO back to primary position in US foreign policy. No doubt in 1949 that treaty which linked American Continent and Western Europe was keystone of US foreign policy. In ensuing years, however, this view of NATO had been more honored in statements than in actions. Important conclusion of group is how US should act on this principle. Many obstacles to this in US as in other countries, especially in implications for domestic policy. Group thought principal points on which difficulties arise are largely in UN, relations with peoples of less developed areas, and formulation military policy.

Group considered problems insoluble unless they fully discussed and talked out. Best place for this in North Atlantic Council where Ambassadors well acquainted with each other and more inclined to talk frankly than elsewhere, live in close proximity with each other and can discuss problems informally prior to meetings, and where security record of organization is very high. US study group was impressed that NATO organization lends itself admirably to consultation on problems arising not only in treaty area but outside. Such consultation in Council did not exclude regular channels of diplomacy which often advantageous.

Acheson pointed out that for fruitful consultation, necessary for participants to listen with view to altering their judgements as appropriate. Also, since NAC is Council of governments, country raising question should have formulated point of view, be prepared to state it, have it criticized and be influenced by views of others.

Acheson emphasized it height of folly for countries to go to UN in times of trouble to have policy made for them. If they had no ideas, policy in UN would be determined largely by new states quite ignorant of subject matter. Moreover, policy is watered down in UN to lowest common denominator. Asserted UN not glittering hope of world as some think, though it plays important role. Stressed NATO, if ready create military and national will for defense, is more likely than any other organization to be central hope of world. Believed it was erroneous to think, as some countries, there is choice between policy of standing by allies and sympathy with people of less developed areas. There is no hope for peoples of these areas unless members of NATO alliance stand together for defense and use economic power to assist less developed areas within framework of free system.

Against this background of ideas, Washington study group agreed NATO should be made central but not necessarily final point of decision. In some cases, agreement might not be possible but unity of alliances should be maintained and point established beyond which disagreement should not go. Also NATO consultation should antici- pate, to extent possible, events before they happen which would make agreement easier when action necessary. Above all, necessary to be practical and not be worried by inability to agree on ideological relation- ships. Important thing is to be together on practical steps that can be taken immediately, e.g. in less developed areas, should be prepared to take action re education, economic development etc., that can exert strong influence in these areas and help choke off impractical resolu- tions in UN. Stressed NATO nations too great and too powerful to be called on to vote in UN on abstract questions having no useful purpose. Also pointed out NATO nations among themselves should not avoid discussing matters for ideological reasons. Pointed out for example, Monroe Doctrine no reason why Cuba should not be discussed in NATO Council.

Turning to military matters, pointed out Soviets now have tactical nuclear weapons and advantage which West had held in 1956–57 now has been equalized. As indicated in various Norstad speeches, West now going back to idea threshold must be raised before nuclear weap- ons used. Important to be able to enforce pause for reflection as to whether nuclear weapons should be used. These questions raised in UK paper on long-range planning. Thinking of Washington group had started at this point with emphasis on necessity to make decision. Felt that if conventional arms must be strengthened, it should be done by modernizing existing forces where needed, making them more mobile, and bringing them to MC–70 goals. Acheson stated this should not be difficult if De Gaulle, as all hoped, secured Algerian settlement and when German divisions brought up to strength. Further effort also re- quired by other members of alliance. Required, however, setting of pri- orities, not to extent of displacement of "other things" (i.e. nuclear weapons) but with a priority on conventional buildup not present in past.

In approaching these problems, Acheson made clear, as President had recently stated to military committee, American forces and nuclear weapons would not be withdrawn from Europe. It was less clear, how- ever, how we should move in nuclear field than in conventional field. There was idea emphasis should be on water-borne rather than land- based missiles. While decision on this point beyond his competence, Acheson stressed we currently have water-borne missiles and not MRBMs and from practical point of view, therefore, should use what we have while we consider other measures.

Turning to question of political control, Acheson recognized na- tional feeling in some countries [that] they must have voice in military decisions re use of nuclear weapons. Question one of establishing general guidelines within framework political authority. Various ideas had been expressed as how this to be done. While stating Ambassador Finletter would convey views, Acheson emphasized there should be no doubt there will be powerful weapons assigned to NATO, that these would be used under circumstances and rules endorsed by Council and that there is absolute certainty that if there is nuclear attack in Europe, US will respond with all weapons at its command. Idea of nuclear war between Europe and USSR in which US would not become involved too fantastic to believe. [1-1/2 lines of source text not declassified] Defense of Europe and US completely linked. Problem is how we must meet such an attack if it occurs, acting rapidly but not too rashly. Acheson emphasized Council must study this with help of military advisers and SHAPE. Stressed that with two times as many people and three times Soviets' industrial production, inability to oppose USSR would be due weakness in will, not resources.

Acheson's statement was well received by all delegations which expressed appreciation clear US statement on determination maintain its forces in Europe and utilize all its power in event Europe were attacked. In other comments, Belgium emphasized dependence of smaller countries on support of their allies in UN and elsewhere, impossibility for smaller countries to maintain all three arms of military defense and suggestion such countries might concentrate on those elements of defense most appropriate. In this connection referred to General De Gaulle's statement[1] but drew opposite conclusion smaller countries alone could not provide for their national defense. Belgium also raised question of leadership, emphasizing need for great powers to let smaller allies know about problems, discuss them and suggest solutions. Rejected idea of any Directorate outside NAC. Acheson, in reply, stated problem of greater integration in military forces had been discussed since May 1950 but with little progress. While US certainly not to blame for this, hoped new Secretary General would take up this problem. Acheson strongly stressed responsibility of NAC, as civilian authority, to take action in these fields and exercise control. Said it was because of default of NAC to do so that SHAPE is only place problem being faced. Pointed out there no possibility of getting defense we need in NATO if each NATO country seeks to become complete military power.

UK expressed essential agreement with Acheson's statement but emphasized in line with previous statements in the Council, that essential thing is to think of deterrent in terms of stopping wars rather than winning them. For this, necessary deterrent be credible, efficient, unified, of correct type and one we can afford. Task of NATO was to decide

---

[1] Not further identified.

how this could be done, keeping in mind necessary balance between conventional and nuclear armaments. Acheson, in response, emphasized danger of attempting distinguish between NATO forces that can deter and those that can win war. Emphasized force that will deter must be in fact force that will win. Must think in terms of force that will inflict great damage in case of attack and suffer as little damage as possible in return.

Greece took opportunity to emphasize need for stepped-up "psychological warfare" on part NATO governments, citing Communist advances in Cuba as case in point. Acheson agreed. French PermRep welcomed Acheson's statement on maintenance US troops in Europe which he felt to be essential element of European security. Indicated, however, De Gaulle difference with Belgium on question of organizing national defense.

Portugal agreed with Acheson's statements reference UN. Took occasion to point out despite several statements made by Portugal in Council and most recently April 20 statement,[2] eight NATO countries had voted against Portugal in April 20 UNGA vote on Angola. Pointed out again this was question of vital importance for Portugal which could have adverse repercussions for overseas territories, for Portugal and alliance as whole. Mr. Acheson expressed his personal agreement.

Norway welcomed Acheson statement as indicating no need for any change in structure of NATO. Norway felt it futile attempt strengthen NATO through organizational devices since present structure entirely adequate. Reference vote in UN, pointed to statement in report to Council on Kennedy–Macmillan talks[3] which indicated there might be some advantage in having divergent views expressed by NATO members in UN. Netherlands called attention to various suggestions which had been made for great integration of defense of Benelux countries. Welcomed Acheson's support of this type of integrated defense, but, in lightly veiled dig at France, said it was impossible to convince populations reference need for integration if no assurance others willing to cooperate.

Finletter

---

[2] The U.S. Mission summarized this statement in Polto 1467, April 20. (Department of State, Central Files, 375/4–2061)

[3] Macmillan visited Washington April 4–9. The statement under reference has not been identified further, but Finletter had reported to the Council on the Kennedy–Macmillan talks on April 12. (Polto 1412 from Paris, April 12; ibid., 611.41/4–1261)

103.   Telegram From the Department of State to the Embassy in the United Kingdom

Washington, May 5, 1961, 9:44 p.m.

5217. London's 4450 rptd info Paris Topol 41.[1] We are concerned re implications of statements reftel that problem of nuclear weapons "partnership" is for exclusive tripartite (US, UK and French) consideration and is not appropriate for NATO consideration. We agree that question cannot be dealt with definitively at Ministerial Meeting at Oslo but matter is clearly of concern to NATO as a whole and US approach to NATO Strategy and Defense Planning (Topol 1526)[2] based on this premise. Statements reftel and other recent public comments this subject by UK also carry unfortunate implication that nuclear weapons policy towards France should now be changed because she has become nuclear power. This is of course not the case. [8-1/2 lines of source text not declassified]

Embassy should use foregoing with FonOff and express hope that UK can see its way in future statements this regard to avoid tripartite connotations and emphasize importance of finding solution to questions within NATO context.

Rusk

Source: Department of State, Central Files, 740.5611/5–361. Secret; Limit Distribution. Drafted by Magill (EUR/RA); cleared with Fessenden, Owen, Furnas, WE, and BNA; and approved by Kohler. Repeated to Paris and Bonn.

[1] Topol 41, May 3, reported various statements made by Gaitskell and Macmillan during the debate in the House of Commons on May 2. (Ibid.)

[2] Topol 1526, April 25, transmitted the text of a presentation to be made to the North Atlantic Council on NATO strategy and defense that was a summary of the Policy Directive on NATO (Document 100). (Department of State, Central Files, 375/4–2561) Finletter made the presentation to the North Atlantic Council on April 26, circulated it as a U.S. paper, and reported that the presentation was generally well-received and regarded as the opening of a new stage of NATO consideration of strategy and defense. (Polto 1501, April 27; ibid., 375.74/4–2761)

104.   Telegram From Secretary of State Rusk to the Department of State

Oslo, May 10, 1961, 6 p.m.

Secto 54. Eyes only for the President. Before going on to Geneva[1] I want to give you some reflections on my first NATO Ministerial Conference and the contacts I have made here in Oslo.

1. I think our decision to encourage effective consultation by talking less about how to consult and just starting consulting has paid off. In my opening statement[2] I tried to be in some ways almost brutally frank about world problems, notably Cuba, Laos and the Congo. My colleagues from the other countries responded in kind. These exchanges were even-tempered and moderated by understanding. The old timers, both US and foreign, say that it is the most open and intimate political discussion in NATO within their memories.

2. On the whole I think there was a sophisticated understanding about Cuba. My frankness with respect to the "failure" may have disturbed them somewhat. Even Canadian Foreign Minister Green, who unquestionably came prepared to be critical, expressed understanding and a willingness to be helpful at the end.

3. The new Secretary General, Dirk Stikker, handled the meetings superbly well both in open session and in behind-the-scenes spade work. I think we can be very pleased and look forward to good results during his tenure.

4. On all sides there were expressions of appreciation for the firm expression of US intent to maintain its forces in Europe and to be prepared to use the nuclear deterrent in defense of the entire NATO area. I had the feeling that European uneasiness in this respect has somewhat lessened.

5. Despite Cuba and Laos I believe basic confidence in our leadership and desire for its vigorous exercise are in no way lessened. In particular almost everyone reflected to me the great impression that you have made in this initial period not only in the foreign field but also in the lines of your domestic program.

6. I leave also with the strong feeling that in NATO we have a really vital asset.

Rusk

Source: Department of State, Central Files, 396.1–OS/5–1061. Secret; Niact.

[1] For the 14-nation conference on Laos, May 12–20.

[2] Verbatim records, U.S. delegation summary telegraphic reports, memoranda of conversations, position papers, and briefings for the North Atlantic Council meeting held at Oslo, May 8–10, are in Department of State, Conference Files: Lot 65 D 533, CF 1855–1867.

105.   Circular Telegram From the Department of State to Certain Missions

Washington, May 12, 1961, 10:02 p.m.

1793. Following guidance for use (along with final Communiqué)[1] in briefing Governments as well as SEATO and CENTO on NATO Ministerial meeting Oslo May 8–10:

1. Oslo meeting was highly successful opportunity for Secretary, representing new U.S. Administration, engage in far-reaching, frank and lively discussion of major international issues with other NATO FonMins. While non-military aspects of internal development of Alliance, including future evolution of political consultation, were discussed, primary focus was on actual practice of political consultation at Ministerial level. Throughout, Secretary stressed US desire that other members freely raise questions and comment on any subject of significance.

2. In discussion of international situation, there was broad acceptance of US view that militant Soviet initiatives stemming from Moscow December 1[2] declaration of Communist parties, and as evidenced in Africa, Southeast Asia, Cuba and UN must be thought of and dealt with as part of overall confrontation. Free world–Soviet bloc issues are now at stake in all parts of world and neither can nor should be thought of in isolation. (Acceptance this thought is reflected in Communiqué.) While making serious, sober appraisal of world situation, US stressed importance disabuse Khrushchev of any idea West would accept additional setbacks. Growing strength of free world provides firm basis for action toward this end and this fact also reflected in Communiqué.

3. Strong Communiqué statement on Berlin makes clear West will insist on Western rights Berlin including access irrespective of Soviet action.

4. Re nuclear test talks, there was clear recognition that Soviets have raised new obstacles to successful conclusion current negotiations, that West must not allow itself to become victim of a hoax and that if talks should fail (despite comprehensive and reasonable draft treaty presented by U.S. and U.K.) it must be made clear to public that responsibility rests fully with USSR. There was also recognition that Soviet in-

---

Source: Department of State, Central Files, 396.1–OS/5–1261. Confidential. Drafted by Lehmann (EUR/RA), cleared by Fessenden, and approved by Kohler. Transmitted to 55 missions.

[1] For text of the final communiqué, see *American Foreign Policy: Current Documents, 1961*, pp. 483–485.

[2] For text of the Declaration of the Conference of Communist Parties, see *Pravda* or *Izvestiia*, December 2, 1960.

transigeance on key issue of international control in enforcing a test agreement does not augur well for disarmament negotiations.

5. Discussion of developments in Congo, Southeast Asia and Cuba was not intended affect primacy of other Organizations (UN, SEATO and OAS) in dealing with situations these areas, but was in recognition of fact these either are or involve manifestations of single world-wide threat.

6. Colonial question was discussed in Council and bilaterally by Secretary with Portuguese and Belgians.[3] While in colonial questions there are bound to be some differences of opinion, result these discussions was improved understanding of issues and viewpoints involved. No commitments re colonial questions were made but U.S. considers that as result these discussions we are in better position than previously to bring our influence to bear constructively on difficulties as they arise.

7. Both general discussion and specific decisions re internal development of Alliance, particularly in political consultation but also in future economic role of NATO, Civil Defense Planning and information field emphasized need for anticipatory consultation on member country policies in order facilitate rapid consultation on specific issues either in or outside of NATO as questions arise.

8. There is general agreement OECD is primary framework for Atlantic Community consultation on economic policies and means increasing development assistance. Recognition of importance NATO member countries attach to increased development assistance also reflected in Communiqué.

9. No discussion future development NATO military posture was contemplated for Oslo and none took place. However, in context Secretary's overall presentation on future development of Alliance Secretary briefly referred to (a) U.S. determination maintain its forces in Europe (b) need strengthen NATO conventional capabilities (c) need maintain NATO nuclear capability and (d) U.S. intention commit Polaris submarines to defense European NATO area. U.S. plans re strengthening Alliance defense posture were presented to NAC by Ambassador Finletter in late April and will require thorough consideration in Permanent Council. Para 11 of Communiqué reflects recognition by Ministers of this fact.

10. *For Ankara and Bangkok:* CENTO and SEATO briefings should be coordinated with your NATO colleagues.

Bowles

---

[3] For a record of the conversation with Nogueira, see Document 338. No record of the discussion with the Belgians has been found.

106. Letter From the Permanent Representative to the North Atlantic Council (Finletter) to President Kennedy

Paris, May 29, 1961.

DEAR MR. PRESIDENT: I am enormously grateful to you for the photograph. Thank you very much.

I think the time has come for me to give you my impressions about NATO and how the U.S. policy in NATO is working.

The new NATO Secretary General, Dirk Stikker, is coming to Washington in mid-June, and I am planning to accompany him. This letter may be of some value to you as a background for the Secretary General's visit.

1. First, as to military policy, and particularly the prospect of getting the NATO Allies to accept your policies on NATO military matters.

I think we can get what we want. I think we can get the changes in NATO military programs for 1962 through 1966, the safeguards against unauthorized use of atomic weapons, the political control over their use, and all the rest of the policies which have come about as the result of the recent review of NATO policy which you approved.

But I think it important to point out that our Allies are not going to follow our suggestions docilely. They have ideas of their own.

Generally speaking, there are two main lines of resistance:

First, a desire not to change the existing political directive or the existing military programs for the years 1962–66. There is a powerful attitude in the national governments, the Standing Group, the Military Committee, and generally throughout the NATO structure which seeks to keep NATO military planning and the control of that planning exactly as they have been in the past. This inertia is strong—more so than I had anticipated. We in the United States are in a new Administration, but NATO is not.

Second, there is a fear in many of the countries that any change in the present arrangements will cost them more money. Most of the countries are satisfied with the military arrangements as they are, and are not convinced that changes—especially those which would increase their national budgets—are necessary. Most of our Allies understand that the most important military goal is not to have a war, and while they do not say so, I have the impression they believe that only the U.S. Strategic Deterrent can do that; and that the Shield Forces are strong enough as

---

Source: Kennedy Library, National Security Files, NATO. Secret; Official–Informal. Finletter sent a copy of this letter to Rusk on May 30. (Department of State, Central Files, 375/5–3061)

they now are to carry out what, to their way of thinking, is a mission of secondary importance.

Certain countries have individual resistances to our proposals. The Germans do not like the idea of the "pause", which we have given as a major reason for the strengthening of the conventional forces. The Germans see themselves, correctly, in the front line of any battle for Europe. They fear the pause we are talking about will be a pause for the rest of the Alliance but not for the Germans. They fear the Russians may get the idea they can attack the NATO German forces with impunity—that is, without fear of being hurt by atomic weapons—if the U.S. views prevail. With time we can talk them out of this unreasonable fear, but it will not be too easy.

The Turks and, to a lesser extent, the Greeks also object to the new emphasis on conventional weapons. Being exposed and away from the bulk of NATO military power, they fear the new U.S. thinking will be a temptation to the Russians to walk over them with conventional forces. They would like to see our policy be to use tactical nuclear weapons from the beginning—for this would make for the minimum of temptation to the Russians to attack them.

The British also will have questions about our new policy. I think their basic purposes are (a) to avoid any further demands for British manpower, and (b) to prevent increases in the U.K. military budget. The British have eliminated conscription and probably cannot make a substantial increase in manpower without restoring it. And they do not want to spend more money on their troops abroad, largely for balance-of-payments reasons. Further, the British are well informed in these matters and will subject every item of our policy to skillful and close examination.

I think there will be French resistance to an increased emphasis on conventional forces. Their determination to have a nuclear force puts them in the position of giving first priority to nuclear weapons.

The Italians, having accepted IRBM's stationed on Italian soil (an important political fact in Italy), also may be lukewarm about our emphasis on conventional weapons.

The Norwegians and the Danes, on the other hand, like our new emphasis on conventional weapons.

I have as yet no clear indications as to the views of the other Allies.

2. More serious than these questions of individual attitudes is the difficulty that we will not be able to put the new U.S. policy into effect unless we can establish workable machinery for civilian political control of the force and manning levels and weapon systems of the NATO defense force.

It is sometimes not easy to achieve civilian political control of this kind within a single country. It is vastly more difficult in an alliance of fifteen countries.

Here we run up against a tradition deeply imbedded in NATO. So far, no system for proper civilian political control has been established in NATO. There has been the appearance of it, but not the reality. It will not be an easy task to achieve it, but I am convinced that with your support, it can be done.

The practice heretofore has been that the North Atlantic Council would write a political directive within which the military authorities (the Commanders, the Military Committee, and the Standing Group) would establish the requirements. In a formal sense, this looks like political control, but in fact it is not. For generalities are not what count in military programming and policy making. What do count are the actual decisions as to the forces and weapons to be provided. The power to decide the application of policy is the power to decide the policy itself.

Unfortunately, there is a tendency to preserve this formal and unrealistic approach to military programming in NATO.

There are two ideas at work which I think particularly damaging. One is that the role of the civilian authorities is to be limited to having the North Atlantic Council adopt "guidelines" or "political directives" which theoretically are to be followed by the military authorities. If this practice is continued, the military authorities will in fact make political policy with little impact of civilian views on it.

The other idea is that civilian responsibility in military programming is limited to fiscal considerations. Under this approach, the military men would make up a list of requirements, and the civilian authorities would say only how much of these requirements the various countries could afford. This view is, in my opinion, wholly erroneous because it omits the most important element of civilian control—the impact of political considerations upon the level and kind of forces and weapons. Political considerations are present in any military planning decision; they are particularly important in the planning of a NATO force. The responsibility for decisions as to these political matters should not be put upon the military men because of a failure of the political authorities to carry out their responsibilities.

What is needed, I think, is clear. It is that some permanent institutional arrangement be set up to carry on a continuing review of NATO military planning by the civilian and military NATO authorities, each applying his own area of expertise and responsibility. Under such a system, the NATO civilians would apply the political and the fiscal considerations, and the military authorities would apply the military expertise; and out of the combined continuing effort should come a composite result which would be militarily sound, fiscally possible, and, politically, would give effect to the policies which you have approved.

How to achieve this combined continuing study of programming is something else. I will not attempt to go into details on the various possibilities in this letter. It is enough to say that I am convinced it should be and can be done.

3. On the question of political consultation, I am pleased with the way the Council is going. As a result largely of the vigorous support you have given to NATO, the practice of consultation has been doing very well. Your policy was stated strongly in Oslo by Secretary Rusk, and I hear on all sides gratification of the U.S. leadership which he showed in this regard at the Ministerial Meeting. U.S. willingness to discuss anything of concern to the Alliance, regardless of what or where it is, has much encouraged the Allies and much strengthened the Alliance.

I must add also that the "backstopping" which we in Paris have had from the Bureau of European Affairs, from Mr. Foy Kohler, head of this Bureau, and from the Office of Regional Affairs, and from Mr. Russell Fessenden and others in this Office has been of great value to us.

Much, however, remains to be done. I am not at all satisfied with present political consultation in the Council. There is too much demand by our Allies for the facts of immediate negotiations. What is needed is discussion of the substance while policy is being developed and before it reaches the stage of negotiation with other countries.

We have accordingly asked the Secretary General to establish agenda items for the Council which will achieve this effect of having policy debated while it is being evolved. I think there is real will on the part of our Allies to do this, but, again, it will take time and persuasion.

4. I would like to say a word about the economic arrangements of this Mission.

The essence of the various policy statements which you have made about the Atlantic community is generally, as I understand it, that we need to bind together the human, material and political resources of the North Atlantic area into a closer and more powerful community—all to the end of bringing its great potential power to bear in the world struggle.

Granted this objective, it is important that all the functions of community be brought together in coordinated power.

NATO has already begun this by adding the political function of consultation to its originally purely military work. It would be a serious mistake, I think, if we were not to bring the economic function also into the common task.

Because of the presence of the five neutrals in OECD (Sweden, Switzerland, Ireland, Spain and Austria), in addition to the fifteen countries which are also members of NATO, it is appropriate that the OECD's part in the economic functions of the North Atlantic be located in that organization. I doubt if the five neutral countries in OECD really feel as much neutrality between communism and non-communism as is sometimes claimed, but I understand the need for this organizational division of economic functions.

Nevertheless, I think it important that a close relation between NATO be maintained with the OECD.

This is true not only because of the importance of coordinated action in the development of the functions of the North Atlantic community, but also because as a practical matter it is extremely difficult to separate the economic functions of NATO and the OECD.

It is sometimes not recognized that even with the OECD in being, NATO must retain those economic functions which involve obvious conflict with the Sino-Soviet Bloc.

For example, on May 18 at a meeting of the Committee on Economic Affairs of the North Atlantic Council, the following items were on the agenda:

a) Credits to the Soviet Bloc;
b) East-West Trade—General Problems of Trade with the Soviet Bloc;
c) East-West Trade—Exchange of Information on Commercial Negotiations with the Soviet Bloc;
d) Report on Heavy Ruble and New Soviet Rate of Exchange;
e) Implementation of Iceland Stabilization Program;
f) UK-USSR Commercial Negotiations;
g) Problems of the Coordinating Committee in Connection with Standards for the Limiting of Strategic Exports to the Communist Bloc;
h) Exchange of Documents with SEATO and CENTO Relative to Trade with the Communist Bloc;
i) Soviet Oil; and
j) Economic Mission to Greece and Turkey.

These agenda items show, I submit, that the NATO functions in the economic field which cannot be handled by an organization with neutrals in it are of considerable importance.

For these reasons I respectfully urge that the present relationship between this Mission (USRO) and the OEEC be carried on with OECD after the OECD is ratified by the other countries and comes into being. The arrangement, as you know, is that although I am accredited to the OEEC as the U.S. observer, Mr. Tuthill of my USRO staff, with the personal rank of Ambassador, represents the United States in all meetings of the OEEC Council (other than ministerial meetings); that I represent the United States in the NATO Council; but that the two operations are within a single mission called USRO, of which I am the chief.

In practice, my relationship to Ambassador Tuthill is essentially that of coordination. I know the broad lines of what are going on, as he keeps me fully informed. We see to it that the economic functions of NATO and the OEEC are carried out in such a way that there is not only no conflict but there is also affirmative coordination. The system is now working well, and I would hope very much that it would not be changed when the OECD is set up.

Respectfully yours,

Thomas K. Finletter

---

107. Memorandum of Conversation

US/MC/4   Paris, June 1, 1961, 3:30 p.m.

PRESIDENT'S VISIT
Paris, May 31–June 2, 1961

PARTICIPANTS

United States   *France*

President Kennedy[1]   General de Gaulle
Mr. Glenn (Interpreter)   Mr. Lebel (Interpreter)

NATO

General de Gaulle opened by mentioning that the questions of Angola and of Latin America had been discussed in the morning meeting.[2] What is now the pleasure of the President?

The President said that an important subject of this session is NATO and the manner in which this Alliance could be made stronger

---

Source: Department of State, Conference Files: Lot 66 D 110, CF 1891. Secret. Drafted by Glenn. The meeting was held at the Elysée Palace.

[1] Kennedy visited Paris May 31–June 2 before his meeting in Vienna with Khrushchev. For a memorandum of his conversation with de Gaulle on the Common Market, see Document 11. For de Gaulle's account of the visit, see *Memoires d'Espoir, Le Renouveau, 1958–1962*, pp. 267–271.

[2] A memorandum of the conversation during the morning, US/MC/3, is in Department of State, Conference Files: Lot 66 D 110, CF 1891.

and more efficient, or possibly, what other instrument might be conceived in preference to NATO to insure common defense.

General de Gaulle said that he wanted to discuss this very important question with utmost frankness. NATO is in fact two different things: first an Alliance, second an organization. No one questions the need for the Alliance. There is complete agreement on this subject. There might possibly be some discussion whether it would not be useful to make it clear that this Alliance which was forged for the defense of Europe extends also to other parts of the world. This, however, is something which it is almost unnecessary to say because it is quite clear that if war were to break out regardless where, the Alliance would still be operative.

The second aspect of NATO is that of an organization which grew upon the Alliance. This organization was based on two principles: First, the fact that at the time, nearly eleven years ago, when the Alliance was established, the U.S. had the practical monopoly of nuclear weapons. Therefore, the essence of the organization was a defense of Europe by American nuclear weapons. There were, of course, also some additional means of defense, a shield of conventional forces, the purpose of which was to gain enough time to permit the deployment of the American nuclear forces. All of this was perfectly natural at the time. The other principle upon which this organization was based was the weakness of the European powers. Speaking for France, the General said that France at that time was weak. She was weak economically, a prey to political disorder and having lost international influence. She was no longer a great power and had no ambitions to become one again. She could not live by herself either in war or even in peace. Germany was in a similar situation. She had been defeated. She was militarily, morally, and politically weak and devoid of national ambition. This still applies to a large extent to Germany because even though Germany is now very productive and economically strong, she has a "broken back" as a nation because of moral condemnation under which she still lives. Likewise for Italy. Italy has also made great progress in production but has not regained national ambition. In contrast to the European powers, the U.S. was intact and strong. The U.S. had the means and therefore the ambition to assume the position of leadership. These circumstances were implemented as two organizational principles. First, NATO was an American defense of Europe. Second, in consequence, such European contributions that could be made to that American defense of Europe were integrated under American leadership.

But the situation has greatly changed since eleven years ago. First of all there is no longer a nuclear monopoly. On the contrary, the Soviets and the Americans are more or less equal and each can destroy the other. As a consequence, the U.S. is now in danger and in consequence of the danger of being destroyed (even while destroying Russia) the U.S. will find it extremely difficult to make the decision to use nuclear weapons. Of course, such a decision will be easy to take if the Soviets do not strike with nuclear weapons then the U.S. might not strike either. It is, in particular, not clear whether if the Soviets launch an aggression by purely conventional means, whether the U.S. will be the first one to use nuclear weapons. Thirdly, the U.S. is committed not only in Europe; alongside with crises such as that of Berlin, there might arise crises in Africa, Asia, in Latin America, and elsewhere. The very simple idea which equated defense with the defense of Europe no longer applies. This has changed the situation in regard to the defense of Europe and Europe herself has also changed. France is now a little stronger than she was (although the General is not under any illusions that she is genuinely strong yet) but the fact is that she has gained some strength in the economic field and in the political field. She even has some means of defense.

(She is, of course, still encumbered by the Algerian situation and by the last stages of decolonization, but this is about over.)

There is also a difference in French psychology. Eleven years ago France had given up all ambition. Today she has again some ambition as a nation. This brings about a need to consider the position in regard to French national defense. The fact that a country with strong traditions and even strong military traditions does not have its own military defense is something which is bound to be greatly disliked. There is no national defense in Europe today but only integrated defense under U.S. command. This is not acceptable to France.

One might think of some incident such as the recent one in which some generals had revolted for a short time against the Government. The causes of the mentality of the generals who disobeyed their Government may be due to the fact that defense had become denationalized and since the generals did not have the responsibility for French national defense (being under international command) they did not see fit to obey a Government to which they were no longer used to be directly answerable.

(The General did not wish to imply that the revolt of the generals was encouraged in any way by NATO or directly caused by NATO but simply that the state of mind of the generals in respect to the Government was to a large extent due to the supranational character of defense in Europe.)

France sees that defense is no longer national defense and France does not accept it. It is difficult for the French to have a stable state and a stable Government under any circumstances and it is almost impossible to have them without a feeling that the Government is responsible for national defense. If the people do not feel that the State and the Government fulfill that part, it will not obey the Government. That is why France cannot continue under a system of integrated defense and without her own responsibility in the field of defense.

What is more, the absence of national defense is not good for the Alliance itself. The war, if it comes, will be terrible and cannot be waged without the full support of the people. Therefore, it is necessary to re-establish national defense. This, of course, within the Alliance and with mutual help between the members of the Alliance. Such help is, of course, traditional in history as the U.S. has shown it at various times. However, the defense of France must once again be French defense.

Of course, we are at present in an atmosphere of an international crisis, at a time when the President is about to see Mr. Khrushchev and where the possibility of unpleasantness over Berlin is very real. France does not have any intention of weakening NATO at this moment but France wishes for a different type of organization for the future.

This also could be based on two axioms. The first one is that it is not certain that the U.S. will strike first with atomic weapons. Second, that in Europe the bigger of the European powers (for the smaller ones do not really count) should have their own national defense.

Of course, in speaking of the nuclear situation one has to take into account the opinion according to which there is a difference between tactical and strategic nuclear weapons and that tactical weapons would be used immediately even if strategic ones were not. The General does not think that this distinction is very real. If it were real, however, then what would be the consequences? Western and Central Europe would be laid waste by Soviet and American tactical nuclear weapons respectively, while both Russia and the U.S. remain unscathed. There is nothing in such a possibility to make Europe very happy. Moreover, it is rather doubtful that once a first step in the use of nuclear weapons is taken, the second one and the last one would not be taken also.

In the last and final analysis, the General believes that American nuclear power remains a major part of the defense of the free world and it would be good that power be not only maintained but even strengthened. It is, however, something to be used only in the last resort. As for the defense of Europe, it should be assured by the European countries, not without the U.S., of course, but not exclusively through the U.S. The major European powers such as France, Germany, and up to a point Italy, should develop their own national defenses. The U.K. already has some national defense of its own. This is what France wants and this is what France will develop as soon as the Algerian business is over. In the European defense (which would receive U.S. help), each major country should play a special part. The smaller countries count for very little and it is a mistake of NATO to assign an equal place to every nation, large or small. The roles of the major powers would be coordinated, Germany being the vanguard, France the second line of defense, Britain covering the northern flank and insuring communication by sea, and Italy covering the southeast in the Alps. As for the U.S., it would be the reserve to be committed fully but not at the first moment. As President Roosevelt had said the part of the U.S. is to be the arsenal of democracy. In each case, each country would be acting according to its nature and its traditions. This, of course, is in the case of a non-nuclear war. There can be no nuclear war, only total nuclear destruction. It is clear, of course, that each country will play its part with the help of the others but, nevertheless, within the system of its own national defense.

The President said that he would like to reply with equal frankness. For the United States, as well as in his own personal opinion, the defense of Europe and the defense of the United States are one and the same thing. The loss of the resources and the manpower of Europe and the possibility that these might be taken over by the enemy would spell a certain defeat for the United States. This was the American position in both World Wars and today this is clear to all Americans. [5-1/2 *lines of source text not declassified*] This is one of the reasons why American troops were placed in Europe so as to make the Soviets understand that any attack by them on the European allies would be physically and automatically an attack on the United States. [4 *lines of source text not declassified*]

[1 *paragraph (5 lines of source text) not declassified*]

It might be true that there are some psychological advantages in strictly national defense establishments. Yet, the problems created by integration could not be solved by national defense establishments. Among the countries of Europe only Germany, France, and the U.K. could possibly afford nuclear weapons. In such a case, this would not resolve the psychological doubts of the other nations which would then tend towards neutralism in such a way that the entire Alliance would fall apart.

General de Gaulle interrupted the President saying that he did not have in mind national defense establishments which would include nuclear weapons. Not only the number of countries which could afford such weapons would be small, but also Germany is legally prevented from having any, and the disadvantages deriving from German possession of atomic weapons would be far greater than the advantages.

The President said that he had inferred that President de Gaulle wanted to see atomic weapons in national arsenals. This is, however, a misunderstanding and, as a result, the President requested that a part of his remarks not be interpreted.

The President asked, however, that some remarks dealing with the possible placing of U.S. atomic weapons at the disposal of the Alliance be interpreted:

There is consideration on the part of the United States to transfer some atomic weapons to NATO control as a means of strengthening NATO unity and mutual trust of NATO members. Such a transfer would create difficult problems of command. Who in fact would give an order that such weapons be used? The President would be willing to see General de Gaulle be the spokesman of Europe in respect to solving this question.

It is only if the will to use nuclear weapons in case of necessity is obvious that the Soviets will believe in the deterrent which such weapons represent. The problem is how to build trust within NATO and deterrents without.

The President said that there are two different questions before us. The first one is the French decision to obtain an independent nuclear capability. A decision seems to have been taken on this point. The second question is quite different. This is the question of defense of Europe. It is quite certain that countries such as Italy, Turkey, and Greece will not have a nuclear capability and, therefore, will have to depend on the guarantee of others for their defense. There is no conflict between the first and the second question. The point is how to strengthen the Alliance. If France has a nuclear capability of her own, she may add her guarantee to that of the United States. The point remains that such a guarantee wherever it comes from must be trusted by friend and foe alike in order to be effective. If there is no trust, the Germans may say that they are not confident that the French will use their atomic bomb in order to protect the Germans in the same way in which it is heard that France does not have the confidence that the U.S. will use its nuclear capability in order to defend France. There is no end to such implications and the problem still remains with us. How shall we solve it?

General de Gaulle said that he quite agrees with the President that it would be good to make the Soviets believe that American atomic weapons will be used in the defense of Europe. The General is by no means certain that the Soviets do believe that. Furthermore, he is not certain that even the United States believes it, or that Turkey and Greece believe it. Likewise, no one believes that any country will place its atomic weapons in the hands of others. This is why he does not ask the United States for atomic weapons, either in the form of a gift of weapons or in the form of help in developing them. France would not either give her nuclear weapons to anyone once she has them. This is simply because those weapons are too frightful.

The President reaffirmed [4 lines of source text not declassified] the defense of Europe is a necessity for the United States. Once again, the problem is how to convince others of the seriousness of one's own intent. When France has nuclear weapons, how will she convince the Germans of her intent to use them in the common cause? How will she create that confidence which we are trying to create now and which is the only thing that can discourage the Soviets?

General de Gaulle said that it was not his impression that the U.S. would never use nuclear weapons but only that the U.S. would use nuclear weapons in the sole case where it felt its territory directly threatened. The same thing in his opinion applies to the Soviets and to France when France has nuclear weapons. Now the President says that for the United States, U.S. territory and European territory are one and the same thing from the point of view of defense. "Since you say so, Mr. President, I believe you," but still, can one be certain? At what moment will the U.S. consider that the situation calls for the use of atomic weapons? One hears that the United States intends to raise the threshold for the use of atomic weapons. This must mean that the United States has decided that such weapons will not be used in all cases. When are they going to be used? This is the question which preoccupies Europe. It is not known at what point they will be used and the General feels that if he were in the President's place, he would not know that either.

The President said that the raising of the threshold for the use of atomic weapons simply means an attempt at obtaining better control of those very widely dispersed weapons. At the present moment, some U.S. companies and certain U.S. battalions have nuclear capabilities. This means that a local unpleasantness, for example Berlin, might lead to the use of atomic weapons. It is only to improve control over the use of such weapons that the U.S. seeks to increase its conventional capabilities and raise the threshold for the necessity of using nuclear weapons [2-1/2 lines of source text not declassified]. Raising the threshold does not mean decreasing U.S. commitments but merely increasing effective control.

The President thanked General de Gaulle for the views which the latter presented with such frankness. He wanted, however, to underscore that there was a great difference between the United States in World War I or World War II and the United States today. Even far in World War II, the United States was still isolationist but at the time of the Korean war, the United States moved in unhesitatingly. This should be a cause of confidence for America's allies and what is most essential now is to strengthen the mutual confidence of the allies because only this could make the Soviets realize that we mean business.

General de Gaulle said that he certainly was quite willing to convince the Soviets of the seriousness of our intent. For the rest, he expressed his appreciation to the President for the frankness and the conviction with which the latter stated the U.S. views. This is something on which conversation should continue in the future or even from now on. There is another point which the General would like to make. That is, that in the present crisis situation, France will do nothing to weaken NATO even though she may have some concern about the overall validity of the way in which NATO is organized.

The President thanked the General for his presentation of this important question of which the President would like to continue discussing the next morning. He would like in particular to come to grips with the question on the manner in which trust could be fostered since the same arguments which are used to say that U.S. nuclear weapons might not be used for common defense can be used also for other cases as, for instance, between France and Germany.

General de Gaulle said that some geographical considerations must be taken into account in the latter case. The Rhine is much narrower than the Atlantic and, therefore, France might feel more intimately tied to German defense than we might feel tied to French defense. It is fine if geographical considerations may make the French guarantee more trusted by the Germans. The fact remains that our problem is how to foster more trust within the Alliance since we cannot suffer from an excess of it.

108.   Memorandum of Conversation

Washington, June 14, 1961, 3:31 p.m.[1]

SUBJECT

NATO Defense Strategy and Planning

PARTICIPANTS

Mr. Dirk Stikker, Secretary-General, NATO
The Secretary
The Under Secretary
Mr. Dean Acheson
Mr. A. Saint-Mleux, NATO International Staff
Ambassador Thomas K. Finletter
Mr. George C. McGhee, Counselor & Chairman of Policy Planning

---

Source: Department of State, Central Files, 375/6–1461. Secret. Drafted by Magill, initialed by Kohler, and approved in S on June 26.

[1] The time of the meeting is from Rusk's Appointment Book. (Johnson Library)

Mr. Foy D. Kohler, Assistant Secretary for European Affairs
Mr. Paul Nitze, Assistant Secretary of Defense
Mr. Russell Fessenden, Director RA
Mr. Robert N. Magill, Deputy Director RA

The Secretary asked Ambassador Finletter for his views as to how he thought the U.S. "Green Book" proposals[2] should be worked out in NATO. Ambassador Finletter characterized existing procedures for the development of military requirements and programs, pointing out that the role of the Council under this procedure was an extremely general and limited one. He said this procedure was in effect being challenged by the U.S. "Green Book" policy. The U.S. approach was one that we wanted to negotiate with our Allies in NATO, not rigidly, but with conviction. These negotiations should not be a general theoretical exercise but should deal with the practical problems involved. The main problem in Ambassador Finletter's view was how to conduct these negotiations and translate agreement on general principles into concrete programs. He and Mr. Stikker were consulting intensively in an effort to evolve a procedure for this purpose. Ambassador Finletter noted that one of the key problems was how the Council should work with the NATO Military Authorities and with which military authorities. He hoped that a dialogue between the Council and the Military Authorities could be arranged and thought that real progress was being made in Paris toward this objective.

Mr. Stikker agreed but said the progress was slow. The problem as he saw it lay in the apparent conflict between existing and proposed military requirements on the one hand, and the application of the U.S. April 26 paper[3] on the other. He pointed out that SACEUR and SACLANT were proceeding to brief Ministers of Defense on their proposed 1966 requirements (MC–96)[4] while the Council was considering the U.S. paper of April 26. This created a confusing situation which should not exist. Mr. Stikker emphasized that he and the Council were not equipped to pass judgment on the relative merits of the April 26 paper and MC–96, and that the Council must have competent advice in order to have a basis for judgment. In the absence of a convincing new judgment, European NATO Governments would not be willing to commit themselves to any significant changes in defense programs. [*9 lines of source text not declassified*]

Ambassador Finletter agreed with these observations but said many countries had not been doing what they should in the past be-

---

[2] Under reference here is the Acheson report (see the source note, Document 100), which had a green cover in the final draft approved by the President.

[3] See footnote 2, Document 103.

[4] Not found.

cause they were not persuaded that the existing military requirements were essential. He thought it was necessary for us to translate the Green Book into new and convincing requirements and said that the U.S. Delegation in Paris was studying this problem urgently with the able assistance of Mr. Levy. If the results of these studies could not be agreed in the Council, the U.S. Delegation would refer the views of other governments back to Washington for further consideration. Mr. Stikker interjected that this process must also involve a dialogue with the military authorities. The Secretary asked Mr. Nitze whether the studies referred to by Ambassador Finletter were being guided by the Defense Department. Mr. Nitze said Defense had issued no instructions to Paris and that the USRO studies were being conducted independently.

Mr. Kohler referred in this connection to Mr. Stikker's observation, made earlier in the day, that he obtained very little information from the Standing Group.[5] Mr. Stikker elaborated this point, explaining that he now obtained almost none of the Standing Group papers that he had previously received as the Netherlands representative. He added that he could not, of course, become an expert on military questions in such a manner as to put him in conflict with SACEUR's judgment. He thought it would be extremely dangerous to degrade SACEUR whose role in Europe was extremely influential and in whom the Europeans rested great confidence for their defense. The Secretary asked whether it was not generally believed in Europe that General Norstad spoke for the U.S. Government. Mr. Stikker said this was not the case at all and that General Norstad was regarded as an international commander with a completely independent status.

The Secretary wondered whether other NATO Governments would be prepared to make their positions known in the Council or would use the existing uncertain situation as an excuse for delaying any increased defense effort. Mr. Stikker felt the latter would be the case. Ambassador Finletter said there was really no alternative but to continue to follow existing procedures for the time being. We must carry forward on the basis of existing requirements until new requirements are developed. Mr. Stikker doubted that any progress could be made on the basis of existing requirements because everyone knew that MC–70 was no longer valid and that the proposed MC–96 requirements would not be approved. The Secretary asked whether we were not working at cross purposes in that the Commanders were pursuing MC–96 while the Council was trying to study the new U.S. approach. Ambassador Finletter reiterated that we should not interfere with existing proce-

---

[5] A memorandum of Stikker's conversation with Kohler is in Department of State, Central Files, 375/6–1461.

dures as this would create a vacuum. He hoped that Secretary McNamara would be able to bring proposals to Paris in July for a modification of MC–96 and that these proposals could then be discussed in NATO. He was sure that the U.K. would also be proposing modifications. Mr. Stikker said that a U.S. paper with concrete force proposals was needed as soon as possible as a means of starting a dialogue. The Secretary asked whether this paper should really be a U.S. paper. He said that he had thought the next move was up to the Europeans. If the U.S. were to submit another paper, he was afraid the U.S. might then be so committed as to confront other NATO members with a "take it or leave it" position. Mr. Stikker said he would like to be able to study the U.S. paper privately before it was submitted to the Council. The Secretary pointed out that the U.S. had not decided whether it should put in another paper as the next step.

Mr. Acheson thought a U.S. paper would be helpful to the Council in coming to grips with the problem in concrete terms. He said that in the past the Council had been able to provide only generalized directives to the Military Authorities and that SHAPE had then gone ahead and done whatever it wanted to do. If the Council and the International Staff were given the competence to deal with the practical aspects of the problem, this process could be reversed. Ambassador Finletter said he shared the Secretary's concern regarding the possibility of undue U.S. pressure but thought this could be avoided through the attitude adopted by the U.S. The U.S. should welcome the concrete views of other members and be prepared to take them fully into account.

Mr. Stikker thought that after the U.S. paper was ready, the International Staff could consider how it might best be presented, either as a U.S. or as an International Staff paper. The Secretary explained that his concern was partly with respect to the scope of the U.S. paper. He thought it would be inappropriate for the U.S. at this stage to be definitive regarding the use of nuclear weapons because we were looking to our Allies for suggestions in this regard. On the other hand, it would be appropriate for the U.S. to be more specific in its views on NATO force requirements. The Secretary asked when the U.S. paper would be ready. Mr. Nitze said it was not due until July 15 in first draft and that it would have to be completed in time for Secretary McNamara to take it to Paris for his July 25 meeting with General Norstad. The Secretary observed that if the U.S. was able to reach solid conclusions in its paper, we would have to press hard to obtain the necessary action from other NATO members. Mr. Stikker agreed but said it was important to remember that each Government had its own parliamentary problems and hard political decisions to make. Ambassador Finletter commented that progress would necessarily be gradual and that we could not assume overnight changes.

Mr. Nitze said he had been thinking the Council should give a directive to the Military Authorities so that they could be working on the problem concurrently with Council consideration of military requirements. The Secretary felt the Council's guidance to the Military Authorities should be clear and precise. Ambassador Finletter agreed with this and said that USRO had been trying to frame careful questions which the Council could use to get the right answers from the Military Authorities. There should be no loopholes. The Secretary asked when the new requirements would replace the proposed MC–96 requirements. Ambassador Finletter thought the new requirements would differ significantly from MC–96, particularly with respect to MRBMs. However, the MC–96 requirements for 1962, which formed the basis for this year's Annual Review, do not involve any significant change as compared with present requirements. He anticipated that it would take some time to negotiate acceptance of the U.S. paper and that there probably would be confusion during this period, but that major changes would eventually be made.

Mr. Stikker thought there would be major problems involved in making basic changes. If certain force requirements were deleted, the Military Authorities would want to offset the reduction with other types of forces and equipment. For example, if MRBMs were sharply reduced, there would be a greatly increased requirement for manned strike aircraft. He pointed out that delays in resolution of these problems would create increasing difficulties and confusion. SACEUR would be persuading Ministries of Defense of the importance of his proposed MC–96 requirements. However, SACEUR must not be inhibited in his efforts as that would derogate SACEUR. Ambassador Finletter agreed fully, but thought the International Staff should be strengthened to play a more important role in the process. Mr. Gregh is now struggling almost alone. The Secretary observed that the central problem seemed to be one of drawing together in NATO national decisions on NATO programs and relating these to a collective judgment regarding the nature and magnitude of the force structure NATO needs. Mr. Kohler commented that we must keep in mind the utility of U.S. military assistance in persuading governments to make an increased effort toward meeting military requirements.

The Secretary asked Mr. Stikker if it would be useful for the U.S. to provide him with someone of great stature who could help him with military planning after the U.S. paper had been made available. Mr. Stikker observed that this was now Mr. Gregh's function. Mr. Kohler said that he admired Mr. Gregh, but that he and his staff were not equipped for the job that must be done. Mr. Stikker thought it would be helpful to have someone at a very high level who could work effectively with him in bringing pressure to bear on governments. Ambassador

Finletter cautioned against derogating the function of the Council, emphasizing that the Council must not be permitted to deal only in generalities but must get down to specific problems. Mr. Acheson thought it would be useful for the U.S. to submit a paper giving a concrete application of its views. If the Secretary-General were then provided with staff assistance competent in this field, he would be in a position to make a realistic assessment for the Council.

109. Record of Meeting Between President Kennedy and the Permanent Representative to the North Atlantic Council (Finletter)

Washington, June 14, 1961, 5 p.m.

Also present: Secretary Rusk, Mr. Acheson, Deputy Secretary Gilpatric, Assistant Secretary Nitze, Assistant Secretary Kohler, Mr. Rostow, Mr. Owen.

1. Mr. Finletter emphasized the need for greater civilian control by the North Atlantic Council over NATO military programs.

2. Secretary Rusk indicated that Mr. Stikker might wish to strengthen his International Staff to facilitate civilian control. Mr. Stikker had spoken of the possible need for a high level assistant who would help him in negotiating NATO military programs with individual NATO countries.

3. Mr. Finletter spoke of the differences between General Norstad's views and the new U.S. policy which Mr. Finletter was representing. The President asked for a fuller description of these differences. Secretary Rusk, Mr. Acheson, and Mr. Nitze indicated that they centered on, but were not limited to, General Norstad's desire for 500 land based MRBMs. This desire was inconsistent with existing U.S. policy, which holds that there is enough nuclear power already programmed for Europe and that a large new MRBM program would absorb such energies and resources as to prevent needed improvement in existing conventional forces.

4. The President stressed the importance of making clear to the Europeans that the projected improvement in conventional forces did not imply any weakening in its use of nuclear weapons. He asked that a letter to General Norstad be prepared making the point.

Source: Kennedy Library, National Security Files, NATO. Secret. No drafting information appears on the source text.

110.   Record of Meeting Between President Kennedy and the Secretary General of NATO (Stikker)

Washington, June 16, 1961, 11 a.m.

Also present: Mr. Finletter, Mr. Acheson, Undersecretary Bowles, Assistant Secretary Kohler, Assistant Secretary Nitze, Mr. Owen.

1.   Mr. Stikker said that it would be hard to get Continental acceptance of the proposed improvement of non-nuclear forces (with which he agreed) unless the Continental countries felt that adequate nuclear power was being deployed on the Continent. He spoke of the need to ensure that the previously proposed Mace missiles would be replaced by more modern missiles, e.g., land based MRBMs.

2.   It was indicated that the Pershing missiles (which have a shorter range than MRBM's, and cannot reach the USSR) would be deployed on the Continent.

3.   Mr. Stikker said that he hoped that the most modern missile system (whatever it might be) would be deployed on the Continent.

4.   The President indicated that the question of MRBM's was for the fairly distant future and that, for the present, the alliance should face up to immediate tasks, e.g., improving existing forces. The President said that we were developing our own views about the specific goals which needed to be attained and would communicate them to the alliance about mid-July. In doing so, we would indicate that our views were of course, subject to change in the light of our allies' desires. He stressed this point.

5.   Mr. Stikker suggested that perhaps the discussion of NATO strategy should be deferred, so as not to create differences in NATO at a time of crisis over Berlin. Mr. Finletter felt the discussion should go forward, and that discussion of concrete programs—rather than generalities—would strengthen the alliance.

6.   The President stressed that the proposed improvement in conventional forces did not imply any weakening of the nuclear deterrent. He asked Mr. Stikker to emphasize this point, whenever he could. The President emphasized that the improvement of non-nuclear forces was not a new policy; it was simply trying to fulfill a policy to which NATO was already committed. No one would argue that existing non-nuclear forces were adequate. The non-nuclear build-up would complement nuclear forces—not replace them. Very great nuclear power was already deployed in Europe.

Source: Kennedy Library, National Security Files, NATO. Secret. No drafting information appears on the source text.

7. The conversation then turned to Berlin. The President suggested that this should be the main issue for all of us in the period ahead. The need for firmness was stressed. There was some discussion of European attitudes and of what Chancellor Adenauer's position would be at the height of the crisis. Mr. Acheson suggested that the Chancellor sometimes seemed ready to accept the division of Germany, and at other times seemed to make German unification a major objective of his policy. It was agreed that the latest Ulbright statement made Communist intentions regarding Berlin more clear than Khrushchev had done.

8. The meeting concluded with Mr. Stikker asking about the President's discussion of NATO with General de Gaulle. The President reported that the General had not changed his basic views about NATO, but that the General had indicated that he would not press his views this year, while the Berlin crisis was festering.

---

111.   Telegram From the Embassy in Germany to the Department of State

Bonn, July 5, 1961, 9 p.m.

21. Paris for USRO. Ambassador Finletter and I called on Chancellor this afternoon primarily for discussion NATO long-term planning. Following points emerged:

I.   After full discussion of subject, it was generally agreed, with strong concurrence from Chancellor, that Berlin Question and long-term planning for NATO were separable problems, and we should not allow Khrushchev's artificial crisis re Berlin to interfere in slightest with our planning for 1962–1966 forces for NATO. Chancellor said latter should proceed serenely and without being disturbed by Khrushchev. He saw no reason why discussion among Allies of their long-term plans should have any result other than to strengthen Alliance.

II.   On organizational side of NATO, Chancellor made quite a point of need for strengthening Secretary General's staff. We pointed out to him that you had already assured Stikker US would do everything it

Source: Department of State, Central Files, 375/7–561. Secret; Limit Distribution. Repeated to Paris.

could to strengthen his staff and generally to assist him. Finletter said he was already in touch with Secretary General in Paris for purpose of working out details of doing so. Chancellor seemed satisfied with this.

III. Chancellor wanted to know if we thought NATO was capable of carrying out its functions properly with present organization. Finletter said he felt organization should be strengthened, but not reorganized. This, by the way, was exactly same answer which Stikker told Finletter he had given Chancellor when question was raised during his visit with Chancellor last week. We both said we felt the important thing was for the leaders of the Alliance to be in general agreement on what they were trying to do, that if they were and if the ideas were good, there would be little problem of the Alliance moving ahead. Chancellor seemed reasonably satisfied with this answer.

IV. We gained impression Chancellor is reasonably well satisfied with US approach to NATO military planning, although, as in other matters, he will need reassurance from time to time. We went into pretty full discussion of purpose of American emphasis on conventional weapons and covered much same ground which Acheson had gone over previously.[1]

One question, however, arose. Chancellor seemed to have misunderstood, or to have remembered incorrectly, a remark by Henry Kissinger re missile gap.[2] While Kissinger was no doubt talking solely about missiles, Chancellor seemed to think that he had admitted there was overall deficiency in American strategic Air Force and accordingly US was vulnerable to a Russian atomic attack during period 1961–1963. Chancellor appeared to be reassured on this point as result of our discussion.

V. Chancellor made flat statement that since death of John Foster Dulles he had not been kept properly informed about condition of American military strength. My impression, after some discussion, was that what Chancellor was really concerned about was our nuclear strength and specifically number and location of nuclear warheads in NATO area, although his remarks referred to American military strength generally. We assured him that within limits of law he would be kept fully informed. This raises question of some importance which we hope you will consider. Meanwhile, I shall follow up with view to obtaining more precise idea of Chancellor's desires in this field.

VI. Chancellor also raised question of de Gaulle's attitude toward Alliance. He said he felt main trouble with de Gaulle was his feeling that

---

[1] See Document 97.

[2] A summary of Kissinger's conversation with Adenauer on May 18 was transmitted in airgram G–1278, May 19. (Department of State, Central Files, 375/5–1961)

NATO had no control over its nuclear forces. Control was, for practical purposes, in hands of Americans, and other Allies had no real say over their own destiny. There followed long discussion of possibility of enmeshing Allies more firmly into Alliance. We pointed out that the President had declared defense of NATO was indivisible, and that he had indicated his willingness to consider any policy which gave credence to this indivisibility. We explained US was taking position it had open mind re any proposals by Allies for NATO control over nuclear weapons. We referred to the President's Ottawa speech,[3] and said US was willing to look at any proposals for creation of NATO MRBM force offered by Allies. We hoped, in fact, there would be suggestions from them, and thereafter discussion of proposals in NAC. Chancellor emphasized that progress must be made in this area. He was careful to stress there was no distrust of US, but he pointed to what he regarded as interregnum during American Presidential elections and at one point reminded US that last President of US had gone so far as to suggest some withdrawal of American forces from Europe as an economy measure.

Chancellor then went on to say he believed if proposals for enmeshment of major Allies into affairs and commitments of Alliance could be put forward, this very well might have effect of breaking de Gaulle's resistance to full participation in NATO. He said FedRep would be anxious to work along these lines with US.

VII. At conclusion of conversation, Chancellor thanked Finletter for coming to Bonn and remarked that this was best discussion he had on NATO in long time.

Dowling

---

[3] For text of President Kennedy's address to the Canadian Parliament, May 17, see *Public Papers of the Presidents of the United States: John F. Kennedy, 1961*, pp. 382–387.

112.　Memorandum of Conversation

Washington, September 9, 1961, 11 a.m.

SUBJECT

NATO Aspects of Berlin Planning

[Here follows a list of participants.]

The Secretary invited Mr. Stikker to discuss Berlin planning, as he saw it, from the NATO point of view. Mr. Stikker said that the Council had been active on Berlin since mid-August following a brief period to digest the Secretary's presentation of August 8.[1] He described the arrangements that had been made for the August 21 meeting[2] on the Berlin military build-up and General Norstad's subsequent briefing of the Council.[3] Mr. Stikker thought that the responses of NATO Governments on defense measures had been rather good thus far on the whole, but said there had been more difficulty on the matter of economic counter-measures.[4] Some of this difficulty was due to the fact that the Council did not like to be confronted with the conclusions of others. However, the Council had created an ad hoc committee to study this problem and was concentrating at the moment on legal questions deriving from bilateral and multilateral trade agreements. Mr. Stikker thought some governments were going so carefully into those legal problem as to lose sight of the basic issues. He observed that this reflected a psychological problem some Council members did not have the same feeling of urgency as the Four Powers and time is required to [illegible text—generate?] the same attitude in other governments. He pointed out that another aspect of the problem is the insistence of certain NATO members on the importance of having a program in the political field to accompany the military build-up. In recognition of this attitude, the Council had undertaken private and informal discussions on the question of negotiations in the hope that points might be developed

---

Source: Department of State, Secretary's Memoranda of Conversation: Lot 65 D 330. Secret. Drafted by Magill and approved in S on October 1. A summary of this conversation, between the Four-Power Ambassadorial Group and Stikker, was transmitted to Paris in Topol 318, September 10. (Ibid., Central Files, 375/9–1061)

[1] A summary of Rusk's presentation on Berlin on August 8 and the discussion that followed was transmitted in Secto 50 from Paris, August 9. (Ibid., Conference Files: Lot 65 D 366, CF 1943)

[2] A summary of the August 21 NAC meeting was transmitted in Polto Circular 5, August 22. (Ibid., Central Files, 375/8–2261)

[3] A summary of Norstad's presentation on August 23 was transmitted in Polto Circular 9, August 23. (Ibid., 375/8–2361)

[4] The NATO Economic Countermeasures Working Group began meeting on August 25. Reports on its sessions and report are ibid., beginning with 375/8–2561.

which would be helpful to the Foreign Ministers Meeting. Reverting to economic counter-measures, Mr. Stikker said the Council had concrete proposals to deal with in this field, and, although it had been asked to sign on the dotted line, it was his duty to do his best to obtain full cooperation from NATO, and he would do so.

The Secretary said he was concerned regarding the Council's attitude on economic counter-measures. These measures might have to be put into effect rapidly in order to obtain maximum impact on the Soviet Bloc, short of resort to military measures. The NATO reaction to the Four Power recommendations was not a new one and illustrated a dilemma frequently facing the U.S. in dealing with NATO. He noted that the U.S. is usually criticized for lack of leadership if it does not put forward firm proposals, but that it is criticized equally for dictating to others when it does submit firm recommendations. The Secretary said that precise proposals do not mean that we want to preclude full consideration by the Council and are not prepared to consult on differing points of view. He observed that the heart of the problem was probably the fact that some other NATO Members may not recognize the full seriousness and urgency of the Berlin situation. He indicated some surprise at the fact that there was a better NATO response on the military build-up than on the problem of economic counter-measures, and wondered if this reflected a belief by some that military action really will not take place and they are, therefore, reluctant to commit themselves on economic measures that could involve sacrifices. The Secretary thought that, if this was a correct appraisal, we might do well to discuss the serious prospects of military action on Berlin. He added that it might be desirable to communicate with Heads of Government on the situation.

Ambassador Caccia said it was important for all 15 NATO Members to be in a position to put economic counter-measures into effect and the Secretary agreed. Ambassador Alphand surmised that some governments are more willing to take military measures, which they can decide as a matter of national policy, than to take economic counter-measures which affect important vested interests. The Secretary observed that it was important to have a full discussion in the Council of economic counter-measures and their effects, because in doing so we would be able to consider what the economic impact would be on some NATO Members. Mr. Stikker thought the problem was one of persuading governments to pass the necessary internal legislation and wondered if it would be useful to have a Heads of Government meeting as a means of exerting maximum pressure for action. The Secretary said he had not meant to suggest a Heads of Government meeting, but rather the usefulness of communicating with Heads of Governments. Referring to suggestions by the Norwegian and Belgian Permanent Representatives, Mr. Stikker thought it might be desirable to have a Council meeting in Washington as the best means of conveying the Washington sense of urgency to NATO. He alluded to the trade difficulties that economic counter-measures would impose on Iceland and Greece and suggested that NATO should develop some formula to compensate for such difficulties when the curtailment of trade exceeded a certain percentage of trade. He said he knew Iceland well and that a definite commitment for economic compensation would be needed before Iceland would agree to engage in economic counter-measures. Mr. Stikker asked that he be permitted to have some flexibility to propose a solution along this line in Council discussions.

The Secretary said he had supposed that the problem of economic compensation would be raised by the countries most adversely affected. He hoped it was not generally assumed that the U.S. would take on the task of protecting all countries from any adverse economic impact. He asked Mr. Stikker how the NATO machinery would handle this question. Mr. Stikker said the Council should first make decisions on the principles involved and that it could then work out the details in the Committee of Economic Advisers. He thought there was no need for new machinery. Ambassador Grewe expressed the hope that NATO Members could be persuaded that economic counter-measures would be better in some situations than military action, or no action at all. He illustrated this by reference to the possibility that civilian air traffic might be stopped by indirect or administrative means and said this would be a situation in which military action should not be taken, but which would require some definite counter-measures. Mr. Stikker noted that the NATO ad hoc committee on economic counter-measures was due to produce its report by September 23 and urged that there be more contact between the Ambassadorial Group and NATO in the meantime. Ambassador Caccia hoped the Ambassadorial Group would be able to report soon to the Council and to invite any ideas that other Council members might have. Ambassador Alphand said that the Ambassadorial Group did not want to [illegible text—dictate?] to the Council, but thought it should be precise as possible in its recommendations. Mr. Stikker said the dominant NATO interest was in the importance of having negotiations first; many members felt that only if negotiations failed should they resort to economic and military measures. Thus it was difficult to get them to focus on such measures. The Secretary said he found it difficult to conceive what arguments anyone could use against resorting to an economic embargo if access to Berlin were actually cut off. Mr. Stikker agreed but said that as of now some members merely talk about the [illegible text—aperture?] profonde.

In response to the Secretary's request, Mr. Kohler described the pattern of activities on Berlin within and under the supervision of the Ambassadorial Group. He said that the Group would soon forward a new report on economic counter-measures but hoped that this would not deflect attention from the decisions in this field already requested of the Council by the Ambassadorial Group. He thought the Group could contribute more to NATO discussions and probably should. Mr. Kohler asked if Mr. Stikker had any suggestions to this and said that the group would be glad to try to implement them. Mr. Stikker said he had two thoughts. One was that he should have more information on what was actually going on, so that he could better guide and influence the Council discussions. His other thought was that the Council should meet in Washington for a few days. Mr. Kohler said the latter was a good suggestion that the group would wish to consider. He asked if it would help if one of the four Permanent Representatives should make periodic reports to the Council, perhaps once or twice a week. Mr. Stikker thought this a useful suggestion and suggested that the reports should be made to restricted meetings of the Council.

---

113. **Telegram From the Department of State to the Mission to the North Atlantic Treaty Organization and European Regional Organizations**

Washington, September 16, 1961, 6:57 p.m.

Topol 365. For Finletter from Rusk & McNamara.

1.   We have been reviewing, in light of recent conversations with you and Stikker, how best to handle further NATO consideration of longer-range military planning. Your Polto 281[1] has been very helpful in this regard. September 18 NAC meeting to consider this subject makes it necessary for U.S. to take position this question. Statement at end this message is for your use in that meeting.

2.   We continue believe it essential that we devote our full attention over the next several months to those urgent measures which are required to improve the manning, equipment, training, reserve stocks and overall quality of existing forces. However we recognize necessity for taking action on the 1966 force requirements providing this can be done without detracting from the Berlin issue.

Source: Department of State, Central Files, 375.75/9–1661. Secret; Priority; Limit Distribution. Drafted by Magill and Fessenden; cleared with Nitze, McNamara, and Kohler; and approved by Rusk. Repeated to SACLANT for Collins.

[1] Polto 281, September 5, reported on subjects that Stikker would raise during his trip to Washington and summarized a paper that the Secretary General had circulated, entitled "The Role of NATO Forces." Stikker's paper recognized the validity of the U.S. position on strengthening conventional forces and recommended that NATO military authorities reconsider and complete the force requirements for MC–96. (Ibid., 375/9–561)

3. We agree with you desirable to take action soon in way that (a) does not prejudice our future freedom of action in respect of matters on which US Government decisions have not yet been reached (b) leaves way open for U.S. making known any further views on force goals it believes should be sought to fulfill Green Book policy—as such views emerge from current U.S. studies of forces now building and underway, from standpoint of balance and capabilities (c) gives NAC key role to play (d) avoids divisive debate on conceptual aspects of strategy, since it is specific military programs that are of greatest importance in governing actual development of NATO force pattern rather than statements of long-range requirements (e) achieves outcome in NAC which appears to justify considerable commitment of U.S. prestige and NATO effort to recent review of long-term strategy initiated by U.S.

4. To this end following procedure seems to us desirable:

(a) U.S. would introduce into NAC statement which it would propose NAC adopt as follow-up to Stikker paper, indicating clearly its view re relative priority of different basic elements 1966 requirements with high priority going to enhancing NATO capabilities for non-nuclear defense of forward areas Allied Command Europe against ground/air attack. NAC would then direct Military Committee to translate this view into specifics, i.e., to assign priority ratings to major 1966 force requirements approved by it. U.S. comments on 1966 requirements would be submitted to Military Committee so as to arrive by the time Military Committee had received NAC instructions.

(b) Upon receipt of directive from NAC Military Committee would approve NATO 1966 force requirements, leaving aside requirements for MRBMs and SSN(B)s, subject to development of a system of relative priorities for these requirements. It would direct Commanders jointly to develop detailed country programs based on this system of priorities.

(c) Simultaneously with transmission of approved requirements and the system of priorities to the NATO Commanders, Military Committee would forward them to NAC for review. Depending upon results of Military Committee action, NAC could conduct separate review of priorities or could review them when Commanders' proposed programs are forwarded through NAC to countries as provided in TAR procedure. By time NAC review took place, current U.S. studies referred 2(b) should have been completed and results of the studies could be put to good use by U.S. Perm Rep in that review.

5. To carry out above procedure we have drafted following U.S. statement to Council which should be made at September 18 NAC session:

"1. The U.S. believes that NAC discussions of long-term strategy have been useful in clarifying thinking and providing a basis for increased effort by all NATO nations to achieve needed military forces. U.S. would like to assert, however, that the importance of discussions of long-term planning and strategy and the forces related thereto has been overtaken by the pressing and urgent need to bring into being immediately, and at the prescribed levels of quality, forces necessary to cope with the developing crisis over Berlin.

2. The U.S. emphasizes again the need to provide now forces adequately manned as to number and technical qualifications, forces fully equipped with weapons, transport and ammunition, forces adequately backed up by spare parts, war reserve items, petroleum and other consumables, forces which are properly supported logistically and by service units, in short, balanced forces fully capable of discharging their responsibilities to defend NATO territories and peoples. This is the immediate and pressing priority to which all of us must direct the best effort of which we are capable.

3. Turning now to the matter of long-term defense planning with which we are dealing today, statements made by the various PermReps have been helpful contributions to the discussions in the Council. The paper prepared by SYG has drawn these contributions together. We note that SYG's paper states necessary to increase capabilities in conventional field, but recognizes difficulty in reaching agreement on exact level to be attained. We recognize such difficulty. However, we consider that any actual increase in our conventional capability will increase proportionately the credibility of our overall deterrent. We hope that NATO will approach this task through a vigorous effort to augment conventional capabilities along the general lines already approved in MC–70, as updated by the proposed 1966 requirements.

4. In this connection, one general point should be made—the U.S. maintains now, and will continue to maintain, nuclear strike force capable of devastating the USSR. The U.S. intends fulfill its treaty commitments to its NATO Allies in all circumstances. Thus, the U.S. will not hesitate to use all means at its disposal including nuclear weapons and its strategic strike forces if such prove necessary to defend the peoples and territories of its NATO Allies, and will not be deterred by threats of a nuclear attack on the U.S.

5. The U.S. has withheld its comments in Military Committee on these proposed MC–96 requirements because these requirements which call for major new nuclear weapons programs, particularly the MRBMs, pose basic political, strategic and resource questions that are difficult to resolve and which require extensive further consideration. As soon as planning for the Berlin crisis has been completed, attention should again be directed to these questions.

6. Meanwhile, we understand that some action on end-66 requirements is needed promptly in order that NATO may proceed with ur-

gent programming for 1963 and 1964 to achieve needed strengthening NATO forces. There seems to be consensus in NAC that we should now move ahead to this end. U.S. shares this view and believes NATO should base its programming for near future on proposed 1966 requirements other than elements referred to in para 5, which require extensive further examination. As part of this urgent programming, U.S. believes NATO should give a high priority and increased measures to building non-nuclear forces and that NATO should fulfill very substantial nuclear programs to which NATO is already committed and which will create even greater nuclear arsenal than very substantial one already existing in Europe.

7. The U.S. believes that NATO procedures to move ahead with this programming should ensure that Military Committee and Military Commanders receive specific guidance from NAC needed to discharge their respective roles in developing military plans and programs.

8. To this end, U.S. would propose that Council adopt following statement: 'North Atlantic Council notes statements made by the SYG and the PermReps in discussion of NATO long-term planning. It requests Military Committee, in its action on NATO Commanders' proposed 1966 requirements, to develop an agreed statement of priorities to govern the development of country programs by the NATO Military Commanders, in accordance with the Triennial Review procedure, which would accord high priority to enhancing NATO non-nuclear ground/air capabilities in forward areas Allied Command Europe. Pending further guidance from the Council, Military Committee should defer action on NATO Commanders' proposed requirements for MRBMs and SSN(B)s. Simultaneously with its transmission to the Commanders, the Military Committee should forward this agreed statement of priorities to the NAC for review.'

9. This procedure would also have advantage of enabling NAC to act in way which would recognize in the long-term planning the gains being achieved currently by short-term Berlin measures."[2]

Rusk

---

[2] On September 19 Finletter reported that he had made the statement as authorized and, in response to a specific question from Stikker, approved the general lines of Stikker's paper. (Polto 348; ibid., 375/9–1961)

114.   **Telegram From the Embassy in France to the Department of State**

Paris, October 16, 1961, 8 p.m.

2054. From Stoessel. General Norstad has asked me to report that in a number of contacts he has had with Europeans since his return from Washington October 4, they have taken initiative in raising with him their concern about seriousness of U.S. in its intention defend Europe if necessary with nuclear weapons. One of recurring points which is noted by Europeans as reason for their concern in this connection is continued emphasis which U.S. continues to place on build up of conventional forces.

[1 paragraph (10 lines of source text) not declassified]

General Norstad comments that he feels most of the representatives who have raised the question with him would be pleased to see conventional build up and are convinced of necessity to maintain balance in conventional and nuclear capabilities. However, they seem to feel that U.S. is overemphasizing one aspect of NATO forces and this is cause of concern to them.

Gavin

Source: Department of State, Central Files, 375/10–1661. Secret; Limit Distribution.

115.   **Letter From Secretary of State Rusk to Secretary of Defense McNamara**

Washington, October 29, 1961.

DEAR BOB: In order to keep open the option of holding to the April 21 NSC policy,[1] I believe that our posture in NATO should continue for the present to be one of reaffirming both our intention to commit Polaris submarines to NATO and our willingness to consider a multilateral NATO seaborne missile force, if this is desired by the other NATO coun-

Source: Department of State, Central Files, 375/10–2961. Secret. No drafting information appears on the source text.

[1] Document 100.

tries, but that we should not approve in NATO any requirement for land-based MRBM's until the political and military aspects of the question have been thoroughly studied in the US Government. For the same reason, I would hope that planned US MRBM development work could relate to weapons suited for sea-based, as well as land-based, deployment and that we could avoid describing this work in NATO in terms so specific as to narrow our later freedom of action.

You will recall that the April 21 NSC policy precludes deployment of MRBM's to the forces of individual European countries—whether or not these forces are committed to SACEUR, calls for commitment of US sea-based missiles to NATO, and holds out the long-term possibility of a multilaterally owned and controlled sea-borne NATO missile force, such as the President discussed in his Ottawa speech.

Sea-based deployment could be reconciled with the concept underlying this policy more readily than land-based deployment, for two reasons:

1.   We could deploy sea-based missiles to US forces in NATO waters without too much difficulty. An attempt to deploy land-based US missiles, on the other hand, would almost certainly move the European countries on whose soil they were to be stationed to seek comparable missiles for their own forces.

If we refused their requests, we would probably fail to secure deployment rights for US missiles. If we acceded to their requests, this action would be viewed as a major step toward creation of de facto national strategic nuclear capabilities, since neither these missiles' commitment to NATO nor planned physical safeguards would likely be considered adequate protection against a determined attempt by a technologically advanced country to divert the missiles to national purposes.

Resulting widespread awareness that several NATO countries thus had acquired the means of independently initiating effective strategic attack on the USSR would make it more difficult to maintain the cohesion of Europe and the Atlantic Community. It would create peacetime divisions within the alliance—particularly in any grave international crisis, as well as greatly lessen our ability to follow a non-nuclear strategy or a centrally controlled nuclear strategy in event of hostilities.

These divisions would be the greater since (i) we might well be unable to deploy these missiles in France without aid for the French national program, which I would consider contrary to our interests; (ii) the German role in any MRBM deployment would have to be substantial and would generate great concern, particularly in the UK. [4-1/2 lines of source text not declassified]

2. The alternative proposal of a multilaterally owned and controlled NATO MRBM force is more plausible in a sea-based than in a
land-based context, since land-based missiles would be clearly vulnerable to seizure by the nations in whose territory they were based. The
fact that the Soviets are deploying a growing number of MRBM's on
land does not seem a good reason for our deploying them there too if US
and multilateral deployment would be more feasible at sea, and still be
effective. I am anxious to hold the proposal for a force open to the Europeans since it may well reduce pressures, particularly in Germany, for
attempts to compensate for the present US atomic monopoly by developing national strategic nuclear capabilities.

I realize that there are economic and military, as well as political,
considerations which bear on the choice between sea- and land-based
deployment. Any economic savings would strike me as a lesser factor,
in view of the grave implications of this choice for our national security.
The military factors are, of course, a matter for judgment by your Department. It does seem to me that any military advantages would have
to be considerable to outweigh the damage that land-based deployment
would do to the alliance in other respects.

It is for these reasons that I am anxious to avoid any actions which
would now prejudice the option of holding to sea-based, rather than
land-based, MRBM deployment in NATO Europe.

Sincerely,

Dean[2]

---

[2] Printed from a copy that bears this stamped signature.

---

116.   Paper Prepared in the Department of State

DNM D–0/1   Washington, December 1, 1961.

NATO MINISTERIAL MEETING
Paris, December 13–15, 1961

SCOPE AND OBJECTIVES

Atmosphere

Although there are very grave problems facing the Alliance, the
general atmosphere in NATO at present is on the whole healthy. There

---

Source: Department of State, Conference Files: Lot 65 D 366, CF 2012. Secret. Drafted
by Fessenden and cleared with Kohler and S/P.

is less of the feeling that NATO is in a state of "disarray" than is usually the case before the December Ministerial meeting. Nevertheless, the problems facing the Alliance are most serious and, as usual, U.S. leadership will be a crucial factor in determining the outcome of the meeting.

Berlin is bound to dominate the Council meeting, with attention focused on the 4-Power Ministerial meetings which will just precede the NATO meeting. A crucial problem will be to give the eleven members of the Alliance outside the Four Powers a feeling of partnership in formulation of Alliance policy on Berlin and avoiding any impression that the Four are dictating to the others.

The Soviet threat in other areas will also be very much in the minds of the Ministers. This will be especially true of the Soviet note to Finland.[1] The residual colonial problems of Portugal and Belgium will also figure largely in the meeting, including the question of NATO country votes on colonial questions in the UN. Other East-West issues, such as disarmament, will preoccupy the Canadians and Scandinavians.

Less evident, but very much in the air, will be the general question of the future of the Atlantic Community. Although such developments as the U.K. joining the European Communities will not be discussed in the meeting, the implications of this and similar developments for the Atlantic nations will be in the back of the minds of the Ministers.

On the military side, the continental countries, led by Germany, and the southern countries will generally press for stronger NATO defenses and for measures leading toward greater integration of the NATO defense effort. The debate on NATO strategy which has taken place in the Permanent Council during 1961 will also be very much in the minds of most NATO members, although it is doubtful that the interested countries will use the NATO meeting to reopen a full-scale debate on these issues. There is also likely to be pressure for a greater involvement of the U.S. strategic capability in NATO defense.

Finally, there may be a recurrence of earlier pressures for holding a NATO Heads of Government meeting sometime in 1962, and particularly in the context of Berlin.

General Objectives

The general U.S. objectives at the December meeting should be:

1) To obtain maximum possible unified NATO support for the U.S. position on Berlin.
2) To stress to our NATO Allies the world-wide nature of the confrontation between the Sino-Soviet bloc and the Free World.

---

[1] For text of the Soviet note of October 30, see *Pravda*, October 31, 1961, p. 9.

3) In order to avoid complete preoccupation with crises and Communist initiatives, to put proper focus on the constructive long-range development of the European-North American partnership.

4) In the military field, to ensure forward development of the Alliance's defenses, building upon actions taken in connection with the Berlin crisis, and to maintain European confidence in NATO defenses by taking steps to make evident the inseparability of the defense of Europe and North America.

Specific Objectives

Below are outlined the more specific objectives arranged in accordance with major agenda topics.

Political (Agenda Item I)—Berlin. On Berlin it will be desirable to obtain maximum possible support for our four-point program (political, economic, military, and psychological) within the limits imposed by Allied unity. Of key importance to obtaining NATO-wide support on Berlin will be the giving of full information on our negotiating position, as well in advance of the Ministerial meeting as possible. The U.S. comments on Berlin should incorporate the assurances given to Adenauer in his recent conversations with the President,[2] since these will be well received by the Alliance as whole. Nearly all members of the Alliance will undoubtedly strongly support our general position on negotiations, which may put the French in an increasingly isolated position. Although this poses dangers of leaks regarding Allied disunity, we should nevertheless not hold back from taking our case to the Alliance as a whole, over French opposition if necessary.

Economic counter-measures have been under intensive discussion in NATO. Although it would be desirable to have final agreement by the time of the Ministerial meeting, this may well not be possible. In this event, we should propose a referral of the question to the Permanent Council for further discussion.

On the military side of Berlin we should continue our efforts to push for greatest possible build-up of Alliance forces, exercising our leadership primarily by demonstrating through our own preparedness measures that we are willing to make the required sacrifices. We must also be prepared to comment on U.S. military aid policy. Berlin military contingency planning should not be discussed in any detail at the Ministerial meeting. We should confine ourselves to commending the progress which has been made in agreeing on NAC directive on contingency planning.

Other Areas. With regard to other areas, the U.S. should stress again the general theme of the Oslo meeting that the Communist threat is

---

[2] For documentation on Adenauer's visit to Washington, November 20–22, see vol. XIV, pp. 590 ff.

world-wide. We should cite Finland in this connection. It is important for the U.S. to stress the threat in the Far East, including Korea, Vietnam, Laos and Taiwan Straits. We should also make a full presentation on the Latin American situation, following up on our full discussions at Oslo on this subject and on the first NATO experts' study on Latin America. We must also be prepared to state our position on colonial questions, particularly as reflected in UN votes.

Long-range Prospects. A major U.S. purpose at the meeting should be to raise the sights of the Alliance from the immediate threats facing us around the world as a result of Communist aggression by focussing due attention on the constructive purposes of the Alliance. We should welcome progress being made in other fields, such as the full use being made of the OECD, the negotiations between the U.K. and the European Community, and other steps to strengthen Europe. We should stress the determination on our part to see a parallel strengthening of the partnership between Europe and America.

Military (Agenda Item II). Our presentation should lead off with a comprehensive review of information on Soviet strategic capabilities against the U.S. and Europe, comparing it with U.S. strategic capabilities. We should then follow with a clear reaffirmation of our assurances regarding the U.S. response to a Soviet attack on Europe and then lead into a discussion of the three major issues.

(a) *Strategy.* While we do not want to open up a major discussion on strategy, we do want to take the occasion to improve Alliance understanding of the issues at stake by bringing out the full implications of the intelligence assessment. There remains a tendency in the Alliance to put sole reliance on the use of nuclear weapons. We should seek to bring home the fact which is still not generally realized: that we are facing a situation in which we may well be going to war. Fuller realization of this fact should have its impact on the strategic thinking of the Alliance. In our handling of the strategy discussions, we should try to do so in a way that, while making our views known and reaffirming the importance we attach to them, will not result in acrimonious debate with the danger of publicity leaks about Alliance disunity on the fundamentals of strategy.

(b) *MRBMs.* We should try through the briefing of the respective strategic capabilities of the U.S. and the USSR, to demonstrate that the Alliance should have full confidence in the present nuclear deterrent and the ability of this force to assure adequate coverage of NATO targets. We should recognize, however, that there are Allied concerns on this last point and should be prepared, in this same context, to take steps to stress again the inseparability of the defense of Europe and North America: We should indicate our willingness to carry through on commitment of Polaris submarines to NATO and to join our Allies in considering establishment of a multilaterally owned and controlled NATO

MRBM force, both of which have already been publicly offered. We should indicate that we consider that a multilateral force would be the means of MRBM deployment most consistent with NATO cohesion, and that we would not be prepared to facilitate procurement of MRBMs for NATO forces not under multilateral ownership and control. We should also indicate our willingness to have the MRBM requirements for 1966 considered early in 1962.

(c) *Control.* Our Allies have also shown some desire to explore means for giving the Alliance a greater role in nuclear matters, quite aside from MRBM deployment. We should indicate a willingness to join them in trying to devise guidelines which would govern the use of nuclear forces committed to NATO. We should also be willing to join them in exploring new means for reaching collective decisions regarding use of these weapons which would be consistent with their credibility as a deterrent.

117. Telegram From Secretary of State Rusk to the Department of State

Paris, December 15, 1961, 10 a.m.

Secto 38. Eyes only for the President. Best wishes to you and Mrs. Kennedy for a deeply satisfying and safe visit to Caracas and Bogota.[1]

Thursday meeting of NATO ministers will I believe prove most productive.[2] Intelligence and strategic discussion by McNamara and me proved to be a sobering and highly appreciated presentation to Allies of facts of life and regarded by them as unprecedented in NATO experience. Now remains to be seen whether they will follow up with increased effort to strengthen Alliance. There seems little doubt about readiness of all but France to rally behind your leadership on handling

---

Source: Department of State, Central Files, 396.1–PA/12–1561. Secret. According to another copy of this telegram it was drafted by Rusk. (Ibid., Conference Files: Lot 65 D 366, CF 2002)

[1] President Kennedy visited Latin America December 15–19.

[2] Reports on the individual sessions of the North Atlantic Treaty Council meetings held at Paris, December 13–15, as well as briefing papers, telegrams sent to and from the U.S. Delegation, and other documents relating to the meeting are in Department of State, Conference Files: Lot 65 D 366, CF 2002–2014.

Berlin question and even France has moved significantly in trying to close that gap. Allies now understand our effort to remove nuclear war from realm of magical incantation for solving problems and our reasons for seeking alternatives between surrender or incineration if enemy leaves us any such choices. Will see Norstad on Friday to clarify any questions remaining in his mind about what is expected of him.

Believe Thompson should have first talk in Moscow before Christmas, perhaps immediately following Bermuda meeting,[3] in order not let that situation drift back into harsh stand off of last summer. It is entirely clear from here that firmness of democratic peoples of Alliance must rest upon their knowledge every reasonable effort being made to find acceptable peaceful solution.

Will make full report your return.

Rusk

---

[3] See Document 387.

---

118. Telegram From the Mission to the North Atlantic Treaty Organization and European Regional Organizations to the Department of State

Paris, December 18, 1961, 8 p.m.

Polto 804. For the Secretary from Finletter. I have just received following letter addressed to you by Stikker which I am sending by telegraphic means because of its importance. As you will note copies of this letter have also been sent to Adenauer and Home (original letter being forwarded by pouch).

"I thought it might be worthwhile as a follow-up to the discussions you and I had during the meeting to give you my personal evaluation of the present feeling in the North Atlantic Council on Berlin.

"The meeting was a useful one. Very frank exchanges took place; and I think we had more of a real discussion—as opposed to a series of prepared statements—than at any Ministerial Meeting I remember. All of us, I am sure, as a result of it have gained a better appreciation of the problems facing us not only in Berlin but all over the world.

Source: Department of State, Central Files, 375/12–1861. Secret; Limit Distribution.

"So far as Berlin itself is concerned I have no doubt that what I call the 'other eleven' in the Council—that is the whole membership less the United States, United Kingdom, France and the Federal Republic—solidly support the four in wanting to take a strong line in defence of their basic rights. Given the attitude of the Russians, no other position is possible. On the other hand, they feel that if they are to maintain public support for a policy which may lead them up to the brink of war and even, conceivably, over it, they must at the same time be able to assure their peoples that nothing is being left undone which might possibly lead to a peaceful settlement. They, therefore, consider that the three responsible powers must do everything they can to settle the Berlin problem by negotiation; and, moreover, that despite the uncooperative attitude of the Russians, the three should individually and collectively do all they can to get negotiations under way.

"You are, in effect, asking the Alliance to arm in order to parley. If we do not parley, not only will it be difficult to induce the other powers of the Alliance to arm effectively, but we shall have real difficulty in holding the Alliance together.

"This brings me to the second thing I want to say. It may be true, up to a point, that the differences which arose over the communiqué[1] stemmed not from a disagreement over the basic question of whether there should be negotiations at all, but from varying appreciations of the desirability of negotiations at this particular moment, and of whether or not a genuine basis for negotiations exists; and clearly this is the only line we can possibly take in public. But the fact remains that on Friday afternoon, the Council came as near as in my memory it has ever come to a public breakdown over a major issue. I am not suggesting that the blame can all be laid at one door. But the fabric of the Alliance will not stand many more scenes like that of last Friday.

"I realise the difficulties. I also realise that this is a problem not only of keeping NATO together—for I truly think it is as serious as that—but of presenting a united three (or four) power front to the Russians. But unless some way can be found of carrying on the dialogue without an open split in the Alliance, and unless the 'other eleven' can be told that this is being done, I foresee the greatest difficulty in obtaining from the rest of the Alliance the political and military support without which Western policy cannot succeed; and we shall enter a period of grave danger for the whole future of NATO.

"I am sending copies of this letter to Chancellor Adenauer and Lord Home."

(Signed) D.U. Stikker.

Finletter

---

[1] See footnotes 1 and 2, Document 119.

119.   Circular Telegram From the Department of State to Certain Missions

Washington, December 19, 1961, 8:05 p.m.

1135. In conjunction final communiqué,[1] following is guidance for use in briefing governments as well as SEATO and CENTO on NATO Ministerial Meeting in Paris December 13–15:

1.   Paris meeting provided valuable opportunity for NATO members to engage in thorough and candid review of political, economic and military problems facing Alliance in light of continued worldwide Communist threat to freedom. Meeting focussed in particular on special problems arising out of Berlin crisis, contemporary Congo situation, NATO military strategy, and progress of allied military buildup to meet Soviet-induced Berlin crisis.

2.   Presence at Paris meeting of Defense Ministers of NATO countries gave Secretary McNamara an occasion to explain US Administration's views on basic NATO military strategy in light of assessment Soviet military strength and capabilities. Secretary Rusk, on basis Secretary McNamara's presentation, summarized US views on far-reaching political implications which should be drawn from assessment Soviet military strength.

3.   In connection with Berlin and Congo, Ministerial discussion was frank and vigorous and highlighted differing viewpoints within the Alliance. Frank exploration of these differences, however, only helped to underline essential vitality of NATO Alliance and its ability successfully to engage in political consultation on controversial issues.

4.   During discussion Berlin question, Secretary Rusk emphasized that Atlantic Community stronger now than year ago both in terms of military and economic strength and political consultation. However, Berlin crisis and other critical spots throughout world underline fact that none of current problems could be treated in isolation. All must be viewed in context of Sino-Soviet program of world revolution backed by resources from Communist bloc.

5.   Secretary said Soviet pressure on Berlin continued unabated. There had been no significant substantive changes in Soviet position although certain procedural improvements had emerged as result discussions with Gromyko. Alliance must be firm and determined in defense

---

Source: Department of State, Central Files, 396.1–PA/12–1961. Confidential. Drafted by Van Hollen (EUR/RA), cleared with Hillenbrand and the Department of Defense, and approved by Kohler. Sent to 54 missions.

[1] For text of the communiqué, see *American Foreign Policy: Current Documents, 1961,* pp. 505–508.

of West Berlin. This firmness of West was in interest of peace because chances of war enhanced when each side thinks other will not fight. At same time, Secretary said that it is important to keep in touch with other side to prevent crisis from developing too far and to avoid miscalculations. Consequently, Alliance should be ready through responsible contacts with Soviets to search for peaceful solutions.

6.   General opinion within Council was strongly in agreement with US viewpoint regarding Berlin although well-known attitude of France renegotiations was re-affirmed. Paragraph 8 of communiqué represents compromise language which would permit resumption of diplomatic contacts with USSR.[2]

7.   As communiqué indicated, Minister considered that USSR's action in constructing wall in Berlin, in brazen disregard its obligations, demonstrated essential nature of Communist system and irresistible attraction of free society. Ministers again emphasized their determination to protect and defend basic liberties of West Berlin despite any future Soviet signature on so-called "peace treaty" with puppet East German regime.

8.   During Council's general review of international situation, developments in Middle East, Southeast Asia, Latin America and Africa were discussed. Re Congo, detailed exchange reflected already familiar differences of view among NATO members. Secretary described situation in Southeast Asia and Latin America, explaining nature of increased US assistance to South Vietnam and developments in Cuba and Dominican Republic. (FYI. Secretary asked Ministers to study how their governments could associate themselves with US in meeting threats to Western positions in these areas. End FYI.) He also informed Council that although US decision to liberalize its trade policies might provoke "Great Debate" in US, President Kennedy believed issue must be faced squarely instead of simply attempting to extend anachronistic trade legislation.

---

[2] The language in the communiqué about negotiations with the Soviet Union on Berlin had been the subject of much discussion, first among the Quadripartite Foreign Ministers on December 11 and 12 and then at the North Atlantic Council on December 15. The language originally drafted by the four Foreign Ministers had not been approved by de Gaulle, and only a telephone call from Kennedy to the French President on December 12 had achieved a minor language change. (Kennedy Library, National Security Files, France) In the discussion of the communiqué on December 15 Spaak stated that the four-power language appeared not to advance the Berlin question at all and argued for negotiations at the earliest moment. Protracted discussions with intermissions in the meeting finally achieved the language for paragraph 8 that appeared in the final communiqué. The U.S. Delegation commented that this was the most difficult communiqué drafting session in recent years, and that only the need to project the unity of the Alliance had saved the division over the communiqué from being forced into the open. (Polto Circular 76, December 16; Department of State, Central Files, 375/12–1661)

9. In course of Ministers' discussion of military questions, Secretary strongly reaffirmed that defense of Europe and North America was indivisible. To underscore inseparability of these two areas, US prepared to join with its Allies in considering: (a) greater NATO collective participation in basic decisions on nuclear policy and (b) creation of NATO MRBM forces. While emphasizing present superiority of American nuclear strength, Secretary urged Allies to continue to reinforce their combat-ready conventional forces.

10. In connection military buildup, Ministers reviewed improvements which had been made by member countries in their force contributions in response to the enhanced military threat arising from the Berlin situation. They observed that state of readiness has been improved, units reinforced and mobile task force established. At same time, in view continual aggressive intent of USSR and its unwillingness consider genuine disarmament, it was recognized that NATO Alliance faced no alternative except to further strengthen its forces and modernize its equipment.

11. During consideration economic questions, Council noted that since Oslo meeting Special Mission had been created to look into the economic problems of Greece and Turkey. This mission will report to the Council before end of April 1962.

12. As reflected in communiqué, there was reaffirmation of belief of NATO member countries that, in view of their stronger economic base, they should continue to cooperate closely on methods of providing expanded aid to developing countries of world.

13. For Ankara and Bangkok: CENTO and SEATO briefings should be coordinated with your NATO colleagues.

Rusk

120. Telegram From the Embassy in Belgium to the Department of State

Brussels, December 19, 1961, 8 p.m.

1108. Paris pass USRO. Spaak discussed recent NATO Ministerial meeting with me last night saying American presentation, particularly that of Secretaries Rusk and MacNamara, was one of most important developments in history of NAC. Whereas past NATO military presentations and estimates of western and Soviet capabilities had frequently been counter-productive in their total concentration on what appeared to be unbridgeable gap between western deficiencies and Soviet military strength, with a discouraging effect on those who wished to see realistic and effective NATO military strength developed, MacNamara presentation had pointed out where we were ahead of the Soviets, where we were behind and where effort was needed.

This balanced presentation was very encouraging because of its overall implications, including western superiority nuclear weapons, and estimate that with somewhat greater effort there is realistic hope we can close gap in conventional forces. Spaak felt it most important that implications of MacNamara presentation be thoroughly studied by NATO soonest with a view to developing "a real and rational NATO military policy which thus far has been non-existent".

He also mentioned that as result of NATO meeting he had felt better equipped to take firm position in Socialist National Congress, that Socialist Party should re-examine its negative policy toward Belgium's defense effort (Embtel 1096).[1]

MacArthur

Source: Department of State, Central Files, 396.1–PA/12–1961. Secret. Repeated to Paris, London, and Bonn.

[1] Telegram 1096, December 18, summarized Spaak's speech on December 17 to the Socialist Party Congress. (Ibid., 755.13/12–1861)

121. Memorandum From the Chairman of the Joint Chiefs of Staff (Lemnitzer) to President Kennedy

CM–470–61   Washington, December 20, 1961.

SUBJECT

    27th Meeting, NATO Military Committee in Chiefs of Staff Session, Summary
    Report (U)

1. Since you unfortunately were able to attend only a portion of the
National Security Council meeting, 19 December 1961, you did not hear
my briefing on the NATO Military Committee meetings of last week.
Accordingly, I take this method of providing you with the highlights of
these important meetings.

Introduction

2. The 27th Meeting of the NATO Military Committee in Chiefs of
Staff Session was held on Monday and Tuesday of last week in Paris. As
you may know, the Military Committee, which is the senior NATO military authority, meets in two types of sessions. The so-called Permanent
Military Representatives, selected by the Chiefs of Staff of the NATO nations, meet regularly in the Pentagon. Additionally, on a twice yearly or
more often if necessary basis, the Chiefs of Staff of the NATO nations
(except Iceland) meet in Chiefs of Staff session. Chairmanship of the
Chiefs of Staff session rotates alphabetically. It being the U.S. turn, I
served in an international role as Chairman of this meeting, having
taken over from Admiral Mountbatten last June. General Ruffner, our
Permanent Representative, acted as U.S. Military Representative. For
the first time in the history of NATO, all of the Permanent Representatives, as well as the Chiefs of Staff, participated in such a meeting.

Formal Session

3. Some of the more important items of the agenda of the formal
session and their related documents were:

    A. *The Intelligence Appreciation,* prepared as a primary function by
the Standing Group, and presented orally by its Chairman. This document is the agreed intelligence estimate upon which NATO military
planning is based.
    B. *The 1962 NATO Common Infrastructure Program.* This item was
consideration of a document which is the submission of the annual military requirement for facilities to the North Atlantic Council.

Source: Kennedy Library, National Security Files, NSC Meetings, 1961. Top Secret.
No drafting information appears on the source text.

C. The most important item on the formal agenda was consideration of the paper, MC–96, *Force Requirements for End-1966 and Tentative
Country Breakdowns Thereof.*[1] This document is the statement of force requirements projected five years ahead, as determined by the NATO
military authorities. This paper includes a break-out of forces on an individual country basis and, although agreement to the document does
not constitute a firm country commitment, it does provide the basis for
force development and it is the standard against which progress is
evaluated. The Committee approved this paper and submitted it to the
North Atlantic Council.

Informal Session

4. This was the third time that an informal session has been held. It
was recognized some time ago that free, frank expression of views was
sometimes lacking during formal sessions. For this reason, we experi-
mentally tried an informal session during our meeting last December. It
went so well on that occasion and again in April and this session that I
believe the informal session will become the most useful reason for the
Military Committee meetings. Incidentally, for the informal session
each principal is permitted only a limited number of subordinates in attendance, and no formal record of the discussion is made.

5. This time our discussion was centered on the current East-West
crisis over Berlin. Four interrelated and complementary items were considered:

A. The NATO Build-up.
B. The Soviet Build-up.
C. Berlin Contingency Planning and Progress in NATO Planning
Related Thereto.
D. SACEUR's presentation on Nuclear Capability.

6. In the following paragraphs certain items from both the formal
and informal sessions are covered in greater detail.

Intelligence

7. Following the presentation of the Intelligence Appreciation by
Admiral Douguet, Chairman of the Standing Group, the German representative, General Foertsch, read a rather long paper. The gist of this paper was that, from German intelligence sources, they had concluded
that the Soviet forces available to oppose NATO are substantially
greater than estimated by the Standing Group. This view was essentially
as expressed by Chancellor Adenauer and Minister Strauss during their
meetings with you in November. In concluding, General Foertsch proposed that countries *not* members of the Standing Group be permitted a
greater participation in the development of NATO intelligence estimates.

---

[1] Not found.

8. You will recall that the second item on the informal agenda was, *The Soviet Build-up*. To key-note this discussion, the Chairman of the Standing Group presented in detail the Soviet build-up since the Berlin crisis. Again the German representative reiterated his view that the estimate was inaccurate, and broader participation in the intelligence field should be considered.

9. In summarizing this item as Chairman, I directed the Standing Group to study this problem in conjunction with the Military Committee in Permanent Session.

MRBM's

10. The matter of a NATO MRBM force was discussed in relation to the committee approval action on MC–96, *Force Requirements for End-1966 and Tentative Country Breakdowns Thereof*. At that time the German representative read a second paper. In this paper he stressed three primary points:

A. It is important that all countries fully meet their requirements.
B. Germany agreed to MC–96 with great reluctance because they consider that the MRBM force had been excluded. (The key sentence in MC–96 upon which they base their view is as follows: [*5-1/2 lines of source text not declassified*].

[*1 paragraph (1 line of source text) not declassified*]

General Foertsch proposed that military authorities study the military and technical problems involved in incorporating MRBMs in NATO forces.

11. Following the German statement, SACEUR, SACLANT, and several countries expressed disapproval of and proposed the deletion from the MC–96 paper of one sentence in paragraph 3 and that part of paragraph 6 which deals with the same point. In their view, these sentences reduced the strength and effectiveness of the document as a valid statement of military requirements. These sentences are as follows: "Nevertheless, it is possible that force requirements for end-1966 may have to be reviewed in the light of the conclusions of the current studies on NATO strategy," and "In developing country breakdowns, the Military Committee is mindful of the numerous nonmilitary factors which, in the case of some member nations, may prevent the early full attainment of the proposed force levels or compositions for the nations concerned. Further, the tentative breakdowns are not necessarily to be regarded as commitments but, rather, as a guide to forward planning."

12. The Military Committee action in respect to this paper was:

A. To approve the MC–96 document without alteration or deletion for submission to the Council.
B. In order to save time, pending receipt of political guidance, to direct the Standing Group to study the military aspects of the integration of MRBMs into NATO.

Control of Nuclear Weapons

13. In keeping with our policy of informing the Alliance of our nuclear capability vis-à-vis the Soviets, SACEUR gave the same presentation he gave to the North Atlantic Council recently. This briefing includes very broad and general coverage of the following:

A. The number and type of nuclear launching vehicles now available to SACEUR. Specific numbers of weapons were not included but the fact that planning for allocation is completed was mentioned.

B. NATO nuclear targeting and the general geographical location of nuclear storage sites.

C. A schematic representation of the atomic strike communications system with its [less than 1 line of source text not declassified] for release purposes.

14. Following SACEUR's presentation, the German representative made a third rather long statement that included three main points:

A. NATO conventional forces are inadequate; nuclear weapons in truly balanced forces are necessary;

B. The key problem of nuclear weapons is the matter of control; and

C. NATO must have the shortest possible reaction time.

He concluded by recommending that "The Standing Group should continue, in greater detail, its study on a suitable system for the control and release authority of nuclear weapons now available in NATO, using MC–95 as a basis." (MC–95 is a document titled, *Military Control of Nuclear Weapons,*[2] prepared by the Standing Group, approved by the Military Committee, and now in the hands of the Permanent Council.)

15. A lively discussion followed which centered primarily upon the matter of political decisions which were necessary before further progress could be made by military authorities in the study of this item.

16. Finally, the Committee agreed:

A. To record recognition of the importance from a military point of view of the subject and the need for political guidance at a reasonably early date so that planning may continue.

B. That the Standing Group should continue study of this subject *after* the Council has acted on MC–95 and issued political guidance.

Contingency Planning—Tripartite Planning

17. I mention a further item to give you a feel for the great interest that exists among the NATO military authorities regarding contingency planning for the use of NATO forces for operations short of general war,

---

[2] Not found.

and particularly the relationship of tripartite planning to NATO planning.

18. On 25 October the North Atlantic Council approved a directive to the NATO military authorities concerning planning for the Berlin emergency.[3] Specific direction was given to coordinate NATO planning with the Tripartite Military Contingency Planning (Live Oak). Prior to the meeting the major Allied Commanders had been requested to report their progress.

19. SACEUR reported first, outlining conceptually the various operations for which his Live Oak "Catalog of Plans" was being prepared. Further, he explained the relationship of Live Oak to SHAPE planning and the degree of coordination which must occur if planning and operations were to be effective. This evoked a lengthy discussion, finally terminated by a request from the Committee that I determine from the Secretary General if SACEUR's briefing could be fitted into the agenda for the Ministerial Meetings. (As it turned out the UK and France disagreed [Secretary Rusk agreed][4] so the Secretary General decided not to include this briefing for the Ministers. Instead, the Military Committee agreed that General Norstad should furnish the members of the Military Committee a sanitized version of his briefing so that all may brief their Defense Ministers on an agreed, accurate basis.)

20. SACLANT reported next. He explained that although his headquarters had only recently received the directive, he had previously on his own initiative prepared suitable plans for most conceivable contingencies. For this reason he was prepared to initiate contingency operations on relatively short notice. However, in that SACLANT forces are earmarked for assignment rather than actually assigned, and since for country reasons his forces are maldeployed, certain practical delays were inevitable.

21. In the discussion following SACLANT's report the main points of interest were:

A. The degree of coordination that is required and occurs between SACEUR and SACLANT headquarters.
B. The mechanics of conveying national forces to SACLANT control during emergencies of less than general war magnitude.
C. Quality and quantity of LANTCOM forces.

In remarking on the last point, SACLANT stated very frankly that his forces were seriously deficient in manning, equipping, and logistic support. He urged action to provide earlier availability of better forces.

---

[3] Not found.
[4] Brackets in the source text.

Portuguese Statement

22. Incidentally, as a last minute addition to the formal agenda, the Portuguese representative, General De Araujo, presented a statement in which it was explained that military operations in Angola required withdrawal of a portion of the NATO committed forces. The forces withdrawn consist of 5 destroyer escorts, 5 infantry battalions, and 2 artillery companies (approximately 50% of the force committed to NATO by Portugal).

Summary

23. You have undoubtedly noted that the Germans were the source of three important initiatives for this meeting. In actual fact, they proposed yet a fourth—that a study of the requirements for conduct of and defense against biological and chemical weapons be undertaken. It appears clear to me that we may expect increasing effort by the Germans to be accepted fully into all aspects of NATO military activity.

24. It was a very useful meeting, I believe, more successful than any of the seven I have previously attended. Particularly noteworthy was the informal session during which the representatives conducted a most comprehensive and frank discussion.

L.L. Lemnitzer[5]

---

[5] Printed from a copy that bears this stamped signature.

---

122. Telegram From the Department of State to the Mission to the North Atlantic Treaty Organization and European Regional Organizations

Washington, December 30, 1961, 8:32 p.m.

Topol 929. Polto 804.[1] [Here follow delivery instructions for Rusk's letter to Stikker.]

Source: Department of State, Central Files, 375/12–1861. Secret; Verbatim Text; Limit Distribution. Drafted by Van Hollen.

[1] Document 118.

"Dear Mr. Secretary-General:

Thank you for your letter of December 18 in which you gave me your evaluation of the present atmosphere in the NATO Council with regard to the Berlin question.

I share your concern about the effect which the continuing differences among us may have upon the solidarity of the Alliance. As I told my French, German and British colleagues in Paris earlier this month, we must give serious thought to the question of mutual confidence among ourselves. I asked them this question: to what extent are our problems related, not to the Soviet Union, but to a lack of mutual confidence as to our intentions and willingness and ability to work together? I continue to feel that we must solve our own internal problems before we can hope effectively to face the Soviets.

At the same time, while recognizing that the NATO Alliance has undergone strain, I am hopeful that we can bridge our differences. Underlying any difficulties on the question of negotiations with the Soviets is the essential unity of the 15 on the non-negotiability of our vital interests in Berlin. This is a critical point to remember when we begin to worry about the cohesion of the Alliance. Furthermore, I agree with you that the Paris NATO meeting was a very effective exercise in political consultation which, in the case of Berlin, provided for a frank and uninhibited consideration of the respective positions of member Governments. It was particularly valuable to me in enabling me to hear the forcefully expressed opinions of those whom you have referred to as the 'Other Eleven'.

While this exchange of viewpoints did not result in much forward motion, we were able to work out an arrangement within the Alliance under which we will resume exploratory contacts with the USSR. The nature and timing of our approach to the Soviets as well as the instructions to be sent to Ambassador Thompson were discussed by the President with Prime Minister Macmillan last week. In the context of the Paris discussions, it was agreed that Ambassador Thompson should seek an appointment with Gromyko as soon as possible after January 1 to attempt to ascertain whether any basis exists for meaningful negotiations. In his initial approach, Thompson will limit himself primarily to exploring Soviet intentions on access arrangements. He will not raise the other major aspects of the Berlin problem such as the status of West Berlin, the relations between West Berlin and the Federal Republic, or the broader questions of Germany including frontiers and reunification. Since it is intended that Thompson's initial probe will be of an exploratory nature only, and will not include negotiations, it should not be of long duration. However, if on the basis of this probe it is decided that grounds for negotiations exist, a Foreign Ministers' Meeting will presumably follow. In any event, we will keep you fully informed regarding the outcome of Thompson's approach and will also ensure that the Council is informed.

In closing, let me say that I greatly admired your firm and skillful handling of the NATO Ministerial Meeting under somewhat trying circumstances.

I look forward to seeing you towards the end of January, at which time we can discuss further these questions of mutual concern. Ambassador Finletter will be in touch with you to work out precise dates for your visit. Meanwhile, warm greetings for the new year. With warm regards, Sincerely, Dean Rusk."

Rusk

123. Telegram From the Department of State to the Mission to the North Atlantic Treaty Organization and European Regional Organizations

Washington, January 8, 1962, 9:12 p.m.

Topol 968. We can expect US being shortly subjected considerable pressure in NAC to participate in consideration of complex of questions relating to NATO nuclear role. It can be assumed FedRep will press for early establishment ad hoc group to study MRBM's. Further, we are committed to discussion end 1966 military requirements early in 1962; Council notation of MC 26/4[1] will not in itself postpone consideration of strategy and MRBM's, to which MC/CS reserved. Also MC–95 on nuclear weapons control has already been postponed for NAC discussion. Finally, Rusk–McNamara presentation in Min Mtg invited Alliance to consider in effect modified strategic concept.

To cope with these pressures you are instructed, subject your concurrence, to make an early statement in NAC along following lines:

"In December NATO Ministerial Meeting Alliance recognized need for continuing prompt consideration of ways and means to estab-

---

Source: Department of State, Central Files, 740.5611/1–862. Secret; Verbatim Text. Drafted by Kranich (EUR/RA); cleared with Fessenden, Nitze, Seymour Weiss, Bowie, and Owen; and approved by Kohler. Repeated to London, Bonn, and Rome.

[1] Not found.

lish further NATO participation and role in use of nuclear weapons. In-cluded in this need is question of whether, and if so how, MRBM's should be deployed on Continent of Europe and/or adjacent waters.

The United States continues in its strong conviction that best inter-ests of Alliance are not served by further proliferation on a national ba-sis of nuclear components or missiles systems serving predominantly strategic purposes. Believe reasons for this conviction well known and US appreciates most members of NATO share this view. US continues to hope this view will come to be shared by all, as intricate problems we now confront are thoroughly studied in period ahead.

It was in recognition of need for progress on constructive approach to these problems consistent with this conviction that Secretary said at Paris meeting that US was prepared to work hard on the questions bear-ing on how best to assure continuance of an effective NATO nuclear de-terrent. US at direction of President is continuing its comprehensive and intensive review of all aspects of question. It is hoped that at end this special study, US will be able to make known its conclusions in course of consideration looking to eventual decisions, some of which might per-haps be taken by time of spring meeting.

In meantime US would not expect NAC to declare moratorium on consideration many issues involved. On contrary believe discussions in NAC should proceed without delay. Believe NAC should know, how-ever, that US participation will during early stages such discussion be designed primarily to elicit and evaluate views of others and to indicate various factors and considerations involved in this range of questions. US continues in its opinion that, although time is of course important in considering these subjects and reaching decisions, fact remains that Western strategic nuclear capability will remain effective. Targets of particular concern to defense of Europe are and will continue to be ade-quately covered by US nuclear forces. Thus, in our view, we can afford time to carefully consider and decide these terribly complex and impor-tant questions relating to NATO nuclear role."

Following your statement to NAC along above lines, it is also de-sired that US take initiative in recommending procedural steps to be taken by NATO. In this regard, we would hope that restricted NAC dis-cussions would serve not only to consider the questions of NATO nu-clear role, including MRBM force and the control issues involved in MC–95, but also to review existing strategic concepts which bear on the MC 26/4 stated requirements for MRBM's as well as the need for con-ventional forces and the concept of graduated action in Berlin contin-gency military planning. Our objective in this discussion strategy would be to follow up on educational process initiated by Rusk–McNamara presentations and to set stage for consideration of MRBM and related issues in framework of revised strategy.

In substantive discussions you should avoid giving impression US nuclear policy, per se, undergoing fundamental change and be guided by Rusk and McNamara December statements. You should not, if issue US commitments arises go further than to reaffirm past US commitments—notably one in President's Ottawa speech. However, if this proposal is brought up, you might point out US has not yet had formal or definitive comments from its Allies on this proposal and would welcome such comments. You should stress that US would not be prepared to provide MRBM's for any forces not under multilateral ownership and multilateral control.

In all discussion suggested above, we believe that in addition to PermReps, would be useful have certain key individuals in governments engage in restricted NAC discussions. It is asked therefore that you propose that for these discussions on NATO nuclear role, MRBM's, and strategy concepts, PermReps be augmented by country experts, both political and military, from capitals. We plan send separate messages major NATO capitals suggesting key people we would like to see participate.

If a proposal is made in NAC to establish special ad hoc group, we should be prepared to support formation of a group consisting of PermReps membership less than full NAC. Such group should, however, be appropriately augmented by experts from key capitals. FYI Only. We considering desirability having PermReps plus experts visit US after US position established to acquire first-hand knowledge what involved in maintaining and operating highly centralized control over US worldwide nuclear force. End FYI.

Your comments requested.[2]

Rusk

---

[2] On January 9 Finletter replied that he welcomed "enthusiastically" these proposals and suggested some minor revisions in the draft statement. (Polto 872; Department of State, Central Files, 740.5611/1–962) He then arranged with Stikker to have the presentation made to the North Atlantic Council on January 17. (Poltos 921 and 926, January 18 and 19; ibid., 740.5611/1–1862 and 1–1962)

124.   Letter From Secretary of State Rusk to Secretary of Defense McNamara

Washington, January 20, 1962.

DEAR BOB: As you know, I share the concern expressed by the President in our discussion with him yesterday,[1] that no action be taken to effect a reduction in our military forces overseas lest this be construed as a willingness on the part of the United States to diminish its military posture during this period of crises. In this connection, I appreciated the prompt action taken by Mr. Nitze and other members of your Department to correct the misimpression that grew out of the recently issued directive to USAREUR[2] to undertake tentative planning for force withdrawals to begin as early as this February. I am, of course, aware that DOD Fiscal Year '63 budgetary plans do anticipate a reduction in forces, providing international political circumstances permit. Moreover, I presume that there is a point beyond which delay in developing such plans, and more importantly delay in their implementation, creates serious internal administrative problems for the Department of Defense.

Given the foregoing considerations, I believe it would be helpful if we knew present Department of Defense thinking with respect to the alternatives which are open to us in meeting any force reductions which might be contemplated, as well as with regard to the timing of such reductions. In this connection, I would appreciate any information you could give us on the following questions:

1. Under present budgetary plans, how much of a reduction would be required from forces presently in being?
2. What are the alternative possibilities from the Defense Department point of view for effecting such reductions with specific reference to the degree of latitude which we have as between (a) forces overseas and forces in the United States, and (b) forces in the various theaters overseas?
3. For how long a period can we safely put off the decision to reduce our forces without creating unmanageable budgetary and administrative problems for the Department of Defense?
4. Assuming the decision were made not to go through with the force reduction, what would be the budgetary impact and what legislative problems, if any, would we face?

Source: Department of State, Central Files, 740.54/1–2062. Secret. Drafted by Seymour Weiss and Johnson on January 19.

[1] A reference to the meeting on Berlin at 6:05 p.m. on January 18. (Johnson Library, Rusk Appointment Book) No other record of this meeting has been found.

[2] Not further identified.

I will be back in Washington by February 1, and would hope we might together then review this situation to see whether we should make some recommendations to the President on the question.

In light of their interest in this matter, I am sending copies of this letter to Mac Bundy and General Taylor.[3]

Sincerely yours,

Dean Rusk[4]

---

[3] On February 1 McNamara replied that the Department of Defense was "sensitive to the implications involved in any announcement with respect to reductions of troops in Europe" and would discuss the matter with Rusk once Department of Defense plans had been developed. (Department of State, Central Files, 740.5/2–162)

[4] Printed from a copy that bears this stamped signature.

---

125. Memorandum of Conversation

Washington, February 5, 1962, 4 p.m.

SUBJECT

NATO Nuclear Questions

PARTICIPANTS

United States	*NATO*
The Secretary of State	Mr. Dirk U. Stikker, NATO
Mr. Foy D. Kohler	Secretary-General
Amb. Thomas K. Finletter	Mr. George Vest, Special Assistant
Mr. Russell Fessenden	to the Secretary-General

In response to the Secretary's question, Mr. Stikker said that the atmosphere in the NATO Council today is good and progress is being

---

Source: Department of State, Central Files, 375/2–562. Secret. Drafted by Fessenden, initialed by Kohler, and approved in S on February 18. Stikker visited Washington February 5–7; a memorandum of his conversation with Kohler at 9:30 a.m. on February 5 is ibid.; memoranda of his conversations with McGhee and the U.S. Working Group on NATO strategy on February 5 are ibid., 375.75/2–562 and 375/2–562. A memorandum of his conversation with Ball on February 7 is ibid., 375.75/2–762. A memorandum of his conversation with the President on February 6 is printed as Document 126.

made, with the exception of remaining difficulties over economic countermeasures for Berlin. The important discussions of nuclear questions and strategy have started well; however, it will be vitally important that these discussions be pursued to a successful conclusion. Opening up this range of very sensitive questions in NATO requires that there be some form of decision; otherwise, the effect on the Alliance could be very damaging indeed.

Mr. Stikker then described his plans for handling NATO discussion of these matters. Mr. Stikker said that he felt it most important not to challenge the existing Political Directive. He argued for the pragmatic approach, as contrasted with the theoretical. He admitted that it might, after the practical problems of providing for a forward strategy had been solved, be possible to change the Political Directive. Mr. Stikker said that he planned to start the effort to increase the conventional capability of the Alliance by having General Norstad, during his February 14th briefing on Berlin contingency planning, stress the fact that we today have no forward strategy and then to outline the specific steps required to make it a reality.

The next step, Mr. Stikker said, will be discussion of political control of nuclear weapons. In this connection, Mr. Stikker said he hopes it will be possible for the US to agree on something with respect to (a) guarantees on the maintenance of US nuclear weapons; (b) guarantees that the US will take care of targets directly relating to the defense of Europe; and (c) guidelines with respect to the use of nuclear weapons. Prompt agreement on these matters will provide time for more gradual consideration of some of the more difficult questions. Agreement on these matters would also provide something specific for the Athens meeting. Mr. Stikker said that he had also listed for the Council's consideration various ideas which have been proposed on decision-making, including weighted voting and a smaller group. He had done this because he had thought it was necessary for the Council to consider all these matters thoroughly; he did not anticipate, however, that any of these would be agreed on.

[1 paragraph (13-1/2 lines of source text) not declassified]

Mr. Stikker briefly mentioned the mechanism for wartime consultation. He said that he had mentioned this subject to Macmillan, who had told him to discuss it bilaterally with the United States. He had also mentioned it to the French NATO Ambassador twice and had told him that he would be willing to discuss this subject with de Gaulle at any time; however, de Gaulle had shown no sign of interest.

The Secretary asked Mr. Stikker whether it would be desirable for the US itself to come forward with a specific US plan on NATO nuclear questions. The Secretary thought such a move by the US could be deeply divisive within the Alliance. Because of the dangers of the US prematurely backing any specific plan it might be better to have the subject discussed thoroughly by others first.

Mr. Stikker agreed, but added that someone must start matters going and this is what he had attempted to do in his recent paper on political control of nuclear weapons.[1] Mr. Stikker said that he did need to know, however, whether the US attitude on finding a solution to the NATO nuclear questions was a positive one. He also needed more information on these matters which could be obtained only from the US. In this connection, he mentioned a comprehensive list of questions he had submitted on MRBMs.

The Secretary said that there were two matters that he wanted to stress on which the US was very sympathetic:

a) On the exercise of the Presidential authority, we were prepared to agree to the two guidelines which had been cited in the Secretary's presentation to the December Ministerial meeting. We were also prepared to consider very sympathetically any further guidelines which could be agreed among the Allies.

b) We were also prepared to consider with interest and sympathy any proposals on which the Allies could agree, which would be an alternative to the present de facto arrangement in which the decision essentially rests with the US.

The Secretary said that he wanted to comment on European doubts concerning our determination to use nuclear weapons. He said that, if tomorrow all access to Berlin were stopped, he had the feeling that no NATO Government would ask us to go to nuclear war. The Secretary said that he had the feeling—stressing that he was speaking quite informally and unofficially—that the fact of what nuclear war really means hasn't "bitten home" in most NATO countries.

Mr. Stikker said that he felt the uncertainty, regarding our determination to use nuclear weapons, exists in Europe. He agreed with the Secretary that no country would ask us to go to nuclear war if access were blocked in Berlin, but said that it is really a matter of how hostilities develop and how they progress. The uncertainty in Europe today is perhaps addressed more to the question of how far the US would let matters deteriorate before using nuclear weapons. Mr. Stikker criticized recent talk about large-scale limited war in Europe. Mr. Stikker said that something of a paradox exists: If the Europeans are not sure that the US

---

[1] Under reference here is NDP 62/2, January 23, 1962, on the political control of nuclear weapons, which was discussed at NAC meetings on January 24 and February 1, without any definite conclusions being reached. (Poltos 945 and 1003, January 25 and February 1; Department of State, Central Files, 740.5611/1–2562 and 2–162) No copy of the paper itself has been found.

will use nuclear weapons and are not certain that we will maintain and improve those weapons that now exist in Europe, they will not agree to a conventional build-up. If, however, they are reassured about our attitude on these nuclear matters, then the atmosphere will be much better for a conventional build-up.

Mr. Stikker cited again the talk about changing the Political Directive as a cause of the uncertainty. The Secretary commented that he saw a danger in attempting to rewrite the Political Directive because of the effect on the Soviets interpretation of the Alliance's intentions.

126. Memorandum of Conversation

Washington, February 6, 1962.

SUBJECT

    Call of Secretary General of NATO

PARTICIPANTS

    The President
    Dirk U. Stikker, Secretary General of NATO
    Thomas K. Finletter, US Permanent Representative to NAC
    Foy D. Kohler, Assistant Secretary

The President welcomed Mr. Stikker for his second visit to the U.S. and opened the conversation by inquiring about the state of the Alliance.

Mr. Stikker replied that he thought the state of the Alliance was generally good but that there were many problems and some uneasiness and uncertainties. A number of the NATO Ambassadors had approached him before his departure and German Defense Minister Strauss had even flown down from Bonn to express his concern about his upcoming discussions with the President. The latter had referred to them as not only of political but even of historic importance, an exagger-

---

Source: Department of State, Central Files, 740.5/2–662. Secret. Drafted and initialed by Kohler and approved by the White House on April 12. The conversation lasted from 10:31 to 11:30. (Kennedy Library, President's Appointment Book) Finletter left at the end of this part of the conversation. A 3-page memorandum of conversation on Berlin, the Azores, and West New Guinea is ibid.

ated statement which did however illustrate the strength of the concern. He wanted to cite two examples. The first was the range of problems connected with Berlin contingency planning, and the Thompson–Gromyko talks. He had just had a telegram this morning reporting on the Council meeting yesterday at which the US Representative had faced many complaints about the handing over of documents to the Russians which had not been cleared with the Council and about which they had not even been informed. Some countries like Canada were capable of saying that if they were only to learn things post facto which might involve NATO in courses of action then they were not prepared to go along. After Mr. Kohler explained that while these documents had not been submitted to NATO they in fact represented only previously approved positions or matters about which NATO had been informed, the President said that he thought we should have provided these papers earlier. He added that he had great appreciation for the difficulties which faced Ambassador Thompson in the current exercise. It was difficult enough to get agreement among 3 or 4 but with 15 different views we were likely to face paralysis of efforts at negotiation. However he repeated that he agreed that we must do our best to bring NATO along and not give people an excuse to complain that they were not adequately consulted.

Mr. Stikker then said that a much more important problem was that of Germany. He had visited Germany often for speeches and had had talks with top officials, trade union leaders and others. There was clearly a sense of the growing military strength of the Federal Republic and the beginnings of a wave of nationalism. Even Chancellor Adenauer, the most European of the Germans, had recently referred with evident pride to Germany as the second strongest member of NATO. These sentiments were coupled with widespread uncertainty as to United States policy particularly as regards the concept of limited wars on the continent as against the use of nuclear weapons. Mr. Stikker referred to the discussions which had been going on inconclusively during the past year about the NATO strategy. No agreement had been reached. It was important that in the forthcoming discussions agreement be reached if we were not to face serious disunity. [11 *lines of source text not declassified*] Strauss complained about lack of even information with respect to US nuclear capabilities to defend NATO. The President challenged this statement, saying that he was sure the Germans knew a great deal about the nuclear situation. He was sure that what interested them was the matter of the conditions for the use of military weapons. Mr. Stikker responded that Strauss had even cited the fact that there were some 200 nuclear sites in Germany and that he did not really know what was in them and raised the question as to what became of German sovereignty in such a situation. The President said that questions of use and control of nuclear weapons were different from matters of size and location of stocks. However, the fact that Herr Strauss raised questions about lack of information made this a factor which had to be dealt with in itself. Mr. Stikker agreed that this was the case but went on to say that he felt this problem was a manageable one. If the nuclear problem now be approached as he had suggested, by the formalization of US guarantees with respect to the availability of nuclear weapons for the European command and with respect to coverage of targets essential to European defense, this would go far to allay German uneasiness. He also hoped that means could be found to provide more factual information, perhaps to a restricted group. Even more important of course was to give the Germans a share in the decision-making as to the use of nuclear weapons. He referred in this connection to his suggestions that the other countries might delegate authority to the President for the final decision under agreed guidelines. Such guidelines could cover the case of a massive nuclear and conventional attack and then more doubtful cases. In addition to these the Council would be discussing the question of the possibility of NATO MRBM force.

Referring first to the question of a multilateral NATO missile force, the President reiterated the statement in his Ottawa speech and assured Mr. Stikker that the United States was prepared to join in trying to work out plans for this. He understood that a suggested paper had already been put forward on this. Continuing, the President said he recognized that the Germans might well have a "natural concern" as to the circumstances under which the United States would decide, in the face of risk of destruction of its own territory, to use nuclear weapons. In this connection he commented on the difficulties which the French were experiencing in trying to build up a nuclear capability. He thought the French were finding it so expensive that there was some danger of their turning to the Federal Republic for help. [11 *lines of source text not declassified*]

The President then referred to the importance of a build-up of NATO's conventional forces. He felt it essential that the present imbalance be corrected. He realized that some of our partners say that this emphasis on conventional forces means that the US will not use nuclear weapons. He thought however that this was in many cases just an excuse. Mr. Stikker commented that he in fact knew of one country which was deliberately refraining from cooperating in conventional build-up, which it claimed would in fact make the Americans more reluctant to use nuclear weapons. In any event Mr. Stikker said he felt that the Council must take a pragmatic approach and have a factual discussion of these problems. It was necessary to get rid of the prevailing uncertainty. He said there was some difference between himself and Mr. Kohler as to the eventual desirability of amending the existing political directive, but confirmed that this did not affect agreement on the pragmatic approach.

He turned then to the question of "Missile X" which he understood was under R and D in the United States as a possible replacement for existing delivery systems. He said he lacked the technical knowledge adequately to deal with this question, but that he had given a list of questions to Mr. Kohler and Mr. Nitze[1] to which he had requested answers. After Mr. Kohler had indicated we would do our best to respond to these questions, Mr. Stikker said he wanted to be sure that the United States would take a positive approach toward helping to find the answer to this problem.

The President then asked Mr. Stikker how all this would provide the needed reassurances to the Alliance and particularly to the Federal Republic. Mr. Stikker replied that he thought basically if the suggested assurances were given on the part of the United States and guidelines worked out with respect to use of nuclear weapons, this would go a long way toward solving the problem. It was true that Strauss was carrying on considerable agitation but he thought that if Adenauer had solutions to the problems now under discussion this would be sufficient for him to keep control of the situation and for any public opinion to subside. The President commented that in connection with the nuclear question it was necessary to think how an attack would actually take place. If it were not for the exposed position of Berlin the situation would be different and easier to deal with. In any event, control of nuclear weapons must be absolute. Mr. Stikker then cited the possible formulae which had been considered for decision making. He commented that Adenauer, for example, had at one time accepted the concept of weighted voting. Any formula which provided for European participation in the decision would probably be sufficient to contain German nationalism. However he wanted to emphasize that some positive result must be reached.

In response to a question from the President, Ambassador Finletter then referred to the problem of possible amendment of the McMahon Act.[2] He pointed out that while the US veto applied to present stockpile arrangements, a different problem would be presented by a multilaterally-owned NATO force. This implied multilateral control and almost any acceptable formula might go beyond the legal authority of the Act as it now stood. The United States should keep an open mind and the President might want to consider whether or not it might be better to take the initiative and simply go ahead on the US side with having the Act amended. Without commenting directly on this question the Presi-

---

[1] Not further identified.

[2] For text of the Atomic Energy Act of 1946 (P.L. 79–585), August 1, 1946, see 60 Stat. 755; for the amendment of July 2, 1958, permitting the transfer of nuclear materials and information to other nations, see 72 Stat. 276.

dent assured Mr. Stikker that in any event we supported his efforts to arrive at a solution of these problems which would reassure the Alliance. He thought that our own objectives and Mr. Stikker's were fundamentally the same: [2 *lines of source text not declassified*] to achieve strict and responsible control of nuclear weapons, whether this was a question of US control or whether it was a question of others sharing in that control. On the initiative of Mr. Stikker there then ensued a discussion of the question of the US veto on the use of nuclear weapons with both Mr. Stikker and Ambassador Finletter estimating that there might be some difficulties if a US veto were involved. Mr. Kohler said that it was clear that under existing legislation the President alone was responsible for a decision to release nuclear weapons for use and that it would be necessary for the United States to retain a veto over any such decision. In the circumstances the United States Government could not itself make an offer to give up this authority. Indeed to do so could cast some doubt on our own willingness to use the nuclear weapon in defense of NATO. If our European allies did not feel completely assured on this basis then it would be up to them to put forward any proposals which they wanted us to consider. Thus under present legislation the most that could be done would be to say that we would consider such proposals if they were made. The President confirmed this statement and went on to point out that there would be considerable difficulties connected with the amendment of the McMahon Act—indeed there could be a very bitter fight on the subject. While we wanted to do our utmost to reassure our allies he hoped that a solution could be found which would spare us this difficulty.

---

127.   Telegram From the Embassy in France to the Department of State

Paris, February 21, 1962, 8 p.m.

3972. During discussion about nuclear situation in NATO with de Gaulle yesterday,[1] I pointed out the great nuclear strength of NATO and the current interest in a multinational nuclear force and finally the de-

---

Source: Department of State, Central Files, 375/2–2162. Secret; Limit Distribution.
[1] For a report on other subjects discussed, see Document 239.

gree to which such a force would satisfy nuclear aspirations of non-nuclear nations, such as, for example, Germany.

He replied by saying that NATO was General Norstad, he was American, had American weapons, that he realized there were many nuclear weapons available to support NATO and that, in effect, they were American weapons. He then went on to say he did not see how making a multi-national force would make much difference because they would still be American weapons. He added that there would probably be some technical changes in their control but he did not, in long run, think this would make much difference. I did not want to talk about the costing formula or the control problems involved, at this time, and so did not continue the discussion beyond this point.

My own feeling is that as France gets closer to have a nuclear capability, she will be increasingly difficult to deal with on nuclear matters. Unless the US will relinquish veto control over the launch of a nuclear weapon, France will not seriously consider a NATO nuclear force. They are well informed on abundance and variety of nuclear weapons in US stockpile and of solemn intent of US to use weapons in defense of NATO. We seem to accomplish little in reiterating these facts. They still remain skeptical of US willingness to enter into a nuclear exchange with USSR if issue at stake is, for example, West German territory. They feel that survival of France, in final analysis, will very likely depend upon her ability to retaliate against Russia and now that they are approaching a nuclear capability, they will settle for nothing less than this.

Gavin

---

128. **Telegram Topol 1279 From the Department of State to the Mission to the North Atlantic Treaty Organization and European Regional Organizations**

Washington, February 28, 1962, 8:51 p.m.

[Source: Department of State, Central Files, 740.56311/2–1562. Secret; Priority; Limit Distribution. 1-1/2 pages of source text not declassified.]

129. Telegram Polto 1163 From the Mission to the North Atlantic Treaty Organization and European Regional Organizations to the Department of State

Paris, March 6, 1962, 5 p.m.

[Source: Department of State, Central Files, 375.75611/3–662. Secret; Niact. 2 pages of source text not declassified.]

---

130. Memorandum of Meeting

Washington, March 15, 1962, 5–5:30 p.m.

PRESENT

The President
Mr. Robert Bowie
Mr. McGeorge Bundy
Mr. Carl Kaysen
Mr. Robert McNamara ⎱ for about the last
Mr. Roswell Gilpatric ⎰ half of the discussion

Mr. Bundy reviewed the calendar of decisions that are to come to the President with respect to NATO nuclear matters and indicated that none of these can be looked at individually. He mentioned the MRBM decisions, the problem of assisting the French missile development, the dispersion of additional tactical nuclear weapons to NATO strike aircraft. The President then asked whether Secretary Herter had not originally made the Polaris offer and he had not repeated it at Ottawa for two purposes: first, to dissuade the French from their course of building a national nuclear capability, and, second, to deal with the problem of whether the Germans would be stimulated to do the same thing. Since we are clearly failing in our first aim, is it wise to go ahead simply on the grounds of dealing with the Germans? Mr. Bowie responded by saying that he would put it in a somewhat different way. The French were by no means united in their support for a national nuclear capability. This

---

Source: Kennedy Library, National Security Files, MLF. Secret. Drafted by Kaysen on March 16.

was the idea of deGaulle and a rather small group around him. Many other Frenchmen opposed it. One of our aims in making the original proposal to commit a Polaris force to NATO was to offer to those Frenchmen who opposed the present policy an alternative which they could support and which they could offer to France. Mr. Bowie then went on to discuss the technical problems of the French missile and nuclear weapons programs, in particular, the difficulties the French will have in making a warhead small enough to carry on the missile they are now developing. For this reason our own experts believe that it will take three or four years beyond the present target date of 1967 before the French will have a usable nuclear-armed missile. Further, it will cost much more than the French now expect to spend. The President asked whether the continued denial of France's wishes on our part won't simply stimulate the French to combine with the Germans, whatever we offer the latter. Mr. Bowie indicated that he did not think the present German Government would, in fact, behave this way. In his judgment that government was strongly oriented to the notion of collective defense in NATO, and if we could provide a collective nuclear defense, they would welcome it. DeGaulle, on the other hand, was clearly against a collective defense, and it was for this reason that it was no use to attempt to move him toward a more cooperative relationship with NATO by meeting his desires in the nuclear missile field. These desires arise precisely from his preference for individual over collective defense and, therefore, it could not be in our interest if our policy had to be to outwait deGaulle and provide an attractive alternative to individual defense which deGaulle's successors would welcome, especially under the pressures of mounting difficulties and costs in France's own program. The President asked whether we were not offering MRBM proposal basically to the French and Germans and whether the others were simply uninterested. He further expressed concern that we were pouring our money into the ocean in this proposition in order to satisfy a political need whose use was dubious. Mr. Bowie agreed that the need was primarily political and not military but urged its reality and importance nonetheless. The President asked whether the Europeans really would satisfy their political desires through a force on which the U.S. still exercised a veto. Mr. Bundy explained our thoughts on how the processes of discussion in the North Atlantic Council could educate the European governments to the facts of nuclear life in such a way that the force, even though under an American veto, would still meet their concerns. Mr. Bowie pointed out that it was more appropriate to use the term "joint control" than the term "veto." He distinguished the case of response to general nuclear attack in which there could clearly be no discussion, and any other case in which there would be discussion in which the other European powers would certainly want us to join. Secretary McNamara emphasized the consensus that there was no military need for the MRBM. He further stated that those who thought there was military need by this indicated a lack of understanding of the nature of the nuclear control problem which was in itself dangerous. On the other hand, he did grant the political need. He cautioned, however, that there was a possibility that the creation of this force would compete with the increase in Europe in conventional capability that was far more important. There was some general discussion on the relation of this force to stated requirements of General Norstad for missiles and their implication in competing with the conventional forces, and then the discussion broke off.

CK

131.   Letter From the President's Military Representative (Taylor) to President Kennedy

Washington, April 3, 1962.

DEAR MR. PRESIDENT: As you know, I have just completed a two weeks' visit to Europe[1] which included stops at several NATO capitals and discussions with numerous officials, both US and foreign (Inclosure 1).[2] While the purpose of my trip was personal orientation, I should like to report to you my impressions on some of the political-military problems which particularly struck me after an absence of nearly three years from Europe. I have listed them under three heads:

    a. The depressed state of US relations with France, resulting largely from our opposition to the French atomic program.
    b. The problem of keeping West Germany a contented non-nuclear power.
    c. The acceptance by NATO of the "new" US strategy.

To avoid an unduly long letter, I have attached short supporting papers covering each of these three topics. Here I will state only the principal conclusions which I believe these papers to support. The first is that the US, after consultation with Prime Minister Macmillan and Chancellor Adenauer, should open negotiations with President de

---

Source: Kennedy Library, President's Office Files, NATO General. No classification marking. No drafting information appears on the source text.

[1] Taylor visited Europe March 18–31.

[2] Not printed. Inclosure 1 was a list of the U.S. and foreign officials seen by Taylor.

Gaulle directed at changing our policy toward aid to the French atomic program in exchange for loyal French cooperation within NATO, for French participation in a multilateral NATO force, and for an overall normalization of Franco-American relations.

The second is that we should strengthen German ties with NATO by supporting the forward strategy recommended by General Norstad, by giving Germany a voice in controlling the use of any multilateral NATO atomic force and by adopting a statement of principles on the use of atomic weapons similar to the guidelines which Secretary General Stikker is proposing.

Third and last, in the NATO forum we should advance our strategic ideas in a low key without giving the appearance of lecture or exhortation, preferably by way of a NATO comprehensive review of the military requirements for implementing a forward strategy capable of offering some degree of protection to the exposed population centers of West Germany.

My reasons for arriving at these conclusions are set forth in the attached inclosures.

Maxwell D. Taylor[3]

Enclosure 2[4]

THE STRAIN ON RELATIONS WITH FRANCE RESULTING FROM US OPPOSITION TO THE FRENCH ATOMIC PROGRAM

It is impossible to go to Paris today and meet with representatives of the de Gaulle Government without becoming deeply impressed with their bitterness toward the US Government. Their hostility results from our refusal to aid the French atomic program and the extension of this non-cooperation to their missile and nuclear submarine programs and then to remotely related projects in a way which strains the imagination to find justification in the requirements of the McMahon Act.

I found no European officials, US or European, who do not believe that de Gaulle is going to carry out his program to obtain national atomic weapons for France in spite of the cost and in spite of American resist-

---

[3] Printed from a copy that bears this typed signature.
[4] Top Secret.

ance. Most of them apparently believe that even if de Gaulle disappeared from the scene, a successor government would not be likely to cancel the program. In case the French encounter technical difficulties beyond their capability to resolve, it is probable that the French would turn to the Germans for aid, a contingency which the latter do not like to contemplate.

The US can either stand pat in refusing to help the French in all fields however remotely related to the atomic weapons program, can modify its position to one of non-cooperation in the atomic weapons field alone, or can open negotiations with France with a view to trading technical aid in atomic matters for important concessions such as:

    a. A French return to cooperation in NATO;
    b. Commitment of a significant part of French atomic weapons, when available, to a multilateral NATO atomic force; and
    c. An overall normalization of French-American relations.

After exchanging views with Adenauer and Macmillan, I would be inclined to try the latter course, i.e., negotiate with the French, and fall back to the middle course if the negotiations proved fruitless. This suggestion is advanced under no illusion as to the likelihood of de Gaulle becoming a grateful, cooperative partner or a true convert to integration of effort within NATO, but he may be induced to withhold his monkey wrench. Also, I appreciate the argument that the existence of a French national force will whet the appetite of the Germans for one of their own; however I would try to meet this contingency through a multilateral NATO atomic force in the use of which the Germans would have a vote. This possibility is discussed in the following paper.

Enclosure 3[5]

STRENGTHENING WEST GERMAN TIES TO NATO

West Germany is in the geographical front rank of NATO facing (the Germans would say) 92 hostile divisions. Several of their principal cities, notably Hamburg and Munich, lie forward of the main NATO battle position, and the German leaders know it. They hear talk of a forward strategy to defend these centers but do not see the conventional forces to execute it. At the same time, they hear of a "new" American strategy which calls for imposing a pause on these hostile divisions by conventional means without the use of nuclear weapons. In combination, the lack of conventional forces to implement a true forward strat-

---

[5] Top Secret.

egy and the alleged reluctance on the part of the US to use atomic weapons at the outset of an attack are matters which give pause to many German leaders concerned with the long-term security of their country.

If West Germany is to continue to be a contented non-nuclear member of NATO, particularly after France obtains national nuclear weapons, these problems need to be faced before a critical situation arises in the heart of the Alliance. Several courses of action suggest themselves and deserve serious consideration.

The first is to develop the concept and then plan for a multilateral NATO nuclear force which will include Germany among a restricted group of nations controlling the use of this force. The composition of the force should be designed to meet the requirement of giving the Europeans—and particularly the West Germans—a feeling of participating more directly in determining the use of atomic weapons in NATO. The weapons in such a force should be counted against SACEUR's military requirements to strike targets of primary interest to the Alliance and be subject to his control as are his other atomic weapons, but the justification for the force would be primarily political-psychological. It should be set up in business without delay by allocations of existing weapons by the US and UK (and eventually by France); the subsequent modernization of these weapons by the introduction of a new MRBM should be planned as a part of the overall modernization program for all of SACEUR's atomic forces.

West Germans need reassurance not only through the provision of this NATO nuclear force but also through evidence of a determination to use all NATO atomic weapons under certain predetermined conditions which will satisfy German security requirements. For the moment, some declaration of principles governing the use of atomic weapons such as Stikker's currently proposed guidelines, if approved both by the President of the United States and by the North Atlantic Council, seems the most feasible way to give the needed reassurance to Germany.

Finally, there is need to give reality to a forward strategy which can be executed for the duration of a significant pause without a general employment of atomic weapons. In the eyes of the Germans, means for such a strategy do not exist now. The first step is to agree within NATO upon what these means should be; in short, to embark on the NATO military review which is discussed in the following paper.

The foregoing actions are affirmative suggestions to tie the West Germans more tightly to the West. There are some negative actions which would work strongly against this objective if the Europeans—particularly the Germans—became aware of them. They include any action which might suggest that the multilateral NATO force is a device to remove atomic weapons from Europe or to deflect a general modernization of NATO atomic forces. Another would be to advocate a pseudo-forward strategy based on an obviously fragile defensive shield without the depth, durability, or logistic means to support sustained combat. The Germans know too much about war and the facts of life to be taken in for long.

Enclosure 4[6]

THE "NEW" US STRATEGY

General Norstad feels, and I agree, that the sure way to defeat our purpose of gaining NATO acceptance of our reoriented thinking on military strategy is to present it as something new and extraordinary, made in the USA. He points out that many of the cardinal points, particularly the increased emphasis on conventional weapons and the concept of creating a pause before using atomic weapons, have been a part of NATO thinking for a long time. In his recent Emergency Defense Plan[7] now disseminated to NATO commanders, there is recognition of the possibility of a conventional conflict in resisting an aggression less than general war.

In listening to the views of General Norstad and the SHAPE staff, I was struck both by their support of the need for a forward strategy to reassure the Germans and by what I view as their reluctance to face up to the need for larger forces to give reality to such a strategy. One thought was advanced that the pause imposed on the Soviets might occur prior to firing a shot, presumably while they contemplated the consequences of an attack on NATO forward positions. This would be accomplished by placing a sufficient number of NATO ground forces far enough forward to oblige the Soviets to mass for a major military thrust thereby exposing their forces at the outset to the possibility of effective use of nuclear weapons. If the attack then came, the NATO forces would be expected to expend themselves on these forward positions, since their numbers would not permit anything like an effective resistance forward and a defense in depth as well. In the background of these views, I detected a fundamental disbelief in the practicability of getting an increased NATO contribution to support a forward strategy with adequate forces.

Returning to the problem of influencing our NATO allies in the direction of our strategic thinking, if direct explanation and exhortation must be avoided, it remains to find a better way. I would recommend a

---

[6] Top Secret.
[7] Not found.

comprehensive NATO review of the requirements for an adequate forward strategy as a vehicle to argue the case for the modified strategy. To do such a job in a professional military way, it would be necessary to give to the Allied planners—and through them their governmental leaders—much of the new information on weapons effects, targeting plans, and enemy capabilities which would be otherwise suspect if suddenly released to support US arguments on NATO strategy. In this NATO forum, we could thrash out the differences in assessing Soviet capabilities which now plague our international discussions.

In passing, I would mention that the assumptions for such a review would, as always, largely control the outcome. I would suggest the inclusion of the following assumptions if the end product is to have the desired value:

a. NATO should defend far enough forward to cover the main population centers of the exposed member nations.
b. NATO forces should be sufficient to prevent without the general use of atomic weapons any serious inroad into NATO territory for at least _____ days (the exact figure to be based on a political estimate of the time requirement).
c. SACEUR should have operational control of all the weapons necessary to strike the principal targets primarily threatening Western Europe, to include the Soviet MRBM deployment.

The establishment of agreed NATO requirements for a forward strategy would have generally good consequences apart from the progress which it might make in educating our Allies. One result would be to require SHAPE to justify the need for NATO MRBM's both as modernization of existing bomber and cruise missile forces and as a contribution to the NATO nuclear force previously discussed. Another would be to establish the role for very low yield atomic weapons in extending the capability of conventional forces. Such matters could not be considered without getting into questions of NATO organization, command and control. In the full context of Western European defense and in the relatively cool atmosphere of military planning, we might hope for more progress than in high temperature political discussions, where these intricate matters are often considered in isolation.

On the negative side, it is probable that an honest study of requirements would be opposed, possibly frustrated, by national interests desirous of controlling the end result. If this result is a requirement for a greatly increased contribution to NATO, efforts will be made to discredit and bury the review. Nonetheless, even in this case, it would have important collateral benefits and is, I am convinced, worth giving a sincere try. There is not much likelihood that the project will be started—certainly its conclusions will not be adopted and implemented—without vigorous US backing all the way.

132.   Memorandum From Secretary of State Rusk to President Kennedy

Washington, April 13, 1962.

SUBJECT

General Taylor's Comments on His Recent Visit to Europe

You requested my reactions to General Taylor's report on his recent trip to Europe, as set forth in his April 3 letter to you.[1] I have omitted reference to the French nuclear and the NATO multilateral force issues, except as they relate directly to other views of General Taylor.

Strengthening West German Ties to NATO. I concur generally in General Taylor's comments on strengthening West German ties to NATO. There are several observations, however, that I would make.

First, although I fully agree that we must develop a multilateral NATO nuclear force as one answer to German concerns, I do not concur that such a force should be justified on the basis of SACEUR's military requirements. I feel that the basic need for the NATO multilateral force is political; it would have military utility, but not necessarily for SACEUR's requirements, which the U.S. has not accepted. I also do not concur in General Taylor's view that the force should be set up without delay, drawing on existing weapons of the U.S. and the U.K. and eventually of France. I believe that a multilaterally owned, controlled and manned force is essential to meet the political requirement.

Secondly, I agree with General Taylor that the guidelines currently being developed in NATO are needed to give the Germans evidence of our determination to use nuclear weapons. Although there may be a problem in obtaining French agreement, the current discussions in NATO on these guidelines promise that something can be worked out which will meet some German concerns. Language in the guidelines as presently drafted states that nuclear weapons will be used in the event of (i) an unmistakable nuclear attack, in which case the possibilities for consultation will be limited; and (ii) a full-scale Soviet conventional attack, in which case it is expected that time will permit consultation. In a situation involving less than unmistakable nuclear or full-scale conventional attacks, but nevertheless involving a threat to the integrity of NATO territory, the decision to use nuclear weapons would be subject to prior consultation in the Council. Although we do not have formal

---

Source: Kennedy Library, National Security Files, Maxwell D. Taylor Trip to Europe. Top Secret. No drafting information appears on the source text.

[1] Document 131.

German approval, the indications are that these guidelines will be acceptable to the Federal Republic.

Thirdly, we also concur with General Taylor that there is need to give reality to a forward strategy which can be executed for the duration of a significant pause without general employment of nuclear weapons. We feel, however, that the problem here has two aspects: (i) The first aspect is to explain the basis for U.S. thinking on this issue, as Secretary McNamara began to do at Paris in December and as we hope to continue to do through the U.S. information program in the NAC. Only when the process is further underway will we be able to judge whether it would be useful to have a general NATO review of military requirements. (ii) The second aspect is to fill the large gaps which presently exist in NATO forces. The fact is that the Alliance today is deficient in the forces required to fulfill immediate needs and first priority must be given to filling these deficiencies.

As for the negative actions to be avoided, I agree that the multilateral NATO force should not be portrayed as a device to remove nuclear weapons from Europe. On the contrary, we are presently engaged in NATO in developing formal assurances that an adequate level of nuclear weapons will be maintained in Europe and that targets of concern to the Europeans will be covered. Furthermore, these assurances will be reinforced by the program for giving our NATO Allies full information, in general terms, on targeting and on the numbers and deployment of nuclear weapons.

Although the issue of our nuclear policy toward France is being covered separately, I would like, in commenting on General Taylor's recommendations regarding Germany, to make the general point that a change in our policy of non-cooperation with France in nuclear or missile matters would basically contradict the objective of tying Germany into NATO more closely. A change in our policy of denying the French help for a national nuclear or missile program would inevitably lead, sooner rather than later in my view, to German pressures for similar treatment. However we responded to these pressures, such a development in Germany would make far more difficult the task of tying Germany more closely into the Alliance. We have made clear to the Germans why we do not provide help for the French missile or nuclear program, and any change in our posture would be taken by them as a sign of a basic shift of policy—in whose fruits they would expect to share.

The "New" U.S. Strategy. General Taylor's comments on the "new" U.S. strategy are also, generally speaking, in conformity with my views. I agree that we should generally advance our strategic ideas without giving the appearance of lecture or exhortation. This does not mean, however, that we should not continue to make our case for a conventional buildup and for a strategy that does not rest on use of nuclear weapons from the outset. Although General Taylor's proposal for a comprehensive review of military requirements in SHAPE might be a desirable technique, at some point, as indicated above, I believe it also important that there be discussion in the NATO Council so that the political authorities may be given a fuller comprehension of all factors involved in our thinking. In this connection, I am concerned that there be an adequate flow of information to our NATO Allies, both on the facts of conventional requirements and on nuclear matters.

On the conventional side, I am concerned that there appears to be a serious difference of view between the U.S., the Germans, and SHAPE, on the magnitude of the threat we face in Soviet divisions. You will recall that this difference came out sharply at the briefing of Adenauer last November. It has not been resolved. The same U.S. figures used in the Adenauer briefing were used in Secretary McNamara's briefing of the NATO Council last December. The Germans again challenged our figures, as did Norstad privately. The JCS is currently studying the matter, but so far has not been able to provide us with the data required. This has seriously hampered our efforts to follow up on Secretary McNamara's presentation at the December NATO meeting. I am informed that Defense is now working to remedy this deficiency.

On the nuclear side, I am concerned that we be in a position to give in the NATO Council as full information as is necessary to convince our Allies that there is adequate protection for them against the Soviet threat to Europe. Any failure on our part to provide the information necessary can undermine our basic purpose: to give the Europeans enough confidence in nuclear defense to head off pressures for independent national nuclear programs. Again, I believe that Defense is seeking to bring together the information necessary to meet this need.[2]

Dean Rusk[3]

---

[2] In an April 25 memorandum McNamara commented on the 3d and 4th enclosures to Taylor's report. Stating that he shared Taylor's appreciation of the German concern and that a NATO nuclear force was justified by political-psychological factors rather than military, he stressed that the Germans should be given reassurances about the NATO response to an attack on Germany. McNamara also shared Taylor's view that the new strategy should not be represented as something novel, but speculated that it was too early to tell if NATO conventional forces would be strengthened. (Kennedy Library, National Security Files, Maxwell D. Taylor Trip to Europe)

[3] Printed from a copy that bears this typed signature.

133. Minutes of Meeting

Washington, April 16, 1962, 10:30 a.m.

PRESENT

The President, Secretary Rusk, Secretary McNamara, and Mr. McGeorge Bundy

The meeting opened with discussion of the question of possibility of assistance to the French in nuclear and missile fields.

Secretary Rusk explained that this is not essentially a matter of our having a special policy toward the French. We have rather a standing policy which de Gaulle is now trying to get us to change, although neither he nor his Foreign Minister has ever asked for nuclear help.

Secretary Rusk believed that centrally de Gaulle is in favor of a Directoire—the U.S., U.K., and France. In his pursuit of this objective he was standing alone among the six in Europe, and in NATO he had been 1 against 14 on negotiation with the Soviets, as he was now 1 against 14 on guidelines for the use of nuclear weapons. He had gone so far as to hold up the installation of tropospheric scatter facilities for US/NATO communications through France.

The Secretary believed we must recognize that if we go in de Gaulle's direction in these matters we will have very great difficulties with our other Allies. The Germans would not like it in the long run; the Italians would be strongly opposed, as would others, such as Canada. Moreover, we must consider this matter in the light of our overwhelming problems with the Soviet Union. We now have a chance of dealing with the USSR, and nuclear help to the French would run against this effort.

At the same time the Secretary believed that our existing policy should be carefully delineated. He had restrained some of his own people who wished to extend a policy of non-cooperation beyond its relevance to French nuclear delivery systems. In particular, the Secretary hoped there might be means of cooperation in outer space activities.

As for consultation, the Secretary felt that de Gaulle consulted only on matters that were of primary interest to others. There had been no consultation on such matters in his own sphere as Bizerte or Algeria. In Southeast Asia he wished consultation without responsibility, since de Gaulle himself had explained to the President that there would be no French troops in that part of the world.

Source: Kennedy Library, National Security Files, Meetings with the President. Top Secret.

In summary, the Secretary believed that France was not de Gaulle, and that we could not and should not treat this country with the trust and confidence that we show toward the United Kingdom.

Secretary McNamara, after remarking that he agreed that changing our attitude on nuclear weapons would not change de Gaulle, advanced his position in terms of what he called a "narrow military view." The Defense Department believed that France is capable of having a nuclear force and will have one. By 1965 she will have an effective fission-bomb aircraft force, and by 1970 she can be expected to have thermonuclear weapons with a missile delivery system. She will do this with or without de Gaulle.

At the same time, the French posture has three disadvantages from the point of view of the Department of Defense. First, there is a persisting weakness in French conventional forces which they will not be able to remedy as long as the burden of their nuclear effort is not lightened. Second, the French have failed to help in the balance of payments problem created by American forces in France. Third, the French have refused to cooperate on NATO nuclear guidelines and on the NATO MRBM problem. Secretary McNamara did not know how much the French might change these three policies in return for nuclear help, but he thought that they might and that we should find out.

There followed some discussion of what the Germans and British might think. The President's attention was called to Adenauer's recent expression of concern to Stikker about any help to France, and the President himself remarked that he doubted if the British Government could face the political consequences of nuclear assistance to the French.

Secretary Rusk reiterated his view that de Gaulle's basic purpose was the development of an independent capability, so that it was most unlikely that he could accept a real commitment to NATO. Mr. McNamara then stated in essence the position presented in the Defense paper of April 11[1] on this point and repeated his view that the present situation is unsatisfactory and that the French could be expected to proceed and develop a force of their own whether or not we help them. To this the Secretary replied that costs are the one great barrier to nuclear diffusion. If we should now be willing to help the French we should be blackmailed into helping others when they reach the point of heavy financial pressure, and in effect we should be reducing the price of entry into the nuclear field. The Secretary's view was that we should instead seek a way to reduce our special nuclear relation to the British. The reestablishing of such nuclear sharing with the British in 1958 had been a mistake.

---

[1] Not found.

The Secretary of Defense asked if we could not undertake a probing discussion to see what we might obtain. The Secretary felt that it would be disastrous to do this bilaterally since it would have a very heavy impact on our other allies.

The President indicated his own belief that it was wrong to move on this matter now. In the light of these conflicting considerations he was not prepared to authorize any change in our policy. He thought the only thing we could be sure of getting from the French was money. He believed therefore that it was in our interest to have public speculation die down and he asked that guidelines be prepared accordingly.

The discussion then turned to the problem of MRBM policy. The Secretary of State, in urging adoption of the proposed policy, agreed with Mr. McNamara that NATO would not be able to settle on any other controlling agent than the President. He then briefly discussed the guidelines stated in the paper[2] and indicated his belief that from a political point of view it was most important to go through the exercise of ways and means of controlling such a force and to find out that there is no one but the President. The Secretary also thought multilateral manning was of great importance, especially as it might prevent a row with the Soviet Union over German activity in this field. He also emphasized his conviction (not shared by all his colleagues) that the Europeans should pay the bulk of the price for this force. The President energetically agreed with this last sentiment.

Secretary McNamara registered four points:

1. The Joint Chiefs of Staff strongly disagree with this paper.
2. He himself would disagree if there were to be a NATO control separate from the President.
3. He believed that we must indeed get off dead center in discussion of these issues.
4. There was a danger that in following this policy Europeans might come to take nuclear weapons as a substitute for necessary conventional forces.

Secretary McNamara believed for himself that there is no military requirement for such an MRBM force, but he pointed out that the Joint Chiefs and General Norstad disagree strongly. As to the cost of such a force, he thought it might run to about 2 billion dollars. The U.S. might contribute 600 million dollars, and the Germans 400 million dollars, but he could not see who would pay for the other billion. Nevertheless, he was very enthusiastic about submitting the proposal for its political values.

Secretary McNamara then expressed his own preference for an American-manned and American-financed force which would be a

---

[2] See the attachment to Document 135.

genuine part of the American strategic deterrent. He thought such a force would be more justifiable in economic and military terms, and he believed that it might in the end meet the European political requirement too.

At the President's request, Mr. McNamara detailed the opposition of the Chiefs as follows:

1. The Chiefs object to the transfer of information. Mr. McNamara strongly disagreed and believed that it was important to communicate views and figures which would show that a nuclear war would be indivisible, that it would be catastrophic, and that the deterrent power of the U.S. is and will remain overwhelming.
2. The Chiefs deny the notion that there was no military requirement for MRBM's.
3. The Chiefs strongly object to any notion of multilateral control of Polaris.

On this third point, Secretary McNamara agreed with the Chiefs, and with Secretary Rusk's concurrence the decision was made not to approve this paragraph 2 d. of the document.

The President indicated that any greater degree to NATO control would be hard to accept. He further believed that as much as possible we should state the matter in such a way that the Europeans would come to us with their ideas. We must not seem to be proposing a flat American position.

It was agreed that each Secretary would explain these matters to his own subordinates, and later the President approved the attached guidelines as guidance for all concerned.

McG. B.[3]

---

[3] Printed from a copy that bears these typed initials.

---

134. Telegram From the Department of State to the Mission to the North Atlantic Treaty Organization and European Regional Organizations

Washington, April 16, 1962, 8:31 p.m.

Topol 1579. Subject: Multilateral MRBM Force. You are authorized make following statement at earliest opportunity to NAC, which should

---

Source: Department of State, Central Files, 375/4–1662. Secret; Priority; Limit Distribution; Verbatim Text. Drafted by Fessenden and Kranich; cleared with Nitze, Seymour Weiss, and Owen; and approved by Kohler. Repeated to Bonn, Brussels, and London.

be represented not as US proposal but as a US contribution to the resolution of the issues involved in the question. We leave tactical handling to you,[1] but suggest you may wish arrange in advance support of Spaak, de Staerke, Stikker and others.

Begin text: During the course of the past several months the NAC has been engaged in the consideration of many facets of the problem of NATO's nuclear role. These discussions have centered around provision by the US of nuclear weapons information to NATO, assurances of the US that it will maintain adequate nuclear capability at the disposal of the Alliance and guidelines for the use of nuclear weapons. We hope these measures will go far toward meeting our allies' concerns in this field. We are prepared to go further, however, if they desire. We are prepared to join our allies in creating a genuinely multilateral NATO MRBM Force, if they believe that such a Force is needed. We are also, as a separate measure, prepared to commit additional external forces to NATO.

Within the US an intensive review of this question has now been concluded and the US desires to place a résumé of its conclusions before the NAC at this time. This is not done in order to precipitate immediate discussion, but rather to provide the NAC with a body of US conclusions which other countries can review and consider, in order that the Alliance can give early attention to the questions involved soon after the Athens Ministerial meeting, perhaps in a committee established especially for this purpose. It is not intended that this presentation should in any way disrupt the Council's present schedule for discussion of items other than the two steps I am about to discuss between now and the Athens meeting.

To take the more immediate of these two steps first: The US is prepared to commit to NATO US nuclear forces outside the European continent, additional to those already committed. In this connection, the US will provide NATO at the Athens meeting with a schedule calling for progressive commitment of Polaris submarines as the total submarine force grows.

As the second step the US is prepared to join its allies in developing a modest sized (on the order of 200 missiles) fully multilateral NATO sea-based MRBM force. We do not urge a NATO MRBM force on the Alliance, in view of already programmed US strategic forces, but we are prepared to proceed with it in view of the recognized need for greater

---

[1] On April 19, however, the Mission to NATO was informed that the "highest levels" in Washington did not want to be in a position of trying to push its MRBM proposal on the Alliance, but rather wanted to be in a position of responding to Allied desires. Because of this Washington wanted the subject handled in a way not likely to give rise to press reports that the United States had submitted a proposal for adding MRBMs to Allied forces. (Topol 1607 to Paris; ibid., 700.5612/4–1862)

sharing of nuclear responsibilities within the Alliance and the fact that such force would have military utility.

This conclusion is consistent with past indications of our views. The US is on clear record, in President's Ottawa speech and elsewhere, that it is prepared to join with its NATO allies in considering creation of a truly multilateral sea-borne NATO MRBM force, should the Alliance desire such course, as means for providing allies with greater participation in Alliance's nuclear role. The US has on several occasions indicated, as for example in statements of Secretaries Rusk and McNamara in Paris in December, that the US would only facilitate procurement of MRBMs for NATO if these missiles were to be placed under multilateral ownership and control.

I should like now to indicate some of our specific thoughts as to the nature of this NATO MRBM Force.

First, It would be under multilateral ownership, being financed, both for continuing cost and operation, through infrastructure principle, under formula to be determined. Costs would be equitably shared, with greater part of costs being borne by our allies.

Second, It would be subject to multilateral control as to use in accordance with NATO agreed guidelines or any agreed formula for consultation and decision-making.

Third, There would be sufficient degree of mixed manning to ensure that no single nationality is predominant in the manning of any vessel, or of the missiles aboard any vessel, in the multilateral force.

Fourth, This initial force would be sea-borne in order to avoid the political problems associated with land-based deployment, facilitate multilateral control, minimize collateral damage if attacked by enemy nuclear fire, and lessen vulnerability.

Fifth, This force would come under appropriate NATO commanders' command.

Sixth, Since defense of NATO area is indivisible a NATO MRBM Force, if one is created, should not fragment this unified task. Planning for its use should, therefore, assume that it would be used in integral association with other allies' nuclear forces. Construction of such a Force along the lines suggested above would thus not imply that the separate defense of Europe was its purpose or likely effect. On the contrary, US willingness to join in creating such a Force should be dramatic evidence of US unconditional commitment to defense of the entire Alliance.

Seventh, US would be prepared to furnish warheads. Ways should be found to safe-guard design data, e.g., US custodians could remain aboard any multilaterally manned NATO vessel with standing orders to release the warheads in case a properly authenticated order to fire was received through agreed channels.

Eighth, Targeting of the force and the kind of missiles and vessels to be used in the force would be determined at an appropriate time in the light of our continuing consideration of NATO strategy, of the role of this force in that strategy, and other relevant factors.

The US would welcome the views of its allies concerning the formula for multilateral control of this force. A formula which would involve transfer of warheads or procedures for using the force without US concurrence would require amending existing US law and could well entail other obstacles, depending on the character of the arrangements. The US is willing, however, to consider any proposal which is put to it by a clear majority of the Alliance.

The above described multilateral MRBM force, together with the other steps that we have mentioned, would represent an effective program for sharing nuclear responsibility within the Alliance. This program would, we believe, respond to allied concerns in a way which would ensure that nuclear weapons become a force for cohesion, rather than division, in the Alliance. It would provide substantial impetus to the forces of integration within the Alliance. The multilateral force, in particular, would represent a bold and affirmative action toward greater Atlantic interdependence. It would provide our allies with a role in strategic deterrent which should effectively deflate Soviet attempts at nuclear blackmail. It would thus create an alternative to national development of nuclear capabilities which would make sense from both a military and political standpoint. We repeat that these views are outlined not as a US proposal but as a US contribution to resolution of the issues involved in this question. While this resolution will obviously take time, we would welcome any expression of views, either before or at the Athens meeting, and would be prepared to join our allies in considering it in more detail thereafter.

Rusk

135.   National Security Action Memorandum No. 147

Washington, April 18, 1962.

TO

The Secretary of State
The Secretary of Defense

SUBJECT

NATO Nuclear Program

The President has approved the recommendation of the Secretaries of State and Defense that U.S. policy on MRBMs be governed by the provisions of the paper entitled "Suggested NATO Nuclear Program," dated March 22, 1962; except that Paragraph 2(d) should not be volunteered by the U.S.

In handling the MRBM issue in the North Atlantic Council, the U.S. should outline its views in accord with the contents of this paper, not as a U.S. proposal, but as a U.S. contribution to the resolution of the issues involved in this question.

The Secretary of State will have the responsibility for handling tactics on this topic, consulting with the Secretary of Defense as appropriate.

McGeorge Bundy

[Attachment][1]

Paper Prepared by the Departments of State and Defense

Washington, March 22, 1962.

SUBJECT

Suggested NATO Nuclear Program

After approval by the President, the United States should outline the following elements in NAC, at appropriate times and in suitable detail. These elements should be discussed in the context of revised strat-

---

Source: Department of State, NSAMs: Lot 72 D 316. Secret.

[1] Secret. No drafting information appears on the source text. This paper was originally submitted to the President under cover of a March 29 memorandum from Rusk and McNamara, which explained that paragraph 2(d) was unagreed. (Kennedy Library, National Security Files, MLF)

egy. Within this framework, the need for improved conventional forces should be stressed and elaborated in necessary detail, and the extent to which the nuclear proposals are dependent on an adequate conventional program should be made clear.

1. *NATO Participation:* Measures should be instituted to give NATO greater information about US nuclear strategy, and greater participation in the formulation of that strategy. (Specific actions to this end currently under study by the State and Defense Departments should be included, if they are found to be useful.) As part of these measures:

(a) Procedures should be instituted under which we would share information about our nuclear forces and consult about basic plans and arrangements for their use in the NAC and the Standing Group–Military Committee. Although we should withhold highly sensitive operational information concerning sorties commitments, time on target, penetration tactics and the like, we can and should provide a considerable body of information, including targeting policy, nuclear force strengths, analysis of the force capabilities, some intelligence on Soviet Bloc strengths, and constraint policies. In putting forth this information, the US would stress the extent to which planned uses of this US strategic force are devoted to European as well as North American interests, the importance of responsible, centralized control over nuclear forces, the strength of the present and future nuclear capabilities of the US, and the probable consequences if a nuclear war were to occur. To facilitate this enlarged participation by NATO in over-all nuclear planning and operations, increased functions regarding these matters could be assigned to appropriate bodies, such as a small special group and the NATO Standing Group–Military Committee.

(b) An attempt should be made to work out NATO guidelines, which the US President would agree to observe, regarding use of all US nuclear weapons in defending NATO.

2. *US Forces Outside the Continent:*

(a) The US should indicate to its allies that an appropriate portion of US external forces will be directed against targets of special concern to Europe.

(b) The US should state that it is prepared to commit to NATO US nuclear forces outside the European continent (additional to those US forces already committed, in amounts to be determined). This might be the force indicated under (c).

(c) To meet on an interim basis any political need for having MRBM's based in the European area which would come under NATO wartime military command, Polaris submarines should, as promised by the President in May 1961, be committed to NATO. The US should furnish NATO with a schedule calling for the progressive commitment of Polaris submarines as the total Polaris force grows.

(d) To meet on an interim basis any political need for multilateral political control over MRBM's based in the European area, the US should indicate its willingness to consider proposals for some form of multilateral NATO control (such as indicated under 3(g) below) over the Polaris submarines committed to NATO, if this is strongly desired by our allies. It should make clear that it could not consider proposals which would limit the operational effectiveness of this vital element of the free world deterrent or prevent the US from using these submarines in self-defense whenever it felt compelled to do so. The US should also make clear that the timing of any institution of any agreed multilateral control would have to be determined by the US in the light of operational considerations at the time the proposals were made. Any multilateral control over these Polaris submarines would lapse when they were replaced by a multilateral MRBM force.

3. *Multilaterally Manned NATO Force:* The US should indicate its willingness to join its allies, if they wish, in developing a modest-sized (on the order of 200 missiles) fully multilateral NATO sea-based MRBM force. It should not urge this course, and should indicate its view that MRBM forces are not urgently needed for military reasons, in view of already programmed U.S. strategic forces; it should make clear that it would be prepared to facilitate procurement of MRBM's only under multilateral ownership, control, and manning.

(a) *Targeting and Weapons.* The question of the targeting for a multilateral force, and the question of the kind of missile and vessel to be used in the force, should be determined in the light of NATO's continuing consideration of strategy, the role of the force in that strategy, and other relevant factors.

(b) *Participation.* The US should only be prepared to proceed if the venture had adequate allied participation, so that it did not appear to be a thinly disguised US-German operation.

(c) *Costs.* The costs should be equitably shared. The US should make clear that it would not be prepared to make a major contribution to the cost but would expect the greater part of the burden to be borne by the allies.

(d) *Mixed Manning.* The US should require a sufficient degree of mixed manning to ensure that one nationality does not appear to be predominant in the manning—and is not, in fact, in control—of any vessel or of the missiles aboard any vessel in the multilateral force. Members of the mixed crews would be recruited from national armed forces into the NATO MRBM force and would thereafter be under the control of that

Force; for trial and punishment of major crimes, they would be returned to their country of origin.

(e) *Custody*. Ways should be found to safeguard design data, e.g., US custodians could remain aboard any multilaterally manned NATO vessels, with standing orders to release the warheads in case a properly authenticated order to fire was received through agreed channels (see g, below).

(f) *Centralized Command*. In presenting these views, the US would stress its belief that the defense of the NATO area is indivisible and that a NATO Force, if one is created, could not fragment this unified task. Planning for its use should, therefore, assume that it would be employed in integral association with other Alliance nuclear forces. Construction of such a Force along the lines suggested above would thus not imply that the separate defense of Europe was its purpose or likely effect. On the contrary, our willingness to join in creating such a force should be dramatic evidence of our unconditional commitment to the defense of the entire Alliance.

(g) *Control*. The US should indicate that it wishes to ascertain the views of its allies concerning the control formula. In the ensuing discussion, it should be receptive to a control formula along the lines of that on which they are most likely to agree:

(i) Advance delegation to some person or group of authority to order use of the MRBM Force (in conjunction with other nuclear forces available to NATO), in the clearly specified contingency of unmistakeable large scale nuclear attack on NATO.

(ii) Agreement that the decision to order use of the force in other contingencies should be based on a prearranged system of voting in the NAC, which a majority of our allies will almost certainly wish to provide for voting by unanimity or by a group including the US.

In connection with NATO consideration of the multilateral force the United States should make plain that transfer of nuclear warheads or procedures for using the force without United States concurrence would require amending existing United States law and could well entail other obstacles depending on the character of the arrangement. The United States should indicate, however, that it is willing to consider any proposal which is put to us by a clear majority of the Alliance.

136.   Telegram From Secretary of State Rusk to the Department of State

Athens, May 6, 1962, 4 p.m.

Secto 70. Eyes only President and Acting Secretary. There is general consensus among Ministers and US Delegation that this has been most successful NATO meeting of Kennedy Administration. There was genuine satisfaction our handling Berlin problem to date and, despite minor needle from Luns and expected reservation from Couve de Murville, agreement on basis on which we plan to proceed.

My bilateral talk with Schroeder was friendly and relaxed as was quadripartite dinner on Berlin.[1] Couve took initiative to tell me he appreciated accuracy of US background press briefing and recognized error Drew Middleton story was solely matter *New York Times*.

Two US statements on defense, especially additional information provided by McNamara, made profound impression not only because of what was said but because US took unprecedented step to demonstrate its seriousness and solidarity with respect to Alliance problems.

Only serious frictions my visit Athens were as anticipated problem of West New Guinea with Netherlands which I hope to resolve this afternoon, and colonial questions with Portugal which will require further careful nursing. Luns told me privately he had been "rather unfair" in his speech on WNG at NATO table and certain other members of Six who supported him at table told me privately his language had been excessive. I am convinced that it was wise not to permit matter to become bitter Donnybrook at NATO table set off by a sharp reply by me to Luns and I know that other members appreciated this restraint.

[1 paragraph (7-1/2 lines of source text) not declassified]

Minor potential storms such as Greek revolt against wisemen's report[2] and Italian rejection of nuclear guidelines were successfully resolved and meeting ended this morning in atmosphere of harmony and confidence which erased memories of the communiqué battle which marred December meeting in Paris.

Source: Department of State, Central Files, 396.1–AT/5–662. Secret; Priority; No Other Distribution. Rusk was in Athens for the North Atlantic Council Ministerial Meeting, May 4–6. Summary and verbatim records of the sessions, telegrams to and from the U.S. Delegation, memoranda of conversations, briefing papers, and the texts of Rusk's statement on the political situation and his and McNamara's statement on NATO defense policy, are ibid., Conference Files: Lot 65 D 533, CF 2095–2103.

[1] Memoranda of these conversations on May 5, US/MC/30 and US/MC/21, are ibid., CF 2095.

[2] Documentation on the "Report on the Special Economic Problems of the Less Developed Member Countries" is ibid., CF 2103.

Will background American press this afternoon but cannot guarantee they will reflect the boredom of serenity as contrasted with the high news value of even bits and pieces of disagreement.

Rusk

---

137. Circular Telegram From the Department of State to Certain Missions

Washington, May 9, 1962, 9:26 p.m.

1920. Subject: Summary of NATO Meeting in Athens. NATO Ministerial Meeting Athens May 4–6 one of most successful in history of Alliance, resulting in solid accomplishments. Highlights of meeting were (1) full political consultation on East-West problems, particularly Secretary's statement on Berlin and Germany, disarmament and other major East-West issues; (2) in defense field Ministerial confirmation of guidelines, assurances and nuclear information program; (3) Secretary McNamara's statement on defense, which contained fullest factual information on nuclear matters ever given Alliance; and (4) approval of resolutions on Greece and Turkey,[1] which provides basis for Alliance-wide efforts to assist Greece and Turkey in meeting their special economic problems.

1. *Political Consultation.* Secretary Rusk's statement on Berlin very well received by Alliance. Secretary said Soviets up to present had made no significant move to meet West's vital interests, i.e., continued presence Western forces in Berlin, free access, and maintenance relations between West Berlin and FedRep. At same time, Soviets seem to desire continuation talks and to avoid moving Berlin toward military crisis or diplomatic impasse. Secretary said discussions with Soviets have taken place on three levels: (1) permanent solution German question, which Soviets view in terms their proposals for free city and to which West has

---

Source: Department of State, Central Files, 396.1–AT/5–962. Secret; Limit Distribution. Drafted by Fessenden and approved by Kohler. Sent to New Delhi, Tokyo, and 19 missions in Europe.

[1] Texts of the resolutions on Greece and Turkey are ibid., Conference Files: Lot 65 D 533, CF 2103.

counter-proposed German reunification on basis free elections; (2) facts of situation today, re which Soviets stress existence of two Germanies and to which we respond in terms of Western responsibilities for Berlin, the presence of Western forces there and Western access; and (3) finding means of dealing with facts of disagreement, i.e., setting aside points of disagreement and recognizing points of agreement. Secretary said we believe some progress has been made in getting across to Moscow that West is determined to preserve its vital interests in Berlin. Soviets have also shown some, but not much, interest in third level of approach. US believes coming weeks might indicate whether anything in nature of modus vivendi possible. US believes effective contact should be maintained with Soviet Union on Berlin.

Other Ministers, except French, endorsed US position and continued contacts, some giving enthusiastic endorsement. French did not disagree with US position and in fact approved modus vivendi approach. French, however, warned against dangers of prolonged negotiations and particularly dangers of being drawn toward recognizing GDR and neutralization of Germany.

On nuclear tests, Secretary stressed our disappointment over failure achieve nuclear test ban treaty and described US-UK efforts at Geneva to reach satisfactory agreement. Explained that US policy continued be based on President's March 2 statement.[2] Emphasized difficulty making any headway on either nuclear testing or disarmament as long as Soviets continued to be obsessed with secrecy.

Others Ministers endorsed US position, none taking issue with US resumption of tests.

On general disarmament, Secretary stressed US desire make some real beginnings toward disarmament. Stressed considerable negotiations ahead and that we must be certain impact of disarmament in total situation will result in giving no military advantage to either side. Other Ministers also endorsed US position disarmament.

In summarizing East-West relations generally, Secretary stressed difficulty in appraising Sino-Soviet conflict, but pointed out Free World could not derive comfort from Sino-Soviet conflict which in last analysis is difference of view as to how communist world should accomplish its objective of world domination. Secretary said general atmosphere East-West relations improved with respect to techniques, methods, tactics and discussions. Warned, however, against being misled by any atmosphere of détente. Underlying policies of Soviets remain same. Building

---

[2] For text of the President's address to the American people on nuclear testing and disarmament, March 2, see *Public Papers of the Presidents of the United States: John F. Kennedy, 1962*, pp. 186–192.

up Soviet strength is continuing and West must therefore still look to strength which is necessary for its security.

On Far East, Secretary covered briefly West New Guinea in response to strong statement by Dutch, critical of US policy. On Laos Secretary said US is doing its best to persuade Phoumi to negotiate seriously and stressed that US does not have preconception on exact pattern of coalition government but believes satisfactory cabinet might be achieved with serious effort. Secretary said alternatives to successful coalition not attractive. Concluded by saying in future may be faced with serious decision on question of putting forces into Laos or increasing aid. Secretary distinguished situation South Vietnam from that in Laos and explained US had greatly increased aid to help South Vietnam win its own war. Explained function US military personnel and our belief there has been some improvement in Diem's domestic and foreign policy, although he still has long way to go. US commitment to South Vietnam different from Laos because military factors more favorable and Vietnamese themselves heavily involved. Only other major comment on Far East was strong Netherlands statement, largely attacking US. Secretary avoided direct rebuttal to Netherlands. Other members of Six spoke up in quick succession after Dutch, generally although not fully endorsing Dutch position.

Secretary commented on Latin America describing progress in attitude of Latin American Governments and peoples toward Castroism, as evidenced by Punta del Este. Although tension remains in Latin America on Cuban question, US believes Castro communism being isolated in hemisphere. Secretary said US making great effort on Alliance for Progress. If it moves rapidly, tensions will develop within Latin American countries and between them and US, but we hope adjustments will be by democratic means. Secretary urged Europe give increasing attention to Latin America not only in aid but in trade and wide range other relations so as to tie area closer to Europe.

Africa discussed by Belgians, British and Portuguese. Latter gave lengthy statement painting gloomy picture of deteriorating Western position in all areas uncommitted world, especially Africa. Only response to Portuguese by UK, which pointed out such states as Nigeria and former French colonies, which are sympathetic to West.

Middle East discussed very briefly by Turks.

2. *Defense Policy.* In defense field, NATO took major step forward in acting on paper (NATO Document C–M(62)48)[3] concerning NATO nuclear policy which had been worked out by Permanent NATO Council since December 1961 Ministerial Meeting. By carefully worked out

---

[3] Not found.

procedure developed by Stikker to take account of French and Italian problems, Ministers "confirmed" statement of factual situation in conclusions of paper which covered following topics: (1) assurances by US that it will make adequate nuclear weapons available for NATO defense and assurances by the US and UK that their strategic forces will continue to cover as fully as possible all key elements of Soviet nuclear striking power, including MRBM sites, giving equal priority to those threatening Europe as to those threatening US and UK; (2) undertaking by the US and UK to furnish fullest possible amount of information on nuclear weapons and external forces in order give whole Alliance full insight into problems of NATO nuclear defense (NATO nuclear committee established for this purpose); (3) guidelines regarding the use of nuclear weapons by NATO in self-defense [4 *lines of source text not declassified*]. NATO action on these matters represents significant step forward in enhancing NATO's nuclear role and hence heading off pressures for independent national nuclear weapons capabilities.

French had reservations on points (3) and (4) above and Italians, because Presidential elections in progress, unable take definitive action at time of NATO meeting. French reservation handled by Stikker asking Ministers to confirm above as statement of factual situation and expressing hope that French could eventually see way clear accept guidelines. Stikker also said that French would be welcome participate in any consultations that might take place. Italian temporary reservations handled by Stikker pointing out that internal constitutional arrangements prevented Italian Government taking definitive action at this time, but that such action anticipated shortly. In discussion French explained their reservation as due to fact that guidelines in no way change existing situation and that nothing new really embodied in document on which Ministers acting.

3. *Secretary and Secretary McNamara's Statements on Defense.* In very restricted session with no notes to be taken, Secretary and Secretary McNamara gave major statements on US defense policy. Secretary led off, setting forth basic principles of US position on NATO nuclear defense policy and NATO strategy. Secretary McNamara then gave to Council fullest statement it has ever received on basic facts in nuclear field. (This message will not attempt to summarize Secretary McNamara's statement; we are exploring with Defense best means for informing key members addressee NATO posts of content of Secretary McNamara's speech.) Major purpose was to carry forward process of educating Alliance in basic facts of nuclear warfare and rationale of US views on strategy. General impact of statement seems to have been very favorable and it is our hope that future discussion in NATO Council will follow from principal topics in Secretary McNamara's statement. French Defense Minister struck only dissenting note in attempting to re-

ply to Secretary McNamara's criticism of small independent nuclear forces. Germans expressed strongly favorable reactions in comments after meeting.

US commitment of Polaris submarines had major favorable impact. Effective immediately, 5 presently operational submarines are earmarked for assignment to SACLANT. By end 1963, US expects to have committed 12, with 2 withdrawn for overhaul, leaving net of 10.

Subject of MRBMs discussed only briefly, with Secretary making clear our willingness, if our Allies desire, to join in possibility creating sea-based MRBM force which would be under fully multilateral ownership, control, financing and manning. Secretary McNamara supplied technical data on new missile being developed by US. Subject of MRBMs not pressed by other Ministers at meeting, although it is expected that it will be pursued subsequently in the Permanent Council.

4. *Special Economic Problems of Greece and Turkey.* After considerable last-minute discussion with Greeks, Council acted on resolutions concerning special economic problems Greece and Turkey. (NATO Doc. CM(62)53)[4] These resolutions important because they call upon countries willing and in position to do so to assist Greece and Turkey economically, both bilaterally and multilaterally, and in particular to examine urgently establishment of consortia. Secretary in his statement on this subject, urged that steps be initiated looking toward early establishment of consortia for Greece and Turkey in OECD. Passing of NATO resolution should assist us in efforts obtain larger contribution than heretofore from other NATO Allies, in meeting economic needs of Greece and Turkey.

Statements attributed to Secretary in foregoing are uncleared by Secretary.

Ball

---

[4] Not found.

138.   Letter From the Deputy Under Secretary of State for Political Affairs (Johnson) to the Assistant Secretary of Defense for International Security Affairs (Nitze)

Washington, May 23, 1962.

DEAR PAUL: On the basis of previous discussions, I understand that you have been asked by Mr. McNamara to follow up on the Department of Defense proposals relating to the withdrawal of certain U.S. forces now in Europe. These proposals are presumably the ones contained in the attachment to the memorandum from the Secretary of Defense to the President, dated April 23,[1] which identify force adjustments designed to alleviate U.S. balance of payment problems while at the same time correcting certain force mal-deployments, particularly in non-combat units. In recognition of the serious implications of the payments deficit it is our desire to cooperate in this effort in every possible way. However, whatever action is decided upon must be carefully arranged to avoid what could be very adverse political and psychological repercussions. At this juncture in our Berlin negotiations we would not wish to risk conveying an incorrect impression to the Soviets or our Allies as to the firmness of the U.S. intention to insist on our vital interests in Berlin, even at the expense of employment of force if the situation so demanded. Our build-up actions of last Fall had this as a principal objective and this objective is no less valid today.

Consistent with the foregoing, we have worked out a series of political criteria which we desire to see applied to proposals for withdrawing any major numbers of U.S. military personnel from Europe. These are attached. As can be seen from the list of criteria, our objective is to handle any withdrawal of forces which may be militarily justified in a manner least likely to create political problems. In this connection, we wonder whether the Department of Defense would not find it feasible to consider converting a portion of the support forces currently being proposed for withdrawal into a combat unit, for example, an additional division, for retention in Europe. General Norstad has suggested such an approach and we gather that the Ailes Committee considered a similar proposal to be feasible. If the Department of Defense determined that a portion of the forces identified as surplus in their current capacities could, with military advantage, be transformed into a combat element, this would have an immense positive political benefit. Under these circumstances the return to the U.S. of significant numbers of military per-

---

Source: Department of State, Central Files, 711.5/5–2362. Secret. No drafting information appears on the source text.

[1] Neither the memorandum nor the attachment has been found.

sonnel could be more easily portrayed as a hardening of U.S. combat posture rather than as a retrenchment or wavering in our commitment to European security. Moreover, the provision of an additional division, even if coupled with still sizeable force withdrawals, could serve as a valuable negotiating lever with our Allies to secure a further force commitment from them to the forward strategy concept advanced by General Norstad. We might make our additional division contingent upon added European contributions toward the forward strategy goals.

We are prepared to work with the Department of Defense to facilitate as rapid a redeployment of excess forces from Europe as is feasible. I suggest that after you have had an opportunity to consider the attached criteria we might then meet for the purpose of jointly considering specific force adjustment proposals.

Sincerely,

Alex[2]

[Attachment][3]

Paper Prepared in the Department of State

POLITICAL CRITERIA TO BE APPLIED IN EFFECTING ADJUSTMENTS IN U.S. FORCE DEPLOYMENTS IN EUROPE

I. *Objective.* In order to assure that recommended withdrawals of U.S. forces from Europe are accomplished with a minimum of adverse political repercussion and without degradation of U.S. combat capability, the Department of State proposes that the criteria identified in paragraph II below be adhered to.

II. *Criteria.*

a. Force withdrawals shall, to the maximum feasible extent, avoid creating the impression among our Allies or on the part of the Sino/Soviet Bloc that the object or effect of the force withdrawal is in any way to decrease U.S. ability to support its security commitments.

b. So long as the Berlin crisis continues, no combat forces, or support forces essential to combat effectiveness of deployed forces, shall be withdrawn.

---

[2] Printed from a copy that bears this stamped signature.

[3] Secret. No drafting information appears on the source text.

c. It is the view of the Department of State that adverse political consequences of force withdrawals can be substantially moderated if the action can be portrayed as an adjustment which does not detract from, but even improves, U.S. combat potential. Accordingly where militarily feasible withdrawals of support forces should be accompanied by adjustments or reorganizations which add to combat strength.

d. Where determined by the Department of State, as necessary, specific negotiations or advance consultation with foreign nations will take place prior to the announcement of withdrawal intention or prior to the taking of any specific withdrawal action.

e. The Department of State does not object to the shift to the U.S. of any military activity which the Department of Defense determines can just as readily be performed in the United States as overseas, such as training, so long as it is consistent with the preceding criteria.

f. Similarly, the Department of State does not object to the withdrawal of support forces which are considered by the Department of Defense as excess to requirements in Europe, subject to the preceding criteria.

III. *Procedure.* Appropriate staffs of the Departments of State and Defense will work out specific arrangements for effecting recommended withdrawals.

---

139. Circular Telegram From the Department of State to Certain Missions

Washington, May 25, 1962, 3:36 p.m.

2005. In aftermath of very successful NATO Ministerial Meeting, Department believes we should consider next steps to be taken in North Atlantic Council to consolidate and follow up on gains made at Athens.

Defense

In field of defense policy, Athens meeting marked end of important phase of Council activities, phase which has absorbed attention of Alli-

---

Source: Department of State, Central Files, 375/5–2562. Secret; Limit Distribution. Drafted by Fessenden and Van Hollen; cleared by Johnson, Kohler, Schaetzel, Seymour Weiss, Rostow, Owen, UNP, ARA, RPE, AF, FE, and the Department of Defense; and initialed by Rusk. Transmitted to missions in 14 NATO countries.

ance for more than year. We are hopeful that "Athens package" re guidelines, assurances and information will prove adequate to satisfy for time being desires for greater sense of participation in nuclear matters. (This will, however, require energetic follow-up by US in supplying meaningful information to NATO nuclear information committee.) We can anticipate, however, that guidelines-assurances information package will not suffice permanently to satisfy pressures for nuclear role. Multilateral MRBM issue in particular must be dealt with. Following next steps appear required:

(a) We should immediately undertake necessary action to make nuclear information committee work and work well. This will entail, first, assuring that CABAL system and US security arrangements are reconciled. Most important, however, we should continue process begun in December and continued in May of supplying significant information to the Alliance.

(b) Multilateral MRBM force question should be dealt with in a constructive framework with US prepared to participate in accordance with outstanding instructions.

(c) We should continue our efforts to implement NATO's forward strategy and to build up NATO forces to meet non-nuclear part of MC 26/4 goals.

(d) Discussion of NATO strategy should be appropriately pursued, with US continuing to advance its views for Alliance consideration in manner not calculated to provoke divisive debate, but nonetheless designed to advance educational process. We should resist efforts to invoke Political Directive to oppose US views. It should become increasingly apparent that US no longer accepts fundamental basis of Political Directive. At same time, we should not ourselves initiate efforts to revise Political Directive. In brief, Political Directive should be "set aside" for present. Constructive interpretation of Directive should be governing principle.

Political

In political field, we believe we should encourage NATO members to step up consultation, taking lead from Stikker's Annual Report reinforced by Secretary's comments at Athens that there is room for improvement and that US hopes to increase number of close exchanges between NAC members and senior US policy making officials. Seems to us that in addition to strong US support and initiative, Stikker and Hooper are keys to more effective political consultation in NAC and POLAD respectively. USRO therefore at early date should discuss possibilities of improving NAC and POLAD political consultation with Stikker and Hooper, drawing at your discretion on results of recent analysis prepared by Department for Secretary which points up poor record of other larger NATO countries; i.e., not only French, but also British, Germans and Italians. (This analysis contained Athens position paper NMA–D–1/7.[1])

Urge Stikker and Hooper to attempt in both NAC and POLAD meetings, as well as private conversations with NATO delegates, to point out need for broadening and deepening consultation, specifying if possible those areas in which consultative process can be strengthened.

Although we recognize sensitivities involved, suggest you also sound out Stikker re possibilities his suggesting that NATO representatives of Six as well as UK provide Council with reports on various Heads of Government meetings re European political and economic integration. In past, this has not been an area either for political consultation or for exchange of information. We should not initially expect more than token reports from participating countries. However, seems to us that although these reports might contain limited amount of substantive information, they might serve several purposes: they would help establish principle that all members of NATO Alliance have legitimate interest in being kept informed on developments in field of European integration; such manifestation of collective NATO interest would help in offsetting French separatist tendencies re NATO; they would help to establish consistent policy under which all NATO member countries would be expected fill in Council on significant Heads of Government meetings, practice US has been following in case of major meetings such as President's talks with Adenauer, Shah of Iran, Macmillan, etc. On basis Stikker's reaction and USRO's assessment of practicality, we will decide whether to pursue this possibility further.

You should also advise Stikker that in keeping our desire to consult Council even more fully re US policy developments, if Council wishes we will arrange for Assistant Secretary Harlan Cleveland again to consult with Council re major issues at forthcoming UN General Assembly. (At present late June seems most feasible date.) As feasible, other senior officers from the Department might also be able to visit Council for policy consultations. We hope that Stikker will request other delegations to send top officials to Council to consult on special or regional problems, hopefully at same time as comparable US officials attend.

In field long range planning and in keeping with Secretary's statement at Athens, we hope USRO can get together at early date with UK colleagues and with Stikker in order to launch Atlantic Policy Advisory Group. We suggest first organizational meeting of APAG be scheduled within next few weeks in order consider methods of approach and topics for consideration. Advise Stikker that Walt Rostow, Chairman

---

[1] A copy of this paper is ibid., Conference Files: Lot 65 D 533, CF 2101.

of Policy Planning Council, has expressed willingness to attend organizational meeting of APAG and recall for Stikker that two subjects have already been suggested for APAG consideration—"Neutralism" (by Lord Home) and "Sino-Soviet Conflict" (by Secretary Rusk). Both through Stikker and directly, US should stress to key Allied Governments need for effective high level representation on APAG, as per US lead in this respect.

Science

Finally, we hope that progress can be made on International Institute of Science and Technology, proposal which Secretary and a number of other FonMins endorsed at Athens. While we do not expect any formal NATO action, believe informal discussions which will in first instance result in approach acceptable US and UK should be pursued and idea of Institute generally promoted and publicized.

Rusk

---

140. Memorandum of Conversation

Washington, June 9, 1962.

SUBJECT

Strategy of the Western Alliance and Berlin

PARTICIPANTS

U.S.	Germans
The Secretary	Defense Minister Strauss [1]
The Under Secretary	Ambassador Grewe
EUR—Mr. Kohler	Mr. Schnippenkoetter, Counselor,
GER—Mr. Stalder	German Embassy

At the conclusion of his meeting with Minister Strauss, Mr. Kohler escorted him to his appointment with the Secretary.[2] Mr. Kohler briefly informed the Secretary of this meeting as well as of Minister Strauss' earlier meetings with the President, Defense Secretary McNamara, and Deputy Defense Secretary Gilpatric.[3]

Source: Department of State, Central Files, 375/6–962. Secret. Drafted by Stalder on June 9 and approved in S on June 16 and in U on June 14.

[1] Strauss visited Washington June 7–8. A summary of the visit was transmitted to Bonn in telegram 3388, June 13. (Ibid., 375/6–1162)

[2] A memorandum of Strauss' conversation with Kohler is ibid., 375/6–862.

[3] No records of the meetings with McNamara and Gilpatric have been found; a memorandum of Strauss' conversation with the President, which covered material similar to that with Rusk, is ibid., 033.62A11/6–862.

The Secretary mentioned his forthcoming trip to Europe and said one of the things he hoped to learn in Paris is what is meant by the French when they speak of a "reorganized NATO" and of "changes in the situation since 1948". While a "reorganized NATO" is spoken of, no proposals have been put forth; nothing has been spelled out. Yet this might have a bearing on a NATO MRBM force. The Secretary inquired whether Minister Strauss knew what the French had in mind.

Minister Strauss said he had not been able to get any clear answers. However, President DeGaulle's recent press conference[4] made evident at least the outlines—the contours—of French thinking. The French appear to be saying that a defense of the West based only on the United States is a thing of the past; there must be a new system based more or less on a coalition of national armies with a low degree of integration. Such a system—as Minister Strauss interpreted French thinking—must include national nuclear components, a flexible arsenal (not necessarily flexible within the US understanding of this term), and a stronger French position in NATO command posts. Minister Strauss said he did not think the French extended this latter point to include the NATO top side, i.e. to an integrated NATO General Staff.

The Secretary went on to say that one of the purposes of his forthcoming visits to Paris, Bonn, and London was to see whether elements of pure misunderstanding can be removed and whether, where real differences exist, these differences can be identified more precisely and, if possible, resolved. In inquiring of Minister Strauss what he understood the feelings in Paris to be, he would not wish to seem in any way to appear to be separating one ally from another. He inquired because it is important to know.

The Secretary said he thought one element of misunderstanding with Paris arose from what he understood to be President DeGaulle's feeling that the civic morale of France—(and of the army, interjected Minister Strauss)—must be rebuilt. Recalling DeGaulle's personal experiences of 1940, this was understandable. The point of misunderstanding, however, arises when this rebuilding takes place at the expense of one's friends. If DeGaulle seems to be saying that France must do X, Y, or Z because it cannot rely on the US, this is one thing. But if he says he must make it possible for France to assume a larger share in resolving the common problems of the West, this is another matter. The Secretary repeated that we do not feel we know enough about what DeGaulle has in mind.

---

[4] For a record of de Gaulle's press conference on May 15, see *Major Addresses, Statements and Press Conferences of General Charles de Gaulle, May 19, 1958–January 31, 1964,* pp. 172–184.

Mr. Kohler said specific questions had been asked but that there had been no answers.

Minister Strauss said the French system of priorities—force de frappe, corps d'intervention, territorial defense army—does not fit into the NATO concept.

The Secretary agreed that there appeared to be certain apparent contradictions. He hoped Minister Strauss had gotten the impression in Athens that the US was moving rapidly in the direction of a multilateral sharing of the great issues and problems in the nuclear field.

Minister Strauss said he had; he considered Athens to have been a turning point.

It was an anomaly, the Secretary continued, that as we move in a direction which we would have supposed the French wanted, the French are moving in another direction.

Minister Strauss said it was all the more important, therefore, that more be learned of what France has in mind before NATO document 26/4 is discussed. Returning to the French system of priorities, he said French planning means that no more than four French divisions can be contributed in the future. At the present time, the French contribution was only 1-1/2 divisions and these were equipped with obsolete matériel.

Minister Strauss expressed his surprise at having learned from Secretary McNamara yesterday that the US had offered to reequip the first two divisions returning from Algiers but that this offer had been rejected. He would be very pleased, Strauss went on, if the US could persuade the French to accept.

The Secretary expressed his hope that a common ground could be found. He had no doubts about the essential commitment of all the NATO countries to basic principles. The differences we were experiencing are rather in the nature of family differences. But it was to be hoped these would not grow. To the press, agreement is boring; disagreement is "news". Thus, these much publicized differences could have unfortunate effects on public opinion.

Minister Strauss thought there were, nevertheless, strong differences. He then expressed his appreciation—not merely as a "foolish compliment"—for the speeches of the Secretary and Defense Secretary McNamara at Athens. For the first time in NATO, there had been put forward for discussion a strategic concept.

The Secretary said Athens had been important because, by making the facts known, it was possible to explain how we had arrived at our strategic concept. Perhaps because of this the Minister felt that the NATO MRBM idea was dead.

Minister Strauss did not consider the idea dead. He thought rather in terms of its having failed up to now. This failure could not be ascribed to a lack of effort. A too optimistic view of the legal, technical and other problems had, however, been held.

The Secretary inquired whether these were real obstacles, or were they more in the nature of political differences among the capitals. Would France, for example, sit down and work out the legal and technical problems?

Minister Strauss thought France would sit down but would not give in. The establishment of a multilateral MRBM force would not satisfy France now.

The Secretary thought it possible that if the UK joins the Common Market without a serious dilution of the Rome Treaty, these problems might diminish. Meanwhile the US was prepared to get into these questions to the extent that our allies wish us to. We had started with the hope that our allies would discuss this matter and work it out, but there had been no progress. We continue to hope this matter will be discussed, although we would not want to table a US plan.

Minister Strauss went on to say that it was possible to distinguish two aspects of a multilateral MRBM force—the military and political. First, was it merely military; does NATO need this force to fill a gap—to have a differentiated weapons system. If the answer is yes, such an MRBM force could be set up with no changes in the present nuclear set up. Nuclear weapons would be immediately under SACEUR and control would be under the US. The Pentagon, Strauss said, appeared not to think of the MRBM force as a strong military requirement.

It was perhaps a political rather than a military requirement, the Secretary said.

Minister Strauss thought it had elements of both. Discussing the second aspect—the political—he said the question is whether the MRBM force is a good object with which to demonstrate the existence of a multilateral force. It would not change the weapons system, only command and control.

The Secretary expressed the hope that our friends in NATO realize that what has been said to the NATO Council about consultation is an attempt to go as far as possible multilaterally, subject to the physical circumstances at the time decisions must be made.

Minister Strauss inquired whether it could not be said that there are short and long run tasks to be taken up. The short run task is to work out practical guidelines to make a consultation system workable and to prove that consultation is possible. If this is not the case, the idea of a multilateral force should be dropped.

The Secretary referred to what had for a time been a matter of mis-understanding between Washington and Bonn. This related to our ref-erences to a buildup of conventional forces. Bonn had not realized that this was being thought of in the context of forward strategy.

Minister Strauss agreed and said that discussion in Bonn had been directed at identifying the borderline between conventional and nuclear weapons. Was it between conventional weapons and *all* nuclear weap-ons (including, for example, the Davy Crockett), or was the borderline somewhere within the range of the nuclear arsenal short of general war. There was no experience upon which to base an answer. There was now a new problem; how strong must our conventional forces be and at what point—i.e. in what types of conflict—would the lowest yield nuclear weapons be called into action. In other words, how can the nuclear de-terrent be made more credible and how long can the use of nuclear weapons be postponed when the conventional fail. This was a matter of concern in Germany. There was every wish to avoid the use of tactical nuclear weapons. Yet Germany could not watch the Soviets overrun part of its territory—the Ruhr or Hamburg—and accept the concept that negotiations proceed from the status quo once the conflict has been stopped.

The Secretary said he could agree with this. It was, he went on, very hard to write a scenario which includes another actor who may not play. One could imagine, on a purely theoretical basis, in the case of a block-ade of West Berlin, the commitment of a small force to probe Soviet in-tentions, followed by a conventional, a tactical, and finally by a strategic force. The difficulty was that this theoretical circumstance might last only five minutes. We have no illusions about this. In speaking of credi-bility one must, however, also look at the other side of the coin. The con-text must be considered. A threat, for example, to invoke the deterrent if one of our jeeps is not permitted to pass through a checkpoint would, of course, not be taken seriously.

The Secretary went on to say that we should have the obvious means thoroughly to engage the two systems—NATO and Warsaw Pact—so that they (the Soviets) know the issue is nuclear war. We do not propose to accept deep intrusions into NATO territory by conventional forces. In an aside about *The Guns of August,* which the Secretary com-mended to the attention of Minister Strauss, the Secretary spoke of the breakdown of understanding among the European capitals in August 1914. A way must be found not to let this happen again. As he had told the Chancellor, we want to have clear agreement on what our vital inter-ests are and what must be done if these are undermined. We must be sure that if we do what must be done, we can face our people and say that we had done everything possible at the diplomatic level and that our actions in no way were the consequence of negligence or inactivity.

It was this that was very much in the mind of the President. Thus far, however, there are no indications that the Soviets accept or recognize our vital interests.

Minister Strauss said the "fatal thing" was that we are fighting with our backs to the wall. If we had on our side an arsenal of negotiating issues—concessions to trade for concessions—things would be less difficult.

It was true, the Secretary said, that there existed a whole range of matters which are no longer negotiable as a result of what has happened along the way. With respect to our rights in Berlin, there is nothing to bargain with.

Minister Strauss said the Soviets had dropped all hope of controlling all of Germany. This had been what lay behind the various pre-NATO and post-NATO plans for neutralized zones and the like in Central Europe. Such plans would have meant the dissolution of Europe. However, this period was now ended. The Soviets cannot afford to attack Central Europe. But with Berlin the difficulty is the unfavorable geographic location.

The Secretary spoke briefly of his itinerary. He would visit Berlin very briefly; both Berlin and Bonn had urged him to do so despite the fact that his tight schedule permitted only a few hours there. In Bonn he hoped to have some fundamental talks. Such misunderstandings as existed were, in his view, not serious. There was close to complete agreement on policy and full agreement on all the underlying issues. With respect to the role of East Germany in the Access Authority, the Soviets, upon reading this, said they would not have West Germany a member of such an authority. There could, therefore, be no differences with Bonn on this.

Minister Strauss thought an international access authority would be an improvement over the present state of affairs, inasmuch as the East Germans now control most of the traffic.

The Secretary cautioned Minister Strauss not to speak of East German "control". So long as we are in Berlin—as he had told the Soviet Ambassador on several occasions—they do not have control.

Minister Strauss recalled in this connection having received a less than perfect grade in an English examination some years ago, because he had translated the word "control" incorrectly; in German the word has a somewhat different meaning.

The Under Secretary inquired whether any serious thought had been given to Franco-German nuclear cooperation.

Minister Strauss stated that France had made not the slightest overture—nor had the Germans. Germany, he said, was not concerned for reasons of prestige. Moreover, the right to produce nuclear weapons had been renounced.

The Under Secretary said he was, of course, thinking of peaceful uses, although some of these might at some point have military applications.

Minister Strauss said with respect to peaceful uses, German cooperation was 80 percent with the US, 15 percent with the UK and 5 percent with the French.

Referring to his earlier meeting with the President, Minister Strauss spoke of the President's evident concern over a further diffusion of nuclear capabilities; after France more and more NATO, as well as non-NATO, countries could be expected to develop their own capabilities. Sweden, the Minister thought, would have its own capability by 1970.

Turning then to what appeared to be the French arguments for its own nuclear capability, Minister Strauss said these included an apparent belief that the US deterrent is not a reliable one. In addition, there appear to be considerations of prestige involved and, closely related to this, the feeling that what is legitimate for the UK cannot be denied to others.

This, interjected the Secretary, could be extended indefinitely.

Another apparent French argument, Minister Strauss continued, was of a more objective nature. Would not the deterrent be more credible if it consisted of a number of separate deterrents rather than of a more centralized one?

The Secretary asked to what extent, in the Minister's opinion, was it believed in Europe that the defense of the United States and Europe is indivisible.

Minister Strauss replied that Secretary McNamara at Athens had pointed up a matter of concern. It was that a first nuclear strike by a country such as France would not do too much damage and that such a country would then in turn be wiped out. There would then be the choice for the allies of leaving such a country to its deserved fate or of going to war without regard to whether its action had been right or wrong or the fact that its action had not been given allied approval.

It was difficult to identify any nuclear issues for NATO members, the Secretary said, which was not a nuclear issue for the US.

Turning again to the apparent French belief that nuclear diffusion is desirable because of US unreliability, Minister Strauss said the argument is at times posed in terms of what will happen in 1966 when a US-USSR nuclear stalemate will have been achieved. What then will be the strategic concept? In Athens—so this argument runs—the US spoke of an overwhelming arsenal in terms of numbers and ranges of weapons, an indestructible means of delivery, and an indestructible second strike

406   Foreign Relations, 1961–1963, Volume XIII

capacity. The USSR cannot yet match this. This—to interpret this French argument further—gives the US strong feelings of superiority and the conviction that it is in full control of the world. But will this US concept remain fully as reliable after 1966, or will there have to be expected a modification? It is on this basis of the post-1966 US-USSR nuclear stalemate, Minister Strauss said, that the French argue openly for the creation of their own nuclear deterrent. And this concern is not entirely absent in the UK.

If the talk was about 1966, the Secretary noted, this was really a very short time period in the historical context. If there was one thing evident, it is that there is deeply entrenched in the US on the basis of the most selfish, elementary and national considerations, the conviction that there is no security for the United States without Western Europe.

For this reason, Minister Strauss added, one European concept must be rejected as completely wrong—that of Europe as a third force. To support Europe as a third force is to dissolve the bloc of the free world and to establish in its stead two separate centers—Europe and the United States. All steps toward European unity should rather be viewed as part—a slice—of the Atlantic Community based upon increasing interdependence. Success in achieving European unity would mean establishment of an entity of comparable size to the US. This in turn would lead to an Atlantic Community supported by, or based on, two solid pillars. The existence of such an Atlantic Community would represent a meaningful deterrent.

The Secretary agreed that a third force was not feasible. It overlooked the fact that Europe cannot be a third force inasmuch as it is Europe which is the issue between Washington and Moscow.

Returning to another facet of the French argument about the reliability of the US concept in the post-1966 period, Minister Strauss referred to the concern about placing the release of nuclear warheads exclusively in the hands of the US President. In the event of a conflict— so the argument runs—the Soviets may then attempt to blackmail the President by informing him that the release of tactical warheads to defend certain territory would be considered a casus belli. This would place the US President under severe pressure not to release, say, ten warheads, and to accept a Soviet penetration rather than expose the US to danger.

The Under Secretary noted that this was precisely the kind of blackmail the Soviets had attempted over Berlin.

If the Secretary could overcome the French arguments while in Paris, the Minister said, we will have come closer to an understanding.

The Under Secretary thought much of the French (and European) thinking along the lines outlined by the Minister was based upon a cultural lag. It was the US of the 1930's which was still in the minds of many Europeans—a United States which had never made a total commitment. The US mood and mentality had undergone a great change. Finally, the nature of nuclear war appeared not fully to be understood in Europe.

Minister Strauss expressed his appreciation for the extremely useful talks he had had in Washington and said he hoped to see the Secretary in Bonn.

This was also his hope, the Secretary said.

---

141. Telegram From the Department of State to the Mission to the North Atlantic Treaty Organization and European Regional Organizations

Washington, June 14, 1962, 7:56 a.m.

Topol 1922. Eyes only for Ambassador Finletter. To Ambassador Finletter from the President. I have just approved the long cable of instruction[1] to you on MRBMs but I would like to give you this short additional statement of my own views for your guidance.

First, you should make it very plain that the military need for this force is not proven. Seen from the center rather than from a theater command post, the Western military need for this force in undemonstrated.

Second, the cost of this undertaking is great, and the main burden must necessarily fall on European members. No advocates of this force should neglect or underrate this problem of cost.

Third, the United States would strongly oppose the substitution of this force for needed efforts to strengthen conventional forces. Our support for a multilateral MRBM force will be contingent upon adequate efforts in the conventional field, and so our allies should understand that the cost of this force would be an addition and not merely a substitution in relation to existing programs.

Fourth, my estimate is that in the light of these factors, the probability of final affirmative action on this MRBM force is low at present. Nev-

---

Source: Kennedy Library, National Security Files, MLF-Instructions to Finletter. Top Secret; Niact; No Other Distribution. Drafted by McGeorge Bundy and cleared with Kohler.

[1] See Document 142.

ertheless, I strongly support discussion and examination in NATO, for its educational effect and as a basis for any action our allies may, in fact, wish to take. As I see it, your job is to communicate our central position while keeping it clear that if Europeans do want this force, we will firmly support it and pay our proportionate share.

John F. Kennedy

Rusk

142. Instructions for the Permanent Representative to the North Atlantic Council (Finletter)

Washington, undated.

MRBM Instructions. Eyes only Ambassador Finletter.

At the recent Athens meeting, the U.S. presented its views on the most central military issues facing NATO. It also provided information on a number of the major weapon programs the U.S. is carrying forward in order to support the Alliance. Today, my government would like to address again the subject of nuclear forces in relation to the defense of the European part of NATO and, in particular, the need for a new MRBM force.

It is our view that major nuclear war is the only kind of war in which 1000 to 2000 mile range MRBM's would be likely to be used. We cannot conceive of a significant exchange involving weapons of this range and character being a partial or limited one.

Major nuclear war, in turn, would be basically a single operation involving an over-all series of attacks against an over-all target system.

Source: Kennedy Library, National Security Files, MLF-Instructions to Finletter. Secret. The source text, which was attached to Document 141, bears the notation "Final Version." On June 2 the Department of State sent a 15-page telegram to Finletter containing a preliminary draft of these instructions and asking for his comments. (Topol 1853; Department of State, Central Files, 700.5612/6–262) The following day Finletter replied that he was "delighted" with the instructions and offered a few comments on the draft. (Polto 1611; ibid., 700.5612/6–362) On June 8 a revised text, approved at the staff level of the Departments of State and Defense, was forwarded to Secretary Rusk and to the White House for final approval. (Memorandum from Kohler; ibid., 711.5611/6–862) Omitted here are sections on Soviet nuclear and other forces, alliance systems, and costs.

In this context, the requirement for a major NATO nuclear weapons system—such as the proposed MRBM—can only be evaluated as a component of all the nuclear assets available to NATO, including external as well as committed forces.

The evaluations which the United States has made of over-all nuclear requirements and the programmed forces support the view that the presently programmed system is adequate, and is appropriate to handle the opposing nuclear forces—whether they threaten Europe or other Alliance territory outside Europe. We conclude, therefore, that MRBM's are not urgently needed for military reasons. Nevertheless, MRBM's would have some military utility and they could be of considerable political importance. The U.S. is willing, in any case, to continue to bear the primary responsibility for providing the nuclear support of the Alliance. However, other members of the Alliance may wish to participate in the building of a NATO MRBM Force to contribute to this mission; if so, the U.S. is prepared to join in creating such a Force.

I shall outline the basis for these views concerning the proposed military requirement for MRBM's in Allied Command Europe. I shall deal with the adequacy of programmed forces in terms of, first, countering major Soviet nuclear forces and, second, countering other Soviet military forces. Then I shall discuss the types of systems which make up the longer range elements of the programmed forces and the criteria which are relevant to their selection, so that you can judge why we believe that the programmed mix is appropriate for the purposes which these longer range elements are designed to serve.

[Here follow sections on other subjects.]

Summary on Military Need

To sum up our view on the military requirement. The Alliance position on the MRBM should be viewed in the context of global nuclear war. In this context, the U.S. believes that already programmed, rapidly growing, nuclear forces are adequate to meet Alliance needs, and the U.S. is willing to continue to bear the responsibility of dealing with targets which its forces plan to cover, if the other members of the Alliance do not wish to take part in the building of a NATO force to deal with some of these targets.

—We believe that these programmed forces are sufficient to deter any rational Soviet initial resort to nuclear weapons or all-out non-nuclear attack.

—If deterrence fails, these programmed forces have the capability to destroy the greater part of Soviet nuclear forces, albeit at high cost in terms of possible resultant damage to the West.

We believe that such a devastating nuclear exchange would bring any advance of Soviet ground forces toward Western Europe to a halt. If not, the capability of programmed forces of varying kinds and ranges to master their Soviet counter-parts and to attack Soviet ground forces and supply lines would meet the Alliance's tactical needs.

Therefore, the coverage of Soviet targets, including SACEUR's threat list, will remain effective, despite the fact that Europe-based strike aircraft will be declining in utility during this period as a means of delivering nuclear weapons.

And we believe that the alliance forces which can accomplish these tasks represent about the right mix of different systems.

The U.S. does not believe, therefore, that MRBM's are urgently needed for military reasons.

The Multilateral Force

We realize that our views may not be wholly shared by all members of the Alliance. This difference need not prevent the Alliance from taking useful action in the MRBM field, if a sufficient desire for such action exists in the Alliance. Such a program for expanding our nuclear striking power would, of course, have military utility; and it could have considerable importance politically.

If our allies wish to add MRBM's to NATO forces and to participate in an MRBM force, the U.S. is prepared to join them in creating a multilaterally owned, financed, controlled, and manned sea-borne MRBM force. The force should be sea-borne to avoid the political problems associated with land-based deployment, to minimize vulnerability and collateral damage, and to permit genuinely multilateral control and manning. When we say a multilaterally manned force, we mean that the manning of each vessel, and of the missiles aboard each vessel, should be genuinely mixed; obviously, this does not mean that each vessel need have fifteen nationalities aboard—three nationalities should suffice to create a balanced crew in which no single nationality is predominant.

If such a force were established, presently programmed alliance nuclear forces should, of course, be reviewed from the standpoint of possible resultant reduction in these programmed forces.

Planning for the use of any such MRBM force could be worked out by the Alliance in the light of its continuing consideration of strategy, the role of the force in that strategy, and other relevant factors. In this process the views of SACEUR—especially concerning targeting—would naturally be taken carefully into account.

It would be essential that construction of such an MRBM force, if it should take place, be undertaken parallel to a continuing vigorous buildup of NATO non-nuclear forces. Establishment of such an MRBM force would be contra-productive if it diverted resources from that buildup. There would, of course, be substantial costs to NATO associated with an MRBM program, even if we cannot now estimate this magnitude with precision. Because of these substantial costs and the availability of other forces which I have mentioned, we do not believe that an initial sea-based MRBM force should be larger than about 200 missiles. Whether further steps might eventually be useful is a question which the Alliance need not decide now.

FYI: You will have to evaluate in light of tactical situation at the time how to introduce additional elaboration of U.S. views on MRBM force set forth in earlier instructions. We wish to avoid appearance of U.S. taking initiative to submit "U.S. plan." We do not wish, however, there to be any misunderstanding re U.S. unwillingness consider any mode of allied deployment other than multilaterally owned, manned, and controlled sea-based force of size approved by President, and you may include this point in above initial statement, in language of Presidentially approved policy paper, if you believe this useful. With this exception, we believe preferable that additional views be advanced subsequently, after others (e.g. Belgians) have taken initiative on multilateral MRBM force.[1]

---

[1] On June 15 Finletter reported that he had read the instructions to the North Atlantic Council that morning and distributed copies to the other delegations, the International Staff, and the Standing Group. (Polto 1675; Kennedy Library, National Security Files, MLF)

---

143. Telegram From the Delegation to the North Atlantic Council Ministerial Meeting to the Department of State

Paris, June 20, 1962, 10 p.m.

Secto 12. Brussels for Embassy and USEC. Following is fuller report on Secretary's discussion MRBMs in informal meeting with NAC permanent representatives.[1]

Source: Department of State, Central Files, 740.5612/6–2062. Secret; Priority; Limit Distribution. According to another copy, this telegram was drafted by Fessenden and approved by Kohler. (Ibid., Conference Files: Lot 65 D 533, CF 2122) Repeated to the other NATO capitals.

[1] Secretary of State Rusk visited Europe June 18–28. Background and briefing papers for the visit, a chronology, telegrams, and memoranda of conversation are ibid., CF 2121–2127. A summary report on the meeting was transmitted in Secto 11, June 20 (ibid., Central Files, 762.00/6–2062); a memorandum of the conversation at the meeting, SET/MC/9, is ibid., 110.11–RU/6–2062.

Secretary explained he wished try to clarify certain aspects MRBM question, without going into question in any great detail. US has been faced with rather difficult dilemma on MRBM issue. We are aware of interest in this question in the Alliance and, after Ottawa speech by President year ago, had hoped NAC would pick up question largely without US. Later became apparent that more facts were needed by Alliance and US tried provide some of this at Athens. June 15th statement by Ambassador Finletter[2] further step in same direction.

Secretary also stressed that MRBMs are only part of picture. US is trying move on broad multi-lateral front on all nuclear questions. Secretary also stressed that US wants avoid presenting US plan and that June 15th statement not presented in "take it or leave it" spirit. Sole purpose was to give our views such as they are until we hear views of our allies. We had hoped that there would be thoughtful examination by NAC of MRBM question, process which might take some time.

Secretary finally stressed by no means US intention to kill MRBM idea. Wholly incorrect to conclude this our motive. Citing text of US June 15th presentation, noted that we said there was "not an 'urgent' requirement." We did say that MRBMs would have military utility. We also feel that costs are another factor which must be put into scales by Alliance. Our whole purpose, in short, was to make a responsible and full reply to many requests for our views on MRBM question.

Following points came out in ensuing discussion:

Belgium opened with praise for Rusk/McNamara Athens statements and expressed approval US June 15th MRBM presentation. Stressed two points: (1) Hope all Alliance members will participate fully in MRBM question, and (2) need is to find compromise between exclusive US nuclear capability and desire by Europeans to participate in decisions. US June 15th statement contained a possible compromise to meet these two points. Stressed also political questions involved. Belgium concluded by saying had read US statement carefully and noted that it does not deny military requirement.

Belgium then alluded to relationship MRBM question to Common Market negotiations. Great decisions pending on UK joining EEC are bound have profound effect on Alliance, just as child's growth in a family often disturbs its surroundings.

Netherlands fully seconded Belgian point on Common Market negotiations and suggested MRBM question not be precipitated too soon, because of its obvious relationship to Common Market negotiations. Would be wrong to overload governments with two such basic decisions as UK-EEC negotiations and MRBM question at same time. Sug-

---

[2] See footnote 1, Document 142.

gested might take several months, or even years, before MRBM/nuclear question could really be dealt with.

Secretary fully agreed on timing of MRBMs, indicating US not pressing. Said we are nevertheless making certain preparations, such as decision make development studies of missile X. Secretary added that we understand fully relationship of MRBM question to Common Market negotiations and future organization of Europe in political/defense fields which might result from UK entry.

Secretary also said Stikker's proposed order for discussion MRBMs seems satisfactory i.e., discussion of military aspects, followed by discussion of costs. Main US purpose has been to relieve ourselves of any responsibility for holding back discussions.

Secretary said he also wanted lay special stress on importance of buildup in conventional capability of NATO forces. This may lead to certain questions as to relative priority for MRBMs and conventional forces. Fact is that conventional capability of Alliance continues to deserve much greater attention and effort than has been case to date.

Should be noted that UK, French, and German permanent representatives made no comment on MRBM question.

Rusk

---

144.   Memorandum of Conversation

SET/MC/20   Paris, June 20, 1962, 3 p.m.

SECRETARY'S EUROPEAN TRIP
June 18–28, 1962

PARTICIPANTS

United States

The Secretary of State
Ambassador Gavin
Mr. Bohlen
Mr. Kohler
Mr. Manning
Mr. Hillenbrand
Mr. Cleveland

France

Foreign Minister Couve de Murville
M. Lucet
Ambassador Alphand
M. Laloy
M. Barduc
M. de Margerie

SUBJECT

NATO Nuclear Problem

Source: Department of State, Central Files, 110.11–RU/6–2062. Secret. Drafted by Cleveland and approved in S on June 26. The meeting was held at the French Foreign Office.

The Secretary asked the Foreign Minister whether he had given further thought to the questions which were discussed in Athens, particularly to the proposals regarding guidelines and nuclear information, etc. Couve de Murville said he was not quite clear whether there was anything new about these proposals. His impression was that the guidelines, for example, were just a matter of carrying on the previous practice of the NATO Council but registering it on paper. The American suggestion for giving fuller information on nuclear matters was essentially a unilateral decision by the U.S., and so far as France was concerned it "raised no problems."

The Foreign Minister then asked what the British attitude on these subjects appeared to be. Mr. Kohler replied that the implication of the proposal which the British themselves had made for a NATO Atomic Committee was that they were prepared to go along.

Couve de Murville continued that the question which was in fact on the agenda of the NATO Council was the MRBM question, which frankly he had never understood. So far as he could see the problem remained the same—that is, who possesses nuclear weapons, who controls them, and who makes the decisions about their use?

The Secretary replied that so far as the U.S. is concerned, our position is that we have a situation in NATO which is not unsatisfactory from our point of view. However, it has been suggested that others do not feel the same way. Our view is that if our Allies in NATO believe the situation with regard to nuclear weapons in NATO should be changed, they should get together and come up with a concrete proposal. We had taken the initiative in the matter because we had the impression that this would not happen otherwise. At the same time we did not want to propose a "U.S." plan. Therefore we put out certain ideas as a basis for discussion. The difficulty is an old one—it is hard for us to float a tentative proposal without the others assuming that this is something we want to push. It is sometimes hard to consult about these important matters while ideas are in the stage of formation if the reaction of other countries is to say "How dare you put forward your ideas without consultation?" As soon as we express a few opinions, we found, for example, that some have misunderstood us when we pointed out certain problems which are raised by a multilateral force; some of our NATO colleagues have assumed—wrongly—that this means we are opposed to a multilateral force, whereas in fact what we wanted to do was to lay the problem out clearly so that intelligent discussion could take place on it. Another misunderstanding arose when we said there was no urgent military requirement for MRBMs in Europe. What we mean is that the targets are generally covered already, and that in addition we (the U.S.) have a strong second-strike capability. At some later time there would perhaps be an urgent requirement, and there may be some requirement now. As to the cost of a NATO force, our view is that these weapons should be paid for on a multilateral basis.

Finally, the Secretary said, we have not vetoed a multilateral MRBM force. If there were an alliance proposal, we would want to consider it, and we could even consider if necessary going back to the Congress to change our existing legislation.

In summary, the Secretary said, we are not crusading for a particular proposal nor are we vetoing any proposal. If the matter is not moved forward, we believe it will not be our fault.

The Foreign Minister commented that perhaps until other urgent questions are settled, in particular the question of the political organization of Europe, it might be better not to pursue the MRBM question in NATO. He added that he was not sure if any country except the U.S. knew what a multilateral European weapon really means. The idea has never been a very precise one.

What is likely to be the central political question, the Secretary said, is whether a government can delegate to international machinery or to a group a decision which involves the very life and death of the nation. The U.S. in a sense has this decision now, not by any group election but by the fact of our having developed the nuclear weapon. But to resolve the problem on a broader basis in peace time is extremely difficult. He said the dilemma involved the question of decision by unanimity or by majority. Unanimous decision would mean no action, but majority decision is also hard to accept—can a country accept a majority decision on a matter of life and death when it does not take part in the majority?

The real question, Couve de Murville continued, is "What is an alliance?". There are two possible concepts: a) The philosophical concept—the purpose of the alliance is to insure collective defense at the lowest possible cost. b) The concept that an alliance is not something in itself but rather a collection of countries, with each doing things in its own way. If we consider the question of the Atlantic Alliance from the viewpoint of the second concept, then we must take into account principles other than simple efficiency. Nevertheless, even from the viewpoint of efficiency, the notion of a national deterrent is defensible. The defense of a country means the defense of its life, and its life is bound up with its nationhood. Therefore national forces also are efficient.

The Secretary replied that an American, of course, cannot disagree with the view that an alliance is an alliance of states. But it cannot be an alliance of separate defense policies, nor can it involve separate decisions on war and peace. It is not necessary that we should hold identical views on policies regarding defense outside of Europe and the North Atlantic area, but within that area agreement is necessary. It is this approach which lies behind the principle of guidelines which would help to define circumstances in which the atomic weapons would be used.

He was concerned, the Secretary continued, about the use of the term "modern" weapons when referring to nuclear weapons. To use this term seems to reduce the importance of conventional force. The United States, with a *million men overseas*, cannot see why conventional forces should be considered infra dig. On the contrary, these forces are in our view necessary to maintain the forward strategy.

Furthermore, in the face of a single enemy, our defense must be considered indivisible, especially in the nuclear field. It is difficult indeed to conceive of a partial or separate nuclear war. In fact it is technically impossible. So we cannot see how it is possible to think of a series of nuclear forces in the Atlantic area independent of each other. In our view it is possible to find common policies within an alliance of states.

The Foreign Minister replied that we all agree on that. There is no question, he said, that common defense is necessary. The French also agreed that conventional forces are not outmoded. Rather, they consider that conventional and atomic forces are parts of a single force.

But, Couve de Murville, continued, some countries in the alliance, including the United States, have interests outside the NATO area. More than that, none of us can organize their entire national life and the military organization within the North Atlantic Alliance. The alliance is of great importance, but it cannot be exclusive; for example, France cannot deny itself part of the weaponry of a modern army simply because one of its allies has enough or more than enough of this type of weapon to take care of everybody. Any country has a present and future position, and must consider both of them in its policies. This is a fact of life.

The Secretary replied we could agree that the objective of an alliance like NATO should be an efficient defense of the area viewed as a whole. It is for this reason that we need a common defense effort. The Foreign Minister agreed, but added that this should not exclude consideration of national interests.

The Secretary asked if the end of the Algerian war would make a difference in terms of France's ability to contribute to NATO forces. The Foreign Minister somewhat evasively replied that it would make it possible to completely reorganize the army, in order to train it for modern warfare. In particular the Army could be brought back to France; the term of compulsory military service could be reduced; the army could be re-equipped with modern weapons as fast as possible.

The Secretary asked Couve de Murville how the French see the problem of the diffusion of nuclear weapons. The Foreign Minister replied this is indeed a big question. At the beginning—in 1945—only the United States had atomic weapons. They appeared something fantastic and out of range for everybody but the United States. The Americans thought so too. But four years later, the Russians had their weapon. Then the United Kingdom followed suit and then came France, whose program was initiated as far back as 1954. There seems little question that the Chinese are working on atomic weapons, and if they succeed it will be impossible for India not to follow suit. Even certain highly-industrialized small countries like Sweden and Israel might follow.

Then there is the problem of Germany. The Germans have respected so far the agreement which involved a German renunciation of atomic weapons but they are showing increasing signs of being obsessed by the problem. Indeed, the proposal for a NATO multilateral nuclear force derives from this German obsession and the hope that it could be met in this way.

Finally, Couve de Murville said, there is of course the idea of Europe. If something can be done to create a political union of Europe, which would also involve coordination in the defense field, then the nuclear problem would arise in this context, between France, the United Kingdom, and Germany. (At a different point in the meeting, in the context of a discussion of the UK-EEC negotiations and the future of Europe, Couve de Murville remarked that despite the problem of less cohesion which would be raised by having a larger number of members in a political union, the nuclear problem could be dealt with more easily in the context of a Europe which included France, the United Kingdom and Germany, than in one which had in it only France and Germany.)

In conclusion, the Foreign Minister raised the question of whether in fact there is any way to stop proliferation. The Secretary asked whether in the French view a nuclear test ban might not make a contribution to this process. The Foreign Minister replied he was convinced the Chinese would not accept a test ban. This was a matter essentially between the United States and the Soviets.

Referring to an earlier remark by the Foreign Minister to the effect that the Soviets might accept a test ban when they felt they were not too far behind the United States in nuclear weapons development, the Secretary wondered whether there was not also the problem of the burden on the Soviet Union of extended competition in the nuclear weapons field, as indicated by recent Soviet economic measures. The Soviets might feel that a continuation of the nuclear arms race involved a continued investment of economic resources in nuclear weapons for a marginal military contribution. Mr. Couve de Murville agreed, giving it as his opinion that the United States could in fact stand the arms race longer than the Soviets. The Secretary remarked that this consideration of the use of resources might also be a discouraging factor for the Chinese and the Germans.

The Secretary then turned to the question of the meaning of an "independent" nuclear strike force. He asked the Foreign Minister if he could envisage the idea of allied nuclear forces acting differently from each other, rather than in an indivisible manner. The Foreign Minister replied that theoretically this was not impossible but practically and politically it was very unlikely. One theoretical possibility: assuming the takeover of all of continental Europe by the Russians based on a fully conventional war, with Britain then facing invasion from the continent. Under these circumstances the British might want to use their nuclear capability. The Secretary said that in such a case a nuclear war would in fact have started at a much earlier stage.

The disturbing thing, the Secretary continued, is the notion that a strike force should be national rather than within the alliance. The Foreign Minister replied that the strike forces would be national just as all forces are national, including those assigned to NATO. The French strike force would be independent until there are agreements which settle its use.

The Secretary asked if the French would envisage their own strike forces as being at least as multilateral as the United States taking into account, for example, the proposed NATO guidelines and atomic information program. The Foreign Minister replied that the United States force is at the President's disposal. The United States he continued, is committed to use its own nuclear weapons as is necessary in the defense of Europe. But such a commitment is not the same thing as multilateral planning. There is, of course, nuclear planning which takes place in SHAPE, but on the atomic side, General Norstad takes his orders from the President of the United States. The Secretary referred to the NATO alert list, but the Foreign Minister replied that this list is British and American.

Mr. Kohler asked how the French strike force would be targeted. The Foreign Minister replied that this is a different area from that in which General Norstad operates, because on the American side the parallel organization is SAC. The French strike force, he said, should be considered as parallel to SAC, not to the tactical nuclear weapons which were in SHAPE's area. It would be independent in the same way that SAC is independent, if there were no coordination.

The Secretary asked if the Foreign Minister saw any difficulty with a combined target list for the French strike force. The Foreign Minister replied that in realistic terms the French strike force would not add much to the striking power of the United States; as to the suggestion for a combined target list, he said he was ready to have it considered. The Secretary said that the problem of independent employment of nuclear force needed study. The Foreign Minister agreed that it needed study, and repeated that he was prepared to have it studied. He added that this idea had never been discussed before between the two Governments.

Proceeding on the same line, the Secretary said it was difficult to see any issue which would be nuclear for the French but not for the United States.

Mr. Couve de Murville agreed. He said it was normal that we should raise the question. It was not, of course, an immediate question, in view of the development of the French strike force, but he would think it over and discuss it further with the Secretary.

The Secretary asked if he were correct in assuming the French would *not* conceive the function of their strike force in terms of using it as a "trigger" in case of a nuclear war. The Foreign Minister replied emphatically: "No. We're not that silly." The French reason for wanting a nuclear strike force is the same as that of the British: since these arms exist and form part of the normal armament of a modern army, there is no reason why a country with the necessary resources should not try to have these capabilities.

---

145.   Memorandum of Conversation

SET/MC/25   Bonn, June 22, 1962, 11:30 a.m.

PARTICIPANTS

United States	*Germany*
The Secretary of State	Chancellor Adenauer
Ambassador Dowling	Foreign Minister Schroeder
Mr. Bohlen	Dr. von Eckhardt
Mr. Kohler	Dr. Carstens
Mr. Manning	Dr. Krapf
Mr. Morris	Dr. von Hase
Mr. Hillenbrand	Dr. Osterheld
	Dr. von Braun
	Dr. Reinkemeyer

SUBJECT

NATO Nuclear Problems

Source: Department of State, Central Files, 110.11–RU/6–2262. Secret; Limit Distribution. Drafted by Hillenbrand and approved in S on June 28. The meeting was held in the Chancellor's Conference Room at Schaumburg Palace.

After discussion of the Berlin situation had been concluded,[1] Foreign Minister Schroeder raised the question of the NATO nuclear problem. He noted that in Athens the Ministerial Council had received impressive statements from the Secretary of State and Secretary of Defense. The Federal Republic largely shared the US strategic assessment but considered that the political and psychological problems were somewhat greater than US spokesmen had indicated. If there were nuclear possibilities on one side and the nuclear reaction on our side was in the hands only of the strongest partner, this created problems. In Athens the UK and French positions had seemed clear. Retention of their own nuclear capacity was given a greater priority than any contribution to a shared deterrent. The Federal Republic saw no better solution to the psychological and political problems involved than cooperation with the US proposal on MRBMs. This cooperation plus exchange of information and the working out of an integrated strategy would be the best course, even if it ultimately depended on one nuclear power. To ask a speculative question, Schroeder continued, he wondered whether the United States considered that the UK and French nuclear problem could be better worked out in the context of general European developments.

The Secretary said the nuclear problem is made especially difficult because it is not always easy to deal with the harshest realities of the harshest thing in the world today within the framework of friendly discussions in the Alliance. We do not underestimate what is required for a nuclear force if it is to have any effectiveness whatsoever. The US had made an enormous investment in its nuclear deterrent for more than 16 years. The Soviet strength in this field was only a fraction, although a substantial one, of US strength. We have been trying to bring the US deterrent capability within a multilateral framework by the provision of guide lines, by our commitments to consult and by coordination of policy. We realize this arrangement might not be good enough for the governments in the Alliance. We can see that those who might be incinerated will want to take part in this regardless of the size of the nation involved. We do not believe that national nuclear capabilities are the way to solve this problem. We have not said to the French that they cannot have a nuclear force. France has not asked us to help it. There has been no intergovernmental argument on this point. We cannot, of course, accept the idea that there could be any relatively small national nuclear force which for decades would make any difference to the military strategy of the Alliance. The idea that such a force might be used independently of the Alliance is frightening. The indivisibility of the nuclear defense of the West is fundamental. This is a harsh reality. Beginning in 1945 our policy against further expansion of these weapons in

---

[1] A memorandum of the conversation on Berlin, SET/MC/24, is in vol. XV, pp. 196–200.

the hands of national governments has been constant. Not every government is constituted the same. He had to say frankly that, when we send envoys to some capitals, we are doubtful whether to send an Ambassador or a psychiatrist. These weapons are not toys. They relate to the chief end of man and to all that is worth living for. Their possession has made us as old as Methuselah.

We had hoped that the Allies would be able to talk out the problems of a NATO multilateral force. We have now concluded that we must participate in these discussions. We have stated some views on the subject but have not taken a final position and have put any proposals forward on a take-it-or-leave-it basis. We have emphasized certain elements: (a) that the US should not pay a disproportionate part of the cost of a multilateral force which is being built for political reasons arising elsewhere, and (b) that measures should be taken to ensure that the force is genuinely multilateral, for example, by multiple manning and by basing of the force at sea. The US, which is responsible for the nuclear defense of the Alliance, has had to go on its knees to plead for the deployment of its weapons on behalf of the Alliance. Half of the countries have said no, sometimes for trivial reasons. This has not been a pleasant experience for us.

There has been some feeling in NAC, the Secretary continued, that we had delivered a mortal blow to the multilateral force. This was certainly not because of any US policy opposed to such a force. If the serious problems involved dealt it a mortal blow, this is another matter. However, its failure is not inevitable. It should be fully discussed and we will participate in this discussion. If, of course, two leading NATO countries are opposed, this might be decisive. Attitudes on this subject as well as the form of the problem itself might change after a solution is obtained to the question of UK relationship to the Common Market. We hope that the UK will enter the Common Market. If the Rome Treaty were to provide more cohesion than now exists on political and defense matters, this would be relevant. We will provide all the information we can so that the discussion in NAC can proceed on realistic grounds.

Another aspect, the Secretary went on, was that we support a forward strategy and have many divisions on the German front. We would not like to see other countries fail to carry out their conventional force commitments in order to build up a nuclear force which has no military significance. The Secretary added that, although he had spoken vigorously on this subject, his views were not aimed at the Germans.

Schroeder said that the Federal Republic was convinced that a certain conventional strength was absolutely necessary. He agreed it was wrong to say, as some did, that we must have a nuclear force and therefore do not need conventional divisions. The Federal Republic would contribute her fair share of 12 divisions in the build-up of NATO forces.

The problem of a multilateral nuclear force was complicated by the fact that the UK explicitly and the French implicitly, argue that they must first have national nuclear forces before making contributions to a multilateral force. Therefore, the burden falls on the US. The Federal Republic had a common interest with the US in this connection. The association of the US with the Continent was proved by the fact that there were large US troop contingents on the front lines. When, however, the question of political prestige was involved, the Federal Republic had no lesser interests than other countries. The Federal Republic thought the best way to satisfy this political aspect was by a multilateral project. The Germans would, therefore, proceed on this line in the NAC discussion.

The Chancellor remarked at this point that he appreciated this was a difficult subject for the US. He remembered how, in 1954, when at the Lancaster House meeting he had renounced the manufacture of ABC weapons in the context of the Nine Power Agreement, Secretary of State Dulles had said to him that the *rebus sic stantibus* doctrine would of course apply. The Chancellor said that he had indicated his awareness of this to Mr. Dulles.

[1 paragraph (3 lines of source text) not declassified]

Commenting on the question of UK entry into the Common Market, he [Adenauer] saw the negotiations as difficult and protracted. The British elections would come within at most two years. If Labor won, one could not forget that this party had originally ended conscription and that the Conservatives had not felt able to restore it.

The Chancellor referred to the plan which he said General Norstad had put forward late in 1960 at the Stikker residence on Lake Como.[2] However, in view of the elections, the Eisenhower Administration did not feel itself able to push this plan. He then alluded to the fact that while he had confidence in the US President, the possibility might arise where the latter would be incapable of taking a decision on the use of nuclear weapons. He knew that the President had tried to reassure him on this point during his Washington visit last November. He, therefore, thought that the military aspect, rather than prestige and political aspects, was all important since a matter of survival was involved. The Federal Republic seeks a solution that will unite NATO and not split it.

The Secretary said we agreed the question should be intensively studied. He understood that this would start with the military aspects, but he recognized that there were also political problems involved. Since the proposals of 1960 to which the Chancellor has referred, there had been substantial changes in the nuclear field which affected the problem, for example, the great increase in our Polaris Program.

---

[2] Presumably this is the meeting described in Stikker, *Men of Responsibility* (New York: 1965), pp. 333–334.

146.   Telegram From the Embassy in the United Kingdom to the Department of State

London, June 26, 1962, 8 p.m.

Secto 81. Followed based on uncleared memcon.[1] Secretary and Lord Home discussed on June 25 MRBMs and related nuclear questions. Discussions continued subsequently by Kohler with Shuckburgh and Ramsbotham. Below is summary.

Home said British felt military need for MRBMs should be discussed first in NATO and this discussion might take some time. British feel ultimate form multilateral force might take, whether NATO or European, should be left open for moment. Main point is to wait to see developments growing out of UK entry into Common Market.

Secretary said he essentially agreed British views on timing MRBM discussion. Felt we should proceed "with all deliberate speed". Stressed US did not want to seem to be holding up Alliance consideration MRBMs. We had earlier remained silent on subject, which had been interpreted by some as US holding up NATO action. Secretary also stressed we have no intention presenting "US plan". In Ambassador Finletter's June 15 statement to NAC,[2] our sole purpose had been to raise certain questions which we felt required meaningful consideration MRBM question. Definitely not our purpose, as some appear to have thought, to veto MRBMs entirely.

Home said British felt Athens package of guidelines, assurances, and information had gone long way take care of German concerns. In recent discussions with Germans, British had impression they were quite satisfied, at least for present.

Secretary said he believed this was true, adding that recent Washington talks with Strauss[3] had further useful effect on Germans, but fact that Germans are satisfied for present is not by any means whole story. Secretary said his recent talks with Adenauer[4] left him with strong impression that future German pressures for nuclear role bound to be very strong. Secretary gained clear impression Germans want to reserve their position on nuclear question for future. Their strong opposition to any

---

Source: Department of State, Central Files, 110.11–RU/6–2662. Secret; Limit Distribution. Repeated to Paris, Bonn, and Rome.

[1] SET/MC/36, June 25. (Ibid., 110.11–RU/6–2562)

[2] See footnote 1, Document 142.

[3] See Document 140.

[4] See Document 145.

nuclear non-dissemination provision in Berlin package further evidence of this.

In subsequent discussion, Kohler reiterated Secretary's point re German position, stressing that multilateral solution must be found if German pressures for national solution are to be headed off. Kohler also stressed that Germans had made strong point of non-discrimination. Any ultimate solution found must avoid discriminatory treatment of Germany in nuclear matters. Kohler also pointed out that French had spoken of German interest in nuclear matters as "obsession". Furthermore, Germans themselves in Bonn had been careful say there were no pressures for national program "as of now". Also significant was Chancellor's statement that original WEU declaration by Germany based upon *rebus sic stantibus*. As result, US convinced that pressures for national program inevitable in Germany if alternative not found. Kohler also pointed out Germans made quite clear they do not propose to add in any way to their existing undertaking in the unilateral WEU declaration.

Ramsbotham said, based on their talks with Balken and other Germans, they have feeling additional reason in German mind for avoiding further undertaking on non-dissemination is that Germans want to avoid giving Russians right of interference in future.

Ramsbotham said UK at earlier stage multilateral MRBM force discussions had understood we had no idea diluting unilateral US control. More recently British had heard from Stikker and others that US position on this was not so categoric.

Kohler said that we do in fact want to leave impression conveyed by Stikker and others that we have open mind on control question. We believe would be politically very unwise for us to make flat statement at outset that we insist on unilateral US control. We of course have no present intention change existing system and, indeed, do not have any legal authority to do so but we do not want to rule out possibility considering situation if it develops our Allies wish to see some change. Key to control problem is really targeting. We want to bring about realization by all that nuclear war is in fact indivisible and to demonstrate that control must be based on really integrated targeting and strategy.

Ramsbotham asked for confirmation that, if MRBMs are provided for NATO, they would be provided only to multilateral force. Kohler confirmed that this is case.

On MRBM requirement, Kohler explained importance of full sharing targeting info in NATO. Only in this way, in our view, can we reach understanding of MRBM requirement. Information on targeting will demonstrate that many of targets for which MRBMs said to be needed are already taken care of. Result may be that only 200 or so will remain for coverage by Polaris and another 200 plus battlefield targets and the like could be dealt with by other means, one of which might be missile "X", another V/STOL aircraft, etc.

Ramsbotham said he believed UK generally agrees with US views on military requirement, although they also feel something is to be said for having MRBMs for deterrent effect. There is place for some MRBMs to fill in complete spectrum of nuclear weapons from small tactical to major strategic. Nevertheless, UK agrees with US view that inconceivable that MRBMs will be used except in general war situation.[5] Ramsbotham said this type of question which UK wants Standing Group to look into.

Bruce

---

[5] Kranich underlined this sentence in the source text and wrote beneath it: "Why do we keep raising this straw man?"

---

147. Paper Prepared by the Secretary of State's Special Assistant (Bohlen)

Washington, July 2, 1962.

IMPRESSIONS IN REGARD TO UNITED STATES-EUROPEAN RELATIONS

As compared to previous times that I have been to Europe in the last few years, this was the first time that we went to various capitals in the same visit, which gave me an opportunity to judge some of the general questions which will be of importance for our relations with that continent in the fairly immediate future.

It is perhaps difficult for an American fully to understand how much their dependence upon the United States in the immediate post-

---

Source: Department of State, Conference Files: Lot 65 D 533, CF 2124. Secret. The source text, which bears no drafting information, was attached to a brief memorandum from Bohlen to Rusk, July 2, stating that these impressions were in response to a request by the Secretary of State.

war period was resented by the Europeans. These nations, and I am now speaking only of the larger ones—in particular France—have a long tradition of independent political and economic action and occupied a primacy of place in world affairs, which it is extremely difficult for them to forget. In the case of France, there is also the element of a guilt complex arising from the fact that it was only thanks to the efforts of the United States and the United Kingdom that France survived the war at all. The defeat of 1940 has left a very definite psychological influence which affects, in no small measure, the policies of France at the present time. Added to this is the memory of Suez in 1956 and the unbroken string of French postwar defeats in Colonial questions. Sentiments which are psychological and subjective, have found their true expression in General de Gaulle. His own writings reveal how much he bitterly resented the necessity of being dependent on the United States and the United Kingdom during the war years, and how vigorously he sought to circumvent or overcome this dependence whenever possible. To some extent, this feeling of now being in a position to get out from under the tutelage of the United States, which in European eyes was always tremendously exaggerated, is present in all European countries in varying degrees. I am sure that we all recognize the fact that Europe is now a self-supporting entity and we must expect, therefore, that they will be much more inclined not to accept American views on international questions. I am not speaking here of the specifically European differences which we have had in the past, such as on the Colonial question, but rather a change in European psychology brought on by European recovery and the consequent watering-down of the American predominant position in the world.

It is against this background that we should look at what unquestionably will be the biggest single political issue in the not-too-distant future; namely, that of the ability of some of the European countries, individually or together, to produce a nuclear capability. I say in the relatively near future since the question of England's joining the Common Market will undoubtedly have a major effect on the development of this question, but also because a certain amount of time will be necessary before any such nuclear capability appears on the continent. The main choice that we will have to think about is whether or not this capability is to be on a purely national basis or whether it can be directed into some all-European form; in other words, multinational. In either case, this will require a very careful study on the part of the United States as to our relationship to this capability, and keeping in view the very real possibility that some changes will have to be made in the McMahon Act if we are to preserve good relations with the European community or the individual members thereof.

In addition to the historic and traditional reasons which will impel Europe towards this capability, there are some of a more practical nature, involving the whole complex of defense and armaments. While it may not be immediately apparent, there is, in my opinion, unquestionably a connection between the development of the nuclear arm and the development of conventional forces. While Europe was weak and in the process of recovery, this factor did not emerge. But if nations are told that they will have no voice in the major weapons of war upon which their security and future depend, they may well tend to regard the money and resources required for the development of conventional forces as not worthwhile. There is some truth in the thesis that the ability to act in its own defense is an attribute of sovereignty and that if nations are told that their real defense, which will be in the nuclear field, will be in the hands of others, they will recoil from the sacrifices necessary to build up the conventional forces. I do not mean this as an absolute thesis because there will, in any event, be a considerable European conventional force in being, but merely as a intangible factor which does play on the whole complex of an adequate defense. This is particularly true in Europe proper since it is extremely difficult to see how conventional forces on the continent of Europe, given its division, could ever play an important part in an actual war—almost certain to be nuclear from its inception.

France

The attitude of the French, and especially your talk with de Gaulle,[1] seems to indicate a certain relaxation in their attitude to many of the international questions. This seemed to be true particularly in regard to the Berlin discussions and I imagine that de Gaulle's statement to you that these talks had not produced the dangerous reaction in Germany that he had expected, is probably a true expression of his views. In addition, there may well be the feeling that France was being left out of a process in which the United States was, in effect, carrying the ball for the whole Western world. It may, therefore, be that France will be more disposed to enter into the Berlin discussions with us and the British than has been the case for almost the last year.

On the nuclear question, there was uniform conviction from everyone I talked with in Paris, whether French or foreign, that France was going to go ahead with the development of a nuclear armament no matter what the cost in the way of diversion of funds and resources from other tasks which we might consider more urgent. While in theory and in practice this small and ineffective nuclear capability is folly, stemming primarily from the particularly French subjective attitudes out-

---

[1] See Document 255.

lined above, I don't see what we could do to prevent it without doing mortal damage to the whole concept of the Alliance.

In your talks with Couve de Murville,[2] he was not quite definite that the nuclear arm would, under all conditions, remain completely independent and completely national, and it may be that we might direct our policy with a view to having France, once she has obtained some nuclear capability, work towards its eventual integration into a European complex. This will be extremely difficult and probably impossible as long as de Gaulle is in power, and obviously as long as France continues to work on national lines, she will, by the development of certain patterns as well as a technical civil service in the nuclear field, tend to freeze herself in the direction of the maintenance of a purely national force. I don't think, under the circumstances, we could, with any wisdom, agree to assist her in the development of this force along national lines, if only for the eventual and inevitable effect on West Germany. Since we must accept the fact that France will sooner or later have this nuclear force, there might be certain elements of inducement which we might be able to use to bring her around to the idea of an integrated European nuclear capability.

Germany

With Germany, the main question at the moment is that of Berlin and particularly those elements of any conceivable Berlin settlement which would deal with the problem of Germany as a whole. It seemed to me at Bonn that the Germans are very reluctant to contemplate any agreement on nondiffusion of nuclear weapons which might, in any conceivable circumstance, apply only to Germany. They also showed a good deal of reluctance to any nonaggression arrangement between Warsaw and the NATO Pact for the same reason. The question of frontiers did not arise in any of the meetings at which I was present. On the other hand, there are tendencies in Germany working towards the modification of the Hallstein doctrine which will undoubtedly come about certainly no later than the departure of Adenauer.

The Chancellor's reference to the alleged Dulles remark on "rebus sic stantibus" in 1954, at the time of the German signature renouncing the manufacture of ABC weapons, was of considerable interest in connection with the nuclear question.[3] It seemed to me that the Germans would prefer to be equal participants in any European multinational force but, failing that, would sooner or later begin to move towards a national nuclear capability.

---

[2] See Document 144.

[3] For a memorandum of Rusk's conversation with Adenauer on June 22, see Document 145.

Schroeder is obviously a very intelligent and effective man, and I certainly gained the impression from the talks with him that he thinks much more along our lines than does the Chancellor; but, in general, Germany seems to be in a kind of an interim situation and will be as long as Adenauer stays on, since all of the leading candidates for his post will undoubtedly be influenced in their thinking on any question by their estimate of its effect on their chances of getting the job.

At the moment, with the talks with the Soviets on dead center, there would appear to be no great problems of an immediate nature with the Germans, but if, as is always possible, there should be some shift in the Soviet attitude, we will have, I imagine, considerable difficulties with the Germans, especially if the shift is in the direction of some compromise arrangement on Berlin.

Italy

I did not find in the conversations I attended in Rome any great, major problems of a European nature, except that of the activities of Mr. Mattei and the inherent problems of the "opening to the left."

England

While the conversations in England were very agreeable and, in general, satisfactory, I was again struck by the curious fixation that the top British seem to have in regard to the necessity of making additional moves or even concessions towards the Soviets at this time. (Lord Home's remarks about the need to take advantage of the lull in order to put forth new concessions on Berlin and the insistence of Mr. Godber that it was up to the West to make some new moves in the disarmament field.) I imagine this is probably due to certain domestic currents and with the government clearly worried about the internal situation, it is probably natural, but I think we should stand very firm, particularly in disarmament, against yielding to any British attempts in this direction.

The general sentiment in Paris, Bonn, and Rome seems to be that, in the last analysis, Great Britain would join the Common Market and this sentiment seemed to be shared by Heath in London. It is obvious, however, that the French accept this probability with some reluctance since it seems to cut across the idea of a French-dominated European community. But certainly my impression in Germany and, of course, in Rome, was that the governments were strongly in favor of Britain's adherence. I did not talk enough with Adenauer, however, to get any impression of what his real views on this subject are, but certainly Schroeder and his associates were definitely in favor of Britain's joining.

Since there seems to be a general consensus that no serious discussion in regard to the question of the nuclear factor in the European picture could be dealt with until the decision had been reached in regard to

Great Britain's joining the Common Market, we have a period of a number of months in which we can attempt to sort out our views in regard to this question before it becomes actual. I would only make one suggestion, and that is preferably we would avoid any public statements on the subject during the coming months and, above all, avoid the term "the indivisibility" of nuclear power, which to any European is merely a euphuism for absolute American control. If we do use the term, we should know how it will be interpreted abroad.

I fully realize how immensely complex and difficult the entire question of the nuclear factor in our relations with Europe is and will be. There are obviously many facets of the subject which I do not know, but I am convinced, from a political point of view that we will be faced with some form of European nuclear capability—at best or at worst, a number of independent national nuclear capabilities, with all the consequences that this would entail for the Alliance and for the security of the United States. I would think it might be well to institute a very high level group, particularly from State and Defense, which would examine very carefully, and with some urgency, all the aspects of this problem so that we would be ready to meet it when it arises in our relationship with Europe.

148. Memorandum for the President

Washington, undated.

SUBJECT

General Norstad's Trip

1. *Background.* General Norstad is visiting Washington against a background of concerns over US policy which he has expressed to US officials who have visited him recently. These concerns reflect, in part, the fact that in past years General Norstad has been a strong, able, and unquestioned leader of the alliance on matters of politico-military policy. This situation resulted partly from tradition (beginning with Gen-

Source: Kennedy Library, President's Office Files, NATO/Norstad Meeting. Secret. The source text, which bears no drafting information, was attached to a memorandum to the President from Rusk and McNamara, dated July 14, and was intended as a briefing paper for the President's meeting with Norstad on July 16. No record of that meeting has been found, but the President's Appointment Book records a meeting with Norstad from 4:07 to 5:27 p.m. (Ibid.)

eral Eisenhower in SHAPE) and partly from his own considerable talents of leadership and diplomacy. The advent to power of a US administration with its own ideas on strategy necessarily produced a new situation. The General's reaction to this situation is a natural one, and is compounded by differences of view regarding some tactical, as well as substantive, issues. He may raise two of these tactical issues while he is here:

(a) The General indicates that, although he is in general sympathy with the views of the new administration, he believes that we have presented these views badly—thus antagonizing our allies. (He may refer here to US discussion of this strategy in NATO in terms which make clear that some of its aspects are a departure from the strategy that our allies support and have followed so far under General Norstad's leadership. This US discussion has undoubtedly generated some allied questioning but, on balance, we believe that it has had a constructive educational effect. German Defense Minister Strauss indicated, when last here, that he welcomed the detail and candor with which the new administration's strategy had been discussed in recent US speeches to NATO; he spoke feelingly of the silence with which US had veiled its views on basic strategy in the past.)

(b) The General is also reported to be disturbed by the practice of sending visiting experts from State and Defense for short tours of duty with Ambassador Finletter's staff. He believes that this has caused confusion and misgivings among our allies. (These experts were sent at Ambassador Finletter's request, so that his staff and other national delegations might be made more familiar with US thinking. The views which they have expounded have naturally not always coincided with those of our allies or of the General, but their presence has helped to ensure useful and meaningful communication between Paris and Washington thinking. The fact of the matter is that some of the thinking results from complex, new studies generated here in Washington. The only feasible way to make the necessary information available, fully and expeditiously, is by supplying key personnel who were involved in making the studies.)

2. *June 15 Statement*. The source of greatest concern to the General at the moment, however, is the June 15 statement of Ambassador Finletter concerning MRBMs—both because he was not consulted about it, and because of the issue which this statement takes with the MRBM requirement, of which he has long been the principal exponent.

3. *Procedure*. We should have consulted General Norstad about the June 15 statement, as a matter of courtesy, although his basic views were known. He can be assured that in the future, whenever time permits, we will seek and welcome his views.

4. *Substance.* On the substantive question, the basic MRBM differences are as follows:

(a) *Requirement.* General Norstad wants 450 MRBMs to replace
strike aircraft in Europe, which will become increasingly obsolescent.
(The basic question is one of developing a logical strategy. To a considerable extent there is a difference between US policy and General
Norstad's views as to whether a modernization of the NATO strike
force or an expansion of its strategic nuclear capability[1] is justified. The
US position is that planned alliance forces are adequate, but that a multilateral MRBM force would have some military utility and might have[2]
considerable political importance; we are prepared to join in setting up
such an MRBM force if our allies desire, provided that it[3] does not unduly divert resources from non-nuclear programs.)

(b) *Manning.* General Norstad probably prefers MRBMs to be deployed under existing procedures, i.e., US MRBMs, and nationally
manned allied MRBMs with US warheads under "joint control". However, in the case of MRBMs the warheads would, for technical reasons,
be contained in the missiles, instead of being stored in igloos. (Deployment to nationally manned forces of missiles capable of reaching the
USSR and containing their own warheads would, even with planned
technical safeguards, be regarded as close to creation of de facto national
strategic nuclear capabilities by many countries, including the USSR.
German participation would, therefore, create severe divisive strains
within NATO and in East-West relations. Moreover, a national pattern
would have been set for the future shape of allied nuclear efforts, which
we hope increasingly to channel into multilateral forms. For all these
reasons, the US position is that allied MRBMs should be under multilateral manning, ownership, and control.)

(c) *Sea vs. Land.* General Norstad wants MRBMs to be both land-
based and sea-based. (We believe that land-basing would involve serious political problems.) Governments would demand a special national
role in the peacetime deployment and control of any missiles on their
territory, and the possibility of national seizure of such missiles in wartime would frustrate the whole point and purpose of a multilateral
force. Serious European and Soviet concerns would be generated by the
prospect of deployment of MRBMs on German territory. The evident
presence of MRBMs with the warheads aboard travelling about European roads might stimulate neutralist and anti-nuclear sentiment and

---

[1] McNamara added by hand "or an expansion of its strategic nuclear capability."

[2] McNamara added the words "might have."

[3] At this point in the source text McNamara struck out the words: "is of a size, i.e.,
about 200 missiles, which."

demonstrations in some countries. If an accident, possibly induced by sabotage, involving even the threat of nuclear contamination occurred on land, the political damage to NATO would be serious. For all these reasons, the US position—since it was first made public in the President's Ottawa speech—has been that a multilateral MRBM force should be seaborne.

5. *Tactics.* These differences are of long standing. The US Government reached its position in full awareness of General Norstad's views and the reasons for them. He, in turn, has known of our views, and the reasoning behind them, and has not been moved to change his own position, which antedated them.

It is doubtful, therefore, that a detailed substantive discussion will narrow the difference. Indeed, a discussion based on the premise that the US position was open to substantial early change might do more harm than good by causing the General to engage in arduous and hopeful debate.

It is also doubtful that it would be desirable or appropriate to try to suggest to the General the course that he should follow in discussing these issues in his July 25 appearance before the NAC. He is dedicated to the larger interests and cohesion of the alliance, anxious to avoid a divisive confrontation, and likely to handle himself in the NAC with restraint and statesmanship. He has, moreover, traditionally been sensitive to attempts to dictate his course as an international commander.

More useful than either of these courses may be to discuss with General Norstad the considerations which suggest that the difference between his position and ours is one that we can both live with, since the US position will partly meet his immediate needs. A suggested outline for a discussion along these lines follows:

"We appreciate that General Norstad's views on the military requirement for MRBMs are rather different from those which the US holds and which the President instructed Ambassador Finletter to present on June 15. We also know that the General's views are based on long and thoughtful examination of the questions involved. These views have received the most careful consideration here in our review of theater and global factors bearing on this problem.

"In terms of end results, the difference in views between General Norstad and the US may not be critical. Our approach to military aspects of the problem, as set forth in Ambassador Finletter's presentation, is to consider that problem from the point of view of the objective which both the US and General Norstad share: to ensure that there be the best possible coverage of all targets, with full account taken of political and military factors.

"If agreement were reached on a sea-based multilateral MRBM force, with 200 missiles, this could go a long way toward covering many of the targets involved. Remaining targets can, we believe, be adequately covered by external or other forces. We will have this problem under continuing review in the future, to ensure their coverage with the best possible weapons. Whether further steps are needed is a question which the Alliance can continue to study. In order to keep open the possibility of future action as may be required, we are continuing research and development on a wide range of items.

"In addition, Ambassador Finletter's statement said that, although the US does not feel there is an urgent military need for MRBMs, we do feel that MRBMs would have military utility and could be of considerable political importance. In his meeting with the Permanent Representatives on June 20,[4] Secretary Rusk sought to make clear that the US is prepared to go forward. We do have some firm views on the need for a genuine multilateral approach to the MRBM problem for political reasons, and believe that the Alliance should have full information on such factors as costs before arriving at decisions. But, as Secretary Rusk explained to the Council, we certainly are not seeking to 'kill off' MRBMs as such.

"As for timing, we look forward to a careful, meaningful discussion of the MRBM question in the upcoming months. We do not expect, and other countries do not appear to expect, the Alliance to rush into a decision. We sense that there is within the Alliance a desire to give priority attention to the negotiations between the UK and the EEC, after which we will have a better picture of the shape of Europe and of the resulting relationship between Europe and North America. The general framework of that relationship was laid out in the President's July 4 speech at Philadelphia.

"We are keenly aware of the great services General Norstad rendered and is rendering the free world in giving vital and effective leadership to its military efforts in the crucial European area. We wish to support and strengthen that leadership, on which we set great store. We are most anxious that US handling of the MRBM issue not have a contrary effect. The US will do what it can to avoid or minimize any divisive effects in continuing NAC discussions. We believe that action on this issue can have a vital bearing on the political future of the Alliance, and we are anxious that it be approached in a way that lays a sound basis for the larger partnership which we see ahead."

---

[4] See Document 143.

149. Telegram From the Department of State to the Mission to the North Atlantic Treaty Organization and European Regional Organizations

Washington, July 19, 1962, 5:32 p.m.

Topol 128. Brussels for Embassy and USEC. Personal from Secretary to Finletter.

1. I appreciated your thoughtful Polto 21.[1] Such analysis and projection is most helpful, and I hope you will continue to favor us in this way from time to time. In re your suggestions, in para 8–10:

2. *Atlantic Interdependence.* I agree (your 8B) we must try to shape events so that the partnership takes forms which, in the military and other fields, foster Atlantic unity. We want to make clear, in every way we can, that US strategic power not only is adequate to allow the time essential for settling nuclear issues in a wise and orderly way, but also is tightly linked to the defense of NATO Europe. We wish to educate our allies to military fact that the defense of the entire NATO area is an integral problem and not divisible; we wish to reaffirm by U.S. actions and statements that the U.S. commitment to this collective defense is complete and unreserved. This seems to me essential:

(a) to maintain allied unity, confidence, and cohesion;
(b) to minimize pressures for hasty or unwise allied action;
(c) to ensure that a multilateral force, if one is created, does not fragment the unified defense of the NATO area and that planning for its use assumes that it would be employed in integral association with other alliance nuclear forces;
(d) to ensure that our allies, if a multilateral force is created, do not consider that it—rather than the total Western nuclear complex—is the instrument on which they must place primary reliance militarily for their nuclear defense, and are not moved by this view to divert unduly large resources from non-nuclear programs to building it up.

I should be most interested in any specific suggestions you may have concerning further actions to strengthen this allied awareness of Atlantic inter-dependence. Creation of the NATO nuclear committee and commitment of Polaris submarines to NATO were intended to serve this purpose.

3. *US Posture Toward MRBM's.* I agree (your 8C) that we should make clear to our allies that they err if they believe that we oppose a multilateral MRBM force.

Source: Department of State, Central Files, 375/7–562. Secret; Priority; Limit Distribution. Drafted by Owen and Kranich; cleared with Kohler, Nitze, Fessenden, Weiss, Kohler, the Department of Defense, and the White House; and approved by Rusk. Repeated to Bonn, Brussels, Rome, The Hague, and London.

[1] Polto 21, July 5, examined the role of NATO after the United Kingdom, as seemed probable, joined the Common Market. (Ibid.)

This is not our view, and there is everything to be gained by making that fact clear. I recognize that in the end our allies may not settle on a NATO force, and may conceivably find themselves inclining instead to a so-called "European" multilateral force, but these possibilities do not make the education re advantages of multilateral approach and indivisibility of nuclear defense referred to in para 4, below, any less important. On the contrary, such education is essential, to ensure that whatever force may be set up is genuinely multilateral and linked to other alliance forces; and this educational purpose will only be served if our allies take current discussion of multilateral approach seriously. To get them to take this discussion seriously, you should stress political and military reasons US is willing to go forward with multilateral force, if our allies desire:

(a) *Political.* I am prepared to see us lean quite hard on the political importance of multilateral force, in view of the impressions of German attitudes which I formed in Bonn. Schroeder was quite explicit on the point that the best approach to the German situation lies through a multilateral approach. You can make clear to our allies that we are prepared to accept, as legitimate in political terms, an allied desire for a greater role in the nuclear field, provided that the role is fulfilled in a military framework which links it to other alliance nuclear forces and through a genuinely multilateral form, and provided that it is fulfilled without detriment to non-nuclear programs.

(b) *Military.* The U.S. has said that the programmed force is adequate, on present assessments, to carry out the necessary and feasible strategic missions. Within the aggregate force which is now planned, however, substitutions are possible, and a satisfactory multilateral force might, therefore, permit some adjustments in presently planned force programs. You can stress, therefore, that if other members of the alliance would like to participate more directly in the alliance's nuclear mission through multilateral force, this can surely be arranged in a way that would be militarily useful.

4. *Educational Work re Multilateral Concept.* I wholly agree with your proposition (para 9) that in explaining the basic principles on which a genuine and effective multilateral force would be built we can exert a powerful and constructive educational effect on European thinking in nuclear field. We should use this discussion, therefore, to get across to our allies (i) the feasibility and necessity of a genuinely multilateral rather than national approach to allied nuclear problems; (ii) how a genuinely integrated force would differ from essentially national forces under a thin veneer of multilateralism; (iii) indivisibility of nuclear defense, from a military standpoint. This education will be of value as background for the consideration of nuclear policy by our allies which lies ahead.

For this reason among others, you can be most forthcoming and aggressive in setting forth our views both re practicality and advantages of having any allied MRBM force under multilateral manning, ownership, and control, and re need for linking that force to other alliance nuclear forces. You should indicate, as I did at Bonn, that such a force must be so integrated as to preclude withdrawal of national forces, and thus alert our allies to the distinction between genuine and phoney multilateral alternatives.

All this can best be done in bilateral talks at present time, and I hope that you will act aggressively to this end.

While we do not want now to create debate in the NAC which would compel other countries to take positions on this issue before the UK-EEC negotiations are completed, we do want to make the U.S. position on genuine multilateralism and on indivisibility of nuclear defense wholly clear. More than this, we want to present to other countries the basic facts and analyses which are relevant to that position, so that they will be most likely to reach sound conclusions when they do begin to grapple with these nuclear issues.

As further step to this end, we hope to make available the studies you ask for in Polto 22,[2] plus appropriate back-up personnel as necessary, by September. If an NAC sub-committee could be established by then—without any policy commitment by other governments concerned—to collect and study for Council the facts about how a genuine and effective multilateral force might be set up, this could be a useful means of education. Such a technical study for the Council would not require the UK and others to take positions on policy issues till after the EEC negotiations, and could provide sound basis for eventual decisions by Council. If de Staercke is now to ask in NAC for further information of technical nature about the principles of multilateral force, therefore, I hope that he will indicate (i) that he does not expect U.S. answers until September; (ii) that even then he looks to thorough study rather than early policy decisions by other member governments; and (iii) that he proposes NAC sub-committee be set up by then as useful means to this end.

5. *Control.* I agree (your para 10) that it is of utmost importance we convince our allies that they are free to explore the control issue on its merits. You can certainly stress, as I did to Couve, that we are open to allied proposals and that we do not exclude the possibility of a change in the law.

In re your request for specific examples of possible control procedures, I suggest that you hold to those cited in the Presidentially-approved policy paper[3] which you have. I should think these would be

---

[2] Polto 22, July 5, reported that de Staercke would propose to the North Atlantic Council a study of the principles for an MLF. (Ibid., 375/7–562)

[3] Document 135.

specific enough to get allied discussion going, without appearing to foreclose U.S. government position on proposals allies might eventually make to us re issue and manner of U.S. participation, since these examples would be relevant regardless of U.S. role. These examples would also serve additional purpose we have in discussing control issue, i.e., making clear that multilateral control is feasible, in terms of both political and operational needs, contrary to French argument (Paris A–2419)[4] that only national control can really meet these needs. I hope you will have this purpose well in mind and will work actively in bilateral discussions to fulfill it.

Once the allies thus begin to consider control of a multilateral force on its merits, I hope they will be able to focus on the facts—instead of the slogans—involved, and thus begin to take the indivisibility of nuclear warfare more seriously. A continuing objective of our educational efforts, should be to lay before them the facts and analyses which are necessary to this understanding.

But the only way in which we will get them to grapple with these facts and analyses is through a really free and serious discussion, and I doubt we'll get such a discussion until the misapprehensions concerning our position on control to which you refer are removed. So I hope you will treat clarifying allied thinking on this latter point as a matter of the first importance.

6. I trust you will continue to keep us well informed about technical-level discussions of multilateral concept, as it proceeds, and your judgments thereon. I regard these discussions as of great importance in trying to guide and influence allied thinking along constructive lines. I hope you will take lead in such educational discussions, both in bilateral side-talks and in technical discussions, in elaborating and discussing the matters referred to above. I take it you are aware that you do not need specific instructions in pursuing this educational end within framework of approved U.S. policy. You should of course bear in mind that U.S. has agreed with what appears to be NAC consensus that NATO multilateral MRBM force concept should not be pursued at policy level in full NAC discussions while UK-EEC negotiations undecided. I am following your labors closely; you have my full support, as well as my best wishes for success, in this important endeavor.

Rusk

---

[4] Airgram 2419, June 28, summarized a discussion on June 25 between French and U.S. officials about French nuclear policy. (Department of State, Central Files, 375/6–2662)

150.   Letter From President Kennedy to Prime Minister Macmillan

Washington, August 7, 1962.

DEAR PRIME MINISTER: Thank you for your message of August 3.[1] The thoughts you express therein in many ways parallel the conclusions I had reached regarding the use of nuclear weapons in the European theater. One of the first things I took a hard look at last year was precisely this question. It seemed clear to me that we must arrange for a more effective control over the nuclear weapons already in the theater and that we must achieve the capability of a balanced and flexible defense which would enable us to deal with any military aggression in such a way as to give us the possibility of engaging military forces to bring about a pause which might give a last clear chance to avert the danger of nuclear war and to resume negotiations. This seemed to me also to require a really substantial build-up of conventional forces since it was not credible to me, and I am sure would not be credible to Moscow, that we would go from relatively limited surface probes directly to nuclear warfare as contemplated under the prevailing NATO strategic doctrine. As you know, we have been moving, without directly challenging that doctrine (CM–56),[2] toward bringing our allies toward a recognition of both aspects of this matter. This effort has stirred some criticism and encountered some opposition.

On the question of achieving better control of the nuclear weapons stockpile in Europe, we have moved ahead toward the installation of permissive links to enable us to exercise a centralized control over their use. I think this is an important first step. I agree that it is desirable to consider in due course other methods of strengthening controls, including your idea of a tactical nuclear command directly under SACEUR. But I think it would be premature to go very far with this at the present time, since very complex questions about the organization of Europe and of NATO would arise. Further, if it were even known that we were considering such an organizational step at this moment, it would immediately give rise to further suspicions and speculations, some of which would be attributed to the forthcoming change in the Supreme Command.

Source: Department of State, Presidential Correspondence: Lot 66 D 204. Secret. No drafting information appears on the source text.

[1] In this message Macmillan expressed his growing concern about the diffusion of tactical nuclear weapons in Europe, advanced the idea of a tactical nuclear command directly under SACEUR, and informed the President of the British decision to cancel its Blue Water missile. (Ibid.)

[2] Not found.

Another reason for waiting a while on this matter, from my standpoint, is that Secretary McNamara has begun a careful review of our whole policy on tactical nuclear weapons. It is a tangled subject, and one on which feelings run high, but we hope by the end of the year to have a much better grip on it than we now have, and so to be in a position to join in forward steps of the sort which are implied in your letter. But before this study is completed and the argument thrashed out among us, it would not be easy for us to take a clear position.

We have tried to see to it during the past year that NATO received a considerable education with respect to nuclear weapons. You will recall the speeches which have been made in the NATO Council by Secretaries Rusk and McNamara. For your convenience, I am attaching a portion of Secretary McNamara's speech in Athens[3] which bears directly on this problem. Efforts of this kind have been beneficial, I am sure, but the educational process is still continuing. At the moment the discussion tends to focus on the question of an MRBM force and, as you know, we have agreed to soft-pedal this in order not to cause complications to your Common Market negotiations. Meanwhile what we need, I believe, is more education and less controversy. For this reason I would suggest the omission, in the statement you propose to make about Blue Water, of the first phrase in the fourth sentence reading, "whatever the ultimate NATO decisions may be on the concept of large-scale use of tactical nuclear weapons in support of land forces in a continuing battle." I fear that this particular phrase would stimulate public discussion of this complex and controversial issue at a time and in a way which would not be helpful to the continuing consideration of broader nuclear issues in the NATO forum.

As to the decision you are making not to proceed with the development of Blue Water, I appreciate your reasons for this and feel they are right. I welcome the suggestion that the savings in this respect can be devoted to speeding the build-up of your conventional force.

In summary, then, let me say that I was very glad to get your letter and that I think we are much of one mind on these matters. For a number of tactical reasons—the current situation in NATO, the Common Market negotiations, and the timing of our own internal studies—I believe that major new departures should wait until 1963. But I remain very glad that you have opened this subject with me, and I hope that we can work closely together in pressing forward to a better posture at the right time.

With warm personal regards,

Sincerely,

John F. Kennedy[4]

---

[3] Not printed, but see the source note, Document 136.

[4] Printed from a copy that bears this typed signature.

151. Telegram From the Embassy in France to the Department of State

Paris, August 17, 1962, 9 p.m.

865. Policy. From Stoessel. General Norstad visited Bonn August 16 at invitation of Chancellor. Visit grew out of discussion on July 14 in Paris between Chancellor and Norstad. During Bonn visit, General Norstad had approximately 2 hours private talk with Chancellor. During this talk, Chancellor personally gave General Norstad Grand Cross of Order of Merit of FRG. Following talk with Chancellor, General Norstad attended luncheon hosted by Chancellor at which Strauss, Carstens, US Chargé Morris, among others, were present. General Norstad saw Strauss for a brief talk after luncheon and then had meeting with press.

[2 *pages of source text not declassified*][1]

Stoessel

Source: Department of State, Central Files, 611.00/8–1762. Secret; Limit Distribution. Repeated to Bonn.

[1] For text of President Kennedy's July 19 letter accepting Norstad's resignation, see *Public Papers of the Presidents of the United States: John F. Kennedy, 1962*, p. 563. He was succeeded by General Lemnitzer.

---

152. Telegram From the Department of State to the Embassy in France

Washington, August 23, 1962, 9:28 p.m.

Topol 259. Re Polto 180.[1] Question of how to proceed in September, both in terms objectives and tactics, with NAC consideration nuclear

---

Source: Department of State, Central Files, 375.75611/8–1062. Secret. Drafted by Kranich; cleared with Weiss, Bundy, Owen, Popper, and the Department of Defense; and approved by Tyler.

[1] Polto 180, August 10, reviewed the sensitivities of Alliance members to U.S. statements and suggested areas in which the United States might make proposals to allay their concerns. (Ibid.)

matters and MRBM question, as well as our Defense Data Program, must be related to three factors:

(1) UK-EEC negotiations have not yet proceeded to point where we can see clear image of shape of UK tie to continent which may emerge sometime this Fall after negotiations resumed. This fact, plus strong UK objection, pending completion negotiation, to any NAC discussion of basic political issues involved in consideration multilateral force, must be recognized as powerful constraint on further policy debate, although not on discussion and examination relevant data and analyses for purposes of education.

(2) At moment Europeans generally are hard pressed to catch breath in area of nuclear strategy. Our June 15 NAC statement,[2] several major speeches on strategy, etc., have not yet clarified in minds of Europeans our objectives and proposals sufficiently to provide basis for Alliance consensus. In addition, changes in US military high command have evoked considerable speculation as to our intentions (see Paris 857).[3] This lack of consensus and mood of uneasy suspicion is certainly in part attributable to widespread European lack of basic orientation to nuclear facts of life which US largely alone enjoys. On other hand we must recognize that deep differences on basic strategy may still exist after conclusion our "nuclear education program", due to simple fact that Europeans have different political responsibilities and attitudes stemming from heritage of ideas and experiences which lead to positions which cannot be quickly shaken by rational argument. Obviously process of achieving consensus on strategy likely to be long drawn-out.

(3) NATO is now faced with several competing requirements: air defense, MRBM force, NADGE, conventional forces for forward strategy, etc., which in aggregate represent enormous costs and certainly raise issue of priorities in applying limited European resources. We have not yet focused on costing and related problems, some of which are subject current studies to be concluded in September–October period. It unlikely, however, that all these priority problems can be sorted out and decided upon in NAC prior to December Ministerial Meeting.

In light these factors our objectives for coming NAC discussions of MRBM force should be, as indicated in Polto 128,[4] to provide technical

---

[2] See footnote 1, Document 142.

[3] Apparently a reference to telegram 865 (Document 151), which, as transmitted, was incorrectly numbered 857 and subsequently changed to 865.

[4] Presumably a reference to Topol 128 (Document 149) since Polto 128, July 25, summarized an NAC meeting on that day dealing with Berlin and disarmament. (Department of State, Central Files, 375/7–2562)

data on weapons systems; to set forth our views on military aspects of requirement; to demonstrate technical feasibility of multilateral ownership, control, and multi-national manning; to dispel allies' misconceptions US policy does not leave them free to discuss control issue on its merits; and to make clear distinction between genuine multilateral force and disguised national forces under multilateral veneer. In addition, we should in light studies mentioned above try to answer any questions of technical nature concerning June 15 or other statements. By such multi-faceted educational process we would hope to increase understanding relevant fact and issues and thus ensure that future allied policy debate on NATO nuclear role which seems likely to follow outcome UK-EEC negotiations is as solidly grounded in such understanding as possible.

Defense Data Program is designed to provide to Europeans nuclear information needed by them to understand evolution our policy in direction less reliance on nuclear weapons. We still working on content and scope of next presentation (presently only one of limited scope planned prior to December NATO meeting); however, doubtful whether this one presentation will in itself provide sufficiently broad factual base to accomplish seven tasks re policy clarification you enumerate in reftel.

We believe September through December is time to "make haste slowly". We should not try to force conclusions or decisions concerning US policy views, nor should we conduct our presentations or technical discussions in manner which seems to call for early policy decisions on issues about which Europeans disagree with us. Nor is this time for new US policy initiatives, i.e. for new proposals not yet made known to allies. On other hand we want to provide as rapidly as NAC et al. can assimilate those analyses, facts, and findings which have led US to its policy conclusions set forth in Ministerial Meetings and NAC, particularly June 15 statement. Several important studies will provide substance for Defense Data Program. In short, our aim at this point is to provide facts and analyses for educational purposes, not to force decisions.

We agree completely your views re UK proposal for consultative role for NATO Nuclear Committee. We have repeatedly told UK Embassy here we see no urgency in matter, and Committee should address problem not only after but in light experience it has not yet had.

Finally, believe NAC should make special effort to maintain highest degree of secrecy about upcoming NAC talks. You should make strong intervention on this point, pointing out much harmful uncertainty and misunderstanding re NATO strategy directly traceable to attempts individual governments "smoke out" others through inspired commentaries and press leaks. Only Soviets benefit.

Above and other thoughts will be gone over with Amb Finletter this week in Washington.[5] Any further comments by you by then would be appreciated.

Rusk

---

[5] No record of Finletter's discussions in Washington has been found.

---

153.   Telegram From the Mission to the North Atlantic Treaty Organization and European Regional Organizations to the Department of State

Paris, September 18, 1962, 9 p.m.

Polto 309. Reference: Topol 344.[1] NAC discussion NATO defense policy ended in no formal agreement on conclusions Stikker paper NDP/62/10, but general consensus discussions defense policy should move deliberately in coming months without pressing for decisions. Main effort should be put into working group with expanded terms of reference made up of committee of whole of PermReps. Conflicting views expressed as to extent to which working group should concentrate on study multilateral forces as distinct from other ways providing MRBM's. Stikker will prepare paper proposing procedures for forthcoming NAC and working group discussions to be circulated early week September 24 and discussed NAC meeting Thursday, September 27. Norstad appearance before NAC was generally welcomed but no date set.

Most PermReps participated in extended discussion to be reported in detail in separate message.[2] Stikker opened by centering discussion

---

Source: Department of State, Central Files, 740.5612/9–1862. Secret; Limited Distribution. Pouched to the other NATO capitals.

[1] On August 30 Stikker gave Finletter a copy of NDP/62/10, August 29, a paper that the Secretary General had drafted dealing with NATO defense. No copy has been found, but on September 1, Finletter characterized it as proposing an active study of the complicated military problems facing the Alliance. (Polto 241; ibid., 375.75/9–162) In Topol 344, September 15, the Department of State transmitted instructions to Finletter for dealing with NDP/62/10. (Ibid., 740.5611/9–162)

[2] Transmitted in Polto A–354, September 22. (Ibid., 375/9–2262)

on procedure and suggesting possibility expanding terms of reference working group proposed paragraph 45 his paper. UK called for a limited step by step approach to discussion of Stikker's paper and urged initial emphasis on use of NATO Nuclear Information Committee to get better understanding present and planned nuclear capability Alliance. Italy urged basic re-examination NATO strategic concepts and political directive, but gon [got no?] support.

Belgium (de Staercke) then made strong plea for NAC to undertake concrete study of the multilateral force idea advanced by US June 15 and listed a number of organizational military and financial aspects requiring careful study. French expressed interest in Stikker's concept of possible special role three nuclear powers in paragraph 36 and possibility stress on conventional build up might weaken credibility strategic nuclear deterrent. Agreed policy debate not wise at this time when negotiations under way to decide political framework and shape Europe will take as well as role UK in Europe. Willing have working group study military and technical questions but not political ones. Canada supported Belgium on focusing on study of multilateral force in working group and both Canada and France indicated interest receiving more briefings in NATO nuclear committee as proposed by UK. Netherlands, supported later by UK, questioned focusing on multilateral sea borne forces because prejudicial to eventual decision as to how MRBM's might be provided and de Staercke disclaimed any desire to prejudice decision stating wanted only give concreteness and focus to work of coming months.

Germany stated imperative give continuing attention NATO defense policy and promised submit detailed comments. Believed urgent strengthen SACEUR shield forces but also wanted go ahead with working group study technical aspects MRBM force. States Germany prepared participate in integrated NATO missile force and to contribute funds and personnel if NATO decides establish such a force. Force must have Atlantic character and participation United States absolutely indispensable. Further study needed however whether force should be exclusively sea borne or whether some missiles should be deployed on land. Felt command and control problem less urgent since NATO Athens guidelines and present custodial arrangements could serve on interim basis. Favor a number of experts groups drawing on personnel from NATO capitals. Suggested immediate establishment separate legal experts group.

US (Finletter) spoke along lines instructions Topol 344 and supported de Staercke on expansion terms working group and specific attention multilateral force. Recognized Nuclear Information Committee proper channel for sensitive information but main focus should be working group of committee of whole of NAC making appropriate US experts, sub-groups, and government contributions. Stressed importance secrecy NAC discussions this subject.

UK warned should not be assumed any MRBM's required and expressed doubt military requirement existed for MRBM's. Suggested this question of requirement might be first point of study. French disputed this, arguing requirement for MRBM force could not be settled on purely military basis. Stikker then summarized outcome discussion as in first paragraph this telegram.

Finletter

154.   Editorial Note

On August 11 Secretary of Defense McNamara wrote to Secretary of State Rusk proposing a series of limited attendance conferences between the two Departments to concert the planning with respect to NATO. (Department of State, Central Files, 110.11–RU/10–462) Rusk agreed to the idea in a letter of September 5 and the first meeting was scheduled for October 11. (Attachments to McNamara's letter of August 11)

In addition to the two Secretaries, the meeting, which was held in Rusk's conference room beginning at 10 a.m. and running through lunch until 4 p.m., was attended by Generals Taylor and Lemnitzer, Nitze, Johnson, Bundy, Tyler, Schaetzel, Bowie, and Finletter. In the course of the session the participants discussed MRBMs, forward strategy, application of the Political Directive, MLF, force goals, and NATO reorganization, and concluded that until the question of British membership in the Common Market had been decided, no initiative should be taken in NATO on any of these questions, but further education of the Alliance on the trends in U.S. thinking should be continued. A 30-page record of the meeting, drafted by Schaetzel, is ibid., 740.5/10–1062.

At a second meeting on November 30 the Secretaries discussed the strategy for the forthcoming NATO Ministerial Meeting. In the discussion on the MLF McNamara stated his belief that the position of the United States was ambiguous since some officials were selling it, while others were pouring cold water on the idea. At the same time Rusk stressed that the Allies had not faced up to the problems of control and command, and he foresaw great difficulties ahead. According to Lemnitzer's notes on the meeting, McNamara stressed repeatedly that the United States was weakening its position within the Alliance and not giving it proper leadership. The Allies would not buy both a conventional build-up and an MRBM force. (National Defense University, Lemnitzer Papers, Box 29, L–216–71)

155.   Telegram From the Mission to the North Atlantic Treaty Organization and European Regional Organizations to the Department of State

Paris, October 18, 1962, 9 p.m.

Polto 476. Policy. Herewith short report Norstad Council briefing 17 Oct. Full report for security reasons being transmitted Polto A–438[1] (Limit Distribution S/S, Pouch No. 2–4600, invoice C–172; ETA Washington 21 October).

SACEUR wanting to keep "temperature" low stated he not arguing or opposing anything, merely wanted state most plainly urgency and reason for MRBM requirement.

He listed in substantial detail extent and nature of priority threat list of targets bearing on defense of ACE.

He detailed weapons systems available to his command to meet this threat.

He noted potential of external strategic forces but questioned their direct relevance because of time and other considerations.

He stated that he had no bias in favor of any method for fulfilling requirement, be it under bilateral arrangements or multilateral arrangements. He is trying to keep his mind open on question of nature of MRBM deployment but admitted to being partial to a mix of sea land based systems suggesting that land basing might be even more survivable a system than sea basing.

He stressed importance of relationship between range and accuracy and demonstrated nature of his constraint policy with chart show-

Source: Department of State, Central Files, 740.5611/10–1862. Secret; Priority; Limit Distribution.

[1] Dated October 17. (Kennedy Library, National Security Files, MLF)

ing increase in civilian casualties which would result from taking out an airfield in vicinity of a city by means of high yield intercontinental system as opposed to low yield more precise medium-range system.

He concluded with equation no MRBMs in a relatively few years equal no defense equal no NATO.

Questions from UK, Germany, France, Denmark and Canada and SACEUR answers reported fully in airgram.

Comment: General Norstad's presentation was most able and had considerable effect on PermReps. Its main conclusion was there was an important military requirement for MRBMs in ACE not only to replace existing weapons but also to handle more effectively than is now possible numerous targets, notably Russian IRBMs, of especial importance to Europeans.

I believe difference between General's presentation and June 15 US paper is one of degree only, for two reasons. First, General's presentation dealt primarily with existing state of affairs whereas thrust of June 15 paper is almost wholly on programmed forces, that is, on conditions in the future as they will be as result of increases in external forces now programmed but as yet in important measure not in being. And, second, June 15 paper recognized that "regardless of any feasible addition to programmed forces, a variety of Soviet weapons of different ranges would survive that could threaten both Europe and the US" and that "surviving Soviet forces would be great enough to inflict heavy civil damage on both European and North American NATO no matter what additions we might make to programmed nuclear strength."

Furthermore the US position on subject of MRBMs has been based largely on position that quite apart from question of extent of any requirement, US is opposed to introduction of nationally-owned and operated MRBMs into ACE system; will not assist in any such introduction; and that if "Allies wish to add MRBMs to NATO forces and to participate in an MRBM force, US is prepared to join them in creating a multilaterally owned, financed, controlled and manned seaborne MRBM force."

For these reasons seems to me that we should now wait for any initiation by other delegations or by International Staff looking to reviewing discussion of NDP/62/10. My recommendation that no such move be initiated by US. Our position has been stated quite fully already in June 15 document, and I think we should stand on it unless and until initiative to dispute it is taken by someone else.

Finletter

156. Telegram From the Department of State to the Mission to the
      North Atlantic Treaty Organization and European Regional
      Organizations

Washington, October 31, 1962, 7:27 p.m.

Topol 594. 1. As reported telecon, Nitze regretfully unable schedule visit to Paris at this time.

2. Reviewing Poltos 513 and 518[1] Department struck by tendency number of members to cite lessening of tension because of immediate Cuban denouement as ground for slowdown in meeting shortfalls in force levels and equipment and, prior to today's meeting, for delay in approval Bercon–Marcon plans. We wish to urge caution against assumption that critical period is past. We note with approval U.S. Perm Rep statement (Polto 518) opposing relaxation. Indeed, this is moment to press ahead with the unfinished business of the Alliance. Improvement in our defense posture is indispensable to subsequent utilization of situation to seek new openings in disarmament and other East-West problems.

3. We get impression sense of euphoria could, if it makes headway, result in rapid destruction of impressive Alliance solidarity achieved during crisis last week. This points up need for further improvement consultation procedures in order to capitalize on backing we now enjoy in NAC. We know you have this requirement very much in mind, and we ourselves are searching for ways in which we can maintain psychological momentum. As appropriate, we still hope to create sense of immediacy among Perm Reps by occasionally sending senior officials intimately involved in handling of Cuban crisis to brief NAC.

4. Meanwhile, however, we hope you will react quickly and often against any suggestion that Alliance can let down its guard because of immediate outcome of Cuban situation. In Cuban affair we have had virtually all military chips in our hands: geographical proximity; land, sea and air superiority; and SAC readiness. No reason to believe Soviets would have withdrawn so quickly if crisis had come over Berlin or other area considered vital to their security and geographically closer to them

---

Source: Department of State, Central Files, 375/10–2962. Secret; Priority. Drafted by Popper; cleared with Thompson, Hillenbrand, Nitze, and Schaetzel; and approved by Tyler.

[1] Polto 513, October 29, summarized that part of the NAC meeting on October 29 at which the Acting Secretary General had read from a paper urging all countries to meet the shortfalls in force levels. (Ibid.) Polto 518, October 29, reported that at the session on October 29, de Staercke, speaking for his government and as Dean of the Council congratulated "President Kennedy for clear-sightedness, courage, firmness, as well as moderation, with which he handled most difficult and serious Cuban situation." (Ibid., 737.56361/10–2962)

than to us. Consequently, NAC must beware of assuming that in any confrontation outside Western Hemisphere and in the absence of further NATO strengthening Cuban result would necessarily be duplicated.

5.   Cuban affair strengthens our conviction that firm but moderate posture which is best calculated to restrain Soviet adventures can be maintained only if it is backed by adequate level of armed force in high state of readiness. U.S. was able last week to prepare for wide range of possible military actions; it was not constricted by need to rely unduly on this or that particular arm or weapons system. Conclusion as related to Europe would seem to be that Alliance should accelerate, not relax its efforts to build up spectrum of forces permitting flexible response to Soviet initiatives.

6.   At same time it is noteworthy that succession of U.S. moves on Cuba flowed from intensive contingency planning which helped to clarify objectives to be sought and instrumentalities to be used. Similar process as applied quadripartitely to Berlin and presented to NAC seems to us already to have paid large dividends and to be necessary for enabling NAC to face up to all eventualities. If we can maintain our military readiness and keep our plans up to date, we need not fear ability of Alliance to measure up to future tests; we will indeed thus help to avoid them.

7.   Paras 4 through 6 can be used at you discretion with NAC.

Rusk

157.   Memorandum of Conversation

Washington, November 14, 1962.

SUBJECT

Cuba, Berlin and NATO (The President's Meeting with Chancellor)[1]

Source: Department of State, Conference Files: Lot 65 D 533, CF 2181. Secret. Drafted by Tyler and approved in U and S on November 19 and in the White House on November 29.

[1] Adenauer visited Washington November 13–16; see footnote 1, Document 51.

PARTICIPANTS

US	Germany
The President	Chancellor Adenauer
The Secretary of State	Foreign Minister Schroeder
Under Secretary Ball	Ambassador Knappstein
Ambassador Thompson	State Secretary Carstens
Ambassador Dowling	State Secretary von Hase
Mr. McGeorge Bundy	Dr. Reinkemeyer
Mr. William R. Tyler	

[Here follows discussion of Cuba.]

The Chancellor said that he thought a major problem was a reorganization of NATO, which he said left room for much improvement. He said he had talked with Secretary General Stikker before his recent illness, and praised his qualities of reliability, persistence and thoughtfulness. However, it was no secret that Stikker had not felt very happy in his NATO role, and now he had had this serious illness. This meant that one must envisage a replacement for Stikker in the foreseeable future. Norstad was also of this view. The Chancellor said he felt that the Secretary General of NATO should be an American citizen and that this would give the Council an entirely different character. He rapidly characterized the role of Ismay as having been that of housekeeper for the organization, while Spaak loved to talk and indulge in fascinating discussions. Stikker, on the other hand, had ideas with regard to reforming NATO, and had felt keenly the absence of a military adviser.

The President said that we were not so much disturbed by the organization of NATO as by its military weakness. Europeans already considered the organization to be too much dependent on the US, and an American Secretary General would merely increase this feeling. The real problem, said the President, was that we should increase our forces and strengthen their conventional capability.

The Chancellor said he could not agree with the President that a NATO military build-up was something that could be considered separate from reorganization. He felt that if there had been an American Secretary General, de Gaulle would never have avoided receiving him personally, as had been the case with Stikker until the Chancellor had personally spoken to de Gaulle about the need of doing so. The President commented that perhaps de Gaulle would have received the Secretary General if he had been German.

The President went on to say that the number one task of the Alliance was to strengthen our forces and that this was the most convincing way in which we could impress the Russians.

The Chancellor engaged in a somewhat lengthy analysis of de Gaulle's personal position in France, pointing out that the latest assassination attempt had been planned and carried out by military personnel in active service. He recounted the anecdote of de Gaulle's having avoided shaking hands with a French General at a reception at the Elysée when Adenauer was last in Paris. This particular General had been relieved of his duties on the following day, and had evidently been invited because he had been on the list of people who would normally be there. This was the kind of thing which de Gaulle was up against, and the Chancellor felt that the Algerian question had not at all been settled yet in certain military circles. All this imposed restrictions on de Gaulle's freedom of action.

The President said that what was needed was not merely diplomatic strength and initiative but military strength as well. Both were needed. Of course, we all had worries. De Gaulle had his; we had ours—among them our balance of payments problem. However, we were all faced with the Soviet threat in equal measure, and appropriate means must be taken to enable us to face up to it.

In the light of this, it was strange to hear de Gaulle talking about the battle of France beginning after the battle of Germany had ended. This was a totally outdated and unsound strategic concept for the defense of the Alliance. We needed to have our troops as far forward as possible in as great strength as was required. The Chancellor defended de Gaulle by saying that in 1958 de Gaulle said he was for the reunification of Germany because he did not want the Soviets on the Rhine.

Turning to the UK, the Chancellor said that it did not have conscription. As a result, we did not really know how many troops and reserves the UK had, and the British Armed Forces certainly contained too high a proportion of civilians and half-trained personnel. However, he wished to say that he agreed in the main with the President and that he would try to have a conversation with de Gaulle about military matters and Europe when he sees him again.

The President came back to the need for more conventional troops to meet the Berlin situation. While you could defend Western Europe as a whole with nuclear weapons, this simple concept was not relevant to the Berlin situation. The plain fact was that Europe was not doing enough in 1962. The President compared figures of the US military and aid efforts, in relation to population and resources, with those of the Federal Republic. We were faced with a situation in which the UK refused to do more, and de Gaulle refused to do more. This meant that the Federal Republic of Germany must make a greater effort. In addition, we must have sufficient military strength to defend Berlin and to give us an alternative to nuclear war or surrender. The Chancellor asserted that the Federal Republic stood shoulder to shoulder with the US. The Chancellor then introduced the subject of tactical nuclear weapons and the difference between US troops, which had tactical nuclear weapons in the field, and German troops, which did not. The President said that the point was that we needed to have greater conventional power so as to be able to give a convincing military reply to aggressive actions by the Soviets before having to move into the area of tactical nuclear weapons. Once the latter were used, you ran the danger of rapid escalation. The Chancellor said that modern tactical nuclear weapons were very small and sophisticated. One must assume that the Soviet troops also had similar nuclear weapons. Thus, a situation had arisen in which German troops were standing face-to-face against Soviet troops, and that the latter were better armed. He said the German troops should be armed with tactical nuclear weapons so as not to be at a disadvantage in the face of Soviet aggression. The President returned to the subject of the need for more conventional divisions in Europe, which, in addition to our nuclear strength, would put us in a good position. The Chancellor said that the major question was whether troops in the front line should be equipped with small nuclear weapons so that they could stand up against Soviet troops which had similar weapons. The current situation was that German troops did not have such weapons and were in a position of inferiority. The President said that the reality of the situation was that once you get to the point of using small nuclear weapons, you are very close to the big blow-up. So what we must do was to strengthen non-nuclear forces and give ourselves more flexibility of response. He said that, as things are now, we have enough troops armed with nuclear weapons. The Chancellor said that he could not share the President's view that once you get into the front you start using small nuclear weapons and are necessarily doomed to move into big nuclear warfare. He quoted General Heusinger as subscribing to his view. The fact was that German troops felt uncomfortable when neighboring troops were better equipped than they were. The President returned to the subject for the need for larger conventional forces and said this was the single most important need for the defense of the Alliance, and in particular to meet the requirements of the Berlin situation.

The Chancellor said he agreed with the general proposition that more forces were needed for NATO, and that General Norstad had recently complained publicly about the present shortcomings.

The Chancellor said that General Norstad and President Eisenhower had both warmly praised General Lemnitzer as a successor to Norstad, and the Chancellor wanted to make it clear that he and everyone else knew that General Lemnitzer was a most highly qualified and respected successor to General Norstad. He said he would be speaking with de Gaulle again about all the matters that had been discussed. He said there were some very real differences of opinion within the Alliance on the nuclear question and the composition of forces, and that the French Permanent Representative, Ambassador Seydoux, had recently been strongly criticized in the Council by the Belgian Permanent Representative because of France's military policies in relation to NATO.

The meeting broke up at about 1 o'clock.

---

158. Scope Paper Prepared for the NATO Ministerial Meeting

LSP/S–3   Washington, December 6, 1962.

NATO MINISTERIAL MEETING
PARIS, DECEMBER 13–15, 1962

The December Ministerial Meeting assembles at a moment of transition and flux. While it may serve as a vehicle for stimulating movement in beneficial directions, it is unlikely to provide an occasion for major decisions. The dominant note may be a sense of elation and relief at the outcome of the Cuban crisis; there will surely be satisfaction at the demonstration of Allied solidarity the crisis has provoked. On the other hand many questions will be raised regarding the next phase of Soviet-American relations, East-West negotiations in general, and the shape of future developments within the Communist bloc. Perhaps more than at any time in recent years, the United States will be expected to provide leadership and guidance in these matters.

In this outward-looking sense the general condition of the Alliance is good. The same cannot be said, however, of its inner cohesion. While the long-term perspectives of Western unity have not changed, the pace at which it is being achieved has undeniably slackened. The critical negotiations between the EEC and the UK have lost momentum. De Gaulle's political triumph will hardly contribute to greater flexibility on the side of the EEC or to a venturesome approach to closer European unification. Indeed, it may result in a greater degree of French obstruction both to European integration and to joint efforts in NATO.

All of the Ministers will be addressing themselves in one way or another to these matters. At the same time, they will wish to exchange views on other important political problems of concern to the Alliance,

---

Source: Department of State, Conference Files: Lot 65 D 533, CF 2204. Secret. Drafted by Popper and cleared by Tyler, Schaetzel, Seymour Weiss, Owen, and the Department of Defense.

notably the future of Berlin; the prospects for limited measures of disarmament such as a nuclear test ban, denuclearized zones, and measures to reduce the risk of unintentional war; residual colonial problems of NATO members, particularly Portugal, and the unsettled Congo question; the evolution of relations with the less developed countries; the implications of the Sino-Indian hostilities; and other matters of similar import. In discussing these subjects the Ministers will recognize that, as the Cuban affair demonstrated, NATO's interests are affected by developments which take place outside as well as inside the NATO area.

On the military side NATO is moving slowly toward a resolution of great issues of basic strategy. The Cuban crisis demonstrated the value of a broad spectrum of military power—power which permitted the application of a carefully measured response sufficient to deal with imminent danger without triggering a nuclear exchange. Certain European members, however, will be inclined to attribute the American success mainly to nuclear superiority. It will be important to set the record straight on this matter, because it will profoundly influence NATO's actions across the board in the military area.

In this context, the Ministers will doubtless wish to consider future force requirements, the level of defense efforts, and the apportionment of defense expenditures among the Allies. These subjects are of special concern to the US at a time when balance of payments and budget problems are in the foreground. The US will wish to reiterate its views on these matters, particularly on the continuing major importance of strong conventional forces in the types of confrontation likely to occur in the years ahead. Firm but moderate statements in this area will set the stage for comprehensive military studies the US will present to NATO in 1963 as a basis for a thoroughgoing joint re-evaluation of Alliance defenses. Among the specific strategic problems under review will be the question of the MRBM requirement for European defense. There will be some informal discussion of the Ottawa-type, multilateral seaborne MRBM force, now for the first time under serious review by European members. Finally the problem of financing the Greek defense effort may be added to the agenda.

General Objectives

At the Ministerial Meeting the general US objectives should be:

1. To preserve the heightened Alliance solidarity visible as a result of the Cuban experience.
2. To urge improved consultative procedures and to clear the way for ultimate organizational changes designed to increase NATO's effectiveness in reacting to East-West confrontations wherever they occur.
3. To avoid divisive action or debate which could prejudice our discreet efforts to encourage UK-EEC negotiations.

4. To extend the range of Alliance support already attained on Berlin.

5. In the military field, to demonstrate to the Europeans the need for larger and better non-nuclear forces adequate for a prolonged defense in forward areas; to induce them to assume their fair share of the Alliance military burden; and to reiterate the US willingness to move forward toward a multilateral, sea-based MRBM force, if our Allies desire.

There are listed below some of the major issues likely to be raised at the meeting, with an indication of the recommended US attitudes.

Political Issues

1. *Cuba and Consultation*

The Allies will no doubt be principally interested in the effects of the Cuban crisis on the Communist world, and in the next moves in Soviet foreign policy. They will expect a full exposition of US thinking on these subjects, and particularly of their impact on the Alliance. Though highly satisfied with the outcome so far, they will recall that circumstances did not permit consultation when the quarantine was imposed. They will be asking whether the US means what it says when it stresses the need for more effective political consultation in NATO.

In his political review the Secretary should be prepared to deal with these matters. Statements should aim at preserving the improved morale resulting from the Cuban affair, without inducing complacency or relaxation. While the NAC has already been briefed fully on Cuban events, there is now an opportunity to present a longer range view of Alliance prospects. The difficulties of crisis management in a coalition will be appreciated even if not explicitly explained. There will probably be a generally favorable response to our advocacy of more effective consultative arrangements. There will also be lively interest in tentative proposals for organizational changes pertinent to this problem, although there is no sign that any action of this kind is immediately practicable.

2. *Berlin*

Though temporarily quiescent, the Berlin problem will remain a primary focus of Allied concern. The states represented in the Quadripartite Ambassadorial Group will be expected to express their views on future Berlin developments. Recent NAC action on contingency plans has eased some of the disagreements on Berlin within the Organization. The US statement should stress the continuing long-term threat to Berlin, as well as the desirability of effective alert measures, to prepare for possible eventualities.

3. *Arms Control*

The Allies will also be eager to receive our assessment of the prospects for arms control measures in the wake of the Cuban crisis. While the French and Germans will be sensitive to anything resembling denuclearization or disengagement in Europe, the Scandinavians and Canadians will press for greater accommodation to Soviet views for the sake of agreement. A full exposition of our estimate of the prospects for initial measures to reduce the risk of war and for a test ban will be useful, and will allay apprehensions without arousing false hopes.

4.   *Other Area Problems*

The Allies will await the Secretary's assessment of the Sino-Indian situation, with particular reference to its implications for future relations between China and the Soviet Union. Questions may also be raised regarding developments in Southeast Asia, though for the moment relatively little is heard on this subject. The Secretary will probably not be expected to dwell heavily on African, Middle-Eastern and other Asian problems, but his views may be sought on the question of the Portuguese colonies and the Congo. If the Portuguese continue to be unwilling to extend the Azores base agreement, the Secretary may wish to raise the matter in bilateral conversations.

5.   *Integration and Partnership*

Because the UK and the EEC negotiations are at so delicate a stage, it will be advisable to touch on them only with great circumspection in full meetings. In bilateral conversations the Secretary will wish to point out that all those concerned, the United States included, have a major stake in the success of the negotiations. While the reference to Atlantic Partnership may be muted, no one should be left in doubt that it remains an ultimate objective of American policy.

Military Issues

The US objective in military matters should be to have NATO come to grips in 1963 with issues of basic strategy, future force requirements, the level of the defense effort and national defense contributions, and the future of the Alliance nuclear deterrent including the organization of a multilateral MRBM force. The indications are that this will not be easy. Despite the Cuban experience, it is not at all clear that the European Allies will be willing to alter the current strategic concept, with its heavy emphasis on deterrence entailing the early use of nuclear weapons in major operations. Nor have they been willing to contemplate a conventional force build-up to meet established force goals or an increased level of expenditure comparable to that of the US. Moreover, recent European press comment emphasizing American opposition to individual national nuclear forces in Europe has heightened European sensitivity on this matter, especially among the French.

The US presentation on these matters will lay emphasis on the following factors: (1) the contingencies NATO forces are most likely to be called upon to meet will dictate the use of non-nuclear rather than nuclear forces; (2) conventional forces adequate for a prolonged defense of Europe in forward areas are well within NATO's economic and social capabilities; (3) the European Allies can and should shoulder a greater proportion of the burden of meeting NATO force requirements; (4) there should be systematic coordination of strategic objectives, force levels, and budget outlays among the Allies on the basis of long-term, integrated plans; (5) the US is willing, if the Europeans so desire, to facilitate the creation of a multilateral, sea-borne MRBM force, provided such a force is coordinated with other NATO deterrent forces in regard to military planning and does not displace or reduce the level of conventional forces. While the US will not press for specific decisions on these matters at the Ministerial Meeting, it will want to stimulate Alliance efforts to deal with them expeditiously, on a cooperative basis.

The US effort in this regard will be supported by the presentation of comprehensive back-up studies demonstrating the cogency of its approach. Such studies are now in preparation. It will be useful to announce at the meeting a firm date for delivery of the information on the use and effects of nuclear weapons (Defense Data Program), to which the US was committed at the Athens meeting last spring. We should bring to the attention of our Allies the MRBM force educational effort now under way. We should also be prepared to exploit the planning cycle now about to begin in the NATO Military Committee, looking toward end-1969 force goals, to propound our views on strategy questions. As a related matter we should carry on the effort initiated during the recent triennial review of the status of NATO forces, to work out more satisfactory methods of bearing the burden of sustaining balanced forces capable of meeting Alliance requirements, without impairing the military task of formulating such requirements.

---

159. Telegram From Secretary of State Rusk to the Department of State

Paris, December 15, 1962, 9 p.m.

Secto 22. Eyes only for the President and Acting Secretary. This meeting of NATO has been marked by an almost "intolerable serenity", as one delegate put it, but I wish to report certain personal impressions.

Source: Department of State, Central Files, 396.1–PA/12–1562. Secret; Priority. According to another copy this telegram was drafted by Rusk. (Ibid., Rusk Files: Lot 72 D 192, Chron)

(1) Central theme of meeting has been deep satisfaction your handling of Cuban crisis, without criticism about lack of prior consultation. For first time in many years U.S. Secretary of State did not raise hand and swear that U.S. would indeed faithfully meet its solemn NATO commitments; no one noticed the omission in atmosphere of general confidence.

(2) McNamara and I hit conventional force deficiencies very hard.[1] My impression is that other Ministers are getting seriously concerned, partly because they sense that U.S. patience is running out. Whether this will result in effective action remains to be seen.

(3) General de Gaulle's interest in NATO continues at most minimum level. It was obvious however that his esteem for you had gone up many notches over Cuban affair and that atmosphere our relations has been significantly improved. For first time French passers-by waved to me on the street.

(4) Perfectly clear that Nassau meeting will become Skybolt Summit[2] and that British will make major effort to insure that we take whatever steps necessary to insure they have independent nuclear deterrent. McNamara and I should have chance to go over this with you at earliest opportunity.

(5) NATO unanimous (except France) that open channels should be maintained between Washington and Moscow with minimum of nervousness about our exploration possibilities agreement on any subject but especially Berlin.

(6) Have given drafts non-transfer nuclear weapons to British, French and Germans.[3] British fully agree. Germans will agree if Peiping's adherence is required. French are studying and will let us know. Am slightly encouraged that we have not had oracular rejection from Paris.

(7) Spaak has been working hard and courageously on Congo. Believe our future course should be taken in closest consultation in view large number Belgians in Congo and Spaak's ability to keep our NATO Allies reasonably quiet.

---

[1] The texts of Rusk's and McNamara's statements on the military situation were transmitted as enclosures to CA–7291, January 10, 1963, and CA–6769, December 21, from Paris. (Ibid., Central Files, 396.1–PA/1–1063 and 12–2162) A summary of the discussion of the military situation was transmitted in Poltos 697 and 698, December 15. (Ibid., 396.1–PA/12–1562)

[2] For documentation on the discussion of the Skybolt missile at the Nassau meeting between President Kennedy and Prime Minister Macmillan, December 19–20, see Documents 402–407.

[3] Not found.

(8) Am encouraged by talk with Nogueria about Azores bases.[4] As minimum solution, I pressed for either a clear and simple one-year extension of existing agreement or an arrangement by which they would give us six months notice before the six months expiration period would begin to run. Nogueria seemed to understand the practical problem which force us to need definite assurance rather than to leave the agreement subject to cancellation on a day-by-day basis. Elbrick will follow up promptly.

Rusk

---

[4] See Document 349.

---

160.   Telegram From the Department of State to the Embassy in Italy

Washington, December 18, 1962, 8:17 p.m.

1151. Eyes only for Ambassadors Reinhardt and Hare. Subject: Jupiter Missiles.

1. This message is strictly FYI. No distribution should be made of this message and tight security should be maintained.

2. The Secretary and Secretary McNamara, in separate conversations at Paris discussed subject of removal of Jupiter missiles from Turkey with Sancar and Erkin, and McNamara discussed removal of Jupiters from Italy with Andreotti.[1]

3. Proposal advanced by McNamara was for dismantling of the Jupiters by April 1, with these missiles to be replaced by Polaris stationed in Mediterranean. [1 line of source text not declassified]

4. Proposed replacement was explained in terms of a desire to modernize Alliance missile capability removing a highly vulnerable

---

Source: Department of State, Central Files, 740.5611/12–1862. Top Secret. Drafted by Seymour Weiss and Johnson; cleared with Kitchen, NEA, EUR, and the Department of Defense; and approved by Johnson. Also sent to Ankara.

[1] Memoranda of conversation with Erkin (US/MC–2) and McNamara's conversation with Sancar (US/MC–20) and Andreotti (US/MC–21) are ibid., Conference Files: Lot 65 D 533, CF 2198.

system which, during the Cuban crisis, provided inviting target to the Soviets should US have been forced to undertake military action against Cuba. In view of high vulnerability and advancing obsolescence, these systems should be replaced with more modern and effective system prior to onset of any new crisis which might, for example, occur in the near future over Berlin. In this way Alliance would have benefit of more effective deterrent force while denying to the Soviets an opportunity to bring political pressures to bear by threatening attacks against vulnerable Jupiter missiles.

[1 *paragraph (5 lines of source text) not declassified*]

6. McNamara also indicated to Andreotti that while US was of view that SETAF should be taken over by Italians, US was prepared to continue support for at least an interim period and that we would be prepared to modernize SETAF by replacement of Corporals by Sergeants, such action to be related to Jupiter removal.

[3 *paragraphs (23 lines of source text) not declassified*]

10. Following McNamara's talk with Defense Minister, Erkin mentioned matter informally to Secretary in a friendly and relaxed mood saying that he saw no difficulty provided ways and means were found to make it clear that US was continuing a military presence in Turkey and was firmly committed to Turkey's defense.

11. Importance of maintaining strictest security was emphasized in conversations with Turkish and Italian governments. Should you be queried by representatives of Turkish or Italian governments, Secretary does not think it advisable for you to attempt to amplify US proposal. We are now working out next steps for following up on US proposal. For example, we have in mind that Secretary of Defense McNamara might soon visit Southeast Asia and would stop off in Ankara for discreet talk with highest Turkish officials. If, therefore, matter is raised with you suggest you merely refer to talks in Paris and indicate will request further instructions.

Rusk

161.   Circular Airgram From the Department of State to Certain Missions

Washington, December 20, 1962, 12:47 p.m.

CA–6704. Subject: Summary of NATO Ministerial Meeting. NATO Ministerial Meeting, in Paris December 13–15, although without dramatic results, provided valuable opportunity for full political consultation on East-West problems in light Cuban crisis and for examination of military posture of Alliance. Highlights of meeting were: 1) Secretary Rusk's political presentation[1] which analyzed Cuban crisis and current Cuban situation in terms of confrontation between East and West and prospects of negotiations with Soviets, together with fundamental questions raised by recent events; 2) on military side, statements by Secretaries Rusk and McNamara emphasizing importance of conventional buildup of NATO forces so that Alliance would have capacity for wide range of military responses in case of need; emphasis also placed on importance of equitable sharing defense burden among NATO countries; 3) deep satisfaction expressed over US handling of Cuban crisis; 4) careful optimism regarding current status of Alliance in view Soviet setback on Cuba, continued strength and confidence in West, and Soviet internal problems as well as further deterioration in Sino-Soviet relations. In view of NATO Secretary General Stikker's continuing convalescence, meeting chaired by Acting SYG Colonna (Italian).

Political Questions

1. *Cuba:* In opening statement on political issues, Secretary provided Ministers with analysis of Cuban crisis, observing that unity of NATO and OAS at height of crisis was undoubtedly significant factor influencing USSR. Secretary stressed point that Soviet intention to establish at least 72 MRBM's and IRBM's in Cuba represented potentially significant shift in balance of power which US could not ignore. Cuban episode raised number significant questions, Secretary said, including: question of how Soviets' inability to respond on the spot in Cuban situation except through nuclear action affected range of choice NATO Governments would have before them elsewhere; implications for NATO's role in crisis management; whether there could be serious Communist-Free World confrontation anywhere which was not of vital interest to

---

Source: Department of State, Central Files, 396.1–PA/12–2062. Secret. Drafted by Van Hollen; cleared by Popper, Swank (S), and the Department of Defense; and approved by Schaetzel. Sent to the other NATO capitals and Moscow, Stockholm, Madrid, New Delhi, Tokyo, Geneva, Bangkok, and Berlin.

[1] A copy of this statement was transmitted as an enclosure to CA–6800, December 21. (Ibid., 396.1–PA/12–2162)

NATO. In terms present situation in Cuba, although missiles and IL 28 bombers have been removed, there remained substantial Soviet presence in Cuba, including military personnel estimated to number at least 12,000.

Other Foreign Ministers indicated strong approval of US handling of Cuban episode. Majority agreed that as result Western position was stronger than before in relation to Communist bloc, but Portugal emphasized that crisis was still dangerous because of Communist regime in Cuba.

2. *East-West Negotiations:* Secretary emphasized that peaceful negotiation other East-West issues must await resolution of Cuban conflict. Assured Ministers that in private conversations with Soviets, there was no elaboration of general language used in public exchanges about relations between NATO and Warsaw Pact countries. We believed this was matter which could best be approached through practical steps in disarmament field. With regard Berlin, Secretary said that in limited recent references to Berlin by Soviets, there had simply been reaffirmation existing positions, with no indication urgent negotiations were either promising or desired. On disarmament, Secretary was not optimistic re prospects in immediate future but felt perhaps nuclear test ban represented most likely area of agreement.

Among other Ministers certain division of opinion about desirability of broad East-West negotiations in near future was evident, with Belgium and Canada advocating Western initiative toward such negotiations and UK and France urging West should wait for favorable opportunities. Unlike December 1961 NATO Meeting, however, question of stance of Alliance re future negotiations did not cause controversy over Communiqué[2] language. Ministers agreed in Communiqué to their "readiness to examine any reasonable possibility of reducing international tension".

3. *Longer Range Matters:* In his statement, Secretary stressed intra Bloc problems contrasting them with opportunities for increased Western strength through economic integration, US Trade Expansion Act and outward looking Common Market perspective. Emphasized that Cuban crisis and other developments underlined importance of improved NATO consultative procedures particularly in field of contingency planning. Secretary's views on need for improved political consultation supported by several countries, including Italy and Belgium. Luxembourg and Danish Foreign Ministers spoke in favor of economic cooperation and enlargement of EEC.

---

[2] For text of the final communiqué, see *American Foreign Policy: Current Documents, 1962*, pp. 570–572.

4. *Other Areas:* Discussion of situation in other areas covered Congo, Middle East and Latin America with Belgium leading off with review of recent history Congo developments. Said past efforts seemed to be showing results and to offer hope of avoiding grave dangers of alternatives to conciliation. Portugal said Communist penetration Africa far deeper than generally believed in West, praised stability and good government in Katanga and thought Congolese should be left alone to settle own problems. In only rebuttal UK said could not agree with Portugal's outlook for somber future of Africa. Secretary paid tribute to diligence and courage of Spaak in working toward peaceful settlement in Congo.

Discussion of Middle East limited to recital by Turkey of developments during past year. Recommended against hasty recognition of Yemen revolutionary government, underlined improved relations between Syria and Turkey and took pride in Turkish role as conciliator in Indo-Pakistan dispute.

Re situation in Latin America, Italy pointed to OAS support for US in Cuban crisis. Emphasized serious economic problems Latin American countries and said Europe could help in making Alliance for Progress succeed. Was important to let Latin America know that Western Europe sympathetic with their problems and wished to help. Secretary associated himself with these comments and stated we wished be certain that NATO friends understood we supporting strengthening of LA-WE ties.

Military Questions:

5. *Commanders Briefings:* In an innovation, prior to Ministerial consideration of military questions three major NATO commanders— SACLANT (Admiral Dennison), CINCHAN (Admiral Bingley), and SACEUR (General Norstad)—provided useful briefings of current military situation in their respective commands, each highlighting shortfalls between military requirements and forces actually in being. There was also military intelligence appreciation given by General Strother, Chairman of Standing Group and statements re NATO deficiencies by General De Cumont, Chairman of Military Committee.

6. *Secretary's Statement:* Following commanders' briefing, Secretary made opening statement under discussions of NATO Triennial Review, noting review had highlighted NATO shortfalls. Said NATO should undertake thoroughgoing re-examination of strategic doctrine and, on basis this re-examination, decide how best to meet military requirements. Regarding NATO strategic policy, Secretary said US believed Alliance must progress beyond automatic reliance on use of nuclear weapons from outset and toward capability of wide range of responses. Immediate objective should be attainment of current force

goals. At minimum, governments cannot permit percentage of gross national product devoted to defense to decline.

With regard MRBM's, Secretary said US thought sea-borne MRBM force multilaterally manned, owned and controlled, offered useful way to deploy MRBM's. Would be normal expectation that such multilateral force would be NATO force with US participation. However, we would look with sympathy upon multilateral European force if our Allies preferred, but such force should be intimately coordinated with all NATO deterrent forces. US would bear cost its own participation such force but major burdens would be borne by other states. Expenditures for MRBM force would be an addition to Alliance military budget.

7. *Secretary McNamara's Statement:* Secretary McNamara gave lengthy presentation on relationship between Alliance strategy, defense budgets, and military forces. Said NATO's problems in 1960's were radically different from late 1940's and it was therefore necessary to discard solutions and strategies which were no longer in tune with current conditions.

McNamara said that Alliance expenditure in strategic nuclear field ($15 billion per year for US alone) remained adequate for contingencies of general nuclear war. On other hand, there was need for expansion of consultation for handling of strategic deterrent and exploration of means by which Alliance as whole could share more effectively in operations and support of deterrent. Emphasized that it was US intention to maintain and to increase tactical nuclear weapons in Europe although doubted such weapons could compensate for non-nuclear weaknesses.

McNamara said that in view of adequate nuclear power available to Alliance, basic need was to strengthen conventional NATO forces which would confer large political benefits on Alliance, especially its European members. It was essential to deploy and use non-nuclear strategy locally in forward defense of Europe particularly in view of possibility Soviets probably could deploy total of about 60 Soviet divisions on Central Front within 30 days. Consequently, US studies indicated that NATO forces should consist of about 60 divisions by M plus 30 days in addition to substantial strengthening of Alliance tactical air posture (Allied D-Day force would approximate MC 26/4 goal of 30 divisions).

McNamara said that to remedy most important weaknesses in present forces over 5-year period would cost about $1.7 billion per year, in addition to current Western European and Canadian expenditures of $18 billion per year. US believed it was doing more than its part for defense of Alliance but other NATO countries would be required make additional effort. Using GNP as rough measure of individual nation's defense contribution, recent trend in NATO has been to spend declining percentage of GNP on defense although GNPs have been rising rapidly.

McNamara concluded that Alliance needed tools for extensive forward non-nuclear action to add to defense posture and resources to bring such defenses into existence. Proposed that Alliance examine these theses and, if found convincing, they should be carried out as highest priority. If Alliance did not find theses convincing or did not provide requisite resources, would be necessary to reconsider forces, budgets and strategy that were appropriate and formed consistent whole.

8. In general, other Defense Ministers did not reply directly to Secretary Rusk's and McNamara's presentations but their remarks indicated continuing basic divergencies within Alliance on military questions. While agreeing in principle to need for improved NATO military effectiveness, several other Ministers (including UK, Italy, Canada, and Turkey) stressed political and economic problems which made it difficult to increase level of defense expenditures. UK said either NATO must be content with gap between present forces and military requirements, or reconcile strategy with resources available. Italy supported multilateral MRBM force but noted that in view Italy's low per capita GNP, its contribution to defense was reasonable. German representative endorsed all proposals for clarifying strategy but questioned whether forward strategy could be effected with conventional weapons alone. This connection, drew attention to General Norstad's assertion that post-1964 plans cannot be carried out effectively without MRBM's. Canadian representative said Canada had no firm position on MRBM question, while Belgian Defense Minister said that, although Belgium gave first priority to conventional forces, it was quite interested in multilateral MRBM force. France did not speak during discussion military questions.

At conclusion discussion, Council adopted resolution on Defense for 1962 drafted to include reservation by Greek Government. Greeks indicated that as soon as problem of aid to Greece settled, they would notify SHAPE of their firm force goals for 1963.

Other Issues

9. *Research and Development:* In separate meeting, Defense Ministers reviewed and approved report of working group created at Athens meeting to seek methods of improving cooperation among member NATO nations in research, development and production of military equipment.[3] Defense Ministers reaffirmed their willingness to cooperate in translating report's recommendations into positive action.

---

[3] A copy of this report, C–M(62)114, is in Department of State, Conference Files: Lot 65 D 533, CF 2202.

10. *Aid to Greece:* With regard to assistance to Greece to meet its defense goals, special working group achieved solution which involved additional finance effort from Greeks supplemented by aid from other countries.

For Addressees:

A. Foregoing, in conjunction with NATO final communiqué, may be used on selective basis in briefing governments as well as SEATO and CENTO (Ankara and Bangkok should coordinate CENTO and SEATO briefings with your NATO colleagues).

B. Final texts of Secretary Rusk's two statements (on political and on military questions) and Secretary McNamara's statement will be sent under cover of airgram to certain posts.

Rusk

---

162. Telegram From the Department of State to the Embassy in Germany

Washington, December 21, 1962, 5:32 p.m.

1436. For Ambassador. Info Paris USRO for Finletter. A central element in our approach to the Skybolt problem has been to see that the agreements reached gave full account to the interests of our other European allies and particularly to the Germans. It is therefore of the greatest importance that you see Schroeder and convey this message to him, covering the following points.

1. A major aspect of the Nassau agreement[1] is to commit both the US and UK to the development of a NATO multilateral force. While this does involve American assistance on the missile component of the British strategic force it does not involve the provision of warheads and it is dependent on the British construction of the submarines.

Source: Department of State, Central Files, 740.5611/12–2162. Secret; Priority; Limit Distribution. Drafted by Schaetzel, cleared with Rostow, and initialed by Rusk. Also sent to Rome and repeated to Paris.

[1] For documentation on the Nassau meeting, December 18–21, between President Kennedy and Prime Minister Macmillan, see Documents 402–410. For text of the Nassau Agreement, see *American Foreign Policy: Current Documents, 1962*, pp. 635–637.

468 Foreign Relations, 1961–1963, Volume XIII

2. But the point to be stressed with the Germans is that a major new line of policy has been unfolded at Nassau with both Britain and America, quoting article 7 of the agreement, "Agreed that the purpose of their two governments with respect to the provision of the Polaris missiles must be the development of a multilateral NATO deterrent force in the closest consultation with other NATO allies and that they will use their best efforts to this end."

3. You can tell Schroeder that we contemplate that participation in the proposed multilateral force may be available to non-nuclear member nations of NATO through the contribution of personnel and resources for the operation of nuclear facilities, including submarines, manned by units of mixed nationality. An early invitation will be extended to such countries to participate in the discussion and development of such units.

4. Schroeder will also be interested in the fact that we have offered the French Government an opportunity to engage in a similar undertaking to that which we have agreed at Nassau with the British. We do not, of course, have any French reaction, but in any event the US and the UK would not make their own interest contingent on France. But we will of course seek French participation.

Finally, advise Schroeder that we intend to keep in close touch with him for we would hope that Germany will be in the forefront in the discussions within NATO which will lead to the development of the multilateral force. We intend to pursue actively the multilateral approach ourselves and expect to initiate discussions of the subject in NATO in January.

For Reinhardt:

You should draw on the foregoing in briefing Piccioni.

Rusk

---

163. Telegram From the Department of State to the Embassy in Germany

Washington, January 10, 1963, 9:05 p.m.

1569. Ref: Embtel 1686 and previous.[1]

Source: Department of State, Central Files, 611.41/1–363. Secret; Priority; Limit Distribution. Drafted by Popper; cleared with OSD/ISA, GER, Seymour Weiss, Schaetzel, and Owen; and approved by Tyler. Repeated to London, Paris Topol, Rome, and Brussels.

[1] Telegram 1686, January 3, reported that the German reaction to the Nassau agreement was "one of considerable caution, bordering on downright reserve." (Ibid.)

1. Dept has found most helpful your detailed reporting on German reactions to Nassau agreement and is taking it fully into account in preparing for Under Secretary's presentation in NAC.

2. For your information we expect Under Secretary, while following same general line in Bonn as in Paris, to cast his special comment to German officials along lines indicated below.

3. We can understand German concern that Nassau may freeze FedRep in second-class position, fortifying distinction between present nuclear powers (including France) and non-nuclear states, prolonging far into missile era independent deterrent for former, and preventing equivalent status. We know, too, that Germans resent, as discriminating against non-nuclear participants in multilateral force, right of withdrawal from NATO nuclear force of assigned national contingents. Finally, we are aware of their sensitivity to the implication in the Nassau context that a US-UK-French directorate may come to assume a predominant position in NATO and in determining the fate of Europe.

4. To meet these concerns we are suggesting that Under Secretary urge Germans not to be unduly swayed by immediate press reactions in UK and France or by ex parte interpretations of general language of Nassau communiqué. Basic point we hope Germans will keep in mind is that Nassau blocks out general framework containing within itself greatest possibilities for evolution and growth. Opportunity exists for all interested NATO members to participate in shaping institutions envisaged at Nassau. What is required now is intensive study and consultation to ensure that action in NATO responds to long-term needs of Alliance and its members.

5. We hope FedRep will from outset play active role in deliberation and action on Nassau follow-up. We hope they will express their views on aspects of Nassau communiqué of interest to them, and that they will let us have their thinking on the creation and organization of the NATO nuclear force. In this connection, we draw attention to portion of Under Secretary's NAC statement[2] relating to inclusion of tactical nuclear forces in NATO nuclear force.

6. FedRep will note that Nassau permits immediate start on multilateral mixed-manned component of nuclear force. This means that Germans and other countries most directly interested (notably US, Italy and Belgium) could promptly make a preliminary agreement permitting an early start on selection and training of manpower, ordering equipment and facilities, and creating the international agencies to administer and command the force. At the same time, participating countries could reach agreement on long-term arrangements for all aspects of this mat-

---

[2] See Document 164.

ter. Germans should bear in mind in this respect that rapidity with which they are ready to act, along with other expected participants, i.e., Italians and Belgians will in considerable measure determine how rapidly force will come into being. Ball speech will indicate U.S. willingness to begin work on concrete measures at once. Under these circumstances multilateral force might well come into existence within same time frame as UK and French forces.

7. Germans should also recognize that multilateral mixed-manned component could, if vigorously and imaginatively supported, come to be a principal element in NATO nuclear strength in longer term future. It can be no secret to Germans that British and French may one day conclude they simply do not have resources to maintain both nuclear and delivery components of an effective national deterrent system. While we can obviously give no assurances on this matter, we think it quite possible that in ten years or less, if European trend toward integration continues, British and French will be putting more and more of their nuclear eggs into multilateral mixed-manned basket. And in proportion as this occurs, any element discrimination against Germany will be correspondingly reduced.

8. In this respect we would urge Germans not to be mesmerized by notion that they are in second-class status. All of us must start from where we are; and fact is that UK has and France is obtaining nuclear weapons. What we are trying to do is to create a structure in which others can be dissuaded from doing likewise, and UK and France can be offered long-term alternative to national programs, so as to limit national nuclear proliferation. Whether this structure comes into being will depend, in good measure, on how vigorously the FRG is now prepared to move on the multilateral mixed-manned force. If this is their disposition, we are prepared actively to join them and other interested countries.

9. Finally, we recognize that creation of a multilateral mixed-manned NATO force will in long run raise fundamental questions regarding political control of its use. In discussing control of a multilateral force last fall we indicated we would give consideration to proposals for control supported by Allied consensus even if they did not provide for a U.S. veto. This position remains unchanged. At same time, we are sure Germans would agree that questions of veto or no veto may prove a highly over-simplified approach to problem of preventing irresponsible use of NATO nuclear power while permitting its rapid employment when necessary; we are prepared actively to cooperate with them in studying necessary arrangements to this end.

10. FYI: Under Secretary will make clear, if Germans ask, that our policy of not facilitating MRBM procurement for nationally manned and owned forces remains unchanged outside of agreements concluded

at Nassau. We realize it is of utmost importance to be clear on this point, if there is to be any interest by Germans and other non-nuclear powers in possibility of multilateral mixed-manned force. In this connection, we will refer to:

(a) Distinction, which we hope will be transitional, between arrangements for nuclear and non-nuclear powers.
(b) Importance of getting multilateral mixed-manned force under way quickly, as element of Alliance cohesion and viable alternative to national programs.
(c) Fact that only in case of multilateral mixed-manned force could we envisage possibility of U.S. considering control arrangements which might involve changes in U.S. law and which majority of Allies favored.
(d) Fact that need for mixed manning is relevant to all non-nuclear powers not just FRG.

We hope Germans will perceive, without explicit U.S. statement, that their national manning and ownership of MRBM's, even with U.S. warhead custody, would involve us in serious problems, in terms of both Allied cohesion and East-West relations. We know Germans are aware of unsettling effect such a development would have. End FYI.

Rusk

---

164.   **Telegram From the Mission to the North Atlantic Treaty Organization and European Regional Organizations to the Department of State**

Paris, January 11, 1963, 9 p.m.

Polto Circular 27. Department pass information SACLANT for POLAD. Attention Kitchen. Department Circular telegram 1192.[1] Under Secretary began presentation to NAC January 11 with brief review of US/UK decisions on Skybolt and Hound Dog at Nassau, and UK proposal on Polaris. Consideration of this latter British proposal, Ball said, had given whole new dimension to Nassau discussions, for Polaris un-

---

Source: Department of State, Central Files, 375/1–1163. Secret; Niact. Also sent to EUCOM, SHAPE, SACLANT, and USAREUR.

[1] Circular telegram 1192, January 8, asked for a telegraphic summary of Ball's address to the North Atlantic Council on January 11. (Ibid., 375/1–863)

like Skybolt and Hound Dog had probable effective life through decade of 70s; consequently any decision make Polaris available would necessarily influence structure Western defense well into future.

Ball said both governments had recognized this fact and had felt grave responsibility to take no steps re Polaris which would be prejudicial to ability of whole alliance mobilize full potential for nuclear defense.

Certain basic principles and goals emerged from consideration these problems, Ball said. First was that nuclear defense of West is by nature interdependent and indivisible. Ball said US had become convinced in years since 1945 that security of US meaningless if it divorced from defense of Europe. He said that other nations, as they studied this question thoroughly, would be led to same conclusion.

Therefore it had seemed imperative at Nassau to make nuclear defense arrangements in such way as enable alliance as a whole to evolve common nuclear defense policy. Such common policy would not only ensure most rational use Western resources but would also discourage proliferation and make progress toward arms control manageable. Consequently goal should be arrangement permitting increasingly cohesive effort in nuclear defense by European countries which effort would be intimately associated with US strategic forces.

Ball said these considerations had led two governments at Nassau to agree to work for creation of a multilateral nuclear force in which any interested NATO member whether or not a nuclear power could play important role in manning, equipping and controlling a force devoted entirely to alliance purposes. In developing these proposals we could not of course ignore fact that some members of alliance are nuclear powers; our offer of Polaris to UK and similar offer to France reflected this fact. But design of nuclear force was task for all interested NATO members, and speed with which it developed would depend on initiative of NAC governments. US for its part was prepared participate fully in what can be great common enterprise.

Under Secretary then outlined some of implications of Nassau agreement with respect composition, command and control of nuclear force. Concerning composition of force he said: 1) Elements from US strategic nuclear forces and UK bomber command, together with selected tactical nuclear forces in Europe (i.e., pre-targeted weapons, not battlefield weapons at present), might be immediately assigned to proposed NATO nuclear force; 2) UK Polaris force will be assigned as it becomes available, together with equal US force; 3) two governments would also cooperate with other NATO countries in developing multilateral force, which US assumes would be based on principle of mixed manning, to which all interested NATO members could contribute.

Concerning command Ball said US believed NATO nuclear forces should be under SACEUR. In any event, it seemed essential to US both nationally assigned units and mixed-manned forces be responsible to same commander. However, we would not rule out establishment of strategic force at same level as present Supreme Commanders.

Concerning control, Ball noted there were critical problems. Said Secretary Rusk, Ambassador Finletter and other spokesmen of US administration have stated US views these problems and have made clear US prepared consider any proposals desired by consensus of alliance. He wished make only these comments:

1) Nuclear force, both with respect nationally assigned forces and mixed-manned components, should be governed in its use by guidelines agreed at Athens; 2) Alliance must face possibility of East-West confrontations outside NATO area which would involve use of such force. To meet this contingency alliance must develop as quickly as possible same kind of political consensus on world basis as now exists for example re Berlin. In this connection Ball said it is hope of US Government that over months and years ahead NATO political consultations will develop to point where Nassau agreement provision for withdrawal of national components of nuclear force would never arise as a real question. In light of this US hope US is anxious to explore all possible means to strengthen political consultation and will elaborate its views on this question at appropriate time.

Re mixed-manned component of nuclear force US believes more strongly than ever that this component is essential. In addition its military values, mixed-manned force provides opportunity for non-nuclear powers to play important role in nuclear defense. Moreover we look on this force as ultimate embodiment of integrated NATO effort in area of security vital to all. To support these views US prepared make substantial financial, technological and equipment contributions to this force.

Concerning targeting of force Ball said this was subject for continuing exchanges within alliance. US felt there exists greater common agreement than is generally realized on how such force should be used. It will of course be essential to coordinate targeting as between NATO forces and massive external forces in hands of US.

Ball pointed [out] that two governments at Nassau had stressed need for flexible balanced defense which could not be achieved by nuclear capability alone. Would be highly imprudent to concentrate on nuclear force at expense of adequate conventional strength.

Ball then made some observations concerning procedure for further NATO consideration these questions. Said he realized that the proposals would require most careful study and consultation. Within near future US and UK hoped to make recommendations re size and composition of certain immediate elements of proposed nuclear force, and also intended develop series of questions to which other countries would wish to add. In near future various working groups might be set up to refine questions for study and recommend procedures to advance NATO consideration. US hoped alliance would be in position soon, perhaps by Ottawa Ministerial meeting, to develop steps and proposals looking [toward] establishment of nuclear force, including multilateral component, which force represents step along road to long-term organization NATO's nuclear power.

In summing up Ball reemphasized it was fundamental US policy that security of Western Europe is a basic national interest of US. Problem before NATO was how to fit technology of nuclear arms into larger objectives of our partnership. In US view Nassau agreement moved nuclear question much farther toward alliance solution.

Problems were not easy ones. Scientific progress had been much more rapid than changes in political institutions. This was a pioneering enterprise requiring all energy and imagination alliance can command.

Full text pouched.[2] Addressees may use its substance in discussions with Foreign Offices. US/UK texts not distributed here but will be made available to NAC in due course by IS. Separate telegram[3] summarizes UK statement and Council discussion.

Finletter

---

[2] A copy of the full text is ibid., 375/1–1163. Polto 775, January 11, reported on the atmosphere of the meeting, which was described as "highly successful," noting that the "general atmosphere of meeting was to welcome strongly Nassau agreement as providing opportunity for a most important step forward." (Ibid.)

[3] Polto Circular 26, January 11. (Ibid.)

165. Memorandum for the Record

Washington, January 12, 1963.

SUBJECT

Meeting with the President, January 12, 1963, 11:00 AM,
(President's Office)—Nassau Implementation

OTHERS PRESENT

Vice President, Secretary Rusk, Secretary McNamara, General Taylor, Director McCone, Assistant Secretary Nitze, Assistant Secretary Tyler, Mr. McGeorge Bundy, Mr. Jeffrey Kitchen, Mr. John McNaughton

Secretary Rusk gave a brief report on Under Secretary Ball's presentation to the NATO Permanent Representatives in Paris.[1] He described the allied reception of Ball's summary of our views on the Nassau Agreement as friendly but reserved.

Secretary Rusk said the British would, for political reasons, push very hard publicly the concept of a British independent nuclear force. He said Macmillan will be emphasizing a national nuclear capability and understanding the multilateral aspects of the Nassau Agreement.

Secretary Rusk expressed his hope that de Gaulle would not reject the Nassau offer until we had had time to explain to him what it entailed. He noted that de Gaulle had asked for a study of the existing French nuclear program and its prospects. Thereafter, de Gaulle would decide where the Nassau offer fitted into the French program. He mentioned reports that de Gaulle, at a press conference on Monday, would reject the Nassau offer.

With respect to Germany, Secretary Rusk said we must push immediately for discussions in NATO of a multilateral force in order to meet Adenauer's demands for German equality. He called attention to German opposition to a three-power (U.S./U.K./France) directorate. Germany, he added, wants quality of treatment and would oppose any arrangement which did not provide equal status for Germany. Italy will also be interested in ensuring that its participation in the nuclear deterrent is on the basis of its status as a big power.

Secretary Rusk thought that one way to meet the political side of the problem would be to initiate a NATO training program at once, even before there was progress on working out problems of the control of multilateral nuclear force.

Source: Kennedy Library, National Security Files, Meetings and Memoranda Series, Meetings with the President. Top Secret. Prepared by Bromley Smith on January 15. A copy of Kitchen's notes on this meeting, which give more detail on the work of the Steering Group, is in Department of State, Conference Files: Lot 66 D 110, CF 2217.

[1] See Document 164.

Mr. Kitchen made a progress report on the activity of interdepartmental groups engaged in planning further steps to implement the Nassau Agreement.[2]

a. Ambassador Reinhardt had opened discussions with the Italians and further discussions would take place during Prime Minister Fanfani's visit to Washington.[3] The Italians, in giving up their Jupiter capability, will try to establish some bilateral nuclear arrangement with us.

b. Ambassador Hare will initiate discussions with the Turks this weekend.

c. General Lemnitzer, who has taken a negative view of the removal of the Jupiters,[4] will be talked to by Mr. Nitze, who is leaving shortly for Europe.

d. Technical talks with the British on proceeding smoothly and a U.S./U.K. agreement is being drafted following a strict interpretation of the Nassau Agreement. A second paper is being prepared which will present the alternative of widening U.S./U.K. cooperation beyond that envisaged in the Nassau Agreement.

e. No interdepartmental agreement has yet been reached on the U.S. nuclear force to be assigned to NATO. It is hoped that by next week a paper listing the types of U.S. forces to be assigned to NATO will be ready for Presidential consideration.

f. As regards negotiations with the French, a study is being made of what we can offer to the French with and without changes in the legislation. In response to the President's question as to what we would offer to the French, Mr. Tyler said that if de Gaulle accepts the concept of a multilateral NATO force, then we might give the French nuclear submarines and nuclear warheads, but if de Gaulle opposes the multilateral concept, then our position will be considerably different.

There ensued a general discussion of the problem of negotiating with the French. Secretary Rusk called attention to the importance which the Joint Committee on Atomic Energy attaches to any U.S. offer of nuclear assistance to France and urged that any offer to the French be kept in phase with the known views of the Congressional committee members. He foresaw serious difficulty if our talks with the French include offers of assistance which were unacceptable to Congressional committee members. He said he agreed that, if the committee members approved, we could give nuclear technological information to the French equal to that which we know the Russians already have.

---

[2] Documentation on the work of the Steering Group on Implementing the Nassau Decisions is in Department of State, Conference Files: Lot 66 D 110, CF 2217–2219.

[3] Regarding Fanfani's visit to Washington, January 16–17, see Documents 312 and 313.

[4] On January 11 the Embassy in France had reported that Lemnitzer, on military grounds, could not support the substitution of Polaris submarines for Jupiter missiles since this would result in a net reduction in the total strike capacity of ACE. (Telegram 2758; Department of State, Central Files, 740.5611/1–1163)

Secretary McNamara said de Gaulle might take the offer, he might charge us with bad faith by making the offer because the French could not take advantage of it since their program was not far enough along, or he could turn down the offer on grounds other than French technical inadequacy.

The President thought that we should push ahead on the Skipjack project because it was not directly related to Nassau. He recalled that he would be meeting with the Joint Committee on Atomic Energy members next week to discuss both the Skipjack project and the Nassau Agreement.

Mr. Bundy said that if the French accept fully the concept of a multilateral nuclear force, then the case for giving the French real nuclear assistance is very strong.

Secretary Rusk urged that in our talks with the French we emphasize all of the Nassau Agreement, not just the offer to them. He recalled that the French have not been helpful to us and in fact have left the alliance as far as all matters are concerned except full support in the event of the outbreak of war. If we give the French nuclear assistance in these circumstances, he added, and do not insist that they join with us in all matters involving the alliance, other alliance members will think that the way to get assistance from us is to behave as the French are now behaving.

The President asked that General Norstad's views be heard by those working on the Nassau followup. He reminded the group that in his view we were engaged in negotiating a multilateral force because of the German problem.

Secretary Rusk said that possibly a way to satisfy the Germans would be to create an Executive Committee of NATO composed of the five major powers, with representation on a rotational basis of the smaller powers.

The President stressed the importance of developing our plans for control of the multilateral force.

Mr. Bundy emphasized the importance of the management of this force and thought that it was important that we move promptly so that the British will not slip away from their commitment to a multilateral force. If the British move away from the multilateral concept, the Germans will create major difficulties.

It was agreed that a letter from the President to Adenauer[5] would be prepared and sent in an effort to reassure the Germans that they

---

[5] Dated January 12 and transmitted to Bonn for delivery to the Chancellor in telegram 1589, January 12, it stated that the United States was prepared to join Germany and any other interested country in preliminary steps leading to a multilateral sea-based MRBM force. (Ibid., 740.5611/1–1263)

would have meaningful participation in any arrangements arising out of the Nassau Agreement.[6]

Bromley Smith[7]

---

[6] In a January 14 memorandum Kitchen wrote the following about this meeting:

"The Secretary said he thought the meeting with the President had gone well and that we had succeeded in conveying to both the President and Secretary McNamara the necessity for keeping an open and flexible approach to following up on Nassau and especially in our approach to the French." (Department of State, Central Files, 740.5611/1–1463)

[7] Printed from a copy that bears this typed signature.

---

166.   Telegram From the Embassy in Germany to the Department of State

Bonn, January 14, 1963, 7 p.m.

1791. Paris also for Stoessel and McGuire.

1.   Under Secretary Ball met with Chancellor, Schroeder, von Hassel and others for two hours this morning in meeting devoted exclusively to Nassau Agreements. Chancellor did all the talking on German side. General impression conveyed by Chancellor that although Germans had many questions they wished discuss in connection Nassau Agreements, they were prepared to cooperate fully in NATO study and, as he put it, "with vigor."

2.   Under Secretary began with presentation similar to one given before NAC,[1] stressing heavily our determination to proceed with planning multilateral force with other interested countries NATO Alliance. He said that Nassau decision to supply Polaris to British and similar offer to French affected shape of Western deterrent into 1970s and therefore it was our firm determination not to freeze pattern in such a way that major Western Allies could not work with US in control of such a force. Indivisability of Atlantic defense meant that there must be participation on equal footing of FedRep and others. He put great stress on bringing FedRep into arrangements on basis of full and equal participa-

---

Source: Department of State, Central Files, 375.75611/1–1463. Secret; Priority; Limit Distribution. Repeated to London and Paris.

[1] See Document 164.

tion. He said that our first preference had been to have British contribution solely to a multilateral force but that we recognized special problems of the British Govt and had therefore settled on an intermediate position whereby our agreement to supply Polaris to British was tied to their contributing that force to NATO and to supporting US in an effort to create a multilateral force. He said that we would be willing to proceed immediately to work on creation of this force as rapidly as possible. It is our hope that in long run we would be able to transform existing national forces into a multilateral force which would give effect to the principle of indivisibility and prevent nuclear proliferation.

3. Ball indicated that he hoped major countries would begin a study of structure of such a force. Problems of mixed-manning, financing and control in which all major countries could contribute. He referred to the President's letter[2] which had suggested possibility of an executive committee in NATO as one solution to control problem. He also placed great stress on necessity for NATO Alliance to consult on all areas of confrontation, even beyond the geographical limitations of Alliance itself.

4. We have been talking about a multilateral force for some time but the principal difference in our position after Nassau is that we no longer are waiting for a European initiative but are now forced by decision to use Polaris to take initiative ourselves in proposing plan to key European countries. We are no longer prepared to proceed in leisurely fashion but wish to proceed as soon as possible. We are not prejudging final form that such a force would take, but we are willing to engage in free discussion promising substantial contributions and technical information, hardware and financing.

5. We feel that seaborne force whether surface or submarine is best. Presently we tend to favor a submarine force because of its greater security from a military point of view. However, surface force is cheaper and not subjected to some of mixed-manning difficulties of submarine force.

6. Chancellor thanked Ball for his presentation and the President for sending him and said that Prime Minister must have "launched his attack suddenly because there seemed to be many gaps in our plan." He stressed, however, that this was a great project for the Alliance and these gaps would have to be discussed. He said that he would cooperate fully in this study but wished to make several observations. First, he wanted to point out the international commitment of the FedRep not to produce atomic weapons. He assumed, however, that this scheme is not prejudiced by that commitment. Second, he welcomed the change from a pas-

---

[2] See footnote 5, Document 165.

sive role in US position because he knew that Europe alone could not come up with proposals for a multilateral force. Third, he recalled that last US proposal made by General Norstad in 1960 had been shelved prior to last election. Fourth, he pointed to presence of large Soviet forces on the Eastern frontier including 22 well-trained reliable Soviet divisions and stressed German view that NATO planning must include use of intermediate range and tactical nuclear weapons. He raised question of whether or not creation of seaborne force might not call into question continuation of NATO forward strategy.

7. Ball immediately answered this observation by stating there was no intent on part of United States to diminish battlefield tactical use of nuclear weapons but that our strategy remained that we would use force necessary to stop and eject any move into NATO territory. He stressed that we would hope that this would not escalate but that we accept consequences of our strategy and are prepared for nuclear conflict.

8. Chancellor recalled recent letter from Premier Khrushchev[3] in which he had promised immediate use of nuclear weapons in any conflict in Central Europe and said it must be NATO plan to retaliate with both tactical and strategic forces. Ball again replied it was not our intent to withdraw all nuclear forces to the seaborne force, that we must regard new multilateral nuclear force as an addition to European forces and not substitute for existing forces.

9. Chancellor then referred to position of General de Gaulle and Mr. Ball replied that we, of course, did not know what his final position would be but that we hoped France would cooperate. If not, we cannot wait and must proceed to plan a multilateral force. British understand this and understand that there is no condition of French acceptance for further planning.

10. Chancellor then referred to right of UK and of France to withdraw in event of national emergency. He assumed that this meant they could each order independent use of force and that all others would become involved if there were to be such a confrontation. Ball replied that problem at Nassau was to recognize fact of British independent capability and that French are determined also to have such capability, and yet to plan for future in such a way as to seek merging of these national forces into a multilateral force. Macmillan had recognized that there was little possibility of withdrawal and independent use, but he had public problem of past history and British image of 1940 to deal with. Our view is that by creating multilateral force as quickly as possible we will show example and actually attract national forces. Chancellor then com-

---

[3] Not further identified.

mented that 1940 was a bad historical example and Ball replied that we all have to deal with tendency of people to deal in terms of past history and not appreciate change brought about by new technology.

11. Chancellor agreed that there was new element in situation but speaking frankly wondered whether Secretary McNamara's statements about increasing conventional forces reflected understanding new strategy. Ball replied in long interchange that increasing conventional forces in the US view was a way of giving additional strength to the nuclear deterrent. We saw that as only way to stop any temptation to nibble away at NATO territory. Chancellor then referred to Cuban situation which he said was opposite of present European state of affairs. There in Cuba US had preponderance of strength. Here Russia has bulk of divisions, perhaps better equipped and tougher than German and American forces. Conventional war would mean defeat in Europe. Ball replied that building of conventional forces would mean that Russians would be less tempted to try any advance in Europe because they would be certain that response would escalate quickly and they could not have cheap victory. Chancellor then said real danger of nibbling was in Soviet economic offers of trade to West and in spy infiltration in Western Europe.

12. Chancellor ended by saying that he wished to make two points. First, he agreed with our Paris statement on importance of placing these forces under SACEUR, and second, on question of ordering use of forces, he recalled discussion he had with President[4] in which President had said if he could not be reached others would always be available to give command for use of American nuclear power. Chancellor hoped same response arrangement could be made for multilateral force. Ball replied we would be willing to begin immediately to plan control mechanism. Perhaps along the lines of executive committee, which could act under appropriate guidance without any delay. He hoped that Ambassador Grewe would be given prompt instructions to begin work in Paris. Chancellor promised full cooperation in multilateral project, implying that Under Secretary had answered main faults which he had had in mind. After luncheon with Chancellor there was meeting with Defense Minister and members of his staff in which much of same ground was covered, and in which Germans raised several technical questions. To these, Ball replied that US had no preconceived notions and suggested that answers could appropriately be found in NATO consultation.[5]

---

[4] Presumably a reference to the conversation on November 14, 1962, see Document 157.

[5] A 7-page memorandum of Ball's conversation with von Hassel is in Department of State, Central Files, 375.75611/1–1463.

Hassel agreed, and reiterated that Grewe would cooperate in immediate, intensive NATO consultations.

Dowling

167. Telegram From the Department of State to the Embassy in Germany

Washington, January 18, 1963, 1:49 p.m.

1646. For Ambassador only. Please deliver the following letter from the President to Chancellor soonest.

"Dear Mr. Chancellor:

I greatly welcomed your letter and the expression of your determination to participate with us in the creation of a multilateral nuclear force within NATO.[1]

I regard the establishment of such a force, with the Federal Republic as a full participant, as having great significance for the alliance and for the entire West. You have my assurance that we intend to press toward this objective with the utmost vigor.

This American intention reflects the full commitment of my country to the support of European integration and Atlantic partnership. Our security is identified with that of Western Europe for reasons of the most basic character: Only if the resources of a uniting Europe are joined to those of the US in needed tasks can you and we look forward to success either in defending the free world or in ensuring its continued progress. Developing Soviet weapons technology does not weaken this proposition, but reinforces it. Europe or the US, if split from one another, would be that much weaker in confronting this threat; acting together, I am confident that we can continue to deter aggression.

Source: Department of State, Central Files, 740.5611/1–1863. Secret; Eyes Only. Drafted by Owen and Ball; cleared with Bundy, Rusk, and Ball; and initialed by Rusk.

[1] Undated, but transmitted to the President by Knappstein on January 17, this 4-paragraph letter repeated what the Chancellor had told Ball, that the Germans were prepared to participate in the creation of a multilateral NATO nuclear force. (Ibid., Presidential Correspondence: Lot 66 D 204)

For these reasons, the interdependence of the Atlantic Community is in my country no longer a matter of debate. Our forces—both nuclear and non-nuclear—will remain in Europe and will be used, as necessary, to meet any threat to NATO from whatever quarter. Against the background of this interdependence, I believe that the period immediately ahead will be one of growing opportunity for progress toward greater European and Atlantic cohesion—in the political, military, and economic fields.

I am glad that my suggestion of a possible executive mechanism within NATO seems interesting to you. As I wrote you[2] and as Mr. Ball further explained, such a mechanism might well be the best means of providing political direction of the multilateral force, while at the same time making possible effective consultation—which seems increasingly essential—regarding problems that lie both within and beyond the NATO area.

In the military field, the creation of a seaborne MRBM force—under multilateral ownership, manning, and direction—would bring interested European countries and the US together in a program that would meet immediate allied nuclear aspirations and promote the cause of European and Atlantic cohesion. If we miss this opportunity for constructive action, and try instead to deal with the nuclear issue on a disunited basis—e.g., through spreading independent national efforts, this cohesion could be gravely threatened—and our enemies would make the most of it.

Similarly, in the economic field an opportunity is at hand to complete the European Community through successful conclusion of the current UK-EEC negotiations. Although this is, of course, for the countries directly concerned to work out, I am sure you share my own view that the failure of these negotiations would represent a setback of major proportions in our mutual efforts to develop the unity and strength of the free world in the face of the common danger. I am greatly concerned by the course which events in Brussels are taking.

It occurs to me that during your forthcoming trip to Paris you will have an opportunity to do some very useful work on behalf of the kind of Europe which has been your own central objective and to which you have given great leadership.

Meanwhile we have been having good and useful talks with Signor Fanfani in Washington.

We have talked about a NATO executive mechanism, about the EEC negotiations—which he views much as you and I do and about the need which he also sees for early action on the multilateral nuclear

---

[2] See footnote 5, Document 165.

front—as a step toward both greater political cohesion and modernization of alliance nuclear forces. As part of this modernization we also discussed replacement of obsolete IRBM's in Italy and Turkey by Polaris
submarines in the Mediterranean, which are a more effective and modern weapons system, until a multilateral MRBM force came into being.

I am hopeful that this Italian disposition to move vigorously will
permit early action toward our common objectives. I shall continue to
keep in close touch with you as the situation develops, so that we can
concert our actions to this end.

In conclusion, let me say quite earnestly that the United States is not
interested in encouraging or promoting differences among our Allies.
On the contrary our great preoccupation is—as it has been for fifteen
years—to see the evolution of an alliance in complete unity—within
Europe and across the Atlantic."

Rusk

---

168. Remarks of President Kennedy to the National Security Council Meeting

Washington, January 22, 1963.

The President began his discussion of national security problems
by calling attention to the worldwide responsibilities of the United
States. While we fully recognize our responsibilities, other states are not
carrying their fair share of the burden.

Cuba

The major lesson of the Cuban crisis, the President said, was the
paramount importance of timing. Both sides, the United States and the
USSR, need sufficient time to consider alternative courses of action. Our
objective was and is to protect our national interests while trying to
avoid a nuclear exchange which, if it happened, would be a defeat for
both sides. In handling crises, it is important that the Russians have

---

Source: Kennedy Library, National Security Files, NSC Meetings 63. Secret. No
drafting information appears on the source text.

enough time to debate their action. If they are forced to react in an hour or two, they may react in a spasm and resort to nuclear war. We, too, looking back on the quarantine vs. air strike decision, took several days to discuss and understand the advantages and disadvantages of the alternatives. The reason for building up NATO conventional forces is to gain greater control over the timing of a showdown in Europe provoked by the Russians.

[1 paragraph (6-1/2 lines of source text) not declassified]

Western Europe

Turning to Europe, the President recalled that de Gaulle's current policy is no different than that he has been advocating since 1958 when he first proposed to President Eisenhower a U.S.-U.K.-France directorate giving France, in effect, a veto on our use of nuclear weapons. The suggestion was turned down because it would have broken up NATO. This Administration agrees it was a correct decision. The turndown of de Gaulle's proposal was not, however, the reason why he is behaving as he now is. Even if we had given France nuclear weapons, de Gaulle would have tried to restore France to a predominant position in Europe. For years, in speeches and in his memoirs, de Gaulle has expressed his view that France must be a dominant power speaking to the USSR and the West as an equal, dependent on no one.

In analyzing de Gaulle's present actions, the President said de Gaulle did not question our support of Europe. The proof that he does not fear we would desert him is the deployment of only a small number of French troops opposite the Russians in Germany. He relies on our power to protect him while he launches his policies based solely on the self-interest of France. Having been turned down by the U.S. and U.K. on the directorate, de Gaulle turned to Germany. This helps to keep Germany from looking to the Russians. It does threaten NATO which de Gaulle strongly opposes.

As to the Common Market, the President said that if Great Britain joined, Europe would be strengthened and stabilized. We favor the U.K. joining even though it will cost the U.S. considerable trade. If France keeps Britain out, this will be a setback for us but a more severe setback for the U.K.

Our interest, the President continued, is to strengthen the NATO multilateral force concept, even though de Gaulle is opposed, because a multilateral force will increase our influence in Europe and provide a way to guide NATO and keep it strong. We have to live with de Gaulle. One way to respond is to strengthen NATO and push for a multilateral nuclear force which will weaken de Gaulle's control of the Six. We should not be overly distressed because the problems caused by de

Gaulle are not crucial in the sense that our problems in Latin America are.

U.S. Trade Negotiations

The President then summarized the guidelines for forthcoming trade negotiations. In the present situation, we must be very careful to protect U.S. interests. Our balance of payments problem is serious, it is not now under control, and it must be righted at the latest by the end of 1964. If we do not do so, there will be pressure against the dollar and Congress will be demanding reductions in our foreign programs.

One effort we must make, the President continued, is to seek to prevent European states from taking actions which make our balance of payments problem worse. For example, we maintain large forces in Germany. We must firmly oppose West Germany if it increases its agricultural production to our detriment. We have not yet reached the point of wheat against troops but we cannot continue to pay for the military protection of Europe while the NATO states are not paying their fair share and living off the "fat of the land." We have been very generous to Europe and it is now time for us to look out for ourselves, knowing full well that the Europeans will not do anything for us simply because we have in the past helped them. No longer dependent on the U.S. for economic assistance, the European states are less subject to our influence. If the French and other European powers acquire a nuclear capability they would be in a position to be entirely independent and we might be on the outside looking in. We must exploit our military and political position to ensure that our economic interests are protected.

[Here follow sections on the Attitude Toward Neutrals, Assistance to Foreign Countries, and Domestic Issues.]

Defense Problems

Recalling recent decisions limiting or halting certain military programs, e.g. the B–70, Skybolt, and Nike–Zeus, the President said we are going forward with large defense and space programs. If the necessity develops, we will do even more, but there is a limit to how much we can do.

One of our big tasks is to persuade our colleagues in Europe to increase their defense forces. If we are to keep six divisions in Europe, the European states must do more. Why should we have in Europe supplies adequate to fight for ninety days when the European forces around our troops have only enough supplies to fight for two or three days? Our forces in Europe are further forward than the troops of de Gaulle who, instead of committing his divisions to NATO, is banking on us to defend him by maintaining our present military position in Europe. While recognizing the military interests of the Free World, we should consider very hard the narrower interests of the United States.

[Here follows a section on Test Ban Negotiations.]

169.   Summary Record of NSC Executive Committee Meeting No. 38 (Part II)

Washington, January 25, 1963, 4 p.m.

[Here follows a list of participants.]

(Attached to these notes is a copy of the intelligence report which prompted the President's discussion of European policy.)[1]

At the conclusion of the discussion of Cuba, the President asked the members of the Executive Committee to remain for a discussion of our policy toward Europe. He said that our relations with de Gaulle during the next few months may be in for very heavy going. Now that de Gaulle will soon have his own nuclear force, he may make major policy changes, including possibly a French/Russian agreement. During the past few days he has tried to lock the British out of Europe and he may begin shortly trying to lock us out. At present de Gaulle is cooperating with us in none of our policies.

The President said that in the past we had two sanctions which could be applied against European states. The first was financial assistance. Now that we are no longer giving aid to Europe, this means of exerting pressure has disappeared. The second was our military defense of Europe. This sanction is wasting away as the French develop their own nuclear capability.

The President thought that we should look now at the contingency of de Gaulle trying to run us out of Europe by means of a deal with the Russians. He thought we ought to think now about how we can protect ourselves against actions which de Gaulle might take against us.

The President said that if de Gaulle did make a deal with the Russians, it is possible that the Germans would go with the French. He

---

Source: Kennedy Library, National Security Files, Executive Committee Meetings. Top Secret.

[1] Not found.

noted that in the present situation we cannot help the Germans very much. He referred to Ambassador Dowling's report of a conversation with Adenauer upon the Chancellor's return from his discussions with de Gaulle in which the Chancellor reported that de Gaulle had said the British had turned down his suggestion that their nuclear deterrent be committed to a European defense system and instead, at Nassau, had agreed to turn over their nuclear force to the U.S.[2]

The President said he was disturbed by Adenauer's reference to a European defense system. He did not know what this was. Possibly he was referring to a defense system in which only the Six would benefit.

De Gaulle may be prepared to break up NATO. He may be thinking of neutralizing Europe by supporting a plan similar to the Rapacki Plan.[3] If the French do move in this direction, we must be prepared to react immediately. For example, the French may suddenly decide to cash their dollar holdings as a means of exerting economic pressure on us.

The President said he had tried to understand de Gaulle's reaction to Cuba. He thought that the only logical way to explain de Gaulle's reaction was French belief that their support of us in the Cuban crisis involved a commitment which might get them into war arising out of American actions not directly involving French interests. He said that de Gaulle may have come to the conclusion that the security of France would increase if the French had no ties to the U.S. If there were no U.S. ties, U.S. difficulties outside of Europe would not endanger French security. The President asked Secretary McNamara to look closely at any U.S. funds being spent for NATO, including our share of infrastructure costs.

As soon as the French have a nuclear capability, the President continued, we have much less to offer Europe and the Europeans may conclude that continuing their ties with us will create a risk that we will drag them into a war in which they do not wish to be involved. If we are not vital to Germany, then our NATO strategy makes no sense.

The President said we must not permit a situation to develop in which we would have to seek economic favors from Europe. He thought we should think now about how we can use our existing position to put pressure on the Europeans if the situation so demands. De Gaulle now banks on our protecting him. We should be thinking of how we can react in an effective way in Europe; for example, withdrawing our tactical air force to bases outside France. He asked the Defense Department to look

---

[2] Not further identified.

[3] First enunciated in an address to the United Nations General Assembly on October 2, 1957, this plan called for a denuclearized zone in central Europe. For text, see U.N. doc A/PV.697.

very carefully at current proposals to provide additional planes to French forces and to other NATO powers. He thought we should be prepared to reduce quickly, if we so decided, our military forces in Germany.

The President summarized by repeating that de Gaulle may have thought during the Cuban crisis, that he was tied to the U.S. and that the Skybolt decision which resulted in the Nassau agreement had tied the U.K. to the U.S. Therefore, since the U.K. had chosen the U.S., France could keep the U.K. out of the Common Market as a non-European power.

The President concluded by asking that the Departments of State, Defense and Treasury look at all aspects of the possibilities he had described so that we would be prepared in the event any of these contingencies became reality.

Secretary Dillon referred to the President's statement that France was opposing every U.S. policy and noted that in the financial field there was no lack of cooperation by French financial officials. He said the explanation for this may lie in the fact that de Gaulle pays very little attention to economic matters.

The President recalled the U.K./France cooperation in the research and development of a supersonic airplane, the Concord. He said he had appointed a group to review the question of whether or not we should set out to develop a supersonic air transport. In this connection, if the French initiate active measures against us, he did not want our air transport companies to have to go begging to France for a supersonic transport.

Secretary Rusk said that de Gaulle's reaction to Cuba may have arisen from a sudden realization that the French "might fry" as a result of their commitment to us, which was called into force as a result of a non-NATO situation. He felt that de Gaulle's present fever might be short-lived. He said no sensible person failed to realize that Europe is lost to the Communists if Europe, without our strategic missiles, confronts Soviet missiles.

The President repeated again his concern that we may be facing very heavy weather in our relations with Europe. He recalled that de Gaulle had mentioned to him that France would be making some proposals about NATO, but that we had never received these proposals. Perhaps de Gaulle would be confronting us with a plan to set up a European defense system in which we would have no part. He repeated that we should get ready with actions to squeeze Europe. He said there is not much we can do against France, but we can exert considerable pressure on the Germans. We should make no threats to any European state but merely act in such a way as to convey our intentions. For example, we might close down U.S. installations in France and Germany. Perhaps de Gaulle is not interested in a multilateral NATO force if he succeeds in obtaining a treaty with Germany. The President doubted that Germany could participate wholeheartedly in a NATO multilateral force at the same time it was so intimately tied to France.

The President urged that we take a cold, hard attitude toward the situation which may develop in Europe. He said we can take care of ourselves and are not dependent upon European support.

Ambassador Thompson said he wished to discuss at a later time with the President his view that the situation described by the President might call for us to adopt an entirely opposite course of action. The President said that he thought we should look at all possibilities, as far as he was concerned, the way he had described his thinking was the only speculation which made sense to him.

Secretary Ball said he wished to point out that Adenauer was entirely out of tune, not only with other Germans, but with other European countries. He said that the treaty with France means everything to Adenauer. However, Adenauer may soon be out of power, sooner than he had planned. In addition, the German legislators may refuse to ratify the treaty with France if de Gaulle insists on keeping the British out of the Common Market.

The President said the next three months would be a crucial period and he wanted us to be prepared to respond immediately if de Gaulle and those tied to him act against us.

Secretary McNamara said there were two ways of dealing with such a development. One way would be to disengage entirely from Europe. The other would be to tie ourselves much more closely to the European powers other than France. He said that there were certain actions we could take in the immediate future which would contribute to either of the two courses of action he described. These actions include disparaging French nuclear capabilities; pulling our tactical fighters out of France and basing them in the U.K. or Spain or returning them to the U.S.; and drastically reducing our logistical base in France.

Mr. Bundy said he wondered whether we should move the headquarters of NATO and thought that a location in one of the low countries might be preferable.

The President said that if it appears that the Europeans are getting ready to throw us out of Europe, we want to be in a position to march out. Secretary Rusk said that de Gaulle's view is not the view of most Europeans. He recalled that during the Cuban crisis de Gaulle had immediately and flatly given us the fullest support in the event our actions resulted in war.

The Attorney General asked whether we actually thought we would be better off if we got out of Europe. He suggested that a paper be written stating the advantages and disadvantages of our leaving Europe. Secretary Ball said the State Department is already preparing a paper on this subject, and he recalled that our policy has always been one of removing our troops from Europe as soon as we were certain that Europe could defend herself.

The President concluded the discussion by saying we should look now at the possibility that de Gaulle had concluded that he would make a deal with the Russians, break up NATO, and push the U.S. out of Europe.

Bromley Smith[4]

---

[4] Printed from a copy that bears this typed signature.

---

170. Memorandum From the Assistant Secretary of State for European Affairs (Tyler) to Secretary of State Rusk

Washington, January 28, 1963.

SUBJECT

The Attitude of our Allies Toward our Pressure for Increased Conventional NATO Forces

I would like you to have my own personal estimate of how our European allies see this question, and of their reasoning.

First of all, I think we have failed to convince governments of the soundness of our arguments. Europeans believe that any Soviet aggression against NATO forces on the European front would escalate rapidly and automatically to general nuclear war. In other words, they do not accept the premise of the possibility of a limited military engagement with Soviet forces in Europe. This leads them to look for some explanation other than the one we give, for our pressure in favor of increased

---

Source: Department of State, Central Files, 375/1–2863. Secret. Drafted and initialed by Tyler. The source text bears the notation "Secretary Saw."

conventional forces. Generally speaking, they read into our arguments a reluctance on our part to commit ourselves to the use of nuclear weapons for the defense of Europe in the event of Soviet aggression. They attribute this reluctance to a US desire to find a way to reach a compromise with the Soviet Union short of general nuclear war, and worry lest this should take the form of some kind of a deal over Europe. Furthermore they reason that a NATO defense strategy which envisages dealing with a Soviet non-nuclear aggression, however limited, by conventional forces only, has the effect of encouraging the Soviets to believe that there is a possible area of military conflict in the heart of Europe in which they can engage with impunity in so far as nuclear warfare is concerned. While the Germans are the most vocal on this aspect of the subject, it is my impression that the peoples of Europe in general do not believe that an increase in the NATO conventional potential would add to the degree of security which they now enjoy.

The consequences of this general state of mind are that neither governments nor public opinion are likely to make the effort required to bring their conventional forces up to the NATO force goals.

Whether they would do so if faced by the alternative of US withdrawal of troops, I do not know, but I have my strong doubts.

---

171.   **Editorial Note**

Presumably as a result of the National Security Council Executive Committee meeting on January 25, a European Policy Review Group began meeting on January 28. Chaired by Ball and including Thompson, Rostow, Kitchen, Nitze, Kaysen, and from the Joint Chiefs of Staff, General Goodpaster, the group met "to review procedures for political consultation and the military relationships of the US and Europe." Only records for four meetings of the group (January 28, 29, 30, and 31) have been found and they show that a wide variety of opinions were expressed on changes that might be made in the political, economic, and military relations between the United States and Europe. (Department of State, S/S–S Files: Lot 66 D 219, Special Study Group) No report of the group or records of further meetings have been found.

172. National Security Action Memorandum No. 218

Washington, January 30, 1963.

TO

The Secretary of State
The Secretary of Defense

SUBJECT

Implementation of the Nassau Agreements

Following a discussion on the implementation of the Nassau agreements, the President:

1. Approved the general framework of negotiations with the British, including the proposed Memorandum of Agreement (prepared by Sub-Group I) and the Aide-Mémoire and Instructions to the U.S. Negotiators (prepared by Sub-Group II).[1]

2. Approved in principle the proposal for proceeding with negotiations for the establishment of a Multilateral Force (recommended by Sub-Group IV).

3. Specified that the Multilateral Force negotiations not be linked directly to the conventional force buildup or budget. However, the President expressed the view that Multilateral Force effort should not result in diminution of the present conventional programs, and he directed that in the course of negotiations it should be ascertained how governments intended to pay for participation in the Multilateral Force on a long-term basis.

4. Agreed that insofar as the control mechanism of Multilateral Force was concerned, it should be our present objective to obtain agreement on voting unanimity.

5. Emphasized that in the course of negotiations, U.S. should not become engaged in such a way that failure to achieve agreement would seriously damage U.S. prestige.

6. Directed that he be given frequent and continuing progress reports on the foregoing.

McG Bundy

Source: Department of State, NSAMs: Lot 72 D 316. Secret.

[1] Documentation on the work of the various Sub-Groups of the Steering Group on Implementing the Nassau Decisions, including texts of the aide-mémoire, instructions, and memorandum of agreement referred to here, is ibid., Conference Files: Lot 66 D 110, CF 2218–2219.

173.   Summary Record of NSC Executive Committee Meeting No. 41

Washington, February 12, 1963, 10 a.m.

MULTILATERAL NUCLEAR FORCE

The President said he wished to discuss the question of a multilateral nuclear force for NATO. We first needed to agree on what it is we will propose to NATO, how soon we should initiate these discussions, and how much success we expect to achieve in the political area as a result of our offer. He asked Ambassador Merchant, who is to be the chief negotiator, to state his views on this problem.

Ambassador Merchant said he approved in general of the basic document. (A copy of the document entitled "Integrated Seaborne Polaris Force" is attached.)[1] He said he believed that the sooner he began discussions with the NATO powers in Europe the better. He acknowledged that further guidance was needed on two questions: (a) control of the multilateral force, and (b) whether the force should consist of submarines or surface ships. Personally, he recommended that the President stand by a statement made by U.S. officials to NATO on October 22nd to the effect that the U.S. would consider any proposal for control of this force suggested by the Europeans, including the possibility of no U.S. veto over the firing of the missiles of this force.[2] He urged that this offer be left open-ended.

With respect to the choice between submarines and surface ships, he said he favored giving the Europeans an option to choose surface ships if they so desired.

Describing his forthcoming European trip as a reconnaissance in force, Ambassador Merchant requested latitude in discussing both the control and subs vs. surface ship questions.

The President summarized his recent conversation with Admiral Rickover[3] who opposed our offering to put Polaris subs in a multilateral force because:

Source: Kennedy Library, National Security Files, Executive Committee Meetings. Top Secret.

[1] Not printed.

[2] On October 22, 1962, Acheson had briefed the North Atlantic Council on the Cuban situation. A report on this meeting was transmitted in Polto 502 from Paris, October 23. (Department of State, Central Files, 611.3122/10–2362)

[3] The meeting with Rickover took place February 11 (Kennedy Library, President's Appointment Book), but no other record of it has been found.

1. The Polaris submarine is a dangerous instrument which requires highly trained crews. We have had several close escapes even with U.S. crews.

2. There is a grave danger of compromising our nuclear reactor technology. We are ahead of the Russians in this field and cannot afford to take the risk of losing our secrets by offering to allow the Polaris submarines to be operated by mixed European crews.

The President recalled the opposition of the Joint Atomic Energy Committee to our offer of Skipjack to the French. He felt that the Committee might strongly oppose our offering Polaris submarines to the Europeans. He did not wish to get into a position of making a proposal to the Europeans on which we could not deliver because of Congressional opposition. He felt that the problem of security could be dramatized by opponents of a multilateral NATO Polaris force.

Secretary McNamara said he favored proposing a NATO surface force for the following reasons:

1. A submarine force would cost almost twice as much as a surface force.

2. The survivability of a surface ship is one-half to two-thirds that of a submarine.

3. Admiral Mountbatten has stated to General Taylor his belief that a mixed crew could not operate a Polaris submarine efficiently, although Admiral Anderson has said, in opposition to Admiral Rickover, that a mixed crew could be trained to operate a Polaris submarine.

4. The attraction of a surface force could be increased by offering the new MRBM missile now under development which is expected to be better and cheaper than the Polaris.

Secretary McNamara concluded that in his view we should lay out all the arguments in favor of a surface force and seek to present the subject in such a way that the Europeans will choose a surface force.

Secretary Rusk said that we must support a multilateral force in order to avoid the development of national nuclear capabilities. Political as well as security reasons require us to seek some form of multilateral force acceptable to the Europeans.

The President pointed out that Congress felt it had practically invented the Polaris. If we did decide to offer the Europeans a surface force, we would have greater latitude than if we had to ask Congress to make Polaris submarines available to NATO.

Secretary McNamara reflected his deep concern about current Republican efforts to dictate military policy to the Administration. He said he had originally opposed the surface force concept, but he had now come to the conclusion that we should offer the Europeans a surface force rather than take on a major fight with the Republicans who would be quick to exploit a proposal to share Polaris submarines with European members of NATO. He doubted that it would be possible to sell

Congress on a NATO Polaris multilateral force. He recounted his unsuccessful effort to convince a Republican Congressman that our present nuclear strategy was not a "no win" policy or an "underdog" strategy.

Mr. Bundy said another additional advantage of proposing a surface force now is that we can have an operational surface force much faster than a submarine force.

The President concluded the discussion of this question by saying we should limit our offer to that of a surface force.

Mr. Bundy said the next question involved the control of this force. Everyone agreed that the U.S. must retain an authoritative voice in the control of the force, but there were differing views as to whether we should support a European force without a veto or an Atlantic force with or without a veto.

The President recalled that de Gaulle had told someone that one way to deal with the problem of control would be to give the Germans control of nuclear weapons upon the outbreak of war. The President asked what we could offer the Europeans to convince them that they had a substantially increased voice in the control of nuclear weapons.

Ambassador Merchant said we would be offering the Germans the following:

1. Reassurance that the U.S. was staying on the European Continent.
2. Participation in the control of nuclear force. Possession of nuclear weapons has become the touchstone of political power and greatly overemphasized.
3. An alternative to de Gaulle's plan for Franco-German cooperation.

Ambassador Merchant said he believes that the multilateral force would have strong appeal for the Europeans. We would be able to make more nuclear knowledge available to them at the same time as we were giving them a sense of participation in the nuclear field. In the course of this activity, the European leaders would face some of the problems of nuclear warfare which are not now understood by them. It is possible when they see the price tag and all of the problems involved in a multilateral nuclear force, they may lose interest in it.

Secretary Acheson agreed with Ambassador Merchant's statement that the problem of controlling a nuclear force had been blown up by the Europeans out of all proportion to its importance. He said the discussion of a "voice" in the use of nuclear weapons had become a catch phrase. The question was a "voice" in what? The "voice" that is meaningful involves the question of whether or not to go to war, not whether or not to use a specific weapon. He stated that in his view a nuclear force without a U.S. veto on the use of that force made no sense. He believed we should tell the Europeans that if they contributed to the nuclear force they would be given a "voice" in decisions involving its use. He urged that we avoid discussion of ultimates and start immediately to get Europe mixed up in the process of learning the facts about nuclear war. He urged that we tell the Europeans we had concluded that a surface force was the best and that we were prepared to start training their nationals to participate in the operation of such a force at once. During this process, their military officers would learn the facts of nuclear war. We could also tell the Europeans, if they insisted on discussing the question of control, that control would depend on what they put into the nuclear force, i.e. if their contribution buys 2% of the force they would have a 2% voice in deciding when it would be used.

Secretary Acheson's view was that our offer of a nuclear surface force would be meaningful to the Europeans because de Gaulle had no alternative to offer, i.e. his proposal would not be realized for a long period of time.

Secretary Rusk pointed out that in his view, when the Europeans learned the facts of nuclear warfare, they will discover that it makes no sense for them to launch nuclear weapons without the U.S. In addition, he believed that the Russians would be reassured if we insisted on a veto over the use of a nuclear NATO force because the Russians have an overriding fear that the Germans will somehow manage to obtain control of nuclear weapons which they can fire on their own decision. For these reasons, Secretary Rusk said he opposed a European force in which we would not have a veto.

Ambassador Bruce pointed out that if the Europeans actually come to the conclusion that nuclear war is indivisible and that it makes no sense for them to think of a force which could be used independently of the U.S. force, he believed that the Europeans would then say there was no point in paying for a multilateral force. Possibly we should not go down the road of a multilateral force but place our emphasis instead on the Paragraph 6[4] or "first" phase force.

General Taylor reported that both the Germans and the British military wanted to talk about Paragraph 6 forces immediately. The Germans appeared ready to put into Paragraph 6 forces their F–104s and their Mace missiles. Firing of this force would be done under the same rules which now apply to NATO forces, i.e. SACEUR. A Deputy SACEUR nuclear commander would control the multilateral nuclear force. All participants would thus be brought into training and planning activity quickly in Omaha and in the SACEUR staff.

Secretary Ball said that the State Department sees the political problem first while the military stresses the practical aspects of the military

---

[4] Reference is to paragraph 6 of the Nassau Agreement.

force. He said he believed that Paragraph 6 forces would probably satisfy military officers, but he did not believe that it would satisfy the politicians to a degree which would prompt them to oppose de Gaulle's plan.

The President reminded the group that more than a year ago we had asked the Europeans to come forward with their proposal for the control of nuclear forces. We now have to take the initiative because the Europeans did not come forward and de Gaulle has forced us to advocate a particular plan. He repeated his question as to what the Germans will see in the force control proposal being discussed.

Ambassador Dowling said the Germans will see these advantages:

1. The answer to de Gaulle's allegations that the U.S. will leave the European Continent.
2. Equal status in the nuclear field with the British and the French.
3. Participation in a nuclear force which will meet the immediate need because the Germans do not yet expect to share in controlling the trigger.
4. The appearance of immediate movement toward participation in a multilateral force.

He added that the multilateral force proposal provided for mixing Atlantic nationals together promptly in the development of a NATO system based on nuclear warfare.

Mr. Murrow, citing Secretary McNamara's comment that the surface system would in effect be a second-rate system, expressed his view that a surface system would not give the Europeans a true sense of participation. They would feel that we were below the water with the real weapon and they were on the surface with a facade weapon. He feared the Soviets would exploit this situation.

Secretary McNamara replied by saying we could offset such reactions by stressing to the Europeans the new missile which they would use in the surface force. We have $800 million in the FY '64 budget to develop this missile, which will be more accurate than the Polaris, and, when in production, will cost less per missile.

Ambassador Dowling said he did not feel that the surface force would be unsaleable to the Germans.

Mr. Bundy said that if the British support a surface force, the Europeans would be more favorable toward it. In addition, he said the true test would be whether we were buying the weapon. The reason Skybolt was unsatisfactory was because the Europeans knew we did not think enough of this weapon to purchase it for our own forces.

Secretary Rusk said we may have been overestimating the Europeans' desire to share in the control of the nuclear force. In his view, the Europeans did not expect equality with the U.S., but they did want equality with their neighbors. He hoped that our emphasizing Paragraph 6 forces might take the steam out of their desire to participate in the control of a multilateral force.

General Taylor hoped that Ambassador Merchant could relate the Paragraph 6 forces to the second-phase forces in such a way as to encourage the Europeans to accept a surface force.

The President asked whether we could respond to the fear of the Europeans that the U.S. will withdraw from Europe by making an agreement with them that if we do withdraw we would not do so before we had assisted them in developing their own nuclear force. In addition, he wondered whether we could not satisfy the Germans by agreeing to reduce the time between the use of non-nuclear forces and the firing of nuclear missiles. We could overcome their doubt that we would fire nuclear missiles by making clear now when we would resort to nuclear warfare in a given situation.

Secretary Rusk expressed his doubt that the Europeans would ever support a purely European nuclear force.

Secretary Acheson expressed his view that it was hopeless for the Europeans to have a nuclear force without the U.S. He said we must get additional conventional forces in Europe within the next five years because it made no sense whatsoever for the U.S. itself to attempt to defend Europe on the ground. Our purpose, he said, was to increase allied power, not divide it. He urged again that we offer to the Europeans a surface force which is soon realizable—as soon as the Europeans are trained to participate in its manning. As to the use of the force and its control, he said we should tell the Europeans it will be used as any other weapon now in the NATO combined force. The Europeans know that the use of any weapons, even rifles, makes no sense unless we too are involved.

The President asked Secretary Acheson how we would avoid the European reaction if what we are proposing is not a real force but merely a facade.

Secretary Acheson repeated his earlier statement that the concept of a "voice" in the use of the force is merely an illusion—the question is one of going to war, not the use of nuclear weapons. He repeated again his view that we must consider the use of nuclear weapons the same as non-nuclear weapons now under NATO control. He pointed out that what we were offering was something meaningful while de Gaulle has nothing to shoot now and only a hope of getting something later.

Secretary Rusk said the Europeans do not really understand what nuclear war means. The idea that de Gaulle wants a nuclear force for the purpose of triggering our nuclear force is silly because it means that de Gaulle's use of nuclear weapons would result in the total destruction of

France. Hence, what they are really talking about is destroying all of France to get the U.S. into a nuclear war.

Ambassador Dowling felt that our present proposal should go only as far as is necessary to answer the questions which the Europeans now have in their minds. As they learn about nuclear warfare, we can go forward with plans which would be more acceptable to them because of their acquired knowledge.

In response to the President's request for his views, Governor Herter made the following points:

1. We are committed to discuss a multilateral force with the Europeans, even if our hope is that the Europeans would not accept it.
2. We should initiate consultation with the Europeans and bring them in to participate in nuclear force planning in every way we can.
3. We should consult with them on how we can add to a nuclear force.

Ambassador Bruce said it was most important for Ambassador Merchant to know what type of a nuclear force he is to offer to the Europeans. It is only fair that the Europeans know what we are asking them to join. If it is our view that we are not going to offer them Polaris submarines, then we should tell them now so that they cannot in the future say that we promised something which we did not carry out. The President thought that one way of moving from a submarine to surface force would be to have the British and the German military officers consider which force was preferable and, if, as we anticipate, they would conclude that a surface force is preferable, then politically it would be easier for us to tell the Europeans that we favored a surface force. Convincing the Germans would be the key to this situation. The Italians have already discussed the use of the Garibaldi in a surface force.

In response to his question, Secretary Acheson was informed that the security factor with respect to the nuclear reactor would disappear after four or five years, even though Admiral Rickover believed it would always be with us.

Ambassador Merchant said we might get the military to say that mixed manning of submarines was impossible and dangerous. However, we must avoid the Europeans then asking for Polaris submarines nationally manned. He felt that if we think we cannot deliver Polaris submarines because of Congressional opposition, we ought to tell the Europeans so.

Secretary Rusk cautioned that we must move off the submarine offer with great care.

Secretary Ball said we should advance the reasons why a surface force is preferable, i.e. we can get it faster, it costs less, and it will have new missiles. This would appeal to the Europeans who want something fairly fast.

In response to the President's question, Mr. Bundy said no legal problem was involved in offering a surface nuclear force if the U.S. keeps custody of the nuclear warheads. If the Europeans ask for control of the weapons, then we could not give this to them without changing the existing law or by a treaty.

Ambassador Bruce doubted that there would be any difficulty in Europe because the British would have the Polaris missile and no other Europeans would. He said the Europeans realized that they would never be able to build up sufficient nuclear forces to ask for control of the firing of NATO weapons because we will always have overwhelming military power. Our problem is to figure out some way to make it possible for the Europeans to live with this fact, [1 line of source text not declassified]. We must find a way of giving them a means, even a façade, of answering de Gaulle's argument. What we are seeking is a political solution, not a military answer. No solution will be perfect. No solution can allow the Germans to gain possession of nuclear weapons. What we are trying to do is to overcome the present political uneasiness about the nuclear force problem in the hope that the uneasiness will vanish within five years. Everyone in Europe knows that Europe is not going to be able to build a huge nuclear force. Ambassador Merchant should not leave for Europe until he has our full answer to this existing situation.

The President repeated his view that if military officers, including Germans and Italians, would tell us we should go for a surface force instead of submarines, it would be much easier to change our offer.

Secretary McNamara suggested that State and Defense work out the tactics before Ambassador Merchant leaves for Europe. In his view he said we must decide whether we do or do not want a multilateral force. If we do, we may well have to help Europe pay for the cost of this force. If we decide to pay the cost, then we ought to draw up a package offer which is truly attractive to the Europeans.

Secretary Rusk expressed his doubt that security problems raised by Admiral Rickover and Congress should control our policy.

Secretary McNamara said it was not the security problem which had prompted him to shift from favoring a submarine force to favoring a surface force, but rather the domestic political problems which he had encountered so forcibly during Congressional hearings in the past week.

The President asked that a brief of the advantages of a surface force be drafted by Defense. He believed that we must, with great caution, shift from the submarine offer to a surface ship offer, primarily because of the ease with which the submarine offer could be attacked in Congress.

Secretary Acheson suggested that we tell the Europeans now we are prepared to support a surface force and that we will talk to them about submarines later.

The President hoped that the surface force decision could be held very tightly so that when we do make the offer we do so in a clean fashion.

Mr. Bundy said the problem for consideration by the group at its next meeting would be that of the control of the Paragraph 6 forces.

Bromley Smith[5]

---

[5] Printed from a copy that bears this typed signature.

---

174.   Memorandum of Conversation

Washington, February 18, 1963, 4 p.m.

PRESENT

> The President
> Secretary Rusk
> Ambassador Bruce
> Ambassador Merchant
> Mr. Walt Rostow
> Mr. Gerard Smith
> Mr. Jeffrey Kitchen
> Admiral John Lee
> Mr. John McNaughton
> Mr. McGeorge Bundy
> Mr. Carl Kaysen

SUBJECT

> The Merchant Mission and the Multilateral Force

The President opened the discussion by expressing his deep concern about the multilateral force project, and particularly the fact that the United States might be tying itself too closely to a project that might fail. He said it was his impression that the British were not for it; the French were clearly against it; and the Italians did not have a deep-seated interest in it. The Germans reportedly were interested, but once they realized how little they were getting for their money, they might look at it differently. Moreover, he wondered whether the multilateral

---

Source: Kennedy Library, National Security Files, Meetings with the President. Secret. No drafting information appears on the source text. The meeting was held in the President's office.

force could have any real attraction unless the United States was prepared to give up its veto, and at this point he saw no justification for relinquishing the veto.

The Secretary of State said the problem at issue came right out of
Germany, and how it was resolved was a matter of intense interest to the
Germans as well as their neighbors. [2 *lines of source text not declassified*]
At this juncture the alternative to the multilateral path seemed to be the
development of national deterrents and proliferation. If the U.S. did not
take the initiative, we could expect greater Franco-German collaboration and a considerably more complicated problem. The Secretary
agreed that if the Europeans were not interested in the multilateral
force, there was nothing we could do about it, but felt that because of the
vital issues at stake, a try had to be made.

The President returned to the question of control, citing Ambassador Bohlen's view that unless the United States was prepared to give on
the control issue, the concept of the multilateral force would collapse
[5-1/2 *lines of source text not declassified*]. Clearly this was not something
which could be given away easily. Therefore, the multilateral force and
possible alternatives had to be carefully considered. The President suggested that an alternative might be the par. 6 forces. These would not
require large financial outlays, and, therefore, the Europeans would not
have any real basis for insisting upon the relinquishment of U.S. control.
Moreover, the principle of multilateralism could conceivably be established through the par. 6 forces.

With reference to the par. 6, Ambassador Merchant thought this
could provide us with a fall-back position in the event that the MLF
failed. He said it was difficult to judge the situation until we knew better
what the other people wanted. His mission—which he considered a reconnaissance in force—should give us a sounder basis for assessing the
depth of interest in the multilateral force than we now had. At this juncture he did not feel the U.S. needed to relinquish the veto. It could insist
upon the rule of unanimity for the MLF, which in effect meant the reciprocal relinquishment of the veto by all.

The President indicated he remained concerned that we might be
identifying ourselves too closely with a proposition (MLF) that might be
rejected. Rather than take this risk, he thought we might better focus on
some version of a multinational force, operated through an Executive
Committee.

Secretary Rusk said that something more was needed since we had
committed ourselves at Nassau to go the multilateral force route.

The President, however, continued to insist that the United States
should not be placed in the position of attempting to force the sale of the
MLF. [3 *lines of source text not declassified*] He did not see why the Europe-

ans should have more confidence in each other than they had in us. Wasn't there something that could be done for the Germans—who are on the front line—without giving away our control? [2 *lines of source text not declassified*]

Mr. Bundy interjected to say that that matter had to be looked at in a time context. He appreciated the President's concerns but felt the multilateral force could be tied to other arrangements—monetary, economic, etc.—of importance to us, and although there were obvious dangers in relinquishing our monopoly, 10 years from now it would be difficult to see the Europeans willing to leave it all in our hands.

Secretary Rusk agreed, adding that in his view, as the Europeans looked more closely at the problem they would see the impracticability of de Gaulle's views and join us.

Mr. Bundy said this was an important factor. However, if the Europeans rejected de Gaulle's concepts, that was one thing; if we did, it was quite another.

The President again returned to the question of the risks in the MLF, saying he hated to see the French and the Soviets stirred up by a proposition that could flounder on the issue of the U.S. veto. The Secretary said he did not quite see the problem that way. In his view, the question was really whether or not we wanted to toss Europe into de Gaulle's lap. And the principal antidote to de Gaulle at this time was organizing Europe along the lines of the multilateral force.

Ambassador Merchant returned to the question of the German interest in the multilateral force, saying that although he was not optimistic about the project he thought it was worth a serious try. If the multilateral force was established, it would be a major step forward in creating the kind of Atlantic Community we wanted. Moreover, he thought the Germans had a greater interest in the project than the President seemed to imply. He inclined to the view (which he said was also Ambassador Dowling's) that the Germans would be willing to pay a lot of money for first-class citizenship and, therefore, the MLF could have real and considerable appeal for them. In any event, he felt that in a month we would have a better notion of the depth of European interest and if the MLF worked, we would have extricated the Germans from the exclusive French embrace. If it didn't, we would have given up nothing. Future decisions were not foreclosed and, given its potential value, the MLF was worth a trial. If it failed, we could always come back to par. 6.

The President was not quite sanguine about this tactical approach. He did not want to find himself in a position of supporting a par. 6 as a fall-back proposition after an MLF failure. Rather, he preferred that the par. 6 and MLF projects be handled together so that, regardless of how it worked out, we would always end up with a multilateral force. Perhaps by identifying both the par. 6 forces and the MLF as multilateral arrangements, we would never be in a position of having the principle of multilateralism rejected.

Mr. Bundy thought the thing to do was to put both these proposals under a single umbrella, the basic concept being shared responsibility of the Allies.

[3 paragraphs (23 lines of source text) not declassified]

The President [2 lines of source text not declassified] went on to describe a possible framework for par. 6 forces—a U.S.-U.K. nucleus, plus an Executive Committee, with access to Omaha, minus multilaterally owned and operated ships and submarines. [less than one line of source text not declassified] And if MLF was not workable, it might be worthwhile going this route, which, at least, did not require our giving up control. The relinquishment of the veto, in his view, in effect meant an acknowledgment on our part of the fact that European interests were different from ours—and this he was not prepared to do.

Merchant said he too opposed giving up the veto at this time. He thought it most important we make clear to the Europeans that the MLF is a serious proposal which we wanted to discuss with them; that we were interested in their views; and that if they had alternative proposals, we were prepared to consider them.

The President again emphasized that although we wanted to get a multilateral force organized and to sea, we wanted to do so without giving up our control.

Mr. Rostow interjected at this point to say that he thought that, although Ambassador Bohlen accurately reflected Paris' view of the control problem, Bonn's view of the situation was probably very different. Rostow said he did not believe the control question was an important one for the Germans at this time. The Germans do not trust the British or the French or the Italians; in fact, what they seem to be looking for is an arrangement which would keep us, the United States, inextricably tied to them. And in this context, the control problem does not arise as an urgent issue.

In answer to the President's question as to why the Germans then were looking for something new if they trusted us so much, Rostow said the Germans merely wanted first-class citizenship, and participation in a nuclear force was symbolic of that class of citizenship.

Still on the control problem, the Secretary said he did not feel this was an issue that would face us immediately. At best, he said, it would take us a year to succeed with the MLF, and at least two to fail. Nothing would collapse in a short term.

Mr. Bundy stressed that, in any event, we wanted to avoid a repetition of last June's performance, in which we seemed to have had the worst of both possible worlds. It was important, he said, to avoid giving the impression that we did not believe what we were saying. By the same token, we did not want to be in a position of forcing a proposition on others without giving them a fair chance to question and discuss it.

In answer to the President's question on the cost factors, Ambassador Merchant said he lacked precise figures, but his working estimates were $1.8 billion for a multilateral force of 8 submarines and a little more for a force of 25 surface ships. Merchant also thought that he had fairly impressive arguments to justify the use of surface ships in the MLF in preference to submarines. These included such factors as cost, availability, training requirements, and the fact that the surface ships could be built abroad while the submarines had to be built here, in the United States.

Insofar as his immediate schedule was concerned, Merchant said he planned to leave for Paris on Friday morning (February 22), spending a week there to discuss the MLF with NAC and the Permanent Representatives of the interested countries, and at the same time stopping in to see Couve so that the French would not feel that his principal mission was to encircle him. After Paris, he planned to go on to Rome, Brussels, possibly The Hague, and then London.

As for possible French reaction to the MLF exercise, Mr. Bundy expected the French, in the first instance, to be quite wary.

The President agreed, but thought that the moment the French latched on to the control problem they would begin to fire back. He thought that perhaps one way to deal with this problem was to explain to all interested participants that they would be better off with the MLF which would be a step forward in bringing the United States and Europe closer together and giving the Europeans a greater voice in managing the Alliance's security problems. However, the President again cautioned against trying to over-sell the MLF and to assure the Allies that this was the cureall for all our problems. The important thing, he emphasized, was not to stick to the MLF too long if it seemed to be a losing proposition but to assure that we had a multilateral formula at hand that had a chance of success.

Insofar as Ambassador Merchant's immediate mission was concerned, the President indicated he was prepared to issue appropriate instructions along the lines Ambassador Merchant had requested, including Ambassador Merchant's proposals for dealing with the control question.

David Klein[1]

---

[1] Printed from a copy that bears this typed signature.

175. Memorandum for the Record

Washington, February 21, 1963, 12:20 p.m.

Those present were: The President, Ambassador Merchant, Mr. Gerard Smith, Admiral Lee, Mr. John McNaughton, and McG. Bundy.

The purpose of this meeting was to review and give final approval to instructions to Ambassador Merchant's negotiating team. The President did review and approve these instructions in the form in which they are attached hereto.[1]

The President reported that he had learned from Mr. McCone of Mr. McCone's own doubt that the submarine form of the MLF represented a significant danger from the point of view of possible penetration of U.S. reactor technology, and that he had asked the Secretary of Defense and Mr. McCone to review the matter for him. He asked Ambassador Merchant what his own plan for presentation on this matter was, and Ambassador Merchant replied that he expected to proceed in terms of a clear U.S. preference for surface ships, on a number of grounds: manageability, earlier readiness, operating economy, and the general value of a new weapons system. The President remarked that the pursuit of the *Anzoategui* indicated that it would not be easy to keep track of a fleet of surface missile ships.

On the control issue, the President reviewed and approved the new language in the attached paper, after revising it to insure that it did not give an implication that the U.S. would necessarily be more flexible in later discussions. The significant point about this language is that it makes no apologies for advancing and defending a position of unanimity. Mr. Smith, who has had the longest and the closest experience of what has been said to Europeans in the past on this matter, expressed his satisfaction with these instructions.

It was at this meeting that it was first made clear to the President— and this is a matter which I myself did not clearly understand before— that the plans for the MLF would require changes in the legislation affecting the custody of warheads. This matter came up as part of a discussion of Ambassador Merchant's rather testing two hours before the Joint Committee the previous day, and the President asked whether in fact under a rule of unanimity legislative changes would be necessary. Mr. McNaughton said that there were a number of points on which indeed changes would be needed, and said that the men working on the

---

Source: Kennedy Library, National Security Files, Meetings with the President. Secret. Prepared by Bundy on February 23. The meeting was held in the Cabinet Room.

[1] Not found attached, but printed as Document 176.

MLF had reached a clear and unanimous conclusion that it would be a much more marketable enterprise if in fact there were symmetry of responsibility, so that U.S. control was exercised at the summit, like that of other participants, rather than all the way along the line in terms of a special monopolist's relation to the warheads. The President at first appeared to feel that it might be better not to propose arrangements which would require a change in the law on custody, but after hearing strong argument from Mr. Smith and Ambassador Merchant to the effect that the political effectiveness of the proposal would be gravely compromised if there were no modification of our existing practices, and after weighing the argument that the Congress might well find modifications in the law quite acceptable as long as the principal of unanimity was maintained, he appeared to accept the proposed position. Later in the day, at his press conference,[2] he confirmed and supported the position which Ambassador Merchant reported that he had taken the day before—namely, that any arrangement as important as the proposed MLF would of course be sent up for Congressional review and approval in the appropriate way.

The President repeated his frequently expressed concern for the preparation of an effective and presentable alternative in the event that the MLF did not make good progress, and it was agreed that such an alternative would have to combine the processes of consultation, participation and representation—of which Mr. Acheson is a notable advocate—with larger emphasis on the so-called paragraph 6 forces. Responsibility for prompt preparation of such a fallback position was assigned to Mr. Kitchen.[3]

McG. B.[4]

---

[2] For a transcript of the President's press conference, see *Public Papers of the Presidents of the United States: John F. Kennedy, 1963*, pp. 201–209.

[3] On February 25 Bruce and Thompson discussed Merchant's instructions further with Bundy and the President. (Kennedy Library, President's Appointment Book) According to Schaetzel, Bruce reported that the President was "still deeply worried about the multilateral force; primarily that the project might abort with subsequent discredit to the United States." Before the United States became too deeply committed, he wanted Merchant to visit Europe, and then return to Washington for a general review of the project. (Memorandum of a telephone conversation, February 26; Department of State, Central Files, Def(MLF).

[4] Printed from a copy that bears these typed initials.

176. Memorandum From President Kennedy to the Members of the MLF Negotiating Delegation

Washington, February 21, 1963.

MEMORANDUM FOR

Ambassador Livingston T. Merchant
The Honorable Gerard C. Smith
Rear Admiral J.M. Lee, USN

1. I instruct you, under the general direction of the Secretary of State, as a matter of urgency

(a) to investigate, through consultation within the NATO framework in Paris and in appropriate NATO capitals by direct discussion with interested governments, the possibility of an international arrangement along the lines set forth in the Steering Group report of February 7, 1963 (IND/P/7).[1]

(b) if two or more other governments display the necessary interest, to negotiate a Preliminary Agreement along the lines set forth in paragraph 14 of that paper.

2. You should be guided by the following additional considerations:

(a) You should pursue the line taken in U.S. presentations to the North Atlantic Council in 1962 which indicated the substantial advantages and therefore the clear U.S. preference for surface ships for an initial multilateral force, a preference confirmed by further studies in Washington.

(b) U.S. policy regarding the U.S. share of financing of the force and other relevant financial and hardware elements on which allied views are expressed will be reviewed in the light of your reports.

(c) The control of this force is a subject for final settlement in the Preparatory Commission—which is the stage at which countries will be called upon to put up sizeable funds. But obviously you will have to dis-

---

Source: Kennedy Library, National Security Files, MLF. Secret. No drafting information appears on the source text. An earlier draft of these instructions had been approved in principle at a meeting at the White House on February 13. (Memorandum IND/M/17, February 14; Department of State, Conference Files: Lot 66 D 110, CF 2218) Paragraphs 1–2b and 3–7 of the February 14 draft are the same as the source text; paragraphs 2c i–iv were not present in the draft. No other record of the meeting at the White House has been found.

[1] A copy of this 6-page paper, which outlined various aspects of an integrated seaborne Polaris force, is in Kennedy Library, National Security Files, MLF.

cuss this issue in general terms in exploring a preliminary agreement. In these conversations you should proceed as follows:

(i) You should offer the concept of a committee made up of at least the larger participants in the MLF, which would decide on firing by unanimity. It could act on other issues by less than unanimity.

(ii) You should not hesitate to press the concept of unanimity on the war issue as the tradition of NATO. You should argue our belief that no major participant will wish to abandon the right to approve a NATO decision for nuclear war, and you should emphasize that unanimity offers equal control to all major participants and does not simply perpetuate a U.S. monopoly. You should ask our friends to consider whether in fact they would ever wish to send off a NATO force if the strategic nuclear forces of the U.S. were being withheld.

(iii) You should seek to ascertain from our allies their views as to a desirable control formula. You should state that if our allies favor some system other than (i), we shall of course consider any alternatives they have in mind.

(iv) You should point out that any initial arrangements reached by the Preparatory Commission about control, as about other aspects of the force, could of course be re-examined and reopened as we all gain experience with the MLF. If our allies thus feel that they need not regard the initial control arrangement as immutable, they may be the more willing to settle on a unanimity control mechanism ad interim, since several years will elapse before the force takes to sea. Throughout this period, planning for the MLF will permit us to engage in serious and low key discussion with our allies about matters of strategy, targeting of nuclear forces, and similar issues, in the context of discussing the concrete problems of the MLF. If properly exploited, this opportunity may yield with time a consensus on strategic views and the interdependence of all nuclear and other allied forces, which will have a constructive effect on their attitudes toward the control issue.

3. In the interest of promoting NATO solidarity, you should seek maximum support within NATO in Paris for the concept of an MLF but seek to avoid procedural obstructions to rapid and effective progress, such as might be raised if formal NAC approval were sought for the opening of negotiations on a preliminary agreement.

4. During discussions in NATO you will assist Ambassador Finletter; on your bilateral discussions with governments you will keep him fully informed.

5. You should arrange to be kept continuously informed on negotiations arising from Paragraph 6 of the Nassau Agreement and on the development of policy decisions relating thereto in order to ensure that such negotiations are consistent with the effort to create an MLF as early as possible.

6. You should so conduct this mission as to avoid serious damage to U.S. prestige if our allies do not wish to proceed with an MLF.

7. You should keep me and as appropriate the Secretary of Defense currently informed of your progress by reports through the Secretary of State.

John F. Kennedy

---

177. Memorandum of Conversation

Washington, February 25, 1963, 5 p.m.

SUBJECT

Tour d'Horizon

PARTICIPANTS

Germans
Defense Minister Kai-Uwe von Hassel
Ambassador Karl Heinrich Knappstein
Minister-Director Franz Krapf, German Foreign Office
Mr. Horst Blomeyer-Bartenstein, German Embassy
Mr. Fruedenstein, Interpreter

Americans
The Secretary
Assistant Secretary William R. Tyler, EUR
Mr. Robert M. Brandin, EUR/GER

The Secretary opened the conversation by saying that we had been disturbed by events of the past month or so, but that our compass bearings were being clarified. We were distressed by our problems with de Gaulle. Keeping to defense questions for the moment, we were surprised by de Gaulle's January 14, 1963, press conference.[1] At Nassau we thought it important, after settling the Skybolt question, to get UK support for a multilateral force. If Europe wanted to be partners in this force, we were ready to cooperate. For over a year we had been asking for European views and were perhaps optimistic in expecting that the various European countries could agree on a proposal. Therefore, it

---

Source: Department of State, Central Files, Pol Ger-US. Confidential. Drafted by Brandin and approved in S on March 1.
[1] See Document 57.

seemed to us that the agreement with the UK was an important step. At Nassau it was also our intention to bring the French into the picture. We talked to de Gaulle and thought he would examine the Nassau Agreement in the light of France's own nuclear program, capabilities and requirements. In the meantime, we would have worked out our agreement with the British, which we have been trying to do this past week. It was our thought that on the basis of the agreement with the UK and the French study, we could then have talked with the French. These talks would not have been circumscribed in any way and we had hoped they would develop the relevance of the French nuclear program to the Nassau Agreement. As it has turned out, however, we know very little about the French program, in some ways less than we know about the Russian program, although NATO knows all about ours.

The Secretary went on to say that since the French had indicated they would study the Nassau Agreement and discuss it further, de Gaulle's press conference came as a shock. We had reason to believe this matter would not be settled without warning at a press conference. De Gaulle's action limited the possibilities even from the French point of view. We did not consider the conversations closed however. We were where we were before January 14, but it is more difficult to proceed now.

Minister von Hassel said the multilateral force had not been discussed in his meetings earlier in the day at the Pentagon, but it would be discussed during his trip to SAC the following day.[2] The discussions at the Pentagon concerned German military procurement in the US, cooperative logistics and cooperative R&D.

Minister von Hassel said State Secretary Carstens had informed the Secretary of the German position on the Franco-German Treaty. As regards de Gaulle's press conference, Germany was also caught by a surprise. The Chancellor attached the greatest importance to UK entry into the EEC. Prior to and during the Franco-German discussions in Paris, the Chancellor tried to influence de Gaulle regarding this matter.

Minister von Hassel emphasized that, as the Chancellor and he had said to Mr. Ball, who happened to be in Bonn on January 14,[3] Germany would fully support the multilateral force. Afterward in Paris de Gaulle said he fully understood the German attitude toward joining the multilateral force, although the French attitude differed. During the Paris talks de Gaulle also said he fully understood the German intention to give 100% support to NATO. The Germans made it clear they supported

---

[2] A memorandum of von Hassel's discussions with Secretary McNamara on the plane trips to and from Omaha is in Department of State, J/PM Files: Lot 69 D 258, McNamara/von Hassel.

[3] See Document 166.

the NATO strategy and political concepts and that these would be the guidelines of German policy. The Franco-German Treaty would be within the framework of the Alliance and could not be interpreted as affecting NATO or any other treaty commitment of Germany.

Minister von Hassel said the military part of the Franco-German Treaty covered four points. First, an effort would be made to reach as much common ground as possible on strategy and tactics. Second, there would be an exchange of officers, instructors, trainees and units up to the company level (the last for a week or so). Third, there would be joint development of weapons where this was appropriate. Fourth, there would be cooperation on civil defense.

Minister von Hassel acknowledged that the first point raised the question of whether France and Germany intended to develop their own separate strategy. The answer, as the Germans made clear to the French, is that the German strategic concept will continue to be based on NATO. As the map shows, however, there is a strategic relationship between Germany and France. France is essential to Germany as a rear area, particularly as concerns logistics. Germany is important to France as a forward area. For the first time France has now agreed (in writing) to support the forward defense strategy. France will move one division from Trier to Bavaria and will set down logistic support for a third division inside Germany as a basis for wartime deployment. Another French home division will be moved to Alsace. It is the German view that France now agrees to the concept of forward defense. This change in the French attitude can be attributed to the excellent relations between France and Germany.

Minister von Hassel then turned to the discussions with the French on joint R&D. The French originally proposed that all R&D be on a joint basis, but the Germans would agree only to joint R&D where appropriate. The agreements clearly reflect the German viewpoint. The Germans made it clear that the Franco-German Treaty could not disturb Germany's arrangements with the US and the UK on cooperative logistics and cooperative R&D. Consequently, there would be no sudden diversion of German military procurement from the US to France. The US would continue to be the main source of German foreign military procurement.

Minister von Hassel said Mr. Gilpatric had told him of meeting the Italian Prime Minister Fanfani who had said that all the laws and regulations now being drafted in the Common Market—e.g., common agricultural policy—would make UK entry more difficult. Minister von Hassel said he had discussed this with Hallstein who denied that this was the case. In fact, Hallstein maintained the reverse was true. Minister von Hassel said that in talking to de Gaulle he had made the point that he favored Franco-German reconciliation, but such reconciliation would have a solid basis only if the UK were in the Common Market. De Gaulle, however, thought the UK was not ripe for membership in the EEC. Nevertheless Germany would do everything to bring the UK into the EEC. Public opinion and all political parties in Germany favored this step.

Turning to the NATO nuclear force, Minister von Hassel said he was looking forward to meeting Mr. Merchant to see what could be done in creating this force and how Germany could contribute. From a political and military viewpoint, Germany supported the NATO nuclear force as a vital instrument of NATO policy. It was difficult to answer the question of whether France would eventually participate, but a start should be made. When the NATO nuclear force was in being perhaps France would reconsider its attitude, particularly when it saw that there was genuine sharing. De Gaulle was clearly worried about a US-Soviet deal at European expense. The creation of a NATO nuclear force might help dispel this fear.

Minister von Hassel then assured the Secretary that Germany would not do anything to help France develop its own independent nuclear force. This had not been discussed with the French. They were going ahead on their own initiative.

The Secretary said he would like to make a few remarks preparatory to Minister von Hassel's meeting with the President.[4] Concerning our reaction to the Franco-German Treaty, Germany should be aware that Franco-German reconciliation had been an objective of US policy for 17 years. To illustrate the problem in our mind, however, we knew what the German attitude was on the larger issues at stake because we had been in close touch with each other. We did not know what de Gaulle had in his mind; nor did his own Ministers apparently. In this marriage of a known and unknown therefore, we wondered what the children would look like. During 1947–1949 the US made the basic decision that its own defense required concerting US and European defense. US troops in Europe were not there as tourists or as a gesture to Europeans; they were there because it was basic to our own defense and the defense of US and Europe together. It was our impression, however, that de Gaulle intended to participate less and less in NATO. This raised the question of what was in his mind. We had the impression that he made a distinction between the Atlantic Alliance, which he supported, and NATO, about which he had reservations. His reservations about NATO might have something to do with its organization. The French had proposed establishing a tripartite directorate in NATO, which the

---

[4] A memorandum of von Hassel's conversation with the President on NATO strategy is in Department of State, Central Files, Def 4 NATO; a memorandum of their conversation on the Nassau Agreement is ibid., Def 12 NATO.

US had refused in deference to Germany and others. The French had also made some references in Paris to the reorganization of NATO, but had said nothing positive. The central point in our mind was that the US and German lines of policies on defense were clear, but we did not know about the French line.

The Secretary pointed out that if things were said from across the Atlantic which gave the impression that the US was no longer needed in Europe, the instinctive reaction of the American people would be to bring our troops home. This was not yet a serious problem, but it could be one. For this reason, the strong reaction of the Five at Brussels was very important.

Turning to the multilateral force, the Secretary said we had noted Paris press stories discounting the Merchant Mission. The fact was, however, that the US has moved from a position of neutrality on this matter. After Nassau we considered we had an obligation to try to develop such a force. We did not intend to be dogmatic and we recognized the necessity of consultation to give Germany and others a chance to express their views. The multilateral force in our opinion could strengthen the Alliance. It would also convey the right signals to Moscow. There was a danger that the wrong signals were being received in Moscow since January 14. There was no real difference in the West regarding the USSR, but the Soviets might get the wrong idea. If a genuine opportunity opened up for discussions with de Gaulle on the multilateral force, we would not reject it. It seemed to be difficult to establish contact however.

The Secretary then asked Minister von Hassel if the Germans thought there was any difference in the French mind between the Atlantic Alliance and NATO.

Minister-Director Krapf said the Foreign Office had never thought about this and he wondered how the two could be regarded as separate.

Mr. Tyler said de Gaulle was opposed to political integration because it diluted sovereignty and to military integration because it diluted the patriotic spirit. Hence, he might be opposed to NATO as a sort of military equivalent of the UN in which national identity was lost. His effort to establish tripartism in NATO was not successful. He did not like the integration aspects of the NATO multilateral force. Although the French had recently been stressing cooperation between Europe and the US and their loyalty to the Alliance, they said nothing about NATO.

Minister-Director Krapf observed that the French seemed to be taking a similar attitude in the European community toward political integration.

Minister von Hassel said de Gaulle had a problem of restoring the morale of French troops and modernizing the French Army. The French

Army in fact had to be rebuilt. This would only be possible by stimulating patriotism. De Gaulle realized Europe would be lost if left alone by the US, but he feared a US-Soviet deal at Europe's expense and wanted to take measures to offset it.

The Secretary said it was important to the Alliance that we try to banish a number of historical ghosts, such as de Gaulle's fear of US-Soviet deal, the US fear of a European third force, Germany's fear of a Franco-Soviet deal, etc. Ghosts could be manufactured at will, but if we all made clear our commitments, they would not materialize.

With respect to negotiations with the USSR, the Secretary said we did not see any basis for any agreement at this time. There was no indication that the USSR was ready to recognize our vital interest in Berlin; the prospects for an agreement on nuclear testing were gloomy; there were difficulties in Laos because the Pathet Lao was not performing as it should; there was no significant movement in the disarmament field; and Cuba would remain a major issue as long as there was a single Soviet soldier there.

The Secretary observed that whenever the Soviet pressure rose, quarrels seemed to break out in the West.

The meeting concluded with Minister von Hassel referring to his forthcoming trip to SAC in Omaha. The Secretary took the occasion to note that there had been a massive increase in nuclear deployment in Europe since 1961. Minister von Hassel responded that this information had been given to the Germans by the Defense Department.

---

178.   Memorandum for the Record

Washington, February 28, 1963.

SUBJECT

Joint Chiefs of Staff Meeting with the President, February 28, 1963—Force Strengths in Europe

The President pointed out to the Joint Chiefs that we must now examine the question of "how much we can reduce our forces in Europe in the next twelve months."

The President stated that by the time we have the NATO meeting in Ottawa in May we must have some specific plan in this regard. He feels

---

Source: Kennedy Library, National Security Files, Clifton Series, JCS/Kennedy. Top Secret.

that it is incongruous for us to be planning on ninety days of conventional warfare in Europe when the other allies have such varied capabilities of four to thirty days. He mentioned that Secretary McNamara is working on a reduction of the "backup." He mentioned that the French, acting up as they are, and Lord Mountbatten's promotion of a "plate glass" concept, it did look like an appropriate time for us to reconsider our position. Fundamentally, the question is this: If no one else is going to do it, why should we? The President feels that May would be a likely time for us to face our allies with our decisions on the matter.

General Wheeler pointed out some of the dangers inherent in a heavy reduction of forces. We might entice the Russians to take a venture like Cuba. They might be tempted to seize Hamburg or Munich. This is the hostage city concept. There was conceivable discussion about the doubt of the Europeans of our will and determination to defend Europe, and that if they seized a city like Hamburg or Munich, a doubt that we would ever use nuclear weapons to force the Soviet Union back.

The President pointed out to the Joint Chiefs that there was also a great danger of doubt in the Soviet Union about whether or not we would use nuclear weapons and that it would be unlikely that the Soviet Union, with this doubt in their minds, would take up a venture such as the seizure of a city in Western Germany. The President expressed in no uncertain terms that de Gaulle has money and not much else on his side and that it is absolutely essential for us to protect our monetary position. Otherwise, we might be so poor that we would have to withdraw everywhere, not just reduce our forces in Europe. He challenged the Joint Chiefs to think in terms of using our military strength to get an economic adjustment that, in the long run, would protect our interests vis-à-vis our allies. The President stated that as far as he could see right now, Europe was probably about eighth on our list of dangers. The President assured the Joint Chiefs that we should do more than they do in Europe, but not so much more as we are doing now.

General Taylor said that this was the area to explore. One point is that we are giving a great deal of direct support to the allies for which we do not charge them. We furnish manpower and money to pipelines and other support operations which have grown up over the years when they desperately needed it, and it is time to examine this area to see how much money we could get from them. The President pointed out that we lose money via tourists, a factor which is almost impossible to control. We lose via investments and these we are doing something about. This leaves us only the military as our major expenditure in Europe. Eventually we will have to confront them with the fact that either they must pay or we will have to cut back.

Strategically, the President said that the Joint Chiefs are faced with this problem: if others aren't going to do their conventional tasks, we should examine our own to see that it makes sense. He stated that he felt that we were caught by habit in Europe in our thinking of our support and force levels. He directed the Joint Chiefs to think of this problem in terms of the funds available to us vis-à-vis our really pressing dangers. He pointed out to them his own grave doubt that our most pressing dangers are now in Europe. He gave as an example the danger of the Chinese Communists taking India and the whole subcontinent of Asia while all our money was being directed toward the support of Europe and a conventional war, which would more than likely not occur.

Except for the specific decision on the Berlin garrison, the President gave them no other guidelines but left the clear impression that the Joint Chiefs were to come up with a reappraisal of the conventional force structure in Europe, including our own, in time for specific government proposals for the NATO meeting in Ottawa in May.

C.V. Clifton[1]

---

[1] Printed from a copy that bears this typed signature.

---

179.   Memorandum of Conversation

Washington, March 6, 1963, noon.

SUBJECT

NATO Matters

PARTICIPANTS

The President
Mr. Stikker, Secretary-General of NATO
Elbridge Durbrow, U.S. Representative to NAC
George S. Vest, Staff Aide
J. Robert Schaetzel, Deputy Assistant Secretary for Atlantic Affairs

The President welcomed the Secretary General and asked him to comment on some of the major problems which the Alliance would face in the next 12 months.

Source: Department of State, Central Files, Def 4 NATO. Secret. Drafted by Schaetzel and approved by the White House on March 19. The meeting was held at the White House. For Stikker's account of the conversation, see *Men of Responsibility*, pp. 375–377. Memoranda of his conversation on NATO questions with Tyler on March 4 and with Rusk and Rostow on March 5 are in Department of State, Central Files, Def 4 NATO; a memorandum of his conversation with Hillenbrand on Berlin on March 5 is ibid., NATO 8–3. Memoranda of his conversations on NATO military matters with McNamara on March 7 and Rusk on March 8 are ibid., Def 12 NATO.

The Secretary General said that as a result of Brussels there was an evident need to make progress. He himself had not favored the rather vindictive position taken by Spaak and did not believe there should be a slowdown in the Common Market. He thought we should keep in mind the possibilities in GATT and also the fact that there will be an opportunity for the other five members of the Common Market to make progress in 1965 in the field of outside tariffs. The key thing was to go on with whatever progress was possible.

In the field of political consultation NATO had just had an excellent presentation by Assistant Secretary Martin on the Latin American situation and it would be useful to have further exchanges. He had talked to Mr. Rostow about some of Rostow's ideas as to how political consultation could be improved; he was worried about any development which would not maintain the Council as the center of things and so he would not want to move fast along some of the lines advocated by Mr. Rostow.

In the field of defense, as Secretary General, he had to keep in mind the whole picture of NATO's defense needs, which included the Interallied Force, the Mixed-Manned Force and conventional forces. He had to keep in mind how the available funds might be divided, because after all Finance Ministers would look at it just that way.

As for the Nassau communiqué, he urged that the US should cooperate in moving ahead with para. 6 or the Interallied Force just as rapidly as with the para. 8 or Multilateral or Mixed-Manned Force. As they knew, he had always favored the MLF. It was needed to meet the needs of an evolving Europe and particularly of Germany and Italy. Countries like these two needed to be included in the nuclear world and at the moment they, as well as a number of other European countries, did not have sufficient knowledge of nuclear facts and nuclear planning. To the extent that there was ignorance or dissatisfaction in these countries, de Gaulle could play on nationalism. Nationalism was always latent in France, but now it was blatant. Frenchmen who used to discuss subjects objectively were now falling into line solidly behind de Gaulle positions; he regretted that it reminded him of similar episodes which he could recall in the early Hitler days in Germany.

The President noted that after years of difficulty France was finally back in the world of power and prosperity, but de Gaulle's focus is entirely on France and not on Europe. He talks about the French nuclear force, not a European force; and if you followed de Gaulle's reasoning to its logical end, we would come to a situation where each country would want its own national deterrent, with all the dangers which this entails for Europe as a whole. He suggested that de Gaulle was not offering Europe very much.

The Secretary General said that in talking to de Gaulle he once asked him: if you had the bomb, could you assure me that you would use it for the rest of Europe. De Gaulle had replied No.

The French were going to go on being difficult, he thought, but there was an area in which the other members of WEU could exert some pressure; namely, under the Brussels Treaty the level of atomic stocks that any one of the partners can hold on the mainland of Europe has to be decided by a majority vote of the WEU Council. This was something to keep in mind, especially since what France did in the field could have its repercussions on later developments in Germany.

On the subject of Germany he thought that the West had been fortunate in the emergence of Schroeder and von Hassel, the latter, although new, seemed to be a good man too.

The President commented that von Hassel had made an excellent impression on his recent visit to Washington.

The President asked how the Merchant presentation had gone. Mr. Stikker said it had been a good one; it began in a quiet vein and this was the right way to start.[1] The President said that the US hoped to begin with the Mixed-Manned Force. This naturally had its limitations initially, but it still had the potential to grow into a European deterrent in due course, but it could not start on this basis. One could not now, for instance, answer the question, "Who decides for Europe?". The President suggested that the first objective was to get the force at sea as an important symbolic move.

The Secretary General agreed, but said that it might take some time to get this force organized and in the meantime there were other things that could be done right away, such as the Interallied Force. The President asked what it was that could be done right away.

The Secretary General explained that there were three components of the Interallied Force which derived from para. 6 of the Nassau communiqué:

1. Pretargeted tactical weapons,
2. U.K. Bomber Command and the U.S. equivalent,
3. U.S. Polaris subs replacing Jupiters.

The first two elements existed at the moment and so it should be possible to move ahead rapidly in organizing them into an existing force. In doing so it would not be necessary to give too many rights or to introduce changes of command, but at least the work could begin.

On the MLF he thought he could predict the European response along the following lines: Cooperation and financial contribution from

---

[1] Reports on Merchant's presentation to the North Atlantic Council on February 27 were transmitted in Poltos 1067 and 1068, February 28, ibid., Pol 7 US/Merchant.

Germany and Italy; some money and a base from the Netherlands; interest but little money from Belgium; and finally possibly something from the Canadians. He believed the Canadian attitude was definitely changing and had heard indirectly, from recent conversations in London, that Diefenbaker and Churchill were looking into the possibility of nuclear arms for the 8 squadrons of F104–G's which were based in Europe for NATO. If this first step were taken, he then thought the second and third would follow for NORAD and perhaps MLF.

The President interjected that the US would have to be very careful not to step in in any way during this preelection period.

The Secretary General thought that it was a poor idea to stress the rule of unanimity to a Mixed-Manned Force. [*1-1/2 lines of source text not declassified*] For his part, he hoped that the members of the force would be willing to delegate the responsibilities for its use to four people, the US President, the Prime Minister of the UK, the Prime Minister of Italy and the Chancellor of Germany. There was some chance that this idea might be accepted.

The President asked if the group would decide on the basis of unanimity?

The Secretary General continued his explanation that, although he could see some cause for worry about other governments in the future, he was not worried about the US 10 years hence. The US, he thought, would not refuse if the European allies asked that the force be used because if it did so, the European countries would rush to Moscow. It was possible that there could be developed slowly an acceptance of the idea of a system of weighted voting. This would ease US Congressional attitudes; the practical result would be that no one European country would initiate the use of the force or could veto its use when it was needed. Once the European officials and authorities were more familiar with all aspects of the nuclear world, such a system might be acceptable. However, the nuclear secrecy of the US, while understandable, had been a major cause for the malaise in the European partners of the Alliance. This was of course notably true of the French, but in other capitals as well he encountered from time to time the complaint of chiefs of staff and other officials that they did not know what their own forces were to do in case of war.

[*1 paragraph (6 lines of source text) not declassified*]

The President suggested that the United States saying "no" was not the problem of control. In any event he said he wanted to wait until Ambassador Merchant returned from Europe and review the situation in light of his report. He also said he did not want to take up the difficult questions that must be resolved with the Congress until the general situation was clearer.

President Kennedy asked what would have happened if the US had assisted de Gaulle a few years ago in his nuclear program. The Secretary General said that if de Gaulle had had atomic weapons it would have made no difference; he would not have been more helpful in NATO. He would have wanted the veto for himself but he would not have wanted anyone else to have it. His motivation is French nationalism pure and simple.

President Kennedy said that the debates in the atomic area are rather like arguments in a rich man's club; while we discussed nuclear sharing, the rest of the world stood around hungry and waiting. There was an enormous aid job to be done and the US would like to coordinate aid activities among the members of this club. The Secretary General pointed out that it had to be recognized that France was doing a very large job in the aid field although in a specialized area. The President agreed but said that it was very difficult to coordinate anything with the French. While on the subject of French expenditures, the Secretary General noted that France has had to reorganize its army, which takes time and money; officers have had to be shifted and it is a difficult and expensive undertaking.

The President explained that, after talking to Admiral Rickover, he had concluded that the Polaris submarine as contrasted with reactor technology was so advanced in relation to the Soviets, that it might well have raised excessive problems with Congress to make it the base for the Mixed-Manned Force. He described the virtues of a Polaris surface force with considerable enthusiasm: The surface ship was safer mechanically. There were less US problems politically with Congress since the Polaris sub is an extraordinarily vital development for US security. The surface force was not vulnerable as was evidenced by the 2-1/2 days the US spent searching for the *Santa Maria* in friendly waters.[2] It could be more rapidly produced than submarines and could be built in Europe. Mixed-manning would be simpler, and physical command and communication would be easier.

The Secretary General said that he had received a good briefing from Admiral Ricketts the day before and found it even more convincing than he had expected.

The President observed that the Polaris MLF would be linked with the external US nuclear force. The Soviets would not strike at the MLF alone since it would be 40% US manned and the US would certainly be immediately involved. Hence the MLF would be an essential additional element to the indivisible defense for the West; and if the Soviets touched it, it would thus initiate general war.

---

[2] See footnote 2, Document 342.

The President asked Dr. Stikker for his reaction to General Norstad's suggestions regarding a control body. The Secretary-General replied that triumvirate control would not work and went on to refine his own thoughts somewhat. He explained that Belgium had indicated, for example, that it might be willing to allow a smaller executive group to decide the use of the force by simple majority. In such a case he thought the Dutch would follow suit and thereafter it would be most unlikely that the Greeks and Turks could ask for a better status since, if they participated, they would do so chiefly on the basis of outside financial assistance. Canada, which was beginning to show some interest, would, he thought, follow the same path. The result was, he thought, a fair chance that the members of the Mixed-Manned Force might agree to delegate authority to the US, UK, Germany and Italy. In that connection he agreed with the thought advanced by General Norstad that the Secretary General should be included but without a vote.

The President commented that there was a widespread myth in America that there was a single entity called Europe and de Gaulle spoke for it. The Secretary General said that this was totally wrong of course. Europe would not accept such a situation. The President said perhaps this was a point which would emerge when the Secretary General spoke to the press. He thought that it was an excellent idea that a distinguished European would be in a position to set the record straight.

President Kennedy said that the US was watching carefully the evolution of trade negotiations between the US and Europe. If the US was not able to maintain markets there, if it should be locked out of Europe or if it was not earning as much as it now does, then the US would certainly have to do something about it, perhaps a withdrawal of some sort from Europe or a cut in activities in India and elsewhere, actions which were really contrary to the national interest. He hoped there was some comprehension of these considerations in Europe.

The President went on to say that it would be helpful if the Secretary-General could, in the course of his public statements, say a "few kind words" about the multilateral force. He observed that splitting the atom politically was more difficult than physically.

The Secretary General concluded with a final emphatic plea that the US not hold back in moving forward on all aspects of the Nassau communiqué where possible.

180.   Memorandum From the President's Special Assistant for National Security Affairs (Bundy) to Secretary of State Rusk and Secretary of Defense McNamara

Washington, March 11, 1963.

It may be useful if I circulate this brief summary of the conclusions reached in the meeting with the President on Saturday, March 9, at noon.[1]

1. It was agreed that the United States will give energetic support to the Paragraph 6 forces, along the lines of the agreed and approved guidelines worked out after the Tyler–Greenhill discussions.[2] In particular, it is the object of the United States Government to reach announced agreement on the institution of the Paragraph 6 forces not later than the Ottawa meeting in May. The State Department will retain coordinating responsibility for this effort, while the Defense Department will undertake the direct task of negotiating these new military arrangements, involving, as they do, intense discussions with SHAPE and with Defense officials in other countries.

2. The further assessment of the multilateral force and its prospects must await the return of Ambassador Merchant, but the President has reaffirmed the definite preference of the U.S. Government for surface vessels as against nuclear submarines. It was agreed that an intensive effort should be made to bring to the attention of our allies the professional judgment of outstanding military men of several countries that in the case of a mixed manned force, surface vessels are strongly preferable. It was further agreed, subject to any difficulty that might be discovered in further study by the officers directly charged with the enterprise, that we should arrange for an extensive program of visits to Washington by well-qualified defense and military officials of NATO countries, so that the case for the surface force can be fully presented on the widest possible base here. We do not wish to use a flying squadron, like the Merchant mission, in this case if it can be avoided.

McGeorge Bundy

Source: Department of State, Central Files, Def(MLF) 3. Top Secret.

[1] No other record of this meeting has been found.

[2] Records of Tyler's meetings with Denis Greenhill of the British Embassy, February 18–21, concerning the implementation of paragraph 6 of the Nassau Agreement are in Department of State, Central Files, Pol US-UK.

181. Memorandum for the Record

Washington, March 14, 1963, 5 p.m.

SUBJECT

Minutes of the Meeting with the President, March 13, 5:00 P.M., on NATO
Nuclear Forces

PRESENT

The President, Secretary of State, Under Secretary of State, Mr. William Tyler,
Mr. Jeffrey Kitchen; Secretary of Defense, Deputy Secretary of Defense,
Chairman, Joint Chiefs of Staff, Mr. Paul Nitze; Mr. McGeorge Bundy, Mr. Carl
Kaysen

The meeting was devoted to further consideration of what should
be done about the paragraph 6 forces pursuant to the discussion between the President, the Secretary of State and the Secretary of Defense
on March 9.[1] Three documents were before the group: Memorandum,
Nitze to Bundy, March 12; Memorandum, Kitchen to Bundy, March 13;
and Merchant's views of paragraph 6 forces, as registered in London
3534 of March 13.[2]

The meeting opened with a statement of the problem by the President: What should we do to get the paragraph 6 forces under way and
make what we could of this part of our post-Nassau plans. Messrs.
McNamara and Nitze stated that our objective should be to get the military command structure under SACEUR for the paragraph 6 forces organized and agreed in time to be certified at the Ottawa meeting in May.
In addition, we should explore the question of the political control
group which would direct the use of these forces.

Mr. Kitchen raised some questions about how this letter could be
done without suggesting to the Europeans that we were once again
changing our direction, and that we had given up our interest in the
multilateral force in favor of the paragraph 6 forces. Further, the paragraph 6 forces imposed no price of admission comparable to that required for the MLF and was therefore a most unsuitable basis on which
to deal with the control issue. This view was endorsed and reinforced by
Mr. Ball. Mr. Ball cited Merchant's report as evidence that our concept of

---

Source: Kennedy Library, National Security Files, Meetings with the President. Secret.

[1] For a summary of the conclusions reached at this meeting, see Document 180.

[2] Bundy's 4-page memorandum discussed what the United States could make out of
paragraph 6; while Kitchen's memorandum stated that the question was not "what" but
"when" should the United States act. (Department of State, S/S–NSC Files: Lot 70 D 265,
NSC 3/13/63) In telegram 3534 Merchant expressed his concern that discussion of paragraph 6 forces could adversely affect negotiations on political control of the MLF. (Department of State, Central Files, Def(MLF))

the MLF was meeting considerable favor in Europe, and that it would be dangerous to do anything which would signal another change in direction. Secretary McNamara argued the advantages of getting something done and indicated his view that the military command structure alone offered very little in the way of additional substance to the Europeans beyond what they already had, unless we discussed the political control issue.

The President expressed a desire that we put ourselves in a position to make as much of the paragraph 6 forces as possible, in the event our proposal for a MLF was not acceptable to the Europeans. In his own view our present proposal on the MLF, in which we continued to require unanimity on the political decision, as we should, and in which we offered merchant ships instead of submarines, did not represent anything very attractive to the Europeans.

Secretary Rusk argued the importance of careful timing on the whole process of decision. In his view, the right thing to do *now* was to stop at the discussion of the military command structure, leaving the political issue until later. In two or three weeks, we would have Merchant's assessment of what could be done on the MLF and, accordingly, we should defer any consideration of the political control issue until we had Merchant's judgment on how successful our efforts to create the MLF were likely to be. The President agreed that we should follow the course that Secretary of State recommended, and asked him to sum up his view of what Mr. Nitze should do now. The Secretary said that in effect Nitze should *talk* about the first question, the military command structure, and *listen* to what others had to say on the second, the political control issue. In response to observations of Secretary McNamara and General Taylor, the Secretary agreed that Nitze should not say anything that would stop us from coming back to a discussion of political control, based on the paragraph 6 forces, if in two or three weeks we judged that that was desirable in view of the prospects of the MLF as seen then.

Mr. Nitze then summarized his own understanding as follows:

a. He would negotiate on the military command structure for the paragraph 6 forces on the assumption that there would be a European four-star general as commander or chief staff officer of the NATO Nuclear Force under SACEUR.
b. He would not raise the issue of the political control of the nuclear commander, but he would be receptive to what was said on it, especially to what was said in response to the British, who would undoubtedly raise the issue.
c. He would so conduct his discussions that we would not be barred from coming back to the question of political control.
d. He would meet with the NATO Nuclear Committee and explain what we were proposing in terms of paragraph 6 forces and how this related to the problem of further transmission of information to NAC.

The President closed the meeting by remarking that the Secretary of State had two or three weeks to sell his MLF proposal.

CK

182. Telegram From the Department of State to the Embassy in the United Kingdom

Washington, March 14, 1963, 5:59 p.m.

4851. For the Ambassador from the Under Secretary. Paris for Ambassadors Finletter and Merchant; Bonn for Chargé. I note in your 3510[1] that Macmillan stated inter alia that he regards the Nassau Agreement "as a whole and stood by it entirely."

Against that background, this may be an appropriate moment to try to put the nuclear issue in its widest context and especially its relationship to broad European and Atlantic developments in discussions with UK in aftermath of Merchant mission.

Reports from Merchant supplemented by Chayes suggest Merchant's team made gratifying progress in Bonn and also in Italy. We appear to be farther along in getting a firm footing with the Germans than we might reasonably have hoped a month ago.

This raises question as to UK role. Not only would the political impact of the Multilateral Force be enhanced, but course of European and Atlantic development might be given a new lift if Macmillan Government could be persuaded to take more enthusiastic position on MLF.

As your own analysis here in Washington so clearly indicated, the key to constructive developments in Europe and to an effective mutually supporting European-US relationship is Germany. If ultimate UK entry into Europe is to be possible, German leadership to this end within the Community is essential. Moreover, whether Europe proceeds in the pattern of the last ten years, or moves toward autarky and the third

---

Source: Department of State, Central Files, Pol US-UK. Secret; Priority. Drafted by Schaetzel and Ball; cleared with Tyler, Kitchen, Furnas, Owen, Popper, and BNA; and approved and initialed by Ball. Repeated to Paris and Bonn.

[1] Telegram 3510, March 12, reported that Bruce, Finletter, and Merchant had spent a half hour with Macmillan at the latter's invitation discussing Nassau and the MLF. (Ibid., Def 12 NATO)

force delusion, will depend on the German role and the ability of the Five to work pragmatically with Britain.

The danger of the present situation is that the stiff-upper-lip mien of the British in the aftermath of January is less a policy than a respectable diplomatic reaction. For the sake of Europe as well as Britain, I think it would be useful for the British Government to take positive steps that will line them up solidly with the FRG and give the lie to de Gaulle's contention that they are not genuinely European. Just as Schroeder and von Hassel are committing themselves to the MLF so there is an opportunity for Britain to commit itself to the "new Germans." And, as you will have learned from Livie, this is exactly what von Hassel hopes to persuade them to do, by committing themselves on a substantial scale to MLF. This could be venture that brings British and Germans closer together. It could lead to close and mutually beneficial relation between Germany and Britain devoted to building new Europe and stronger Atlantic partnership which was so well begun by Schroeder when he led the Five in support of British entry on January 28 and 29.

Great advantage of substantial UK MLF participation is that it would put UK at heart of a venture in which it would be participating on terms of equality with continental countries; para 6 implementation is necessary and useful but, by itself, probably insufficient. If British preclude UK role in genuine nuclear sharing with Germany and Italy, they may well end by isolating themselves further from Europe and Germany. A more open-handed British support of the MLF, on the other hand, could provide an outlet for the talent and experience of the British in naval and nuclear affairs.

I fear that, if the Macmillan Government cannot be brought to see these larger issues of UK's relation to the continent, the natural evolution of events may conspire to damage British basic interests and position in the world. They cannot profitably re-establish policy on classical balance of European power, playing with pragmatic bilateral political and economic arrangements while hoping that somehow European developments will work in their favor. And a continued sense of drift and lack of purpose could encourage Little Englanders and niggling and sterile anti-Gaullism.

I recognize British have conditioned reflex against mixed manning. But this is not instinct to be encouraged. In fact, attitude it reflects may well be the principal cause of British post-war failure to understand significance of forces at work in Europe. I have no specific suggestions as to any action to be taken but have set forth the foregoing thoughts in the hope you may find them useful to draw on in your conversations with key members British Government during critical next few days and weeks.

Rusk

183. Memorandum From the Head of the MLF Negotiating Delegation (Merchant) to Secretary of State Rusk

Washington, March 20, 1963.

This memorandum is intended to provide a summary of my visit, together with Gerard Smith and Admiral Lee and other members of the Team to Paris–Rome–Brussels–Bonn–London–Paris between February 22 and March 17. It will be supplemented by more detailed reports and recommendations.

I return encouraged over the prospects for an MLF, of a character which is sufficiently responsive to certain of our European allies' desires and at the same time acceptable to the United States. A substantial element of the leadership of important members of the Alliance wants an MLF—and any doubts on this score in the United States should be set at rest. If the United States does not move with this European pro-MLF drive, Gaullist forces will be encouraged and Atlantic Community hopes set back.

In response to pressing invitations, we have scheduled visits beginning early in April to The Hague, Athens and Ankara. I think it is important to accept their invitations. We may well encounter serious interest on the part of one or more. None of these countries, however, in my judgment is crucial to the establishment of an MLF and none is in a position, with the possible exception of The Netherlands, to make any significant contribution of resources. Therefore, the next round of capital visits should not be the cause for any delay in the United States Government reaching a definitive position re MLF.

On this second trip it will probably be desirable to return to one or more capitals covered in the first circuit, as well as stopping in Paris to reassure NAC that it is being kept abreast of significant developments. In this connection, Stikker now appears to be an outspoken advocate for the MLF, although he has serious reservations concerning several aspects of our concept. If he can be kept in this constructive frame of mind, to which his Washington visit contributed so much, he will be a valuable ally.

As you know from reporting telegrams, I made clear that we were on an exploratory mission to ascertain whether the basis for the negotiation of an agreement existed. In every capital I emphasized that, as a re-

---

Source: Department of State, Central Files, Pol 7 US/Merchant. Secret. Initialed by Merchant. In a March 20 covering memorandum, which indicates that Secretary Rusk saw it, Merchant suggested a limited distribution within the State Department and "strongly recommended" that a copy be sent to McGeorge Bundy, a recommendation that was approved by Rusk.

sult of our deepened and intensified studies in recent months, we had reached certain conclusions which we desired to share with our allies and exchange views.

Certain aspects of our concept gained ready acceptance by all. Among these were that an MLF would be managed and controlled by its owners, assigned to NATO and fitted appropriately into the NATO military command structure. Another was that an MLF should be created by Charter or Treaty, in a form suitable for ratification by governments, in accord with constitutional requirements, and that it should be open for later adherence by all NATO members prepared similarly to accept its obligations and responsibilities and contribute a fair proportionate contribution to the enterprise. No single member should contribute more than 40 per cent to the total cost of creating and operating the fleet. An administrative organization, with an Executive, would need to be established to handle budgetary, administrative and similar matters.

The concept of mixed-manning was generally accepted and there was general agreement on its practicability, particularly in surface ships. There was also general acceptance that the MLF should not be created at the expense of conventional forces.

Crucial Elements in Our Concept

Three elements in our concept which are crucial and still not fully acceptable abroad:

1. The Force should be a surface force;
2. Whereas many administrative decisions might be taken by a vote less than unanimous, the vital decision to grant political authority to use the nuclear weapons of the Force should be taken by unanimity of the principal owners in a political committee representing all the owners; and
3. Specific shares of the cost of creating the fleet, with its necessary supporting establishments, and the recurrent expenses of operating and maintaining it, including possible later modernization.

On costs, we used the round figure of $500 million a year over a ten-year period, pointing out (in considerable detail) that this figure was incomplete in that it did not take into account past R&D (which would run in the neighborhood of half a billion dollars) or modernization costs. The latter would be designed to take later advantage of developments in the art of missilery and similar future developments in technology. This item of modernization, I said, might amount to something like $1 billion over the ten-year period, with the bulk of such expenditures naturally coming toward the end of the period. I pointed out such additional capital investments would be the subject of future decisions of the owners. Past R&D we would want to discuss in more detail but I said I thought we would be disposed to be generous in the treatment of this item when it came to costing.

On the question of cost sharing, I spoke at all times of a U.S. contribution of the order of one-third. I think some made an unwarranted reference that we might be prepared to go to 40 percent. In Bonn, I made clear that I would expect the Germans to match our contribution. In Rome, I talked in terms of Italy taking on 15–20 per cent. With Spaak I spoke of a Belgian contribution of the order of 5 per cent. In London, I talked of a British contribution of 5 to 10 percent.

The Nature of a Preliminary Agreement

I am convinced that before we enter a Preparatory Commission or Conference to draft the Treaty, the participants in such a body must have reached specific advance agreement on the following key elements, in addition to an agreed declaration of intent to proceed with the creation of an MLF:

1. A mixed-manned surface fleet of X ships and Y missiles to be assigned to NATO and appropriately fitted into the NATO command structure;
2. The Force should be created at no prejudice to the conventional buildup in NATO;
3. The political decision to authorize the use of the weapons would be made in a committee of the owners (on which all major owners would sit), voting by unanimity of major owners or some other specific formula which would safeguard our interests;
4. A specific agreement on the percentage of the total cost which each participant would bear, with the total amounting to 100 per cent; and
5. Some provision authorizing detailed multilateral planning and possibly other preliminary steps in advance of the Treaty coming into force.

I think it would be foolhardy to enter a Preparatory Commission unless prior agreement had been reached on these key points. It is possible that further examination will indicate other points or elements which should be similarly covered in the Preliminary Agreement.

Reaction by Countries

Italy

Fanfani expressed great surprise at our stated strong preference for surface ships. He claimed that he had presented the MLF to the Cabinet and to the Parliament as a concept which Italy supported on the assumption that it would be composed of submarines. How much of this was bargaining, how much due to prior exchanges with the Germans, how much to the fact that the *Garibaldi* is a political liability and also a surface ship, and how much due to a desire to find a justification (during the election period in which the Government is paralyzed) for stringing out technical talks is hard to say. I do doubt, however, that his surprise was entirely genuine, and I suspect in some degree all of the reasons I have cited played a part. Compared to this issue, the other elements of our concept as presented did not seem to give great difficulty to the Italians who appear to be prepared to support the MLF with substantial resources.[1]

Belgium

I saw only Spaak (with de Staercke) in Brussels and found him somewhat preoccupied with domestic political problems related to the MLF but still full of enthusiasm for it. He did raise the serious point of the Belgian Government's belief that something had to be done to make their conventional forces combat worthy and that it was hard to see how funds could be found for an MLF over and beyond those needed for improving their conventional forces. I think Belgium will continue to give loud vocal support to the MLF without commitment. However, if an MLF is in certain process of creation with the US, Germany and the UK among its founding membership, I believe Belgium will scramble aboard the bandwagon.[2]

Germany

Our discussions in Bonn were in greater depth than in any place else and, on the whole, quite satisfactory. The Germans are strongly pro-submarine but I think it is significant that von Hassel, during the course of our visit, took public credit for having originally suggested the surface ship. Unanimous political control by the major owners is the other point which gives them difficulty. I believe they genuinely fear the risk in years to come of a leftist or neutralist government in one or two other countries which would be members of the MLF. Privately, they spoke of both Italy and the UK in this connection. The Germans do not want to contemplate the Force being paralyzed for use in the supreme crisis by one weak member. The control issue I think can be worked out with them but it is a real problem in their eyes. On all the other points in our concept, I think they are all right. They give clear evidence of willingness to match any US share in the cost of the MLF.[3]

United Kingdom

The attitude of the British in the first meeting was decidedly tepid. Lord Home's first reference to it was in terms of "the UK not necessarily being opposed in principal to the MLF". Later in the day Macmillan was more forthcoming but showed an alarming sensitivity to the possible ef-

---

[1] Merchant reported on his meeting with Fanfani in telegram 1752 from Rome, March 3. (Ibid.)

[2] Merchant reported on his discussion with Spaak in telegram 1350 from Brussels, March 6. (Ibid., Def(MLF) 3)

[3] Merchant reported on his discussions with Adenauer and von Hassel in Bonn in telegrams 2293 from Bonn, March 6 (ibid., Pol 7 US/Merchant), and 3471 from London, March 9 (ibid., Def(MLF) 3).

fect on innocent merchant shipping coming into British ports in a crisis (such as the recent one over Cuba) if there were merchantmen armed with missiles and intermingled with this commercial movement in the sea lanes.

The second day went very much better and ended up with the British talking in terms of how they could help with other allies and where they might find the money in their budget to finance a 10 per cent interest. They even spoke of UK commitment of nuclear warheads to an MLF. If this occurred, I believe the UK move toward the continent would be clear to all. It should also make our case with Congress go better.[4]

Summary of Reactions

In summary, I think the Germans are genuinely enthusiastic; and I think the British will find great difficulty in staying out of a nuclear venture like MLF lest it become a new US-FRG "special relationship". These two countries, with the U.S., would certainly be an adequate starting nucleus and sufficient to avoid the charge we were working on a bilateral nuclear deal with Germany. If Britain did decide to join, Italy in my judgment could not stay out. We must recognize, however, that it is highly improbable that the new Italian Government arising from the elections will be in a position, even if so minded, to sign a preliminary agreement along the lines sketched above until early or mid-June at the earliest. If the UK should hang back and if the Italian elections should indicate a Government of appreciably different complexion from the present, then we would be of course in some difficulty to find the necessary additional political membership to add to Germany's as well as to finance the balance of the cost. Greece and Turkey in my judgment by themselves or in combination would be inadequate on both scores. Belgium and Holland, while probably adequate politically, would probably find little enthusiasm for joining a project in which the UK and Italy were doubtful starters, leaving only Germany and the U.S.

As one can see, the UK and/or Italy are key to the enterprise. I believe strongly, however, that we should not delay our decisions, reserve our attitude or otherwise act on the assumption that the worst and least likely combination will develop. My belief is reinforced by the leverage we possess with the British to prevent them wrecking our policy in so vital a matter as the MLF.

---

[4] Merchant reported on the first meeting with the British in telegram 3523 from London, March 12 (ibid., Pol 7 US/Merchant); on the second in telegram 3549 from London, March 13 (ibid., Def (MLF) 3); and on the meeting with Macmillan in telegram 3510, see footnote 1, Document 182.

Some Opposition and Minority Reactions

In France as you know, I saw Couve de Murville. He was amiable but repeated deGaulle's decision that France had no interest in joining the MLF. (Adenauer told me that deGaulle said he understood Germany's interest in the MLF and made no objection to Germany's planning to enter it.) A day or two before I left Paris, Ambassador Bohlen told me that he had had an indirect indication that General deGaulle might want to see me. I do not think this means anything in terms of change in France's policy at this time. In Paris, I also spent two hours alone with Monnet.[5] He is a great enthusiast for the MLF and very hopeful for its success. He thinks it essential since he foresees no real movement for some time on British entrance into the Common Market, and he fears a period in which divisive forces will be active. Incidentally, he was insistent that the U.S., at this stage, not contemplate abandoning a veto over the use of the MLF.

In Rome, I was struck by the fact that Piccioni during the entire meeting lasting four and one-half hours never opened his mouth. Fanfani did practically all the talking and Andreotti was vocal and an active participant in the discussion toward its end. What Piccioni's silence meant, I will have to find a Florentine or Sicilian to explain to me.

In Bonn, I had a long, private lunch with three members of the Bundestag Commission. Erler of the SPD was one, and he indicated support for the MLF.

In London, I had a long talk (at his request) with Patrick Gordon Walker, the Foreign Minister in the shadow Labor Cabinet and a friend of a number of years standing. He said that the leaders of his party were skeptical of the MLF to the point of outright opposition but at the end of our talk he said he had been impressed and that they would have to do some re-thinking on this subject.

The foregoing are odds and ends of impressions for what they are worth. All of them, I believe, were reported separately by our Embassies or in the Merchant Team's own reporting telegrams.

The Press

On such a complex project as the MLF which has a number of difficult hurdles to clear, I did not find the negative press coverage a serious handicap. On the contrary, more glowing press coverage would have concerned me.

As the reporters get a better grasp of the immense political opportunities that would crown a solution of the large technical difficulties on which they heretofore have tended to focus, I look towards a warming

---

[5] A memorandum of Merchant's conversation with Monnet on March 2 is in Department of State, Central Files, Def(MLF).

up of the press to the MLF. There will be needed a well-planned, phased information plan and this we are already working on.

In conclusion, before my next departure (about April 1), there is need to re-examine and re-affirm or modify our position on the key elements in our concept and also to review our suggested timetable and procedures. There is also a good deal in the way of further technical work to be put in hand. The status of consultation with Congress and a systematic plan for further action in this respect is also needed.

In my own view, the key questions and the ones causing the greatest difficulty are: (1) submarines vs. surface and (2) political control by unanimity.

On the former, I urge that we close out the submarine alternative definitively at the present time. The acceptance of surface ships would be more palatable, however, if we could hold out some legitimate hope that in a later modernization program or for a later additional increment to the fleet, submarines could be seriously contemplated. We would, of course, have to be sure that we were in a position to properly hold out such a hope, however cautiously and carefully phrased the language would be.

On political control, I am frankly increasingly more concerned over the question of "positive control" (by which I mean degree of assurance that MLF would be fired if we should want it to be) than "negative control" (assurance that it could not be fired over our veto alone). In the first situation, I am concerned that there might be in the crunch a timid partner who would veto. This risk both reduces the credibility of the MLF as a deterrent to the Russians and lowers its value to us as a reliable coverer of targets. I am not so much concerned that we would stand alone in voting to withhold firing under any imaginable circumstance, particularly were the UK a member. It is almost inconceivable to me that under the circumstances when all the other partners knew that we were not prepared to loose our own retaliatory forces there would not be at least one partner who would see the lunacy of acting under those circumstances without us. This, however, is a matter on which the President's judgment must prevail as to what the Congress at the present time would accept. If one assumes we must retain our veto, then I think "the rule of unanimity" should be coupled with agreement to re-examine the voting question at a started future time or times, any change of course being determined by unanimity.

I think we are far enough advanced to take final decisions on all these and on some less important and less controversial points which require re-affirmation of past decisions. The returns are not yet in from The Hague, Ankara and Athens, but none of these will crucially affect the prospects or the outcome. Hence we need not wait for the results. The Scandinavian countries, Portugal and Luxembourg, I consider out and in my own judgment Canada is dubious as even a delayed starter, irrespective of whether Diefenbaker or Pearson forms the next government.

We will have further papers coming to you posing choices and making recommendations, but I thought the foregoing draft which I have dictated hastily might be helpful setting of the stage. Both Gerry Smith and Admiral Lee concur in it though each of them would modify some of my formulations.

Recommendations for Action Now

The Administration up to now has only given conditional endorsement to the MLF, pending the development of concrete evidence of European interest. Mr. Smith, Admiral Lee and I believe that the Team's visit to capitals during the past month has produced sufficient evidence of European interest to warrant an unconditional endorsement by the Administration of the MLF. In view of the Congressional atmosphere, I appreciate that it will not be easy for the Administration to make a deep commitment to the MLF now—a commitment which will not permit any early change to some other policy.

In the event of such affirmative decision, all appropriate resources of the Federal Government should be devoted to the success of the MLF. Public and Congressional relations must be handled at the highest level and the people of the United States should be brought to realize that the Administration means business about the MLF.

If the President takes this affirmative decision, we should also move promptly to end any European expectations that the United States would supply to the MLF nuclear propelled submarines for the initial force. In view of the past participation of the President in this question it is suggested that an appropriate communication from the President to the Heads of Government of appropriate countries be promptly forwarded. (Drafts are being prepared.)

As an earnest of our serious purpose to try to mount follow-on squadrons of the MLF submarine, we should propose after appropriate consultation, to the Germans and the Italians and other contributors to the MLF a program of cooperation in submarine technology aimed at ultimately putting the MLF in a position something like that of the UK in December, 1962 when it elected nuclear propelled submarines as the platform for Polaris missiles. It is believed that meaningful cooperative agreements could be made with the MLF in the nuclear propelled field without compromise of the most sensitive information referred to in the recent memorandum from Secretary McNamara and DCI McCone on this subject.[6]

---

[6] Not further identified.

Since the Nassau Agreement was reached at the Heads of Government level, it is recommended that a Preliminary Agreement to establish the MLF could appropriately be signed by Heads of Government. An especially appropriate occasion would be President Kennedy's pending visit to Rome in June of this year. I believe this timetable could be met if the necessary underlying decisions are made promptly and we move ahead vigorously on all fronts.

Livingston T. Merchant

---

184. Memorandum of Meeting

Washington, March 22, 1963.

MLF

PRESENT

> The President; the Secretary and Under Secretary of State, Ambassador Merchant, Mr. William Tyler, Mr. Jeffrey Kitchen, Mr. Gerard Smith; the Secretary of Defense, Deputy Secretary of Defense, Mr. Paul Nitze, Mr. John McNaughton, General Maxwell Taylor, Admiral John Lee; Mr. John McCone; Mr. Carl Kaysen

Secretary Rusk asked Mr. Nitze to report on the discussions in Paris. Mr. Nitze reported along the lines of his memorandum to Mr. Bundy of March 22.[1] At present, the Dutch, Belgians and Germans were eligible to contribute to the Paragraph 6 forces, in addition to ourselves and the British. Soon there would be a total of eight or nine countries. With our new dispersal the French would become eligible, and after their elections it might be possible to take up the subject with the Canadians. There are still some technical obstacles to Italian participation, and Belgian participation is waiting on treaty ratification. The discus-

---

Source: Kennedy Library, National Security Files, Meetings with the President. Top Secret. The meeting was held in the Cabinet Room.

[1] Not found, but Nitze transmitted a summary of his discussions with Stikker on March 20 regarding paragraph 6 in Polto 1190, March 21. (Department of State, Central Files, Def 12 NATO)

sions in Paris revealed some problems with the British on how arrangements would be described, and with Lemnitzer on the details of the command arrangements. These can be worked out in two weeks.

In response to the President's question of when we would announce this, Mr. Nitze said that we would announce it at Ottawa and we could give it whatever color we wanted to in terms of wording of the communiqué and any accompanying statements made by ourselves. Secretary Rusk commented that, presented as the first step in implementing the Nassau Agreements, these arrangements would appear more important than they would viewed simply in themselves. The Secretary indicated to the President that he would like to raise with the French the subject of possible assignment of their forces when he is in Paris on April 8. The President indicated that this would be appropriate if the dispersal had already been made.

The President approved the next steps on the Paragraph 6 forces as set forth in Mr. Nitze's memorandum.

Ambassador Merchant summarized the conclusions to which his exploratory discussions in Europe had led. There was no doubt that there was a genuine interest in the MLF in Germany and Italy and even the UK was willing to support it, though not so strongly. The prospect of getting a Preliminary Agreement by the end of June was sufficiently good that we should now make the decision to go ahead. Further, we now have the advantage of momentum; delay will lose this advantage. While he is committed to making a tour of the smaller NATO countries he has not yet visited, these visits are not essential to the decision, which can be made now. Ambassador Merchant asked for new instructions authorizing negotiations for a Preliminary Agreement, and Presidential action with Adenauer, Fanfani and Macmillan to close out the submarines as a possibility at present. This involves the risk of making the MLF non-salable, but we must face it. Ambassador Merchant argued that we can and should mitigate the risk by expressing a willingness to consider at a fixed future period the possibility of another increment to the force in the form of submarine-launched missiles. In addition, it would also be helpful to suggest the possibility of present or future cooperation in the field of nuclear propulsion. Mr. Merchant recommended that the President should inform the Congressional leaders on these points now.

Mr. Merchant noted that there is already agreement on some of the essentials involved in the Preliminary Agreement. These are mixed manning of ships, membership open-ended in NATO, the force to be assigned to NATO, and ownership and operation by a separate organization set up by treaty (or joint resolution in the U.S.). On the vital points of costs and control, further negotiations were necessary. We had to preserve the veto in some way, but this could be done not only through unanimous decision, but also through various weighted voting schemes. Ambassador Merchant suggested that the control issue be reviewable in five years when the NATO Treaty itself is up for review. There had to be an agreement on costs. Ambassador Merchant had already told the Europeans that the U.S. was willing to pay up to 40%, and that our treatment of overheads of various kinds would be reasonable. Ambassador Merchant stated that the minimum membership had to be the U.S., Germany and one of Italy or the UK. He judged that if Germany agreed, Italy would follow and if the UK joined, both Holland and Belgium would join. Greece and Turkey were eager to join, but could not presently meet the cost. Secretary Rusk endorsed Ambassador Merchant's judgment on membership. In his views, if Germany joined, both Italy and the UK would feel constrained to join. Ambassador Merchant observed that Italy could not make a commitment before June. He went on to say that we must formulate our views somewhat differently than we had in the past; namely, that, after considering the views of our allies, we had decided that this was a desirable force. We were giving it our backing. We were prepared to amend the Atomic Energy law and get a treaty or whatever was necessary to bring the force into being. It is clear that there were obstacles in European opinion to the success of this effort, especially their concern with submarines which he thought reflected German-Italian collusion. If this effort were successful, it would add strength to NATO and counter DeGaulle's appeal. In its absence he saw no other course which promised a tolerable result for us. In the short run, there would be great pressure in Germany for land-based MRBM's. In the long run we would have a problem of Franco-German nuclear arrangements.

Ambassador Merchant felt that we could get an exploratory agreement ready in time to be signed in Rome by the President, and the heads of other European governments involved. On this basis the Preparatory Commission could go to work on 1 July, and the final agreement would be ready to give to the Congress this Fall. Ambassador Merchant pointed to the undesirability of putting this agreement before the Congress in a Presidential election year. If we do not take the opportunity now, it will fail. Secretary Rusk raised the question as to which was preferable, a treaty, or a joint resolution plus an amendment of the McMahon Act.[2] In response to the President's question on what amendment to the McMahon Act was required in order to put the MLF into being, Ambassador Merchant pointed out that the ownership and custody of the warhead would lie with the MLF rather than with the U.S., with arrangements to protect the design data.

---

[2] For text of the Atomic Energy Act of 1946 (McMahon Act), see 60 Stat. 755.

The President and Mr. Merchant, after a brief discussion of the advantages the Europeans saw in this arrangement as against the present arrangement, moved on to the problem of control. [*6-1/2 lines of source text not declassified*]

[*2 paragraphs (21 lines of source text) not declassified*]

The President asked how we have made the argument in Europe with respect to submarines. Ambassador Merchant responded that he had emphasized the positive case for surface ships in terms of ease of operation, economy in cost per ready missile, and date of availability. In response to a private question by Von Hassel, Ambassador Merchant had admitted that there were political difficulties but stated that these were not controlling. Ambassador Merchant's impression was that the Germans had made their own head count in the Congress and had come to the conclusion that we would have a hard time offering submarines.

The President then decided that if the Europeans are not ready to accept surface ships, we cannot go on with the offer. Ambassador Merchant urged the need for some language permitting a re-examination of this issue at a later date. The President noted that this would not make sense economically before the 70's. There was some further discussion of the vulnerability of surface ships versus submarines and of the relative costs of the two modes, taking vulnerability into account, and omitting it. There also was some discussion of the costs of detecting and tracking a surface force. Secretary McNamara, General Taylor and Admiral Lee indicated that in the particular circumstances of European waters, a surface ship force had a real military value. [*3 lines of source text not declassified*]

Secretary McNamara said that if the MLF were accepted by the Europeans, he would recommend in the FY 65 force structure that we reduce the goals of our Minuteman force by a number of missiles equivalent to those that the MLF would provide. [*8-1/2 lines of source text not declassified*]

[*1 paragraph (3 lines of source text) not declassified*]

The President asked whether we should now write to the Germans and the Italians, defining our stand on the surface shipping control problem. Ambassador Merchant responded that, while he needed to make a second trip, it was desirable that we should make up our minds as soon as possible on the main issue and tell the Germans and Italians that we are now prepared to sign a Preliminary Agreement on a surface-ship force, with the possibility of additional submarine-launched missiles to be examined at some future date, and a control formula, [*less than 1 line of source text not declassified*].

Secretary Rusk raised the question of timing. Ambassador Merchant has returned from Europe, and must consult with Congress. Secretary Rusk suggested that he make an interim report to the Congress now; consult with the Germans again after his trip to the other European countries; and then come back for final approval of Congress. Ambassador Merchant again emphasized the need for us to be able to say to the Germans that we would like to endorse the proposal because we believe in it, and we are prepared to move ahead on the basis specified, if they are willing. What Congressional consultation would we need before we could say this? Mr. Gerard Smith raised the question of the dangers of an adverse press playback in Europe of any consultation here. The experience of our first consultation with the Joint Committee exemplifies these dangers.

In response to the President's question of what we should do if the proposal for an MLF dies, Mr. Ball argued that if we present it in a positive way, it won't die. As a great power, we should know what we want, the Europeans are accustomed to our leadership, and they have been looking for it. He urged that Ambassador Merchant be given a positive instruction to go ahead. The Secretary asked how we could go ahead unless we are sure the Germans are interested. Mr. Ball responded that their interest would depend on our attitude.

The President, after reviewing the attitudes of other governments and the moderation of his own enthusiasm for the proposal, agreed that we should put it to the Germans strongly before the next week was out. He wanted to write to the Germans and the Italians on the basis outlined and leave the matter of Congressional consultation until later. Congress should be given our proposition on what was essentially a take it or leave it basis. The communication to the Germans should invite immediate technical consultation on any problems that remain if they accepted our basic principals.

The President asked whether Ambassador Merchant agreed with this formulation. Ambassador Merchant demurred on the question of Congressional consultation and urged the President to talk to the leadership, and at the same time check on European desire to act on what we consider a good argument. The President again expressed his desire not to consult with the Congress now. When the Secretary pointed to his commitments to make an interim report to some committees, the President suggested that Ambassador Merchant say that he was too ill to meet anybody for a week.

The Secretary raised some of the mechanical problems involved in communication by letter, Adenauer in particular. The Italians obviously could not answer a letter now. After some discussion, it was agreed that the Italians had to be informed of what we were getting from the Germans, but we could indicate that we expected no action from them now before their elections. Our emphasis must be on the Germans. For this it might be desirable to find some device for getting Schroeder and Von

Hassel to go down to consult with Adenauer when he got the letter. The President and the Secretary agreed that the essential point was German agreement.

In response to the President's question, Secretary McNamara agreed that this was the best course of action, both with respect to European governments and the Congress.

The President then raised the question of how he should explain our failure if we got a negative response from the Germans and asked both Departments to suggest how we might be prepared to deal with this. Mr. Nitze expressed his fear that we would get no definite answer. Messrs. Merchant and Ball shared this expectation. The President disagreed and asked State to deal with the how and when of communication. He wanted a plan which had a definite control scheme that would be clear and defensible and agreeable to the Germans. If Congressional pressure for consultation appeared to be irresistible, he requested that he be consulted before any appearances or discussions with the Congress. He also requested the two Departments to examine what can be done with Paragraph 6 as an alternative in the event that the Germans did in fact fail to respond.

C.K.[3]

---

[3] Printed from a copy that bears these typed initials.

---

185. Telegram From the Department of State to the Embassy in Germany

Washington, March 29, 1963, 9:01 p.m.

2336. Following is text of letter which Tyler is carrying from President to Chancellor.[1] In your discretion this text can be given to Chancellor's office for transmission to the Chancellor prior to Tyler's call Tuesday.

Source: Department of State, Central Files, Def 12 NATO. Secret; Verbatim Text; Priority. Drafted in EUR and the White House, cleared in draft with the President, and approved by Tyler.

[1] On March 29 the President signed a memorandum instructing Tyler to visit Chancellor Adenauer for the purpose of obtaining an early German decision on the MLF. (Kennedy Library, National Security Files, MLF) A similar letter was drafted for delivery to Fanfani (ibid.), but Tyler, using discretionary power, decided not to deliver it during his meeting with the Italian Prime Minister on April 3.

Begin Text. March 29, 1963. Dear Mr. Chancellor:

Ambassador Merchant has given me a full report of his conversation with you in Bonn and his discussion with other high officials of the Federal Republic.

I am glad to know that your Government supports the concept of a multilateral force and is prepared to join in its development.

Your country and mine—along with other members of the Alliance—have the opportunity to mount a powerful military force of a nature unique in the history of the world—one which would respond to the increasing threat of Soviet nuclear capabilities.

Such a force—organized on a multilateral basis—would have more than military significance. It would meet the healthy desire of the great nations of Europe for a larger role in nuclear defense without contributing to the dangerous situation in which many nations throughout the world would own separate national nuclear forces. It would make a long further step toward effective Atlantic cooperation, and give body and substance to the Atlantic partnership. I am happy to think that Germany and the United States can act together with other allies in the creation of this great enterprise.

My Government is prepared to join in pressing ahead with this venture immediately, and it has occurred to me that you and I and the other heads of governments might be able to sign a general preliminary agreement during my forthcoming visit to Europe. Our two Governments and others have already been discussing the possibility of reaching such agreement in June, and if we can meet this schedule I think we can sustain the sense of momentum which is essential in these great new international ventures.

But for me there is one important political problem here at home. The multilateral force will require major legislative action in this country, and before I can properly sign a general preliminary agreement, I must have thorough consultation with the Congress and indeed with the American public as a whole. I am ready to undertake this consultation promptly, and, as I say, it is a necessary step on the way to the preliminary agreement which we envisage for June.

But for this consultation to be effective, I must be able to say firmly that this proposal will in fact meet the requirements of the principal prospective participants—and most of all of the Federal Republic. The Congress will be much more likely to accept the principles of this radical development in our own policy if it can be confident that the prospect of the multilateral force is real and the need in Europe urgent.

On the basis of what you and your colleagues have stated in messages and discussions in recent months, I believe that I might now give this assurance, but I would not think it proper to do so without your express approval, especially with respect to two specific questions which were not fully resolved during Ambassador Merchant's visit. One of these is the mode of deployment of the force—whether on surface ships or submarines—and the other the mechanism for political control. Let me set forth my thoughts on each of these issues for you.

I am sure you know that arrangements governing nuclear weapons have been a matter of great national sensitivity in this country from the beginning. We have invested tens of billions of dollars and two decades of effort in the development of our vast atomic arsenal. The American people have learned to think of the American strategic force not only as a great national asset but also as the principal bulwark of Free World defense.

I can lead them to understand that the time has come—for many reasons—when we must begin to share nuclear military responsibility with the now strong nations of Europe. But I know that you will appreciate how great a change in traditional American habits of thought is involved in the kind of sharing of nuclear responsibility envisaged in the multilateral force.

Against this background I have given the matter careful thought. I am convinced that the initial force should be based on surface vessels. I am convinced further that from the point of military effectiveness we can build a first-class force in this manner. Secretary McNamara—who has made the most thorough analysis of the problem—has advised me that, for the uses intended, the balance of advantage clearly weighs in favor of a surface-borne system—particularly when the factors of timing, ease of operation, and costs are taken into account.

The multilateral force would operate in an environment quite different from that which dictated the design of our United States Polaris submarine system. That system was developed to meet the problems of operating over long distances and in all geographical and military situations around the world. But, in our view, the multilateral force should be specifically related to the defense of Europe. It would deploy in a highly favorable situation where its operating areas would be behind the shield of NATO. It would thus automatically be protected by distance, and by the full air, surface, and anti-submarine defenses of the Alliance, including the Greenland-Iceland-UK barrier. Further, the areas of its intended operation have extensive shallow-water zones, straits, inlets, islands, and long, irregular coastlines. All of these factors could be used to advantage by surface forces.

I recognize that some commentators in Europe are suggesting that surface ships are somehow inferior to submarines and that, therefore, the multilateral force may seem to be a second-class force. I want you to know that our own conviction of the quality of the surface force is so clear that we expect, if this force is agreed on, to be able to make substantial savings in the provision of additional U.S. strategic striking forces which might otherwise be needed to cover the same targets. This Government would not consent to the very substantial investment which it is now willing to make for this force except on the basis of a clear conviction of its first-rate quality.

In order to make progress with this matter, I propose that we now agree on surface ships for the initial multilateral force. The number of ships can be mutually agreed, the force must make a substantial contribution to the Alliance deterrent in order to support the objectives we both have in mind, but the figure of twenty-five ships and two hundred missiles is not immutable.

A decision to go forward now with a surface force would not preclude consideration of submarines at a later stage, if this seems wise, after we have gained operating experience in mixed-manning and other features of joint ownership and control.

Let me turn to the second issue, the question of political control. Ambassador Merchant has already discussed with your Government the method by which the political decision would be taken to release the force for military use. The proposal we have made would call for the unanimous agreement of all major participants. In view of the enormous importance of any decision to use strategic nuclear weapons in the NATO area, it has been our belief that every government playing a major role in the provision of such forces would wish to have a right of concurrence in any such decision to fire. Obviously each government must make its own best judgment on this important matter, but speaking for my country, I must say that in our judgment it is essential that a decision to fire should have the concurrence of the United States. In this judgment I am greatly influenced by the fact that any use of the multilateral force would almost inevitably require the immediate support of the full strategic strength of the Alliance as a whole. Since the overwhelming proportion of this total strategic strength is American, the American Government must have a particularly intense concern with any decision to fire any NATO strategic forces.

Let me point out here that this right of concurrence is one which I should think that your Government too will wish to insist on for itself. In the light of the substantial proportion of the force which your Government is thinking of contributing, and in the light of the exposed forward position of Germany, I should think that any German Government would wish to be assured that the multilateral force would be fired only with its consent. In this respect, I think it is clear that in the current stage of the affairs of the Alliance our two Governments must have a most powerful concern with any decision to use such a force.

But within this limit, I can tell you that we are quite prepared to accept whatever arrangement best suits the other major participants. One method would be the unanimous decision of the major participants which Ambassador Merchant has already suggested. But if other major participants do not insist on the right of concurrence that such a procedure would give each of them, we would support an initial control scheme which required the concurrence of the United States and any combination of the other participants. All that is necessary at this stage, I think, is that our two countries should be prepared to move forward on this problem on the broad basis which I have outlined above.

With these considerations in mind we have prepared a list of points to be covered in a preliminary agreement, which I am asking Mr. Tyler to show you.[2] I hope you will let me know promptly and candidly whether your Government can go ahead with an agreement along this line. If so, I would be glad immediately to undertake the necessary discussions with Congressional leaders that would make it possible for me to be able to conclude a preliminary agreement in Europe in June.

I have read with interest comments of all sorts on the multilateral force, and I know how easy it is to find weaknesses or limitations in any new arrangements for the nuclear defense of the Alliance. But in these matters it is much easier to be a critic of any proposal than it is to produce a better one, and all of the alternatives which I have heard of seem to me to be much less satisfactory in the long run for the Alliance in general and for our two countries in particular. Thus, it seems to me that it is the proper course now for us to move firmly forward on the basis of a proposal which is clearly good, and not to get bogged down in a profitless search for ideal answers which do not exist.

I am convinced that if we can act promptly together we have a chance now to set in train an enterprise that can fix the direction of nuclear defense along safe and sound lines for future generations—a direction that will assure the security of the West while, at the same time, preventing developments that might undermine the safety of the world. In addition, we may recapture the momentum toward trans-Atlantic unity which has unhappily been arrested by recent events.

It is my deepest hope that you and I can now join in this common effort which has such portent for the Atlantic Community as a whole.

Sincerely, John F. Kennedy. *End Text.*

Rusk

---

[2] Not found.

186. Summary Record of the National Security Council Meeting

Washington, April 2, 1963, 10 a.m.

The meeting opened in the absence of the President with Secretary Rusk reviewing the current situation in Europe. Referring to a paper (copy attached)[1] which had been circulated to the Council, the Secretary called attention to the fact that several of the NATO countries are facing elections in the near future and others have problems connected with the replacement of aging leaders. France is the only country which will have a reasonably stable political situation in the immediate future. Secretary Rusk commented that because the British did not tell us as much as they knew prior to de Gaulle's action in vetoing British membership in the Common Market, we had overestimated the odds that the Common Market negotiations involving UK membership would be successful. Most countries in Europe do not want the U.S. to leave, but all want their relationship with the U.S. to appear to be less one of dependence. There is popular support for de Gaulle's position insofar as it expresses the European desire to be independent of the U.S. and to reduce U.S. presence in Europe.

In the light of the present situation, Secretary Rusk said that there are no new major changes in our European policy which we must make. As to the Paragraph 6 forces, we seem to be moving ahead and probably we can reach agreement in Ottawa in May as to how these forces will be organized and controlled in NATO. It is even possible that the French might be prepared to contribute some of their forces to the Paragraph 6 force.

As to the MLF, Secretary Rusk reviewed briefly the points which Assistant Secretary Tyler would be making to Adenauer tomorrow in Italy. On the basis of Tyler's preliminary discussions with German officials in Bonn, the major problem appears to be German concern about the survivability of surface craft as opposed to submarines. The problem of controlling the MLF can probably be dealt with by indicating, without making a commitment, that in the future we would be prepared to consider changes in the control arrangements, if such changes were desired by those contributing to the MLF. In effect, we would do no more now than promise to review control arrangements at a later time.

Under Secretary Ball reported on a meeting he attended recently in Cannes, France,[2] which brought together for the first time since de

---

Source: Kennedy Library, National Security Files, Meetings and Memoranda Series, NSC Meetings 1963. Top Secret.

[1] Not printed.

[2] Not further identified.

Gaulle's press conference of January 14 the leaders of the major European States. As a result of numerous informal conversations, Mr. Ball said he was impressed with the lame duck character of most of the member governments of NATO. He referred to the "air of death" which surrounded the Macmillan government and noted that the schedule for the replacement of Adenauer is apparently unchanged. He predicted that Erhard would succeed Adenauer.

Mr. Ball said that de Gaulle is isolating himself more and more, and that he does not have a "grand design," or even a clear European policy. All de Gaulle can really do is to oppose the initiative of others by being negative. He cannot build the Europe he desires because his actions are conditioned by his overriding desire to build the predominance of France. As a result, he has nothing to offer other European States.

Mr. Ball said Ambassador Bohlen agreed with the analysis that de Gaulle cannot organize a European nuclear force. De Gaulle still yearns for a U.S./U.K./France directorate in which France would speak for all of Europe. However, Europeans are not prepared to have de Gaulle speak for them. Except for de Gaulle, most Europeans do not want the U.S. to get out of Europe. It is unlikely that the British will be admitted to the Common Market as long as de Gaulle rules France. Furthermore, prospects for making something of the Western European Union are not good.

Mr. Ball said that six months from now Europe would look different and twelve months from now it would look quite different. Adenauer will be gone, and, as a result, de Gaulle's power in Europe will be greatly reduced and limited primarily to France itself. A Labor government will probably take over in the U.K. (In this connection, Mr. Ball said we should start planning now how to avoid a damaging effect on sterling in the event the Labor government did gain power in the U.K.) There will be a strong tendency in Europe to fall back on nationalism as a result of de Gaulle's recent actions.

In conclusion, Mr. Ball said that the momentum toward the unification of Europe has slowed down. No new initiatives are required now, but we should play by ear a decision as to whether at a later time we should put forward a new political suggestion around which "good" Europeans could rally in opposition to de Gaulle. One suggestion to think of in the effort to restore progress toward an Atlantic Community would be a political executive committee for NATO.

In the interim period, Mr. Ball said there were several problems which we should watch carefully:

a. *East-West trade*—The British oppose our policy and the Germans are not happy about the embargo on large diameter pipe. Our attitude toward East-West trade is not understood in Europe. The time might be coming when our effort to push Europe to support our East-

West trade policy may not be worth the cost. He recommended that we consider a revision of our policy.

b. *Conventional force strategy*—Despite our efforts to explain our conventional force strategy, the Europeans are not convinced. This strategy is being used effectively to undermine the European faith that the U.S. is resolved to use nuclear weapons when required.

c. *Nuclear industry*—The Europeans are worrying that if they do not have nuclear weapons, they, as a result, will have no nuclear industry. We must think of ways to overcome this European concern.

d. *Agriculture in trade negotiations*—Despite the very difficult problems caused by the impact of European agricultural policies on trade negotiations, the situation is not entirely without hope. The fact that the British will not now be in the Common Market has eased for the present some of the agricultural trade problems.

Secretary Rusk added two points:

a. The Atlantic alliance policy is a bipartisan policy in almost all NATO countries. Therefore, in the present election uncertainty, there is no fundamental threat to the continuance of the alliance.

b. The Soviets may act in such a way as to put an end to present divisions in NATO and reunify the alliance. He cited the current Berlin airplane incident, reports of which were circulated to Council members.[3]

Mr. Murrow commented that so far there was no political base for our MLF proposal. He feared that if the MLF concept was not explained adequately to the Europeans, we would be caught in a cross-fire in Europe.

Secretary Rusk replied that during the talks which are now going on, we have not been in a position to take a firm stand on the various matters connected with the MLF. He expected that in a very short time, our government, as well as the European governments, could take the lead in explaining to their people the multilateral concept, thereby overcoming the present difficult situation as regards public understanding.

The President joined the Council members, accompanied by the Attorney General.

Secretary Rusk and Under Secretary Ball reviewed their presentations. Mr. Ball emphasized de Gaulle's negativism, i.e. he can wreck the Common Market and upset NATO, but he cannot build a European force. Mr. Ball commented that the British Conservatives might panic and take reckless nationalistic actions in an effort to hang on to power. Labor politicians feared the Conservatives might go all out for a purely British national nuclear deterrent, thereby downgrading the NATO alliance.

---

[3] On April 2 a Soviet fighter plane had fired warning shots at a private plane in the Berlin air corridor. The reports under reference have not been identified further.

The President commented that Diefenbaker may win in Canada. We can expect a similar anti-American line to develop in the U.K. He asked what we thought de Gaulle was likely to do in the event that he saw he could not have his way in Europe.

Under Secretary Ball doubted that de Gaulle would take any dramatic action and pointed out that he may have serious domestic trouble in the months ahead in connection with the miners' strike and the possibility of inflation.

Secretary Rusk reminded the Council that we must be very careful to continue to deal with the British government of the day. We must avoid talking to Wilson as if he were the British Prime Minister or appear to be negotiating with him. He may not become the British Prime Minister and we must be careful not to appear to believe that the Labor government has already taken over in the U.K.

In concluding the discussion, Secretary Rusk asked whether it would be possible for us to offer the French a Polaris package similar to that which we are offering the British this week.[4] He suggested we should consider the Nassau offer to France still open. In connection with suggestions that we start new discussions with de Gaulle, Secretary Rusk said he was seeing de Gaulle in Paris next week, but that other than Viet-Nam, he had little he could now discuss with de Gaulle.

Mr. Bundy said he judged that on the basis of Ambassador Bohlen's review, and of the Department's review, the lines of our European policy required no change. However, he suggested that because of the period we are now entering, it might be helpful if the officials concerned met often to discuss informally the current developments in Europe.

At this point Assistant Secretary Martin and Mr. Dungan joined the group at the President's request to discuss the current status of the Cuban raiders who have been arrested by the British in the Bahama Islands.

Mr. Martin said the present plan was for the British to turn the raiders loose on their boat three miles off the Bahamas. The U.S. Coast Guard would pick them up there. If they refuse to go to Miami, the question before us is what do we then do?

After a discussion of the legal points involved, the President expressed his view that we should ask the British to take away from the raiders all their ammunition, and that we would ask the leaders to come peacefully to a U.S. port. If they refuse to come into the U.S. territorial waters, the U.S. Coast Guard ship would follow them but not fire on them. We would soon know the names of the raiders on the ship and

---

[4] For text of the Polaris Sales Agreement between the United States and the United Kingdom, signed at Washington April 6, see 14 UST 1431.

would seek to apply pressures on them to agree to enter a U.S. port. If a threat to prevent them ever again from entering the U.S. was not effective, the Coast Guard would report the situation to Washington for additional guidance.

Bromley Smith[5]

---

[5] Printed from a copy that bears this typed signature.

---

187.   Telegram From the Department of State to the Embassy in Germany

Washington, April 5, 1963, 8:09 p.m.

2408. Following is unofficial translation of text of letter from Chancellor to President delivered to White House today by German Embassy:

Begin text. April 4, 1963

Dear Mr. President:

"I thank you for your letter of March 29,[1] which Mr. Tyler handed over and explained to me in Cadenabbia on April 2nd.[2] I welcome the opportunity to enter into a frank exchange of views with you on the question of the multilateral MRBM-force, which is, also in the opinion of the Federal Government, of very great importance for the alliance, and which should come into being as soon as possible.

"Members of my government and I, myself, have had talks with Ambassador Merchant, talks which have strengthened the conviction of the Federal Government that the multilateral force is a grand opportunity to further the cohesion of NATO and to counter the threat to Europe brought about by the increasing nuclear potential of the Soviet Union.

Source: Department of State, Central Files, Def 12 NATO. Secret. Drafted by Brandin, cleared by the White House and Tyler, and approved by Creel.

[1] See Document 185.

[2] In his report on the meeting with Adenauer, Tyler stated that the Chancellor was convinced of the military and political value of the MLF. (Telegram 2049 April 2, from Rome; Department of State, Central Files, Def 12 NATO)

The Federal Government is determined to participate in the realization of this project and to share to a large extent the considerable burden connected therewith.

"I welcome your intention to sign, during your forthcoming visit to Europe in June of this year, a preliminary agreement of the heads of government of those states which want to participate in the multilateral force. The Federal Government will do everything in her power to bring about, by that time, a clarification of the problems still open.

"I share your view that, after the previous contacts between our two governments, there are only two important points left that need clarification.

"The first point is the equipment of the MLF with surface ships or submarines. Certain arguments brought forward by Ambassador Merchant for the military usefulness of surface ships are being recognized by my government as justified. With regard to some points we still have doubts, especially in assessing the survivability of surface ships and the efficacy of enemy submarines. These questions need further discussion by our experts. I suggest, therefore, that as soon as possible a group of high ranking German experts discuss thoroughly with American experts the military aspects of the MLF. In these discussions, it might also be possible to examine the military as well as the financial implications of your proposal to consider surface ships for an initial phase and to include submarines into the MLF at a later date, should this seem appropriate in the light of the experience collected.

"In the public opinion of the Federal Republic and of other European countries, there are certain reservations concerning the assignment to the MLF of surface ships, because these vessels are considered as second rate and as a mere stop-gap. Should the discussions between experts which I have suggested lead us to the conviction that surface ships are the most qualified carriers for the MRBM's of the MLF, my government will use all the means at its disposal to secure the approval of this solution by Parliament and public opinion in Germany.

"The second point discussed in your letter, namely the unsolved question of how to settle the final control, has found even more interest in the public opinion of the Federal Republic and of other European states. The Federal Government recognizes the validity of your argument that the use of the multilateral forces would most probably necessitate the aid of the strategic potential of the USA and that, therefore, a decision on the use of the MLF contrary to the wishes of the United States would be problematic.

"On the other hand, we have the responsibility to build up the MLF in such a way that it is regarded by public opinion as a genuine participation of the European NATO partners in nuclear responsibilities and that it offers a stimulant for other NATO states to participate in the MLF at a later date.

"I believe that the differences in opinion of our two governments are not unsurmountable and that a compromise can be found. The Federal Republic has already proposed to provide the principle of unanimous decision for a transitory period and only after some years to proceed to a system of majority decision. On the other hand, Ambassador Merchant has stated that the American Government is ready to re-examine, in the light of the experience gained, the system of unanimous decision after several years. I think that these two proposals can be harmonized and I might suggest that this problem be discussed between our two governments without delay.

"I have read with interest the list enclosed in your letter of the points to be included in a preliminary agreement about the MLF. The draft is a good basis for further negotiations between the interested NATO states during the next weeks. It is acceptable for us in principle subject to clarification of the two problems of the MRBM carriers and of the control.

With kindest regards,
Adenauer"

Rusk

---

188. Memorandum for the Record

Washington, April 5, 1963.

SUBJECT

The MLF and the IANF

PARTICIPANTS

The President; Undersecretary Ball, Messrs. Tyler, Merchant, Smith, Weiss and Admiral Lee of the Department of State; Messrs. Nitze, McNaughton and General Goodpaster of the Department of Defense; Mr. Bundy

Bill Tyler reported to the President on his MLF discussions with the Germans and the Italians.

Source: Kennedy Library, National Security Files, MLF. Top Secret. A longer, but less detailed record of this meeting, drafted by Seymour Weiss, is in Department of State, President's Memoranda of Conversation: Lot 66 D 149.

He was optimistic about possible German participation. The Germans are supporting the MLF for political reasons. (According to Ambassador Dowling, Schroeder told Adlai Stevenson that if the MLF did not materialize, the Germans would be forced to seek equal status with the British and French.) However, to make the MLF politically viable, the German Government has to be able to make a convincing case for a surface as opposed to a submarine force.

As for the Italians, Bill Tyler felt the principal consideration was German participation. So long as there is no German decision, the Italians will continue to agitate on the issue of the surface vessel vs. the submarine. Bill Tyler said Fanfani also had reservations about mixed manning. He appears particularly concerned about the possible distribution of tasks and wants some assurance that Italian mariners will have the same opportunities as the others.[1]

To deal with the problems created by submarine vs. the surface vessel debate, the President approved a suggestion that Admiral Ricketts lead a mission to Bonn early next week for technical discussions with German officialdom—to make the case for the surface ship MLF and give the German Government the arguments it needs to rally the necessary political support for the MLF. The President agreed to Mr. McNaughton's joining Admiral Ricketts and added that Ambassador Dowling should provide the political guidance for the group. He asked also that the Ricketts' mission be adequately staffed with submariners.

To avoid a combined German and Italian maneuver against the surface force, the President decided against joint technical briefings for the Germans and Italians. In fact, the question of arrangements for technical discussions with the Italians was left open since the Italians, unlike the Germans, have not asked for them and in this pre-election period seem reluctant to have them.

Mr. Merchant asked for and was given authority to resume his visit to capitals, going to those he did not reach the last time. The President, however, asked him to by-pass Paris on this round to avoid resurfacing the MLF in NAC at this time.

In view of continued Congressional interest in the Merchant mission, Mr. Bundy undertook to inform the Chairman of the Joint Committee and the Senate Foreign Relations Committee, at an appropriate time, about Merchant's plans to return to Europe.

---

[1] Tyler discussed the MLF with Fanfani on April 3, stating that the President was prepared to proceed if the major European allies were interested in proceeding with the MLF. Fanfani stated that he had been and still was a strong supporter of the MLF, but that Italy believed that a submarine force was better than a surface fleet. (Telegram 4000 from Paris, April 4; ibid., Central Files, Def(MLF))

Before leaving the MLF and the question of the survivability of the surface vessel, there was an inconclusive discussion about the possibility of substituting a Savannah type ship or a conventionally powered submarine for the surface vessel. However, DoD undertook to discuss the security problems of a nuclear powered surface vessel with Admiral Rickover.

It was also agreed to cease calling the surface ships merchant ships and instead refer to them as "surface missile warships". In this connection, Bill Tyler indicated that in his talks with the Europeans, he left open the possibility of considering at a later date—after the MLF was operational—the possibility of including nuclear powered submarines in the MLF.

Mr. Nitze took the opportunity to bring the President up to date on the progress of the IANF negotiations. He said he felt the formula now under discussion eliminated the control problem and was less likely than the earlier British blueprint to encounter French obstructionism. In response to the President's question about making the IANF more attractive, Mr. Nitze said he would recommend against considering any changes in the IANF plans prior to the Ottawa meeting, although expansion and/or modification could be considered after that meeting, and particularly if MLF seemed to be failing.

The President also asked about possible tactics for dealing with French obstructionism in NATO. Mr. Nitze said a scenario was under consideration calling for Mr. Finletter to do some preliminary work with the French and for Secretary Rusk to follow through when he reached Paris.

As a result of this morning's meeting, John McNaughton was asked to prepare necessary instructions for the Ricketts' mission and to send them to the President for approval after the details were worked out by State and Defense.

The Department of State was asked to notify Ambassador Dowling immediately of the Ricketts' mission to assure there was a clear understanding that these meetings would be held in Bonn, rather than in Washington, and get from the Ambassador some sense for timing and arranging the mission.

David Klein[2]

---

[2] Printed from a copy that bears this typed signature.

189.   Memorandum of Conversation

Paris, April 7, 1963, 5–7 p.m.

SEATO COUNCIL MEETING
Paris, April 8–10, 1963

PARTICIPANTS

United States

The Secretary of State
Ambassador Bohlen

France

Couve de Murville
Charles Lucet

SUBJECT

France's Attitude towards the IANF

The Secretary inquired what was the French attitude towards the assignment of their two squadrons in Germany with American warheads to the inter-allied nuclear force.

Couve de Murville replied that his difficulty was to understand what our policy was. He could understand the British point of view but not that of the U.S. The British wanted to try and dilute the Nassau Agreement to make it more supple and to utilize emergency arrangements to keep control over their own force while at the same time supporting NATO. The U.S. realized that the problem of Europe was becoming more important and possibly this IANF was a mechanism to permit some appearance of European participation in the nuclear mystery. What he really didn't understand is what change this force would produce in the NATO set up and he did not understand the feasibility of a Dutch general in command. He thought that he wished to make as little disruption as possible in NATO arrangements as well as in our individual bilateral arrangements with other countries. Ambassador Finletter had told him that France would be welcome to come in but if they didn't nothing much would be changed.

The Secretary said that up to the middle 50's the U.S. had had a monopoly of nuclear power but that since that time the Soviet capability had grown and therefore it was understandable that nations that could be struck wanted to have some knowledge of and participation in nuclear matters. Previous to that the question had not arisen since it would

---

Source: Department of State, Secretary's Memoranda of Conversation: Lot 65 D 330. Secret. Drafted by Bohlen and approved in S on April 10. The meeting was held at the Quai d'Orsay. On April 8 Rusk briefly discussed the same question with de Gaulle. A memorandum of their conversation is ibid.

have been the other side that would have been struck and hurt. He said Nassau under Paragraph 6 introduced a new element into NATO, namely that by introducing the V bombers from the UK and Polaris missiles from the U.S., the strategic factor had been introduced and that it was therefore desirable that the entire targeting system for NATO should be worked out as a unit in close association with Omaha, and that European targets should be under NATO control.

Couve de Murville said he thought this changed nothing, and as far as the battle of Europe that the targeting was perfectly okay but that what he was interested in was the question of the use of these weapons and not so much the targeting, and he did not quite understand the difference between the strategic and tactical elements.

The Secretary replied the dual role might shift and the definition of tactical as the first step in any nuclear exchange might become more important. For example, airfields, anti-aircraft sites and missiles would have to be redefined. This would increase the mix and if NATO did get in on it it would be a very good thing. The U.S. did not wish to see a NATO nuclear club with France outside. He mentioned that of course the French national force was different and he was not referring to that.

Couve de Murville said he understood but he still did not see much to be changed and was rather afraid of an element of deception which would bring up the problem of the NATO organization. He said that the targeting for the French F–104's was already done and it would not add anything new but might merely complicate the work of General Lemnitzer.

The Secretary said he thought that something new had indeed been added. He said the introduction of Polaris weapons and V bombers would provide NATO with something that it did not have, namely a strategic element and this should be combined with what already existed in other weapons.

Couve de Murville said that this raised a different question. He said that at present the weapons assigned to Europe had U.S. warheads as distinct from British V bombers. He then referred to the political problem which the Secretary had mentioned. He pointed out that not many of the Europeans really wanted to join in and were in effect indifferent to the nuclear problem. He mentioned Italy, Belgium, Norway, the Netherlands, etc.

The Secretary objected to the inclusion of Italy.

Couve de Murville said we will say that Italy is half interested but in reality there was only England, France and Germany. This was quite normal since they had traditions of defense responsibility. Apart from these countries, leaving aside Italy, the others do not count. Germany, however, remains the main problem. He was somewhat afraid that these proposals (he was now referring to MLF) would merely increase Germany's appetite for nuclear weapons.

The Secretary said in regard to the MLF this was up to the NATO countries, specifically Germany and Italy to decide.

Couve de Murville said "we don't object, this has no inconvenience for us".

The Secretary then said, referring back to Paragraph 6, that the NATO commander should have responsibility to coordinate the various elements involved in targeting.

Couve de Murville said he could accept this idea but he did not think a Dutch officer could do it. He said that the Dutch had no experience in this field and he doubted if they could coordinate planning.

The Secretary said he did not wish to go into nationalities but felt that the problem was one of competence.

Couve de Murville said he still did not see what it did to the planning staff. What was needed was experience and capability and what should be considered was the efficiency, and that we should do what was technically necessary to try to avoid bringing in organizational disarray.

The Secretary inquired as to where they would put the Polaris and V bombers in the NATO structure.

Couve de Murville agreed that they should be in the NATO structure.

The Secretary then said he did not see why some tactical forces should not be added.

Couve de Murville said this is what the British originally wanted but we had differed; but now we agreed.

The Secretary said it was a problem of long-range and battlefield weapons. The Secretary, referring back to targeting, said it was very important that Europe should know that the targets vital for Europe were not being neglected.

Couve agreed.

The Secretary said that the Paragraph 6 Forces really did not make any startling and new change in the NATO force structure. However, the MLF might if the Germans agree. He would leave the question at this stage.

Couve de Murville said possibly the military technicians should study this question and that his reaction might change with further knowledge.

The Secretary said he hoped that the French would come in.

Couve de Murville said that this matter had now turned into a maneuver whereby if France refused she would be isolated and if she accepted would be accused of having retreated from her position.

The Secretary repeated that the assignment of French 104's under Paragraph 6 would not produce any major change any more than the agreement to give these forces warheads, which the American newspapers had got all wrong.

Couve de Murville agreed that efficiency should be the criterion but did say that if the French assigned the F–104's it would be interpreted as a retreat.

190. Circular Telegram From the Department of State to Missions in the NATO Capitals

Washington, April 15, 1963, 7:06 p.m.

1773. Department has noted substantial confusion in minds Embassy and other observers here re relationship between Inter-Allied Nuclear Force (IANF) and Multilateral Force (MLF). Following may be helpful to addressees in dealing with similar confusion which may arise in field.

1. IANF is name for those nationally-owned nuclear delivery forces (including UK V-bombers and US Polaris subs) which are assigned by member governments to NATO and which constitute those forces committed to SACEUR's Scheduled Program, i.e. which are pre-targeted by SACEUR as opposed to battlefield weapons systems. "Membership" in IANF would be automatic for all such forces unless individual country explicitly withdraws forces from SACEUR's program. These forces will continue under national ownership, may be withdrawn from NATO assignment in accordance with regular NATO procedures, and will be equipped with US- or UK-owned warheads which will remain under present custodial arrangements—i.e. weapons will not be owned by nation assigning delivery systems (except for US forces and for UK forces equipped with UK warheads) or by NATO as a

Source: Department of State, Central Files, Def 12 NATO. Confidential. Also sent to CINCLANT for POLAD. Drafted by Spiers; cleared by Weiss, Furnas, and Owen; and approved by Popper.

whole. IANF will be under SACEUR command and no new command or NATO political control arrangements will be set up, although some staff reorganization will take place in SHAPE (see Circular 1729)[1] as well as certain possible adjustments at Omaha and Norfolk, all of which designed to increase European participation in NATO nuclear affairs. IANF thus is evolutionary development of NATO nuclear organization rather than radical new departure.

2. MLF will be seaborne MRBM force to be multilaterally owned and manned by founding governments and assigned by them to NATO. When assignment made SACEUR will have same command and targeting authority over MLF as he will have over IANF forces: force would be part of SACEUR nuclear strike plans and committed to Scheduled Program. MLF and IANF together will constitute NATO Nuclear Force (NNF): whether new command arrangements under SACEUR or new political arrangements in NATO will then be required for NNF not a matter for decision at this time. MLF will have political governing body of its own to perform those functions with respect to MLF which are now performed by national governments with respect to nationally owned and manned forces, i.e. basic political decision re release, use of nuclear weapons and all logistic, administrative, etc., decisions now taken by national governments. Warheads in MLF will be under multilateral ownership and custody and not retained under exclusive US ownership or special US custodial arrangements aboard vessels. MLF would be at disposal owning governments under terms to be agreed among themselves, and could not be withdrawn from NATO except by decision among owners. MLF would be "open-ended" and any NATO member who wished contribute necessary resources would be able to join—purpose is not to set up inner circle or "Alliance within an Alliance." In introducing principle multilateral control, manning, and ownership of nuclear weapons MLF would be means of giving non-nuclear powers more basic participation in nuclear deterrence and would thus be important new departure, both in military and political terms, in NATO affairs.

Ball

---

[1] Dated April 7, it outlined the status of the consideration of IANF forces based on various discussions that had taken place up to that time. (Ibid.)

191. Memorandum for the Record

Washington, April 24, 1963, 10:30 a.m.

SUBJECT

Meeting with the President on the Multilateral Force, Wednesday, April 24, 1963, 10:30 A.M., in the Cabinet Room

PRESENT

Secretary Rusk, Under Secretary Ball, Messrs. Tyler, Chayes, Kitchen, and Gerard Smith; Messrs. Nitze and McNaughton, Admiral Ricketts, Admiral Anderson; Mr. Bundy and Mr. Kaysen

The President opened by praising Admiral Ricketts and Mr. McNaughton for their effective missionary work in Germany.[1] In response to Secretary Rusk's suggestion, Admiral Ricketts said that he had no doubt that the German Navy and the Ministry of Defense were both unequivocally behind the surface ship mode. This was also true of the Deputy Foreign Minister. The Germans were sending a team of technical people, both military and civilian, who will arrive on Monday to look into matters of ship construction, equipment, costs and training. They are doing this for technical reasons and because they need material to convince the German legislature. Admiral Anderson observed that underlying all the discussions in Germany was the hope that in the future the door could be opened for the additional nuclear submarines in the force. Admiral Ricketts observed that he had told the Germans that, although he had no authority to commit the government on this point, he was sure that there could be a future evolution of the force. However, the immediate issue was the surface ships, and he had urged the Germans to go ahead with the surface ships now without worrying about how it would evolve. Mr. Tyler pointed out that his instructions[2] had directed him to say the same thing and that, in speaking with Schroeder and Adenauer, he had. Secretary Rusk remarked that it was clearly necessary to hold out this hope. The President observed that there was a delicate matter of wording involved, and we had to be careful just how we said what we said, but he agreed that something had to be said. Admiral Ricketts said that in his discussions he had put no date to the process of evolution into another mode—neither five, nor seven years, nor any other time.

The President turned to the question of size of the force. Did we need to maintain 25 ships for technical reasons, and would this be a

---

Source: Kennedy Library, National Security Files, MLF. Secret.

[1] Ricketts and McNaughton had begun discussions in Bonn on the military aspects of the MLF on April 17. Reports on these meetings are in Department of State, Central Files, Def 12 NATO, and Pol 7 US/Merchant; a copy of Ricketts' instructions, dated April 9 and approved by the President the following day, is ibid., Def(MLF).

[2] See footnote 1, Document 185.

sticking point? Secretary Rusk said that he could not speak to the technical point, but that politically there was no need for a force as large as 25 ships, carrying 200 missiles. We wanted to be sure that the cost question wasn't a barrier to membership in the force, especially for the Italians and the Germans, and that therefore it might be desirable to have some flexibility on the size of the force. Mr. Nitze observed that the vulnerability problem, which was related to the size of the force, affected its political credibility. If the force were too small in technical terms, then the political effect we were seeking would be lost, because it would not be considered an effective force by the Europeans. Secretary Rusk asked whether we could at some later stage talk of a range of 15–25 ships, rather than stick with 25 as the necessary minimum size. Mr. Nitze wondered whether 15 ships were enough from the military point of view. Admiral Ricketts said that as long as we talked in terms of a pure surface ship force, a force of fewer than 20 ships raised technical questions.

The President asked how important in mathematical terms was the increase in vulnerability if we talked about a smaller force as compared to a 25 ship force. Admiral Ricketts said that he could not give a precise answer. Many variables, including the ability to deploy ships in different kinds of waters, make 20 a good minimum figure. The President asked for a detailed examination of the relative vulnerability of 15, 20 and 25 ship forces, and Admiral Anderson agreed that the Navy would be responsible for one. Mr. Bundy suggested that we stay with 25 as a number for public discussion now, but we take no fixed positions within the Departments concerned as to whether, how, and when to fall back to a lower number.

Secretary Rusk said that the next step was to see what points had to be covered in a preliminary agreement, and he went over the nine points of Mr. McNaughton's draft memorandum.[3] Our immediate problem was the question of consultation with Congress. He expected that he would have a response from Adenauer on May 3. He thought that we should talk with the Congressional leaders, at least, before that. The President asked whether Adenauer's response on control would be satisfactory. Mr. Bundy replied that he was certain it would be, and that what we had to say to Congress is that we had agreement on unanimity, or, if there was something less than unanimity, the change would be on the European side and would in no way limit the U.S. veto. The President asked again whether the Germans would agree to this, and Mr. Bundy said "Yes." Mr. McNaughton observed that perhaps the Germans were not quite as firm as was suggested. The conversations on control in Germany took the shape of Ambassador Dowling's asserting

---

[3] Not found.

the U.S. position, and the Germans offering no objection. This was a shade less affirmative than a position in which the Germans had spoken out positively on the issue. Mr. Bundy observed that the Germans, however, had no worry about the U.S. veto. Any worries they had about unanimity arose from the possibility of a Harold Wilson veto. Secretary Rusk said that he had put our position perfectly plainly to Schroeder in a private conversation in Paris, and Schroeder had expressed no objection. The President said he did not want to talk to Congress until the German agreement was in hand. He feared the discussion with the Congress would leak, and the Germans would react to the reports by denying that what they heard was what they had agreed to. Therefore, he wanted to wait on Adenauer's letter.

The President then turned to the questions of ownership, custody and security of the warheads, and asked whether they would continue to be in U.S. custody. Mr. Chayes said "No." The whole crew would in effect be the custodians. It was clear that we would want to have a transfer in ownership, and this would require legislation. We had a semantic problem of how we wished to describe the new situation. Secretary Rusk said that it was much more desirable for the warheads to be owned by the force as such, and not by any of the individual nations in the force. It was certainly clear that in relation to the Soviet Union, we didn't want a situation in which the Germans own warheads themselves. The President asked whether it was necessary to transfer ownership explicitly. Messrs. Chayes and Smith both responded strongly that it was. There was a great expectation in Europe that ownership would be transferred. Meeting this expectation was a necessary condition for a political deal. Mr. Nitze observed that the Europeans wanted the transfer of ownership, and that of course the Russians would be content to see us continue ownership. Secretary Ball and Mr. Chayes remarked that what we wanted was corporate ownership by the MLF as such, rather than a partnership in which each partner participated in ownership. Mr. Bundy remarked that Congressman Holifield would probably be on the side of the Russians in respect to ownership, and that this was a symbol of the problems we have to deal with in changing the law. Mr. Smith observed that we would probably have to have agreements with the MLF similar to the agreements we had with some of our NATO Allies. We would probably have to have an atomic energy agreement with the MLF which provided for the disclosure of certain restricted data to the MLF.

The President asked whether we could give ownership to the MLF which in turn would entrust custody to the United States. This appeared to be excessively complicated to several in the group. Admiral Anderson observed that the process of inspection and maintenance of the warheads would have to remain in U.S. hands. Mr. Chayes pointed out that there were various technical guards that were possible against tampering, photography and the like while the warheads were on the ship.

The President asked what provisions for security would be made on the ship itself, in the way of custodial guard. Secretary Rusk and Mr. Chayes pointed out that U.S. personnel could continue to be part of the custodial group. Mr. Smith emphasized that there was a difference between the question of legal custody, which should be in the MLF as such, and the practical involvement of U.S. officers and crew members in the custodial and safety forces aboard the ship. Secretary Rusk said that the indirect method of U.S. involvement was preferable from a political point of view. Mr. Bundy asked whether the physical security of the warheads and design data would be as good in the MLF as under present NATO arrangements.

There was a great deal of discussion on this point between Messrs. Chayes, Smith and Bundy. The President remarked that it is clear that we need to be well prepared on this matter in detail before we go to the Congress, and we have to compare the risk potentials in the present NATO arrangement with those in prospect under our proposed arrangements with the MLF. We must respond in some detail on matters like photography, opening of the warheads and the like. Before we went to Congress, we had to settle at least the political control question with the Germans and, if possible, the Italians, and we had to be fully prepared on the issue of security. He asked who should do it. Mr. Bundy observed that the matter should be under the general direction of Ambassador Merchant, but that on the security and design consideration, it would be most helpful to involve Commissioner Ramey as a participant. The President agreed on this point. He asked Secretary Rusk to organize a meeting to cover these points with him before there was any Congressional consultation.

Mr. Bundy observed that in addition to this question there is a further question of just what we should set as a goal for June—achieve the preliminary agreement on the detailed observations by Mr. McNaughton, or something less. He remarked that Ambassador Finletter and Ambassador Merchant had certain differences of view in this matter, and that they should be heard. The President responded that he would like to hear them next week when they are both here. He remarked that we have open to us a choice in the whole range from a communiqué to a detailed preliminary agreement as a goal to achieve by the time of his visit, and we need not necessarily choose now.

The meeting ended about 11:00 o'clock.

C.K.[4]

---

[4] Printed from a copy that bears these typed initials.

192. **Telegram From the Department of State to the Embassy in Germany**

Washington, May 2, 1963, 7:50 p.m.

2673. Eyes only for Chargé. Following is unofficial Germany Embassy translation of letter from Chancellor to President transmitted under covering letter dated April 30 from German Ambassador:

Begin text.

"My dear Mr. President:

I would like to revert again to the question of creating a Multilateral Nuclear Force which you discussed in your letter of March 29.[1]

The Federal Government appreciates that you have sent to Bonn, in accordance to the suggestions I made in my letter of April 4,[2] a group of experts headed by Admiral Ricketts. The instructive explanations given by Admiral Ricketts on the question of survivability of surface ships have to a large extent dissipated our doubts with regard to an initial equipment of the Multilateral Force with surface ships. The Federal Government is therefore in agreement with your proposal, that the Multilateral Force should in the beginning be equipped with surface ships as carriers for the Polaris A–3. However, the Federal Government wishes to emphasize that a subsequent examination of equipping the MLF with submarines is reserved, should this seem appropriate in the light of past experience.

Moreover the Federal Government has examined your proposals as to political control of the Multilateral Force. It agrees that in the beginning an arrangement may be provided under which the decision to permit the use of the Multilateral Force requires the consent of the major participating countries. However, the Federal Government deems it necessary that this arrangement too should be re-examined after some years in the light of past experience and that a change to a different arrangement should not be excluded.

The Federal Government would appreciate if a provisional agreement on the MLF could be signed by the Federal Republic of Germany and other interested NATO states already during your visit in Europe next June. The Federal Government is prepared to enter immediately into discussions concerning such an agreement. The list of points en-

---

Source: Department of State, Central Files, Def 12 NATO. Secret; Verbatim Text. A copy of the German-language original of the Chancellor's letter was attached to the source text.

[1] See Document 185.

[2] See Document 187.

closed in your letter of March 29 which would have to be dealt with in a provisional agreement on the MLF offers a good basis for these discussions.

On this occasion, those technical and financial questions which according to the enclosure to your letter should be dealt with already in the provisional agreement, and which are still not decided upon, should be settled. Among these questions is the decision concerning the number of ships and rockets with which the MLF should be equipped. Moreover, the share which the participating states should contribute towards the expenditures of the force has to be determined. This should be based on a still more precise summary of the overall expenditures.

The Federal Government is prepared in principle to assume an essential share of the costs of the MLF. It would, however, prefer if the United States as the leading power of the alliance would make in the financial field and in that of personnel a somewhat larger contribution to the MLF than the Federal Republic of Germany. The Federal Government is of the opinion that this could promote the willingness of other NATO states to participate in the MLF.

The previous discussions have already led to a consensus in principle between our two governments. The Federal Government deems it necessary that now also other NATO states are won over to pledge their participation in the Multilateral Force. The Federal Government proposes that the future talks in preparation of a preliminary agreement should as soon as possible be held with other interested NATO countries participating. The Federal Government shares your wish that after signing a preliminary agreement, negotiations for a formal treaty should be carried on and concluded by fall of this year.

The Federal Government notes with deep satisfaction that the project of a Multilateral Force, to which the Federal Republic attributes great political and military importance, now is getting close to realization. I am very grateful to you for the emphasis with which your Government and you personally support the idea of the Multilateral Force. I am convinced that the obstacles still existing on the way towards the Multilateral Force can be overcome and that the Multilateral Force will contribute decisively to the military strength and the political unity of the alliance.

I am looking forward to your visit in June.

With kindest regards

Yours, (signed: Adenauer)"

End text.

Ball

193.   Memorandum for the Record

Washington, May 3, 1963.

SUBJECT

> Meeting with the President on the Multilateral Force, Friday, May 3, 1963 in the
> Cabinet Room

PRESENT

> Secretary Ball, Ambassadors Merchant and Finletter, Messrs. Tyler, Rostow,
> Chayes, Smith, Admiral Lee, State; Secretary McNamara, Under Secretary
> Gilpatric, General Taylor, Admiral Ricketts, Messrs. Nitze and McNaughton,
> Defense; Commissioners Palfrey and Ramey, AEC; Mr. Bundy

Secretary Ball opened the discussion, listing those MLF problems which needed early decisions. These included Congressional consultation; approaches to the British; key elements to be incorporated in the final MLF charter; and Greek, Turkish, and other participation in the Force.

Secretary Ball said the State Department did not think Congressional consultation could be deferred much longer. Congress was becoming restive about the MLF and the situation would not be eased by the Bundestag discussions on the MLF which were due to get underway next week in Bonn.

Secretary McNamara disagreed. He said he was unaware of Congressional restiveness and questioned the wisdom of engaging the Congress, at least until an attempt had been made to bring the British on board.

After a further exchange, the President said discussions on the Hill were certain to leak and this would put the British in an embarrassing position. He therefore thought it best to delay the discussions on the Hill until after an approach had been made to the British Government. Moreover, the Administration then would be in a position to go to Congress with British and German commitments in hand.

Mr. Bundy asked whether discussions with the Joint Committee could not take place anyway. These would focus on the technical shape of the Force rather than the diplomatic progress of the exercise and provide a technical foundation that would be helpful later. The President agreed these would be useful but asked that they also be held in abeyance until after the British talks.

Source: Kennedy Library, National Security Files, Meetings and Memoranda Series, Meetings with the President. Secret.

Addressing Commissioners Ramey and Palfrey, the President went on to say that when talks with the Joint Committee got underway—and he felt that talks with Senator Pastore and the Staff would be extremely useful—it would be important to stress the fact of British and German participation to counter the arguments that the MLF was a "nutty" venture; and remind the Committee that the Administration, with considerable effort and apparent success, had met two of the Committee's principal concerns—mode and control.

Commissioner Palfrey pointed out there was still the matter of custody but the AEC felt this was manageable. Commissioner Palfrey also brought to the President's attention the Commissioners' statement on the warhead and design data security problem. The President said this statement, as well as that of the JCS, which Secretary McNamara gave the President, was helpful. (The JCS document had a paragraph for everyone, but in effect said the MLF was feasible, useful, and desirable.)[1]

On the diplomatic side the President felt getting U.K. participation in the MLF was the most urgent item of business. This was particularly important to avoid giving the MLF the appearance of a U.S./German arrangement. Moreover, the British might be reminded that the MLF was an integral part of the Nassau commitment.

After some discussion it was agreed that discussions with the British would get underway next week in London, with Secretary Ball, Admiral Ricketts, and John McNaughton joining Ambassador Bruce for these talks. To keep the noise level down, Secretary Ball would travel to London alone, (ostensibly to discuss trade problems) while Admiral Ricketts and John McNaughton would travel a separate route, via Paris.

In this connection, Secretary McNamara raised the question of the British financial contribution. He felt this should be no less than 10% of the total. Given other commitments, he thought 10% might impose a very heavy financial burden on the British. He therefore felt we would have to help the British and suggested this might be accomplished by revising other arrangements we had with them. He proposed looking into these possibilities immediately after the meeting.

The President agreed with this general approach, but said he wanted to clear in advance the instructions for the British talks, including the proposed financial arrangements.

---

[1] Presumably a reference to JCSM–350–63, May 2, to the Secretary of Defense, which began with a statement that there was no military need for a seaborne MLF, but that, given adequate participation and support by the Allies, it was feasible and would be an effective and useful supplement to NATO nuclear strength. (National Archives and Records Administration, RG 218, JCS Files)

The President then turned the discussion to the Italians. After some discussion of the political uncertainties in Rome, the President suggested a message go forward to Fanfani, urging early Italian commitment to the MLF. He was prepared to leave the form of the message to Ambassador Reinhardt's discretion to avoid putting Fanfani in an embarrassing position.

In reply to the President's question as to what might be done for Spaak, Walt Rostow undertook to speak with Spaak next week—since he will be in Brussels then on other business. He also agreed that he would keep these discussions on a very general plane.

The President then returned to the subject of Bundestag discussions on the MLF. He wondered whether Adenauer could not be asked to have them postponed until we talked with the British and were ready to start our own consultations with the Congress. Mr. Bundy thought this was feasible, especially since Adenauer left this possibility open in his letter. The President asked that Adenauer be told we were delaying our consultations with the Congress, pending talks with the British and hoped the Germans would do the same.

Ambassador Merchant mentioned that the Greeks and Turks were anxious to participate in the MLF. Their principal problem was money, but he felt some formula could be found to meet this problem. If they joined, control arrangements probably would have to be modified.

Mr. Bundy then raised the question of the negotiating timetable. He thought we should move ahead as quickly as possible, but did not think it would be useful to be tied to a fixed and arbitrary schedule. We did not want to feel we were defaulting if we did not have an agreed treaty by September.

After an exchange on the Rockefeller/Nixon nuclear ploy, the President said it was necessary to make our political case clear and convincing. Mr. Merchant said such a paper was in preparation in State, and Mr. Bundy asked that it be fully coordinated with the White House, Defense, and AEC.

In conclusion, the President reiterated that the first order of business was trying to get the British on board. Congressional consultations would follow.

D.K.[2]

---

[2] Initialed by David Klein.

194. Memorandum of Conversation

Washington, May 6, 1963.

SUBJECT

Multilateral Force

PARTICIPANTS

Assistant Secretary Tyler
Ambassador Merchant, S/MF
Mr. Spiers, EUR/RPM

Mr. Denis A. Greenhill
Minister, U.K. Embassy

Mr. Greenhill reported that when Ambassador Ormsby Gore saw President Kennedy[1] subsequent to the Ambassador's meeting Friday with Under Secretary Ball,[2] he had advised the President of the U.K. views on the MLF as they had been transmitted to the State Department. The President told the Ambassador that, given the situation resulting from the Italian election, U.K. participation in the MLF was more desirable than ever and he hoped the UK would be prepared to make a statement of its position. The Ambassador had noted that, while the US wished to proceed apace in order to achieve a treaty by September, the UK had to go slow. The President had agreed to provide the U.K. Embassy "this week" with a paper setting forth what the UK could contribute to the MLF and what "price tags" could be assigned to various items and facilities which the UK could make available. The President wanted to send this paper to the Prime Minister to reflect on in the hopes of gaining an early U.K. decision. The President had spoken to the Ambassador of the UK taking a 10–15% share of the MLF. The President reportedly had not realized that the Prime Minister believed that the UK's Nassau commitment was to contribute Polaris submarines to the NATO Nuclear Force and not necessarily to participate in the mixed-manned element of this Force. The Prime Minister understands the U.S. desire for U.K. participation but believes that this would require a *new* U.K. decision. The Macmillan government is already under attack on this general question. This is why a U.S. paper such as the President promised would be invaluable in helping the UK make up its mind.

Source: Department of State, Central Files, Def 12 NATO. Secret. Drafted by Spiers.

[1] Gore met with the President from 4:02 to 4:30 p.m. on May 3 (Kennedy Library, President's Appointment Book), but no other record of this meeting has been found.

[2] Memoranda of Ball's conversation with Gore on the MLF and IANF are in the Department of State, Central Files, Def 4 and Def 12 NATO.

Ambassador Merchant reviewed the highlights of his talks with Lord Home and Prime Minister Macmillan in London which covered the possibilities of U.K. contributions "in kind" to minimize cash requirements. He recalled that the communiqué[3] issued at the end of his talks recorded the hope of HMG to find the means to participate in the MLF.

At Mr. Greenhill's request Ambassador Merchant reviewed present U.S. thinking on the schedule of activities on MLF negotiations and Congressional consultations between now and September, including the concept of working out agreed instructions for representatives of governments who would participate in a drafting group. Mr. Greenhill expressed alarm at the time schedule contemplated. He asked whether we considered that agreed terms of reference would be recorded in a common document and signed by governments. Ambassador Merchant noted that there were a variety of ways in which the objective could be accomplished. In substance, what we sought was agreement by governments to assign representatives to the negotiation and to give them common instructions on certain basic issues. This would not constitute a commitment to sign the agreement resulting from the negotiations. We hope that this stage of agreement in principle could be reached by the time the President goes to Europe (about June 20).

Mr. Greenhill said that this schedule would give the UK "big trouble." He could not judge how amenable the Prime Minister might be to these suggestions since this is clearly a very sensitive political issue: Macmillan is under attack both from the opposition and from elements of his own party. Ambassador Merchant noted that while the treaty would be open-ended, the US preferred that the UK be in as a founding member. He estimated that we would be able to give the UK a paper confirming the time schedule he had outlined, the nature and content of the terms of reference, an indication of what we would hope the UK would find possible to contribute as its share, and that payments could be made, in part at least, "in kind."

Mr. Tyler said that he had passed on to the White House and to the Acting Secretary the suggestion that Ambassador Ormsby Gore go to London to work this problem out. Mr. Greenhill noted that Ormsby Gore had not been thinking of going so immediately as next week, and that the Ambassador would be away from May 10–14. He said the Ambassador expressed the hope that he might look over the papers which we would send to the Prime Minister before they are despatched, since he might advise on the best way of presenting the issues involved.

---

[3] Not found.

In response to an observation by Mr. Tyler, Mr. Greenhill noted that there would be a useful impact on the British Labor Party if "Willy Brandt and Company" came out in favor of the MLF. He said that the UK was quite prepared to continue with talks on the technical level between the US and UK Navies while the basic political consideration was going on.

---

195. Message From the President's Special Assistant for National Security Affairs (Bundy) to Prime Minister Macmillan's Private Secretary (de Zulueta)

Washington, May 10, 1963.

The President has asked me to report that in sending the following message on the MLF, he does not mean in any way to put this topic ahead of the test ban matter on which he has just read the Prime Minister's last message. He will be replying to that at the first of the week, and while his own reading of the Khrushchev letter is somewhat less optimistic than the Prime Minister's, he has given instructions that there be as few gloomy rumors as possible until the next move has been agreed between the Prime Minister and himself. Message follows:

Dear Friend:

I have talked with David Gore about recent developments in our plans for a multilateral nuclear force, and at his suggestion I am writing directly to you to ask your support at a point that I may be decisive in the progress of the large-scale undertaking we began at Nassau.[1]

In spite of all the criticism and lack of understanding with which the Nassau agreement was met at first, it has weathered the winter very well. The Polaris agreement between our two countries is clear and good, and I would not want to have the job of opposing it in either country. The inter-allied nuclear force is well on its way; if we can judge by the latest discussions in NATO, its real values are going to carry the day; the French have been reduced to haggling over names, mainly because their own best people know that the idea is a good one for them as well as for NATO. So two of our three projects are pretty well settled.

Source: Department of State, Presidential Correspondence: Lot 66 D 204. Secret; Eyes Only.

[1] See footnote 1, Document 194.

There remains the multilateral force. As I said to David, the Germans have now come aboard in terms that are very satisfactory indeed, although there is still some bargaining to be done about costs and shares. I enclose a copy of the Chancellor's last letter[2] to show just where matters now stand. Between the Germans and ourselves much more than half of the total effort is assured, and some of the smaller poorer cousins like the Greeks and the Turks are waiting only for a complimentary ticket.

But what this club now needs most is the joint support of the Nassau partners. I believe that with such support, the MLF will be sure of success. And what is much more important is that with the U.K. as a charter member the enterprise will serve the larger ideas of a big Europe, an Atlantic partnership, and a reconciliation of independence with interdependence. And these, as we both know, are very large prizes indeed.

I recognize fully that in your country as in ours there are honest sceptics about the MLF—though I'd be glad to turn some of our zealous admirals loose on Admiral Mountbatten. I recognize also that many Englishmen think the Germans should be kept quiet in other ways. But your reports from Bonn will probably run with ours in expressing the depth of the German desire for nuclear reassurance through a shared enterprise. What is encouraging about this German desire is that its basis is *not* an ambition for independence, but a deep need to feel sure that the nuclear powers will be there when needed—with the result that as far as we can tell the Germans actually prefer to keep our finger on the trigger, at least for the present.

Finally, I recognize that your commitment to British Polaris submarines puts a limit on the funds available for a British share in the MLF—and I understand also that while you gave a fair wind to the project, from Nassau onward, there is no contract that binds you to any specified share of it.

But I have watched with interest and respect the serious and growing support which you and your colleagues have given to the MLF idea through the winter—in your own statement of January 30, in Shuckburgh's statement in Paris on February 27, and in the March meetings in London between your Government and Merchant's mission.[3] This sup-

---

[2] See Document 192.

[3] For text of Macmillan's statement to the House of Commons, see House of Commons, *Parliamentary Debates*, 5th Series, vol. 670, cols. 955 ff. A summary of Shuckburgh's statement to the North Atlantic Council was transmitted in Polto 1068 from Paris, February 28. (Department of State, Central Files, Pol 7 US/Merchant) Regarding Merchant's talks in London, see Document 183.

port has been of great importance already, and I think it is well understood in Germany, as it is here.

Meanwhile, General de Gaulle's insistent and self-imposed isolation has been matched by his even more determined commitment to an independent force. In a queer way he, who appears to dislike Nassau, has made all three of its parts more important: your Polaris force because it is not easy to see how Britain could be without an independent force while France insists on having one; the inter-allied force, because it holds the gate open for some real French participation in NATO; and the MLF, because it is the best available way of making it clear that the French force in its present form is not the only—or the best—way of giving the Continent a real share in the most modern form of deterrence.

Through the winter and spring our own thinking and planning for the MLF have been greatly refined. We are now clear about the value— and the preferability, for these purposes—of surface ships; we are clear about the things we do and do not need to ask of our own Congress; we are clear that control should be unanimous among the major participants; we are clear that the whole idea—complex and demanding as it is, and hard to understand at first—offers a new hope for unity in NATO and a path to safe partnership with the Germans.

And while the Russians write about it in their usual unhelpful way, Thompson and our other interpreters report that their noises are significantly mild, for them—and that they do seem to understand the enormous difference between a thoroughly mixed force that simply cannot be fired without the consent of its nuclear members and a force that might go off on the unauthorized whim of some "revanchist." And indeed the truth of the matter is that the MLF will be at least as safe from this standpoint as the nuclear weapons now deployed to German forces, under our custody, on the Central Front.

So I return to my main purpose, which is to ask if you and your colleagues can now make a definite commitment to participate in the multilateral force. We do not need to decide exact shares at this time, but as I understand it what has been discussed among our colleagues is a possible contribution on the order of 10%. I myself strongly believe that whatever the immediate hazards or costs may be, the long-range interest of your country, as of ours, lies deeply in the assured success of the MLF, along with the well-started inter-allied force. We must show all Europe which are the nations that really care for the common interdependent interest.

What does not go forward eventually slips back—so I believe we ought to do all we can to keep the momentum we now have on all aspects of Nassau. What I would hope is that your Government might see its way in the next few weeks to a clear decision in principle. Such a decision would pave the way for prompt negotiations looking toward a basic understanding among prospective participants.

A British decision to join will be immediately helpful in Italy, where it is more important than ever that there be encouragement to a reaffirmation of support for clear commitment to NATO and an active role in its affairs. What is more important still, your decision would confirm the Germans in the responsible choice they prefer to make, and it would put an end to what is otherwise the very real possibility of a Franco/German cooperation in nuclear weapons systems in the narrow Gaullist spirit.

I understand that on the naval side our experts are already in touch with each other, and I am making arrangements to insure that David Bruce is kept fully up to date on our thinking. I do want you to know once again that while I see the costs as well as the opportunities, for us both, I am convinced that the moment for a determined advance together is here.

With warm personal regards,

Sincerely,

John F. Kennedy[4]

---

[4] Printed from a copy that bears this typed signature.

---

196.   Strategy Paper Prepared in the Department of State

Washington, May 17, 1963.

NATO MINISTERIAL MEETING
Ottawa, May 22–24, 1963

1.   Salient Features of the Current Situation

As Ministers gather for the meeting at Ottawa, five factors dominate the Atlantic scene:

Source: Department of State, Conference Files: Lot 66 D 110, CF 2260. Secret. Drafted by Popper and cleared by Tyler, Schaetzel, Seymour Weiss, Owen, Nitze, BNA, GER, and WE.

a. Gaullist opposition to an expanded EEC and an effective NATO has had a depressing influence on the Alliance. The crisis provoked by the French in January has been succeeded by a search for ways to cope with French intransigence, without sacrificing all possibilities for progress in Alliance and Common Market matters.

b. As the Cuban crisis has receded into the background, East-West relations, except as regards Laos, have moved into a calmer period; the Soviet bloc, like the West, seems to be undergoing a period of reassessment or consolidation.

c. Western Europe has entered on a period of governmental instability and change; Italy is in the midst of an interregnum while opposition parties in Germany and the United Kingdom appear to be approaching power. Accordingly, the governments concerned are becoming more reluctant to take hard decisions.

d. The Nassau Declaration has stimulated new developments in NATO's nuclear arrangements, the end results of which cannot yet be discerned.

e. The continuing disparity between accepted NATO force requirements and the force contributions of certain member nations remains a potential source of serious inter-Allied discord.

In these circumstances there would seem to be more need than ever for firm leadership to inculcate a sense of purpose among statesmen unsure of the trend of events in national and international affairs. As is customary at NATO meetings, the United States will be expected to strike the keynotes for NATO action and to establish guideposts by which Allied statesmen may steer their courses.

2. *General Objectives*

At Ottawa the general US objectives should be:

a. To maintain Alliance solidarity and morale in the face of the French onslaught against a cohesive and effective NATO structure and against an integrated Western Europe. More specifically, to avoid a direct confrontation with the French which would have the effect of aligning them against other NATO members in a divisive conflict; instead, to devise means to carry forward Alliance activities despite French reluctance to participate.

b. To continue to broaden the dimensions of the consultative process in NATO by full and frank exchange of views on political and military problems which should be of interest to all the Allies.

c. To extend the progress now beginning to be made in sharing nuclear responsibility within the Alliance, through decisions on arrangements for the Inter-Allied Nuclear Forces and through private, expository conversations on the Multilateral Force.

d. To set the stage for a sustained US effort in NATO to persuade the Europeans of the need for improved conventional forces capable of prolonged operations in forward areas, thus making practicable a strategy of measured response to Soviet aggression.

3. Political Issues

a. *Consultation.* Pursuing its recent efforts, the United States should carry the process of frank exchange of views on political problems, both general and specific, even beyond the point hitherto reached. It would be appropriate for the Secretary frankly to explore the nature of the ties binding the Alliance together; the meaning and consequences of independence and interdependence; the effect of preponderant US military power and our wide-ranging interests and responsibilities; the relationship of NATO to East-West confrontations in areas distant from Europe; and similar matters of fundamental concern to NATO. While admitting the difficulties of dealing with crisis situations to the satisfaction of all concerned, the United States can legitimately seek Allied cooperation in building a more generally acceptable structure of consultative practice.

b. *East-West Problems.* Relatively little need be said in the meetings with regard to specific East-West problems. It will be helpful to explain the situation as regards Laos and Vietnam and to present a brief progress report on the positions in Cuba and Haiti and their implications for Latin America as a whole. On other areas such as Berlin, however, there will be little to add to what Ministers already know. Our views will be sought on prospects for a test ban agreement, on a declaration on the non-dissemination of nuclear weapons to states not now possessing them, and on measures to reduce the risks of war including direct communication between US and USSR Heads of Government. A sober enumeration of the difficulties standing in the way of any further East-West accords on these subjects at this time will help to dissipate any false optimism on these matters. At the same time, it should serve to counteract French insinuations that the United States is planning to dispose of European interests in direct bilateral dealings with the Soviet Union. On a more general plane, the point should be made that recent developments in the USSR—notably, ideological differences internally and vis-à-vis the Chinese Communists, leadership problems and economic difficulties—suggest that Soviet foreign policy may be moving into a period of greater intransigence.

c. *Integration and Partnership.* The French would be antagonized and nothing substantial would be gained, if the United States were too pointedly to reassert its support for European integration. We should, however, continue to emphasize in NATO that our goal is Atlantic partnership. In bilateral conversations, US spokesmen should stress both the continuity of American policy on these two main themes of American policy and the firmness and reliability of the American commitment to Europe. A principal objective in these matters should be to set at rest any doubts about our intention to fulfill our commitments to the common defense, in the nuclear area and in others.

4.   *Military Problems*

a.   *IANF and MLF.* We should evaluate fairly the moderate progress incorporated in the organizational arrangements concerning the Inter-Allied Nuclear Force, resisting any French effort further to denature the concept while restraining the British or others from provoking an open fight with the French. Careful press briefing will be required to maintain a balanced public view of the post-Nassau decisions on this subject, which after all represent the only specific accomplishment we now expect the Ministers to approve at Ottawa. It will also be appropriate for the United States briefly to report on the status of the Multilateral Force discussions; others will no doubt do so as well. While Ministerial action on the MLF will be premature and should be discouraged, US spokesmen should convey an atmosphere of confidence and momentum in their comments. Bilateral discussions on the status of MLF negotiations with the UK, German and Italian Foreign Ministers should be useful. Moreover, we should note the increase in information we are making available to NATO nations on nuclear matters and specifically the imminent submission of a proposed new Agreement for Cooperation regarding Atomic Information under section 144(b) of our Atomic Energy Act of 1954,[1] as amended, which will permit us to extend this procedure still further.

b.   *NATO Defense Policy.* The US should continue to expound to the Allies the need for a strategy of flexible response to Soviet aggression which will avoid the necessity to resort prematurely to nuclear warfare for the protection of NATO territory. It should urge the Allies to augment their conventional forces and adopt the necessary budget levels and planning practices for this purpose. The objective of US discussion on this subject should be to inaugurate study and action in NATO along these lines after the Ottawa meeting, so that measurable progress may be made this year toward acceptance of more equitable sharing of the NATO defense burden by the Allies.

c.   *American Military Retrenchment.* Allied Ministers will come to Ottawa with suspicions nurtured by press reports to the effect that the United States intends to reduce its conventional forces in Europe, either because of dissatisfaction with Allied performance or because of balance of payments difficulties. Any American comment giving currency

---

[1] For text of the Atomic Energy Act of 1954, see 68 Stat. 919.

to these suspicions would have disruptive effects running far beyond the meeting and in fact, in Western Europe generally. It is essential to avoid any reference to American planning on these matters pending completion of the President's trip to Europe and high-level policy decisions in the US Government as to whether or to what extent the American force structure in Europe should be altered.

---

197. Memorandum of Conversation

US/MC/14   Ottawa, May 23, 1963, 6:22 p.m.

UNITED STATES DELEGATION TO THE THIRTY-FIRST MINISTERIAL MEETING OF THE NORTH ATLANTIC COUNCIL
Ottawa, Canada, May 22–24, 1963

PARTICIPANTS

United States	United Kingdom
The Secretary of State	Lord Home, Secretary of State
Mr. William R. Tyler, EUR	Mr. Peter Thorneycroft, Minister of
Mr. Gerard C. Smith, S/MF	Defense

SUBJECT

Multilateral Force

The Secretary opened by stating that we wished to clarify the nature of what the US was proposing in regard to a commitment towards the MLF. He stated that we are suggesting now that the prospective MLF members agree to enter into a drafting group looking to the writing of a treaty. While no financial commitments were expected at this time, it would be understood that if practical arrangements satisfactory to the parties could be worked out, they would enter the MLF force. In other words, there would be a conditional commitment in principle.

Lord Home asked if we could not take this in two steps: first, have a group examine such things as the military requirement and possible

Source: Department of State, Conference Files: Lot 66 D 110, CF 2263. Secret. Drafted by Smith and approved in S on May 29. A conversation along similar lines was held May 20. (US/MC/7–D; ibid.)

ways of meeting it and, after agreement had been reached on these matters, then go into a drafting stage. He said that in any event, they could give no decision until after a Cabinet meeting next Thursday, and perhaps more than one Cabinet meeting would be necessary.

There was some discussion about the degree of commitment which a country would be expected to make merely by entering into a drafting exercise.

Lord Home pointed out the great difficulty which this decision presented to the Macmillan government, stating that all of the military were solidly opposed.

There was a discussion of the possible Ricketts mission, and Mr. Thorneycroft stated that he understood this was now cleared with London.

The Secretary pointed out the solid German interest in the MLF but pointed out the Germans and the US did not want to have a bilateral MRBM arrangement. He said the Italians have a lively interest. It is extremely important to have the UK in MLF—important both to us and to the Germans. Lord Home said the drafting problem was not difficult; he could draft a treaty right now if there was agreement on all of the substantive issues. He said there had been no joint US-UK technical study as yet. He said he did not understand the need for all the hurry.

Mr. Thorneycroft, with some heat, said the UK had never promised to subscribe anything to the force.

The Secretary answered Lord Home's question about hurry by pointing to European concerns that the US might be cooling off on the MLF concept, and he said that there was a need for early Congressional consultation in the US, as well as a hope that a treaty could be drafted in time to submit to Congress this session.

Lord Home questioned whether the Macmillan government could get this proposal through Parliament. He said, of course, they would try to do their best if an affirmative decision were made.

The Secretary pointed out the problem of committing the President's prestige in advance of good assurance that important European countries were with us. There would be little sense in engaging in a useless struggle with elements in Congress who would be opposed. Lord Home said that they had the same problem with their Parliament.

Mr. Thorneycroft asked if the US would be "hurt" if the UK finding was negative on the basis of a failure to find any military utility for the force—saying that this was a conclusion that Secretary McNamara told him he had reached. The Secretary answered that in this extremely regrettable contingency he thought it was likely that the US would go ahead anyway with other nations interested in the MLF.

Lord Home reverted to the need for further technical study, citing the possibility of flat-bottom monitors and also whether MLF ships would need escort vessels.

There was more discussion about the nature of the military requirement. It was pointed out that the US Joint Chiefs of Staff had found that the MLF force could become an effective combat force which could be a significant increment to the nuclear deterrent of NATO. The Secretary pointed out that this whole problem had originated with the felt military need contained in SACEUR's MRBM "requirement" which we had downgraded for political reasons. Mr. Thorneycroft urged that we re-study the whole matter in the context of the balance between nuclear and non-nuclear weapons systems and try to look at this thing from a purely military point of view. He said that UK military thought that it was "monstrous" that the UK should be asked to spend money on what they considered a very low priority weapons system.

Lord Home said the thing to do is to find out how we can do SACEUR's job with less resources.

The Secretary felt that the European urge to have access to a weapons system to match the Soviet MRBMs was a legitimate one and he thought that a seaborne system was preferable to land-based missiles—especially in Germany.

Mr. Thorneycroft asked about the possibility of a mixed air squadron. It was pointed out to him that convincing Europeans that surface ships were effective after Nassau was difficult enough. It would be impossible to persuade them that, in the time frame being considered for MLF, an aircraft system could be an effective military force.

The Secretary pointed out that the US had proposed surface ships long before Nassau, and the Nassau agreement which had concentrated on the submarine Polaris system had caused some degree of confusion in our European friends' minds. Lord Home asked what about four Polaris submarines if you could mix-man them. The Secretary pointed out the insufficiency of such a force in the face of such a large and growing MRBM deployment in the USSR. He felt that this Soviet system needed to be matched, to some extent—especially for psychological deterrent reasons. He urged Thorneycroft to obtain a current briefing on this Soviet build-up.

Mr. Thorneycroft pointed out the illusory nature of some military "requirements". The Secretary said he felt that the European part of NATO would be more "serene" if Allied Command Europe felt that it had missiles of its own.

Lord Home wondered if we could not make a new start, since the surface concept has been so downgraded in Europe and since one could expect large-scale public attacks on the concept.

The Secretary again stressed the importance that the UK be in as a founder of the MLF and pointed out the small percentage which participation would add to the UK defense budget—less than 1%. He said that he was surprised at the UK feeling that this matter had not been studied enough yet, that these problems seem to come to the UK as problems of first impression. He pointed out that we have been studying the matter for a long time. Lord Home felt that this was "made in America" package and it would be better to start again and try to jointly construct an acceptable system. It was pointed out that this matter had been studied internationally for many months and the first proposal for surface ships had in fact been contained in a German paper early in 1962.

Lord Home acknowledged the strength of the political arguments in favor of the MLF, as did Thorneycroft, but speculated about great Parliamentary difficulties.

The Secretary pointed out that the US did not consider this project as military nonsense. He stated that the missiles would cost the US more than the charge which the US would make to the MLF.

The Secretary concluded by urging the UK to come to an affirmative conclusion and indicated his understanding that the President would communicate further with the Prime Minister on the account.

Lord Home said they would do their best.

---

198. Memorandum of Conversation

Washington, May 28, 1963, 5–6 p.m.

SUBJECT

European Situation

PARTICIPANTS

President John F. Kennedy
Foreign Minister Paul Henri Spaak of Belgium
Mr. Edmond Glenn, Interpreter
Mrs. Sophia Porson, Interpreter

The President asked Mr. Spaak whether he wanted the Belgian Ambassador to join in the conversation.

Source: Kennedy Library, National Security Files, Belgium. Secret. Drafted by Glenn and Porson. The meeting was held at the White House. Spaak was among a group of NATO Foreign and Defense Ministers who visited various U.S. military installations following the NAC meeting in Ottawa and then met with the President. A memorandum of the group's conversation with the President on May 29 is in Department of State, Central Files, NATO 8–2.

Mr. Spaak said that he wished to speak to the President alone and to speak very frankly about the situation which has developed within the Alliance. Difficult decisions will have to be taken. The primary fact is that of French policies. These policies are extremely bad and have brought about great changes within the Alliance, affecting both the European Community and the Atlantic Community.

The French are preoccupied with the question of nuclear weapons. Two points might be made in this respect. The first is that General de Gaulle has made a syllogism: a great country must have nuclear weapons, France is a great country, therefore it must have nuclear weapons. He holds very rigidly to this idea and he will not change. Secondly, he sincerely believes that the U.S. is going to withdraw from Europe, and this imposes upon him the duty to be prepared for such a possibility. He is not too unhappy about such a possibility, because if the United States withdraws from Europe and if France has a nuclear force, then the hegemony of France in Europe will be assured.

This attitude was reflected in his actions on January 14 when he delivered a severe blow to both the Atlantic and European Communities. His method in doing this was entirely unacceptable, as he had not warned either the British or his own partners at the Brussels negotiations of his intentions. De Gaulle forced a change in policy by a simple statement to the press. Resentment over these tactics is very strong in Europe and has created in Europe an atmosphere in which trust is lacking. It is in this context that the questions of the multinational and the multilateral forces have to be considered. France will not accept this multilateral force. French actions create doubt as to the very principle of the unity of the defense of America and Europe. General de Gaulle believes that the U.S. may lose interest in defending Europe, and therefore it is up to France to insure that defense. This is a false idea, but he cannot be convinced of that fact. Therefore, it is up to the other members of the Alliance to insure its unity by standing together.

The President asked Mr. Spaak whether he thought that helping France in the development of its nuclear force might be a good step if it were feasible. Should the US consider, as a possible policy for the future, a withdrawal from Europe? We would, in these circumstances, announce in advance that the US would turn over to the Europeans the nuclear weapons necessary for the defense of Western Europe.

Mr. Spaak replied negatively to this suggestion. He does not believe that any such policy would be likely to improve the situation within the Alliance. De Gaulle's ideas are based on false premises and moving in the direction of accepting them would amount to moving in the wrong direction. Minister Spaak could not imagine who would attack France alone. If war comes, all of Europe will be involved—not just France.

A multilateral nuclear force could have been the solution to the French and German problems, but it seems almost impossible to achieve at this point because France wishes to pursue its own policy. The result of France's policy has been to make Germany the number one country within the European Community, and should the Germans participate in the multilateral nuclear force, it will become the United States' number one ally on the European continent.

Another problem is that France can create serious difficulties in the economic relations between the United States and the European Community. Mr. Spaak mentioned that during the last EEC meeting, the French attitude had been such that he had feared it might seriously affect the GATT meeting in Geneva.

Having weighed all the pros and cons of the MLF, Minister Spaak recommended that we go ahead with it, but we must realize that France will create more and more difficulties.

The President asked Minister Spaak whether he thought the United States should give nuclear aid to France. Spaak replied that he would have said yes but for the fact that France has not shown itself to be an unconditional ally of the United States. De Gaulle maintains two positions which make it impossible for the United States to give France nuclear assistance: 1) He has often referred to the Atlantic Alliance as being a momentary, transitory thing, and 2) he often alludes to his vision of the Europe of the future extending from the Atlantic to the Urals.

President Kennedy commented that we have no assurance that if we help France become stronger it will be our ally. Having studied de Gaulle's policy, he does not consider de Gaulle a good risk.

President Kennedy said he was sure Spaak knew why we had put forward the MLF concept. There is a divergency of opinion about the MLF in Europe (for example Adenauer says one thing and Schroeder and Strauss say another). Furthermore, the President indicated he was not certain whether the MLF will ease those pressures.

Minister Spaak said that the MLF, if accepted by Germany, will solve one problem, because then Germany will not ask to have its own nuclear force. Naturally, if France refuses to participate in the MLF system, the system will not be perfect. The real question, however, is to solve the German problem, and to do that the MLF must be developed. The Foreign Minister noted that de Gaulle says he will not help Germany build up its own nuclear force, but it is very possible that he may some day offer to create a Franco-German atomic force.

President Kennedy said that if the MLF fails, then the warheads will remain under exclusive US control, which in the long run is bound to be an irritant.

President Kennedy said that he believes de Gaulle's policy of attacking NATO is a bad example to the rest of Europe. Taking Italy as a case in point, the President said that it would be most unfortunate if every Italian government were to have to decide on whether or not to support NATO.

Turning to Britain, he said that the British are reluctant about joining the MLF because the present government has been promoting the idea of a national deterrent and this will be a serious issue in the coming electoral campaign. President Kennedy and Prime Minister Macmillan have been corresponding on this question, and we are sending Admiral Ricketts to the UK to discuss it. We feel we should proceed with the MLF. Adenauer has agreed to surface ships and the concept of unanimity in firing. If the UK, Italy, Germany, and, we hope, the others agreed to the MLF this would be a joint enterprise with the Germans for the sixties.

President Kennedy said that he knows the concept of the MLF bothers de Gaulle, but isolated or not, de Gaulle will make difficulties anyway. Minister Spaak thought it better to have de Gaulle isolated and sulking than to give up the MLF. After all, the situation in France can change.

The President asked Mr. Spaak whether he thought de Gaulle would be in power for the next four or five years. Minister Spaak answered that de Gaulle's term of office may end sooner than that, but it would not necessarily solve the problem, since the question of de Gaulle's successor is an extremely dangerous one owing to France's domestic political situation. It is not certain that a succeeding government would be more sympathetic to the United States or the UK than the present regime. Moreover, de Gaulle's policies have already created a serious internal situation by causing a rapprochement between the Socialists and the Communists. However, there are other political figures in France who do not share de Gaulle's thinking. Debré, for example, does not have de Gaulle's prejudice against "les Anglo-Saxons". In Mr. Spaak's view Debré would not follow de Gaulle's policy towards them if he were chief of state.

The President asked whether the six countries of the EEC might develop a joint military policy. Spaak replied that this would be unwise because the defense of Europe and the United States must be indivisible. Moreover, why should Europe seek to develop its own nuclear force when it has the strength of the United States behind it. The only reason for having a separate force would be if Europe were to be engaged in a war by itself—and if the Communists start a war it will be directed against the United States more than against Europe. It will be a total war, involving Europe and the United States, and the defense of Europe would just be part of the overall defense of the West.

President Kennedy then asked to what extent de Gaulle's syllogism that France must have its own nuclear force and his statements that the United States might not defend Europe have gained support in Europe. Mr. Spaak answered that de Gaulle's ideas have some support in all parts of Western Europe, but only among a small minority. The great majority of Europeans have faith in the United States. The United States must avoid being influenced by de Gaulle's repeated statements that the United States will abandon Europe. The people and governments of Europe do not share de Gaulle's feeling.

President Kennedy asked Mr. Spaak what points he should make in his statements during his German and Italian visits this June. Mr. Spaak suggested that the President reiterate what Secretary Rusk said in Ottawa, i.e. that we are bound to Europe and to its defense not out of sentimentality but owing to the political and historical facts of life. Some Europeans still think of war in terms of 1914 or 1939—but the next war would not be over Alsace-Lorraine or a border dispute, but rather for world domination.

The President remarked it was unfortunate that with people like Pearson, Erhard, Luns, Fanfani and Moro as national leaders, all committed to cooperate within the Atlantic Alliance, one man could block the flow of history. Mr. Spaak expressed the belief that de Gaulle can do great harm by awakening nationalism in France, because this can lead to a rebirth of nationalism in Germany. In Britain the political campaign will be waged on the issue of a national deterrent.

Mr. Spaak said he fears Franco-German relations will worsen. He does not think that there is much substance to the Franco-German treaty as it is, and the idea of meeting every three months to discuss points of disagreement, such as defense, Britain, the Common Market, and so forth, is a very poor one, since, in fact, there are no major points of agreement. In this connection, the President said he felt that Adenauer, deep inside, had supported de Gaulle's stand on Britain's entry into the Common Market.

Mr. Spaak commented that there are now two policies in Germany, that of Adenauer and that of his successor. The policy of the latter is much less "Frenchified". He mentioned that during a recent talk Erhard had clearly shown that he was aware of the danger of a rebirth of French nationalism, which would inevitably lead to revival of German nationalism.

If we were to make a choice, the President asked, between the concept of the American-British-French triumvirate or the Franco-German alliance, which would be more dangerous? Mr. Spaak replied that both are bad, as either would destroy the Atlantic Alliance and lead countries like Belgium and the Netherlands into neutrality.

President Kennedy observed it is regrettable that there are such problems with and in Europe, because today's struggle does not lie there, but rather in Asia, Latin America, and Africa. The whole debate about an atomic force in Europe is really useless, because Berlin is secure, and Europe as a whole is well-protected. What really matters at this point is the rest of the world, and what we need is the type of cooperation shown by Belgium, the United States, and others in attempting to solve the Congo problem.

Mr. Spaak agreed with the President, but emphasized that de Gaulle does not see the world in that way. He sees it as it was in 1914 or 1939 when the state of Franco-German relations meant war or peace. Mr. Spaak commented that he could not imagine who would want to attack France today, but de Gaulle reasons in the past and talks as though World War II were yet to come. It would be so much better if de Gaulle could see the value of joint diplomacy, but he will not, and we must face that fact because "he is there."

One danger that we must watch for in economic negotiations, said Spaak, is that de Gaulle might push the Common Market countries into a protectionist policy. President Kennedy stated that the economic problem is crucial to the West, because this is where our position can be weakened, viz. the U.S. balance of payments situation. It is essential that we succeed in economic matters, because a failure for the United States is a failure for Europe, too. He said he was pleased that the "Kennedy round" would not take place until later, because he did not think that the current atmosphere is favorable.

---

199.   Circular Airgram From the Department of State to Certain Missions

Washington, May 29, 1963, 11:35 a.m.

CA–13427. Subject: NATO Ministerial Meeting, Ottawa, May 22–24, 1963. Ref: Sectos 8, 12, 13, 14, 17, 18 and 19.[1]

Source: Department of State, Central Files, NATO 3 Can(OT). Secret. Drafted by Kranich and van Hollen (RPM) and transmitted to 22 missions and commands in Europe and to USUN.

[1] None printed; dated May 22–24, they summarized various sessions of the Ministerial Meeting. (Ibid.)

This airgram briefly summarizes topics discussed and outcome of the NATO Ministerial Meeting, held at Ottawa, May 22–24, and encloses texts of statements by Secretary Rusk and Secretary McNamara and of the final communiqué.[2] A fuller record of the proceedings is contained in the referenced telegrams which have been pouched to all NATO capitals.

I.   Defense Subjects

1.   *IANF.* Without accepting the concept of a separate force, the Ministers approved: (a) assignment of the V-bombers and Polaris submarines to SACEUR; (b) establishment by SACEUR of a nuclear deputy; (c) arrangements for broader participation by non-Americans in nuclear activities in SHAPE and at Omaha; (d) more extensive nuclear information to be provided national political and military authorities.

The French, both during and before Ottawa, made it clear that they could not condone representing the organization of SACEUR's nuclear forces as the creation of a new entity.

The above steps are significant in that they provide SACEUR with more nuclear power and make possible greater European participation in nuclear affairs.

2.   *MLF.* Secretary Rusk outlined the status of discussions on the proposed NATO multilateral force and expressed the hope that the terms of reference for the treaty negotiations would soon be ready. The other Ministers informally noted the efforts of several countries in considering the possible establishment of a multilateral nuclear force. The UK indicated that it saw formidable problems in the MLF, particularly of cost.

3.   *Special Force Review.* The Ministers agreed in principle to a special NATO force review to start during 1963 which would be designed to bring into closer alignment forces, strategies, and budgets. It is hoped that at the conclusion of this review a more satisfactory balance between nuclear and conventional arms will be achieved, and a more equitable sharing of the defense burden realized. The modalities of the review are yet to be worked out, and in this connection Sec-Gen Stikker has agreed to draft some concrete proposals for NAC consideration.

4.   *Consequences of Armaments Race.* Although speaking on the subject of disarmament, Lord Home reverted to the question of NATO nuclear strategy by raising the question of the consequences of a nuclear armaments race and asking whether in building up its tactical nuclear forces "at back-breaking expense" the West was not preparing for a war which could not be fought because the "overkill" capacity of both sides

---

[2] The statements are not printed. For text of the communiqué, see *American Foreign Policy: Current Documents, 1963*, pp. 408–409.

would totally destroy both the West and the USSR. He suggested the possibility of establishing "a minimum deterrent."

II.   Political Subjects

1. Secretary Rusk discussed "State of NATO Alliance" making following points: (a) despite talk of "disarray", NATO countries are united on basic purposes for which NATO founded, i.e., defense against USSR; (b) US continues to believe firmly in indivisibility of defense of Europe and US and in interdependence between two areas, including equitable burden-sharing; (c) NATO interdependence applies to economic and political field as readily as to military area; therefore, there is need for increased political consultation on emerging problems and potential crises outside treaty area; (d) US hopes European nations will participate fully in Alliance for Progress. Several of the Ministers, including those of Canada and the Netherlands responded positively to the invitation to share responsibilities in Latin America and other underdeveloped areas.

2. Several Foreign Ministers, including Martin of Canada, Home (UK), and Haekkerup of Denmark, stressed the importance of continuing to seek to reach an agreement in the disarmament field.

3. *NATO–Warsaw Non-Aggression Pact.* Following Secretary Rusk's report that Dobrynin had shown considerable interest in the possibility of a NATO–Warsaw Non-Aggression Pact, Lord Home, seconded by Spaak (Belgium), suggested that the pact proposal had attractive aspects, provided the problem of recognition of East Germany could be overcome. Negative and cautionary views were expressed by Couve de Murville (France) Schroeder (Germany) and Averoff (Greece).

4. West German Foreign Minister Schroeder reported on Berlin and German-Soviet relations, explaining in particular the situation in East Germany and Eastern Europe, including West German-Polish Trade Agreement.

5. Couve de Murville (France) indicated that it was unrealistic to talk about equal partnership or burden-sharing between US and Europe because there was no such thing as European unity. Some progress had been made toward unity in economic field, but little progress in political or military areas.

6. Number of Foreign Ministers of smaller NATO countries endorsed Secretary's comments on US-European interdependence and also supported Secretary's views re closer political consultation. Turkish Foreign Minister Erkin emphasized problems in the Middle East and Greek Minister Averoff stressed need for greater external financing to assist Greek economy and to support Greece military burden.

Rusk

200. Telegram From the Department of State to the Embassy in the United Kingdom

Washington, May 29, 1963, 5:22 p.m.

6389. Following for your information is text of letter dated May 28 from the President to Prime Minister, which was transmitted through White House channels.

"Dear Friend:

Thank you for your interim answer to my message about the MLF.[1] I have now heard also from Dean Rusk about his conversations in Ottawa with Alec Home and Peter Thorneycroft.[2] We appreciate the frankness with which they have conveyed some of their preoccupations with the course we are urging, as well as their recognition of its major political advantages.

Let me begin by saying that I think strictly military preoccupations can and should be dealt with by the technical people. The military case for the MLF is a good one and can be fairly represented as such. Our own conviction of the quality of the surface force is so clear that we expect if this force is agreed on, to be able to make substantial savings in the provision of additional US strategic striking forces which might otherwise be needed to cover the same targets. This Government would not consent to the very substantial investment which it is now willing to make for this force, except on the basis of a clear conviction of its first-rate quality. So we are glad that further arrangements have been made for Admiral Ricketts and his staff to talk with your people in London. Any improvements that emerge from these conversations in the basic military design can only be of advantage to all of us.

Meanwhile, every day that passes makes it plainer that a clear move from the United Kingdom toward participation in the MLF will be a major forward step in our joint effort to bind the alliance safely and strongly together, in the face of General de Gaulle's opposite course. The Germans are the heart of the problem, and I simply cannot escape the conclusion that of the courses available to us in dealing with them, the MLF is the only safe one. [8-1/2 lines of source text not declassified]

[6-1/2 lines of source text not declassified] I am sending separately a report of a recent interview by von Hassel[3] which shows how difficult it

---

Source: Department of State, Presidential Correspondence: Lot 66 D 204. Secret; Priority; Eyes Only.

[1] Macmillan's message, May 20, stated that the British Government needed to hold Cabinet meetings before a decision could be taken on the MLF. (Ibid., Central Files, Def 12 NATO) The President's message, May 10, which pressed the British to participate in the MLF, is in the Supplement.

[2] See Document 197.

[3] See the final paragraph of this telegram.

would be for German politicians to defend a policy of nuclear restraint without the political answer of German partnership in the MLF.

So I believe that our two countries must go ahead on this. Just the same, I recognize that you have a political problem of timing. What seems to us essential is that we should go forward in such a way as to maintain continuous momentum. It is not critical that definite agreements should be announced during my European trip, but we do think it important to have the work completed in 1963 so that Parliaments and our Congress can act early in the new year. In our own case, political attention will necessarily begin to turn toward the nominating conventions and the election campaign well before summer next year, and Congressional action should come as early as possible in next year's session.

I believe that one good way of meeting these goals and taking account of your own problem of timing would be to begin the treaty negotiations in a less formal manner than we previously had in mind. Instead of setting up now a formal Drafting Group that would doubtless result in some fanfare, we and the other interested countries could pursue discussions, technical talks, and negotiations at this stage by using space at NATO headquarters in Paris, and using normal diplomatic channels as necessary. By this process, we could move forward toward reaching a detailed consensus and reducing it to the written terms appropriate for a treaty. Given the necessary energy and political determination, a sufficient consensus could in this way probably be developed by August or September to justify convening a multilateral drafting group at that time to put the treaty into final form.

As I see it, the indispensable ingredient of the process I have outlined is a firm political will to come into it with the object of creating a multilateral MRBM force along the lines we have been discussing and to join and support such an MLF if a satisfactory treaty emerges.

I understand that your Cabinet will consider the MLF matter this week and I hope that you will decide that this procedure is within the bounds of your already expressed policy favoring the MLF. Decision by the participants now to join in this next phase will permit final adherence to be reserved until each country has a chance to review the Charter, but it will also maintain our momentum toward an agreement.

With warm personal regards,

Sincerely,

John F. Kennedy."

Included as attachment to message to Prime Minister was text of interview on May 24 with von Hassel by *Frankfurter Allgemeine Zeitung*, which we assume you have or can obtain from other sources

Rusk

201.   Memorandum From the President's Special Assistant for National Security Affairs (Bundy) to President Kennedy

Washington, June 15, 1963.

SUBJECT

The MLF and the European Tour

I think we now need a sharp change in planning for the political discussions of the MLF in Europe. In Bonn, Rome, and London this will be a major topic, and I think it is important to switch from pressure to inquiry. I also think that quite possibly this shift should be signaled before we leave Washington. I reach this conclusion because a close look at the most favorable result of the opposite course is not encouraging.

Assume that we can swing Macmillan on board; David Bruce thinks we can. It will be slower, in the wake of Profumo, simply because the government will take a while to pull itself together; but I do not quarrel with David—though one could.

Assume further that the Italians follow suit at some point (in August or September at the earliest). There is reason to doubt this result, because of Nenni's difficult and focal position, and more deeply because of the lack of real enthusiasm for the MLF anywhere in Italy outside of a few pro-American diplomats. But the Italians have tended to do what we wanted if we wanted it loud enough, and the assumption is not wild.

Assume further that there is enough agreement, soon enough, for a drafting group to complete its work in '63. This involves more speed than anyone really wants, outside the U.S. Department of State, but again it is conceivable.

Assume finally that in 1964, early in the session, we muster support for an amendment of the McMahon Act and a new MLF treaty. We have a very long road to go in educating the Senate to this point, and we should have to do it in the face of reluctance and even opposition on the part of some of those who are normally our friends. Moreover, the problem of coordinating a really effective exposition of the case for the force would be formidable. Still, if it is worth it, it may be that it can be done.

On all these four assumptions, do we want it? My present conclusion is that on the evidence in Europe, in the Soviet Union, and here, we do not. In Europe the successful pressure for an MLF decision would have these clear consequences:

In France, there would be increased hostility; this does not mean de Gaulle, who is probably fixed in his anti-Americanism for some time to

---

Source: Kennedy Library, National Security Files, Regional Security Series, MLF. Secret.

come, but rather other Frenchmen who are clearly with him in their conviction that an MLF, subject to U.S. consent, is an attack on the French nuclear effort, which has support that goes far beyond de Gaulle.

In Great Britain, where almost no one with any political standing is personally favorable to the MLF, the decision would be regarded as an extraordinary case of subservience to U.S. pressure. We should not believe those who tell us that the Foreign Office is favorable; in unguarded remarks to others, Home and other Englishmen have indicated their doubts, and the few who are for it are for it because we are, and they wish to be loyal Allies.

In Germany, the justification most frequently given for German approval would be—as it is now -that the Germans must do what is necessary to keep the Americans happy; that will make a poor impression here. There is no strong affirmative German sentiment for the MLF as something the Germans themselves want.

In Italy, the issue will be divisive, and it will not make us friends. Among Italians there is no enthusiasm for the MLF as such; at best, there is a willingness by some who are strongly pro-Western in personal orientation to walk with American leadership and to keep up with the Germans.

In the rest of NATO, except for Turkey and Greece, political support for the MLF would be scanty at best. In Turkey and Greece the concept is approved, but on the clear assumption that we would pay the Greek and Turkish bills.

Only among the passionate pro-Europeans like Monnet is there real sentiment *for* the MLF, and this sentiment itself is conditional upon a clear offer to abandon the veto at an early stage if a genuinely European force becomes practicable. While I believe in making this offer, I am more and more clear that it is a debating trick, for the present.

If we press the MLF through in the next 12 months, we shall have only grudging support among the very people in whose interest the force has been designed.

Underlying all this European reluctance is an increasing realization that the MLF is not merely a concept but a cost. The cost is so moderate in comparison with our budget for nuclear weapons systems that we have tended to discount it in thinking about what Europeans themselves would want. But it is striking now that such support as the MLF has is almost always in Foreign Offices and very seldom in Treasuries or Ministries of Defense, where the resources must be found.

In the U.S.—Here in the U.S. the political cost of amending the McMahon act for the purpose of arming people who are themselves uncertain and divided on the need would be very great and it would draw deeply on the kind of personal leadership you may well need to limit testing, or to get ratification of a test ban agreement, or to press forward with the "Kennedy round," or to continue the defense of foreign aid. The drain will be directly upon the Presidential account, since the State Department has no leverage and the Defense Department will not be able to make the case on straight military grounds. Indeed it will be necessary to admit that on straight military grounds this force is not necessary; we have said this too often—and it is too plainly the fact—for us to change our tune now.

In the Soviet Union—and this, I think, is a new factor of real importance—the MLF will be increasingly held up as a militaristic maneuver which prevents serious progress toward peace in Europe. If we press it through, I think it is predictable that we will not get many of the things we now hope Harriman can talk about. We may not get them anyway, but with the MLF moving into action, we should be vulnerable—rightly or wrongly—as the nuclear rearmers of Germany. Moreover, this charge will add to the disenchantment of many Europeans with what we are pressing upon them.

If this is an accurate picture of the troubles that lie ahead with the MLF, you may well ask how we got as far in as we have. The answer, I think, is a double one: one turns on people and the other on policy. It happened that the people with the direct responsibility here (Ball, Merchant, Rostow, Schaetzel and Owen) were and are passionate believers in the MLF as a means of blocking national deterrents, General de Gaulle, and all other obstacles to European unity. They have pressed the case more sharply and against a tighter timetable, at every stage, than either you or the Secretary would have chosen. I myself have not watched them as closely as I should have, and more than once I have let them persuade me to support them where I might well have been more skeptical.

But the more important answer, I think, is that in fact it was necessary, after Nassau, to take a direct initiative in favor of the MLF and to find out, by making it a U.S. proposal, whether in fact there was real support for it. The MLF is in trouble now, and we have a real problem in framing our next steps with it, but I think we would be in worse trouble if we had made no proposal designed to meet the nuclear ambitions of Europe. Then indeed we would have left General de Gaulle a free field. And the charges of American monopoly and insensitive domination would have been redoubled in strength.

There is much more that could be learned here by a close review of our past policy, but the real problem now is what we do next.

It is essential that we not back away too sharply from the MLF. A hasty reversal would not only be wrong on the merits but very damaging to our prestige. We can and should continue to make clear our own conviction that this force will work; it can carry its share of the military load, and it represents a serious forward step toward NATO nuclear partnership. We can and should urge continuing study of this proposal, by an international planning staff in Paris; we should not at all abandon our readiness to bear a full share if adequate European participation is developed; we should welcome and even encourage comparative studies of the MLF as against alternative ways of dealing with the needs of our Allies.

But at the same time we should take off any sense of a deadline, and I think we should try to widen the discussion to include other elements in the nuclear problem, such as consultation, control, alternative weapons systems, coordination of existing nuclear forces in the West, and non-proliferation. We should, if possible, seek a framework of discussion in which the French would be willing to participate, and we should capitalize on one of the great facts which underlies European reluctance to pay for the MLF: namely, serene confidence in our own present strategic superiority and our will to use it in defense of Europe.

In other words, instead of pressing in a somewhat nervous and narrow way for a single specific solution, I think we should seek to widen the discourse to include more people and more problems—in Monnet's phrase, we should line the people up on one side of the desk and the problems on the other, and spend a long time looking at them together. Monnet's phrase is aimed at the MLF alone, but I think it makes more sense in a wider framework.

If this course makes sense, the place to decide on it is Bonn, and the man to back it is Adenauer. If the German Government is firmly favorable to the course, no one else will criticize it in any major way, and we shall be able to change the course of negotiations with very modest damage to the U.S. or her President. There would be a certain loss of face for the passionate MLF salesmen, but they are not the U.S. Government.

If this is to be done, then I think we need to decide whether or not there should be some public hint of it before we go to Germany. I began thinking that there should be, but on reflection my belief is that it may be better to discuss this problem with the Chancellor personally. The real question then is whether we should give him a hint of it before you arrive and, if so, by what kind of messenger.

Can we talk about this on Monday?[1]

McG. B.[2]

---

[1] No record of a meeting on Monday, June 17, about this memorandum has been found. On June 20 Bundy sent the President a second memorandum on the MLF, this one specifically directed to discussing it with Chancellor Adenauer. After stressing the need to reassure him and sketching the U.S. and German views on the MLF, Bundy suggested that if the Chancellor agreed to proceed with the MLF, then there should be studies by working groups on the technical aspects of the project. Finally the President should talk about France and the U.S. desire to keep the door open for French participation. (Ibid.)

The same day, in response to a request from the President on June 19, Rostow transmitted a 9-page memorandum on how to handle the MLF on the President's European tour, which included draft language for communiqués in London, Bonn, and Rome as well as draft language for a speech in Frankfurt on the subject. (Department of State, Conference Files: Lot 66 D 110, CF 2280)

[2] Printed from a copy that bears these typed initials.

202.   Circular Telegram From the Department of State to Missions in the NATO Capitals

Washington, June 18, 1963, 8:07 p.m.

2173. Ref: Deptcirtel 1996.[1] Subject: U.S. Troop Withdrawals in Europe. Responses DeptCirTel 1996 greatly appreciated. U.S. forces commitments in relation balance payments problem under study. Secretary has provided following views to DOD:

(a) major troop withdrawals from Europe would, in current political context, be contrary to U.S. interests;
(b) such withdrawals would not appear warranted on B of P grounds alone and certainly not in advance of previously exhausting other possible solutions; and,
(c) no withdrawals for any reasons should be considered pending outcome of Special NATO Force Review.

The foregoing would not, however, preclude relatively minor force adjustments for modernization or other technical reasons.

For background information Posts status of troop withdrawals is as follows:

During Berlin crisis Army strength increased from 228,700 to 273,400. It was reduced to 256,000 during FY 1963. DOD has programmed further reductions to 240,000 during FY 1964. However, only non-combat portion (9,700) of this reduction agreed of which 7,400 represent personnel in units and 2,300, personnel spaces. Possibly 1,000 of the personnel in units may move in June with the balance (6,400) phased over the first quarter FY 1964. Decision for balance of withdrawal (combat units) has been deferred until after President's trip Europe. Separate message provides guidance for public affairs treatment withdrawal 7,400.

Tactical fighter squadrons in USAF in Europe numbered 21 prior to Berlin crisis. Increased by 11 National Guard squadrons during Berlin crisis. Seven of these have now been withdrawn, with remaining four scheduled for departure during first quarter FY 1964. However, pre-Berlin level has been indefinitely "augmented" by earmarking three high performance squadrons in U.S. for rapid deployment Europe.

Source: Department of State, Central Files, Def 6–8 US/NATO. Secret. Drafted by Kranich on June 13; cleared with Seymour Weiss, EUR, and the Department of Defense; and approved by Tyler.

[1] Circular telegram 1996, May 20, reported that the Department of State had received reports from Europe that there was widespread concern over the possibility of troop cutbacks in the NATO area and asked for judgments on the consequences of any U.S. force reductions. (Ibid., Def 6 US/NATO) Replies, which indicated that any cuts would be likely to have unfavorable repercussions, are ibid., and Def 6–8 US/NATO.

Separate from above action is Reorganization of Army Division structure (ROAD concept) involving replacement of battle groups with battalion/brigades. Despite withdrawal bulk of augmentation forces, remaining U.S. Army forces in Europe will still be larger and have marked increase in capability over pre-Berlin forces as consequence reorganization plus other measures to increase combat power and flexibility.

Rusk

203.   Telegram From Secretary of State Rusk to the Department of State

Wiesbaden, June 25, 1963.

Secto 8. Berlin for USDel. Paris for USRO. Reference Secto 7.[1] First subject raised with Chancellor by President in afternoon general discussion was how we should state our position re status of MLF.

President stated it had been our view last winter that both Italians and British should be participants. Now picture had become somewhat obscure but we did not wish cease our efforts. What should our position and posture, both public and private, be over next six months?

Chancellor said he felt there would be new elections in Italy before very long. As for UK, no one knew what would happen there. He thought best position to take was precisely that set forth in communiqué which had just been approved.[2] Believed that was all could be said now, with final note being that negots would continue.

In response President's inquiry where negots would take place, Secretary said he had told Schroeder in morning meeting[3] that we

---

Source: Department of State, Central Files, Pol 7 US/Kennedy. Secret; Limit Distribution. Repeated to Berlin, London, Rome, and Paris. No time of transmission is indicated on the source text.

[1] Dated June 26, it transmitted a general summary of President Kennedy's conversation with Adenauer and Rusk's conversation with Schroeder on June 24. (Ibid.) President Kennedy was in Bonn as part of a trip to Bonn, Berlin, Dublin, London, and Rome, June 23–July 2.

[2] For text of the communiqué, see *Documents on Germany, 1944–1985*, pp. 848–849.

[3] A summary of Rusk's conversation with Schroeder was transmitted in Secto 11, June 25. (Department of State, Central Files, Pol 7 US/Kennedy)

would be discussing matter shortly with British in London and Italians in Rome and then would have further discussions with Germans. There had been no talk in specific terms where these subsequent negots would be held. We had felt we could come back to this question later.

Chancellor suggested these further discussions be held in Washington.

President said there was not much practical likelihood that British would be willing do more than merely discuss MLF. Brit Govt was faced with coming elections, critical labor attitude, criticism from Mountbatten, etc. Italian internal political situation was not good. He therefore doubted if much progress could be made in near future. But it was necessary to keep concept alive for a year or maybe more, even though there were just two of us participating. Meanwhile we should put flesh on other mechanisms which would be suited to needs of FedRep; otherwise we might be faced with situation in fall where we had vacuum, particularly if Italian elections did not turn out well. What was needed was period of time to consider building up of alternatives as well as strengthening of existing mechanisms. In other words, we should continue discussions of MLF through summer and fall and review situation at that time. If outlook then not good, we should consider such things as how we might strengthen IANF and improve coordination in field of nuclear policy and control over nuclear strategy. In this way we would know best way to proceed if we should fail in MLF project—which he hoped we would not.

Chancellor said Germans interested in seeing MLF established, but had no great illusions they were making any terribly significant contribution to it. US was leading power in project and had all the experts. Chancellor reiterated suggestion for Washington as place for further discussions. President said he agreed; we would go ahead with talks in Washington and then consider in fall where we stood. Chancellor added that advantage of talks in Washington would be to emphasize to British and Italians this was serious business and they would be more likely participate than if talks scheduled in Bonn.

Rusk

204. Memorandum of Conversation

PET/MC/17   Sussex, England, June 30, 1963, 10 a.m.

PRESIDENT'S EUROPEAN TRIP
June 1963

PARTICIPANTS

United States

The President
The Secretary of State
Ambassador Bruce
Mr. McGeorge Bundy
Mr. William R. Tyler

United Kingdom

Prime Minister Macmillan
Lord Home
Sir David Ormsby Gore
Lord Hailsham
Mr. Peter Thorneycroft
Sir Harold Caccia
Mr. Philip de Zulueta

SUBJECT

MLF

The Prime Minister said there was a political problem of presentation rather than a military problem. He explained to the President the position of HMG on the eve of the House of Commons debate on Tuesday and Wednesday, July 2 and 3. He said the mood of the House was confused and that unless he had a clear statement of the Government's position he didn't think that the Government would survive. He said that he intended to "attack the attackers" of the surface mode, for example, Field Marshal Montgomery and others. The Prime Minister was satisfied on the basis of the findings of the experts that the MLF plan was workable and "not to be laughed out of court." He had always said that sooner or later the question would arise whether the alliance would be able to survive, while its members were growing in strength, on the basis of nuclear forces being only in the hands of the two major parties. The problem was, he said, "how to NATOize the atom." The Prime Minister recalled the British commitment at Nassau to assign bombers to NATO. The MLF had also been discussed and the problem was a difficult one, but, he said, we must maintain our general attitude and go forward.

The Prime Minister said that it would not be possible for HMG to participate in a conference which discussed only the MLF. He said HMG could not take this politically. On the other hand if the talks were so gen-

Source: Department of State, Central Files, Pol 7 US/Kennedy. Secret. Drafted by Tyler. Approved by the White House on July 12. The meeting was held at Birch Grove. A memorandum of Rusk's conversation with Lord Home on June 28, US/MC/6, on the MLF and other subjects is ibid., Conference Files: Lot 66 D 110, CF 2275.

eralized that it looked as though the MLF were being dropped, that would be bad for the President of the United States. He said he thought the best thing would be not to hold a formal conference with a lot of admirals in uniform present "to launch the fleet." He hoped it would be possible to create a framework of discussion within which each participant would explain what was on his mind in relation to the total NATO nuclear problem.

The President expressed understanding for the political situation in which HMG found itself. He said that the discussions at Nassau had their origin in the problem posed by the decision to give up Skybolt. He noted that people still talked of US bad faith with regard to Skybolt, but they did not realize how much money the US had put into Skybolt, roughly $350 million. The President recalled that we had offered to participate with the UK in the cost of continuing Skybolt, that we had offered Skybolt to the French, and that we had developed the thought of the MLF as a step forward in the circumstances. The President said that maybe the MLF was not a satisfactory solution. However those who say this haven't come up with a better alternative. He said the UK Labor Party wanted a NATO solution but never seemed to provide any details of how to achieve one. He thought it was desirable to continue to study the possibility of a NATO solution. He hoped that HMG would be prepared to study with other NATO powers, including the US and the FRG, along what lines progress could be made. The President said we were not thinking of a formal meeting in August, but rather how to keep the discussion going. It was important to agree on what the UK relationship to the US-FRG study would be. We were not pressing HMG necessarily to be part of this study.

The Prime Minister said he agreed that HMG did not want to participate in a regular conference. He thought he would say that the UK had long recognized that the basic problem which confronts the NATO powers is that of the relationship of non-nuclear powers to the nuclear deterrent. Nuclear weapons for the alliance were needed. He thought the thing to do was to study the problem of the organization of the nuclear deterrent and its relationship to the alliance. This would include a study of various solutions of which the MLF is one. At this point the President tried to get the Prime Minister to agree to saying that HMG was prepared to join in a study of matters "relating to problems connected with the MLF" but the Prime Minister said he couldn't go as far as this. The Prime Minister then outlined what he intended to say in Parliament in the following week, so as to avoid being pinned down on joining a study concerned exclusively with the MLF.

At this point Lord Hailsham said he thought it should be possible for HMG to say that it would be prepared to discuss matters relating to the MLF, without prejudice to the question of HMG participation. The Prime Minister said he would do what he could in this general sense.

The President said that unless it were properly handled, the present situation could develop analogously to the Skybolt problem. If the MLF were to fail, the Germans would then say that they must have land based MRBM's, to which the US was opposed.

(At this point it was recognized that there was a problem of language of the communiqué,[1] and that this had to be faced immediately. The President asked Mr. McGeorge Bundy to go off and draft some language with the British, which would be mutually satisfactory.)

Secretary Rusk warned against linking the MLF to the Moscow trip of Lord Hailsham and Under Secretary Harriman,[2] lest this matter create the impression in the minds of the Soviets that the MLF was negotiable.

---

[1] For text of the Joint Communiqué, June 30, see *American Foreign Policy: Current Documents, 1963*, pp. 503–505.

[2] Harriman and Hailsham visited Moscow July 11–17 to negotiate a nuclear test ban treaty.

---

205. Telegram From Secretary of State Rusk to the Department of State

Rome, July 1, 1963, 10 p.m.

Secto 31. Following based on uncleared memcon,[1] subject to revision, and not to be discussed with foreign officials:

July 1 morning private meeting talk between President and Segni touched on MLF, FGR and Italian internal situation.

On MLF, Segni said even though Leone govt nominally "provisional," it stood good chance getting Parliamentary approval for Italian go-ahead. On this issue, Leone could get support of party groups which do not support his govt. Segni personally was strongly in favor of MLF.

Source: Department of State, Conference Files: Lot 66 D 110, CF 2279. Secret; Eyes Only.

[1] US/MC/25. (Ibid., CF 2275)

If British stayed out entirely, this would make problems for Italians. Otherwise, Leone govt faced fewer obstacles on this issue than Macmillan's. President said U.S. aware of limitations and weaknesses of MLF when it was first proposed. Our general intention was to give non-nuclear countries like Italy and Germany stronger role in deterrent aspect of NATO defense. We wanted to be sure Italy and Germany were not just accepting membership out of sense of partnership, and that there is real need for MLF and MLF meets this need. He then described plans to carry on technical talks on MLF in Washington and expectations British would participate. Even if they didn't, talks would proceed. These talks also open to Italians. President said he hoped that prior to his departure either in final communiqué[2] or in other public statement, Italy would announce intention participate in such technical talks.

On Germany, Segni said very important not let FGR stand alone. France should not be only close friend. French had overcome previous bad relations, and so could Italians. Segni pointed out he due visit President Luebke soon and he hoped for better German-Italian relations. Closer European relations with FGR had to be built around solid US-FGR relationship. President said he very pleased with his visit Germany. New team of Erhard, Schroeder and Von Hassel could be expected to work hard for European and Atlantic unity.

On internal political scene, Segni said fate of center-left formula depended on outcome Socialist (PSI) congress in October. Recent effort detach PSI from Communists (PCI) and lead them into democratic camp had led to strong PCI pressure on Lombardi faction of PSI. Opposition of majority of PSI Central Committee to Nenni's agreement with Moro for a new center-left government had resulted from combination two factors: PCI pressure and fear within PSI ranks that renewed association with Christian Democrats (DC) would cause PSI further loss of strength. Leone govt would last at least until budget vote deadline Oct 31. Continuance beyond that date also depended on PSI congress. Another possible factor was skill Leone had shown in dealing with different Italian parties. As with MLF, he might find on other issues more support in Chamber from other groups than these supporting govt. President said he was interested in internal situation various countries in view U.S. impression that threat of Soviet military takeover had receded to be replaced by political and social moves. Segni said he agreed with this view.

Rusk

---

[2] For text of the final communiqué, see *American Foreign Policy: Current Documents, 1963*, pp. 493–494.

206. Memorandum From the President's Special Assistant for National Security Affairs (Bundy) to Secretary of State Rusk

Washington, July 11, 1963.

SUBJECT

The Next Steps on the MLF

The President has read and approved your undated memorandum to him on the subject of follow-up on the June 24th meeting with Chancellor Adenauer.[1]

I reported to the President your supplementary comment that it would be useful in these discussions to keep before the participants the set of considerations from which the proposal of the MLF has emerged. The President expressed his cordial agreement with this view. He believes that lack of enthusiasm for the MLF in many cases can be traced to a failure to work through the alternatives, and he believes that alternative proposals should be tested by discussion in the same way as the MLF itself, wherever there is apparent support for them.

The President desires that these talks be conducted in such a way as to fulfill all the understandings into which he entered in his European trip. At the same time, he does not wish the negotiations to go forward in a way which would recreate any impression that the United States is trying to "sell" the MLF to reluctant European purchasers. We support the MLF and believe that it is a sound answer to a very difficult political-military problem; we have taken the leading role in developing and testing this proposal which our special responsibilities make necessary; we will continue to use our best efforts in support of this proposal; but the decision on participation will have to be made by each nation for itself.

The President wishes us to be particularly on guard against the development of any notion that if the MLF should fail, there might be some implied obligation to proceed with land-based MRBMs. Our negotiators should make it very clear that in the view of the United States land-based MRBMs are not a good answer to the problem of deterrent missile strength for NATO.

Source: Kennedy Library, National Security Files, Regional Security Series, MLF. Secret.

[1] A copy of this undated memorandum is attached to a July 7 memorandum from Smith to Ball, which bears a notation that the Under Secretary carried it to the President on July 10. The memorandum envisaged low level informal talks with the Germans and Italians and any other interested countries on key aspects of the MLF, hoped that the British would participate, and attached a paper entitled "Basic Elements of Future MLF Agreement." (Department of State, Central Files, Def(MLF))

Washington, Paris or elsewhere. Stated SecGen would be informed of status these discussions.

Greek Ambassador raised question earlier stated Greek reservation re its inability to make financial contribution to MLF and was disturbed that US paper did not seem to take this into account. US Reps stated we familiar with Greek position and that this question was matter for discussion among all potential participants during current meetings. Mentioned possibility of contributions in kind. Turkish Rep associated himself with Greek views.

Re press treatment, we agreed no effort should be made publicize discussions. On other hand no effort would be made to keep it secret.

US reported that Belgian and Dutch Embassies had not yet received instructions re their participation. Canadians had advised us they did not wish associate themselves with these talks although they retain interest in MLF project and its progress and wish keep informed on developments. Said British had not closed door on future participation although Embassy had been instructed not to attend present session.

Date of next meeting will be arranged when comments on US paper have been received by Embassies.

USRO may draw on above to brief SecGen.

Rusk

---

209.   Notes on a Conversation

Washington, August 30, 1963.

SUBJECT

Notes on Conversation re the MLF with Mr. McGeorge Bundy

PARTICIPANTS

Mr. McGeorge Bundy
Ambassador F. E. Holting, Jr.
EUR—Mr. J. Robert Schaetzel
S/MF—Mr. Howard Furnas

In the conversation with Mr. Bundy the following were the principal points which emerged:

1. On the basis of two years experience with Adenauer and one week in Germany, the President as never before is convinced that Germany is essential to United States foreign policy.

Source: Kennedy Library, National Security Files, MLF. Secret. Drafted by Furnas. The meeting was held at the White House.

2.   Germany now is committed to the MLF. It is conceivable that in about a year's time, if it proves impossible to interest other major countries (e.g., United Kingdom, Italy) in the MLF, the United States and Germany might go ahead with the MLF on a bilateral basis.

3.   While no perfect solution, the MLF is the best available one to deal with the problem of German participation in the nuclear strategy of the West.

4.   We should begin quietly consultations with the foreign affairs committees of Congress and specifically on the mixed-manning experiment, and should inform Senator Pastore of the Joint Committee on Atomic Energy. However, any formal consultation would seem to be premature.

5.   The President believes we are now in the correct posture on the MLF. Last spring we were too far out ahead of our allies in trying to "sell" the concept. On the other hand, Mr. Bundy showed some concern about the slow pace of the September work program.

6.   While agreeing about the crucial importance of Italy to the MLF, if any further "selling" is needed, we should leave this primarily to the other potential participants. For example, the Germans might make an effort with the Italians at the time of Adenauer's planned farewell visit to the Pope.

7.   The British will not come in so long as Macmillan is pinning his election hopes on the results of Nassau and on the United Kingdom's national nuclear program. After the election a change may be possible. The United Kingdom Treasury is opposed because of the expense and Mountbatten (who is increasingly irresponsible) and some of the British navy and defense officials are against the MLF because it's a new concept and they didn't invent it. Also they cannot face giving up the prestige that nuclear weapons presumably gives them.

8.   The schedule which we have in mind for further multilateral conversations in Washington, including passing out the scope paper,[1] and for convening an MLF Working Group in Paris the first of October is satisfactory. So are the proposed arrangements for the military planning sub-group to meet in Washington at the end of September and to begin its work with a war-gaming exercise on the survivability of surface vessels.

9.   The mixed-manning experiment is approved if our allies can be interested in proposing it. The President would authorize necessary supporting actions to conduct the experiment. State should, through diplomatic channels, prepare the way.

---

[1] A copy of this 2-page paper, "Multilateral Force Discussion: Suggested Terms of Reference," is attached to a memorandum from Furnas to Ball, August 26. (Department of State, Central Files, Def(MLF))

210.   Telegram From the Department of State to the Mission to the North Atlantic Treaty Organization and European Regional Organizations

Washington, September 11, 1963, 6:18 p.m.

Topol 292. Suggestion has been made within US Government that it would be helpful to future of our efforts on MLF if beginning could be made in mixed-manning somewhere in existing NATO forces. Study within government confirms it would be feasible to institute such a project on US Naval vessels. Subject has been broached through diplomatic channels with Germans, Italians, Greeks and Turks as possibly meriting study provided interest of these governments is such to warrant further exploration. Germans particularly have asked for US ideas in writing as basis for such study. Following aide-mémoire has been prepared for this purpose and is being transmitted these four governments September 12.

Begin verbatim text.

AIDE-MÉMOIRE

The United States has been giving preliminary study to the suggestion that one or two ships of the United States Navy might be designated as mixed-manning training facilities for the purpose of obtaining actual experience in mixed-manning afloat. This concept might constitute a useful step which could be taken in the early future and give those nations presently interested in the Multilateral Force both an opportunity to benefit from lessons learned during the operation and a head-start on the training of initial crews for assignment to the Multilateral Force, if and when agreement to establish this Force is reached among the governments participating in the forthcoming negotiations. Such a project could also serve as a concrete demonstration of the practicability of the principle of mixed-manning.

For the purpose of facilitating the consideration of this suggestion on the part of its partners in the Multilateral Force discussions, the United States sets forth the following points:

1. The United States would be prepared to designate a Guided Missile Destroyer (DDG) and, concurrently if desired, a naval auxiliary ship for this purpose. The sophisticated weapons systems of the DDG would enable personnel from potential Multilateral Force participating countries to become proficient in the maintenance and operation of complex missiles, fire control and electronic systems, a proficiency which would be an asset to those countries in connection with the future

---

Source: Department of State, Central Files, Def(MLF) 9–5. Confidential. Drafted by Spiers; cleared with Furnas, Schaetzel, Chayes, S/P, and the Department of Defense. Also sent to Bonn, Rome, Athens, and Ankara and repeated to The Hague, Brussels, Ottawa, London, and CINCLANT.

provision of personnel to the Multilateral Force vessels. A naval auxiliary type, on the other hand, is a comparatively simple and easily manned ship for which adequately trained personnel are readily available in all navies.

2. Apportionment of personnel could be made so that non-United States officers and enlisted personnel would be represented in all departments as far as possible. The ship or ships concerned would operate as an integral part of the U.S. Sixth Fleet in the Mediterranean and the Second Fleet in the Atlantic, participating in United States and NATO exercises as appropriate. For this reason the commanding officer would continue to be a United States naval officer. Although it is understood that in the Multilateral Force itself no single nation would have a majority of the personnel, it might be desirable that not less than one-half of the crew of the U.S. ship be United States nationals. It would be feasible to have four or five nations represented in the ship's crew. The ship would remain in its present command organization and would not be employed in contingency operations wherein the United States acts unilaterally without the prior agreement of the participating nations.

3. If this project is deemed desirable, a number of English-speaking personnel could be immediately assigned into those billets requiring no specialized training and assignment of training quotas for those billets requiring specialized training could be made. All personnel would remain members of their national navies, ordered by their parent navy for duty to the mixed-manned ship, would wear their own national uniforms and be subject to the orders of superior officers. Each participating nation would be responsible for pay and allowances for its personnel and would also pay for necessary training and subsistence. All personnel would need adequate English language qualifications. Integration of crews would be accomplished on a time-phased schedule. Full integration of a naval auxiliary could be completed in about four months. A DDG could be about 80% integrated in four months and fully integrated in about twelve months; the additional time being required for specialized training for about 20% of the crew.

The United States is prepared to discuss this matter in further detail if desired by the participating governments. If the other governments concerned consider it useful to pursue this idea, the suggestion could be placed on the agenda of the meetings to be held in Paris commencing October 7. The United States would welcome an expression of views of the Governments of Germany, Italy, Turkey and Greece. It would be understood that, while such a project would be related to the Multilateral Force in the manner indicated, it would not have a formal connection and the participants would not, by the fact of their participation, be undertaking any commitment or obligation with respect to the Multilateral Force.

End verbatim text.

Rusk

---

211. Circular Telegram From the Department of State to the Embassy in the Netherlands

Washington, September 11, 1963, 7 p.m.

474. The Hague's 321.[1] Following is Department's assessment of UK's position re MLF which has been discussed with Ambassador Bruce and has his concurrence.

Important fact current British attitude toward MLF is conviction of Macmillan that independent nuclear deterrent is an issue which will help Tories in upcoming election. We see no possibility UK will change now negative position regarding membership in MLF or even agree to participate in MLF discussions until British go to the polls, an event not likely to occur before spring.

In addition to this immediate consideration, UK policy and tactics vis-à-vis Europe over last 15 years indicate that British decisions to play role on the continent almost invariably have been reactions to European determination to proceed with given programs, if necessary, without UK. In our judgment, therefore, whether post-election government in England is Tory or Labour, participation by Britain in MLF will depend in substantial part on quiet but determined efforts of Europeans and US to bring force into being and likelihood of these efforts succeeding.

In the present election impregnated atmosphere in the UK it is to be hoped that Europeans, particularly Dutch, who have been most favorable to British entry into Europe, would devote energies to constructive European developments. MLF is such a project. We see German overtures to Belgians and Dutch as a worthy effort on part Germans to further a positive enterprise at a time when European progress other avenues stalemated in face of French obduracy or objection.

Source: Department of State, Central Files, Def(MLF)3. Confidential. Drafted by Schaetzel and cleared in draft with Furnas, Owen, Popper, Bruce, and BNA. Repeated to Brussels, Paris, Bonn, London, and CINCLANT.

[1] Telegram 321, September 5, reported that the Netherlands believed the British would not participate in the MLF and asked the Department of State for its estimation of British intentions. (Ibid., Def(MLF) 12)

In course informal discussions with Dutch officials Emb may draw on foregoing and emphasize participation in Paris MLF working group would not involve Dutch commitment to subsequent treaty drafting or force itself.

Rusk

---

212.   Memorandum of Conversation

Washington, September 23, 1963, 4 p.m.

SUBJECT

Atlantic Solidarity and Multilateral Force

PARTICIPANTS

Italy	*United States*
Foreign Minister Attilio Piccioni	The President
Ambassador Sergio Fenoaltea	Acting Secretary Ball
Minister Piero Vinci, Foreign	Assistant Secretary Tyler
Ministry	Mr. William J. Tonesk, U/PR
Minister Gian Milesi Ferretti, Italian	Mr. Galen L. Stone, WE
Embassy	Mr. Neil Seidenman, Interpreter

The President said that we were interested in the progress of the multilateral force. We hoped that the United Kingdom would come in. We thought that we ought to proceed with the establishment of such a force. Possibly this was the only way we could prevent a very sharp division in the NATO Alliance. If we proceeded to organize the force with the Germans and Italians, the President said he felt the U.K. would join.

Foreign Minister Piccioni said that Italy had made it clear that she completely adhered in principle to the concept of the multilateral force. Eventually they would like to see such a force constituted with all the members of NATO. There was a certain perplexity, in their view, of the British attitude. Perhaps this was due to internal politics. He said they were bewildered to see this shift in the British position. The position of France, however, surprised them less. German participation was of great importance. The Italians did their best to bring about the best solution from the technical point of view. They hoped the other members of

---

Source: Department of State, Central Files, Def(MLF)3. Confidential. Drafted by Stone and approved in the White House on September 27. Piccioni was in the United States to attend the meeting of the U.N. General Assembly.

NATO would also appreciate the need for setting up such a force so it would not be a "little lateral" force.

The President said it was important to get the force started. Once it was started others would join. Any such agreement was uncertain in the beginning but it then became more desirable as it got underway.

The President said he had talked in the past of the possibility that a multilateral force would evolve if Europe so desired it. The problem now was that the organization of the structure of such a force still had some time to go. It was our feeling that Europe and the United States would coordinate closely together until there was a significant détente. Foreign Minister Piccioni referred to the French proposal to call a meeting of the four nuclear powers for October to work toward disarmament. He said it remained to be seen what were the concrete possibilities that the French had in mind. He thought the United States might be able to do something to build the complete frame of nations on this fulcrum of Europe.

The Foreign Minister said that there had been certain problems between the Common Market and the United States and pointed out that Italy had always worked to overcome these problems. He was personally convinced of the approach advocated by the President in his speech at Philadelphia.[1] We must ask ourselves on both sides of the Atlantic how fast we could arrive at solutions.

The Foreign Minister said that during his dinner with Secretary Rusk he had raised the possibility of the future of a multilateral force in a European context. He felt the possibility should exist for Europe to dispose of a purely European multilateral force. This should not be taken as a contrasting of an European initiative with that of the United States. However, he felt we had to be realistic about this matter. The President said he agreed that the United States position ought to be to support whatever arrangement the Europeans arrived at. The problems we had in the 60's might be described as follows: there was much less chance of a military attack from the Soviets; Europe was more secure than it had been in the past; Berlin also was more secure; the problem was political and monetary. We had to give stability to Germany. We also had to give an effective answer to the Communists in Italy and in France. We were moving toward the general lines of collective policy. It was now a problem to draw together for common purposes. This was the only question he had about de Gaulle. De Gaulle's attitude divided Europe and the United States. The President said he did not think the situation with the Soviets was such that we should be divided. A few years ago all the premises on the defense of Western Europe were based on the monop-

---

[1] For text of the President's address on July 4, 1962, see *Public Papers of the Presidents of the United States: John F. Kennedy, 1962*, pp. 537–539.

oly of nuclear weapons by the United States. Now that the Soviet Union had achieved a nuclear capability there was some feeling that this changed the fundamental assumption on which the defense of the West was based. The acquisition of nuclear weapons brought with it a terrible responsibility. The effect had been that the Soviet Union was somewhat bolder in the 50's than it was today. Some thought that Europe was in greater danger today than before and that our strategy was outmoded. No Soviet leader would be insane enough, however, to launch an attack on Europe, just as we would not launch an attack on the Communist Bloc. There was too much danger. The problems that we would be facing in the 60's would consist of trouble in Latin America and Algeria. These were the trouble spots.

The President said that Italy had given us support when we needed it. If we proceeded with the multilateral force on a limited basis of participation by the Germans, Italians and the United States and got one ship on the ocean and showed that it could work with a multilateral crew, then the British would come in. The British would not join up now but they would when the force became a reality. The President said that Admiral Mountbatten was opposed to the concept but this would not be a fleet that would be manned by the military—politicians would man this fleet.

---

213.   Memorandum of Conversation

Washington, October 4, 1963, 10:30 a.m.

SUBJECT

The MLF

PARTICIPANTS

United States	UK
The President	Lord Home, Foreign Secretary[1]
William R. Tyler, Assistant Secretary	Sir Davis Ormsby Gore,
European Affairs	Ambassador to the U.S.
Thomas M. Judd, EUR/BNA	Oliver Wright, Foreign Office

Following the discussion of Gromyko's claim that the MLF was blocking a worldwide non-dissemination agreement (see separate Memcon),[2] the President inquired as to the thinking in London on the

---

Source: Department of State, Central Files, Def(MLF). Confidential. Drafted by Judd and approved by the White House on October 15. The meeting was held at the White House.

[1] Home was in the United States to attend the U.N. General Assembly.

[2] Not found.

MLF. He knew that Thorneycroft was opposed. Who were the other opponents? Lord Home replied that one of the problems was that the MLF at the moment did not have a single friend in Parliament. The MLF would cause the Macmillan government additional problems in Parliament. The President said for that matter he did not know how it would go with Congress. We hadn't done much work on it as yet.

The President then inquired as to the British thinking on the proposed experiment in mixed manning on a single ship. Lord Home quoted Montgomery's statement to the effect that the battle would be inside the ship rather than outside. The British might be able to provide some men for the ship. He thought that we should move slowly on the MLF question.

The President said there was no hurry. The Germans were in no rush as long as they could see progress being made. The ship could sail around for as much as a year and a quarter or a year and a half and the Germans would be satisfied. By then we should know what the situation was. It was better to get the ship sailing than to try to get agreement on a blueprint for the MLF.

Lord Home remarked that it might be better for both of us to hold off on the MLF until after our respective elections.

---

214.   **Telegram From the Mission to the North Atlantic Treaty Organization and European Regional Organizations to the Department of State**

Paris, October 11, 1963, 10 p.m.

Polto Circular 33. Summary: First Paris meeting MLF working group held October 11 attended by permanent representatives Belgium, FRG, Greece, Italy, Turkey, UK, and US. As result extensive informal consultations among delegations and with SYG, as well as several informal preliminary working group meetings, this first formal meeting went smoothly. Military sub-group constituted, with first meeting Washington October 18 under permanent chairmanship Admiral Ward, USN. Germany, Greece and Turkey approved US proposed mixed-manned demonstration in principle and stated ready to participate but at request Belgium, Italy and UK, military sub-group initially asked to consider technical aspects proposal and report to working group. Press

---

Source: Department of State, Central Files, Def(MLF) 3. Confidential; Priority. Repeated to the other NATO capitals.

release concerning convening working group and establishment military sub-group agreed for use by each delegation.[1] End summary.

At request other delegations, initial session MLF working group convened October 11 in US delegation conference room. US permanent representative, as host, welcomed SYG underlining importance working group attached to his interest and attendance even though NATO not immediately involved in present discussions. Recalled that discussions had been conducted in Washington over several months among five interested countries and that Belgium and UK had joined group at final Washington meeting October 7[2] when decision taken to shift discussions to Paris. Since present meeting represented continuation discussion already underway, formalities were dispensed with. US permanent representative then summarized agreements as to arrangements worked out in several informal meetings of national representatives, who were all permanent representatives, and in informal consultation with SYG. Only previous formal act had been invitation by Belgian permanent representative to SYG at NAC meeting October 9 to attend working group as observer in personal capacity, which SYG had accepted. No chairman of working group would be designated, even on rotational basis; meetings would be held in various delegation conference rooms with host representative taking lead in discussion. (*Comment:* Informal chairmanship arrangement arrived at because of unwillingness Belgian Government on instructions from Spaak to have Belgian permanent representative be chairman even on rotational basis and because of desire avoid any procedure in which all permanent representatives could not participate equally.)

US permanent representative continued that meetings would provide for two places at table for each delegation with not more than three additional seats per delegation. SYG would also be at table. While informal Secretariat arrangements expected to become necessary, these would be deferred until shape of work more clearly seen, but informal contact points for communications among delegations would be designated. No formal meeting record would be kept for time being.

US permanent representative said contemplated committees or sub-groups would be established as needed. Discussions in Washington had resulted in apparent consensus military sub-group would be needed, which would work in Washington except as otherwise agreed, would function under the supervision of the Paris working group and would report to the working group. Since it was desirable to proceed rapidly, October 18 had been suggested as first meeting date. Admiral

---

[1] Not found, but see footnote 7 below.

[2] A summary of this meeting was transmitted in Topol 429, October 7. (Department of State, Central Files, Def(MLF) 3)

Mixed-Manned Demonstration.

US permanent representative recalled US offer of September 12[4] and asked whether countries were interested. He suggested per Topol 453[5] that assuming desirability project generally agreed, it should go ahead with execution by US Navy in conjunction other navies and with military sub-group as consultative and advisory body. Italian permanent representative expressed interest in proposal but urged technical aspects and implications be first referred to military sub-group for study and report back to working group. Commented Italians consider mixed-manning feasible and experiment not needed though they would not object to having it organized. UK supported Italian request for technical study by military sub-group before those WG members who decide to participate decision and Belgium said for "known reasons" probably could not take part but encouraged study. Greek, German and Turkish permanent representatives stated agreement in principle and readiness to participate while willing to have examination technical aspects by military sub-group; despite US efforts to get more clear-cut action, consensus of working group was military sub-group should first examine and report to working group.

German permanent representative raised again MLF war game, stating it was important and relevant to subsequent operations. Assumptions on which war game conducted would have political implications and he proposed assumptions be reviewed in working group. UK permanent representative again raised question of meaning of "war game", which he confused with proposed US demonstration. Belgian permanent representative observed phrase "war game" had undesirable connotations and suggested better term might be "exercise d'état major". Admiral Ward made clear that while US would provide computing facilities, all participants would contribute to inputs and results would be evaluated by full military sub-group. Italian asked what type of vessel would be studied, urgent that three or four types rather than only US surface ship proposal be examined. It was left that this point would be among those considered when military subgroup submitted assumptions for war game to working group for approval.

Future business.

US permanent representative noted that purpose working group discussions was set forth in "purpose" section of terms of reference developed in Washington[6] and suggested next step for working group was to get down to business. Since Belgian unable host meeting at pres-

---

[4] Presumably the aide-mémoire transmitted in Document 210.

[5] Topol 453, October 10, transmitted suggestions for the handling of a mixed-man demonstration. (Department of State, Central Files, Def(MLF)3)

[6] The terms of reference were transmitted in CA–2557, September 4. (Ibid.)

ent, German delegation turn came next and German permanent representative should set date next meeting himself or call meeting at request any delegation. German permanent representative asked for suggestions and Greek permanent representative suggested should be informal discussion among permanent representatives before setting precise date, time and agenda.

Press Relations.

US permanent representative commented all would perhaps prefer pay no attention to press but this was impossible in view of stories already being published and unfortunate content of press treatment if nothing positive was done. As for working group meetings themselves, however, we understood it was agreed that content of meetings should be treated in same way as privacy of NAC meetings so that representatives could continue to speak freely without fear of being quoted in press and thus maintain good working relations. Draft press release (Polto 418)[7] reviewed and a few textual changes made. Turkish permanent representative pointed out letters "M.L.F." were easily confused with "Mobile Land Force" and accordingly full phrase "Multilateral Force" was used throughout. It was agreed each delegation should release text at 4 p.m. Paris time, avoiding giving impression this would be first of series of releases.

Finletter

---

[7] Polto 418, October 9, transmitted the text of a draft press release that had been circulated to the other MLF delegations. (Department of State, Central Files, Def(MLF)3)

---

215.   Memorandum of Conversation

Washington, October 16, 1963, 10 a.m.

SUBJECT

Problems of the NATO Alliance

PARTICIPANTS

United States

The President
Ambassador Finletter
Mr. J. Robert Schaetzel, Deputy
    Assistant Secretary, EUR
Mr. Christopher Van Hollen,
    EUR/RPM

NATO International Staff

Mr. Dirk U. Stikker, NATO
    Secretary General
Mr. John Getz, Special Assistant to
    Mr. Stikker

Source: Department of State, Central Files, Def 4 NATO. Secret. Drafted by Van Hollen and approved in the White House on October 19. The meeting was held at the White House.

NATO Force Planning Exercise

The President opened the substantive portion of the conversation by asking Mr. Stikker about the status of the NATO Force Planning Exercise. The Secretary General replied that although the French had vetoed the initial concept of this exercise, a compromise had been reached and some progress was now being made. As a result of the compromise, the NATO Council would be much more directly involved from the start. This procedure had certain advantages, but it might also mean that the problem of handling the French could become more difficult. The purpose of the exercise, Mr. Stikker said, was to reconcile NATO strategic requirements, force levels and military budgets. However, the French position was that the work on the basic NATO strategic document [MC 100/1][1] must be completed first. If the French adhered to this position, difficulties would arise because they would have prematurely fixed one of the three elements which were to be reconciled as a result of the entire exercise.

France and NATO

On the broader question of France's role in NATO, Mr. Stikker said that he did not think that as Secretary General he could subject himself to a open conflict with the French. Instead, the task was to find some system of "mutual forbearance". If General de Gaulle wished to hold full responsibility for France's defense and for the deployment of French forces, and if he wished complete independence within the Alliance, there was no chance that the General's viewpoint could be changed. However, the business of the Alliance must be carried forward and not threatened by all-out French obstruction. Therefore, an understanding should be reached with the French that despite France's position the other members of NATO would be permitted to continue to work toward a system of closer integration. The problem was how to obtain such an understanding from de Gaulle. Mr. Stikker suggested that since the NATO Secretary General did not exist in de Gaulle's eyes and since the Secretary General also had no real contact with the French Government, an understanding regarding France's role in NATO could only be reached at the Chief of State level. Noting that he was planning to visit Bonn later in the month, Mr. Stikker said that he planned to raise the possibility of a policy of "mutual forbearance" with Chancellor Erhard.

The President said that while he could see the advantages of such an agreement for other members of the Alliance, he was not certain that General de Gaulle would see any advantages in it for him. It would reduce France's opportunity to exert its influence within NATO. Mr. Stik-

---

[1] Brackets in the source text. MC 100/1 has not been found.

ker commented that a substantial segment of French opinion did not approve of de Gaulle's views on a French force de frappe and many Frenchmen were unhappy about France's isolation.

NATO Force Planning Exercise (continued)

Reverting to the NATO Force Planning Exercise, the President said that he was aware of de Gaulle's attitude toward NATO and toward the purportedly dominant US influence in NATO. However, he wondered about de Gaulle's objection to the strategic studies which were proposed. He presumed that de Gaulle did not wish anyone to sit in judgement on what he considered to be the sovereign prerogatives of France. Mr. Stikker agreed that this was the basis of the French objections and explained that, at present, the problem was in the hands of the NATO Standing Group. The Standing Group must give instructions to the major NATO Commanders. But the French insisted that, before any definitive instructions could be given, some decision must be reached on the basic NATO paper, MC 100/1. Here, problems arose because the French wished to use the bomb sooner than others. Thus, the French were in a position to exercise a veto on the entire NATO Force Planning Exercise unless the others acceded to their request that agreement first be reached on the strategic studies.

The President said that it seemed to him that it would be better to have the strategic study undertaken in line with the French desires rather than to have nothing at all accomplished. He asked what Mr. Stikker's reaction would be if the French insisted on pursuing their study. Mr. Stikker replied that he would be compelled to accept this approach. Ambassador Finletter explained that the Ottawa agreement[2] placed stress upon the inter-relationship between forces, strategy and resources as well as the inter-play between various risks involved. Thus the fulfillment of this goal would help to break down the conflicts between the US and its European Allies and would also contribute to the overall political cohesion of the Alliance.

NATO Forces vs. Resources

The Secretary General said that last year his NATO Staff had made a study of the gap in dollar requirements in NATO and had concluded that over a two-year period NATO countries should spend $7 billion more than they were now spending. Subsequently, there had been a $2-1/2 billion increase in expenditures which represented some improvement. Another study was designed to determine what European countries were buying in Europe for their troops and what the US was buying as well for its troops. This study revealed that the US was spend-

---

[2] See Document 199.

ing approximately $12 billion on 25 M+30 divisions while the Europeans were spending $6.8 billion on 75 M+30 divisions. In other words, for one half the money the Europeans were able to support three times as many divisions, a discrepancy which related largely to the higher basic US costs, wages for troops, etc. This discrepancy and the reasons for it was the type of subject which would be carefully examined during the Force Planning Exercise.

Multilateral Force (MLF)

Asked by the President about the status of the Multilateral Force (MLF), Mr. Stikker said that he wished to make two points: first, regarding the veto and, second, relating to the MRBM question. With reference to the veto, he said that present plans would give every country a veto over the use of the force. He was worried about this procedure, [4 *lines of source text not declassified*]. At the same time he was convinced that the US at present should not give up its veto.

With regard to the MRBM question, Mr. Stikker said that he hoped that if the MLF came into being, it would take care of General Lemnitzer's MRBM needs. He recalled that in his paper to the Standing Group,[3] General Lemnitzer had requested 568 MRBMs which he considered necessary to cover targets vital to Europe. At present, Mr. Stikker continued, the US had three submarines within the NATO framework and the UK had four submarines, providing a total capacity of about 120 MRBMs. If the MLF added 200 more MRBMs to the overall NATO total, there would still be a gap of about 260 MRBMs. Despite this gap, Mr. Stikker said, he did not believe that any European leaders would wish to accept 260 MRBMs within their territory. On the other hand, European countries would not accept the gap involved and it was therefore important to insure that this gap could be closed in such a way to get rid of the MRBM problem which had been hanging over the Alliance for some time.

The Secretary General suggested that when he went to Bonn he might explore on a personal basis with Erhard would not accept whether he would be prepared to accept 260 MRBMs on German territory. He had the strong impression that Erhard would not accept MRBMs and that it therefore might be useful to sound out the Germans on this subject. The President asked what would happen if Erhard responded affirmatively, noting that this was a subject which would have to be handled carefully. He agreed that NATO should try to get rid of the MRBM problem, noting that it tended to whet appetites and that the required targets were already covered. The important thing however was the symbolic aspect of the MRBM requirement and he hoped that this symbolism could be transferred to the MLF. With regard to the veto

---

[3] Not further identified.

problem, the President noted that [*1-1/2 lines of source text not declassified*] the actual formula for control would have to be negotiated out among the participating countries. From the US viewpoint, Congressional attitudes must be considered.

Ambassador Finletter commented that Mr. Stikker had put forward the idea under which the US would have a veto while the other European countries collectively could work out arrangements for a form of European veto rather than to permit individual European countries to exercise a veto. Such a concept would fit in well with European desires and with the Atlantic Partnership concept. The President said that some formula might be worked out on the basis of contributions to the Force under which, for example, 100 might be required to fire out of a total number of 130, with the US and Germans making up 40 each and with the US retaining the veto.

Asked about the current interest of various European countries in the MLF, Mr. Stikker said that the Germans were definitely interested, the Italians had been interested up to the present time, the Greeks and Turks were interested but lacked money, while the Dutch and Belgians remained doubtful. In response to the President's inquiry as to whether the experimental ship could become operational before a final decision was reached on the MLF, Ambassador Finletter replied affirmatively noting that the MLF group in Paris had agreed at its first meeting to proceed with the experiment using a U.S. guided missile destroyer and a supply ship. Mr. Schaetzel commented that at the recent Ditchley Conference on strategic problems, which was attended by about 20 Britishers, the initial British reaction to the MLF was quite negative. However, in the course of three days intensive discussion in which the origin of the MLF was explained, the political and military aspects reviewed, and all alternatives considered, the attitude of the British participants toward the MLF changed 180 degrees. However, the main problem was still the extremely difficult position of the British Government.

Possible French Action in 1968

The President asked whether it was true that France was prevented from changing NATO before 1968. Ambassador Finletter explained that there was some confusion on this point. The situation was that in 1968 any country, after giving one year's notice, could get out of NATO. But this did not mean that the year 1968 necessarily had further significance in terms of a basic NATO reorganization. Mr. Schaetzel commented that when France's future attitude toward NATO was discussed while Couve de Murville was in Washington recently, Couve left the impression that France had no specific plans to seek a change in NATO at this time.

Position of NATO

At the conclusion of the meeting, the President commended Secretary General Stikker for his strong leadership in NATO, observing that although commentators continued to write about NATO's "disarray" the organization was still strong. As an example, the President cited Italy, stating that without the NATO tie it was quite likely that Italy's entire political orientation might have already shifted to the disadvantage of the West.[4]

---

[4] Near the end of a luncheon for Stikker, Rusk and the Secretary General discussed the December Ministerial Meeting and France's attitude toward NATO. A memorandum of their conversation is in Department of State, Central Files, NATO 3.

---

216. National Security Action Memorandum No. 270

Washington, October 29, 1963.

TO

The Secretary of State
The Secretary of Defense
Chairman, Joint Chiefs of Staff

SUBJECT

Meeting with the President, Thursday, October 24, 10:30 a.m., in the Cabinet Room, on European Matters

1. Based on Secretary Gilpatric's summary of recent Presidential decisions concerning the redeployment of US military forces from Europe and the schedule for implementing the approved actions, the President reaffirmed that:

a. Possible redeployments of US forces under consideration within the government should not be discussed publicly nor with our allies until a decision has been made and a politico-military plan for action approved. Following these steps, we should consult as appropriate with our allies before any public announcement is made, and then proceed with our intended actions. Wherever possible action of low visibility should be taken without public announcement.

b. The United States will maintain in Germany ground forces equivalent to six divisions as long as they are required, and this policy is to be reaffirmed by Secretary Rusk in Frankfurt.

Source: Kennedy Library, National Security Files, Meetings and Memoranda Series, NSAM 270. Top Secret.

2. The following actions were approved by the President, to take place under the above guidelines.

(1) The three C–130 squadrons permanently stationed in France will be returned as scheduled; two squadrons will be maintained in France on rotation.

(2) US Army lines of communication forces in France will be reduced by approximately 5400 as scheduled.

(3) The inactivation of the Lacrosse and 280mm gun battalions will proceed as scheduled.

(4) A plan for the further reorganization of the Army's European logistics forces, entailing an additional reduction of about 30,000 personnel over the next two calendar years, will be developed by the Department of the Army for review by the Joint Chiefs of Staff and the Secretary of Defense.

(5) The specific 10% reduction in headquarters staff of 7th Army and USAREUR and the over-all 15% reduction worldwide in headquarters staffs (which may involve further adjustments in Headquarters, 7th Army, and USAREUR) will go forward as scheduled.

(6) The President approved the return to the United States, commencing early in 1964 and to be completed within FY 1964 with the minimum explanation practicable, the six Berlin "Roundout" units consisting of three artillery battalions, two armored battalions, and one cavalry regiment, with its support units. The schedule of this action and the manner of disclosure to the FRG were left for later decision by the President.

(7) The redeployment of the second Long Thrust battle group will not be discussed until January, although planning should go forward for its probable return to the United States in early spring.

(8) B–47 units will be withdrawn from Spain and the United Kingdom as scheduled by the spring of 1965. The President reaffirmed this decision after being informed that although the Joint Chiefs of Staff recommended against this action the Deputy Secretary and the Secretary of Defense strongly supported it.

(9) The President approved in principle the proposal to withdraw three fighter squadrons from France and seven fighter squadrons from the UK by the end of FY 1966. Defense should urgently prepare, in connection with State, a plan of action to carry this out, with an estimate of the political and military problems (including the views of the Joint Chiefs of Staff) involved for final approval of the President before any implementation.

3. On the basis of the above guidelines and decisions, section IV of Secretary Rusk's draft speech for Frankfurt on 27 October was reviewed and appropriate modifications were made.[1] The President approved the attached revised draft.

4. At the conclusion of the meeting, the President set forth the following rationale for use by US officials publicly, with the guidance that

---

[1] For text of Rusk's speech at the dedication of a memorial to George C. Marshall, see Department of State *Bulletin*, November 11, 1963, pp. 726–731.

it should be used only as required, and only in such detail as is necessary.

a. The United States intends to keep the equivalent of six divisions in Europe as long as they are required. The United States will continue to meet its NATO commitment.
b. Operation Big Lift should be viewed as an example of our ability to add rapidly additional forces to Europe. Were it a replacement division, it would use the equipment of one of the divisions now in place. Instead, it is using one of the two division sets of equipment prestocked in Europe. In reality, the US thus will have over seven divisions in Europe over the next month or more.

McGeorge Bundy

---

217. **Memorandum From the President's Special Assistant for National Security Affairs (Bundy) to Secretary of State Rusk and Secretary of Defense McNamara**

Washington, November 21, 1963.

I have read the letter of November 17 from the Secretary of State to the Secretary of Defense,[1] and I think it important to note, in the absence of the Secretary of State, that letter does not fully reflect the most recent discussions between the President and the two Secretaries.

It is the President's view that we should not undertake a sharp confrontation with the Germans or the French over NATO strategy in future weeks. The President does not desire that any members of the government should undertake extensive argument with the Germans on strategic concepts during the Erhard visit, because he intends to review this matter himself with Secretary Rusk, Secretary McNamara, and General Taylor in preparation for the NATO meetings. In these circumstances it does not seem to me that there should be serious discussion with either Schroeder or Von Hassel on the problems of NATO strategy, and in particular I think it would be a mistake for officers of the United States Government to assume that a policy paper of April 1961 is Holy

---

Source: Department of State, Central Files, Def 4 NATO. Top Secret.

[1] In this letter Rusk suggested that the United States needed a "solid presentation" on strategic policy for the NATO Ministerial Meeting in December and stated that Erhard needed to be briefed during his forthcoming visit on the outlines of this presentation. (Ibid., Def 1 NATO)

Writ. If Chancellor Erhard desires a military briefing it would of course be valuable for him to have one, but this briefing should be guided more by Secretary McNamara's speech of November 18,[2] which had explicit approval, than by any other document.

Finally, I believe that time will be saved in the long run if detailed staff discussion of the plans for the NATO meeting can be held in abeyance until the President has a chance to discuss these matters with Secretary Rusk, Secretary McNamara, and General Taylor.

McGeorge Bundy

---

[2] For text of this speech, see Department of State *Bulletin*, December 16, 1963, pp. 914–921.

---

218.   Memorandum of Conversation

Washington, November 27, 1963.

SUBJECT

U.S. Policy in Europe; U.S.-Soviet Relations

PARTICIPANTS

Jens Otto Krag, Prime Minister of Denmark[1]
Count K. Knuth-Winterfeldt, Ambassador of Denmark

The Secretary
Eric V. Youngquist, Officer in Charge Danish-Norwegian Affairs

The Secretary assured the Prime Minister: 1) that while President Johnson was still Vice President, he supported President Kennedy's foreign policy not merely because he felt that he was called upon to do so, but from a sense of conviction; and 2) that there would be no reduction in the sense of U.S. commitment and involvement in Europe. In fact, he said, we are prepared to go farther in a partnership with Europe than Europe itself is.

Source: Department of State, Central Files, Pol 1 Eur-US. Secret. Drafted by Youngquist and approved in S on December 9.

[1] Krag was in the United States to attend the funeral of President Kennedy who was assassinated on November 22 in Dallas. A 2-page memorandum of his conversation with President Johnson later that day is ibid., NATO 3.

The Secretary said that most of the questions that seemed to be trans-Atlantic in character turned on issues which could be settled only by Europe itself. The most important of these is the question of what structural and formal developments will take place in Europe. The differences in conception as to the future structure of Europe have caused us difficulties. For example, he said, we could have had a love affair with France had we been willing to accept the idea of a *directoire*, with the UK, France and the United States sitting as co-equal heads. This concept was rejected by both Presidents Eisenhower and Kennedy. Until there is some settlement of this question of form or structure trans-Atlantic relations will remain unsettled.

The Prime Minister, referring to talk of dissension and disunity within NATO, suggested that a meeting be held, on a higher level than the forthcoming NATO meeting, where the allies could talk about the things on which they are agreed rather than on those which divide them. Such a meeting would solve no problems, but could have an important psychological effect. The Secretary replied that the idea was rather persuasive, particularly since major changes had recently taken place in the leadership of four of the NATO partners, and added that we would give it serious thought.

Continuing on the subject of NATO unity, the Secretary said that it was almost a tragedy that, at a time when the Communist world has been racked by uncertainty about its own structural arrangement and when important changes were taking place within the Communist Bloc, there had not been sufficient unanimity in the West. Had there been this unanimity, then the contrast between the free world and the Communist world would have been dramatic.

The Prime Minister observed that France was both a loyal and a difficult ally, to which the Secretary replied that both words were very true. The Prime Minister concluded by suggesting that it might be possible to adopt deGaulle's own recipe in dealing with deGaulle himself, that is, try to live with the problems rather than solve them. Specifically, why not leave the question of atomic defense and control of atomic weapons where it stands?

Regarding the French attitude toward MLF, the Secretary observed that deGaulle's ideas on nuclear defense were not really in conflict with the idea of the MLF. DeGaulle has not rejected MLF; he has merely said that he has other things to do. To the Prime Minister's query whether deGaulle regards the MLF as useless, the Secretary mentioned that this could hardly be the case, since it would be some time before deGaulle had two hundred missiles, whereas MLF would have that striking power immediately.

To Ambassador Knuth-Winterfeldt's observation that deGaulle appeared to object to the MLF because he felt that it would only be an extension of U.S. control, the Secretary replied that the U.S. would only be one member of the force. The Secretary said that the U.S. of course wants to participate in any decision, regardless of who makes it. This in itself can hardly be called a monopoly. The only way Europe could have a force without U.S. involvement would be to have Europe completely independent of the U.S., because it would be impossible for a decision to be taken involving us where we would not insist on some participation.

The Prime Minister then said that Europe could not be defended in any other way than through participation by the U.S. To this, the Secretary demurred, saying that Europe could defend itself without the U.S., but that it did not have to do so. We would, of course, not object if the countries of Europe were to decide to create their own defenses, and devote an additional 25% of their budgets to defense, but we would regard it as wasteful. We consider the defense of Europe equivalent to the defense of the U.S., said the Secretary. It is as simple as that.

Reverting to the subject of NATO unity, the Secretary said that the U.S. realized that developments of recent years make necessary some reorganization of the NATO framework. All we ask, he said, is that, pending this reorganization, the members of NATO give NATO their full support. Without a pledge of such support, then uncertainty and difficulties naturally will arise.

To the Prime Minister's statement that Denmark regarded presence of U.S. troops in Europe essential, the Secretary noted that there were domestic political problems in a situation where the U.S. was the only member of NATO which had met its force goals completely. Given the U.S. balance-of-payments situation, there might be congressional pressures for some reduction in U.S. military presence in Europe. In reality, however, there will be no problem, said the Secretary, because of the basically strong general support for NATO which exists among the general public in this country.

[Here follow 4 paragraphs on U.S.-Soviet relations, civil aviation, and shipping.]

219.   Telegram From the Embassy in France to the Department of State

Paris, November 30, 1963, 4 p.m.

2610. Eyes only Secretary. Finletter and I lunched with Couve de Murville, Lucet, and Seydoux at Couve's invitation today to discuss French attitude and probable next moves on NATO planning.

The lunch was against the background reported in previous cables from Finletter of apparent French concern that France might find herself isolated in NATO discussions this topic and even possibility that France might wish to block whole exercise.

Lunch successfully dispelled any such notions. Finletter emphasized that U.S. did not wish in any way to see France isolated; but on contrary to find formula which would permit French participation.

Couve asked what was the purpose of this exercise, holding forth at great length the French view that nothing would be changed by its results except that there might be some disagreeable friction within Alliance. Finletter said he saw considerable value in the possibility that exercise would afford for communication and exchange of views on subjects concerning which there had been considerable lack of understanding. He emphasized, with my support, that while it would be hoped that the discussions taking place in NFP would produce greater understanding of all factors, including strategy, nevertheless he agreed with Couve de Murville that political consequences of this most important element, and therefore discussion on strategy undesirable. Should be handled with great care in order to avoid confrontation.

Comment: It appears to me that purpose of lunch was to endeavor to sound out in private, amicable conversation difficulties which could have produced friction in NATO. I ventured purely personal tentative suggestion that at some time preceding NATO Ministerial Meeting it might be useful for FonMins and DefSecs of four principal allies to have a quiet lunch or dinner to discuss some larger aspects of this basic problem without any attempt at conclusions or decisions. This suggestion, although recognized as completely informal and personal, seemed to be well received by Couve.

Bohlen

Source: Department of State, Central Files, Def 4 NATO. Secret.

220. Memorandum of Conversation

Washington, December 2, 1963, 3 p.m.

SUBJECT

Preparations for December 1963 NATO Ministerial Meeting

PARTICIPANTS

(See attached list) [1]

Secretary Rusk asked to turn first to the "concept" of the Ministerial Meeting. The events of the last 10 days have given what otherwise would be a routine session more importance. It would provide a useful opportunity for mutual reaffirmations of faith in the Alliance, more significant now both because of President Kennedy's death and the numerous other governmental changes in the Alliance since the Ottawa meeting. Secondly, we need to seek a common assessment within the Alliance of several key questions, e.g., what is going on in the Bloc and how this affects East-West relations; the military and strategic questions treated in Secretary McNamara's November 18 Economic Club speech; economic developments. He was doubtful that we should try to grapple with NATO strategy or let the December meeting become the scene of a sharp and acrimonious debate on strategic choices. The bilateral discussions would be more important in this area as well as in others, such as the successor to Stikker. Generally, the meeting should be used to consolidate, rather than to air differences. It is evident that the Alliance has the will to respond to external threats. The question for future discussion is whether the military posture is appropriate for the best response.

Secretary McNamara said he agreed with these comments. Specific matters which he agreed we should not raise would be, first, the potential withdrawal of U.S. air units from the UK, Spain and France and, secondly, the current difference with France on strategy. Skill will be required to avoid being drawn into the latter but we must make an effort, since only a sharp conflict will result.

Secretary Rusk said that in his view the prime objective was to avoid getting pinned to a single strategic plan, as the French had done, for example, in World Wars I and II. In his view the function of our defense establishments was to provide to heads of government the capabilities for alternative military responses to be used as situations required. We cannot know in advance what is going to be called for and we need a wide range of alternatives, not automatic action. Secretary

---

Source: Department of State, Central Files, NATO 3. Secret. Drafted by Spiers and approved in S on January 6, 1964. The meeting was held in the Secretary's office.

[1] Not printed.

McNamara said this was exactly the essence of the U.S. strategy and precisely the area of our greatest differences with France. He read excerpts from a recent Gallois statement showing that the French were locked into a strategy of massive retaliation. At some point, however, we will have to have a confrontation with France. Otherwise the Alliance will be led step-by-step into a force structure which would prevent us from having the alternatives to which Secretary Rusk referred.

Secretary Rusk asked whether Secretary McNamara could give NAC a more detailed analysis of the Soviet military position and its strategic implications along the lines of the Economic Club speech. Secretary McNamara said he would like to do this at the right time, but felt that now such an analysis would lead us directly into a discussion of strategy; therefore, he would like to play it down.

Secretary Rusk asked whether we could give some advance thinking on our next year's military budget. Secretary McNamara said he would do so. He viewed this as another installment in a progress report to the Alliance, the first chapters of which were given at Athens and Paris last year. This time he wished to review our latest force plans and the implications thereof. He would want to deal with our strategic nuclear power and our tactical nuclear power in Europe. These should be placed alongside estimates of the Soviet military position and we should draw appropriate conclusions about strategy, but not in a way that would provoke the French. However, the French may be forced to respond, since this analysis will undermine their strategic concept completely. He intends to raise this matter with von Hassel tomorrow[2] and to point out bluntly that the French are proposing a bankrupt strategy with great consequences for the FRG. He will urge the Germans to bear a greater part of the burden in dealing with the French on this issue.

General Lemnitzer expressed the hope that Secretary McNamara's comments would emphasize that there was no justification for relaxation in our efforts to meet conventional force goals. In some quarters in Europe the wrong conclusion had been drawn from the Economic Club speech: that we were in a good position and could relax.

In connection with his own proposed remarks Secretary Rusk said that he would hope to extract a reaffirmation of commitment to the Alliance from others as well. This was not a matter for just the US to make pledges about. He also intends to go over frankly the questions which arise in the US on the double standard within NATO. Without actually saying so, he wants to give the impression that if we did what the others are doing we would be charged with abandoning Europe.

---

[2] No record of a meeting with von Hassel on December 3 has been found, although it is referred to again in Topol 733 to Paris, December 3 (ibid., Def 4 NATO), which summarized the conversation in Rusk's office described here.

General Lemnitzer pointed out there is still an inclination in Europe to overestimate the détente. Secretary Rusk said he would go over this subject in detail at the meeting, reviewing East-West developments in both the multilateral and bilateral spheres, and show why there were very narrow limits of validity in any talk about détente. There was nothing to justify relaxation. General Lemnitzer said there were many who will seize on any alibi to rationalize reducing our efforts. The UK as well as others had been "hurt" by a message he had sent to MOD's expressing his concern about the dangerous "trend" in NATO, citing various force withdrawals and numerous reductions in terms of service.[3]

Secretary Rusk noted that we would prepare a brief statement from President Johnson to the Ministerial Meeting. Secretary McNamara expressed the hope that we would be in a position to exchange drafts of the two speeches before either he or Secretary Rusk departed for Paris. He wanted to get General Taylor's views on his own statement before the General departed for Paris on the 11th.

Secretary Rusk raised the question of relocation of the Military Committee and Standing Group, noting that others may bring this question up in Paris. Secretary McNamara said he would like to avoid making any changes of this nature before fully considering our long-range objectives. We are not prepared to do this yet. General Taylor noted that the JCS has no objection to relocation if this would mean a great deal to the Alliance, but that they are not pressing for such a change. Personally, he sees no real advantage to be gained. He did believe there was room for greater staff internationalization than the modest measures now under consideration contemplated. He would, however, like to talk to the State Department about where we want to end up with all of this. General Lemnitzer noted that the Secretary General had a legitimate problem in that he had no place to turn for international military advice. Accordingly, he has to go to SACEUR, even though this does not meet his broader requirements. However, even if the Standing Group moved to Paris tomorrow the SYG could not get anything but three separate national views. Right now his only sources of international military advice are the major NATO commanders. In any event, on the question of reorganization there is insufficient unanimity of opinion in any single area to let us come up with an agreed step within the Alliance. Reorganization will raise problems immediately with the French, who occupy a large number of important positions, even though their contribution is limited to two divisions and 10 air squadrons. The Germans, with a much larger contribution, have a far less important role.

---

[3] Not identified further.

Secretary Dillon raised the question of Finance Ministers representation at Ministerial meetings. He noted that we were trying to shift the discussion of Annual Review questions from the morning to the afternoon of the 17th so that it would not conflict with the meeting of the Group of Ten. It was important to bring the Finance Ministers into discussions so that they will have a stake in budget proposals which arise at a later stage. This was particularly a problem in the case of coalition governments, where the Defense and Finance Ministers might be from different parties. He noted, further, that room should be made for Finance Ministers to attend restricted sessions so that they would not get bored with the meetings and refuse to come. This had been the problem in the past.

Ambassador Finletter supported Secretary McNamara's ideas on what should be avoided. We do not want to break new ground at this meeting, and specifically, he hopes nothing comes up on NATO Force Planning. General Taylor noted that the subject of the impasse on NFP would inevitably be discussed in the MC/CS, and would have to be included in its report to the Council. Secretary Rusk agreed that all reference to this could not be avoided.

Secretary Dillon noted that Secretary McNamara had referred to the balance of payments problem in the outline of his remarks. He expressed the view that we should not make this a NATO-wide problem, since we could only lose. Secretary McNamara agreed that we would not want a multilateral analysis of our balance of payments problems, but that we should explain our difficulties and what we are trying to do.

Secretary McNamara said that he proposed to send MC 100/1 to State for official review. Since this will be the formal basis of our disagreement with the French, he wished to have this checked out with the political authorities. He would also send a revised copy of the Joint Chiefs' new paper on U.S. strategy.[4] He believed this was a good statement, the first of its kind, and said that he would be discussing it with von Hassel tomorrow. Nevertheless, he would like to send it to the Department for review and whatever comment we might have.

---

[4] McNamara sent Rusk a copy of CM–1044–63, November 29, under cover of a letter dated December 3. (Department of State, Central Files, Def 1 NATO)

221. Scope Paper Prepared in the Department of State

TNT/B–1   Washington, December 6, 1963.

NATO MINISTERIAL MEETING
Paris, December 16–18, 1963

1. The Current Situation

The Ministerial Meeting takes place this year in an atmosphere not of crisis but of uncertainty. The following factors dominate the scene:

(a) Although the Johnson Administration does not intend to change the course of American foreign policy, our allies will be carefully examining our day-to-day actions to discern any differences in content or style in the new U.S. approach to international problems. The December Ministerial Meeting will provide the first occasion since the tragic death of President Kennedy to give the NATO Foreign Ministers a considered review of U.S. policy.

(b) The meeting occurs at a moment when new governments are applying themselves to NATO problems for the first time in Italy, Germany, and the United Kingdom. Thus, of the five major NATO powers, only France enters the meeting with the same leaders as it possessed at the time of the Ottawa meeting last spring.

(c) French opposition to the organizational features of the NATO Alliance—that is, to integrated military command and planning and to more intensive political cooperation—is now more clearly revealed than ever before.

(d) Initial apprehensions regarding the outcome of East-West negotiations, particularly those of the Germans and French, have been allayed. While no immediate action is in prospect on an East-West non-aggression arrangement, an observation post agreement, or a non-dissemination accord, resumption of negotiations on any of these matters will revive underlying differences of approach in NATO.

(e) Nevertheless, the atmosphere of détente following conclusion of the Limited Test Ban Treaty has already impeded efforts to strengthen NATO forces in Europe. The recent Annual Review disclosed a gradual downward drift in strength.

(f) This situation highlights the long-standing problem of the proper distribution of the burden of maintaining NATO armed forces, as between the U.S. and its allies. U.S. moves dictated by balance of pay-

Source: Department of State, Conference Files: Lot 66 D 110, CF 2341. Secret. Drafted by Popper and cleared by Tyler, Schaetzel, Owen, Rostow, Weiss, GER, WE, and the Department of Defense.

ments considerations will be subject to very close scrutiny, particularly by the Germans.

(g) The control of NATO's nuclear strength continues to pose a fundamental challenge to the Organization, despite the progress which is being made in preliminary discussions on the Multilateral Force.

The foregoing circumstances seem to call for a more than ordinarily firm expression of American leadership in NATO. Our allies will be expecting the U.S. to buttress the Organization and to give it a sense of direction in coping with its immediate difficulties. A Presidential statement pledging continuity of policy on vital issues could be effective in maintaining Alliance confidence both in the constancy of the American purpose and in the solidarity of NATO itself. Such a statement, from President Kennedy, was read to the Permanent Council on February 15, 1961.[1]

2. *Objectives*

The general U.S. objectives at the meeting should be:

(a) To sustain Allied confidence in the constancy of U.S. policy and strength.

(b) To fortify NATO morale through reaffirmation by Member Governments of their reciprocal obligations to maintain the vitality of the Alliance.

(c) To create the broadest possible area of agreement on future East-West relations, through consultation in the meeting and bilaterally and through assurances as to continuing consultation in future.

(d) To avoid, if at all possible, a disruptive confrontation with the French over NATO's powers and functions, without sacrifice of fundamental NATO principles.

(e) To seek the most effective means of proceeding with the analysis of Alliance strategy, forces, and resources which is required if the Organization is to deter or to respond rationally to Soviet aggression, whatever its scale.

3. *Political Issues*

(a) *East-West Relations.* The Permanent Council has, of course, been informed and consulted frequently on East-West negotiations since the Limited Test Ban Treaty was signed on August 5. The current meeting, however, will provide the first opportunity to discuss with Ministers collectively not only past developments but, more important, what we believe may lie ahead. It will be advisable for the U.S. to maintain a balance between wishful thinking on the so-called détente, on the one

---

[1] For text, see Department of State *Bulletin*, March 6, 1961, pp. 333–334.

hand, and opposition to all discussion with the Soviets as dangerous or pointless, on the other.

Ministers will expect a review of the prospects for and obstacles to a non-aggression arrangement, a system of observation posts, a non-dissemination agreement, a reduction in military budgets and other measures proposed by the USSR to reduce the risk of war. We might usefully present as well a brief status report on our bilateral negotiations with the Soviets on wheat sales, the use of outer space, a consular agreement, cultural exchanges and civil aviation.

A realistic survey of this negotiating scene, sketched against the background of the potentially inflammatory situations in Berlin and Cuba, comes appropriately from us as the prime mover of the Alliance and its principal exponent of political consultation. It provides a setting for efforts to induce the British to join in forestalling a harmful, competitive relaxation of credit terms for trade with the Soviet Bloc. And it helps to dispose of allegations that the U.S. would be willing to reach security agreements with the USSR over the heads of its allies.

(b) *NATO and Atlantic Partnership.* In the unlikely event of a direct French attack on NATO, we shall have to make a firm but moderate reply. To remain silent could cause serious injury to the Alliance. The real though limited degree of military integration and political cooperation thus far attained in NATO is the cement of the Alliance; without it there is no assurance of NATO's utility in a crisis. In any event, we will wish to make clear our continued commitment to the goal of creating an effective Atlantic partnership. Our objective in this regard assumes both a vigorously functioning Alliance and further progress toward European integration.

(c) *Organizational Matters.* Recognizing that an organizational change may sometimes help to reinvigorate what many consider a static or dispirited agency, we have nevertheless concluded that no significant initiative of this character could be successfully pressed at this time. At this stage it is preferable for us merely to discuss any ideas we or others may have, for future disposition.

In two respects, however, we must contemplate more immediate action. First, we must begin now to search for a candidate of suitable stature and dedication to Alliance objectives to replace Dr. Dirk Stikker when he relinquishes the post of Secretary General next year. Second, as a long-term objective, we could encourage the trend toward creation of a NATO international military staff, which could provide military staff advice on a non-national basis to the Military Committee and replace the tripartite Standing Group. This development would have far-reaching organizational implications and would, inter alia, have the additional advantage of permitting the more equitable representation of

German and Italian officers, as well as those from the smaller NATO countries, in the higher military activities of the Alliance.

4.   *Military Problems*

(a) *NATO Force Planning Exercise.* It is now apparent that this exercise may well provide the only means of reconciling NATO strategic doctrine and the force structure and military outlays of NATO members in a more fully consistent pattern, within a relatively short time. Increasingly stiff French opposition to the exercise confronts us with a dilemma. Yielding to it could result in the long run in stultifying NATO's ability to engage in long-range military planning and coordinated defense; resisting it might provoke a much more serious French estrangement from NATO than anything we have yet observed. Our primary objective at this meeting must, therefore, be to seek some compromise permitting the exercise to proceed, if not with French participation, then at least with French acquiescence or benevolent abstention. If this proves impossible, we shall ultimately have to decide whether to carry on the exercise outside the NATO framework. However, we must avoid promoting or dramatizing French isolation on the procedural and strategic issues involved at the Ministerial Meeting.

(b) *The American Military Commitment.* With the change in the Presidency, Europeans worried at the prospect of cutbacks in American force levels in Europe for balance of payments or other reasons will seek reassurance at the meeting. Discussion on this subject should be cast in terms of the need for common effort by all the Allies to carry the burden of NATO defense.

At the same time, this would be a poor moment to initiate general discussion of further retrenchment measures now being planned for possible future implementation. Any such discussion would be construed as forecasting a new direction in American military policy; as a justification of the de Gaulle thesis on American undependability; and as an open sesame to force cuts by every NATO country. We should, however, bear in mind the utility of laying the groundwork for the return, as early as politically practicable, of those combat units we are maintaining in Central Europe over our NATO commitments. This consideration is in no way inconsistent with assurances as to fulfillment of the commitments themselves.

We can perform a useful service to the Alliance by providing a thoroughgoing analysis of the military needs and defensive potentialities of the Alliance as we see them, along lines forecast in Secretary McNamara's address on November 18. Beginning with our estimate of Soviet capabilities, we can espouse the principle of a measured response adjusted to the scale of a Soviet aggression; stress the prospects for non-nuclear resistance short of an all-out war; and set in proper perspective the effects of recent technological and strategic developments. The main thrust should be to demonstrate the utility of adequate general purpose forces, and not to encourage a reduction in their numbers.

(c) *Nuclear Problems.* While the basic problem of nuclear responsibility and nuclear control in the Alliance is still very far from solution, there is likely to be less emphasis on it at the pending meeting than in past years. No aspect of this subject is ripe for action at this time. We should refer realistically to the status of the preliminary discussions on the Multilateral Force now in process in Paris and Washington, making clear our continuing support and, in bilateral discussions, our willingness to proceed toward establishment of the Force whenever the Germans and Italians are prepared to do so. Moreover, we can as desired cite the nuclear planning, targeting and assignment arrangements completed as a result of the decisions taken at Ottawa last spring. Only if the French precipitate a debate on national nuclear forces should it be necessary to intervene in a major way on the nuclear issue.

---

222. Editorial Note

The 32d Ministerial Meeting of the North Atlantic Council was held at Paris, December 16–17. Leading the U.S. Delegation to the meeting were Secretaries Rusk and McNamara who presented the Council with a message from President Johnson. In two restricted sessions on December 16, the Council discussed the international situation. At the third and fourth sessions on December 17, the Ministers considered military questions and adopted a final communiqué. The U.S. Delegation reported on these meetings in Polto 864 and Polto Circulars 49–51, December 17. (Department of State, Central Files, NATO 3 FR(PA)) Memoranda of the conversation between members of the U.S. Delegation and foreign officials together with the telegrams to and from the delegation are ibid., Conference Files: Lot 66 D 110, CF 2345, 2346, and 2354. The text of Rusk's remarks on the international situation was transmitted as an enclosure to circular airgram 6352, December 20 (ibid., Central Files, NATO 3 FR(PA)); the texts of his remarks and those of Secretary McNamara on the military situation were transmitted as enclosures to circular airgram 6354, December 20 (ibid.). For texts of President Johnson's message to the Council and the final communiqué, see *American Foreign Policy: Current Documents, 1963,* pages 436–439.

a European power, but as an African, Asiatic and Oceanic power which we are and which we want to remain." To this he added on April 7, 1954, that "for lack of atomic arms, of which we have let others have the monopoly, our forces, dear as they cost us, do not constitute a whole, and that automatically reduces them to the rank of auxiliaries. On the other hand our African and home bases have been handed over to the Americans, joint commands have been assigned to them, without French Governments demanding for France a share in the plans and decisions concerning atomic war."

These views are directly reflected in the actions of General de Gaulle over the past two and one-half years. They were also shared by many French political leaders, and difficulties had developed particularly in the nuclear field with the last several governments of the Fourth Republic, which had bargained for information in the nuclear field by withholding permission for the US to introduce nuclear warheads into France. The white paper issued by the French Government after their first atomic explosion indicated that the basic decisions to proceed with military applications of nuclear energy were taken during 1955–56. Undoubtedly the French leaders resented the declaration of common purpose by President Eisenhower and Prime Minister Macmillan on October 25, 1957,[2] which included the statement that "we regard our possession of nuclear weapons power as a trust for the defense of the free world." The French first revealed to us early in 1958 that they had been secretly working on an atomic bomb project for several years.

In his first meeting with Secretary Dulles in July, 1958,[3] General de Gaulle reiterated the French determination to develop nuclear weapons and French insistence upon custody over any nuclear warheads stationed in France, as well as his beliefs that the US influence in NATO was too preponderant and that the leading NATO powers should develop a "global" strategy. General de Gaulle also indicated that he would submit three papers to us, on nuclear matters, on revision of the North Atlantic Treaty and its command structure, and on the broad strategy of the Three Powers. We have never received the first two papers. The third paper is the memorandum of September 17, 1958.

Tripartite meetings

After consultation with the British, we held a series of tripartite meetings with the French at the ambassadorial level in Washington, in an endeavor to learn from the French what General de Gaulle had in mind. We made clear, both privately and in the press, that we would not agree to any institutional arrangements among the Three Powers, that

---

[2] For text, see *American Foreign Policy: Current Documents, 1957,* pp. 643–646.

[3] For documentation on Dulles' visit to Paris in July 1958, see *Foreign Relations, 1958–1960,* vol. VII, Part 2, pp. 52 ff.

would in any way derogate from the institutions established under our series of multilateral treaty arrangements. We also endeavored to make clear to the French that we could not enter into any special arrangement giving them any veto right over our use of nuclear weapons anywhere in the world, although we probably failed to dispel their illusion that such an arrangement exists between ourselves and the British. [*2 lines of source text not declassified*]

We did agree, however, to hold a series of informal and ad hoc consultations of the Three Powers at the Secretary and Under Secretary level. The first consultation was on the Far East and the second on Africa. There was to be a third consultation on military contingencies and planning for Africa, but the French side collapsed at this point and no further meetings were held in this series. General de Gaulle wrote further letters to the President and the Prime Minister, indicating that these meetings had not realized the purposes he had in mind. We reiterated our position about his original proposals, and the matter remained dormant. Meanwhile the French Mediterranean fleet was withdrawn from wartime earmark to NATO command, nine USAF squadrons were withdrawn from France so that they could be armed with nuclear weapons, and the French proceeded with their own atomic energy program.

After the Congo situation developed last summer, General de Gaulle again complained about the lack of tripartite consultation and proposed a meeting of the three heads of government. However, the French had very little to say when a preliminary tripartite meeting was held at the Foreign Minister-Secretary of State level in September in New York. President Eisenhower indicated that he would not again visit Europe during the remainder of his presidency, and further tripartite meetings were therefore limited to the Under Secretary and Secretary levels just prior to the NATO ministerial meeting at Paris in December. These meetings considered not only such matters as the Berlin question, Soviet intentions, and Laos, which the Three Powers have been discussing for many years in view of their historic involvement in these issues, but also such subjects as the Congo and the Caribbean. It developed shortly thereafter that the French had passed to the Belgians an agreed tripartite paper on the Congo, although we have insisted to the other NATO powers all along that these informal tripartite consultations have merely constituted exchanges of views on matters in which the Three Powers had special responsibilities.

Conclusion

Quite aside from the special tripartite meetings that have been held over the past two years, we have of course continued our close tripartite consultations on all aspects of the German question, flowing from the special responsibilities of the Three Powers in Germany. Prior to the meeting of the four heads of government at Paris last May, meetings were held of the three Western heads of government in December 1959 and May 1960.[4] All of these meetings have flowed from our established responsibilities. Our endeavors to mould consultations on other subjects to a special tripartite framework have been less than successful because such a framework has been contrived and has not been a normal diplomatic development. We have not satisfied the basic proposals set forth by General de Gaulle in his original memorandum on this subject, although President Eisenhower endeavored to assuage him by establishing a special communications arrangement following his visit to France in September 1959.[5]

The French effort to establish a new form of Triple Entente with the British and ourselves has in our view failed to take account of the reemergence of Germany and Italy from the war period, ignores the geographic and military importance of the smaller NATO members, and would tend to undermine our framework of mutual defense treaty arrangements. Tripartitism is also believed to be most unpopular with the Afro-Asian countries.

Under these circumstances you might wish to raise the question of tripartite consultations with the French Ambassador at the first opportunity. You could speak along the following lines: You have reviewed the course of our tripartite consultations at all levels over the past two years and it appears to you that the special meetings which have been arranged have not been particularly fruitful; and that the full utilization of our normal diplomatic facilities would seem to be fully adequate for purposes of information, review and consultation on most questions in which we are both interested. Moreover, our impression has been that the French Government has not been satisfied with these discussions, which began as a result of French initiative. Therefore, if the French desires are in fact unfulfilled, perhaps these discussions might be terminated.

You could then suggest that Ambassador Alphand advise his government of the foregoing and obtain their views on this matter, adding that if Couve de Murville and General de Gaulle believe that the tripartite meetings held over the past two years have been really fruitful, we could consider their continuation. We would in any event continue our special arrangements where they have always existed, such as on Germany or in preparation for four-power meetings.

We should mention this to the British only after we have taken it up with the French.

---

[4] For documentation on the Heads of Government meeting in December 1959, see ibid., Part 1, pp. 527 ff. For documentation on the meetings that preceded the abortive summit conference in May 1960, see ibid., vol. IX, pp. 159 ff.

[5] For documentation on Eisenhower's visit to France in September 1959, see ibid., vol. VII, Part 2, pp. 253 ff.

224.   Memorandum of Conversation

Washington, February 28, 1961.

SUBJECT

Tripartitism

PARTICIPANTS

The Secretary	The French Ambassador
Ambassador Gavin	M. Lebel
Mr. McGhee, C	M. Winckler
Mr. White, EUR	M. Pelen
Mr. McBride, WE	
Mr. Beigel, WE	

Ambassador Alphand referred to the tripartite relationship which exists between the French, British and ourselves. He said that the French wish to improve this consultation and to continue the ad hoc meetings of the three Foreign Ministers which have been going for some time. He said that in the past one official in each Government had been in charge of following and organizing these meetings and that in the US case it had been Under Secretary Merchant. The French also hope that the three Heads of Government could meet from time to time and noted that this had taken place during the last US Administration. He said the French believe it most important that this precedent be followed up. He said the French also thought that tripartite discussions between the Secretary and the two Ambassadors here were important for the conduct of our day-to-day common business. Ambassador Alphand said that unfortunately the decisions reached in tripartite discussions were not always implemented. General de Gaulle hoped that the machinery could be improved. He stressed that the French did not have any desire to establishment of a formal institution or for setting up a directorate to impose tripartite decisions. [sic] He said that the French did not through this mechanism hope to obtain a veto over US policy. He said the French hope that matters could be discussed and agreements reached, or that the three could agree to disagree.

Ambassador Alphand continued, saying that the French believed that if there were tripartite agreement on the policies to be followed, NATO and SEATO, for that matter, would usually follow the lead of the three. This would also greatly assist in presenting a solid front to the Soviets. He noted that the three countries involved had interests in virtually all major problems throughout the world. There were also

---

Source: Department of State, Central Files, 396.1/2–2861. Secret. Drafted by McBride and approved by S on March 17.

important traditional aspects of influence of each of these three countries outside of Europe. He noted this was not the case with other countries such as Germany which was not interested in participation in world-wide problems other than those such as Berlin which affected her directly. Ambassador Alphand said de Gaulle attached ever more importance to tripartite consultations, especially in view of the decline of the United Nations.

The Secretary asked if the French thought that the tripartite talks which had taken place over the past few years had been satisfactory and had been what the French had in mind. Ambassador Alphand said they had been the minimum which the French desired but that they had not been sufficient to prevent a fait accompli in many cases, such as Lebanon. He noted that the French had also been guilty in the same sense in the Suez case. He said in the past de Gaulle had sometimes been disappointed because he had thought he had reached an agreement with us and the British in the tripartite forum, but these agreements had not been implemented. Ambassador Alphand summarized that the French wished to continue what already existed in this field but to improve it.

The Secretary said that we considered tripartite solidarity important too and would like to find the best means to keep close to the British and the French. He said there were certain procedural problems involved. Sometimes it was preferable to have simple, quiet, and informal meetings and not to have any publicity which might lead to complaints from other NATO members and from other countries as well. The Secretary said tripartitism would work well if the policies of the three countries agreed but that it was hard when our policies disagreed, and in these cases our commitments to formal tripartite consultative procedures would not help. The Secretary said he thought that tripartite Foreign Ministers' meetings from time to time were helpful and that they would undoubtedly meet together during the forthcoming SEATO meeting. The Secretary said he did not know currently of any plan which was likely to bring the three Heads of Government together. He expressed willingness to continue tripartite meetings here. He thought we should identify our differences and see if we could devise means on how to deal with them. On some subjects such as Berlin and Germany it was natural to have tripartite conversations before discussing these matters with the Germans. However, there was no particular problem in harmonizing our policies here in this field.

Ambassador Alphand said that the French did not desire any publicity regarding tripartite talks and agreed generally with the Secretary's comments. The Secretary added that in some areas we undoubtedly had different approaches but that our national purposes were the same. Ambassador Alphand agreed, saying that in Laos and Africa, for instance, the French and ourselves had the same aims. The questions which we should discuss tripartitely were how to reconcile our tactics and methods. The Secretary said that the procedures of the US Government were, of course, complex and that one of the questions was when, in our own internal processes, we should insert consultations with our allies. He recommended that if there were questions that the French wished to bring in to us at an early stage they should do so, even if we were not entirely ready to comment.

The Secretary thought that we should let tripartite consultations develop naturally over the coming weeks and months and that we should not now institute any stylized code of procedure. He said he expected to see Couve in the last part of March at SEATO. He said there should be maximum tripartite consultation possible in order to reach accords whenever feasible.

Ambassador Alphand said the tripartite meeting with the Secretary a few days previously to discuss instructions to Ambassador Thompson had been very helpful.[1] He thought it well that there was a common tripartite view before Ambassador Thompson saw Khrushchev or Gromyko. He also thought it essential that the three Ambassadors in Moscow should speak the same language to the Soviets.

Ambassador Alphand then asked whom the Secretary would appoint as his Deputy to meet with Lucet and Hoyer-Millar for discreet advance preparations for further tripartite ministerial meetings. The Secretary said that this function might well devolve on the Deputy Under Secretary who had not yet been named. Ambassador Alphand said that Lucet had the equivalent rank of a Deputy Under Secretary.

Ambassador Alphand then passed to the military field and noted that de Gaulle had covered tripartite global strategy in his memorandum of 1958. The French had proposed tripartite military discussions in Washington including the British and French members of the Standing Group. He said there had thus far been no tripartite military planning which de Gaulle thought was essential in view of the many strategic changes since NATO had been formed in 1949. He said de Gaulle attached great importance to the military side of these consultations. The 1958 memorandum clearly involved defense all over the world. De Gaulle particularly had in mind military planning for the African-European area. Nowhere did a Western body to study these problems exist. Therefore, the French thought some tripartite study of the general strategy concept was essential. This would mean an extension of the role now played by the Standing Group, though not necessarily with the same personnel. It was understood, for instance, that the US would not

---

[1] According to his Appointment Book, Rusk discussed Thompson's instructions with Caccia and Alphand at noon on February 22. (Johnson Library). A memorandum of this conversation is in Department of State, Secretary's Memoranda of Conversation: Lot 65 D 330.

be represented by its member of the Standing Group. The Secretary said he did not think that talks of this type should be identified with the Standing Group.

The Secretary concluded on this subject saying that he would revert to this point at the end of our talks, when we would pick up specific questions which had not been answered. Therefore he would defer further comment on this point until a later date when he would hope to respond to the French proposal.

---

225. Memorandum of Conversation

Washington, March 10, 1961.

SUBJECT

Tripartite Consultation between France, the United States and the United Kingdom

PARTICIPANTS

United States	*France*
The President	Mr. Chaban-Delmas, President of
Foy D. Kohler, Assistant Secretary	the French National Assembly
(present during second half of	Hervé Alphand, French
conversation)	Ambassador (present during
Edmund S. Glenn, Interpreter	second half of conversation)

After greetings by the President, Mr. Chaban-Delmas said that he was glad to be able to see the President alone, because as President of the National Assembly he is not a member of the French Administration; he has nevertheless been entrusted with a personal mission from President de Gaulle to President Kennedy and will present General de Gaulle's thoughts.

The recent assumption by Mr. Kennedy of the Presidency of the United States creates an opportunity which may never recur to carry out some fundamental changes and improvements in the working methods

---

Source: Department of State, Central Files, 611.51/3–1061. Confidential; Limit Distribution. Drafted by Kohler and Glenn and approved by the White House on March 17. Chaban-Delmas visited the United States March 2–16, and in a memorandum to the President on February 16 Rusk had recommended that the President receive him. (Ibid., 033.5111/2–1661)

of the Western Alliance. Four or eight years from now it may be too late to proceed with such changes in methods, and thus to reverse the flow of events which, according to General de Gaulle, has been consistently favoring the Communists during the last eight or ten years. It is necessary to build up the West into a team within which the positions of Washington, London, Paris and the other Western capitals would be intimately coordinated. Mr. Chaban-Delmas alluded to a conversation he had with Chairman Khrushchev, in which the latter, after a lengthy exchange, lost his temper and in a cold anger stated that he could always win against the West because there was no coordination between the policies of the Western nations and he could play them one against the other. This is also the opinion of General de Gaulle, who sees the danger deriving from such a lack of coordination as threatening the West not only in regard to concrete political situations but even more in the struggle for the minds and hearts of man, a struggle which may be lost because of a lack of a clear common position on the part of the West. The need for a fundamental reconstruction of the Western procedures will be presented to President Kennedy by General de Gaulle when the two of them meet, which should be in the near future. It has already been presented in Washington by Ambassador Alphand and is now being presented by Mr. Chaban-Delmas acting as a personal emissary of General de Gaulle.

The most complete coordination should exist between the three Western Powers which have responsibilities extending beyond their own borders. These are the United States, which is the leader and the greatest power of the West; the United Kingdom, which has special ties with the Commonwealth; and France, which has special ties in Africa and some other areas of the world. The three powers must consult jointly before taking common decisions on the major aspects of world politics. Such consultations should be carried out without irritating the sensitivity of the other Western nations and therefore on an informal basis. The method by which such consultations are to be carried out can be determined easily, because the reason for the inefficiency of the consultations as carried out up to the present, is not caused by the mechanism employed but rather by the absence of a strong determination to arrive at unity. It is only President Kennedy who can provide the will and the determination in question; administrations and governments will follow his leadership. The French realize that this may not be easy: The United States is the first power in the free world, and without its help France would have already been swallowed by the Communists. This preeminent position of the United States may lead to the temptation for the United States to take the position that major decisions belong to the United States alone. This would amount to being tempted by the devil; the United States must instead derive the logical consequences of its own successes. The United States has rebuilt Europe and thanks to the United States Europe has taken on a strength and an importance which warrant that it be consulted. France, in particular, has been strengthened thanks both to U.S. aid and to the coming into power of General de Gaulle. General de Gaulle is working for a united Europe and is in constant touch with West Germany and the other nations of Europe. This makes France a natural channel for the coordination of policies on the continent in the same way in which the United States and the United Kingdom are the natural channels for the coordination of policies in other geographical areas. France asks for an understanding of her position in moving towards the absolutely necessary goal of having Western policy coordinated by decisions taken beforehand at the level of the conception of policies and not belatedly at the level of their implementation.

It is up to President Kennedy to choose the approach; if he does so the difficulties which exist will be overcome. The policies of the West may be carried out through the United Nations or through NATO or any other channel; the important thing is that the decisions be taken together and before starting in any one direction in any particular case. President de Gaulle is not against any channel of policy or any organization, and the President will find him a partner very easy to get along with, once a policy of consultations is inaugurated. It is, however, only a personal agreement between the three heads of government which can give substance to consultations carried out by the foreign ministers and the diplomats.

The President reviewed the various issues of French-American relations. There is today complete accord on Berlin and also on the French policy in Algeria;[1] in the latter respect the United States greatly admires the policy and the efforts of General de Gaulle's Government. There is some disagreement on the Congo; there, however, the situation is so confused and changing so constantly that such a lack of complete agreement is relatively unimportant as any policy tends to be overtaken by chaotic developments. There are two other areas where differences of opinion exist. One of these is nuclear arms policy and the other one is Laos. In regard to the former there is no urgency, as there is still time to coordinate policies and arrive at complete mutual understanding. The situation is different as respects Laos, in regard to which agreement must be obtained urgently.

Summing up the conversation, the President said that he saw two major areas in it: one, the opinion of the French that the policy of the three principal Western powers is insufficiently coordinated; the Presi-

---

[1] Following the conversation reported here, the President and Chaban-Delmas discussed Algeria at some length. A memorandum of this part of the conversation is ibid., President's Memoranda of Conversation: Lot 66 D 149.

dent greatly desires to improve this coordination and would be interested in hearing suggestions from the French side as to the manner in which this could be done; and, two, the question of Laos. The latter is a very urgent question in regard to which something must be done right now; there exists the possibility that the United States may be drawn into a military action in Laos, that is to say in a country in regard to which the major responsibility was placed on France by the Geneva Conference. There are divergencies between the American and the French policy in regard to that question and in particular in regard to Souvanna Phouma. An agreement between the two countries must however be obtained, since without agreement success in Laos hardly appears possible.

Mr. Chaban-Delmas stated that he would return to the question of Laos later. At the present moment he wishes to continue on the question of the general methods to be followed in coordinating the policies of the West and on the necessity of a coordination in this area. The West is facing two types of difficulties: those which are due to the common enemy and those which are due to lack of coordination among the Western powers and the lack of prior policy decisions preceding any action taken by the West. The West may be compared to three medical doctors who come in only after a crisis in the health of the patient has arisen and who prescribe often incompatible medicines even before consulting among themselves. What they should do is to get together on preventive methods before any crisis arises. Let us take Communist China as an example. There exists an American policy in its respect. The United Kingdom does not oppose this policy openly, but follows a policy which differs from the American one at least to the extent of 50%. As for France, which could be helpful as it has some points of contact in the Far East, it simply looks from the outside in. Anther example is the Congo. If the Big Three had studied together the situation in that country during the last few years, ever since signs of unrest appeared there, and if they had made common approaches to the Belgians telling them that a change in policy was necessary and that that change could not be a sudden withdrawal without any serious preparation for Congolese independence, it is possible that the Congolese crisis would have never arisen. Of course, what is being suggested is not that the three main powers of the West dictate to the other Western countries. General de Gaulle would never wish to suggest in regard to other countries something which he would not accept in regard to France. The point is that common studies by the United States, British and French Heads of Government, who have at their disposal the experience and the means which can enable them to understand the global consequences of any particular policy, would lead to suggestions which the other Western nations would find it easy to follow. Such suggestions might be transmitted to the other nations through the natural channel of that member of the Big Three which has the most intimate associations with any particular geographical area. For example by the French in Bonn—where the United States and the United Kingdom also have Ambassadors who could make it clear that the policies presented by one of the Three is indeed the common policy of all Three; by the United States in Tokyo (which may be subjected to very severe pressures in the near future); and by the United Kingdom in its own area of direct association.

Mr. Chaban-Delmas repeated that the decision on this point is up to President Kennedy. If the United States continues its present policy of deciding policies alone, the French will remain good friends of the United States, as the friendship and the mutual understanding of the two countries, and as a matter of fact all of the Western countries, derive from an extremely deep community of ideas; but the policies of the West will in such case be carried out inefficiently and Khrushchev will continue to be able to carry the ball through a disorganized Western team. If on the contrary the President decides to change the methods of Western policy towards work and preparation in common it will certainly be easy to arrange for meetings of the three chiefs of government in a way which will not frighten Chancellor Adenauer or any other Western Chief of Government. For example, such meetings might take place at the occasion of broader meetings of NATO or other groups of Western powers. The same thing may apply to meetings of Foreign Ministers and of diplomatic representatives, which will become fully useful only if prior agreement on the broad ranges of policy is obtained among the Chiefs of Government. As for what such decisions would be, there is no need for prejudging. General de Gaulle is not against using the United Nations as a channel for policy—for example in regard to the Congo—but he is of the opinion that this, as any other channel of policy can be useful only if a common stand is first of all determined between the Western powers. In the case of the Congo such a common stand might have resulted in different actions on the part not only of the Belgians but also of the Soviets and therefore to an entirely different situation within the UN.

Another example of an area in which a common policy should be determined is that of aid to underdeveloped countries. Thanks to General de Gaulle's policy France has a very strong position in Africa, where she had given independence to twelve nations without friction and in full amity. There are, however, some countries of Africa which mistrust France but which trust the United States which has no colonialist past. A coordination of policies between the two countries could take advantage of the privileged position of each of them.

Mr. Chaban-Delmas again insisted on the importance of arriving at a coordinated policy at the present moment. He had been receiving invitations to come to the United States for the last twelve years. He did not accept those invitations until now because he felt that in the past the political situation either in Paris or in Washington or in both capitals was such that he could not accomplish much by coming. He feels that at the present moment favorable conditions exist both in Paris, where General de Gaulle has put the French political house in order, and in Washington where a vigorous administration is in office. Such a combination of favorable circumstances may not recur again. The West cannot afford four more years of drift.

The President thanked Mr. Chaban-Delmas for presenting to him General de Gaulle's ideas. He himself feels the need for more harmony in French-American relations and has been discussing with the French Ambassador the methods for obtaining such harmony. He intends to improve the necessary exchanges of ideas. Two main areas must, however, be distinguished one from [the] other. One of these is that of a variety of problems on some of which agreement exists (as on Berlin) while on some others there is as yet no agreement but there is at least time for seeking and obtaining an agreement. This is the area in regard to which improved techniques on consultation and exchanges of ideas may be developed. The other area is one in which agreement between the two countries must be obtained immediately. This is Laos. The President would like Mr. Chaban-Delmas to be thoroughly acquainted with the American position and the American thoughts on Laos so as to be able to present this position and these thoughts to the French Government on his return to Paris. The President asked Mr. Kohler to arrange for briefings of Mr. Chaban-Delmas on this question in the Department of State.

Mr. Chaban-Delmas said that he would be happy to discuss the Laotian question as suggested by the President. He would be accompanied by Ambassador Alphand in his conversations in the Department.

---

226. Telegram From the Department of State to the Embassy in France

Washington, April 26, 1961, 9:58 p.m.

4541. Embassy requested deliver following Presidential message to de Gaulle. Advise time date delivery.

Source: Department of State, Presidential Correspondence: Lot 66 D 204. Official Use Only; Niact. For text of an April 24 message sent to de Gaulle on Algeria, see *Public Papers of the Presidents of the United States: John F. Kennedy, 1961*, p. 315.

"Dear General de Gaulle: I want you to know how deeply gratified I am with the success you have achieved in mastering events in recent days.[1] I know that the American people join me in this feeling of gratification knowing that, if the result had been any other, the tragedy would have been for all of us and not for France alone. The steadfastness you displayed in the face of the hazards was inspiring and in full accord with firm, unswerving devotion to your nation which has been your role in France's difficult days.

I must add, as well, that I was particularly heartened by the splendid manner in which the entire French people and the great majority of the French armed forces responded to your leadership.

With warmest personal wishes,

Sincerely yours,

John F. Kennedy"

We do not intend publish but have no objection should de Gaulle wish to do so. If de Gaulle wishes publish, inform Department in advance, if possible, to permit simultaneous publication by White House.

Bowles

---

[1] The President is referring to the military coup that began in Algeria on April 22, but was successfully put down by April 26.

---

227.   Telegram From the Department of State to the Embassy in France

Washington, May 5, 1961, 10:07 p.m.

4770. Embassy pass USRO and Thurston. Personal for Ambassador from Secretary.

I am grateful for thoughtful analysis reflected in your 4479,[1] and believe it might be useful spell out my own thinking these issues.

Source: Department of State, Central Files, 611.51/4–1861. Secret; Limit Distribution. Drafted by Owen; cleared with RA, S/AE, WE, Acheson, and Kohler; and approved by Rusk.

[1] Telegram 4479, April 18, reported that Gavin was becoming convinced that some basic changes were required in U.S. policy toward France and, in particular, recommended that the United States cease preventing export to France of technical information and materials applicable to rocketry and offer to help the Europeans technologically to develop a second-generation vehicle launcher. (Ibid.)

1. Our policy of trying to slow down acquisition nuclear weapons capabilities is based on view that such acquisition will increase risk of war by accident or miscalculation, diminish possibility controlled nuclear response in event of hostilities, raise new obstacles arms control, and pose very grave threat to allied political cohesion. The more rapid and extensive any additional acquisition of nuclear capabilities, the greater will be these dangers.

2. Policy of trying to slow down nuclear proliferation precludes US assistance not only for development nuclear warheads but also for development ballistic missile systems, since such systems represent an essential and politically most sensitive aspect of effective nuclear strike capability.

3. We recognize that provision info on ballistic missiles might be of only limited importance in overcoming formidable difficulties France faces in trying create militarily meaningful missile capability. But experience to date suggests provision any kind of aid only leads to requests more extensive assistance. Refusal of these further requests (unavoidable under existing national policy) then leads to more friction than if no aid had been granted in first place.

4. Recognize that France will nonetheless continue its missile program. But cost and time required for France to prosecute that program will surely be greater if we do not provide help than otherwise. This cost and time may eventually tend discourage French from pursuing present path, in post-de Gaulle period, if alternative means of responding to basic French concerns are developed by US (see para 6, below).

5. We also recognize that French will probably develop nuclear strike capability with manned aircraft, even if they do not develop effective ballistic missile capability. Their national nuclear program will be less promising in this event, however, than if they have missile capability, since aircraft less effective delivery means. Thus French will be less apt, if dependent on aircraft delivery, to consider they have achieved such success in nuclear program as to justify continued national effort in this field in post-de Gaulle period. And Germans will also be less likely, in this event, to consider that such striking success has been achieved in French nuclear program as would justify their trying to follow in French footsteps.

6. Key question throughout, in my view, is not so much whether France will achieve some sort nuclear weapons capability but effect on German aspirations and thus on NATO of US posture of encouraging French nuclear effort. The French will face a most serious resource problem in trying to prosecute a national missile and nuclear program alone. They may well seek German aid at some point. The Germans would not now wish to be drawn into such a venture and would be unwilling to grant aid under present circumstances. But if US signifies it approves

French program and helps that program, German resistance to joining it may be greatly weakened. Even possible that, despite Chancellor's desires, Germany might eventually be moved to seek US aid for its own program in this event. Any such German effort create or join in creating nuclear capability would shake NATO to its foundations. For this reason I am not aware and would not approve any assistance to Germans or any other country for development of national ballistic missile capability.

7. In light these factors, and after most careful review different considerations, I believe US should proceed along lines laid out in Acheson recommendations concerning US policy toward Atlantic nations, which President approved April 21:[2]

(a) not help France achieve nuclear weapons capability or produce or acquire MRBM's;
(b) seek to respond reasonable French interests and concerns through such steps as more intimate political consultation with France, guarantee to maintain US nuclear capability in Europe for life of treaty, commitment US Polaris submarines and UK strategic forces to NATO, greater allied and particularly French participation in planning and decision regarding use nuclear weapons committed to NATO, and other measures to same end now under consideration here.

Rusk

---

[2] See Document 100.

---

228. Talking Points

PDG–A/2   Washington, May 27, 1961.

PRESIDENT'S VISIT TO DE GAULLE
Paris, May 31–June 2, 1961

Talking Points (Summary of Scope Paper)[1]

The President will have five sessions with de Gaulle, totaling seven and a quarter hours (approximately 50% of the time probably required

---

Source: Department of State, Conference Files: Lot 66 D 110, CF 1895. Secret; Limit Distribution. No drafting information appears on the source text but like the scope paper, referred to below, it was probably drafted in the Department of State.

[1] Dated May 15, a copy of this 8-page paper, PDG A/1, is ibid.

for interpretation). Four of these meetings are alone with interpreters. De Gaulle has given only general ideas on agenda. Hopefully at the first half-hour meeting on Friday, May 31, at 12:30 de Gaulle may indicate in what order he would like to raise subjects. Since, however, he has not done so to date, the following talking points follow the order of the Scope Paper which was discussed with the President.

1) *East-West Issue:* Large community of interest exists between U.S. and France and there are few disagreements on nature of threat. Stress identity of U.S. and French views on this most fundamental issue as overriding intra-alliance problems which we may have.

2) *Berlin:* This is only specific subject which de Gaulle singled out for discussion. He considers it of paramount importance and strongly favors maintenance of status quo. Stress here again our community of interest and fact both U.S. and French prestige committed to maintenance of Western position on Berlin and express agreement with de Gaulle's very firm position on Berlin. Reference could be made to need to get ahead with contingency planning in Washington and fact that French representative here may need fuller instructions from Paris.

3) *"Europe":* Another area where we are largely in agreement. Emphasize U.S. support for broad political objectives of EEC (de Gaulle's support for European integration is likewise best means to avoid resurgent German nationalism).

4) *Africa:* Another area in which our interests and policies largely coincide. Stress our support for French policy of self-determination as implemented throughout Africa south of Sahara by French and which French now seeking to implement in Algeria. We are well pleased with progress which states in Africa of French persuasion are making and orderly way in which they came into independence. While we have some minor differences regarding aid (particularly military) to the African states and a few minor divergencies elsewhere, by and large we are in accord. We strongly believe France should continue to play a major role in Africa especially in the former French territories and we emphatically do not seek to displace her. We are impressed with the strength of the cultural and other relationships between France and these territories and consider their continuation in our common interest.

5) *U.N:* Here is an area of disagreement. De Gaulle's distrust of the U.N. is widely known. He considers the U.N. Congo operation a failure which should be terminated. While there is no hope of converting de Gaulle into a U.N. supporter, we probably should review for him reasons why we consider the U.N. so important to Western policy. It could be added that without the U.N., the chaos in the Congo would have been much worse.

de Gaulle the basic assurance on nuclear weapons which Eisenhower gave the British and which you have confirmed to them. This understanding is "that the United States would, of course, in the event of increased tension or the threat of war take every possible step to consult with Britain and our other allies." This is understood to mean consultation in advance of the use of nuclear weapons. We have a supplementary understanding with the British under which there must be joint agreement on the use of nuclear weapons based in the UK, but there is no occasion for parity here because we have no nuclear weapons based in France. So in the current circumstances, the general offer of consultation is equal to what the British have.

4. On the question of providing inertial guidance systems to the French, I am still unable to get clear information after a day of telephone calls. I am giving this to Paul Nitze as an item of first priority for a full report, and he will bring it to the plane tomorrow.

5. The attached memorandum (3) gives the background of the French decision on withholding jets to Morocco. It appears that the French were simply annoyed at some earlier difficulties with the Moroccans. The State Department points out that this is an illustration of French failure to consult with us, and if we had known of their decision, we might have been able to act in time to prevent acceptance of the Soviet offer.

6. What we want to persuade the French to persuade the Portuguese to do in Angola is a matter of some argument in the Department, but on the whole the dominant view is that we should simply ask de Gaulle himself to communicate in his own way to Salazar the importance of reform and gradual decolonization. Since de Gaulle himself has exemplified this policy in his relations with former French colonists in Africa, it seems wise to us to leave the initiative to him in framing precise proposals to Salazar. In any event, we have nothing very precise to propose. I will have the latest cables from our Consul in Angola tomorrow if you want them.

7. On the Moroccan bases, our position is clearly stated in the annexed cable to Ambassador Bonsal. (4) In essence, this cable tells Bonsal to make a real study of the whole matter with the King and his Ministers. We are currently committed to a withdrawal by the end of 1963, and Bonsal is authorized to explore both special arrangements that may be desirable and possible before and after this deadline. He is also instructed to press for the withdrawal of Soviet technicians in Morocco, in accordance with assurances from the King and his grandfather.

8. On an arms embargo in Africa, the view of the State Department is mainly negative, in contrast to that of Senator Fulbright in a letter which I attach at Tab 5. The State Department believes that for us to attempt an external agreement on arms limitation would be resented in

most of the African states as a form of paternalism and neocolonialism. They also believe the initiative would fail and that Khrushchev is quite capable of using the UAR or Ghana as a conduit. Further, Khrushchev would probably reply by proposing a nuclear-free Africa, and until we can dispense with our bases in Morocco and Libya, this would be a good ploy for his side. De Gaulle has occasionally hinted at an arrangement under which the United States and the USSR would refrain from shipping arms, while former colonial powers continued their kindly relations as suppliers—but no one else seems to think this has any chance of success with any party. There seems to be no alternative to a careful policy of ad hoc decisions aimed at avoiding both arms races and Soviet penetration wherever possible.

9.   On the preferences between the European Common Market and the Brazzaville group, and the effect of these preferences on Latin America, the first memorandum from the Department is unintelligible, and Walt Rostow is rewriting it.

10. American aid as against French aid to Africa—Williams is preparing a new memorandum which will be at hand tomorrow. He misunderstood your request the other day and supposed that the quantitative material on French aid in the briefing papers was what you wanted.

11. On French flights over Libya, there is an appendix in the briefing papers which explains that they have been a matter of reconnaissance in connection with the Algerian struggle. As far as we know, they are not going on now, and none are scheduled for the next several weeks, but they could be restarted at any time if the French become suspicious about nationalist activity on the Libyan side of the frontier.

12. The present consulting machinery with the French in relation to Africa is being improved, we think, by the efforts of Assistant Secretary Williams and his associates. He has arranged a meeting at the Assistant Secretary level for the latter part of this month, and the Department also hopes that DAG will be increasingly helpful in this area as its members exchange information. A comment on this point may be helpful, because in the past France has often been the least communicative member of DAG.

13. Finally, I enclose copies of the memoranda of conversations between Eisenhower and de Gaulle at meetings of September 1959, April 1960 and May 1960.[3]

14. There is no formal agenda for the de Gaulle session, and we hope you may be willing to work one out with de Gaulle in your first

---

[3] For records of these conversations, see *Foreign Relations*, 1958–1960, vol. VII, Part 2, pp. 255 ff., 343 ff., and 364–365.

short session before lunch on Wednesday. Gavin has earlier reported that de Gaulle is interested in Africa, Asia, Latin America and Europe. He has also expressed particular interest in Berlin, and some concern for economic relations between the United States and Europe.

15. We are sending for de Gaulle's press conference on the UN and for the full text of his War College speech about NATO and the French Army. Meanwhile, the Department assures me that the best quotations from both are in the French briefing book at Background Paper B.

---

230. Memorandum of Conversation

US/MC/7   Paris, June 2, 1961, 11:30 a.m.–1 p.m.

PRESIDENT'S VISIT TO DE GAULLE
Paris, May 31–June 2, 1961

PARTICIPANTS

US	French
The President	General de Gaulle
The Secretary	M. Debré
Ambassador Gavin	M. Couve de Murville
Mr. Bohlen	Ambassador Alphand
Mr. Kohler	M. de Courcel
Mr. McBride	M. Lucet

General de Gaulle opened by saying that he would sum up the discussions which the President and he had had. The President was of course free to interrupt at any time.

With regard to Berlin General de Gaulle said the two Presidents had been in agreement.[1] President Kennedy will see Khrushchev and it depends on the latter whether there will be any Berlin crisis. De Gaulle said the President could tell Khrushchev for him that France agreed with us that the Berlin statute should not be modified by force. Perhaps

---

Source: Department of State, Conference Files: Lot 66 D 110, CF 1891. Secret. Drafted by McBride. A summary of this conversation was transmitted from Paris in Secto 9, June 2. (Ibid., CF 1892) The President visited Paris on his way to the summit meeting with Khrushchev in Vienna.

[1] For memoranda of the Presidents' discussion of Berlin, see vol. XIV, pp. 80–86.

one day the German question would be reopened but certainly not now in the cold war period. Any change must be approved by the four powers. De Gaulle said he also agreed with the President that our military experts should concert closely on Berlin contingency planning.

President de Gaulle said that President Kennedy and he had also had a frank talk concerning Laos.[2] He said he understood the US commitments to Thailand, Vietnam and the Philippines. He agreed that the situation was bad. If US honor and prestige forced us to intervene militarily, France would not oppose. On the other hand, France would not intervene herself. He considered Southeast Asia a bad terrain militarily, politically and psychologically to fight a war. France has long experience in Indochina fighting against Communism. She had been partly successful. However, the situation had become worse as more and more outside effort was poured in. De Gaulle repeated his thesis that India and Japan were the most important free nations in Asia but that most of the other nations of the area are fictitious.

The President said he had explained that while we realized France would not intervene in Laos, it was essential to keep this position quiet. The possibility that the US and two or three other countries might intervene remained a factor in the situation which would be adversely affected should the French position be publicized. The President said he was not absolutely certain what we would do until we see what happens in Geneva. He mentioned opposition of the US to intervene in Laos.

De Gaulle said he agreed entirely with the President regarding not publicizing the French position. With regard to the Geneva Conference, General de Gaulle thought it was best to return to the 1954 accords. In Laos itself the need is for a new government and Souvanna Phouma seems the most qualified and least bad person. The French would not hide their support for him.

The President agreed that the military situation was so bad that Souvanna Phouma was really the only hope but wondered if the situation had not gone even too far for him to be acceptable. The President said that our relations with Souvanna Phouma were bad while those of the French were good. Furthermore, France has some responsibility under the 1954 agreements. He hoped France would use her influence. France can play a role which we cannot.

De Gaulle asked if Souvanna Phouma planned to go to Washington. The President said we had wanted him to come there from Moscow but the Cuban matter had intervened and he had decided not to come, partly as the result of misunderstanding and partly because of his decision against it.

---

[2] For text, see vol. XXIV, pp. 214–220.

General de Gaulle then said that the disappearance of Trujillo had given President Kennedy the occasion for a rundown on Latin America.[3] He said France considered the US should have a dominant role in the hemisphere and anything we can do for Latin America is to the good. He had thought that Latin America should be left alone with the US. However, the President had stressed that there should be a constructive European role in this area so the French will do what they can in the cultural, economic and even political field so that the Latin Americans can see they had another valid interlocutor, and he thought this was important because of the evolution of Latin America in the political field, the poverty of the area, Soviet propaganda and the example of Cuba. He thought assisting Latin Americans in selling their raw materials was particularly important.

De Gaulle said President Kennedy had referred to the July OAS meeting in Montevideo and to invitations to the United Kingdom and the Community of the Six. He said France would send an observer to Montevideo and he would also ask that Latin America be put on the agenda of the meeting of the Six Heads of Government in order to study how Europe can help in this area.

De Gaulle said that he and the President had discussed principally the Congo and Angola as African problems. He said President Kennedy had explained that US policy in the Congo was still acting via the United Nations. France did not believe the United Nations was either impartial or effective in the Congo and expected little good to come from its activity. He saw some elements of hope in the Congo situation and believed some form of government was developing. France would encourage Kasavubu through her friends in Africa. He felt the UN was too divided to be of much help but concluded he had no opposition to US policy in the Congo. He noted overt Soviet intervention would, of course, change the situation.

De Gaulle then said both he and President Kennedy felt the Angola situation was serious. Portugal was behind the times in Black Africa. Portugal has a certain concept of her relations in this area but he agreed that bit by bit the Portuguese should take a constructive line. However, Salazar should not be pushed. Pushing him too hard might cause a revolution in Portugal and it would be dangerous to have a Communist state in the Iberian peninsula. He thought the UN attitude towards Portugal was wrong.

De Gaulle then said that in response to the President's request France would encourage the Portuguese to make a constructive ap-

---

[3] A memorandum of the discussion on Latin America, US/MC/3, is in Department of State, Conference Files: Lot 66 D 110, CF 1891.

proach. He said France wanted a solution to the Angola problem and agreed that repressive measures would fail.

The President concluded by saying the longer the present situation went on, the worse it would be. He agreed military means would not succeed. Some political advances must be made. He thought because of the constructive French influence in Africa, France could be helpful with the Portuguese.

General de Gaulle then said he hoped he had clarified the French position in defense matters, especially NATO.[4] He said the President had certainly clarified the US position. De Gaulle reviewed what he had said to the President. Eleven years ago NATO had been created in a certain situation. The US had a nuclear monopoly. The European states were in decline. For example in France the economic situation was poor and politically the country was confused. France had no defense but the US and was furthermore engaged in the decolonization struggle. The important nations of Europe—Germany, Italy and France—were all in a defeatist mood psychologically. US nuclear weapons covered Europe, so integration under US command was natural.

De Gaulle said that now the situation had changed. The US had kept nuclear weapons but the Soviets had developed them too. It did not matter who had more, since each can kill the other and either could kill Europe.

Europe has made progress, he went on. This should not be exaggerated but there had been some achievements and political stability exists. The European countries are stronger economically and are terminating the colonial problem. They should, therefore, have a role in Europe itself. Furthermore, France will have a modest nuclear force. Both Germany and Italy are firmer now than before. Of all the European countries, France especially has the air of a nation. France wants to express her personality in defense matters.

Therefore, De Gaulle went on, integration can no longer satisfy France. France, of course, cannot defend herself alone and there is no question that the Atlantic Alliance is essential. However, in defense organization France wishes a national defense posture. France will not tear down or demolish NATO now in an international crisis. But NATO cannot go on as it is indefinitely and France wants to reaffirm this.

De Gaulle then passed on to the question of use of nuclear weapons. He said he had insisted that President Kennedy define the US position because Europe needs to know when and how the US will use nuclear weapons and under what circumstances. He quoted President Kennedy as saying, and invited him to interrupt if he was mistaken, that US secu-

---

[4] See Document 107.

rity was tied to Europe and that US security would be wrecked by a Soviet takeover in Europe. [2 *lines of source text not declassified*]

[4 *paragraphs (1/2 page of source text) not declassified*]

De Gaulle then said he and the President had discussed how to arrange the use of nuclear weapons by the three countries in the West which would have them. These weapons are of a world-wide scope and might be used in the off-shore islands, in the Far East or even Cuba. It was not the affair of NATO to decide the use of nuclear weapons but a tripartite affair to settle how under different circumstances the three would deploy their weapons. One day there should be a tripartite plan in this sense. A small standing group should be created to apply this plan and develop it. De Gaulle said he had expressed this idea and the President did not seem to oppose it.

The President said he had mentioned to General De Gaulle it was important to consult on all matters in which the three countries were involved all around the world. He said that in the case of Laos he had not realized there were such divergencies of view until this exchange of correspondence with General De Gaulle. This showed a need for better consultation. The President added that it was also a matter of concern that the non-nuclear members of NATO should not feel that they have no voice in their security. He mentioned Turkey and Germany as examples. He thought that there was need for better consultation, not only with regard to the use of nuclear weapons. The President then said he believed that the US should consult Great Britain and France on the use of nuclear weapons. He said he hereby extended to France the guarantees given to the United Kingdom by his predecessor that he would consult France regarding the use anywhere in the world of nuclear weapons, unless an attack were so imminent that our survival was threatened.

The President wondered whether our arming NATO with submarines did not help to meet the French view regarding national defense. He agreed that the present tripartite consultative arrangements were not satisfactory and said he would nominate someone to meet with the British and French to maximize the arrangements for agreement and in the case of disagreement, at least define quickly and well in advance what disagreements existed. He added that French and British opinion would also be given much weight when he consulted them regarding the use of nuclear weapons anywhere in the world.

The President added that if Khrushchev should present us with a Berlin crisis following the German elections, perhaps the Heads of Government should meet.

De Gaulle said he was very favorable to the statements the President had made with regard to consultation. He thought close contact to be highly desirable. He added that if subjects of direct interest to countries such as Germany or Turkey were discussed, they should be consulted. However, only the Three have world-wide responsibilities. Those of the United States are enormous but France and Great Britain have some as well and therefore there should be tripartite consultations on a world-wide basis, while the other countries might be consulted at the local echelon.

De Gaulle said he was, of course, favorable to the President's position on consultation with regard to the use of nuclear weapons. He said perhaps the President had not quite decided with regard to the tripartite military group suggested by the French to study this nuclear weapons program along the same lines the President had suggested for tripartite consultation.

De Gaulle said that with regard to NATO he had no objection to furnishing Polaris to NATO but this, of course, did not change things fundamentally for Europe since these are US nuclear weapons which would of course remain under US control. He thought this quite normal.

The President said there had been little time this morning for detailed discussions on consultations and proposed a further meeting at 3:45 p.m. on June 2[5] in order to take some concrete decisions to obtain the advantages of a greater tripartite intimacy without the disadvantages of upsetting other countries.

De Gaulle concluded the meeting by saying he had been genuinely pleased to see the President who had a great future which he, De Gaulle, obviously did not have since he would be passing on the reins to younger men. He thought perhaps the President and he himself would be taking certain dramatic actions together although he of course did not exactly know what the future would hold. He thought the atmosphere of the talks had been excellent. The Franco-American alliance is fundamental to the French people on the basic issues and all the rest is mere mechanism and machinery. Never have the common destinies of the two countries been closer.

The President thanked General De Gaulle and said that not even the magnificence of Versailles was his most vivid impression of France, but rather French vitality. Never has he seen more vigorous people. Although we may not agree on all matters, he thought these talks were most helpful.

He closed in expressing his greatest confidence in General De Gaulle.

---

[5] See Document 11.

231. Memorandum of Conversation

Washington, June 6, 1961, 4:30 p.m.

MEMORANDUM OF CONVERSATION WITH THE PRESIDENT AND THE CONGRESSIONAL LEADERSHIP

PRESENT

> The Vice President, Senators Mansfield, Humphrey, Russell, Fulbright, Dirksen, Saltonstall, Hickenlooper, Wiley
>
> The Speaker, Congressmen McCormack, Albert, Vinson, Morgan, Arends, Chiperfield, Hoeven, Byrnes (Wisconsin)

I. General de Gaulle

The President opened the meeting by expressing appreciation to the Leadership, and explained that his object was to bring them up to date on the events of his trip to Europe. The President first discussed his meeting with de Gaulle. Although there was much discussion in the papers about trouble with the French, he found the differences of secondary importance compared to the agreement and to the common interest which he found between the United States and France, especially on policy toward Europe.

Disagreements had turned on two subjects—NATO and de Gaulle's desire for a nuclear deterrent of his own. His grievances go back to World War II when he had difficulties with Churchill and Roosevelt, and the meeting was worth it in moderating this part of his attitude. Another element in his attitude was his resentment of the fact that nuclear help had been given by the United States to the United Kingdom and not to France. To these unexpressed grievances should be added his stated view that the whole position in Europe has changed since NATO was founded. Then there was a nuclear monopoly; now there is a nuclear balance. The United States could say that it was prepared to act by trading New York for Paris, but would we really do so? In addition, General de Gaulle was opposed to integration, which he thought ruined the morale of the armed forces and was one reason for the recent trouble with his generals in North Africa.

Nevertheless, the General agreed to make no attack on NATO, now, although he will want to act later after the present Berlin crisis ends and after he gets his army back from Algeria. But he is alone in this posture toward NATO and his position does not bother the President

---

Source: Kennedy Library, National Security Files, Meetings with the President. Secret. No drafting information appears on the source text. Printed in part in *Declassified Documents, 1986,* 2256.

much. Moreover, de Gaulle himself had said that what would settle the position in Europe was not what he, de Gaulle, said, but what happens in West Berlin.

The President reported general agreement with de Gaulle on Africa and Latin America. To a question from Senator Fulbright on Laos, he said that de Gaulle's position was good with respect to the present conference in Geneva and that he was prepared to go back into Laos, but not to take military action there. To a further question, the President said that de Gaulle appeared to expect an Algerian agreement by the autumn, although other Frenchmen were not so optimistic. The General seemed to have no interest in a transfer of Polaris weapons to NATO since they would not reinforce French forces. He was for the alliance but against integration. He was agreeable and friendly in every way, although he treats the press as only Sam Rayburn does in Washington, The President read from his talking paper most of items 1–11 on pages 3 and 4 (attached)[1] and reported that he had given the French the same assurances as he had the British with respect to consultation on the use of atomic weapons, if time permitted.

The President reported that the French seemed to him a long way from having a nuclear force of their own.

In response to a question from Senator Fulbright, the President indicated that in his judgment General de Gaulle does not really want the British in the Common Market. He appears to believe that they will not make the necessary political commitment, and in any case de Gaulle prefers the present situation in which he is the dominant figure. To a question about de Gaulle's successor, the President said Debre seemed to him a fine fellow without much political stature who does at present appear to be de Gaulle's favorite.

The President said there had been no discussion of the test ban—de Gaulle had not raised it and the President had followed the same course because the prospects for the test ban seemed so dim at present. De Gaulle seemed to want help from us on missile guidance systems, but there had been no discussion on the point.

[Here follows discussion of the President's meeting with Khrushchev in Vienna; see volume V, Document 66.]

---

[1] Not found.

232.   Telegram From the Department of State to the Embassy in France

Washington, July 2, 1961, 4:28 p.m.

16. Eyes only Ambassador. [Here follow instructions for classifying and delivering this and a second letter transmitted in telegram 17, Document 233.]

"June 30, 1961

Dear General de Gaulle:

It is almost exactly a month since we met in Paris. Much has happened in that time, and while many members of our two Governments have been in touch with each other on special problems, it seems to me time to write you again. I have the better occasion to do so because I am now able to send the enclosed formal statement confirming the understanding and assurance which we agreed upon with respect to the use of nuclear weapons. This assurance is parallel to the one which has been in force between this Government and Great Britain.

Obviously, the biggest issue before us now is Berlin. Fortunately, as we discovered in our first conversation, you and I see this problem in essentially identical terms. What has happened in June simply shows that we were right to take it seriously. We, for our part, are closely engaged on serious planning of all sorts to meet a crisis which seems to us to be more serious than any before it. Ours is a large and complex Government, and clear decisions on concrete steps do not come as quickly as I would like. But the direction in which we shall move is just like yours in the movement of a division from Algeria to France. It is action and not appearances that will be effective in our judgment. We shall also move to insure agreement and understanding in this country as a whole, and while there are occasional voices, even in my own party and in the Senate which sound an uncertain trumpet, I can assure you that they do not represent the Government or the people of the United States on this issue.

In this atmosphere of serious preparation for a test in Berlin, the notion of effective negotiation towards disarmament seems somewhat unreal. Mr. McCloy has been meeting with the Russians because it seems to us important not to be hasty in breaking off discussions on which there was agreement some months ago. But we are simply repeating over and over again that there can be no discussion of substance except after a new agreement on an appropriate forum. The time may come, I believe,

---

Source: Department of State, Central Files, 700.5611/7–261. Secret; Verbatim Text. Drafted by Beigel and cleared by Kohler and Tyler.

when it will be possible and useful to have such serious discussion in a very small circle, but I must say that time does not seem to be now.

I am personally disappointed that we have not made more progress in this last month toward the establishment of stronger processes of consultation in the intervals between our personal meeting. I do not think either of our foreign secretaries has been idle, but we must not allow the pressures of the day to prevent preparations for continued close consultation, even though some of these pressures are those of the consultation which does in fact go on regularly at many levels. I have talked with Dean Rusk again about this, and he tells me that he is planning to talk about ways and means today through Ambassador Alphand and Ambassador Caccia, as agents of their two foreign secretaries.[1]

Meanwhile, one of the lessons which I draw from our meeting in May is that there is a sense in which no other consultation can substitute for direct encounters between chiefs of Government.

It seems to me that if the crisis in Berlin becomes more serious, and perhaps on even more general grounds, it may be useful if you and Prime Minister Macmillan and I can have a meeting at some convenient time in the autumn. I should be glad to know whether this seems a reasonable idea to you.

May I conclude by sending my warmest personal regards, in which Mrs. Kennedy joins, to you and to Madame de Gaulle.[2]

Sincerely,

John F. Kennedy"

Rusk

---

[1] Rusk met with Caccia and Alphand at 3:05 p.m. to discuss consultations. According to a memorandum of conversation they agreed to discuss in Washington Laos, the Congo, Africa including Algeria, disarmament, and Southeast Asia. Rusk asked the Ambassadors to seek the opinions of their Foreign Ministers with respect to a pre-September meeting. (Ibid., 396.1/6–3061)

[2] On July 6 de Gaulle responded saying that he too believed Berlin was the essential problem and agreeing on the desirability of a meeting with Macmillan. (Ibid., Presidential Correspondence: Lot 66 D 204; printed in part in Charles de Gaulle, Memoires d'Espoir, Le Renouveau, 1958–1962, p. 272)

233. Telegram From the Department of State to the Embassy in France

Washington, July 2, 1961, 4:29 p.m.

17. Eyes only Ambassador. Re: Deptel 16.[1] Reftel forwarded text of Presidential letter of June 30 to de Gaulle and indicated second Presidential letter of same date to follow. Text of second letter is quoted below. Delivery instructions contained in reftel.

"June 30, 1961

Dear General de Gaulle:

I wish to refer to our recent conversation on the use of nuclear weapons.[2] With regard to the use by the United States of any nuclear weapons, I give you the following assurance, which is, of course, not intended to be used publicly. In the event of an emergency such as increased tension or the threat of war, the United States will take every possible step to consult with France and other allies unless an attack were so imminent that our survival was threatened. The channel of direct telephone communication between us is intended for this purpose, if necessary.

This assurance is, of course, in addition to the written understanding contained in the exchange of letters between Ambassador Dillon and Minister of Foreign Affairs Bidault of April 8, 1954,[3] concerning the use by the United States of bases in France. That understanding provides that "the use of the bases and installations placed at the disposition of the United States Government in Metropolitan France and French North Africa will, in time of emergency, be a matter for joint decision by the United States and France in the light of the circumstances prevailing at the time." I confirm the continuing validity of this written understanding.

I am happy to give you the foregoing assurances in the interest of the common defense and in the spirit of the close relationship which exists between our two countries.

Sincerely,

John F. Kennedy"

Rusk

Source: Department of State, Central Files, 700.5611/7–261. Secret; Verbatim Text.

[1] Document 232.

[2] See Document 230.

[3] Not found.

234. Telegram From Secretary of State Rusk to the Department of State

Paris, August 7, 1961, midnight.

Secto 36. Eyes only for the President. At dinner this evening with Lord Home and Couve de Murville alone we had good discussion of Tripartite consultative machinery. I expressed your keen interest in improving such consultation, along the lines of your discussion with General de Gaulle, but also emphasized the need for discretion in order not to stimulate bad feelings from other countries both within and outside NATO. Couve expressed a complete understanding of problem of discretion and stated that both the Italians and Germans had already registered with him their sharp reaction to the rumors they had already picked up on the subject. I asked Couve frankly whether the General's interest in tripartite consultation was primarily to obtain greater harmony of policy or whether his purposes depended upon making the existence of such consultations generally known. He smiled but did not reply directly but simply reaffirmed their understanding of need for discretion.

I then proposed that we arrange more effective consultation within framework of existing machinery which could provide adequate cover. I suggested that British and French Ambassadors in Washington meet regularly with Secretary or appropriate deputy and that there be someone designated from one of three governments to serve as a secretary. I then proposed that, for military discussions, French and UK insure that they have on NATO Standing Group officers who would have their complete confidence who could be drawn aside by the tripartite political group for discussion of strategic problems beyond NATO.

Couve accepted with alacrity but I am not at all sure that this will fully satisfy General de Gaulle. Lord Home went along graciously in order to accommodate US and France but I have no doubt that he would not consider this arrangement an adequate substitute for our bilateral relationship. In view of fact that all three governments will be in continuous contact over next several months because of Berlin and other problems, I believe that this is as far as we should now go about consultative machinery. At Foreign Minister level I am convinced this is entirely adequate but there may be special problems upstairs which we shall have to deal with if they are raised. In any event, I believe we have made a reasonable response to your conversation with General de Gaulle.[1]

Rusk

Source: Department of State, Conference Files: Lot 65 D 366, CF 1943. Secret. Drafted by Rusk who was in Paris August 4–9.

[1] On August 23 Alphand, who was in Paris for consultations, discussed the French position on tripartitism with de Gaulle. An account of this meeting is in Hervé Alphand, *L'etonnement d'etre*, Paris, 1977, p. 366.

tainment such goal is bound to revive independence of ideas as to how matters should be run and to bring forth statesman such as de Gaulle with views different from ours. These differences we must begin to live with even though France and continental Europe are not yet sufficiently strong or unified actually to impose them.

2. Foremost among many things that concern de Gaulle in Europe today is future of West Germany. More than any European statesman he has worked to bring Western Germany into intimate association with all facets of Western European life. At same time I am inclined to believe that he thinks first object of Soviet strategy in Western Europe today is disarmament of West Germany. If Soviets succeed in this they may well feel confident of outcome of struggle between free world and Soviet system. Further in evaluating their prospects they must be impressed with basic distrust of Germans that exists in so many places in Europe. De Gaulle therefore has consistently sought to integrate Western Germany into Western European Community as a strong contributing member. When one realizes this one understands his attitude on Berlin situation. Any suggestion of examining "European security" as part of an overall examination leading to solution of Berlin problem is a suggestion directly pointed towards partial or complete disarmament of West Germany. "European security" is a euphemism used by Soviets to cover neutralization of Western Germany. At this juncture in European affairs French feel that Soviets have achieved many of their chief objectives in Berlin. Through the erection of the wall they have stopped the flow of East Germans into West Berlin and through varying approaches to salami-slicing they will achieve some form of de facto recognition of East Germany. Soviets had hoped to get US sit down and discuss "European security" in bartering over West Berlin rights that were in fact already ours. Thus far they have not achieved this objective. Now they have for moment moved pressure center to Finland with view to forcing Finland into some kind of accommodation to Soviet designs: very likely recognition East Germany and possibly further neutralization that would place Finland more securely under thumb of Soviet Union. They may wish also to block improvement of German relations with Scandinavia and push toward neutralization of area after which they would again try to examine "European security" with a view to extending neutralization pattern to Germany.

In any event it clear that discussion of prospects for German acceptance of disengagement or thinning out of inspection zones would be strongly opposed by de Gaulle who continues to believe that strong West Germany participation in strong European community is basic to our posture in dealing with Soviets and even to any equilibrium on which secure détente might rest.

While we may not agree with this view we cannot reject it out of hand without jeopardizing Western Alliance and our own survival. Tactical differences which arise from this extreme reluctance of de Gaulle to get involved in negotiating this concept with Soviets may be regrettable but I cannot see anything unhealthy in his basic view on Germany. In last analysis it may be something we could live with more easily than a certain softness in UK viewpoint (understandable in view British special vulnerabilities) even though differences with UK are masked by more relaxed and empirical "Anglo-Saxon" approach to daily business which we instinctively find more congenial.

3.   What is frustrating and humiliating for de Gaulle is that as he himself quite frankly said on September fifth[3] France still lacks means to translate these concepts into reality and to make voice felt. Despite strides in economic field her modernization is just getting underway and she is still wasting manpower and money in Algeria. She has not yet succeeded in achieving de Gaulle's goal of balancing out her commitments at new level as continental rather than colonial power even though transition is obviously underway. And on top of this comes Soviet created crisis in Europe for which France's military and other resources are not properly mobilized and oriented. This frustration inevitably translates itself into glacial manifestations of displeasure which find their way into Franco-American relations. We on our side tend to cultivate image of France still exploiting her indispensable geographic position and the considerable remains of her influence in Africa and Asia in ways which obstruct and annoy us and which we find negative and at times absurd. But in reality there are obvious signs that these attitudes are changing and I think de Gaulle is just as conscious as we of global nature of Soviet threat. Moreover I believe that if France gets her feet on new ground she can and will confront this threat and make positive and solid contribution to Western cause.

4.   Meantime I think de Gaulle while understanding our basic problem in US with respect to public support during present danger, may feel that US is rushing too fast at Berlin crisis and concentrating its strength a bit too rapidly in area where Soviets may suddenly decide slacken pressure for time being and try diversionary tactics as in pressure on Finland and Scandinavia or possible acceleration efforts in Africa or Asia. This may partially explain current difficulties over troop ceilings which I hope to clarify soon, as well as difficulties over less important matters.

---

[3] For a transcript of de Gaulle's press conference on September 5, see *Major Addresses, Statements and Press Conferences of General Charles de Gaulle, May 19, 1958–January 31, 1964*, pp. 140–150.

5. In long run I think we have everything to gain from paying as much attention as we can to French counsels in areas where they have long experience and in acting on basic assumption that France will ultimately have even greater contribution to make and that de Gaulle's long view of things may have something to be said for it as in past, annoying though his short-term sensitivities may be. For this reason I hope two Chiefs of State will be able again to meet face to face and get tuned in again on same wave lengths as they did in May.

Gavin

237. Telegram From the Department of State to the Embassy in France

Washington, November 29, 1961, 8:42 p.m.

3090. Paris pass Stoessel and USRO for Ambassador Finletter. Personal for Ambassador Gavin from the Secretary. I appreciate your thoughtful consideration of problem discussed in your 2542.[1] Upon reflection here I believe that to furnish enriched uranium to France for military applications would lead to other French requests relating to production of nuclear weapons and would be in contradiction to US policies which we have already clearly decided and in part announced. We have made clear to all governments that we will engage in no activity and undertake no action which would be likely to assist any new nation to acquire or develop an independent nuclear weapon capability. Significance of present legislation in this respect is that it is designed to limit such cooperation to the one other country allied with us that had already achieved such capability.

Source: Department of State, Central Files, 751.5/11–1461. Secret; Limit Distribution. Drafted by Beigel and Williams (S/AE) on November 22; cleared by Tyler, Owen, the President (through Bromley Smith), and the Department of Defense; and approved by Rusk.

[1] Telegram 2542, November 14, reported that Gavin, after the most careful consideration, believed that the United States should offer to provide France with enriched uranium for military purposes. (Ibid.) The previous day he had written along similar lines to the President. (Kennedy Library, National Security Files, France) On November 15 and 20 respectively, Norstad and Finletter, for different reasons, opposed Gavin's idea. (ALO 1074; ibid., President's Office Files, France, and Polto 677; Department of State, Central Files, 751.5/11–2061)

I also believe it is already clear to French that we will undertake no action likely to result in any direct or significant aid to France in developing or securing independent nuclear warhead or effective nuclear weapon delivery capability. As you have just reiterated to French Defense Minister, we otherwise stand ready to continue our mutual cooperation with France in scientific matters and in peaceful applications of atomic energy as well as in such mutual defense matters as recently signed 144(b) Atomic Cooperation Agreement with France.[2] I believe French recognize that cooperation in mutual defense matters can proceed only in conjunction with full cooperation by France as NATO partner, and I recognize you will continue pursue this line with Messmer. We shall also press this point with him during his forthcoming visit here.

I believe you are already familiar from our earlier exchange of telegrams[3] in this general field that we are profoundly convinced that not only would assistance along lines your 2542 confirm and encourage presently independent course followed by France but would lead to increased pressures in Germany and elsewhere for national nuclear programs. It would be divisive force within NATO. We consider best way to handle problem within NATO is through our multilateral MRBM offer, which I plan to renew at NATO Ministerial Meeting in December,[4] and through possible other means to give Alliance a larger NATO nuclear role, if our allies so desire.

We all realize that our position on this subject may hamper development of closer relations with France and we are striving in other ways to overcome this handicap. You of course realize difficulties raised for all of us by French position on variety of important military questions affecting NATO security, and we fully endorse and support your efforts to bring greater measure of French cooperation in these questions.

In view of President's great interest this general subject he has also reviewed this message and has approved it.

Rusk

---

[2] For text of this agreement, signed at Paris July 27, see 12 UST 1423.
[3] See Document 227.
[4] See Documents 116 ff.

238. Letter From the Assistant Secretary of State for European Affairs (Kohler) to the Ambassador to France (Gavin)

Washington, February 2, 1962.

[Source: Kennedy Library, National Security Files, France. Secret; Personal. 2 pages of source text not declassified.]

---

239. Telegram From the Embassy in France to the Department of State

Paris, February 21, 1962, 8 p.m.

3973. During tour d'horizon with de Gaulle yesterday, I stated I was particularly interested in political union of Six and military significance of that union, specifically the relationship it would have to NATO.

De Gaulle said that purpose of political union of Six was to form a concert of nations, to establish a common view on political matters of concern to all. One purpose also is to encourage cultural and economic exchanges. He said that there is no doubt that it has defense implications but these have not been seriously considered so far. In time they will be but French thinking has not gone very far on military matters. They have not examined relationship of Six to NATO, but in any case, he said, the political union would strengthen the Atlantic Community. He obviously did not want to go any further in discussing the problem with me.

The foregoing is in essence what he said on Six although we talked about it for quite some time. I am satisfied that de Gaulle's thinking as expressed in his memorandum of 25 Sept 1958 and, in part, reaffirmed in his last letter to the President,[1] remains unchanged. He considers NATO inadequate to deal with prevailing conditions affecting the vital

---

Source: Department of State, Central Files, 375/2–2162. Secret; Limit Distribution. In addition to this telegram, Gavin reported on his discussion of NATO in telegram 3972 (Document 127), and of Algeria in telegram 3857, February 20. (Department of State, Central Files, 611.51/2–2062)

[1] Dated January 11, it primarily discussed the question of negotiations with the Soviet Union on Berlin, but also devoted 2 paragraphs to the differences between France and the United States on atomic weapons. (Ibid., Presidential Correspondence: Lot 66 D 204)

interests of US, UK and France and, when all is said and done, he considers NATO to be a US headquarters in Europe. Now, whether or not we respond to his desires for a triumvirate organization he will proceed to organize Europe on his own, insofar as he can do so.

In Sept 1958 memorandum he envisioned the organization of theaters of operation with, I believe, responsibility for these areas being given to specific great powers. Europe, he believes, should be the responsibility of France. It is for this reason therefore that he has taken initiative, repeatedly, in European affairs. I am convinced that his thinking on subject of Six has gone far beyond what he was willing to discuss with me yesterday and, further, that he does foresee clearly organization of Six as ultimately a strong military bloc.

I base this upon discussions with his Ministers and with others here in France. Looking back on his handling of Algerian situation, for example, one is impressed by his cleverness in moving inexorably towards his objective, while at the same time giving out only as much information as was necessary, from time to time, to meet a particular tactical need or to satisfy insistent demands that would not be denied. It seems obvious to me that he will now devote most of his time to strengthening France in a unit of Six and strengthening the Six politically, economically and militarily. If these views are valid then it will avail us little to continue to try to persuade him and prevail upon him to be more cooperative in NATO affairs. Realistically, we should realize that as long as he is President of France we are going to have to be prepared to deal with Six in which France is playing a powerful role on economic and political matters and anticipate the military relationship which ultimately may come into being. It is very likely that other members of Six will oppose the French initiative and they will continue to support fully their commitments to NATO. I doubt that this will deter de Gaulle and further, I doubt also that he will attack NATO or take any overt actions against NATO. In fact, for tactical reasons, he will continue to give lip support to NATO while he moves toward his own objective, a strong European power bloc in which France will play leading role. He believes that this will best serve the interests of France in opposing Soviet power and, finally, he rationalizes this view to point where he believes it best serves the interests of NATO and Atlantic Community. To his mind, there is no dichotomy in this thinking. With an awareness of this, as one course of action de Gaulle is likely to follow, we should conduct our relations within NATO and with NATO powers, other than France, in such a manner as to maintain close ties with NATO and its individual members. In this respect, Germany is in a particularly sensitive position from the viewpoint of her relations with the USSR and her nuclear aspirations.

Our relations with Germany should be such in my view that whenever she is confronted with a choice between aligning herself with France or the US, she should choose the US. This would obviously influence our discussions with Soviets on broad problems of European security as well as role Germany would play in a multi-national NATO nuclear force. (The foregoing goes well beyond the current day to day situations with which we normally deal here in Paris, but I believe it deserves our careful thought. To continue to deal with de Gaulle in anticipation that he will be responsive to our current diplomacy, seems to be unrealistic to me. Our own interests will best be served, as well as those of our Allies, when we understand where de Gaulle is going and then, while not ignoring him, nevertheless take such actions as we consider adequate to serve our interests and those of our Allies without necessarily being too concerned with or responsive to intransigence of de Gaulle or to roadblocks he may place in our way. When Algeria is settled, he is going to be far more difficult to deal with and this, if we understand it, should not in any way disturb us. Our own objectives can be sought and our own interests served effectively despite difficulties he may interpose.)

Gavin

---

240. Memorandum of Conversation

Washington, February 28, 1962, 9:45 a.m.

SUBJECT

US-France Divergencies: Berlin, The Nuclear Question and NATO

PARTICIPANTS

U.S.	France
The President	Edgar Faure, former Premier of
William R. Tyler, Act. Asst. Sec.,	France
EUR	Hervé Alphand, French
	Ambassador

Mr. Faure expressed his warm sentiments of admiration for the President's speeches during his campaign in 1960, and for the spirit and the goals of the New Frontier. He said this term was difficult to render in the French language, as in French a frontier is something which marks a boundary or limit, whereas the New Frontier opens up new horizons.

Source: Department of State, Central Files, 611.51/2–2862. Secret. Drafted and initialed by Tyler and approved by the White House on March 7. The meeting was held at the White House.

The President acknowledged Mr. Faure's remarks and said he was glad to have this chance of talking with him. He noted that the United States is very much interested in developments pertaining to France, and sets great store by Franco-American relations. Unfortunately, he added, there seems to be a general sentiment that these relations had become less close of late.

Mr. Faure said that there had been no substantive change in the situation to justify this, but several articles in the press had magnified difference of views between France and the United States out of all proportion.

The President said that we fully endorse the French Government's policy with regard to Algeria, and that what differences of opinion there had been with regard to the Congo were not really important. There remained the areas of divergencies of views concerning Europe. If these were to continue, it would be unfortunate. Among the major problems of concern to us was that of the possibility of the Germans acquiring nuclear weapons for themselves. The President said that this was most undesirable and would doubtless not be desired by other European countries. The Soviets would probably be inclined to view such a development as a provocation. Then, the President continued, there was the question of Berlin. The talks in Moscow had not so far shown any disposition on the part of the Soviet Union to meet us on a basis which would make fruitful negotiations possible. The Berlin crisis might well become critical this spring or summer, and there was the question of what steps we might have to take.

Mr. Faure replied that with regard to Berlin, the vast majority of French political and public opinion is in favor of the United States approach, and not of that of de Gaulle. There was a question in his mind whether de Gaulle's tactics reflected his real belief or whether they constituted a tactical position designed to remind the military that France was faced by other and even graver problems than that of Algeria. He also thought that de Gaulle liked to cast himself in the role of a mediator, and that he had been disappointed at not being able to play this role. However, he was sure de Gaulle had not given up this idea, and his tactics reminded him of Richelieu's remark that some people liked to move toward their goal in the position of a man rowing a boat, i.e., with their back turned toward the direction in which they were going. He also said that de Gaulle was like the Knight on a chessboard: He was inclined to take a couple of steps in one direction before moving finally in the direction in which he wished to go.

Mr. Faure said he did not think that the nuclear question was insoluble. He was convinced that France would not provide, or encourage Germany to obtain, nuclear weapons. He said the French people would not favor this, if only because of the effect it would have on the Russians.

Mr. Faure pointed out that the protocols to the Paris Agreement of 1954[1] absolutely prohibit Germany from manufacturing or acquiring nuclear weapons, as well as biological and chemical weapons. He thought that the French nuclear program would certainly continue in its present form until after an Algerian settlement, but he thought that there might be a subsequent evolution in French willingness to work with the United States through some cooperative arrangements which would preserve French national nuclear capabilities.

Ambassador Alphand said he thought de Gaulle was absolutely sincere, both with regard to the tactics which he had followed on the Berlin question, and with regard to the French nuclear program. He said he did not agree with Mr. Faure's interpretation of de Gaulle's thinking on these two subjects.

The President referred to the danger of Germany ultimately acquiring control over nuclear bombs through a joint Franco-German program.

Mr. Faure emphasized that he did not believe that such a program was contemplated nor that it could ever be carried out, because of the limitations already imposed on Germany by international agreements, to which Germany had subscribed.

The President said he was anxious to re-establish personal contact with de Gaulle at an appropriate time, and he speculated that this might be sometime after the settlement of the Algerian problem.

Mr. Faure thought this was most desirable. He was convinced that the President's personality and authority would have a profound influence on de Gaulle in the direction of finding a solution to outstanding differences between our two countries.

The President observed that before arranging a meeting, there would first have to be some preparation, and an indication that our views were moving closer toward each other; otherwise there would be a damaging let-down if he and de Gaulle were to meet only to disagree. Mr. Faure said he shared the President's opinion.

Turning to the question of an East-West conference, Mr. Faure said he was very much in favor of maintaining contacts and exchanges of views with the Russians. He thought that if a Heads of Government conference were held, the Russians would be more likely to make some concessions before or after, than during, the conference. He recalled that the Summit conference in 1955 had been preceded by the unexpected Soviet agreement to an Austrian State Treaty, and had been followed by some liberalization measures in Poland and Hungary. He observed that the

---

[1] For text of this protocol, signed at Paris, October 22, 1954, see *Foreign Relations, 1952–1954*, vol. V, Part 2, pp. 1435–1457.

Soviet psychology is such that they do not like to yield or make concessions during actual negotiations, but are rather inclined to do so before or after them.

Summing up, the President said that the three major issues over which the United States and France had at the present time far-reaching divergencies of views were: Berlin, the nuclear question, and NATO. These were important areas of disagreement, but he hoped it would be possible to make a move toward reconciling our views on these subjects, after a settlement of the Algerian problem.

Mr. Faure thanked the President very much for the conversation and said that, if the President had no objection, he would like to report the President's views re the subjects they had discussed informally to de Gaulle, on his return to Paris. He thought this would be of great interest to de Gaulle, and that it would be helpful to the cause of Franco-US understanding.

---

241. Telegram from the Embassy in France to the Department of State

Paris, March 9, 1962, 7 p.m.

4219. Embassy telegram 4041.[1] Called on PriMin Debre this morning to discuss among other things his press conference of last week in which he was quite critical of US nuclear policy vis-à-vis France.

I began by telling him I had intended to see him before I returned to Wash but knowing how busy he was I hesitated to ask for appointment. I told him that although I realized that differences of views existed between our govts on some problems, I was anxious to work closely with his govt with a view to keeping to a minimum such differences as may exist. For this reason, I was a bit disturbed to read of press backgrounder he had in which he had been critical of US nuclear policy. I added that when I was in US and talked to President, President had read article in

---

Source: Department of State, Central Files, 611.51/3–962. Secret; Limit Distribution.

[1] Telegram 4041, February 27, reported that Debré had invited four U.S. newsmen to Matignon on February 26 for an interview during which he stated that Franco-American relations had badly deteriorated. He characterized many American actions as "stupid," and singled out U.S. attempts to prevent France from becoming a nuclear power. (Kennedy Library, National Security Files, France)

New York Times by Doty and asked me about it.[2] I informed Debre I told President I would discuss it with him upon my return here.

Debre replied by saying that press always dramatizes and exaggerates news. He said primary purpose of getting four members of US press together was to talk about Algerian situation. After talking to them about Algeria, Debre was asked by correspondent if he thought Atlantic Community would be stronger and more effective after Algeria was settled. He replied by saying as everyone knows, there are differences of view about what is best for Atlantic Community. From point of view of France one fundamental fact is that the great strength of Atlantic Community is in atomic power. The US supports NATO with its atomic power. It shares nuclear info with UK. He then went on to say fundamental nature of nuclear power is real to France also, and that just as US thinks it should have nuclear power to defend itself, France believes it should have nuclear power to defend itself and Europe. Debre said it was unfortunate that US has not been of more help to France, but France is going ahead with her own nuclear program. He added that France and Germany and all of free Europe had to have capability of defending itself with nuclear weapons.

I told Debre we were aware of importance of nuclear weapons in defense of Europe and it was for this reason we are trying to provide for this through NATO. He did not reply directly to my comment and made reference again to Franco-German situation. I asked him then if he foresaw likelihood of French-German nuclear weapons program. He said that Germans could not make weapons because they were forbidden to make them by treaty, and further that nuclear weapons in German hands would be a catastrophe for Soviets and would cause very dangerous conditions to arise. He avoided answering my question and I did not press him further. Our conversation lasted over one-half hour and at no time did PriMin admit to the strong criticism of US nuclear policies as reported to us by journalists who had been present.

Gavin

---

[2] Gavin talked with the President on March 1, but no other record of the meeting has been found. (Kennedy Library, President's Appointment Book) The Doty article appeared in *The New York Times*, February 27.

242.   Letter From the Ambassador to France (Gavin) to President Kennedy

Paris, March 9, 1962.

DEAR MR. PRESIDENT: In our meeting last week, you suggested that I send you a memorandum listing the problems on which a fundamental difference of view exists between the United States and France. I am attaching such a list.[1] It covers only military and technological matters but its very length, for which I apologize, emphasizes the magnitude of the problem.

Our basic differences with France today lie in the military field. France's determination to build a modern military force clashes with our policy not to assist the development of independent nuclear deterrents. Our policy starts with the Atomic Energy Act by prohibiting assistance relating to nuclear weapons and has been extrapolated into other technical areas, notably the missile area.

Here are some of the effects of this policy difference. France will spend at least $700 million to build a gaseous diffusion plant which will produce enriched uranium by 1965. We sell enriched uranium to the United Kingdom. We have failed to give France any assistance in building a nuclear submarine despite Secretary Dulles' offer to do so to de Gaulle in 1958. We are asking France to help us in redressing our balance of payments by making more military purchases in the United States, but we will not sell the very items France wants because they are associated with modern weapons systems.

France for its part is extending the range of non-cooperation with us into a variety of areas only remotely connected with modern weapons, as for example, seismographic test detection and military communications systems. There is in my opinion a real danger that this non-cooperation may extend into the economic field and could, as I mentioned to you, raise increased difficulty for us in the future both in trade relations with France and in our negotiations with the EEC.

It seems to me that it would be in our own best interest to enter into broad discussions with the French Government on this entire problem of military cooperation. We should seek to deal with France on a quid pro quo basis, and as pointed out above and in the attached memorandum, there is ample basis for both discussions and exchange. I believe we should take a close look at France's nuclear program by the test of

---

Source: Department of State, Central Files, 611.51/3–1262. Secret. The source text was attached to a letter from Gavin to Tyler, which stated that Gavin was enclosing it for Tyler's information.

[1] Not printed.

"substantial progress" in our Atomic Energy Act. I have considered the merits of offering to sell enriched uranium to the French Government beginning at the time they would be producing their own but I believe it may be too late now for this offer to be attractive to them. There may be other areas, [such] as sale of U.S. missile technology, where we can narrow the gap between U.S. and French policies.

In conclusion, Mr. President, I believe that our own interests must come first and that they can best be served by developing a national policy that will enable us to take such actions with France as will serve our national interest while at the same time they are helpful to France. This seems to me to be entirely possible.

I appreciate the opportunity to present these views to you.

Respectfully yours,

James M. Gavin[2]

---

[2] Printed from a copy that bears this typed signature.

---

243. Telegram From the Department of State to the Embassy in France

Washington, March 14, 1962, 9:25 p.m.

4920. Eyes only from Acting Secretary for Ambassador. Our relations with the French on nuclear questions are obviously at a very low ebb. This has been made clear by your recent conversations with Debre and others, and by Debre's remarks to the American correspondents. The bitterness shown by the French on this subject makes it plain that very little can be gained by discussing the subject further with the French at this time.

The President believes therefore that it would be best for the present to avoid being drawn into further discussion of nuclear questions with French officials which could only further exacerbate our bilateral relations generally.

Ball

Source: Department of State, Central Files, 700.5612/3–1462. Secret. Drafted by Fessenden; cleared by Tyler, Owen, Beigel, and Bundy (in substance); and approved and signed by Ball.

244. **Summary of Discussion Between President Kennedy and Prime Minister Macmillan**

Washington, April 28, 1962.

SUBJECT

Meeting with de Gaulle

The President asked whether there was any point in a meeting between the Prime Minister, de Gaulle, and himself, not necessarily as a prelude to a four-power meeting. He doubted that a bilateral meeting would produce anything useful, but perhaps it was desirable just to keep in touch with him.

The Prime Minister remarked that he had tried to keep in touch with de Gaulle, drawing on their war-time association, etc. After the Algerian question was off de Gaulle's mind and the French Army was back in France, de Gaulle might be more receptive to consideration of other problems. The Prime Minister commented that his instinct was not to disturb de Gaulle until after the EEC negotiations were completed.

In the afternoon meeting on April 28, the President remarked that he had talked to the Prime Minister about de Gaulle in the morning. They had decided to wait until after the Prime Minister's meeting with the General in June before deciding about a tripartite meeting.

[Here follows a list of participants.]

Source: Department of State, Central Files, 396.1/4–2862. Secret. No drafting information appears on the source text. The meeting was held at the White House. Regarding Macmillan's visit to Washington, April 27–29, see Document 391.

245.   Telegram From Secretary of State Rusk to the Department of State

Athens, May 4, 1962, 5 a.m.

Secto 24. Following based on uncleared memcon.[1] Secretary in bilateral talks with German and Canadian Foreign Ministers today has drawn on following points in explaining rationale US policy toward nuclear sharing with France. Secretary also plans draw on same points in conversations with various other Foreign Ministers:

1.   US policy is strongly opposed to nuclear sharing with France. The rationale for this policy is not based solely on opposition to the diffusion of nuclear weapons. Nor is it based mainly on our negotiations with the Soviets regarding non-transfer of nuclear weapons.

2.   The major bases for our policy are the following considerations bearing directly on France itself. In the first place, the French Government has not asked the US for nuclear assistance at a high level. In fact, De Gaulle has made quite clear that he does not intend to ask for nuclear assistance. Lacking such an authoritative approach, we have no real basis for acting in any case, and no opportunity to discuss on basis of all the relevant issues, such as those noted below:

A)   French today are making proposals in field of European integration which are being vigorously opposed by other members of Six. These French proposals run counter to concept of true integration which US has long supported.

B)   French have made proposals for reorganizing NATO which run directly counter to concepts of other members of Alliance. French changes run in a nationalistic direction; US and other members of the Alliance support organization of NATO along lines of collective defense.

C)   French continue to press vigorously and inflexibly for 3-power directorate concept. This is unacceptable to US and to other members of Alliance. It would also create obvious great difficulties for us in our relations with countries outside Atlantic area.

D)   French by various actions have shown their contempt of NATO and UN, both of which are fundamental to US policy. Specifically in NATO they have withdrawn their Mediterranean fleet; denied US nu-

---

Source: Department of State, Central Files, 711.5611/5–462. Secret; Limit Distribution. Also sent to the other NATO capitals.

[1] Rusk, who was in Athens for the North Atlantic Council meeting, May 4–6, met with the German and Canadian Foreign Ministers at 1 and 4:15 p.m., May 3, but the memoranda of their conversations do not deal with France. (Ibid., Conference Files: Lot 65 D 533, CF 2095. Regarding the Council meeting, see Documents 136 and 137.)

clear storage rights in France, made integrated air defense system less effective; and more recently refused to give us permission to establish tropospheric scatter link from low countries into nerve center at SHAPE.

E) French are not pulling their weight in difficult and dangerous questions of Berlin and disarmament.

F) France was paralyzed recently for several days by fear of military coup d'état; on other hand, France has large and powerful communist and extreme left group which is possible successor government.

G) French made clear that their purpose for establishing national strategic deterrent is not to cooperate with US and the Alliance, but to ensure France's independence of US and Alliance.

For all these reasons, therefore, it would be most unwise for US to grant any kind of assistance to France for their independent nuclear capability. It is far more than question of whether or not France qualified under McMahon Act. There are whole range of other considerations which are main bases of our policy.[2]

Rusk

---

[2] On May 4 Gerard Smith and Bowie sent a memorandum to Kohler stating that this telegram presented an inadequate rationale for the U.S. non-sharing policy. They believed it was "based on the *principle* that spreading national capacities" was "bad per se—not on *expediency* aimed at leveraging better behavior of an ally." (Department of State, Conference Files: Lot 65 D 533, CF 2100)

---

246.   Telegram From the Department of State to Secretary of State Rusk, at Athens

Washington, May 5, 1962, 8 p.m.

Tosec 95. For Secretary from Acting Secretary. President mentioned to me this past week his concern re the increasing isolation of de Gaulle and his wish to find some mechanism for bringing France back into the community of western nations. In view this opinion, I am concerned as to his possible reaction to your Secto 24[1] when he returns from Palm

---

Source: Department of State, Central Files, 711.5611/5–562. Secret; Priority; Eyes Only; No Distribution. Drafted and initialed by Ball.

[1] Document 245.

Beach Monday. The reported conversation particularly with Schroeder will presumably be communicated to De Gaulle through German transmission route and might be interpreted by the General as disclosing a United States Government policy of systematic opposition to him and his govt.

I am fully sympathetic with your impatience with Gaullist negativism. [2 lines of source text not declassified] Nevertheless I think it important we appear to aim our attacks at specific policies of Gaullist govt without giving impression we are opposed to whole spectrum of Gaullist policy.

This is a personal cautionary note I am expressing only to you. My apprehensions re the President's possible reaction may be unfounded. I recognize that Secto 24 was based on an uncleared MemCon. It may well have stated your position too bluntly and with exaggerated emphasis, or there may be other surrounding circumstances it would be useful for me to know in case President raises question. As against that possibility you might if you think it desirable send me before Monday suggestions as to line I should take.

Ball

---

247. Telegram From Secretary of State Rusk to the Department of State

Athens, May 6, 1962, 4 p.m.

Secto 69. Eyes only Acting Secretary. Bear in mind that Secto 24[1] was uncleared memcon and indicated that I had "drawn on" certain points in telegram in discussing question. Further, telegram standing naked and alone does not contain other information affecting atmosphere which I had not planned to put in cable traffic.

In view President's reference to hope I could visit Adenauer on return from NATO, a suggestion which I could not fit with commitments present trip, I responded positively to Schroeder's hope that I could come to Bonn some time in June if schedule permits. I also had friendly talk with Couve de Murville suggesting that we arrange for tour d'horizon on bilateral basis beginning with Alphand and possibly topped off with a visit by me to Paris. Thus Paris and Bonn could be covered same time with, hopefully, a few days vacation and acceptance Oxford honorary degree.

Source: Department of State, Central Files, 711.5611/5–662. Secret: Priority; No Other Distribution.

[1] Document 245.

Couve and I agreed that there are major elements of agreement between our two governments and that, in his words, "differences are largely of a tactical and procedural nature." I told him that our tour d'horizon ought to cover policies toward NATO, UN and other points where divergencies have appeared.

It has been obvious at this NATO meeting that Couve has tried to be as helpful as possible and that he understands we are trying to move same direction. Examples are our willingness forego any reference nuclear testing in NATO communiqué[2] to meet his view, and his care in handling press despite certain stories which exaggerated extent of agreement on Berlin procedures. Incidentally, we understand he was quite upset about remarks his own Defense Minister in commenting on McNamara speech.[3]

Must emphasize that points mentioned in Secto 24 are additional to basis of US policy on nuclear sharing with anyone. McNamara's speech to NATO made elemental basis of policy quite clear. I am getting out supplementary comments for those receiving Secto 23 to put matter into better perspective.[4]

Finally, I did not use materials Secto 24 as systematic attack on France in conversations with Schroeder or Green but as passing references to difficulties we find with French policy in self-imposed isolation from important tasks Alliance. Nor did I pursue these matters with other Foreign Ministers except Home and, to limited extent, with Spaak. Spaak is somewhat nervous lest we seem to support French attitude within Six and in NATO.

My own view is that we must press our problems with France through systematic, careful and sympathetic bilateral talks to see how far we can go within limits permitted by De Gaulle. We should not assume that Algerian settlement should make him more intransigent but should assume the opposite for purposes of full exploration. Pompidou as more man of the world than Debre could have constructive influence (obviously Couve thinks so). However, in view my conversations with Couve, I doubt that any trickling back which might occur would be interpreted as deliberate backbiting.

Please show the President this telegram.[5]

Rusk

---

[2] For text of the NATO communiqué, May 6, see *American Foreign Policy: Current Documents, 1962*, pp. 541–542.

[3] A copy of McNamara's speech on defense policy is in Department of State, Conference Files: Lot 65 D 533, CF 2101.

[4] Transmitted in Secto 80 from Athens, May 6. (Ibid., CF 2104)

[5] On May 13 Rusk called Alphand and reviewed his conversation with Couve de Murville. The Secretary of State suggested that the bilateral talks begin in Washington, and Alphand agreed to cable Couve for clearance. (Ibid., Rusk Files: Lot 72 D 92, Telephone Conversations)

248.   Telegram From the Department of State to the Embassy in France

Washington, May 9, 1962, 6:17 p.m.

5984. Eyes only Ambassador from Acting Secretary. President today asked that I communicate to you his deep concern about appearance here within last three days of articles by two well-known columnists on USG responsibility for rapid deterioration our relations with France. May 7 column by Sulzburger concludes that "Franco-American relations are at a low ebb and nothing is being done to improve them." And includes such statements as "compromise can salvage something; obstinacy leads only down blind alleys." Joseph Alsop article today speaks of the "ugly relationship between France and US" and of the two governments "doing their best to inflame the situation still further by all sorts of calculated slights and petty persecutions." Both articles castigate nuclear policy issue.

Appears to President that these stories part of a systematic campaign to present state of US-GOF relations to American public in most unfavorable and distorted fashion.

President asks that you caution your staff that in their contacts with French officials and the press they make every effort reflect spirit of Athens discussions in their portrayal US position on outstanding issues. With such care and diligence our representatives can assist in counteracting and offsetting misleading press stories.[1]

Ball

Source: Department of State, Central Files, 611.51/5–962. Secret; Priority. Drafted by Springsteen (U), cleared with Tyler and the White House, and approved by Ball.

[1] On May 10 Gavin responded that he shared the President's concern, and since Debré's press conference, had cautioned the Embassy staff to support U.S. policy both in spirit and to the letter. Gavin stressed further that although the Embassy was doing everything possible to put U.S. policy in a good light, the fact remained that the French in their contacts with the press were doing the opposite. (Telegram 5295; ibid., 611.51/5–1062)

249. Memorandum of Meeting

Washington, May 11, 1962, 4:30 p.m.

PRESENT

The President, Ambassador Alphand, M. Malraux,[1] M. Lebel, Mr. Bundy

After pleasantries about M. Malraux's visit to the National Gallery, the President asked M. Malraux if he would like to state the general views of his government on major problems. M. Malraux answered that in talking with the press he had already found that there were certain mistakes with respect to French policy. First, France was not opposed to entry of Great Britain into the Common Market. There was a misunderstanding here which could be cleared up in Paris.

The President interjected that as he understood it, the French thought that the British should choose between the Commonwealth or the Common Market. A sharp choice here would make things difficult for Prime Minister Macmillan, who had to contend with his Labor opposition. The United States itself had urged that those applying for membership in the Common Market should pay the full entrance fee, but the question in his own mind was whether in fact General de Gaulle did not fear and oppose British entry into the Common Market.

M. Malraux replied that while the formulation of the press made the question impossible, the President's formulation was no more than difficult. Without denying that General de Gaulle might desire to keep the British out of the Common Market, M. Malraux remarked that in affairs of state the French would not act according to their desires any more than the Americans. If England really wished to join the Common Market, nothing could prevent her. The President said that one does deal in terms of desire in these matters, and that this was exactly what troubled him. The United States favored British entry into the Common Market not as a matter of simple U.S. interest. Indeed British entry would be against the economic interest of the United States and was desirable only on the larger political ground of holding the Germans as a part of Western Europe.

Source: Kennedy Library, National Security Files, France. Top Secret. The meeting was held in the Cabinet Room. A memorandum of Malraux' conversation with the President along these same lines on May 13 is in the Johnson Library, National Security Files, Aides Files, Bundy. A memorandum with Rusk the following day is in Department of State, Secretary's Memoranda of Conversation: Lot 65 D 330.

[1] Andre Malraux, French Minister of State for Cultural Affairs, visited the United States May 10–16 at the personal invitation of President and Mrs. Kennedy. (Memorandum for Bundy, May 10; ibid., Central Files, 033.5111/5–1062)

M. Malraux asked whether the British would come with or without the Commonwealth (thus formulating the question in just the fashion the President had described as worrying.)

Ambassador Alphand contended that the French reservations on this matter were no different than the American. The President said that it was difficult to force a man to choose between an old wife and a new mistress, to which Alphand remarked that except for a short period one might keep both, while Malraux contended that to arrange one's affairs with both might involve boring troubles. The President repeated his view that the Common Market would be helpful in tying the British in, but said that perhaps in the French view this additional attraction was no longer needed—perhaps the French believed that the Germans were already safely attached. He repeated again that if the United States could support the entry of the United Kingdom at a time when it was losing gold on the balance of payments, it was a fair question why the French should be so reluctant.

The President continued that our feeling was that General de Gaulle apparently preferred a Europe without Great Britain and independent of the United States—a powerful force which France would speak for. This view brings France and the United States into conflict. We have felt that the defense of Europe was essential to the United States. A Europe beyond our influence—yet counting on us—in which we should have to bear the burden of defense without the power to affect events—would not be desirable. General de Gaulle should make no mistake: Americans would be glad to get out of Europe. Just before the President took office, President Eisenhower had recommended to him a cut of 2/3rds in the number of U.S. divisions in Europe—although of course the nuclear guarantee was to be maintained. The President instead had built up American strength. He wondered whether General de Gaulle's fundamental attitude was based on his experience with Americans in World War II, and he repeated that Americans would be happy to leave Europe if that was what the Europeans wanted.

M. Malraux replied that the President had quite naturally spoken purely as an American and he would like to reply in strictly French terms and take the President's propositions in inverse order. The President was more sure of the idea of Europe than the Europeans were. The Europeans dream of Europe and they talk of it, but the reality is very difficult and very uncertain. It is possible that de Gaulle does have a certain mistrust of England as a part of Europe. The President must understand that for a very long time in European history England had been a marginal part of European affairs. But if England really means to join Europe, then on balance France would like it. M. Malraux felt that he himself could hardly be charged with a lack of sympathy for the British—he was the only French Cabinet Minister with a DSO. But there was a fear that this would not work.

If General de Gaulle now looked toward Germany, it would be precisely because he sees the possibility of a real understanding with the Chancellor. For all Europeans, progress toward the reality of Europe was a matter of trial and error, enacted wherever they could make a breakthrough. De Gaulle in his attitude towards Germany had shown that he was not inflexible, and it was harder for him to change his basic view towards the Germans than it would be for him to change in his view of England.

Returning to the United States, M. Malraux began with the nuclear problem. The U.S. position had initially been based on the fact that the U.S. was the only nuclear power. The U.S. had not merely leadership but complete responsibility. From the time of the first Soviet development of atomic weapons, the problem changed its shape. From the American point of view there was now a real question about a third force. For M. Malraux this was a purely verbal notion.

The President interjected that we did not fear that such a third force would be neutralist. We were concerned, instead, about whether there was to be a wholly separate, independent force unrelated to American responsibility and interest.

M. Malraux indicated his own view that such a force would have a convergence with the U.S. in military and economic affairs—with probably some formula of association.

The President said that we have no sense of *grandeur*, and no tradition of leadership among the nations. Our tradition is fundamentally isolationist. Yet since World War II, we have carried heavy burdens. In our international balance of payments we have lost $12 billion, and the drain on our gold continues. We have engaged in a heavy military buildup, and we have supported development of the Common Market. When there was trouble in Berlin last year, the burden came on us. We have called up 160,000 men while France brought in two new divisions, and now France was reducing the period of military service. We find it difficult to understand the apparent determination of General de Gaulle to cut across our policies in Europe. If it is desired that we should cease to carry the load in Europe, nothing could be better from our point of view—it has now cost us about $1, 300,000,000 to maintain our forces in Europe and the savings on these forces would just about meet our balance of payments deficit.

The President said that he and all of the leading members of his Administration were great admirers of de Gaulle—and also of Adenauer. Yet there seems to be a conscious French effort to eliminate us from the affairs of Europe. After Vienna, the President had increased the defense expenditure by $5 billion and unbalanced his budget. Yet on a whole series of matters—Congo, NATO, and Berlin itself—the French were pursuing an opposite policy. Apparently there was a fear that the U.S. wished to dominate Europe. Yet such an idea was wholly wrong. As for the atomic difficulty, that came because on every other matter there was trouble. The reason seems to be a basic French drive to be wholly independent of the Anglo-Saxons. The President is not an Anglo-Saxon but he would be glad to take the U.S. out of Europe if that was what the Europeans wanted.

M. Malraux remarked that he did not think that de Gaulle's feelings toward either England or the U.S. were derived essentially from his experiences in World War II. The President replied that he had read General de Gaulle's books.

M. Malraux said that France had lived in the presence of real threats to its existence for all of its national life, while the U.S. had had no such experience until very recently. France had experienced disaster in 1940, and for many years after 1945 there was in France the absence of the feeling of a State. At practically no point was the French State in operation. For the President of the U.S. in the same period, the idea of the American State was clearly based on his capacity and responsibility for the defense of the nation. The French Army of today had faced twenty years of fighting all over the world without defending France, and that is why it has gone mad. What is now needed is to re-create a State in which the orders of the government are carried out. To do this, General de Gaulle must have a fundamentally national idea, and this idea is the idea of self-defense. Wherever the American line of thought crosses this purpose, the dialogue between the two countries becomes unreal. (The French word which M. Malraux used repeatedly was "faussé.") It was essential that the French should understand the position of the U.S., but the Americans also must understand the French complex on self-defense.

The President replied that the Americans also were committed to the defense of the West. The line of defense for all of us was in Germany. How could each country defend itself merely by its own means within its own borders? We must defend our interests together at the place where defense is necessary.

M. Malraux answered that his point was not military. It was a point about the nation itself, as a nation under a State. If this nation under a State could not defend itself, it would be liquidated at once under pressure.

The President asked how American policy cut across this basic French purpose.

M. Malraux asked whether our policies do in fact cut across each other. He agreed that we had some quite serious problems, but he thought also there were a considerable number of misunderstandings. What were the real problems?

The President said he had been speaking of the defense of Europe. M. Malraux repeated that he thought there were a number of misunderstandings. He would not wish to discuss such specific problems because obviously he was not the Foreign Minister. He would instead like to find out what were the basic American perspectives and purposes. He had read the President's books but in France he thought people did not understand just what American policy was.

The President said that our policy is very simple: it is to sustain and to assist countries which wish to be independent. This effort was going on all over the world and it placed a great strain on the resources of the United States. We would like to have the help and support of our friends in Europe in this work. But the President repeated that he did not see how this work could go forward if, in fact, General de Gaulle's dream was that of independence from the United States and Great Britain in a Europe in which France was the leader. The President repeated that if this were to be the policy of the European continent, the United States would like nothing better than to leave Europe. M. Malraux said the President might be right about the dream of de Gaulle, but that a dream is not the same thing as what one does in reality. He asked, speaking not as a Cabinet Member but as a historian, whether the United States could in fact leave Europe. The President replied that we had done it twice and that to stay there even now was very expensive. We were there now because of our obvious responsibilities, but some Europeans seem to regard our presence in a more sinister light, as a kind of unwarranted interference in their internal affairs. M. Malraux remarked that when the United States left Europe before, Russia was not a threat.

The President replied that certainly the Russian threat is the reason that we stay. He then reviewed his own personal experience since becoming President. We had made a tremendous effort after Vienna and the President believed it was these military efforts which had led Khrushchev to veer away from the showdown which had loomed in Berlin at the end of the year. Yet General de Gaulle seemed to say it was his determination which had produced the results. The President did not enjoy making these great military efforts. The United States was carrying a very large load, and in particular he found it very hard to understand this latent, almost female, hostility which appeared in Germany and France, and an apparent sentiment that we might not be reliable in keeping to our engagements.

M. Malraux interjected that de Gaulle does not believe at all that it was his statements of determination which had stopped Khrushchev. He did not think any French member of government had this kind of hostility toward the United States. The President interjected that there might not be so much of this now (probably referring to the change of Prime Ministers). M. Malraux repeated that France simply must recreate her nationhood and cannot endure to have her defense entirely in the hands of another nation, however friendly. The question of re-creating a nation was the immediate question for France. M. Malraux thought the matter of mistrust was a deep question to which he would wish to address himself further.

The President asked why these French requirements made it necessary to oppose NATO and to oppose the diplomatic probes. What was the reason that we always wound up in such sharp disagreement? The President believed that given the dangers and the heavy responsibilities which the United States faced in Berlin, we must make an effort to talk. Such talks might not work, but we ought to find out. The President did not find an overwhelming determination in other members of the alliance. He had asked the Chancellor how many divisions he would have in the first fighting in Germany, and the Chancellor preferred to talk about a naval blockade. Now we read in the papers of a Franco-German axis. If there was to be such an axis, the President would be glad to let it try to handle the Berlin affair. The President repeated that we do not understand the posture of France.

M. Malraux said that we could make a list of disagreements and work on them but that what he was really trying to do was to get to the center of the matter. His feeling was that the dialogue between the two countries was completely at cross purposes. The President repeated that we have done the military work while France had opposed probes, and this opposition had spread to Bonn. So we wind up with the alliance in disarray. The feeling in Bonn and Paris appears to be that the United States is not standing firm, and the President is getting tired of it.

M. Malraux replied that he did not think France had ever opposed the probes. He was familiar with General de Gaulle's January letter to the President,[2] in which France had said she did not believe in the success of the probes, but this was not the same as the President's accent of conflict on the matter.

The President thought it was much more than that. The French position had indeed been regarded as opposition. If the U.S. were not carrying the load, then the President could understand a policy of every man for himself. But he knew from General Clay's cables that whenever there was trouble the call went out for the U.S. Yet he could get no cooperation from General de Gaulle. Back in December he had telephoned asking for a change of a few words in a communiqué—with no result.[3]

---

[2] See footnote 1, Document 239.

[3] See footnote 2, Document 119.

The only reason the President could find was that somewhere deep down inside, General de Gaulle does not want the Americans in Europe—perhaps, the President again suggested, as a result of his experiences in World War II.

M. Malraux said that if that was what the President thought, then the end of the conversation was quite opposite from the beginning. We should start all over again. But what is important is that that is what the President thinks, and we can start again from there. The President replied that all the difficulties in communication were due to him and not to Ambassador Alphand, who, he was sure, had communicated the President's feelings very accurately. The President reminded M. Malraux that his wife is deeply Francophile, and that he himself had a great respect for General de Gaulle. De Gaulle had done two great things: first, he had achieved the Franco-German rapprochement; second he had handled the French withdrawal from the colonies in such a fashion that it was a victory for France. He thought that General de Gaulle was right 80% of the time, but he did wish that de Gaulle might say that we were right 20% of the time. Alphand said with a smile that perhaps the proportions were reversed. To make his basic point more sharply, the President said that we feel like a man carrying a 200-pound sack of potatoes, and other people not carrying a similar load, at least in potatoes, keep telling us how to carry our burden. If others would carry their share, the President could understand it. But we had done most of the work and now we were carrying most of the burden of criticism. The President was not going to do both.

M. Malraux said that while the President might believe in some Bonn–Paris axis, he himself did not believe in it at all. The President repeated that when we ask what others will do, we get a poor answer. They will make no military effort, and we must make no diplomatic probe. We are told that we ought not to speak for others, but only for ourselves. Yet the others do not make a corresponding effort. In these circumstances, should we continue?

M. Malraux replied that while he recognized that the President was carrying the potatoes, others had their own burdens, a point which the President had said he understood and recognized. M. Malraux agreed that any misunderstanding was not due to the Ambassador, and concluded by saying that we should direct our attention in the next discussion not to minor troubles but to the major central question.

The President agreed, saying that his whole object was to find out what the central difficulty was in our relations with France.

McG. B.[4]

---

[4] Printed from copy that bears these typed initials.

250.   Telegram From the Embassy in France to the Department of State

Paris, May 16, 1962, 7 p.m.

5425. At family luncheon with de Gaulle today he took me aside at once and after usual amenities suggested that I come by and see him after his return to Paris Sunday night.[1] I will make an appointment for some time next week. He asked about my visit to Washington and I told him I had discussed quite extensively all the matters of common interest to our two countries with the President.[2] I made specific reference to the need for understanding about our desires to cooperate with France's support of emerging African countries. I then reminded him of discussion with President last May in which he expressed an interest in cooperating more closely with us in Latin America.[3] Nothing significant came from our discussion and by implication it is to be continued next week.

After lunch he again took me aside and remarked he had been kind to US in his press conference yesterday.[4] I replied that I in a way felt so too but added that I should be frank with him and tell him that the press conference will be seen in different light in Washington than in Paris and undoubtedly there will be people in US who will not think he was particularly kind to US. He said he was used to that. (J'ai l'habitude.)

De Gaulle then went on to talk about organization of Western Europe remarking as he did that US should not be mixed up in Western European difficulties and should keep itself apart only bringing its weight to bear in case of necessity. It would suffice for Western Europe to know that if war were to start it could rely on US. In reply I told him that for many years US remained, in effect, isolated from Europe but we had then participated in WW I. After that war feeling of isolationism grew considerably, particularly in our midwest and, in fact, up until Pearl Harbor there were many who felt US should stay out of WW II. Nevertheless, out of deep conviction we entered that war and we left thousands of our sons buried in Europe. WW II brought an end to isolationism in US and we feel that now we should share burdens of Atlantic

---

Source: Department of State, Central Files, 611.51/5–1662. Secret.

[1] May 20.

[2] Gavin met with President Kennedy on May 2, but no other record of their meeting has been found. (Kennedy Library, President's Appointment Book)

[3] See Document 230.

[4] For a transcript of de Gaulle's press conference on May 15, see *Major Addresses, Statements and Press Conferences of General Charles de Gaulle, May 19, 1958–January 31, 1964,* pp. 172–184; see also *American Foreign Policy: Current Documents, 1962,* pp. 600–603.

Community wherever those burdens take us and in doing so we will strengthen free world.

In final analysis, fulfilling role that we do in Europe is an alternative to isolationism and, except for a small extreme right political bloc, isolationism is antithesis of present administration. He nodded, seemingly in understanding, and had nothing to say. But I was almost startled by cold harshness of his unqualified statement that US should stay out of affairs of Europe.

Reference was made to his emphasis yesterday in his press conference on balancing of Western Europe against Eastern Europe. He said that all depended on whether or not we had war. If we had war, no one knows what would happen. If we did not have war, people should become accustomed to living in peace and the only way this could be brought about was through the balance of Western Europe against Eastern Europe. It was suggested that modern, rapid communications had shrunk the world so that it would seem impossible to set Europe apart from rest of world, let alone Eastern Europe from Western Europe. The Atlantic was no longer a division. Again, he nodded but made no comment and left me with clear impression that he thinks a Western Europe organized, undoubtedly under leadership of France, will be able to checkmate Eastern Europe.

I will continue this discussion with him next week. I would again like to press him on his concept of how a Europe of Six would accommodate to or within NATO.

I told de Gaulle that President had had good talk with Minister Malraux and he had made certain suggestions to Malraux (ref Deptel 6133)[5] which he will be bringing back to General de Gaulle. Since I did not know what latter were and de Gaulle did not query me about them we did not discuss. In view my meeting with de Gaulle next week it would be most helpful if I had some information of suggestions Malraux will bring back to de Gaulle. I would appreciate as much information as it may be appropriate to have as soon as possible.

Although five MRP members had resigned this morning, de Gaulle made no reference to this. He was calm, relaxed and in a thoroughly agreeable mood.

Gavin

---

[5] Telegram 6133, May 15, informed Gavin that, at his discretion, he could brief de Gaulle on the U.S. position on Laos and should tell the General that the President had had a good conversation with Malraux. (Department of State, Central Files, 751J.00/5–1562)

251.   Telegram From the Department of State to the Embassy in France

Washington, May 18, 1962, 4:46 p.m.

6203. Eyes only from President for Gavin. I have read your interesting report of your luncheon talk with General.[1] When you see him again, I hope you will spell out our inability to accept the notion that we should stay out of all of Europe's affairs while remaining ready to defend her if war should come. We cannot give this kind of blank check. In Berlin and Germany, in particular, all major questions of policy relate directly to the confrontations of the Soviet Union and therefore to questions of war and peace. General European policy in turn relates directly and sharply to the problem of Germany. We cannot and will not stand apart from these questions as long as our strength and will are committed to the defense of Europe against any Soviet attack. If Europe were ever to be organized so as to leave us outside, from the point of view of these great issues of policy and defense, it would become most difficult for us to sustain our present guarantee against Soviet aggression. We shall not hesitate to make this point to the Germans if they show signs of accepting any idea of a Bonn–Paris axis. General de Gaulle really cannot have both our military presence and our diplomatic absence, and you should make this point with emphasis. I am sending you by pouch copies of my conversations with Malraux in which you will find this position developed at greater length.

Rusk

Source: Department of State, Central Files, 611.51/5–1862. Top Secret; Priority. Drafted by Bundy and approved by Rusk.

[1] See Document 250.

252. Telegram From the Embassy in France to the Department of State

Paris, May 28, 1962, 1 p.m.

5700. Eyes only Secretary. I called on de Gaulle as scheduled Saturday morning.[1] I presented him with copy of personally autographed book from President Kennedy *To Turn the Tide* which I had been holding for appropriate occasion. He received it, nodded, laid it aside.

De Gaulle said he realized we did not complete what we had to discuss at luncheon last week and he welcomed opportunity to exchange views with me. I began by drawing upon Deptel 6203,[2] once again pointing out that we have had to take active part in combat in Europe in two World Wars, which we did at great sacrifice, and now we felt we believe we have responsibilities in Europe and as member of Atlantic Community we want to take active part in affairs of Europe, that to us, it was not enough to assume we would merely become active in European affairs in event of war. De Gaulle replied by repeating almost word for word my statement, then saying that he realized isolationism was a thing of the past, that NATO in fact does now exist. Further that he was aware of important role U.S. had played in First and Second World Wars. In First War U.S. did not enter until 1917 after much had happened. Again the U.S. did not enter Second War until 1941, after France had been defeated. He said that he noted too that U.S. did not enter war until Pearl Harbor was attacked. He said France is not likely to forget contribution made in both wars by U.S. Now, however, situation is entirely different. The U.S. is committed beforehand and he considers it essential that she be so committed since if Western Europe is lost then U.S. will not last long. He said his fears are not that US will not be committed in time, nor that it will not play an active role in European affairs. He said he fears exactly the opposite, that U.S. will play a somewhat excessive role in European affairs. He said he realizes that U.S. enjoys a very great superiority of weapons, that it is by far the most powerful nation but nevertheless there are other countries. If U.S. assumes total responsibility in matters of defense this then becomes total political responsibility. Other nations, in fact, become protectorates. The Alliance will then break down within itself. If U.S. continues to exercise excessive leadership this will occur. He said he is not at all sure that our policy vis-à-vis Germany

---

Source: Department of State, Central Files, 611.51/5–2862. Secret; Niact.

[1] May 26.

[2] Document 251.

was most appropriate. He said he tried to present this view to President Kennedy last spring.

I replied by saying we considered NATO a very valuable instrument of the Atlantic Community and we wanted to fulfill our obligations in NATO. With this in mind we were curious about his thinking regarding role that Six would play in NATO. We were aware of growing importance of Six and of significant role he was playing, and I told him I would appreciate talking with him about relationship between the two as he must have foreseen it. He replied by saying that when NATO was created that was one thing but now situation is different.

Role that U.S. is now playing in Europe, and in NATO, will only contribute to breakdown within Alliance. He said he was disturbed by our excessive leadership and then said he would cite two specific examples.

First, he said we entered into negotiations with USSR on Germany. He said U.S. obviously wanted to do this and that Allies did not. Nevertheless we went ahead. Result was to commit France and Germany to course of action they could not agree to. U.S. entered into negotiations despite views of her Allies. I did not have opportunity to mention U.S. soundings with USSR are supported by British and certain other Allies.

Second, he said that official view of U.S. borne out by President himself, was that France should not have an atomic force.[3] He said that this attitude shakes very foundation of our Alliance in public mind. France is responsible for herself, it is responsibility that she cannot delegate and her people know this. If U.S. persists in this attitude then there is nothing to do but for each country to act in its own best interests.

Before I could reply he brought our meeting to a conclusion by saying he appreciated my coming in and did not want to impose on my time any further. Note of finality in how he expressed this thought made it quite apparent to me that "exchange of views" had come to end. I had number of items yet to talk to him about, so as tactful approach I expressed my appreciation to him for time saying I did not want to leave before telling him we have been sympathetically following his determined efforts to put Algerian situation under control. I told him that we hope he will achieve his goals and further that we would like to be of every possible help to him. He merely acknowledged what I had said and I then went on to say I was anxious to have an opportunity to discuss with him role that he saw UK playing in Europe particularly in the Six. I added that if he did not have time now perhaps we could talk

---

[3] At his press conference on May 17, President Kennedy had stated that he did not agree with France's decision to go forward with its own atomic force. For a transcript of the press conference, see *Public Papers of the Presidents of the United States: John F. Kennedy, 1962*, pp. 400–408.

about it another time but if he did have the time now I would like to discuss it. On this note he began to rise from his chair making it evident meeting had come to an end and so I took my departure. I have never seen de Gaulle in more unfriendly and tense state of mind. I would attribute it among other things, to Salan verdict[4] and Malraux's report to Cabinet. Salan verdict was shock to everyone and to de Gaulle particularly it was a personal and political blow.

When Malraux reported his conversations in Washington to Cabinet, reaction was highly critical of U.S. I will report on this separately.[5] Obviously de Gaulle's attitude changed greatly between our luncheon of about ten days ago and this meeting. At luncheon he was willing and anxious to talk and, in fact, asked me to return but on this occasion told me what he thought of our own policy and would receive no comment. Gap between our two governments is now farther apart than it has been in a long time. As seen from here likelihood is that this will widen unless a change, not now foreseen, takes place.

Visit of Secretary Rusk to Bonn will be considered against the interests of France and in fact an effort to isolate France. Long-range implications of our widening differences with France to our own country are deeply disturbing, particularly in realm of economics where it could hurt us at time when we need cooperation of France and European Common Market. If there ever has been need for an agonizing reappraisal of our policy vis-à-vis Europe certainly it is now.

Gavin

---

[4] On May 23 General Raoul Salan had been sentenced to life imprisonment rather than given the death penalty.

[5] Telegram 5706 from Paris, May 28, reported that the French Cabinet was deeply disturbed by Malraux's report on his meeting with Kennedy. (Department of State, Central Files, 751S.00/5–2862)

253. Memorandum of Conversation

Washington, May 28, 1962, 11 a.m.

SUBJECT

US-French Exploratory Talks; First Session

PARTICIPANTS

French	*US*
Ambassador Alphand	The Secretary
Minister Claude Lebel	Mr. William R. Tyler, EUR
	Mr. Johannes V. Imhof, WE

The Secretary's trip to Europe

The Secretary said that he regretted press speculation from Bonn concerning his visit there. He said he had discussed the possibility of a European trip with Couve de Murville in Athens. No firm date had been set as yet for the trip but the Secretary was thinking of leaving in the third week of June. His tentative plans would be to visit Paris, the UK (to receive an honorary degree at Oxford) and Bonn. Ambassador Alphand said that he would inform Couve de Murville.

Procedure

The Secretary suggested that the present talks should consist of several shorter sessions rather than one long one. Ambassador Alphand agreed.

The Secretary asked Ambassador Alphand whether he had seen Secretary McNamara's statement at Athens.[1] Ambassador Alphand said he had not. The Secretary said that Ambassador Alphand should be provided with a copy of Secretary McNamara's statement. (*Note:* We took this action on May 29.)

Third Force

Ambassador Alphand said that he thought one of the principal purposes of this discussion was to separate misunderstandings from real differences and to find a formula which would make it possible to live with some of the real differences. He said some of the misunderstandings arose from the press treatment of de Gaulle's statements. The press had exaggerated and distorted some of de Gaulle's recent statements. The press had ignored repeated references by de Gaulle to the Atlantic Alliance. The French continued to consider NATO as essential and there

---

Source: Department of State, Central Files, 110.11–RU/5–2862. Secret. Drafted by Imhof and approved in S on June 12.

[1] See footnote 3, Document 247.

was no change in France's basic alignment with the West. The Secretary recalled that in the discussion of the communiqué[2] during the President's visit with General de Gaulle, de Gaulle had not liked the statement that NATO was the basic element. Ambassador Alphand said that the form of the Alliance was not basic, that the structure might change, but that the principle of the Alliance with the West remained firm.

Ambassador Alphand said that it was necessary to remember that de Gaulle often spoke from the point of view of an historian. For instance, his recent references to a balance in Europe certainly did not mean that he would enter into negotiations with the Soviets tomorrow. This statement merely reflected his belief that in the long run serious negotiations leading to a real détente might take place. The press had distorted all this to make it appear that de Gaulle was anti-NATO, anti-US and toying with an independent policy toward the Soviets. Nothing could be further from the truth.

The Secretary asked whether de Gaulle had used the term "third force." Ambassador Alphand said he had not. He said that General de Gaulle was opposed to the concept of a neutral Europe. For this reason, de Gaulle was against negotiations on Berlin now, precisely because he feared this might lead to a neutral Germany, and by extension to a neutral Europe. Ambassador Alphand said that de Gaulle had in mind a modified relationship between the US and Europe. Europe should be less dependent on the US. The Alliance must continue although its form might change.

Ambassador Alphand said that General de Gaulle believes that an effective defense must be national and that the entire Alliance would be less effective if there was a high degree of dependency on the US. The Secretary said that without any briefing on our part the press had begun to talk about the concept of a "third force" in connection with de Gaulle's press conference.[3] This touched a very sensitive nerve. The concept that Europe could be the arbiter between the US and the Soviets was basically fallacious. Europe was the key issue outstanding between the US and USSR. If ever Europe decided to play an independent role, issues between the US and the USSR would be greatly reduced. In a sense, the US rather than Europe was the "third force" in this combination.

Ambassador Alphand reiterated that there was no question of a neutral posture on the part of France, nor flexibility in dealing with the Soviets.

---

[2] For text of the joint communiqué, June 2, 1961, see *American Foreign Policy: Current Documents, 1961*, p. 535.

[3] See footnote 4, Document 250.

Structure of NATO

The Secretary said we had accepted the concept of defending the principle of the Alliance in the remotest corners of the world. He wondered whether de Gaulle took the same view and equated such a commitment with the defense of France. Ambassador Alphand repeated that it was the form rather than the substance of the Alliance that was an issue. General de Gaulle fully accepted the principle of the Alliance. France and the US would stand together in any real crisis. Ambassador Alphand cited as an example the present relationship between the French Mediterranean Fleet and the Sixth Fleet which, according to Admiral Anderson, was better than ever despite the fact that the French Fleet had been withdrawn from NATO. He said that units currently being withdrawn from Algeria might not be integrated in NATO but would be available in case of need. Mr. Tyler asked whether these units would be stationed in Germany. M. Lebel said that it might not be possible to station these troops in Germany unless they were integrated into NATO.

The Secretary asked Ambassador Alphand to comment on General de Gaulle's views regarding a reform of the structure of NATO. Ambassador Alphand said he could discuss this only in the most general terms. This topic should be reserved for discussion on the Ministerial level. In general, the greater role of Europe and the US loss of its nuclear monopoly must be taken into account. He said it was difficult to discuss this question in detail as de Gaulle's precise views were unknown to him.

The Secretary asked whether Couve de Murville would be prepared to discuss the nature of changes in NATO which the French might propose. Ambassador Alphand said that he would mention this to Couve.

The Secretary said that we had gone far to reduce our special position in NATO and to underline NATO solidarity. We were taking up many issues in the North Atlantic Council. We had promised at the last meeting to consult about the use of nuclear weapons anywhere in the world. It must be borne in mind that the reaction in NATO to this might not be uniform. For instance, some governments might prefer not to be consulted about this problem.

Ambassador Alphand said that de Gaulle wanted closer consultation between the big Three and some tripartite organization to back up these consultations. The Secretary said that the implications of a special position of the Three would create problems in NATO. Ambassador Alphand said that de Gaulle's January 11 proposal[4] for regular meetings of representatives of the Three and for a small organization to prepare

---

[4] See footnote 1, Document 239.

planning for military and strategic matters had never been answered. The Secretary said that if Bonn and Rome agreed to a special position of the Three we would have less of a problem. Closer consultations among the Three were desirable if not accompanied by a public posture showing that the Three were acting as a kind of directorate.

Ambassador Alphand noted that there had been no tripartite consultations recently except on Berlin. He regretted that the French had not been invited to participate in the recent consultations on the Congo and said that it would be useful in general to have consultations on strategic planning. The Secretary said that the main purpose of the Congo talks had been to induce financial interest to bring pressure on Tshombe. As to strategic planning, the Secretary thought that some of this might be useful but that there would be no point in conducting contingency discussions, e.g. the circumstances under which nuclear weapons would be used. There were limits inherent in this problem which inhibit detailed discussions not only with foreign powers but even within our own Government. We should be under no illusion that by having a paper we also have a policy. As an illustration, the Secretary mentioned the 1948 events in Korea.

The Secretary asked Mr. Tyler to cite a specific problem, the tropospheric scatter system, which was important to the Alliance but to which the French had thus far refused to agree. Ambassador Alphand said that he was not informed about this problem but would have himself briefed.

The Secretary asked to what extent the French had taken into account the views of other members of NATO with respect to tripartitism. Ambassador Alphand said there should first be a discussion with the French and then with the British and then with the others. He said experience in NAC had shown that if the US, UK and France agreed, the others concurred. The Secretary wondered whether this was still true. The new strength which Europe had acquired affected not only France but other countries as well. Ambassador Alphand agreed and said that this issue was closely linked with the organization of Europe. If the European Community included an agreement relating to defense, the Alliance would have to take this into account. The French were now actively considering this problem, which could be an additional topic for discussion with Couve.

The Secretary said that we were not frozen to any form. It seemed to him that much of the discussions in NATO in the past had overlooked the fact that the US was also a member. Discussion had generally centered on the three European fronts, the central front and the northern and southern flanks. Targeting for instance must take into consideration the problems of all members of the Alliance. Fortunately there was as yet no competition on this but differences might arise in the future.

Organization of Europe

Ambassador Alphand said that de Gaulle was not opposed to British entry into the Common Market. The economic problems involved posed no essential differences from those confronting the US. The UK must enter without the Commonwealth although there could be a period of adjustment. At the end of this period the Commonwealth should be in the same position as the US.

The Secretary asked how this would affect the former possessions in Africa. Ambassador Alphand said that there might be a longer period of adaptation for political reasons until there was some global arrangement to develop their resources. Although admitting that there were some practical problems, Ambassador Alphand said that in the economic field we were much closer than the press would lead one to believe.

Ambassador Alphand referred to a statement made by the President to Minister Malraux[5] that the US was in favor of British entry despite the fact that this was against the economic interest of the US. He thought it should be recalled that trade between the US and the Common Market had tripled since 1952. He said the Common Market would not be protectionist. Admittedly, differences (wage scales, etc.) for the moment were too great to permit the creation of a free trade zone but the Common Market was not protectionist and would on the contrary attempt to establish closer economic relations with the US.

On the political side, on the other hand, Ambassador Alphand felt there might be problems. It was questionable whether the European spirit was compatible with the British outlook. Certainly the Europe of the Six would be more coherent than a Europe of the Seven or Nine. Ambassador Alphand wondered in this connection why we wished Britain to become politically a member of Europe.

The Secretary said that this was the trend of history. The Commonwealth no longer really constituted an operational unit. Britain belongs to Europe and the Channel was less of an obstacle than former French-German antagonism which had been liquidated. UK membership would contribute to the cohesion of Europe in the long run and would also help to reassure Germany. Furthermore, joint French-UK efforts, especially in Africa and in the UN, could be extremely effective and would be most helpful to the US. In reply to the Secretary's question Ambassador Alphand said that there was no basic disagreement between France and the UK outside of Europe. The main problem was the

---

[5] See Document 249.

UK position on relations with the Soviets and doubts whether the UK was really European minded. Ambassador Alphand said that he himself believed in European integration. He felt at the same time that de Gaulle's concept of European unity was a step in the right direction. Certainly de Gaulle's concept suited the British better than the concept of European integration.

Relations between the US and Europe

The Secretary said unnecessary theoretical debates about the US relation with Europe should be avoided. The practical fact was that we had given up sovereignty in many fields and would continue to draw close to Europe.

Ambassador Alphand said that de Gaulle did not suggest that we should get out of Europe but rather that we should not get into details, and should permit Europe to establish its own organization. The Secretary said that we had no blue print for Europe, nor did we desire a controversy about our relationship with Europe. European solidarity was in our national interest. There would be less controversy the more cohesive Europe becomes. Ambassador Alphand observed that the US would sometimes be accused of playing one European power against the other, sometimes of favoring a united Europe in order to be able to dominate it better.

---

254. Memorandum of Conversation

Washington, May 31, 1962.

SUBJECT

US-French Exploratory Talks; Second Session

PARTICIPANTS

French	*US*
Ambassador Alphand	The Secretary
Minister Claude Lebel	Mr. William R. Tyler, EUR
	Mr. Johannes V. Imhof, WE

The Secretary's Trip to Europe

The Secretary said that he hoped to be in Paris on June 19 and to have dinner with Couve and additional conversations on June 20 and

---

Source: Department of State, Secretary's Memoranda of Conversation: Lot 65 D 330. Secret. Drafted by Imhof and approved in S on June 15.

June 21 if possible. Ambassador Alphand said that he would confirm these dates with Couve de Murville.

Couve de Murville's CBS Interview

Ambassador Alphand gave the Secretay an advance copy of Foreign Minister Couve de Murville's interview with CBS, to be broadcast at 10:00 p.m. on May 31.[1] He said he was happy to note that Couve de Murville's statements support the arguments which he, Alphand, had made in the meeting with the Secretary on May 28.

Nuclear Policy

Ambassador Alphand noted that the next point on the agreed agenda was nuclear policy. He felt that again it was necessary to clarify certain misunderstandings. There had been numerous reports in the press that the French desired an independent nuclear force as a kind of trigger, to force the US to use their own nuclear weapons. Nothing could be further from the truth. There were also allegations that France desired an independent nuclear force to pursue a neutral policy. Ambassador Alphand noted that he had already refuted the argument of neutralism in the previous meeting. A typical example of distortion was the sudden reprint, in *The Washington Post* of May 29, of an article by Defense Minister Messmer on nuclear policy which had actually been published on February 15. *The Washington Post* had made it appear as if this article had just been released. Alphand said he had talked to *The Washington Post* about this.

Ambassador Alphand said that there were two main reasons why the French were determined to have an independent nuclear force: (1) the need for a deterrent against a Soviet threat directed specifically against France or French interests. Although it might be argued that France was amply protected by the US deterrent, it was impossible to tell what conditions would be in ten years from now and France would therefore not feel safe without having a deterrent of her own, and (2) France must have modern weapons if she wants to be a modern country.

Ambassador Alphand noted that France had never requested nuclear aid from the US. General Lavaud's visit was concerned with a quid pro quo on a purely commercial basis. No political considerations had entered into this discussion. Also, all talks that the French were looking to aid from the British in this field and would exact British nuclear aid as a price for British entry into the Common Market was absurd and without any foundation.

---

[1] Not found.

Ambassador Alphand said that it might be argued from the technical point of view that the French nuclear program represented a duplication of effort and that the French would not be able to develop a fully effective force. The fact remained that politically France required such a force. The nuclear program had been started before de Gaulle came to power and would be continued after de Gaulle had left the scene.

The Secretary said that he wished to explore some peripheral questions for the purpose of further clarification: (a) For example, it had been argued that it was necessary to give the French army a new mission in order to improve its morale. The Secretary asked whether this consideration played a role in the French nuclear program. Ambassador Alphand said this was a contributory element. He said the army was in a state of despair. It had fought in distant areas and must be brought to realize that its primary mission was the defense of the nation. The army must feel that defense is a national responsibility. Ambassador Alphand noted parenthetically that, in Europe, only General de Gaulle agreed with the US that Europe should bear a heavy defense burden.

(b) The Secretary said that the costs of a nuclear program and of space research were of course enormous, but that there was a feedback into the economy as a result of technological and other advances. He wondered whether this consideration had a bearing on the French nuclear program. Ambassador Alphand said that this was indeed a very important reason to which he had meant to refer when he had said that France wants to be a modern country and therefore must have modern weapons.

(c) The Secretary asked whether the French Government had considered the effects of its nuclear program on Germany and eventually on other countries. Ambassador Alphand said that he hoped a further spread of nuclear weapons could be controlled. In the case of Germany, there was, in the first place a legal obstacle. Furthermore, Germany had no uranium and no launching sites. M. Lebel added that he recalled that General de Gaulle told President Kennedy that he understood our position because if he had the bomb he would pursue exactly the same policy, particularly vis-à-vis Germany. Ambassador Alphand said that once the French had acquired a nuclear force the French would cooperate in preventing the further spread of nuclear weapons.

The Secretary said that all of our allies in the West would be concerned if the Germans moved into the nuclear field and the Eastern bloc would be particularly concerned. Ambassador Alphand said that the Germans had thus far not exercised any pressure on the French to acquire nuclear weapons and asked whether we were under such pressure. The Secretary said that they were not pressing us either, but our problems with Germany would be multiplied if we cooperated with the French nuclear program. Ambassador Alphand said that our non-cooperation extended to fields not covered by the McMahon Act and mentioned as an example missile guidance systems.

(d) The Secretary asked whether an agreement on disarmament would reduce pressures in France to acquire a nuclear capability. Ambassador Alphand said this would be the case if existing stocks of nuclear weapons were destroyed or fully controlled. On the other hand, if it were simply a question of a nuclear test ban, the French would remain determined to acquire a nuclear capability. The Secretary said that at Geneva we had proposed a 30 percent reduction in nuclear delivery substance in the first stage of a disarmament program. The Soviets had proposed a 100 percent reduction. Because of the great Soviet superiority in conventional forces it would be necessary to increase the conventional forces in NATO before such a proposal could be seriously considered. It would also be necessary to take a hard look at Communist China. The Secretary said that it was regrettable in this connection that the French had been absent from Geneva. Ambassador Alphand said that he felt that the Geneva Conference did not provide the kind of forum in which real progress could be made. The Secretary agreed that no real progress had been made but pointed out that the forum itself was immaterial. The decisions would be taken by the Big Powers and the other nations were merely onlookers.

Reverting to the policy issue in the nuclear field, Ambassador Alphand asked why we objected to France having a bomb and why we had no such objections with regard to Britain. The Secretary said that our policy was not directed against France as such but against the proliferation of nuclear weapons. We consider this weapon to be indivisible. The Secretary said that in his discussions in Paris on this subject[2] he had obtained the distinct impression that the accent was placed not on cooperation, but on independence which implied independent action. Ambassador Alphand quoted from President de Gaulle's letter to President Kennedy in which de Gaulle referred to the coordinated use of Western nuclear forces.[3] He recommended that this be discussed with Couve. The Secretary asked whether this might open the way for a NATO nuclear force. Ambassador Alphand said that coordination should take place between those Western powers which possess this weapon and not with those which did not possess it. It was desirable to correct this situation. The Secretary said that it would be necessary to

---

[2] Presumably Rusk is referring to conversations he had in Paris at the time of the North Atlantic Council Ministerial Meeting December 13–15, 1961, but no specific record along these lines has been found.

[3] The pertinent phrase in the January 11, 1962, letter is: "When the time comes it will no doubt be advisable to organize the combined use of the Western nuclear armaments." [Footnote in the source text.]

include some of the powers which while they did not have nuclear forces would suffer equally from the effects of a nuclear war. We were therefore giving consideration to a multilateral NATO nuclear force. Ambassador Alphand said that there was nothing new in our NATO proposal except that it perhaps served to appease the Germans if indeed they wanted to be appeased. Our proposal did not provide an answer to the sharing of controls.

The Secretary asked why the French were opposed to the stationing of our nuclear forces in France. Ambassador Alphand said that this was connected with de Gaulle's 1958 memorandum and that there existed a clear link between the agreed use of nuclear forces and permission to station them on French territory.

Ambassador Alphand asked whether our position on proliferation of nuclear forces was perhaps linked to our disarmament talks with the Soviets. The Secretary said that our position went back to the earliest period when the bomb was first employed. It was then realized that possession of this weapon might lead to uncontrollable consequences. It was frightening to think what might happen if Israel, Egypt, or China had the bomb. Ambassador Alphand said that once the French had reached an agreed position with the US on nuclear policy they would cooperate to prevent the spread of nuclear weapons.

The Secretary asked whether in the French view there was an organic connection between possession of the bomb and tripartitism. If there was, he could not agree. Naturally there would be a relationship between the Three on nuclear questions but there would not be tripartitism on political issues. Ambassador Alphand said that this problem would have to be placed into the column listing US-French disagreements. The Secretary said that the Three could no longer impose themselves on the rest of the world. Ambassador Alphand said that the French did not wish to impose themselves but that they did want to have their own say on important political and strategic matters. Ambassador Alphand repeated that he was convinced France would coordinate the use of its nuclear forces with ours.

The Secretary said that an independent nuclear force seemed to imply an independent use of such a force and this in fact could act as a trigger on our forces. He said it was difficult for him to envisage a situation under which the French would be prepared to use nuclear weapons and we would not. Ambassador Alphand cited as a example Soviet blackmail aiming at the establishment of a pro-Soviet regime in France. The Secretary said that our presence in Europe was precisely designed to prevent such a blackmail. Alphand said it was difficult to foresee what the situation in this respect might be ten years from now. The Secretary said that he had come away from his last discussion with de Gaulle with the feeling that France doubted our determination to defend Europe. He had felt like saying that if such a situation ever arose it would be because Europe had made it impossible for us to defend her.[4]

---

[4] At their third meeting on June 9 Alphand and Rusk agreed to group the problems they had discussed into those where there was: 1) basic disagreement, 2) no longer any need for discussion because they had resolved the misunderstandings, and 3) discussion was still needed. These problems would comprise the topics addressed by Rusk and Couve de Murville in Paris. (Telegram 6631 to Paris, June 9; Department of State, Conference Files: Lot 65 D 533, CF 2124)

---

255. Telegram From Secretary of State Rusk to the Department of State

Paris, June 20, 1962, 10 p.m.

Secto 13. Eyes only for President and Acting Secretary. Following is complete account of Secretary's conversation with de Gaulle June 19 which included Ambassador Gavin, Mr. Kohler, Couve de Murville, and Mr. Andronikov, interpreter. As this is complete cleared report, no mem/con will be prepared.

Begin text.

The Secretary opened the conversation by expressing his pleasure at meeting again with President de Gaulle and of having an opportunity to continue with M. Couve de Murville the tour d'horizon which the two Foreign Ministers had initiated on the occasion of the NATO meeting in Athens. He told de Gaulle that he had been specially charged by President Kennedy to express his warm regards and his admiration for the wisdom and courage with which President de Gaulle had conducted his French policy toward Algeria and to express President Kennedy's sincere wishes for a successful and peaceful conclusion of these efforts.

The Secretary said that at present time the United States felt that Allied solidarity was of the utmost importance. It was for this reason that he and Couve felt that it would be useful to sort out and narrow down any areas of difference between the two governments. He mentioned the known U.S. interest in the question of solidarity as involved in such

---

Source: Department of State, Central Files, 110.11–RU/2062. Secret; Niact; No Other Distribution. Relayed to the White House. Rusk visited Europe June 18–28.

discussions as the organization and possible enlargement of the Common Market. We are not interested in details of intra-European arrangements but have a vital interest in Alliance unity. For this reason the Secretary had been greatly distressed by press gossip that he was coming to Europe to play one capital against another. Any such behavior would be fundamentally contrary to U.S. interest and policy.

He felt that there had been some misunderstanding and misinterpretation of each other's position and that much of this could be cleared away through friendly discussion. He was satisfied that our basic purposes were in fact identical. It seemed quite possible, the Secretary continued, that we are approaching a climactic situation. It is clear that on the Soviet side they are facing many problems. After Stalin's death and Khrushchev's proclamation of a policy of peaceful coexistence, Khrushchev had been under constant pressure to prove that his policies would be effective in extending the Communist empire. However the Soviets had been faced during this period with the emergence of a strong Europe and by the unexpected resistance to their influence which they had encountered in the newly emergent nations. Differences and disputes had developed between Moscow and Peiping as to the means to be used to promote Communist purposes. A debate is now in course and a big decision may well be pending.

The Secretary said he would illustrate his views by referring to the specific question of Berlin. We had been discussing this question for a year now with the Soviets. After Soviet Ambassador Dobrynin had made his statement during their last conversation, the Secretary had asked him frankly whether he had said anything new. Mr. Dobrynin had admitted he had not said anything new but had simply summarized the Soviet position. In turn, after the Secretary's reply, Dobrynin had asked him whether he had said anything new, to which the Secretary had also responded in the negative. These talks with the Soviets, the Secretary continued, had produced no basis for negotiations. It had become clear that the central issue was the Western presence in West Berlin which we did not regard as negotiable. In the past months, apart from the central issues, the U.S. had introduced a few subjects of a broader nature in which the Soviet side might have an interest such as nondiffusion of nuclear weapons and nonaggression arrangements between the members of the NATO and Warsaw Pacts. However there had been no real discussion of these questions. And there had been no progress on the central point because the Soviets had not withdrawn their demand for liquidation of the occupation forces and we could not concede on this subject.

Despite this lack of progress, the Secretary said, the Soviet side had indicated that they did not wish to produce an early crisis or bring the talks to an open impasse. However there had been several opportunities for them to do so. They seemed to be as anxious to keep the conversations going as were many in the West, in which we did not, of course, include President de Gaulle.

The Secretary was aware that the question arises as to why these talks should take place. When he had seen President de Gaulle before, he had indicated that President Kennedy considered that he had a political problem both as respects the American people and the people in the free world generally. The President continued to feel it essential that contact be maintained. The Secretary recognized that the French view had been that no basis for negotiations would be found and that this view had proved to be correct up to present. Nevertheless we felt that the talks had been useful. Khrushchev had used the fact of the talks as an excuse whenever called upon to explain why he had withdrawn deadlines or desisted from harassments. For President Kennedy, who had been asking the American Congress and people for funds for a military build-up for an extension of aid, it was important to let the people know that diplomacy had not been idle in seeking peaceful resolution.

In sum, the Secretary said, we had reached no agreements of any kind with the Soviet side and there had been no withdrawal of the Soviet demand for the ouster of our troops from West Berlin. We were in a nose-to-nose confrontation. We had made it clear to the Soviets that Berlin is a war issue. However they did not seem to be moving the situation either toward a crisis or toward a diplomatic impasse. This could, of course, be different tomorrow since Moscow could make a decision one way or the other.

President de Gaulle said he wanted to say to Mr. Rusk that the French were informed through Ambassador Alphand. As we knew, there had been no reason for the French to object to the talks though they foresaw no result from them except perhaps talking for the sake of talking. He said that he had to recognize that while there had been no result, still the French apprehensions as respects the Germans had not been justified. He had thought that the Germans would react strongly but they appeared not to have been unduly concerned. On the question of Berlin, while the U.S. had got nothing, neither had the Soviets. The Germans had not been upset and there had been no upheaval in Germany as the French had feared. However he wondered whether the United States did not fear that if the talks were prolonged there would be engendered in the Germans and in the other European Allies as well a new political attitude. They would get used to the idea that all these things are to be negotiated between the Soviet Union and the United States even if there are no results from these negotiations. Eventually the impression would grow that these two were the only important powers and that there is nothing else to negotiate. He wondered whether this was good for the state of mind of an Alliance. He could see that the U.S. was concerned by a loosening—he would not say distortion—of the Alliance. He wondered whether we were right in pursuing our present line. As regards the Franco-American relations, he could understand what we had in mind and what our policy is. Everyone knows that there are in fact two centers of power in the world. But the question is whether there is an Alliance or whether there are only the two powers facing each other with the result that in the end there will either be war between the two or peace between the two. This approach to the situation is to be seen in statements of our leading figures. Even President Kennedy says that the U.S. has the power so it is up to them to act. Defense Secretary McNamara says that since overwhelming nuclear power is in the hands of the U.S. others should not have it. In this case why should there be an Alliance?

The Secretary said he wanted to comment on President de Gaulle's statement. He said the U.S. does not claim or seek the role of spokesman for anyone. Neither do we think it is possible for two powers to dispose of all questions. He wanted to point out that the U.S. has practically no bilateral problems with the Soviet Union. The real issue between the two is in fact the safety of places like Berlin and Western Europe. We have committed ourselves to their defense and have so informed the Soviet Union. Berlin might well lead to a nuclear war so it was prudent and necessary that contact be maintained so that if war should result we could say that we had done everything reasonable to avoid this result. We were conducting our talks with the Soviets on the basis of policies agreed in the Alliance. He would concede that France had not participated and we had made it clear to the Soviets that others were not committed. However we had conducted these explorations on an agreed basis and fourteen members of the Alliance were anxious that we continue them.

The Secretary said he would cite one other instance—that of Laos. After the new administration had come to power President Kennedy had carefully reviewed the situation there. He had concluded that it was unfortunate that in 1960 the U.S. had broken from the position of the UK and France. He in fact agreed with the views of these great friends. President Kennedy had discussed this question with Chairman Khrushchev in Vienna. However he had not attempted there to talk for the Alliance. The actual negotiations had occurred in Geneva and taken place in full concert between the Western Allies (though some of our Asian friends had been pained). The Secretary emphasized that we had no intention of negotiating alone without our Allies on these great questions.

President de Gaulle replied that he wanted Secretary Rusk to understand him well. He had not said that U.S. policy was not wise but only that the manner in which it was conducted risked inducing the frame of mind that he had described. He himself understood U.S. policy and did not fear that the U.S. and the Soviet Union were going to partition the world. However, our Allies might be led to believe that this was the case, particularly since this was exactly what the Russians wanted. Turning again to the McNamara speech,[1] he asked how it was possible to explain in France statements by leading members of the U.S. administration that it was dangerous to have nuclear weapons in the hands of countries other than the U.S.

The Secretary commented that no American had said it was dangerous to have nuclear weapons in the hands of any other countries; some countries have them now. This was the problem, he said, which our two governments had never really discussed. The U.S. had gone very far in the NATO Council in giving the basic information required to explain why we sincerely see these problems as we do. We think that it was generally felt in the NATO Council that this exposition as such had been helpful. The Secretary felt that we should go as far as possible (as an Alliance) in discussing nuclear strategy. During the past year we have made great strides in developing guidelines for the use of nuclear weapons, assurances as to availability of these weapons for use and in discussing target coverage. We have taken these initiatives because we thought that if we should find ourselves in a nuclear war, those who will suffer have the right to be consulted. We have also been asked to participate in discussion of a multilateral NATO nuclear force. In this connection we have put forward facts to be considered with respect to political and military factors and to cost. However behind all this it must be taken into account that U.S. policy with respect to diffusion of nuclear weapons is deeply rooted. Ever since we produced the first bomb the U.S. has sought ways to limit the extension and multiplication of this weapon, for example in the Baruch Plan.[2] There is nothing attractive in the prospect of widespread development and diffusion of nuclear weapons. We also have in mind the impact on the possibilities of disarmament. A real problem is how to deal with several hundred nuclear missiles coming at a speed of 1200 miles per hour against us or against the great Alliance. The nuclear arms race requires of necessity staggering resources and the concentration of scientific talents on a vast scale to get at problems threatening to surpass the mind of man. We hope to turn this course downward. That is why we were interested in the end of nuclear testing. Otherwise we are faced with the need for a fantastic effort with mounting instability and danger.

---

[1] See footnote 3, Document 247.

[2] For text of this plan, June 14, 1946, see Department of State *Bulletin*, June 23, 1946, pp. 1057–1062.

As to national nuclear forces in the Alliance, the Secretary continued, we on our side are trying to commit our nuclear capability as fully as possible to examination and judgment by the Alliance. Far from being able to act independently, we find that with the possession of nuclear weapons we have less freedom of action than ever before. If there are nuclear forces within the Alliance which might move separately, then we are faced with a whole series of most difficult problems. Defense in NATO must be indivisible. We must act together. It is impossible for us to act separately. There are delicate problems of common action but this is fundamental.

President de Gaulle replied that he fully understood Secretary Rusk's position.

These problems were not only difficult but perhaps unsolvable. The U.S. has fantastic means and faces the enemy with similarly fantastic means. Therefore, the U.S. considered that strategy and defense policy belonged to it. Any other power in the place of the U.S. would probably do the same. However, the problem is how to reconcile this policy with the need to maintain the Alliance. States like France must have their own personality and must be their own masters. He was not angry with us ("je ne vous en veux pas"). He did not see how the problem could be settled. Perhaps it was best for each of us simply to play his own game and live with the situation. This was not a deadly matter since our aims are the same.

The Secretary said that he wanted to ask a question—not that he thought that this would solve the problem. He said it was hard for us to imagine a nuclear war issue for our friends in Europe which would not also be a nuclear war issue for us. He said he could not exaggerate the fundamental change which had come about in American thinking since World War I. The American policy was based on national interests and American interest is not separable from that of Europe. We, therefore, find it impossible to understand or even to conceive the possibility of a separate action. The unity of strategy is the central problem.

President de Gaulle asked what the Secretary meant by speaking of "acting separately". Surely he did not believe that the French were going to go on their own. The Secretary replied that we had not discussed this question and then he did say frankly that some of the public debates and press comments were confused and confusing. Much of it seemed to indicate distrust in Europe as regards the U.S. commitment, a matter on which we were very sensitive. He thought separate action was impossible in this situation, whether by President Kennedy or by Prime Minister Macmillan or anyone else. In a nuclear issue with the Soviet Union we are all involved. The atmosphere of some public discussion left quite another impression.

President de Gaulle commented that the French could not do much about this problem nor could the Americans. The Soviet Union has now developed enormous nuclear capability and naturally enough this had changed American psychology. No one could be sure what could be done. The French do not believe that the Americans would abandon Europe even as Europe would not abandon the U.S. in case of a Soviet attack. However, one could not be sure as to the timing and the conditions and the extent of the decisions the U.S. would take for all parts of Europe. The U.S. does not know the answer to this itself. It was impossible to know the answer. For example, if Germany should be lost France could not remain without any French national defense. So France is building the means for such defense, however modest. The French simply do not know what would happen and neither could the Americans. The fact that the U.S. has not made these decisions was shown by the fact that we did not give nuclear arms to our Allies since that would involve us. The U.S. does not want to give help to France since that would involve it. The very fact that we feared such involvement showed that we were not decided.

The Secretary replied that it was clear that we must talk these questions out more between us. The U.S. was involved much more than President de Gaulle might imagine, since we consider ourselves a part of Europe from the point of view of our safety and our defense. He considered it important that what is in fact indivisible be thought about as such. Perhaps the forthcoming debate in the NATO Council would begin to open the question for some solution.

President de Gaulle replied what Secretary Rusk conceived of as indivisibility seemed to him to amount to integration which meant American control. For the French this no longer corresponded to what is necessary. Of course, we must be ready and if a fight should come we would stand together.

End text.

Secretary will comment on above by separate telegram at first opportunity.[3]

Rusk

---

[3] See Document 256.

256. Telegram From Secretary of State to Rusk to the Department of State

Bonn, June 21, 1962, 10 p.m.

Secto 27. Eyes only for President and Acting Secretary. Eyes only for Ambassador Gavin. Following are my principal impressions after brief talks with DeGaulle and Pompidou and several talks with Couve de Murville.[1]

1. The motive of DeGaulle's determination to acquire a national nuclear capability is primarily psychological and subjective. It is in part based upon his desire for status to place France on roughly the same level as the United States and clearly distinctive from other European countries. We must, I believe, accept as a fact, in current situation, the French intention to develop a national nuclear capability from which there will be no weakening even though means were found to accord them more status. I think we must also work on the assumption that France will continue its nuclear program whether DeGaulle is at the helm or not.

2. A derivative of the above is DeGaulle's relative contempt for smaller and weaker countries. His aversion to the UN, disrespect for a majority of NATO, objection to disarmament negotiations in front of eight neutrals are symptomatic.

3. He is asking for a status which he apparently thinks we and the British can confer upon him if we were only well disposed toward France. The fact that we cannot do so without deep injury to the sensibilities of other allies, including his neighbors Germany and Italy, he chooses not to understand.

4. His general attitude toward the United States is nevertheless friendly and derived from a combination of his respect for American power and his personal liking for President Kennedy with whom he is obviously deeply impressed.

5. It seems to me that practically everyone beneath DeGaulle would like to work with us as closely as he will permit. But this should not be exaggerated because he keeps these matters under rather close reins.

Source: Department of State, Conference Files: Lot 65 D 533, CF 2122. Secret. Drafted by Rusk and cleared with Kohler and Bohlen. Repeated to Paris.

[1] A report on the meeting with de Gaulle is printed as Document 255; a report on the one with Pompidou on June 20 was transmitted in Secto 23 from Paris, June 21 (Department of State, Central Files, 611.51/6–2162); memoranda of the conversations with Couve de Murville are ibid., Conference Files: Lot 65 D 533, CF 2122 and Central File 110.11–RU.

6. A line of argument which will be impossible on its face for us to meet is that no one can surely foresee the future, therefore France must be in a position to uphold the interests of France whatever comes. This leads him to be skeptical about flat commitments for the immediate future which might seem to be dangerous for French freedom of action for the longer range.

7. DeGaulle's remark that France must have nuclear weapons for its own defense "if Germany falls" seems to me to reveal the narrowness of his approach and the serious limitations on his appreciation of the nuclear weapon. I think we must continue to make major efforts to educate both DeGaulle and other French officials on the nature and indivisibility of nuclear warfare.

8. I was somewhat surprised by the affirmation of interest in European unity and solidarity which I met on all sides. On Common Market, for example, I clearly had the impression that France will not offer any overriding political objection even though they still have regrets about what they think will be the change in a united Europe introduced by the presence of Anglo-Saxon Islanders. It seems clear that this is partly because DeGaulle had hoped that eventually France would in fact be the spokesman for a united continental Europe.

9. We succeeded in removing a good many impressions based upon gossip and rumor. We have underestimated the fact that Paris has even more active centers of gossip, bons mots, and barbed wit, than we find in Georgetown cocktail parties. I am taking up with my colleagues special steps to moderate the effect of this static upon our official relations.

10. Pompidou is a very impressive man and it might be that some occasion could be found for him to have an informal talk with President Kennedy.

11. Couve de Murville and I agreed that a meeting between President Kennedy and DeGaulle could be advantageous if it could be informal and could close without an impression of serious disagreement, but both of us agreed that the time was probably not yet.

The resistance to DeGaulle's attitude toward European unity will not, I believe, be a major factor because DeGaulle will probably accept a high degree of European integration if Britain joins the Common Market on the political terms set by the present six. Further, I would suppose that France is relatively united behind the French nuclear program, partly because of the special quality of French nationalism and partly because it represents a declaration of independence from the US, at least symbolically. Questions about integration of French nuclear forces with us or with NATO will probably be deferred until France has something operational.

12. I believe the French must still come clean in their attitude toward Germany. There is on the one hand a desire to have an intimate relation with Bonn but, on the other, a desire to insure that France is clearly the senior partner. This may change after Britain enters the Common Market (which the French expect) but it will take some time. I found Couve de Murville wishing to be as helpful as possible, and this was made manifest on a large number of questions such as Laos, Algeria, UN matters, etc. It is rumored Couve will be replaced possibly in July. If his successor is a pure DeGaullist without the European experience of the past decade which Couve has had, Couve's departure would be a loss.

13. I do not believe we should attempt to solve major problems of present disagreement before Common Market discussions have come to a conclusion one way or the other. These would include nuclear relations, methods of consultation, NATO multilateral force, NATO organization.

14. We have had the usual difficulty with the press which has tried to deal with questions which cannot be resolved at present and on which the press would like to sick France and the United States on to each other. But I am quite sure that we made some headway during my short visit in reducing Washington–Paris temperature somewhat and in clarifying points of difference and the far more numerous points of agreement.

Rusk

257. **Telegram From the Embassy in France to the Department of State**

Paris, July 6, 1962, 6 p.m.

86. Eyes only Secretary from Ambassador.

(1) I have been reflecting on conversations you had here with de Gaulle, Couve de Murville and Pompidou and read with keen interest your telegram Secto 27 from Bonn.[1] Below I am submitting some of my

---

Source: Kennedy Library, National Security Files, France. Secret.

[1] Document 256.

views on present situation in France, particularly as it affects Franco-US relations and on developments which we foresee in rapidly evolving "Europe".

(2) Most important difference between France and US is certainly centered on French nuclear deterrent. I fully subscribe to view expressed paragraph 1 your tel that France will continue its nuclear program whether de Gaulle at helm or not. As for de Gaulle's motivation in pursuing his program, I am convinced it fundamentally political and skepticism on flat commitments certainly plays important part in de Gaulle's thinking as does desire create position of strength which will enable France have greater degree of independence from US. Added reasons are possession of nuclear deterrent would give France stronger voice in world councils and give her clear advantage over countries not possessing such weapon. Also de Gaulle believes no great power can voluntarily accept status which would leave it in permanently inferior position. Moreover I believe that de Gaulle in no wise constitutes voice crying in wilderness for I find more and more Europeans inclining toward view that some sort of European nuclear force, independent from, but complementary to US and NATO controlled nuclear forces is needed at present stage in European development.

(3) I believe de Gaulle's remark quoted in paragraph 7 of your telegram that French must have nuclear weapons for its own defense "if Germany falls" is not based so much on unawareness of military realities as on belief USSR, like Hitler in Czechoslovakia, might be successful in absorbing Germany through non-military means or perhaps in neutralizing Germany, and that France must keep herself in position of sufficient power resist USSR encroachment and blackmail. However that may be I believe we must not only work on assumption France will have bomb but I have strong feeling that in spite of possibility of a multilateral NATO deterrent (to which de Gaulle opposed on grounds it would merely be means for sharing costs of disguised purely American control force) we must regard as a possible, even probable, contingency development sooner or later of independent "European" deterrent mentioned above. Logic would seem argue that from closely integrated economic organization of Europe, including UK, and from integrated political organization, presumably less closely integrated, would flow common defense organization with coordination and pooling of material, scientific and industrial resources. It seems difficult envisage any such defense organization encompassing two independent and uncoordinated nuclear forces—UK and France. There certainly many in France who are beginning to think along these lines and it is development we must watch carefully. In this connection I was interested note comment

by Macmillan's Private Secretary (Secto 82 from London)[2] that he felt ultimate solution might involve pooling UK and French deterrents in some kind of European force.

(4) Complementary problem is how de Gaulle might envisage control of any such European deterrent. I think he would want it independent though closely coordinated with US deterrent under NATO umbrella. Within Europe he would probably wish control limited to major powers, i.e., France, UK, Germany and Italy. This would be consisent with contempt of small power mentioned paragraph 2 your tel. His whole reasoning on this nuclear problem is, I believe, based on assumption there will not be war. In the meantime he knows he can and must rely on US strength and will continue support Atlantic Alliance.

(5) Other major but related subject which can be expected hold center of stage in France when, [garble] Algeria out of way will be development of "Europe". As you point out in your paragraph 8, it seems France will not offer any overriding political objection UK entry into Common Market and to subsequent entry into political organization of Europe. This will profoundly affect de Gaulle's position of leadership but at same time it seems reasonable think de Gaulle believes UK accession would over period of time fundamentally dilute US-UK intimate relationship and that France would be able play major role in a Europe on par with US. De Gaulle is realist and I expect he has already adjusted his thinking to this prospective new power relationship.

(6) De Gaulle's view of "Europe" is I believe based on his historical concept of French position in world and on his view of Europe's future. His view is long-range and is motivated I think only in part on desire for European policy which can be independent of US. In this connection I thoroughly agree with your comment in paragraph 4 your tel re de Gaulle's general attitude of friendliness towards US. I have had feeling some people have made mistake of interpreting many of General's actions as being in some sense directed primarily at US. I do not believe this is true in most instances. Fundamentally his concern is French national interest which, on basic issues, he regards as largely same as that of US. He seeks a Europe in form of loose confederation of states guarding their sovereignty jealously but I am convinced he regards this as a stage in development over long run of increasingly close political association which can develop only in time as policies become more closely coordinated and individual powers rid themselves of problems particular to each, i.e., Belgium and Congo, France and Algeria, Germany and unification. Sense of European nationalism will grow but only slowly.

---

[2] Not printed. (Department of State, Conference Files: Lot 65 D 533, CF 2122)

(7) I am in full agreement with your view in paragraph 13 that we should not attempt to solve major problems of our disagreement until Common Market discussions have been brought to conclusion one way or another. However, in meantime we must anticipate that problems of nuclear deterrents and of economic political and defense organization of Europe will put serious strains on NATO and on our desire for close consultation and coordination of policy. While it true many beneath de Gaulle would like to work with US as closely as he willing permit (paragraph 5 your tel) we should not exaggerate this tendency or overlook fact that many of these men share certain of de Gaulle's views, particularly as they relate to unwillingness place France in position where, as they see it, US would maintain predominant role enjoyed in 1950's. US will be faced with many thorny and sensitive problems and movements may develop which are irresistible. A European deterrent may be one of them.

(8) As regards French I believe we must continue to cooperate and consult in all possible areas of mutual concern, refrain from showing our displeasure too openly or too often and reserve use of strong influence or pressure for a limited number of selected objects of principal importance to us. Chief among those is of course maintenance strong NATO with unified control over European deterrent, should it develop, and a clearly coordinated position with our Allies on East-West questions, especially Berlin.

(9) As regards NATO, establishment of political organization of Europe and development of European defense policy will certainly affect it and should be expected make necessary some sort of reorganization of machinery of North Atlantic Alliance. If we take initiative on reorganization it should help ward off undesirable initiatives taken for example by de Gaulle who so far has kept his ideas on reorganization of NATO to himself. Plans for any new institutions of North Atlantic Alliance should be designed to encourage full and intimate French cooperation, coordinated with and through Europe.

Gavin

258. Memorandum of Conversation

Washington, July 20, 1962, 6–6:50 p.m.

SUBJECT

Payments Arrangements Among the Atlantic Community

PARTICIPANTS

U.S.	French
Acting Secretary Ball	M. Giscard d'Estaing, French
Mr. Johnson, E	Finance Minister
Mr. Tyler, EUR	M. Pierre-Brossolette, Finance
Mr. Beigel, WE	Minister [Ministry]

The French Finance Minister was invited by the Acting Secretary to meet in the Department. He said that the purpose of the recent French gold purchase was to raise the gold ratio of the French reserves from 65 to 70 percent, in order to bring it into line with the recently prevailing ratio of 70–75 percent. He said that France preferred not to have had a public statement but recognized its usefulness to the U.S. The French Government was nonetheless surprised by some of the adverse press reaction. He said that he had indicated this to the President in their talk this morning[1] and that he was pleased to see that the President understood that the French intention was primarily to contribute to the stabilization of the U.S. balance of payments.

The Acting Secretary said that the President is preoccupied about raising the consideration of this general problem from the level of central bankers to the level of political management, as a way to give meaning to the Atlantic partnership in this area of our relations. He said that thinking about details here is still somewhat rudimentary, but the principle we have in mind is to seek political agreement to stabilize payments among the major industrialized countries. He said that we hope to prepare some suggestions in this direction.

M. Giscard d'Estaing said that in his view any unilateral action by either side to deal with this problem would be undesirable, either to devalue or to change the dollar parity. He said that the comment in this direction seemed mostly to be in the British press with a little in France.

Source: Department of State, Secretary's Memoranda of Conversation: Lot 65 D 330. Confidential. Drafted by Beigel.

[1] Giscard d'Estaing talked with the President at 10 a.m. (Kennedy Library, President's Appointment Book), but no other record of the conversation has been found. In a memorandum to the President, July 18, however, Ball recommended that, without prejudice to any solution of the problems discussed, the President welcome Giscard's initiative and his desire to explore the balance-of-payments problem. (Department of State, Central Files, 033.5111/7–1862)

He thought that such a move would be disastrous and would impair any possibility of increased confidence in the stability of the dollar. He went on to say that any change in the parity would only lead others to follow suit or even go further.

The Acting Secretary said that official opinion is quite clear here that any unilateral action is undesirable.

M. Giscard d'Estaing went on to say that there must therefore be a multilateral approach, and the question is, which one? He said that it is important to consider the subject with great secrecy, not like the experience of the IMF expansion last year. He said a discreet procedure must be found to work out an agreement. He said that he had spoken along this line to the President and had suggested that discussions go forward under cover of the OECD, with a restricted number of countries and with ministerial contacts as well. He thought that the countries should probably be the U.S., the U.K., France, Germany and Italy. He thought that to include the Benelux would be too many.

The Acting Secretary agreed that discussions could very well take place among the representatives to Working Party 3 as well as on the occasion of ministerial meetings, and that the four countries represented the most important interests.

M. Giscard d'Estaing said that the behavior of the creditor countries will be important while the U.S. is taking actions to bring its external accounts into equilibrium. He said that the restricted group of countries could consider a common balance of payments policy which would involve abstention in gold purchases on the creditor side. They should in his view also consider rates of interest, capital flows and regulation of capital markets, but they should particularly develop a multilateral attitude not to utilize their dollar reserves for a certain period. He said the problem will be what attitude should be taken toward those who might not be willing to accept such discipline. He thought that there would be a problem with the U.K. in this regard, but went on to say that the U.K. is likely to cooperate in view of its desire to join the Common Market, provided a discipline is reached among the Six in this matter.

The Acting Secretary said that we have in mind such possibilities as minimum gold reserves and an agreement regarding the ratio of gold to dollar holdings above the minimum. He said that the Finance Minister's presentation was very close to our own thinking. He went on to say that if we remain under constant pressure of unilateral action from abroad, while we continue to run substantial deficits, the pressures here to institute restrictive trade measures will be much more difficult to resist. He said that the U.S. is now undertaking certain measures that are certainly not to his liking, such as the military Buy American measures that have been announced within the past week. He said that in his view we should endeavor to solve our basic payments deficit through non-restrictive measures. He reiterated that if the possibility of unilateral action abroad is removed it will be possible to eliminate the restrictive measures and instead seek a solution through an expansionist approach. He said that the solution of course partly depends upon the actions of others, in such fields as capital exports. He said that if we can move this entire subject into the forum of multilateral decisions the results should be beneficial to all concerned.

Mr. Johnson said that the U.S. could of course bring its over-all payments position into equilibrium rather quickly if it were to institute measures that we do not wish to undertake and which would be undesirable.

The Acting Secretary noted in this connection that the U.S. had an ascending tariff level up to 1933 which in part contributed to the worldwide depression. He said that if this general problem is to be solved through sound, expansionist means it will require multilateral political decisions, which will be a good test of the Atlantic partnership.

M. Giscard d'Estaing said that the determination of the President and the principal officers of this Government to deal with the problem in this manner was in his view not well known abroad. He said that he intends to report to the French Government the strong determination voiced to him by the President. He said that if there is an occasion to do so, it would be desirable for the U.S. to make its attitude better known abroad.

The Acting Secretary drew attention to the President's balance of payments message to Congress in February, 1961, in which the first point was the statement of determination to defend the dollar through expansionist measures.[2]

M. Giscard d'Estaing wondered how the present press campaign could be accounted for and Mr. Ball suggested that the New York financial community frequently expressed views that were not in accordance with the thinking of the Administration. M. Giscard d'Estaing said that their views were not without influence in the European financial community.

The Acting Secretary said that there is not the slightest sympathy within the U.S. Government for the views appearing in the press regarding devaluation.

M. Giscard d'Estaing thought that it would be very useful to make more widely known in Europe that many other measures would be taken by the U.S. before consideration would be given to any devaluation.

---

[2] For text of the President's message to Congress, February 6, 1961, see *Public Papers of the Presidents of the United States: John F. Kennedy, 1961*, pp. 57–66.

The Acting Secretary said that in looking at the foreign reserve situation, such as the German position with some $2.5 billion in dollar holdings, it is apparent that our exposure to these holdings is not really serious. He said that the loss, for example, of twenty percent on balances of this size would be very small in terms of the size of the American economy. He said that in face of these realities, it should be possible to work out multilateral political decisions which could involve our giving the kind of assurances necessary to other Treasuries, thereby enabling the U.S. to resolve our basic payments problem in an orderly and non-restrictive way.

M. Giscard d'Estaing said this should be possible if everyone cooperates and that it seemed to him to be worth the risk. He said a problem would arise for him if the French were to see the British or the Swiss managing their reserves differently. Mr. Ball said that perhaps the Swiss would have to be included in the discussions among the other four.

Mr. Johnson said that we must also find a method to handle situations in the future that may arise in the case of other countries.

M. Giscard d'Estaing said that he agreed to this in principle but that it did not seem possible to him that both the immediate and the long-term aspects could be dealt with at once. The long-term aspects could only be considered over time in view of the several approaches that had already been suggested and the need to involve many other countries as well as the IMF. He said that we now need time to help the U.S. solve its problem and then turn to broader questions of international liquidity. He said that the solution that might be adopted by smaller countries, such as devaluation, cannot be adopted by the U.S. He noted that if the U.S. went very far in this direction it would soon face the question of gold parity. He thought that in three or four years a more general study of gold versus liquidity proportions in reserve holdings would have to be made, which would inevitably raise broad questions of devaluation or other measures to increase the liquidity base for the industrialized countries as a whole.

Mr. Johnson said that we would agree it is not desirable to inject discussion of the various plans for international liquidity into the present situation.

The Acting Secretary said that we are thinking of an agreement among the major countries on something that would at first be much more limited in scope, and that we could thereafter turn our consideration to more permanent solutions on a broad scale. He asked whether the position of the pound is likely to become an important element in negotiations between the U.K. and the Common Market.

M. Giscard d'Estaing said that the former Chancellor of the Exchequer had in fact invited him to London this weekend to discuss this question. This was prior to his dismissal. He said that the agenda suggested by the British had begun with an item on the consequences for the pound of U.K. entry. He said that it may seem too much to the British to solve this as well as the other problems they face in connection with entry into the Common Market, and they may therefore like to see the pound become the currency of the Common Market. He said the Common Market has no monetary problems of this nature now but that the U.K. is undoubtedly interested in such matters.

The Acting Secretary recalled the discussion at lunch in which the Finance Minister thought that effective tariff negotiations, including some zero rates, would require a greater concerting of economic policy. He said that while we agreed with this in principle, to the extent it would involve planning of the allocation of production it would be very difficult for us. He said that this would run counter to the history and assumptions underlying the U.S. economy. He said that we do recognize that a concerting of domestic economic policies in general is important, and perhaps inevitable with the growing degree of interdependence among the advanced countries. He said that the more this concerting develops the greater is the tendency for it to continue. He thought that this could go forward on a broad basis without getting involved in any planned allocation of resources.

M. Giscard d'Estaing said that the success of new tariff negotiations would probably depend upon the economic situation prevailing while the negotiations are taking place. He said that if the situation is less expansionist than today, which he felt is likely to be the case, it would be difficult for the European countries to go very far in the absence of other kinds of economic action. He said that it would be difficult to advocate a further opening of the Common Market unless there were other measures of discipline that could be undertaken.

The Acting Secretary suggested that the Common Market does not have a central direction in this respect. M. Giscard d'Estaing agreed with this but said that discipline prevails to avoid unfair competition. He said that he felt the regularity of growth that has been achieved among the Common Market countries has been due to the coordination that has taken place under the Rome Treaty, and he will be interested to see if historical analysis bears out this belief. He said that the test may come as we head for more troubled times. Mr. Ball noted that there is nonetheless very little dirigisme as such in the institutions of the Common Market.

259. Telegram From the Embassy in France to the Department of State

Paris, September 20, 1962, 4 p.m.

1408. I began farewell call on President de Gaulle today by touching rather lightly on his attitude towards possibility of meeting with President Kennedy about second week in November. He did not seem surprised and promptly replied that he would welcome very much indeed an opportunity to meet again with President, but that there were two questions on his mind. First, with regard to locale, he was afraid that a meeting in Washington would involve too many ceremonies, etc. I replied by assuring him that the President disliked spending time at needless ceremonies, etc., and that what would be more suitable would be a working visit, and that I thought this could be handled in Washington as well as any other place in US. I did ask him if he had another locality in mind, and he replied that he did not, that he was just concerned in principle with too many ceremonies. Secondly, and even more important, de Gaulle felt that unless there was something specific that needed discussion at this time on which we could find common understanding, there was some danger that public would be expecting great things from meeting and then would be disappointed. I told him my government would understand his concern about lack of specific achievement.

He then gave a hasty tour d'horizon from Berlin to disarmament and commented that while we are in general agreement on most things, we frequently do not find common meeting grounds on specifics.[1] He repeated his concern that if a meeting were to occur, there would be considerable public expectation over results and that if nothing unusual were achieved, ensuing letdown would be of negative value. He repeated several times great pleasure it would give him to see President again, and that he would welcome a visit with him. He was quite sincere on this latter point.

Comment: De Gaulle was obviously trying to make it clear that he was not being difficult and that he would really like to see President but he was genuinely concerned lest the meeting end on a negative note. Couve yesterday also said this to me.

Based upon my experience here, and a belief that psychological value of such a meeting would be very good for both of our countries,

---

Source: Department of State, Central Files, 611.51/9–2062. Secret; Priority; Limit Distribution.

[1] In telegram 1400 on the same day, Gavin reported that he had also emphasized the U.S. support for NATO and the effectiveness of the U.S. deterrent force. In turn, de Gaulle had been enthusiastic about his recent trip to Germany. (Ibid.)

and an awareness of value of a good and productive atmosphere here in immediate future when we will be concerned with implementation of a new U.S. trade legislation, I believe it would be good policy as well as good business for our Presidents to meet. De Gaulle's preference for informal type weekend meeting has been exemplified in Rambouillet and Birch Grove meetings and I think a meeting in that pattern would be welcomed and most useful. I would like to suggest therefore consideration of a meeting at, for example, Palm Beach. If a meeting were to take place at Palm Beach, I would further suggest brief visit to Cape Canaveral. De Gaulle continues to show unusual interest in new technology. For example, he is attending dedication of Telstar site in Brittany next month. I believe brief visit to Canaveral would please him and would contribute to overall psychological impact which we should seek to achieve. [2]

Gavin

---

[2] On September 24 Tyler sent Rusk a memorandum commenting on this telegram and stating that in the present circumstances, he did not think there was anything the United States could or should do to promote a meeting in 1962 between the two Presidents. (Ibid., 611.51/9–2462)

---

260. Instruction for the Ambassador to France (Bohlen)

Washington, undated.

1. *Basic Objective.* Our policy in the nuclear field reflects our basic objective in Western Europe: To work for an ever closer partnership between an increasingly integrated Europe and the US. This objective would be prejudiced by US aid for politically divisive national nuclear programs; it would not be prejudiced by US aid for a genuinely multilateral effort which brought the European countries together in a common enterprise closely linked with the US.

Source: Department of State, Central Files, 123–Bohlen, Charles E. Secret. No drafting information appears on the source text, but it was attached to a memorandum from Rusk to the President, dated October 16, which stated that he had approved it and that he believed it would be helpful to Bohlen. Also attached to the instruction was a 5-line memorandum for Rusk, stating that he had given Bohlen oral instructions on the general nature of his mission and now wanted to add specific instructions on the nuclear issue.

2. *Basic Tactic.* Your posture in regard to matters nuclear should reflect US confidence that the movement toward greater unity in Europe and toward a closer US-European partnership will eventually make itself felt in the nuclear field, as elsewhere. In the meantime, we should not seek out debate, which would be as useless as it would be harmful, on the nuclear issue with the French. We should be clear as to our own policy, and equally clear that French policy is for France to decide.

3. *Substance.* In making clear our own policy, you should indicate:

(a) *General.* We recognize that a Europe reviving in strength and confidence may wish to play a greater role in the nuclear field. We are ready, if our allies desire, to join them in examining steps to this end. We are not, of course, ourselves pushing for change in this field. Nevertheless, if it should turn out that a NATO or European force—genuinely unified, multilateral, and effectively linked with our own—is what is needed and wanted, we would be prepared seriously to consider this possibility. The most tangible manifestation of this basic posture is our willingness to facilitate creation of a multilaterally manned, owned, and controlled MRBM force, if one can be set up in a way that makes political and military sense, and if our allies are prepared to shoulder the very substantial burdens involved.

(b) *Strike Air Force.* If the French ask what would become of their intended national strike air force, in the event they join a multilateral MRBM force, you should answer that this is for them to decide. As General Norstad has pointed out, aircraft are phasing out as an effective Europe-based system for delivering nuclear weapons. We can let time do its work—here as with the British V-Bombers. We should, therefore, neither provoke needless controversy about an obsolescing program by denying aid for the production of aircraft nor needlessly enhance the status of that program by seeking French agreement regarding future uses of their intended strike air force before that force has even come into being.

4. *Aid for National Programs.* It follows from the basic policy described in paragraph 1 that we should not now provide aid for French national production or procurement of warheads or of the missiles to carry such warheads. If the French argue this involves discrimination between France and the UK, you may answer that:

(a) In respect of MRBM's, our policy is symmetrical between the two countries. You may refer to Secretaries Rusk and McNamara's statements to NATO that we would not facilitate MRBM procurement for allied forces which were not genuinely multilateral.

(b) In respect of warheads, there *is* an asymmetry and it is to be explained—as the French know—by historical circumstance. If there is a fault in this asymmetry it lies in what was done in 1958, rather than in what has not been done since. We do not intend to aggravate the situation by extending the special nuclear bilateral relation with the UK to new fields, or by extending it to other countries. Rather, we look to the long-term possibility that this relation may eventually be subsumed in a comparable relation with an integrated European effort.

5. *Timing.* The policy outlined above will, we recognize, not lead to an early and radical change in French policy. Time will be required for European-minded groups in France, which favor the multilateral over the national approach, to continue to grow in strength; for the repercussions of continuing progress toward European integration to make themselves felt; and for the difficulties, costs, and limited advantages of a national program to become more widely appreciated. While this is going on, France may or may not participate in a multilateral MRBM program; in any event, it will continue its own national program and a great many people in France will assure us that this program is here to stay.

Through this transitional period, we should bear in mind that the nuclear issue is one on which we and the French have agreed to disagree, and we should have both the tact to avoid reopening this difference and the patience to await the verdict of history upon it. We should be clear that our view of the matter reflects neither doubts as to the constancy and stability of France nor an insistence on relegating Europe to second class status. We should seek the closest and most confident relations with France in all other respects, and make clear our willingness to treat a uniting Europe as a full nuclear partner whenever it manifests the will and resources to act as such.

---

261. Telegram From Secretary of State Rusk to the Department of State

Paris, December 13, 1962, 11 a.m.

Secto 8. Secretary,[1] accompanied by Bohlen and Tyler, called on de Gaulle at 3:30 pm Dec 12. De Gaulle said he was glad to see Secretary and had written to President to congratulate him on handling Cuba crisis.[2] The successful outcome had been result of President's "firmness and lucidity." De Gaulle said he did not know how things now stand but essential objective had been reached of withdrawal missiles and bombers. Secretary conveyed warm personal greetings from President and

---

Source: Department of State, Central Files, 751.11/12–1362. Secret; Priority; Limit Distribution.

[1] Rusk was in Paris for the meeting of the North Atlantic Council December 13–15.

[2] A copy of this message, November 2, is in Department of State, Presidential Correspondence: Lot 66 D 204.

congratulations on support he had received from French people in recent elections. Secretary expressed our pleasure at prospect visit by "Mona Lisa" to Washington and added we would greet her safe return to France with sense relief. De Gaulle said he was sure no harm would come to the lady and wanted Secretary to know that France would not have entrusted her to any other country. Secretary expressed appreciation for de Gaulle's remarks about Cuba and for his firm support at the time. The Secretary then gave de Gaulle extensive account present Cuban situation, stressing that problem not yet resolved. De Gaulle thanked Secretary and said French support had amounted to little because it had been principally a US affair. If world war had resulted, France would have been at the side of United States. Secretary said we hoped that Cuba had been wholesome experience for Soviets and had removed any illusions they might have entertained as to any US hesitancy in comparable circumstances. Should crisis occur over Berlin we feel most important we should be in best position to meet it. This would require increased consultation to harmonize our policies and to organize ourselves so as to be able to respond quickly and efficiently. De Gaulle agreed and revealed some familiarity with contingency planning. Asked Secretary what he meant by saying that we should go further in our preparations. Secretary gave example of better and faster communications in crisis, need to speed up military moves envisaged under Live Oak, and to be prepared to apply rapidly economic and other counter measures. De Gaulle concurred in need for developing and refining agreed measures for execution of plans. Said we had to foresee three categories of events with regard to Berlin: (1) Soviets might harass and threaten Western [Sectors] to point barring ground access short of hostilities. In this case we should apply counter measures. (2) Soviets might cut off West Berlin from rest of world. In this case we should cut off Soviet links with rest of world. (3) There might be Soviet military attacks on Berlin. This would mean all-out war. Said that if question of completing plans for counter measures, he agreed we should do this and if Soviets want to make things rough for us in Berlin, we should react with appropriate measures. Secretary said question was how we could prevent Soviet leaders from miscalculating in Berlin as they had in Cuba. All reports received by Moscow should be such as to bring home to them our determinations. De Gaulle agreed and said if Soviets miscalculate it is their business not ours. This was why he had never been very happy about interminable talking and probing by US and British Govts on Berlin. This made it seem as though we thought that some agreement could be reached, whereas all we have to do is to wait until Soviets realize that they cannot obtain anything by their pressure. Secretary said the issue was really one of credibility about intentions. We had always stressed to the Soviets that presence Western troops Berlin non-negotiable. However it was fact that we are short of our force goals in NATO. If we had too few forces, Soviets could expect they could not last more than a few days. Thus we must reconcile our public actions with our private words. Secretary stressed that we had not discussed other questions than Cuba with the Soviets either in New York or with Mikoyan in Washington. Our impression from latter's visit was that Soviets not prepared to talk seriously at this time. De Gaulle picked up reference to deficiencies in NATO. He agreed that Soviets may be impressed by thought that forces of Alliance couldn't last very long. France was very conscious of this fact. Whole NATO military planning was based on the assumption of one battle which would be over very quickly, whether waged by nuclear or conventional weapons. France was concerned about her own defense, had felt she must have defense in depth. As things stood, everything would be destroyed after the first onslaught. "Norstad might well be wiped out." France could not accept this situation and had to assure her own defense in depth to the extent she could. Secretary said we were proceeding on assumption that Soviet offensive on such large scale as to break through Western forward forces would lead us directly to a nuclear war. De Gaulle said President Kennedy had also said this to him but things go fast and France ran the risk of being invaded. France was not the only country which did not have all her forces committed to defense Germany. US and British did not have all their forces on German soil either. Secretary pointed out we have substantial forces in Germany. De Gaulle said he did not know what kind of battle would take place there nor what United States would do. Should events develop in such a way as to justify it, France would possibly be prepared to throw her troops into the battle for Germany. Secretary asked what greater certainty we can give as to our role than our 400,000 troops committed to NATO and our solemn commitments to Alliance. He said we were not concerned with what we would do in the event of Soviet attack, but rather about the kind of signal we are sending to Moscow in advance. NATO had planned for thirty divisions and this figure had not yet been met. The question [is] what inferences the Soviet Union would draw from this deficiency. De Gaulle said Soviets could not doubt that France would defend herself. She was increasing and modernizing her forces and was developing a national nuclear force. However the number of divisions assigned General Norstad was a different matter. Secretary insisted that we must all together bring Moscow the conviction of our determination. De Gaulle said that we must face the fact that the Western Alliance was an alliance of individual states. This might have certain theoretical disadvantages though he wasn't sure. At any rate the joint power of the West was what counted. He was sure of one thing which was that integration is not a good solution. The Secretary said we had been concerned by what Khrushchev had been saying to his numerous visitors. He frequently attributed varying attitudes about Berlin to individual states. It was important we should all think this over so as to make Khrushchev convinced that there is no doubt about our resolve. With a faint smile, de Gaulle said it was possible that Khrushchev sometimes indulged in "wishful thinking" (in English).

Turning to Africa the Secretary stressed the importance of aid to the less developed countries. There was need for increased consultation among the major industrialized powers of the West—US, UK, France and Germany—on discharge of their responsibilities in this field. The industrialized countries should work more closely together. Our thoughts were moving toward the idea of a better division of labor or apportionment of responsibilities. We should work out a more efficient basis for certain countries to play a more prominent role in given areas in which historical and other circumstances gave them the best chance of being effective. He said that we have no desire for competition. We really needed to create a basis for a more efficient utilization of our resources. De Gaulle said he had taken note of the Secretary's views. He thought that the major difficulty came from the less developed countries themselves, which tended to shop around to get aid from whatever they could. He agreed that we should try not to "eat the wool off of each other's backs," and that there are situations where individual countries were in a position to play a primary role.

Comment: De Gaulle gave impression of being relaxed and, for him, relatively forthcoming and receptive to discussion of views expressed to him. His tone was friendly, if not cordial, throughout. He concluded the meeting, which ended shortly after 4:30, by thanking the Secretary for having come to see him and saying that he hoped things would go well at the NATO meeting.

Rusk

262. Telegram From the Department of State to the Embassy in France

Washington, January 1, 1963, 6:49 p.m.

3198. Personal from the Secretary for the Ambassador. Eyes only.

1. The principal objective of your initial exchange will be to impress on the French that the decision to offer them the Nassau proposals[1] represents a major turning point in United States policy. It implies a willingness to recognize France as a nuclear power and to bring substantially to an end the exclusive quality of the US-UK relationship. With the offered help France should be in position to contribute the kind of nuclear capability to Western defense that will be relevant to the 1970s.

2. At the same time it must be made apparent to the French that the offer cannot be considered apart from the principles of Nassau, which are founded on the propositions of interdependence and the indivisibility of Western defense and which include, as an essential element, the creation of a multilateral force, the assignment to that force of missile systems provided under the Nassau proposals and an equitable sharing of the burden of conventional defense.

3. In essence, therefore, the points that should be given particular emphasis are, first, that the United States is prepared to make a major decision of policy and to accord to France—at least so far as the Nassau proposals are concerned—the same status as Britain, but only on the understanding that the French themselves revise their policy to accept that multilateral principle.

4. In your initial conversation you should, of course, make it apparent that you recognize the importance of this matter to both sides and that it cannot be resolved over night. What is involved, after all, is the shape of the alliance, including the organization of the nuclear power of the West, and the major decisions under discussion cannot possibly be translated into force in being before 8 or 10 years from now. The United States is prepared to examine this problem in all of its aspects. However, the French cannot at this juncture be apprised of the exact nature of further US assistance, beyond the offer of a "similar

---

Source: Department of State, Central Files, 741.5612/1–163. Secret; Niact. Drafted by Schaetzel, cleared with Kitchen and Bundy, and approved and initialed by Ball.

[1] For text of the Nassau Agreement, December 21, 1962, see *American Foreign Policy: Current Documents, 1962*, pp. 635–637.

arrangement" as suggested by the President in his letter to de Gaulle.[2] As you know, we are developing urgently with Defense and AEC possible lines of US aid to France, what political, legal and Congressional problems such aid would entail, and finally, the reciprocal cooperation we would require from the French.

5.   Against this background it would seem desirable in your initial exchanges with the Foreign Minister and subsequently President de Gaulle to cover the following points:

(a) We are not pressing for a French reaction to the President's proposal; a proposal has been put forward and we shall assume that in due time the French reaction will be forthcoming.
(b) It should be stressed that the public documentation is the totality of the Nassau agreement. In this connection you may make available to the French on a confidential basis the two Minutes (the President's Minute of December 21 to the Prime Minister and, secondly, the memorandum by the Prime Minister of December 20)[3] should you consider this desirable.
(c) The French will undoubtedly realize on the basis of your outline of the Nassau agreement that much work remains to be done in developing the broad principles and courses of action settled upon at the meeting between the President and Prime Minister Macmillan. The French may therefore have questions to which there are no answers yet. But you should indicate willingness to forward any questions that occur to Washington for further guidance.

6.   You should concentrate during your first conversation on preventing Couve[4] from reaching a negative conclusion based on an inadequate understanding of the full implications of the American decision and the Nassau arrangements. It is recognized that you may feel it tactically desirable to say less to Couve in your initial conversation than you would be prepared to say in the course of subsequent talks with General de Gaulle.

Rusk

---

[2] Transmitted to Paris in telegram 2 from Nassau, December 19, the letter reviewed the agreements that had been reached with the British at Nassau and concluded "that the United States is prepared to join with you in an arrangement on the same basis as with the British." (Department of State, Central Files, 375.75611/12–1962) Telegram 2 also contained a similar letter to Adenauer without the offer of an arrangement similar to that offered the British.

[3] Documents 409 and 408.

[4] In a meeting with Couve de Murville on January 2 Bohlen followed these instructions with particular emphasis on paragraphs 1 and 4. The French Foreign Minister's only question was whether congressional action would be needed on the agreement with the British. In commenting on the meeting Bohlen stated that, as expected, the conversation offered no concrete indication of French thinking, but did confirm that they were not closing the door to further discussions on the question. (Telegram 2654 from Paris, January 2; Department of State, Conference Files: Lot 66 D 110, CF 2217)

263. Telegram From the Embassy in France to the Department of State

Paris, January 4, 1963, 7 p.m.

2684. Eyes only for President and Secretary. In a forty minute interview this afternoon I discussed with de Gaulle the various aspects of the Nassau offer and agreement with the British. I began by saying that since both our countries obviously considered that the Alliance was of vital importance to the defense of the West any general problem which concerned the Alliance should be of interest to both of us. I mentioned that the Nassau Accords with the British, which as de Gaulle knew, began with the decision of the U.S. to cancel the Skybolt Operation, represented in themselves a new approach to the problem of nuclear armaments and the Alliance and represented for the U.S. a considerable major shift in its attitude towards this question. I said that the problem obviously was one of the reconciliation between nuclear powers, of which I listed the U.S., U.K. and France, and the non-nuclear powers on the other. At this point de Gaulle interrupted to say that France was not yet a nuclear power but was determined to be one. I continued by saying that this was a very real problem for the future of the Alliance and had particular relevance to the question of Germany since that country had the necessary scientific, technical and industrial resources to become a nuclear power but that it was very much part of the problem that had been discussed. De Gaulle admitted that such a problem existed but said in regard to the Germans that for the immediate future there would seem to be no danger of Germany becoming a nuclear power although he himself was convinced that at some time in the far distant future Germany would also have atomic bombs. When I asked him whether France accepted this he immediately replied no, that France, because of past history and other reasons, would never be in favor of Germany acquiring the atomic weapon on a national basis but he merely felt that in the long run it was inevitable. In reply I stated that we did not regard this as entirely inevitable but that if it did happen it would cause great divisions in the Alliance and would be a subject of great concern to the Communist Bloc, with which de Gaulle agreed.

Returning to the question of the Nassau Accords and the offer which had been made, de Gaulle said that the French Government had no intention of closing the door on future discussions but that he did feel, given the French circumstances as compared to those of Britain, that there was very little that could be done in the immediate future in

---

Source: Department of State, Conference Files: Lot 66 D 110, CF 2217. Secret; Niact. A note on the source text indicates that it was passed to the White House on January 4.

regard to this offer. He said that Great Britain, who had always participated with us in nuclear matters with the exception of a short period
immediately after the war, was in a very different situation than France
in regard to the Nassau offers. For example, he understood that the British were much nearer to the completion of a suitable submarine and
would be able to manufacture the warheads, whereas France did not
and would not have this capacity for a considerable number of years
and that therefore the offer had very little immediate practical value to
France. I told him I could see his position if he was operating simply on
the bare basis of the Nassau offer, but that we regarded this as a beginning and not an end in itself. De Gaulle replied that they could only go
on what had been offered at this time, to which I repeated that as far as
the U.S. was concerned there was no aspect of the entire problem of nuclear weapons and the effect on the Alliance which we would not be prepared to discuss with France. De Gaulle went on to state that as we well
knew he had a very poor opinion of the possibilities of a multilateral
force which he said would be merely the present situation under a different guise since it would inevitably be an American commander. I
took him up on this point and told him that for the future there could be
absolutely no certainty that it had to be an American commander in any
form of multilateral force and that this indeed was one of the questions
which could be discussed. I asked him, leaving aside for the moment the
particular interests of France, how he envisaged the nuclear problem for
the Alliance as a whole, particularly the difference which would certainly arise in the future between the nuclear powers and the non-nuclear powers.

De Gaulle replied that for the immediate future he thought the Germans would confine themselves to "grumbling" but that he had always
thought that Germany should be regarded as a forefront of the Alliance
and the place where the first attack from the East would be received. He
said he had always thought that the solution was to make provision for
all weapons, including nuclear weapons, to pass over to German command at the moment of the outbreak of war but he did not favor the
turning over of any nuclear weapons to Germany during peacetime. I
inquired whether he felt that in regard to modern warfare that there
would be time to make the transfer in the event of a Soviet attack, but he
tended to wave this aside saying that if proper precautions were taken
in advance this could be done. He then went on to develop an already
well-known thesis to the effect that if he had been an American he
would have adopted the same policy as had President Eisenhower and
President Kennedy; that we had felt it necessary in our own interest to
safeguard our atomic secrets, which he well understood, but the fact remained that this had created a difference between England and France
in the atomic question.

He then developed at considerable length his view of the Cuban developments, which I find of considerable interest although full of holes. He said that the events in Cuba had brought to his attention a factor in regard to the American defense policies which he had thought about but had not fully accepted. He said the U.S. had suddenly found itself with a menace on its doorstep in Cuba and had taken swift and energetic action to force its removal, of which he was very complimentary. He said, however, the lesson he had drawn from it was that the U.S. had given greater priority to matters affecting its own immediate security than for example the defense of Europe. He said up to this time he had generally, along with other Europeans, felt that the U.S. had given number one priority to the defense of Europe as a means of defending the U.S. I took issue with him on this point stating I did not think it was a question of where the menace lay. I said that I thought it was a mistake to assume that because we reacted so vigorously in regard to a Soviet base in Cuba that we would not have reacted equally as vigorously, in fact probably more so, if the menace had been as direct to Western Europe. I told him I thought this was merely a manifestation of the simple fact that the U.S. had commitments of interest which were global; that we had alliances for defense in South Korea, Formosa, the Philippines and Japan and places in the Far East which we would most certainly honor if threatened. That the real issue here I felt was that the U.S. with these global commitments could at any time find itself menaced by Communist action and that our reaction thereto could always bring with it the threat of general war. I said that this aspect of the matter stemmed largely from the fact that the North Atlantic Treaty did not cover all the U.S. engagements indeed as it did not all of the involvements of Great Britain or France. De Gaulle seemed somewhat impressed with this analysis of the problem I had presented and did not pursue the matter any further.

I told him during the conversation that we were particularly pleased that France had not shut the door on further discussions of this matter, but I had no success in drawing him into any specific suggestions for the continuation of these discussions. In regard to the technical aspect he said that France had had a number of hints from the U.S. which had led them to send missions to Washington to discuss certain technical questions but as soon as any matters touched on atomic affairs the discussions were halted by the U.S. I told him that while for the moment I could not go beyond the terms of the Nassau offer that these were considerations which applied primarily to the past and I could only tell him that we were prepared to discuss any aspect of the atomic question and its relation to the Alliance. I pointed out to him, however, that the Nassau Accords contained some commitment on the part of Great Britain to the multilateral principle, but exactly how this would be applied was a matter for further discussion.

De Gaulle throughout was extremely amiable and indeed for him cordial, but obviously had no intention of committing France even to any definite form of negotiation or discussion. It was quite clear to me that he definitely had decided that the advantage to France in the Nassau offer is not sufficient to bring him to any degree of commitment to the multilateral idea. It also seemed clear that he was holding back with a view to having us make the next move of a somewhat more concrete nature, particularly on the question of submarine construction and possibly the question of warheads. He spoke several times of the period of seven to eight years which would be required before France would see anything particularly to her advantage in the Nassau offer and also was quite clear on his opposition to the multilateral force. He seemed to be less sure in his outline of how to handle the German problem and I imagine he will be giving further thought to the idea of multilateral force as a means of dealing with the problems of the Alliance in the immediate future.

At the close of the meeting he told me that if I had anything further I wished to say to him on this question that he would be very glad to see me.

Bohlen

---

264.   Telegram From the Department of State to the Embassy in France

Washington, January 19, 1963, 3:47 p.m.

3528. Paris pass USRO. Department appreciates your analysis in Embtel 2804[1] and fully agrees with your assessment situation. We therefore believe that in present circumstances we should press forward with

---

Source: Department of State, Central Files, 751.11/1–1563. Secret; Limit Distribution. Drafted by Spiers on January 18; cleared with Owen, Popper, Bundy, Kitchen, Schaetzel, Tyler, McNaughton, and WE; and initialed and approved by Rusk. Repeated to London, Bonn, Rome, and Brussels.

[1] Telegram 2804, January 15, reported that de Gaulle's views on the subjects treated at his press conference the previous day were fairly well known and had been reported before. The only surprise was that he had stated them publicly with such brutality and frankness. (Ibid., 375.800/1–1563) For a transcript of the press conference, see *Major Addresses, Statements and Press Conferences of General Charles de Gaulle, May 19, 1958–January 31, 1964,* pp. 208–222; see also *American Foreign Policy: Current Documents, 1963,* pp. 378–380.

UK on Polaris agreement and on immediate assignment of contingents to NATO Nuclear Force as well as with other NATO powers on multilateral mixed-manned force. We also agree that in light De Gaulle press conference we should not now undertake new initiative with French that would lead them to expect that we would sweeten Nassau offer without any concomitant change in French policy, since at this juncture such change seems highly unlikely.

We believe it is more than ever clear that De Gaulle will not contemplate any fundamental changes in his policy or move to our view re desirability increasingly united Europe working in ever closer partnership with US in nuclear and other field, until and unless march of events and attitudes of other countries suggests that basic policy of interdependence is likely to prevail. While keeping firmly on our present course we wish to make sure that France is at all times aware that door is continuously open and that we are ever ready to discuss new arrangements in which we cooperate, both bilaterally and in a multilateral framework, more closely with France and in which France cooperates more closely with movement toward European unity and Atlantic partnership.

It is important however that French understand that our larger objectives are inconsistent with the concept of help to a French nuclear policy that is not evolving in directions which will contribute to, rather than detract from, the cohesion of the European Community and the Atlantic partnership.

As our discussions with UK unfold and as we develop more precisely our ideas with respect to development mixed-manned component of NATO Nuclear Force, our intention is to instruct you to keep French, at whatever level you deem appropriate in light of developing situation, abreast of our thinking so that French do not get impression it is object our policy to freeze them out; French exclusion, it must be clear, is strictly a consequence of their own continuing wish to be excluded and any forthcomingness on French part with respect cooperation in these endeavors would be fully reciprocated by us.

Rusk

265. Memorandum of Conversation Between Secretary of State Rusk and the French Ambassador (Alphand)

Washington, January 19, 1963, 3:07 p.m.

Ambassador Alphand came in alone, at his request, for an informal talk on the present situation. Upon my request that he lead off, he said there seemed to be two separate problems—the nuclear problem and the Common Market situation.

On nuclear matters, he said that President de Gaulle had taken into account the fact that France was far behind the United Kingdom in nuclear development and that the Nassau offer, therefore, did not mean anything to France. Further, France has made it clear to us all along that they were determined to develop their own national nuclear force; the cost of this national force would make it impossible for France to participate in a multilateral force. He pointed out that President de Gaulle in his press conference[1] had referred to the coordination of the nuclear forces of NATO and had referred to "technical and strategic" cooperation. He indicated that France expected to have perhaps 50 nuclear bombs in 1964 carried by Mirage aircraft and that they were working on their own missile and missile nuclear warhead. He said that they did not yet have a thermonuclear device nor did they anticipate having a warhead of sufficient sophistication in time to take advantage of the Polaris offer. He strongly intimated that it would be desirable for the United States to talk further with France about the possibilities of cooperation in the nuclear field.

With regard to the Common Market, he made the point, not very convincingly, that these discussions had been going on for more than a year, that they had made no significant progress and that it was obvious that Great Britain was not able or willing to accept the Treaty of Rome as it stands. This was what President de Gaulle meant by saying that the United Kingdom was not ripe for entry into the Common Market. He said that if Britain were tomorrow to accept the view of the Six on the remaining points of issue, France would not and "could not" prevent Britain from entering the Common Market. I told him that I had some impression that the nuclear question and the Common Market discussions were in effect linked and that perhaps the Nassau Agreement had been used as an additional reason for raising political objections to the entry of the United Kingdom into the Common Market. I told him that I

Source: Department of State, Rusk Files: Lot 72 D 192, Chron. Secret; Eyes Only. Drafted by Rusk.

[1] See footnote 1, Document 264.

had the impression that President de Gaulle was going to take his time before coming to a final decision on the Nassau discussions in order that a careful examination of the situation on both sides could be made to ascertain the relevance of a "similar arrangement" with the French. He confirmed his own personal understanding (and recommendation to Paris) that he had expected President de Gaulle to take considerable time before replying and that this was the sense of de Gaulle's letter to the President[2] on the subject. He indicated that he, personally, had been caught by surprise by the negative approach in de Gaulle's press conference. I pointed out to him that we had supposed that, following Nassau, further elaboration on our side would be necessary both to go forward with the British and to talk in more detail with the French. The relevance of the Nassau offer to France could not really be determined without the French having more information about what we had in mind and our having more information about the French nuclear program and planning. We have given the rest of NATO much more information about the US nuclear program than we ourselves know about the French program, and, indeed, we feel we know more about the Soviet nuclear program than we do the French program. On the multilateral force, he indicated that the French understood that the multilateral force could and would go forward without French participation. I confirmed that we were prepared to discuss a multilateral force with the members of the Alliance who express an interest in it and that indeed several of them had expressed a very lively interest.

On the Common Market, I told him that it seemed to me that President de Gaulle had raised a major political objection to the UK entry and that this was not just a matter of failure of agreement on the remaining technical and economic points. When President de Gaulle said that the UK was not ripe for entry into the Common Market, this can only mean that France is not ready for the UK to enter the Common Market as only the British themselves could say that they are unable to accept the conditions for entry. Alphand attempted once again to reject this interpretation and repeat his conviction that the UK could enter tomorrow by accepting the Rome Treaty. I told him I could accept this as his own view as a Frenchman but I found it hard to believe that this was what President de Gaulle meant in his press conference.

I then mentioned to Alphand a number of disturbing reports which we have about rumors or charges emanating from French official

---

[2] Dated January 2, it thanked the President for his offer to extend to France an arrangement similar to that made with the British at Nassau, and stated that France was studying the content and implications of the offer "with keenest interest." (Department of State, Presidential Correspondence: Lot 66 D 204)

sources about the position of the United States.[3] I mentioned, among others, (a) the report that we were withdrawing nuclear weapons from NATO; (b) that the President and the Prime Minister had made some sort of deal on Berlin at Nassau and (c) the report that we were trying to encircle France or somehow embrace or smother Western Europe by the American presence. He was obviously interested in my factual statement of the great increase in American conventional and nuclear strength in NATO in the past two years and the reminder that Secretary McNamara and I had made this information available to Foreign and Defense Ministers in NATO. He did not respond to my reference to other rumors on the basis that he was uninformed but did point out various references in President de Gaulle's press conference which indicated friendship, solidarity and cooperation.

I emphasized the importance of atmosphere and the intangible psychology factors which could be so disturbing to the unity of the Alliance. I said, for example, that the general impression in the French handling of the force de frappe was not that of an assumed unity of the Alliance to which France wished to make a contribution but the assumption of disunity and the possible need for a separate force through the unreliability of the United States. He admitted the accuracy of the impression but disclaimed the point of view as the official French position. I spoke of the impression being created from Paris that President de Gaulle looks upon Europe as threatened both by the Soviet bloc and by the US and that it was not always clear which of these threats was considered to be the more serious. I reminded him of the American presence in Europe in 1946, 1947 and 1948 and told him that no one has welcomed more than we a strong and vigorous Europe assuming control of its own affairs. For several years after 1945 the "Twenty Mule Team Wagon" was pulled largely by one mule, with the other mules in the wagon. Since then, the other mules had become revived and had been getting more and more into harness. No one welcomed this more than we: if we had to pause for a vigorous discussion among ourselves about which way we should all be going, this is nothing at all surprising given the nature of mules and sovereign states.

The above summarizes the principal elements in an hour and a half conversation in which Alphand disclaimed any instructions, indicated that he did not anticipate making a full report to the Quai d'Orsay and

---

[3] At 6:34 p.m. on January 18 Bundy had called Rusk to tell him that the President was angry about "what the French have been putting out in Brussels." Rusk suggested that Bohlen might talk to the French and tell them that among friends this was an "outrage." Bundy replied that the "Pres' first impulse was to have B call Alphand and raise ———." Bundy and Rusk agreed that Rusk should talk to the President about the President seeing Alphand on the matter instead. (Ibid., Rusk Files: Lot 72 D 192, Telephone Calls)

during which he did not make any proposals or seek to draw any from me. He did leave the impression that he hoped we would take fresh initiatives with Paris, particularly in the nuclear field, but I did not pursue the matter beyond saying that, although it appeared that President de Gaulle had rejected the Nassau proposals, the Nassau statement still stands as our own policy.

[1 paragraph (3 lines of source text) not declassified]

Dean Rusk[4]

---

[4] Printed from a copy that bears this typed signature.

---

266. Telegram From the Embassy in France to the Department of State

Paris, January 24, 1963, 5 p.m.

2947. Brussels for Embassy and USEC. The real reason for de Gaulle's rejection of the Nassau offer so flatly at his January 14 press conference remains somewhat obscure. In his conversation with the British Ambassador on January 2 and with me on January 4, and indeed in his interim reply to the President on this subject, de Gaulle generally took the attitude that the matter be kept open for further discussion despite the obvious non-acceptability of the offer as made. In fact he was explicit with the British Ambassador (Embassy telegram 2664)[1] in saying that at his press conference he intended to be very "prudent" in answering questions.

French officials with whom I have discussed this are extremely vague as to the reasons for his shift in posture although all admit that some event had occurred between January 7 and the time of this press conference which caused him to take a position contrary to the previous line. Malraux, with whom I had a long talk yesterday, was quite definite in stating that de Gaulle's shift of position had come as a surprise to him; that he had seen de Gaulle just prior to his departure on the 7th for Washington and that de Gaulle had told him then that while he in-

---

Source: Department of State, Central Files, 375.75611/1–2463. Secret; Limit Distribution. Repeated to London, Bonn, Rome, and Brussels.

[1] Not found.

tended to maintain the principle of a national nuclear deterrent he was disposed to leave the door open for further discussion with the American Government. Malraux said he so informed the President while in Washington[2] and was somewhat surprised to find that de Gaulle had shifted his position at the press conference. He believes that the statement made by Ball during his visit to Paris may have been the factor that caused de Gaulle to change, but beyond this opinion he had no definite information as to the genuine cause of de Gaulle's shift.

Lucet at the Foreign Office, whom I saw yesterday also, confessed complete bewilderment and said that de Gaulle's attitude on this subject at the press conference had come as a complete surprise to the officials at the Quai d'Orsay. Lucet, however, obviously attempting to soften the impact of de Gaulle's objection, said that he thought de Gaulle's willingness to consider cooperation in "technical" and "strategic" matters represented an advance over the French position on the subject of targeting which had been brought up by the Secretary with Couve last June.[3]

Comment: The reference by Malraux of Ball's visit is interesting. It is conceivable that the post-Nassau development of our thinking in regard to the immediate implementation of the genuinely multilateral force in NATO may well have been the reason why de Gaulle shifted his posture on this question. It will be recalled that in his conversation with me de Gaulle had stressed the fact that the question was not urgent since it would permit ample time for discussion, whereas Couve de Murville expressed surprise (Embassy telegram 2762)[4] in learning from Ball of our intentions in this regard, at the same time making it very plain that France would not participate in any multilateral force. It is entirely possible that de Gaulle realizes as a result of this that France would be forced very soon to disclose its attitude towards a multilateral force and therefore chose his press conference as a means of making his position entirely clear.

Bohlen

---

[2] On January 8 Malraux had accompanied President and Mrs. Kennedy to the unveiling of the "Mona Lisa" at the National Gallery of Art in Washington.

[3] See Document 256 and footnote 1 thereto.

[4] Telegram 2762, January 12, reported on a conversation between Ball and Couve de Murville on January 12 during which the Under Secretary of State outlined the statement he would make the following day to the North Atlantic Council on MLF. (Department of State, Central Files, 375.75/1–1263)

267.   Memorandum for the Record

Washington, January 28, 1963.

Ambassador Alphand came in to see me at 7:15 this evening. He had been asking for an appointment all day and I had told him that I would call him after a meeting which I had to attend with the President at 5:30. I did so, and he came.

He began with the statement that we were going through difficult days and that in his opinion we would get through them. He said that they reminded him of the days in which the European defense community was coming to a crisis, days which he remembered because he had been the principal French negotiator in favor of this community. He recalled the period in which Mr. Mendes-France had opposed the EDC, and then there had followed the negotiations looking toward a different solution, in which the Germans joined NATO. At the time he, Ambassador Alphand, had been opposed to this second arrangement, but since then he had concluded that it was right. Similarly he hoped that the current differences might lead to a good solution. In particular he sought to press upon me the possibility that if the British should not get into the Common Market, an alternative arrangement could in fact be worked out, in terms of association—and on reflection I believe that it was this idea, the promotion of a British associate membership, which was at the root of his visit.

Ambassador Alphand continued with an expression of his great concern over the degree to which the press had interpreted General de Gaulle's press conference and other recent events as implying a deep division between the purposes of the French Government and those of the United States. He said that he thought there might be differences in emphasis, but no difference in fundamental purpose. He said that he had brought me the recent speech of Couve de Murville in the French Chamber and that he had read and studied this speech and the General's press conference with great care and he thought that American press was emphasizing—indeed greatly overemphasizing—points of difference, and ignoring the numerous olive branches which he, the Ambassador, was able to find in these speeches.

I then allowed myself to say to the Ambassador that I thought the world, the press, and the United States Government were in very little doubt as to the purposes and meaning of the press conference of the President of France. We had reached the conclusion that the President of

Source: Kennedy Library, National Security Files, France. Confidential. Dictated by McGeorge Bundy at 9:45 p.m. on January 28.

France did not want Great Britain in the Common Market and had decided to prevent British entry. I did not think that it would be a great contribution to Franco-American understanding to attempt to obscure this opinion of the President of France, and I was willing to venture the opinion that if General de Gaulle were with us he would agree that this was his purpose. Ambassador Alphand replied rather stiffly that he did not so interpret the press conference of President de Gaulle. We danced around this problem for a few minutes and then I said that since it was not a matter of immediate and direct interest to the United States, I was prepared to rest my own opinion upon the judgments which had been expressed by so many Europeans in recent days. Ambassador Alphand said, again rather stiffly, that he thought we must indeed have an opinion, since we had been expressing it so strongly with the Government of the Federal Republic of Germany. I said that I did not think he should suppose that the opinions of the Federal Republic were different from those of Europeans as a whole.

Ambassador Alphand then reverted to the broad question of the purposes of our two countries and repeated his view that there was no serious difference between us. I said that I would like nothing better than to accept this opinion, but that what limited my acceptance of his proposition was the fact that General de Gaulle had so often expressed purposes and attitudes which seemed to me not to be consistent with the view of the Alliance which I believed to be that of my Government—and so far as I knew that of Ambassador Alphand himself. I read to the Ambassador certain striking passages from the third volume of General de Gaulle's memoirs, passages in which General de Gaulle put forth clearly his intent to establish France as the leading force in a third world power—a continental European group so situated as to play the role of arbiter between the Anglo-Saxons and the Soviets. Ambassador Alphand asked me when this opinion had been expressed, and I told him. I also said to the Ambassador that in a search of General de Gaulle's writings I was unable to find any passage in which he had indicated any approval of the continued presence of American troops in Europe. The Ambassador's reply was that, so far as he knew, General de Gaulle had never expressed his opposition to this presence.

Somewhere along the line, Ambassador Alphand asked me why the Americans should be so concerned about exaggerated press reports of this sort. I made it clear, in reply, that the United States did not feel that the position taken by General de Gaulle could or should be allowed to interfere with the basic development of the Atlantic Alliance. I made it clear that whatever might happen at Brussels, and whatever might be the opinion of the Elysee, the United States would naturally wish to continue with the basic policy and purpose which had governed our affairs for fifteen years, and which, to the best of our knowledge and belief, corresponded with the desires and purposes of the majority of the people of Europe. In the course of this argument I said to Ambassador Alphand that we did not suppose that Europe and the Elysee were precisely the same thing—to which he said that he entirely agreed. In repeating my concern about General de Gaulle's possible desire to eliminate the American presence from Europe, I stirred Ambassador Alphand to remark that not as an Ambassador, but as an inspector of finances, he was himself of the opinion that we could not indefinitely sustain a large internal deficit, a deficit on the balance of payments, and four hundred thousand men in Europe. He thought that we would wish to withdraw some men from Europe, but that everything depended upon the way in which these rearrangements were worked out within the Alliance. And I said that I agreed on this last point, although I thought he should understand that in our judgment large deficits were now a clear source of national strength.

Ambassador Alphand kept repeating that the General was entirely loyal to the Atlantic Alliance and that we need have no fear of any reversal of alliances. I said that I was not disposed to disbelieve him, but that I did think there was a likelihood that General de Gaulle might have a concept of the Alliance which was old-fashioned and in fact unworkable. It appeared to me that he might believe that the Americans could be persuaded to remove their forces from Europe, and keep out of European affairs except in the event of emergency, in which case they would be reliably at hand, with their strategic nuclear strength. I said that I thought this was not a workable idea, and that if French diplomacy should seem to seek an American withdrawal of this sort, it would be foolhardy to suppose that the guarantees of Article 5 of the North Atlantic Treaty could remain reliably in force. I did not add that there was an obvious inconsistency between this apparent long-term goal of President de Gaulle's and his repeated current assertions that there could be no guarantee of American reliability in the present situation.

In this connection I had occasion to remark to Ambassador Alphand that while we recognize General de Gaulle's right to pursue the goal of an independent nuclear deterrent, and could only regret our own difference of view, without bitterness, we did find it troubling to learn from Chancellor Adenauer that General de Gaulle had spoken to him of the French nuclear deterrent as a good means of triggering American nuclear forces in time of need. It did not seem to us that this concept was likely to lead to fruitful or mutually confident relations among nuclear allies. Ambassador Alphand said that the General had never said anything of this sort to him; I charitably changed the subject.

Ambassador Alphand did recognize that both the President and the Secretary of State had behaved in a most correct fashion and had in fact avoided saying anything which could add to misunderstanding.

Since he said this in what seemed to me a patronizing tone, I told him of my regret that I could not make the same comment about the press conference of President de Gaulle. He stiffened again. I tried to give him relaxation by repeating my view that the opinions and attitudes of the Government of France would not in fact disturb us in our effort to continue in a pattern of trust and cooperation with Europe as whole.

McG. B.[1]

---

[1] Printed from a copy that bears these typed initials.

---

268. Telegram From the Embassy in France to the Department of State

Paris, February 16, 1963, 2 p.m.

3293. Eyes only for President from Ambassador. Reference: Deptel 3900.[1] Many thanks following your kind words. I believe for purposes this message and to save space it would be best to concentrate on last question in your message, namely, whether De Gaulle is planning a systematic campaign to reduce American influence and presence on continent. In effect, answers to this question embrace the ones asked earlier.

You will of course appreciate extreme difficulty of getting any exact evaluation of future policies or actions of General De Gaulle. One of the characteristics of French scene at present time is absence of any certain knowledge of De Gaulle's intentions even on part of Ministers closest to him. It is possible, however, based upon his writings, public statements and actions to set forth certain general considerations.

I do not believe that De Gaulle has a calculated deliberate aim to eliminate American influence and presence on the continent. This, however, requires a definition of what we mean by "American influence". There is, I believe, in his mind a definite distinction between the normal policy activities of a particular non-European country in Europe as

---

Source: Department of State, Central Files, Pol 15–1 Fr. Secret.

[1] In telegram 3900, February 14, the President asked Bohlen for his current evaluation of de Gaulle's present policy and future purposes, and in particular wanted to know whether he was "planning a systematic campaign to reduce American influence and presence on the continent, and if so, what steps he might be likely to take next." (Ibid.)

against what he would regard as temporary excess of control and direction. He will not in my opinion be inclined to oppose or work against as a matter of principle the first type of American influence. It does follow however that there will be many fields in which our interests would be opposed, i.e., in certain economic matters. I believe that we can count on continued French opposition to the exercise of what he would regard as excess American influence or control, particularly in the military fields. De Gaulle has consistently held the belief that the only permanent unit in international affairs is the nation. He is prepared to combine French power with that of friendly nations but not to integrate it. He believes that nationalism expressed in the leadership of essentially one man is a permanent element in the world. It was for this reason that he opposed so vehemently any supranational authority in Europe and has been and is continuing to work for a Europe which would be a union of states. I should say that his strong support of nationalism and opposition to any integrated collective organization (heavily accentuated by his memories of France's humiliation in World War II which I might add is shared by virtually every French person) lies at the bottom of the differences we have and will continue to have with De Gaulle. He obviously envisages at some time in the far distant future a return to a situation in Europe in which there will be no Soviet menace and consequently no need for American military presence. Until that time he most certainly believes in US military presence in Europe. This I am convinced does not stem from any inherent hostilities toward the United States (although there are undoubtedly certain hang-overs from the war) but it is primarily his belief in the future course of events.

It is in the political implications of our military policy that we find the chief application of his views and contradiction to our own. He has made it abundantly plain that he will not participate in any multilateral force under the NATO umbrella which he regards as a mere disguised version of American control of European (in this case French) atomic power as well as our own. I think therefore we can count on his opposition to the MLF although I do not believe this will be very blatant or very open. What however remains the big question is whether or not he envisages at some future date a coordinated European atomic capability of which his force de frappe would be the nucleus or whether he intends firmly to retain this force de frappe entirely in French hands and under French exclusive command.

As to US action in the face of this situation, I shall leave to others any recommendations in the economic field since I see little that we can do [to] avert from dealing with current matters.

I do however have a number of views in regard to our policy in pushing forward with the MLF. It would seem to be extremely unwise for us to push with our like-minded allies on this matter until we have thoroughly thought through how far we ourselves are prepared to go. There are of course many aspects to this program but the chief one in my opinion is one that should be settled at least by the executive as soon as possible, i.e., whether we intend to request legislative changes which would remove our control over the use of the weapons for the MLF. If we intend to leave present presidential authorization for use of this weapon as is, then I believe the multilateral force will soon be exposed as a fraud. On the other hand if we are determined to give the multilateral force, whether under NATO directly or under purely a European component, a genuine automony in the atomic field, I believe we have a proposal which would certainly enlist the support of all of the European members with the exception of France and which would bring to bear on that country very strong pressures indeed. In short, without going into all of the aspects at this point raised by your questions, I would strongly urge, Mr. President, that we do not proceed very much further with our allies until we have come to our own conclusion on the central point of the right to use the weapon without specific US control. I would think that this aspect of the situation would fall well within the problems of the tasks which you have given Ambassador Bruce.

I have not attempted in one message to cover entire subjects raised in your telegram. I can however add any particular point you might desire.

Bohlen

---

269.   Memorandum of Conversation

Washington, February 28, 1963, 5 p.m.

SUBJECT

U.S.-French Relations

PARTICIPANTS

The Secretary
Ambassador Hervé Alphand, French Embassy
Mr. William R. Tyler, Assistant Secretary, EUR
Mr. Johannes V. Imhof, WE

Ambassador Alphand referred to discussions with the Secretary and with the Attorney General on US-French relations and on the lack of

---

Source: Department of State, Secretary's Memoranda of Conversation: Lot 65 D 330. Secret. Drafted by Imhof and approved in S on March 6. At 2:56 p.m. on February 28 Tyler had called Rusk and said that Bundy had been talking with Alphand about seeing the President. Bundy reported that he had discouraged the idea, "but not entirely," since there was not much to talk about at that moment. Rusk told Tyler that there was no problem if the Ambassador wanted to drop in on him. (Ibid., Rusk Files: Lot 72 D 192)

communications between the two governments.[1] He said he had written about this to Couve de Murville and had received a reply. Couve de Murville had said that he did not feel that this was a problem. Ambassador Bohlen was an excellent ambassador and would have access, whenever he desired, to the French Government and to General de Gaulle. Ambassador Alphand said he hoped that this would also apply to him. If we had something we wished to discuss we should avail ourselves of these channels.

The Secretary asked whether this meant that we were supposed to take the initiative. Ambassador Alphand replied evasively. He referred to the exploration which took place after the Nassau conference, pointing out that Ambassador Bohlen was immediately received by Foreign Minister Couve de Murville and by General de Gaulle but that there had been no indication of a special offer to France. Ambassador Alphand added that of course the French had not asked for anything. The Secretary said that we had no information that a different offer to France would have been appropriate. We had expected that there would be a discussion. There had been none. Ambassador Alphand said that the French Government had made its position clear. After General de Gaulle's press conference, the Prime Minister, the Foreign Minister and he (Alphand) had repeatedly clarified the French position. Ambassador Alphand referred to the positive points in President de Gaulle's press conference, including de Gaulle's offer to cooperate in the strategic and technical field, if asked. Ambassador Alphand said that with regard to the multilateral force the French had informed us that they would not block the discussion. On the other hand, it was not appropriate for the French to make proposals of their own.

The Secretary said that as a result of recent French decisions, France now had some difficulties in her relations with some of her allies, including the U.S. Nevertheless, it seemed to be the French position that all the others would have to come to Paris and that it was not up to France to take the initiative. The Secretary noted that General de Gaulle had often made a distinction between the Atlantic Alliance, the importance of which he recognized, and NATO which he felt should be reformed. Nevertheless, General de Gaulle had never made proposals concerning a reorganization of NATO. Ambassador Alphand said he thought that the French had no blueprint for a reorganization of NATO. He also thought that everybody agreed that NATO was in need of reform but that it was difficult to decide precisely what to do about it. He added that the French had taken the initiative many times and had made a great number of suggestions in the past but that most of these suggestions had not been considered, an exception being the case of Laos.

---

[1] For a memorandum of Alphand's conversation with Rusk, see Document 267; no record of the discussion with the Attorney General has been found.

270.   Letter From the Ambassador to France (Bohlen) to the President's Special Assistant for National Security Affairs (Bundy)

Paris, March 2, 1963.

DEAR MAC: I am writing you directly because of the subject matter which I am particularly anxious should not in any form leak out but do wish to get it to the eyes of the President.

You will have seen the telegram that I sent Eyes Only for the President concerning an extremely confidential conversation I had had with Louis Joxe, giving a few of his personal opinions in regard to the present state of mind of de Gaulle.[1] I certainly hope that this message will be kept as labelled since any leakage would be ruinous for Joxe.

I had lunch with Joxe last Tuesday following his talk with de Gaulle on Monday. The first item of direct interest to us is that Joxe is cancelling his proposed trip at the end of March to New York under the auspices of France-Amérique, during which he expected, as you know, to come to Washington to see you and presumably the President. The reason for the cancellation was obviously his talk with de Gaulle who seemed to have objection to his going to Washington on the grounds that a visit by a French Cabinet Officer might give rise to speculations of an unnecessary character. This is obvious nonsense and Joxe virtually admitted it to me and in the circumstances asked my opinion of the desirability of his making a trip just to New York. I told him that I thought it would be better to cancel the entire trip since to go only to New York and not to Washington would create more speculation than if the entire visit were cancelled. He is sending a message to Bill Burden in New York giving the excuse of some general work here and holding out the hope of some future date later on.

I hate to belabor the point but I do wish to emphasize how extremely important it is that the de Gaulle element in this matter be kept quiet since, as Joxe told me, should it leak he would be in very serious trouble with the General.

In addition to this, Joxe told me he found General de Gaulle in a very bad humor; he seemed to be suspicious of virtually everyone and

Source: Johnson Library, National Security Files, Aides Files, Mc G Bundy. Secret; Personal. No drafting information appears on the source text. Also printed in part in Charles E. Bohlen, *Witness to History, 1929–1969*, p. 502.

[1] Telegram 3360 from Paris, February 23, which, in addition to the points noted in Bohlen's letter, reported that de Gaulle had been brooding for some time and at a Cabinet meeting on January 9 had spoken with considerable violence about the United Kingdom. (Department of State, Central Files, Pol 15–1 Fr)

everything and appeared to be brooding about something. Joxe said he was unable to extract from him any information of any value on international affairs and was of the private opinion that de Gaulle is thinking of some move in this field. Joxe admitted that he had no evidence or reason to support this view which appeared to have been based entirely on his past knowledge and association of de Gaulle's character. He, however, ruled out completely again any question of any "deal" with the Soviet Union unless de Gaulle became absolutely convinced that a US/USSR deal was about to be announced, in which case, according to Joxe, he might try and move first. However, this probability was dismissed as a complete fabrication by both of us.

We ran through a number of other subjects which might be conceivable, such as some move for the reorganization of NATO, some move towards the Six or even one toward England, but could find no satisfactory explanation. The only thing that is certain is that according to Joxe de Gaulle was in an extremely bad frame of mind and seemed to be brooding over some possible move.

The thing that strikes me most about the present governmental situation in France is the extraordinary ignorance of de Gaulle's Ministers, even those with whom he has had long and relatively intimate association, and who like Joxe have performed great services for him, of de Gaulle's intentions on any given question, particularly in international affairs. This certainly goes for Couve de Murville, who is extremely agreeable personally but obviously has very little knowledge as to what the General will or will not do. This, as you can well imagine, sets up a situation which makes it very difficult for a foreign diplomat, especially in present circumstances an American one, to operate at all with this government.

I have, I suppose, talked in the last month with at least ten Cabinet Officers in general on the subject of French policy and the General's intentions and have received almost as many different interpretations as there were people asked.

1) I am reasonably convinced, however, that our estimate of de Gaulle is not perhaps as accurate as it could be. He is not, I am convinced, a Machiavellian plotter who thinks through his various moves in foreign affairs with any calculated purpose to be immediately achieved in mind. He has, as demonstrated by his various writings, particularly "The Edge of the Sword" written in 1932, and his "War Memoirs", set forth I think in considerable clarity some of these simple conceptions that he has in mind. In the first place it is important to remember that de Gaulle is distinctly a part of that half of France (or less than one-half) which has been since 1789, and still is, conservative, hierarchical, religious and military. This was one of the reasons for his bitterness against Petain. He is also the product of French military training

pre-World War I and II in that he tends to approach a given problem from a highly analytical and rather simple point of view. His ignorance of the operation of other countries is, I would say, very great, and this is particularly true of the United States. I am sure he has no understanding or indeed interest in the constitutional structure of the United Sates and its bearing on foreign affairs. He is a man of considerable natural courtesy on the surface but extremely cold-blooded and even brutal in his handling or dismissal of immediate subordinate officials if he considers that the need of the country or of the regime requires it. His central thought seems to be that the State (Etat) is the natural and indestructible unit in national affairs. Ideologies—le communisme passera mais la France restera—are passing phenomena which change, but the State as an entity as it has been understood in Europe, is the infrangible permanent unit upon which I would say all of de Gaulle's policy is based.

2) It follows from this conception that he would be very much against any form of integration—anything that would water down the authority of the fundamental unit. He is, as I have said in an earlier telegram, prepared to combine French power with that of other countries in the classic form of alliance, but is *not* ever disposed to merge or share French power with the power of others, especially if the latter is superior.

3) He views the present situation in Europe as an abnormal one stemming from the particular circumstances of World War II. He unquestionably looks forward to some distant time in the future when there will be a disappearance of the Soviet menace as it is today, i.e., the ideological content will gradually pass away from the Russian scene and Russia the State will resume the normal pursuit of its national interests. At that time de Gaulle envisages the retreat of the United States from Europe since the need would no longer exist. Whether this will take 10, 20, 30 or 40 years, I think to de Gaulle it is relatively unimportant. This habit of talking in general terms about the future with no indication of time is one of de Gaulle's puzzling habits. The press and many people often think he is speaking of actual policy when he is really talking about events which may be half a century off. When this happens it would be extremely important for France to have its own nuclear power which, in my opinion, he envisages not so much for eventual use against Russia but as a means for French security and assurance against Germany. And it is here that I believe that the least thought out or the least deeply felt of de Gaulle's policies is to be found. He obviously believes in Franco-German cooperation and harmony with, however, a healthy dose of suspicion stemming from the past. He believes this union or cooperation to be the cornerstone of the future Europe, but he has not fully thought through or indeed in all probability does not have any definite clue as to the resolution of the nuclear problem with Germany. As you

will recall in his interview with me in early January[2] he spoke of the inevitability of Germany acquiring the bomb, but here again the time element was extremely fuzzy and the circumstances even more so.

4) On the subject of his opposition to Great Britain's entry into the Common Market, this is certainly no new factor in his thinking, but I now believe it possible to set forth relatively clearly why he chose January 14 to announce this fact to the world. It must be remembered that de Gaulle found upon his return to power in 1958 France already engaged by the Rome Treaty. He therefore accepted the situation which would have been too difficult to have attempted to change. He did, however, successfully veto the institution of any supranational authorities in Europe (again because of his belief in the eternal, basically unalterable nature of the State). In short, I am convinced that by January 14 he had come to the conclusion (in part because of the Nassau Agreement) that England was not genuinely ripe to become part of Europe and he was definitely concerned lest the other five members of the Common Market for political reasons were prepared to compromise the one economic aspect of the Common Market which was of genuine interest to France, namely agriculture. What was surprising about this press conference was less the content than the tone and final brutality with which he raked Great Britain over the coals and the general nastiness of his comments about the United States. The Nassau shift is more difficult to analyze, but my best guess is that it was George Ball's statements re MLF, plus the President's background press conference in Palm Beach.[3]

As to Franco-American relations and American relations to Europe as a whole, I would like to make a few observations which really are for your and the President's eyes, although I certainly have no objection to your showing this letter—indeed I wish you would—to Dean Rusk personally.

Insofar as Franco-American relations are concerned, I see very little that can be done at the present time to improve them. My relations as far as I can make out with all the French officials continue to be good, and it is, of course, possible for me to see de Gaulle at any time when I have anything particular to take up with him. On the other hand, I think it would be a great mistake to endeavor to see him just for the sake of seeing him when I would have no particular subject for discussion to bring up. Therefore, insofar as France and the United States are concerned, for the immediate future I can see no particular moves that we can make

---

[2] See Document 263.

[3] For Ball's report to the North Atlantic Council on January 11, see Document 164. For a partial transcript of the President's press conference on December 31, see *Public Papers of the Presidents of the United States: John F. Kennedy, 1962*, pp. 913–915.

beyond going on with day to day questions and matters as they come up. I see no prospect of any real dialogue developing between the President and de Gaulle and I am reasonably certain that de Gaulle does not wish to meet with the President because he is not by nature a dialoguist or a discusser. He apparently will often listen to his Ministers but does not ever seriously discuss questions with them, and in his meetings with Macmillan and Adenauer the circumstances have been so different that they would not be applicable to a Kennedy/de Gaulle encounter. Insofar as Europe as a whole—and particularly NATO—are concerned, I would strongly agree with the merits of a multilateral nuclear force, but only if we are able to obtain from Congress the abolition of the American veto power inherent in the idea of unanimity in the body that would exercise supreme decision over the use of that force. As I have already said, if this veto remains, it will be regarded by every European (even though some governments for political and other considerations find it desirable to go along with us) as confirming the correctness of de Gaulle's view about American monopoly and control of nuclear matters. It seems to me so obvious that it must be just as apparent to you as it is to me.

The French have constantly maintained and many Europeans believe that there will be American *reluctance* to use the nuclear weapon in the event of a Soviet attack on Europe because increasingly nuclear conflict would mean the destruction of many American cities. Therefore, anything that gives us the power to *prevent* nuclear action under certain circumstances feeds this thought and tends to confirm it. The fact that our veto over the use of a multilateral force would be shared with other members of the Council or command structure would not affect this basic principle. It is no longer as it was several years back—the European fear that American "irresponsibility" or "hot headedness" would lead us to premature use of the nuclear weapon, but rather the opposite.

I fully realize how terribly difficult it may be to obtain any Congressional consent to the removal of the veto and, as reported in my discussion with Livie Merchant and others with him, I gather this came out rather bleakly in the Congressional discussions they had before coming over. In fact, you will have seen it has appeared already in the French press as part of the American existing position. But it seems to me that we should be very careful that we do not get ourselves out on any limb if in our very best and considered judgment it is impossible to remove the veto. Any other form of voting, whether by three-fourths majority or majority vote minus one, or any other gimmick of this nature, would resolve the problem since it is not the operation of the system in the real event of war that is of importance but its appearance and the interpretations that might be read into it in time of peace. I merely state this as a serious warning and one to be kept in mind as we go down the road.

It seems to me that basically the difficulty of our policy in regard to Europe is that we have not fully adjusted to the fact of European recovery. I do not mean only the economic and financial recovery, but also the moral and spiritual vigor that seems to have accompanied this process, coupled with a very serious but nonetheless real line of thought to the effect that the danger of a Russian attack (particularly after the Cuban crisis) had greatly diminished and, in fact, is non-existent in the eyes of many Europeans. Incidentally, I am sure that it is a factor in de Gaulle's thinking which tends to regard the Cold War as over and the beginnings of the process that he sees for the long-distance future as already in operation.

I have also heard the arguments, and they are extremely convincing, of those who believe that to let Europe leave the existing situation unchanged from a military point of view (i.e., abandon the MLF if we can't get the veto removed) would be a dangerous if not suicidal policy on the grounds that sooner or later we would find ourselves building for the Germans the medium ranged ballistic missiles which they would then man while keeping control of the warheads, as is now the case with tactical weapons in some countries. This is conceivably true but I am not quite able to understand why we would have to agree to make available MRBM's to the Germans although admittedly there are some six hundred Soviet missiles that could rain down on Europe. It should, however, be possible to offset the effect of the Soviet missiles with the increase of our Polaris submarines and, of course, further and continued evidence of our willingness to go to general nuclear war in the event of any attack on Europe. I do not for one minute suggest the withdrawal of any of our forces from Europe unless our dollar balance position makes this an absolute necessity and the Europeans genuinely welsh on their defense commitments. We would still have the problem of the French force de frappe but I am afraid this will be a problem no matter what we do, whether we succeed with the MLF or not. I am well aware of the President's thinking, as it was up to the time I left Washington, on the consequences of a French force de frappe, with which I fully agree, but this will take a good many years to develop and there are also all sorts of possibilities that might occur in the intervening period.

In other words, what I am suggesting as a possible alternative in the event that the MLF, because of the presence of the American veto, proves to be unworkable is really in effect to leave Europe alone politically and, in large measure, unchanged militarily. I would not continue to press the Europeans hard for an increase in conventional forces because certainly conventional and nuclear forces are very closely interrelated.

The question of conventional forces by themselves is very little understood or appreciated by European governments who merely see in them (the nuclear situation being as it is) an element of increased costs without any really convincing military advantage. It is a very hard point to argue since it is extremely difficult to see that there is any probability at all of a Soviet military action (short of an accidental brush of no consequence) which is likely to occur. I realize, of course, the importance of the Berlin question and the need for a certain amount of conventional forces in order to carry out existing plans. I have just seen a summary of Paul Nitze's speech, made out West somewhere, on this subject and it seemed to me that it represents a viewpoint which will have little positive effect here.

I have not dealt with the aspect of the European picture insofar as economic matters are concerned or, in fact, in general with the problem of Great Britain (since I think we can accept as reality that there is no prospect of Britain's joining the Common Market within any reasonable future). Others I know are working very closely on this problem. There is one possibility in regard to France which I have considered somewhat and which might help matters, but I am by no means sure on this point. This would be for the President to sit down and write a very thorough and detailed analysis of United States policy towards Europe which would deal very thoroughly and very carefully with:

1) Our entire defense interests and posture in regard to Europe;
2) Our economic policy present and future in regard to the "Atlantic Community". It would be very important in this point to make clear in irrefutable terms that we had no hidden purpose of domination of European markets, etc., etc.
3) Some thoughts on the problem of the Soviet Union. If there is one factor that seems to crop up rather continuously in French thinking it is that the U.S. and U.S.S.R. are in some fashion either actually negotiating under the table or definitely intend to. I fully realize the difficulty of disproving something that does not exist by mere words, but I would think it would not be too difficult to work out something in this field.

In short, what I have in mind now is the trying out of a dialogue in writing between the President and de Gaulle, not so much for the purpose of attempting to change de Gaulle's attitude but rather to attempt to avoid a deepening of his suspicion and an increasing tendency to take every minor action of the United States and feed it into a preconceived pattern. This is somewhat of an afterthought to the rest of this letter but I would appreciate very much your views and, of course, those of the President on any such possibility.

I hope you do not think that my analysis of de Gaulle in any sense means that I agree with him, because I distinctly do not, but he is, however, a factor which we will have to contend with for a good many years to come and the better we can understand him, the better off we will be.

I am sure there are absolutely no new thoughts in this letter but I wanted to get it off my chest.

I am completely recovered now with only a slightly dimmed sight in one eye, but otherwise just as well as have ever been—in fact possibly better since I am off smoking.

Incidentally, I was very pleased to see the nice article in *Newsweek* on you which I read with great pleasure.[4]

Yours,

Chip

---

[4] On March 7 Bundy replied that he and the President had read this letter "with great interest," and that the President was quite willing to consider a written dialog with de Gaulle. (Johnson Library, National Security Files, Aides Files, Mc G Bundy)

---

271. Memorandum of Conversation

Washington, May 25, 1963, 11 a.m.

SUBJECT

Review of French Foreign Policy

PARTICIPANTS

US	France
The President	Foreign Minister Couve de Murville
William R. Tyler, Assistant Secretary	Ambassador Hervé Alphand
	Charles Lucet, Director of Political Affairs, Foreign Office

The President greeted the Foreign Minister and said he was glad to see him. He asked how things were going on in France. The Minister said the economic situation was generally favorable, but there was a danger of inflation. The government was taking certain measures such as limiting credit, increasing taxes, and liberalizing imports. The President stressed the importance the United States Government attaches to

---

Source: Kennedy Library, National Security Files, France. Secret. Drafted and initialed by Tyler. A memorandum of Ball's conversation with Couve de Murville on the same day covering trade, monetary policy, and nuclear matters is in Department of State, Central Files, Pol Fr-US.

increasing the volume of trade. He said he thought so long as the interest rates and the costs of France and the United States remained relatively stable, we could look forward to such an increase. The Foreign Minister said he thought that the greatest need of the West was to have a sound monetary policy. This aspect of the common interest of the West was not being adequately discussed. The President agreed and said that matters of this sort tended to be treated too technically and to remain too much in the hands of the bankers, who do not see them in terms of the national interest.

The President then turned to the US balance of payments difficulties. He said that the United States would be short another $2.5 billion this year. The danger was not so much a matter of loss of dollars, as the possibility of a run on gold. This was our big problem. The President said that every time it was proposed that we take some steps to bring our payments into balance, we were exposed to loss of confidence in our currency which took the form of a run on the dollar. Couve asked whether the United States Government had ever considered changing the international price of gold. The President asked in turn whether this would not cause a run on the dollar. Couve said it would not, because everyone would have already agreed on the new price beforehand, and each currency would be pegged to it when it came into effect. He went on to say that he thought that the United States was dealing with the problem of the balance of payments piecemeal. The United States, he said, does not have a real deficit. It has a foreign trade surplus. He said he thought that tourists should be counted under trade. He said the real trouble was that there was too much export of US capital abroad. The President agreed that tourists are a form of trade. He pointed out that we lose $1.5 billion under this category in addition to our expenditures for military and foreign aid programs. Couve observed that tourists represented something more than trade, that they played an important political and psychological role in international relations.

The President asked the Foreign Minister what are the objectives of French foreign policy. Couve replied that France's first task was to bring about some kind of union of Western Europe. A start had been made with the Common Market and other international institutions. In the long run one must foresee the existence of the two big powers, the United States and the Soviet Union. The Soviet Union, as the result of the last war, now found itself partly in Europe. It was important that Europe help to keep the balance with the assistance of the United States. He thought that the present Soviet position and role in Europe would not last forever, perhaps 50 years or 20 years. In any case the only thing to do was to build up European unity and strength. Europe would never be able to fight alone or to provide by itself for its security. It would always need US support. Eventually, there would have to be some form of accommodation in Europe by the Soviet Union. This was what General de Gaulle meant when he said "Europe from the Atlantic to the Urals." He said Europe had begun the process of unification in the economic field and this would be followed by progress in the political and military fields, but this would not be outside the framework of the Atlantic alliance. It was important that ties within Europe between the various countries be multiplied. The Franco-German pact[1] was an example of such drawing together. Couve said that the pact itself added nothing substantive to the relations between the two countries but tied them more closely to one another. He said that the object of French policy in Europe was to link Germany so tightly to the West that she would never be in a position to fight a war in Europe without French consent. There was increasing training of German troops, and stockpiling of supplies for the German armed forces in France. Couve said that the UK was part of Europe and in the long run must join Europe. The breakdown of negotiations in Brussels had been unfortunate but the real reason for this was that the EEC did not want the participation of the United Kingdom to change the nature of the European Economic Community. The UK was still subject to a conflict between its relations with the EEC, with the Commonwealth, and with the United States. Couve said he had already felt as long ago as last October that the UK would find itself unable to join the Common Market.

Couve then discussed the charges which were frequently aired publicly that France was promoting an inward-looking Europe. Some people continued to say this and thereby created misunderstanding. The facts were that Europe was only inward-looking politically to the extent that it was trying to find itself and to create its unity. In the economic and commercial fields, however, Europe was outward-looking in relation both to the liberalization and increase of trade, and its responsibilities toward the less developed countries. He pointed out that the common external tariff of the EEC was lower than that of the British, and relatively lower than the US tariff average. Couve then repeated again that Europe could only be said to be inward-looking in a very limited sense, and that in any case the United States could not be left out of the life of Europe in the political and defense fields.

The President thanked the Foreign Minister for his remarks and asked why it was that these thoughts which all sounded very reasonable seemed to take the form of being directed against the United States. The President mentioned specifically General de Gaulle's press conference of January 14, which had created this impression over here. The Presi-

---

[1] For text of the Franco-German pact, January 22, 1963, see *American Foreign Policy: Current Documents, 1963*, pp. 486–488.

dent said that the danger of a Soviet attack against Europe nowadays was minimal. He thought that Europe was quite secure militarily now. The Soviet Union's problem, he said, lay in the direction of Communist China rather than Europe. There were really no problems of major importance between the United States and France, and yet the general atmosphere seemed to reflect a situation in which there were basic differences and disputes between the two countries.

Couve agreed that the interests of France and the United States were essentially the same. He said he thought the only area in which there was a real dispute was in the nuclear field. He said that the United States felt that since it had more than enough to deter the Soviet Union, it was a waste for others to build nuclear weapons. France also understood the US position on the nonproliferation of nuclear weapons. However, France had a different position because France is a different country, and because she must herself look to her own future. From the French point of view there was a strong argument to be made in favor of her having nuclear weapons, just as the British had them. France, he said would never help the Germans to make nuclear weapons.

The President said he understood that these were the reasons why France had made the decision to be a nuclear power. We recognized this fact of life and he wondered just where it was that France and the United States were at odds. Couve said he did not think they were. The President said Western Europe was as militarily secure as any place could be these days. The nuclear matter has been settled. It is now merely a question of whether the United States was right or wrong. He didn't think there was any dispute at this time. Monetary policies were much more important. He thought the thing we must do a little later was to agree on the coordination of our nuclear forces. The President said that it seemed to him that the US decision to make an offer to the French on Skipjack, plus the open door held out to France at the time of the Nassau meeting represented a beginning of movement on what might have been a useful road of cooperation in the nuclear field. He said that the United States also felt that the concept of the MLF was responsive to major German and Italian concerns and desires to play a part in nuclear defense. The Nassau Agreement[2] was not preventing Prime Minister Macmillan from fighting a campaign against Harold Wilson on the basis of maintenance of the national nuclear deterrent, which was what de Gaulle himself would be arguing for.

The Foreign Minister said that there was a basic difference in psychology between France and the UK. The French agreed to, or disagreed with, a proposition on the basis of principle. The British, on the other

---

[2] For text of the Nassau Agreement, December 21, 1962, see ibid., *1962*, pp. 635–637.

hand, made the decision on the basis of convenience, and then made the adjustment of a factual situation so as to conform to principle. The President pointed out that Macmillan had had a problem on his hands as a result of the failure of Skybolt. He had come to Nassau with a statement by over a hundred backbenchers protesting against the cancellation of Skybolt. Couve said France had nothing against the UK's special relationship to the US, which was understandable because of the special ties of language and tradition between the two countries. It was only when this special relationship intruded into problems of immediate concern to the UK and to Europe that there were difficulties. Ambassador Alphand at this point injected the remark that France does not oppose the idea of nuclear cooperation with the United States. Couve said that France did not wish to join the MLF, but was not opposed to it. The President mentioned the value of the idea of the MLF in relation to the German problem. Couve said he had misgivings on this point because he thought the MLF would look increasingly like an essentially US-German business, with a few other much less important countries "such as the Italians" added. He was not sure that the MLF really met German requirements, and feared that it would rather whet the German appetite in the direction of an increasing nuclear role, particularly in view of the size of the German contribution. The President observed that he thought the French force de frappe was a far greater incentive to Germany to play a national nuclear role, than the MLF. Couve said he was convinced that the Germans with their twelve divisions and their important share in the MLF would want to increase their nuclear role. He said it might be true that France was giving Germany a bad example, but France had done everything by herself and on her own. How could Germany do likewise? Where could she get uranium or testing sites? The President said that Israel was able to get uranium. Couve said that even if the Israelis get an atomic device they would be able to make trouble but they would not be able to wage nuclear war in the real sense of the word. The President asked Couve if it was his judgment that we would do better not to go ahead with the MLF. Couve said that from all the reports he had of what the Germans were saying about the MLF, he had doubts and apprehensions about it. The President asked if France would help the Germans in the nuclear field if the US gave up the MLF. Couve replied certainly not. He said that people speak about a European nuclear force but this could only happen if there existed a European political power. This might perhaps come about in 10 or 15 years' time. In that event the German problem would be a different one and Germany would be part of the European political power. In the meantime, there are the French and the UK independent deterrents with national vetos on their use.

The President said he hoped one day we could discuss with France what should be done about China. He asked what was the view of General de Gaulle. Couve said the French Government thinks that China's rift with the Soviet Union will develop and increase and will be a major factor in the next ten years. The President asked Couve what he thought the policies of the West should be in SEATO and in Southeast Asia. Couve said one should also consider the role of Japan, which considers herself as being the most knowledgeable of the Western-oriented powers about China. The President asked what should be done about Southeast Asia, and whether India should be built up. Couve said France did not think that China wanted to take over Southeast Asia but rather to establish a buffer region between the United States and China. If this view was correct, the best thing would be to achieve a political solution of the problems in that area. The President asked about Laos and what should be done there. He said that if things went on deteriorating as they are now we would all be in serious trouble. Couve said he did not think that much could be done other than to go on "with patience and modesty." He did not think that it was possible to pursue a major policy or that there was much that could be done.

The President brought up again the Israeli nuclear problem. He said he hoped that Couve would have an opportunity to discuss it with the Secretary of State. Couve said that France [*1 line of source text not declassified*] was only leasing, and not selling, uranium to Israel. He went on to say that the "only cheerful area" was Africa. France had recently signed a good agreement with Guinea. He thought that things were going along pretty well with Algeria. The President mentioned that there were great difficulties in Haiti and asked about the French position there. Couve said there were several hundred French nationals in Haiti. He said that the message which de Gaulle had sent to Duvalier in reply to his letter had been sent off by coincidence at the time of the crisis. The President said we were watching the situation closely and that we could not allow the creation of another Castro-type regime in this hemisphere. Should this occur, we would have to intervene.

The President again asked the Foreign Minister what could be done to improve the image of our relations with France. He referred to the recent GATT Ministerial Meeting,[3] and said that that had finally gone off all right after some difficulties. The President referred to rumors that France was contemplating taking more of her ships out of NATO. The Foreign Minister refrained from commenting on this last remark by the President, but said that France attached very great importance to the GATT meeting and to the trade field as a whole. The President recalled

---

[3] May 16–21 at Geneva.

that he had told General de Gaulle when he had seen him in Paris in 1961 that the United States would welcome an increased European role in Latin America, and that France, because of her great cultural tradition, as well as her economic and commercial role, could play a considerable part in our efforts to improve and stabilize economic and political conditions in that area. The Foreign Minister agreed that this was in France's interest as well as ours.

The conversation came to an end at about 12:15.

---

272. Circular Telegram From the Department of State to Certain European Missions

Washington, June 15, 1963, 6:12 p.m.

2155. 1. US has been officially informed that France will shortly withdraw from earmark remainder its naval forces committed to NATO. This action would conclude process started by French in 1959 when they withdrew French Mediterranean Fleet from NATO earmarking. Objective of present step very likely de Gaulle desire avoid even appearance of impairment full freedom of action for French naval units in war.

2. Not clear whether forces to be withdrawn include units earmarked for both Channel Command and SACLANT. If former, seven destroyers involved. If both, action could involve one aircraft carrier, 21 destroyers and destroyer escorts, 5 submarines, as well as several squadrons maritime aircraft. We understand withdrawal these units from earmarked category would have no appreciable military significance so long as French Naval forces continue their present cooperation with other NATO forces in planning and training through informal bilateral arrangements. French informant has indicated such cooperation will continue.

Source: Department of State, Central Files, Def 6–8 Fr/NATO. Secret. Drafted by Kranich and Popper on June 14, cleared with WE and the Department of Defense, and approved by Tyler. Sent to 15 missions in Europe.

3. Political implications of contemplated French actions are far more serious. They are sure to be interpreted by press as blow to Alliance military effort and its prestige unless action taken to counteract such impressions. Much will depend on how French publicize withdrawal, since if de Gaulle desires he could make action appear as significant slap to NATO. On other hand, if French willing to restrict announcement their action to NATO military and political channels, and simply list zeros under earmarked forces columns in Intermediate Review submission, political effect may be minimized. To date we have impression French as desirous as we to have minimum of publicity.

4. Accordingly, we plan to say in NAC and official circles that we regret French action. Even though under present circumstances it may not have great military significance, it cannot help but affect adversely solidarity and psychological well-being of Alliance. NATO military structure raison d'etre is to plan and conduct if necessary military operations on basis of national commitments of forces. Adequate forces are essential to this purpose. National commitment of forces to NATO, both through earmarking and assigning, is means whereby active cooperation in NATO military planning and training is best assured. Withdrawal of commitments greatly decreases extent to which Alliance can count on quick and effective reaction to attack, and informal bilateral arrangements however useful in training, etc., are no substitute for this assurance.

5. Publicly in response to questions we would say that while we of course regret French action, it has no great military significance, since most important point is whether French Naval forces maintain adequate capability and are in fact available for defense of West in event of war. We assume this to be the case.

6. Above represents Dept views. JCS now considering specifically military implication of expected French action

Rusk

273. **Telegram From the Embassy in France to the Department of State**

Paris, August 20, 1963, 6 p.m.

808. Pass Defense. From Burns.[1]

1. Following constitutes informal views to questions raised in Deptel 734[2] regarding withdrawal from NATO certain earmarked units of French Fleet.

2. After French withdrew their Mediterranean Fleet from NATO in 1959, SHAPE attempted to develop co-operation agreements with French authorities but suspended talks in February 1960 when became apparent that no formal agreement could be reached. At present time, therefore, no formal agreement exists between SACEUR and French for either peace time co-operation or war time missions. Nevertheless, U.S. 6th Fleet has in the past conducted many bilateral operations in conjunction with French naval forces involving temporary commitment of forces for specific training exercises.

3. COMSIXTHFLT and ALESC (Commander Toulon Squadron) have prepared peace time bilateral instruction for conduct of simple US/French exercises of opportunity between units of 6th Fleet and Toulon Squadron. It is primarily communication plan to provide for conduct of typical exercises that can be undertaken on short notice whenever US or French units join up at sea without resorting to elaborate preplanning and lengthy operations orders. This agreement has been prepared but is unsigned, intended date of promulgation is 1 Sept 63 under joint signatures of COMSIXTHFLT and ALESC. No other formal bilateral US/French agreements exists.

4. For information, similar US/UK agreement between COMSIXTHFLT and CINCMED has been in effect since 1960 also. Preliminary steps have been taken to establish such agreements with Italian and Hellenic Navies.

5. In addition to foregoing, bilateral exercises of larger scope are conducted from time to time. No standing agreement exists, however, to conduct such exercises. They are planned for on case-by-case basis and, as in case of recent US/French Fairgame exercise, a jointly agreed, one

---

Source: Department of State, Central Files, Def 6–8 Fr/NATO. Secret. Repeated to CINCLANT for POLAD.

[1] Robert Burns, Second Secretary at the Embassy in Paris.

[2] Telegram 734, August 8, asked for a summary of agreements between the French Fleet and the U.S. Fleet in the Mediterranean. (Department of State, Central Files, Def 6–8 Fr/NATO)

time instruction from COMSIXTHFLT and Alesc was issued to guide participating forces.

6. Moreover, French naval forces continue to participate in numerous NATO exercises both in Mediterranean and Atlantic. French officers customarily attend AFMED training conferences and obligate their forces in specific exercises.

7. From record of recent debate in NAC, cannot be determined whether French are willing merely to establish some form of peace time co-operation or are willing to discuss war time missions with SACLANT. While SHAPE does not exclude possibility that French may now be willing to work out an agreement on war time missions with SACLANT, based upon SHAPE's experience to date, it feels improbable that negotiations with SACLANT will extend beyond memorandum of agreement for record.

8. Subordinate ACE commands particularly AFMED, believe that existing co-operation in Mediterranean between ACE and French Fleets is excellent and that renewed attempts to reach written agreement would probably jeopardize this co-operative atmosphere. SHAPE would therefore prefer not to initiate talks with French on peace time co-operation. If SACLANT is successful in working out peace time co-operative arrangements with French, SACEUR would of course be very interested to know details thereof.

9. SHAPE does not object to any informal or formal written agreement between French and SACLANT as a NATO commander which pins down specific missions for French vessels in war time. In fact, written agreement should strengthen present imprecise relationship. SHAPE could not agree in advance, however, to such an instrument which might extend to operations in SACEUR's area of responsibility. If, however, during the forthcoming talks between SACEUR and French authorities any areas of interest to SACEUR are raised on war time missions, SHAPE will be pleased to send representatives and to participate as appropriate.

10. SHAPE feels that it is important to obtain written agreement from French for war time missions, particularly timing and extent of actions, but at same time believes this should be accomplished without establishing or formalizing new category of assignments as suggested by Stikker.

11. SACEUR is of course, aware that French have announced that they intend to concentrate their naval forces in Atlantic and moreover that MOD Messmer recently stated that French no longer attach great importance Mediterranean lines of communication. Situation with respect to French Fleet is, however, definitely not clear. For example, French reply to 1963 Intermediate Review which projects French plans

through end 1964, states that from January 1, 1964 French forces organized so as to be concentrated and reinforced in North Atlantic. In same reply, however, French list forces that will be available for cooperation with NATO forces in SACEUR's area under national command. These are essentially the same as those forces listed last year and exceed requirement set forth in MC 26/4.[3] There is some evidence that French do not expect to move their forces from the Mediterranean to Atlantic until second half of 1965 in which case Intermediate Review would be accurate in showing no change from previous reports. This move is probably tied to completion of land division, which will be base for aircraft on carriers *Foch* and *Clemenceau*, whose home port being changed from Toulon to Brest. Other forces involved are detroyers associated with these aircraft carriers. However, info available here indicates that French Naval Forces adequate to establish an effective wartime barrier against enemy submarines attempting to enter the Mediterranean at Gibralter will continue to be based in the Mediterranean. These forces include submarines, destroyer escorts, maritime patrol aircraft and the light carrier *Arromanche* which will shift from a training role to ASW.

12. Regardless of degree to which French wish to shift focus their strategy from Mediterranean to Atlantic, SHAPE believes there will continue to be national considerations which will necessitate French presence in sizable numbers in Mediterranean. For example, there exists at Toulon an important industrial establishment and various training facilities including a naval missile range which will inevitably cause return of units to Mediterranean should the French so desire. Marseilles is one of more important French ports, Corsica is French territory, and Algeria represents potential vacuum which neither French nor Alliance can allow be dominated by Communists. In addition, port of Gabes in Tunisia is an important northern terminus of French Sahara pipeline. Inherent mobility of naval forces will permit new concentration of French Fleet in Mediterranean at any time. In this connection although French may expect to station their major naval units at Brest, it is noteworthy that they are able to reach Mediterranean or other ACE waters within 48 hour leeway to be on station under definition of Category A forces. Thus although French can disclaim for political reasons any vital interest in Mediterranean, they cannot separate themselves from economic or military reality.

13. Question of withdrawal French aircraft from NATO assignment will be subject separate message.[4]

Bohlen

---

[3] Not found.

[4] Not further identified.

274. Telegram From the Embassy in France to the Department of State

Paris, September 15, 1963, 5 p.m.

1455. For Secretary. I asked Couve de Murville this morning if there was anything he could tell me on his talk with Schroeder and what views if any that he had in regard to post-Adenauer Germany from the point of view of foreign policy. Couve de Murville said in his discussions with Schroeder in regard to the talks with the Soviet Union it was his impression the Germans were primarily interested in not appearing to block the possibilities of a "détente" (a view which Couve said did not trouble the French Government), but in order to protect German interests would always insist that reunification figure as the purpose of any discussions with the Soviets on German matters. He said he had told Schroeder that he would be interested to know what success he would have with Rusk or Home in adopting this procedure with the Soviets. In regard to post-Adenauer Germany he said that all of the difficulties which might arise in this field were largely due to domestic German politics within the CDU.

At this point Couve on his own initiative launched into quite a complaint in regard to U.S. policy in regard to Germany. He said that American policy was entirely directed to presenting Germany with a choice between France and the U.S., that we were conducting a major propaganda campaign in Germany against France and Franco-German association, that these "activities" in Germany were causing resentment here in Paris since the French thought that the real choice for West Germany should always be between Western oriented policy or Soviet Union, etc., etc. I told Couve that I did not know where he got this information, that we had no policy or propaganda in Germany designed to interfere with Franco-German collaboration and would be very interested to have him give me some specifics in support of his charges. I also suggested that he might care to discuss this with you and even the President. Couve de Murville then made the remarkable statement that he was sure that the President and you would deny it and be in completely good faith but that activities of this nature were going on in Germany (his implication being that some American services there were acting in contravention of governmental policy). When I pressed him further on his statement he had no evidence or information to support it beyond saying it was what some Germans had told him. He maintained throughout that U.S. policy

---

Source: Department of State, Central Files, Pol US-WGer. Secret; Limit Distribution. Repeated to Bonn.

in Europe was directed primarily to weaning Germany away from close association with the French.

We then had rather a lengthy discussion in regard to Franco-American problems. I pointed out that most of the questions that had caused difficulties between us had been on French initiative, mentioning in this connection French actions in NATO, statements by de Gaulle giving as an example de Gaulle's statement of mid-August in regard to Vietnam which will be covered in a separate message.[1] Couve de Murville continued to maintain that the purpose of U.S. policy in Europe was to prevent the serious consolidation of Europe and to retain for the U.S. a position of authority in defense, economics, and elsewhere. It was quite easy to make a case against this view but what was curious was the persistency with which Couve de Murville maintained his attitude.

Comment: Since it is relatively uncharacteristic of Couve de Murville to launch into such a statement I would be inclined to attribute it to some special concern in the French Government over their relations with Germany. It has become clear that the discussions with Schroeder last week did not produce any real agreement, particularly on East-West issues, and that the French therefore are attempting to blame the U.S. and its policy for a lack of development in Franco-German relations. He also took mild exception to a speech of mine in Bordeaux last weekend in which I said the U.S. was for a liberal "open" Europe as against a closed inhibited one. Couve said it was critical of French policy. In any case it will be extremely interesting to see what line Couve de Murville will take when in Washington.[2]

Bohlen

---

[1] Not found. For text of de Gaulle's statement on Vietnam, August 29, 1963, see *Major Addresses, Statements and Press Conferences of General Charles de Gaulle, May 19, 1958–January 31, 1964*, p. 241; see also *American Foreign Policy: Current Documents, 1963*, p. 869.

[2] In a separate message to Rusk on September 25 Bohlen reported that it was clear to him that Couve de Murville was very concerned about the state of French policy and sought to throw the blame onto the United States for the difficulties France was encountering with Germany. Bohlen suggested that it would be very useful for Rusk and the President to have a "frank and serious conversation" with Couve de Murville during his visit to Washington. (Telegram 1465; Department of State, Central Files, Pol Fr–US)

275. Memorandum of Conversation

Washington, October 7, 1963.

SUBJECT

    Franco-American Relations and Europe

PARTICIPANTS

US	France
The President	Mr. Couve de Murville [1]
Mr. Ball	Ambassador Alphand
Ambassador Bohlen	Mr. Lucet
Mr. Tyler	

The President asked the Foreign Minister about the state of Franco-American relations and whether they were improving. The Foreign Minister said that a greater degree of mutual understanding was required on methods and procedures rather than on questions of substance with regard to East-West relations. He also said that the European relationship should be looked at, not merely Franco-US relations. The President asked how the Foreign Minister thought that our approaches differed. Couve said the main question was whether Europe was going to be a going concern with her own policy, including her own means of defense. There was a strong inter-relationship between Europe and the United States in trade and economic problems. This was reality and was in no way dramatic. If there were questions which arose these should be discussed so as to find a way of promoting unity. It was important that Europe and the United States work together with regard to LDC's. Couve pointed out that US trade with Europe had increased greatly in the last few years. In the political military field there was a change going on compared with the immediate post-war situation. Europe was now able to offer and accept a greater share in the burdens of the world. This meant two things: (1) Europeans must reach agreement among themselves on how to unite; (2) they must adjust their relations with the United States in such a way as to reach agreement across the Atlantic. He said there had been increasing economic unity among the Six in the last five years. He said there were still intra-European differences but as the Common Market developed, these would be discussed increasingly with the United States. The major problem, he

---

Source: Department of State, Central Files, Pol 1 Fr-US. Secret. Drafted and initialed by Tyler; approved by U on October 11 and by the White House on October 15. The meeting was held at the White House on October 15.

[1] Couve de Murville was in the United States to attend the 18th session of the United Nations General Assembly.

said, was that of defense, in particular the nuclear problem which is very difficult and important. At the moment he could see no solution. There was the great problem of Germany, also the Soviet Union. Intra-European ideas on defense were not all identical. He was not able to offer any solution but the problem was there and must be discussed within Europe and with the United States. Europe was prepared to accept her share of the burden of expenditures and defense. With regard to Germany, French policy was based on the idea that Germany must be on the side of the West as part of Europe and of the Free World. Germany should be powerful enough not to be submerged and this meant that she must be an ally of the United States, and attached to the Western world. France's major preoccupation was to try to prevent anything which would detach Germany from the West, for this would lead to neutrality and to an eventual takeover by the Soviet Union. This was why France was so careful in the field of negotiations with the Soviet Union. The Soviet proposals were designed to create doubts among the Germans. These doubts were only increased when France and the United States appeared to be quarreling with each other. This was very bad for common interests and anything which we could do to avoid conflict, or the appearance of conflict, between our two countries would be most helpful.

The President said that one of the unintended results of the Franco-German Treaty of last January was that it made it appear as though France and the United States had basically different aims. The treaty really looked as though it were something more than the healing of old wounds, but rather as though it were outside of, and directed against, NATO. The President said he shared the desire to bring Franco-US relations closer. If these appeared to diverge on defense and European problems this was certainly bad for Germany. It would be good if we could normalize our relations on NATO and economic matters. The President asked how far apart we really were.

The Foreign Minister said that the treaty had in fact been signed outside of NATO, but Franco-German relations in themselves, and the grouping of six countries in Europe, are outside of, and not part of, NATO. He felt that the Franco-German Treaty strengthened the Alliance but was different from NATO. He agreed with the President that the divergencies between us are bad for Germany. With regard to NATO, everybody knows that since the war the United States had assumed almost the entire burden of defense. This was the case in 1949 and the situation was almost the same today, fourteen years later, even though the problem had basically changed. The reason why most countries in NATO were satisfied with the present situation was because sacrifices go together with responsibilities. NATO was adopted when Europe was flat on her back. Today European countries should have a greater share in defense. The nuclear problem was a special problem, he said, but it should be dealt with in this same spirit. NATO was based on US command because it was normal that it should be in the hands of the most powerful country in the Alliance. However NATO had been created at the moment of the greatest crisis that the West had faced in Europe. Now there was less danger of aggression from the Soviet Union. However today NATO was still on a war footing which was difficult to sustain. It was very difficult for countries that have a tradition of responsibility for defense to bring contingents into an international army without being given a greater share and a greater role. This applied not only to France but also to the UK and Germany. Formerly when the danger was greater, France had no desire to assume responsibilities. Now the converse was true.

The President said that whenever we even looked as though we were contemplating reducing the extent of the US contribution this had gotten us into difficulties with our allies. The Foreign Minister agreed that this was the case with regard to Germany. He said the Germans were apprehensive and unhappy. The President referred to the concern in Germany at the prospect of our withdrawing a cavalry regiment which had only represented part of the increase at the time of the Berlin crisis. The Foreign Minister agreed that there was a real problem. What difference, he asked rhetorically, does the withdrawal of 3000 men make to the defense of Europe? Turning to economic matters, he said that the major problem was not that of chickens but of agriculture. He thought that in this field, too, there was no basic contradiction between French and US interests and policies. Mr. Ball referred to the recent measures which the French government had taken facilitating US exports of fruit to France. He said that these had been very helpful. The Foreign Minister referred to the "Kennedy Round." He said we would have very vigorous discussions, no doubt, but apart from inherent difficulties France was of the opinion, contrary to what was often said, that it would be a good thing to liberalize trade and lower tariff barriers. The Common Market must not be protectionist but rather more liberal than individual countries were. Ambassador Alphand complained that the press continued to talk about Europe being "inward looking." The Foreign Minister said this was a British invention. The President said that what really mattered was not so much trade as the problem of the balance of payments. For the United States, foreign trade was, relatively, less important than this. He said that we should create a system within the West which would result in a relatively even flow of international payments. He said, for example, that France was increasing her reserves by $25 million a month. We should look to see what can be done to avoid this kind of situation. New steps were needed to bring the balance of payments problem under control. He said that it was of course related to trade. The

Foreign Minister said that he did not think that trade played such a big role. What the President was referring to was the international monetary problem. He did not intend to go into this complicated matter at this time. He agreed that balance of payments problem was a major one. He said he had had no more success in persuading us to accept his ideas on what should be done to remedy the situation, than in persuading his own government (the Foreign Minister was alluding here to his recommendation that the price of gold be raised). The President said that US foreign investment was an American problem but he asked what about tourism. The Foreign Minister said that the United States and France did not have to worry about individual payments, but that the important element in the situation was that of the flow of long- and short-term capital. The President said we had tried to do something about long-term investment abroad. This was very difficult because every time we did something it had caused widespread concern. He said we had increased interest rates domestically which should help the problem. The Foreign Minister asked what Europe could do about American investments: To forbid them would be regarded as an anti-American action ("Inward looking," quipped Ambassador Alphand).

The President went back to the subject of NATO and said he could not see where the disagreement lay. He did not disagree with anything Couve had said about NATO so far. He said it was true there was less danger of war but at the same time it was difficult to do anything in the way of reduction of forces because of German nervousness. He wondered where all this took us in our relations with France. The Foreign Minister said that with regard to France and NATO there was only one sensible thing to do: To leave things as they were and never to speak about them. France was being reproached for having only two divisions instead of four and for having a nuclear program. But this did not weaken NATO. If war were to come, French divisions and her ships would be fighting on the side of the United States. The President said that when the United States does anything people worry about it. He thought that this principle should work both ways and not just against us. Ambassador Bohlen said that what really counted were new acts by France taken without consultation with her allies and contrary to the spirit of NATO, e.g., her latest withdrawal of ships, and earlier initiatives. Mr. Ball said that this point should be stressed. If we move or shift troops, then we do it against a considerable background of doubt and apprehension which has been stimulated by France claiming that we have it in mind to withdraw from Europe. The Foreign Minister denied that this was so. He said that France felt that her defense arrangements could not be based on the assumption that the United States was going to be militarily present in Europe forever. Mr. Ball said that one of the difficulties with General de Gaulle's statements on the defense of

Europe was that although they sounded precise, the time factor was not defined, so that he made it sound as though the United States was going to pull out now.

The President asked the Foreign Minister about the significance of the recent speech by the State Secretary in the Foreign Office, Habib-Deloncle.[2] The Foreign Minister replied that he thought the excitement it had caused was due to the workings of "complicated British minds," which chose to see in it a French plot to make things more difficult for the MLF. He said that General de Gaulle never saw the speech before it was delivered, but that he himself had seen it. The only significance it had was that if the UK was prepared to join Europe in the nuclear field, this could lead to an agreement with the Community. The President asked how Europe was going to organize herself in nuclear matters. The Foreign Minister referred to his own remarks at the Ottawa meeting in May.[3] He said NATO had shown that in order to organize defense you have to have valid political power to control it. If Europe were to achieve political unity then her resources could be put at the disposal of a nuclear force. The President said he didn't see on what we differed with France. Was it deficiency in liaison? Why do we give the appearance of having friction with France, which is an unhealthy condition? He said he thought that we were quite close on Laos, but General de Gaulle's statement on Vietnam had been unhelpful, particularly with regard to its timing. The Foreign Minister said that it had not been General de Gaulle's intention to do anything unhelpful. France had been in a position at the time when she had to say something. France had never had very good relations with the Diem Government. There was a French interest in developing economic and cultural, rather than political, relations. He felt that in the long run, evolution seemed to lead in the direction of the unification and neutrality of Vietnam. He said that he was aware that the statement had been badly received in Washington, but it had been no better received in Moscow or Peiping. Mr. Ball repeated that the timing had been unfortunate. The Foreign Minister said he did not know what the real situation was in Vietnam. The President said he thought it was being made to appear worse than it is. The Foreign Minister said France had been in Indochina during a period of some ninety years and her experience had always been that any problems must be discussed with the Chinese. He thought that this held true today also. He said the Russians were out of Vietnam and Southeast Asia in general and that they have almost no influence there. He said

---

[2] The text of Habib-Deloncle's speech before the Council of Europe, September 23, was transmitted in telegram 1421 from Paris, September 24. (Department of State, Central Files, Pol 3 Council of Europe)

[3] Regarding the North Atlantic Council meeting at Ottawa, see Documents 196, 197, and 199.

they were in roughly the same position as the UK: both were getting less and less influential, whereas the Chinese influence was increasing.

The President asked about the possible nuclear role of Israel, and the French position. The Foreign Minister said France had not changed her policy and was following the situation closely. France wanted to prevent Israel from acquiring MRBM's. He said they now have only small missiles of the "Véronique" type for use with conventional warheads.

The President asked the Foreign Minister how he suggested that France and the United States manage their affairs in the next few months to indicate a greater harmony between them. He said he thought that this would be useful for France too. The Foreign Minister agreed and said it would also be useful to Germany. He said the US and French would be meeting in Paris within the next two months (NATO meeting) and that more talks would then be held. It was a matter of discussing outstanding problems of mutual interest and trying to dispel suspicions and grievances. The President asked what Prime Minister Pompidou had meant when referring to a certain "economic press" being sold out to US interests. The Foreign Minister brushed this aside and said that this was merely a matter of French domestic politics.

276.   Memorandum of Conversation

Washington, November 25, 1963.

SUBJECT

French-American Relations; Forthcoming Visit of General de Gaulle to the United States

PARTICIPANTS

US	France
President Johnson[1]	President de Gaulle[2]
The Secretary	Foreign Minister Couve de Murville
Assistant Secretary Tyler	Ambassador Alphand
E. S. Glenn (interpreter)	

Source: Department of State, Presidential Memoranda of Correspondence: Lot 66 D 149. Confidential. Drafted by Glenn and approved in S on November 26 and by the White House on December 2. The meeting was held in Rusk's office. A memorandum of de Gaulle's conversation with Rusk along similar lines on November 24 is ibid., Secretary's Memoranda of Conversation: Lot 65 D 330.

[1] President Kennedy was assassinated November 22 in Dallas, Texas.

[2] De Gaulle was in Washington for President Kennedy's funeral.

The President thanked General de Gaulle for having crossed the ocean to express the sympathy of France for the United States in this hour of need. He expressed the great personal admiration he has for General de Gaulle and mentioned their conversation in 1960.[3] General de Gaulle spoke of the emotion of the French people at the news of President Kennedy's death. President Kennedy was extremely popular with the French people. General de Gaulle feels that we owe it to President Kennedy's memory to proceed along the path which he had traced. This path is that of continued mutual trust between the United States and France. The difficulties between the two countries have been greatly exaggerated. One can say in fact that many of the descriptions which have appeared referring to tensions between the two countries were descriptions of something that didn't exist. In reality those difficulties are minor and are the result of a change in the reciprocal situations of the two countries, whose relative circumstances have somewhat changed, mainly from the military point of view but also, up to a point, from the political one. This calls for some adjustments, but for no major change. What is important is that France knows perfectly well that she can count on the United States if she were attacked. Likewise, if the United States found itself at war, France would come in with such means as she possesses at the side of the United States. President de Gaulle had sent a telegram to that effect to the late President.[4]

President Johnson (speaking before the interpretation had been completed, and in particular before General de Gaulle's statement about Cuba was mentioned) stated that the attitude of France at the time of the Cuban crisis proved that France would stand by the United States. The question is simply one to make all the necessary arrangements for mutual benefit. The President said he hoped that General de Gaulle would go on with his plans and return in the near future to the United States. His great wisdom will be of great help to us, and Americans admire him very much.

General de Gaulle thanked President Johnson for his kind words. President Kennedy had paid him a visit in Paris[5] and he intended to return it. At that time he intended to speak very frankly of all questions of mutual concern.

As to what France is trying to do, it is to organize Europe—continental Europe—from an economic point of view and after this is done, perhaps also from the political point of view. To do so will be difficult, but President de Gaulle is hopeful. The organization of Europe is something of the greatest importance for the relations of the continent with

---

[3] Not further identified.

[4] Not found.

[5] See Document 230.

the entire Free World. When this organization is completed, Europe will open negotiations with the United States on economic questions. The intent in regard to these negotiations is to take a very liberal attitude; Europe does not aim at autarchy; on the contrary she intends to keep all windows open, and considers this to be of the greatest importance.

President Johnson said that he felt sure that General de Gaulle knows that the obligation of the United States is absolute, and that we are fully committed to common defense. This is the most important. The United States has also the firm belief that France is likewise committed. We may have some problems but we will find a solution to them. It is easier to knock somebody's barn down than to build one but it is not the right way of acting. The President feels no doubt that if General de Gaulle puts his great mind at the service of the common interests of the two countries all the difficulties will be overcome. He hopes therefore to see the General back in the United States in February or at such time as will suit the General. At that moment we will work together not only to consolidate each of our nations separately but to consolidate both of them together.

General de Gaulle thanked the President and said that he did not wish to take any more of his time. He just wanted to add one word. What he had seen on this day in the United States greatly encouraged him and made him feel that we will be able to fulfill the obligation which we all have to President Kennedy. General de Gaulle has seen a great display of unity among the American people and he can assure President Johnson of the sympathy and the friendship of the entire world to the United States. This is very good for our common interests.

President Johnson thanked General de Gaulle for having crossed the Atlantic on this day. This is something which the American people will not soon forget. They are grateful that General de Gaulle has placed his great name and his great leadership at their side on this day.

On the way to the elevator President Johnson reiterated his hope to see General de Gaulle in the United States in February. General de Gaulle said that the details can be discussed through the usual diplomatic channels.

277. Memorandum From the Ambassador to France (Bohlen) to Secretary of State Rusk

Paris, December 13, 1963.

I am setting forth a number of conclusions which I have reached after a year in this country in regard to the foreign policy of France (or rather of de Gaulle), its relations to the U.S., and a number of suggestions for U.S. attitudes. While this memorandum is primarily prepared for your use as background material in your talks with French officials here, it may be, if you consider it wise, worthwhile taking back to Washington for presentation to President Johnson. I shall endeavor to be as brief as possible.

1. The character of de Gaulle is completely formed by his education, experience and his own characteristics, which are highly egocentric [*less than 1 line of source text not declassified*]. Insofar as I can ascertain from conversation and reading, he has never been induced to change any of his basic views by conversations with others nor as a result of concessions or favors done him by other countries. The only conceivable circumstances that can produce a shift or change in his policies, if not his attitude, would be an actual change in the conditions under which he is operating. (This was noticeable in the case of the Algerian question.)

2. The relations with the U.S., as unsatisfactory as they are to us, are in my opinion the way that de Gaulle wants them. Given his strong emphasis on the nation as the only real international unit, and his deep dislike for this reason of any form of integration or any other association which waters down the sovereignty of a country, it is natural that he should stress the *independence* of France in all matters. In some inherited matters where he believes that France in her "weakness" of the post-war period allowed her sovereignty to be subscribed, he has sought to disengage the French Government from these commitments wherever possible, i.e., NATO. He undoubtedly feels that *too close* a relationship between a relatively small country (which he bitterly recognizes to be the case in regard to France) and the U.S. could in his view lead only to an actual derogation of the weaker country's sovereignty.

3. Therefore (leaving aside what conceivably might have been the result of an early agreement by us to provide France with atomic secrets), I am quite convinced now that de Gaulle is not interested in any conceivable offer we might make on atomic matters. I do not mean that he would not perhaps be willing to pick up items here and there which

Source: Department of State, Conference Files: Lot 66 D 110, CF 2350. Secret. Rusk was in Paris for the North Atlantic Council Ministerial Meeting December 16–18.

would have some immediate value to the French atomic program and might save France some money, but rather that France's policy under de Gaulle would not be changed in any important aspect by a major concession in this field.

4. It is noteworthy that the relationship of France has not improved with any country in the world since de Gaulle came to power. The Franco-German Treaty is in a sense an improvement but has been extremely soured by recent German attitudes towards the U.S., and in particular by the current Common Market quarrel. This, I feel, is part of de Gaulle's emphasis on independence and a genuine preference in many ways for going it alone, and I consider that many of his acts, particularly in some of his public statements—where action is not possible for France—have been motivated purely by a desire to strike out on a difficult line for French policy than that pursued, for example, by the U.S. or even by other allies. His statement on Vietnam of last August I believe falls into the first category and his refusal to talk to the Soviets with the British and ourselves into the second.

Having outlined what might be called negative elements in de Gaulle's policy, I should like to counterbalance these now with some of the positive ones which I do not feel are widely understood and are certainly not accepted in the U.S.

1. De Gaulle does not for the foreseeable future desire in any way to see the U.S. leave Europe, especially militarily. We have some 180 installations in France and approximately 35,000 troops, and apart from current problems which arise in any country there has been no sign of any concerted French move to push us out or to make life difficult for our forces here.

2. De Gaulle believes very strongly in the Atlantic Alliance, but for the reasons given above in view of his dislike of integration he does not like the NATO organization as it now stands. It is by no means clear what he has in mind, if indeed he has anything in mind, in regard to the reorganization of NATO. I am inclined to believe that he simply does not like a NATO Supreme Commander (especially if he is an American), the international staff and the elements of integration.

3. I believe personally that there is no possibility that de Gaulle would try to double-cross the Alliance by a deal with the Soviet Union. He undoubtedly looks forward to a time many, many years hence when the Soviet Union will cease to be a cause and merely become a Russian country. At that time obviously he would expect France to welcome Russia back into the community of European nations. This, however, is problematical and so far into the future as to be unnecessary even to consider.

4. In keeping with his desire to show independence he is undoubtedly at the moment creating at least the impression that he is contemplating some move in regard to Communist China. I do not think at the moment that this involves any conscious step in the direction of diplomatic representation but merely some developments in trade and cultural affairs. This in part is again based upon his desire to show independence from the U.S. and also is connected with his belief that a settlement in Southeast Asia is only possible with the consent of Communist China.

There are in fact about four levels in France in regard to relations to the U.S. which can be discerned.

1. There is first of all General de Gaulle himself, operating from the Elysée and basing his actions on his own thoughts, his own instincts, analysis of information received, and according to all reports withdrawing more and more from any intimate contact with his colleagues. He quite literally has no close friends or even associates.

2. There is the Government, and I would say by and large, with particular reference to the Foreign Office, that the members of the Government are on the whole favorably disposed towards the U.S. They are disquieted and some are alarmed by de Gaulle's attitude and frequently go out of their way personally to show that they do not share his attitude.

3. There is a particular vicious and uninstructed group, in the UNR especially, who swallow 100% the worst features of de Gaulle's attitude towards the U.S. (This includes a very small number of ministers, [less than 1 line of source text not declassified]. Their views are expressed in numbers of speeches and also have a certain penetration in the state-owned RTF and very much less so in the press.

4. Finally, there is the great mass of French people, and I would like to state that in all the times I have been in France I have never seen more genuine pro-American sentiment among the people of France as a whole. This was completely borne out by the strong reaction and the nature of the reaction to the assassination of President Kennedy.

Conclusion

I have sought here to set down very briefly the pros and cons of current French policy, but it seems to me that they add up to the following considerations as far as the U.S. is concerned:

1. To recognize that no concession or courtesy or personal contact will have any effect upon de Gaulle's policies or attitudes, that the relations with the U.S. are about where he would like to have them, that he will accept any concessions or courtesies as a natural right and as a recognition of his "greatness." However, he should be at all times, as indeed should the French Government, treated with the utmost courtesy. I

would recommend great care in the avoidance of any derogatory statements in regard to de Gaulle which he will be able to use for his own purposes.

2. Attempt to avoid wherever possible action which would cast doubt upon the U.S. determination to defend Europe in the event of war. In this, I should tell you that I believe that the theory of the "pause", introduced in the spring of 1961, has more than any other factor played into the hands of de Gaulle in promulgating the theory that the U.S. could not be relied on to use nuclear weapons in Europe if necessary because of the threat to our states. I shall be very glad to discuss this at further length with you.

3. We should continue of course to work for our own interests with France, keeping in mind that apart from the attitude generated by de Gaulle and a number of key questions, i.e., atomic defense and the formulation of European unity (to which should be added the French refusal to talk on Germany, although this seems to me to be a rather empty subject for the moment), the working relations between France and the U.S. are not any where nearly as bad as they are frequently painted in the press.

Finally, I should do nothing, repeat nothing, about the question of a meeting between de Gaulle and President Johnson and I would certainly be strongly against any possibility of President Johnson coming over to visit de Gaulle (unless of course he is planning for other reasons a European trip, which I imagine would be very difficult in view of the election).

The foregoing deals only with the immediate prospects for 1964, assuming of course de Gaulle is still in power, and does not go into the post-de Gaulle events.[1]

Charles E. Bohlen[2]

---

[1] Secretary Rusk met for 40 minutes with de Gaulle on December 16, but their conversation was confined to a discussion of Southeast Asia. (Secto 25 from Paris, December 16; ibid., CF 2345)

[2] Printed from a copy that bears this typed signature.

Italy

278. Memorandum of Conversation

Washington, January 26, 1961, 4:30 p.m.

SUBJECT

Survey of Italian Problems with the Secretary

PARTICIPANTS

The Secretary
Ambassador Manlio Brosio, Italian Embassy
Mr. Carlo Perrone-Capano, Minister, Italian Embassy
Mr. William L. Blue, WE

The Italian Ambassador expressed his appreciation for the opportunity to review Italian-American relations with Mr. Rusk and said he looked forward with pleasure to his association with him. The Secretary responded that he shared the Ambassador's pleasure and added that the new administration hoped for the closest possible relations with Italy.

Ambassador Brosio informed the Secretary that there was a possibility that Mr. Segni, the Foreign Minister of Italy, might visit the United States during the U.N. General Assembly meeting beginning in March and hoped to meet the Secretary informally during his stay in the United States.[1] The Secretary said he would very much like to see Mr. Segni, but would request that the meeting be on a very informal basis because of the chain reaction which might result from a more formal visit. The Secretary also indicated that he would like to have the Foreign Minister for lunch while he was here. The Secretary asked that the necessary arrangements be made for Mr. Segni's visit to Washington at the appropriate time.

Ambassador Brosio opened the substantive portion of his remarks by saying that there were no major problems between Italy and the United States, but that he would like to outline for the benefit of the Secretary some of the problems which were current.

1. *South Tyrol*—The first subject was that of the South Tyrol, a question which Italy would have to live with for a long time. He ex-

---

Source: Department of State, Central Files, 611.65/1–2661. Confidential. Drafted by Blue and approved in S on February 4.

[1] No record of a meeting between Segni and Secretary Rusk has been found.

pressed his appreciation for the support given to Italy by the United States during the last U.N. General Assembly meeting. He mentioned the meeting between officials of Italy and Austria taking place in Milan and stated that the United States could be assured that Italy would approach this meeting in a spirit of cooperation within the framework of the Gruber–de Gasperi agreement.[2] He made it very clear, however, that Italy was not prepared to allow any separatism between the Italian and German communities. In a later comment he deplored the injection of racialism into this issue. The Ambassador assured the Secretary that the Italian Government was prepared to negotiate in a generous way and asked only for United States understanding and support. The Secretary said that he hoped that the talks in Milan would be fruitful. He added that the United States would be more comfortable if we were not confronted with a problem of this kind between two good friends. He added that he saw no reason to think that the United States would change its position on the Alto Adige question.

2. *Common Market*—The Ambassador mentioned the February talks of the Heads of Government of the Six.[3] He indicated that they would be discussing certain French proposals, some of which might be acceptable to Italy. He added that Italy would also like to see something done to accommodate the U.K. He concluded with the statement that U.S. policy toward the Common Market had always been farsighted and that he would only hope that this policy would not change but would continue. The Secretary responded that, as the Ambassador knew, there has always been strong bipartisan support in the United States for European unity. He added that the United States Government wished the Common Market well and hoped that the two parties would work out their difficulties in such a way as to increase the flow of trade and economic growth.

3. *Spaak Resignation*[4]—The Ambassador then mentioned the reports of the resignation of Mr. Spaak, who would be in the United States

---

[2] On June 23, 1960, the Government of Austria requested that the General Assembly place the question of the "Austrian minority in Italy" on its agenda. The issue was referred to the Special Political Committee on October 10, 1960. On October 31, 1960, the General Assembly adopted Resolution 1479 (XV), which called on Italy and Austria to resume their bilateral negotiations over means to implement the 1946 De Gasperi–Gruber agreements. The United States supported an Italian suggestion that the matter be adjudicated before the International Court of Justice at The Hague and voted in favor of the October 31 General Assembly resolution. Representatives of the Italian and Austrian Governments discussed the South Tyrol question at Milan on January 27–28, 1961. For text of the De Gasperi–Gruber agreement, signed on September 9, 1946, and included as an annex to the Treaty of Paris, signed February 10, 1947, see 61 Stat. 1245 or TIAS 1648.

[3] The EEC heads of government met in Paris February 10–11 with the objectives of improving their political cooperation and creating a single European market.

[4] See Document 95.

in the near future. He referred to a communication of January 25 from his Foreign Minister to the effect that Mr. Spaak's decision to resign might be dependent on the outcome of discussions in Washington on the subject of consultation within NATO. The Ambassador went on to say that the Government of Italy hoped that Mr. Spaak would not resign for various reasons, one being that it would be very difficult to replace him. He also was of the view that the publicity which would grow out of reports that he was resigning over the question of political consultations in NATO would be unfortunate. He concluded with the statement that Mr. Segni had expressed the hope that the United States would discourage Mr. Spaak's resignation. The Secretary asked the Ambassador if Mr. Segni's information had grown out of a recent contact with Mr. Spaak. The Ambassador replied that he thought the information was from their Mission in Paris. The Secretary said he asked this question as he had information from private sources contrary to that reported by the Ambassador. The Secretary agreed with the Ambassador that Mr. Spaak's resignation would be unfortunate, but indicated that the United States could not commit itself without knowing what Mr. Spaak's conditions were. He made it clear that there were no reservations with reference to Mr. Spaak on the part of the United States, but that we could not give him a blank check without knowing what was on his mind.

4. *Nuclear Arms to NATO*—The Ambassador introduced this subject by saying that he realized that it was very early in the new administration to bring this up, but he wondered if the administration planned to continue the policy of the former administration on nuclear arms to NATO. In response the Secretary said that the matter was under study. When Ambassador Brosio mentioned an A.P. report that Lord Home had informed Parliament that the new administration intended to continue the policy of the previous administration in this field, the Secretary said that he could not believe that the Foreign Minister had made any such statement. He stated that the U.S. had taken no steps inter-governmentally in this matter in view of the brief time which has elapsed since January 20th. The Secretary went on to say that despite any current impression to the contrary, his appointment and that of Mr. Bowles and Ambassador Stevenson did not represent any lessening of interest in NATO. He said it was true that all three had on occasion been involved with matters concerning other parts of the world, but this did not mean that they were unaware of the importance of NATO. He added that not only they, but the President himself regarded support of NATO as fundamental to U.S. policy. He stressed that we must reinvigorate the NATO alliance, but also work for good relations between the NATO countries and the other nations of the world. It was no secret, he stated, that at times the United States was torn between our friends in NATO and those in other parts of the world and that we cannot always accept

the views of our NATO partners as regards the rest of the world. However, we certainly should do everything possible not to allow our differences in viewpoint to weaken the unity of NATO.

The Secretary commented that if the Ambassador found that his reactions to any of the specific problems which he had raised were too general, he hoped that he would please let him know so that he could make them more specific. The Ambassador responded that he understood the Secretary's position and that he did not expect specific answers to all of the questions which he had raised, but merely wished to review for the benefit of the Secretary some of the issues which were important to Italy at this time. The meeting was concluded after further pleasantries.

---

279. Telegram From the Embassy in Italy to the Department of State

Rome, February 1, 1961, 7 p.m.

2956. Embtels 2908 and 2909[1] described our difficulties in achieving removals by GOI of remaining discrimination against dollar imports of agricultural commodities, and recommended continuing US pressure on GOI within limitations of political tolerance. Purpose of this postscript is to call attention to these limitations.

Present government, formed last August as reaction to Communist inspired mob violence which was culmination of six months of political maneuvering following fall of Segni government early in 1960, remains an uneasy coalition of four center parties. It has considerable potential for constructive achievement but is subjected to continuing strains. Three months after local elections early in November, many city and provincial administrations have yet to be formed. Very delicate operation is involved of trying to enlist cooperation of Nenni Socialist Party on limited local scale without disturbing national government coalition, which contains substantial forces implacably opposed to agreement with Nenni on any level. While involving serious short-term risks, entire operation is probably in long-term interest of Italian democracy but, in any case, it is made necessary by arithmetic of election results, and their political effects.

Source: Department of State, Central Files, 765.00/2–161. Confidential.
[1] Both dated January 30. (Ibid., 465.006/1–3061)

Embtel 2868[2] described high point of near-crisis through which government has just gone, and subsequent messages have reported its gradual attenuation. Main strength of present government is lack of viable alternative, vividly demonstrated last year when almost all other possible combinations were tried, and failed. Unfortunately, energies of government leaders are largely absorbed by continuous factional and party maneuvering which daily confronts them. As result they have too little time for planning and execution of current and new programs. In any case, their margin of political power is so slight that they dare not make moves significantly vulnerable to partisan attack. Decision-making power of government is thus inhibited and this is seen with particular clarity in matters which involve special appropriations and in sensitive political sectors such as those of Somalia (Embtel 2877)[3] and agriculture, described in Embtel 2908.

We thus cannot for present realistically expect GOI to make "courageous" decisions which their friends and indeed they themselves, would like to see made. We should by all means keep up pressure on liberalization but in our judgment, agricultural situation is sufficiently delicate that, under present circumstances, it might be used to precipitate a political crisis. Apart from political results if this happened, there is no assurance that GOI would not adopt new protectionist policies in agricultural area harmful to our broader interests in Europe.

Horsey

---

[2] Telegram 2868, January 26, reported on the formation of a center-left city government in Milan and its impact on relationships among Italian parties on a national level. (Ibid., 765.00/1–2661)

[3] Dated January 26. (Ibid., 700.5–MSP/1–2661)

---

280. Editorial Note

Ambassador at Large W. Averell Harriman visited Rome March 8–11 for meetings with Italian Government officials and party leaders. In a March 9 meeting with Prime Minister Amintore Fanfani, Harriman outlined the foreign policy objectives of the new administration, and the two men discussed relations with the Soviet Union. At Harriman's request, Fanfani gave his opinions on the upcoming Italian presidential election. Fanfani suggested that Harriman meet with Enrico Mattei, chairman of the Italian state oil company, ENI, to discuss oil policy. Harriman also met with President Giovanni Gronchi at which time he reaffirmed U.S. pledges of cooperation with Italy and outlined Kennedy administration policy. At Harriman's request, Gronchi discussed his February 1960 visit to the Soviet Union and his impressions of the Soviet leadership.

On March 10 Harriman met with Foreign Minister Segni for a discussion of Mediterranean issues, particularly Algeria, and the Portuguese colonial situation. He also held a meeting with Mattei, who "spoke with burning indignation of the discrimination practiced against Italy and against his group in particular by the main US and British oil companies. He said that Italy had begun its industrialization much later than the other nations because during the 19th century, when the main source of power was coal, Italy had no coal and a ton of coal on the dock at Genoa cost twice as much as it had in Britain, France or Germany. Italy's industrialization had only recently gotten under way after the development of hydro-electric power, and then like magic, a whole chain of industries had sprung up in the Po Valley. He had made deals with the Soviet Bloc simply because the Western oil companies pursued a blind policy of short-term profits without regard to the long-term effects thereof. He again expressed his indignation at this treatment saying 'we too are allies, we too are part of the West, and want to remain with the West.' He said that the attitude of these petroleum companies in the producing areas was equally blind. They did not realize that the world had changed and that the peoples of these areas were no longer content with a 50 percent share of the profits and the oil companies telling them not to meddle in the oil business because they knew nothing about it. It was not merely the profit that they were after but was a sense of participation. Therefore, in his dealings he had introduced a new formula. Fifty percent of the net profits to the local government and of the remainder, 50 percent to the associated national oil enterprise, which to join him invested no money and which paid off his initial investment out of their 50 percent of the profits over a 12 year period. This gave them a direct interest in the production, and this sense of participation which was so essential." (Memorandum of conversation; Department of State, Central Files, 110.15–HA/3–1061)

Harriman met with the leader of the Italian Social Democratic Party, Giuseppi Saragat, on March 11. On the issue of possible participation by the Italian Socialist Party in a government, Saragat noted that his party had made gains in the November 1960 elections "which coincided with Nenni Socialist setback" and "categorically opposed PSI entry in government because of present Socialist participation with Communists in trade unions and numerous local governments and their foreign policy views." (Telegram 3520 from Rome, March 11; ibid., 765.00/3–1161)

On March 11 Harriman met with Fanfani for the second time (see Document 281).

At the conclusion of the visit, the two governments announced that Harriman had extended an invitation to Prime Minister Fanfani on behalf of President Kennedy to make an official visit to Washington at a future date to be agreed upon. Memoranda of conversation between Harriman and Italian leaders are in Department of State, Central File 110.15–HA.

281.   Memorandum of Conversation

Rome, March 11, 1961.

PRESENT

    Prime Minister Fanfani
    Ambassador Harriman
    Colonel Vernon Walters

The conversation opened with Mr. Harriman reading to Prime Minister Fanfani that part of a statement covering the announcement that he had delivered a message that President Kennedy was anxious to meet and confer with Prime Minister Fanfani. The Prime Minister was pleased and agreed with the text read to him.

Mr. Harriman indicated that he was pleased to have heard Pella, after his somewhat conservative picture of Italian finances, agree with a large investment program in the south and the islands.

The Prime Minister said he was happy that the three Ministers had a chance to present their views to Mr. Harriman and that he had certainly drawn the conclusion that, considering what was available and what was planned within Italy, there was certainly a margin for Italy to carry her share in a coordinated plan of assistance to the under-developed countries.

Source: Department of State, Central Files, 110.15–HA/3–1161. Secret. Drafted by Walters. The meeting was held in the Prime Minister's office at Viminale Palace.

Mr. Harriman then said that he had seen Mr. Saragat and had told him that he was disappointed that the Social Democrats had not been able to attract more votes from the left, and, in fact, had lost some. Mr. Saragat pointed out that he had, in fact, gained some at the last elections and Mr. Fanfani confirmed this.

Mr. Harriman said that Saragat felt he was being badly treated by the British Labor Party. Mr. Fanfani replied that the British Labor Party, and also the French Socialists led by Mollet, were anxious to see Nenni's Socialists detach themselves from the Communists. The Prime Minister said that, in his opinion, what should be done was to use the Liberals on the right under Malagodi to attract votes from the right, and the Social Democrats under Saragat on the left, to attract votes from further left.

With regard to detaching the Socialists from the Communists, he felt that there were three conditions: the possible, the imminent, and the probable. Certainly, such detachment was not imminent, everything was possible, and as to the probabilities in the future, one could only speculate. In a limited way, in some city governments they were attempting to show the Socialists that there were advantages to cooperating with the democratic majority. This was being done cautiously and with prudence. Saragat was obviously anxious that the Socialists not be brought into the majority against him but with him, and Malagodi was fearful that if the Socialists came in, the Liberals would be pushed out in the cold. He feared this might happen after the Socialist Party Congress in Milan later this month. The Prime Minister said that there was no chance of this happening. At a later date, possibly after the elections, consideration might be given to Socialist participation in the government, providing that they detach themselves from the Communists on foreign policy, on NATO, and in labor.

Speculating on the future prospects of his own government, he did not feel that the Socialists or the Republicans wanted to bring the government down, nor did Malagodi, but he had to fight against the right wing of his own party, and he foresaw considerable longevity for his own government.

Mr. Harriman said that he feared Nenni had been too closely associated with Togliatti for too long, and that attempts should be made to win over the Socialist electorate, rather than Nenni himself. The Prime Minister agreed and said that this was what they were trying to do.

Mr. Harriman then spoke of the policies of the new Administration, saying that there was a new spirit, that they were concerned with expanding the economy and correcting unemployment, as well as protecting against inflation. The Prime Minister said that he was particularly grateful to President Kennedy for his courtesy in sending Mr. Harriman, who was a proven friend of Italy and who knew conditions in this country so well, to talk with the Italian government leaders.

Minister Horsey and Ambassador Vanni then joined the Prime Minister and Ambassador Harriman and the text of the two statements was agreed upon.

---

282. Despatch From the Embassy in Italy to the Department of State

No. 961   Rome, April 26, 1961.

SUBJECT

American Posture Toward Italian Socialist Party

Despatch No. 899[1] described developments in the Italian Socialist Party (PSI) in the last six months, the results of the recent Congress of the Party in Milan,[2] and the position of the right and left wings of the Party on key issues. The present despatch draws certain conclusions and makes recommendations concerning the desirable United States posture toward the Party, and as to actions which should be taken to encourage complete independence from the Communists and the adoption of a pro-western foreign policy, as requested in the Department's A–233 of March 17.[3]

The Congress produced no dramatic developments but it had the useful result of bringing out clearly the positions of all concerned, stripped of much of the evasion, euphemism and ambiguity which had covered public statements of Party policies in the past. A tenuous majority was obtained for an affirmation of the policy followed by Nenni and the autonomist majority during the past two years. Nenni personally moved further than he had in the past, publicly expressing readiness to

---

Source: Department of State, Central Files, 765.00/4–2661. Confidential. Drafted by Horsey.

[1] Dated April 11. (Ibid., 765.00/4–1161)

[2] The Italian Socialist Party held its National Congress in Milan March 15–20.

[3] This airgram requested the Embassy to "submit urgently" a review of developments within the Italian Socialist Party together with recommendations regarding desirable U.S. policy for the "immediate future." (Department of State, Central Files, 765.00/3–1761)

cooperate with the DC Party as a whole, not only, as in the past, with the "Catholic workers" or the "democratic elements" of the Party. (Ricardo Lombardi, coming from the Action Party and with the extreme anti-clericalism which is its hallmark, held back on this point and still views cooperation with the DC in terms of liberating the "Catholic workers" from the "domination" of the Church and the rest of the DC Party, i.e., of splitting the DC Party.) Most observers agree, however, not only has "autonomy" made no progress at the Congress but that, in terms of policy positions and of party following, it suffered a slight set-back. There was no sign of a favorable change on the key issues of internal security and foreign policy which still create a wide gap between the PSI and the "center" parties. The PSI autonomist majority was weakened by a slight reduction in its percentage vote, now only 55 percent. It was weakened also by the retreat of Lombardi to a position nearer the center, close to the ground previously occupied by Nenni.[4] This division in the autonomist ranks deprives Nenni of full control of the formal party organs, reducing him to the rank of a factional leader, and, at least for the present, Lombardi seems to hold the balance of power among the autonomists, and in the Party as a whole. This situation was recently illustrated in the Chamber debate on Cuba, during which Lombardi spoke for the PSI. He saw no blemish whatsoever on the Castro record and his performance, seeming as it did to flow from full "autonomy", did far more damage to the United States position and to the Italian Government than the shrill routine of the PCI.

Opinion in the "center-left" area of the democratic parties is now, finally, virtually unanimous in the realization of the difficulties facing the PSI autonomists and of the unlikelihood of substantial progress at least until after the next national elections. [Here follow a discussion of press commentary and an analysis of the history and current policy positions of the PSI.]

What is likely to happen for the next two years or so is that the PSI will continue to remain suspended between Communism and democratic socialism; that the habit of cooperation with the PSI and the DC at the local government level will grow, and that it will exert a spreading influence in both the PSI and the DC Parties. Before the local elections last fall, most observers over-estimated the electoral appeal of the PSI and it is likely that the contradiction in its present posture, i.e., cooperation with the DC (the traditional enemy) in some places and with the Communists in others, will lead to further losses. If the PSDI gains in this process, as it did last fall, there will be a *reliable* strengthening of the

---

[4] The satisfaction of the PCI with the outcome is evident from the analysis in Despatch No. 938 of April 18. [Footnote in the source text. Despatch 938 is ibid., 765.00/4–1861.]

democratic area and a sure basis for further progress in the process of slow reform and social change which is now under way.

The "American ideal" or the "American purpose" exercises a certain attraction in the PSI, as it does in all constructive sectors of Italian society, and the composition and tone of the new Administration in Washington greatly helps the projection of this image. This disposes PSI autonomists more favorably toward the United States and we can and do see that this influence is brought to bear in every possible way. All this, however, has little if any effect on the *pace* of the development of PSI "autonomy" because it is only remotely related to the reality of the problems faced by the autonomists. Our posture toward the PSI should continue to be one of sympathy with the objectives of moving away from the Communists, of strengthening democracy and of adopting foreign policy positions in tune with the harsh realities of the day. Our interest lies in the systematic encouragement of this trend, in such a manner and to such an extent that what we do does not significantly contribute to governmental instability or give the impression that we believe that PSI support can yet safely be considered a determining factor in a governing majority. If such an impression were to be created, it would almost certainly lead to the fall of the government and to a prolonged period of paralysis and crisis with unpredictable but certainly very serious consequences, for the reasons analyzed at length in Despatch No. 257 of September 12, 1960.[5]

We should change the visa regulations in the way, and for the reasons, suggested in Embassy Despatch No. 241 of September 17, 1959,[6] so that our policy will not be burdened by the adverse consequences of the present presumption that we think past or present membership in the PSI is the same (for purposes of US national security and the Immigration Act of 1952)[7] as membership in the PCI.

We should continue to urge on political leaders in the four parties supporting the Government the importance of further reform measures. The present Government has plans for many, and has made a start on some of them, continuing the slow but unspectacular progress of the last ten years. Most importantly, we should continue to encourage and support the kind of management of the national economy which has led to Italy being in the lead of all industrialized Western countries in the rate of expansion, creating the new national wealth which is essential for the

---

[5] Despatch 257 assessed the "Prospects for Italian Political Stability." (Department of State, Central Files, 765.00/9–1260)

[6] Despatch 241 discussed visa policy regarding members of the Italian Socialist Party. (Department of State, Central Files, CA)

[7] For text of the Immigration and Nationality Act of 1952 (P.L. 414), approved June 27, 1952, see 66 Stat. 163.

financing of most of the necessary reform measures and which is leading to rising standards of living all over the country.

Primarily, however, our efforts to influence and accelerate the process of "autonomy" should be in the continuation and expansion of the activities described in Despatch No. 931,[8] being alert to new opportunities and means of pursuing the same objectives, in political, labor, cooperatives, cultural and other fields, all under the tactical guidance of the Ambassador. Although the basic structure has been generations in the making, great change has taken place in the last five years and we can confidently expect further change.

Outerbridge Horsey
Chargé d'affaires ad interim

---

[8] Despatch 931, April 17, reviewed the evolution of U.S. policy toward the PSI and its specific recommendations: "(a) Broadening of existing contacts with PSI autonomists; (b) Inclusion of PSI autonomists in social functions; (c) Invitations to PSI autonomists for USIS cultural programs; (d) Contacts with PSI journalists, labor leaders, and communal officials in fields such as education, together with presentation of books and other USIS materials; (e) Loan of USIS films and equipment to PSI groups; (f) Development of low-key programs in USIS branches aimed at attracting labor audiences, particularly PSI; (g) Sponsorship of labor grants for PSI autonomists to visit the United States." (Department of State, Central Files, 765.00/4–1761)

---

283. Editorial Note

In April 1961 the President's Special Assistant, Arthur Schlesinger, Jr., accompanied by James E. King, a senior analyst at the Institute for Defense Analysis, attended a Bologna conference on the subject of U.S. foreign policy. The meeting was sponsored by a group of Italian intellectuals, organized around the journal *Il Mulino*, which favored Socialist Party participation in Italy's Government. Following the conference, King met with a number of senior Italian Government and party leaders together with Chargé Horsey to explore their views on the possibility of an opening to the left, by means of the inclusion of the Italian Socialist Party in a governing coalition. Although King explained his status as a private citizen, both U.S. and Italian officials regarded him as an unofficial emissary of the Kennedy administration.

In addition to his meeting with Nenni, King was received by President Gronchi, Prime Minister Fanfani, Christian Democratic Party secretary Aldo Moro and a number of senior parliamentary leaders. In a 40-minute discussion with King, Nenni expressed generally favorable views of the Kennedy administration's policies and sought to explain the current positions of his party on entry into government and Italy's foreign policy. As a result of these talks, King concluded that an opening to the left was probable and that it was unlikely to destabilize the Italian Government. He also noted a strong desire among proponents of the opening for some form of active support from the U.S. Government. King forwarded a copy of his report to Walter Rostow on the National Security Council on May 3. (Kennedy Library, National Security Files, Italy—Notes on Italian-American Relations) Horsey's comments on the King visit together with his response to King's recommendations is in telegram 4320 from Rome, May 8. (Department of State, Central Files, 765.00/5–861)

According to Arthur Schlesinger (*A Thousand Days*, pages 877–878), he and Robert Komer of the NSC staff hoped to utilize Fanfani's June 1961 visit to the United States as the platform for a formal statement of U.S. support for the opening to the left. On June 8 Schlesinger met with William Knight and William Blue of the Department of State for a discussion of the respective positions of the Italian Socialist and Italian Communist Parties. A memorandum of their discussion is in Department of State, Italian Desk Files: Lot 68 D 436, Pol 7 Visit—Fanfani—1961. In a June 9 memorandum Komer outlined the rationale for including the PSI in a governing coalition:

"The only thought I would suggest adding on the 'Opening to the Left' would be that Italy's series of delicately balanced Centrist governments, hobbled by barely half of the parliamentary votes, have been characterized by a form of 'immobilismo' which has hampered dynamic movement toward reform. Meanwhile, Communist strength has been inching up on the Left. A final break between the PCI and the PSI, which would result from an opening to the Left, would destroy Communist hopes of achieving a parliamentary majority and create a dynamic non-Communist alternative." (Kennedy Library, National Security Files, Italy—General)

284. Memorandum of Conversation

Washington, June 12, 1961, 5 p.m.

SUBJECT

NATO Strategy

PARTICIPANTS

US Side
The President
The Secretary of State
Mr. Nitze, Assistant Secretary of Defense
Ambassador Reinhardt
Mr. Tyler, Deputy Assistant Secretary
Mr. Schlesinger, Special Assistant to the President

Italian Side
Prime Minister Fanfani[1]
Foreign Minister Segni
Ambassador Fenoaltea, Italian Ambassador[2]
Mr. Fornari, Director General of Political Affairs
Mr. d'Archirafi, Diplomatic Adviser to the Prime Minister

The President asked the Prime Minister if he was satisfied about the US strategic approach. Fanfani said he had discussed this question at length with Ambassador Harriman[3] and Mr. Acheson.[4] He approved of our desire to increase conventional weapons. He thought there was some concern lest increasing conventional weapons might mean raising the threshold to a point where this might mean hesitation on the part of the United States in using nuclear weapons. He pointed out that Italy was the only power which had carried out in practice the December 1957 NATO resolution.[5] He said that Italy recognizes the difficulty of the problem of command. Fanfani said that Italy was geographically extremely exposed to potential aggression, and was the power which had accepted most risks. This entitled her to be most consulted. The President asked Fanfani whether the US proposals with regard to Polaris

---

Source: Department of State, Central Files, 375/6–1261. Secret. Drafted by Tyler. Approved in S on August 4 and the White House on August 11. The meeting was held at the White House.

[1] Fanfani made an informal visit to the United States June 11–16.

[2] The Italian Government announced Fenoaltea's nomination as Ambassador to the United States on April 28; he presented his credentials to President Kennedy on May 26.

[3] Presumably during Harriman's March 1961 visit to Rome.

[4] Presumably following Acheson's April 1961 participation at the Bologna conference on U.S. foreign policy.

[5] For text of this resolution, see Department of State *Bulletin,* January 6, 1958, pp. 12–15.

were of interest to Italy. Fanfani replied that since mobile bases are now technically possible, the US had been wise in having made the proposal. The President said that he understood the problem of not decreasing Italy's sense of security. Fanfani asked if Foreign Minister Segni might speak to this point. Segni said that in 1958 Italy had assumed grave responsibilities in having agreed to the installation of IRBMs. Now we have proposed Polaris missiles, which means mobile sea-bases. Italy feels that there should be an appropriate degree of control by the Italian government with regard to the use of these weapons. So far, he said, only two powers have accepted IRBMs, and if this remains the case it should be easy to work out the decision-making process. He said that there was no problem with regard to tactical weapons such as Nike and Honest John, which were merely a form of artillery. These should remain under military command.

The President commented that General de Gaulle was still dissatisfied with NATO and integration of Western defense, and that he may make a proposal this fall or winter for reorganization of NATO. The President said he hoped that it would prove possible to work out something.

---

285.   Memorandum of Conversation

Washington, June 13, 1961, 10:15 a.m.–noon.

SUBJECT

Economic and Military Aid to the Somali Republic

PARTICIPANTS

US Side
The President
Under Secretary Ball
Mr. Schlesinger, Special Assistant to the President
G. Frederick Reinhardt, American Ambassador to Rome
William R. Tyler, Deputy Assistant Secretary
William Witman, Director, AFN

Source: Department of State, Central Files, 777.5–MSP/6–1361. Secret. Drafted by Tyler. Approved in B on August 10 and by the White House on August 15. The meeting was held at the White House. The President and Prime Minister also discussed aid to less-developed countries, Soviet oil, Iran, and South Tyrol. Regarding the South Tyrol issue, Segni spoke of the meetings between Italy and Austria and noted that some of the Austrian proposals implied a "considerable weakening of Italy's northern frontier" with implications for Italy's and NATO's security. He felt that Italy might have to turn to the International Court of Justice. (Ibid., 663.65/6–1361)

The two nations failed to reach agreement, and on July 17 Austria again requested General Assembly discussion of the South Tyrol issue. On November 11 the General Assembly adopted Resolution 1661 (XVI), calling upon Italy and Austria to continue their talks.

Italian Side
Prime Minister Fanfani
Foreign Minister Segni
Amb. Fornari, Director General of Political Affairs
Mr. Sensi, Chief of Cabinet to Minister of For. Affairs
Mr. Manfredi, Counselor, Italian Embassy
Mr. Perrone Capano, Italian Minister
Amb. D'Archirafi, Diplomatic Adviser to Prime Minister
Amb. Fenoaltea, Italian Ambassador

The President gave the reasons why we would like to see the Italian Government provide military aid to the Somali Republic. [1] He said that it was not something that we were prepared to do because it would create an adverse reaction by Ethiopia and jeopardize retention of our military facilities in Eritrea.

The Prime Minister asked Foreign Minister Segni to comment. He said that Italy had already given substantial financial aid to Somaliland in order to help it to balance its budgets for 1960 and 1961. For the latter year alone Italy was giving the equivalent of 3-1/2 million dollars for budget purposes in addition to 2-1/2 million dollars in aid. The President asked Mr. Witman to present the U.S. view. Mr. Witman pointed out that in spite of the aid which the Italians had given, there would be a deficit of about 2 million dollars, which meant there was a danger of a crisis at the end of this year, and of the Somalis turning to enemy sources for financial aid, unless they received it from the West. The President suggested that a memorandum be drafted setting forth U.S. views on this matter which would be given to the Prime Minister before he leaves. In the ensuing discussion concerning the granting of military aid, Foreign Minister Segni said that Italy could not do it alone, and that the UK contribution had been inadequate. The Prime Minister outlined the Italian arguments in favor of tripartite aid. He stressed the political problem and said that if Ethiopia receives military aid from the U.S. while only Italy and the UK give military aid to the Somali Republic, it would look as though Italy and the UK were championing the Somali Republic while the U.S. was championing Ethiopia. He suggested that the U.S. give consideration to providing some surplus military equipment to enable the Somali Republic to maintain an appropriate force (6 to 7,000 men) to assure internal order. He said that the Italians had given the Somali Republic the equivalent of $22 million in total aid while the UK had provided only about 150,000£. The tensions between the Somali Republic and Ethiopia were great and it was important that nothing be done which might precipitate or encourage clashes. He mentioned that the

---

[1] Somalia was formed on July 1, 1960, by the fusion of colonial territories formerly held by Italy and Great Britian.

Somalis had wanted the Italians to supply two patrol boats against contraband activities and arms smuggling. The Italians did not have these and thought the U.S. might be willing to spare two as a sign of friendliness to the Somali Republic. In further explanation of the extent of the Italian sacrifices in favor of the Somalis, the Prime Minister mentioned that the Italians had even trained themselves to eating the inferior bananas of the Somali Republic to help their exports, instead of getting better bananas from elsewhere, including the U.S. Mr. Witman explained that the U.S. was even willing to go to the Ethiopians and tell them (although this would be distasteful to us to have to do) that we hoped they would understand that it was better for the Somalis to be armed to an appropriate degree by the Italians and British than having e.g.: the Chinese Communists supply them with arms. The whole situation was not made easier by the fact that this little Somali Republic was laying claim to approximately one-third of Ethiopian territory.

The Prime Minister said that this was a most difficult situation. He repeated his feeling that if the U.S. refused to share in providing military aid to the Somalis it could not help but be interpreted as an anti-Somali course of action. The President agreed that the problem was an important and difficult one and said there was tripartite interest in this situation. He said that while we could, as appropriate, provide economic assistance and help to a certain extent with the police, we would not give military assistance because of Ethiopian sensitivity. He suggested that Italy and U.K. provide the required military aid and that we continue to see what we could do to help in other fields. Foreign Minister Segni commented that the current total Italian financial contribution to the Somali Republic amounted to $7 million and that there would be difficulties in the Italian Parliament if more aid were requested to cover the financial deficit.

---

286. Editorial Note

During a luncheon conversation between President Kennedy and Prime Minister Fanfani on June 13 in Washington the following exchange took place:

"The President inquired about the geographical strength of Communism in Italy. Mr. Fanfani replied that the Communists derived much of their strength from the central and northern parts of Italy and that as a result of the increasing migration from the rural areas into the urban areas, there was a danger that a large part of the migrating workers would be won over by the Communists.

"The President asked Mr. Fanfani what effect the opening to the left would have on the political balance of power in parliament. Mr. Fanfani analyzed the various shifts of votes which would result from the opening to the left and concluded that in the end the Socialists would be left with 60 deputies and the Democratic Center would gain 30. The final outcome would be a Chamber of Deputies whose composition would give the Communists 30% of the deputies and the Democratic Center 65%.

"The President raised the subject of Nenni and Mr. Fanfani remarked that no one as yet knew where Nenni would go and that it would be best to let Saragat solve the Nenni problem. The President made no comment." (Memorandum of conversation; Department of State, Italy Desk Files: Lot 68 D 436, Italy—Nenni's Possible Visit—1962)

---

287. Editorial Note

On July 5 the Department of State forwarded to the White House a paper entitled "Outlines of U.S. Policy Toward Italy." Among its recommendations regarding Italian political affairs was:

"We should encourage the evolution of the PSI toward greater and more effective political independence of the Communists, being careful not to move too far ahead of the line being followed by the responsible progressive leaders of the DC Party. The choice of specific actions to be taken to achieve this objective should be kept under close review and at any given moment should reflect our current assessment of the opportunities and dangers inherent in the situation. Our influence should be directed towards encouraging the party to break its ties with the Communists in every possible field, particularly within the CGIL labor organization, to form local administrations with the democratic parties rather than the PCI and to modify its fundamentally neutralist foreign policies." (Department of State, PPS Files: Lot 67 D 548, Italy)

In a July 6 memorandum to Walter Rostow, Schlesinger commented on the paper, stating that it "in the main, is harmless." Schlesinger continued:

"The critical issue in Italian policy continues to be our attitude toward the 'opening to the left.' In this respect, the paper shows a definite advance over past State Department thinking on the subject. However, it still adopts the attitude that the PSI is engaged in a unilinear drift toward the west and implies therefore a passive, wait-and-see policy on our part—i.e., it implies that it is OK for us to stand by until the situation has evolved, at which time we are then free to accept or reject the possibility of CD–PSI collaboration.

"In my judgment, this is a misreading of the situation. The pace of events has been quickening steadily this spring; and the evidence shows clearly that the PCI is engaged in a massive effort to isolate and discredit Nenni and to wreck his position and influence. [*1-1/2 lines of source text not declassified*] we may find that, instead of gradually evolving toward the west, the PSI will be cut to pieces in the Communist counteroffensive." (Kennedy Library, National Security Files, Italy)

---

288. Telegram From the Embassy in Italy to the Department of State

Rome, July 15, 1961, noon.

160. Embtel 103.[1] Fanfani received me last night (July 14) at his home. I reviewed considerations set forth Deptel 53.[2] Fanfani said he had given much thought to problem since Horsey saw him on July 8 and rationalized issue under following three headings:

1. Original Soviet insistence on July 13 date was presumably motivated by desire to confuse parliamentary situation in Italy. This obstacle had now been passed. He had impression Soviets expected him, following their planted story in *Paese Sera* (Embtel 120),[3] to deny to Parliament story of his intention visit Moscow. This he had avoided simply by saying he would not discuss matter in his speech. Communists had subsequently cancelled inscribed speech wherein they had presumably intended to attack him for the expected announcement, since had they done otherwise he would have had them in a box.

Source: Department of State, Central Files, 033.6561/7–1561. Confidential; Limit Distribution. Also sent to Moscow.

[1] Telegram 103, July 11, reported that Fanfani had "personally" assured Horsey that "no decision yet made on dates of proposed visit to Moscow." Reinhardt also reported that he had talked about the visit with Foreign Minister Segni the previous evening. Segni "mentioned the proposed Moscow visit in strictly confidential terms and seemed unhappy about it" while confirming that the Italian Government had taken no decision on the dates of a visit. (Ibid., 033.6561/7–1161)

[2] Telegram 53, July 7, expressed Rusk's concern over the proposed Fanfani visit to Moscow in the face of a renewed Soviet challenge to Berlin and Soviet efforts to create the notion that NATO countries were not united on the Berlin issue. Rusk asked that Reinhardt convey his concerns to Fanfani and ask him to defer his visit until the Berlin question was resolved. (Ibid., 033.6561/7–761)

[3] Telegram 120, July 7, reported that the left wing daily *Paese Sera* had printed a story that Fanfani would announce a visit to the Soviet Union the following day and that the United States was in agreement with the trip. (Ibid., 033.6561/7–1261)

2. For internal political reasons he was convinced, as were other party leaders of the convergence, that he could not refuse invitation. This was true for general reasons, but particularly because of importance that, should Berlin crisis require some degree of mobilization or other emergency measures in Italy, government be in position to insist that it had taken every possible step in interests in peace. Fanfani expounded at length on this point. This consideration he thought would indicate desirability of visit taking place sooner rather than later.

3. Third element was international psychological factor raised by you. He did not seek to rebut importance of this element, but pointed out that problem for him was relative importance of external and internal considerations. It was his view that Italy's continuing ability to neutralize its large Communist element was important part of her contribution to NATO defenses.

Another factor uppermost in their minds, Fanfani asserted, was problem of Soviet return of President Gronchi's visit to Moscow.[4] If Prime Minister should visit Moscow it would at least serve purpose of precluding Soviet insistence that in absence Prime Minister's visit Khrushchev come to Rome. It was Fanfani's belief that no Christian Democratic government could accept visit of Soviet Prime Minister to Rome, and he recalled Pope's reaction to Adolf Hitler's visit.[5] Furthermore, he doubted Khrushchev would be satisfied with Italian visit which omitted Rome.

Fanfani said Soviet Ambassador had been pressing to see him for several days, presumably to propose another date. He had been avoiding him and would continue to do so until next week. He expected to be able to postpone date beyond first of August, but might well find it necessary to accept a later date if offered. In any event, he intended to be as dilatory as possible. He promised to keep me informed of developments and, should the Moscow visit be decided upon, he would ask us for all information and advice we wished to provide, commenting that he had never been in the Soviet Union and that present Soviet Ambassador Kozyrev was the first Russian he had ever really talked to.

On July 12 British, French and German Ambassadors were informed by Catani of possibility of visit. Palewski thought visit a poor idea but was particularly incensed that Segni had not raised it with his colleagues during Foreign Ministers' meeting of Six. I understand German Ambassador thought visit not a bad idea, but am uninformed as yet with respect to British reaction.

---

[4] President Gronchi visited the Soviet Union February 6–11, 1960.

[5] During the 4 days of Hitler's May 1938 visit to Rome, Pope Pius XI left the city for the papal retreat at Castel Gandolfo and ordered the closure of the Vatican museums.

I would assume that matter will now become subject of discussion at Bonn meeting July 18. Department may wish to ascertain what British, French and German reactions are, with a view to using that forum to bring further pressure on Fanfani if you deem it advisable.[6]

Reinhardt

---

[6] On July 17 the Department of State replied:

"Continue believe Fanfani visit Moscow unwise under circumstances. However if PM believes cannot be avoided we are of opinion should occur soonest and be brief as possible. Secretary conveyed this thought to Italian Ambassador seventeenth but you should personally convey it also PM soonest." (Telegram 154 to Rome; Department of State, Central Files, 033.6561/7–1561)

---

289. Memorandum of Conversation

Washington, July 17, 1961.

SUBJECT

Consultation and the Fanfani Visit to Moscow

PARTICIPANTS

The Secretary
Ambassador Sergio Fenoaltea, Italian Embassy
Mr. William L. Blue, WE

The Ambassador opened by saying that this was his first business call on the Secretary, as his previous visit had been a courtesy call just prior to the Fanfani visit. He then stressed the need for Italy to count on U.S. support, as the Italian Government was faced continually with great difficulties. He said that even after a hundred years of unity, Italian leadership had to work almost hourly to keep the democratic establishment going against a strong Communist party on the one hand and rightist elements on the other. He mentioned as one of the problems facing the government the economic conditions in Southern Italy. He said

---

Source: Department of State, Central Files, 765.00/7–1761. Confidential. Drafted by Blue and approved in S on August 9.

that in a certain sense Italy was still somewhat of a frontier fighting to maintain democracy on a daily basis. The Secretary stated that, as the Ambassador knew, the United States had a lively interest in supporting Italy as had been expressed to Mr. Fanfani while he was here.

The Ambassador went on to stress the problems facing the Italian Government in connection with NATO. He said that the IRBM launching pads had been introduced only against strong opposition.[1] He added that the support required was not only economic support because Italy had always had this, but also moral support. The Ambassador then mentioned the necessity for consultation with Italy. He said that all too often Italy was left in the dark. He added that the question of consultation was not one of vanity, but of necessity to help the government cope with anti-NATO forces within Italy. He emphasized it was absolutely essential that the government be able to say it had been consulted and not as a secondary power but because of its importance to the Alliance.

The Secretary responded to the effect that, as the Ambassador knew, the United States has a great problem on the question of consultation. He said he wished to consult our allies whenever possible. He assured the Ambassador that during the past few weeks we had been consulting certain countries on a response to the Aide-Mémoire.[2] He added that there had been no consultation on where we go next, as the United States had not developed its own position yet, but, when we did, our allies would be consulted. He added we had also been consulting the French on problems where there were differences in policy between the United States and France.

The Ambassador cited as a small indication of what he had in mind the fact that no one had come to Rome to brief the Government there on the Khrushchev–Kennedy talks.[3] He said that he knew this was a small matter and perhaps even a matter of appearances, but this type of consultation was very important to the Italians. He added that he hoped the Secretary would allow him to come by from time to time to discuss problems with him, as after all, this was bilateral consultation.

---

[1] On September 30, 1958, during a debate in the Italian Chamber of Deputies, Foreign Minister Segni announced that Jupiter missile bases would be established in the Puglia region, in response to the decisions taken at the December 1957 NATO heads of government meeting. On March 30, 1959, the Department of State announced an agreement with Italy covering the apportioning of costs and the status of U.S. forces assigned to man the missile bases. The accord was approved in the Italian Senate on April 17.

[2] For text of the Soviet aide-mémoire of June 4, regarding a German peace treaty, see Department of State *Bulletin,* August 7, 1961, pp. 231–233.

[3] June 3–4 in Vienna; for documentation on this meeting, see vol. V, Documents 57–64.

The Secretary then raised the subject of the Fanfani visit to the Soviet Union. He said the U.S. was aware of the Prime Minister's domestic problem, but was concerned about the international aspects of the visit and believed that if he must go, the sooner the better. The Ambassador said that he had nothing definite on this visit. The Secretary then informed the Ambassador that we had word from Rome that there had been such an invitation and that there was some inclination to accept it, but the timing had not been set. The Secretary said we had indicated that we were skeptical of the usefulness of such a visit at this point on the part of a high statesman of a NATO country, but he reiterated that if the Prime Minister felt he must go, it was better to go now than later. The Ambassador indicated some skepticism that such a visit would be made. He assured the Secretary that we would be informed if Fanfani did go and that there certainly would be no problem, in view of Fanfani's background, that he would not demonstrate moral firmness during the visit. The Secretary indicated that this aspect was certainly not a matter of concern to the United States.

The Ambassador then turned to the Alto/Adige question. He began by tracing some of the history of the recent talks and mentioned the terrorism which had broken out about the time of the talks in Zurich which he termed very unfortunate.[4] He said that the Italian Government was still agreeable to referring the matter to the ICJ, which had originally been a United States suggestion and wondered if this was still the U.S. position. The Secretary said that this was correct and he hoped that resort would be had to the ICJ rather than having the question thrown into a "wild and free-swinging" meeting in the U.N. General Assembly. The Italian Ambassador added this was not a political matter as the Austrians claimed, but a legal question. The Secretary then stated that he wanted to say that we thought the Italian Government had acted with great moderation in this dispute and this was appreciated by the United States. He added he only hoped this moderation could be continued so that "you can talk it out between you". He said he presumed the terrorists had pushed the Austrian Government further than the Government would have liked.

The Ambassador said there was one point which he wanted to make entirely clear, i.e., mediation was out of the question as far as the Government of Italy was concerned. He said that the U.S. should impress on the Austrians the necessity for moderation. He added that they were now openly encouraging terrorism and bombs made in Austria had recently been found. He said that many of the leaders of the Tyrol movement were former Nazis and that the Deputy Mayor of a South

---

[4] In July 1961 a series of seven foiled bombing attempts by German-nationalist groups in the South Tyrol left two dead.

Tyrolean town had recently made a speech in which he had declared that one of these days all of the Tyrol would be united and would be a part of one great Reich.

The Ambassador indicated that one of the most tragic aspects of this whole affair was the effect on relations between the Federal German Republic and Italy. He then referred to the support being given to the Austrians by the Bavarians. These pan-German manifestations are particularly deplorable, he added, when we are all uniting to support Berlin. He said unfortunately these developments played into the hands of the Communists in Italy who exploited them against NATO and the European Community. He also indicated Italian policy had always been strong in support of NATO and EEC and the idea of tying Germany to Europe, but this policy might be affected by these manifestations of pan-Germanism.

The Ambassador then queried the Secretary as to whether some approach could be made to the Chancellor to bring him to disassociate his Government from the Tyrol question. He said he was not asking the United States to go to Adenauer and say that the Italian Government had made this proposal, but he was throwing this out as a personal idea which might possibly have merit. The Secretary asked if Segni had mentioned this to von Brentano and the Ambassador said he did not know. The Secretary manifested some interest in this proposal and said it would be studied.

The Ambassador then raised the subject of Berlin and Mr. Khrushchev's intentions. The Secretary said that we would be in touch with his Government on this subject before too long. He added that Mr. Khrushchev was serious in his determination to exploit the Berlin question and he would continue to press the matter. He also said that Khrushchev was anxious about East Germany and wanted to strengthen it. He said he presumed that negotiations would take place at some stage, but before we negotiate we want to make it clear to him that we are firm. In conclusion we are making a total review of our policy and would be in touch with his government soon, the Secretary said.

The Ambassador said at the end of the conversation that if Fanfani went to Moscow, he hoped that we would recall that he was about the last to make the pilgrimage.

290.   Letter From Prime Minister Fanfani to President Kennedy

Rome, August 26, 1961.

MR. PRESIDENT: Upon my return from Moscow, I provided you, through diplomatic channels as early as August 5, and then through Mr. Salinger on August 8, and through Secretary of State Mr. Rusk on August 9 with the information I obtained in my talks from August 2 to 5 with Mr. Khrushchev and my evaluation of that information. [1]

In substance, I considered that (1) Negotiations between the Allies and the U.S.S.R. should be opened as soon as possible, not later than immediately after the West German elections; and that (2) It was necessary to begin at once a confidential exploration of topics, procedure, time, and location of the negotiations.

I pointed out the need for such an immediate exploration not only for the constructive preparation of the negotiations, but also (1) To induce the U.S.S.R. immediately not to initiate avoidable and deplorable political-and-diplomatic castling maneuvers; and (2) To prevent a chain reaction at the end of which, at any unexpected moment, an incident might arise, and from that, a catastrophe might develop.

The deplorable measures adopted and announced by the Communists for Berlin on August 14[2] and subsequently, the countermeasures that the members of NATO have had to take or announce, confirm the validity of my above-mentioned evaluation.

Therefore, in line with our common political and ideological principles, our joint responsibility for the fate of our people, and our duty to seek, in an atmosphere of peace, to extend free progress throughout the world, I again request you, Mr. President, and your Government to take, and cause to be taken, all appropriate steps to prepare, from now on, to announce as soon as the preparation will give sufficient assurance, and to initiate, possibly immediately after the West German election, constructive and conclusive negotiations.

Source: Italian Foreign Ministry Files. No classification marking. The source text is a 1993 Italian Foreign Ministry translation. A similar Department of State translation is in Department of State, Central Files, 611.65/8–2661.

[1] Prime Minister Fanfani and Foreign Minister Segni visited the Soviet Union August 3–5. Fanfani personally briefed Secretary of State Rusk on the results of his Moscow meetings on August 9 when Rusk visited Rome. A memorandum of their conversation is ibid., 611.61/8–961.

[2] On August 13 the East German Government sealed off its borders with the Federal Republic of Germany and the Soviet Union sealed off its zone from the Western-administered zones of Berlin. For texts of notes exchanged between the Allied powers and the Soviet Union, together with a declaration by the Warsaw Pact, see Department of State Bulletin, September 4, 1961, pp. 395–401; or Documents on Germany, 1944–1985, pp. 773 ff.

To add to the information available to you on the situation, I believe it is my duty to inform you that on the night of August 24 I received a letter from Mr. Khrushchev, dated August 22, confirming my evaluations, as can be set forth at your request.[3]

I trust that you will consider this letter as an additional evidence of my respect for you and a genuine, friendly contribution to whatever action the special, grave responsibilities we assumed in NATO may compel you to take.

I renew the hope that farsighted action may enable us, for the good of our peoples, to overcome our trials and to be successful in attaining peace, freedom, and security. I beg you to accept the assurances of my very high consideration.[4]

---

[3] According to a September 1 memorandum from Tyler to Rusk Fanfani subsequently forwarded a copy of the Khrushchev message to President Kennedy through a personal emissary. (Department of State, Central Files, 765.00/9–161) No copy of this letter has been found.

[4] Printed from an unsigned copy.

---

291.   Telegram From the Embassy in Italy to the Department of State

Rome, October 28, 1961, 2 p.m.

1475. Dept A–98.[1] We are in agreement with Dept that Lombardi's speech was disappointingly rigid expression of PSI desire to see definite change of direction in GOI foreign policy. Even allowing for tactical and personal elements (need to placate PSI left wing, circumstances of delivery by opposition party in parliamentary debate, and Lombardi's own polemical style and predilection for theory), fact remains that text stands as an official expression of long-range PSI on objectives in foreign policy.

Source: Department of State, Central Files, 765.00/10–2861. Secret; Limit Distribution.

[1] Airgram A–98, October 18, expressed disappointment with the tone and substance of the statement by Socialist Party leader Ricardo Lombardi on foreign affairs before the Italian Chamber of Deputies. It advised the Embassy: "If DC–PSI cooperation is tried and fails, it must not seem to have failed because of American opposition. Would be counterproductive to identify ourselves with those who oppose DC–PSI cooperation for domestic policy reasons. However, we are considering desirability of expressing to our PSI autonomist contacts in Italy disappointment that Lombardi statement of policy in foreign affairs debate has by silent acquiescence of autonomists, been permitted to stand as official position of Party." (Kennedy Library, National Security Files, Italy)

As Dept has pointed out, speech constitutes catalog of implications for US which might ensue from PSI influence on government, and no doubt if PSI were admitted to government support it would press for action to reach these ends. Also appreciate risks inherent in continuation of such pressure over period of time. We do not believe, however, that PSI would be able to oblige GOI to accomplish these objectives, and we doubt that they need be taken as literal statement of what we should expect to happen in short-term if PSI voting support accepted by future coalition. Our reasons for doubting PSI ability to reach stated goals derive from divisions within PSI itself and from potential opposition of center parties.

Lombardi's stress on doctrinaire objectives is not shared by all elements of PSI. His approach is more moderate than left wing would like and more drastic than Nenni's. While Nenni's report in PSI Central Committee meeting on October 19 (A–324)[2] endorsed Lombardi's speech, it then proceeded to modify tone of latter and to stress theme of practical short-term objectives rather than of PSI's long-term aims and neutralist policy. Latter were absent from Central Committee's October 12 resolution. Embassy officers have found in conversations with autonomist leaders Demartino, Pieraccini, Cattani, and Bensi that they were dismayed by tone of Lombardi's speech and do not realistically expect center-left government to have much more effect on foreign policy than reinforcement of such initiatives in favor of negotiations and détente as have characterized recent Fanfani actions. We are inclined to think that division in PSI itself would hamper concerted pressure by PSI on center-left government to accomplish long-term policy objectives and that some compromise of these aims with Christian Democrats would be likely, both because of PSI desire to make cooperation in center-left government work and as consequence of any advance that might be made in measures for social problems in domestic field, which are of particular importance to PSI.

PSI ability to push national government toward its long-term foreign policy objectives would also be qualified by potential opposition within DC and other parties composing center-left coalition. If difficult issues of foreign policy should arise, we believe there would be sufficient support for Western objectives, particularly from Saragat in PSDI and from many elements in DC, to resist PSI pressure and even bring government down rather than move toward neutralist position. Reluctance of DC majority to engage in center-left experiment would accentuate this resistance, and assistance might be obtained from group of six pro-NATO ex-PDI deputies close to DC who could provide a DC–PSDI–

---

[2] A–324, October 19, analyzed Nenni's report on foreign policy to the PSI Central Committee. (Department of State, Central Files, 765.13/10–1961)

PRI government with a majority if PSI should balk on a key foreign policy issue.

As Dept has observed, clarity of Lombardi's statement in parliamentary foreign policy debate has done nothing to settle issue of PSI suitability for voting cooperation with center-left government. We do not think that government based on PSI support is inevitable alternative to present formula. Administrative government or prolonged crisis with present government continuing in caretaker position, with or without national elections, are other possibilities. Also we do not think that present international situation makes this a propitious moment for center-left experiment with PSI to be attempted, for very reason that it might founder on foreign policy question.

No doubt Fanfani, Moro, and other DC leaders are fully aware of foreign policy implications which formation of center-left government would have in terms of questions it would raise in minds of Italy's allies. They are also aware of inevitable divisions that foreign policy issue would create domestically within DC. Although Fanfani and Moro may be favorably disposed toward eventual opening to left, they are sufficiently astute to realize that alliance with a party whose stated long-range foreign policy aims with respect to NATO are so glaringly disparate from those of the DC would be particularly difficult to justify at present time. Even if center-left alliance could be rammed through, intra-DC dissension would probably doom it to eventual failure, with consequent damage to Fanfani and Moro personally. Accordingly, both these leaders, privately and publicly, have maintained that prior to embarking on center-left, PSI would have to commit itself to support DC foreign policy.

Center-left issue appears, however, to be absorbing attention of all political figures, and many seem to believe that time is running out and experiment must be tried soon or indefinitely deferred. It is possible that government may be brought down even before November 11 date on which President's power to dissolve Parliament expires.[3] If this should happen, center-left experiment probably has been talked about too long and exerts too great a political attraction for it to be prevented by efforts on our part except such as would go far beyond measures proposed in A–98.

As opportunities have presented themselves, Embassy officers have expressed negative reaction to Lombardi's speech in conversations with PSI autonomists Demartino, Pieraccini, Cattani, Bensi, and Vit-

---

[3] Under the Italian Constitution, the President of the Republic may not dissolve a government during the 6-month period immediately preceding the election of a new President.

torelli, and with some exponents of center-left in PRI, PSDI, and DC. We have, for example, on occasion politely questioned whether Italy's own best interests in security and international relations would be served by a PSI-influenced foreign policy, and we have asked whether period of international tension would be propitious for launching of center-left experiment, in view of Nenni's own statement in June television interview that atmosphere of international détente would be more conducive to the operation. Further, with foregoing individuals and with opponents of center-left, who are also anxious for statements which could be utilized as US support for their views, we have taken line that despite our doubts on international grounds, US neither favors nor opposes creation of center-left government.

Thus, we believe that we have already taken action similar to that contemplated in A–98. We have proceeded cautiously, for we believe that we should avoid impression of conducting campaign and that we should not go so far become publicly identified with opposition to center-left, thus damaging our position in Italy. Without seriously running these risks, however, we could discreetly do more, if Dept desires that we do so, we would appreciate instructions, indicating as completely as possible position we should take.

Reinhardt

---

292. Memorandum From the President's Special Assistant (Schlesinger) to the Under Secretary of State (Ball)

Washington, November 1, 1961.

SUBJECT

　Meeting on Italian Policy

This memo is for your private contemplation. I don't think it would serve any useful purpose to send it down the line.

The policy laid down in Airgram A–98,[1] sent to Rome under the signature of Secretary Rusk, is as follows:

Source: Kennedy Library, National Security Files, Italy. Secret.

[1] See footnote 1, Document 291.

Unless PSI as organization is willing and able to disavow or decisively to modify Lombardi line we would be forced to consider formation of government subject to PSI influence (that is, depending on PSI support even if it did not participate directly) as potentially very serious for West.

This is a demand for a formal public recantation by the PSI as condition precedent to US acceptance of an Italian government dependent on PSI support.

From the statement that, without such recantation, such a government must be regarded as "potentially very serious for West," there presumably follows:

a) we should actively oppose the formation of such a government [1 paragraph (2 lines of source text) not declassified].

All this raises at least two questions:

1. Is the policy laid down in Airgram A–98 a sensible and realistic policy? is the prior public recantation "as organization" demanded by Airgram A–98 a condition that can be reasonably met? or will it have the effect of locking us back into the Luce–Dulles policy of rigid opposition to the "opening to the left"?

2. Should so important a policy decision be taken without consultation in the highest levels of the State Department—especially when it runs contrary to the evident line of thought in Amembassy Rome (see Airgram A–324)[2] and when its spirit would seem to conflict with the spirit of President Kennedy's assurance to Prime Minister Fanfani that we had no objections to his exploring the possibilities of a center-left coalition?[3]

Arthur Schlesinger, Jr.[4]

---

[2] See footnote 2, Document 291.

[3] Reports of a Kennedy statement of support for the formation of a center-left government led the Embassy to request clarification from the Department. In a December 28 letter to Horsey, Tyler noted that "to the best of our knowledge the President made no comment of his own but merely asked unslanted questions and listened to the answers." (Department of State, Italian Desk Files: Lot 68 D 436, Italy—Nenni's Proposed Visit—1962)

[4] Printed from a copy that bears this typed signature.

293. Telegram From the Department of State to the Embassy in Italy

Washington, November 8, 1961.

1401. Embtel 1475.[1] Department has exhaustively reviewed question of position US reps should adopt re possible government dependent on PSI support. Position should be as follows:

A. In discussions with top level Demochristians, particularly Fanfani and Moro, Embassy reps should confidentially state we are alive to possible advantages in isolating Communists and strengthening Italian democracy which might result from obtaining PSI support for government, provided, however, that this could be accomplished without any compromise whatsoever with PSI on foreign policy. Embassy should emphasize however that we would consider it serious development for West if formation of such government with PSI collaboration were to result in any change in Italian support for NATO or in Italy's foreign policy in general. (*Begin FYI*. Will be noted this approach leaves to CD leaders question of public or private assurances or guarantees on foreign policy to be required of PSI as price of formation of government dependent on PSI support. *End FYI*.)

B. In discussion with PSI Autonomists US reps should confine selves to reiteration of our concern over and disagreement with current PSI foreign policy positions and our hope that Party will move to wiser positions in future. Should make clear we share wish of most Italians for dynamic, "positive" domestic program which would accelerate existing pace of reform, improvement in material conditions and social change. As friends of Italy, we would welcome PSI support for such program, although this question does not of course involve US directly. Same comments could be addressed to other figures in PSDI and Republican parties who favor opening to left. (*Begin FYI*. Will be noted that specific reference to our attitude towards government with PSI support, as outlined in preceding para, would be omitted from these comments to PSI, PRI and PSDI figures. Should US reps be pressed for statement of specific US attitude toward such Govt, they should turn question aside, avoiding reply. *End FYI*.)[2]

Rusk

Source: Kennedy Library, National Security Files, Italy. Secret; Limited Distribution. Drafted by Knight, cleared by Tyler, and approved by Ball. The time of transmission is illegible.

[1] Document 291.

[2] On December 3 Foreign Minister Segni called Reinhardt to his office to express concern over the political impact of a proposed visit by Nenni to the United States. In the course of his response, Reinhardt conveyed the substance of paragraph A of telegram 1401 to Segni. (Kennedy Library, National Security Files, Italy)

294.   Editorial Note

The question of the United States attitude toward an opening to the left publicly surfaced on January 13, 1962, when the Turin newspaper *Gazzetta del Popolo* published a report stating that President Kennedy had discussed the issue during a January 9 White House meeting with Giuseppi Codacci-Pisanelli, president of the Interparliamentary Union and a Minister without portfolio in the Fanfani government. According to the memorandum of conversation of this meeting:

"The President opened by referring to the Italian political situation and asking what was going to be done about Nenni. Mr. Pisanelli said this was the great question in Italy at the moment but that those who hoped by making a deal with Nenni to isolate the Communists were doomed in his opinion to disappointment, witness, he said, the recent statement to this effect by Riccardo Lombardi of Nenni's party. The most difficult aspect of this problem was accordingly foreign policy." (Department of State, Presidential Memoranda of Conversation: Lot 66 D 149)

In telegram 2041, January 17, the Department of State informed the Embassy in Rome: "If questioned by Italian correspondents White House will reply as follows: *Begin text.* Reports that President Kennedy in his discussion of January 9 with President of Inter-Parliamentary Union Giuseppe Codacci-Pisanelli expressed an opinion on the question of the so-called Opening to the Left in Italy are without foundation. The question of the political debate now underway in Italy was briefly touched upon, but the President expressed no opinion whatsoever on either side of the various points of view under consideration. *End text.*"

It added that the Embassy could make a "similar clarification" if questioned by the local press. (Department of State, Central Files, 033.6511/1–1962)

---

295.   Editorial Note

The Christian Democratic Party's National Congress met January 27–February 1, 1962. During these meetings, the Christian Democrats approved a plan for the formation of a government led by Prime Minister Fanfani and enjoying the external support of the Italian Socialist Party. On February 2, Fanfani presented the resignation of his government to President Giovanni Gronchi. After discussions with party leaders, Gronchi asked Fanfani to form a new government on February 10. On February 16, the Christian Democratic, Social Democratic, and Republican parties announced agreement on a program for a new Fanfani government of the center-left. The Socialist Party gave its approval to the government's program on February 18. In telegram 2485, February 19, the Embassy in Rome submitted a lengthy analysis of the new government and its program. (Department of State, Central Files, 765.00/2–1962)

On February 21 President Gronchi swore in a new Fanfani government that included 19 Christian Democratic, 3 Social Democratic, and 2 Republican Ministers.

---

296.   Memorandum From Secretary of State Rusk to President Kennedy

Washington, February 20, 1962.

SUBJECT

Our Assessment of and Actions with Regard to a Possible Italian Government Supported by the Socialist Party

Christian Democrat Party leaders of Italy seem to be following a correctly cautious policy in their approach to the formation of a government depending on the support in Parliament of the left-wing Italian Socialist Party of Pietro Nenni. (The recent evolution of this question is described in enclosure 1.)[1] This could constitute a turning point in Italian political affairs, for better or for worse. Present Italian policies would probably not, however, show a significant change in the immediate future.

Cooperation with the PSI, if wisely pursued, could bring impressive long-term gains for Italy. It could add to the ability of Italian Governments to adopt much-needed constructive programs. (Among the measures advocated by the PSI there are many that Italian moderates

---

Source: Kennedy Library, National Security Files, Italy. Secret.
[1] Not found.

favor.) It could broaden the "area of democracy" in Italian politics. It could lead to the political isolation of the Communist Party. (Communist leaders are now feverishly developing tactics designed to discredit the new formula or, better yet, to convert it into a vestibule for a new Popular Front.)

However, the ultimate risks of such an association for Italian democracy and for the United States are also impressive. Forty percent of the PSI Party continues to favor close unity of action with the Communists. Even under its present "Autonomist" leadership the PSI urges a greater degree of "independence" vis-à-vis the U.S., confesses to a tendency towards neutralism, favors a disarmed and neutralized Germany and would probably oppose controls over strategic trade with the Soviet Bloc. In domestic affairs it opposes discriminatory measures against the Communists, and favors the reestablishment of labor unity in an organization including the Communists. (It continues to collaborate with the Communists in trade unions, cooperatives and many local governments.) Its potential influence in these directions would be compounded by the fact that some of these views are shared to a greater or lesser extent by certain elements of the center parties, and their currency has of late, if anything, been increasing.

The fear that the issue of collaboration with the PSI might endanger Christian Democrat Party unity has for the moment been attenuated by the handling of the party's recent National Convention by Party Secretary Moro. Moro formulated a cautious step-by-step approach to collaboration firmly rejecting any change in foreign policy or in the party's attitude toward the Communists. He also urged the continued participation in the Party leadership of those opposed to the PSI "experiment". The Convention endorsed this formulation by an 80 percent majority.

United States Actions:

Our actions have been taken in the framework of the policy set forth in the Policy Guidelines paper on Italy (enclosure 2).[2] Although this paper has not yet been "promulgated", the sections on Italian internal political affairs have been fully approved in the Department of State. [*3-1/2 lines of source text not declassified*]

Our fundamental hope, as this movement has almost inexorably developed, has been that its fruits might be harvested without the surrender of any of the major gains already made by Italy in both foreign and domestic affairs in recent years. During the past year we have avoided taking a clear-cut position for or against PSI collaboration insofar as Italian internal issues were concerned, stating that this was a ques-

---

[2] Not printed.

tion that the Italians themselves should decide. In confidential conversations we have stated that we were alive to the possible advantages in isolating the Communists and strengthening Italian democracy which might result from obtaining PSI support for the government, and that we shared the wish of most Italians for a dynamic "positive" domestic program which might accelerate the existing pace of reform and of social change, and the improvement of material conditions. However, we have placed our primary emphasis on the need to ensure that Italian foreign policy was not affected by the formation of such a government. We have made no secret of our concern over and disagreement with the PSI foreign policy positions, or of our hope that the PSI would move to wiser positions in the future.

[1 paragraph (5-1/2 lines of source text) not declassified]

In recent weeks we have been particularly careful to avoid any action which might seem an attempt to intervene in the "great debate". We rejected a suggestion that Nenni be officially invited to the United States before the Christian Democrat Convention, believing that the PSI would use such an invitation as the basis for claiming that we favored an opening to the Left with or without further modification of PSI foreign policy positions. We have since agreed, however, that Nenni might well be invited to visit this country by a private organization after a new government has been confirmed.[3]

Now that the crisis has formally begun, we have taken the position with the press that: 1) we deferred to the judgment of our Italian friends as to the type of government best suited to strengthening Italy's democratic institutions and economy; and 2) we were confident that Italy would continue to lend its whole-hearted support to NATO and European integration.

For the future, we are in fact by no means reassured that should a government dependent on the PSI be formed Italy's policies would not as a result gradually evolve in directions unfavorable to us. PSI influence could very well, unless the center parties held completely firm, affect Italy's support for NATO, Italy's primary reliance on ties with the U.S., the position of Italian free trade unions and cooperatives vis-à-vis cooperation with Communist organizations, Italy's contribution to Western defense with particular regard to its defense budget and to the stationing of U.S. forces in Italy, Italian support for controls by NATO countries over strategic trade with the Bloc, and Italy's role in the U.N.,

---

[3] Senator Humphrey, who met Nenni September 30, urged in a November 6 letter to Rusk that Nenni be officially invited to visit the United States. (Department of State, Central Files, 033.110–HU/11–661) In early December Nenni indicated his interest to Embassy officials through an intermediary. Documentation on Nenni's interest and the Department's decision to withhold an official invitation pending political developments in Italy are ibid., Italian Desk Files: Lot 68 D 436, Italy—Nenni's Proposed Visit—1962.

with particular reference to its relations with the uncommitted and emerging nations.

Conclusion:

We do not, in conclusion, feel justified in advancing a categoric judgment on whether the "opening to the Left" will eventually prove a favorable or an unfavorable development for us and for Italian democracy. Everything will depend on its implementation. (We are at the moment encouraged by the caution that Italian leaders are currently displaying in their approach to the question.) We are, however, certain that such collaboration will usher us into a period of greater uncertainty in our relations with Italy. Our task will be one of helping our Italian friends to reap from the situation the benefits that we and they hope for (in isolation of the Communists and the strengthening of Italian democracy) and to avoid the dangers, both in foreign and internal affairs, that we and they fear.

Dean Rusk

---

297.   Editorial Note

On February 21, Presidential Special Assistant Arthur Schlesinger, Jr., met with Pietro Nenni in Rome. According to Nenni (*Anni di Centro Sinistra*, pages 213–214), Schlesinger stated U.S. approval of Italy's political evolution, comparing it to the knocking down of gates that had prevented participation by Italy's masses in the governing process. Nenni in turn underlined the limited nature of the new governing arrangement, indicating it was the first step in a process, and stressing the tenuous nature of the experiment in an opening to the left. Nenni also explained the PSI's neutralist position on foreign policy and its incompatibility with Atlantic policies. Schlesinger, according to Nenni, stated his agreement. Nenni than added that his party's stand was not incompatible with a Western policy of reduction of tensions and expressed the PSI's hope that the West was seeking to pursue such an approach in its relations with the Soviet Union. Nenni also recorded that in seeking to explain U.S. policy, Schlesinger stated that he understood the PSI's point that it could be loyal to NATO while critical of certain Alliance policies.

Schlesinger reported on this meeting in *A Thousand Days*, pages 803–804, and in a memorandum to President Kennedy. No copy of the memorandum or other record of the meeting has been found.

298.   Memorandum of Conversation

Washington March 17, 1962.

SUBJECT

Mattei and ENI

PARTICIPANTS

Mr. Ball
Mr. McGhee
Mr. Johnson
Ambassador Reinhardt
Mr. Tyler
Ambassador Achilles

Mr. West
Mr. Knight
Mr. Schlesinger, The White House
Mr. Komer, The White House

Summary:

Following an exhaustive reassessment of the position of Mattei in Italian politics and in the international oil industry it was agreed that we should examine the possibility of encouraging one or more of the major Western oil companies to reach an accommodation with him. Mr. Walter Levy will be asked by Mr. McGhee to come to Washington to canvass the situation. Jersey, Socony, or other companies might be interested in considering such an arrangement.

Mattei's General Position:

Ambassador Reinhardt said that the problem of Mattei was a long-standing one and that there were no particularly new elements in the situation other than the evergrowing magnitude of his activities. Mr. Ball commented that new elements might be found in his alleged responsibility for the establishment of the new Fanfani Government dependent on the PSI, and the possibility that he was becoming a front for the Chinese Communists and an agent for the Soviets in the sale of oil.

Ambassador Reinhardt said that even Mattei's power had its limitations. Last summer when he seemed to be bidding for a special role to help the Iraqi oust the British oil companies, the Italian Government had forced him to back down. Similarly, when he gave evidence of attempting to develop special relationships with the FLN with a view to obtaining special concessions in Algeria after the liberation, the Government had again forced him to back down. The Ambassador noted the opinion of the French Ambassador to Rome, M. Gaston Palewski, who believed

---

Source: Department of State, Secretary's Memoranda of Conversation: Lot 65 D 330. Secret. Drafted by Knight and approved in M on April 2 and U on April 5.

that Mattei was undoubtedly the most powerful single individual in Italy and was strong enough to force others not to interfere in his operations but by the same token was not strong enough himself to exercise control in other fields.

The Ambassador said that Mattei's "power" had to be kept in perspective. When he claimed to have masterminded the opening to the left this was pure nonsense. Certainly he had long been in favor of it, but so had many others. He was a highly unstable person and the term megalomania was the only one that suitably described him. He had only two obvious interests: the oil industry and salmon fishing.

Mr. McGhee said these considerations limited the problem but did not change the fact that this government-owned Italian organization was doing things in many areas of the world that were most harmful to our interests.

Ambassador Reinhardt agreed, but pointed out that Italy had a long-standing complex about being short of energy. ENI and Mattei had become Italian institutions answering the Italians' national desires in the energy field, as well as their wish to be "big time" in general. Mr. Schlesinger suggested that Mattei had become a great symbol of economic nationalism in Italy. Mr. McGhee noted the disruptive effect of Mattei's operations in third countries and in our relations with the bloc. As an oil company, however, he said Mattei's operations had been a failure. He had not found oil in Italy, his development of gas supplies had been made possible by a discovery made by American companies, and the cost of the oil he produced himself was uneconomically high by any objective standard.

What the United States Should Do About Mattei:

Ambassador Achilles then raised the question of what we should do about Mattei in the future, [1-1/2 lines of source text not declassified] we could try to win him over. [1-1/2 lines of source text not declassified] to the U.S. and give him the red carpet treatment; or b) we could involve him in profitable oil operations in the Middle East, Africa or elsewhere to provide him with sources of oil other than the Soviet Bloc.

Ambassador Reinhardt could not say whether we would be able actually to take Mattei into camp. Mattei thought he was going to succeed in developing other sources of supply (in the Near East, Africa, etc.) for his distribution network. On the question of his purchases of Soviet oil the Ambassador noted Mattei's own statement that as a percentage of his total consumption during the next few years these would decrease to perhaps half of their present relative level. The Ambassador said he did not believe Mattei wanted Soviet oil because it was *Soviet* oil but merely because he could get it at a lower price. He was completely one-track-minded in his concentration on the oil business.

Mr. McGhee asked whether there would be any basis for reaching a deal with him. He personally thought it would be worthwhile for the American oil companies, for example, to offer him participation in the Iranian consortium, or other first-rate oil fields. Mr. Ball asked whether, in connection with any such deal, we could achieve an acceptable degree of cooperation with Mattei on restraints in purchases of Soviet oil. Ambassador Reinhardt was of the opinion that the price of the oil involved would be an important factor. Mr. McGhee asked whether Mattei and his organization disposed of large sums of capital. He noted that the oil companies were usually happy to distribute the risks of their operations but that such an arrangement would presumably require substantial capital from Mattei. Ambassador Reinhardt commented that Jersey seemed to be trying to reach some sort of arrangement with Mattei on the lawsuits currently before U.S. courts. He noted that some time ago Mattei was said to have stated to a friend in response to a question as to just what he wished that, "All I want is 10% of the European market".

Mr. Tyler said that in his opinion there were two sides to the question: the matter of Soviet oil and the free world petroleum industry, and the existence of an extremely powerful individual in Italian politics who could, if he so decided, exert tremendous pressure on the Italian Government for a given line of policy. Ambassador Reinhardt said that Mattei did not appear to have any particular bias in favor of the Communists and he cited Mattei's history in leading anti-Communist partisans at the end of the last world war. It was Mattei's pride that he had succeeded in keeping his organization entirely separate from the Communist partisans. The Ambassador suggested accordingly that Mattei was not political in his orientation but was an opportunist whose interests were focused on the oil and related industries. Mr. Ball said that if this were the case, it might be possible to dissuade him from some of his more harmful present pursuits by involving him deeply in the free world oil industry. Mr. Schlesinger asked whether he was the type of person who would, in fact, wish to be tied down in this way.

Mr. McGhee thought there would be no problem on the question of sharing the sources of oil with Mattei. The problem would be on the marketing side. The oil companies would be well advised to cut Mattei in on their good concessions. Insofar as the markets were concerned the situation was one of dog eat dog and Mattei might compete to his heart's content. In any case, he would not be able to cut prices beyond a certain minimum since he would then also face the same economic facts of life that the other companies faced. Jersey itself was large enough to make an arrangement with Mattei.

Mr. Schlesinger and Mr. Ball both said they thought such an operation worth trying. Mr. Ball said, however, that it would be necessary for Mattei to behave like a member of the club if he were, in fact, admitted.

Perhaps he would not wish to be domesticated but we would lose nothing by trying.

Mr. McGhee suggested that an arrangement with Mattei would presumably have to include some undertakings on his part such as: 1) that he would not interfere with the percentage split with the governments of producing countries; 2) that he would be "fair" to the Western oil companies in Italy itself both with regard to markets and exploration; and 3) that he would reduce his trade in oil with the Russians.

Mr. Ball said the net result of such an arrangement, if it could be accomplished, would be to remove Italy from the category of oil-short countries. It was entirely possible that this would basically change Italian actions and attitudes in this entire field for the better.

Mr. McGhee suggested that Department representatives discuss this question quietly with Jersey. Mr. Ball agreed and suggested that Walter Levy be asked to come to Washington in a few days to discuss the possibilities. (Mr. McGhee will arrange this.) [1-1/2 lines of source text not declassified] Ambassador Reinhardt suggested that if such an attempt were made Egidio Ortona (Director General for Economic Affairs in the Italian Foreign Ministry, and favorably disposed toward the United States) might be helpful. Mr. Ball agreed.

Possible Meeting of the Under Secretary with Mattei

Ambassador Reinhardt suggested that before any approach on the possibility of an accommodation were made to Mattei, Mr. Ball should meet with him on a social basis without raising substantive matters. He said that if Mr. Ball did, in fact, visit Rome this month, an inconspicuous luncheon could be arranged at the Villa Taverna. It was agreed that it would be undesirable for such a visit to take place under circumstances making it seem that Mr. Ball had gone primarily to see Mattei. If, however, other business took him to Rome a talk with Mattei might be made to seem incidental. The Ambassador pointed out that a visit to Rome by Mr. Ball would in any case be useful from the point of view of our overall relations with Italy. Mr. Ball concluded, however, by saying that it was not yet clear whether he would be able to go in the immediate future.

ceremonial office and Fanfani is too young, active and ambitious to agree to accept such a sterile position. There are three likely possibilities mentioned for the Presidency, Gronchi, Segori [*Segni?*] and Saragat. However, Parliamentary elections are extremely hard to predict, and it is very likely that someone other than one of these three will be elected.

General Decker inquired about the status of the NATO Atomic Stockpile Agreement, and Ambassador Reinhardt said that it had been signed in January although the implementing technical agreements still are not signed. Each service has a technical agreement to be signed and he and General C.D. Palmer had agreed that since the language in each agreement was quite similar, one standardized agreement should be drafted to cover all three services. Work had begun on this problem at EUCOM and the draft should be about ready for discussions with the Italians in Rome. In reply to a question by General Decker, Ambassador Reinhardt said that he did not foresee any difficulty in completing action on the agreement.

General Decker asked the Ambassador's views on the continuation of SETAF in Italy under present arrangements. Ambassador Reinhardt said that U.S. military presence in Italy is very important. The Italians respond well to demonstrations of strength and friendliness and the great majority of Italian people are delighted at this guarantee of U.S. support. SETAF has a high value to the U.S. in political terms and any change in its organization or size should be gradual. This is particularly true in light of the present political situation. [3 *lines of source text not declassified*] He noted that the Italian relations with SETAF were unexcelled. Ambassador Reinhardt said that he had been most impressed by the cordial relations that exist between SETAF and the Italian Armed Forces.

General Decker asked what the Italian reaction would be to a phase-out of the UK Thor force. Ambassador Reinhardt said that this problem caused him great concern. There is a great deal of feeling among professional military and political people in Italy that the Jupiter program was not a wise one and that the Italians were hooked on a poor weapon. However, they feel that they must make the best of a bad situation. Undoubtedly, in time, this will become a public issue as will the question of the necessity of a follow-on weapon for the Jupiter. The phase-out of Thor might bring these problems out into the open sooner than under normal conditions. We must have some rationale for the Jupiter if we do permit the phase-out of Thor. The Italians do not have a position on the MRBM, but the Jupiter problem will make them focus on the subject. General Decker said that Jupiter is a first generation weapon and that the MRBM is presently under discussion and the USAF has been charged with developing a weapon. If the program is carried out then some weapons could be deployed to Italy. In reply to Mr. Johnson's question, Ambassador Reinhardt said that the Italians view the presence of Jupiter both as a positive deterrent and as a lightning rod. General LeMay said that the MRBM is the only practicable replacement for the Jupiter, and he believed that we should go all out on the MRBM program including deployment of it to Italy. The Thor and the Jupiter will wear out in time, and we cannot logically replace them with Titan, Polaris or Minuteman. Thus the MRBM is the only answer. Ambassador Reinhardt said that if other missiles become operational in the Mediterranean area, the Italians probably will be agreeable to removal of the Jupiters. Mr. Nitze stated that the Thors will phase out in 1964 unless action is taken to extend them. General Decker pointed out that if the Thors are to go out in 1964 we can expect a leak when Parliament is informed. General LeMay said that the Thor program in the UK was entirely political; there was no military requirement for it and the RAF had never wanted the program.

Ambassador Reinhardt closed by stating that the Italians have an increasing awareness of space activities and they are very happy with our successes. Mr. Johnson noted that this is true throughout the world among nations friendly to us.

[Here follows the remainder of the memorandum.]

---

301.   Telegram From the Embassy in Italy to the Department of State

Rome, April 25, 1962, 11 a.m.

2899. Eyes only for Under Secretary McGhee. Ref Deptel 2668.[1] It is encouraging that ESSO willing seek rapprochement with Mattei, and I hope this will lead eventually toward the broader objectives of containing Soviet oil and promoting harmony among Western oil companies.

Source: Kennedy Library, National Security Files, Italy. Confidential; Priority; Limit Distribution.

[1] Telegram 2668, April 23, reported that McGhee met on April 19 with W.R. Stott of Standard Oil of New Jersey to discuss the elements of a possible accommodation with Mattei, that Stott "sizes up Mattei very much as we do," and that he believed that a basis for accommodation existed. It requested the Ambassador's views on a démarche with the Italian Government aimed at reducing points of friction between U.S. oil companies and ENI, at limiting ENI's purchase of Soviet oil, and at ending unfair discrimination against U.S. oil companies in Italy. (Kennedy Library, National Security Files, Italy)

I had thought it generally agreed that, given the psychological problem of Mattei personality, a helpful first step would be accord him some recognition, on theory that this might facilitate subsequent efforts by our oil companies to reach some accommodation with him or at least assuage his sense of damaged ego sufficiently to minimize future polemics. I continue think such recognition would be useful, especially if it could be arranged before rather than after the proposed approach by ESSO. (Despite an ESSO approach, Mattei would doubtless still seek a meeting with U.S. officials, but a meeting then would be of different character, tending to involve our spokesman directly in the negotiations perhaps even at Mattei's behest.) If a prior meeting is now ruled out by Stott's proposed approach to Mattei this week (I assume ESSO continues to oppose what they consider build-up of Mattei by any semi-official "recognition"), then I believe best course would be to limit the U.S. Government role strictly to one of encouragement toward harmony without any direct intervention such as suggested in ref message.

I think that any official U.S. approach to the Italian Govt regarding our relations with Mattei should follow rather than precede an attempt at rapprochement in the commercial field through ESSO or other majors. It seems to me that an official US approach to Italian Govt seeking specific limitation on oil imports (and below the 14 percent limit which has been self-imposed), coming before inter-company negotiations had revealed a basis for agreement and before U.S. had "recognized" Mattei, would surely appear to Mattei as an attempt to bludgeon him into an agreement unfavorable to his interests. (The same would be true if Stott should appear to be speaking for US Govt, and particularly if Mattei got impression that he had to meet Stott's terms before "recognition" by US Govt would be possible.) To protect his negotiating position Mattei would doubtless pressure Italian Govt not to make any commitments.

An official US approach to Italian Govt, moreover, does not seem called for at this stage, I assume that ESSO proposes to offer Mattei sufficient inducement to help resolve immediate problems between the two companies and to contribute to a satisfactory understanding with Mattei at company level concerning future ENI purchases of Soviet crude and ENI attacks on operations of the majors. We would not expect Mattei to back down immediately and openly (to his own govt) from positions he has long espoused, or from his existing contracts to purchase Soviet crude, but the availability of alternative sources of low-priced crude (from ESSO and others who might follow) should in itself operate against any increase in ENI's purchases of Soviet crude and might even lead to a commitment in that sense.

In light of foregoing, I suggest that Stott be advised before his meeting with Mattei this week that he should not expect an official US démarche to Italian Govt at this time (seeking agreement that ENI will not increase its purchases of Soviet crude) since such approach in our view would stiffen Mattei's resistance and reduce the possibility of any agreement being reached. I think Stott should also be told that we remain receptive to a meeting between Mattei and State Dept officials as soon as convenient. (In my view, it would be better to have this meeting in Washington as initially suggested rather than to have UnderSec Ball come here, unless ESSO negotiations have proved fruitful by that time.)

Although this might appear as inadequate US Govt support for ESSO negotiations, it should be recognized that pressures on Italy by other govts for limitation of Soviet oil imports (through NATO oil study) produced few results and were interpreted by Italians mainly as an effort to defend interests of "petroleum cartel" and to limit Mattei's bargaining power with Western companies. An official US intervention for the same purpose at this time, even though related to ESSO's new offers, could be similarly interpreted. And If ESSO's initial negotiations were unsuccessful, influence of US Govt toward an eventual agreement would have been dissipated prematurely.

As I see it the purpose of this exercise, which may well be prolonged, is to encourage rapprochement with Mattei, leading to more harmonious relations among oil companies and to cooperation on Soviet oil, to exert direct bilateral US Govt pressure at this stage, especially to achieve a specific limitation which we have failed to obtain in NATO, seems premature and could work against the broader objective.[2]

Reinhardt

---

[2] Telegram 2695 to Rome, April 25, reported that Reinhardt's objections to the proposed strategy for dealing with Mattei had been raised with Stott. Since Stott maintained his view, McGhee had urged him to meet with Reinhardt prior to any discussions with Mattei to reach agreement on tactics. (Kennedy Library, National Security Files, Italy) Telegram 2935 from Rome, April 28, reported that Reinhardt and Stott had reached agreement that an official U.S. approach to the Italian Government at that point was impractical and might be counterproductive. (Ibid.)

302. Memorandum From the President's Special Assistant (Schlesinger) to President Kennedy

Washington, April 27, 1962.

SUBJECT

[less than 1 line of source text not declassified]

1. As you know, the Italian political situation has entered a new phase of moderate left-of-center government. This experiment is generally agreed to be in our interest (a) because it gives the middle-of-the-road group a working majority and thereby makes for political stability in Italy; (b) because it means the defection of the Socialist party (PSI) from the pro-Communist left and thereby promotes the political isolation of the Communists; (c) because it makes possible programs of social and economic reform and thereby opens up an attack on the conditions which breed communism.

2. This new political situation, though promising, is still fragile. The Italian Communist Party (PCI) is doing its best to prevent it from succeeding. Pro-Communist elements in the PSI are fighting the Nenni policy of collaboration with the Christian Democrats. The PSI Congress will take place this winter; a general election impends next spring. It is essential to the success of the Fanfani experiment that Nenni maintain his leadership in the PSI and that the PSI do well in this election and not fall on its face, as a result of its new policy.

[Here follow paragraphs 3–5.]

[2 paragraphs (11-1/2 lines of source text) not declassified]

[Here follows the remainder of the memorandum.]

Source: Kennedy Library, National Security Files, Italy. Secret. Drafted by Komer.

303.   Telegram From the Embassy in Italy to the Department of
State

Rome, May 27, 1962, 3 p.m.

3134. For Under Secretary. Following is résumé of conversation at
luncheon at Villa Taverna May 22 attended by Under Secretary Ball, Enrico Mattei, President of ENI, Colonel Vernon Walters, Brazza
Savorgnan (Mattei's interpreter) and myself.

Mattei stated at length and with some emotion that his only aim
was to provide Italy with a cheap power source and to put Italian labor
to work. He repeated over and over that the major oil companies would
have to treat him like a human being and realize that he was here to stay.
He said that up to now they had fought him at every turn and tried to
keep him out of several countries. He had had to take leftovers but he
had brought in oil in commercial quantities in some of these leftovers
(Sinai, parts of Iran, etc.). Mattei said that now however there were some
indications that there was a change of heart on the part of the oil companies. A British company was holding out an offer of crude at a lower
price than Soviet crude and he had a useful talk with Mr. Stott of Standard Oil of New Jersey. Secretary Ball said that the US Government had
no special brief for the oil companies other than where US vital interests
were concerned and recognized that relations between them and ENI
had not been good in the past and that we welcomed what appeared to
be an improvement of these relations. We recognized what Mattei had
created and how important it was to Italy and were anxious to keep
communications open to him.

Mattei said that in many of the newly developing areas of Africa
and Asia there was distrust of the US, UK and France and that his presence there had prevented Bloc countries from moving in. He cited an
appeal by Castro last year which he had not answered and said that as a
result the Czechs had moved in. He said that he too was of the West and
it was better for ENI to be there than for one of the Bloc countries. He
said that he attempted to bring the local countries and people in not only
in matters of financial participation but also in training indigenous personnel in oil techniques. In a refinery which he owned jointly with a US
corporation he had been forbidden to train Italian personnel. The British
did not do this and he said that if he published the letter from this US
corporation it would have a very bad effect on Italian public opinion. In
reply to a question as to whether this might not be a regular commercial
practice to protect patents he said that this was not the case as this refinery was outmoded and no new processes were in use there.

Source: Department of State, Central Files, 110.12–BA/5–2762. Confidential; Priority; Limit Distribution.

In reply to a question by the Under Secretary regarding pipe he said that he had made a deal with the Soviets to supply them with 250,000 tons over 5 years in return for crude and that other countries such as West Germany and Japan were supplying them with larger quantities every year. With regard to crude imports into Italy he said that he was buying Soviet oil because it was the cheapest he could get. It was his duty to provide Italy with the cheapest possible sources of energy. In reply to a question by the Under Secretary, he said that he had been asked by Chancellor Raab of Austria to look into the construction of a pipeline from Trieste to Vienna to lessen Austria's dependence on Soviet sources. He avoided commenting on the possibility of an eventual extension to Bratislava that the Under Secretary had raised or on the possibility that Soviet crude might flow in the opposite direction to Trieste.

Mattei then spoke of China and said that there was great resentment there against the Soviet Union and the other Bloc countries as the Chinese had found out that they had been overcharged for much of the equipment that they had been furnished by these countries. He said that two months ago the Russians had practically moved out of China and there had been a vacuum but that the Russians had realized how dangerous this might become and had moved back in; in fact the Soviet Minister of Foreign Trade Patolichev had been there. It was to apprise him of the importance and extent of this vacuum that had led Mattei to try to see President Kennedy at the time. He himself was doing some work with the Chinese and exhibited a friendly letter from Marshal Chen Yi suggesting further cooperation. Mattei implied that he might be useful in China but did not put forth any definite suggestion. From cheap industrial machinery exported to other Asiatic countries and remittances from the overseas Chinese they had about $350,000,000 in foreign currency. He was doing a hundred million dollars worth of business with them which was as much as he could handle. In reply to a question by Ambassador Reinhardt as to what type of goods the Chinese particularly wanted he replied vaguely "industrial plants". Mattei expressed the belief that China would be increasingly influential in world affairs.

Asked by the Under Secretary how he felt about the Common Market, Mattei replied that by extending his present practices to the whole of the Common Market he could survive and prosper and lower the price for petroleum products throughout the area.

The tone of the meeting was friendly and Mattei seemed appreciative of this opportunity of setting forth his views to the Under Secretary.

Detailed memorandum follows by pouch.

Reinhardt

304. Memorandum of Conversation

SET/MC/19   Rome, June 23, 1962, 5 p.m.

SECRETARY'S EUROPEAN TRIP[1]
(June 18–28, 1962)

PARTICIPANTS

United States	Italy
The Secretary of State	Prime Minister Fanfani
Ambassador Reinhardt	Foreign Minister Piccioni
Colonel V. Walters	Minister Marchiori

SUBJECT

Fanfani Tour d'Horizon

The Secretary opened the conversation by saying how happy he was to have an opportunity to talk to the Prime Minister. He brought greetings from President Kennedy for the Prime Minister and regretted the shortness of his stay in Rome. The Prime Minister said that he understood the Congressional commitments of the Secretary[2] and he too was happy that they had this opportunity to talk.

The Secretary said that he would be happy to know what the principal concerns of the Prime Minister were at this time on the international scene, on the repercussions that Italian internal politics might have on Italy's foreign policy and on those actions of the United States which might be of concern to the Prime Minister. The Secretary added that he knew that President Kennedy would be extremely interested to know the Prime Minister's feelings. President Kennedy, who had to live 24 hours a day with his responsibility in the field of nuclear weapons, lived 24 hours a day with the hope that peace could be consolidated.

Prime Minister Fanfani referred first of all to the situation in Berlin and said that he felt that all things considered there had been some relaxation of the tensions that had previously existed there. Whether this was part of Khrushchev's tactics or not was difficult to see. Khrushchev had accustomed the world to his sudden storms of ill humor, followed by periods when he was in a more benign mood. He had, however, been

---

Source: Department of State, Conference Files: Lot 65 D 533, CF 2123. Secret. Drafted by Walters and approved in S on June 26.

[1] Secretary Rusk visited Rome, June 24, during a trip to Belgium, France, Greece, Luxembourg, the Netherlands, and Italy.

[2] Rusk testified before the House Foreign Affairs Committee on July 2.

very tough on Berlin when talking to Minister Preti in Moscow recently. The Prime Minister then showed the Secretary a long three-page letter reaffirming the Soviet position on Berlin and disarmament. The Secretary thanked the Prime Minister for showing him the letter (Piccioni had not yet seen it). The Secretary commented that when Khrushchev was talking about Berlin by indirection, that is through third parties, he was invariably a great deal more violent than when talking to us. In our talks with Dobrynin, these had always been conducted in a business-like, quiet atmosphere, without threats of war or use of hydrogen bombs.

Mr. Fanfani then said that a curious phenomenon was taking place in regard to the attitude of the Soviet Union toward the Catholic Church. He had recently had private indications that the Soviets were prepared to let all Catholic bishops in the Soviet Union take part in the Ecumenical Council to be held in Rome in October and this might well be true for the other satellites. There were indications in Czechoslovakia of a less rigid attitude toward the Catholic Church. The Prime Minister felt that this might mean that the Soviets feared that the Council might eclipse them in matters of peace and relaxation of tensions. For this purpose they were calling the Council of Friends of Peace in July and were making great efforts to insure its success.

The Secretary then asked what the Prime Minister thought of the situation in Poland and Mr. Fanfani said that the situation there was a good deal different than in other satellites, and the Church enjoyed greater freedom. He had the feeling that the Poles had been counselling moderation to Khrushchev. The Secretary said that he felt there was a great deal which the Italians might do in Warsaw by encouraging the Poles along this line and added that recently he had a long talk with Mr. Rapacki in Geneva. Foreign Minister Piccioni broke in to say that Rapacki had lived in Italy for ten years as a workman, spoke excellent Italian and had a rather pleasing personality. The Secretary said that he had told Rapacki some simple truths such as the fact that we are in Berlin, that we intend to stay in Berlin for the foreseeable future in view of the world situation, and that, if anybody tried to throw us out, there would be war. This might not seem rational to Khrushchev (namely that we were prepared to fight over Berlin) but he would have to consider the risk that we might be a "little crazy", and would fight. Furthermore, the presence of the Western garrisons in Berlin was a stabilizing factor and in a sense a reassurance for Poland. The Secretary added that as Rapacki had left him he had smiled, shaken hands and said "Good luck to you," and as he went out the door, he had turned back and smiled an even broader smile and said, "I mean good luck to both sides, of course."

Prime Minister Fanfani said that the situation in Berlin might again become grave, as Khrushchev had indicated that he would not countenance the presence of Western garrisons in Berlin and talked as though he were determined to get rid of them.

Mr. Fanfani said that the Polish Ambassador had been trying to see him for three months. He had refused because he knew what the Polish Ambassador wanted to do. He wanted to invite Fanfani to go to Warsaw, and he asked what the Secretary of State thought he should do. The Secretary said that he wanted to review the question in all its aspects. He said he felt that it might perhaps be wiser to invite Rapacki to visit Italy first if he went to Geneva to sign the agreement on Laos. The Italian Prime Minister and Foreign Minister seemed to like this idea.

Mr. Fanfani said that it would be very interesting to observe further actions of the Soviets toward the Catholic Church and also to see whether or not they would send observers from the Russian Orthodox Church to the Ecumenical Council. Mr. Fanfani said that it was his belief that the Vatican would shortly invite the heads of all states to attend the opening of the Council and it would be embarrassing if the Soviets were to reply affirmatively before the nations of the Free World. He did not know what this change in attitude meant toward the Catholic Church. The impression that the Italians had derived from one of the smaller satellite states was that they would like to leave the Orthodox Church free to do what it wanted.

Mr. Fanfani said that in regard to differences between the Soviet Union and China, he did not believe that these would lead to an immediate break in the Sino-Soviet bloc. This was something that might come about in the much more distant future.

The Prime Minister then said that Italy was still a devout supporter of the cause of European economic and political unification. Italy had always supported Britain's entry into the Common Market, and he was happy to reaffirm this fact to the Secretary. He expressed fears that Germany and France might get together and attempt to set up Europe on the basis of their two countries, or three or four, if the others did not join. He discussed his concern in this regard at some length and the Secretary said that he did not believe this was the intention of Adenauer and de Gaulle.

Mr. Fanfani expressed the belief that we must try to bring the Benelux around to be more helpful. He felt that the Germans had always favored British entry into the Common Market and de Gaulle was now resigned to its inevitability. (The Secretary said he thought this was a rather apt way to put the matter.) Fanfani said de Gaulle had asked him at Turin whether he thought it would simplify the integration of Europe if the British were brought in. The Italians had replied affirmatively and de Gaulle had said that they were deluding themselves. He, therefore, seemed to have moved from this position at the present time.

Mr. Fanfani expressed the belief that one of the reasons why General de Gaulle wished to develop a nuclear weapon was that he felt that this might be attractive to Chancellor Adenauer. The Secretary said that both Adenauer and de Gaulle were deeply concerned with the importance of a true understanding between their countries and Foreign Minister Piccioni commented that today they were standing watch on the Rhine together. The Secretary smilingly added that in this brotherhood it would be interesting to see who would be the older brother. He added that he greatly appreciated all that the Italians had done to support constructive developments both in the field of European economic and political integration, as well as in NATO.

Mr. Fanfani then spoke of the internal difficulties which Khrushchev was having within the Soviet Union and said that he did not believe that he was quite the all-dominant dictator that we sometimes thought outside. There were forces at work within the Soviet Union.

On the way over to the dinner at Villa Madama, Prime Minister Fanfani, in the car without the presence of Minister Marchiori, said that he would reply to the other question which the Secretary had asked him concerning the impact of internal political developments in Italy on the foreign policy of that country. He had not been concerned when he last saw the Secretary about such possible effect of the opening to the Left; he was now even more relaxed about this problem. In the recent debate in the Senate on the budget of the armed forces, Minister Andreotti referred to the Athens agreement and even the Socialists had voted to approve the defense budget. Fanfani expressed his confidence that similar approval under similar conditions would be obtained in the Chamber of Deputies. He said that the Socialists had been an opposition party for almost all of the 70 years they have been in existence. They did not understand the responsibilities of power and in some ways it might be easier to have them in the Government than out. Sometimes in discussions they asked almost childish questions. Recently they had finally agreed to the Christian Democrat formula for the nationalization of electricity in Italy. Mr. Fanfani felt that the Italian Socialist Party was moving toward a more positive participation in the democratic life of Italy and that the Socialist Parties of Europe were moving in a similar direction. They were now becoming more concerned with freedom than with material improvements, perhaps because substantial gains had been achieved in the latter field. The Secretary felt that perhaps one of the reasons for this was that the Soviet bloc countries had failed to perform the miracles they had promised.

After dinner the Secretary mentioned the question of the Voice of America relay station in Sardinia. The Prime Minister replied that the situation on this was presently very bad. Italian law reserved the middle band of frequencies for the Italian radio-television monopoly. The

United States interest was in the use of the short-wave bands and the Italians had previously felt that this would be possible, but subsequently they had discovered that on the books there was an old piece of Fascist legislation by which all broadcasts on short-wave bands were reserved for the Italian state. The Italian Government had sounded out the Supreme Court on this matter and it appeared that they could not give us what we wanted short of a state treaty between the two nations which would have to be subject to Parliamentary ratification. He felt that it might not be wise to attempt to do this at this time. The Secretary asked whether this difficulty still held even if the station still were the property of the Italian Government. The Prime Minister replied that these difficulties still held. The Secretary said he would like to reflect on the situation a little bit and the Prime Minister then changed the conversation to pleasant amenities.

---

305. Telegram From Secretary of State Rusk to the Department of State

London, June 24, 1962, 7 p.m.

Secto 59. Eyes only for President and Acting Secretary.

1) Visit to Rome was more than worth the few hours I was able to give it. Detailed reports on group discussions coming separate telegrams.

2) I had a most satisfactory private talk with Segni who may be counted upon as firm and loyal friend. He seemed in fine fettle and his presence in the Italian Presidency for the next seven years, God willing, is reassuring.[1] He is concerned about the possible longer range impact of the "opening to the left" on Italian foreign policy and believes it bears close watching. He knows that if he wishes to say anything quite privately to us on this or any other subject Ambassador Reinhardt has a special channel to the President. I was happy to hear him say that I could deal with Foreign Minister Piccioni on the same basis of utter confidence

---

Source: Department of State, Central Files, 611.65/6–2462. Secret; Priority; No Other Distribution. A note on the source text reads: "Relayed to White House, 6/24/62 5:55 p.m." Memoranda of Rusk's conversations with Italian leaders are in Department of State, Conference Files: Lot 65 D 533, CF 2123.

[1] On May 6 the Italian Parliament elected Antonio Segni President of the Italian Republic on the ninth ballot.

and trust as had been possible with Segni himself. In view of known Segni–Fanfani tensions, I thought this especially significant. There is no doubt that Segni will fully support NATO solidarity, close friendship with the United States, and the kind of European unity and North Atlantic Community which have been objects of US policy.

3) [*3-1/2 lines of source text not declassified*] but he insisted that the opening to the left would make no difference to Italian foreign policy and cited Socialist support in the Parliament for increased military budgets on the basis of the Defense Minister's report of the Athens NATO meeting.[2] He said all the right things for my ears but I could not help thinking of Frondizi.[3] [*3 lines of source text not declassified*]

4) The new Foreign Minister, Piccioni, seems to be solidly Western-oriented, conservative in his views, interested, well informed and articulate. I have the impression he will prove to be a good anchor to windward, especially with Segni in the background.

5) It is worth noting that Segni, Fanfani, and Piccioni each seemed to attach the greatest importance to private talks with me without the others being present. [*less than 1 line of source text not declassified*] it clearly is a situation we must watch very closely.

6) During our discussion of the US-Soviet talks on Berlin, Piccioni invited my comments on a study prepared "by a friend of ours" on Soviet motives and intentions. This study, according to Piccioni, set forth the thesis that practically all aspects of Soviet international behavior, including the drive on Berlin, can be explained by our frustration of their desire to expand their trade with the United States. (This sounded to me like Mattei, but the Embassy is looking into this further.)

As you will learn from the record of the talk, I came back very hard on this, since the Italians have clearly been tempted by the possibilities of increased trade with the USSR for themselves. I was as emphatic as I knew how to be in puncturing this thesis, and I must say for Piccioni that he seemed both satisfied and relieved.

7) I was greatly encouraged to find Italy a strong adherent to the broadest concept of the Common Market in political as well as economic fields. While favoring UK admission, they do not wish to dilute Treaty of Rome. I think they can play a useful middle-man role in all this, and encouraged them to do so.

8) All high officials went out of their way to express appreciation for the job Reinhardt is doing as Ambassador.

Rusk

---

[2] See Document 304.

[3] Arturo Frondizi, President of Argentina, 1958–1962, was overthrown in a March 1962 military coup.

306. Editorial Note

On August 2, Presidential Assistant Schlesinger, NSC Staff member Komer, and Assistant Secretary Tyler met in Washington with Giovanni Pieraccini, editor of the Italian Socialist Party's daily, *Avanti!*. In response to Schlesinger's questions about the current relationship between the Communist and Socialist Parties,

"Mr. Pieraccini indicated that the situation had changed very much. The only way to overcome the Communists was not through violent opposition but through a vast-reaching program of effective social reforms. At the present time, with a left of center Government built around a grouping of Socialists and Social Democrats, the Socialists and the Communists find themselves for the first time in diametrically opposed positions as regards their support of the Government. And this diametrically opposed stand is stronger than may transpire in the news. The Communists, in their campaign against the Socialists, which is even stronger than that against the Christian Democrats, loudly proclaim the Socialist betrayal and selling out to management and U.S. interests, thereby labeling themselves the true representatives of the workers. The recent election results, showing slight losses for the Communists accompanied by slight gains for the Socialists, indicate the need to carry forward the policies of social reform advocated by the Democratic Socialists and which are aimed at the very heart of the basic political problems. Since the left of center Government has been in power the Communists have been in an awkward position, as they would lose strong arguments in their favor if they were to oppose frontally such measures as the nationalization of electric power. At the same time they fear that the workers may become convinced that Democratic Socialism can strike effectively against the forces of reaction."

Pieraccini then outlined the difficulties that the PSI faced in breaking its ties with the Italian Communists. He noted, in particular, the perilous condition of *Avanti!*, and the PSI's reliance on its newspaper to present its views to the Italian people.

"In reply to a question about possible sources of assistance, Mr. Pieraccini indicated that any help from Government enterprises such as ENI and IRI was rather minimal. He also contrasted the meager budget resources of the Socialists with the abundant ones of the Communists. The yearly budget of the Socialists has been around 500 million lire, part of it coming from contributions by workers and part from a yearly campaign organized by *Avanti*, which last year netted 200 million lire for the Party. Until now the Party has been operating at what might be called the subsistence level, and even though there seems to be no possibility of collapse—with victory assured at the next Party Congress—unless the Party is helped in carrying out an independent policy aimed at the consolidation of democracy, it shall have to limit itself to a defensive type of action. At the present time the Italian Socialist Party is in a difficult position, as it encounters varying kinds and degrees of opposition from all shades of the political spectrum. Yet it may well become the strongest party in Italy. Democracy can only win out in Italy if the Socialist Party becomes strong and effective. At the present time only a strong Socialist force can attract and enlist the support of Italian workers. But if this Socialist force does not become a reality, then the country will be split between the Communists and the extreme right. An effective strengthening of the policies advocated by the present Government will bring about unification within the Socialist Party. In order to carry forward policies likely to attract the workers economic help has to be found, but this help has to be without strings. It is necessary that the true friends of Italy understand fully the political situation, show their trust in the Democratic Socialists and give help without listening to those who consider the Italian Socialist as unsafe for democracy.

"Mr. Schlesinger asked whether those were also Mr. Nenni's views. Mr. Pieraccini answered in the affirmative, and added that the long range policies of the Socialist autonomists were the only ones that could hold the workers in a democratic structure, even though it would be of course a Democratic Socialist Party. He recalled in this connection that the net result of the coming into power of center-oriented governments in the past had been a strengthening of the Communists. So the effort of the autonomist Socialists together with certain Catholic groups must be understood and helped."

Regarding *Avanti!*'s financial difficulties, see Nenni, *Anni di Centro Sinistra*, pages 52, 87, 91 ff. [*text not declassified*]

At the conclusion of the meeting, Schlesinger and Pieraccini discussed the possibility of a Nenni visit to the United States during November 1962. (Department of State, Central Files, 765.003/8–2262)

307.   Memorandum From Robert W. Komer of the National Security Council Staff to Vice President Johnson

Rome, September 5, 1962.

SIR: Further on Italy's new left-center cabinet. I believe it fair to say that we in the White House, including the President and Mac Bundy, are more enthusiastic about this new reformist government than the cautious types in State and the Embassy.

We see in it the best opportunity, after over a decade of weak center governments, to translate Italy's economic miracle into more for the people through social and economic reform. We also see in it the best way to isolate the extreme left (which got 37–39% of the vote in the last national election) by consolidating the split between the Communists and the left Socialists (who now back the government). The Embassy is more concerned than we are lest the left Socialists under Nenni drag Italy in a neutralist direction. We think attractive pull of European unity far outweighs this tendency.

Many Italians still wonder whether the US looks with approval on a government supported by Socialists. So, if at luncheon or dinner, you can inquire about this government, and perhaps indicate our general approval of social and economic reform, it could do much to encourage the most desirable political trend in Italy in years.[1]

Bob Komer

Source: Johnson Library, Vice Presidential Security File, VP Johnson's Trip to Middle East. Secret; Eyes Only. Vice President Johnson visited Italy on September 5 at the conclusion of a trip to Greece, Cyprus, Turkey, and Iran. Komer accompanied him.

[1] Telegram 541 from Rome, September 6, reported that during a conversation with Fanfani, Johnson told him that the U.S. Government was watching with interest the reform programs he was trying to establish. Fanfani responded that although it was too soon to expect concrete results, the fundamental "objective of his government was to develop a democratic form of economic planning which would not be compulsive but would seek to orient resources of the nation in most productive and progressive direction." (Department of State, Conference Files: Lot 65 D 533, CF 2149)

308. Editorial Note

In a September 12 memorandum to Schlesinger and Bundy, Komer reported:

"My impression from my talks with Embassy Rome is that we are moving toward consensus on the matter of enhancing the split between the Italian left Socialists and Communists. Ambassador Reinhardt claims that any remaining differences are essentially those of timing rather than viewpoint. Although I wouldn't put it quite this strongly, my brief talks with Reinhardt, Horsey, and Baker (the political officer following the left parties) convince me they're a good deal less negative than before."

He concluded:

"All in all, I'm convinced that the WH effort to stir up movement on this front over the last six months has been most useful. We have made progress in getting State and CIA to look forward instead of backward on what is essentially a question of opportunities versus risks. To me, the translation of Italy's economic miracle into meaningful political and social terms is essential to future Italian political stability, and to the final disappearance of a serious threat from the extremist left. These potential gains far outweigh the risks of undermining the center party or encouraging a neutralist trend. Such fears were legitimate in the late Forties and early Fifties, but I just can't give them the same weight in the prosperous Italy of today. Moreover, what price neutralism in a country which is the most enthusiastic exponent of the European idea because it has the most to gain." (Kennedy Library, National Security Files, Italy)

---

309. Editorial Note

In an October 17 speech before the Socialist Party's Central Committee, Nenni indicated the PSI's readiness to enter into a governing coalition. In an October 18 analysis of the Nenni speech, the Embassy in Rome commented:

"Nenni's speech, intended chiefly to outline PSI political platform for next elections, contained many positive aspects, particularly what is generally interpreted as a firm commitment not to form regional governments with Communists in areas where PSI and PCI would together have majority. DC spokesmen, including Party Secretary Moro, have been pressing PSI strongly on this issue in past weeks and failure of Nenni to make commitment of this kind (assuming it is confirmed by Central Committee) might have caused serious trouble for government. However, refusal to call for isolation of PCI and failure to state position on labor leaves still unclarified PSI ambiguities in two vital areas." (Department of State, Central Files, 765.00/10–1862)

In a memorandum for Bundy, October 19, Schlesinger commented:

"During this period, practically *all* the evidence, I believe, has supported our view that the Nenni Socialists have split irrevocably from the Communists and are determined to bring the PSI into the democratic orbit."

He continued:

"I still consider it to our interest [*less than 1 line of source text not declassified*] to manifest a sympathetic interest in their problems and future:

"1) the hardest and most costly stage yet of the PSI disengagement effort—that is, disengagement at the local level—is now upon us. (This will be followed in due course by disengagement in the labor movement—which will be even harder and costlier.) It is essential that Nenni win this fight—and it must be remembered that the Autonomists, handicapped in the next months by Nenni's uncertain health, will consequently need help more than ever.

"2) the success of the Italian experiment has a larger significance. If a CD-Socialist coalition can work in Italy, it may very likely provide an important model for France after De Gaulle, Germany after Adenauer and Spain after Franco. If the Italian experiment fails, the most hopeful formula for political stability in Western Europe will be discredited—perhaps beyond repair." (Kennedy Library, National Security Files, Italy)

---

310. **Telegram From the Embassy in Italy to the Department of State**

Rome, January 9, 1963, 9 p.m.

1336. Paris pass Finletter and CINCEUR. Embtel 1327.[1] When I saw Foreign Minister Piccioni this afternoon I covered Jupiter proposal and asked for his reactions.[2] He said he had met with Fanfani and Andreotti at noon, that they had discussed problem in some detail, but agreed that

Source: Department of State, Conference Files: Lot 66 D 110, CF 2221. Secret; Priority; Limit Distribution. Repeated to Ankara and Paris.

[1] Telegram 1327, January 9, discussed the replacement of Jupiter missiles in Italy. (Ibid., Central Files, 765.56311/1–963)

[2] In a conversation with Italian Defense Minister Andreotti during the December 1962 NATO Defense Ministers meeting in Paris, Secretary McNamara suggested the early replacement of Jupiter missiles with Polaris missiles to be installed on three U.S. submarines assigned to the Mediterranean. McNamara stated the first of these submarines would be on station in the Mediterranean by April 1, 1963. The U.S. proposal was outlined in a letter from McNamara to Andreotti, January 5, 1963. A copy of the letter is ibid., Italy Desk Files: Lot 68 D 436, Prime Minister Fanfani's Visit to U.S.

it should be carefully studied before formulating position. He said Fanfani had reserved to himself to express Italian reactions when he reached Washington early next week.[3]

I have just come from Fanfani who said he understood importance of proposal and whose preliminary opinion was that from military and technical point of view it posed no insuperable problems. Yet he was, he said, much concerned with relationship of the exercise to forthcoming Parliamentary elections here. If elections were to be held early in April and Jupiter replacement could be postponed until just after that date, there would be no problem. Unfortunately however date of elections was still uncertain and could conceivably be later in spring. He said he wanted to ponder matter for few days and would be prepared to discuss it fully upon his arrival in Washington. He had a few detailed questions but nothing that went beyond my instructions.

I intend to try to see him again before his departure for Washington, to ascertain results of his reflections. If he seems inclined to postpone implementation of plan I would point out that given improbability that it can be withheld indefinitely from public domain, it might be politically advantageous to be able to announce an early decision and thus preclude left and right opposition from reaping benefits of long drawn-out and built-up propaganda campaign.

Reinhardt

---

[3] Telegram 1242 from Rome, December 21, reported on a meeting with Fanfani during which he expressed concern about the international situation and indicated his desire for a meeting with the President. Reinhardt endorsed the idea of a Fanfani visit. (Washington National Records Center, RG 84, Rome Post Files: FRC 68 A 5612, 320 Italy) President Kennedy's invitation for a visit was delivered on January 8, 1963. Fanfani accepted on January 9.

---

311.   Telegram From the Embassy in Italy to the Department of State

Rome, January 12, 1963, 2 p.m.

1362. Embassy telegram 1342.[1] Prime Minister Fanfani's forthcoming visit to Washington offers us an opportunity to stimulate the Italian

---

Source: Department of State, Central Files, 033.6511/1–1263. Confidential; Priority. Repeated to Bonn, Brussels, London, and Paris.

[1] Telegram 1342, January 10, reported on the subjects that the Italians were likely to raise during Prime Minister Fanfani's discussions with U.S. officials. (Ibid., 033.6511/1–1063)

Government toward further activity and initiative in a useful direction. It comes at a moment of unusual fluidity in the Western political scene and at one in which the Italians, bestirred to play a more important role, seem uncertain regarding specific lines of policy they should follow. Accordingly, in addition to the usefulness of discussing specific subjects the Prime Minister and we may wish to raise (see below), helpful results may be obtained if we can use the opportunity of the visit to build up the prestige and self-confidence of Italy, thus helping her to overcome her chronic worries about the role of a second rate power in Europe, and at the same time encourage the Italian Government to set a course we believe to be in our own and general interest of the West.

In recent years, as it has played a growing role in the Councils of Europe, the United Nations and in certain areas around the world, Italy has shaken off some of its postwar sense of inferiority. But the Italians now fear that the balance within the NATO Alliance is about to undergo a new change. Many believe that although Britain may have lost its "special inside track" with the United States, it is nevertheless about to assume a primary role in a new nuclear relationship, which France might conceivably join. This conjures up the specter of the directoire,[2] and the Italians are again wondering and worrying whether they are about to be frozen into a new and more permanent state of inferiority within NATO.

There is throughout the greater part of the Italian political spectrum an inherent tendency toward neutralism which has been more in evidence under present Italian leadership than for some time past. (Some of this, of course, is for internal tactical reasons.) Yet, the Italian center left government and its political and press supporters appear to be moving closer to United States views with respect to certain elements of foreign policy than are anti-communist center and conservative elements, which traditionally support us here. For instance, the center Left spokesmen emphasize the dangers of nuclear proliferation, the importance of the development of an Atlantic community, and are more ready to accept United States leadership and control of Western military forces in a multilateral framework, while at the same time, of course, also seeking an enhanced role for Italy. Their support for British entry into the European community has been quite articulate.

Recognizing the dangers for us implicit in certain foreign policy views of the present Italian leadership and the inclination of some of its members toward neutralism, we believe we should encourage the Italian Government to play an increasing role in NATO and to make its

---

[2] A reference to de Gaulle's 1958 proposals for a reorganization of NATO and the establishment of a U.S.-British-French directive committee. For documentation, see *Foreign Relations*, 1958–1960, vol. VII, Part 1, pp. 314 ff.

weight increasingly felt both there and in the EEC, where it generally advocates policies we favor. The recent stir caused by La Malfa's alleged plan for a Rome-London axis has moved Italy into a more exposed and possibly stronger position favoring United Kingdom membership and progress toward the political unification of Europe. Fanfani has given some evidence of wanting to make these major points of Italian policy.

Italian doubts about the Nassau agreement[3] and whether this condemns Italy and other non-nuclear states to second class NATO status (Embassy telegram 1334)[4] makes such encouragements as we can give Italy at this time even more important.

We therefore see the visit as an opportunity to overcome some Italian doubts and complexes and to get Fanfani and the Italian Government committed privately and publicly (e.g., through the communiqué and presumably inevitable press interviews) to policies and principles which we favor.

As for specific subjects which the Prime Minister may raise in Washington (Embtel 1342), we have the following suggestions:

1. On the post-Cuba and post-Nassau military and political outlook, Fanfani will primarily want to hear the views of the President and the Secretary: and it seems highly important that this opportunity be taken to clarify Fanfani's (and Martino's and Fornari's) thinking on the main political implications of the Nassau agreement. Suggest it also be stressed that the results of the Cuban affair were obtained by a show of United States determination and strength, and not because both the President and Khrushchev are peace-loving, as Fanfani has put it publicly here.

2. On United Kingdom membership in the EEC, although Italy has already taken a strong position vocally, it might be useful to press the Prime Minister on what specific measures he has in mind to facilitate United Kingdom accession to EEC. We understand the Italian delegation has often been less than forthcoming at Brussels when its own interests were involved. It might also be useful to explore with the Prime Minister what his views are on ways to advance European political unification and his attitude toward, for instance, the La Malfa–Lippmann thesis that the only alternative to a "Gaullist Europe" is the spread of center-left type of governments based on collaboration between European DC and Socialist Parties.

---

[3] For text of the Nassau agreement, see *American Foreign Policy: Current Documents, 1962,* pp. 635–637.

[4] Telegram 1334, January 8, reported on discussions with senior Italian Foreign Office officials regarding the Nassau agreement on a multinational nuclear force. (Department of State, Central Files, 375.75611/1–863)

3. On East-West problems, we understand Fanfani is especially interested in knowing more about our Berlin strategy, and this interest may be heightened by the fact that Khrushchev will be in East Berlin while Fanfani is in Washington. (It might be useful to give opportunity to the Prime Minister to make some public statement of Italian views on Berlin at this juncture.)

4. On disarmament, we should be prepared for a question from Fanfani as to whether postponement of the reopening of the Disarmament Conference in Geneva has some specific significance, as is currently thought by some Italian Foreign Office officials.

We have already forwarded our suggestions about the Civil Air Agreement if that subject arises (Embtel 1343),[5] and the Pollaiolo paintings are sure to be mentioned (Embtel 1342). We feel it is very important because of internal political factors that the Unites States not overlook some mention in regard to neutralist pressures on the Italian Government, evident during the Cuban crisis. We should, for instance, while expressing our sympathetic interest in the center-left experiment, express concern about the possible long term impact of neutralist views held by some influential members of the Socialist Party (and by the implication of the left wing of the DC itself), in view of the fact that the Socialist Party is a potential member of a future Italian Government. The United States will, of course, wish strongly to express hope for increased Italian aid to LDCs (Embassy views on this have already been forwarded separately), and increased military contribution to Western defenses.

Reinhardt

---

[5] Telegram 1343, January 10, reported that Fanfani had received recommendations from members of his cabinet to denounce the U.S.-Italian Civil Aviation Agreement. (Ibid., 033.6511/1–1063)

312. Memorandum of Conversation

Washington, January 16, 1963, 11:30 a.m.–1 p.m.

SUBJECT

   Modernization of Nuclear Missiles in Italy and the Mediterranean

PARTICIPANTS

Italy	United States
Amintore Fanfani, Prime Minister of the Italian Republic	The President
	Mr. Neil A. Seidenman—LS (Interpreter)
	Mr. McGeorge Bundy (for last few minutes of the meeting)

The President indicated his willingness to discuss any of a number of topics under the headings of political, economic, and defense problems and deferred to the Prime Minister as to which should be their main topic of discussion.

The Prime Minister chose to talk about nuclear weapons and the missile bases in Italy. He also thought that attention should be given to what should and what should not be included in the communiqué, and to the timing of an announcement of agreement.

The President, noting the Prime Minister was still scheduled to see the Secretary of Defense,[1] pointed out that the Jupiter missile should be replaced, since, like the Thor missile, it was only a "first-strike" weapon, and that a much more modern weapon should replace it. The Corporal missile was also dated and should be replaced by the Sergeant. The Jupiter should be replaced by the Polaris, which could be fired from a surface vessel, such as the *Garibaldi,* or from submarines. Another point to consider would be the question of what course to follow in regards to the use of U.S. Polaris submarines in the Mediterranean, and also the

---

Source: Department of State, Conference Files: Lot 66 D 110, CF 2222. Secret; Limit Distribution. Drafted by Seidenman and approved in the White House on January 29. The meeting was held at the White House.

[1] Fanfani met separately with Secretary McNamara and Secretary Rusk during the afternoon. In a January 16 memorandum to Secretary Rusk summarizing the President's morning discussion with Fanfani, Bundy reported: "The President asked Bob McNamara to press home with Fanfani this afternoon the degree of military advantage that would come from getting the Jupiters out and getting on with other and less vulnerable weapons systems. Bob plans to do this especially by emphasizing how much of a hostage the missiles are at a moment of tension. The President's view is that we should go hard down this line, on the ground that we shall never have a better chance to get these dangerous weapons off the scene before a new crisis, and he believes that we should continue to emphasize with Fanfani the advantages of a firm and early decision." (Ibid.)

setting up a multi-lateral nuclear force. Should emphasis be given to undersea or to fixed surface systems?

The President suggested that nothing final should be stated before the Prime Minister had conferred with Secretary McNamara, since this was a complex question of defense, of special interest for our two countries, as well as for other countries, and of the greatest significance after the Nassau talks. But the President stressed that the two leaders indeed should achieve a meeting of minds in Washington at this time, and ensure that there would be no loose ends remaining.

The two leaders therefore decided that it would facilitate their exchanges to set the appointment with Secretary McNamara after the meeting with Secretary Rusk, on the same day, to be able to arrive at definite conclusions in their second talk on the following day.

The Prime Minister pointed to what he termed a political problem; namely, the question whether or not a solution relating to the "termination" of the Jupiters was near. This, he said, would have to be announced.

The President hereupon expressed the position that the approach should preferably be in terms of a package. We would say that the Jupiter should be replaced, in order to modernize our missiles and defense, replacing the Jupiter with the Polaris and Corporal with Sergeant. We would be saying that we are in agreement in favor of continuing work toward a multi-lateral force. And if we can agree to this, there would be further exchanges on a technical level in regard to details and specific roles; surface or sub-surface deployment; and the part to be played by Italy. Also, the U.S. would have Polaris submarines in the Mediterranean, for 1963–1964. We would also be talking about an improvement in the political control (of European defense), over the European nuclear force—in which Italy would have an important part. If there is agreement on such a package basis, the meeting would end in decisions for the strengthening and modernization of our forces, and better political control over these weapons. But it should be given out, whenever an announcement were to be made, as a whole package. We certainly would not wish to have the different points of decision simply leak out, without coherence and possibly at the wrong moment.

Prime Minister Fanfani said that he had discussed the proposal with the President of the Republic, the Minister of Defense, and the Minister of Foreign Affairs, and all three posed the objection that to announce it before the elections might unloose a grand scale debate. This would appear to suggest the conclusion that it would be better to wait until after the elections.

The President replied that he could not know the intricacies of the Italian political scene as closely as the Prime Minister, as to the various political forces at work and the different stands. He did emphasize, however, that in his opinion our approach could be enhanced at this time, since the basic content of the package would seem to offer comfort to most political groups. It aims at the setting up of a multi-lateral force in which Italy would participate. Hence it strengthens Italy militarily and gives Italy more significant voice in the control of European policies. It provides for the presence of American Polaris submarines in the Mediterranean, which means greater security for the southern European area and hence for Italy as well. It would call for a "multi-nationally manned" nuclear force, in which Italy would take part with surface weapons and perhaps with the *Garibaldi*,[2] to the further strengthening of Italy. It would also call for taking out the Jupiters, which may not be entirely pleasing to all, but the package on the whole should meet with general approval within most groups. There could be some objection on the left (*sic*) to the part about the Jupiters, but certainly the Right would be pleased with the prospect of continuing U.S.-Italian cooperation with the newer Sergeant missile; with the strengthening of both nuclear and conventional forces for Italy in the multi-lateral set-up; with the *Garibaldi*, and especially with the fact of a formal agreement for Italian-American cooperation.

An important aspect of the decision, of course, would be to ensure that it was taken as a compact unit and presented as such at the appropriate time, and not to allow it to become a matter of public domain, piece-meal, through the Italian newspapers, subjected to varying interpretations according to the political affiliations of the press. Indicating his receptiveness to the Prime Minister's views on the matter of timing, against the background of Italian internal politics, the President stated his conviction that in the course of these meetings, five or six points should be formulated and brought together to form a decision in which each aspect would be cast in its proper light. This would constitute a real advance in our mutual cooperation, and would avoid having each point come out in isolated fashion, by driblets. With all of the points bound together as a unit and thus presented, our mutual positions would be much strengthened.

---

[2] It may be of interest to note that Prime Minister Fanfani himself did at no point in the discussion make mention of, or allude to the *Garibaldi*, nor even express himself in any way in response to the President's mention of its possible use. [Footnote in the source text. In a telephone conversation with Rusk at 9:56 a.m., January 16: "B [Ball] said before he sees Fanfani with the Pres—did Sec or McNamara talk about *Gharibaldi*? Sec said yes—and it is all right to be sympathetic and work something out. Sec replied re some submarine that that is for the future and we would need to check with the Comm. B said also we would have to decide re going ahead with the French. Sec said to take it easy. B mentioned saying something about Jupiters in the communiqué. Ball would like to keep it out. Sec prefers not to refer to names." (Department of State, Rusk Files: Lot 72 D 192, Telephone Conversations)

The Prime Minister agreed with the President's reasoning for ensuring the effectiveness of decisions taken by them. But there were two possible avenues of procedure: 1) to make a decisive announcement at the appropriate time, or 2) to announce that he had accepted the request made by the U.S., that he would submit the proposal to the Government, and that the terms of the proposal would be subsequently announced. He added, however, that there would be a need to define certain elements of the understanding.

The President replied that in his view it would not be desirable to allow for prolonged discussion over these things. It would be better to try to conclude an agreement on the various aspects of the proposal as one piece, and to act upon it quickly. If we make a suggestion and this were submitted to debate, it might take far too long. If four or five points could be brought together into a complete proposal, rather than submitting this to a debate at the risk of losing too much time, it would be better to take a decision quickly and that would be all. To submit it to Parliament, even as a unit, would make it vulnerable; some may not like certain parts of it. Some may not go along with the multi-lateral idea; others may be opposed to Polaris; and still others may have doubts about letting go of the Jupiters at all.

The British, the President pointed out, had the Thor missile after Jupiter, and now they've apparently decided that manned bombers will do the job better than the Thor until 1970; and after all the British have been in the nuclear business for some years now. So that if we are to increase the strength of the West, now is the time to decide. We have the Atomic Energy Committee [Weapons Analysis Report] from [January],[3] 1961, which said at that time that the Jupiter was unsatisfactory. The President again recognized that the Prime Minister undoubtedly knew the political problems of his country better than anyone else, but re-emphasized the significance of the British decision on the even more efficient Thor missile, in relation to the concept of "strengthening and modernizing" forces as soon as possible.

The Prime Minister, indicating his concurrence, asked the President to define what the point relating to submarines in the Mediterranean would consist of.

The President explained that this would involve patrol missions by United States Polaris submarines in the Mediterranean, equivalent to those presently carried out in northern waters. A submarine station similar to the one at Holyloch is being constructed in the Iberian Peninsula, and the submarines will be supplied from Holyloch until completion of the other station. Meanwhile, the submarines would run their missions in the Mediterranean, each mission lasting 45 days, where they

---

[3] Brackets in the source text.

would gain access to additional targets and offset the present range limitations of the Polaris. This would begin in 1963. But in addition the question of the multi-lateral force would be taken up, and the determination made as to whether this would be primarily surface or sub-surface.

The Prime Minister said he would act in favor of supporting the multi-lateral force decision at the next meeting of the Atlantic Council. He mentioned that at the January 11 meeting the Italian NATO delegation declared its concurrence with this approach. The next step would be that of taking decisions pertinent to the formation of the NATO Committee on the multi-lateral force, and there seemed to be increasing difficulty in these decisions.

The President observed that beyond the problem of the Jupiter, which could no longer be considered as a deterrent weapon but simply a target for the Soviets, there was in addition the need to give attention to other points: 1) There should be a mobile force. A land-based force would pose a given set of problems; it would be hard to imagine hauling these weapons through the streets of Italian or French cities, which goes back to the proposal once put forward by General Norstad. This would also entail potential political as well as military risks. 2) If the mobile force is sea-based, then it must be determined whether it is to be sub-surface or surface. A "multi-nationally manned" submarine is of course a complex matter. If it is to be surface, this would be costly and also complex; it would require very complicated firing mechanisms. However, it can be done. It may not be simple, but it certainly can be done by the European countries. But, the President assured, we are ready to consider either way.

We definitely feel, the President continued, that this is the best time to act, when attention to these matters is made easier by the present period of relative relaxation between East and West. At this time we see the need for change and improvement of the position of the West, and this is the way to do so. We shouldn't forget the decision made by the British, who think the manned bomber is better than Thor, when Thor was better than Jupiter—and now Polaris is better than all three!

The Prime Minister said that there was no disagreement as to the status of Jupiter. There were only certain problems on his mind of a psychological nature. The people in Italy feel bound up in this question, which also involves the prestige and strength of the Italian armed forces. The Prime Minister asked whether or not the President could for example conceive of announcing that these bases, presently to be used to launch Jupiter missiles in case of war, could be subsequently used for cooperative peaceful space efforts. The President indicated lively interest in this idea. The Prime Minister added that it would seem a shame to allow all that had been built up so far at these bases to fall to ruin.

The President responded reassuringly that the idea might well be an asset to this proposal as a whole, which by all means should be clearly seen as a source of strength for Italy. So that with these different points joined to form a whole unit, the proposal would be more satisfactory. Then as to the mode of presentation, this should also be agreed upon between the two leaders, for if it were revealed as anything less than a joint decision, there would be political difficulties, with some in favor and some against, for one reason or another. This is why it would be far better to present it as a joint proposal formulated by both governments on a level of equality, thus giving it the maximum degree of force—with both parties in agreement, tying it together and wrapping it up so that it could contribute toward the strength of Italy.

Prime Minister Fanfani recalled that attention should also be given to the element of timeliness.

The President fully agreed. But he again stressed the view that any combination of decisions to be outlined in the proposal taken as a matter of joint interest—towards modernization of weapons, the use of the Sergeant missile, the multi-lateral force, joint space efforts—should clearly point to a strengthening of Italy's position. Meanwhile, the President recommended that they should continue to think about the "package", until the following day, after the Prime Minister had consulted with the Secretary of Defense, and of course to the question of maintaining a balance of interests in Italy against the background of political problems at home, which the President again conceded were more familiar to the Prime Minister.

The President showed the Prime Minister the page of the Atomic Energy Committee report from early 1961, containing three paragraphs concerning the inadequacy of the Jupiter missile, which the President encouraged the Prime Minister to read. The Prime Minister did so, and in concurrence with the point made in the text pointed out that this had been the conclusion of Italy's Chief of Staff as well. The President commented in passing that the Italian Chief of Staff was indeed recognized as a knowledgeable man on the subject of missilery.

The President again stressed that by the following morning they should be able to combine four or five points into a proposal that would strengthen the Italian and American position within the framework of the Alliance, thus making this meeting a gain in its cohesiveness and hence political strength. Not to accomplish this now and to leave the announcement for another future occasion, with the coming elections in May or June, when our position would not be as strong as it can be at the present moment would be wrong. This is a very important factor from the political as well as the military standpoint.

Prime Minister Fanfani expressed agreement with the views of the President, and, thanking him for his clarifying statements, he promised to bear them in mind for his talks with Secretary McNamara, and to give special thought to the problems involved in this approach, notably the matters of substituting a future formal agreement; mode of presentation; and timing of the announcement.[4]

The President called Mr. McGeorge Bundy into the room during the last few minutes of the talk.

---

[4] On January 24 the Italian Government announced that it had agreed with the United States on a plan for removing the Jupiter missile bases. The Chamber of Deputies voted its approval the following day. An exchange of diplomatic notes on the Jupiter withdrawal took place on March 22. The notes were forwarded to the Department of State in airgram A–1368 from Rome, March 28. (Washington National Records Center, RG 84, Rome Post Files: FRC 68 A 5612, 430.1 IRBM) The agreement called for the removal of the Jupiter missiles 25 days after the first Polaris submarine arrived on station in the Mediterranean on April 1.

---

313. Memorandum of Conversation

Washington, January 17, 1963, 10 a.m.

SUBJECT

Europe's and America's Role in Aid to Less Developed Areas

PARTICIPANTS

Italy
Amintore Fanfani, Prime Minister of the Italian Republic
Sergio Fenoaltea, Ambassador of Italy
Edoardo Martino, Under Secretary of Foreign Affairs
Giovanni Fornari, Director General of Political Affairs
Carlo Marchiori, Foreign Policy Advisor to the Prime Minister
Umberto La Rocca, Chief of Secretariat to the Under Secretary
Giuseppe Bartelomei, Chief of Secretariat to the Prime Minister
Gian Luigi Milesi Ferretti, Italian Minister

United States
The President
Secretary Rusk
Under Secretary Ball
Ambassador Reinhardt
Mr. McGeorge Bundy, The White House
Mr. Arthur Schlesinger, Jr., The White House
Mr. Pierre Salinger, The White House
Assistant Secretary Tyler

Source: Department of State, Central Files, 611.65/1–2363. Secret; Limit Distribution. Drafted by Gammon and cleared in S on January 25 and at the White House on January 28. The meeting was held at the White House. The President and Prime Minister also discussed the Common Market, conventional arms build up, the Berlin situation, and French nuclear policy. (Ibid.)

Mr. Francis E. Meloy, Jr., Director, WE
Mr. Samuel R. Gammon, WK, Italian Desk
Mr. Neil Seidenman, Interpreter
Mr. Jose De Seabra, Interpreter

The President remarked that in 1961 he and the Prime Minister had discussed assistance to Somalia.[1] The US has been limited in what it could do there by its special relations with Ethiopia. However, he had recently told the Somalia Prime Minister that the US was prepared to give some arms aid. The President hoped that Italy would continue to help exclude the Soviets from Somalia by helping that country, particularly in its desire for an effective air line. The President noted that the West is currently doing well in Africa; the Congo was improving and France was making a vigorous effort in African development.

Prime Minister Fanfani thanked the President for America's efforts with Somalia. He had seen the Somali Prime Minister both before and after his recent visit to the US. The Prime Minister had made clear to him Italy would welcome all of his requests including any for aid in economic development. In fact Italy, had granted all of the requests made during his initial stop in Rome. Action was now in train regarding them. Prime Minister Fanfani believed that the Somali tendency to turn toward the East was now partially halted. He pointed out that all of the new countries really want aid from the West without renouncing the prospect of aid from the Soviets. He warned that the West needed to act rapidly in playing this game, which all the new countries engage in, and that we were sometimes too slow in responding. He noted, however, that the West must be careful how it acts in this competitive game.

Under Secretary Martino then brought up the subject of training for Somali pilots. He said that the Somali were very sensitive to their need for an airline which would permit them to connect their communications net more effectively with the outside world. Pilot training had both civil and military implications, since military pilots were ultimately available for civilian purposes. Germany had offered to train Somali pilots, and Italy had offered to train a small number also. This training was to have begun at the end of this month and had at first been accepted by the Somalis, but they had recently reversed their position. This was the current status on this matter.

The President stated that he wished to raise another matter—IDA (the International Development Association).[2] The US supports IDA

---

[1] Document 285.

[2] Telegram 1338 to Rome, January 18, reported that in Secretary Dillon's meeting with Fanfani Dillon expressed U.S. interest in bringing IDA negotiations to a successful conclusion and noted that Ambassador Leddy would be going to Rome to discuss this with Carli next week. (Department of State, Conference Files: Lot 66 D 110, CF 2222)

strongly and believes that other countries should also do so. However, he pointed out, with our balance of payments problem (even though it was alleviated by Italian military offset purchases), we hope that Europe will be more forthcoming in the aid field notwithstanding European countries internal development problems with their own South. The President stated that we could not continue to help on our present scale too long. Our gold reserve is flowing out to Europe. Although it was natural for Europe to be slow to react to this relatively new phenomenon and natural for the US to be slow, perhaps too slow, in responding to its gold reserve losses, action needed to be taken by both sides.

The President pointed out that our aid effort in Greece and Turkey and, to a certain degree, in Spain, made no sense. They are *European* countries.

The President commented that Latin America is the most dangerous region of the world. Argentina, Brazil and all the other countries were in difficulties. France's special tie with Africa has drawn EEC assistance to that continent, but we hope that Italy will help secure a helpful European attitude toward Latin America, where the situation is growing worse. The President pointed out that the capital flight from Latin America had exceeded our own very substantial aid. There was a real danger that we might confront a Communist Latin America in the future.

Prime Minister Fanfani reminded the President that Italy in general works in the aid field through the use of export credits. This device had been criticized as being an excessively commercial attitude, but the criticism was not valid. In the first place the recipient countries liked this device, and secondly, there were many recipients which never paid their bills anyway! Argentina has had much Italian export credit assistance and now has a half billion dollar debt which is not paid. Brazil also has a large unpaid bill.

The President interjected that we would be happy to exchange a few unpaid debts with Italy! Prime Minister Fanfani wondered if it were really better to tell the recipients these were not outright gifts. He noted that the Italian aid effort thus far has cost 240 billion lire and might rise to 300 billion lire this year. The Director of the Bank of Italy was highly critical of this increase and of Italy's system of aid.

Prime Minister Fanfani also pointed out that Italy made a substantial contribution through enabling borrowers to obtain loans at a rate of interest below four per cent as in the case of Argentina and Yugoslavia. In addition, Italy made some outright grants as in Somalia, where it provided budgetary assistance and both development and military aid. The Prime Minister said Somalia cost Italy more independent than it had as a colony. Nevertheless, Italy did not grudge this assistance, since Somalia was a responsible and cautious country unlike some of the more reckless new ones such as Morocco.

With respect to Greece, Italy had undertaken a defense subsidy of $2.4 million there and had removed its right to have .8 billion lire of the Italian war indemnity to Greece spent exclusively within Italy.

The Prime Minister stated that with respect to aid we would have to see what the future holds. Italy is studying the problem to see what it can do. He noted that aid also had political implications. Prime Minister Fanfani continued by saying that Italy's real economic miracle is its transition from an alms beggar to an alms giver. Italy hopes to double its national income per unit of population in the coming years, which will enable it to do better in the aid field. He assured the President that Italy would do its best to help others.

The Prime Minister mentioned that India had recently solicited military aid in the form of mountain howitzers. Italy's problem there was in transferring to India the patent rights for producing these guns.

The Prime Minister recalled his long talk with President Kennedy in June 1961 concerning Latin America.[3] There the situation was still bad notwithstanding US assistance. Italy had tried to help the Latin American countries, the Christian Democratic parties, and their labor movements to develop middle level leadership to fill the gap between the top and bottom strata of society.

The Prime Minister noted the accuracy of his 1961 forecast, in which he still believes, that the Soviet Union is making Latin America and not Africa its prime target. The Soviets' shift of emphasis from Berlin to Cuba recently proved this. The Prime Minister believed the Soviets would leave Africa alone. He considered that the Soviets believe Africa is not ripe for the class struggle and therefore, though the USSR remained interested in African developments, it would wait for an opportunity for intervention to mature. He noted that both in Italy and in the world in general the Communists always placed their emphasis on areas other than the most depressed. They sought to pit the have-nots against the haves in areas where the former had something but not enough. Therefore, he felt the Soviet Union was concentrating on Cuba and Latin America in general. He reminded the President that in 1961 he said the front between the West and the Soviet Bloc was not Berlin but Latin America. It remained the front line today.

Under Secretary Martino noted that Italy has had many requests to lend assistance not only in backward areas but in NATO countries which were more developed. He cited military assistance given by Italy

---

[3] A memorandum of this conversation is in Department of State, Conference Files: Lot 65 D 366, CF 1912.

to Greece of $1.2 million this year with the promise of the same next year. He pointed out that Italy was also giving $10 million in aid to Turkey. Both countries were, of course, near neighbors of Italy.

The President interjected that these figures did not correspond to Italy's $3–5 billion gold reserve. The US has lost $1 billion from its reserves in the last year. Italy was in a stronger position than the US. The US was pouring out its reserve and Italy was building its up. He urged Martino to think in bigger terms.

Prime Minister Fanfani hailed the President as his ally on this point in the internal argument within Italy over what to do with its surplus. He noted Italy was fighting increases in the cost of living. Some of the surplus was also being spent abroad. Italy's 1962 reduction by 10 per cent of its customs duties would also affect Italy's balance of trade. Last year Italy's trade deficit increased from 500 billion lire to 800 billion lire.

The Prime Minister explained that the Italian reserve was built up from three sources; by tourism from the US and especially from the Nordic countries of Europe, which he characterized as the sale of sunshine; by ship chartering, which was a highly competitive business; and by remittances from Italian emigrants, particularly Italian workers in Northern Europe. This last source would diminish as Italian workers returned home to the expending Italian economy. Therefore, the Italian balance of payments would have a smaller margin, and Italian reserves would tend to fall. The Prime Minister admitted that most any outflow would go to the common market countries and Northern Europe, from which Italy buys a great deal. He noted that within the last few months Italy also had reduced its duties on meat and on petroleum and that it would have to take further similar steps in the future.

The President pointed out that the annual addition to the world gold supply is only $700 million. There is not enough gold to go around. Therefore any countries accumulating a surplus are basing their gains on the deficits of others. The President stressed that gold flow must be reciprocal. He characterized the accumulation of a gold reserve by countries which then hoarded it as the path to the panic of 1929. The world gold supply was inadequate for trade requirements if countries hoarded reserves. He drew on the analogy of the plight of the Roman Empire when its silver mines were exhausted. The President noted that we have attained a certain stability in our handling of the atom in the modern world but that we have not yet learned to manage our economy. He emphasized that the US cannot continue to bear the burden of a billion dollars a year loss to its gold reserve, nor could Latin America continue to build up Europe's reserves by a flight of capital. This was a most important subject he concluded and noted emphatically that Spain had a $1.2 billion gold reserve.

The Prime Minister agreed with the President's concluding remarks. He pointed out that Italy was moving toward a new agreement between ENI, its national petroleum authority, and US oil companies, which would be of help to the United States. He noted a new trend toward Italian purchases in America which would also help. He recalled that he had told Ambassador Reinhardt that Italy's $124 million arms purchase in America was made under an arrangement which helped both the US balance of payments situation and also helped Italy. He recalled also that he had told Secretary Dillon last June that the defense of the dollar was the defense of the West. He pointed out that Italy had last summer repaid in advance some US loans. Italy planned to continue its efforts and its work to help our bilateral trade relations and would welcome American initiatives.

The President in conclusion acknowledged Italy's helpfulness in this problem.

314. Memorandum of Conversation

Washington, February 15, 1963, 12–1:10 p.m.

SUBJECT

Italian Political Developments

PARTICIPANTS

Italy	*United States*
The Honorable Giuseppe Saragat, Leader of Italian Democratic Socialist Party (PSDI) [1]	The President LS–Neil Seidenman–Interpreter

The President asked about the effectiveness of the center-left government, which Mr. Saragat helped to create.

Source: Department of State, Central Files, Pol-Italy. Confidential. Drafted by Seidenman and cleared in the White House on February 26. The President and Saragat also discussed French plans for European unification, aid to less developed nations, and relations between Europe and Latin America. Memoranda of these portions of their conversation are ibid., Pol 14 Italy.

[1] Saragat visited the United States on a USIA leader grant program.

Saragat in response noted that the center-left formula is an attempt to carry out social reforms and provide for the welfare of the people in order to draw the laboring class away from the extreme left and into the democratic area. He pointed to the analogy of the President's efforts to win the developing nations to democracy by the same formula. In Italy this approach has caused the Italian Communist Party (PCI) such problems that it is at a loss how to respond. Unlike ten years ago, today a dictatorship in Italy is absolutely inconceivable, since labor now has developed faith in democracy and in republican institutions.

Regarding the Italian Socialist Party (PSI), Saragat pointed out that while its policy on internal problems is coming closer to the democratic parties, it must still be brought to shift its foreign policy from neutralism to support of the Atlantic cause. PSI leader Nenni should be given every assistance in breaking away from the Communists, short of any concessions in matters of foreign policy. There our attitude must be absolutely firm. He forecast success in winning the PSI over to democracy, if relations with it are conducted with courage and firmness.

The President asked what part of the electorate could be expected to vote Communist, and what proportion of this vote was truly Communist. Saragat noted that the PCI vote would not exceed twenty-five per cent; the majority were not Communists, but, he observed, the strength and organizational skill of the party was such that it appeared that they all really were. Saragat said that even in the South of Italy, enlightenment of the voters was leading to the beginning of a shift of voter support away from the traditional parties of the Right. He asserted that the PCI would make no gains in the coming elections and might even lose votes for the first time since World War II.

The President noted the analogy of our efforts in Latin America to promote reform governments of the center-left which would undercut the Communists' appeal to the poor. He asked if the PSI and Saragat's Democratic Socialist party were not the true voting alternatives on the liberal left for those who wished to protest the Christian Democrats (DC) identity with business interests. Saragat denied that the DC party was conservative and observed that Premier Fanfani and DC Party Secretary Moro were quite close to the socialist movements. The DC Party stood to lose some votes to the Right but not to the Left, since it is as a whole oriented to the Left.

The President pointed out that NATO ties also have important implications in reinforcing a country's internal political stability, since a foreign policy consistent with international security has a steadying influence. Saragat agreed.

315. Letter From Prime Minister Fanfani to President Kennedy

Rome, March 6, 1963.

MR. PRESIDENT: Last Friday I received your letter of February 28 calling my attention to Mr. Merchant's forthcoming visit and asking me to let you know what I thought of it.[1]

Mr. Merchant's visit took place the day before yesterday and I had a conversation with him together with two of my colleagues, Mr. Piccioni (Minister of Foreign Affairs) and Mr. Andreotti (Minister of Defense). After thinking over what was said, I can now accede to your request. I do that with the traditional cordial sincerity of an ally and friend, who wishes to make a contribution to constructive mutual decisions.

Mr. Merchant stated beforehand that he would dwell only on the American plans concerning the proposed establishment of the multilateral NATO nuclear force, without going into the other question of replacing the Jupiter fixed bases with Polaris submarines. For the latter ones the agreements reached between us on January 16–17 and approved by the Italian Government on January 24 and by the Chamber on January 26 remain in effect.

As to the American plans concerning establishment of the multilateral NATO nuclear force, Mr. Merchant told us, in short:

(1) That, in addition to being made up of Polaris submarines, planes and tactical nuclear forces contributed by the participating countries, the multilateral NATO nuclear force should include also a certain number of surface ships of the merchant-vessel type, covertly armed with Polaris missiles and manned by crews from several different countries, with a maximum of 40% of the crew from any one country;

(2) That the multilateral NATO nuclear force would be placed under the organizational control of a Commission composed of all the NATO members and deciding by majority vote, and under the operational control of a small Commission including at least all members participating in the ownership of the nuclear weapons, and deciding by unanimous vote;

(3) That the cost of establishing, operating and modernizing the multilateral nuclear force (exclusive of the cost of the preparatory plans contributed by the USA) should be borne by the countries participating in the project;

(4) That the planning should be concluded after June 1 next with a multilateral agreement regarding the above-mentioned problems.

Source: Italian Foreign Ministry Files. Secret. The source text is a 1993 Italian Foreign Ministry translation. A similar Department of State translation is in Department of State, Presidential Correspondence: Lot 66 D 204, Italy.

[1] On January 24 the White House announced that President Kennedy had appointed former Under Secretary of State for Political Affairs Livingston Merchant to head up a special team to prepare U.S. proposals for a NATO multilateral force. As part of the consultative process, Merchant visited Rome on March 3.

In concurrence with my colleagues, Messrs. Piccioni and Andreotti, I made the following comments to Mr. Merchant:

(A) Italy confirms that it is in favor of the establishment of a multilateral nuclear force, believing that it can promote a more organic, economical and efficient defense and prevent the risks and weaknesses of a nuclear proliferation and dispersion;

(B) Italy recognizes that the countries adhering to the establishment of the multilateral nuclear force must share the necessary costs (each in proportion to its ability);

(C) Italy believes that, once the multilateral nuclear force is placed under NATO (SACEUR), it will be necessary to define the political body that will control the organization of such a force as well as the political body that will have control over its use. Italy considers that while the former, with jurisdiction over organizational matters, can decide by majority vote, the latter, with jurisdiction over final use of the force, must necessarily decide by unanimous vote;

(D) In so far as the structure of the multilateral nuclear force is concerned, it is obvious to Italy that it can include Polaris-armed submarines and nuclear tactical forces; but the inclusion also of surface ships, even those of the merchant-vessel type, as suggested by Mr. Merchant, is not considered to be advantageous.

The good reasons adduced by you and Secretary McNamara, during our talks in Washington, against the use of surface vessels armed with Polaris missiles, and in favor of using instead submarines armed with Polaris missiles, remained deeply impressed in our minds. And on February 11 we had the pleasure of hearing Mr. Gilpatric repeat to us that these reasons were still valid.[2]

You will understand how surprised we were to hear Mr. Merchant argue in favor of using surface ships of the merchant-vessel type armed with Polaris missiles, not only because this was in conflict with the arguments that we had considered together but also because of other politico-military reasons which I shall explain to you below just as I explained them to Mr. Merchant the other day.

Replacing the Jupiter nuclear defense with the Polaris submarine system has the advantages which you and Mr. McNamara explained to me, and of which you convinced me. Acceptance of Polaris-armed surface ships of the merchant-vessel type, says Mr. Merchant, would afford greater speed in making them ready and would involve a smaller training and operating cost.

We wish to point out, however, that the new system loses the defense factor consisting of the ability to submerge and retains only that of mobility. The importance of the latter feature increases in direct propor-

---

[2] Under Secretary of Defense Roswell Gilpatric visited Rome February 11–13, and held talks with Fanfani and Defense Minister Andreotti.

tion to the possibility of its being used in the open sea. Conversely, it decreases when the system must be used in enclosed waters. Now, most of the seas within the NATO orbit (the Baltic, the North Sea, the Mediterranean) are enclosed waters, and therefore the use of Polaris-armed surface vessels in these seas would be subject to the worst possible conditions. If anything, nuclear strategy should deem it advisable, first of all, to continue to prefer submarine over surface vessels. Should a choice have to be made in order to reduce the over-all cost of defense, then NATO, with its enclosed or almost enclosed bodies of water, should be assigned submarine forces, while surface forces should be assigned to operations in the open sea where they can make full use of their mobility factor.

Mr. Merchant mentioned another element in defense of surface ships: the fact that they would be undistinguishable (because of their merchant-vessel feature) from the thousands of vessels of the same type plying the sea lanes every day, even in enclosed waters.

Permit me to say that the merchant-vessel appearance required of Polaris-armed surface ships presents very grave disadvantages, which lead to the rejection of such vessels as efficient media for the common defense. In fact, first of all such vessels, in order not to be identified and recognized, and hence for their own protection, must be able to mingle with the other similar vessels. But how can this necessity be reconciled with the (carrying of) armaments and above all with the military multinational make-up of the crews? Do the laws and treaties on merchant shipping permit such camouflaging? For how long can we expect the non-NATO countries (I refer, of course, to friendly or neutral countries, and not to enemy countries) to approve such camouflaging? And how will the anti-NATO countries themselves react, and indirectly cause other peoples to react, even in peacetime against all the merchant ships of the NATO countries (which would be) suspected, until proof to the contrary was established, of being surreptitiously armed with Polaris missiles? And what will be the reaction of the private shipowners in all NATO countries who could easily find themselves faced with the necessity of having to give their passengers and shippers explicit assurances that their vessels are not among those secretly armed with Polaris missiles? And at the sounding of the first alarm, what will the enemy do to prevent action by the said surface ships of the merchant-vessel type armed with Polaris missiles? Does not the camouflaging justify a preventive action (by the enemy) against all surface vessels, equally under suspicion, and all ports harboring them? Would not the terrible moments—which, I was told in the USA, were experienced last October because of the reactions that were foreseen, under certain circumstances, against the Jupiter land bases—be repeated, extending the anxiety to every maritime city or locality suspected of sheltering a surface vessel that might be secretly armed with Polaris missiles?

On the basis of all these considerations, you will see that the conclusion to be reached is quite simply: the participation of Polaris-armed surface ships, especially of the merchant-vessel type, in the make-up of the multilateral NATO nuclear force would reduce by about one-third the expense as compared to submarine forces, but it would create such difficulties and such dangers that even in peacetime it would weaken the entire economic and military system of the NATO countries, striking at the heart of their trade and normal life and bringing them to the brink of war under the worst possible conditions.

These considerations lead me to say, Mr. President, that the plan submitted by Mr. Merchant must be reviewed in so far as participation of surface vessels in the composition of the multilateral nuclear force is concerned. Should such a review not take place, Italy, being a country situated within an enclosed sea, provided with many harbors and committed to the development and unhampered use of a considerable merchant fleet operated on behalf of her nationals and of foreigners all over the world, would have to further consider the proposal relating to the use of surface vessels armed with Polaris missile. And I believe that in view of the present politico-parliamentary circumstances she would not be able to reply (at this time), but would have to wait until the new Parliament is elected on April 28, meets in opening session on May 16, and proceeds to choose and confirm the new Government.

From what has been explained to us it appears that a more efficient multilateral NATO nuclear force can be established with the Polaris submarines without the use of surface ships, of the merchant-vessel type or other. We know that it would cost more; but it would provide better conditions of security and employment and would not carry with it the political, economic, and strategic consequences I have mentioned, which would weaken the NATO system from the very beginning, rather than strengthen it. And Italy prefers to shoulder higher costs rather than accept, for reasons of mistaken economy, a weaker system.

At this stage of the planning, I wished, in accordance with your request to make whatever contribution I could with these observations. Let me assure you that they are the result of careful thought and are made in pursuance of our pledge that we must in all conscience strive to fulfill our duties toward our fellow countrymen and our Allies, by advising both the former and the latter to seek, not the least expensive way but first and foremost the way which is in all respects the safest for the defense of our common freedom and peace, without unwittingly giving our enemies pretexts and reasons for strengthening themselves psychologically, economically, and strategically at our expense.

I trust that you will study my comments in the same spirit of respectful friendship which inspired me in formulating them, and then consider adopting these suggestions for modifications that you are so wisely seeking by means of a consultation of opinions which, through Mr. Merchant's mission, you have undertaken with your characteristic courage.[3]

With assurances of my high esteem, I send you friendly and cordial greetings.[4]

---

[3] In a March 14 reply to Fanfani, President Kennedy responded that U.S. studies indicated a surface force would offer real technical and military advantages and assured the Italian Prime Minister that the MLF plan did not include an effort to disguise the ships. (Department of State, Presidential Correspondence: Lot 66 D 204, Italy)

[4] Printed from an unsigned copy.

---

316. Editorial Note

Parliamentary elections in Italy April 28–29 showed a continuing swing to the left on the part of the Italian electorate. The Christian Democratic Party lost 750,000 votes and 13 seats in the Chamber of Deputies. The Social Democrats gained 11 seats and the Socialists 3. The Italian Communist Party made a significant advance in its total vote, winning over one-quarter of all votes cast and picking up 26 seats in the Chamber of Deputies. In telegram 2302, May 1, the Embassy in Rome reported:

"As politicians begin agonizing examination of just what happened in these elections and what possibilities are now open to democratic forces in Italy, only fact immediately apparent is that there is no pat explanation of disappointing results and no easy solution to what may become prolonged period of governmental instability."

The telegram continued:

"First attempt will probably be to regroup center-left, but it will be delicate operation. DC is far from united and, particularly if PSI attempts press advantage in terms of 'unreasonable' program demands, new center-left combination might easily fall apart before it began. Other possibilities include single-party governments enjoying negotiated support from other parties or depending on support first of one and then another. It would probably be difficult, however, to find anyone willing to try to head so inherently unstable a government.

"Outlook then is for protracted and delicate negotiations with usual accompaniment of offers, statements of position, trial balloons and backroom deals." (Department of State, Central Files, Pol 14 Italy)

In telegram 2416, May 13, the Embassy further reported that the results of the election had probably derailed plans for an immediate entry by the Socialist Party into a governing coalition. (Ibid.) Two days later, May 15, with the parties deadlocked on the choice of a new government formula, Prime Minister Fanfani handed in his resignation to President Segni. The Italian President then asked Christian Democratic Party Secretary Aldo Moro to begin negotiations aimed at the formation of a new government.

The uncertainties attending the formation of an Italian Government, together with reports that Pope John XXIII was seriously ill, caused a change in plans for President Kennedy's projected visit to Italy. Originally the President had planned to visit Rome near the beginning of his June 23–July 3 trip to Europe. In view of the complications arising from negotiations over a new Italian Government and the Pope's illness, the White House delayed the visit until the end of the President's European trip. On June 3, upon news of the death of Pope John, the Department of State formally instructed the Embassy in Rome to propose July 1–2 to President Segni as the dates of the Kennedy visit. It also instructed the Embassy that in the event of the election of a successor to Pope John prior to the President's visit:

"President would not wish be in Rome during coronation itself but above schedule might well fall between conclave and coronation and thus give him a chance for informal meeting with new Pope." (Telegram 2422 to Rome, June 3; ibid., Pol 7–US–Kennedy)

In telegram 2746, June 19, the Embassy reported that Moro's efforts to form a government had collapsed after a June 16–17 revolt against PSI participation in the government led by Nenni's rival for leadership of the party's autonomist wing, Riccardo Lombardi. Nenni had submitted his resignation to the PSI central committee. Nevertheless, Segni, who was the foremost proponent of the visit, assured U.S. officials that a government, "albeit perhaps a minority one," would be in office when the President arrived in Italy. The Embassy further reported that a number of "Italian leaders friendly to us" were counseling either postponement of the visit or a meeting outside of Rome, warning that any new government formed prior to the President's arrival would lack a parliamentary mandate. (Ibid.)

On June 21 Giovanni Leone formed a minority government of Christian Democrats. The same day a conclave of the Cardinals of the Roman Catholic church elected Giovanni Battista Montini, Archbishop of Milan, as successor to Pope John. The new pontiff took the name Paul VI. Following instructions provided in telegram 2422, the Embassy arranged for an informal meeting with the new Pope during the President's Rome visit.

317. Briefing Paper Prepared in the Department of State

PET/BI–1   Washington, June 14, 1963.

PRESIDENT'S EUROPEAN TRIP
June 1963

Bilateral Background Paper: Italy
U.S. Views on Center-Left Experiment

The crucial question in Italian politics in recent and coming years is the extent of Socialist separation from the Communists and the dependability of Socialist orientation in defense of democratic ideals in Italy and in NATO. A principal objective of Italy's first center-left government (March 1962–May 1963) was to assist the Socialists in completing their withdrawal from cooperation with the Communists, with whom they had a unity of action pact until early 1957. We cannot say yet whether the experiment has been a success. The effort has been criticized as too risky and the chances of success too slight. The recent Communist electoral gains and the state of confusion in the Socialist Party after the election are adverse factors. Under the center-left government, however, the Socialists increasingly oriented themselves toward European unity, accepted Italy's NATO role, although with limitations, and showed willingness to explore Italian participation in the MLF. We believe that only Italians are in a position to decide about the center-left. During the period before the center-left government was formed and during its existence, the U.S. Government has therefore refused either to press for or to counsel against the experiment. Both advocates and opponents of the experiment have criticized this posture, but we believe that it was and remains the correct position for us to take.

In the immediate post-war period the alternatives in Italy were communism or democracy. [*1-1/2 lines of source text not declassified*] The present choice in Italy, however, is between a liberal democratic coalition and a conservative democratic alternative, both of which are threatened by the Communists. These two democratic alternatives between them gained nearly 70% of the votes this year (excluding the Communists and neo-Fascists), whereas in 1958 the single democratic possibility won only 58% (the Socialists then being in opposition). Under these circumstances, our most effective efforts should be directed to encouraging all democratic parties to strengthen their efforts against Communism, without favoring one party, faction, or solution among the democratic alternatives.

Source: Department of State, Conference Files: Lot 66 D 110, CF 2274. Secret. Drafted by Gammon. Cleared by Tyler and Brandin. This paper was included in the President's European trip briefing book.

318. Memorandum of Conversation

Rome, July 1, 1963, 10:45 a.m.

PARTICIPANTS

President of the Republic Antonio Segni
President of the Council of Ministers Giovanni Leone
Vice President and Foreign Minister Attilio Piccioni
Under Secretary of State Edoardo Martino
Foreign Office Secretary General Attilio Cattani
Ambassador to Washington Sergio Fenoaltea
Diplomatic Adviser to the President of the Council Carlo Marchiori

The President [1]
The Secretary
Embassy Chargé d'Affaires Francis T. Williamson
Mr. McGeorge Bundy, White House
Mr. Theodore Sorensen, White House
Mr. William R. Tyler, Assistant Secretary of State for European Affairs
Embassy Political Counselor William N. Fraleigh, Rapporteur

In the afternoon the following joined the conference:

Foreign Office Director General for Political Affairs Giovanni Fornari
Foreign Office Director General for Econ. Affairs Egidio Ortona
Mr. Francis E. Meloy, Director, Office of W. European Affairs, Department of
    State
Embassy Economic Counselor H. Gardner Ainsworth

Time & Place: Quirinale and Palazzo Madama, July 1, 1963

PART I—Morning Discussions at Quirinale Palace

Introductory and Preliminary Remarks

Segni said it was a great pleasure to have President Kennedy in
Rome. The pleasure of the Italian people at having him here had been
demonstrated by the warm reception the President had seen on his way
in from the airport.

Segni then cited some of the ties that unite the US and Italy. He mentioned that so many Italians live happily in the US, as the President had

---

Source: Department of State, Conference Files: Lot 66 D 110, CF 2280. Secret. Drafted
by Fraleigh and transmitted as enclosure 1 to airgram 63 from Rome, July 17.

[1] President Kennedy arrived in Milan the evening of June 30 and flew to Rome the
next morning for a meeting with President Segni. For text of Kennedy's statement at the
airport, see *Public Papers of the Presidents of the United States: John F. Kennedy, 1963,* p. 545.
Kennedy and Segni met alone while Rusk held talks with Prime Minister Leone. Memoranda of their conversations are in Department of State, Conference Files: Lot 66 D 110, CF
2275. Rusk, Leone, and other senior U.S. and Italian officials joined the Presidents at the
conclusion of their private meeting.

already observed in his arrival remarks. US and Italian history also have in common their respective people's struggle for independence. Segni said that although Italy achieved freedom later than the US did, there was nothing more alien to the Italian character than lack of freedom. Italians are more than advocates of independence, they are strong individualists. They admire the progress made in the US without sacrificing freedom. Italy has obtained material progress, too, especially since the war, and also without sacrificing freedom.

Segni then mentioned other ties recalling that it was an Italian who discovered America.

Segni said, "I have known Presidents Roosevelt, Truman, Eisenhower, and now you, Mr. President." (Segni said Rockefeller for Roosevelt and hastily corrected himself. Everyone enjoyed the slip, which helped to give the meeting a lighter note.) Segni congratulated himself on knowing American leaders, and so many of them, over a long period. He reiterated a warm welcome to the President on his own behalf and that of the Italian government. It was their desire to make US-Italian ties even closer.

President Kennedy thanked President Segni for his kind remarks. He said his visit to Europe had resulted from President Segni's invitation to visit Italy extended to him last winter. He had wanted to come to Europe because he believed it desirable to demonstrate the solidarity of the Atlantic Community, the solidarity of the US with Europe. If that solidarity was to be kept sound, there were two particular questions which needed to be dealt with: (1) how to divide the power of the atom between the countries of the Alliance; (2) how to organize the economic relations of the countries of the Alliance. All the disasters of the 1930's were the result of economic failures in the 1920's. Stability in Europe and in the US would be damaged if there were any economic setback in the U.S. Therefore the U.S. and Europe needed to work together on trade matters, monetary policy and all the rest. Close collaboration was necessary.

The President expressed his special appreciation to the Italian President and other Italian officials present for the cooperation Italy had given to NATO, to the Atlantic Community, to the US and to other countries having a common view of the future.

Leone then spoke in the name of the Italian Government strongly supporting President Segni's earlier remarks. He also spoke of the enthusiasm of the Italian people over the President's visit. He thanked the President for all the US is doing for the world. He said the Italian Government and people look forward to the President's state visit next year, accompanied by Mrs. Kennedy.

President Kennedy then said there was little time left for the morning session of their talks since they were already behind schedule. He suggested they might take up two matters on which he would like to have the views of the Italian Government, to wit: MLF and the coming trade negotiations.

MLF

On the MLF, the President said the idea had been put forward some years ago to meet the needs of countries not having a voice in the use of nuclear weapons but entitled to have such a voice. There had been much criticism of the MLF idea but no better scheme had yet been put forward. When some people speak of forming a committee to handle the atom it is necessary to have also an analysis on how this would work. De Gaulle has said in criticism of the US proposal that every monopolist considers that his monopoly should be satisfactory to all. But the US considers that its proposal would give Europe real participation in nuclear power and avoid the danger of every nation acquiring its own nuclear force.

The US accepts the fact of the existence of a French nuclear force. But it has put forward the MLF idea to work out the needs of Italy and Germany as great powers. As members of NATO, Italy and Germany have a right to join in such a force. But the US does not want Germany and Italy to give their support to the MLF just to please the US, but only if they really want the MLF. The US does not want the MLF unless it is of real value and interest to Italy and Germany.

The UK had accepted the MLF at Nassau, where they had also supported the idea of a multi-national force. But since then there had been much criticism of MLF from such leading UK personalities as Lord Mountbatten, Lord Montgomery and others, partly on grounds of expense, partly because they seemed concerned that Germany would get too much of a role in the control of the weapons, and partly because they considered that participation in such a force would mean a diminution of British national power. Macmillan has thus far been unable to get much support for MLF.

In Germany the President had agreed with the German leaders to study the MLF question further in Washington this summer. In the UK the President had agreed with Macmillan that the British would participate in this study but that they would be unable to say as of now whether they would join in the force when it is created.

The President said he hoped that Italy would join in this study. The US wanted Italy to know that perhaps the UK would never participate in the force itself. In that event Germany, Italy and the US might decide to go ahead with it anyway. They could decide about that in the fall. Now it was a matter of deciding on whether or not to go ahead with a special study, and on the degree of Italian participation in such a study. The President said that the US wants to give Italy a maximum share of participation in the common project.

Leone replied that he would like to make the Italian position absolutely clear. He pointed out that his Government had not yet obtained a vote of confidence. It was, therefore, in a precarious position. The Italian Government had hoped to obtain a vote of confidence before the President arrived but was unable to do so. He paid tribute to Segni for having tried his best to make it possible for a government to be in office by the time the President arrived.

Leone said that that very day he would present his Government's program to Parliament and on the following Wednesday the debate would begin. Perhaps there would be a vote in the Senate by Friday and if the Senate voted its confidence then the debate would go into the House. Leone said that while his Government was in a sense a limited government, and a single party government, depending for its support on the abstention of the Socialists, it would nevertheless assume very definite tasks. It would not act like a caretaker government but like one with definite powers and responsibilities, particularly in the field of foreign policy. He was going to speak plainly on this matter, foreign policy, this very day in Parliament.

Against this background of realities, Leone said he would like to discuss the US proposals which President Kennedy had just outlined. With regard to the MLF the President had stated very well how it could prevent proliferation of nuclear weapons. The Italian Government was very anxious to avoid such proliferation. This had also been the view of the Fanfani Government. Even Italians opposed to the Government held a similar view. The Italian Parliament and public were thoroughly in favor of such policy. The Communist Party of course opposed any policy based on NATO. But on the Atlantic policy in general there was a wide range of agreement among the other Italian parties beginning with Saragat on the left and continuing through the DC, Republicans, Liberals, Monarchists and MSI. All these were for a policy of Atlantic decision and unity. The Socialist Party of Nenni had a special problem in regard to foreign policy. In fact, foreign policy was at the base of the disunity within the Socialist Party.

The Socialist Party was under pressure from the Communists and was going through difficult times. Some Socialists did not want to be cut off entirely from the Communist Party and this attitude was reflected in their views on foreign policy. Other Socialists were ready to break completely with the PCI. This, Leone said, was one of the profoundest problems in Italy.

But, Leone said, this Government was determined to maintain Italy's established foreign policy. Maybe the Socialists would side with the Communists. Maybe not. President Segni who had been Foreign Minister and had long stood by the US and NATO, felt the same way as he, Leone, did. Leone said, "We are not going to yield on foreign policy, even at the cost of difficulties in our internal affairs. We know that if we yielded we could get the Socialists into the government and, under cover, the Communists also."

Leone then said that Italy stood by its agreement in principle on MLF. There remained questions of detail. One of these was the question of submarines versus surface vessels. It was hard to get an exact idea of what this problem involved. This should be studied further. There had been talks already between President Kennedy and Fanfani during which submarines were agreed on as the best carrier for the nuclear weapons. While this was being studied, there had been a change of view by the US in favor of surface ships. He just mentioned this to illustrate the Italian concern about certain details. He, Leone, and his Government accepted the principle of MLF just as the previous government had done. It did so not as an act of friendship for the US but because it believed that the MLF will be useful for the Atlantic Alliance. Italy was disposed to join in the studies that were proposed especially on the technical side.

At the same time, however, Leone said he must reiterate that because of precarious position of his Government, which had not yet obtained a vote of confidence, he would hope that as little as possible would be said publicly about the Italian Government having assumed any commitments until after the vote of confidence had been obtained. His Government did not intend to be as undecided as had been the case with the UK. It just wanted to be cautious. President Kennedy said he entirely understood and agreed with this.

President Kennedy said he would like to ask the Foreign Minister, whose opinion he valued highly, whether he feels that MLF meets the problem confronting the Alliance—i.e., of giving other powers a voice in the control of nuclear force, or whether he thinks some other system might be better.

Piccioni said that before answering he wanted to associate himself in complete support of all the Prime Minister had said.

He wanted to go even further to clarify the Italian Government's position. He did not stop to recall the need for NATO and Italian loyalty to NATO. Italy had been one of the founders of NATO and NATO was one of the bases of Italian foreign policy. All Italian Foreign Ministers had supported NATO as the basis of Italian foreign policy. The reason for this was of course the world situation. The late Prime Minister De Gasperi was the first to realize that the West had to raise and maintain its defensive strength to be able to oppose any aggression; but for this bloody events would have followed. It was for such reasons that Italy had decided to join an alliance like NATO. Moreover, NATO was no ordinary alliance. It was not designed merely to use its power in a positive sense. It was established as a defensive force, as the shield of liberty and the independence of the West. This was the line in which Italy participated.

Then there had been an evolution in armaments and the advent of atomic power produced a new problem. The Alliance had to face the problem of having its own nuclear armament or to use such an armament belonging to someone else. Piccioni said, "We are grateful to the US because despite its independent position in the atomic field it decided to open the possibility of sharing its nuclear power with the Atlantic Alliance."

The question was how to share this force. It was not feasible to distribute nuclear secrets, or for each member of the Alliance to have its own nuclear power or to create another international Alliance within NATO disposing of nuclear armament.

Piccioni said from the time NATO was set up he had agreed on close control over the nuclear weapon.

He said Italy had always agreed on the aim desired. The only question was of how to achieve it. Then came the questions of MLF and MNF. Piccioni described the MNF as subordinate and related to the question of MLF.

Here the President interjected that it was already past the hour for lunch. He said he appreciated the points the Foreign Minister had made, especially about US willingness to share its nuclear power. Piccioni apologized for having gotten somewhat carried away with his thoughts. He felt he had spoken too long. The President said he was very eloquent, and must be a good speaker in Parliament. The meeting was then adjourned for lunch.[2]

Part II—Afternoon Discussions at Palazzo Madama

The discussions were resumed at about 3 p.m. Piccioni was the first to speak, desiring to conclude his remarks begun in the morning.

He said the countries concerned were in the phase of developing the MNF and MLF proposals, following Ottawa where such work had been started. He said the Italian Government had at previous NATO meetings expressed a questioning view about MNF as a phase to MLF. He said the Italians had repeatedly expressed themselves in this way at

---

[2] Italian and U.S. officials lunched at the Palazzo Madama, the offices of Italy's Prime Minister. According to a memorandum of conversation, the luncheon discussion focused on issues relating to the opening to the left. (Ibid., Central Files, Pol 1 U.S.)

Following lunch the President drove to the Piazza Venezia for a wreath-laying ceremony and meeting with the Mayor of Rome. He also made brief remarks to a large crowd of Italians. For text of his statement, see *Public Papers of the Presidents of the United States: John F. Kennedy, 1963*, p. 546. The President then returned to Palazzo Madama where the U.S. and Italian delegations resumed their discussions.

Ottawa and would do so again. Italy was prepared to adhere to the MLF. But it was never pleased at the idea of having to pass to the MLF through other stages.

On the other hand, certain technical preparations were needed. These were the responsibility of NATO. NATO was more than a traditional alliance—it was a community. So he would underline again the necessity for adequate preparations. And so Italy would request an adequate and responsible study to be made of all aspects of the problem. Italy would ask also that any NATO member not able to accede immediately to the MLF should at least have the right to adhere to it in principle and leave the matter of the solution of the establishment of the force to NATO, thus avoiding proliferation.

Having given its adherence to the principle of the multi-lateral idea, Italy now expressed itself in favor of an adequate study.

Piccioni discussed at some length the technical question of submarines vs. surface vessels, recalling how first one and then the other had been advocated as more suitable. He reiterated that this was one of the reasons why Italy saw the need for serious study.

He recalled that Admiral Ricketts had been in London recently.[3] He suggested that the Admiral should perhaps come to Italy.

In Ottawa two groups had been formed to continue studies. These also should continue their work. Piccioni said, "We must arrive at an understanding on how MLF can function effectively and within the aims of NATO."

Beyond this he said he had nothing to add except to express again Italy's fidelity to NATO, to the power of NATO, and to the concept of the Atlantic Alliance and the idea that it should be reinforced by a nuclear deterrent. Italy was disposed to support this principle when the studies were completed.

President Kennedy said this was excellent. He thought they would go ahead with the study. Admiral Ricketts could come to Italy whenever convenient for the Italian Government. The President suggested that the study be begun in Washington. It could be continued later in Paris under NATO auspices if anyone felt that would be useful.

Test Ban Talks

The President then spoke about the mission of Governor Harriman and Lord Hailsham to the Soviet Union to try to negotiate an end to nuclear tests.[4] He said he did not know what method it might be possible to

---

[3] Admiral Claude V. Ricketts visited Bonn April 17–18 and London June 4–5.

[4] In June the United States, United Kingdom, and Soviet Union announced that Lord Hailsham, President of the Council and Minister of Science, and Under Secretary of State for Political Affairs Harriman would visit Moscow for discussions on a nuclear test ban treaty. Hailsham and Harriman arrived in Moscow on July 15. They concluded discussions and initialed a treaty banning aboveground nuclear tests on July 25.

agree upon or whether indeed such talks would be successful. Two or three possible methods had been suggested by the Soviets. In any case the effort must be made. China might explode its first atom bomb in about a year, and while it would be some years more before China could have sufficient bombs to try to attack anyone, the attainment of the atom bomb by China would complicate the situation in Asia. It would increase China's prestige; it would cause other countries to want to have their bombs. India might want its bomb. Israel and the UAR might also want to construct bombs.

So, the President said, this might be the last chance to achieve a test ban. He was not very optimistic about the chances of success. But it had to be tried. The US and the West would be better off with a test ban. They could then maintain their lead in the nuclear field. The Soviets could of course conduct small underground tests, but these would probably be discovered. If the situation remained in status quo, the US would stay ahead in the nuclear race. If the Soviets made tests in secret, they might catch up but the West would know about it.

Also if the West could agree with the Soviets on something so important as this, there might be important consequences upon Chinese-Soviet relations. The Soviets would perhaps be moved more towards the West because of fear of China. If the US could reach agreement with the Soviets on anything as important as this, that fact could be useful for a wide range of reasons.

Leone said the Italian Government shared the President's ideas completely. A test ban agreement should definitely be tried. It was a worthy effort. All Italy could do was to offer its best wishes for success. He would talk about this in Parliament and before the Italian people.

Piccioni said the Italian Government had shown its support for this aim at Geneva. There were great expectations for concrete results in this field.

President Kennedy reiterated that he thought the probabilities were against success. There was no evidence that the Soviets would accept such guarantees as the West considers essential. There was also much opposition in the US to the US joining in a test ban agreement with the Soviets. But the judgment of the US Government was that Western security would be strengthened by a nuclear freeze.

Economic Problems

The President then turned to the economic problem. He said it was the most difficult problem the West faced. With the large Communist vote in Italy, the question of the future in France after De Gaulle, and the uncertain situation in Spain, Portugal and Greece, there were many points of instability in the West which would be greatly accentuated if there were any important economic recession. The US had suffered two recessions in the late 1950's; US unemployment was still too high, around 6 per cent. The US was trying to carry out steps to strengthen the economic situation in the Western community, such as by managing successfully mutual monetary affairs. Otherwise each country would soon restrict the movement of trade and the clock would be turned back to the 1920's. This would bring about a very serious situation.

The President said the West should put economic affairs at the top of its agenda—not leave them just to economic and trade ministers, however capable they might be. Economic problems involve security, military and political affairs. They are the West's biggest problem in the 1960's; a problem not only for the US and Europe but for the US and Europe with respect to the rest of the world.

Basic producers had undergone a further drop in world prices of raw materials recently. This was causing worry.

Economic matters were more important than the nuclear problem, because in the nuclear field the US commitment is clear and the Soviets know it. If the West fails to establish an MLF, it will not really be any worse off. But if it fails in the economic field, it will be very badly off.

It was important that the Dollar keep its strength and usefulness. If the Dollar failed, the West would need something else in its place or Communism would win an easy victory. Western countries should work hard on the achievement of agreements on trade and commercial exchange.

The President said the Italian Government had been very helpful on these matters. He mentioned Italy's help in the matter of offset purchases. He also mentioned Italy's helpfulness on certain technical arrangements with US Treasury Department representatives. He reiterated that the economic question was the priority issue.

Leone called on Minister Ortona to state the Italian view.

Ortona said that for the Italian part, negotiations on tariffs were being given the greatest importance. He said Italy had given proof of this at Geneva where it had done its part within the framework of the European economic community. It had tried to arrive at useful compromises. A good beginning had also been made in the work of the OECD. Such negotiations were constantly moving ahead in spite of difficulties. For important economic and political reasons it was necessary to arrive at further agreements between the governments concerned.

As for the Dollar, the President had mentioned some of the things Italy had done. Italy had also done other things lately to help to strengthen the Dollar. The Italian economic situation and balance of payments were causing some concern and problems. They were certainly not better than last year. But Italy was doing its best and wanted to help to keep the pre-eminence of the Dollar because of its importance for Italy's trade and for that of other countries, and indirectly for the LDC's.

President Kennedy said the point is that every nation cannot hope to build up its balances every year. Only so much increased wealth is coming into the West each year. Countries could either build up their reserves of Dollars or gold, or exchange fully back and forth. The West needed a common understanding about what would be best for all. The situation was like that of a bank. If all members assume some risk, there is no risk. But if everyone wants to take care first of his own interest, there is risk for all.

The President said that the US monetary position had improved. There was no longer a too great outflow of short-term loans. Especially if the desired tax cut would be approved, the US economic position should be good. The Dollar has proved its liquidity in Europe for years. This problem, too, would be met. But again if every country wanted to increase its trade balances every year, the West would be weakened.

Continuing on the question of trade balances, the President said that in spite of the French argument that the US is advocating agreement with the EEC because it is trying to dump American goods abroad, the fact remains that the US domestic market is much greater than its foreign market. The US would have no problem of balances if it were not for its aid and defense commitments. The US loss has been Europe's gain. For instance, the US loses a billion and a half dollars in tourists' payment balances annually.

The President reiterated that this whole economic question should be at the top of the agenda. It is not a question of losing trade. It is a question of balances. If everyone were again to adopt restrictive trade policies, this would adversely effect the economic development of the West and of the LDC's.

The US appreciates what Italy had done and wishes other European countries would do the same. The US wants Italy's continuing understanding. The French, too, have been helpful on some matters such as monetary policy though on trade they have been more restrictive than they have needed to be.

Ortona spoke again for the Italian side. He said that on the question of conversion of dollars for gold, Italy has not converted any dollars into gold since 1960. Also, Italy's percentage balance in gold is less than that of the UK, the Netherlands or Belgium. He said this is proof of Italy's good intentions.

The President said Italy's balance in gold is also less than that of Spain.

The President said he thought that there was general agreement. The policy which the US had followed and which has resulted in a drain of US reserves has been a useful policy. The US does not expect Europe to do its work for it. But it is up to Europe to take the long view in its own self-interest, just as the US has done.

The meeting then ended with some discussion about the content of the communiqué which would be issued. It was suggested that, when asked, spokesmen for the two sides would say to the press that the talks had concerned NATO, economic matters and test ban talks, without going into any details.

319.   Memorandum of Conversation

US/MC/29   Rome, July 1, 1963.

THE PRESIDENT'S TRIP TO EUROPE
June 23–July 2, 1963

SUBJECT

Italian Domestic Political Scene

PARTICIPANTS

Italy	*United States*
Communist Party Secretary Togliatti	The President
Christian Democratic Party Secretary Moro	
Socialist Party Secretary Nenni	
Former Prime Minister Fanfani	

As the President strolled through long lines of people, Americans and Italians, who were waiting in the garden to greet him, he was introduced to Mr. Togliatti. The President told him that he was glad to see him there, and that he was enjoying the visit to his country. (A photograph of this meeting was retrieved from an Italian photographer at the President's request.)

The President subsequently asked Nenni many of the questions he had earlier put to the Prime Minister and the speaker of the Chamber about the vagaries of Italian election results in a situation of growing prosperity. Nenni gave him essentially the same answer: there were too many people left behind, which the President would clearly see for himself if he could stay a few days and visit the countryside, and the slums.

Source: Department of State, Conference Files: Lot 66 D 110, CF 2275. Confidential. No drafting information appears on the source text. Approved in the White House on July 22. These discussions took place at a reception following an official dinner hosted by President Segni at the Quirinale Palace. For text of President Kennedy's public remarks at the Segni dinner, see *Public Papers of the Presidents of the United States: John F. Kennedy, 1963*, pp. 547–550.

The President asked Nenni if he thought it possible for the PSI to cooperate with the majority. Nenni gave an unreserved "yes."[1]

Fanfani, who was at the dinner, also dropped by. The President expressed the hope that he would attend the Democratic convention, which will be held in Atlantic City.[2] Fanfani said he appreciated the invitation. The President told Fanfani that he was sorry that his visit was taking place at a time of such confusion. Fanfani quickly said something signifying resignation to circumstances and wished the President success.[3]

---

[1] According to Nenni (*Anni di Centro Sinistra*, pp. 288–289), during their conversation the President stressed the importance of Italy's role in Europe, especially as a balance on the ambitions of General de Gaulle's France. They also discussed the importance of continuing dialog between the United States and Soviet Union prior to their conversation of the prospects of the center-left. Nenni also stated that the President extended an invitation to visit the United States.

[2] The President's initial meeting with Fanfani occurred during the 1956 Democratic national convention.

[3] Commenting on the President's discussions with the party leaders the Embassy reported: "In general, we have good grounds to believe that all secretaries were impressed by President's personality, his interest in and knowledge of Italian as well as European situation, his willingness to listen and to consider their opinions. We can only hope that President's (and US) readiness to stand up and be counted as particularly friendly to so-called democratic sector of Italian political opinion will have also left its mark on government leaders who so quickly caved in to threats of extremist reactions." (Telegram 64 from Rome, July 6; Department of State, Central Files, Pol–7 U.S./Kennedy)

---

320. Memorandum of Conversation

Washington, October 4, 1963, 6:10 p.m.

SUBJECT

Italian Political Situation

PARTICIPANTS

Italy

Emilio Colombo, Minister of
    Treasury
Sergio Fenoaltea, Ambassador,
    Italian Embassy
Gian Luigi Milesi Ferretti, Minister,
    Italian Embassy

United States

The President
Neil Seidenman—Interpreter

Source: Department of State, Central Files, Pol 1 Italy. Confidential. Drafted by Seidenman, cleared by Stott, and approved in the White House on October 14. The meeting was held at the White House.

Senator Merzagora, after saying that he was deeply touched by President Johnson's words, emphasized that he was not only confident, but certain, that the line which had been pursued in Europe by President Kennedy, a line of attentiveness, vigilance and generosity, would be continued in the period ahead.

President Johnson assured him that it would, and if there were any changes they would be for the good.

Senator Merzagora went on to say that while Italy was going through a process of political transition at the moment,[3] he could assure the President that there would be no change in the relationship and in the feelings between Italy and the United States, a feeling of friendship and consideration for the United States in all those organizations in which our two countries share a common cause.

Secretary Rusk added that, as we try to decide how to write the coming chapter, Italy's steadfastness in NATO and as an ally constitute a source of strength for the free world, and this will be of extreme importance for the future. We thus rely heavily on Italy. In this context, he was looking forward to seeing Foreign Minister Piccioni at the forthcoming NATO meeting in two or three weeks.

Senator Merzagora recalled his words to the Secretary in Rome last summer, to the effect that Italy would be unfailingly watchful that no change could come about to affect either the existing structures of common policy or Italy's absolute, unconditional, unqualified friendship with the U.S. He yielded to Foreign Minister Piccioni for confirmation of what he had said.

Foreign Minister Piccioni confirmed that he was very solidly behind everything the Senator had said. He pointed out that his authority is "shaken" now, on the eve of a "complete change" in the Italian Government. He could, however, absolutely assure the President that the new government would be absolutely firm in the principles of foreign policy that have been upheld over the past two years; and above all, it will not fail to reaffirm Italy's friendship toward the United States in all the organisms that form the living structures of our relationship. The Minister concluded by saying that political talks between Italy and the United States could be broadened in January (a reference to the State visit of President Segni scheduled for January 13–18, 1964).

President Johnson closed by saying that this meeting had been a great reassurance to him.

---

[3] On November 11 Prime Minister Roumor presented his resignation to President Segni. The following day Segni asked Aldo Moro to form a new government. Moro announced that he would seek Socialist Party participation in this government. Moro completed his negotiations on November 23. The program of the new government, announced November 25, underlined Italy's loyalty to the Atlantic Alliance and its readiness to participate in the MLF.

323. Telegram From Secretary of State Rusk to the Department of
State

Paris, December 16, 1963, 6 p.m.

Secto 22. Secretary called on Italian Foreign Minister Saragat at Italian Embassy, Paris, afternoon December 15. Saragat referred to fact he had not been able see President Kennedy during President's visit Italy in July. President had thereafter written Saragat. Letter[1] has been great inspiration to Saragat and to his work. Foreign Minister emphasized Italy shares US grief at loss of President Kennedy.

Secretary told Saragat US pleased to see him named Foreign Minister and he was looking forward to working closely with Saragat.

Foreign Minister said new Italian Government has good parliamentary majority.[2] Italy's position remains unchanged. Nenni Socialists have accepted Italian policy with regard to NATO alliance and Western orientation. Only small fringe likely detach themselves and go over to Communists.[3] Nenni Socialists naturally emphasize matters closest to their interests and convictions and while accepting national defense policies, place stress on continuing dialogue with Soviet Union and on peace. Nenni Socialists accept MLF in principle but have asked for complete plan before giving final acceptance. When one thinks that only three years ago PSI was pro-communist and now is participating in government and had accepted NATO and Western obligations, one realizes what a great step forward has been made in Italy. There has been great strengthening of forces favoring the West. Saragat said he fully realizes things will not be easy. Many battles must be fought but he is very optimistic regarding the future. He believes ultimate result in Italy will be foundation of strong Social Democratic Party like that in Austria, but not so strong as in UK. In response to Secretary's question, Saragat said process formation such a party would take considerable time but irreversible trend has set in. Secretary said in view many changes in Gov-

---

Source: Department of State, Conference Files: Lot 66 D 110, CF 2345. Confidential. Drafted by Meloy and concurred in by Gordon and Little. Rusk and Saragat were in Paris to attend the North Atlantic Council Ministerial Meeting, December 16–17.

[1] Not found.

[2] On December 4 Prime Minister-designate Aldo Moro presented his new government to President Segni. The government included 16 Christian Democratic, 6 Socialist, 1 Republican, and 3 Social Democratic ministers. Pietro Nenni assumed the position of Vice President of the Council of Ministers. The government won a vote of confidence in Parliament on December 17.

[3] On December 27, 27 Socialist Party deputies belonging to the leftwing "carristi" faction broke with the party to form an Italian Socialist Party of Proletarian Unity (PSIUP). The new party was led by Lelio Basso and Tullio Vecchietti.

ernments represented at forthcoming NATO sessions, we hope this meeting will be one of consolidation and not stimulate points of difference. It is important that press not have the feeling we are going away with great controversies raging around us. Points of difference such as those concerning NATO strategy and force goals should be left to discussion in PermReps meetings. Saragat entirely agreed.

Secretary referred to new U.S. administration and emphasized President Johnson is strong individual who will be a strong President. President Johnson has rural liberal background and tradition of support for Roosevelt and Truman policies. He participated in Kennedy administration's decision making and can be counted on to give strong leadership to continuing liberal policies.

Rusk

Portugal

324. Telegram From the Department of State to the Embassy in Portugal

Washington, March 4, 1961, 4:55 p.m.

471. For Ambassador Elbrick and Barbour from Secretary. Elbrick should seek soonest feasible interview with Salazar in order make following presentation. (I plan parallel approach to Fernandes here when you inform me you have appointment with Salazar.) Barbour should inform UK Government at high level of US démarche to Portuguese indicating we would welcome similar British approach. NATO discussion of this problem as recommended by Embassy Lisbon may at appropriate stage also be most useful. These are lines which Elbrick should use in discussion with Salazar:

1) We are deeply concerned over deteriorating position Portugal in United Nations and in Africa, and over growing difficulties in UN in connection with its overseas provinces. Accordingly we wish talk frankly and in friendly spirit with Portugal as ally with view to improving mutual understanding our position and, we would hope, influencing Portugal to undertake major adjustments in her policies which as presently constituted seem to us headed for very serious trouble.

2) Most immediate problem is Liberian move place Angola question on Secretary Council agenda. In view our traditional position on inscription of items we shall vote in favor inscription. If you think it useful you may recall that we agreed to inscription last year of various items directed against us, e.g., U–2, RB–47, Cuba. We have long held that inscription on Security Council agenda does not in itself constitute position on substance of item inscribed, nor can it constitute intervention in internal affairs of member state.

3) In view US worldwide commitments and responsibilities we find it increasingly difficult and disadvantageous to Western interests publicly to support or remain silent on Portuguese African policies and have come to the conclusion that more public clarity on US position on these particular issues of overseas provinces is required. FYI. In general,

---

Source: Department of State Central Files, 753.00/3–461. Secret; Niact; Limit Distribution. Drafted by McBride; cleared with Chayes, Bowles, Ball, Cleveland, Kohler, McGhee, AF, ARA, the White House, and the Department of Defense; and approved by Rusk. Also sent to London; repeated to Paris, USUN, Rio de Janeiro, Luanda, and Lourenco Marques.

we are greatly concerned that because of our close association with Portugal, which we value as ally, we shall come under increasing criticism from Afro-Asian countries which will, rightly or wrongly, tend to hold us responsible for Portuguese actions and inaction in connection with overseas provinces which clash with America's traditional position in regard to colonialism and self-determination. End FYI.

4) US feels that it would be remiss in its duties as fellow NATO member of Portugal if it did not point out its conviction that step by step actions are now imperative for the political, economic and social advancement of all inhabitants Portuguese African provinces towards full self-determination within realistic timetable. Conversely attempt maintain status quo may lead to maximum disadvantage. We would be lacking in candor if we did not express our serious and sober conviction on basis most sympathetic examination Portuguese African policies, that those policies are so totally out of step with political and economic advancement elsewhere in Black Africa that unless Portugal adjusts her policies to African realities, increasingly serious outbreaks in her territories may be expected in future.

5) In accordance above thoughts, we believe it would be very helpful if Portugal were willing announce decision to submit information to UN on overseas territories in accordance with Article 73e of the UN Charter. We feel that such action, coupled with effective steps by Portuguese advancing the inhabitants of Portuguese African provinces towards full self-government with self-determination, would go long way to reducing pressure upon Portugal in UN, and avoidance creation more Congos. More importantly we are convinced that such reforms would in long run constitute best assurance that Portugal could maintain mutually beneficial ties with overseas provinces. FYI. Conceivably if Portugal feels she cannot report to SYG, she could report to certain UN nations such as SC members. End FYI.

6) We are fully aware of economic importance of overseas provinces to Portugal and of great potential cost of their development towards responsible self-government. This process of readjustment may initially be economically costly. Accordingly we are prepared to extend important bilateral assistance to Portugal and to her overseas territories and in addition to explore possibilities unilateral aid program with selected NATO countries in order minimize economic consequences for Portugal. While these territories presently economic assets, continued political deterioration could quickly turn them into liabilities. Furthermore history shows British-Indian type relationship in long run much more profitable economically than where colonial relationship abruptly and bitterly terminated as in Guinea case. FYI. I am fully aware distasteful nature above line to Salazar regime but feel frankly this approach required especially since no real effort along these lines previously

made. We have few illusions here that Portuguese Government in the near future will change its policies toward African possessions, especially in light their previous intransigeance. However if as result this démarche, and hopefully similar approach by British, and perhaps Brazilians at some later stage, Portuguese can be brought to accept at least fact that we must "agree to disagree" on their African policies, we will have taken forward step in what will probably be long and difficult road toward necessary changes. Similar developments will occur in UN context. At present time we wish primarily alert Portuguese to problem, and we wish avoid appearance of "take it or leave it" attitude which would only invite Portuguese precipitate counter-action which we do not want in connection with NATO or Azores where we believe retention of base rights very important.

Immediate purpose of your démarche is to make Salazar understand that he cannot reasonably expect us to support Portugal in forthcoming SC debate or in GA on this issue, while in longer term we would hope effect change in their policies which although heretofore rigid in extreme may be open to change among certain elements at least. Meanwhile welcome your comments on what useful further steps we could take in case there is further deterioration in Portuguese territories which would doubtless result in sharply increased pressures in UN. We have also in mind possibility trouble at any time in Portuguese Guinea fomented by Republic of Guinea. In short inaction to us seems likely to lead to catastrophic upheavals of Congo type or worse. End FYI.

Elbrick should coordinate with Rio so that Rio may inform Brazilian Government for its information only either simultaneously or immediately after démarche made.[1]

Rusk

---

[1] In telegram 567, March 7, Elbrick reported that he had met with Salazar for 1-1/2 hours and presented in detail the views set forth in this telegram. Salazar was relaxed and friendly but "deeply concerned over what he considers self-defeating policy of US with regard to Africa." (Ibid., 753.00/3–761)

325.   Telegram From Secretary of State Rusk to the Department of State

Oslo, May 8, 1961, 4 a.m.

Secto 10. Secretary, accompanied by Kohler and McGhee, met with Portuguese Foreign Minister for hour and half May 7, discussion centering entirely on Portuguese African colony question. Following based uncleared memorandum of conversation. Complete memorandum being prepared.[1] Secretary opened by assuring Foreign Minister that fundamental US objective was to prevent Soviets from seizing leadership of peoples striving for expression of nationalist feelings and seeking economic development. If Soviets are able to convince new nations that they are in best position to fulfill such aspirations, Communist power would be in position to leap over peripheral free world defenses and flank the NATO citadel. Secretary emphasized US has no desire get Portuguese out of Angola; on the contrary we hope they will be able make arrangements with local inhabitants which will permit them to stay to their mutual benefit. Secretary assured Foreign Minister US desires support Portugal in its problems with its African territories if Portugal will give us something more to support. Crux of matter is not passing public opinion or UN majorities but whole relationship of West with Afro-Asian world.

Foreign Minister gave long, able and occasionally emotional exposition familiar arguments Portuguese African colony case. He voiced complete lack of confidence in UN as forum for dealing with such problems. Since West does not possess parliamentary majority on such issues, UN has become instrument for achievement Soviet policies. Soviets, when out-voted, have no hesitancy in failing to comply, which puts nations of West who do comply in serious disadvantage. If we continue allow UN to solve such problems today, UN will tomorrow be solving such world problems as disarmament and Berlin.

Only after SC action did serious incidents arise in Angola. Although Foreign Minister admitted local participation, he asserted incidents had no relation indigenous nationalism but were direct result invasion from Congo. In granting African countries independence West is not able to impart to them our values, but make them easy prey for

---

Source: Department of State Central Files, 753.022/5–861. Secret. Repeated to Lisbon, London, Paris, Rio de Janeiro, USUN, Lourenco Marques, and Luanda. Rusk was in Oslo for the North Atlantic Council Ministerial meeting, May 8–10.

[1] US/MC/1, not printed. (Ibid., Conference Files: Lot 65 D 366, CF 1862) On May 9 Rusk and Nogueira again discussed the Portuguese colonial question. A memorandum of their conversation, similar to that recorded in this telegram, US/MC/17, is ibid.

Communist exploitation as in Ethiopia, Mali, Guinea and the Sudan. Story is not finally told in Congo which is key to Africa. If Angola through premature grant of independence goes Communist, US should consider strategic consequences loss of roads, railroads, mines and other facilities there and in Mozambique.

Foreign Minister then advised that Portuguese Government had on its own initiative and before US démarche of March 7[2] been aware of "winds of change" in Africa and had prepared and was ready to advance far-reaching reforms which would have been very impressive even to Afro-Asian nations. Such plans include:

(1) Economic development, new roads, ports, et cetera;
(2) Increased education of all types and at all levels;
(3) Granting of full political and social rights to all regardless of color.

Because of strong Portuguese public reaction to US position in UN and impossibility of appearing to yield under pressure, Portuguese Government had been forced postpone announcement of these reforms. Foreign Minister asserted that present Portuguese Government is last that will cooperate with West. If Portugal loses its colonies, it will be succeeded by a Castro-type government.

In response to question by Secretary as to future Portuguese intentions Foreign Minister replied that Portuguese Government hopes, with end of rainy season which is nearly over and with help military reinforcements now being sent Angola, restore order and then to publish and carry out reforms. This would not be possible, however, if there is in the meantime any additional international criticism or pressure against Portugal. Foreign Minister requested that US in meantime make no public pronouncements regarding Portuguese African colonies and that any further discussions this question be confined to bi-lateral talks or to regular NAC meetings. Secretary expressed appreciation statement Foreign Minister and suggested they hold another discussion before current meeting over. We wished learn more details of Portuguese plans so we could be helpful. Both agreed unnecessary for colony issue to be raised in current meeting. Full minutes follow.[3]

Rusk

326.   Telegram From the Embassy in Portugal to the Department of State

Lisbon, June 8, 1961, 9 p.m.

998. Re Embtel 990.[1] I have just delivered Secretary's letter to Foreign Minister Franco Nogueira.[2] He read it calmly without any visible emotion but he became more and more depressed as we talked.

His reaction was as expected. He said he failed to see logic of US position and proceeded to expound familiar views on motivation of ASAF and Soviet Bloc attacking Portugal and attempting to fragmentize Africa. He understood that US reasons for voting for resolution[3] entirely different from those of Soviet but world would be impressed by fact we vote with Soviet Bloc. This particularly true of African countries arrayed against Portugal, all of which would see in SC resolution a "green light" to step-up terroristic attacks. Portugal will stand its ground, he said, and result will be "a blood bath". At a time, he said, when Western World is beset with so many crises, it is ill-advised of US to antagonize a friend (Portugal) and undermine an alliance (NATO), in an effort to curry favor with countries whose reliability is at least questionable.

I expanded on reasons for our attitude, assuring him US was not aiming at objection of Portugal from Africa. We are interested in seeing Portugal grant the peoples of overseas territories greater voice in their own affairs and we felt Portugal could avoid disaster in those territories only by taking measures to accomplish this end quietly. I thought this would not be too difficult in view of fact he had already told me government was prepared to institute far-reaching reforms. I said that this was a most critical moment in Portuguese history and that extraordinary measures were required to meet situation.

Nogueira agreed that far-reaching reforms were necessary but said that these could not be introduced overnight. He said if ASAF resolution passed in present form it would be impossible for Portugal to cooperate with GA committee. In keeping with its previous stand, Portugal Government would ignore such resolution.

Source: Department of State Central Files, 753.022/6–861. Confidential; Niact. Repeated to USUN.

[1] Telegram 990, June 8, reported that Elbrick had an appointment with Nogueira at 5:30 p.m. (Ibid.)

[2] Dated June 7, it was a reply to a letter from Nogueira of June 2 (telegram 966 from Lisbon, June 2; ibid., 110.11–RU/6–261), which urged the Foreign Minister to consider reforms for Portugal's African colonies. (Ibid., 753.022/6–761)

[3] For text of the draft resolution on Angola, June 6, see U.N. doc. S/4828.

On parting Nogueira said he feared that US vote for present ASAF resolution would provoke another wave of anti-Americanism in Portugal.[4]

Elbrick

---

[4] On March 27 Elbrick had telephoned McBride and reported that a demonstration was going on in front of the chancery. Elbrick commented that U.S.-Portuguese relations had reached a low point, and in his opinion the U.S. position was "so unenviable" that nobody could say anything that would be influential or that would even be listened to. (Memorandum of telephone conversation; Department of State, Central Files, 611.53/3–2761) Later that day the Embassy reported that the crowd of 15,000 to 20,000 people had demonstrated in front of the chancery for more than an hour, breaking some windows, before being dispersed. (Telegram 677 from Lisbon; ibid.)

---

327. National Security Action Memorandum No. 60

Washington, July 18, 1961.[1]

TO

   The Secretary of State

SUBJECT

   U.S. Actions in Relation to Portuguese Territories in Africa

The President reviewed the report of the Presidential Task Force on Portuguese Territories in Africa, dated July 12, 1961,[2] and approved the following recommendations for action:

1. Send a special envoy to Portugal to talk with Salazar and inform him the U.S. is convinced Portugal must without delay institute basic and far-reaching reforms for her African territories. The scope of these reforms should be such as to lead eventually to self-determination. Inform the UK and France in advance, and Spain when the action is taken.

Source: Department of State, NSAMs: Lot 72 D 316. Secret. No drafting information appears on the source text. Copies were sent to the Secretaries of Defense and the Treasury, and the Directors of Central Intelligence, Bureau of the Budget, U.S. Information Agency, and the International Cooperation Administration.

[1] Originally dated July 14; July 18 is cited as the "revised" date. The earlier draft did not contain the final phrase in paragraph 12 beginning with "recognizing."

[2] Not found.

2. Consult with the UK and France concerning further coordinated pressure on Salazar.

3. Explore with the Vatican, Spain, and Brazil the possibility of their interceding with the Portuguese.

4. Begin immediately to formulate a U.S. course of action to be used in connection with the Portuguese African territories problem in the UN.

5. Unless the results of step one above make it unnecessary or undesirable, raise the problem in the African subcommittee of NATO and subsequently in the NAC, with the objective of impressing upon Portugal the importance attached by its NATO allies to the need for a major change in its colonial policy.

6. Make all possible efforts to insure that MAP equipment supplied to Portugal is not being diverted to Africa in contravention of existing agreements.

7. Deny authorization of licenses for the commercial export of arms from the U.S. to either side.

8. Expand U.S. assistance to refugees suffering from the Angolan conflict.

9. Expand the U.S. educational programs for Africans from the Portuguese areas.

10. Provide U.S. economic assistance, primarily in the form of manpower training, to help develop the technical and administrative skills of the Africans essential in the event reforms are introduced.

11. If Salazar embarks upon a more liberal colonial policy, grant reasonable requests for economic assistance in accordance with existing commitments.

12. Implement the foregoing quietly insofar as possible and in a manner designed to bring about basic and far-reaching reforms in Portuguese colonial policy, and to minimize the possibility of losing the Azores; recognizing the grave military consequences which would attend such a loss.

Accordingly, it is requested that the Department of State initiate the appropriate actions in collaboration with the other responsible agencies to carry out the recommended actions. It is further requested that the President be kept informed, through this office, of significant developments in the implementation of these recommendations.

McGeorge Bundy

328. Telegram From the Department of State to the Embassy in Portugal

Washington, September 1, 1961, 10:23 p.m.

253. Paris for Embassy and USRO. Based on uncleared memorandum of conversation:[1] Secretary had second discussion with Portuguese Ambassador at working lunch August 31.[2] He used occasion to discuss Western position on Berlin and Germany at some length and to stress importance Portugal in NATO. Secretary explained need for build up in conventional weapons and said would be discussing opening negotiating position with NAC during next few weeks. Secretary said he expected negotiations with USSR to take place some time between mid-September and mid-October. He expressed hope that Portugal would not allow attitude on Angola condition participation in NATO. Said he had detected certain withdrawal from NATO on part Portuguese since Angolan question came to fore. Hoped Ambassador could use personal influence to reverse this trend. Secretary also stressed importance US attaches to closest relations with Portugal and assured Ambassador NATO members shared this sentiment. Also stated Angolan situation was as painful for allies as for Portuguese.

Secretary told Ambassador that US necessarily views questions such as Angola as peripheral and marginal when compared to Berlin crisis although he realized this question central in Portuguese thinking. Secretary also suggested Portuguese might well establish constructive relations with certain of Afro-Asians particularly Africans of the Monrovia group such as Nigeria. Ambassador seemed to appreciate value this suggestion.

Secretary welcomed Pereira's assignment to Washington and said believed much could be accomplished through frank and relaxed discussions of mutual problems. Told Ambassador that at one stage consideration given to sending special envoy to Lisbon but he opposed this on basis envoy was coming here in person Ambassador Pereira.[3]

Source: Department of State Central Files, 611.53/9–161. Confidential. Drafted by Blue and cleared with Tyler. Repeated to Paris, London, Madrid, Luanda, and Lourenco Marques.

[1] Not found.

[2] In Rusk's first substantive meeting with Ambassador Pereira, August 22, Rusk reiterated the importance that the United States attached to a program of reform for Angola, while the Ambassador said that the situation in Angola was coming under control. (Telegram 213 to Lisbon, August 23; Department of State, Central Files, 611.53/8–2361)

[3] On July 21 Tyler had sent a memorandum to Rusk expressing his and Kohler's skepticism about sending a special emissary to Salazar even though the President had expressed his approval for the idea. (Ibid., 611.53/7–2161)

Ambassador expressed appreciation frankness of Secretary's remarks and thoughtfulness in seeing him during this busy period. Assured Secretary he would convey these and any views in future to his government. Also said he was particularly appreciative Secretary's kind remarks about importance his mission. Ambassador seemed particularly concerned over critical public opinion in US which he said it was important to change. He hoped friends in US and abroad would show more understanding of Portuguese position in Angola now that reforms announced. Assured Secretary importance Portugal attaches to NATO alliance in present crisis and said Portugal would do her part. Added although appreciative US stress on Berlin crisis he hoped US would understand Portugal faced with great problem in Angola which she considered vital.

Secretary emphasized this one of a series of meetings and that he hoped inform himself more on Angola situation and discuss it further with Ambassador at early date.

Rusk

---

329.   Memorandum of Conversation

Washington, November 7, 1961.

SUBJECT

Portuguese Overseas Policy

PARTICIPANTS

United States	*Portugal*
The Secretary	Mr. Franco Nogueira, Portuguese
Ambassador Elbrick	Foreign Minister [1]
Assistant Secretary Kohler	Ambassador Pereira, Portuguese
Assistant Secretary Williams	Embassy
Dep. Assistant Secretary Tyler	
Mr. L. Dean Brown, WE	

The Secretary opened the luncheon discussion by reassuring the Foreign Minister that the U.S. is not conducting any secret discussions

---

Source: Department of State, Secretary's Memoranda of Conversation: Lot 65 D 330. Secret. Drafted by Brown and approved in S on November 14.

[1] Nogueira was in the United States to attend the U.N. General Assembly.

with the Germans, French and British here in Washington of which the other allies are not fully informed. Now that a German Government has been formed, however, we may be able to move forward.

The Secretary asked Mr. Nogueira about his impression of the U.N. The Foreign Minister said that Portugal supported the U.N. as it had been constituted and was in full agreement with the Charter. Portugal had seen the U.N. grow in a different manner than expected. The new membership is largely irresponsible. The U.N. has diverted its attention from major problems which confront all nations, such as disarmament or nuclear testing, to matters which affect the national interest of individual members. Portugal cannot permit the U.N. to take actions with regard to its national interests. The Soviets, of course, pay no attention to the U.N. when it concerns itself with the Soviet Union's national interests. Soviet influence in the U.N. has grown. Once it was virtually isolated; now the Afro-Asians join it in denouncing the West.

The Secretary said we cannot consider the U.N. and the real world as two completely separate entities. It would be dangerous if the Soviets and Afro-Asians got together on an anti-Western position in the world itself.

The Foreign Minister discussed the reforms program. These are now being implemented. Municipal elections will be held in February. In Angola, Mozambique, and Portuguese Guinea about a million people will vote.

The Secretary said these elections are perhaps the most significant part of the program. If the government which exists is supported by the people—as in Puerto Rico—then the basic problem has been coped with. He thought the Portuguese had gone quite far with their program. What remains now is to tell the U.N. and the world what is being accomplished. He hoped the elections would provide a means whereby Portugal could make its case. He emphasized the fact that the U.S. is not crusading in the U.N. However, it has to deal with the situation as it has arisen there. That is why it hopes the Portuguese can take a positive position in the U.N. which will enable its allies to give support.

Reverting to the elections, the Foreign Minister said observers could come freely in to see the election process. These could be journalists or government officials, but not U.N. representatives as such. He said that it was difficult to make the Portuguese case in the U.N. As soon as the Portuguese said anything at all then they were, in a sense, "reporting" within the context of 73e. This they wanted to avoid. In addition, Portugal is automatically attacked by the Afro-Asians no matter what is said.

The Secretary said that not all Africans react in the same way to the Portuguese problem. Many are concerned by what is happening in the

331. Telegram From the Embassy in India to the Department of State

New Delhi, December 5, 1961, 8 p.m.

1611. Pass to White House for President. Paris for USRO for Finletter. The recurrence of concern here for Goa problem makes timely a new look at Portugal and problem of Portuguese colonies. The purpose of this telegram is to urge that both the reputation of the administration and the larger purposes of our foreign policy require a bolder and more dramatic stand on this issue than we have taken so far.

May we assume the following truths to be reasonably self evident:

1. That the Portuguese empire has survived not by peculiar merit but for a combination of reasons remarkably related to backwardness, tenacity and pure accident.

2. That its hour, especially in Africa, is approaching and that few will come forward to stake their reputation on the durability of these last colonies in otherwise independent Africa. We are duly agreed, in principle, on anticipating change rather than being over-taken thereby.

3. That as a contributor to NATO, the Azores Base apart, Portugal has never been of importance. SACLANT, one assumes, does not float or sink according to the Portuguese contribution.

4. That Portugal's colonial conflicts, if they continue, will increasingly swallow her resources and these could indeed develop an indirect claim on aid for the purpose of postponing, however briefly, the inevitable.

5. That the antipathy to colonialism is profound, and that Portugal, as the last colonial power, is thus an increasingly prickly companion.

6. That to the extent that we support Portugal, actively or even passively, we find ourselves compromised in much the same position as the French, Dutch or Belgians. We get no credit for helping end colonialism. We are remembered as resisting exit at five minutes to twelve.

7. That the Kennedy administration ought, on this matter, to see the brilliant lessons of the Roosevelt administration. Even during a war, even in face of close friendship for Churchill, and even given the far greater stakes, Roosevelt came out for an independent India. He thus procured for himself an unparalled position of prestige and leadership not to mention an enviable position in history. All servants of the pres-

---

Source: Department of State, Central Files, 753D.00/12–561. Secret. Repeated to USUN, Paris, and Lisbon.

ent President will hope, naturally, for a similar stance and reward. They will note that Roosevelt's was not earned by an excess of conservatism. And it is the present good fortune that with Portugal nothing comparable is at stake. They will note, finally, that Roosevelt's support of an independent India won him the affection of all colonial peoples without costing him friendship of the British or even of Churchill.

8.   That we should like to have the issue of Portugal's colonial territories resolved without avoidable violence, force or bloodshed and without postponement until that explosive last moment when the largest number have come to believe that Communism is the only alternative to the older colonialism.

9.   That our problem with Communism is not in Europe, where our position grows increasingly strong and Communism is increasingly an academic force, but in the erstwhile colonial world—South Viet Nam, Laos, the Congo, Ghana. Portugal, the Azores apart, has no serious relation to the problem of Berlin, the point of Communist pressure in Europe.

10. That the present Portuguese regime, under an aged dictator, has most of its future behind it. If our experience elsewhere is a guide, support of this regime, however plausible it seems in the short-run, is earning us no Portuguese friends for the longer-run and could be cultivating the anti-Americanism which has elsewhere been so often the fruit of our support to obsolescent despotism.

As to action: In supporting the recent GA resolution to check compliance on ending colonialism, we took the position without its profit. Now, on an early occasion, I urge that the President make clear that our position Portuguese colonialism is no longer passive but active. This should be done in a speech before some responsive forum. It would make clear that we are specifically and unqualifiedly for the early independence for these territories and will press Portugal by all peaceful means to this end. Our concern for the defense of Portugal no longer can imply any defense of Portugal's colonial possessions.

He would also note that France and Holland have been vastly strengthened by the loss of dissident colonial possessions and that Belgium is recovering quickly. In all cases, friendship with the US has been strengthened and, without the drain of dissident colonialism, the countries in question have been able to participate much more fully in the Western Europe renaissance.

Our announcement should also note that Goa and the other Portuguese enclaves remaining in India are as much a part of the Indian subcontinent as British India, the princely states, or Pondicherry. With the ending of Portuguese-African colonialism, this problem will be solved.

Thus any justification for resort to force as recurrently here discussed is eliminated.

It will be suggested that this might cause Portugal to withdraw from NATO. We would be sorry but the major misfortune would be Portugal's for we contribute more to her protection that she to ours. Our treaty on the Azores Base runs through next year. We should hope and expect to have it extended, but we must, as in all matters, deal in the calculus of gain and loss. There are no absolutes in these matters. No one in the Defense Department would argue for the world-wide weakening of the political and military posture of the United States because of the inability of our services to circumvent the need for a few acres of asphalt. None would wish to say our services are so impoverished in their planning as to be unable to do so.

In announcing this policy we should indicate our serious concern for the problems of transition that will be involved in Angola and Mozambique, our desire to see the settlers there protected, and our belief that by preparing now, effective international means can be found to safeguard and police the transition and protect the Portuguese there from the anarchy of another Congo.

The Asian enclaves, though a relatively minor aspect of the larger problem, are a recurrent and major issue here. We would derive great credit were we to be clear-cut on the issue and we would end a source of considerable comfort to the Communists. At present, Communists and fellow-travelers are able to divert attention from Chinese Communist frontier intrusions by whooping it up against Portugal, and, inter alia, her allies.

There will be wide agreement with this recommendation from all who over the years have been singed either in reputation or conscience by too prolonged dalliance with decayed dictators or enfeebled strong men—with Peron, Perez, Batista, Trujillo and, most recently, one fears some in Southeast Asia. So disagreeably lucid has been this lesson that we can only assume that it has been wonderfully well-learned. There may remain perhaps some slight resistance arising from conservatism and an affection for the status quo, or the feeling that even the least or most out-moded of Europe is to be preferred to the most of Asia and Africa. But one doubts that these positions will be strongly defended in light of the great gains that will come from Rooseveltian boldness, clarity and liberalism. May I assume agreement?

Galbraith

332.   Telegram From the Embassy in Portugal to the Department of State

Lisbon, December 8, 1961, 9 p.m.

617. Reference New Delhi's 1611 to Department.[1]

1. This Embassy does not agree with assumptions, analysis or recommendations of reference telegram as they concern conduct of our relations with Portugal.

2. "Goan problem" would appear more of Nehru's making than inspired by any genuine desire of Goans be annexed into Indian union. It would seem that a look at Nehru's reasons for creating issue at this time is equally as important as any "new look at Portugal and problem of Portuguese colonies".

3. It would appear fairly self-evident that Nehru, faced with embarrassing incursions by the Chinese Communists on Indian soil, and with elections next spring, has decided he must find some heady diversion, and has created psychological campaign on Portuguese Goa for this purpose. At same time, Nehru is saddled with commitment to AFAS members of unaligned powers at recent Belgrade Conference to "liberate Goa" as first step in dissolution of Portuguese empire in Africa. With re-establishment of order in Angola, and lack of any manifest interest in Goan population by becoming part of India, Nehru is confronted with choice of embarking upon naked aggression in Goa in order achieve his ends (which at variance with his stated policy of peaceful solution to international problems) or risk losing his status as AFAS leader.

4. Larger purposes our foreign policy require us to consider strategic defense US rather than solution to Nehru's internal domestic problems and his commitments to AFAS powers.

5. From reference telegram it would appear that Embassy New Delhi is not in possession of recent military evaluation of Azores base. What is dismissed as "few acres of asphalt" is evaluated by recent Presidential Task Force on Portuguese territories as "single most valuable facility which the US Government is authorized by a foreign government to use." Task Force report[2] states further that its "loss would require a major overhaul of US wartime plans" and that "there are no suitable alternatives for the Azores route".

Source: Department of State, Central Files, 753D.00/12–861. Secret; Priority. Repeated to Paris, New Delhi, USUN, Oporto, and Bombay.

[1] Document 331.

[2] Dated July 12; a copy of this report is in the Kennedy Library, National Security Files, Angola.

334.   Telegram From Secretary of State Rusk to the Department of State

Paris, December 15, 1961, midnight.

Secto 44. Re Secto 37.[1] Secretary had further talk with Nogueira today prior latter's return to Lisbon.

Nogueira raised recent démarche by Ambassador Elbrick,[2] clearly under instructions perhaps sent after Secretary's departure, in which reaffirmation US support Portuguese against forceful aggression on overseas territories linked to "prompt and dramatic" declaration on Portuguese acceptance self-determination.

After Secretary confirmed his awareness démarche, Nogueira expressed surprise this action which negated assurances support against use of force. Secretary replied by repeating Portuguese depriving selves of best defense by withholding "Regerias." Nogueira said he might accept this as respects Angola, but not Goa, where political life already advanced, elections having been held last month with nearly 80 percent participation. The only step left in Goa would be to turn it over to Indians. Secretary commented that if comparable vote proved Goans chose remain Portugal, this would be best defense, to which Nogueira responded along lines taken yesterday (reference telegram). Thus second half Elbrick démarche demolished first part. If Portuguese follow this advice, no question but that Goa down drain in three months. Secretary cited US approaches to Nehru and U Thant, and assured Nogueira we considered our views in Portugal's own long-range self-interest in overseas possessions, to which Nogueira expressed appreciation. Secretary added no one but Portugal was going to fight India for Goa. This was fact of life which made political solution essential. He agreed with Nogueira India no more likely to pay attention UN action re Goa than re Kashmir. To Nogueira's urging put teeth into warnings to Nehru against use force, Secretary commented no question Indian relations with US and others would suffer, even though not in sense specific sanctions, and Indian world position would be tarnished.

Nogueira argued if US believed in Portugal's serious purpose, as he believed case, must give them confidence. Repeated if they followed our advice, would have several "Congos" in six months. Secretary insisted

---

Source: Department of State, Central Files, 753D.00/12–1561. Secret. Also sent to Lisbon, New Delhi, and USUN.

[1] Secto 37, December 14, reported that Rusk, who was in Paris for the North Atlantic Council Ministerial meeting December 13–15, had discussed with Nogueira various possible courses of action on the question of Goa, including an approach to Nehru. He stated that the United States was doubtful that any of these steps would have any real restraining effect on India. (Ibid., 753.00/12–1461)

[2] Not further identified.

Portuguese not making their best case and case others could support. Nogueira replied Portuguese in fact taken many steps and under US insistence considering departure from their established principles. If they did so, what would US in fact do? Would US support Portugal as having made good case? He wondered.

Secretary responded Portuguese entitled to answer this question. He did not want to answer offhand, though we could say reform program should be given chance. However, he asked Nogueira to give Elbrick full outline so he could consider in detail our return Washington.

Nogueira agreed to this, but repeated Portuguese regarded last démarche as great step backward, offsetting previous assurances. This matter great concern to GOP. They had taken steps as urged but need something on other side. If Nehru takes Goa there will be grave repercussions in Portugal and Portuguese Government and possibility fundamental change in foreign policy.

Rusk

---

335. **Telegram From the Embassy in Portugal to the Department of State**

Lisbon, December 18, 1961, 1 a.m.

654. I was summoned to Foreign Minister's office at 11 p.m. tonight. He had been closeted with Prime Minister Salazar and returned to his office a few minutes after I arrived. I was unaccompanied but Secretary General Archer and Director Political Affairs Themido were present "to record conversation".

Nogueira's demeanor reflected gravity of situation. He was calm and deliberate as he delivered following message to be transmitted immediately to Washington: Portuguese Government had considered carefully message I had given him yesterday re US attitude toward possible meeting of SC to consider Goa question. He then repeated very accurately message I had given him (Department telegram 553)[1] received

---

Source: Department of State, Central Files, 753D.00/12–1861. Secret; Niact. Repeated to New Delhi, London, Madrid, Paris, and USUN.

[1] Telegram 553, December 16, reported that the United States was not encouraging Portugal to bring the question of Goa to the United Nations, but, if it did, the United States would support the calling of a Security Council meeting. If Portugal did bring the issue to

Continued

last night. He noted particularly that US would consider itself obliged to treat possible introduction of broader issues in accordance with policy previously adopted in UN (i.e., "colonial aspects"). Portuguese Government had been prepared to request SC action immediately upon outbreak of hostilities in Goa, but he said final decision had yet to be made. This decision would probably be made tonight or tomorrow morning. Meanwhile government had taken decision to inform US Government through me that if Goa issue is considered by SC and US Government should adopt same position with respect to Portugal which it had adopted in previous UN actions this year, Portugal would be obliged to reconsider its relations with US and this would necessarily involve a complete change in status of those relations. He did not mention NATO relationship or Azores base, but there was no misunderstanding as to exact meaning of his declaration.

I said his message was of gravest importance and would be received with great concern in Washington. While I had not been authorized to reveal contents Department telegram 554,[2] I felt it necessary to inform Nogueira that US had made clear to GOI position it would take in event latter resorted to force over Goa. I reminded him that yesterday we had been considering question of preventative meeting of SC; now hostilities had actually taken place. I would not, however, make any definitive reply to his remarks and limited myself to saying I would transmit message immediately to Washington.

Nogueira said he hoped US Government would understand Portuguese Government's position. He had often warned us that pursuance of our present policy re Portuguese overseas territories could have dire consequences in Portugal itself and could well lead to "Castro-type" regime here. Portugal, he said, did not want support of US if it were to lead to Portugal's destruction.

Our reaction to this declaration of intention will be of utmost importance to Portuguese in making their decision re UN action. Department's instructions urgently requested.[3]

Elbrick

---

the United Nations, it would be impossible to prevent discussion of the more general question of Portuguese overseas territories, and on this issue what the United States said and how it voted probably would be "unpalatable" to Portugal. (Ibid., 753D.00/12–1661)

[2] Telegram 554, December 16, reported that at a meeting that day with the Indian Ambassador, Ball had made very clear the concern of the U.S. Government over the Indian threat to resolve the question of Goa by force. (Ibid.)

[3] On December 19 Tyler telephoned Rusk to say that the Portuguese Ambassador had called to express the thanks and appreciation of Nogueira for U.S. support in the Security Council during the discussion on Goa. "He said that the Portuguese Government realizes the United States did everything it could within the limits open to it." (Ibid., Rusk Files: Lot 72 D 192, Telephone Conversations)

336. **Telegram From the Embassy in Portugal to the Department of State**

Lisbon, January 12, 1962, 6 p.m.

745. For the Secretary. I spent an hour with Franco Nogueira last night in an effort to learn what moves Portuguese Government might make next, particularly in connection with UN. As I had expected, I found him extremely bitter and unreconstructed (though at no point did he renew Salazar's threat to withdraw from UN).

I asked him how he expected to deal with Angolan item to be debated this month in UNGA and I inquired particularly whether he expected to attend. He said he would not be present and would leave Portuguese representation entirely up to Garin.[1] I told him I was sorry to hear this, referring to your conversation with him last November[2] and hope expressed at that time that Portugal would make forthcoming statement in GA re overseas reforms and their intentions for future. I reminded him that such a statement would make it possible for Portugal's friends to offer some support against attacks of extremists. This produced an immediate and unpleasant reaction. Nogueira said US has been constantly pushing Portugal to take various and successive steps in connection with overseas territories, but so far had offered nothing in return. He said he had asked you in Paris[3] and had subsequently asked me exactly what US would be prepared to do to help Portugal and had never received any definitive reply. He saw no purpose, therefore, in following our suggestions re tactics in UNGA. Speaking personally, he said that Portugal has lost all confidence in US. He said our "carrot and stick" tactics had thoroughly antagonized people here. Fact is, he said, encouragement we offer Portugal on one hand is always nullified by unfriendly acts on the other.

It is apparent that our vote on December 19 on resolution condemning Portugal for failure to cooperate with UN in overseas matters, coming immediately after our efforts to prevent forcible take-over of Goa, rankles greatly. Moreover, Nogueira feels that we did not bring sufficient pressure to bear on Nehru and that outcome of Goa affair would have been quite different if we had. He read to me excerpts from a report (source unknown, but it was written in French) which alleged that Ambassador Galbraith, by expressing to Nehru sympathy for Indian cause,

---

Source: Department of State, Central Files, 611.53/1–1262. Secret; Priority.

[1] Vasco Vieira Garin, Portuguese Representative to the United Nations.

[2] See Document 329.

[3] See Document 334.

had actually encouraged Indian invasion of Goa. Nogueira expressed interest in seeing copy of letter which he understood had been transmitted by Galbraith to Nehru,[4] setting forth US Government's concern over threat to use force. I said letters to and from heads of government cannot be released to third parties, as he knew. I told him, however, as I had told him before, that concern of President and Government of US over use of force had been expressed most clearly to Nehru.

I again asked what course Portugal would follow in UN. I pointed out it would serve no purpose for Portugal to boycott UN proceedings which would only result in even greater isolation and more violent attacks by some UN members. Nogueira said this seemed to worry US, but did not worry Portugal. He did say Portugal, realizing it cannot "go it alone" with any success, will take other actions in its defense, but he refused to describe them.

Nogueira was in a very unreasonable frame of mind. He said he felt US was working against Portugal, that dialogue which had begun so promisingly between us last year had produced nothing, that US is trying to achieve economic domination of Africa by its present policies, and he would not be surprised if US were trying to bring about political change in Metropolitan Portugal. I rejected these statements emphatically and pointed to fact we had always expressed desire to be of help to Portugal in most difficult situation. Nogueira merely replied he could no longer give any credence to such assurances. I asked him if Portuguese Ambassador in Washington were being instructed to present these views to you. He replied in negative, saying this was personal conversation and should be considered off the record. He saw no particular reason to express these views officially, since views of Portuguese Government in past had made no impression on US Government.

Toward end of this long and highly disturbing conversation, I pleaded again with Nogueira to reconsider position re handling of Angola item in UNGA. I said I thought he should appear personally in New York and that he should not dismiss so casually need for some forthcoming statement from Portugal. As I had indicated in past, US Government most anxious for Portugal to do something in its own behalf which US could support. Nogueira said he did not believe such statement would cause US to change its attitude in any respect. US would, he thought, continue to vote for resolutions condemning Portugal's practices overseas, regardless of facts as presented by Portugal. He understood we were already working with others on so-called "moderate" resolution re Angola and claimed he had already seen text (source un-

---

[4] Not further identified.

known). He was caustic in upbraiding US for not having had courtesy discuss such resolution in advance with Portuguese Del in New York.

Before leaving, I again expressed hope Nogueira would attend UNGA and I presented as vigorously as possible arguments in favor of full and forthcoming statement re overseas territories. Nogueira said it might be possible for him to attend end of Angola debate, though thought obviously did not please him.

Nogueira has just telephoned me to say government has decided to make lengthy statement at outset of Angola debate. This statement would include, inter alia, chapter on overseas reforms, their significance and Portugal's intentions for future. I said I was very glad to hear this. Apparently some of my arguments did not go unheeded. I can only hope that this effort will serve to close somewhat the gap between us.

Elbrick

---

337. Telegram From the Embassy in Portugal to the Department of State

Lisbon, February 13, 1962, 8 p.m.

825. For the Secretary. Reference: Department telegram 649 and Embassy telegram 822.[1] Following his reply to my démarche today (which he emphasized was all he could say to me officially), Nogueira proceeded to discuss overseas problems and Port-American relations at length. He was careful to label this discussion "personal and informal". While some of his remarks, for this reason are far more extravagant than would normally be the case, I think they give a fair indication of problem we face here.

Source: Department of State, Central Files, 611.53/2–1362. Secret; Limit Distribution.

[1] Telegram 649, February 9, noted that the recent vote in the United Nations indicated that the opposition to Portuguese overseas policy was nearly unanimous and asked Elbrick to urge Nogueira to change it. (Ibid., 611.53/2–962) Telegram 822, February 13, reported that Elbrick had an appointment to see the Foreign Minister. (Ibid.)

338. Memorandum of Conversation

US/MC/24   Athens, May 5, 1962, 8:30 p.m.

TWENTY-NINTH MINISTERIAL MEETING OF THE
NORTH ATLANTIC COUNCIL
Athens, Greece, May 4–6, 1962

PARTICIPANTS

United States	*Portugal*
The Secretary of State	H.E. A. Franco Nogueira
Mr. Kohler	H.E. V. de Cunha
Mr. West	Mr. P.P.B. de Sousa Pernes

SUBJECT

Portuguese Foreign Minister Nogueira's Allegations Regarding Anti-Portuguese Attitudes and Activities of U.S. Government and American Private Groups

This subject constituted the major topic of discussion of the meeting, which took place at a dinner given by the Secretary and which lasted over three hours. Foreign Minister Nogueira repeated many, but not all, of the complaints which he and other members of the Portuguese Foreign Office have made to our Embassy in Lisbon. (The only complaint with which all of the American participants in the discussion were unfamiliar was that concerning American relief activities in the Congo.)

Minister Nogueira's approach to the subject was somewhat oblique, but later he became more specific. For example, in a discussion of the African independence movement, Minister Nogueira said he wondered whether the Secretary really thought some of the recently created African countries were really independent. He, Nogueira, considered that the Congo was not really independent but largely subject to UN and US direction. When the Secretary expressed his qualified agreement with the Minister's statement, the latter then asked why the United States did not exercise more control over certain activities of the Congo Government. (The context of much of the conversation which followed indicated more clearly that the Foreign Minister was referring, albeit obliquely, to activities concerning Angolan rebel elements in Katanga.)

The Secretary brought up the question of the "forged letter" that the Minister had raised with Ambassador Elbrick earlier,[1] and concerning

---

Source: Department of State, Central Files, 611.53/5–562. Secret. Drafted by West and approved in S on May 15. The meeting was held at the Ambassador's residence. A summary of this conversation was transmitted to Lisbon in telegram 847, May 23. (Ibid., 611.53/5–2362)

[1] Elbrick reported his conversation with Nogueira on February 20 concerning the "forged letter" in telegram 840, February 21. (Ibid., 611.53/2–2162)

which the Secretary had spoken to Ambassador Pereira earlier.[2] The Secretary assured Minister Nogueira that a very careful study had been made by the United States Government and that the letter was an obvious forgery. He pointed out that there were powers who resorted to such devices to sow mistrust and dissension among allies. Minister Nogueira politely but firmly insisted that his Government knew that the letter in question was not a forgery. He was at liberty to discuss this letter because the source through which it had been obtained had since dried up. He had, however, many other documents which constituted proof of the role the United States was playing vis-à-vis Portugal. The Secretary stated that the United States Government would like to refute the Minister's suspicions and, if necessary, would send a top member of J. Edgar Hoover's staff to Lisbon to work with the Portuguese experts. Minister Nogueira was unresponsive to this specific suggestion.

The question of visas for American diplomatic couriers traveling in Portuguese Africa was also discussed. Minister Nogueira alleged that many of our couriers had not confined themselves to courier duties and that Portugal did not have enough PIDE agents to cover the activities of the number of couriers for whom visas had been requested. He suggested that one courier a month should be enough. The Secretary made it clear to Minister Nogueira that in diplomacy it was the prerogative of a country to determine what its own courier needs were, that the United States did not attempt to prescribe how many Portuguese couriers were needed for the Portuguese Embassy in Washington and that it was up to the United States to determine how many couriers it required in Africa. Mr. West pointed out that, in order to permit flexibility in the operation of the American courier system in Africa and because of the time required to obtain visas, it was necessary to obtain visas for more couriers than would actually be used. The Secretary invited Minister Nogueira to submit any evidence he might have of irregular activities by American couriers.

Minister Nogueira also raised a question of Ambassador Gullion's request for visas to enable him and Mrs. Gullion to visit Luanda. He said that the Portuguese Government had been prepared to consider this request sympathetically, but when it was advised that the Gullion party would also consist of various military attachés, it became obvious that recreation was not the object of the trip. Mr. West pointed out that it was not unusual for American Ambassadors to employ the aircraft assigned to their Air Attachés for periodic recreational visits to points outside the countries to which they were accredited and that, for someone stationed

---

[2] A memorandum of Rusk's conversation with Pereira on March 9 is ibid., 611.53/3–962.

in Leopoldville, Luanda was an understandable choice. The Minister's only comment was that obviously Ambassador Stevenson did not have the same appreciation of the attractions of Angola.

Minister Nogueira raised the subject of the Methodist missionaries who had been arrested in Angola and sent to Portugal. He alleged that the Portuguese Government had acceded to requests from the American Embassy in Lisbon for the release of these persons on the condition that they would not engage further in anti-Portuguese activities but that, as soon as the missionaries in question returned to the United States, they commenced a campaign of public speeches misrepresenting conditions in Angola and designed to create hatred of Portugal. The Minister also complained about the activities of the American Committee on Africa. When the Secretary pointed out the difficulties under the American system of controlling the activities of religious and other private organizations, Minister Nogueira retorted that any nation which can control U.S. Steel is not powerless.

Minister Nogueira raised the subject of Ambassador Stevenson's speech at Colgate University last March[3] and took exception to the comparison between developments in Hungary and Angola. The Secretary pointed out that Ambassador Stevenson was not attempting to compare the two situations but was attempting to make the point that the feelings among black Africans with respect to Angola were in some respects comparable to the feelings which others had with respect to the suppression of the Hungarian people. The Minister also mentioned the portion of the Stevenson speech which pointed out that a U.N. resolution condemning South African racial policies had been supported by the entire General Assembly save for Portugal. The Minister expressed his pride in the Portuguese record of assimilating colored people and affording them equal opportunities. The Secretary expressed his regret that Governor Stevenson's speech had been misinterpreted and assured Nogueira that measures had been taken to prevent the recurrence of such speeches. (The following day a copy of USUN's press release #3934, giving the text of Ambassador Stevenson's speech, was passed by the Portuguese Delegation to the American Delegation.)

The Secretary mentioned Ambassador Pereira's speeches earlier this year before the Press Club of Washington and the Commonwealth Club of San Francisco, and stated that he thought they were useful in telling the Portuguese story to the American public. They had served to bring out the fact that Portugal does envisage eventual self-determination in Portuguese Africa. In replying (to a portion of the Secretary's comment), Foreign Minister Nogueira recalled that at a

---

[3] For text of Stevenson's address at Colgate University, March 6, see Walter Johnson, ed., *The Papers of Adlai E. Stevenson*, vol. VIII (New York: 1987), pp. 213–221.

previous NATO meeting the Secretary had urged him to give attention to telling the Portuguese story. He added that the Portuguese Government was acting on this suggestion. In discussing Portuguese problems at the UN (see separate memorandum),[4] the Secretary suggested the usefulness of putting various UN Delegations and key American political figures on the Portuguese mailing list. The Secretary and the Foreign Minister agreed that some progress had been made in telling the Portuguese story, but the latter said many difficulties were being encountered. Mr. West cited the objective treatment given to Angola by a series of articles by Estabrook in *The Washington Post*. Nogueira agreed that this series had been helpful but pointed out that after that *Newsweek* had seen fit to publish a completely distorted version of the Estabrook articles and that the Portuguese Embassy had been obliged to protest this treatment. He alleged that "people connected with the United States Government" were preventing the Portuguese story from being told in the United States.

The Minister noted that when order was restored in Northern Angola, in 1961, some 80,000 to 90,000 refugees who had fled to the Congo returned to their homes, as did many more who had gone to Southern Angola. The United Nations High Commissioner for Refugees and the International Red Cross had recognized this situation by cutting off aid as of January 15, 1962, but at that point American aid took over. The American aid program had encouraged refugees to remain in the Congo and had enabled Holden Roberto and the UPA to continue recruiting Angolan youths for the rebel forces. The Americans present for this discussion were not able to respond specifically to this allegation, and the Secretary said he would undertake to furnish Minister Nogueira with information on this subject prior to his departure from Athens. (In the event, it was not possible for the Secretary or other members of the American Delegation to get this information to Minister Nogueira before the latter's departure from Athens and Ambassador Elbrick was asked to convey it to the Foreign Minister upon the latter's return to Lisbon.)

During the course of the long conversation two brief exchanges served to characterize the Portuguese Government's mood and the depth of its suspicions. At one point the Secretary inferred that the Portuguese mistrust of the United States reminded him of that of the Soviet Union. Foreign Minister Nogueira replied that the two extremes (of the political spectrum) tended to think alike. Near the end of the discussion the Foreign Minister stated, in response to the Secretary's question as to what he thought American intentions really were, that he had "no confidence in U.S. intentions".

---

[4] US/MC/25. (Department of State, Conference Files: Lot 65 D 533, CF 2095)

339. Letter From the Ambassador to Portugal (Elbrick) to the Deputy Assistant Secretary of State for European Affairs (Tyler)

Lisbon, May 14, 1962.

DEAR BILL: We have just received today uncleared accounts of the Secretary's conversation with Franco Nogueira in Athens.[1] They certainly offer us no encouragement, although I think it was useful that the Secretary should hear at first hand the charges that have been thrown at me frequently in Lisbon. I am sure that Foy[2] has given you an even more vivid picture of what transpired. Nogueira's comments and attitude give a rather clear idea of how frantic these people are and to what lengths they can go. The local political situation is now adding to the Government's troubles and, bereft as they are of friends, they make no effort to hide their anger and chagrin.

Incidentally, we were embarrassed by the fact that we only received the first account of the Rusk–Nogueira conversation today. I should like to have seen Nogueira immediately after his return from Athens, but I could hardly do so without any knowledge of what had happened there. I shall try to arrange a meeting with him now, but meanwhile some valuable time has been lost as well as some of the atmosphere. It would have been most helpful to us if the memoranda of conversation (or summaries) could have been cabled.

I have just read *The New York Times* editorial entitled "The Tragedy of Portugal," in last Saturday's edition.[3] Coming on top of everything else—particularly the statement that Portugal is "one of the poorest and worst administered nations of non-Communist Europe"—we expect the Portuguese to be even more acid than before. Actually, *The Times* on this occasion went out of its way to be nasty to Portugal for reasons of its own, but I think it was unnecessary to resort to exaggeration. Portugal, like Greece and others, is poor—although this has never been considered a sin—but I would take definite issue with the statement that it is the worst administered. However, *The Times* has always had its knife out for Salazar (as well as for Franco) and apparently had to take this cut at him. I agree that it will be difficult for Portugal to hold on to its overseas territories indefinitely, but the kind of attack Portugal has been subjected to from various quarters recently will only serve to increase the

---

Source: Department of State, Central Files, 611.53/5–1462. Confidential; Official–Informal. The source text was initialed by Tyler and Rusk.

[1] See Document 338.

[2] Foy D. Kohler, Assistant Secretary of State for European Affairs.

[3] May 12.

magnitude of the disaster resulting from the possible loss of the territories.

Jimmy Minotto of Arizona, who was once head of the aid mission to Portugal, has been here recently in the service of Senator Carl Hayden and the Senate Appropriations Committee. In advance notice to me, he billed the visit as a private one and, for the most part, made his own arrangements to call on various people here, including some officials. He turned down an offer to accompany him on these calls, although he did fill me in to a certain extent subsequently.

He is very interested in Portugal and unhappy over the present state of our relations. Having known Salazar fairly well in the old days, he spent an hour and a half with him, having made the appointment himself. He heard the usual story, but in addition Salazar commented that the people of Portugal would not countenance his agreeing to an extension of our Base rights agreement in the Azores under present conditions. This sounds ominous; the most hopeful interpretation may be that it is an expression of gamesmanship, since Salazar could be fairly sure that the word would get back to us. (Minotto said he is making no written report of his visit and hoped we could refrain from mentioning the substance of his talks in official despatches. Actually, he learned little that is new.)

When the Secretary raised the question of the Base negotiations with Franco Nogueira in Athens, Nogueira said it would be up to the "interested party" and refused to be included as an interested party himself. This, too, is not encouraging, though not unexpected. I note that the Secretary told Spaak in Athens that our delay in beginning negotiations was not unintentional.

As I wrote you previously, the delay may have worried the Portuguese Government to a certain extent, but I felt that we should not delay unduly. I still feel the same way. While the indications are all bad, we shall never know how the Portuguese may react until we actually pop the question. I am afraid that nothing that may happen in the near future will make our presence in the Azores any more—or less—acceptable to the Portuguese Government and I am anxious to get started. While the military people here can see no alternative to renewing the agreement, the political people have other ideas which we will only learn about when the negotiations begin.

There is a certain amount of political ferment locally, as we reported. More and more responsible people are beginning to question the course which Salazar seems determined to follow. The handling of the students recently was very ill-advised and the Government has made more enemies in the universities. The military remain quiet, although it is known that some important figures are giving very serious thought to the future. As usual, there are numerous rumors and these have been encouraged by the demonstrations on May 1 and May 8, both of which surprised the Government by the obvious disregard of the demonstrators for police authority. These demonstrations were brief and somewhat abortive, but they may well breed others. If they do and real violence erupts, there is a good chance that any change of government which results may be far to the left and this would be very unhelpful to us, to NATO, and the Western world. We can only hope that wiser and cooler heads, foreseeing some such eruption, will force Dr. Salazar's hand and oblige him to step down. In the latter case, we can hope for a continued tenure of our Base in the Azores; in the former, our position would be most precarious.

This letter has been much too long. I do hope that our negotiating instructions will be forthcoming soon. Many thanks for taking the time to read these lines.

With best wishes,

Sincerely,

Burke

---

340.   Memorandum From Secretary of State Rusk to President Kennedy

Washington, May 23, 1962.

SUBJECT

The Azores

With reference to your memorandum of May 21,[1] we hope shortly to work out a position for our negotiations with Portugal on the Azores base, taking into consideration the useful thoughts contributed by Adlai Stevenson and Dean Acheson.[2] We will, of course, discuss this further with you prior to undertaking actual negotiations which need not be until around the end of June or the first part of July. In this connection, I

Source: Kennedy Library, National Security Files, Portugal, Azores Base. Secret. No drafting information appears on the source text.

[1] In it the President stressed the need to work out a U.S. position on the Azores base before negotiations were begun and to explore the role that NATO countries might play in the discussions. (Ibid.)

[2] In an April 25 memorandum to Rusk, Acheson accepted a connection between the base negotiations and Angola. (Ibid.) In letters to the President on April 26 and May 10 Stevenson stressed the need to separate the issues and involve NATO in the base discussions. Copies of all three documents are ibid.

might note that no revision of the details of the present agreement is desired by us, nor, as far as we know, by the Portuguese. Thus, negotiations on the base agreement itself simply involve a decision by the Portuguese whether they are willing to extend the present expiration date of December 31, 1962.

In the meanwhile, I believe that one of our first tasks is to attempt at least in some degree to dispel the exaggerated Portuguese suspicions regarding our involvement with the Angolan dissidents. I attempted this with Nogueira at Athens [3] and we are following up through Ambassador Elbrick at Lisbon. Perhaps if this miasma of suspicion, little of which is based on fact, can in some degree be dispelled, we can create a slightly better atmosphere for initiating negotiations.

As you know, Dantas, the Brazilian Foreign Minister, is taking a helpful and constructive interest in this whole question of Portugal and the future of its overseas territories. He will again shortly be seeing Nogueira. I am hopeful that his efforts may bear some fruit. In the meantime, forces also seem to be at work in Portugal itself, and, while we cannot be sanguine, there is always the possibility that there might before too long be developments more favorable to our interests.

We also propose taking advantage of all possible opportunities to point out to the other NATO countries the importance to them of the Azores base. We will impress upon them that this is not just a bilateral matter between the United States and Portugal, and that it is just as much in their interest as it is in ours that Portugal be brought around to take a constructive attitude toward the renegotiation of the Azores base agreement.

I agree that we must at least contemplate the possibility that we will not be successful in our efforts to obtain renewal of the agreement. The JCS have made studies of the possible alternatives to use of the Azores base. [3-1/2 lines of source text not declassified] however, they have instructed MATS further to look into the question of alternate routes. I am informing Secretary McNamara of your question and we will be discussing the matter further with Defense.

[Here follows a section on West New Guinea.]

Dean Rusk

---

[3] See Document 338.

341. Memorandum From the Ambassador at Large (Bowles) to President Kennedy

Washington, June 4, 1962.

SUBJECT

The Azores

From all indications we are likely to face a harsh squeeze from the Portuguese in regard to our Azores base-rights which lapse December 31.

Pressures from Lisbon, vigorously supported by pressures from within our own country, already are focusing on the alleged need for a "more reasonable" United States stance in regard to Africa and particularly Portuguese Africa as a quid pro quo for renewal of the Azores agreement.

Portugal's role as a "staunch NATO ally" and the need for all good allies to stick together will be increasingly underscored. In this context I would like to urge that we adopt the following approach:

1. Our African policy has been one of the most successful efforts of your Administration. It has reversed the 1960 tide which was running strongly in a pro-Soviet direction in a number of African countries, won us the friendship and respect of many African leaders, and helped to stabilize several crisis situations.

In my opinion, it would be unthinkable to modify an effective policy in a key continent to fit the 18th century views of the Lisbon Government.

2. At the same time, the loss of our Azores facilities would be an extremely serious blow to our capacity to support our defense forces in Europe and those of our NATO allies.

3. Since the primary function of the Azores facilities is to help us defend Europe, the status of the base there should be changed in any event from that of an exclusively U.S. military facility to that of a NATO base for which all NATO members are responsible.

4. We should, therefore, propose to the North Atlantic Council that the Azores facilities be placed under General Norstad's command as of December 31, 1962. As NATO commander he could then request us

---

Source: Yale University Library, Bowles Papers, Box 498, Folder 297. No classification marking. The copy at the Kennedy Library is not initialed; it was classified secret and attached to a memorandum from Bowles to Bundy dated June 5. (Kennedy Library, National Security Files, Portugal) Drafted by Bowles and also sent to Rusk, McGhee, Tyler, Johnson, Williams, Rostow, Brubeck, and Kitchen.

to operate the facilities on NATO's behalf, with token military contingents from other NATO countries. We could also reserve the right to use the facilities within agreed guidelines for our non-NATO operations.

5. Negotiation for a substitute multilateral agreement should then be conducted by representatives of NATO meeting directly with representatives of the Portuguese Government. Our present bilateral agreement with Portugal could be allowed to lapse as the new agreement took effect.

I believe that we should take every opportunity to challenge the assumption that our European allies are doing us a favor whenever they provide us with the necessary facilities from which to defend their own continent.

This is a clear case in point. If the Portuguese put as much store in NATO as they say they do, let them negotiate in good faith with their partners for the common defense.

More particularly we cannot allow President Salazar to use a facility which is essential to his own defense and that of his European allies as a lever with which to force the United States Government to modify an African policy which has been paying important dividends to the entire Western world.

---

342.   Memorandum From Secretary of State Rusk to President Kennedy

Washington, June 12, 1962.

SUBJECT

Negotiation of the Renewal of the Azores Base Agreement

With further reference to my memorandum of May 21[23],[1] I make the following recommendations for our negotiations with Portugal on the Azores Base Agreement.

A. Current Situation.

1. The portions of our Agreement with Portugal which authorize peacetime use by the United States of military facilities in the Azores

---

Source: Kennedy Library, President's Office Files, Portugal. Secret. No drafting information appears on the source text.

[1] Document 340.

expire on December 31, 1962. The renewal of these rights is important to the maintenance of a strong and flexible military posture for the protection of our national security interests. Prospects for Portuguese acquiescence to the renewal of the Agreement are not encouraging.

2. Historically the primary objective of Portuguese foreign policy has been to preserve the territorial integrity of Portugal, specifically the overseas provinces. The vigorous implementation by the United States since March 1961 of the policy of publicly advocating self-determination for the peoples of Portugal's African territories is regarded by Portugal as directly opposed to its vital national interest.

3. This United States policy shift immediately followed the *Santa Maria* episode,[2] in which Portugal was dissatisfied with the United States role, and preceded the invasion of Goa, where the failure of the United States and the United Kingdom to dissuade India from attacking the territory bitterly disappointed the Portuguese Government. United States attitudes and actions are now being viewed as not only threatening Portugal's territorial integrity but the Salazar regime itself. While in disagreement with the general tenor of United States African policy, Portugal is known to be embittered over the following and other specific manifestations of United States policy or activity in the United States:

a. public statements by United States officials in the United Nations and elsewhere critical of Portugal's policies in its overseas territories;

b. votes in the United Nations for resolutions critical of Portugal;

c. reception of UPA rebel leader Holden Roberto by U.S. officials as well as his visits to this country and extensive contacts with non-official American groups;

d. sponsorship by the United States Government of programs for the education or training of expatriate Portuguese African students either in the United States or elsewhere;

e. financial and material assistance to Holden Roberto and the UPA by such private groups as the American Committee on Africa.

4. Our efforts thus far to dispel Portuguese suspicions with respect to the U.S. Government have been singularly unsuccessful. The Portuguese Government is not receptive to simple denials of their allegations, since it does not want to be convinced in private, but, rather, desires a positive public stance by the United States as evidence of our good will.

5. United States interest in retaining the Azores is the only lever by which the Portuguese can hope to obtain a modification of our African policy. They will attempt to use the lever to maximum advantage. It is

---

[2] On January 23 the Portuguese cruise ship *Santa Maria* was seized in the Caribbean by Portuguese exiles led by Henrique Galvao. The United States participated in the search for the vessel, which eventually was sailed to Recife where Galvao was granted political asylum.

expected that they will not press this advantage to the full immediately, but will maintain constant pressure down to the termination date of the Agreement and beyond in seeking to obtain modification of United States policy.

B. *Specific Points at Issue.*

1. *Our Position* will be to inform the Portuguese Government of our desire for a simple five-year extension of the existing Agreement.

2. The *Portuguese tactic* will be to attempt to obtain a modification of our Portuguese African policy and the adoption of a policy more favorable to Portugal.

C. *The Probable Scenario.*

1. Shortly (this week) we will make a low-key approach to the Foreign Minister in Lisbon by our Ambassador stating our interest in a simple extension of the agreement for five years, to be effected by an exchange of notes.[3] Since the Preambular texts of the 1951 and 1957 Agreements refer to the doctrine and obligations of the North Atlantic Treaty to which both countries subscribed as the basis for the Agreements, we will also propose to the Portuguese Government that we jointly inform the NAC, as a matter of interest to all NATO members, that our two Governments have initiated negotiations for the extension of the current Agreements. By thus jointly notifying the NAC, if the Portuguese agree, we hope to encourage a more positive attitude on the part of the Portuguese, while at the same time preparing the way for such active assistance by other NATO members as we might consider necessary and desirable during our discussions with the Portuguese. The Portuguese Government may not agree to such notification to the NAC on the grounds that the Azores Agreement is a bilateral matter. It may regard and resent our suggestion as a form of pressure. However, to demonstrate that this is not just a bilateral U.S.-Portuguese matter we and Defense have transmitted to our Missions in NATO countries a background talking paper[4] setting forth the facts with respect to the Azores Base, both with regard to NATO as a whole and with respect to the individual members.

2. The approach by Ambassador Elbrick will prepare the way for my visit to Lisbon on June 27–28, when I will hold discussions with Prime Minister Salazar and Foreign Minister Nogueira. By this two-step

---

[3] On June 15 the Embassy in Lisbon was instructed to begin the negotiations with a low key approach suggesting to Portugal a 5-year extension of the agreement. (Telegram 896; Department of State, Conference Files: Lot 65 D 533, CF 2124) On June 18 Elbrick reported that he had made the approach to Nogueira, who "seemed somewhat surprised by our low key opening gambit." (Telegram 1185 from Lisbon; ibid., Central Files, 611.53/6–1862)

[4] Not found.

procedure it is hoped that we can break through the psychological barrier of Portuguese frustration and bitterness and bring out into the open for concrete discussion the differences between us. Until these are fully exposed we are not in a favorable position to move toward their resolution. At the same time, we will avoid the inherent disadvantage of sending a special emissary to initiate the negotiations which could be interpreted as a sign that our initial position is weak. It may be advisable at a later stage of the negotiations to send such an envoy.

3. Should, as we anticipate, Portugal allege that the United States has not been acting like a true ally, we will endeavor to keep separate the Azores negotiation discussions, a matter of Western European defense, from the question of African policy. (Realistically we recognize that we may not be able to separate the two issues of the Azores and our African policy because Portugal will not permit them to be separated. However, for us to initiate negotiations by offering to adjust our actions to meet at least some of Portugal's known complaints would be construed as a position of weakness. The Portuguese have been insistent that they have documentary proof of the role played by the United States vis-à-vis Portugal, the implication being that while outwardly professing friendship we are actually seeking to destroy Portugal's position in its African territories. We must first get at this basic suspicion and expose its unreality before we can advantageously seek to evolve specific solutions to the issues which have strained our relations.)

4. We will point out that, in many spheres, Portugal and the United States have continued to carry on normal relations—"business as usual"—while differing over African policy. We are thinking of our PL 480 agreement,[5] the peaceful uses of atomic energy, and Export-Import Bank loans, for example. We seek to deal with Portuguese requests to us, each on its own merits, without introducing extraneous matters, and we would hope that Portugal would do the same with us.

5. Since the primary Portuguese position will be directed toward obtaining political concessions from us, we will not initially make any offer of monetary or economic assistance to Portugal in connection with the initiation of discussions. However, the Department of Defense is working on a military assistance package under the existing MDA Agreement[6] calculated to meet probable requests for such assistance. Our offers of economic assistance to Portugal tied to its reform program in Africa have thus far evoked no positive response, despite repeated

---

[5] For text of the commodities exchange agreement, signed at Lisbon November 28, 1961, see 12 UST 3051.

[6] For text of the mutual defense agreement, signed at Lisbon January 5, 1951, see 2 UST 438.

approaches by us here and in Lisbon. Any specific Portuguese request for economic assistance directly related to the Azores negotiation will be given full and prompt consideration.

6. We will point out that our support for the principle of self-determination is fundamental and it would be misleading for us to give the impression that it is subject to bargaining. However, in our conviction that the self-determination of peoples is an inevitable process which has accelerated greatly in our time, we do not conceive that we are in fundamental disagreement with the Portuguese Government. Rather, we view our differences as being those of how and when rather than why. Under these circumstances, and with full and sympathetic understanding of the problem facing Portugal, we are firmly convinced that in frankly discussing these differences in order to resolve them in a manner equally acceptable to all elements involved, we will find in them a factor binding us closer together rather than dividing us. In this connection we could refer to and renew our previous offers to consider with Portugal how we could be helpful in raising the level of education in Angola. Now as always the United States is ready to assist Portugal, as it can, to reach a mutually satisfactory resolution of our differences, as we must.

7. We might at some stage send a special envoy from you to the Prime Minister to break a possible impasse in the negotiations. However, no decision need or can be reached at this time.

8. We will meanwhile be maintaining close contact with Brazilian officials who have recently been taking constructive and imaginative steps to promote a solution to the problem which Angola (and by extension the other Portuguese African territories) poses for governments friendly to Portugal.

9. If Portugal continues to insist on concessions to which we cannot agree, we will be faced with the necessity of withdrawing from the Azores. While thus losing our peacetime rights, we would continue to have wartime use of the Azores and the right of transit for the life of NATO. Under these circumstances our last resort would be to propose to the Portuguese and to the NAC that a NATO presence be established in the Azores to assist in maintaining the facilities there at their operating optimum. This NATO presence is no precedent for such an arrangement in NATO and its accomplishment would require a considerable change in the attitudes and policies of a number of NATO governments. It is not anticipated that Portugal would permit the United States to use these facilities under a NATO arrangement, if they would be unwilling to do so bilaterally. Therefore, since what we seek is the continued right to station tankers and other vitally needed equipment, supplies and personnel in the Azores, such a status for the base would fall short of meeting fully our national security interests. In this event every effort would

be made through the NAC to secure the optimum use of the Azores facility.

10. Our negotiating posture should be characterized by utmost patience, as a long drawn-out negotiation, with appropriate temporary extension of the Azores Agreement, might not be to our disadvantage. The Portuguese might refuse to sign even a temporary extension of the agreement but simply keep us dangling on a month-to-month basis. We should be prepared to face this possibility.

Dean Rusk

343. Memorandum of Conversation

SET/MC/46   Lisbon, June 28, 1962, 11:30 a.m.–1:25 p.m.

SECRETARY'S EUROPEAN TRIP
(June 18–28, 1962)

PARTICIPANTS

United States:
The Secretary of State, Dean Rusk
Ambassador Elbrick
Counselor Xanthaky (interpreter)

Portugal:
Dr. Antonio de Oliveira Salazar, President of the Council of Ministers
Dr. Jose Manuel Fragoso, Director General, Political Affairs, Foreign Office

SUBJECT

Portuguese-American Relations

[Here follows discussion of East-West relations, Berlin, and Laos.]

The Secretary then turned to bilateral problems, stating that the United States had always considered itself a friend of Portugal and wished to continue on this basis its relations between the two countries.

Source: Department of State, Conference Files: Lot 65 D 533, CF 2123. Secret; Eyes Only. Drafted and initialed by Xanthaky and approved in S on July 5. The meeting was held in Dr. Salazar's office in the National Assembly Building.

He was aware that in the last year or so certain difficulties and misunderstandings had arisen. The Prime Minister inquired whether in fact these were misunderstandings. The Secretary replied that he was not sure on this point and therefore believed it important to review the present state of our relations. He had talked to the Foreign Minister, Dr. Franco Nogueira, as to the possibility of the two countries recognizing the advantages of a joint "tour d'horizon" on a systematic basis.[1] He believed that three points would then become clear, i.e., 1) the degree of agreement on many subjects on which we can continue to cooperate closely; 2) some unnecessary misunderstandings which would become identified in frank conversation and subsequently eliminated; and 3) some points of disagreement which may be singled out and identified better as a result of frank conversation than they have up to the present time. This would be done with the idea of managing them without their affecting the general relations between the two countries.

Concerning point number three, the Secretary stated that the accomplishments of Portugal in Angola, the reforms, the economic and social development plans, and cooperation with specialized agencies of the United Nations such as ILO and WHO, and the recent declarations of Ambassador Teotonio Pereira, would seem to indicate that Portugal does not object to the principle of self-determination although insisting that this must come about by internal evolution and not due to external pressure. All of this seems to indicate that the gap is not as great as one might believe.

Dr. Salazar interrupted the Secretary to inquire whether he was aware of the real significance of the expression "internal self-determination" as used by Ambassador Teotonio Pereira. The Secretary replied that that was exactly one of the points which he would like to clarify. In questions of that nature among nations having well established historical traditions, although different, different points of view will probably prevail. He believed, however, that there were certain points of friction which could be eliminated. For example, it is not the objective of the policy of the United States to see Portugal removed from Africa or substitute the United States in the Portuguese possessions. Dr. Salazar expressed the opinion that such expressions were not entirely clear, since the practical results of the policy the US does follow may entail the removal of Portugal.

---

[1] In conversations at 11 p.m. on June 27 and at 9:55 a.m. on June 28 Rusk and Nogueira went over much the same ground that Rusk and Salazar did in this conversation. (SET/MC/44 and 45; ibid.) In commenting on the state of Portuguese-American relations, Nogueira told Rusk that he could not conceal the "gravity and seriousness" of the present state of affairs. (SET/MC/44)

The Secretary observed that although the American people were attached to the tradition of self-determination, the American Government
has not made a crusade of this. He reminded Salazar that the United
States had never requested the inscription on the United Nations
agenda of any problem of this nature. If the question of Angola had
never been raised in the United Nations it certainly would have been
more convenient for the United States. This was an observation which
he believed important. The United States is confronted with problems
which are not of its own making. As to how these problems should be
handled in the United Nations, he agreed that there had been differences and it was this subject that he wished to discuss in a more detailed
fashion with the Minister of Foreign Affairs. The Secretary said that we
had worked hard to moderate the handling of certain questions affecting Portugal in the UN with prejudice to our own political position. The
results obtained have not given satisfaction to Portugal but he could assure that the situation would have been much worse without American
efforts. The Secretary believed it was important that there was a growing sentiment of moderation in the UN even among those who had formerly taken extreme views. As an example he cited the UAM group and
Nigeria, who are preoccupied with the possibility of a situation of chaos
and violence continuing on the African continent. The Secretary believed that this moderating tendency would soon carry weight.

The Secretary also commented that it did not appear to him that the
Portuguese cause had always been well presented. This was principally
because the Portuguese Government refused to accept the jurisdiction
of the United Nations with respect to Article 73 of the Charter. Thus the
debates were based half on ignorance and half on knowledge. He believed that the Portuguese decision to have recourse to the specialized
agencies of the United Nations would serve to help the Portuguese
cause in the future. In his conversations with the Foreign Minister he
had endeavored to become better acquainted with the real Portuguese
position on furnishing information.

Dr. Salazar then inquired whether the United States believed that
the international treaty which set up the United Nations should be
changed at the will or desire of the General Assembly. He asserted that
at times the United Nations takes decisions based on new interpretations of the Charter without these new interpretations having been debated. The Secretary recalled that in the course of the debates leading to
certain resolutions, interpretations of the text of the Charter were discussed. Continuing, the Secretary confirmed that while there had been
different points of view between the two countries on the subject of submitting information to the UN, he was encouraged by his conversation
with the Foreign Minister because he saw that in this field much depended on interpretations of terminology. On the other hand there had

been small points of misunderstanding or the allegation of certain incidents. If we could discuss these on a basis of confidence it was probable that incidents a, b or c would not correspond to the truth. It might also happen in connection with incident b, error would be admitted. For example, he did not know that among diplomatic couriers sent to Angola one was not really a courier, and he immediately put a stop to this. He believed it was important that we should not become involved in fighting against shadows and he could assure that, faced with concrete complaints, everything would be done to eliminate the cause.

The Secretary said Dr. Franco Nogueira had told him of his conviction that our differences were not in matters of substance but more as to methods and techniques. In the light of what the Secretary had said regarding American intentions toward the Portuguese presence in Africa, he believed that the two countries in the ensuing weeks could undertake frank conversations with a view to clarifying one by one the points of friction. As a member of the United States Government he could not deny the principles on which our country was constructed. They are the same which enable us to confront the Soviet Union today in the name of the free world and they are the same with which we are confronting the racial problem in the United States. But in the last 18 months we have seen a tendency on the part of Portugal with respect to Angola which we believe is very constructive: the reforms, the Regedoria elections, the economic and social development programs, and the desire to open up Angola to those that wish to see and obtain information. All of this reduces the gap existing between our two policies. The Secretary repeated that the United States wishes to march with Portugal as a friend. He said Portugal is not considered as a satellite of America and we do not wish to be a satellite of Portugal. The Secretary remarked that if we tackled our problems as friends we may find here and there a stubborn pocket of resistance but not an irreducible one. He mentioned that he was in the State Department when NATO was created and had worked with General Marshall and Mr. Acheson and Mr. Lovett and that the development of the recent misunderstanding and difficulties between us had caused him pain. He was confident, however, that if we entered into frank discussions our troubles will be overcome although he admitted that it may not be possible to overcome them all. What was essential, however, was good will and understanding on both sides. In such an atmosphere we should manage to settle our disputes. Dr. Salazar inquired of the Secretary whether he did not think he was being too optimistic. The Secretary replied that it was the obligation of a representative of an allied government to proceed with optimism. "Even when the results are not encouraging?" questioned the Prime Minister. The Secretary assured Dr. Salazar of his belief that the results will be good.

Returning to the question of Angola, the Secretary expressed the opinion that with the programs in course, Portugal could state that what she was undertaking was what the people of Angola desired and supported. This, in the knowledge that there are always those who desire more. The Secretary remarked that although there may be differences between us, there was a wide field of understanding in the practical course of our affairs. Because of this he believed that there is a great advantage in continuing systematic conversations here and in Washington. Dr. Salazar agreed entirely, explaining that there were certainly many pending problems and added that we should not waste our time with problems of the past. The Secretary thanked the Prime Minister for these views and stated that the United States was prepared to go forward, with no idea of influencing or bringing pressure upon Portugal, in the field of social and economic development in metropolitan Portugal as well as in the overseas, adding that we were ready to discuss these matters as they came to the mind of the Portuguese Government. The Secretary explained that US cooperation might be more easy on some points than on others. With respect to the problem of education in Africa, for example, it would be difficult for us to surmount the language problem but if Portugal has a lack of teaching personnel perhaps the Brazilians could cooperate, since they are also greatly interested in defending Lusitanian culture in Africa.

Dr. Salazar observed that this Brazilian interest did not mean that their interest was identical with that of Portugal in respect to Africa. Brazil is especially interested in Angola as that territory was reconquered from the Dutch with forces coming from Brazil after the Portuguese War of Restoration in the 17th century. Brazil therefore has a "moral" interest in Angola. The Secretary clarified that he had never been under the impression that there was any nationalistic interest in Africa on the part of the Brazilians. As he saw it that interest springs from Brazil's desire to avoid any reduction of Portugal's influence in Africa. Dr. Salazar agreed with this thesis and stated that at a certain moment Brazil thought it could be an intermediary between the West and the new African countries. He believed, however, that the doors of Africa only open to Brazil in exactly that part of Africa which is Portuguese and as a consequence of the existence of the Luso-Brazilian community. That was a much easier door than those of the small independent countries.

Continuing, the Prime Minister commented on the Secretary's allusion to the possibility of Portugal obtaining Brazilian technicians and teachers and expressed the opinion that this would not be easy since Brazil will be needing all of these for her own development for many years to come. Dr. Salazar stated, however, that Portugal would attempt to resolve that problem once it has the means to carry out an overall plan. With respect to the Secretary's statement that the United States had manifested a desire to help Portugal if a way could be found, Dr. Salazar agreed that this assistance could have taken place. He remarked that when Ambassador Elbrick had presented this idea sometime ago, educational and highway plans for Angola and Mozambique had been drawn up. It had been the intention to submit these to the American Government for consideration but when they were preparing to do so a policy took shape in the American Delegation in the United Nations with respect to Angola which was clearly contrary to Portugal. Portugal therefore believed that the offer for assistance envisaged the same aims as that policy: the expulsion of the Portuguese from Africa and under such circumstances it would not have been decent to present plans to the United States.

The Secretary declared once more that the two countries should consider all these problems. He had spoken to the Foreign Minister in order to see how this could be worked out in practice. If the two countries could place these problems on a plane of cooperation and trust it would be a great relief to both parties.

Dr. Salazar thanked the Secretary very cordially for his visit and said he regretted exceedingly that he could not remain here a few days longer.

---

344. Telegram From the Embassy in Portugal to the Department of State

Lisbon, July 23, 1962, 8 p.m.

66. Embassy officer called at Foreign Office today at request Director General Political Affairs Fragoso who opened conversation by stating he was sorry he had very serious matter discuss which had pained GOP. He then said rather sarcastically that Mr. Williams during his recent trip had made no speeches but had held private talks with high officials.[1] During one of these talks he stated US wished have independence Angola and Mozambique speeded up and once they were independent would provide all possible economic aid. He said that he was aware dif-

---

Source: Department of State, Central Files, 033.1100–WI/7–2362. Secret; Priority; Limit Distribution.

[1] Assistant Secretary of State for African Affairs G. Mennen Williams visited Europe July 9–20.

ficulties this separation would mean for Portugal mainly of economic and social character, but that US was ready help Portugal. He reiterated that there could be no deviation in US policy toward Africa.

Fragoso asserted with some feeling that this statement was inconsistent with what Mr. Rusk had come to Lisbon to say. Indeed this statement by high official USG was complete denial recent talks. He said that Mr. Rusk and the Ambassador had reiterated on many occasions that US was interested maintenance Portuguese presence in and ties with African provinces, and he wondered what ties and what presence they had in mind in view of Mr. Williams' remarks.

He termed this a step backward and said that it was unfortunate this position was expressed same time Secretary was reaffirming to Portuguese Ambassador what he had said here,[2] indeed at very time when US and GOP were on point of opening talks on differences. He reiterated that after Secretary's visit there had been an improvement in atmosphere but that this statement on part of high official USG again raised question of confidence and good faith.

Fragoso insisted there could be no doubt as to accuracy Williams' statement and that US would not be able offer any denial.

Embassy officer during conversation reiterated several times USG's interest in maintenance Portuguese presence Africa and that talks between two governments directed to this end.

At one point in response Fragoso said that Williams' statement made clarification nature this presence imperative.

Fragoso also indicated Foreign Minister would want discuss above matter with Ambassador July 24.[3]

Elbrick

---

[2] A memorandum of Rusk's conversation with Pereira on July 18 is in Department of State, Secretary's Memoranda of Conversation: Lot 65 D 330.

[3] Elbrick reported in telegram 67, July 24, that Nogueira had repeated the charges to him, and while the Foreign Minister was calm and affable, it was clear that he was very upset. (Ibid., Central Files, 033.1100–WI/7–2362)

345. Telegram From the Department of State to the Embassy in Portugal

Washington, July 24, 1962, 10:42 p.m.

35. For Ambassador from Williams. Reference: Embtel 66.[1] Portugal's trouble is not that they don't know things but that they know too many things that aren't so. Following is for your background information:

As my cables indicated, our allies, particularly French, Germans and Italians, worried about Portugal's African posture and were eager to discuss, sometimes initiated the discussion on Portuguese Africa.

In each case I followed outline agreed with Secretary before leaving:

1. Winds of change we believe will not bypass Portuguese Africa.
2. US believes continued European presence in Africa helpful to Africans as well as Europeans and that British and French have worked this out.
3. If Angola independent tomorrow there would be difficulties.
4. Only ones who can immediately help evolution of Portuguese Africa are Portuguese and maybe Brazilians.
5. US is working to persuade Portuguese to act in their self-interest by moving toward self-determination and Secretary Rusk's talks and Ambassador Pereira's speeches have shown Portuguese making some progress.
6. We have offered aid for education and are prepared to consider offering more.

As a matter of fact I gave Europeans a more hopeful picture of Portuguese Africa than they had had before.

Ball

Source: Department of State, Central Files, 033.1100–WI/7–2362. Secret; Priority; Limit Distribution. Drafted by Williams and cleared by Tyler and Meloy. Repeated to Geneva.

[1] Document 344.

346.   Memorandum of Conversation

Washington, September 5, 1962, 10:15 a.m.

SUBJECT

Portuguese-American Relations

PARTICIPANTS

The President

C. Burke Elbrick, Ambassador to Portugal[1]

The President asked about recent development's in Portuguese-American relations. Ambassador Elbrick said that the situation had eased temporarily, and that Secretary Rusk's visit to Lisbon at the end of June had provided an opportunity to make some progress in resolving some of the problems. The Portuguese Foreign Minister in response to a suggestion from the Secretary, had submitted to us a list of the problems[2] as seen from the Portuguese side and this list was now being studied in the State Department. It was expected that instructions would be sent shortly to Lisbon to guide the Embassy in its conversations with the Portuguese.

The President expressed interest in the Portuguese list. He said he would like to see the list and would also want to see the Department's instructions before they are sent to Lisbon.[3]

The President then turned to the subject of the Azores base negotiations and asked about the prospects for an agreement. Ambassador Elbrick said the base is the only trump card the Portuguese hold in their relations with us. In his opinion, the Portuguese would probably stall for some time, agreeing only to temporary extensions of the agreement while watching our performance in the UN and elsewhere on Portuguese African problems. It must be assumed that they realize that once the card is played it cannot be used again and therefore they probably intend to keep us dangling.

The President said he thought we should make another study of the Azores base question and determine whether there is a feasible alternative.

Source: Department of State, Central Files, 611.53/9–562. Confidential. Drafted by Elbrick and approved by the White House on September 16. The meeting was held at the White House.

[1] Elbrick was in Washington for consultations September 5–10.

[2] The list, covering what Nogueira characterized as past, present, and future problems, was transmitted in telegram 140 from Lisbon, August 17. (Department of State, Central Files, 611.53/8–1762)

[3] A copy of the instructions was transmitted as an attachment to a memorandum from Ball to the President, September 29. (Ibid., 611.53/9–2962)

The President asked about the situation in Angola. Ambassador Elbrick said it had been more or less stabilized but renewed guerilla activity could be expected. The Portuguese would find a highly organized guerilla campaign more and more difficult to combat.

---

347. **Telegram From the Department of State to the Embassy in Portugal**

Washington, September 15, 1962, 5:47 p.m.

136. Eyes Only. Personal for Ambassador from Secretary. The moment is fast approaching when negotiations will begin with the Portuguese Government for continued use of Azores base facilities during peacetime. Present agreement expires at end of this year. As you are aware, we regard these facilities as of very great importance to our national security interests and are anxious to obtain renewal if possible.

At the moment our prospects for doing so are problematical. They might be much better were we willing to back away from the position we have taken on the right of the peoples of the Portuguese territories to self-determination, but this we have no intention of doing.

There will be some unpalatable things to be said to the Portuguese during the months to come, but wherever possible we intend to balance these with attempts to be positively helpful to them. I wish to give them every possible chance to work themselves out of the corner into which they have been put by a combination of their outmoded colonial policy and the strongly-expressed anti-colonial policy of their Afro-Asian critics.

During these negotiations, it will be highly important that we all watch closely whatever we say or do which might affect the Portuguese attitudes, as well as attitudes Afro-Asian Countries. I am asking all the

Source: Department of State, Central Files, 611.53/9–1562. Confidential. Drafted by Starrs (WE); cleared with Tyler, Meloy, and NEA; and approved by Rusk. Also sent to USUN, New Delhi, and Paris. Attached to another copy of the source text is a memorandum from Tyler to Rusk, September 14, which stated that the telegram was occasioned by a speech Galbraith had given on August 8 on Goa and the Portuguese colonial question which was angrily attacked by Nogueira. Tyler believed that the speech "opened a wound in Portugal that may have begun to heal" and argued for the need for speeches on these topics to be cleared with Washington. (Ibid., 611.53/9–1462)

people in the Department and in the field whose responsibilities touch even collaterally on this problem to help me get this job done if it can in fact be done.

I request that during this period statements on Portuguese problems be checked with Department.

Rusk

---

348. Memorandum of Conversation

Washington, October 24, 1962.

SUBJECT

Portuguese Negotiations

PARTICIPANTS

United States	Portuguese
Mr. William R. Tyler, EUR	Foreign Minister Franco Nogueira
Ambassador C. Burke Elbrick	Ambassador Theotonio Pereira
Mr. Francis E. Meloy, Jr. WE	Mr. Jose de Meneses Rosa, Counselor

Mr. Tyler asked Ambassador Elbrick if there were any points he would like to make at the beginning of the conversation.

Ambassador Elbrick said that in the preliminary conversation with the Secretary upstairs[1] the subject of the Portuguese list had been broached. He could assure the Foreign Minister that the list had been most carefully considered here by many officials as well as by the Secretary himself. We would hope to be able to cover the list thoroughly both

---

Source: Department of State, Central Files, 033.5311/10–2462. Secret. Drafted by Meloy.

[1] Rusk gave a luncheon for Nogueira at 1 p.m., and in a memorandum to the President that day he wrote:

"At luncheon today I discussed with Nogueira the fundamental crisis in which we are involved and told him that I thought that you would much appreciate an assurance from him that at this time of crisis there would be no problem about the Azores bases, and that there will be full opportunity for long-term discussions looking toward a solution." (Kennedy Library National Security Files, Portugal)

The 2-page memorandum of Nogueira's conversation with the President at 4:45 p.m. on October 24 deals only with a repetition of the Portuguese position on Africa and attempts by the President to get Portugal to acclaim publicly its support for self-determination. (Department of State, Central Files, 611.53/10–2462)

here and in Lisbon. As the Secretary had said, however, Portugal has included on the list past problems which we feel have been covered in Lisbon, in Athens in a conversation between the Secretary and the Foreign Minister, and here in Washington. We do not believe a purpose would be served in going over these same points here and now. Further certain points were raised on the Portuguese list on which we feel we can not be any more responsive than we have been for legal and constitutional reasons. We would like to be as thorough as possible without going over past problems, where we can not be more helpful.

The Foreign Minister asked what sort of problems did the Ambassador mean. Mr. Tyler pointed out that we had in mind such items as the charge that the U.S. attitude on the problem of refugees in the Congo was instrumental in preventing them from returning to Angola. Full facts as to our part in Angolan refugee relief were fully explained in writing in Lisbon after the Foreign Minister returned from Athens where he had raised this question with the Secretary. Further we had in mind the concern of Portugal over views expressed or alleged to have been expressed by Governor Williams and other U.S. officials. We have already given the Government of Portugal a full and accurate account of what Governor Williams said at stops during his European trip. There is nothing more we can add. In general we doubt that it is useful to discuss matters where there is no reciprocity. We do not intend to monitor statements of Portuguese officials regarding the United States and protest any that do not appear friendly or any that do not meet our approval and the Government of Portugal can not expect us to accept the protests which it registers regarding statements by U.S. officials. We have tried to set matters straight and we do not feel we can add much more.

Mr. Tyler continued that with regard to visits to the United States by terrorist chiefs, the Government of Portugal must bear in mind that we have certain responsibilities as the host nation to the United Nations. Admission of an individual to the United States does not necessarily constitute U.S. Government approval of the individual or support for his principles, views, or actions. Such admission in short does not constitute U.S. Government endorsement or support. We would hope for understanding by Portugal of the situation in which we are even though Portugal does not agree with what we do. Mr. Tyler pointed out that the United States has attempted to be helpful in connection with the Galvao affair although it was important to remember that there were legal complexities in this problem which made it possible for us to keep Galvao from coming to the U.S.

The Foreign Minister said when Portugal raised these points they did not intend to indulge in a display of resentment or recrimination. Instead they wished to see if we can find a basis for cooperation and agreement. Having taken certain positions which Portugal considered harmful to her interests, they wanted to see if the U.S. Government were disposed to change its attitude. He said he perfectly well understood the legal and constitutional limitations on the U.S. Government but Portugal is not satisfied that the U.S. Government has exhausted the legal and constitutional means available to it to control the activities of groups and individuals. In particular, there is the U.S. attitude toward Angolan refugees in the Congo.

It is true that Portuguese officials may have made statements displeasing to the United States but it is not the Portuguese Government and people who are guilty of carrying out policies detrimental to the vital interests of the United States. It is rather the United States which is carrying out policies harmful to the vital interests of Portugal. The Foreign Minister did not think that reciprocity was involved. The United States should bear in mind that what it says and does is so important that it carries great weight throughout the world.

The Foreign Minister said he recognized the obligations of the U.S. with regard to the UN but he would like to make certain points on which he would expect Mr. Tyler to comment. He must point out that not only did the United States allow these people to enter the U.S. but they were in contact with members of the U.S. Delegation to the United Nations, they were received by high U.S. officials, they were permitted to establish offices in the United States and were allowed to receive support.

With regard to the American Committee on Africa, Portugal does expect reciprocity. Recently the U.S. asked its allies for solidarity on the Cuban shipping problem. It is only right and proper that the allies of the United States should give this solidarity and full support would be given to the United States by Portugal. On the other hand, however, when the American Committee on Africa sent two members clandestinely to Africa who entered Angola without visas and without official permission who then submitted a report highly detrimental to Portugal and were thereafter appointed to high advisory positions with the U.S. Government, the U.S. can not expect the Portuguese Government to be pleased. If U.S. position is that it can not be any more responsive than in the past on such matters as these, a serious issue is raised and the Foreign Minister would have to be more explicit than in the past as to the effect of this attitude on U.S.-Portuguese relations. He would like Mr. Tyler to comment.

Mr. Tyler said he believed the Foreign Minister was under a misapprehension. Appointment to the Advisory Committee on Africa was not a high government appointment nor did it give the individual concerned an official position with the government.

The Foreign Minister asked if the U.S. feels a special responsibility for refugees throughout the world or just in the Congo. Mr. Tyler replied that the United States has an interest in refugees and we have been very active in refugee relief through such organizations as the UN and the International Red Cross. The Foreign Minister rejoined that the Red Cross was ready to let the Angolan refugees in the Congo go back to Angola but U.S. groups intervened at this moment with assistance to the refugees which encouraged them to remain in the Congo. Ambassador Elbrick pointed out that there was no direct U.S. Government aid to the Angolan refugees in the Congo.

Mr. Tyler said that with regard to the question of Holden Roberto's reception by U.S. officials, the United States in an effort to accommodate the Government of Portugal will not receive Roberto at our UN Mission in New York and officials of our UN Mission will not seek him out for conversations. Roberto furthermore will not be received at the Department of State. We would not change this practice without first notifying the Government of Portugal that we are doing so. Mr. Tyler said he hoped that the Foreign Minister would realize that in giving this assurance we are making an effort to meet Portuguese problems. The Foreign Minister rejoined by asking if this really required a great effort on the part of the United States. Mr. Tyler replied with emphasis that this indeed required an effort on the part of the United States Government since such a procedure is contrary to our general practice.

Franco Nogueira said what about Holden Roberto's activities in this country, establishing an office and printing propaganda? Was the United States Government prepared to do anything about that? Mr. Tyler replied that so long as Holden Roberto does not violate the United States law there is nothing the United States can do.

Ambassador Elbrick pointed out that a previous reference by the Foreign Minister to Holden Roberto's travelling on a false passport did not correspond with the facts. Holden Roberto has come to this country only on a passport officially issued to him by another Government. Mr. Tyler pointed out that if Holden Roberto were traveling on fraudulent papers, he would not have been admitted to this country.

Mr. Tyler said it was clear that the United States and Portugal have certain differences and have different views on how to reach the same goals. We should not gloss over this fact. The U.S. position has not been taken lightheartedly and we have not casually and thoughtlessly taken positions which are not pleasing to Portugal. Our U.S. positions have been taken because they conform to basic convictions and principles held by this country. In spite of our differences and within the limitations set by these differences we wish to work as closely as possible with Portugal. We are not working against Portugal but do what we deeply believe is best for all of us. We want to find a basis even with our differences for cooperation as allies and old friends. Franco Nogueira said Portugal deeply desires to have the most cordial and friendly relations with the United States and believes that its past performance has shown this. The best judge of the vital interests of the United States is the United States. The same is true for Portugal and Portugal is the sole judge of what is best for Portugal. The question is how to harmonize these views. If the U.S. Government pursues a policy hostile to Portuguese vital interests (and Portugal is the only judge as to what its vital interest may be), what does the U.S. expect of Portugal?

Mr. Tyler said that the issues here are greater than either the U.S. or Portugal can control or influence. We believe that forces are at work in the world beyond the control of either of us. We are not working against Portugal. We would hope that if the Portuguese do not like our policies they would still understand we are not against the vital interests of Portugal but would hope the result of our policies would preserve the interests of all.

Franco Nogueira said that only Portugal can decide its vital interests. What is happening in Africa must be seen in a global context. We have already seen in the Cuban crisis the extent of the Communist threat. We can not separate these elements.

The Foreign Minister said he had been told by Ambassador Elbrick and by the Secretary that U.S. policy is to see that Portuguese presence and influence should be maintained in Africa. Portugal has never been told, however, how the U.S. expects to achieve this end. When Portugal acts in the light of what it considers to be its own vital interests, the United States does not seem to agree with Portuguese policies. What does the United States suggest?

Mr. Tyler pointed out that the Portuguese Government has in the past year undertaken far-reaching reforms. The Government of Portugal had been vindicated by the report of the ILO Committee which visited Angola. It seems to us the more Portugal opens up to the rest of the world and to the UN what it is doing in its African territories, the better its position is. We praised Portuguese reforms at the time they were announced and since as steps in the right direction. We continued to believe progress along this line provides the best assurance for a continuing constructive Portuguese position in Africa.

Mr. Tyler said that he did not wish to minimize what Portugal has done but there appears to be almost a difference of scale. The presence here in the United States of people who are anathema to Portugal or statements by individuals which are displeasing to Portugal are in U.S. terms explicable and understandable to us. These isolated irritations do not symbolize the attitude of the U.S. toward Portugal or its problems, or the efforts that Portugal is making. We laud and praise progressive steps Portugal is taking. We are with Portugal and sympathize with Portugal to the extent of the efforts Portugal is making to meet the problems created by the aspirations of the peoples of Africa. Portugal has taken far-reaching steps already. We would hope she would continue this course.

The Foreign Minister returned to the subject of Angolan refugees in the Congo. He said he believed about 190,000 to 200,000 refugees were present in the Congo. Approximately 90,000 had returned to Angola when at this point U.S. organizations intervened with aid and thus stopped the return of the rest. The refugees know they can return without reprisal. They fled only to escape terrorists. They are now being used by Roberto and by others against Portugal. The Foreign Minister did not believe the U.S. has any responsibility to help these refugees. It should not harm the U.S. position to stop aid to these refugees. Ambassador Elbrick pointed out that such aid as went from the U.S. to these refugees was not unilateral and was given in response to an appeal from an international organization.

Franco Nogueira said it is a well known fact that the U.S. is deeply involved in the Congo; that the U.S. is behind the UN forces in the Congo; that the U.S. is behind the Congo administration; and that the UN forces in the Congo are largely supported by the U.S. The Congo Government has established a base for the training of terrorists near the Angolan border. The U.S. should say to Adoula, "Stop" or the U.S. should say publicly that it does not approve. The silence of the U.S. is a matter of great surprise to the Portuguese Government. This silence is one of the "irritants" to U.S.-Portuguese relations. The Foreign Minister did not believe that the U.S. silence had anything to do with the principles to which Mr. Tyler had previously referred. Mr. Tyler replied that it is true we have a great stake in the Congo but this is a stake for the free world not for the U.S. alone. However, we do not have absolute power in the Congo. Moreover, the United States Government has spoken to Adoula about this camp.

The Foreign Minister said that the conversation so far had developed certain positive facts and certain negative facts. He wondered tentatively if it would not be a good thing to have a written statement from the United States Government regarding the positive facts. Regarding Portuguese presence and influence in Africa, he said he seemed to detect that the U.S. feels we can pursue a cooperative policy. Couldn't the U.S. say so publicly? The Foreign Minister stressed that this was not a formal request—that he was merely raising the point. He understood that the United States approves a policy of reforms by the Portuguese Government and also approves Portuguese cooperation with the ILO and other international organizations. With regard to the UN, the Foreign Minister said he understood the U.S. respect for the UN but Portugal attaches less importance to this organization. The trend seems to be substantiating the Portuguese view.

Ambassador Elbrick referred to the fact that the Committee of Seventeen had produced such an extreme resolution that the United States had not been able to go along with it. Franco Nogueira replied that he had not underestimated the value of this U.S. attitude toward Portugal but to be helpful such an attitude must be a more permanent part of U.S. policy.

The Foreign Minister asked if the United States had added any subjects to the list which he had given Ambassador Elbrick in Lisbon?

Both Mr. Tyler and Ambassador Elbrick said that we had added nothing and Ambassador Elbrick commented that the list appeared long enough to us as it was. Franco Nogueira said that he was not at all sure that the list was long enough and that he personally had deleted a number of items before handing it to Ambassador Elbrick. Ambassador Elbrick said that if the Foreign Minister were inclined to delete items perhaps this was a hopeful sign. The Foreign Minister said that Mr. Tyler had referred to the free world. Portugal wants to support the free world but if the free world exists only to destroy Portugal, the Portuguese would feel differently.

349. Memorandum of Conversation

US/MC/13   Paris, December 15, 1962, 5 p.m.

UNITED STATES DELEGATION TO THE THIRTIETH
MINISTERIAL MEETING OF THE NORTH ATLANTIC COUNCIL
Paris, France, December 13–15, 1962

PARTICIPANTS

United States	*Portugal*
The Secretary of State	Foreign Minister Nogueira
Ambassador Elbrick	Ambassador Dr. Cunha
Assistant Secretary Tyler	Mr. de Sousa Pernes
Willis C. Armstrong, BNA	

SUBJECT

Portuguese Problems in the UN; Situation in Angola; Azores' Base Discussions; US Policy Towards Portugal

Source: Department of State, Conference Files: Lot 65 D 533, CF 2198. Secret. Drafted by Armstrong and approved in S on January 7, 1963.

[Here follows discussion of other subjects.]

The Secretary turned his attention to the United States base at the Azores, and said that he understood that the Foreign Minister had indicated that current base arrangements could be extended pending the conclusion of the talks which had been proposed.[1] The Secretary pointed out that a day to day extension is not very manageable and that it left us in a position in which our rights could be cancelled on a moment's notice, if the Portuguese government concluded that the negotiations were not getting anywhere. Mr. Nogueira said that the position of his government was that the United States could stay as long as conversations continue and after negotiations are finalized unless we do not reach agreement. In the event of a recognition that agreement had not been reached, a six months period would start, and at the end of that six months the base arrangements would be terminated. The Secretary pointed out that we have very large commitments and the base is a very large operation. If we are legally subject to change at any moment, it is very difficult to operate. We would like to have some idea of the time we can stay and otherwise we are on shifting sands. As far as we are concerned, the question of the base arrangements becomes relevant as to how the talks go on other matters. It is difficult to see how to discuss all other matters while the tentative nature of the base arrangements hangs over our heads. We have to make contracts, order troop rotations, etc. We can not really be expected by an ally to be subject to unprecedented interruption in the operation of an important military facility. The Secretary wondered what kind of letter could be written by the Portuguese government, so that we could continue to work at the base. He wondered if we could have a one year extension or an agreement from the Portuguese that they would give a six months advance notice of the date on which the six months termination period could begin. Mr. Nogueira said he perceived the problem and would try and write something which would reach our point.

The Secretary asked whether the Foreign Minister had any comments on the other aspects of our discussions, and Mr. Nogueira said that the Ambassador always says that United States policy is not going to change. This is the policy of self-determination and Portugal does not expect this policy to change overnight or radically. The United States is entitled to its own position on such matters and there is no objection to the position, which is understood. Nevertheless, there are frequent occasions when the United States, through officials and other speakers, appears to single out Portugal for criticism. Also the United States ap-

---

[1] On December 11 Elbrick had reported this in telegram 435. (Ibid., Central Files, 611.537/12–1162)

pears to find it necessary to encourage people who work against Portuguese policy. The Secretary asked how the speeches had been on the sanctions resolution and Mr. Nogueira said that the speeches had been quite satisfactory, because they referred to a decision to integrate into another country as a form of self determination.

Mr. Nogueira went on to another point which was that general United States' propaganda appeared to condemn Portugal, and often in circumstances when the net advantage for the United States was imperceptible. The impression conveyed by much of United States propaganda is that it is doing everything possible to make Angola and Mozambique collapse.

The Secretary asked the Foreign Minister what he felt about the aide-mémoire which was recently given to him,[2] and he said there were some exceptions to be taken, which would be done in writing in due course. The Foreign Minister went on to say that if in fact the United States wishes to control or to destroy Portugal, this could be understood but each time Portugal is told of United States policy, it finds some bit of evidence which tends to contradict the statement of policy. President Kennedy had said that we should avoid friction and irritation, but irritation comes from the United States side, and tends to undermine the Portuguese position. Mr. Nogueira said he had been very pleased to note that the Secretary had spoken of Soviet threats as being global in nature, and that he had also included Africa as a part of Western security. Portugal felt that its position was more important than many people realized.

The Secretary said that he had two or three comments. In the first place, it was not the United States which raised the Portuguese question in the United Nations or anywhere else and the question comes up as a result of other initiatives. If we are asked how we feel, we must say that the Portuguese presence in Africa depends on the attitude of the people in the area they control. If the local people do not want the Portuguese, they will bleed them white and throw them out. The United States believes both in self determination and a continuing Portuguese presence in Africa. The Foreign Minister said he agreed that people could not be held against their will. The Secretary said that some of the things that bother Portugal involve private people or organizations, and we can not do anything about them. He wondered if Portugal had any complaint about statements made by the President or the Secretary of State, and Mr. Nogueira said no, but that sometimes other government people speak and criticize Portugal, and no correction is made. This seems to be a lack of good faith, because there is no clarification and no correction,

---

[2] Presumably this is the aide-mémoire of November 14, which apparently made a commitment to issue a high-level statement condemning attacks on overseas territories. No copy has been found, but it is described briefly in aigram 465 from Lisbon, March 6, 1963. (Ibid., Pol Port–US)

despite the fact that the speeches are frequently contrary to the stated policy. The Secretary said that he was responsible for what government officers said, although he did not always know what this was. The Secretary added that we had worked very hard to assure fair treatment in the General Assembly, and Mr. Nogueira agreed. The Secretary asked how many allies had voted against the sanction resolution[3] and Mr. Nogueira agreed there have been only four besides the United States. The Secretary said that our position on this matter was not contrived. The resolution was wrong and we said so. Mr. Nogueira conceded that there have been helpful remarks by the United States in the United Nations, but went on to say that the more outside pressure there is on Portugal, the slower it is likely to move in the direction in which the United States wants it to. The Secretary said he could see this point. Mr. Nogueira said there is a Portuguese public opinion and there can be no harm in Portugal's pressure upon the United States but it is hard when there is pressure on Portugal. The Secretary said it is hard to be a satellite of forty-two allies.

The Secretary said that we agree with the Portuguese Ambassador in Washington in his comments about self determination in which he recognized that motion towards self determination should be from people inside a country not from the outside. If it were from the outside we agreed it should not happen and the UN and the Congo could not afford to have the kind of thing go on which had been described by Mr. Nogueira a little earlier. Mr. Nogueira asked whether the Secretary had read a recent interview of Salazar in *Life* magazine, in which Salazar had said that the United States believes in self determination, not necessarily independence. Puerto Rico, for example, is self determining but not independent.

Mr. Nogueira wondered how Portugal could be sure that the United States was not working behind its back. The Secretary said that we have to continue to work at credibility, separating fact from fiction, and suspicion from fact. Mr. Nogueria said that there is a difficulty in the tendency of many Americans, including officials, to talk like Afro-Asians, and what he would like is a denial by the United States of their assertions. The United States, according to Mr. Nogueira, has supported the thesis that Portugal is a threat to international security and this is pretty intolerable. Portugal had expected better from the United States. Sometimes the United States appeared to be talking principles and sometimes it appeared to be talking interests. The dialogue appeared to get rather confused sometimes, and Portugal had difficulty knowing which we were discussing.

---

[3] For text of Resolution 1807 (XVII), December 14, see U.N. doc. A/5349; printed in *American Foreign Policy: Current Documents, 1962*, pp. 198–200.

The Secretary asked about self determination for South Katanga and Mr. Nogueira said that this was a matter for the Congolese since Portugal has no opinion on the subject. He said that for 700 kilometers of Portugal's frontiers in Africa there is trouble, and on the other 1,000 all is secure. One can not expect Portugal to feel like having the chaos extend over the other 1,000 kilometers as well. The Secretary said that if we were convinced that everybody could get out and stay out of the Congo and a line could be drawn around it, we would all be happy, but this does not seem to be the case. Mr. Nogueira agreed and said he realized the problem. He said that Portugal is not a champion of secession for Katanga. The Secretary said that unfortunately integration in the Congo determines what kind of government it will have.

Mr. Nogueira said that there were Americans working against Portugal in the Congo and the Secretary asked what kind of Americans they were. He said that Mr. Nogueira should tell Ambassador Elbrick about them.

The conversation ended with reiteration of the following points:

1) How can we be more precise in stating our policy so that the Portuguese can understand it?
2) We will proceed with the UN resolution on rapporteurs.
3) The Secretary will look at the Bingham speech.
4) Mr. Nogueira will see what he can say about the base so that there will be more stability of tenure and operation.
5) Both the Foreign Minister and the Secretary agreed that they would tell the press, if asked, that they had discussed a wide range of problems of mutual interest in the context of the Alliance.

---

350. Letter From Secretary of Defense McNamara to Secretary of State Rusk

Washington, July 11, 1963.

DEAR DEAN: In connection with the U.S. position on possible UN Security Council resolutions calling for severe measures against Portugal and the Republic of South Africa, we understand that these proposals could include economic sanctions, arms embargo, and even expulsion from the UN itself. We have given serious attention, from the standpoint of military security, to such resolutions, and this letter is to indicate my conclusions and recommendations.

Source: Kennedy Library, National Security Files, Portugal. Secret. No drafting information appears on the source text.

Any position taken by our delegation will very likely alienate in some degree either Portugal and South Africa on the one hand, or the African bloc on the other. As the attached memorandum from the Joint Chiefs of Staff makes clear, we have significant military interests, immediate and long-term, which could be jeopardized either way.[1] [5 lines of source text not declassified]

In the Republic of South Africa we presently operate only the Atlantic Missile Range tracking station near Pretoria. As Ros Gilpatric wrote to George Ball on 9 April 1963,[2] this station has contributed greatly to our missile development and other space programs and will continue to be important after 1963, although not vital. In addition, we must take into account the reaction of our NATO allies, and the possible divisive effect upon the alliance, should we give support to a strong African resolution on this subject. Consequently, any course of action which we may envisage should be coordinated in advance with at least the United Kingdom, France and Belgium.

As the attachment indicates, the military assets we derive from Portugal and South Africa must be weighed against those now available to us in the "African bloc". The communications station at Kagnew, Ethiopia, is of critical importance to a variety of communications and intelligence objectives. As we have pointed out before, there is no practical alternative to this facility. Wheels Air Base in Libya is particularly significant for air transport and training operations for our fighter aircraft assigned to NATO; its replacement would be difficult and expensive. In Morocco, despite the phase-out of the SAC bases, we have important communications facilities for which there is presently no substitute. Furthermore, in these countries and in the remainder of the North African and sub-Saharan area, we would attach long-term strategic importance to the preclusion of any Soviet Bloc foothold for military, political, and economic reasons.

Given these considerations, it should be our basic objective, to the extent that it is possible, to avoid prejudicing our relationship with either side in this dispute.

Thus, we recommend that the United States clearly state its strong objections to apartheid in the Union of South Africa and its criticism of the policies of Portugal in the Portuguese Territories. However, I hope it

---

[1] JCSM–528–63, July 10. In it the Joint Chiefs of Staff concluded that for the foreseeable future, U.S. requirements in the Azores were of primary strategic importance by comparison with those in Sub-Saharan Africa and that in order to protect vital U.S. strategic military interests in the Azores and avoid further poisoning of the NATO Alliance, the United States should resist the institution of strong measures against Portugal. It was felt that such a course of action would be justified by the improvement in Portuguese policy and progress made in Angola and Mozambique. (Ibid.)

[2] Not found.

will be possible to avoid a vote in the UN in favor of economic sanctions, arms embargo, or expulsion in the cases of Portugal and South Africa. In any event, I believe the decisions on these issues should be based on general considerations of foreign policy.

I hope that you share the views I have expressed and that we can work on this basis toward a joint State–Defense recommendation to the President as to how we can meet this difficult problem without serious damage to our military position.

Sincerely,

Bob

351.   Telegram From the Embassy in Portugal to the Department of State

Lisbon, July 12, 1963, noon.

49. Recent conversations high-ranking officials Portugal armed forces suggest attitude this normally pro-U.S. group may now be hardening as result resentment over U.S. policy on Portuguese Africa. While too early draw definite conclusions, following two conversations reflect this sentiment and I believe Department should be aware that attitude of influential officer group, which likely dominate political scene here after demise Salazar regime, may be seriously affected.

1. On July 2 Air Force Chief of Staff General Mira Delgado told chief MAAG he found difficult understand how U.S. could expect free use Azores base while at same time supporting, encouraging and financing Portugal's enemies such as Congolese and Angolan rebel groups. Spoke strongly about George Hauser whom he termed U.S.G. representative aiding and abetting African rebel groups. Claimed Communist coloration on part Tanganyika-based groups operating against Mozambique and produced list of USSR propaganda publications found in possession agitator in northern Mozambique. Reverting to Azores negotiations General Mira Delgado admitted probably mutual

Source: Department of State, Central Files, Pol Port-US. Secret. Repeated to Madrid and Paris.

military advantages attached to conclusion new agreement but professed see little or no political advantage to Portugal in view untrustworthy actions U.S.G.[1]

2. Chief Portuguese Naval Staff Vice Admiral Roberedo on July 9 bluntly asked Naval Attaché explain U.S. policy toward Portugal and its struggle in Africa. Professed see U.S. turndown Government of Portugal application purchase 20 rubbber boats as latest evidence real U.S. attitude toward Portugal. Termed it impossible Portuguese officials continue accept fallacy of U.S. as friend and ally who says one thing but does quite another. Heatedly said Portugal could no longer continue accept "always being distrusted and doubted by an unfaithful friend". Chief Naval Staff made quite clear that aspects U.S. policy to which he taking exception would henceforth affect personal relationship between self and Naval Attaché. (ALUSNA 101137Z).[2]

Comment: Air Force Chief of Staff has on past occasions waxed emotional on subject but this is first time Vice Admiral Roberedo has expressed self in this way. U.S. officers participating both conversations have definite impression Portuguese spokesmen though highly agitated intended convey exact message which came through. It may be that in face burgeoning difficulties Government of Portugal has purposefully decided employ military channels as one more avenue through which pressure U.S. for increased consideration Portuguese needs. Whether this true or not, we believe Portugal's officer corps probably does feel strongly let down by supposed ally and could in future turn increasingly against U.S. in direct proportion to deterioration military situation in Africa or increasing conviction that U.S. committed to sacrifice of Portuguese interests for sake African policy considerations.

Elbrick

---

[1] On July 30 Elbrick reported that the MAAG Chief had advised Delgado that the United States could not approve transfers of Military Assistance Program equipment to Africa. Delgado stated that "he found our reply very offensive" especially given the military cooperation that Portugal had offered during the Cuban crisis. Delgado went on to say that Portugal could expect no further cooperation from the United States. (Telegram 113 from Lisbon; ibid.)

[2] Not found.

352.   Memorandum of Conversation

Washington, July 31, 1963, 5:30 p.m.

SUBJECT

Rejection of Portuguese Government's Charges

PARTICIPANTS

Ambassador Pedro Theotonio Pereira, Portuguese Embassy
Governor W. Averell Harriman, Under Secretary for Political Affairs
Mr. Francis E. Meloy, Jr., WE

Governor Harriman said he had asked the Portuguese Ambassador to come in at the instruction of the President. This morning our Ambassador in Lisbon had reported by telephone that he had been summoned to the Foreign Office just before lunch, Lisbon time, by Mr. Fragoso.[1] Our Ambassador reported that Fragoso said that from all information and evidence available the Government of Portugal is convinced that the objectionable resolution presently before the UN Security Council is the work of the United States.[2] Fragoso said that whether the United States votes for this resolution or abstains, Portugal will regard this as being the same thing. Portugal will hold the United States responsible for the results.

Governor Harriman said the President is outraged by this message. It is a matter of fact that the resolution before the UN Security Council was an African resolution. The United States had been attempting to modify this resolution by seeking to eliminate its most objectionable features and had succeeded to a considerable extent. The resolution in its final form was still not acceptable to the United States and therefore it had been the President's personal decision that the United States should abstain. To be accused of responsibility for the African resolution is something which the President cannot tolerate. The President wished this message to be conveyed to the Portuguese Government promptly.

The Portuguese Ambassador said that he was unaware of Mr. Fragoso's démarche. He believed that Foreign Minister Franco

---

Source: Department of State, Central Files, Pol Port-US. Confidential; Limit Distribution. Drafted by Meloy and approved in M on August 2. The meeting was held in Harriman's office. A summary of the conversation was transmitted to Lisbon in telegram 86, July 31. (Ibid., Pol 10 Port/UN)

[1] A memorandum of Elbrick's telephone conversation with Meloy during the morning of July 31 is ibid.

[2] For text of this resolution as adopted, see American Foreign Policy: Current Documents, 1963, pp. 156–158. It was adopted on July 31 by a vote of 8 to 0, with 3 abstentions (U.S., U.K., France).

Nogueira, who is in New York, was also unaware of Fragoso's representations to Ambassador Elbrick. Ambassador Pereira said the Foreign Minister is a man of integrity and a friend of the United States. The Ambassador had been with the Foreign Minister in New York during the Security Council meetings at which the Foreign Minister had made two or three interventions. Portugal had been attacked savagely in the Security Council. The Foreign Minister had invited the African leaders to visit the Portuguese African territories to see conditions for themselves but this invitation had not been accepted. Portugal had also, last year, shown its good will by agreeing to the rapporteur suggestion but this proposal had come to nothing. Now a very strange thing has been going on in New York. Portugal is being attacked while her NATO allies stand by.

Governor Harriman interrupted to say that he had not called in the Portuguese Ambassador to argue about or discuss the situation in Africa. The purpose of this conversation was to inform the Portuguese Ambassador that the President had been outraged by the reported démarche by Mr. Fragoso to Ambassador Elbrick. If Fragoso's démarche represents the Portuguese reaction, the President wonders if there is any use in his trying to work constructively for Portuguese interests. Governor Harriman said he understood Ambassador Stevenson had talked with Foreign Minister Franco Nogueira in New York.[3] Although a full report had not yet been received, we were informed that the conversation had been unsatisfactory. Governor Harriman asked the Ambassador to convey to his Foreign Minister and to the Portuguese Government the outrage of the President at the representations made by Mr. Fragoso and the fact that the President cannot tolerate being accused of responsibility for the African resolution in the United Nations Security Council.

The Portuguese Ambassador said this was a most unfortunate message. He could only present his respects and take his leave.

---

[3] A memorandum of Stevenson's telephone report on this conversation is in Department of State, Rusk Files: Lot 72 D 192; a more extensive report was transmitted in telegram 309 from USUN, July 31. (Ibid., Central Files, Pol 10 Port/UN)

353.   Memorandum From President Kennedy to Secretary of Defense McNamara

Washington, July 31, 1963.

As the Portuguese situation may get increasingly complicated and as they may tend to strike out at us as time goes on I think we should develop a contingency for the loss of the Azores base. Will you give me your thoughts on this in detail.

Source: Kennedy Library, National Security Files, Portugal. Secret. No drafting information appears on the source text.

354.   Memorandum of Conversation

Washington, August 2, 1963, 2:15 p.m.

SUBJECT

Portuguese Explanation of Fragoso Démarche

PARTICIPANTS

The Secretary

Mr. Alberto Franco Nogueira, Portuguese Foreign Minister
Ambassador Pedro Theotonio Pereira, Portuguese Embassy

Mr. William C. Burdett, EUR
Mr. Francis E. Meloy, Jr., WE

The Portuguese Foreign Minister, accompanied by Ambassador Pereira, called on the Secretary following intimations given Ambassador Stevenson in New York that he would welcome an invitation. Franco Nogueira said he wished to come directly to the matter on his mind. He had jotted down a few points on the plane coming from New

Source: Department of State, Central Files, Pol Port–US. Confidential. Drafted and initialed by Meloy and approved by S on August 8. The meeting was held in the Secretary's office.

York so that he would not forget. He was sure the Secretary said he was aware of the "misunderstanding" of the last few days. The Secretary said he was aware of the démarche made by Mr. Fragoso and of the shaking repercussions it had caused in Washington. Franco Nogueira said he was referring to this. He wished to make a matter of record that both he and Portugal had the highest respect and consideration for the President not only as the leader of the Free World but also as a person and an individual. He was not saying this just because of this misunderstanding. He hoped Ambassador Elbrick had reported previous conversations in Lisbon in which he had said the same thing. He has always had such views. The Secretary could ask Burke Elbrick to confirm this. He was not trying to patch matters up or to flatter the President. Franco Nogueira said "let me put a question to you. Do you think it in our interest to offend the President or to offend the United States? Surely not! If this was done it must have been done inadvertently".

Franco Nogueira said he was sure the United States has confidence in Ambassador Elbrick. Portugal also has confidence in him. There must, however, have been some reporting error. He was sure Fragoso was speaking of the overall situation in the United Nations. Portugal holds the United States largely responsible for this. There was no intention of offending the President. Franco Nogueira said: "This I would like to have the opportunity of saying in person to the President". It is unbelievable that we intended to affront the President or that he should be offended by remarks made by the Director General of Political Affairs in the Portuguese Foreign Office even though this man is a responsible official.

The Secretary rejoined that the President did not believe that the remarks had been directed at him personally. Franco Nogueira said "not even officially as President"? The Secretary said the President has been working hard personally to ameliorate this situation. The problem has posed itself in more acute form since the Addis Ababa Conference.[1] As the result of discussions the Africans have cut back their position but not far enough in our view. The African resolution before the Security Council, however, was a far cry from what started out at Addis Ababa. The United States took lots of lumps and bruises and expended much credit but it was in the direction of ameliorating the resolution. To hold the United States responsible for the African resolution before the Security Council is not acceptable.

The United States does take responsibility for the improvement in the African position and for the difference between the African views at

---

[1] The Conference of African Heads of State and Government held at Addis Ababa, May 22–26.

Addis Ababa and the resolution passed by the U.N. We still did not find the resolution acceptable, however, and we could not vote for it. The Portuguese should realize that the President had intervened on several occasions to try to moderate the African position. For example, he had spoken to Nyerere.[2] Hence it was only natural that he should have a strong reaction to the fact that Portugal blamed the U.S. for the African resolution. The Secretary said he had spoken frankly to make the Foreign Minister understand.

Franco Nogueira said he had not known the history in such great detail. The Portuguese may be suspicious, but the impression at the U.N. and in the press was not precisely in keeping with what the Secretary had said. Serious newspapers like *Le Monde* and *Figaro* had said that the USUN delegation wanted to go much further but that the Department and perhaps the White House had restrained the U.S. delegation. Frankly, Portugal had the same impression.

The Secretary said "do you mean we were trying to strengthen the African resolution"?

Franco Nogueira said not the U.S. Government, not the U.S. Delegation, not Ambassador Stevenson. However, we believe the U.S. Delegation or some members of it let it be known they would support a strong resolution. "There are ways of doing this indirectly". There are always "ghosts" who can let this word get around. Other delegations, including the Venezuelan Delegation had this impression. This was the general impression of the U.N. delegations and of the press and Portugal shared this view. However, if the Secretary told him this was not so than it was not so and this would end the conversation.

The Secretary said it was true that the Venezuelan resolution was an improvement but it was still not enough of an improvement for the U.S. to accept. Franco Nogueira said it may have been "better" but not from the Portuguese view. He said Portugal must understand U.S. policy and the U.S. must understand Portuguese policy. You wanted to moderate the resolution, we wanted as extreme a resolution as possible so that it would be rejected. We are not accusing Ambassador Stevenson but it was the impression in New York that some members of the U.S. Delegation were ready to support a strong resolution. We do hold the U.S. responsible for the overall situation in the U.N. This is what was meant by the Fragoso démarche.[3]

---

[2] President Julius Nyerere of Tanganyika visited Washington July 15–16.

[3] Rusk and Nogueira also discussed the U.S. attitude on self-determination and the possibility of the United States sending a special Presidential envoy to Lisbon to talk with Salazar. Memoranda of these parts of the conversation are in Department of State, Central Files, Pol Port-US.

355. **Memorandum From Secretary of Defense McNamara to President Kennedy**

Washington, August 14, 1963.

This is in response to your memorandum of July 31, 1963,[1] requesting my thoughts on what action we would take in the event of the loss of the Azores base.

I can see three possibilities with respect to the continued use of the Azores base: (1) that its use would be limited solely to NATO related activities both in peacetime and wartime; (2) that its use would be restricted to serious crises involving NATO, and (3) that we would be denied its use for all purposes. I have assumed Case (2), that it would be available to us in case of a serious NATO crisis but not in peacetime. Since we may become involved in non-NATO contingencies in which we now plan to use the Azores, this memo deals mainly with those actions which would be necessary under this possibility.

Present Facilities and Uses

Our facilities in the Azores consist of the major Air Force Base at Lages, Naval Air Facilities at Lages and at Santa Maria, port and support facilities on Terceira, Santa Maria, San Miguel and Graciosa Island. We have 3323 personnel manning these facilities, 1763 of them are U.S. military. The facilities provide for an en route MATS stop in support of its peacetime and wartime airlift responsibilities, a base for tankers used in air refueling of strategic and tactical aircraft, CINCLANT's anti-submarine warfare and surveillance operations, en route air-ground communications and an alternate route for trans-Atlantic communications.

Air Operations—Peacetime, Wartime—Near and Long Term

There has been a downward trend in our use of Lages in the past several years which stems from the increasing range of our transport aircraft and the greater use of air refueling of our tactical and strategic aircraft from CONUS. During the 12-month period ending March 1962 the monthly average number of landings at Lages was 537, while in the 15 months through June 1963 this figure dropped to 442. We can, in any case, expect a continued gradual reduction in the future.

The most important planned usage of the Azores base is in the event of a limited war. The planned usage, in support of 20 separate contingency plans in Africa and the Middle East, would involve about 2800

Source: Kennedy Library, National Security Files, Portugal, Azores Base. Secret. The source text bears no drafting information.

[1] Document 353.

landings during a 30-day period based on the movement of one Army division-air wing personnel and equipment.

If we were denied the use of the Azores we would re-route much of our peacetime and crisis traffic along the northern route. Part of this traffic would pass through our Newfoundland bases (Harmon, Argentia and Gander) to Prestwick, Scotland, and thence to European, Middle East or African destinations. Some aircraft such as the C–130 would be routed non-stop from Newfoundland bases to Continental destinations. (Even with the Azores available a large proportion of these aircraft would follow this non-stop route.) South Atlantic re-routing is quite inefficient. There is a loss of about 50 percent of the airlift capacity quite apart from anticipated difficulties with base and overflight rights in South America and Africa.

[Here follow details on the impact of re-routing and sections on tanker aircraft and ASW operations.]

Communications

The communications facilities in the Azores provide a significant portion of the Atlantic area air-to-ground coverage in conjunction with stations at Harmon; Croughton, England; Torrejon, Spain; and Kindley, Bermuda. This coverage includes control of aircraft, weather-reconnaissance reporting, search and rescue transmissions. In addition, long-range point-to-point communications facilities are used for the control and movement of aircraft across the mid-Atlantic, weather reporting and relay, support of SAC alerting and control systems and as an alternative routing of communications traffic when trans-Atlantic cables are inoperative or when atmospheric disturbances preclude transmissions in the North Atlantic.

Denial of the Azores would necessitate increasing the capacity and extending the coverage of the four remaining air-to-ground stations, mentioned above, to compensate for the loss of the Azores; reallocation of frequencies from the Lages facility to these other stations; renegotiation with nations concerned to clear frequencies for use in their areas; and realigning North Atlantic weather reconnaissance tracks to insure communications coverage now provided by the Lages facility. The long-range point-to-point communications capability at the Azores could be replaced by expansion of the existing high frequency radio systems connecting the North American continent with Europe and Africa, complementing the present submarine cable routes and the North Atlantic tropospheric scatter system.

Manpower

An initial look at the manpower situation indicates that the increased requirements at alternate locations which would be involved in our withdrawal from the Azores could be accommodated by reallocation of personnel resources from the Azores, and Bermuda, where a reduction in activities will result. However, if we wish to retain a ready capability for using the Azores in NATO contingencies, we might keep the base on a standby status which would involve keeping some personnel there for caretaker duties.

Availability of Spanish Bases

The loss of the Spanish bases in addition to the Azores facilities, following the evacuation of the Moroccan bases, would pose additional problems. For example, TAC fighters flown non-stop from the U.S. to European and Middle East bases over the generally favorable mid-Atlantic route would be re-routed over the North Atlantic with attendant weather and air space saturation problems. Recovery of tankers, now accomplished at Spanish bases, would have to be done at Wheelus or on French bases. The Navy would be forced to operate its ASW carriers and patrol aircraft and support them from the Western Atlantic, Iceland and the U.K. The loss of Spanish bases would further exacerbate the communications problems produced by the loss of the Azores.

Summary

In summary, if we lose the Azores base we will re-route our transport aircraft via Newfoundland bases to Prestwick, or to European destinations if they have non-stop capabilities. Tactical aircraft will be flown non-stop over the mid-Atlantic route and refueled en route by a buddy KC–135 tanker. ASW activities will be moved to Rota. Air-ground communications capabilities at Lages will be absorbed by stations at Harmon, Croughton, Torrejon and Kindley. Point-to-point communications capabilities will be compensated for by expansion of the existing high frequency radio system from the North American continent to Europe and Africa.

[1 paragraph (3 lines of source text) not declassified]

Detailed actions, costs and timing involved in this planned contingency for the loss of the Azores base are being prepared.

Robert S. McNamara

356.   Telegram From the Embassy in Portugal to the Department of State

Lisbon, August 29, 1963, 10 p.m.

213. For Secretary from Ball.[1] Please pass White House. Following is summary of luncheon meeting with Foreign Minister today at which we had frank preliminary exchange of views. Fuller version will follow August 30.[2]

I opened by setting our position toward Africa in context of East-West struggle and defining differences between premises of Portuguese approach and our own.

I assured Foreign Minister of US interest in preservation Portuguese presence Africa. I said there seemed be measure of agreement on question of self-determination, but after lengthy consideration was of view key element of disagreement was time factor. I said we shared Portuguese objection to equating self-determination with independence which had effect of prejudging exercise.

Foreign Minister stated Portuguese did not fear power African nationalism but considered issue being exploited by communists and implied US policies aggravate problem. He said that unfortunately it was his impression present US administration felt it was working in favor Portugal because their policies more realistic.

He said he considered that Ben Bella threats to send volunteers and arms were empty. I disagreed and told him threats such as those made by Ben Bella might be prompted by demagoguery, but could be effective and could cause increasing trouble in Portuguese Africa as even moderate leaders would have to adopt like measures in order preserve their own position. I reminded him that even most responsible African leaders today were under compulsion to consolidate positions at home by taking strong position against Portuguese, South Africans, etc. I said that even if US accepted hypothetical position that it could cease support African aspirations in Africa such action would result in destruction moderate leaders and takeover by extremists.

During conversation Foreign Minister announced that Portuguese Ambassador at UN today handed U Thant invitation to come to Lisbon

---

Source: Department of State, Central Files, Pol 19 Port. Confidential; Priority.

[1] On August 15 Elbrick was informed that the President had decided to have Ball visit Lisbon. (Telegram 134 to Lisbon; ibid., Pol 7 US/Ball) Ball's instructions, which stated that his mission was to explore relations between the two governments with particular reference to the problems raised by the Portuguese territories, are ibid., Conference Files: Lot 66 D 110, CF 2301.

[2] Transmitted in telegram 985 from Paris, August 31. (Ibid.)

for discussions. He said Portuguese had initiative and intended to keep it, citing invitation to SYG and other steps which they intend to take. I agreed that initiative was important in that it created atmosphere of credibility to declared Portuguese intentions and gave sense of motion but told Foreign Minister in all frankness Portuguese would have to think in terms of some practical time schedule such as outside figure 10 years and make consistent and visible progress during interim. This prompted Foreign Minister to go into rather lengthy presentation as to why it would be impossible for Portugal to think in terms of self-determination within such a time framework. He insisted that responsible whites and blacks in Angola and Mozambique, for example, would not accept such proposal and that this was a matter that even Salazar could not control. I told him that I had heard similar views expressed by the French both in the metropole and in Algeria, Morocco and Tunisia during years before independence. I mentioned that the French also had had deep sense of civilizing mission. I pointed out that events had brought about a change even in Algeria, but, unfortunately, it had come about only after a long and agonizing struggle which had left us with Mr. Ben Bella. The Foreign Minister assured me that the two situations were not at all comparable but gave no facts to support this position.

In conclusion, Foreign Minister indicated his view that US policies in Africa and elsewhere were detrimental to the position of the West and that as a result the West was weaker rather than stronger. I, of course, took issue with him on this, stating that the wave of anti-colonialism was a political fact that could not be ignored. I described its origins. I said that it had developed momentum during difficult time of East-West competition. It was proceeding at fast pace, and some breakage was inevitable. I told him that I thought that because Portugal was one of the last remaining European powers in Africa to give effect to change pressure was being concentrated on it and that pressure would increase. The Foreign Minister professed to see the only way out of the situation as I outlined it was the abandonment of their overseas provinces. I termed this a bad rather than a good way to terminate the unfinished business.

Toward close of conversation Foreign Minister delivered lengthy statement on difficulty of any progress being made on territories problem in UN. He said concession there only led to further impossible demands from the insatiable Africans who equated self-determination with immediate independence for peoples unprepared to govern. He said that when serious problems arose between the great powers—the US and USSR principally—they were settled outside of UN. He said that in settling such problems outside of UN, result was that difficulties on them within the UN settled themselves. He then suggested rather clearly that if Portugal and the US could reach an understanding on the territories problem outside of the UN, UN difficulties would disappear.

I felt he was suggesting a possible approach, but subsequent probing revealed no details, and he did not pursue matter further.

In conclusion, I told Foreign Minister I did not despair of ability two governments come to agreement although it would be difficult. If we could agree on program and timing of action, US prepared absorb some damage to our other interests in order be helpful. I said, however, that our two views still seemed far apart, particularly on timing question. I also added that I would like to think over our conversation overnight and see Foreign Minister again tomorrow before my departure.[3]

                                                                    Elbrick

---

[3] In their second conversation on August 30 Ball and Nogueira went over much of the ground covered in their first. Ball also asked the Foreign Minister to look into the question of military assistance material being used in Portuguese African territories. (Telegram 987 from Paris, August 31; ibid.)

---

357. Telegram From the Embassy in France to the Department of State

                                            Paris, August 31, 1963, 3 p.m.

986. For Secretary from Ball. Pass White House. Following is report Under Secretary Ball's August 29 talk with Salazar. Also present were Ambassador Coelho of Foreign Ministry, Ambassador Elbrick and Counselor Xanthaky.

The Under Secretary expressed his appreciation to Salazar for receiving him and handed him a letter from President Kennedy[1] which the Prime Minister read. He said that he had just recently discussed with President Kennedy and Secretary Rusk the question of Portuguese/American relations and misunderstandings which had arisen. Portugal

---

Source: Department of State, Conference Files: Lot 66 D 110, CF 2301. Secret; Priority. Repeated to Lisbon. For another account of this meeting, see George W. Ball, *The Past Has Another Pattern*, pp. 276–279.

[1] Presumably a reference to President Kennedy's letter of August 27, which thanked Salazar for receiving Ball. (Department of State, Conference Files: Lot 66 D 110, CF 2301)

and the US had enjoyed a long and close friendship and it is important that we clarify any misunderstandings and, while we may not be able to agree on all points, the Under Secretary said, it is probable that we can agree on a substantial number and make cooperation between the two countries more fruitful. If it was agreeable to the Prime Minister, he would endeavor to sketch for him the basis for the position adopted by the US regarding African problems. Ball realized that the two governments have different views and he wished to make it clear that the policy of the US must be considered within the framework of our overall responsibilities and the East/West conflict. After the Second World War, the US felt obliged to move into certain power vacuums created by the retirement of certain European countries from areas in which they had previously been vitally interested, e.g., Viet Nam, Laos, etc. In addition, the US had given billions of dollars to India and Pakistan to protect the sub-continent from communism and to meet what had previously been a British responsibility. We had considered it essential to move into these situations to prevent the communists from doing so.

The Under Secretary emphasized that the continent of Africa was only of marginal interest to the US as far as American national interests are concerned. We feel that commercial possibilities in Africa are limited and we have no large economic ambitions there. We have, however, taken an active interest in African affairs for fear that the continent might be subjected to communist penetration. He said he would like to emphasize again that of all the areas in the world Africa was the least important from the point of view of American national interests, but our role there must be viewed in the light of the East/West struggle. The Under Secretary recognized that the Portuguese Government adopts a different approach and has a long-standing vital interest in Africa after 500 years of occupation and a sense of mission in the area. We felt it is very useful to define clearly our separate points of departure, emphasizing that everything we do in Africa is in the fundamental interest of the protection of the free world.

The Under Secretary said that world political evolution since the Second World War has been greater than that of the previous three centuries. With the dismantling of colonial arrangements that existed for many years, a marked change occurred in the relations between the metropolitan powers and those colonial areas. He cited developments in north and central Africa affecting France, and developments in various areas which affect Great Britain. This movement of political evolution has achieved considerable momentum and must be regarded as a political fact of life. The speed of the movement has been fantastic and the change of relationships between the metropolitan powers and the indigenous peoples has been profound. Admittedly there has been considerable "breakage" in connection with these developments, but the amount of bloodshed involved has been very limited. In the development of our own foreign policy this nationalism has had to be recognized and an attempt made to exercise a certain control in order to channel the movement into useful directions. For this reason, the US could not permit itself to take rigid positions. There is no doubt that the communist powers are eager to exploit the situation for their own purposes. We do not say that we have been wise in everything we have done and we have probably made mistakes, but we have made a serious effort to employ such resources and influence as we possess in an effort to give direction to this evolution.

With regard to Portugal's overseas problems, the Portuguese Government has managed to maintain its relations with the overseas territories with the least possible change. This very fact tends to concentrate pressure on Portugal at this time. The Under Secretary said that one point is very clear as far as President Kennedy is concerned, namely that Portuguese interests and influence in Africa should be preserved. It would be catastrophic if Portugal abandoned its territories there, and the agony which attended the birth of the Congo Republic should be avoided at all costs. France has been able to maintain with the countries of the UAM extremely useful and profitable relations and has also retained a large part of its interests in those countries. In like manner we feel that we should seek to help ensure the continuation of Portuguese influence in Africa.

The Under Secretary pointed out that the ideal of self-determination is a part of our constitutional heritage and that the idea of the consent of the governed is rooted in our past. It is true that in the UN, self-determination is frequently equated by many with independence—a thesis which we do not accept because it prejudges the ultimate outcome of self-determination. We must, however, encourage the operation of the principle of self-determination. As Ambassador Theotonio Pereira had pointed out in at least two speeches in the US, the Portuguese Government recognizes this principle as a matter of internal evolution. The Under Secretary had discussed this with the Foreign Minister today and President Kennedy and Secretary Rusk had also spoken to him about it.

The Under Secretary said that from the point of view of our long-term objectives he felt there was a large area of agreement. The major point which presented the greatest possibility of disagreement relates to the sense of urgency and the speed with which the evolutionary process takes place. We are persuaded that if this evolutionary process is to be channeled in a useful way some arrangement should be made for accelerating it and for telescoping the necessary actions into a fairly short period. The Under Secretary was not thinking in terms of months or even a year or two, but if we wished to avoid a situation where forces may get out of hand actions must be taken in a reasonable time span which would permit the evolutionary process to move very quickly by historic standards.

The Under Secretary assured the Prime Minister that the US Government is unhappy to be in opposition to Portugal, an old friend and NATO ally. We are prepared to assist and defend Portugal in accordance with our own constitutional principles and our analysis of the situation as it exists in Africa.

Dr. Salazar agreed that we seemed to proceed from different premises. He said the evolution in French and British overseas territories followed what the people themselves desired or what the metropolitan powers wanted. He had heard it said that the abandonment of India by Great Britain was a great piece of business because it relieved the British of the expense involved in maintaining the economy of the country and commerce between the two had increased. In Africa, however, the British found a very different situation. Indian culture was highly advanced and there existed a very fine civil service, which was not true in the African territories. Therefore, applying the same principles gave different results.

He did not propose to discuss French or British policy, however, but would confine his remarks to the Portuguese territories. There are several small territories and two large ones. The UN apparently considers all the territories to be equal and asserts that all should be independent (he noted in passing that the US had voted for a resolution which called for independence of all Portuguese territories). He said that the Cape Verde Islands have a population of 180 thousand; Portuguese Guinea, 500 thousand; Sao Tome, 100 thousand, and Timor and Macao with very small populations. It has always been the contention of the Portuguese Government that these territories could not maintain their independence but would be quickly annexed by neighboring states as in the case of Goa. Portuguese Guinea, for example would probably go either to Senegal or the Republic of Guinea. The UN demand for independence of these territories, therefore, can only mean annexation or absorption by others. It is not reasonable to maintain that one-half of the Island of Timor can be independent—but would automatically be absorbed by Indonesia which occupied the other half, and this is also true of Macao and Communist China.

The two large territories, however, Angola and Mozambique, could be independent nations. There is no problem here of lack of physical resources but only of human elements to maintain the territories as independent countries. The populations of both territories are made up of numerous tribes which the Portuguese Government has succeeded in encouraging to live in peace. These territories are not sufficiently developed, however, to offer a guarantee that they would not return to their previous primitive state if cast adrift. The situation in Africa has often been compared to the American revolutionary experience. Salazar felt that this was an absurd comparison because in the US it was the colonizers themselves who achieved independence whereas in Africa it is the colonized that are in question. There is no doubt that Angola and Mozambique may become independent states in the future but the question is when and how. The US is known to be greatly advanced in the science of social psychology but Salazar felt that we had not applied the principles we had learned to underdeveloped peoples. Angola is a very large area. Even if there were three to four thousand trained individuals capable of administering the territory, this would be inadequate for such a large area. He felt that if Angola were to become independent now the situation would be worse than that which had existed in the Congo.

Salazar felt that the US is partly responsible for the condition of African states today (which he described as chaotic). Ball had spoken of the winds of history, alluding to African nationalism.

He believed that in the greater part of Africa there is no nationalism. In Angola there is Portuguese nationality or nothing other than tribal identity. He felt that the problem is extraordinarily difficult and lamented the fact that the UN seemed to have been transformed into a forum for African representatives to call for independence which, in reality, does not exist in the African countries. He said this is perhaps just as well because the Africans could not administer themselves without outside assistance. There seems to be an illusion that an elite exists in such countries but it is actually very small. Europe and America furnish the technicians and administrators required but he did not believe that this is necessarily a good solution.

Salazar said that for many centuries the Portuguese have considered the overseas territories to be part of their country and they feel that the cutting off of those territories would leave no Portugal. Ball had spoken of maintaining Portuguese influence in Africa. If the territories became independent and if the new leaders would respect the Portuguese properties this might be possible but he pointed out that the French and the British had the financial "resources of the city" and the "bourse" in Paris to fall back on. Portugal, a poor country, could not compare with these two. He said that it is alleged that Portugal cannot develop the overseas territories but this is not true. In addition to Portuguese resources used for the purpose, foreign resources would be available and would be guaranteed by the Portuguese Government. If a political link continued to exist between the overseas territories and the metropole the government could continue to guarantee such investments but would not do so with [without] such a link.

Salazar said that the work of development of the African territories had only started at the end of the nineteenth century, unlike Brazil which had been developed by the Portuguese for 300 years before its independence. He said the US has a particular addiction to the idea of self-determination but before this principle can be applied the peoples themselves must be in a position to "determine". The Africans seem to think that self-determination is the same thing as independence and have said so in the UN. Actually the self-determination that the African countries have in mind would be imposed from outside Angola and Mozambique. He could not understand, for example, why the African countries should wish to impose independence, through the UN or by force of arms on the two Portuguese territories.

Salazar said he was in agreement with the Under Secretary on the principle of self-determination which he interpreted as responding to the "consent" or "sentiment" of the people of the areas concerned. He did not know that he could agree with the other point regarding acceleration of the process. Are the inhabitants of the territories in a position to express their wants? While a certain number are entitled to vote in national and local elections, the electoral list is still small. As education increases and the economy develops, these lists will become larger. In metropolitan Portugal itself, he said, only 10 to 15 percent of the population is qualified to vote. He remarked that any election not complying with the fixed views of the African nations would not be recognized by them in any case. The Government of Portugal works in its own way and is attempting to raise the standard of living up to the point where the people can express their preference. The USG has great faith, he said, in the idea of the quick development of administrators, but Portugal, with its long experience in Africa, does not believe that this can be done. He said he was not absolutely certain that the natives of the African provinces could all be raised to the level of the white population, although it will be possible to create an elite to take over the administration.

Salazar said what we see now by way of administrative talent in Africa is pathetic. He said the mailman is now a Minister of Transport, a nurse Minister of Health, and a process server a high judge. He said he would like very much for the USG to use its influence to instill some sense of responsibility in the African countries, though it appeared that the US, like the UK, did not want to annoy the new countries. The new nations have no sense of responsibility and it seems imperative that someone call them to account. Portugal, a small nation, cannot do this, but the US supports some of the African Governments and could have some influence.

Salazar repeated that he agreed with Ball on the principle of self-determination and that the expression of the sentiments of the people involved could lead to a possible federation or confederation, or to other forms. The UN, however, is not in agreement and therefore Portugal's only defense in this situation is to deny the UN the right to judge and to continue to disregard the African views in the UN. Portugal wants to save western civilization in Africa, but not to the extent of adopting precipitate political formulas for which the people are not prepared.

Salazar felt political changes will continue to occur in Africa and the powerful will absorb the weak, a solution which will give rise to a long period of war. He felt the western powers should think of safeguarding those territories which still remain intact.

Salazar said that he made this lengthy exposé to show the Under Secretary the problem and difficulties facing Portugal in Africa. He asked if the USG really believes that there is an internal nationalist movement in Angola. He said that the Portuguese Government had noted no such movement but had experienced invasions by terrorists from the Congo. On such a long frontier, he said, Portugal cannot prevent entry and departure of these individuals and he compared the situation with that which at one time existed between Algeria and Tunisia.

The Under Secretary said he was grateful for Salazar's exposition and could agree with much of what he said. By way of illustrating what we have in mind with regard to self-determination, he cited the case of Puerto Rico which, until the 1930's, had been neglected by the US. Under President Roosevelt, however, there had been a high level of development and a commonwealth relationship had been established which had been voted by the people of the area. He felt that if the people of Angola and Mozambique should choose some similar arrangement with Portugal it would be very beneficial. But like the Puerto Ricans they should have the option of independence open to them.

The Under Secretary said he agreed that self-determination is an objective and that the full and adequate expression of self-determination is not a possibility at the present moment. If 95 percent of the natives of Angola, for example, are illiterate, an expression of their views would mean little.

The solution seems to lie in the principle of evolution and education and in the progressively larger participation in local government. The fundamental point of difference he felt is the matter of timing, as he had told the Foreign Minister earlier in the day. He agreed that it was not possible to solve this problem overnight and that many new nations have been born prematurely, but the speed of evolution at this juncture is of great importance.

Salazar said that the US makes the African problem a political one whereas, for Portugal, it was a sociological one involving the proper preparation of the people of the areas. The Under Secretary said that we have already suggested we might assist in the problem of education and Salazar acknowledged that such an offer had been made, but that the Portuguese Government had not submitted detailed plans to the USG. These plans, he said, had been drawn up for both Angola and Mozambique but, because of complications in the UN, Portugal had seen fit to withhold them. Portugal is a poor, modest country which does not ask for help, he said, and he cited the fact that the Portuguese Government had refused economic aid in the first year of the Marshall Plan. He assumed that the American offer of assistance in education and in highway construction still stood, even though the Portuguese Government had not yet responded.

The Under Secretary said that we have discussed this matter of assistance in the field of education though pointed out the US did not furnish teachers in view of the language difficulty. Salazar said that money is important to build schools and to train personnel and to purchase school supplies. Salazar said that unfortunately Portugal was spending a great deal of money on defense, money which could otherwise be spent for more productive projects, and implied that progress in the field of increased education fell far short of his desires.

Under Secretary Ball said that he would like to clear up some apparent misunderstandings which had arisen recently. He said that the impression seemed to have gained ground in Portugal that the US is supporting Holden Roberto and he wanted to make it quite clear that this was not the case. He said that certain private organizations in the US had voiced support for Roberto but they had no connection with the Government and, he believed, had made no great financial contributions to Roberto. He wanted Salazar to understand that the USG had no jurisdiction over such groups.

Another misunderstanding concerned the recent action of the Leopoldville Government in recognizing Roberto's group as the Angolan Government in exile. The Under Secretary understood that Youlou had said that we had suggested that Adoula recognize Roberto. The fact is that we had advised Adoula not to do so very strongly but he had gone ahead anyway.

Salazar said he believed the Under Secretary's explanations of these matters but he found it difficult to understand why the USG could not oblige Adoula to follow US guidance. The Under Secretary said this would not be possible. We have had many difficulties with Adoula but from our point of view he is the best leader available for the Congo. For example, he had resisted efforts by the Soviet bloc to infiltrate the Congo. Adoula lives in a highly political atmosphere marked by great irresponsibility but if the US imposes its will on him, Adoula's government would fall.

We must, therefore, handle him very gently. We try through persuasion to keep him on a sensible course and we find that sometimes he is reasonable but that sometimes he is an African politican.

Salazar found it strange that countries which had previously supported the MPLA should now recognize the Roberto exile group. He remarked that Roberto is a foreigner in Angola and that he does not even speak Portuguese. Therefore, he has no particular attraction for the Angolan people. He said perhaps recognition of Roberto might not be such a bad thing after all since he had no following in Angola.

Salazar spoke of the danger occasioned by the presence of UN troops in the Congo and the fact, as he stated it, that UN forces are giving or selling arms to Holden Roberto. From his point of view, he said, it would be preferable for the UN forces to leave quickly. The Under Secretary said that the USG is anxious to see the UN forces remain in the Congo for six months beyond the end of this year because the Congolese army is not reliable and the UN forces will have an important role in training that army.

It was agreed that the Under Secretary would meet again with Salazar at 11 a.m., Friday, August 30.[2]

Lyon

---

[2] In their second conversation Ball and Salazar continued the discussion and agreed that Ball would return for further talks on September 6 and 7. (Telegram 988 from Paris, August 31; ibid.) In commenting on his discussions in Lisbon, Ball stated:

"As anticipated Salazar has strongly defended Portuguese colonial practices and his instincts on these matters are far different from ours. At the same time he is showing signs of recognizing need to move. He wants US friendship and support and I believe I have established basis of confidence with him without yielding any points of principle." (Telegram 979 from Paris, August 30; ibid., Central Files, Pol 19 Port)

---

358. Telegram From the Department of State to the Embassy in Norway

Washington, September 10, 1963, 9:05 p.m.

171. Eyes only for Vice President.[1] On his return visit to Lisbon Sept 6–7, Under Secretary Ball met separately with Foreign Minister and

---

Source: Department of State, Central Files, Pol 19 Port. Secret; Priority.
[1] Vice President Johnson visited northern Europe September 2–17.

Salazar.[2] Discussion centered around secret paper[3] (existence of which being closely held) which Portuguese Govt had prepared following previous week's discussion. Paper contained general observations relating principally to discussion of self-determination, statement on time factor, and section purporting to be a proposed program. In his final meeting with Salazar Under Secretary Ball gave his preliminary reaction to key points in paper. He said paper would be studied further in Washington and reactions conveyed through one means or another. Made following four points:

1. With regard to meaning of self-determination, Mr. Ball said in extreme African and some UN circles, self-determination regarded as synonym for independence. Appeared, however, that Portuguese have gone to opposite extreme, excluding from self-determination the option of independence but allowing other options.

2. US hoped Portuguese relations with peoples of their African territories could evolve so that Portuguese "presence, influence, and interests" might be continued in some form. Portuguese interpreted this as requiring continuance of political control. While US did not exclude possibility of preserving strong political connection, such as that between US and Puerto Rico, US would regard this as compatible with self-determination only if it represented free choice of peoples through mechanism under which other options also available. US could not agree that direct political control was essential to maintainence of Portuguese influence. Cited UK, French experience where overseas territories had become juridically independent states, yet metropoles were able to maintain presence and preserve commercial and economic interests. Cited French relationship with UAM states as example which might be a form through which Portuguese could maintain influence in overseas provinces.

3. US felt strongly that election rolls in countries with Negro majority should be expanded to ensure that that majority had adequate right of expression. Obviously, expansion of voting rolls could be achieved only over period of time and with intensive education.

4. Mr. Ball indicated there was a basic difference in US, Portuguese analysis of forces at work in Africa. US believes there are still moderate elements on the African scene who must be strengthened so as to check drive of extremists and radicals, but time is short. Might be possible to enlist support of moderates in progressive program towards self-

---

[2] Memoranda of Ball's conversations with Salazar and Nogueira on September 7 are in Department of State, Central Files, Pol 7 US/Ball and Pol 10 Port.

[3] A copy of this paper was attached to airgram A–135, September 18; ibid., Pol 19 Port.

determination within 10-year time span. Moderate elements do not wish to move too fast in Angola and Mozambique for fear of another Congo; however, if moderates cannot see in Portuguese plans type of progress they can support in order to restrain extremists, they will be silent. Under resulting chaos, within 5 or 6 years Portugal might find it too costly in lives and money to maintain its presence in Africa. Such an event would be catastrophic for all of us.

Salazar thanked Ball for frank reactions to Portuguese paper, but questioned some interpretations. Responded along following lines:

1. Portuguese did not exclude independence from consideration of self-determination. He said that the greatest difficulty was that the Africans, within a certain time limit, are not in a position to opt for anything of substance. If allowed to develop peacefully, everything was possible, including independence.

2. Portuguese believed their presence, influence and interests cannot continue in Africa without political link between metropole and overseas territories. Said link between French and British and their former colonies depended on funds available to be expended in now independent countries to maintain link. Previously he had indicated Portugal has no such resources.

3. Cited large Negro majority in Mozambique and Angola, predicting that eventually electoral lists would reflect this situation. If multi-racial society could proceed in peace, should be possible for whites to vote for blacks and blacks for whites. If not, racists would take over and whites would be excluded from government. Portuguese system was to require minimum of education or some economic position before allowing people to enter electoral rolls. Under this system, would take some time for reversal of majority on rolls to take place. On the other hand, if Portugal proceeded with any other system, the new self-governing territories would fall into the hands of a dozen leaders very quickly and the electorate would vote for something they did not understand. Would be impossible to expand electoral lists quickly without prejudice to the future of Angola; Angola could not remain as a unit if lists expanded quickly, even with UN forces there, but would be quickly divided on tribal basis into "many Katangas." Portugal still defends its desires to continue multi-racial society in which best people will be chosen to run; in Africa now only the African is chosen.

4. While he understood US preoccupation with the fate of moderate leaders in Africa, before US or Portuguese could take action, there would be no more moderates left. Cited recent plot against Houphouet-Boigny, and ouster of Youlou, saying this would happen to all moderates as long as natives believe they must have democratic system without preparation. Said populations of countries where moderates are in control are being poisoned by vicious elements, including Com-

munists, while extremists (Nkrumah, Nasser, and Ben Bella) hold complete power in their countries. While US stressed necessity of having support of moderate elements, he could reply only that soon they would not exist. Portuguese consider extremism has no roots among great majority of African peoples but was caused by small number of agitators. If there were true spirit of national independence, would not be possible for army of 40-thousand to resist more than 4-million. Portuguese considered most African peoples perfectly in accord with Portuguese position. Claimed Holden Roberto would not live for five minutes after arriving in Angola.

Salazar acknowledged that he was a conservative—a reactionary—who believed all South America had become independent earlier than it should have and that the US was now suffering the consequences of this premature independence. He asked what we could expect in Africa which was two-to-three-hundred years behind South America. He opined that, if present trends continued, Africa would either return to the jungle or be recolonized—he saw no escape from these consequences.

Salazar understood Ball had reacted only to brief study of Portuguese paper and hoped he would give Portugal his views after careful study. Expressed his gratitude to President for sending Ball to carry on discussion with Portuguese. Under Secretary assured Salazar he would give careful study to paper and to Prime Minister's views which had been helpful in clarifying paper. Said problem was a serious matter for the US which he would discuss with President Kennedy and Secretary Rusk. Expressed appreciation of the President and himself for Salazar's kindness in giving him so liberally of his time. It was agreed US and GOP would continue these discussions in Washington when Foreign Minister comes to US for UNGA sessions.

Rusk

359.   Memorandum of Conversation

Washington, September 12, 1963.

SUBJECT

Ambassador Anderson's Meeting with The President

PARTICIPANTS

The President

George W. Anderson, Ambassador to Portugal

At 10:30 on Thursday, 12 September, I called on the President in anticipation of my departure for Lisbon as United States Ambassador to Portugal.

The President stressed the importance and the difficulties incident to this position at this particular time, complicated as the relations between the two countries are over the Portuguese situation in regard to Africa. The President pointed out the importance of the Azores Base to United States security at this time and the overall position of the United States in regard to the African countries. He stressed the trend of world events which made it necessary in his opinion for the Portuguese to take a positive and affirmative attitude which could be supported by the United States in the United Nations.

I indicated to the President that I recognized the difficulties and the challenge of this particular assignment. I expressed the feeling that in advocating our position to the Portuguese, we were not without assets in our efforts to convince them the change is indeed necessary. The first of these assets is a strong moral position which should have some impact on the Portuguese because basically they are a people who recognize high spiritual values. Secondly, the force of world opinion which will progressively leave the Portuguese in a position of isolation which certainly should have its effect hopefully to the point of transcending their strong emotional considerations. Thirdly, the apprehension that unless the Portuguese do take action leading to self-determination, the inevitability of brutal conflict in Africa which will lead not only to the destruction of property but the loss of many lives of Portuguese people. I also stressed the point that in the event it was possible for the Portuguese to take a position which the United States could fully support in the United Nations and in the World Forum, the Portuguese should know that the United States would use its influence and position to prevent terrorism within the Portuguese territories from being supported from bases in adjacent African states.

Source: Department of State, Central Files, Pol Port–US. Confidential. Drafted by Anderson on September 13 and approved by the White House on November 19.

The President inquired whether policy would permit me to travel in Africa. I informed him that this was my intention at the earliest practical time provided that it meets the approval of Secretary Rusk. I pointed out that the Portuguese themselves and the Assistant Secretaries in the Department felt that this would be extremely valuable. Hence, it was my hope to make an extensive visit to these critical areas during the coming fall.

I assured the President that I would give my maximum effort to support the United States policies with respect to Portugal, to maintain friendly relations with them and to persuade them that it was in their interest to take an enlightened attitude toward the African problems. The President reiterated the difficulties of the assignment particularly as it affected United States ability to retain our base in the Azores and, therefore, it was important that I submit my best judgment as to the limits the United States could go in the forthcoming discussions in the United Nations without losing the Azores. He said that he did not believe that the Portuguese really wanted us out of the Azores and certainly we wanted to stay, but we had to consider the total picture including the attitudes of all of the African countries. The United States had to use its best influence to support the moderate elements in Africa and to restrain the more radical ones.

The meeting concluded at approximately 1100.

---

360. Editorial Note

Following his return to the United States Ball reviewed his conversations with Salazar and Nogueira with the President and Secretary of State. In light of these discussions, on October 17 he drafted a letter to Salazar to continue the dialog begun in Lisbon. Copies of the draft were sent to Bundy, Williams, Tyler, and Rusk for comments. Following minor drafting changes, the letter, which comprised 15 pages and expounded at length on the U.S. view of the transformation taking place in Africa, was sent to Salazar. A copy of the draft letter is in Department of State, Central Files, Pol 10 Port; a copy of the letter as sent is in the Kennedy Library, National Security Files, Portugal.

On February 27, 1964, Salazar replied, reiterating his position as summarized in his conversations with Ball in Lisbon. (Department of State, Central Files, Pol Port-US) For Ball's account of this correspondence, see *The Past Has Another Pattern*, pages 279–282.

361.   Telegram From the Department of State to the Embassy in Portugal

Washington, November 9, 1963, 3:43 p.m.

318. Following FYI only. Based uncleared memcons and subject amendment on review memcons.

During Nov 6 and 7 visit to Washington, Portuguese FonMin received by Under Secretary, Secretary and President.[1] On Nov 7 he addressed National Press Club and answered questions. In these conversations FonMin repeatedly stressed following points:

(1) Difference in attitudes of moderate Africans in private talks with Nogueira and in their public statements. Privately moderates willing to admit that what Portugal said in New York was satisfactory and that Portuguese claims of good conditions in African territories were valid. They did not hesitate criticize extremists such as Ben Bella. In public, however, they dominated by extremists, who insisted only their point of view acceptable.

(2) Lack of Portuguese surprise at communiqué issued Nov 6 by African group in UN. Communiqué reflected extremism of radicals and showed Africans continued insist only independence acceptable as outcome self-determination.

(3) Disadvantages of premature independence as conducive to communism in Africa and detrimental interests of people.

(4) Disagreement on urgency of situation and on premise that tidal wave running in Africa. If so, it is only because US supports it. A timetable not possible. One starts with period of 10 years and ends up with 10 months.

(5) Stability, both political and economic, in Portuguese African territories. Situation far more encouraging than 2 years ago.

(6) Unlikelihood that Africans could in final analysis turn to Sovs for help. Latter could not support burden.

(7) Unjustified nature Congolese charges of Portuguese planning aggression. US should tell Congo (Leopoldville) its fears groundless. Portugal would continue try to be patient.

(8) Consonance between program outlined in talks with Africans and self-determination. Was not self-determination result of such things

---

Source: Department of State, Central Files, Pol 7 Port. Confidential. Repeated to USUN, Luanda, and Lourenco Marques.

[1] Memoranda of Nogueira's conversations with Ball and Rusk on November 6 are ibid., Secretary's Memoranda of Conversation: Lot 65 D 330; a memorandum of the conversation with the President on November 7 is ibid., Presidential Memoranda of Conversation: Lot 66 D 149.

as increased franchise, elections, plebiscite, acceleration of economic development plans and education?

(9) Adoption by Portugal of US definition of self-determination. However, Portugal refused to accept African definition, i.e., that only one option—independence—is possible.

Under Secretary stressed advantages to Angola of UN presence in Congo. Re self-determination, said full range of options needed together with recognition of right of majority rule and freedom of choice in form of government. Emphasized need to compress and telescope time to accommodate great rush of events of modern world. Ten years with urgent educational program would seem be maximum period for creation conditions necessary to exercise self-determination. Secretary pointed out value of words "self-determination" and urged Portuguese champion them.

President agreed US bore some responsibility in Security Council matters and said this was reason we interfered to extent we do in Portuguese affairs. We have been attempting find a way in which we can be more helpful to Portugal. FonMin's optimism re conditions in African territories and problems regarding timing showed we not in complete accord. We did agree that in exercise of self-determination all options should be open. Anticipating UN debate and resolution, President said we shall exert moderating influence and try make the resolution as restrained as possible. We will keep in close touch with Portuguese. President pointed out this debate likely to be difficult, for discussion such issues in UN becoming more extreme.

Full memcons pouched when cleared.

Rusk

362.   Memorandum of Conversation

US/MC/9   Paris, December 16, 1963.

UNITED STATES DELEGATION TO THE THIRTY-SECOND
MINISTERIAL MEETING OF THE NORTH ATLANTIC COUNCIL
Paris, France, December 16–18, 1963

PARTICIPANTS

United States	Portugal
William R. Tyler [1]	Franco Nogueira, Foreign Minister

SUBJECT

US–Portuguese Relations

At lunch today, and again at dinner, Foreign Minister Nogueira expressed himself with great bitterness with regard to the role and attitude of the United States Government in the recent Security Council session in New York. He said that the resolution[2] was worse than the previous one of July 31. He rejected all attempts to persuade him that on the contrary it had represented progress in the direction of moderation, and by keeping open the possibility of renewing talks with the Africans. He complained specifically that Ambassador Yost had been much more forthcoming in his remarks addressed to the African representatives than when he mentioned the Portuguese Foreign Minister. He also complained that Ambassador Yost had volunteered the statement that the United States had not sold any arms to Portugal and would not do so in the future, but had omitted to ask that no one should sell arms to the terrorists who were training on the soil of the Congo. He railed against the United States for insisting on the return of the F–86's from Portuguese Guinea.

I have never known Nogueira to speak more bitterly than he did to me on these two occasions. Several times he made allusions to (a) a review which the Portuguese Government was undertaking of its relations with the United States and its own position in relation to the Alliance, and (b) to the Portuguese Government having come to the end

---

Source: Department of State, Conference Files: Lot 66 D 110, CF 2354. Secret. Drafted by Tyler on December 17.

[1] Tyler was in Paris for the North Atlantic Council meeting.

[2] For text of the resolution on territories under Portuguese administration, December 11, see U.N. doc. S/5481; printed in *American Foreign Policy: Current Documents, 1963,* pp. 161–162.

of its patience with regard to the Congo. He hinted that his government was considering taking measures to put an end to the present situation which permitted terrorists to operate with impunity from the soil of the Congo. While he was not specific, I inferred that the Portuguese Government is considering armed action.

At the end of the evening, Ambassador de Staercke, in conversation with the Secretary, discussed Foreign Minister Nogueira's state of mind, and said that he also had never known him as violent or bitter. He said Nogueira had also told him that the Portuguese Government had come to the end of its patience and was contemplating some form of military action in the Congo. De Staercke said he had warned Nogueira emphatically of the consequences to Portugal of any such course of action. de Staercke said that Nogueira had asked him if he would come to Portugal and see the Prime Minister (whom de Staercke knows very well) some time soon, but de Staercke was not certain whether it would be desirable for him to go in view of the Portuguese Government's state of mind.

Spain

363. Memorandum of Conversation

Washington, February 7, 1961.

SUBJECT

US-Spanish Relations

PARTICIPANTS

The Secretary
Ambassador Mariano de Yturralde y Orbegoso, Spanish Embassy
Mr. Robert H. McBride, WE

Ambassador Yturralde said that he was going to Spain on consultation for the primary purpose of giving his views regarding the attitude of the new Administration on the relations between the United States and Spain. The Ambassador said that for the past ten years, approximately, relations had been steadily improving and had become excellent. He said that Spain had been very well satisfied with developments in general over the past years and referred to the economic progress made as a result of the stabilization program in which US and international agencies had all been most helpful. Ambassador Yturralde said that there had been some controversy in Spain since the election and some feeling of uncertainty and insecurity both in business and in the Government as to the attitude which the new Administration might adopt toward Spain.

In response to the Secretary's query as to why this feeling had developed in Spain, the Ambassador said that Spanish opinion and the press still remembered that President Truman had made remarks which were critical of Franco. He referred to the fact that in 1946 the United States had gone along with the Polish initiative in the United Nations.[1] This had been a bad moment for Spain, he continued. He said that the Spanish public had attributed the change in US policy to the advent of the Eisenhower Administration but he said he realized that this was not entirely correct since the base agreements signed in 1953[2] were the result

---

Source: Department of State, Central Files, 611.52/2–761. Confidential. Drafted by McBride and approved in S on March 8.

[1] Regarding the Polish initiative in the United Nations in 1946, see *Foreign Relations,* 1946, vol. V, pp. 1062 ff.

[2] For text of the Defense Agreement signed at Madrid September 26, 1953, see 4 UST 1895.

of negotiations which had been initiated in 1951. He said that while he thought Spanish opinion had its facts somewhat mixed up, the feeling did exist. Ambassador Yturralde then said that Spanish opinion had noted that the new Administration had made appointments of certain individuals who had been adverse to the national regime in Spain. This led the Ambassador to a discussion of what he said was the very widespread support for Franco in Spain. He said that in effect Franco was supported by all those who wanted law and order and that only a small minority of youths who had not lived through the civil war were opponents of the regime.

Ambassador Yturralde then described the evolution of the Franco regime in the social and economic fields. He also said that he himself had reported he did not believe there was justification for the nervousness which was now felt in Madrid with regard to the new Administration. However, he said it would be helpful if he could take back personal reassurances from the Secretary.

The Secretary said he did not think he could attach much importance to the fact that our relations with Spain happen to develop favorably particularly during the Republican Administration. He said that he himself had lived through the earlier period of our relations with Spain and he felt that the difficult relationship which we had had with that country was more a result of strong antipathies among the other Western European countries, with whom we were allied, to Spain than through the existence of the independent US policy. The Secretary said that many people in Western Europe had reacted extremely strongly against the Franco regime. The Secretary felt that as Spain's relations in Western Europe had improved, relations with the United States had likewise become better. The Spanish Ambassador inquired if the Secretary did not think that perhaps the reverse sequence had been the case. The Secretary thought there might be some truth in this but that our relations could only really have developed favorably with Spain after Spain had passed a certain threshold with the other Western European countries. The Secretary said he thought it was probably not correct to attribute the evolution of US policy to changes of administration here.

The Secretary then said the new Administration was of course interested in the economic and social revolution all over the world. We wanted to improve the standard of living, education facilities, etc., everywhere. This was in the oldest United States tradition and it was essential to meet the Soviets on this battleground. We must put ourselves in touch with the revolutionary tradition which was in our own traditions as well. The Secretary did not believe that this had any direct bearing on our relations with Spain. He said our objective was to assist people in their development everywhere. The Secretary said on this point that he thought our relations with Spain would remain friendly and cooperative at the government level and that the Ambassador should not communicate any note of anxiety to his Government.

Ambassador Yturralde said that he thought the economic and social goals of Spain and the United States were similar and that the present regime in Spain was making a great effort to raise the standard of living, particularly in the lower classes. The Ambassador thought that he should point out that the Spanish were an extremely proud and touchy people and that it was for this reason perhaps that some anxiety had developed. He noted that any attempt to put pressure on Spain had always been counterproductive.

The Secretary then remarked that we did not necessarily intend to issue any public statements on our relations with Spain or a large number of other countries. He thought that perhaps there had been a tendency to issue too wide a variety in the past and that thus far we had attempted to limit our statements to the most obvious crises situations. The Secretary concluded that he did not see any reason to believe that there would be any change in the direction of US policy towards Spain. As an example of our cooperation with Spain he noted that we had assisted in getting the numerous Spanish passengers off the *Santa Maria*.[3]

---

[3] See footnote 2, Document 342.

---

364.   Letter From the Ambassador to Spain (Lodge) to Secretary of State Rusk

Madrid, March 10, 1961.

DEAR MR. SECRETARY: Before completing my duties as American Ambassador to Spain, one of the main tasks I set for myself was the preparation of the enclosed memorandum[1] containing my colleagues' and my latest thinking on one of the most important aspects of our task here as we see it—i.e., the future of US-Spanish relations. I am sending you a copy in the hope that you will give it consideration in formulating your views and policy in regard to Spain.

Source: Department of State, Central Files, 611.52/3–1061. Secret.

[1] Not printed.

As I wrote to Secretary Herter last December,[2] our relations with Spain have prospered greatly since our agreements were signed in 1953. They have prospered with the government, and they have also prospered with the people, who in general seem to have a natural affinity for "North Americans" just as most of us do for them. The big problem we still have to wrestle with is, of course, what will happen to our relations with Spain when Franco goes, and what we can do now to assure the best possible future in that respect.

Our paper comes up with some hard realities, which in our view need to be faced frankly. Some of these are: [7-1/2 *lines of source text not declassified*] will probably be more democratic but at the same time less friendly to the US than Franco has been for the very reason that, being more democratic, it will include and give expression to anti-US elements (i.e., many elements which are anti-Franco are also anti-US); 3) that while democracy as we know it does not seem practicable for Spain now, the development here of a stable form of government with a capacity for continuity is urgent [2 *lines of source text not declassified*] our main objective, which must be, as we see it, the furtherance of American national security, in the interests not only of the entire non-communist world of which we are the leader but also of the future of democracy itself.

I trust you will find this paper of interest and value. It has the unanimous support of the Country Team here in Spain.

I hope very much that when I am in Washington in a few weeks for debriefing I shall have the pleasure of seeing you.

With kind personal regards,

Respectfully,

John Lodge

---

[2] Not further identified.

365. Letter From the Deputy Chief of Mission in Spain (McBride) to the Acting Assistant Secretary of State for European Affairs (Tyler)

Madrid, September 1, 1961.

DEAR BILL: Many thanks for your letter of August 15.[1] I quite understand how you must be swamped these days.

We have given some further thought to the question you raise of a Don Juan visit to the United States—especially balancing as you suggested the problem of Franco's possible reaction against our possible future interests in Don Juan—and I must say that if we could see how such a visit would in any way advance US interests, we would probably be for it. However, we don't see that it would lead to any such benefit; and it might damage the interests of both the US and Don Juan with Franco, and possibly with Don Juan's standing also with some of the Spanish opposition (as we said in our despatch).[1]

If and when Don Juan raises the matter again—as he may with Burke,[2] perhaps—we think he should be told that of course he can go to the US at any time, and that many people in Washington would be interested in seeing him if he goes, though I think we would hope to avoid any commitments from the very top in this connection. We might also suggest that he might also be asked whether he has considered what effect such a trip might have on his standing with Franco and with certain Spanish opposition groups. Of course, if he insists that he wants to go in spite of this, it would be difficult to put him off without risk of offending him.

As for Franco's possible reaction to such a visit, I suppose that no one can really foretell how Franco would react, not only because he characteristically keeps his thoughts very much to himself, but also because to some extent his reaction might depend on the amount and nature of the publicity attendant upon the visit. It should be borne in mind that, although the new administration has certainly not indicated that there has been any change in US-Spanish policy, no top level US official except for the military has yet officially visited Spain (Secretary of the Navy Connally was here in July and Secretary of the Army Stahr is due in November) while several anti-Franco Spanish personalities (Prieto,

---

Source: Department of State, Central Files, 752.00/7–161. Secret; Official–Informal. Initialed by Tyler. The source text bears the following notation: "Mr. Blue, What *can* we do about promoting a high-level visit to Spain? Do you think Secretary Hodges would be willing to stop off there for a couple of days? Bill 9/12/61."

[1] Not found.

[2] C. Burke Elbrick, U.S. Ambassador to Portugal.

Madariaga,[3] Tomas) have been received on various levels in Washington, and, hence, the atmosphere here is more sensitive than usual to our activities in regard to Spanish affairs. Therefore, if, in addition, Don Juan, whose position is so sensitive and anomalous, were to go to the United States in the near future, Franco might very well be seriously annoyed, and that could entail some risk for our interests here.

We shall be sending you a despatch, in response to your letter of August 11,[4] on the post-Franco outlook which will shed some further light on the factors involved in this question of a Don Juan visit. Please also see our telegram 111, July 28, 1961.[5] In view of all these considerations, we would hope on balance that Don Juan's visit would not take place, at least for some little time yet.

On the whole question of visits by high-level civilians, which is mentioned above, this was raised with me in a letter from Bill Blue on August 8,[6] and I agree with what I take it is his view that it may well be difficult to continue to maintain the kind of atmosphere we need to protect our security interests here without some visits of this kind apart from the purely military which, while welcome here, do not have the same connotation. As you know, the Ambassador thought Robert Kennedy's visit would be useful, and he made an effort to get Senator Fulbright to Madrid, which also fell through. I really think the Department should be making an effort to mount such a visit when possible, but giving us sufficient time to lay it on properly. Yturralde we know has been trying to sell this on his own, and it would, of course, be embarrassing for the Government to raise with us here officially, but they may well be very concerned by the absence of such manifestations. The Ambassador may have further views for you on this subject.

On the further question in your letter about whether, in connection with Angola, we can count on the Spanish to push the Portuguese along or whether they will stiffen the Portuguese against us, I would say that the Spanish are aware that the Portuguese have got to make changes and may even lose out entirely in Angola. But as a Spanish official told us the other day, when their neighbor's house is on fire they are not going to pile wood on it. And there is the further factor, pointed out by Burke that the Portuguese are particularly sensitive to efforts by us to press the Spanish into trying to influence them to accept our views. I think it is important that we keep the Spanish informed as we go along, [1 line of source text not declassified].

---

[3] A memorandum of Madariaga's conversation with L. Dean, Officer in Charge of French-Iberian Affairs, Department of State, on May 25, is in Department of State, Central Files, 611.52/5–2561.

[4] Neither found.

[5] Telegram 111, July 28, reported that the Spanish political scene was marked by political quiet and economic prosperity. (Department of State, Central Files, 752.00/7–2861)

[6] Not found.

Finally, I am glad that you enjoyed your talk with Julian Marias. I find him quite stimulating and I think he both talks and writes well. I also find quite restful his balanced but rather sceptical view of both the regime here and the opposition.

Sorry this letter has been so long.

With all best wishes to you and Betsy from us both, I am

As ever,

Bob

---

366.   Telegram From the Embassy in Spain to the Department of State

Madrid, December 17, 1961, 8 p.m.

786. For S/S. Following is based on as yet uncleared memo of Secretary's conversation with Franco December 16.[1]

Discussion, which lasted more than hour and half and ranged over wide field, dealt mainly with: (1) report by Secretary on NATO Council meeting;[2] (2) relative strength of east and west in which Secretary was able reassure Franco about west's superior nuclear power; (3) cold war problems including some suggestions by Franco about western policy towards Soviet occupied countries; (4) situation within USSR and Sino-Soviet Bloc; (5) Latin America, particularly Dominican Republic, Cuba; (6) importance of western unity, and danger of it becoming divided over problems in Asia and Africa; (7) problems of Goa, Congo and Katanga; (8) future of not yet independent countries; (9) Arab world, and especially Morocco; (10) Morocco's desire for arms and related question of security of Canary Islands and Spanish African possessions (whose strategic importance to west Franco emphasized).

One interesting point unexpectedly raised by Franco was proposal that if and when US is forced out of its bases in Morocco it might usefully establish base in Spanish Sahara where Spain already has air fields, especially near El Aiun. Franco suggested this could serve same strategic purpose as bases in Morocco while avoiding political uncertainties and

---

Source: Department of State, Central Files, 110.12–RU/12–1761. Secret; Priority; Limit Distribution.

[1] In a memorandum to Rusk, dated December 1, Tyler seconded a recommendation from the Embassy in Spain that the Secretary of State visit Madrid on his way back to Washington from the NATO Ministerial Meeting December 13–15. Although Tyler proposed a 24-hour stay, Rusk agreed only to a brief stopover. (Ibid., Conference Files: Lot 65 D 366, CF 2019) A memorandum of the conversation was transmitted as an enclosure to despatch 348, December 18. (Ibid., Central Files, 110.11–RU/12–1861)

[2] See Documents 117–119.

risks arising from population concentrations near Moroccan bases since Spanish Sahara scantily populated and nomads are pro-Spain and west. Secretary did not comment on this idea.

Secretary and Franco agreed that it would be better not to supply arms to Morocco beyond reasonable needs for internal security, but Secretary said heart of problem was not whether or not Morocco would get arms but how to prevent Morocco from turning to Soviet bloc for arms and thus becoming prey to increasing Soviet penetration and influence. Franco replied that if west built dams, reservoirs and otherwise helped Morocco economically Moroccan people would be more contented and would not support demands for arms. Franco emphasized danger to west if Soviet penetration led to Soviet takeover of US bases in Morocco. Secretary agreed and said US and Spain should continue consult together on how to handle Moroccan problem as it evolves.

Re Katanga, Secretary informed Franco very energetic steps now being taken, in which President personally helping, to bring Adoula and Tshombe together to meet and said when they so agreed there would be immediate cease-fire in Katanga. Secretary stressed importance for west and Congo that Katanga not secede. Franco said that experience in Congo showed that best policy in regard certain dependent countries would be to delay granting them independence for determined period of years to allow them to prepare for it, during which time such countries might be given some form of guarantee or trusteeship. Franco did not specify any specific dependent country in this regard, but it seemed clear that he had Angola in mind.

Franco said Spain stands 100 percent with Portugal in its present difficulties. In this connection Secretary and Franco saw eye to eye on need to try to prevent India from taking military action against Goa, but when Secretary suggested that best way to secure peaceful future for Goa might be for Portugal to allow plebiscite there, Franco said trouble with this was India was infiltrating agents into Goa and trying to stir up tension there "to dress up doll," and asked why press Portugal to hold plebiscite in Goa when Soviets were not pressed to hold plebiscites in countries they occupy.

Eastern European countries were evidently much on Franco's mind. He suggested increased assurances to them by US that it still insists upon their independence and is not abandoning them. He said they represent one of major weapons in cold war which US has not used to deserved extent; and in hot war they would constitute important source of weakness and danger for Soviets which west should be prepared to exploit. He also asserted there were signs of increasingly informed public opinion in USSR which Khrushchev was having some difficulty in controlling and that US should try take fullest advantage of this by assuring such public opinion that Soviet Government, not US, is responsible for present danger of world war and that US has no enmity towards Soviet people.

Secretary welcomed these suggestions and reassured Franco about present balance of power between US and Soviet bloc (Franco had suggested that he felt time to be working against US and west since Soviet power seemed have increased greatly in recent years in relation to that of west). Secretary assured him that there was no balance or standoff between east and west in nuclear weapons in which he said US still far in lead. Franco expressed gratitude for this information and said maintenance by US of military superiority was only way to prevent war. Franco made no special comment on Secretary's presentation regarding determination of NATO to stand firm on Berlin and to more than hold its own against Soviet efforts to dominate world except to express agreement and satisfaction. But he said struggle between east and west is primarily political; Soviets have gained much by offering solution to countries which for years had found their positions hopeless and Soviet solution was convincing to many countries and people; therefore only hope in west is to offer another convincing solution preferable to Communism. While searching for this west must not let itself be divided by differences within itself over relatively minor issues.

Re Latin America, discussion of Dominican Republic evoked no significant comment from Franco, but he said US should have acted much more vigorously in Cuba as soon as Castro began expropriating US property and violating human rights. Franco said almost all world would have approved such US initiative. Secretary spoke of increasing Latin American solidarity against Castro and of his hope for important action from January 10 OAS meeting. Franco expressed doubts of efficiency of OAS due to internal weaknesses of some of its members; but he seemed more hopeful Alliance for Progress would prove fruitful. He said, however, US often makes mistakes of considering other peoples comparable to its own in discipline, intelligence and willingness to help themselves, and US should realize all peoples not equal in ability to govern themselves.

There was no discussion of any of Spain's internal problems, although Secretary complimented Franco on success of stabilization plan. Also there was no discussion of future of joint bases in Spain (except that Foreign Minister said in his luncheon toast there should be no difficulty in two countries agreeing on this subject). Atmosphere of Conference was cordial with Franco in increasingly friendly frame of mind as talks progressed.[3]

McBride

---

[3] Telegram 787, December 17, reported that the Secretary's brief visit had been "highly successful," and was most helpful to "over-all US interests in Spain." (Department of State, Central Files, 110.11–RU/12–1761)

367.   Memorandum From the President's Special Assistant (Schlesinger) to the Under Secretary of State (Ball)

Washington, January 8, 1962.

SUBJECT

The Iberian Bases

We are approaching the time when the Spanish and Portuguese bases will have to be renegotiated.

At the moment, the prevalent view seems to be that we must do almost anything necessary to retain the good will of the Franco and Salazar regimes in order not to endanger the base renegotiations.

This view has obviously altered our policy in certain respects from what it would otherwise be, not only in the Iberian peninsula, but in other parts of the world (e.g., the Secretary's Madrid statement suggesting that we are counting on Franco's Spain to play a role in connection with our Latin American policy; our agreement with Salazar not to bring up the colonial context in the UN debate over Goa). It has also hurt the public image of the State Department (cf. recent editorials in such staid journals as *The New York Times* and the *Christian Science Monitor*) and made it look to many, at home and abroad, as if the State Department were still dedicated to diplomacy a la Dulles rather than to the diplomacy of the New Frontier.

It may well be that we have no choice but to sacrifice everything else to the renegotiation of the bases. But we certainly should not accept this conclusion without a careful and critical reappraisal of the base problem. Would it not be a good idea to have a reexamination of the Iberian bases, with particular attention to the following questions:

1) Will impending changes in weaponry and strategy affect the role and value of the Iberian bases?

2) What benefits do these bases bring to Spain and Portugal? We assume that they are doing us a favor for which we must pay through the nose. Is our bargaining position really this desperate? Would not the liquidation of the bases raise economic and other problems for the host countries?

3) If the USSR were to overrun Europe, it is absurd to suppose that Spain and Portugal would be spared. They cannot hope to purchase immunity through neutrality. The bases are as much for their defense as

---

Source: Kennedy Library, National Security Files, Staff Memoranda. Secret. A copy was sent to Bundy.

for ours; and the argument that they are doing us a favor by permitting us to contribute to their own defense is not an impressive one. Yet we seem to be accepting this argument at face value

4) What alternatives are conceivable to the Iberian bases? We saw recently in the case of South Africa that certain military privileges granted to us by the Republic of South Africa were not essential, as we had assumed, but only convenient. Is this the case with Spain and Portugal? If the military were set the problem of carrying on without these bases, would they not be able to solve it?

5) How serious a price do we pay in adopting a posture of cordial association with the Iberian dictatorships? What does this cost us with the anti-Franco opposition? Does it incline them to the Communists? Does it seriously compromise our policy in other parts of the world, especially Asia, Africa and Latin America? Or are objections to these dictatorships now purely sentimental and ritualistic on the part of people whose opinions don't matter much anyway? Do most people accept pro-Franco and pro-Salazar postures as a military necessity, as they accepted aid to Yugoslavia or our wartime alliance with the USSR?

6) If the conclusion is reached that there is no alternative to the Iberian bases, can we not use our relationships with the Iberian dictatorships more purposefully to ease a transition to more liberal regimes? Can we not help bring about a larger measure of economic and social reform? And would it not be possible to do more to cushion the adverse impacts of present policies on liberal, labor, anti-colonial and other forms of disapproving opinion in other parts of the world? Cannot our relations with Franco and Salazar be, for example, correct rather than effusive?

Arthur Schlesinger, jr.[1]

---

[1] Printed from a copy that bears this typed signature.

368.   Letter From the Assistant Secretary of State for European
         Affairs (Tyler) to the Ambassador to Spain (Woodward)

Washington, June 20, 1962.

DEAR BOB: I thought I would give you an account of what went on
when Garrigues presented his credentials this morning. He spoke to the
President at some length and with great earnestness. He started by telling the President how great is his affection for the United States. He
spoke of his family here and of his long association with this country. He
said that he had accepted the post of Ambassador in Washington with
only one aim in view: to strengthen and to deepen the ties between his
country and ours. He was extremely frank, without any trace of embar-
rassment, about his own political position. He said he was not a supporter of Franco, and that he had always remained entirely independent. He
said it was for this reason he had been chosen, and that this very fact was
a certain indication that Franco intended to bring about far-reaching
changes in the social structure of Spain, which were of very great importance, and which would pave the way to a peaceful succession to his regime. Garrigues said that he had been struck by the spate of recent
articles in the American press which heralded the end of the Franco regime. He said he felt that, whatever the emotional justification for this
attitude might be, an abrupt end or collapse of the present form of government in Spain would be disastrous, not only for Spain but for the
West as a whole. He said it was most important that the peaceful
changes which had to be made in the political and social structure of
Spain would be brought about while Franco was still in power. There
was no alternate guarantee of order and stability in Spain at this time,
and the fact that Franco was disposed to prepare for his successor made
it all the more important that his efforts be viewed with sympathy and
understanding by the United States. He felt that the President's own attitude toward these problems was of the greatest importance and he
would like to be able to tell Franco that the President saw these matters
in the same light and would bring his weight to bear in a sense which
would facilitate the course of events which he had just outlined.

The President listened to all this with evident interest, asking one or
two questions here and there. I noticed that the President was careful
not to give a direct reply which constituted a message from him to
Franco through the Ambassador. The President did say that he agreed
in general with the importance of providing for an orderly and peaceful
transition to the post-Franco period, and that he would want to be helpful in this in so far as he could be. I had the impression that Garrigues

Source: Kennedy Library, National Security Files, Spain. Secret; Official–Informal.

had hoped for something more direct and more responsive to his plea for an assurance which he could convey from the President to Franco. However, all in all, I think that Garrigues made a good impression on the President, and that the latter did not mind the "unprotocolaire", directness and intensity with which Garrigues broached this burning subject in his first call on him. I feel that Garrigues is someone with whom we are going to be able to speak very frankly, and that he does indeed have a burning desire to be the architect of a Spanish-American rapprochement, which he identifies with the future of his country. I should add that he stressed the importance of Spain's approach for admission to the Common Market, initially by association, and of the renewal of the base agreement

With best wishes,

Sincerely,

William R. Tyler[1]

P.S. At one point during his talk, Garrigues showed the President a photostatic copy of a newspaper report ("ABC") of a recent speech by Franco, with a headline to the effect that the task before Spain was to effect profound changes in Spain's social structure.

---

[1] Printed from a copy that bears this typed signature.

---

369. Telegram From the Department of State to the Embassy in Spain

Washington, September 21, 1962, 4:18 p.m.

221. Spanish Ambassador saw Deputy Under Secretary Alexis Johnson Sept 19 at former's request to discuss base extension. Garrigues emphasized he not under instructions and merely wished informal exchange of views on his own initiative without commitment either government.

Source: Department of State, Central Files, 752.56311/9–2162. Confidential. Drafted by Matthews and Meloy (WE), cleared by Kitchen, and approved by Johnson.

1) Garrigues believed all three agreements (Defense and Economic and Military Aid) needed updating and renewal. Detailed negotiations required meant one year left before Sept 63 date for "renewal agreements" was not much time. On military side, weapons and situations had changed during ten years since agreements signed so that military strategy now different. Agreements should be reviewed in light changed circumstances; this necessity clearly in Franco's mind. On economic side, Spain receiving no more aid. This perhaps all right, but "miracle of Spanish recovery" unfortunately limited largely to foreign exchange reserves. Personal income for instance about same ($300 per capita) as three years ago. Spain preparing new development plan based IBRD report. Social and economic deficiencies could affect stability of present or future regime. Franco's great authority and prestige should be used to effect major controversial changes. Important that military bases under agreements rest on strong economic and social basis.

2) Garrigues stated perhaps new form of alliance necessary. Imagination should be used to think of ways to improve ten-year old agreement.

3) Johnson stated US viewed question as relatively simple matter. Of three agreements signed in 1953 only Defense Agreement had specified duration and this provided for automatic extension for two additional periods of five years each in absence notification desire to cancel. Ambassador Woodward had indicated to FonMin Castiella US wished Defense Agreement to continue and we understood this also view of Spanish Government. We therefore assumed Agreement itself would be automatically extended for additional period unaffected by fact discussions and possible modifications of Technical Annexes might be required. From US standpoint we quite satisfied with Defense Agreements and Technical Annexes as they stand. We had invited Spaniards to examine them and suggest any changes they thought desirable. With regard conduct of such negotiations as may be necessary, we agreeable to discussions Madrid or Washington, although Madrid seemed more logical, and favored use normal diplomatic channels. In response to question, said State Dept was negotiating agency for US Govt, though military and technical advisors of course would be available to us.

4) Johnson stated we agreed world strategic situation since 1953 had indeed changed. We would be glad have exchange of views with Spaniards and bring them up to date on our thinking on and assessment of world situation. With respect to military and economic aid agreements we had more than fulfilled our obligations. Relations between two countries had happily grown much closer and we are friends and allies with common interests and common problems. Therefore we be-

lieve questions military and economic aid should be considered on their own merits and without reference to base agreement. We would be glad examine Spanish economic plans in spirit helpfulness within our capacity as limited by Congress. Similarly, we would continue review with Spaniards military requirements of Spanish armed forces to meet needs of Spanish defense. However, we wished consider these matters on their merits and quite frankly we did not feel we were "buying" anything. Extension Base Agreement is matter of mutual interests and our relationship with Spain should now be one of mature mutual understanding.

5) Garrigues personally agreed to Johnson statements in 4 above but not certain his government's view. Expressed thought we can be mutually helpful to each other in many fields. For instance Spain might be helpful to US with Portugal or Latin America and US could perhaps be helpful to Spain regarding Common Market. Garrigues said he would report conversation to Ministers Finance and Commerce (who were greatly interested this subject) immediately and they in turn would promptly bring report to Franco.

Comment—Garrigues appeared surprised we regarded base renewal as divorced from economic and military assistance.

Re point 2 above Garrigues not at all specific but appears possible Franco regime may be seeking formal alliance and tangible recognition its greater acceptability internationally.

Rusk

---

370. Memorandum of Conversation

Washington, January 30, 1963, 1 p.m.

PARTICIPANTS

H.E. Antonio Garrigues, Spanish Ambassador
Mr. George C. McGhee

The Spanish Ambassador lunched with me at my request on January 30. The purpose of the luncheon was to make a response to the suggestions he had made in his call on me on December 28, which is described in a memorandum of conversation.[1]

Source: Department of State, Central Files, 375.1–3063. Confidential. Drafted by McGhee.

[1] Not found.

I started by explaining to the Ambassador that we had not taken his suggestions lightly; that our delay in responding had resulted from our desire to canvass our various embassies in the countries concerned to get their best estimate of the position in these countries with respect to Spain's entry into NATO and the Common Market.[2] We had not, in our queries, made any reference to the Ambassador's intervention. We wanted to be as helpful as we could to the Ambassador and the Spanish Government in this matter. We consider one of the obligations of a friend is to be willing to furnish objective advice on request.

I continued that there were two aspects of the problem. One was our direct relations with Spain, which fortunately had been increasingly close in recent years and which had resulted in numerous visits and contacts at various levels in our Governments and numerous cooperative endeavors apart from our use of Spanish bases.

The other aspect was Spain's relationships with Europe and European institutions. Although not ourselves a European nation, we have strong ties with Europe and have been pleased with Spain's interest in a closer association with Europe and its institutions. We are pleased with Spain's membership in OECD and impending entry into GATT. These represented important steps forward.

We are pleased to hear, if it is true, the statement attributed to a high Spanish official that Spain would not welcome an invitation on the part of France to enter into a treaty comparable to that entered into between France and Germany. I pointed out that this would be contrary to the trend in Europe and would be harmful to Spain's ultimate prospects for integration with Europe. France is not in a position to offer Spain NATO or EEC membership. Under such circumstances, a treaty with Spain comparable to that with Germany would be difficult to carry out. Spain would not be operating within the same political framework as France and Germany.

I continued that our ability to assist Spain in its relations with the European countries and institutions was necessarily limited. We have, of course, publicly declared ourselves as being in favor of Spain's entry into NATO; however, there is a limit as to how far we could push Spanish candidacy. It would not be to the advantage of Spain for us to do so in the absence of any hopes for Spain's entry.

With respect to the EEC, there was quite a different situation. Not being a member, we could not openly advocate other countries for membership. Indeed, an open position on our part would probably be

---

[2] On January 5 the Department of State had transmitted circular telegram 1174 to European missions requesting their view of the attitude of their host countries toward Spanish membership in NATO and the Common Market. (Department of State, Central Files, 375/1–563) The responses summarized here by McGhee are ibid.

counterproductive. Although we had attempted to be discreet with respect to the British candidacy, the fact that we supported England probably contributed to her rejection by France.

I then went over with the Ambassador in general terms, country by country, the evaluations which had been received from our various posts as summarized by the EUR Bureau. I indicated that the net of it seemed to be that the present was not a propitious time for Spain's entry either into NATO or the EEC. I pointed out that Spain should not be impatient; that great progress had been made in recent years and that as Spain continued to evolve toward more liberal policies and institutions, as it is currently, the matter of Spain's relationship to Europe and European institutions would take care of itself.

There were many influential countries which were for Spain's entry into both organizations—although they did not appear to believe the present to be propitious, Spain's position in Europe had changed drastically for the better in the last few years. Since the opposition to Spain came principally from the Socialist parties, centering in the low countries and Scandinavia, change in their position would probably be related to the development of the Spanish labor movement.

The Ambassador responded with considerable feeling along lines which indicated great personal and national frustration and resentment of the indignity of Spain's not being considered suitable for closer political association by the Western Nations. He frequently used the words "it is finished" to indicate that the situation had become intolerable. He resented the fact that small Scandinavian nations could block Spain's entry into NATO and that they should be in a position to pass judgment with respect to Spain's internal policies. I pointed out that since NATO and EEC operate on unanimity rule, the decision was, in the final analysis, up to the countries concerned.

He repeated the arguments given to me in previous conversations that Franco was a man of 70 and that Spain should be considered as a country of thirty million people who had much to offer Europe. In his more extreme statements, he indicated that due to liberal pressures in this country we ourselves were aloof from Spain—that we consider her only a useful bit of geography. I attempted to controvert this by disclaiming that our relations toward Spain, which had become increasingly close, were controlled by any such pressure. He deplored the fact that Europeans, although dependent on Spanish bases and defense capability for their security, were not willing to offer Spain any political association.

He had looked to such an association as furthering the evolution which was going on in Spain. Why could they not see this? I pointed out that the governments concerned were probably waiting for this evolution to progress further, before taking the politically difficult step of supporting Spain publicly.

Why should Spain continue the bases? If we could not offer any political help to Spain along the lines of his suggestion in our previous discussion, and could not because of our balance of payments problem offer anything sizable by way of economic help, there was no advantage to Spain for the continuation of the bases.

I pointed out that the bases are of benefit to Spain as well as to us, and should be so considered by the Spanish. Their continued use should not necessarily require an additional consideration as such. Our utilization of the bases had not only contributed to Spanish security but together with our other types of assistance had made an important contribution to the Spanish economy. There had not only resulted improved relations with us but a contribution to the improved attitude toward Spain on the part of many European countries. Any change in the status of the bases would serve to undo the progress made. Spain should continue to be patient and to build on this progress.

The conversation ended in a note of frustration on the part of the Ambassador. He said we must see his and Spain's problem and give him something that he can present to the Spanish Government and people as a justification for our continued use of the bases.

---

371. Memorandum of Conversation

Washington, April 25, 1963.

SUBJECT

Call on the Secretary by Spanish Ambassador

PARTICIPANTS

The Secretary	Don Antonio Garrigues,
H. Freeman Matthews, Jr.—EUR:WE	Ambassador of Spain

The Spanish Ambassador had a one hour meeting at his request with the Secretary on April 25. Garrigues said he was returning to Spain

---

Source: Department of State, Central Files, Pol Sp-US. Confidential. Drafted by Matthews and approved in S on May 9.

on May 4 and wished to be able to convey to the GOS a realistic picture of what could and could not be asked by Spain for extension of U.S. base rights. He asked whether the Secretary had any suggestions he could transmit to the Chief of State. In response to the Secretary's query how he sensed the attitude in Madrid, Ambassador Garrigues said his impression was the situation had deteriorated a little, although it was basically clear the GOS was happy with the Agreements as was the U.S. While he was not speaking under instructions and he did not know whether the GOS had made up its mind on desiderata, three points were clear:

1) Spain's status in the Atlantic Community was unsatisfactory because while Spain shared the risks as much as or more than NATO countries, it had no voice in decisions of life or death involving 30 million Spaniards.

2) Spain's political evolution was underway and he and others were vigorously defending and promoting this trend. Examples of evolution were changes in treatment of the press, of Protestants, and in control over their economy. Furthermore, at its last meeting the Council of Ministers had approved changing the jurisdiction over unspecified cases from military to civil courts. However, to maintain this evolution in the face of the bitter opposition of illiberal forces it was necessary to have signs of the success of this policy by 1) some gesture of friendship from the U.S. (in this connection Ambassador Garrigues mentioned that the President was not planning to visit Spain and that the impression had been created that this Administration was less friendly to Spain than the last) and 2) increased acceptance of Spain in the European "clubs" (EEC and NATO). (Membership in these clubs would be a guarantee of evolution.)

3) Spain's economic development and social readjustments would require outside assistance. He realized U.S. balance of payments problem was severe, but he was hopeful that some means of U.S. assistance not affecting the BOP could be found (contracts, tied loans).

Ambassador Garrigues said the Papal Encyclical's clear endorsement of internal evolution would have profound effect in Spain, but that a gesture of friendship from the U.S. was of utmost importance for evolution. In addition, he personally needed something in hand to bring back to Spain, such as a statement that the President intended to visit Spain in the future.

The Secretary said he wished to make the following informal comments. In the first place he hoped GOS would approach the forthcoming base negotiations in a positive spirit. These Agreements had been of considerable benefit over the past 10 years to *both* countries. Spain's economy and strength had been greatly improved during this period, and the U.S.-Spanish relationship had had much to do with this improvement. The U.S. had supported Spain in a number of international organizations (UN, OECD, IMF, etc.) with gratifying results for both countries. Spain's relations with other Western European countries had also improved, and knowledge of the fact of the U.S.-Spanish relationship had played a role here too. With regard to other European organizations the Secretary was not pessimistic. Finally, while it was true that 30 million Spaniards risked their lives, it was also true that 180 million American lives were in similar danger. The Secretary was sure enemies of Spain knew that when Spain was endangered the U.S. was too, and that this was understood for instance in Moscow. The Secretary concluded therefore that the Agreements had been of great advantage to Spain.

As to a Presidential visit, the Secretary did not want to go over the points already made to the Ambassador by Mr. McGeorge Bundy, but the fact was that the President had visited only two countries in Europe and was now adding only two more (Ireland was a special ancestral case). A visit now was simply not possible. As for a sign of our friendship, it was known throughout Western Europe and Latin America that the U.S. was the friend of Spain and improved Spanish relations with many of those countries was the result. However, the *Secretary would remember Ambassador Garrigues' points regarding Spain's "status", would talk to the President so he would be aware also, and would consider what could be done on that score.*

The Secretary continued that on the economic side Spain was now better off than we were in some respects. He paid tribute to Spain's remarkable recovery. He felt that with normally available credits and Spain's economic reputation, economic development should not be a problem.

With regard to Spain's internal conditions the Secretary said we were pleased to see the direction developments were taking, that we valued the progress made and hoped to see it continue.

The Secretary concluded that over the past ten years both the U.S. and Spain have reasons to approach the forthcoming talks with a positive spirit of friendliness and frankness.

The Secretary felt Ambassador Garrigues should know that the USSR was currently facing many problems—internal political, economic, and with the Bloc and the Chinese. We would be going through a rather severe period in the next few months while the USSR was reappraising its policy. It was of the utmost importance that the solidarity of the West be maintained in this period, lest the Soviets make some dangerous decisions.

Ambassador Garrigues again returned to Spain's "status" in the Atlantic Community and referred to a Sulzberger article regarding "a Maltese Formula for Spain" (association with NATO). Some way must be found to include Spain in the councils of the West and evidence of U.S. friendship must also be shown. The Secretary asked the Ambassador if a Gallup Poll were held in Spain what country Spanish people would pick as their best friend, aside from the special case of Portugal. Ambassador Garrigues said there was no doubt the U.S. would be the choice up to now, followed by Germany and thirdly by France. The Secretary said similarly he was sure some 45 of any 50 Foreign Ministers would say the U.S. was Spain's best friend. Thus U.S. friendship was an evident fact and not something under the bed or in the closet. We have shown our friendship to all the world and do not need to demonstrate it afresh.

Ambassador Garrigues said such amity was not evident enough lately, particularly in view of the questions of the Agreements and of evolution in Spain. Even a six-hour visit by the President would have a greatly favorable effect on our relations, and a 45-minute talk with Franco would be enough to reach complete agreement in principle on U.S. base rights, except for "technical details".

The Secretary said he had benefited from this discussion and would talk to the President about it before his departure for CENTO. The Secretary believed we should discuss the Agreements in the same spirit of frankness and cooperation that has marked their operation over the past ten years, and there would then be no difficulty. There had been a remarkable development of Spain economically and otherwise and in its foreign relations over the past ten years. The Secretary sensed the attitude of the American people toward Spain was also developing well and that the Ambassador must notice this in his travels around the U.S.

The Ambassador concluded by asking whether he perhaps could not carry back a letter from the President to General Franco regretting he could not visit Spain now but would do so later. The Secretary said the possibility of some kind of letter would be considered.

372. Memorandum of Conversation

Washington, May 3, 1963.

SUBJECT

US-Spanish Relations

PARTICIPANTS

The President
The Spanish Ambassador, Antonio Garrigues
Mr. William R. Tyler, Assistant Secretary for European Affairs

The Ambassador opened the conversation with a long statement on Spain's anti-Communism, dedication to close relations with the United States, and unhappiness at not enjoying the international status to which it felt it was entitled, both by virtue of its history and civilization, and of its contribution to Western defense. The Ambassador said that the defense agreement which was about to be renegotiated, provided a good opportunity for the United States to help Spain to meet its desires for more widely accepted international roles in the councils of the West, both politically and militarily. He said Spain was not asking the United States for money but for its support and assistance in the above mentioned respects. He said that Spain had been courageously accepting the risk involved in having US bases on its soil, and felt it was entitled to quid pro quo of strong US efforts in meeting its aspirations.

The President spoke frankly and forcefully to the Ambassador on the nature of the problem we face in relation to our defense commitments, and in the light of our adverse balance of payments problem. He said that the risk to Spain of which the Ambassador has spoken was matched by the risk to the United States and to other Western countries created by the Soviet threat. The President said we could not go on forever pouring out vast sums contributing to the security of other countries, and which have the effect of draining our reserves. Other countries must do more and face up to their responsibilities. We wanted to go on doing what we could, and were prepared to carry a heavy burden in the cause of Western security, but we could not continue forever as we had been doing in the past, incurring heavy adverse balance of payments. The President said if he had to face continuing on this basis or withdrawing US forces from Europe, he would be forced to choose the latter.

Source: Department of State, Central Files, Pol Sp-US. Confidential. Drafted and initialed by Tyler and approved by the White House on May 10. The meeting was held at the White House. On May 2 Ball had sent a memorandum to the President suggesting that he see the Spanish Ambassador for 15 minutes and convey to him an oral message for Franco. (Kennedy Library, National Security Files, Spain)

The Ambassador said that what was most needed was some evidence to his Government that US feelings towards Spain were as friendly and forthcoming as he, the Ambassador, felt that Spain had shown hers to be towards the United States. He said that it was very desirable that there be high-level visits to Spain as evidence of this attitude. The President reminded the Ambassador that President Eisenhower had been to Spain in 1960, and that Secretary of State Rusk had visited Spain as well as Ambassador Stevenson. The President disputed the idea that this Administration was cool or distant in its attitude toward Spain. He reminded the Ambassador of his own efforts in Congress in years gone by in support of the defense agreement with the United States, and of his frequently demonstrated friendly feelings toward the Ambassador's country and people.

The President said he felt sure if there was mutual good will and confidence, a basis would be found for renewing the agreement. The President added that he was personally interested in following developments with regard to the negotiations. He asked the Ambassador to convey his best wishes to the Chief of State, and to tell him of his and the Ambassador's conversation, emphasizing the interest of the United States in maintaining and promoting close, friendly and cooperative relations with Spain.

---

373. Telegram From the Department of State to the Embassy in Spain

Washington, May 9, 1963, 5:09 p.m.

833. Ambassador Garrigues called on Asst. Secy Tyler May 7 for final discussion prior returning Madrid for consultation. Meeting was to have been review of import numerous conversations Ambassador had had last two weeks with most senior USG officials, but developed during course one hour 45 minutes into curious emotional outburst by Ambassador at what he termed "cold" response of Tyler to his attempts to obtain assent to set of principles which in view of US participants would have had effect of giving Garrigues blank check on a new Defense Agreement.

Source: Department of State, Central Files, Def 15 Sp-US. Confidential; Limited Distribution. Drafted by Matthews and Meloy and approved by Tyler.

Discussion began with Garrigues' assertion that senior Pentagon official had suggested that Munoz Grandes be invited to US in very near future in his capacity as Chief High General Staff and that visit be reciprocated later by McNamara visit to Spain. Garrigues took position that Munoz Grandes could leave his higher title of Vice President at home and said he hoped receive official confirmation of invitation when he reached Madrid May 11. Tyler said we had not heard of this project, registered our doubts that such visit could be confined to purely military affair or that Munoz Grandes could leave Vice Presidential hat at home, and believed therefore any invitation would have to come from President or Vice President.

Garrigues then said that as result his many recent conversations he was pleased to have had reaffirmation of US friendship for Spain, particularly the President's assurance that there was no coolness in US feeling for Spain.

As to renewal of Agreements Garrigues described himself as honest broker and not as negotiator. Said he did not know views his Government but said his personal view was that risks Spain was taking by permitting US bases required that Spain be treated equally with any other US ally. He therefore felt Spain should be in NATO. Garrigues said President had agreed there should not be "first class" and "tourist" allies. Garrigues insisted that Spain's "status" with third countries was key point in base renewal and that US *could* do something for Spain vis-à-vis NATO, by bringing pressure on other governments, for example. He indicated belief formula could be found whereby Spain could participate lower level NATO meetings, such as day to day technical discussions. He asserted he not asking US for something it could not do.

Garrigues said that similarly means must be found to elevate bilateral US-Spanish relationship. He complained US met regularly at high level at publicly conspicuous meeting with NATO allies, and said there should be similar formal required meetings with Spain. Spain should receive same information, training, etc. as other allies. Garrigues said he could supply list 20 to 30 things other allies receive which Spain does not. He stated Spanish public opinion required this more elevated US-Spanish relationship.

Tyler summarized situation by stating that we are coming to renegotiation of base agreement in spirit of friendship and cooperation, that GOS has indicated it wishes suggest certain modifications in previously existing agreements, that we are waiting to learn from GOS nature of changes it wishes to suggest and that we will consider these proposals with GOS in most friendly and frank way. We must first know what these ideas are and are therefore eagerly awaiting specific Spanish suggestions; meanwhile it would be inappropriate for us to suggest to Ambassador what he should advise his Government to ask from US. We would welcome any specific ideas, even including what we felt was such nonstarter as Spain in NATO, and would carefully consider them. In our view detailed negotiations would take place in Madrid between GOS and Ambassador Woodward.

Garrigues then entered upon long emotional harangue, good part of it while standing as if about to leave, complaining that our offer to consider suggestions was nothing we would not offer *any* country, and that he could not carry such worthless trophy back to Madrid, particularly as he realized from his conversations here he must advise his Government that economic aid was out of the question. He went on at great length about his personal role, his year-long efforts at great personal financial sacrifice, and his utter disappointment at the cold reception he had received today at Tyler's hands (which he said was in contrast to his treatment elsewhere and on other occasions with Tyler).

Comment: Ambassador evidently hoped obtain our agreement that Spain had been treated unfairly, that present "status" was wrong, and that we were prepared in principle to enter more formal bilateral agreement and to push Spain into NATO. He reacted emotionally when he found he could not get what he wanted (and maybe felt he needed) to bear back to Madrid. He was eventually calmed down, but evident he found meeting a severe disappointment.

Rusk

---

374. National Security Action Memorandum No. 247

Washington, May 27, 1963.

TO

The Secretary of State
The Secretary of Defense

SUBJECT

U.S. Policy Toward Spain

We seem to have the Spanish Government's initial terms for renegotiating our base agreement. As reported by Embassy Madrid

---

Source: Department of State, NSAMs: Lot 72 D 316. Secret.

(Madrid's telegram 1224),[1] these include an undefined combination of military, economic and political assistance and an explicit proviso that unless the United States is prepared "to make certain concessions in various fields to Spain . . . [2] there would not be an extension of the base agreement".

Although the Franco Government clearly does not expect all it is now asking, the President desires that the base problem and the question of negotiation be looked at in their broadest contexts before we go forward with the Spanish, to determine the desirability and utility of maintaining the present arrangements in Spain, as well as the price they may be worth.

He wishes a brief review of our policy toward Spain, in terms of our relationship with the Franco Government and Spain's role in the Western European Community, and with due regard for the fact that Spain may be approaching the end of the Franco era and a succession problem.

In this connection, the President would like answers to the following specific questions:

1. To what extent are the Spanish base facilities militarily essential, rather than merely desirable, for the maintenance of the Western deterrent in the European, African, Middle Eastern areas? Specifically.

> (a) if we were to give up the Spanish bases, either with the Azores available or with the Azores no longer available, what alternative facilities could be used for such operations, as reflex, refueling, recovery, re-strike, Polaris support, communications and logistical support generally?
> (b) to what degree would our ability to respond to contingencies in North Africa and the Middle East be degraded?
> (c) how would the time factor affect these evaluations, i.e., are the bases more valuable now than they will be later or vice versa?
> (d) what effect does the strategic role of Spain's armed forces and territory have on these considerations?

2. Apart from the military considerations, is there a political need for maintaining some or all of the present bases—and through them an American military presence in Iberia at this time?

3. If some or all of the military facilities should be retained, what is the price this Government should pay in terms of military, economic and political assistance and what forms can these take? In this what would be the impact of our actions on our relations with Spain as well as outside of Spain, particularly with NATO Europe? In addition, if any of our forces are to be redeployed or withdrawn from Europe, would it be preferable to have these come from Spain, rather than from NATO?

---

[1] Telegram 1224, May 22, reported that although Franco had no preconceived idea on a quid pro quo for an extension of the Defense Agreement, he did feel strongly that Spain should receive from the United States support in the economic, military, and political fields. (Ibid., Central Files, Def 15–4 Sp-US)

[2] Ellipsis in the source text.

The President would appreciate having responses to these questions not later than June 10. On the basis of these responses he will then wish to determine our negotiating position in consultation with the Secretaries of State and Defense. He expects that there will be no discussions of the base question with Spanish officials until these problems have been considered.

McG. Bundy

---

375. Report on U.S. Policy Toward Spain

Washington, undated.

1. Review of policy toward Spain

During the ten years since the 1953 agreements were concluded with Spain, the Spanish people as well as other Europeans have become increasingly accustomed to the relationship inherent in those agreements. Most NATO countries recognize that our facilities in Spain are valuable assets in the common defense. Almost all European, African and Latin American countries have also improved their own relations with Spain during this period. In no country is criticism of our relations with Spain a serious problem in our bilateral relations with that country. Even among the Spanish opposition to Franco there is understanding of the military basis for our policy toward Franco. Continuation of our relationship with Spain for another five years, even with some concessions of a strictly military nature, would not harm our relations with third countries nor with liberal elements in Spain whose friendship would be important in the post-Franco period. However, this opinion presupposes that the relationship would continue to avoid anything which would be interpreted as indicating a markedly closer political relationship with Franco Spain.

We have been following two parallel policies during this period, (1) having close enough relations with the Spanish Government to assure Spanish cooperation in the current utilization of the military facilities, sometimes far beyond the purposes originally envisaged;

Source: Department of State, NSAMs: Lot 72 D 316. Top Secret. The source text bears no drafting information and is not dated, but it is attached to a June 16 memorandum from McNamara and Rusk to the President that states that it was in response to NSAM No. 247 (Document 374).

(2) avoiding identification as supporting the Franco regime as such, and maintaining contacts with liberal anti-Franco elements. We are placing more emphasis on the second aspect today than was the case three years ago.

While Spanish relations with other European countries have steadily improved, opposition to Franco remains strong among Socialists and labor unions. It seems clear that Belgium, Norway and Denmark would veto Spanish entry into NATO. Spanish application to associate with the Common Market is currently in abeyance. The long-run political interests of both Spain and the US would be served by closer relations between Spain and her European neighbors as well as European organizations. Such close ties would be a stabilizing factor within Spain when Franco departs, which may very well not come before 1968. [*1 line of source text not declassified*] we can not get Spain into either NATO or the Common Market in return for extension of our base rights.

2. Need for Military Facilities in Spain

This can best be covered in terms of the various functions served by our present or planned use of Spanish bases.

MATS/TAC operations: support of the Sixth Fleet: [less than 1 line of source text not declassified] communications. The picture with regard to the first three areas is essentially similar, in that bases in Spain are vastly superior to any alternatives from both a political and military standpoint. Regarding communications, there are no practical alternative locations because of geographical factors.

We envisage continuation, at least over the next five years, of normal peacetime operations by MATS and TAC at about current moderate levels. Even more significant, contingency operations in North Africa, the Middle East, and Tropical Africa, are now heavily dependent on use of Spanish facilities, which have been immediately granted to us in such past crises as the Lebanon. Although there may be future crises in which Spain would have political objections, the likelihood of this seems very much lower than for most European countries, and from an operational standpoint the southern route has major weather advantages. If we could not use Spanish bases for these purposes, our capacity to respond effectively to contingencies in these areas would be seriously degraded. It should be noted that TAC deployment operations require the continued availability of tanker support from Spanish bases.

Support of the Sixth Fleet now involves major logistics facilities at Rota and other bases. [*1 line of source text not declassified*] Removal of all these logistics facilities to any other area would entail very large gold-flow construction costs, probably undesirable concentration, and political risks.

[*1 paragraph (4 lines of source text) not declassified*]

Communications and auxillary requirements in Spanish territory have been steadily increasing, notably through the installation of a European gateway to the Mediterranean tropo-scatter system, transfer of a part of the facilities previously at Kenitra in Morocco, and a number of specialized facilities. With Morocco becoming increasingly uncertain, Spain has become crucial to continuation of adequate naval communication through the Mediterranean and to the east. [3-1/2 lines of source text not declassified] There are no practical alternative locations for the communications facilities in Spain because of geographical factors.

These requirements are substantial in terms of manpower and facilities. [2-1/2 lines of source text not declassified] We regard them as a continuing and essentially irreducible minimum of the base rights we should seek to retain in Spain.

Strategic air operations. The actual conduct of reflex operations from Spain (currently 35 B–47's) is now planned to continue at approximately the same rate until the B–47's phase-out as strategic aircraft in the first-half of 1966. In connection with considerations for early B–47 reflex force phase-out, the Air Force notes that there are serious problems existing in the strategic force [1 line of source text not declassified] which may dictate retention of B–47's in the active inventory longer than now planned. The Secretary of Defense does not believe deferrals of the phase-out of the B–47's will be necessary.

Use of Spanish bases to support reflex and [less than 1 line of source text not declassified] will be a continuing requirement. The Spanish bases support the KC–135 refueling forces [2-1/2 lines of source text not declassified]. The UK bases offer a poor alternative for refueling operations, or for emergency landings when refueling malfunctions occur, due to the high incidence of uncertain weather conditions and operational limitations associated with the UK bases themselves. Spain is well aware of these refueling operations. [3 lines of source text not declassified]

The Joint Chiefs of Staff believe that any actions which reduce or eliminate the use of the Spanish strategic air bases in the near future would impact severely on our over-all military posture and on our strategic force flexibility. These bases, with their excellent facilities (they were specifically designed and constructed for strategic operations), ideal weather conditions, and geographical location, together with the complete lack of Spanish restrictions on type of aircraft, [less than 1 line of source text not declassified] or other operational matters, provide the United States with the most flexible foreign base complex we have.

Air defense of Spain. From a U.S. standpoint, the three U.S. air defense fighter squadrons in Spain are of very limited significance for air defense. [1-1/2 lines of source text not declassified]

[3 paragraphs (26 lines of source text) not declassified]

The most feasible alternative [*less than 1 line of source text not declassified*] in light of the current political climate would be support of the second Polaris submarine squadron from the U.S. This would cause a significant reduction in the number of Polaris missiles on alert (or the time on alert for the total number of missiles on the submarines being supported from the anchorage) at a time when the U.S. is relying heavily on Polaris and the numbers of ready missiles are critical. For example:

Total Missiles				Missiles on alert (average) with anchorage			
No.		*Type*[1]		*US (Max.*[2]*)*		*US (to Med*[3]*)*	
128	(8 SSBN)	A–2	85 (67%)	62	(49%)	56	(44%)
16	(1 SSBN)	A–3	11 (67%)	9	(54%)	7	(44%)
144			96	71		63	

The significance of these differences in alert missiles will decline gradually as additional Polaris and Minuteman missiles become available. No significant decline will occur as a result of the longer range A–3 missile being introduced into operational submarines in August 1964. The advantages [*less than 1 line of source text not declassified*] over U.S. basing apply as well to the A–3 missile as to the A–2, except for the relatively small difference in alert missiles as a result of the shorter transit distance to patrols in the North Atlantic. On the other hand, although the capability to shift rapidly from a follow-on role to an alert role is reduced by U.S. basing, the missiles not on alert because of added steaming time from the U.S. still would be available for follow-on strikes.

[*6 lines of source text not declassified*] A major decision will have to be made on proceeding with the breakwater project (costing nearly $6 million) which has been held up by the Navy pending resolution of the total Spanish base rights problem.

[*1 paragraph (9 lines of source text) not declassified*]

The strategic role of Spain's armed forces and territory. The Spanish Army provides ground security for U.S. facilities, thus obviating the requirement for U.S. troops for that mission. The Spanish Air Force could assume an increasing share of the air defense role by an improvement of its capability. The Spanish Navy can contribute increasingly to the ASW capability in the adjacent areas of the Mediterranean and materially strengthen the defense of the Strait of Gibraltar. The geographic location of Spain and the nature of its terrain provide the best protected area in

---

[1] [*less than 1 line of source text not declassified*]

[2] Assuming SSBNs operate from an anchorage in northeastern U.S. to patrols in the North Atlantic. [Footnote in the source text.]

[3] Assuming SSBNs operate from an anchorage in northeastern U.S. to patrols in the Mediterranean. [Footnote in the source text.]

Europe for U.S. bases. Generally favorable weather contributes to strategic importance in peace or war by facilitating training in peacetime and the execution of flight missions in peace or war. Although Spanish armed forces constitute a potential contribution to the defense of the Free World, the major strategic importance of Spain lies in its territory.

General. The initial cost of construction of U.S. military facilities in Spain exceeded $320 million. A major value of our present base rights arrangements with Spain is the unique freedom of use of all of our facilities. Spain has allowed us to use these bases for practically any purpose the U.S. deemed necessary. This lack of restraints makes our bases in Spain particularly valuable whether in time of peace, increased tension, or war [*less than 1 line of source text not declassified*] and the staging of conventional forces for limited contingencies. In view of the essentiality of certain of our bases and the importance of the others, it would be desirable for the current base rights agreement to be renewed in its present form for another five years. Assuming the availability of acceptable alternative sites, removal of essential operations from Spain to new base facilities elsewhere would require time to negotiate new base rights agreements, construct replacement facilities and achieve an effective operational capability.

3.   *Political aspect of military presence in Spain*

We have considered that our military presence in Spain has been a stabilizing influence and would continue to be so during any transitional period or change in the present regime. [*4 lines of source text not declassified*] On the negative side, we would be caught up in any internal strife in Spain through the presence of our forces.

4.   *The price we should pay*

We have generally taken the line with Spanish officials that we want a simple extension of the 1953 Defense Agreement for five more years, as provided for in the agreement. We have asked them what changes Spain might want in the agreement and have said that we would study any Spanish suggestions. The Embassy at Madrid has not yet confirmed from any other source the allegation by Ambassador Garrigues that Franco himself holds the view that some new quid pro quo is required if Spain is to agree to an extension. We believe it would be realistic to assume that some quid pro quo will be required. Ambassador Garrigues has returned from Madrid with a letter,[4] to be delivered later

---

[4] Dated May 30. (Department of State, Central Files, Def 15–4 Sp-US) A copy of this letter was given to the Department of State on June 14. At a meeting with Rusk on June 17 the Spanish Ambassador officially delivered the letter and discussed how the negotiations on an extension of the Defense Agreement might proceed. Rusk and Garrigues agreed that the discussions would take place in Washington beginning in July with general principles and following agreement on them with technical discussions. (Memorandum of Conversation; ibid.)

this month, which we understand indicates a Spanish desire to negotiate in Washington.

Military assistance. We consider that military assistance will continue to be the basic quid pro quo for extension of our base rights. We have already informed the Spanish that we can visualize a modernization program for their armed forces, based upon their own statement in 1961 of their equipment requirements, of up to $250 million for the five-year period. We have told them that we would be prepared to furnish annual but decreasing programs of grant aid up to a total amount of $75 million over a five-year period, and in return we would expect them to purchase $175 million worth of U.S. equipment toward an offset to U.S. expenditures in Spain. This should be our position in the resumption of discussions with the Spanish even though we have clear indications that they will not agree to offset arrangements of $175 million in purchases. Since the $75 million aid was linked to the purchases of this amount, we could lower the grant aid figure if the Spanish should agree to a lower level of purchases. This would necessarily be at the expense of needed Spanish force modernization and maintenance.

As a fallback formula, in the last analysis, the Department of Defense believes that we should be prepared to offer $50 million outright, with MAP amounts above this on a 1:1 ratio to Spanish military purchases in the U.S., up to a total MAP ceiling of $100 million. In terms of new funds, any amounts arrived at under this formula could be reduced by $22 million, the amount already set aside to fund a Hawk Battalion, which would be a useful and attractive component of any MAP package.

Economic assistance. In 1961 we advised the Spanish Government in writing that because of the great improvements in their economy and in their balance of payments, we would expect Spain to look to conventional sources for any external assistance, such as the Export-Import Bank, the IBRD, and private money markets. We said that we would not expect Spain to apply for long-term low-interest rate development loans from the AID, but that we would be prepared to reconsider this position, should the Spanish economic situation deteriorate. In reply, Spain informed us that once they had developed an economic plan they would seek development loans on soft terms from us. We are not persuaded of the need to change our position. Meanwhile, the Export-Import Bank is continuing its lending program for investment projects primarily in the electric power and steel industries in Spain. Ex-Im Bank loans have averaged $35 million a year over the past four years. The IBRD is about to undertake its first loan to Spain. U.S. private investment in Spain is increasing and has amounted to $50 million during the past three-year period.

While we have had extensive Public Law 480 Title I sales programs in Spain in the past, Spain is no longer considered to be eligible for such concessional sales in view of its balance of payments position and its commercial purchases from the U.S. Spanish foreign exchange reserves have remained stationary at $1 billion over the past six months, and about half of the reserves have been converted to gold. While the Spanish Government predicts a decline in reserves; the short-term outlook is for a further increase arising from the tourist season.

Political concessions. Ambassador Garrigues is anxious to get further international recognition for Spain through some new arrangement with the U.S. and it would appear that his Government has given him a free hand to try, although the Foreign Minister may remain dubious that we will offer any political concessions. A Mutual Defense Treaty would be undesirable from our viewpoint, in terms of its political effect both outside Spain and on anti-regime elements inside Spain. An executive agreement is likewise to be avoided if possible, although this would be less significant than a treaty, if confined to consultation on purely military matters. Any new arrangement should shy away from political connotations. Even if we entered into a military consultative arrangement, we should expect that the Spanish Government would give it maximum publicity, in order to serve its own political ends. The question remains whether we would discuss the defense of Spain in any military consultative arrangement.

From the foreign policy viewpoint, joint military planning with Spain would be undesirable. As a practical matter any discussions relating specifically to the defense of Spain would appear to be unrealistic: in the event of general nuclear attack the full weight of the U.S. would be involved; in a situation short of nuclear attack, NATO defenses would be fully engaged in the defense of Europe against Soviet attack before it became a threat to Spain. The U.S. should not become involved in defense problems relating to Spanish territories in Africa; we should instead be prepared to tell Spain to consult with its neighbors regarding area defense questions involving possible attack from other than Soviet sources. At the same time, we should continue to work together with Spain in such naval questions as ASW defense against Soviet submarines in the Western Mediterranean. With the withdrawal of U.S. aircraft from Spain, air defense discussions would appear to be even less practical, and the purpose to be served by any such joint discussions would have to be examined in light of the changing situation in Spain.

376. Telegram From the Embassy in Italy to the Department of State

Rome, July 2, 1963, 6 p.m.

23. Following message was cleared by Mr. Tyler prior to his departure from Rome:

"Spanish Foreign Minister Castiella called on me yesterday. We had general, cordial conversation lasting 3-quarters hour.

About base agreements Castiella said he felt sure we could reach understanding. It was agreed talks should continue mainly between Garrigues and Tyler. I added I would also give matter my attention from time to time and hoped he would continue to do so with Ambassador Woodward. I said US has no new questions to raise. Castiella commented talks had been slow in getting started. I said perhaps President's trip to Europe had contributed to this. I hoped things would now progress more rapidly. We looked forward to getting specific views and requests from Spanish side. Castiella said Garrigues would shortly have specific instructions to put forward Spanish position.

He said from Spanish standpoint most important matter was to clarify some 'basic principles' involved. These more important than any particular economic or military details. Spain did not want to bargain or ask for anything US could not give. Spain wanted above all to be given 'equal treatment' with other nations participating in Western defense even though Spain is not a member of Atlantic alliance.

He said risks had increased, Soviet propaganda not letting Spanish people forget this, situation now different than in 1953 and constantly evolving. Spain was not afraid of such threats, but in return for cooperation dignity of Spanish people, not just that of any government or regime, required recognition of risks being taken. Castiella said he saw Don Juan in Rome yesterday and he shared this view.

On risks I reminded him US has one million men overseas, takes casualties every week from Communist action. I observed US has almost no bilateral problem with USSR. US is involved in such efforts and risks because it is helping defend free world countries wherever threatened with Communist attack. Castiella said Spain had shown its good will by going beyond texts of agreements in acceding promptly to US

Source: Department of State, Central Files, Def 15 Sp-US. Secret; Priority; Limit Distribution. Repeated to Madrid, Paris, and Rabat. On June 23 the Spanish Ambassador to Italy had urged that during the President's trip to Europe, June 23–July 2, some contact be made between high-level Spanish officials and appropriate U.S. officials at a mutually convenient place. (Telegram 2812 from Rome; ibid., Pol Sp-US) In subsequent exchanges of telegrams a meeting in Rome on July 2 was arranged.

requests, for instance at time of Lebanon crisis and for missile tracking station in Canary Islands. I said this true, both countries had acted in same spirit, each doing more than required to do under terms of agreements. I also said when I was last in Madrid I had given General Franco information about the strategic situation which we had shared with the chiefs of state of only about six countries. We thought General Franco was entitled to this because of the bases in Spain. This led to general expressions of basic good will by Castiella.

Mr. Tyler asked Castiella to tell Garrigues to feel free at any time to take up his problems with him informally. Castiella said Garrigues would shortly give Mr. Tyler an outline of the basic principles Spain is concerned about.

Rest of conversation dealt briefly with following:

(1) Castiella said he had seen Pope Paul who very cordial. Castiella claimed Pope regretted prominence given last winter to his telegram to Franco asking clemency for Spanish student. Castiella said Pope realized his telegram based on misinformation.

(2) Castiella said economic and social progress of Spain is rapid and should make major gains in next five years. One obstacle might be attempts from abroad at interference in Spain's internal affairs. Castiella alleged US trade unions were among those involved in this.

(3) Castiella said King of Morocco would shortly visit Madrid for meeting with Franco. In spite of difficulties, Spain's relations with Morocco were generally good as they were with rest of Africa. De Gaulle had suggested that France, Spain and Morocco were Atlantic countries with many common interests and should try to work closely together. Castiella had been glad to welcome Assistant Secretary Williams recently in Madrid.

It was agreed that if press learned of our talks we would simply say that we had had a general tour d'horizon. If asked we would say that there of course had been some general discussion of the base agreements question but that our discussions on this subject were going on through normal diplomatic channels. Rusk."

Williamson

377. Memorandum of Conversation

Washington, August 30, 1963.

SUBJECT

U.S.-Spanish Relations

PARTICIPANTS

United States

Mr. U. Alexis Johnson, Deputy
    Under Secretary
Mr. William C. Burdett, EUR
Mr. E. J. Beigel, WE
Mr. Frank Ortiz, WE

Spanish Embassy

Ambassador Antonio Garrigues
Minister Emilio Garrigues
Mr. Nuno Aguirre de Carcer
Mr. Juan Duran-Loriga

Mr. Johnson opened the meeting by saying that the memorandum submitted by the Ambassador on July 22[1] had been carefully studied within the U.S. Government, and that he was prepared to give a reply on behalf of the Government. He said that while he would not specifically respond to all of the points in the memorandum, he could assure the Ambassador that the U.S. has taken into account the philosophy expressed in the memorandum. He said that we are prepared to issue a new and significant statement marking our unique relationship with Spain. We have prepared such a document in an endeavor to be responsive to Spanish views.

Mr. Johnson went on to say that in addition to this proposed joint political declaration we would also like to propose an exchange of notes establishing a formal joint Consultative Committee on Defense Matters, to be located in Madrid, in which the United States Ambassador and any other high officials we agree upon could also participate.

Mr. Johnson handed the two drafts[2] to the Ambassador.

Ambassador Garrigues said that in his view the documents contained many positive things in line with the thinking he had expressed. He asked how the proposed declaration would relate to the Defense Agreement.

Mr. Johnson said that the declaration would be in addition to and on top of the Defense Agreement. He said that the two proposals are de-

---

Source: Department of State, Central Files, Pol Sp-US. Secret. Drafted by Beigel and approved in G on September 5.

[1] Not found, but an undated summary of this 64-page memorandum indicated that its principles would have committed the United States to assist Spain in a number of ways. (Ibid., Def 15–4 Sp-US)

[2] Neither printed. Except for minor drafting changes, the declaration and exchange of notes are the same as those signed on September 26. For texts, see Department of State *Bulletin*, October 28, 1963, pp. 686–687.

signed to deal with the matters raised by the Spanish Government in about the only way and to the extent that we believe possible. He said that we had carefully considered both the form and the language and had gone as far as practicable.

Mr. Aguirre de Carcer wondered whether the documents were not similar to the security treaty with Japan and the consultative arrangements with Japan.

Mr. Johnson replied that the documents do not follow any other arrangements, and are intended to provide for mutuality at the political and military levels. He said that the political declaration should be studied carefully, that the language had been carefully weighed in the drafting, and was of considerable significance.

Mr. Aguirre de Carcer said that with regard to political consultations the Department certainly keeps the Spanish Embassy well informed, and he cited recent consultations on the Secretary's trip to Moscow, the Test Ban Treaty, and developments in Haiti. He said that it may be desirable to formalize these political consultations as well as the military consultations. He went on to say that it was of some importance that the reference to "a threat to either country" in the proposed declaration was not limited to threats only of certain specific origins. He added that Spain would also have proposals to make about some of the bilateral technical agreements subsidiary to the Defense Agreement, with a view to adapting them to the pattern existing between the U.S. and the NATO countries.

Mr. Johnson said that we would be glad to receive any specific suggestions that the Spanish Government may have in this regard. He recalled that he had already indicated the U.S. satisfaction with the present terms of the technical and procedural agreements.

Ambassador Garrigues said that the U.S. appeared to have in mind a political declaration on top of the Defense Agreement, to which certain consultative machinery is to be added. He referred to "political, military and economic relations" at the beginning of the proposed declaration and asked what we thought about the economic side.

Mr. Johnson said that in this connection he had reviewed the appendix submitted by the Ambassador on August 27[3] and that he would be glad to comment on it although the appendix would be subject to further study.

Mr. Johnson said that with regard to the suggestion of new PL 480 programs, it should be clear that such sales are made when countries have poor balance of payments positions or are not otherwise able to finance imports of these surplus agricultural commodities through nor-

---

[3] Not found.

mal commercial financing. He said that neither of these situations prevails any longer in the case of Spain and further agreements are not justified.

Mr. Johnson said that the intent of the statement at the top of page 2 of the appendix was not clear to us. He went on to say that in so far as AID is concerned, it was made clear to the Congress in testimony last spring that a number of countries including many participants in the Marshall Plan, as well as Japan and Spain and Lebanon have had substantial economic growth and were no longer dependent upon external assistance. We gave a commitment to the Congress that no AID funds would be required for these countries.

Mr. Johnson went on to say that with regard to other sources of development financing, the Export-Import Bank will continue to be open to Spain. He noted that a very considerable dollar volume of applications was presently under study by the Bank. He said that it is the U.S. view that Spain is quite capable of successfully using funds from such conventional sources. He added that perhaps it would be useful if some kind of general statement could be issued about this Bank financing.

Mr. Aguirre de Carcer said that the Embassy was thinking along this line and that some kind of statement by the Bank would appear to be most useful for optical purposes. He said that from the Spanish viewpoint a continuation of such financing at the average level of recent years was all that was expected, that Spain did not expect any line of credit on top of the normal project financing by the Bank.

Mr. Johnson said that the Export-Import Bank offers real possibilities for Spain and that he would be glad to explore the possibility of a general statement by the Bank. He noted that the Bank was reluctant to give lines of credit, and also noted that there have been difficulties with some underdeveloped countries regarding general statements which were not followed up with satisfactory projects.

Mr. Aguirre de Carcer said that this difficulty would not arise in the case of Spain.

Ambassador Garrigues said that the U.S. position with regard to PL 480 programs is quite reasonable, but that Spain had considered the U.S. economy to be so large in relation to Spain that it had hoped that some channel was possible through which to receive some kind of special assistance. He said that the appendix of August 27 had been prepared merely to mention a few of the possibilities. He said that he had just received a letter from Secretary Dillon[4] which gave a negative reply to his suggestions in every kind of way.

---

[4] Not found.

Mr. Johnson asked about the statement in the appendix that Spain was considering the reimbursement of PL 480 loans in dollars as a friendly gesture. He asked whether Spain intended to accelerate the normal amortization schedule.

Mr. Aguirre de Carcer said that this was not the case, but only to exercise the option of dollar reimbursement.

Mr. Johnson then asked about the reference at the bottom of page 3 to a U.S. suggestion of a blocked account in connection with military expenditures.

Mr. Aguirre de Carcer agreed that this had not been a formal U.S. suggestion but had arisen only in private conversation. He went on to ask about the possibility of U.S. military procurement in Spain.

Mr. Beigel said that a certain amount of procurement may be continuing under the present worldwide regulations governing military procurement overseas, but that the general question of further procurement in Spain of course related to Spanish military procurement in the U.S. and the proposals in this regard that had been made to the Spanish Government in Madrid last January.

Mr. Johnson summarized that we will proceed to consider the possibility of a statement by the Export-Import Bank, which would perhaps be related to the Spanish development plan.

Ambassador Garrigues said that in order to establish a better structure for the future there is need for declarations on other matters, in addition to the political declaration that had been proposed. He said that economic aspects and others had been left out of consideration so far. He said that the Spanish Government may not consider the present documents to be sufficient.

The Ambassador raised the question of the next steps in the discussions.

Mr. Johnson said that we had drafted the joint declaration with a view to signature by the Secretary of State and Foreign Minister Castiella at the time the Minister is in the United States next month. He said that we would expect both the declaration and the exchange of notes would be published at the same time. He said that arrangements could probably be made to sign the documents in Washington around September 26, and that we would intend to have formalities here and not treat this subject casually but in an important manner.

Ambassador Garrigues said that he appreciated the good spirit that underlies the documents given to him today and hoped that we would consider the August 27 appendix further in order to find some formulas aside from the Export-Import Bank statement. He said that the restrictions imposed in connection with procurement or investment in Spain are hard for Spain and mean very little to the U.S., although he admitted that Spain is placing no securities in the U.S. market. He said that Spain is only asking for aid through normal channels. He said that inflationary effects in the Spanish economy arising from the U.S. presence must be alleviated.

Ambassador Garrigues went on to say that on the military side Spain wished to rebuild its armed forces. He said that Spain will look upon the joint declaration as only a platonic declaration without teeth, and it must therefore be complemented with other documents dealing with other sides of our relations in order that something substantive is achieved.

Mr. Johnson said that the MAP agreement will continue in effect.

Ambassador Garrigues asked about information and assistance provided to NATO countries.

Mr. Johnson said that other than Greece and Turkey, there are no new MAP programs for the European members of NATO. He said that some training continues and if Spain has special training problems we would be glad to know about them. He noted that this could be the kind of subject to be taken up in the joint Consultative Committee. He said that as much or as little could be made out of this machinery as the two sides wished.

Mr. Aguirre de Carcer said that Spain would be interested in receiving information on subversive activities in other countries that is available through NATO committees. He said that the Spanish Government hears about this information, such as the management of Soviet funds, from some of the smaller NATO members.

Ambassador Garrigues turned again to the proposed declaration and asked if the last phrase of the first paragraph could be clarified.

Mr. Johnson said that it is important to bear in mind in this connection that the U.S. can only speak for itself, and that the last phrase in the first paragraph had been carefully worded so that we would not appear to be speaking for others.

The Ambassador summed up by saying that Spain continues to look for something on the economic side in addition to the Export-Import Bank, and to the removal of the restrictions he had referred to; and on the military side Spain must be sure to have the same status as other allies, receive the same information and cooperation. He said that the joint committee should in his view include more political ingredients and not be purely military. He said that NATO meetings include Foreign Ministers and this bilateral arrangement needs political membership as well.

The Ambassador said that his Government would consider carefully the documents proposed to him today. He commented on the dispersal of the Spanish Government on vacation, and said that General

Franco would probably not return to Madrid until September 20, although a cabinet meeting would be held in northern Spain next week.

Footnote. On September 1, Mr. Aguirre de Carcer telephoned to Mr. Beigel to say that he was preparing a Spanish translation of the documents for submission to Madrid. He inquired whether "this agreement" at the end of the first paragraph of the Joint Declaration referred to the Defense Agreement and said that this appeared to be the logic of the sentence. Mr. Beigel confirmed that this was the intention. Mr. Aguirre de Carcer also inquired about the intent of the words "continuing" in both the third and fourth paragraphs and said they could be translated two ways in Spanish. Mr. Beigel suggested that when the Embassy has prepared Spanish versions of the documents it may be useful to provide them to the Department, so that a comparison can be made by the Division of Language Services to assure that the Spanish translation conforms to the intent of the original drafts. Mr. Aguirre de Carcer also referred to the phrase "a threat to either country, and to the facilities" and asked whether this meant "or" as well as "and". Mr. Beigel said the use of "and" was deliberate and was intended to imply a general threat to the country in which a threat to the facilities would be a corollary, and not merely a threat to some part of either country.

---

378. Telegram From the Department of State to the Embassy in Spain

Washington, September 24, 1963, 8:47 p.m.

1006. Based on uncleared MemCon[1] there follows highlights Rusk–Castiella meeting in New York September 23, which subject amendment upon review and FYI only. Garrigues and Tyler among those present. FonMin expressed pleasure with manner in which negotiations progressing. Stated Spain had originally planned cancel 1953 Agreement and renegotiate, however new formula permitting new kind of relationship between two countries had achieved principal object of negotiations. Castiella stressed key importance making clear US-Spanish 1025

Source: Department of State, Conference Files: Lot 66 D 110, CF 2315. Secret; Immediate; Limit Distribution. Drafted by Ortiz (WE) cleared by Melot, approved by Tyler, and repeated to USUN for the Secretary, who was there for the meeting of the U.N. General Assembly.

[1] SecDel/MC/5, not printed. (Ibid., Central Files, Pol Sp-US)

"cooperation." Spain desired act with full knowledge of factors affecting Spain. Minister said in extending Agreement GOS must "satisfy" military and Spanish public opinion regarding economic development.

With regard to military assistance, Secretary said US considered it prime importance avoid any possible misunderstanding at any level. GOS must understand that US had severe limitation on what US can do re MAP. Secretary gave Castiella informal draft of secret memorandum indicating level of US military assistance to Spain as presently contemplated and subject to Congressional action at total $100 million. Of this $50 million contingent upon equal purchases in US by Spain.

Spaniards commented on low level MAP. They were told in fact Spain receiving prefered treatment over NATO countries. Garrigues inquired re US possibilities assisting Spain by granting favorable terms and prices in purchases US equipment. We said we would explore these possibilities.

Secretary and Castiella expected to meet in New York September 25 to review latest revisions various documents pertaining to extension Agreement.

FYI Only. In event agreement on extension reached, time has been set aside September 26 for signing ceremony at 1800 New York time.[2] End FYI Only.

Ball

---

[2] Following a further meeting between Garrigues and Tyler in Washington on September 24 (memorandum of conversation; ibid., Def 15–4 Sp-US) and between Rusk and Castiella in New York on September 25 (SecDel /MC/37; ibid., Pol Sp-US), both devoted to suggested drafting changes, the Secretary of State and the Spanish Foreign Minister on September 26 signed the Joint Declaration and exchanged letters and notes on military assistance and the Consultative Committee. For texts of these documents, see Department of State *Bulletin*, October 28, 1963, pp. 686–688.

United Kingdom

379. Message From Prime Minister Macmillan to President Kennedy

London, January 26, 1961.

DEAR MR. PRESIDENT, I was very glad to receive your recent message,[1] sent through Mr. Rusk, about the continuance of Anglo-United States Understandings concerning consultation before the use of nuclear weapons, and the use of bases in the United Kingdom. I am now writing in response to your suggestion that we should communicate with each other about these Understandings immediately after your Inauguration.

These Understandings have their origin in war-time collaboration for production of the atomic bomb and for the liberation of Europe. They have been developed by successive United States Administrations, and now form an essential part of the whole network of Anglo-United States joint defense arrangements which underlie Britain's defence policy and planning. We therefore attach great importance to them. I hope very much that you and your Administration will accept these arrangements and Understandings, and the broad principles upon which they are based, and that, in particular, you will feel able to renew in your own name the personal assurances on these matters given by President Eisenhower and President Truman.[2]

Yours sincerely,

Harold Macmillan[3]

Source: Department of State, Presidential Correspondence: Lot 66 D 204. Top Secret.

[1] On December 19 Prime Minister Macmillan had written President-elect Kennedy a 6-page letter discussing the major problems facing their two countries and proposing a meeting with the President. (Ibid.; and Harold Macmillan, *Pointing the Way*, London, 1972, pp. 309–312) In his reply Kennedy agreed on the need for a meeting, but stressed that further exchanges should wait until after his inauguration. (Department of State, Presidential Correspondence: Lot 66 D 204)

[2] In a February 6 letter Kennedy confirmed the Anglo-American understandings. (Ibid.)

[3] Printed from a copy that bears this typed signature.

380. Paper Prepared in the Department of State

MVK B–III–52   Washington, March 21, 1961.

MACMILLAN VISIT
WASHINGTON, APRIL 4–9, 1961

Background and Objectives of Visit

Genesis of Visit

During the previous administration Prime Minister Macmillan periodically traveled to this country for intimate talks with President Eisenhower. The last such meeting took place in New York on September 27, 1960.[1] Mr. Macmillan wrote you on December 19, 1960[2] how glad he was to accept your invitation to a meeting at your convenience, an invitation which arose from your talk with Ambassador Caccia December 15.[3] The Prime Minister agreed with you on the advisability of starting consideration of our common problems promptly after January 20th through the British Ambassador and the State Department. Mr. Macmillan subsequently suggested a list of topics for discussion.[4] The bilateral talks we have now held with the British served to reduce the number of specific issues requiring discussion at the top level and helped to formulate the agenda of six fundamental items for your talks with the Prime Minister.

British Domestic Situation

Mr. Macmillan will arrive in this country with a solid Parliamentary majority behind him and no obligation to call another election until 1964. The Conservative Government has made a sophisticated and generally successful effort to move with the times. The Opposition Labor Party is split over doctrine and foreign policy and Gaitskell's leadership is under continuous attack. The domestic economy is booming and a sense of affluence is spreading.

This happy surface appearance, however, is somewhat deceptive. There are signs, still small, of boredom with the Conservative admini-

---

Source: Department of State, Conference Files: Lot 65 D 366, CF 1832. Secret. No drafting information appears on the source text.

[1] For a memorandum of this conversation, see *Foreign Relations,* 1958–1960, vol. VII, Part 2, pp. 874–875.

[2] See footnote 1, Document 379.

[3] No record of this meeting has been found.

[4] A copy of the British list is attached to a memorandum from Secretary of State Rusk to the President dated January 28. (Department of State, Central Files, 611.41/1–2861)

stration and restlessness at the absence of drive and imaginative new ventures. The "stale" Conservative Government is being compared unfavorably with the new administration here. Mr. Macmillan cannot ignore an undercurrent of "little islander" or "neutralist" sentiment.

Britain Foreign Relations Problems

In the foreign political field Mr. Macmillan is confronted with the intricate task of harmonizing the Anglo-American relationship with ties to the Commonwealth and Continental Europe. Mr. Macmillan assigns high priority to strengthening NATO and to increased political and economic unity of Europe. But, in his relations with the Continent, he is faced by the revival of Germany, lingering anti-German feeling in Britain, and the nationalism of General de Gaulle. He has basic reservations about the six country integration movement and favors a broader European unity. Britain values the Commonwealth association for reasons of parental pride, the claim it gives to world status and as a link between the West and the underdeveloped world. However, the UK is no longer able to bring to the "club" the accustomed amount of financial assistance, military power and prestige. He is obliged to continue the distasteful business of "unwinding the empire". In doing so he is determined to keep unsullied Britain's remarkable record of leading dependent peoples to independence and not to bequeath to history a Congo. On the other hand, Mr. Macmillan is acutely conscious of the growing pressures for speed coming from Afro-Asian nationalists, given expression particularly in the UN. Mr. Macmillan is under no illusion over the extent to which Britain's fate is bound up with the outcome of the East-West struggle. The communiqué following the Moscow Communist Conference in December and Khrushchev's speech of January 6[5] has resulted in some disenchantment and caution regarding negotiations with the Soviets. Nevertheless, strong pressures remain for exploring every possibility, especially in the disarmament field, for some accommodation and a concomitant nervousness exists about approaching the brink of even local military solutions.

Mr. Macmillan recognizes the UK is no longer a great military power and is able to exert only a marginal effect on the military balance between the US and the USSR. He is concerned that by the acts of others the UK may be drawn into a conflict which could result in its annihilation. This factor together with reasons of prestige lie behind the insistence on maintaining an independent nuclear deterrent which hopefully might give a margin of political independence from the US and make Britain's voice more audible in any US decision on peace and war.

---

[5] For text of the communiqué, see *Pravda*, December 6, 1961; for text of Khrushchev's speech, see ibid., January 7, 1962.

The UK is faced by a steadily worsening international economic position. Exports are meeting increased competition and imports are rising sharply. The UK has a severe balance of payments problem, lately disguised by the recent inflow of "hot money", which is likely to become more acute during the present year. At home there is a low rate of economic growth; inflationary pressures to contend with; and a limited labor supply.

Macmillan's Objectives

The primary objective of the Prime Minister during his visit to Washington, we believe, will be to appraise the climate and judge the prospects for the continuation and value to Britain of the unique Anglo-American relationship. Mr. Macmillan personally was in large part responsible for reviving the Anglo-American relationship after the Suez debacle and for reinstituting the concept of "interdependence". We believe that the conclusions he draws will have far-reaching effects on his decisions and on the degree of cooperation we may expect in months ahead. He will seek to "make his mark" with you and to establish the same close bonds he enjoyed with President Eisenhower. The Prime Minister is an exponent of the art of personal diplomacy and likes to think that "jowl to jowl" he is able to resolve difficult issues. He also has a penchant for soliloquizing in broad and bold historical terms which sometimes turn out to have little bearing on his attitude or that of HMG on specific issues. These monologues can be quite disconcerting if taken too seriously.

Mr. Macmillan's popularity is still high at home, he wields exceptional power and himself makes the big decisions and sets the tone for the government. We attach high importance to a close personal relationship with Mr. Macmillan, but we do not believe he should be encouraged to overburden this channel to the exclusion of more normal diplomatic practices.

We believe he may also have in mind as major objectives obtaining US support in principle for the following:

1) A British role vis-à-vis the Continent which, while furthering the political and economic unity of Europe, would not necessitate an amalgamation of British political personality with the Continent; would retain for the UK a distinctive world-wide role; and would permit a continuation of the Anglo-American relationship and Commonwealth ties. Mr. Macmillan probably will make a special plea for a revision of the US position on Sixes and Sevens in favor of active, or at least benevolent, US support for current British efforts to work out an accommodation between the two groupings.

2) Sympathetic understanding of the practical problems confronting the UK in divesting itself of its remaining colonial territories, espe-

cially in East and Central Africa; acceptance of British good faith in trying to move as fast as possible towards granting independence; and assistance in resisting pressures, especially in the UN, for precipitate actions.

3) A cooperative economic program intended to expand the rate of Western economic growth and to maximize the use of production facilities, and involving avoidance of accentuating each other's balance of payments problem; further liberalization of trade; and the expansion of international credit facilities. Mr. Macmillan probably will emphasize that Western Germany should assume a greater share of the Western burden particularly in aid to the underdeveloped countries.

4) Thorough exploration of the possibilities of an accommodation with the Communist Bloc including particularly suspension of nuclear tests, disarmament, and admittance of Communist China to the UN.

Our Objectives

Our principal objectives might be to:

1) Reassure Mr. Macmillan of the importance we attach to the Anglo-American alliance and to close relations at all levels. The common heritage of our two peoples and the fundamental harmony of our views on world problems form the basis for a relationship which is unparalleled. We think of our ties with the UK as of central importance in building the strength and unity of the Free World in the Atlantic Community and elsewhere. We should eschew ostentation in order to avoid resentment from our other allies. While important differences between us arise from time to time, one of the strengths of our association is that we can agree to disagree.

2) Emphasize the importance of both the U.S. and the U.K. moving toward greater interdependence within NATO and helping to strengthen NATO defenses, with increased emphasis on conventional forces and on NATO political cohesion. Also emphasize the importance we attach to the OECD as a forum for coordinating policies to attain economic growth, while maintaining external payments equilibrium and to expanding aid to the less-developed countries along the lines of our proposal at the London DAG meeting.[6]

3) Emphasize the long term importance of the political and economic strength and unity of the Atlantic Community; the desirability of strengthening British bonds with the Continent; the value we attach to the integration movement of the Six as a step which will tie Germany in closely with the West and reinforce the strength and unity of the Atlantic

---

[6] At the DAG meeting in London, March 18–30, the United States had proposed that Japan, Western Europe, and the United States designate 1 percent of their gross national products for foreign aid.

Community as a whole; our willingness to support a solution between the Six and the Seven provided it does not prejudice progress towards political and economic unity of the Six, is consistent with GATT and does not add to special discrimination against US trade.

4) Stress the need for continuing to move as rapidly as possible to grant independence to the remaining colonies without undue risk to their future stability; to expand the West's economic and technical assistance programs to the underdeveloped world; to create an imaginative public relations program; and to counter Soviet and Communist Chinese influence in Africa, Asia, and Latin America.

5) Warn against any mistaken belief the Soviets are becoming "fat" and therefore less dangerous. While desirous of exploring all substantive and tactical ways of improving relations and eventually of engaging in serious negotiations on basic issues, we are not prepared to make unilateral concessions merely for the sake of an agreement.

6) Bear down on the perils of over precipitate action and the damage to US-UK relations of any campaign to seat Communist China in the UN. Arrangements for the Government of the Republic of China to continue as a member of the UN are a basic essential of our position. It is important that the US and UK concert closely on the tactics to be employed at the UN in order to achieve this objective.

7) Emphasize the need for a realistic combination of military and political steps in Southeast Asia to prevent irreparable erosion of the Western position.

---

381. Circular Telegram From the Department of State to the Embassy in France

Washington, April 8, 1961, 3:56 p.m.

1546. Embassies of NATO countries briefed on Kennedy–Macmillan talks yesterday[1] by Kohler and Sir Frederick Hoyer Millar. Summary

---

Source: Department of State, Central Files, 611.41/4–861. Secret; Niact. Drafted in RA on April 7 and cleared in draft with Kohler and Bundy. Repeated to the other NATO capitals and Moscow.

[1] Macmillan visited Washington April 4–9. Memoranda of his conversations with President Kennedy on various subjects and memoranda of Foreign Secretary Home's conversations with Rusk, together with briefing papers, agendas for the meetings, and supporting documentation are ibid., Conference Files: Lot 65 D 366, CF 1832–1833, and Central File 611.41. For memoranda on their discussion of European economic integration and NATO strategy, see Supplement. For Macmillan's account of the meeting, see *Pointing the Way*, pp. 348–352.

as presented below has concurrence of British Embassy here. US and UK Reps should coordinate presentation to NAC at April 12 meeting.

1. Nature of Meetings. Discussions were informal with no intention of reaching decisions. Discussions were regarded by both sides as useful opportunity to have first exchange of views at highest level on all common problems. Regarded as part of process of exchanging views among allies which is expected as in past to be continuing process.

Dominant theme was need for strengthening unity of West politically, militarily, and economically. General thesis from US point of view was set forth in Vice President Johnson's speech to SHAPE April 6[2] which Kohler commended for reading by all concerned. British were in substantial agreement with this thesis.

2. Economic Problems. Reference was made to efforts now going on in IMF to consider expansion of its scope and increase its effectiveness. It was agreed that US and UK Reps at these discussions should pursue their efforts in this direction. Ways should be found to ease position of member governments encountering international payments deficits.

President brought up problems involved in renewal reciprocal trade agreements act which is necessary for US to play its generally desired role in international trade field. While depending partly on domestic economic situation prospects will be improved considerably if at time of renewal there is no dollar discrimination on part of any of our allies. President asked UK to be helpful in this connection on a few specific items which British are prepared to examine sympathetically. Kohler invited similar action where indicated on part of other allies.

On aid to underdeveloped countries, US cited its determination make OECD effective means for unity in Atlantic Community and for aid to underdeveloped countries. British welcomed this and indicated that they for their own part are prepared to help in developing OECD and DAG. US pointed to strong delegation we are sending to economic policy committee. Both sides hope OECD will deal in future with problems involved in marketing products of underdeveloped areas. Also agreed necessary study methods promote development of production in such areas with ready markets in West not competitive with our own products, such as textiles. With regard to Sixes and Sevens Kohler indicated we must move to solution of problem under OECD umbrella, and move toward ever increasing economic unity of Atlantic Community.

UK comment on this subject was that West must maximize its international trade. No reason why we should not be able to more than hold our own in relation to communist offensive, but can only do so by more

---

[2] The text is in the Johnson Library, Statements File, Box 52.

cohesion economic as well as political and military. However, must work specific problems out properly. UK particularly wishes to be helpful in getting US Government over strain involved in renewal reciprocal trade agreements act.

3. NATO. Kohler alluded to review of NATO within US Government and made reference to general preliminary remarks made on this subject by Ambassador Finletter to NAC. Indicated that generally speaking we are concluding that political consultation should be very considerably strengthened, that all members should be ready discuss problems affecting NATO even if beyond geographic scope and even if differences of view exist. Likely that US will suggest to Council a few procedural improvements, perhaps (1) select committees of NAC which could examine problems prior to full discussion in Council, and (2) small outside "wise men's" group on a continuing basis, point he thought UK did not necessarily accept. UK commented that they entirely agreed with US viewpoint that NATO consultation of basic importance. Kohler indicated in reply to question that our suggestions in this field may be made before end of April to contribute to meaningful discussion at Oslo and expressed hope other members would similarly be making their suggestions with such discussions in mind. Kohler pointed out that while being specific, we do not intend to be dogmatic with regard these detailed suggestions and wish stimulate discussions toward agreed decisions.

On military side our review indicates basically that strategic doctrine and political directive[3] do not need change but rather some interpretation which is part of continuing process. We have strong feeling that alliance is really lagging with regard to conventional forces, that serious steps should be taken to reach presently planned goals both quantitatively and qualitatively in order to raise threshold and be able force significant pause before employment nuclear weapons. This should probably be first priority effort. Our review has led to conclusion that to degree not generally realized NATO has already become very much a nuclear power. We believe it important to maintain effective nuclear deterrent in NATO forces. Can be anticipated that when US Government has officially concluded review it will be made clear that nuclear weapons will remain in Europe for NATO purposes.

With respect to MRBMs this problem still being pursued. Can be expected that Polaris submarines will be committed to NATO in accordance with needs. Interested in hearing views of NATO allies on this subject.

---

[3] Regarding the Political Directive of December 14, 1956, see Polto 14, December 14, 1956, *Foreign Relations*, 1955–1957, vol. IV, pp. 149–156.

UK commented that much of discussion on this topic between President and Prime Minister was exposition of US thinking. Reference was made to UK proposal for strategy review. UK much interested in US current thinking but made no particular comment since whole subject soon to be thrashed out in NATO.

4. United Nations. Full agreement reached on dangers current Soviet campaign against SYG and structure of UN as well as attempt also introduce "three-part" world formula into other organizations, thus obtaining built-in Soviet veto. Touched on question Congo, especially financing of UN Congo operations. Also considered colonial issue as handled in UN. On UK side agreement expressed with constructive Western approach to self-determination, but allusion made to dangers of certain types of resolutions, such as those setting target dates for independence, that might prejudice orderly development. Was agreed that while Allies might sometimes diverge on this issue (might at times be a good thing) should make every effort cooperate re such resolutions to fullest extent possible.

UK commented, on this subject, that PM had said all colonial powers faced with particular problem of timing grant of independence to multi-racial communities, to assure protection minority rights. UK fundamentally anxious be left alone by UN to work out what it thinks best. Glad to see US appreciates UK point of view on this. Want sympathetic understanding and continuing close cooperation between all Western delegations to UN. Don't wish find ourselves in public disagreement merely because of failure make best possible effort at consultation.

Re China, differences of approach acknowledged, since UK recognizes ChiCom, US does not. President pointed to seriousness question of ChiCom admission UN from US viewpoint, since this a prime issue here politically. Essential that matter not merely be handled as credentials question pure and simple, but important underlying questions should be faced. While we recognize that moratorium may no longer be effective procedure, should avoid situation where would be an unthinking substitution of ChiComs for ChiNats. Such eventuality would be great setback for US cooperation generally through UN and otherwise.

UK in course discussion this point first put record straight. Not pressing for Red China in UN or abandonment Formosa. Would rather like help find way out of impasse, and work with US to devise workable course of action. Would at least wish to agree with US on a solution which would have effect of putting Communists in the wrong.

5. East-West Issues. Meetings provided opportunity new US administration explain its basic attitude, cite efforts introduce atmosphere of calm and civility, while having no illusions as to what we can expect from Soviet side. Have therefore made effort remove specific minor obstacles in bilateral relations, as already reported to NAC. Was agreed by

President and PM that Soviet position on various current issues presents little basis for optimism, and in some ways ominous, as re nuclear test conference. Agreed in latter connection US and UK Dels should continue push hard for Soviet reaction to our proposals, so if break comes responsibility will be clear.

6. Berlin. Agreed that two governments, and all NATO, have vital interest in Berlin. Is real danger may be faced with crisis this year, prior to October Party Congress, or timed in connection German elections. Consequently agreed we should now review in tripartite and quadripartite groups, for subsequent customary report to NAC, status contingency planning, which should be firmed up. Should also review various negotiating positions, make sure we have our house in order. UK commented that it has no evidence of imminent Soviet action re Berlin, but should take seriously possibility of Soviet action and be prepared. No reason to be either alarmist or complacent.

7. Soviet-ChiCom Relations. Joint feeling that Khrushchev and Mao agree on objectives but have some disagreement on modalities, with result some pressure on former to be more militant. Situation inside China, notably agricultural difficulties bears watching.

In conclusion, UK commented that PM feels is great opportunity for new US administration, with young President, to take lead and give impetus to greater Atlantic cooperation. UK would for its part be happy see such lead by US.

In reply to question, Kohler pointed out US conclusions its review NATO policies may be presented to NAC piecemeal, some hopefully before end April. While no big decisions expected at Oslo, we hope for meaningful discussion, and perhaps directive by Ministers to NAC re study certain questions.

Rusk

---

382. **Telegram From the Department of State to the Embassy in the United Kingdom**

Washington, April 8, 1961, 8:08 p.m.

4751. Following minute (unnecessary words omitted) agreed to between Secretary and Lord Home sets forth US-UK understanding on

---

Source: Department of State, Central Files, 611.41/4–861. Secret.

follow up actions required as result President's talks with Prime Minister.

Begin text. In course their meetings in Washington from 5th to 8th of April, 1961, President and Prime Minister agreed following action should be taken:

1) Representatives two Governments on Board IMF should continue press enlargement of scope of Fund within existing Articles of Agreement.

2) Officials two Governments should make urgent study longer range problems liquidity. US and UK would not at present initiate steps broaden area international consultation but would be ready listen any views expressed other governments, e.g., at EPC. Action 1) and 2) would be initiated Washington between Dillon, Ball, Heller and Pitblado British Embassy.

3) Two Governments should consult with respect measures designed induce Federal Government Germany make further contribution (whether by purchase arms or overseas aid) to effect foreign exchange cost US and UK of maintaining troops in Germany. Consultation will take place London or Washington as required.

4) Officials two Governments should study in London problems connected with marketing tropical products which would arise from any broadening existing economic associations in Europe.

5) Ball will present the United Kingdom with memorandum on deciduous fruits on which UK will see what can be done liberalize restrictions.

6) Officials two Governments should study feasibility of a plan by which export textiles from Hong Kong to US could be reduced in return for other measures which would diversify economic structure Hong Kong. Study should start in Washington at time of Sir Gorrel Barnes' visit and be transferred if necessary to London.

7) Officials of two Governments should consider problem stabilizing resources countries dependent on one or more commodities on understanding each commodity would need be studied on its particular merits. Consideration this subject will be handled between Ball and British Ambassador.

8) Prime Minister welcomed initiatives recently taken by USG increase effectiveness work of DAG within structure of OECD and undertook UKG would give full cooperation support those initiatives.

9) Existing machinery Washington will consider further what Western negotiating position should be over Berlin if faced by new Soviet move entailing negotiations.

10) Foreign Secretary and Secretary State will arrange for fresh review of contingency planning in respect Berlin. Purpose bilateral review

will be see if Agreement can be reached new instructions to planners both to broaden scope their planning and to authorize training. Bilateral talks would be followed promptly by tripartite talks and subsequently Germans would be brought in on certain aspects. Secretary State will give paper to British Ambassador.

11) Representatives two Governments at UN should consider and report on following problems affecting future UN:

a) Representation China in UN including possibility a delaying resolution linking question with expansion of membership of Councils of the Organization or a "successor States" type resolution on analogy of that passed in respect UAR.

b) Enlargement of composition of Security Council and other Councils of Organization.

c) Position of Secretary-General and structure of Secretariat.

d) Financing of Organization and of operations undertaken under its auspices.

12) Representatives two Governments at UN should consider handling of Laos question at the UN.

13) British Ambassador Washington and Secretary State in consultation with Australian Ambassador Washington should make urgent study the line which three Governments might take with view discouraging Indonesian attack on West New Guinea including possibility of trusteeship so that USG might be in position give suitable warning President Sukarno when he visited Washington later in April.

14) UK agreed look into question providing assistance British-owned railway in Bolivia in light of dangerous political situation that country.

15) UK agreed provide appreciation obtained from President Ayub Khan of situation on Pakistan-Afghanistan border. *End text.*

[Here follows the remainder of the telegram.]

Rusk

383. Telegram From the Embassy in the United Kingdom to the Department of State

London, July 17, 1961, 6 p.m.

229. From Bruce. Re Embtel 218,[1] fol are additional observations:

Obviously, after only few months, residence, my personal estimate of British political scene is impressionistic and perhaps overly subjective. Would seem to me UK now faces three major problems, 1. economic and financial, 2. common market, 3. Berlin.

1. As State and Treasury aware, economic and financial situation UK deeply disturbing. Chancellor of Exchequer's proposals on July 25 will undoubtedly be unpopular, even if sound. Austerity imposed upon seeming prosperity, particularly under conditions full-employment, is politically unattractive. Gaitskell, in speech at Durham miners' gala last Saturday threw down gauntlet, and will capitalize on theme of "we never had it so good".

2. Majority of cabinet has favored UK joining Common Market. Of three objections against such course: a. obligations to EFTA; b. harm to domestic agricultural and horticultural interests; c. reaction in Commonwealth nations, only c. had possible validity, since others could be compromised.

If PriMin had acted nore speedily and ruthlessly perhaps Commonwealth objectives would not have been so serious. Now, his emissaries have been confronted with a shopping list of exceptions and derogations, a press campaign, led by Beaverbrook, traditional champion of imperial preferences, has made some headway. Trade and balance of payments deterioration may provide specious arguments in favor continuing insularity. Outcome will depend on determination by one individual, Macmillan.

3. Berlin constitutes most critical govt concert. In past, it was shoved under rug, or postponed by peripatetic wanderings of Allied statesmen, conferences, and other dilatory maneuvers, but presently there is belief that Khrushchev intends, in absence of settlement favorable to him, to sign separate peace treaty this year with so-called sovereign East German Republic. Consequences of such act literally appal govt and people because of fear of nuclear war ensuing.

Left to own devices, UK Govt, with overwhelming support voters, would, I believe, acknowledge GDR at least de facto, and legalize semi-

---

Source: Department of State, Central Files, 741.00/7–1761. Secret. Repeated to Paris and Bonn.

[1] Telegram 218, July 15, reported that the Conservative Party had hit a relatively bad "patch." (Ibid., 741.00/7–1561)

permanent or permanent division Germany. However, in view contrary American policy, they will align their policies to conform with our own after exhausting arguments against it. They regard our military contingency planning as super hypothetical, and unrealistic, since they consider pol aspects have overriding importance.

The prospect of Berlin crisis provoking, or leading, through inadvertence or accident, to nuclear war, is regarded here with horror. Nor are they unaware that if the West Berliners are forsaken, the monkey will be on the American back and not on their own. Stout as they invariably are in a showdown, their national pol temperament inclines them to compromise, even at expense of principle.

So far I have been speaking of the govt. It is dominated by PriMin Macmillan. He picked up after Suez, and, in Churchillian tradition, made touchstone his own decisions in field foreign policy accommodation with ultimate US positions.

To date, he has, in this respect, carried his cabinet with him. Unlike our cabinet procedure, this is sometimes a delicate task, for if there is much dissatisfaction the govt may fall. The cabinet members are, in distinction to our own, parliamentarians, not simply agents of the PriMin.

The cabinet figure who has latterly most gained in stature is Lord Home, ForMin. This independent Scot, pawky in humor, uninvolved in strict party doctrine, in some degree free of private ambition, has taken a tough line over Berlin. It would be inconceivable for as loyal a man to have done so without the approval of his chief.

I would guess that if the US Govt decides to risk nuclear war over Berlin we would obtain the support of the British Govt at the last moment. I do not think we would get such approval unless we had first negotiated with the Soviets in one or more conferences or confrontations between President and Khrushchev. I say "last moment", I mean after our President had irrevocably decided upon such a course, regardless of foreign expostulations.

The speculations set forth above would appear to any reader of the Brit press to contradict public opinion. This is true. Germany and the Germans are notably unpopular in this country. Selling the whole kit and caboodle of them down any river would not arouse indignation, until later events revealed this had been harmful to the national security.

German bombing of Great Britain, Jewish persecution, and other cruelties, made an indelible impression on the islander. They considered such conduct signally unprincipled and, as applied to themselves, impudent. Unconsciously, they regard themselves as the true Herrenvolk, and the Germans as untrustworthy, unattractive, dangerous and somewhat ridiculous, barbarians beneath a civilized veneer. It should not be overlooked that the word "Hun" still has common currency in England, Scotland, and Wales.

Nor do German prosperity, rates of taxation, comparative superiority in many competing particulars, and tranquil subordination to leadership, endear their citizens and institutions to the British. Joy through work is not a British ideal, as it is in West Germany. Envy of crescent German power is galling to those who for more than a century, considered the exercise of power in Europe their peculiar prerogative. The same reflection applies, in diminished force, to their suspicion and envy of ourselves. Decline of influence is either unnoticed and unacknowledged, or, if publicly manifest, can embitter a proud people against those to whom the torch has passed.

How much attention should we pay to demonstrations against the Polaris base at Holy Loch, unilateralism, banning the bomb marchers, Bertrand Russell defeatism, glorification of Soviet culture as expressed by the admirable Leningrad Kirov Ballet Company, and, in the last few days, by the enthusiastic hysteria over Major Gagarin?

I should like nothing better than to attempt analysis of these and like questions if they had not been, or shortly will be, covered by Embassy reports from which conclusions can be drawn according to one's own interpretation and bias.

Personally, I believe that, realistically, we must deal in terms of power. Power, in this country, resides in its government. That government must conform its policies re Berlin, in the last analysis, to our own (as must Adenauer). Unless our decisions are so adverse to the national security interests as to be unbearable. Probably, conclusions about Berlin will be reached while actual government is still operative; otherwise, similar attitudes will prevail, though accent will be different. It will, I trust and hope, take more than a Berlin crisis to shatter the essential solidarity of informed self-interest between the English-speaking peoples.

Bruce

384. Telegram From the Embassy in the United Kingdom to the Department of State

London, December 12, 1961, 10 p.m.

2295. Deptel 3184.[1] Will answer first paragraph later. Re 2nd paragraph, you have given me a difficult task in asking (1) Macmillan's personal views about topics mentioned (2) evaluating his political future. Let me take up latter topic first.

A. I am neither an intimate nor a friend of the PM. Few apparently are. His play, to use a gambling expression, is close; and his inmost thoughts are seldom open to penetration. He is a political animal, shrewd, subtle in maneuver, undisputed master in his cabinet house. I have never heard of his being addressed with levity on serious governmental matters by subordinates or acquaintances, other than partisan opponents. If so, those heavily lidded eyelids would lift, and a contemptuous glance would stare them down.

His opponents think him a cold-blooded but formidable individual. Some liken him to Disraeli, though he lacks the flamboyance of a man who would change from a morning to an afternoon walking stick as the noon bell tolled at Gibraltar. Nor does he have Disraeli's fondness for exotic dress; rather his clothes are sometimes compared with those of English dukes who have been accused of dressing in the cast-off garments of Irish beggars, though this does Macmillan a sartorial injustice.

At times, he gives the impression of being shot through with Victorian langour. It would be a mistake to infer from this that he is lacking in force or decisiveness, as it would be to deduce from what is called his "balliol shuffle" that he is not capable of swift action. In fact, he can featly spring onto his toes like a ballet dancer, and is quick gun in the shooting field.

Whether his emphasis on the importance of a close American relationship is associated with having had an American mother matters little. Like Churchill, he has made the maintenance of close ties with the US a cardinal point of policy, though occasionally he has departed on an independent course, as when he made a lone wolf journey to Moscow, and returned with an empty sack.

Source: Department of State, Central Files, 611.41/12–1261. Secret; Priority; Limit Distribution. Drafted by Bruce.

[1] Telegram 3184, December 11, suggested that the main topics for the forthcoming meeting between the President and Macmillan at Bermuda should be Berlin, European integration, and nuclear testing. Since this would be an "extremely important meeting" telegram 3184 asked for Bruce's estimate of Macmillan's views on these topics and his political future. (Ibid., 611.41/12–1161)

But this is no mean man. He represents Edwardian and eighteenth century England in the grand tradition of the establishment, and also has an extensive appreciation of contemporary public opinion. He has charm, politeness, dry humor, self-assurance, a vivid sense of history, dignity, and character. To what extent he would bend conviction to comport with expediency one cannot say. He has had long experience in judging men and events. Unable to succeed as middle man between the US and USSR, no longer on a basis of old friendship with the President of the United States, realizing that a revival of the classical balance of power in Europe with Great Britain weighing the scales is no longer possible, my guess is that he will go far to suit otherwise discordant notes to the US President's harmony.

As to his political future, much will depend on Thursday's debate here on the Congo. The Labour Party is in hot and optimistic pursuit of the Tories, many of whom will skirt and babble without joining the pack. This controversy, I was informed today by Harold Wilson, Foreign Minister in the Shadow Cabinet, is the most dramatic parliamentary issue since Suez. Few expect resultant scars to heal quickly, though the Prime Minister has great resiliency, and will remain in command of the Tories unless, as is unlikely, he in overthrown on a vote of censure or no confidence. Undoubtedly, the passions aroused in the UK by the UN policy in the Congo will impair Tory discipline, [and] regardless of the merits or the outcome will probably affect the party's future adversely. This is an instance where, in terms of domestic politics, it is preferable to criticize than to be responsible for decisions.

B. Re PM's personal views on reftel items, I will have to engage in wild surmise.

1. Berlin Complex. He thinks a negotiation is necessary, in order to condition his countrymen to accept sterner measures if it fails. He may believe that the west will come so close to de facto recognition of East Germany that the Soviets will compensate US for it by a paper and plausible agreement over access.

2. (A) European integration and (B) special problems of US-UK relations.

(A) I believe he sincerely desires UK entry into Common Market with concomitant assumption of political obligations. British economy is laggard, and should be improved by membership. Also, he must be conscious of possibility that after Adenauer and de Gaulle pass off scene, UK might well be political spokesman for bloc potentially as powerful as US or USSR.

(B) Believe he will make all reasonable concessions to maintain at least public appearance of US-UK concord on mutual problems, and sincerely holds to close US-UK special relationship.

3. Nuclear Testing. PM wishes to continue test conference. Will argue at Bermuda that resumption by US of tests, unless they are essential, will in world opinion equate US with the USSR. If Soviet tests have demonstrated important progress this would make a difference; it would be easier for the UK if it were plain that Soviet tests had advanced development of anti-missile missiles.

Same applies to Christmas Island. At Bermuda PM will have to be convinced that proposed tests fit the criteria explained by him in the House of Commons debate.

Bruce

---

385. Objectives and Scope Paper Prepared in the Department of State

BMM G–2   Washington, December 16, 1961.

BERMUDA MEETING WITH P.M. MACMILLAN
December 21–22, 1961

Objectives

In the talks, whose scope is sketched below, our objectives are to achieve:

1. Maintenance of the intimacy and dynamism of the US-UK relationship.
2. Sustained British firmness against the Soviet Union. This requires:

    a. A greater UK contribution to the military buildup required by the Berlin crisis.
    b. Full agreement on counter-measures, not just acquiescence.

3. Bring home to the UK our support of its decision to enter the EEC, and stress the desirability of the UK also joining EURATOM and the Coal and Steel Community.
4. Reassure the British on the importance we attach to our existing relationship and indicate that European integration will offer new scope for this relationship.

Source: Department of State, Conference Files: Lot 65 D 366, CF 2025. Secret. Drafted by Sweeney and cleared by Tyler, Bundy, and Nitze.

5. Obtain their agreement and general support for any decision we may make on the resumption of atmospheric nuclear testing, including the details of where this testing will take place.

Scope

Prime Minister Macmillan has indicated in a variety of ways how anxious he is to have the talks with President Kennedy which will take place December 21–22 in Bermuda.

Macmillan desires these discussions not only to exchange and attune views on a common international outlook, but also for British domestic political consumption. Macmillan's Conservative Government won the last general election on October 8, 1959 with an impressive overall majority of 100 seats. Macmillan's leadership progressed impressively upwards from the Suez debacle and his political astuteness gained him the nickname "Macwonder." In recent months, however, this nickname has gone out of vogue, and while Macmillan and his party are not in serious political trouble, they could benefit from the favorable publicity that would follow a friendly meeting with the American President.

Since Macmillan indicated his Government's intention to join the Common Market there have been demands that a general election be held before the final decision. Thus far the Prime Minister has resisted these demands and his resistance has been plausible because the Labor Opposition has not officially opposed entry into the Common Market. The mounting public debate in Britain over Britain's unenthusiastic decision to apply for membership in the Common Market may yet be an influencing factor in a Conservative decision to obtain a new sounding of the electorate.

The Labor Opposition has been so divided in its councils that only recently has Gaitskell commanded full party support. Labor has not been able to persuade British public opinion, according to recent polls, that it offers an effective alternative to the Conservative regime. Labor clearly needs an issue with which to defeat the Conservatives. It is more likely to find its version of such an issue in the foreign rather than the domestic field.

In public comments and asides since Macmillan made some Cabinet shifts last October, he has noted that he was getting along in years (born in 1894) and intimated that the Conservative Party might need younger leadership. These comments suggested to some that he might step down after the next election. No election is required until 1964, but it is obviously advantageous to the party in power to pick the time. In recent months Prime Minister Macmillan has struck observers as appearing more tired than usual, although in the past this weary appearance has been recognized as a pose. Macmillan's personal position of leadership remains unassailed so long as he wants to continue.

There is a strong popular British desire for international action to lessen international tensions, particularly over the Berlin crisis. The British public want to avoid a head-on clash with the Soviet Union which would result in war, if this can be honorably avoided. In the British views the most effective way to avoid such a clash is through East-West negotiations in which Britain would play an important role.

A further important current concern to the British body politic is the developments in the Congo. The British officially see eye to eye with us on the overall Congo picture, and generally look upon the U.S. as the architect of the UN's Congo policy. A sizeable Conservative segment is particularly sympathetic toward Tshombe. British opinion has followed the UN's actions closely and the Government backing for the UN limited military offensive has been upheld in Parliament. Basically, British opinion still prefers a negotiated to a military settlement in the Congo.

Britain's press has recently given greater attention to American criticism of the United Kingdom's failure to meet its share of the Berlin military build-up, particularly with regard to the British Army on the Rhine. This has led to press discussion of the divergence between American opinion that in a dispute with the Soviet Union in Western Europe a "pause" could occur which would see the need for conventional weapons, and the British view that a resort to nuclear weapons in any major dispute with the Soviet Union is inevitable. In the British reading of this divergence, a build-up of the British Army on the Rhine (BAOR), even if desirable, is something the British, plagued by balance of payments difficulties, cannot afford unless they receive assistance from the Germans in off-sets to this balance of payments drain on the continent.

Against this background of domestic political concern and an impressive list of unresolved international problems, the British Prime Minister is most anxious to meet with the President of the United States. Our thought has been that the main discussions at Bermuda should take place under three main headings: first, the Berlin complex; second, European integration and US-UK relations; and, third, nuclear problems.

I. The Berlin Complex

In the Berlin complex of problems the most pressing aspect centers around the question of negotiation of the current crisis, but any such negotiation must be seen clearly in the total German problem. Both the UK and ourselves will be influenced by the recent NATO ministerial discussion at Paris which has shown the differences on the desirability of negotiations. Berlin has become something of a measuring stick of the unity of the Western alliance. From Macmillan's standpoint one of the reasons why he has stressed the necessity of negotiations may be to condition his countrymen to accept sterner methods if it fails.

II. European Integration and U.S.-U.K. Relations

The British decision to apply for membership in the Common Market is one of the most significant decisions that any British Prime Minister has made in recent times. Britain is turning toward Europe. Britain has made clear through the public statements of its leaders that it intends to participate wholeheartedly in the full concept of EEC. In such an integrated Europe, fully capable of playing a major role, it is our hope that Britain would exercise decisive leadership. European integration and the problems that it poses for US-UK relations encompass such dynamic concepts as a realizably strong European unit and the potential of an expanded Atlantic Community. For many British intellectuals the road to Brussels leads to Washington. Between the time of the Bermuda talks and the years before the realization of the goal of a politically integrated Western Europe, many practical things will have to be worked out. We believe it may be premature to embark at this time on too full a discussion of future steps which might dilute the present unique American-British "partnership" as a result of what we contemplate as the political culmination of EEC. Once the political entity that emerges in Western Europe is assessable, we can discuss the desirability and details of transforming American-British special arrangements into an American-EEC cooperation.

It is psychologically important that we emphasize to the British Prime Minister the great value to the United States that comes from existing military and intelligence cooperation with the United Kingdom. We certainly want to see this kind of cooperation continue. This means reassuring the British of our desire for a continuing close association, but at the same time making the point without overtones that neither side can expect the contemporary American-British relationship to be a preclusive one. In terms of the entire Western defense policy in Europe, it is essential that we have full US-UK accord on strategy, as we believe we have. It flows from this that in its European defense posture the UK must demonstrate to the NATO alliance that it not only adheres to overall strategic agreement but is willing to implement it by the necessary build-up in the field wherever that build-up has been agreed upon.

III. Nuclear Problems

The third major heading will concern British support for the U.S. position regarding future atmospheric nuclear testing. There is an idealistic segment in Britain which finds nuclear atmospheric testing repugnant. Although this segment is exploited by Communists it is not predominantly Communist, and it cannot be dismissed out of hand by any responsible politician, because there is strong majority opposition to atmospheric testing for the mere sake of testing. In these nuclear discussions it will be essential that we convince the Prime Minister that if we decide to embark on nuclear atmospheric testing we do so only because it is militarily necessary. This must be made so clear that he will be confident that he can in turn convince the British public that this is the over-riding reason. At the same time we will want British support for a moratorium on the Geneva Conference.

It is to be hoped that the main lines of the Bermuda talks may follow the foregoing three headings. There is, of course, the likelihood that current developments may make it desirable to discuss the Congo or South East Asia, although these have relatively recently been canvassed by the Secretary and the Foreign Secretary.

It is easier for us to be frank and full with the British than with any of our other allies. On so many international problems we find ourselves starting from a point basically similar to the starting point of the British leadership. This similarity of outlook is an important part of the uniqueness of US-UK relations. Furthermore, the British are sincerely desirous of maintaining not only the public image of US-UK accord but want to make the exchange on which this overall accord is based as meaningful as possible.

This similarity of view understandably tends to magnify differences. On the divergences that do exist on aspects of important problems it is in our interests to achieve as close harmony as possible. On the question of the Berlin build-up, for example, the British must be made to see, not only the necessity for their maintaining the BAOR at an effective strength of 55,000, but the importance of showing our other NATO allies that they adhere without reservation to agreed NATO planning. Similarly, it is important that no shading of difference on what is to be done about Katanga should hinder our overall accord on the future of the Congo.

And yet we cannot expect to emerge from the Bermuda talks with all differences solved. The motif should not be obscured, this is a friendly exchange between old friends. Because of the unique closeness of our relations with the British, it will be possible to cover a wide canvas in a comparatively short time. This will be a point of concern to our allies, for the time has passed when Anglo-American decisions can be taken without careful consideration of the views of the other members of the Western Alliance. From the broad discussions that will occur in Bermuda, we will wish to consult with our other allies to maintain the unity and effectiveness of Western policy. Always ready to have a friendly exchange with any ally, but particularly with our oldest and strongest, we realize that it is the unity of the entire Western Alliance that is our shield against the designs of the Soviet Bloc.

386. **Telegram From the Mission to the North Atlantic Treaty Organization and European Regional Organizations to the Department of State**

Paris, December 18, 1961, 8 p.m.

Polto 803. Re Polto 800.[1] In preparation for Bermuda Conf between President and Macmillan, I offer following thoughts for consideration.

We believe UK is one of our most important allies, and indeed, despite some differences, is one, if not the most trustworthy ally to count on when chips are down and fighting in prospect.

Our long-standing close ties with UK, coupled with history of development of atomic weapons, has resulted in UK having been given preferred position with regard to receiving information and equipment from US in atomic and missiles field, particularly strategic area. This has been useful in the past. In the past, Britain has been one of the countries willing to accept the responsibilities and risks of strategic nuclear arms, and is amongst most responsible allies with regard to being entrusted therewith. Question is whether it is in US best interests to continue this relationship at this time and to further foster independent UK strategic missile and atomic strength.

We consider that UK views are clear and that UK strongly desires to maintain present preferred position in this field. Most recent evidence includes UK statements with regard to joining peaceful atomic programs of EEC, seeking to condition participation in EEC on preservation of preferred position on military atomic matters; UK negative attitude of President's Ottawa speech (Secto 47)[2] and generally reflected throughout position taken by UK in strategy discussions in NAC since last spring.

While UK has not stated reasons behind its approach, we consider they probably include following: desire to maintain posture of big power status created by being only other country than US in free world that has some atomic strategic force. We assume British motives are more political than military, for they must realize the additive factor to free world nuclear strength provided by their strategic force is at best

---

Source: Department of State, Central Files, 375/12–1861. Secret; Priority; Limit Distribution. Repeated to London.

[1] Polto 800, December 17, reported various proposals that the British might raise at Bermuda on MRBMs. (Ibid., 375/12–1761)

[2] For text of the President's address to the Canadian Parliament, May 17, see *Public Papers of the Presidents of the United States: John F. Kennedy, 1961*, pp. 382–387. Secto 47, December 16, reported that the British were interested in creating a committee of governments in NATO that would be fully informed about nuclear matters rather than trying to devise some kind of use formula. (Department of State, Conference Files: Lot 65 D 366)

marginal, and they are not likely to become openly dedicated to Gallois theory that motivates French. But, it seems to us, particularly in period when UK reaching for way to join EEC, with concomitant potential considerable degree of loss of independent big power status, UK would wish strongly to maintain some major elements of its old role in the world. Even more importantly, we assume that UK motivated by desire to remain most intimate partner of US in this most important military field, in order to strengthen ties and influence upon US re question of ultimate use of atomic weapons. As stockholding partner in nuclear club, it has greater voice than it would otherwise have.

We are all for maintaining and strengthening US-UK ties. Nevertheless, from long-term point of view, we doubt whether we can continue to do so in atomic missile field without prejudice to bigger game of future. Key job in long run is to ensure GFR remains integrated into West, and we must evolve some way to do so with regard to atomic weapons that will satisfy German demands for equality if we are not to see German effort, or Franco-German effort, ultimately lead to independent German strategic atomic strength or to some arrangement in which US would have no voice at all. This is question of a political rather than a military requirement. Pressures to take action toward that end are in our view no longer something for long-range future but have become a problem that must be tackled now. Only solution that we can see is within framework of some sort of NATO MRBM force in pursuance of policy set down in President's Ottawa speech. Particularly in light of Secretary's remarks at restricted December 14 NAC meeting,[3] and in view our contacts and conversations with Stikker and various Perm Reps, I am convinced Alliance looks to this solution of problem of GFR integration.

If it were not for this problem, I think Alliance would probably by and large be content with present arrangements, but GFR problem now makes this an imperative.

It is submitted it is not possible to give the appearance of wholeheartedly pursuing policy of President's Ottawa speech and at the same time to continue to provide UK with growing independent atomic missile strength. Dept will recall that it was at last Bermuda Conference with UK that US agreed to provide Thors to UK, and that reaction of Europe was that this was step backward in seeking to develop concept of a NATO MRBM operation.

What we really would like from Britain in military field is greater conventional strength on the continent. But the problem here is political

---

[3] The text of Rusk's remarks was transmitted in Polto A–718, December 15. (Ibid., Central Files, 396.1–PA/12–156)

and economic—conscription and a diversion to defense of funds now being devoted to economic growth. We therefore doubt that even if we were to give some further help to UK in atomic missile area that result would be that we would get increased conventional strength which we desire.

As we understand it, UK desires are to see Skybolt developed and made available to them as an interim measure, and thereafter to maintain their atomic strategic role by means of seaborne missiles (later reducing to some degree likelihood of immediate Soviet response against strategic bases in UK itself), coupled with ultimate phase-out of aircraft and missiles in UK. If we were to take on commitments at Bermuda that further fostered this approach, we would not only increase durability of British resistance to idea of NATO multilateral nuclear force, but would once again raise doubts in minds of other allies as to sincerity of our approach to NATO force. We would also give French additional argument in support of their claim that they are discriminated against, which they could use with telling effect, particularly with Germans.

At same time we recognize that UK is at very important and sensitive moment with regard to determining its future policy. It is not yet clear how talks with EEC will go or what new alignments will emerge. We very much doubt that it is in US interests to so reject British approach that it might in long run invite them to participate with EEC, or even with France alone, in further development of strike force as to which US would not even have consultative voice.

On balance, therefore, we recommend frank discussion of various policy motives involved during Bermuda talks in such a way as to let UK know that because of these considerations US at this time not undertaking further specific commitments in nuclear strategic area until we see how discussions in NAC develop. At same time believe we should not slam door of cooperation in these areas in face of UK, since it is difficult to see how things will actually go in future.

In addition, it is for consideration whether the United States should offer some further collaboration with the UK in the nuclear/missiles field in return for a pledge by the UK that a major component of the force that would result therefrom would be placed under NATO command. While this would foster a certain degree of continued independent UK nuclear strength, it can well be argued that it is not realistic to expect the UK to give up all of its independent nuclear strength at this point and that progress must be made slowly. On the other hand, it must be confessed that this would be precedent for the French once they had obtained a "substantial" capability. But it may be the only way to make progress in this area.

Finletter

387. Circular Telegram From the Department of State to Certain Missions

Washington, December 27, 1961, 8:24 p.m.

1172. Following are highlights President's meeting with Macmillan Bermuda December 21–22.[1]

1. Berlin was principal topic. In framework Paris discussions agreement reached Thompson should conduct initial probe with Gromyko primarily regarding Soviet intentions on access arrangements. Other principal aspects of Berlin problem (status of West Berlin including occupation regime, relations with FedRep, etc., and broader question of Germany including frontiers, reunification, etc.) would not be raised by Thompson.

Thompson's instructions will be discussed with FedRep and should arrive in Moscow this week permitting him seek meeting around end of year. Was agreed probe must stop short of negotiations and for this reason should not be prolonged beyond very few meetings. If is thereupon decided that basis for negotiations exists in light our minimum conditions Foreign Ministers' meeting will presumably follow. We will stay in close direct touch with countries directly concerned (UK, France and FRG) and with NATO allies through NAC.

2. Congo: UK reiterated concern at possible prolongation UN military involvement which they believe should be replaced soonest by purely civil affairs training role. We reiterated view Katanga must remain part of Congo, that there must be agreement between Tshombe and Adoula and that fundamental Congo unity must be preserved in framework permitting suitable local powers. We believe role of UN is to keep open path to conciliation and not to impose a political solution.

3. EEC: Discussion brief, being confined largely to Macmillan statement that agriculture constituted principal difficulty and that he could not predict final outcome of negotiations. Said even if all problems resolved the earliest that signature envisaged was one year hence.

Other topics briefly discussed without requiring substantive decisions or containing expressions of fact or opinion departing from standard positions were: Goa, West New Guinea, and Viet-Nam.

Rusk

Source: Department of State, Central Files, 611.41/12–2761. Confidential. Drafted by Knight; cleared with Bohlen, Tyler, and Fessenden; and approved by Tyler. Sent to missions in Latin America, Europe, and the Far East.

[1] Memoranda, background, and briefing papers for the meeting at Bermuda are ibid., Conference Files: Lot 65 D 366, CF 2208–2214. For Macmillan's account of the meeting, see *At the End of the Day,* pp. 145–148; for text of the joint communiqué of the meeting, see *American Foreign Policy: Current Documents, 1961,* pp. 547–548.

388. Memorandum of Conversation

Washington, January 15, 1962.

SUBJECT

> Informal Exchange of Views between the Secretary and Harold Wilson, British Labor Party Leader

PARTICIPANTS

> The Secretary
> Mr. Harold Wilson, Foreign Minister, Labor Shadow Cabinet, United Kingdom
> Mr. Robin Wilson (Mr. Wilson's teen-age son)
> Mr. Joseph Sweeney, BNA

Mr. Wilson, at his initiative, called on the Secretary for an informal exchange of views. According to Mr. Wilson the Labor Party was in accord with the policies of the present American Government. Indeed, Mr. Wilson doubted if there had been such accord on policy between the Labor Party and the American Government in many years. Mr. Wilson was most complimentary about American leadership, particularly at the time of the Congo difficulty. In his view some of the older Tory reactionaries had given the Government trouble. He considered the recent parliamentary debate on the Congo the most important since Suez. He recalled that in talking to Ambassador Bruce at the time there had been rumors that the Government might fall over the Congo. Mr. Wilson had urged Ambassador Bruce not to report this to Washington as a strong possibility because he felt Prime Minister Macmillan would weather the political storm in his own fashion. When Lord Home, the Foreign Secretary, had sent for him to talk about the Congo, it was clear to Wilson that British and American policies on objectives were very close.

The Secretary asked about what Mr. Wilson thought people on the other side of the Atlantic might do to help in repairing the recent damage to the prestige of the UN. Mr. Wilson agreed it was most important that the Labor Party help in this direction and felt that we could count on their cooperation. He jocularly pointed out that many people in the Conservative Party were opposed to the UN "because there were too many foreigners in it."

The Secretary inquired about Denis Healey, Mr. Wilson's predecessor in the Foreign Affairs post in the Shadow Cabinet, who was an old friend of the Secretary's. Mr. Wilson explained that Healey now had the Commonwealth responsibility in the Shadow Cabinet and was at pres-

---

Source: Department of State, Central Files, 611.41/1–1562. Official Use Only. Drafted by Sweeney and approved in S on January 23.

ent touring Africa. The Secretary asked how Mr. Wilson liked his new responsibility, moving from the Exchequer to the Foreign Affairs responsibility? Mr. Wilson explained that he enjoyed the change, that Hugh Gaitskell had decided that the Foreign Affairs responsibility was a heavy one and that he should shift one of the senior officials to this responsibility so that he, Mr. Gaitskell, could concentrate on domestic policy. [2 lines of source text not declassified]

The Secretary asked how Mr. Wilson thought the Common Market outlook appeared. Mr. Wilson said he was not quite sure. There were divisions on this matter in the Labor Party. Douglas Jay and Denis Healey were very much opposed to British membership in the Common Market. He himself had been all over the lot, for it, and opposed to it, and recently he had emerged at the stage where he said "let's see how much we have to pay for the horse, and see the condition of his teeth before we move further." In a view which he had arrived at only since he had been here in America, Mr. Wilson had concluded that what Britain did should depend largely on the size of the external tariff. If, by joining the Common Market, Britain was generally moving toward a free trade area, that would be encouraging, but what we might also be heading for was one of the most restricted trading areas the world had known, and he did not feel that this would be advantageous. Mr. Wilson indicated there might be a general election in Britain before the final decision on British adherence to the Common Market was made, but only if Mr. Macmillan was convinced that a propitious time had arrived for a general election and he felt confident that the Conservative Party could win it. A further concern about the Common Market from his point of view was a series of problems associated with the free movement of capital, which might prove difficult for Britain.

The Secretary inquired if there were any doctrinal restraints on Labor cooperation with the Common Market, in the sense of whether this might be difficult for a Socialist Party. Mr. Wilson felt that there were no such restraints and observed that one of the developments the Common Market permitted and indeed even encouraged was nationalization.

The Secretary explained that he had not read the full text of Lord Home's recent speech on the United Nations, which had been termed "disastrous" by some British papers, but he was curious about what had happened. The first reports in the American press had not indicated any difficulty on the first day but only on the second day did they imply Lord Home had been critical of the UN and caused something of a political outcry. Mr. Wilson explained this had been an interesting development. Lord Home had been speaking in his own home territory to the local United Nations Association. It had been a small audience, not over a hundred and fifty. Lord Home had said all the right things, but he had said several wrong ones in terms of emphasis, and he had made one major blunder. The major blunder concerned the "Colonialism resolution" at the recent session of the UN General Assembly. This "Colonialism resolution" had been hard for the Tories. Lord Home, giving his views to a small group, said he did not believe that anyone who voted for this resolution could really be in favor of peace. The Secretary pointed out that we had voted for this resolution. "Exactly," Mr. Wilson exclaimed, and went on to explain that he had made this point to both Home and the Prime Minister. Mr. Wilson thought this minor tempest would blow over although he did make the point in his insistent way that this was not the only instance in which the Labor Party was closer to American policy than Her Majesty's Government.

In a general discussion of the problems of nuclear weapons the Secretary said that in a sense the possession of nuclear arms imposed limitations on the sovereignty of the United States. Mr. Wilson agreed and observed that the United States had to have nuclear arms, indeed should have them, but the United Kingdom did not really have to have a nuclear deterrent. He noted that British possession of a nuclear capability was most costly and was a major reason why the U.K. could not afford to do more in the way of conventional arms. Mr. Wilson spoke of the Soviet concern about our nuclear capability and a short discussion ensued of the Soviet fear that Western Germany might obtain an independent nuclear capability.

Mr. Wilson referred to his many trips to the Soviet Union and the Secretary asked what he thought was going on in the leadership there at the present time. Mr. Wilson said he was not sure but it seemed clear to him that Mr. Khrushchev had less than absolute control. He suggested further that Mr. Khrushchev had some difficulty with his younger leaders possibly those in the army. He felt the present internal argument might well have had its beginnings in the debate over the decision to set off the 50 megaton bomb, but he felt it was difficult to explain the present situation inside the Soviet Union.

At the conclusion of their discussion Mr. Wilson asked the Secretary if he would sign his son's autograph book. At the Secretary's suggestion arrangements were made for Mr. Wilson and his son to attend the President's press conference which took place a few minutes after this exchange of views.

389. Telegram From the Department of State to the Embassy in the United Kingdom

Washington, February 16, 1962, 8:48 p.m.

4404. Eyes only for Ambassador Bruce. Embassy should deliver following message as early as possible in the morning to Prime Minister Macmillan from President:

Begin text.

February 16, 1962

Dear Mr. Prime Minister:

We have received from your Ambassador a memorandum explaining the White Paper on Defense which I understand you plan to issue February 20.[1] I want to express my real gratitude for the opportunity to comment on this most important matter prior to issuance of the White Paper. Secretary Rusk has already given our reaction to your Embassy, but because of the importance of the matter I want to write directly to you as well.

In all frankness, I must say that I am deeply concerned at this memorandum as it affects Berlin and NATO. I realize that the memorandum may not correspond to what the White Paper will actually say. I realize also that the memorandum and White Paper are intended to present a long-term plan, covering the general philosophy of your Government's defense programs over the next ten years. But here again, I feel that it is very important to take account of the very serious crisis which we face today and I fear that the White Paper, if it follows the shape of the outline, may be subject to most serious misinterpretation by the Soviets, by our other NATO Allies, and by the people of my own country.

My main concerns are three.

First, I feel that a most serious deficiency is the failure to mention any increased build-up to meet the Berlin situation. As you know, we ourselves have taken major measures to increase our combat forces deployed in Europe and to back this up by strengthening our defenses at home. This has required increased expenditures, with a rising percentage of our Gross National Product devoted to defense. It has required

---

Source: Department of State, Central Files, 741.5/2–1662. Secret. Drafted by Fessenden and cleared with the President, Rusk, and McNamara.

[1] A copy of the memorandum is ibid., 741.5/1–962. A memorandum of Rusk's conversation with Hood on February 14 is ibid., 741.5/2–1462. Rusk emphasized the following three reactions to the memorandum: insufficient account of the need for a Berlin build-up, prejudging the need for a build-up of NATO conventional forces, and prejudging the NATO discussion of nuclear forces. The White Paper on Defense was released on February 20.

difficult actions in calling up reserves and maintaining them as long as the crisis demands. I took upon these measures as having one central purpose, and that is to impress upon Mr. Khrushchev and the Soviet leaders the seriousness of our purpose. It is only by this road, I am convinced, that we can prevent what we both want to avoid at all costs—an outbreak of war over Berlin. It seems to us essential that these measures by our Government be reinforced by similar steps by our NATO Allies. Although some countries have responded reasonably well to date, the response on the whole has been less than satisfactory. It is here that your Government's position is pivotal. If Britain were prepared to strengthen its forces, I am sure that the response by other NATO countries would be much more satisfactory. I am sure also that the effect on the Soviet leaders will be very considerable.

Let me say more specifically that, although I welcome the decision to maintain the strength of the BAOR, I also understand that the BAOR is today under the agreed level. We have hoped that the BAOR could at least be brought up to and maintained at the agreed level. We recognize that you, like we, have balance of payments difficulties which impede your ability to bring about a substantial increase in your forces on the Continent. However, Britain's geographical position is such that it should be possible to raise and train forces at home which can be rapidly deployed to the Continent. The memorandum does not indicate that any steps are being taken to give the United Kingdom this capability. The statement that you will continue to rely on regular forces would seem to rule out this possibility. I know that the British effort, as a whole, is not behind that of most European members of NATO, but I cannot help hoping that the White Paper can be used so as to give impetus to others, not encouragement to procrastination.

My second concern relates to NATO strategy. As you know, we have emphasized in NATO and in the context of Berlin the importance of building up the conventional capability of the Alliance. We are firmly convinced that a more adequate conventional capability will contribute greatly to the over-all deterrent of the Alliance. There are signs that our own conventional build-up is already causing some concern to Soviet military leaders. Although the memorandum does not explicitly deal with general NATO strategy questions, the specific lines of action do not seem to provide for any conventional build-up. They thus seem to prejudge adversely the outcome of strategy discussions in NATO, and if the White Paper itself has the same form , the impact on NATO efforts may be severe—with a parallel encouragement to Soviet appetites.

Finally, I must express special concern about the explicit statement that the United Kingdom will "continue to maintain throughout the 1960's" its independent strategic nuclear deterrent. As you know, NATO is going through a basic re-examination of its nuclear policy. The basic objective of that study, which I am sure you share, is to devise means of giving our Continental Allies a sufficient sense of participation in nuclear matters to head off inevitable increasing pressures for independent nuclear capabilities. Our central concern in this is the future course of Germany. I believe that a flat statement by your Government that it will continue its independent deterrent program "throughout the 1960's" may well have the effect of convincing de Gaulle of the rightness of his course and of discouraging the many people in France who have serious reservations about de Gaulle's policies. This, in turn, will hasten the day when Germany will pursue a national program. Alternatively, it will increase pressure for Franco-German cooperation, about which you have already written me.[2] I therefore hope that anything said publicly about Britain's independent deterrent may take full account of these considerations. I would add that we ourselves are prepared to be as forthcoming as possible to meet our objective of finding a NATO solution to head off independent national aspirations.

I know you will understand the spirit in which these remarks are made. Obviously your defense policy is a matter on which I comment with reluctance. Yet I have felt an obligation to speak candidly because of our deep concern about the summary we have seen. Mr. Watkinson, I know, has kept Secretary McNamara broadly informed, but I cannot conceal from you that the summary itself has been a concern to us, especially in the light of the continued dangers in Berlin. In some measure, my comments have related to the substance of your defense policy, but it may be that to some extent our concerns may be met as much by the way in which you state the matter as by the substance of what you mean to do.

I have written with great candor—first, because of the deep concern which we feel here over the possible impact of the White Paper, if we understand it right—but second, because of my confidence that you will not misunderstand this wholly private communication. I could not raise a matter of this sort in this way with any other man—at the head of any other country—and I am sure you know that I do so only because we can both be so confident of our continuing partnership.

With warm personal regards,

Sincerely,

John Kennedy. *End text.*

Rusk

---

[2] Presumably a reference to Macmillan's letter of January 13 describing his talks with Adenauer in Bonn. (Ibid., Presidential Correspondence: Lot 66 D 204)

390. Telegram From the Department of State to the Embassy in the United Kingdom

Washington, February 19, 1962, 7:46 p.m.

4433. For Ambassador from Secretary Dillon. For your information during past few days we have had what could be serious difference of opinion with British over gold purchases. They informed us about ten days ago that they wished to purchase an additional $350 million worth of gold within next 4 to 6 weeks. We were surprised because we did not see how British could possibly have accumulated this many dollars over and above their debt to the International Monetary Fund and their normal working balance of $300 million. We asked Cromer[1] for further information which was furnished us toward end of last week. This information shows that as of February 14 British had total foreign exchange holdings of all sorts amounting to $1292 million. Their current debt to Fund of $1080 million plus their normal working balance in dollars of $300 million total $1380 million which indicates that $90 million of the $350 million in gold which the British purchased from us since last fall came out of the proceeds of their drawing from the Fund. This is completely contrary to the very clear understanding which I reached with Parsons[2] last July prior to the British drawing.

Memorandum of conversation[3] of that meeting prepared by British shows Parsons saying that after their dollar holdings increase above their normal level they would have "the alternative of continuing to hold these extra dollars for the time being or of starting to repurchase sterling in the Fund". This fully bears out our understanding and leaves no room for use of Fund proceeds to buy gold from U.S.

Today Roosa[4] outlined our view in detail to Pitblado who had originally raised matter with him. Hayes, President Federal Reserve Bank of New York, also talked on phone to the Deputy Governor of the Bank in absence of Cromer. In addition at the President's direction I expressed my concern and surprise to Ormsby-Gore during course of small luncheon at White House today for Gaitskell. The President had earlier indicated his concern to Ormsby-Gore who told me that he had reported this to London.

Source: Department of State, Central Files, 841.13/2–1962. Confidential; Eyes Only. Drafted by Dillon.

[1] George R.S. Baring, Earl of Cromer, Governor of the Bank of England.

[2] Maurice H. Parsons, Director of the Bank of England.

[3] Not found.

[4] Robert V. Roosa, Under Secretary of the Treasury for Monetary Affairs.

While current balance of payments situation appears to be seasonally favorable as was the case during first quarter last year, official 4th quarter figures are about to come out which will show substantial losses of short term funds. The loss of several hundred million dollars in gold immediately after publication these figures would obviously be disturbing factor in exchange markets and is so regarded by all Central Bankers on continent who were given preliminary information regarding this matter at the last Basle meeting on February 11. It is also difficult for us to see what advantage there is for British to hold reserve in gold which they owe the Monetary Fund when they could as well pay the Fund off in dollars. This was also personal reaction of Ormsby-Gore.

While we are of course always ready to sell gold against dollars it is clear that if British pursue this matter contrary to their agreement with us last July the repercussions would be extremely serious as it would then become necessary for us to utilize every means in our power to reduce dollar holdings of sterling area since we would have had clear notice that these holdings are now a danger to the dollar. It is our assumption here that this whole matter probably arose as suggestion of certain members of staff of Bank of England and had not been thoroughly thought out at top level. I must say I am surprised at Parsons' role in this since he was the individual who personally gave flat commitment last July.

This message is forwarded for your information since the President felt you should be informed in case matter was mentioned to you in London. No action is being requested as we are handling matter from here. Would appreciate it if you could inform Bean but otherwise should be held very closely because of obvious dangers involved in rumors regarding gold.

Rusk

391. Scope Paper Prepared in the Department of State

MMW D–3   Washington, April 20, 1962.

PRIME MINISTER MACMILLAN'S VISIT TO WASHINGTON
April 27–29, 1962

Our purpose in the Washington talks with the President and the British Prime Minister is clear. We want to be friendly toward the Prime Minister who is under emotional strain on disarmament and nuclear testing and hard pressed politically. We want to listen to his views with sympathetic understanding. We want him to know our thinking on current international issues and project for him our views on East-West matters and European integration. In the process we should make implicit the way we hope U.K. policy will evolve not as a consequence of U.S. pressure, but as a logical result of the forces now in motion. We want him to leave Washington without having induced us to modify our views, but with a satisfied feeling that he has had a very worthwhile and pleasant exchange.

The British need these discussions and we do not. They may well seek to obtain concessions from us which we cannot grant. They may attempt to attach greater importance to these talks than we do.

The fact of the meeting itself reaffirms the special friendship that characterizes the US-UK relationship. The United Kingdom is involved in adjustments of great complexity concerned with its shift from major to lesser power status and its move toward the continent, toward European integration. If our hopes regarding European integration are realized, there will be a challenging opportunity for Britain to exert a position of leadership. Although changes will undoubtedly ensue in the precise nature of the US-UK relationship, as well as in the Commonwealth system, it is early to attempt to define them in detail. What can be said with assurance is that the ties of language, culture and common ideas will endure and continue to be the firm basis for the intimate friendship of our two countries, just as these elements of English history and tradition ensure the continuance of the Commonwealth.

History has pushed Macmillan to very decisive steps. Fundamentally, Macmillan and his group have made the decision about moving toward the continent, but they keep looking back at the US-UK relationship. Any indication at this critical moment that the United Kingdom might be left alone in Europe could provoke a reaction so adverse as to

---

Source: Department of State, Conference Files: Lot 65 D 533, CF 2085. Secret. Drafted by Sweeney and cleared with Schaetzel, Tyler, Ball, and Rusk.

jeopardize British pursuit of the present negotiations with the Common Market. We believe it is inevitable—if not now, then later—that Britain enter the Common Market. Any redefinition of American-British relations should await the larger clarification of the relations between the US and an integrated Western Europe. As this larger pattern develops, US-UK relations, with due cognizance of their special character, will in turn fall into place within the expanded concept. Therefore, we should approach the whole subject matter of US-UK relations in a positive spirit, i.e., focusing on the new US-Europe ties, emphasizing that the US and the UK are both moving into new, changed and closer relations with Europe.

A key part of this positive approach to US-UK relations might well occur in the President painting the kind of integrated Western Europe that we hope will emerge. The leading role of the United Kingdom in such a Western Europe as the President might describe should catch the imagination of the British—for instance, that special political genius of England to which the theory and practice of democracy owes so much.

It is important that the President make no commitments which bind us to perpetuate the present forms of the US-UK relationship. He can understandably respond that we are in a time of great change and look forward to closer US-UK ties with Europe as a whole. The similarity of the US-UK outlook will help us work closely together in Europe and across the Atlantic.

The Prime Minister is well briefed on the intricacies of the Common Market and the precise details of UK-EEC negotiations. The President should seek his forecast of events and make his points in the description of the kind of integrated Western Europe we hope to see emerge, but without himself being drawn into specifics of the negotiations, or of the type of UK-Six settlement we would approve of.

The Prime Minister is too experienced a hand not to make a few skillful tries. Plays which should be guarded against are:

(1) *an appeal for perpetuating Commonwealth preferences in a Common Market* on the basis that without such arrangements the Conservative Government cannot carry Parliament along;

(2) *our support to obtain the association to the Common Market* of the EFTA. Heath recently stated categorically in his otherwise encouraging Western Union speech that association of the EFTA (meaning particularly the neutrals) is "British policy".

On any appeal to acquiesce in perpetuation of Commonwealth preferences the President should indicate a lack of enthusiasm but recognize the importance of the Commonwealth to the interests of the Free World. Any give in our opposition to perpetuating preferences probably will have to take the form of meeting certain exceptionally critical economic difficulties of specific old-line Commonwealth members. The President may wish to refer to our own problems of preference and the domestic political problem this creates for us and possibly imply that we may have to balance our own preference problems and those of the Commonwealth when a specific critical need is evidenced in the EEC negotiations. The President should not offer any encouragement with regard to "association" of the EFTA to the Common Market, but say US policy remains opposed to "association" as the best and certainly as the only answer to what appears to be essentially commercial problems. If the EFTA countries wish to be tied politically but without loss of neutrality, then a Schuman Plan association might be considered—i.e., association with the EEC without preferential trade arrangements. And,

(3) *our help if he runs into opposition from de Gaulle in the larger framework of European unity.* The President might with conviction point out that our influence is limited and only harm could come from the appearance of an Anglo-American gang-up against the French. The President might consider assuring the Prime Minister that he would not be without European allies in such situation and de Gaulle would be particularly susceptible to pressure from a united coalition of his five colleagues of the Six.

The Prime Minister may attempt to throw the responsibility for resolving his nuclear deterrent dilemma on us. He may attempt to elicit an implied commitment that at least in the "holy realm" of military nuclear arrangements the special US-UK relationship will be perpetuated. Nuclear weapons have become a status symbol of international power, and the UK will not give up this symbol easily. The French, however, resent the US-UK nuclear monopoly in NATO and a special nuclear status for the UK within the Community would not be tolerated by the Continental powers. In the long run it may become important to the goal of an integrated Western Europe for Britain to contribute its national nuclear deterrent to the Community as a function of developing a multilateral NATO nuclear deterrent. We might at this juncture concentrate on seeking British support for a NATO multilateral MRBM force and in the process point out the dangers of German and French national nuclear cooperation. We see no reason why the President need conceal his lack of enthusiasm for the Defense White Paper with its failure to support the strengthening of NATO's non-nuclear arm.

We should use the opportunity to steady the British on East-West matters and to induce them to accept the continued necessity of facing up to the unpleasant requirements of the Cold War. We know that Macmillan is terribly worried about disarmament and nuclear testing. We must not underestimate the Prime Minister's concern about the present state of East-West relations, his conviction that he, personally, must do something about it and his desire to go down in history as the architect of an East-West détente. It is important that we counsel him on patience and perseverance.

The discussions will take place in the shadow of resumed Western nuclear testing and possibly a more definite indication of another series of Soviet tests. These developments might possibly pave the way for new proposals on a test ban. The Prime Minister will be most anxious to explore all such avenues. We know that he has a feeling of personal failure that he was not able to come up with some kind of a proposal that would have brought the Soviets around to acceptance of a test ban before the current Western tests.

When most of the wrappings have been removed, the weak spots in the British appraisal of the East-West confrontation concern Berlin, economic counter-measures against the bloc, and a feeling that bringing the Chinese Communists into international affairs is inevitable. On Berlin we may have an opportunity to assess the results of the Secretary's discussions with Ambassador Dobrynin and evaluate whether the Soviets would accept a détente. On the economic counter-measures the Prime Minister of one of the greatest trading nations may be understandably sympathetic to the contention that "the only good Russian is a fat one." With regard to the Chinese Communist role the Prime Minister has indicated he would appreciate information on our views on the future of our relations with the Communist Chinese.

While the discussions with the Prime Minister may convince us that we have reinfused the British with the need to stand firm against the Soviet Union, and we know that in a show-down they would be with us, it is in the grey areas of compromise that might occur at any summit meeting that we have need for concern. It may well be that the purpose of these discussions will be an exchange of briefings for a summit meeting. Against that possibility we want to be sure that the vaunted British spine is stiffened across the board in the day-to-day aspects of East-West confrontation.

In the careful consideration of diplomatic parry and riposte for these talks, it is important that the desirability of acknowledging the special friendship that characterizes the US-UK relationship not be overlooked. Nor should it be labored. Furthermore, a certain amount of reassurance for Macmillan personally is indicated. He has been having a hard time of it. His critics—and even some of his own Tory compatriots—claim he has lost his political magic.

Macmillan and his Conservative Party have had recent political rebuffs. Liberal Party gains in a by-election at Orpington dramatized a decline in the Conservative vote in other recent by-elections. However, the Conservative Party retains its parliamentary majority of over a hundred. The Labor Party has not as yet succeeded in projecting a convincing image of itself as a desirable alternative. On the other hand, the

Conservatives have discovered that the UK move toward Europe may be the key to a positive image for the Tories. But there can be no denying that a certain ferment has disturbed the British domestic political calm. No general election is now expected until next year. While Macmillan undoubtedly intends to guide his party through this next contest, he is again rumored to be stepping down after the elections. This is no new rumor, but there are increasing indications that his tired appearance is less studied pose and more a reflection of reality.

Against this background of a domestic political scene that shows some decline in enthusiasm for Conservative leadership, an increase in the tempo of British public debate over the desirability of entering the Common Market, a lack of success at Geneva in obtaining Soviet cooperation in disarmament or banning nuclear tests, and a threatening host of international problems, the Prime Minister is coming to talk with the President. He is encouraged by the genuine rapport established at the Bermuda talks in December 1961. He would not be averse to parlaying a successful Washington discussion into going with his friends to a summit gathering to try to bring about an overall settlement. He should only be encouraged if there were some tangible indication that equable results might be obtained.

---

392. Memorandum From the President's Special Assistant for National Security Affairs (Bundy) to President Kennedy

Washington, April 24, 1962.

Taz Shepard relayed your question as to why the President of the United States cannot make commitments which bind the United States to perpetuate the present forms of the US-UK relationship. This is a dandy question.

I hope that what the Department means here is what I was trying to say in a memorandum yesterday:[1] that our close cooperation with the British does not depend on British aloofness from Europe or on the existing preferential treatment of the British on nuclear matters. We want the British in Europe, and we do not really see much point in the separate British nuclear deterrent, beyond our existing Skybolt commitment; we would much rather have British efforts go into conventional weapons and have the British join with the rest of NATO in accepting a single U.S.-dominated nuclear force.

Source: Kennedy Library, National Security Files, United Kingdom. Secret.
[1] Not found.

The question of British membership in Europe is now urgent. The nuclear question is less pressing from our point of view, simply because the time does not look right for a solution. Certainly there is nothing for us in any possible British notion that the UK might pay its entrance fee to the Common Market by providing nuclear assistance to the French. In such a case the British would be appeasing the French with our secrets, and no good would come of it for Europe or for us. I strongly agree with Jean Monnet that the Common Market and the nuclear problem should be dealt with one after the other and not both at once. Our discussion of the MRBM problem should fill the gap in NATO while the Common Market and the UK are working out their basic arrangements (everyone is trying not to call it a U.S. proposal but Finletter warns that it will be very difficult to avoid some talk of a U.S. initiative).

So I think the answer is that the President of the United States has every right to sustain the special relationship with the UK as long as the fundamental basis of that relationship is cooperative common effort, and not special preference. After all, we would like a special relationship with the French too, if only it could involve some real cooperation.

McG. B.[2]

---

[2] Printed from a copy that bears these typed initials.

---

393. **Talking Points for the Acting Assistant Secretary of State's (Tyler) Briefing of the Joint Chiefs of Staff on Prime Minister Macmillan's Talks**

Washington, undated.

1. *General*

Talks were informal review of international problems facing US and UK. Major decisions not intended or taken.

Source: Department of State, J/PM Files: Lot 69 D 258, UK. Secret. No drafting information appears on the source text, but it is attached to a May 10 memorandum from Kitchen to Johnson, which states that it was prepared for a Department of State–JCS meeting scheduled for May 11. Prime Minister Macmillan visited Washington April 27–29. Memoranda of his conversations with the President are ibid., Conference Files: Lot 65 D 533, CF 2084; for a memorandum of their conversation on the UK-EEC negotiations, see Document 36.

Subjects discussed include:

Berlin and Germany
Disarmament
Nuclear testing
Possibility of summit meeting
NATO Strategy
Weapons research and development
Meeting with deGaulle
UK-EEC negotiations
US commercial and tariff policy
Britain and Western defense as a whole
Colonial problems and Western unity
Congo
Laos
West Guinea
British Guiana
Shipping

2. Berlin and Germany

Agreed that relaxation of pressure on Berlin made it appropriate to move ahead with talks with Soviets.

Secretary reviewed talks with Dobrynin—we were nose-to-nose on key issues, but Dobrynin did not seem agitated or desire speed things up.

US and UK should point out to Germans and French that we have made no concessions to Soviets, that we are in Berlin to stay.

Prime Minister urged we should press ahead with negotiations when we were not under disadvantage of pressure.

Prime Minister thought instead of agreement, which would involve too much loss of face for Soviets, we might eventually reach some sort of modus vivendi or agreement to disagree.

We noted Soviets are committed to peace treaty and if our rights are not respected when and if treaty is signed a dangerous situation might arise.

3. Disarmament

Agreed that Disarmament Conference should continue after June 1, when interim report to UN Disarmament Committee is due.

We noted that at present Soviets were playing the disarmament conference as a propaganda exercise.

4. Nuclear Testing

We intend wait 3 or 4 months until after our tests and Soviet tests which we expect to follow, and then consider after analyzing results whether we should make another offer for nuclear test ban limited to tests in the atmosphere, or possibly an entire treaty. We would have to take into account pressures in our two countries and around the world.

Prime Minister felt that if we develop new plan of nuclear testing we should present it directly to Khrushchev.

President stressed we should not reveal that we were anticipating another test ban offer. After an analysis of the tests we may find that we cannot make such an offer. Our stand calling for inspection and fixed controls was reviewed.

The Prime Minister was anxious to say that he and the President had worked out the question of tests together and that any changes were made together.

5. Possibility of Summit Meeting

It was agreed that there was no reason for a summit meeting unless there was a prospect of agreement in some important area, such as Berlin or nuclear testing.

It was agreed that bilateral meeting with Khrushchev should be kept open as a possible alternative but that this was not the right time to have a bilateral meeting.

6. NATO Strategy

The President and Prime Minister agreed that Mr. McNamara and Mr. Watkinson were talking about this subject closely and it was better to leave it to them.

President noted that we did have difference of emphasis on question of build-up of conventional forces and asked if the differences stemmed from balance-of-payments difficulties or strategy.

Prime Minister did not think there was a great difference and agreed we must keep up credibility of the deterrent. He agreed on the necessity for a pause before escalation to stress importance not to get the Russians should not think we would not use nuclear force [sic].

The President stressed the problem of Berlin in relation to the justification for the build-up of conventional forces.

7. UK-EEC Negotiations

The Prime Minister told the President at some length how matters stood with respect to UK-EEC negotiations.

Prime Minister stressed the need to take care of interest of Commonwealth and EFTA countries.

President stated his administration like previous one has given strong support to Common Market for political not economic reasons.

President pointed out that UK could not take care of everyone in its wake as it joined the Common Market. The political effect on the UK would be a serious one and would certainly accentuate US balance-of-payments problem, severely affect agriculture and could cause the US withdrawal of forces from around the world.

The President noted that there was an understanding of our respective position if not agreement. The US was prepared make many sacrifices but could not go all the way. He noted that the needs of Commonwealth countries might require preferences for a temporary period, but we were concerned that preferences be terminated by a certain date.

On EFTA neutrals, the President said we have every sympathy with Austria but are not as sympathetic towards Sweden and Switzerland who want the advantages of being in and out.

The President had Secretary Ball explain at length the US position with respect to Commonwealth preferences and the problem of the EFTA neutrals. Mr. Ball also explained the relevance of US commercial and tariff policy.

8. *Britain and Western Defense as a Whole*

President said we were reasonably well informed on each other's position on question of Britain and Western defense as a whole.

It was noted that US had two concerns—first, that NATO should be built up and second, there should be no weakening of British forces elsewhere in order to strengthen NATO.

Prime Minister assured us that Britain would not weaken its forces elsewhere in the world for the purpose of strengthening the British Army of the Rhine. He went on, however, to decry the anti-colonial drive which was exerting pressure on them to leave Hong Kong and Singapore.

[Here follows the remainder of the memorandum.]

394. Memorandum From the Assistant Secretary of State for
European Affairs (Kohler) to Secretary of State Rusk

Washington, May 24, 1962.

SUBJECT

U.K.'s Nuclear Role: A Program of Action

Discussion:

We are increasingly being forced to face up to the issue of the future
of the U.K. independent nuclear capability and the related question of
the U.S.-U.K. special relationship in the military nuclear field.

Our existing policy in this field, as set forth in the April 21 [20], 1961,
Policy Directive,[1] states: "Over the long run it would be desirable if the
British decided to phase out of the nuclear deterrent business." The pol-
icy also states that the U.S. should not prolong the life of the British
V-bomber force, except to the extent of continuing the development of
Skybolt if this is warranted for U.S. purposes.

We have done little to date to implement this policy.

The purpose of this memorandum is: (a) to describe the factors
which seem to be bringing the question to a head; (b) to lay out a suggested program for limited immediate steps to implement the policy;
and (c) to outline some more basic and longer-range actions for further
consideration; (d) to submit a proposed letter to Secretary McNamara
designed to bring about action on the more immediate steps.

1. *Factors Bringing Issue to a Head.* One factor bringing this issue to a
head is the relationship of the U.K. deterrent to the British role in the
European Communities. Present indications are that the issue will not,
at least at present, become directly involved in the U.K.-EEC negotiations. It appears clear that the French do not plan to link the questions at
this time.

[1 paragraph (9 lines of source text) not declassified]

British aid to the French would fragment the European cohesion we
are trying to create by giving preferential status to the French over other
members of the EEC and by stimulating the Germans to want similar
treatment. We should continue to oppose it, if the basic thrust of our
European policy is to be maintained.

The French may, however, not agree to admitting the U.K. to the
European Communities as a full partner and, at the same time, permit

---

Source: Department of State, Central Files, 741.5611/5–1862. Secret. Drafted by Fessenden on May 21, sent through Johnson, and initialed by Kohler and Johnson.

[1] Document 100.

the special and exclusive U.S.-U.K. military nuclear relationship to remain unchanged. The French may argue that the U.K., if it is to join the European Communities, must do so as a complete equal. Maintenance of the special U.S.-U.K. nuclear relationship would, in the French view, preserve a special and preferred status for the U.K. in the most prestige-laden of all fields. If the U.K. is not to extend nuclear aid to France, the French may, implicitly or explicitly, make some assurance that U.S.-U.K. nuclear cooperation is a waning, rather then a waxing, phenomenon the ultimate price of U.K. admission to the Six.

The attitude of the British is a further factor bringing the issue to a head. You will recall that, in the context of the recent White Paper on Defense, the British made clear that they intended to maintain their independent deterrent throughout the 1960s. In his letter to the President,[2] Prime Minister Macmillan justified this decision on the grounds that the independent British nuclear deterrent added to the strength of the overall deterrent of the West. This view runs counter to the U.S. position. Secretary McNamara in Athens[3] made clear our view that relatively weak nuclear forces with enemy cities as targets are not likely to be adequate to perform the function of deterrence. As Secretary McNamara said: "In a world of threats, crises, and possibly even accidents, such a posture appears more likely to deter its owner from standing firm under pressure than to inhibit a potential aggressor. If it is small, and perhaps vulnerable on the ground or in the air, or inaccurate, it enables a major antagonist to take a variety of measures to counter it. Indeed, if a major antagonist came to believe there was a substantial likelihood of it being used independently, this force would be inviting a pre-emptive first strike against it. In the event of war, the use of such a force against the cities of a major nuclear power would be tantamount to suicide, whereas its employment against significant military targets would have a negligible effect on the outcome of the conflict. In short, then, weak nuclear capabilities, operating independently, are expensive, prone to obsolescence, and lacking in credibility as a deterrent."

These remarks, which were generally interpreted at Athens as applying to the French, apply with equal force to the British.

There are also indications, as you are aware, that the British themselves are clinging to the doctrine of first reliance on nuclear weapons and are not responding as well as some other countries to our emphasis on the need for a conventional build-up. This has been evident in both the Berlin and NATO contexts. In the military sub-group on Berlin, the British are continuing to express opposition to our arguments on strat-

[2] Dated February 23. (Department of State, Presidential Correspondence: Lot 66 D 204)

[3] Reference is to the Athens meeting of the North Atlantic Council, May 4–6, 1962; see Documents 136 and 137.

egy. [*9 lines of source text not declassified*] In other words, the U.K. puts so much emphasis on a strategy of early use of nuclear weapons that it is willing to go along with an action which would considerably enhance the Soviet conventional capability.

2. *Program for Immediate Steps.* This situation points to both the correctness of the existing NSC policy regarding the special U.K. nuclear role and the importance of its effective execution.

The heart of the matter is that we should avoid any actions to increase the degree of our special nuclear relationship with the U.K. We should make clear that we are not prepared to extend that relation, notably in regard to creation of a U.K. Polaris missile force. The British will undoubtedly show a continuing interest in acquiring Polaris or other missile-bearing submarines, as they come closer to the end of the effective life of the V-Bomber Force. Even if that life is prolonged through Skybolt, the V-Bomber Force is a wasting asset. (Our information is that development of Skybolt is proceeding and that a production decision will be made one way or the other in July.) If the V-Bombers are not replaced by a sea-borne missile force, the independent British deterrent will expire, since the British have already decided to phase out land-based Thor's by about 1964.

In addition to the basic course of action outlined above, the following supporting actions suggest themselves:

a) We should review and reconsider the extensive collaboration under the Tripartite (U.S.-U.K.-Canada) Technical Cooperation Program (TTCP). [*4 lines of source text not declassified*] The extent of U.S.-U.K. cooperation in the ballistic missile field seems to go well beyond what we would be willing to do with the French and provides a potential unnecessary irritant in our difficulties with the French in the nuclear field. It stems from the Eisenhower–Macmillan agreement of December 20, 1957.[4] This entire range of cooperation needs to be reexamined in the light of the present day situation.

b) We should encourage the British to take part in a NATO multilateral force, if our other allies want to create one. Their present stance is thoroughly negative, but so was their posture toward joining the EEC a while back. In the long run, they may well come to see that a multilateral force is the way of containing German nuclear aspirations which is most consistent with the Alliance's interests.

c) We should instruct all U.S. personnel to take consistently the approved policy line with the British regarding their national deterrent. At present, the U.S. Government may present a rather confused picture to the British. Lacking any clear directive, various lower level officials have been speaking to the British in contradictory terms, sometimes giving the impression that the U.S. favors the U.K. independent deterrent program.

---

[4] This agreement has not been identified further.

3. *Longer-Range Actions.* There are some longer-range and more basic actions which we should consider for future implementation:

a) We should at some not-too-distant date explore with them the possibilities of committing their remaining strategic forces (V-Bombers) to NATO. (This is also existing policy, as set forth in the April 21, 1961, NSC Directive, but has never been implemented.) We should not do this, however, until we have a clearer idea of what we are prepared to do in the way of committing additional U.S. forces to NATO and until we can see how action to this end could be fitted in with the concept of a genuinely multilateral force. We would not want commitment of V-Bombers to substitute for full U.K. participation in the multilateral force or to set a pattern for a multilateral force based on national contingents rather than on units under multilateral ownership, control, and manning.

b) We should launch a State–DOD study of the extent of present U.S.-U.K. weapons cooperation to determine whether there may eventually be possibilities for limiting its scope and/or duration in such a way as to ease the problems referred to above, without generating contra-productive U.K. reactions.

c) Finally we may be forced, in the context of the U.K.-EEC negotiations, to explore with the British the possibility of their offering broad military nuclear cooperation with the European Community as perhaps the ultimate price for their membership therein. This assistance would be to the European Communities, not to a French or other national effort, and would be designed to enable these Communities to mount a nuclear effort whose benefits would only be available to multilaterally owned, manned, and controlled forces. The French could not participate in any way which assisted their national program. If we explore this with the British, we would of course need to be prepared to say that our own close military nuclear cooperation with the British should be gradually transformed into a U.S.-European Community cooperation. This step is not for immediate action, but some basic decisions on this may be forced upon us sooner than we think in the context of the U.K.-EEC negotiations.

Recommendation: In order to move forward with implementation of the more immediate steps and the study referred to under (b), we recommend that you sign the attached letter to Secretary McNamara. (Tab A)[5]

---

[5] Not attached, but see Document 396.

395. **Telegram From the Embassy in the United Kingdom to the Department of State**

London, June 26, 1962, 8 p.m.

Secto 80. Acting Secretary from Kohler. Before leaving for Oxford Secretary asked me to confirm telecon with you to effect he will personally give President and you general flavor of talks here upon return. Meanwhile following are highlights.

(1) Prime Minister Sunday night[1] was in speechmaking mood. Aside from electoral difficulties he was clearly preoccupied by economic and trade difficulties and apprehensive of worse to come. He was alarmed by stock market slump and Canadian financial problem and foresaw crash ahead. He made long speech on his favorite subject of need for "greater liquidity" in support of growing economies and expanding trade along lines he used on first visit to Washington and at Bermuda. Another repeated theme was his thesis that solution of Russian problem and at same time salvation of Britain was trade, trade, trade to make Russians fat and bourgeois. He was impatient with any trade restrictions including COCOM and Cuban limitations though he finally agreed to British acceptance of NATO reporting arrangements.

(2) Secretary gave Prime Minister and later in more detail Home and colleagues rundown European visit along lines reporting telegrams in this series. Home was particularly gratified by impression some improvement in French atmosphere. He again made point British are very concerned that discussion of nuclear questions and NATO reorganization be stretched out or postponed in order to avoid any interference with Common Market negotiations.

(3) While Prime Minister was vehement though vague in saying British Govt would break off negotiations rather than let down the Commonwealth, Heath seemed confident that negotiations are in good course and will be successfully concluded within reasonable time period.

(4) Both the Prime Minister and Home seemed reasonably confident they could deal with parliamentary questions on McNamara speech[2] "one way or another" though they admitted that opposition has

---

Source: Department of State, Central Files, 110.11–RU/6–2662. Secret; Limit Distribution. According to another copy of this telegram, it was drafted by Kohler. (Ibid., Conference Files: Lot 65 D 533, CF 2122) Kohler accompanied Rusk on his trip to Europe June 18–28.

[1] June 24.

[2] For text of McNamara's commencement address at the University of Michigan, June 16, see Department of State *Bulletin*, July 19, 1962, pp. 64–69.

them over a barrel. Secretary stressed that emphasis must be not on independence but on integration of nuclear forces and British assured him they would try find formula along these lines. Result will be reported by Emb.

(5) Home showed normal impatience to move ahead on Berlin and wondered whether new proposals might not be put forward while situation relatively quiet. He suggested conversion of occupation forces to "police forces" and conversion occupation status to "trusteeship status," making clear, however, changes would be verbal rather than substantive. After some discussion he seemed agree these particular suggestions probably not very attractive to Soviets.

(6) Both Prime Minister and Home similarly impatient on nuclear testing. Prime Minister stated flatly he felt only solution to problem of diffusion was conclusion of unpoliced ban for three to five years and then diplomatic pressure on others to adhere. Home put forward a variant of this proposal by suggesting a possibility of one year atmospheric ban with related agreement for joint study of underground testing problem. Secretary told Home we were making thorough study of all possibilities during which we could consider his suggestion.

(7) Question of missiles for Finland was left open for further study on our side.

(8) Home confirmed, subject to securing concurrence of President of Board of Trade, British agreement to NATO resolution on trade and credit relations with Cuba. Emb will follow up.

Full memcon talks with British being prepared.[3]

Bruce

------

[3] Memoranda of the conversations are in Department of State, Central Files, 110.11–RU/6–2462 and 6–2562, and Conference Files: Lot 65 D 533, CF 2123.

------

396. Letter From Secretary of State Rusk to Secretary of Defense McNamara

Washington, September 8, 1962.

DEAR BOB: You will recall the April 21 [20], 1961 NSC Policy Directive,[1] which states that "over the long run it would be desirable if the

------

Source: Department of State, Central Files, 741.5611/5–1862. Secret. Drafted by Owen and Conroy (RPM) and cleared with Tyler, Schaetzel, Weiss, and Popper.

[1] Document 100.

British decided to phase out of the nuclear deterrent business". It also states that the US should not prolong the life of the British deterrent, except to the extent of continuing development of Skybolt if this is warranted for US purposes alone.

The present situation in Europe underscores the importance of this policy. After the UK-EEC negotiations, the special US-UK relationship may have to be closely re-examined in connection with the evolving relationship of the UK to the continent, our own relationship with the new European Community, and our desire to ensure that future European nuclear efforts are based on genuinely multilateral rather than national programs. Pending such a re-examination of the US-UK special relation, which will only be feasible when we can get a clearer picture of the future shape of Europe, I believe it is of the utmost importance to avoid any actions to expand the relationship. Such actions could seriously prejudice future decisions and developments and make more difficult the working out of sound multilateral arrangements.

I know we are agreed, in line with the NSC policy referred to above, that any commitment to aid the British in extending their nuclear delivery capability beyond the present V-bomber force, e.g., through their acquisition of Polaris or other missile-bearing submarines, should be avoided at this time and that US decisions relative to Skybolt should be made on the basis solely of US interest in this missile for our own forces.

Maintenance of this US posture is particularly important at this juncture, since the British are probably now beginning to try to develop some tentative views concerning the nuclear arrangements that they may favor after joining the EEC. They probably feel that the V-bomber force, even with Skybolt, is a wasting asset and that any effective Europe-based deterrence must be based, in the long run, primarily on missiles rather than aircraft. They have shown past interest in the long-term possibility of Polaris missile-bearing submarines. They may be considering whether to try, in this way, to continue a UK national force into the missile era—possibly combined with a French national force under some type of "joint" arrangement. Such an arrangement might be termed a European multilateral force, although it would in fact be neither European (since it would discriminate against the Germans) nor multilateral (since it would involve nationally manned and owned forces). By reason of these facts, such an arrangement would be politically divisive and vastly complicate our efforts to hold pressures for a German national program in check.

British decisions in this field will be a long time in the making and I do not think that we should take remarks which suggest that they are now leaning to such an arrangement—rather than, for example, to participation in a genuinely multilateral force—as necessarily foreshadowing the ultimate outcome. An important factor will be their assessment of possible eventual US willingness to provide aid—by facilitating procurement of MRBM's and Polaris submarines—for an extension of the US-UK special relation into the missile era.

I hope, therefore, that both our staffs can hold to existing policies in discussions with Defense Minister Thorneycroft—avoiding any indication of future expansion in the US-UK special relationship and making clear, if he asks, that we held to the view which we have already expressed that we would only facilitate allied procurement of MRBM's for a program involving genuinely multilateral control, manning and ownership.

I do not believe that we should, however, foreshadow any curtailment of the special relation. This would be contraproductive, in view of the state of political developments in the UK and of the UK-EEC negotiations. I suspect that we can rely on the long-term trends in Europe to bring genuine multilateral courses increasingly to the fore, if we do not indicate a willingness to provide increased aid for less satisfactory alternatives in the meantime.

Thus, if the British raise the question of aid for a hunter-killer (rather than missile-bearing) nuclear powered submarine, such aid would not be precluded by the policy indicated above, in view of our previous sale of a nuclear power plant for a hunter-killer submarine to the UK. In the unlikely event the British raise this question, we might indicate that we would take the matter under consideration and our two Departments could then review timing and other relevant considerations, in the light of pending developments in this field vis-à-vis the French.

In connection with the policy of avoiding any extension of the present US-UK special relation it might also be useful if our staffs could undertake a review of the present extensive collaboration with the British under the Tripartite (US, UK, Canada) Technical Cooperation Program so as to define its scope with greater precision. I understand that this program of cooperation, stemming from the Eisenhower–Macmillan agreement of December 20, 1957, [5 lines of source text not declassified]. I have asked that Bill Tyler's people be in touch with your staff about such a review.

I am sending copies of this letter to Mac Bundy and Glenn Seaborg in view of their interest in the subject.

Sincerely yours,

Dean[2]

---

[2] Printed from a copy that bears this stamped signature.

397. Memorandum of Conversation

Washington, September 14, 1962, 10:30 a.m.

SUBJECT

Courtesy Call by the U.K. Minister of Defense: Relations with the USSR; the
U.K.'s Ability to Put Reserves on the Continent; Relations with France

PARTICIPANTS

British	U.S.
The Rt. Hon. Peter Thorneycroft,	The Secretary
Minister of Defense	Alf E. Bergesen, EUR/BNA
Sir David Ormsby Gore, British	
Ambassador	

Mr. Thorneycroft opened the meeting by saying that he had had a
very useful exchange of views with Mr. McNamara on defense posture.[1]
They had reached complete unanimity. They had discussed the situation in Europe on the defense side and also had lengthy discussions on
the area between Singapore and Suez. They had agreed that they could
not sacrifice efforts in this wide area simply to put another brigade into
Europe.

The Secretary said that the signals that Mr. Khrushchev was getting
on defense matters were most important. He may be putting things off
to November. He might note that the French have no strength in Germany. He might in some strange fashion come to the conclusion that the
West would not fight in Berlin. We were concerned that Khrushchev
might come to the wrong conclusion if the ranks weren't filled and the
forces generally in good trim. Khrushchev may come to the UN this fall
or seek to see the President. As to our bilateral conversations with the
Soviets, we see no way of reconciling our respective views. We have
been expounding the same views over and over again, like a phonograph record. Mr. Thorneycroft said that the U.K. was anxious to avoid
going into something simply to demonstrate strength without considering the problem of how to withdraw or disengage from such a demonstration. The Secretary remarked that the Soviets had just agreed to use
buses for the guard change at the Soviet War Memorial in West Berlin.

Mr. Thorneycroft inquired whether the Secretary thought the Soviets would sign a peace treaty with the GDR. The Secretary thought they
probably would but enforcing such a treaty would be something else.

Source: Department of State, Central Files, 033.4111/9–1462. Secret. Drafted by Bergesen and approved by S on September 27. Brief memoranda of their conversations on
Cuba, Laos, and the Congo are ibid.

[1] No record of Thorneycroft's talks with McNamara has been found.

The Soviets are also building up the GDR forces. The Secretary did not know whether there was any way of determining the reliability of these forces. The Soviets might try to use the East Germans as a front. Mr. Thorneycroft characterized Soviet policy as "terrible brinksmanship". The Secretary remarked that it would be a fine thing for us if GDR troops defected in whole units. He thought there was considerable sympathy for the West in East Germany.

In response to the Secretary's question about Lord Home, Mr. Thorneycroft said that he was firm and very calm. His appointment as Foreign Secretary had been something of a surprise, but he has come up beautifully and is now a model Foreign Secretary, above criticism.

The Ambassador reverted to the German situation. He asked whether the U.K. could play up more the strength of their reserves and the speed with which they could be deployed. Mr. Thorneycroft said that the U.K. could get 60,000 men into Germany in 7 days. More could be done in the way of publicizing the U.K.'s ability to build up troop strength quickly. It might help also domestically as there has been criticism at home (of the U.K.'s contribution to Continental defense). This might also serve as one of the "signals to Khrushchev" to which the Secretary had referred in the beginning of their conversation. In response to the Secretary's question, Mr. Thorneycroft said that he was sure such a (publicity) campaign would be supported by the Labor Party.

The Secretary asked whether they had any word from London whether HMG believed that the French would agree not to transfer nuclear information to countries not having it. The Ambassador replied that they had not heard; Mr. Thorneycroft remarked that his guess was that they would not agree and Mr. Rusk said that that was what we had heard. Mr. Thorneycroft said that the French at some point must choose between the Franco-German alliance and a wider Europe. The U.K. expected to see the cards fall within the next 6 months. Mr. Rusk said that we were concerned about the Chinese Communists' joining the ranks of the nuclear powers.

Mr. Thorneycroft said that the French were in some ways genuinely bitter. They were absolute] ,et on their force de frappe. It was terribly expensive and more than ' :y needed in both fissionable materials and rockets. The Secretary ren.. rked that we could not really discuss most of these questions until the UK-EEC negotiations were completed. Mr. Thorneycroft said that the U.K. hoped to draw France back from its extremely nationalistic point of view. In a small Europe, the French would have to draw on German technicians and German financing for their program. [3-1/2 *lines of source text not declassified*] He pointed out the great desirability of avoiding any unnecessary irritation in relations with France.

398. Department of State Memorandum

Washington, October 31, 1962.

IMPLICATIONS FOR THE UNITED KINGDOM OF DECISION TO ABANDON SKYBOLT

It is understood that a decision as to whether the 1000-mile-range air-to-ground missile Skybolt, which has been under development for some time, is to go into production has either been made or is about to be made, and that indications are that the decision will be not to proceed with production. Our commitment to the British on this weapon is an agreement to sell it to them if we decide to produce it. Discussed below are some of the consequences for the British, and for Anglo-American relations, of a decision to abandon Skybolt. (These are not necessarily in order of importance.)

I. Defense

With the cancellation of its ICBM, Blue Streak, two years ago the UK abandoned its effort to keep up with the US and the USSR in the range of weapons systems available for its defense. It still has, however, the RAF V-bomber force, capable of delivering H-bombs of British design and manufacture against an enemy. The 1962 Defense White Paper, "The Next Five Years," stated as an important principle of Britain's defense that "the efficacy of our deterrent will therefore be maintained throughout the 1960's by using our V-bombers and fitting them with stand-off weapons, Blue Steel in the first instance and later Skybolt." In fact, as the quantity and quality of Soviet SAM's improves, a missile like Skybolt is probably the only real possibility of providing Britain with a modern strike weapon. Cancellation of Skybolt would put in jeopardy not only Bomber Command but a vital element of British defense philosophy, including as it does the future efficacy of the independent nuclear deterrent.

II. Domestic UK Politics

Two of the Conservative Party's talking points (which may or not be valid) are that they have special and superior qualifications, as compared with Labour, for dealing with 1) defense and 2) the Americans. As British defense depends to a unique degree on Skybolt to be manufac-

Source: Department of State, Central Files, 74.5611/11–262. Secret. No drafting information appears on the source text, but it was attached to a November 2 memorandum from Executive Secretary Brubeck to Kaysen, through Bundy, which states that it was in response to a request by Kaysen.

tured by the Americans its cancellation would be a serious blow to the image, both public and private, of Tory competence in these two fields. There will be half-a-dozen by-elections in Britain in November; the results will be scrutinized with unusual attention by political observers to see whether Macmillan's cabinet reshuffle in July has reversed earlier electoral trends which have been against the Tories. Britain's prospective entry into the Common Market and the future of the Conservative Government are bound up to a considerable though unpredictable degree with these by-elections; however, both prognosis and analysis of this relationship are debatable. But the cancellation of Skybolt could be an unmitigated political blow to the Conservatives.

III. The Independent Nuclear Deterrent

As indicated above, cancellation of Skybolt would not only foreshorten the effective life of the V-bomber force but would call into further question the whole concept of the independent British deterrent. It might be noted in passing that the new British Defense Minister, Mr. Thorneycroft, has publicly reiterated Britain's intention to retain this weapon; privately, he has indicated that it has some value as a bargaining counter. Skybolt's cancellation would in considerable measure nullify this value. Whatever our own feelings about the efficacy of the British deterrent, the British could hardly regard our cancelling Skybolt as a friendly gesture in this context, nor is it clear how weakening Britain's bargaining power would be to our advantage. It is not impossible that Britain would undertake the development of a comparable weapon of its own, for reasons of either prestige or survival.

IV. The Special US-UK Relationship

Without beating the drums too much, it might be pointed out that a far more important ingredient in this relationship than the peculiar provisions of our atomic legislation is the degree of mutual trust and confidence which exists between the two countries. In view of the serious consequences for Britain touched on above, it seems probable that Skybolt's cancellation would be a serious blow to this mutual confidence. The British would certainly feel let down—hard. They might console themselves afterwards with thoughts of all the money they were saving; the Labor Party would crow, maybe, that they didn't believe in the independent deterrent anyway; the advocates of interdependence in the hardware field would be permanently silenced, but they were primarily trying to sell British goods anyway; etc. Nonetheless, we still rely heavily on British real estate all over the world, from Christmas Island to Holy Loch; we should carefully consider the possible consequences of an estrangement of this relationship. Finally, if we were to appear to be "double-crossing" our oldest and closest ally—and it might well appear this way—it would be a serious blow to our whole alliance system.

V. Possible Tactics

If it is not already too late, it would of course be preferable to consult with the British, rather than merely informing them, even though we have no legal obligation to do so.

Assuming that a decision has already been made, however, serious and urgent consideration must be given to the manner and timing of informing the British. A letter from the President to the Prime Minister might be appropriate; it should emphasize the military-fiscal aspects of the program which are said to be the basis for the cancellation, without ignoring the repercussions which Macmillan will have to face in the UK. He should have as much time as possible to prepare the ground before an announcement is made.

Again if it is not too late, consideration should be given to the possible bargaining power involved in giving up Skybolt, with the implicit consequences for the British deterrent. Although the British may have in mind the use of their independent deterrent for possible future negotiations with the French involving British entry into the Common Market, or in the evolution of a European deterrent, there might also be the possibility of using their deterrent as a factor in negotiations with the Soviets for a general détente.

---

399. Notes of Conversations Relating To Skybolt

Washington, November 9, 1962.

1. On 7 November I reported to the President, at a time when Dean Rusk was present, that it appeared to me we should consider cancelling the Skybolt program. Because of the serious impact such a cancellation would have on the British Government, I asked the President's approval to discuss the matter with David Ormsby-Gore and Peter Thorneycroft. He agreed that I should do so.

Source: Washington National Records Center, RG 330, McNamara Files: FRC 71 A 3470, Skybolt. Secret. More detailed summaries of the meetings and conversations referred to below are included in *Report to the President, Skybolt and Nassau*, November 15, 1963, by Richard E. Neustadt, a study that was requested by the President in March 1963. (Kennedy Library, National Security Files, Meetings and Memoranda Series, Neustadt)

2. On 8 November I met with David Ormsby-Gore and reported to him that during the past six months the estimated cost to procure the Skybolt missile had risen from $1.4 billion to over $1.75 billion. This increase, on top of a series of previous increases, was causing us to reconsider the worth of the weapon. Two days ago I had referred the matter to the Chiefs and asked for their recommendations. Although no decision would be made on this matter within the next three to four weeks, I wanted his government to be aware that we were reconsidering the program.

3. On 9 November in a telephone conversation. I repeated to Peter Thorneycroft the substance of my conversation with David Ormsby-Gore. I added that in the event it appeared desirable for the U.S. to cancel the Skybolt program, I believed there would be several alternatives that should be considered by the British Government. Further, I stated that prior to any U.S. decision to cancel I would be quite willing to come to London to discuss the matter with Peter. I estimated that the decision would not be made here before approximately December 10. London consultations would probably not be advisable before November 23. He [9 lines of source text not declassified].

Robert S. McNamara[1]

---

[1] Printed from a copy that bears this typed signature.

---

400. Letter From Secretary of State Rusk to Secretary of Defense McNamara

Washington, November 24, 1962.

DEAR BOB: In any discussion with the UK of alternatives to the US Skybolt program, I believe that we should mention these possibilities:

1. British continuation of a Skybolt program, permitting them to attain their required number of Skybolts either (a) through a cut-back production program in the US, or (b) through production in the UK with US technology. Your people tell us that the first alternative might cost about $375 million, or about $175 million more than the UK is now planning to spend on Skybolt.

Source: Department of State, Central Files, 741.5611/11–2462. Secret. No drafting information appears on the source text.

2. Use of Hound Dog on at least some British aircraft. I gather there are various technical problems and uncertainties here. A British decision to study these problems further, before announcing any decision, might give them a much needed breather, domestically.

3. Participation in a sea-based MRBM force under multilateral manning and ownership, such as NATO is now discussing. The UK has made very evident that it would wish to avoid a decision on such participation, however, until EEC negotiations are concluded.

It seems essential that we make quite clear to the British that there is no possibility of our helping them set up a nationally manned and owned MRBM force.

The European countries strongly resent the US-UK special military relation; their resentment has only been kept within bounds so far by indications that this relation would not be extended beyond the V-bombers (which are obsolescing) into the MRBM's which are clearly the next phase in Europe-based nuclear deterrence. We have repeatedly emphasized that we would only facilitate MRBM procurement for a force under genuinely multilateral manning and ownership. If we were now to reverse this policy and extend the special relation into the MRBM period, the continental reaction would be immediate and highly critical, regardless of whether the resulting British MRBM force was to be committed to NATO. Existing continental objections to admitting the UK to membership in the Community on the grounds that its special relation with the US is incompatible with that membership would be heightened; the difficulties of bringing EEC negotiations to a successful conclusion might be significantly enhanced.

Resentment in France, where the US-UK special nuclear relation is a standing irritant, would be particularly strong. The political costs of our continuing to deny MRBM aid to France would be significantly increased.

The German problem would be even more serious. During the Chancellor's visit, members of his party underlined the fact that the FRG simply could not accept new and further forms of discrimination against the Federal Republic in the nuclear field. Given this attitude, US aid for nationally manned and owned British MRBM's would almost certainly eventually lead to German demands for equal treatment. For us to deny these demands would create German reactions which could, over time, weaken both the European Community and the Atlantic partnership. For us to accept such demands would be to stir up very great difficulties both within the alliance and vis-à-vis the Soviets. These difficulties would not be substantially alleviated by use of the permissive link; neither the Soviets nor our allies would have any confidence that German ships with German crews and German MRBM's would not eventually be diverted to national purposes, despite such technical safeguards.

I believe, therefore, that we should limit discussion of alternatives that we would view with favor to a UK Skybolt program, Hound Dog, and the multilateral force. I suspect that, once we have laid out these alternatives to the British, they will need a period of time to decide which, if any, they wish to pursue. In any initial discussion of Skybolt cancellation with the British, therefore, we might inform them that we would be glad to continue consideration of the matter here with Ormsby-Gore, if they wish.

With warm regards,

Sincerely,

Dean

401. Memorandum of Conversation

Washington, December 16, 1962, noon.

PRESENT WERE

The President, Secretary McNamara, Acting Secretary George Ball, Alexis Johnson, Jeffrey Kitchen, Roswell Gilpatric, Dr. Wiesner and McGeorge Bundy

At the President's request, Secretary McNamara opened the meeting by discussing the course of his discussions with Mr. Thorneycroft in London and after.[1] In essence he summarized the discussion as previously reported by cable, noting the insistent desire of the British to obtain a categorical assurance that the United States was in favor of the independent British nuclear deterrent, and his own refusal to give such an assurance. Secretary McNamara remarked that the British had seemed wholly unprepared for his Aide-Mémoire on the technical weaknesses of Skybolt[2] although he had given preliminary notice to

Source: Kennedy Library, National Security Files, Meetings with the President. Top Secret. The meeting was held in the Oval Room of the White House.

[1] Extensive summaries of McNamara's conversations with Thorneycroft on December 11–12 are in *Report to the President, Skybolt and Nassau,* November 15, 1963, by Richard E. Neustadt. For an account by Thorneycroft, see House of Commons, *Parliamentary Debates,* 5th Series, vol. 669, col. 894.

[2] A copy of this aide-mémoire with Ball's handwritten suggested changes is attached to a letter from Ball to McNamara, December 10. (Department of State, Central Files, 741.5611/12–1062) It is also in Neustadt's report.

Ambassador Ormsby Gore on the 8th of November and to Mr. Thorneycroft on November 9.[3] The British had, however, apparently accepted the proposition that Skybolt was in trouble, and their inclination was to seek Polaris as a substitute. The preferred solution would be to buy components for a missile-carrying submarine of their own which might at best be ready by 1969, and Thorneycroft had argued that it was important to have some other instrument between the time at which Skybolt would have become available and that later date. In particular the British had asked to rent Polaris, but Secretary McNamara had indicated his opposition, because of the very great complexity of Polaris submarines and the corresponding difficulty of training effective crews.

Secretary McNamara indicated his opinion that we could consider selling the Polaris missile with its associated guidance and navigation systems. We could link it to the same rules of use and control as those applied to Skybolt and to the existing UK/US mutual defense assistance agreement. Secretary McNamara presented a draft paper indicating the conditions of such an agreement.[4]

Secretary Ball expressed his grave concern with respect to the political implications of any arrangement with the British on MRBM's. He pointed out that any arrangement which appeared to give the British a national capability in this field would lead us at once to the question of what we would do to the French, and so, inexorably, to the question of the role of the Germans. A decision in favor of a national force in this range of weapons would change our entire policy and would represent a major political decision.

There followed an extended discussion of varied aspects of the confrontation of views. The President pointed out that in the eyes of the British there could well be a claim that the cancellation of Skybolt implied some obligation to provide a substitute, on our part. "Looking at it from their point of view, which they do almost better than anybody," he said, "it might well appear to them that since Skybolt was a substitute for Blue Streak, which they had cancelled in reliance on our assurances, we should now provide an alternative." In this connection, Ambassador Bruce indicated that in his judgment this was primarily a political problem—and a political problem which would come to a head on the 29th of January, when Parliament met again. The old question was what would meet the Prime Minister's needs for this hour, and he thought only the Prime Minister could decide this question.

Secretary McNamara argued strongly that the discussions of recent months have demonstrated that our current position with respect to a

---

[3] See Document 399.

[4] A copy of this draft agreement is in Department of State, Conference Files: Lot 65 D 533, CF 2212.

multilateral force simply will not work. He had been told repeatedly by different delegates in Paris[5] that they would be glad to follow the United States if they could only tell what it was that the United States was for. There is no way in which we can persuade the Europeans to buy and pay for both a multilateral force and a full compliance with NATO conventional force goals, but that is what our current policy requires. Secretary McNamara believed that it was time to move on to a more realistic arrangement and one which would better serve our own interests.

Secretary Ball, continuing to urge caution, told the President that this might be the biggest decision he was called upon to make. The President's reply was, "That we get every week, George." Yet the President clearly recognized the complexity of the problem which appeared to involve grave political risks for Mr. Macmillan if we should not help him, and serious risks also for our own policy in Europe if we should help him too much.

Dr. Wiesner argued for the possibility of helping the British, at least in an interim period, by providing them with Hound Dog missiles which could be properly and easily represented as substitutes for Skybolt, while the MRBM problem was being worked through. Secretary McNamara indicated his view that this arrangement would be without military or economic justification. The President interrupted this argument to return discussion to the principal question, and indicated his preliminary view that if we should offer Polaris to the British it must be in the context of a continuation of our undertakings with respect to Skybolt. To this Secretary Ball replied that if we should offer Polaris to the British and not to the French, we would appear to have intensified our special relationship to the British and our refusal to cooperate with the French.

After considerable further discussion, a program which reflected both the desire to be helpful to the British and the requirement of respect for our European allies led the President to approve, for planning purposes, the following general proposal:

1. We would offer appropriate components of Polaris missiles to the British.
2. It would be a condition of this offer that the British would commit their eventual Polaris force to a multilateral or multinational force in NATO.
3. It would be a further condition of this arrangement that the British should undertake to build up their conventional forces to agreed NATO force levels.
4. The terms governing the use of Skybolt would apply also to the use of such Polaris missiles.

---

[5] McNamara was in Paris December 13–15 for the North Atlantic Council meeting.

5. It would be publicly assumed that deliveries might take place effective in 1967, but it would be privately recognized that the probable date of effectiveness of this new system would be 1969.

This conclusion was much influenced by the advice of Ambassador Bruce that since we had told the world we would not help national nuclear forces, we should relate any assistance to the British, in this new field of MRBM's, to a large-scale solution of the broad problem of the Atlantic deterrent. (Ambassador Bruce emphasized this point later in the week by indicating his strong belief that the multilateral and conventional force requirements of the proposed understanding with the British were absolutely fundamental and should on no account be discarded.)

McG. B.[6]

---

[6] Printed from a copy that bears these typed initials.

---

402. Memorandum of Conversation

Nassau, December 19, 1962, 9:45 a.m.

SUBJECT

Skybolt

PARTICIPANTS

U.S.	U.K.
The President	The Prime Minister
Secretary McNamara	Lord Home
Mr. Ball	Mr. Thorneycroft
Ambassador Bruce	Ambassador Ormsby Gore
Mr. Bundy	Mr. de Zuleta
Ambassador Thompson	Mr. Bligh

Source: Department of State, Conference Files: Lot 65 D 533, CF 2209. Secret. Drafted by Thompson and approved by the White House on December 31. The meeting was held at the Prime Minister's house. Briefing papers, schedules, agenda, and a chronology for the Nassau meeting between the President and the Prime Minister are ibid., CF 2208–2214. For Macmillan's account of the meeting, see *At the End of the Day*, pp. 356–361; for Ball's account of the meeting, see *The Past Has Another Pattern*, pp. 264–268. It is also summarized in Neustadt's *Report to the President, Skybolt and Nassau*.

The Prime Minister began the conversation with an expression of appreciation for the handling of the Cuban affair by the United States. In reply, the President expressed his appreciation for the attitude of the Prime Minister and the British Government which was in striking contrast with that of the British press.

The Prime Minister said that he regretted that the wide range of the talks in which he had expected to engage at this meeting had been overshadowed by the Skybolt problem. He thought he was probably the oldest of those present and knew the story from its beginning which he would like to recount. He fully appreciated the U.S. feeling of the danger of doing something which might be considered obnoxious or unfriendly by the other European powers. He did not want to cause trouble with the Germans, the French, the Italians and others or to impede developments which were wanted both by the United States and the United Kingdom.

In the first place, he wanted to mention that the atomic bomb had been developed almost entirely in the beginning by British scientists. The British Isles had been found too small to carry out tests. Churchill and Roosevelt had agreed that the development of the bomb should be carried out in the United States. The whole world knew about the partnership in this matter which was governed by agreement. He was not referring to a legal document but rather to the nature of the agreement. Then there had come the incidents of spies in Great Britain and the McMahon Act. There were many, including some in the United States, who felt that Britain had been treated harshly. Amendments to the McMahon Act had been made which made greater cooperation possible. At this time, the emphasis was on the bomb. Later the emphasis shifted to the means of delivery. Britain had spent about sixty million pounds on the Blue Streak missile. Then there arose the decision as to whether the development of this missile should be continued. Britain was a small and heavily populated island, and the missile would have to be situated near towns where it would be subject to observation and would be exposed to agitators. The Prime Minister had talked to President Eisenhower about the problem and had indicated the British were going to chuck it if they could get anything else.

Then Skybolt came along as well as Polaris. The British made an agreement to buy Skybolt. He was not basing himself on the terms of the agreement but rather on the gentlemen's understanding. Eisenhower had said he wanted something in return, namely the submarine base at Holy Loch. The British had favored another location but had agreed on Holy Loch which was more remote and harder for Lord Russell and his friends to reach. The Prime Minister said that from time-to-time doubts had been cast on the Skybolt development, and he had assumed that in the United States as in England there were always these rumors circulated by rival firms or services. He went on to say it did now seem that Skybolt was in trouble.

The Prime Minister said he understood the U.S. anxiety for the effect any US-UK agreement might have on other allies. He thought the main allies understood the US-UK relationship as a kind of founder company as well as the special arrangement brought about by the amendment of the McMahon Act. He said the other problem was the possibility of bringing into being a larger grouping of powers as well as the possible effect of any such agreement on the Common Market negotiations. The Prime Minister said flatly that he thought the effect of a new agreement on the Common Market agreement would be "frankly, absolutely none." These negotiations now depended on whether the French could maintain the good deal they have in agricultural products vis-à-vis the Germans. If it failed, it would be on that basis. The French and the British have a different concept about the Common Market, the French favoring an autarchical system. There was the question as to what effect an agreement would have on European multilateral arrangements. It was difficult to know what was meant by a multilateral deterrent. The Prime Minister saw no conflict between independent and interdependent forces. Until a supranational authority developed, it did not matter whether it was army troops or air force. Any contribution would be under the control of the Government contributing it. He remarked that the problem of control of allied forces had been with us "since Marlborough" and really was not difficult. He was aware that the French would go on and spend a lot of money. They were grateful for the aid the United States had given, and he had tried to explain this to de Gaulle. He gave the example (which he had not cited to General de Gaulle for reasons of tact) of British forces in the last war which were put under the command of the French General Gamelin, but at a certain time, Churchill had to issue orders to Lord Gort to save the British forces and any French who wanted to come along by going to the channel ports. This enabled the air force to save Britain. Until there was a single state developed, there must be a combination of independent and joint forces. The question was whether the switch of horses from Skybolt to Polaris would upset the principal allies. He thought not.[1] At present, Britain had a powerful bomber force which was important strategically, particularly because of its location in England. If there were to be a role for the bomber in the future, it would probably pass from a strategic one to a tactical one. Why should they not hand over one squadron to SACEUR? They could ask the French to do the same. This would show the purpose of developing the philosophy of building a joint force. They could inform the others what the targets of such a force were to be. He

---

[1] Approximately 2 lines of material deleted at this point in the source text.

thought that at present others were feeling left out and could well be brought in and given more information about these matters. He did not see the difference in principle whether one fired a ballistic missile from the sea or the air. He pointed out that the Skybolt was a ballistic missile. Many in Britain thought that Great Britain should not be in this game, but Britain could not have such a decision forced on them.

The President said he agreed that there was a danger that some would think that cutting off the Skybolt was an effort to cut off the British national deterrent. He pointed out that the United States had alternative means. In considering this matter, we were conscious of the importance of the British to our relationship to Europe. He had told the Prime Minister last night that the United States would divide the cost of Skybolt, which would amount to some $200 million.[2] It was possible that we could use it in the future if we could develop an airplane capable of staying in the sky for several days, but we have no great need for Skybolt. We were prepared to join equally in finishing it. He pointed out that this was a new position beyond that which had been given to Mr. Thorneycroft. All of the U.S. judgments in regard to Skybolt were made in consideration of the existence of our other systems. He pointed out that for $100 million the British could get $450 million worth of work which we had put in it. Skybolt should be capable of deterring Mr. Khrushchev. He pointed out that twenty missiles in Cuba had had a deterrent effect on us. For an amount of money that was not large, the British could maintain a deterrent that would take them through to a later period. For $100 million, they would get a $500 million system.

The second point the President wished to make was that he was aware of the history of the atomic weapon and wished to point out that we were still cooperating.[3] We had supported Britain's entry into the Common Market although this was bound to have adverse effects upon us. The reason was that we felt that British influence was important in the balance and that Britain would contribute to the stability of Europe. We had refused help to the French because of our concern of what might happen in Germany. If we should assist the French, this would not change de Gaulle at all, but pressure in Germany would rise. If we helped the French it meant that any other country which became an atomic power would expect help from us. We hoped that we could use the time available to develop a multinational force.

---

[2] No record of this discussion has been found. The JFK Log Book cites a meeting from 12:51 to 2:40 p.m. but notes no activities after 6:40 p.m. (Kennedy Library) Arthur M. Schlesinger, Jr., wrote about a meeting during the evening of December 18 between Macmillan and the President regarding British conditions for acceptance of Polaris missiles. (*A Thousand Days*, p. 864)

[3] Approximately 4 lines of material deleted at this point in the source text.

The President went on to point out that there was a great difference between Polaris and Skybolt. Moreover, the problem was what these things looked like and not what they were. This point had been illustrated by the introduction of Soviet missiles in Cuba. These missiles had been less a military threat than a major political act. If we join with the British in Polaris and refuse de Gaulle atomic or missile cooperation, we would feed the concept he already has of America and raise new problems. The President said he did not believe that if we went ahead together on Polaris that it would not shake our European allies. All of our people who had recently been in Europe, and this included Secretary Rusk, Mr. Ball and Ambassador Bohlen, were convinced that such action would cause great difficulties. He did not want the British people to think that because of our view in opposition to the proliferation of atomic weapons that we had opposed a British deterrent. If we could work out a solution in regard to Polaris which would move Europe away from national deterrents, we would be prepared to consider such a move but it should be in that context. The President pointed out that all the implications would have to be considered and that was a new problem on which study was needed. The United States had made a fair offer on Skybolt so that the British people should not think that we want to cut them down.[4] The Prime Minister said we ought to think about what a multilateral deterrent is. It need not be one in which the weapons are manufactured by the others.

The President said the question was one of how these weapons should be put in and how they could be taken out. As the Prime Minister had described the matter last night, it seemed rather synthetic. Of course, in extremes they could be taken out. He pointed out that there was a question as to whether we could get the French in and what the effect on the Germans would be of United States, British, and French participation.

The Prime Minister said we would create a force to which the United States, the French, and British would contribute. The President pointed out that if others developed atomic weapons they would expect us to give the delivery system. The Polaris was not just an extension of Skybolt which was not much good after 1970 when bombers would fade out.

The Prime Minister pointed out that Skybolt would be good into the early seventies. The Prime Minister asked if there were a multinational force was it the case that the United States would contribute part of their force while the others would contribute all of theirs?

---

[4] Approximately 4 lines of material deleted at this point in the source text.

1096 Foreign Relations, 1961–1963, Volume XIII

The President replied in the affirmative, stating this was the greatest hope for a Polaris arrangement which would not upset other members of the alliance. He thought we should discuss two possibilities. The first was Skybolt. If the United States did not have Polaris, we would take Skybolt, but we had two other systems. The British did not. We were continuing our bomber force with the Hound Dog missile. He pointed out that we would have to discuss this whole problem with Congress, and he suggested that we and the British should set up a group to discuss these two problems and reach a judgment during the winter.

Mr. Ball said that this should be done in a multilateral context. We had a different concept of a multinational force from the British. We had in mind mixed manning and that the right of withdrawal would not be envisaged, but a commission should consider this problem.

The President said that if after study the British judgment of the effect on Europe was correct we could consider the British concept or that described by Mr. Ball.

Lord Home said he did not share the anxiety the President had expressed. France was going ahead anyway. Even if there were a row with France, it would be far less damaging to NATO than a rift between the United States and Great Britain.

The President asked if we should make a similar offer to the French. Our cooperation with them now was minimal. De Gaulle was beginning to realize that the problem was not the atomic warhead, but the missile. If he asked for the missile, what do we do?

Lord Home pointed out that if the proposal was a multinational force as described by Mr. Ball, it would be voted down because it was impossible to have fifteen fingers on the trigger,[5] He thought that the U.S. and the U.K. and later the French should have a joint force with NATO targets.

Mr. Ball pointed out that we had different assessments of the German problem. We thought that after Adenauer, pressure would mount for some kind of participation.[6]

Lord Home thought that the pressure would be for participation in political decisions.

Mr. Ball replied he thought we should face the situation and enable Germany to have participation in a manner that is controllable.

The Prime Minister asked what we meant by participating. He doubted if Germany would be satisfied with having one of fifteen sailors.

---

[5] Approximately 1 line of material deleted at this point in the source text.

[6] Approximately 2 lines of material deleted at this point in the source text.

The President asked what was the alternative to national deterrents.

The Prime Minister said that he had taken his country a long way in participating in Europe in the economic field. This was not all very agreeable for Britain, but he had done it. But if the whole of Europe was to be dependent upon the United States, why should they do anything? It was not satisfactory to have one out of fifteen sailors.

The President pointed out that Europe could use the same argument against Great Britain, though he agreed there was more logic in the present arrangements than in a multilateral force.

Lord Home thought that the Europeans would be satisfied to see the United States, Britain and France cooperate in a nuclear force if the Europeans knew about the deployment, targeting, etc.[7] De Gaulle had made clear his view that if Germany were to get atomic arms this would unite Eastern Europe. The Europeans did not want Germany to have atomic weapons and were opposed to a multilateral force.

The Prime Minister said that de Gaulle wanted to keep alive his distant hope that the Eastern European satellites, whom Germany had treated badly, could achieve freedom.

The President said Adenauer had expressed the hope that we would not give atomic weapons to France because of the pressure this would arouse in Germany.

The Prime Minister remarked that de Gaulle had quoted Adenauer as saying exactly the opposite.

Mr. Ball said[8] History had demonstrated that we could not keep Germany in an inferior position forever, and any attempt to do so would stir up latent forces in Germany. For this reason we supported a NATO approach.

Mr. Thorneycroft said we should not force the creation of a multinational force which was not wanted, but rather have the Europeans come in at the shallow end of the pool, informing them regarding targeting, etc.

Mr. Ball remarked that this would not work.

Lord Home said we did not have a single ally in Europe that would allow Germany to have its finger on the trigger.[9]

The President referred to the diminishing cost of atomic weapons and said they might become attractive to the Italians and others. If we gave the French Polaris submarines, we would save them a good deal of money and some time. He said that Secretary McNamara did not think

---

[7] Approximately 1-1/2 lines of material deleted at this point in the source text.

[8] Approximately 2 lines of material deleted at this point in the source text.

[9] Approximately 1 line of material deleted at this point in the source text.

the time saved would be very great, but the saving in money would be considerable. Secretary McNamara confirmed this statement. He thought the great protection with respect to delivery systems was their cost. He thought that it was important to keep the attention of the Germans in particular on conventional weapons because of Berlin, although if it were not for Berlin Europe could be defended with four divisions and a nuclear strategy.

The President asked what the argument was against giving such assistance to the French.

The Prime Minister said the British had made a contract which had not worked out.

The President observed that France had objected to our 1958 decision and to the Norstad proposals.[10] Now it was suggested that we come up with a new position which would represent a change of policy, and it would be wise not to hasten this decision.

The Prime Minister said it was simply a question of one horse being lame while the other was able to run. The President rejoined that these were two different races. The Prime Minister said he did not accept this.

Lord Home suggested that if we got a multinational force we could give the French Polaris at a later date.

The President suggested we should consider the whole situation and perhaps have a statement that should state:

1. We had offered to make the Hound Dog missile available and he referred, in this connection, to the treatment of our position by the British and American press, which had made it look as though we were being unfair.
2. We had offered to continue the Skybolt program and to put $100 million more into its development, which would enable Britain to continue its national deterrent.
3. We discussed the problem of Polaris, which was a new field and which should be looked at with care.

The President went on to say that we should look at what we meant by multinational force. How should control be exercised. Whether a similar offer should be made to France? And, finally, we should make judgment on what the effect of our action would be in Europe. The statement he had outlined would answer the charges of United States bad faith, and the charge that Britain was without any alternative. He did not think, however, that we could decide these matters here.[11]

Mr. Ball said this should be on the basis of a private discussion.

The Prime Minister asked that if the present position had not arisen when the Skybolt would have been operational.

---

[10] Approximately 1 line of material deleted at this point in the source text.
[11] Approximately 4 lines of material deleted at this point in the source text.

Secretary McNamara replied that it would have been operational in 1966.

The Prime Minister asked if the Skybolt was likely to be reasonably effective and if it would be safe to carry.

Secretary McNamara replied that it would be safe to carry and would be an effective deterrent, but would have low reliability—something on the order of twenty to thirty percent operational reliability.

The President pointed out that if we did not have other systems available we would go ahead on Skybolt. Secretary McNamara said that in such circumstances we would certainly consider going ahead, but he did not feel that we could do so in view of the availability of alternate systems and the low reliability of Skybolt.

The Prime Minister inquired if the record of failure was worse than normal.

Mr. McNamara replied in the affirmative, stating that this was the most complex system we had yet attempted. He pointed out that an error of one foot per second meant an error of one thousand feet at target.[12]

Mr. McNamara pointed out that he was in a difficult situation in explaining to Congress why we had spent $200 million since 1961. He had asked Congress for $100 million for 1962 and for $130 million for 1963.

The President suggested that these figures might be useful to Mr. Thorneycroft in explaining the situation to Parliament.

Mr. Thorneycroft said that his difficulty in Parliament was that the Skybolt would be late, expensive and unreliable, and these facts had been made public.

The President said the British press had been carrying stories to the effect that our action had not been taken on technical grounds but on political ones.

Mr. Thorneycroft said the British press was looking at the alternative.

The Prime Minister said he agreed that the press must be dealt with and not utilized. He pointed out that the Hound Dog was difficult to use on British planes.

Mr. McNamara pointed out that the Hound Dog could be adapted to British planes, although some changes in the missile would have to be made.

Mr. Thorneycroft pointed out that this would take a long time, and even when accomplished would leave only eighteen inches of clearance at take-off. In any event, this could not be accomplished until about the time when bombers would no longer be used.

---

[12] Approximately 7 lines of material deleted at this point in the source text.

The Prime Minister said the problem was for him as it had been for Britain in 1940—whether to chuck it or go on.[13] He would not engage in anything petty. We could stay at Holy Loch. He pointed out that he had taken big risks in his policies. People had said that Britain was in the front line where they were all targets, but had none of the power. He would be prepared to put in all of his part of a Polaris force provided the Queen had the ultimate power and right to draw back in the case of a dire emergency similar to that in 1940. He thought the United States would do the same if we did not have a superfluity of weapons. Britain could make submarines—not nuclear ones—to carry missiles. This could be accomplished in six years, but the cost would have to be compensated elsewhere. He hoped not in the Far East, where the British contribution was in some ways more important than in Europe. They would have to tax their people more as well. There was no use prolonging the life of the bomber, which was bound to die in any event. Submarines were much more suitable for an island like Britain, which also had a great naval tradition. Such a course, however, would lead to a deep rift with the United States. He said he would not accuse America, and reminded the President that he was one-half American himself.

The President said that in the first place we were prepared to do what we said we would do. He pointed out that we had spent a great deal of money in carrying out the commitment which Eisenhower had made, and that there could be no suggestion of bad faith. We placed great value on our relationship with Great Britain. He pointed out that the British had their own scientists at the Douglas Plant, and asked what they had been saying during the last six months.[14] British scientists at the Douglas Plant were apparently saying that the trouble was not technical but political.

Mr. Thorneycroft suggested that such reports might have come from U.S. personnel, particularly those interested in continuing the project. In reply to a question from the President as to his own opinion on Skybolt, Mr. Thorneycroft said he had to rely on Mr. McNamara's judgment, as he had gone thoroughly into the matter and had publicly said that Skybolt would be late, expensive, and unreliable.

The President pointed out that McNamara's judgment was based on the fact that he had alternative systems. He pointed out that for $250 million investment the British could get a good buy which would deter Khrushchev.

Mr. Thorneycroft pointed out that his own experience was that systems of this kind could be successfully developed only if you went flat

---

[13] Approximately 16 lines of material deleted at this point in the source text.
[14] Approximately 4-1/2 lines of material deleted at this point in the source text.

out in your effort and there was the prospect of a good order at the end of the line.[15]

The President thought our only difficulty was the different judgment we had on the effect a bilateral arrangement would have in Europe, and he repeated that all of our experts thought this would be very serious.

The Prime Minister said this appeared to be based on the assumption that this was a different weapon.

The President said we could not settle this matter today, and then read excerpts from a U.S. draft paper which listed:[16] (1) our offer of Hound Dog; (2) our offer to share equally in cost of completion of Skybolt; (3) a plan for the two governments to cooperate in a NATO missile force.

The President said that after consultation with NATO the two governments might agree (a) that the forces developed under our agreement would be assigned to the NATO deterrent forces and assigned targets under agreements approved by NATO; (b) the U.S. would undertake to make similar assignment of parallel and equivalent forces; (c) the U.S. and U.K. would support the creation of a NATO multilateral force; (d) the U.S. and U.K. forces would be included in such a NATO multilateral force.

The Prime Minister inquired what would happen about SEATO. The British would be contributing all of their force to NATO and he inquired what would happen if the Chinese attacked Hong Kong. He threw out the suggestion that the British contribution might be made proportionate to that of the United States. He said that the British force might be of the most value in the Far East.

The President said the same assistance might be made available to France, which probably would not want it.

The Prime Minister thought the French might be tempted by the time that would be gained.

At this point the meeting broke up for lunch.

---

[15] Approximately 4 lines of material deleted at this point in the source text.
[16] Not found.

403. Memorandum of Conversation

Nassau, December 19, 1962, 4:30 p.m.

SUBJECT

Skybolt

PARTICIPANTS

Great Britain:	United States:
The Prime Minister	The President
Lord Home	Secretary McNamara
Mr. Thorneycroft	Under Secretary Ball
Ambassador Ormsby Gore	Mr. McGeorge Bundy
Mr. Ian Samuel	Ambassador Bruce
	Mr. William R. Tyler

The President read to the Prime Minister the text of the three documents which had been prepared by the U.S. Delegation on a possible substitute for Skybolt.[1] The President emphasized that it was our intention that the details of a multilateral force should be kept private. We should study its possible development and then come to a decision. This much could be said publicly, and meanwhile we would see what the reactions were in Europe. The President pointed out the advantages of the proposal under discussion from the UK view point.

The Prime Minister asked what was really meant by the words "assigned to NATO". He pointed out that SACEUR and SACLANT had forces under their command under double capacity: they are both NATO and national forces. At the time of Cuba, the US itself had withdrawn a number of ships that were assigned to NATO for the special action which the situation required. The fact that these ships were assigned to NATO had not stood in the way of the US. If "assigned" means something like their being part of NATO for ordinary times, for training purposes, maneuvers, and of course joint military operations if the situation should come to that, then this makes things easier. The question was whether units assigned to NATO could be taken out for purposes to which others are not parties.

The President said he understood that it was in the UK interest to define "assigned" as loosely as possible so as to satisfy British opinion with regard to an independent role, whereas from the point of view of the European countries there was advantage in making the work "as-

---

Source: Department of State, Conference Files: Lot 65 D 533, CF 2209. Secret. Drafted and initialed by Tyler and approved by the White House on December 31. The meeting was held at the Prime Minister's house.

[1] Not further identified.

signed" mean a firm commitment which would not be ignored except in moment of extreme national peril.

There followed some discussion with the Secretary of Defense about the distinction between forces which have been "assigned" and those which have been "earmarked for commitment to". The Secretary of Defense said that "earmarked" was usually applied to sea forces, whereas the word "committed" was used for land forces. In any case there was no doubt that national forces which have been assigned to NATO can be withdrawn, with appropriate notice.

The Prime Minister then pulled a paper out of his pocket which he read out and which set forth the British position and reasoning on the question of a substitute for Skybolt.[2] He went on to say that the situation now was that the US had agreed to sell Polaris missiles to the UK, which would construct the actual submarines and the warheads. He said that the primary task of these units would be to contribute to the defense of the NATO area. So the job to be done was to build them, make them available to NATO in all ordinary conditions, and meanwhile see if we could work out some kind of multilateral force. If the UK Government was going to assume these heavy new expenditures, it would have to be in a position to justify the decision to do so. The UK Government would have to explain that the UK was in a period of history between two worlds: the world of independence and the world of interdependence. If the UK was going to undertake this program it would have to have the feeling that it had gained, in the last resort, an instrument which it could use, in certain circumstances, to preserve peace, and in other circumstances perhaps as an instrument of national policy. He said that the UK needed just that degree of sovereignty which would justify making the added effort. If this element were not present, then the question would arise whether the effort was justified, since there were other ways of spending money for the UK Armed Forces, such as making them more mobile, better equipped, and giving them greater support.

The Prime Minister recalled that there had been cases in recent years when it had been necessary to move rapidly to preserve peace:

(1) the UK forces had moved into Jordan while US forces had been sent to Lebanon;
(2) the UK had had to move fast for the defense of the Gulf of Persia;
(3) troops had recently been sent to put down the trouble in Malaysia.

What the UK Government needed was little, but this was "what is needed in order to remain something in the world". This sentiment was shared by the French. The Prime Minister did not think that Germany

---

[2] Not found.

today entertained these sentiments. He thought the Germans were very different people now from what they were under Hitler. He thought that a phrase something like "the primary purpose of those forces would be to contribute to the defense of NATO" would be acceptable. He thought it might be healthy to have this kind of weapon available for special needs in other parts of the world, e.g., the Far East. Then there was the question of the morale of the crews. US submarine crews, for instance, on units assigned to NATO feel strong national loyalties. We would have to see whether and if so how a multilateral force could be created.

The President said that the US has had some rather serious disagreements with the French with respect to their nuclear role, in which the UK has not been involved. Our object is to make the force envisaged as multilateral as possible. We take the view, he said, that this proposal represents a substantial step. He said we do not discount possible difficulties with regard to French and German reaction. These missiles and submarines, said the President, should be available to the UK for national use only in case of dire emergencies. The proposal has the advantage of saving the UK something like $800 million. We recognize that British national forces assigned to NATO could be taken back by the UK in extreme circumstances. The President thought that "ordinary conditions" should cover all situations that could be envisaged short of those which constituted "mortal danger" to the survival of the country.

Lord Home asked whether, if Nehru was in very great trouble, and the UK wanted to put three submarines in the Bay of Bengal, they would be entitled to do so. Mr. Ball said he had been impressed by the Prime Minister's reference earlier in the morning to the situation in which the UK found itself in 1940. That was the kind of desperate situation which in our view would justify the withdrawal of the committed forces. Lord Home said there were other potential crises which should be considered. For example, Kuwait and the UK oil interests there.

The Prime Minister said it seemed to him that what we were saying was that it would be all right for the UK to withdraw its forces if it was a question of absolute survival, but that no situation short of this would justify their doing so. However, there were conceivable situations in which the UK would want to make policy by having Polaris at their disposal for national purposes. Otherwise, the British people might want to do something else with their money. The UK would be committing its entire force, whereas the US would retain a good deal of its Polaris forces outside of NATO. The Prime Minister referred to complications of giving submarines, which was far greater than in the case of aircraft and armies. Submarines would be spoken to but apparently must never answer back. He felt that a British Admiral of the fleet must be in the position of issuing commands to this particular fleet, otherwise the units would "have no life of their own". He added that there was no reason why the British Commander would not be part of a higher command, whether SACEUR or SACLANT.

The Secretary of Defense commented on the very heavy cost involved in the Polaris systems. He said the US and the UK would try not to duplicate overhead costs, and that the UK could share in use of the systems.

The President said that our language was intended to satisfy other members of NATO. After all, we are talking about 1970 for the force to come into being, whereas we are faced with the political requirements of the situation the next two or three years. He said that it was the US and not the UK which carried the responsibility for the situations with regard to France and a nuclear role.

The Prime Minister said he wanted to sum up where we now stood: the UK does not want to go on with Skybolt for the reasons given. Hound Dog would have been absolutely splendid, "were it not for the fact that it would mean practically re-designing the bombers". The Prime Minister said he could see the difficulties facing the US, but if the UK were to acquire the Polaris submarines, it would put them entirely under NATO. The problem was what the word "assignment" really means. The value of the proposal to the UK would be if the British Government in power at the time were able to make use of the British element in the force, should the UK be faced by some national emergency which required its use. The Prime Minister drew a comparison with the US Sixth Fleet, or sending a cruiser or gunboat off to deal with some emergency situation. He said that the UK must reserve the ultimate right to withdraw from the force. The crews must feel that they are the "Queen's sailors" until a supranational organization comes into being. The Prime Minister added that if General deGaulle were prepared to consider joining a multilateral force, he would undoubtedly say the same thing.

(At this point the meeting adjourned, after a brief discussion during which the President and the Prime Minister agreed to keep the Conference going until sometime Friday, December 21.)

404. Telegram From the Delegation to the Heads of Government Meeting to the Department of State

Nassau, December 19, 1962.

1. Eyes only for the Secretary from Ball. No other distrubution. The following two documents are being presented to the British this evening after a day of intense discussion of Skybolt. First document is a draft public statement which might be released, if agreed, tomorrow night or Friday morning. Second is a private understanding of dealing with degree of independence British element of proposed force. Discussion of these documents will resume about ten Thursday morning and we would like your comment and Bohlen's if possible before then:

"1. The President and the Prime Minister reviewed the development program for the Skybolt missile. The President explained that it was no longer expected that this very complex weapons system would be completed within the cost estimate or the time scale which were projected when the program was begun.

"2. The President informed the Prime Minister that for this reason and because of the availability to the United States of alternative weapons systems, he had decided to cancel plans for the production of Skybolt for use by the United States. Nevertheless, recognizing the importance of the Skybolt program for the United Kingdom and recalling that the purpose of the offer of Skybolt to the United Kingdom in 1960 had been to assist in improving and extending the effective life of the British V bombers, the President expressed his readiness to continue that development of the missile as a joint enterprise between the United States and the United Kingdom, with each country bearing equal shares of the future cost of completing developments, after which the United Kingdom would be able to place a production order to meet its requirements.

"3. While recognizing the generosity of this offer, the Prime Minister decided after full consideration not to avail himself of it because of uncertainty regarding the date of completion and the final cost of the program.

"4. As a possible alternative the President suggested that the Royal Air Force might use the Hound Dog missile. The Prime Minister responded that in the light of difficulties in adapting this missile for the British V bombers. He was unable to accept this suggestion.

Source: Department of State, Conference Files: Lot 65 D 533, CF 2213. Secret; Niact; No Other Distribution. No time of transmission is indicated on the source text, but it was received in Washington at 11 p.m., December 19.

"5. The President then proposed a plan for joint action by the two governments in the field of sea-based missile forces in cooperation with other members of NATO. The Prime Minister accepted this plan, and the President and the Prime Minister agreed that it should be further developed on an urgent basis, in the closest consultation with all interested parties.

"6. The role which the President and Prime Minister envisage for their two governments in this undertaking is as follows:

(A) Forces developed by the UK under this plan would be assigned to NATO deterrent forces and targeted under agreements approved by NATO.

(B) The US would undertake to make a similar assignment of forces of at least equal size.

(C) The US and the UK would support the creation of a NATO multilateral force.

(D) The US and UK forces referred to in paragraphs (A) and (B) above would be included in such a NATO multilateral force.

(E) The US under these conditions would make available Polaris missiles (less warheads) together with associated equipment for fire control, launching, guidance and navigation for the British vessels included in the forces referred to in sub-paragraph (A) above. The US would also study the feasibility of making available certain support facilities for such vessels. The UK Government would construct the submarines in which these weapons would be placed and they would also construct the nuclear warheads for the Polaris missiles.

"7. The President and the Prime Minister have as their objective in this new plan strengthening the nuclear defense of the Western Alliance. In strategic terms this defense is indivisible, and it is their conviction that in all ordinary circumstances of crisis or danger, it is this very unity which is the best protection of the West.

"8. The US and the UK agree that in addition to having a nuclear shield it is important for NATO to strengthen its non-nuclear sword. They agree to meet their NATO non-nuclear force goals at agreed NATO standards."

Document two follows:

"Understanding between the President and Prime Minister regarding the answer to inquiries as to the degree of independence of the British element of the proposed force.

Begin text: "Only in the event of a dire national emergency—an emergency which we might have to face alone, which we happily, cannot envisage, and which we must all trust will never occur—would Her Majesty's Government be faced with a decision of utilizing such forces on their own—always, of course, after adequate notice to all their Allies." *End text.*

405. Telegram From the Department of State to the Delegation to the Heads of Government Meeting at Nassau

Washington, December 20, 1962, 2:39 p.m.

27. For Ball from Secretary. As seen from here and in light of previous experience with complex diplomatic arrangements achieved in conferences we attach great importance to making a matter of confidential record the consensus behind critical paragraph 6 of Nassau 1.[1] We are not seeking to go beyond the language of the agreement, i.e., to commit UK to go in the slightest degree further or faster than agreement contemplates. But we do not want to see the UK commitment to NATO multilateral force to lag due to (a) pressure of political in-fighting in England; (b) possible unwillingness of some NATO members to work towards such a force; (c) post-Nassau British public interpretations, in heat of parliamentary debate, of the agreement which might run counter to what both governments now understand to be its substance.

From Tyler–Schaetzel telecon[2] we gather following points may be a part of the US-UK understanding. Would hope that these points could be either made part of US-UK confidential minute or US statement for the record of its interpretation of critical paragraph.

1. The ulimate objective of the agreement will be the development of a multilateral force in which any other interested NATO countries can eventually take part on non-discriminatory basis, without thereby acquiring national nuclear capabilities.

2. The commitment on the part of the British to explore and support such a force is not, however, conditional on acceptance of a similar arrangement by France, nor to agreement by NATO as a whole to a multilateral force.

3. High priority will be given by both governments to the discussion and possible development of the NATO multilateral force. The US and UK agree that early invitation to other interested countries to participate in the discussion and possible development of a multilateral force is indispensable.

Believe we should also make clear, for sake of record in later negotiations with our other allies, that US believes force under multilateral ownership, control, and manning would meet criterion #1.

Rusk

Source: Department of State, Central Files, 741.5612/12–2062. Secret; Priority; Eyes Only. Drafted by Schaetzel, cleared with Rostow, and approved and initialed by Rusk.

[1] Document 404.

[2] No record of this telephone conversation has been found.

406. Memorandum of Conversation

Nassau, December 20, 1962, 10 a.m.

SUBJECT

Skybolt

PARTICIPANTS

Great Britain:	*United States:*
The Prime Minister	The President
Lord Home	Secretary McNamara
Ambassador David Ormsby Gore	Under Secretary Ball
Sir Robert Scott	Mr. McGeorge Bundy
Mr. Thorneycroft	Ambassador Bruce
Mr. Bligh	Mr. William R. Tyler

The Prime Minister recapitulated the UK intentions:

(1) The US Government has very generously made an offer on both Skybolt and Hound Dog.
(2) The UK Government has raised the question of Polaris. The Prime Minister agreed that this was not merely a substitute for Skybolt. It represented something new which marks the opening of a fresh phase in US-UK relationships.
(3) The world has moved on. France is now strong. Germany has a weak government with ambitions.
(4) We are considering organizing a contributory NATO structure, whereby several countries put something into the pool.

"Actually", said the Prime Minister, "the whole thing is ridiculous." What do seven or eight UK units add to the existing nuclear strength, which is enough to blow up the world? So why does the UK want it? It is partly a question of keeping up with the Joneses", which is human. We have not yet reached the point of a melting pot of nations. So countries which have played a great role in history must retain their dignity. This area is not merely a question of difference of degree, but of order. The UK does not want to be just a clown, or a satellite. The UK wants a nuclear force not only for defense, but in the event of menace to its existence, which the UK might have to meet; for example: when Khrushchev waved his rockets about the time of Suez, or when that fellow Qassim got excited and Kuwait was threatened. The UK, the Prime Minister went on to say, wants to do three things: to contribute to NATO, to contribute to the strength and unity of Europe, and to retain

Source: Department of State, Conference Files: Lot 66 D 110, CF 2217. Secret. Drafted by Tyler and approved by the White House on December 31.

an element of strength in its foreign policy in order to maintain the valuation given by other countries to the UK's advice. It was difficult to define what was meant by "withdrawal". You could talk about "dire emergency", but what was meant by "dire" and how much of an emergency would it have to be? It was right, he said, that we should not alarm the Germans or the French—particularly the Germans. We should promote the European concept. It was also necessary that the UK should not have the status of a satellite. The UK should increase or at least maintain the strength of its foreign policy, so that it should not be threatened with impunity. He felt that it was necessary to find language which would take the foregoing into account. The matter under discussion was very serious for the UK, and would be much debated. It would set the tone for the next 15 years. For these reasons, said the Prime Minister, he has asked the Deputy Prime Minister in London to call a Cabinet meeting for Friday, December 21, at 10:30 a.m. Thus there would be a Cabinet decision. He thought it would be useful to hold a drafting session to work out language.

The President agreed that the solution being discussed was, and would be regarded as being a very different question from Skybolt. The US did not want to have similar requests addressed to it, which it would have to refuse. Careful drafting would be necessary. With reference to Kuwait, doubtless the UK Government in power in 1970 would have to decide whether it was still a live issue. He assumed that the UK did not have the intention of using nuclear weapons against Qassim.

Turning to the question of what answer the Prime Minister should give to questions in the House of Commons, this matter would have to be carefully considered. The President said we would have to put something into the agreement on the need to increase conventional forces. So long as Berlin existed as a problem, there was danger of war. He felt that the extra costs involved in building nuclear submarines should not be at the expense of pressing forward toward conventional goals. (At this point, both Lord Home and Mr. Thorneycroft referred to the language in the recent NATO communiqué on conventional forces and suggested that this be used.) The President said the language reached should be such that both countries could defend it. It should include the thought that, having talked together about a multilateral force, both the US and the UK wanted to make such a force a reality. We must not make the multilateral project a mere cover for national deterrents. There was the question of what the Prime Minister should answer to questions in Parliament.

The Prime Minister said he did not like the idea of defining a precise text. He would prefer just to say that the UK force was assigned to NATO. The Prime Minister went on to say that they were talking about a very long time ahead. He suggested making a start by pooling some of the bombers and other aircraft of the US, the UK and France. Thus the multilateral force "would grow naturally, as though from a seed". "Let us do it now, he said, and build up on it."

The President said that pooling bombers might be a good idea, but asked what would the Prime Minister say in answer to questions.

The Prime Minister said this was a hypothetical question. The bombers, then the submarines, would be put into the multilateral force. "Of course", he said, "in the last resort you may be forced to pick up your stick and fight." Moreover, officers of Her Majesty's Navy would expect to take orders from a minister of the UK Government. The President asked the Prime Minister what he would say if people asked whether the UK was retaining an independent deterrent. The Prime Minister said he would say that the UK was making an independent British contribution to the nuclear defense of the West. The President noted that the emphasis was on the words "British contribution", rather than on "independent deterrent". (At this point the Prime Minister distributed a paper with some language.)

The President said that if deGualle were to ask whether the US was prepared to make the same offer to him as to the UK we should say "yes". Of course, he might object to a proposal of this kind. (There followed some discussion of the language proposed by the Prime Minister, and it was decided to recess for one-half hour in order that each Delegation should be able to discuss separately the situation which had been reached.)

The meeting reconvened at 12:00 noon. The Prime Minister objected that the US language went too far in reasserting the very points that had caused him so much anxiety. It did not give him what he needed, which was: "a British force." He insisted that he would have to use the words "supreme national interest." At that point, the President read part of an article in that morning's *Washington Post* to illustrate the difficulties he faced with regard to American domestic opinion. The Prime Minister raised again the three desiderata from the UK point of view: (1) to make a contribution to NATO for joint defense; (2) to give the UK Government authority in international councils; (3) to retain the means of wielding influence in international diplomatic life.

Obviously, said the Prime Minister, he could not say that the British force envisaged would be as British as the Brigade of Guards, but if all this effort and expense were to be borne, it must mean to the British people that they were thereby keeping up with the Joneses. He was sorry, but he could not accept the US paper as it stood. If the US insisted on keeping this language, he would prefer not to agree. It would look as though the US only wanted, "to keep the little boys quiet." DeGaulle would say that the UK had sold out. The Prime Minister said he intended to stress both independence and interdependence together. The

UK was prepared to put the whole force into the pool. The language he had in mind was such as to give the UK Government a "life, and existence" so that it is not merely a client. "I do not believe", he said, "that the Atlantic partnership will ever succeed or be built up except on pooling of equal pride and honor."

The Prime Minister then engaged in a long soliloquy of reminiscences of World Wars I and II. The British troops which had died had done so for their Sovereign, not for just some vague reason which meant nothing to them. He agreed that the force contemplated could be a joint navy for practical purposes, but the British contribution must be the Queen's. In the recent Cuban crisis, he said, the population of the US knew why it was prepared to face war if necessary. These thoughts must be taken into consideration in the agreement which we were trying to reach. If we were to disagree, "we would have to undertake an agonizing reappraisal of our military and political policies."

The President said it was clear that we had somewhat different interests with regard to what should be said after our meeting in Nassau. US policy has constantly been directed toward discrediting national nuclear deterrents, and it was not possible for the US to start saying the opposite.

The meeting broke up at about 1:00 p.m. for further consideration of the language proposed by each Delegation.[1]

---

[1] In subsequent meetings on December 20 and 21 the President and the Prime Minister discussed the Sino-Indian border dispute, the Congo, Yemen, nuclear proliferation, and Japan while members of each delegation drafted the final communiqué and the statement on nuclear defense systems. Memoranda of the President's conversations are ibid.; for texts of the communiqué and statement, see *American Foreign Policy: Current Documents, 1962*, pp. 633–637.

---

407. Telegram From the Delegation to the Heads of Government Meeting to the Embassy in France

Nassau, December 20, 1962.

4. Eyes only Ambassador. Following text letter to de Gaulle from President which you should deliver immediately to de Gaulle, or the

---

Source: Department of State, Presidential Correspondence: Lot 66 D 204. Secret; Priority. Repeated to London, Bonn, and the Department, which is the source text. No time of transmission appears on the source text. A similar letter was transmitted to Bonn in telegram 1 from Nassau for delivery to Adenauer. (Ibid.)

highest official for soonest possible communication to de Gaulle. Time is important since imperative that de Gaulle be informed prior to release communiqué from Nassau.

Begin verbatim text:

Dear General de Gaulle: I wanted you to know that Prime Minister Macmillan and I have had an extensive discussion of the question whether to proceed with the production of Skybolt missiles. I informed the Prime Minister that, having taken all the relevant factors into account, the US Govt does not wish to continue on its own account the production of this missile. However, I told the Prime Minister that, in view of the particular interest of the UK Government with the respect to Skybolt, we would be prepared to complete its development, should the UK so desire, on the basis of equally shared costs. Alternatively, I offered to make available to the UK Government the Hound Dog air-to-surface missiles, should it consider this preferable.

Having carefully considered these two proposals, the Prime Minister decided not to accept either of them.

The Prime Minister then turned to the possibility of provision of the Polaris missile to the UK by the US. We then reached an understanding, subject to approval by the British Cabinet on Friday morning which contains the following key paragraphs:

"After careful review the President and the Prime Minister agreed that a decision on Polaris must be considered in the widest context both of the future defense of the Atlantic Alliance and of the safety of the free world. They reached the conclusion that this issue created an opportunity for the development of new and closer arrangements for the organization and control of strategic Western defense and that such arrangements in turn could make a major contribution to political cohesion among the nations of the Alliance.

The Prime Minister suggested, and the President agreed, that for the immediate future a start could be made by subscribing to NATO some part of the forces already in existence. This could include allocations from US strategic forces, from UK Bomber Command, and from tactical forces now in Europe. Such forces would be assigned as part of a NATO nuclear force and targeted in accordance with NATO plans.

Returning to Polaris the President and the Prime Minister agreed that the purpose of their two governments with respect to the provision of the Polaris missiles must be the development of multilateral NATO nuclear force in the closest consultation with the other NATO allies. They will use their best endeavors to this end.

Accordingly the President and the Prime Minister agreed that the US will make available on a continuing basis Polaris missiles (less warheads) for British submarines. The US will also study the feasibility of making available certain support facilities for such submarines. The UK Government will construct the submarines in which these weapons will be placed and they will also provide the nuclear warheads for the Polaris missiles. British forces developed under this plan will be assigned and targeted in the same way as the forces described above.

These forces, and at least equal forces, would be made available for inclusion in a NATO multilateral nuclear force. The Prime Minister made it clear that these British forces will be used for the purpose of international defense of the Western Alliance in all circumstances, except where H.M.G. may decide that supreme national interests are at stake.

The President and the Prime Minister are convinced that this new plan will strengthen the nuclear defense of the Western Alliance. In strategic terms this defense is indivisible and it is their conviction that in all ordinary circumstances of crisis or danger, it is this very unity which is the best protection for the West.

The President and the Prime Minister agreed that in addition to having a nuclear shield it is important to have a non-nuclear sword. For this purpose they agreed on the importance of increasing the effectiveness of their conventional forces."

I feel that the agreement we have reached can make a major contribution to the cohesion and the effective defense of the West. I want you to know that I would consider a similar agreement with you, should you so desire.

Mrs. Kennedy and I would like to extend to you and Madame de Gaulle our very best wishes for a Merry Christmas.

(Signed John F. Kennedy)

End verbatim text.

Ball

---

408. Memorandum by Prime Minister Macmillan

Nassau, December 20, 1962.

[Source: Department of State, Presidential Correspondence: Lot 66 D 204. Secret. 1 page of source text not declassified.]

409. Memorandum From President Kennedy to Prime Minister Macmillan

Nassau, December 21, 1962.

1. The United States Government proposes to offer to the French Government the opportunity to participate in the multilateral nuclear force envisaged by the Nassau agreement on terms similar to those agreed with the United Kingdom. However, we do not consider that the agreement on the part of the United States and the United Kingdom to support the development and establishment of such a multilateral force is conditional on participation by France.

2. It is also our view that participation in the proposed multilateral force should be available to non-nuclear member nations of NATO through the contribution of personnel and resources for the operation of nuclear vessels, including submarines, manned by units of mixed nationality. I propose that an early invitation be extended to such countries to participate in the discussion and developments of such units.

3. It is agreed that the Polaris missiles and associated equipment to be made available by the United States to the United Kingdom Government under the provisions of Article 8 of the agreement[1] will consist of equipment for fire control, launching, guidance, and navigation.

John F. Kennedy[2]

Source: Department of State, Conference Files: Lot 65 D 533, CF 2212. No classification marking.

[1] Paragraph 8 of the Statement on Nuclear Defense Systems.

[2] Printed from a copy that bears this typed signature.

410. Record of Meeting

Washington, December 28, 1962, 11 a.m.

NASSAU FOLLOW-UP

PARTICIPANTS

State

Secretary Rusk
Jeffrey C. Kitchen
J. Robert Schaetzel

White House

McGeorge Bundy

Defense

Secretary McNamara
Deputy Secretary Gilpatric
John T. McNaughton
Henry S. Rowen

The Secretary remarked that first French reaction to the Nassau proposal was sour according to a report received indirectly from Foreign Office sources. In this connection, he thought we should, as soon as possible, allay French suspicions by making it clearly understood that all that was agreed at Nassau had been made public and there were no secret deals. We should seek to enter a dialogue with the French in which, in effect, we might say "You raise the questions. Which points do you regard as critical and which are those on which you need clarification?" Thus, we could gradually ascertain whether the French were going to change; if they were not, we should not get in a lather. If they were smart they would come to us and ask what a "similar" arrangement really meant.

Mr. McNamara interjected that he thought that as long as the French were willing to commit nuclear forces to a multilateral force under NATO, and if command and control arrangements were satisfactory to us, we should be prepared to supply submarines and war heads to the French. This should be an across-the-board offer provided the French reaction to our conditions was satisfactory. He saw our objective as being to minimize the cost to the Europeans of such nuclear forces; neither the UK nor French should expend funds in duplicating our technology but should shift this increment of military expenditure from developing of nuclear forces to improving and strengthening their conventional capabilities.

The Secretary replied that we should have available a complete framework of negotiating possibilities, backed up by a far-reaching staff review of the alternatives. For instance, he thought a good deal might

---

Source: Department of State, Conference Files: Lot 66 D 110, CF 2217. Secret; Eyes Only. Drafted by Kitchen on December 29.

turn on the non-transfer provision. It might be possible initially to implement the multilateral proposal by utilizing a surface vessel on which a Polaris-type missile could be placed. The next question which might raise a problem with the French would be whether they had a war head which could be mated with a Polaris missile. Throughout any such discussion, we should attempt to steer them in the right direction and we should avoid being negative in the concept of our approach.

Mr. McNamara stated that our objective might become one of getting *both* the UK and France into an advanced nuclear posture if they met our two main conditions of multilateral and command arrangements. We should re-examine all that we have given to the British and consider whether it might not be cheaper over the long-run to furnish new equipment to the French and British rather than simply assist them in various technological processes. This would make them more dependent on us as a source of supply, thus enhancing indirectly our power to control final policies.

The Secretary stated that we have to give careful consideration both to present political issues and those which might arise in the future, and that we must check carefully any penalties we might pay by making premature offers of great dimension. For instance, it was generally agreed that we could *not* get DeGaulle to turn around on some of his policies which are most offensive to us. The question then becomes *what France* are we considering cooperating with? We could not set aside the fact that France was not cooperating with us in NATO, was not cooperating nor paying its share in the UN, was most frequently the difficult partner on Berlin, and had virtually sabotaged SEATO. The present French Government has shown an inclination toward abstention and veto on all major policy efforts and does not constitute a reliable partner.

Mr. McNamara said he should recognize that there might be benefits in leading France to rely upon US technology; by being forthcoming now, we might be able to turn the French in the direction we wanted.

The Secretary said he thought that NATO should get on with its business without letting France interfere but that we should simultaneously try to lead the French in the direction of our long-range goal of multilateralism.

Mr. McNamara said that perhaps a good idea could be achieved by getting enough agreement with the French so that we could get technical groups working together; in the course of these exchanges, we could get the sense of cooperation moved upward to the political level.

Mr. Kitchen said such working together implied an initial contact which developed some degree of understanding—including possible limitations. The problem for us is to obtain engagement so that we may have a dialogue and, subsequently, one of timing and degree in stating what we will or will not do.

Mr. Bundy said he thought this was the heart of the matter and introduced the whole range of possibilities that had been mentioned. We wanted to open negotiations, but even developing an initial understanding or degree of cooperation might take all of 1963. Secretary Rusk said that in this latter connection, we should remind the French that the operational capability envisaged in the British agreement was 1967/68.

Mr. Rusk then directed attention to the list of sub-groups set up under the State–Defense Steering Group.

Jupiters

In connection with Sub-Group V (Jupiters),[1] he emphasized urgency in getting ready a policy package on the removal of Jupiter missiles from Italy and Turkey. Ambassador Hare, who had arrived in Washington for consultation, was relatively relaxed regarding problems we would have with the Turks. The Secretary emphasized however, that, while we could achieve our objective of obtaining the removal of the missiles, a great deal depended on the manner and timing of dealing with this problem so that we did not damage our position with the Turks psychologically and politically.

Secretary McNamara said the President had asked him on Thursday what steps were being taken to obtain removal of the Jupiters. McNamara strongly favored action at the earliest possible date and wondered whether we could set April 1 as our deadline for beginning removal of the missiles.

Secretary Rusk replied that how and when we acted must be dependent on a time schedule to be established on the basis of the consultations we would have this week and next with Ambassadors Hare and Reinhardt. He pointed out that three basic papers dealing with providing a substitute capability for the Turks and Italians were now in preparation by elements of the joint State–Defense group. In this connection, Secretary Rusk said he wanted the Jupiter item removed from the immediate context of work being done by other sub-groups; as a more highly classified matter, it should be treated on a need-to-know basis.

Mr. McNamara said that we must move quickly because (1) he owed an early answer to the Italian and Turkish Defense Ministers, and (2) early action was necessary if we were to achieve anything like an April 1 removal date. Mr. Gilpatric said he thought we should have in-

---

[1] On December 27 the Steering Group on Implementing the Nassau Decisions held its first meeting under Kitchen's chairmanship. Established to review, advise, and recommend policies and programs emanating from the Nassau agreements, its work was divided into the sub-groups described below. Records of meetings and copies of papers and related documentation are ibid., CF 2217–2219 and Central File 611.41.

structions for the Ambassadors by January 3 or 4 so that they could return as soon as possible to Rome and Ankara and begin discussions with the respective governments. Mr. Kitchen inquired if it was still Secretary McNamara's intention to go to Ankara for more extensive military-technical discussions after Ambassador Hare had returned to his post. Secretary McNamara replied that either he or Mr. Nitze would make the trip "if Ambassador Hare thinks this is necessary".

Secretary Rusk said that the approach to the Turks should incorporate his conversations with the Turks on this subject in April 1961,[2] but be conducted on a broader basis. Mr. Bundy said he thought we should take the line, both with the Turks and the world, that we are updating our entire defense strategy and positions of strength with weapons which are more modern and invulnerable.

Secretary Rusk observed that the timing of the public surfacing of these negotiations was very important, both in relation to the allies directly concerned and our other allies in NATO. Special attention should be paid to planning how the release would be made.

Secretary McNamara stated technical arrangements to be worked out with the Turks and Italians for command and control should not be confused with the technical arrangements being worked out for assignment of matching forces to NATO.

While they might be designed to be as complimentary as possible, they could be phased together later and the Jupiter removal not delayed. He thought command arrangements for the Polaris submarines would fall under SACEUR through CINCEUR and the Sixth Fleet. Thus, these boats would clearly be assigned to NATO and substitute for the NATO-assigned Jupiters which would be coming out. These arrangements should be simple and made as quickly as possible. In connection with the US-UK matching forces to be assigned to NATO, thought was being given to including them under a separate NATO nuclear command. Consideration of this latter concept should not have a high priority either in connection with the Jupiters nor in connection with the separate question of getting the matching forces assigned to NATO. In the latter case, it was highly desirable to get some nuclear capability assigned as quickly as possible in order to get the principle established.

Secretary Rusk next invited comments regarding the other Sub-Groups.

Sub-Group I

Mr. McNamara said he thought it would be desirable to have Sub-Group I consider all aspects of future nuclear relationships with Britain, Sub-Group III the same with France, and Sub-Group IV should give pri-

[2] Not further identified.

ority consideration to the question of how we include Germany. Under Sub-Group I he thought an especial effort should be devoted to identification of waste in the UK nuclear program and determination of the extent to which we could reduce such waste by providing technology or end items.

Secretary Rusk agreed we should surface these considerations to see if they were worth the candle politically. In this connection we also should determine what assistance the British could give the French in the nuclear field. Mr. Schaetzel said that this had been looked into previously and it had been determined that very little was identifiable in the British program that was not tied down by the US-UK agreement of 1958. However, he said this would be looked into again, including reexamining the legislative authorization. Secretary Rusk remarked that one way to deal with the problem might be to seek to have existing legislation relative to the UK made applicable to France.

Secretary McNamara said one cost the British might have to contemplate at an early date might be for construction of new warheads for Polaris. In this connection he inquired when it was contemplated implementing conversations might begin with the British. Mr. Schaetzel said he had spoken with Ambassador Bruce about this and the latter thought that no British officials would be ready for definitive talks until after the Government had presented its proposals to Parliament—probably the fourth week in January.

Sub- Group II

There was agreement that considerations applicable to this Sub-Group had been covered in other remarks, but that emphasis should be on early assignment as a first step in firm establishment of the principle.

Sub-Group III

Secretary Rusk said that with regard to negotiations with the French, the first operational question would center around framing instructions for Ambassador Bohlen. This would be followed shortly by the requirement for instructions for George Ball whom we proposed should make a presentation to the North Atlantic Council on January 11. The idea is that Ambassador Finletter and Under Secretary Ball should assure NATO Secretary General Stikker, as well as the member countries, regarding our objectives in framing the Nassau Agreement. Our concept of three types of nuclear capable forces would be set forth, namely 1) national forces outside of NATO, 2) national forces assigned to NATO and 3) multilateral forces developed among NATO countries and assigned to NATO.

Discussion next centered around the exchange of memoranda between the President and Macmillan [1-1/2 *lines of source text not declassi-*

fied] and our proposals to make a similar offer to the French and an offer of assistance to other nations in a multilateral context.[3] It was agreed that the British should be approached right away with a view to making this exchange public and useable in NATO. It was also agreed that Ambassador Finletter should be recalled early in January for consultation prior to Under Secretary Ball's presentation to the NAC.

Secretary McNamara said he envisaged that the work of Sub-Group I should concern itself with the entire range of questions which might arise in subsequent negotiations with the British. He thought that Sub-Group III should concentrate on negotiations with the French although he accepted this might include dealing with other NATO members as necessary. Sub-Group IV should give priority consideration to what type of proposal we intended to make to the Germans. Mr. Schaetzel pointed out that we also should consider how we will deal with the Italians because there is as much anxiety in Rome as in Bonn. Mr. Kitchen said Sub-Group I had been set up primarily as a legal group but that a device could be found for broadening its responsibilities if that was deemed desirable.

Mr. McNamara said the reason he had the Germans so much in mind was not only the political requirements to deal with them in a way that would relieve their concerns and take into account their interest in being a part of a multilateral force but, also, that if they shared in a nuclear force we could press them harder to take a more realistic contribution to conventional capabilities. Our basic objective should be to maximize the military efficiency of the nuclear forces at minimum cost to the Alliance as a whole and to obtain reallocation of the savings achieved to a strengthening of conventional capability.

The Secretary said that under Sub-Group IV we should work hard on the concepts of a future multilateral force as being our ultimate objective but, in the meantime, we had to tailor our policy so as to deal with existing realities. At the present time we could envisage three elements in the nuclear-strategic business. The first was SAC operating outside of NATO. The second would be US, UK and French forces working under assignment to NATO, and the third would be multilateral mixed-manned forces which we should continue to regard as our ultimate objective, but which we cannot realize immediately because neither the French or British are favorably inclined toward its immediate creation. Ultimately, the first two types should wither away and the third type should become the basic force.

---

[3] For texts of these minutes (Memoranda) dated December 20 and 21, respectively, see Supplement.

Mr. McNamara said he regarded a sea surface-borne force as highly vulnerable. He said the British had *definitely* reached that conclusion and would not accept a multilateral force based on the vulnerable merchant ship concept. If this is correct, we should stop advancing that mode as being our leading concept for a multilateral force. A multilateral force could be developed either on a sub-surface basis or on land in either hardened or mobile configurations. If it were a sub-surface force, there would be limited interest in multilateral mixed-manning but that we may eventually get a multilateral force by developing it through a series of bilateral force arrangements. Thus, subs might be jointly manned by the US and respective European countries and assigned to NATO. We could start with such bilateral arrangements with the nuclear powers and try to advance the principles in each case of a non-nationally manned vessel. These were concepts that should be examined. Returning to the possibility of a land-based system, Secretary McNamara said we could place considerable reliance on the Permissive Link. One concept would be to have a multilateral "receiving" command under NATO. This would be multilateral in the upper command levels with ultimate decision to release the weapon still resting with the President, but nationally manned as far as the individual weapons are concerned, controlled by a Permissive Link. The command decision level thus would be multilateral.

At this juncture Secretary Rusk was called from the room.

There was discussion of the state of development of the Permissive Link and Mr. Bundy undertook to check with the Sandia people and perhaps have them come to Washington to make sure they understood not only what was desired mechanically but to give them a better idea of the concept of employment, particularly in a multilateral context.

Mr. McNamara said that in dealing with the West Germans we should require that they raise their strength on an acceptable schedule to a point where they were spending approximately seven percent of their GNP comparable to that now being expended by the British and French. We should make clear that the Germans must get their Army personnel up to level of at least 270,000. Mr. Gilpatric emphasized that there was no use in the US keeping the equivalent of six divisions in Europe with supplies and ammunition for 90 to 120 days of continuous fighting if their flanks were in effect bare because European troops were too few and ill-supplied. The Germans should be brought to choose between a genuine capability or the prospect of American withdrawal.

Secretary McNamara then made a lengthy restatement of his position that we should make clear that we were making fair offers on an across-the-board basis. He reiterated that if the French accepted: 1) multilateral force commitment under NATO and 2) agreed to satisfactory command and control arrangements, we then should be very forthcoming in offering them nuclear technology of all types in order to minimize costs for them and thus reduce waste in the over-all Western defense effort. With regard to Committee V on Jupiters, which was now reached for the second time in the discussion as a result of following the Committee outline, Mr. McNamara said that he hoped our objective was to get the instruction to the Ambassadors by the end of next week so that our dialogue with the Turks might begin no later than January 10.

In the course of the entire foregoing discussion there were several expressions of concern regarding what could and should be said publicly regarding the aftermath of the Nassau Agreement. It was agreed that initially there would be no briefing or backgrounding for the press without checking with Mr. Bundy. Secretary Rusk requested that an agreed guidance for backgrounding the press be developed which would indicate what could and could not be said by officials. In particular he thought we should make clear we were not looking for "crash" results and foresaw long, deliberate negotiations.

411. Memorandum From the Chairman of the Steering Group To Implement the Nassau Decisions (Kitchen) to Secretary of State Rusk

Washington, January 4, 1963.

SUBJECT

Principle Substantive Issues Emerging from Nassau Follow-Up

1. In this memorandum I set forth what appear to be the substantive differences in points of view which are emerging from the work of the Steering Committee and various Sub-Groups which have been organized to provide the detailed follow-up on Nassau.

2. I start from the predominant State Department point of view held by EUR and S/P. This point of view argues that US national interests are deeply involved in the development of an Atlantic Community in which, hopefully, over a period of time political, economic and military interdependence will become an accepted characteristic. This view

---

Source: Department of State, Conference Files: Lot 66 D 110, CF 2217. Secret. Drafted by Weiss and Kitchen. The source text bears a notation that Ball saw it.

holds that events are moving rapidly in that direction. The European Economic Community is perhaps the major immediate stake which hangs in the balance, uncertain as to accomplishment, but with a high probability of its success. This would signify an immense step toward the development of a united Europe economically, which would be one of the prerequisites for interdependent Atlantic Community. However, this point of view also maintains that on military matters, and particularly on nuclear matters, the stakes are at least as high and the issue at least as delicate a balance. Thus, it is the view that our nuclear policy must be focused on our long-range objectives which should be the development of integrated Europeans manufacture, control and use of nuclear weapons. This point of view maintains that such a development can only come about if US policy refuses to support national nuclear ambitions and capitalizes upon the high costs and highly complicated processes of nuclear technology which make it so difficult for powers other than the Soviet Union and the US to develop and maintain independent nuclear capabilities. It believes that we can, and must, use the period of time available to wean Europeans away from the notion of developing nuclear capability, except under a concept of multilateralism in which all who wish to do so may participate in a nuclear force (European if preferred, but hopefully with US participation) but only on a complete integrated basis. In this manner, through mixed manning and other techniques, no one nation could ever withdraw and reserve for itself a national nuclear capability. In the case of Britain it believes that acceptance of the multilateral concept is not far off, viewing the present Conservative Government position as a temporary political expedient. France it accepts as a more difficult problem which will take a longer period of time to resolve but it believes France too, especially under a successor government, will be forced to accept the inevitable course of European multilateralism as the only right course. Finally, Germany represents a key element. This point of view holds that support for any national nuclear force inevitably gives rise to the specter of a similarly re-armed Germany which cannot forever be expected to accept an inferior nuclear position. This, it argues, would be disastrous in the present European political context and would, at this stage in the evolution of German democratic and social life, adversely affect the interests of all of the Free World members.

3. The second point of view is that of Defense as expressed by Secretary McNamara. This point of view appears to place primary emphasis upon the effective utilization of Free World resources for building up its defenses. It argues that resources have and will continue to be grossly mal-used so long as the US refuses to assist its principle Allies with its advanced technology and hardware, while those Allies for their part are equally insistent on developing their own independent capabilities. It

believes that this mal-use of resources will adversely affect not only Allied nuclear capabilities, but far more importantly, the ability of our Allies to contribute to Alliance conventional military strength. On the surface this view appears not to comprehend fully the importance of the political movement toward European integration and the Atlantic Community. However, Defense staff has denied this and offer a different interpretation of Mr. McNamara's views. This argument maintains that we must realistically face up to the fact that the only avenue toward achieving cooperation with our Allies is by our demonstrated willingness to cooperate through our own actions. It hopes that in this way an atmosphere can be developed which will permit the US to have a greater influence than it would otherwise have over the ultimate direction of the Alliance policy. Consistent with the foregoing, the Defense view is that we should proceed with assistance for the development of the British national nuclear capabilities promised at Nassau with all reasonable speed and at minimum cost to the British (two judgments exactly contrary to the prevailing State point of view). It argues that an exactly similar position should be taken toward the French in the belief that this will prove a sufficient inducement to the French to cooperate on nuclear and other matters far more fully than has heretofore been the case (a point of view strongly rejected by the prevailing State judgment). With regard to the Germans (and subsequently the Italians) it would offer them a bilateral participation with the US in a nuclear force at an early opportunity in order to meet the German political problem as well as to gain a maximum German military contribution to the nuclear and conventional forces. And finally, it would continue to support the multilateral force concept for all others in NATO who might be interested, in the hope that over the long run, perhaps the very long run, this would be the accepted avenue for Alliance participation in nuclear affairs.

4. Lastly, there is a point of view which emerges from the White House staff and which presumably is to a considerable extent a reflection of the President's thinking. As we understand it, this point of view holds that Nassau in effect recognizes that there are two paths toward our ultimate objective of European nuclear integration: one multinational, the other multilateral. It argues that it is unrealistic to ignore the fact that our policy in the area of military integration has not achieved success and that we were, and to some extent still are, at odds with our two principal Allies. It accepts the prevailing State argument that multilateralism in nuclear matters must be our ultimate objective but it rejects the State point of view (and in this regard is much closer to the Defense point of view) that this is an objective which can be accomplished at a single point in time and without intermediate stages, or policy plateaus. This point of view reflects the assumption that, like it or not, the sense of national sovereignty remains the determining political force in militar-

ily potent European countries. It places credence in the expression of views by Macmillan at Nassau and DeGaulle everywhere and always as to the importance of the history, culture, tradition, etc., of their two nations and of their unwillingness to sacrifice these features at this point in history to a loyalty to a yet non-existent higher political entity. This point of view would suggest, along with Defense, that we should be prepared to assist in the development of the British national force expeditiously and as inexpensively as possible. It would also offer the French an interpretation of "similar terms" which would bring that nation into an equivalent position with the British during the time span envisioned in the Nassau Agreements, i.e., about 1970. However, unlike the Defense position, it would not accept financial efficiency as a prime determinent in formulating US policy and more importantly, like the State point of view, it would urge the maximum rapid development of the multilateral force concept. This latter it believes important if the Germans are to have "some place to go," although they may not fully share the State concern about the Defense proposal for a bilateral US-German nuclear cooperation. But it would not give a *primary* position to the multilateral force over the multinational force concept, but rather an *equal* status over the next several years.

5. It is apparent that these conflicting points of view are complicated, each with some merit and in toto presenting difficult dilemmas. My own point of view is closest to that which I have attributed to the White House staff. I think that the major weakness in the prevailing State point of view is that it has not taken sufficient account of the importance, be it rational or irrational, of the present force of European nationalism and only dim prospect of a supra-national political authority. I fully share what I believe continues to be a basic tenet of US nuclear policy, namely that multilateralism for Europe and interdependence with the US is the long term objective and the only sane course. But, I doubt that realization of this objective can be forecast in the next several years. Prior to Nassau we could have, as a considered policy, continued our unbending course and played for benefits which time might have delivered to us. Now we have offered the French a formula for ending the special US-UK relationship, and have stated our desire initially to strengthen NATO via multinational nuclear forces and to move from these toward multilateralism. As at least an interim measure, we may have to develop and nurture a feeling within the European Community that the US is not arrogating to itself a judgment as to how outmoded is national sovereignty as a concept for others to live under. The US is not prepared to surrender its sovereign right to control and direct its own national nuclear force, and yet presently it seems to expect this of other nations having histories and cultures pre-dating our own. The requirement therefore is for a policy which carries us through this period of

transition from nationalism to multilateralism. It is difficult to see a clear course between the two which does not dilute and to that extent endanger our ultimate goal, but this I believe we must accept.

My conclusion, therefore, is that the time imperative is such that we should move forward with the British and the French to develop their national capabilities, seeking a firm commitment for their ultimate support of a multilateral force (and without such a commitment from the French, I do not see how we can proceed with them). This will leave us with the problem of the Germans, principally, but of the Italians, the Belgians and others, as well. For them every effort must be made to accelerate the multilateral force. To do this, however, it may be necessary for us to consider whether certain interim arrangements short of the ideal multilateral force might not be acceptable. For example, we have heretofore insisted on mixed crews, represented by no less than three nationalities, with no one predominating. If it would facilitate the technical development of a force, as it might, I am not at all sure that we cannot live with one predominant nationality on a new crew so long as there is some other national participation and so long as the targeting and command structure is multinational. Admittedly, this would involve acceptance of a greater risk that national forces might be withdrawn but it may be an acceptable risk when weighed in the light of realistic probabilities. (Since we argue in support of the multilateral concept, that in time our Allies will come to the realization that small independent forces have no future in the nuclear world, this realization should not be inhibited if the multilateral force is made up of predominately national components. And, if this realization occurs will not the probability of withdrawal be negligible?)

Finally, I think it is vitally important that our policy not be dictated by false notions about maximizing financial efficiencies in defense matters and of radically improving the US balance of payments position through sales of equipment to our Allies, however otherwise desirable both these objectives may be. Especially on this point Mr. McNamara, I believe, tends to greatly underestimate the importance which our European Allies will attach to the economic and technological benefits of national production of nuclear systems, both weapons and propulsion, for reasons exactly like those he does recognize as relating to their force structure preference. While, of course, some sizable purchases will be made from the US, the amount of foreign exchange available to France and especially Britain is likely to be more limited than Mr. McNamara assumes. Moreover, the purchases are likely to be directed toward improving technology and developing independent productive capacity rather than toward purchasing finished US hardware.

6. Finally, while I believe that we should move forward, and in fact are moving forward, with reasonable speed, the problems which face us

are of immense complexity and importance and it would be endangering our best judgments and penalizing ourselves to push the process faster than we are capable of giving it discriminating handling. If only one single agreement were presently possible between State, Defense and the White House, I would hope it would be on this point of a consistent and measured pace, but one which presses to the point where judgments are hurried and ill-taken.

---

412. Telegram From the Embassy in the United Kingdom to the Department of State

London, January 31, 1963, 7 p.m.

2890. Brussels for Embassy and USEC. Paris for Embassy and USRO. Policy. Following Embassy assessment of post-Brussels breakdown situation in UK and suggestions for future policy lines:

1. Statements by PM and other senior Ministers make clear HMG not so far planning to move off in radical new policy direction.

2. While UK for moment buoyed up by support from "friendly Five", this feeling may be replaced when things cool down by further anxiety about British place in the world.

3. With few exceptions, government reactions to collapse of UK-EEC negotiations carefully avoid recrimination and reflect intention to maintain close but informal ties with friendly Five.

4. Unexpected setback at Brussels has left Macmillan Government without mainspring of its policy and seriously damaged its chances of improving its position with electorate in anticipation of general elections in next 12–18 months.

5. Plans announced thus far include full participation in Kennedy round and intensification of effort to strengthen domestic economy.

6. Although Common Market opponents delighted with outcome and cautioning Government about continuing to pursue "will-o-the-wisp" in Europe, there is still surprising degree of support for government's European policy. Some of this due to "closing of ranks" against French but some based on realization that going into Europe right policy for UK (at least no comparable alternative). However, this mood may be dissipated soon and, if intervening election brings labor in, attitude toward Europe likely to be modified.

Source: Department of State, Central Files, 375.800/1–3163. Confidential. Repeated to 19 other European missions.

In light above considerations, we have been thinking along following tentative lines:

1. For psychological comfort and assurance that US will not establish closer ties with Six to neglect of UK, consideration might be given to establishment of joint US-UK Ministerial meetings on trade and economic affairs along lines arrangements with Canadians and Japanese. This suggestion has obvious disadvantage of emphasizing "special relationship" but perhaps presentational benefits for UK may be overriding.

2. HMG determination to pursue expansionary policy at home plus any adverse economic impact of exclusion from EEC may result in balance-of-payments difficulties later this year. If British worried about sterling, we should give assurances of readiness to provide appropriate support.

3. We of course support vigorous implementation of TEA suggested Cedto 700 to Department.[1] As PM indicated in his television speech January 30, liberalization of world trade and payments will have central role in new UK program.

4. On assumption our historical determinism will be proved right, "friendly Five", EEC Commission and UK should be encouraged to look at all future economical and trade policy in terms of avoiding action which will make it more difficult for UK to join EEC at some more auspicious time. Also positive action to bridge gap between UK and Six should be encouraged. For example, UK might, in expectation of compensation in Kennedy round, unilaterally reduce tariff rates above CXT to level of CXT, or make unilateral across-the-board reduction. (Any such course of action would be unprecedented and obviously would require exceptionally bold POL decision). Our actions should also be tailored to same end, especially where EEC decisions likely to be against our own interests. For example, if it appeared agreement on community wheat price probable at substantially above French level, we should press for standstill at expense of immediate progress on CAP. Similarly, move toward projectionist common energy policy should be discouraged. In general, EEC progress in immediate future might be forced on areas which would not ultimately raise great difficulties or UK-harmonization of social charges, mobility of labor, etc., instead of CAP and energy policy.

5. Suggestions have been made that to take advantage of (A) mood for action to minimize blow to European unity and free world (some-

---

[1] Cedto 700, January 23, reported that the British were preparing recommendations on the course of action to be followed if the meeting with the Common Market representatives resulted in a break-off of the negotiations for British entry. (Ibid., 375.42/1–2363)

thing akin to post-EDC situation) and (B) clear division between French and rest on defense policy, UK might be encouraged if it wishes to take initiative in creating including invitation to French a political community. While covering POL and cultural matters, most important feature might be common defense policy developed in context of NATO and supporting Nassau proposals. This approach appears reverse original notion of EEC membership as means of getting UK into European political movement but there seems to be no formal reason for not starting at other end since French blocked economic approach. Since major hurdles to EEC would not be present, opposition might be somewhat reduced and negotiations could presumably be quickly concluded during present government's term of office. HMG would probably not jump immediately into arrangements with large supranational element and majority voting and thus fall short of our long-term objectives in Europe. But agreement could provide for progress in this direction later and, in any event, other avenues of advance toward European POL union apparently not open in present circumstances.

Bruce

413. Circular Telegram From the Department of State to Missions in the NATO Capitals

Washington, February 25, 1963, 5:01 p.m.

1479. In view Washington press stories reporting disagreement between US and UK in Nassau follow-up talks which ended Saturday,[1] and in view numerous separate inquiries from various NATO Embassies re outcome these talks, US and UK gave joint official-level briefing to reps all NATO Embassies except Iceland, Portugal, Belgium and Luxembourg. Following points were stressed:

1. US-UK talks were for purpose discussing respective views on para 6 forces and US-UK Polaris Sales Agreement.[2] They did not get

---

Source: Department of State, Central Files, Pol UK-US. Confidential. Drafted by Spiers and approved by Popper.

[1] Detailed memoranda of the conversations on February 18, 19, and 21, which were chaired by Tyler, are ibid.

[2] Reference is to paragraph 6 of the Nassau communiqué; a copy of the draft sales agreement is ibid., Conference Files: Lot 66 D 110, CF 2219. For text of the final Polaris Sales Agreement as signed at Washington, April 6, see 14 UST 321.

into MLF (para 7) questions, which is to be matter for US presentation in Council February 27. Matters discussed involved those of mainly bilateral concern, including what initial forces would be assigned to NNF by US and UK and various approaches to question of terms of assignment.

2. Contrary to press reports, meetings did not end in disagreement. In fact there was general identity of views although meetings were ad referendum. US and UK Governments each still considering questions involved and it premature to say what instructions will be issued to respective PermReps.

3. US-UK meetings were preliminary to discussion in NAC, since establishment of NNF not a matter for decision by two governments but for Alliance as a whole. Since US and UK were "joint authors" of Nassau, it considered desirable (as suggested by Stikker) that they should give interpretation re what they had in mind in reaching Nassau Agreement. No joint presentation as such would be made to NAC re "results" of US-UK talks since only result would be coordinated instructions to respective PermReps for Council discussion, which in effect began last week with decision re inventory tactical forces.

4. US and UK briefers refused be drawn into discussion details both because these still ad referendum and because proper locus such discussion is NAC.

Rusk

---

414. **Telegram From the Embassy in the United Kingdom to the Department of State**

London, March 27, 1963, 4 p.m.

3744. For the Secretary from Bruce. Paris for Ambassador. I have lately had frank conversations with most of the Labour Party leaders. They are a lively lot, exuding confidence, contemptuous of the present govt, convinced of their ability, if elected, to revive the British economy, and perform other near miracles.

Having long been out of office, and confined to criticism without real responsibility, it will be interesting to watch how, during the cam-

---

Source: Department of State, Central Files, Pol 12 UK. Secret; Limit Distribution. Repeated to Paris.

paign, they develop party doctrines. The thirst for power has already brought about cohesion in their ranks. Former opponents of Harold Wilson now proclaim him peerless. Gaitskell's friend, Gordon-Walker, might well be Foreign Minister in a cabinet of all factions if not of all talents. The discordance of intraparty strife has been muted to a marked degree.

Wilson will, I believe, pursue a generally pro-American line with such reservations as might seem appropriate for a defender of the Socialist faith, and of British national prestige. He is a brilliant debater, persuasive in conversation, affable, seemingly sincere though widely accused in the past of opportunistic insincerity. I think his greatest danger might be a tendency to express his views with unnecessary freedom and verbosity, without having sufficiently weighed the complexities of the problems concerned.

I shall not attempt further comment at this time on Labour personalities and policies. I commend to your attention recent reports and vignettes by Al Irving on these subjects. Sulzberger's *New York Times* column of March 25 is an accurate representation of Wilson's current attitude regarding British nuclear policy. In my opinion, this attitude makes it all the more important that as concerns the multilateral force we continue to consider it, as originally conceived, a possible response to Allied wishes, and not as a project we wish to impose on our partners.

Bruce

---

415. Telegram From the Embassy in the United Kingdom to the Department of State

London, June 15, 1963, noon.

5070. Pass to White House. Eyes only for President and Secretary of State.Whatever estimate I had formed of the political situation in Britain when I left here, six days ago, has been altered by what has occurred during my absence.

The Prime Minister is under heavy attack. On Monday next[1] he must make the most difficult speech, followed by interrogation, of his long career in the House of Commons.

Source: Department of State, Central Files, Pol 15–1 UK. Secret; Priority.
[1] June 17.

It is evident, although I must interpose the caveat that a foreigner is a mediocre judge of British behavior, that in six days the standing of the Prime Minister has undergone a marked diminution. The reasons are not difficult to define.

In the Profumo case, the continuance of that now ruined man in Cabinet office, and his solemn denial to the House of any physical intimacy with Miss Christine Keeler, has given weight to alternative charges against the Prime Minister (1) that he was in collusion with Profumo in the telling of a palpable lie, or (2) that through naivete or stupidity, as well as because of an indolent disregard, or neglect, of the warnings of British security services he took a personal assertion of innocence as an accepted fact. The counter argument of uncritical reliance on the word of a colleague and friend is of little public avail in this connection.

I think few people believe that Macmillan, whose private integrity has not been questioned, would have connived at a clumsy attempt to avoid an almost inevitable disclosure if he had known that Profumo had lied. Nor would it consort with the character of the PM to have done so.

The second charge is more serious. We shall witness the defense against it on Monday. If his dissertation is presented in lofty and persuasive terms (in itself, under the circumstances, no mean feat), in the teeth of impending defections, through some Conservative abstentions in voting, and the certain negative of the opposition party, Macmillan should win through for the evening.

But, unfortunately, for him this would not be a tale that has been definitively told. The laws of libel and slander in the United Kingdom, particularly as affecting a case sub judice, are such that the truth trickles, instead of gushing forth.

No matter what tribunal or special committee may be appointed to review the security aspects of this affair, the UK people, their appetite for sensations already whetted by partial revelations, may reach, if subjected to further shocks, a determination to force out the existing head of government. There are constitutional and traditional impediments to accomplishing this with celerity, but once confidence has been too greatly undermined in rulers, ways of dismissing them are usually devised.

In his vigil this weekend, I do not doubt that the PM, a resourceful man, will draw up a brilliant brief for delivery to the Commons. But even if he gains a personal success, his former prestige will, because of the inexorable impact of events, be beyond complete restoration. Democracies are as cruel as other systems of government in attributing blame to their political leaders. A sacrifice is increasingly demanded here, and the appointed lamb for the altar is the Prime Minister, who must already have appreciated the sad truth that no ingratitude surpassed that of a democracy.

Meanwhile, the lurid details of the involvement of degraded personalities like Dr. Ward, Miss Keeler and other nymphs, fan the popular imagination, inciting both meretricious and wholesome indignation in the public, who feel betrayed by dereliction in official circles.

It is almost impossible, at present, to judge how deeply the moral instincts of the British people are involved. If the actualities concerned private individuals, I would guess that the condemnation now so manifest would later be largely directed toward any other phenomenal scandal. The adventures, or misadventures, of the principals in a recent famous case provided strong fare to newspaper readers, but except as an example of high jinks in high places, were not considered as threatening the national welfare. The esoteric distortions of the sexual impulses of a few self-indulgent, licentious people subjected them to the denunciation of their decent fellow citizens, but had little effect on the political scene.

This present situation is different. A twenty-one year old call girl, of easy and accommodating habits, has precipitated a political crisis. In what seems to have been an eclectic, genial and not disinterested response to admiration, desire, or good fellowship, extended impartially to white, black, and red, she has been the inspirator of the possible downfall of a Prime Minister.

It is ironical and sad that la Keeler, who was led by the sleazy Dr. Ward through London streets, harnessed to a dog collar, might occasion the demise of a government. Her frank predilection for her "hairy chested Russian", her laments over her beloved Profumo, who was less fortunate than her lucky Jamaican lover, do not create the image of a sensitive individual.

No one suspects at worst the Prime Minister of other than gullibility, or stupidity. He must, however, bear the burden of leadership, and concomitant criticism and atonement.

His forensic performance next week will settle the immediate fate of himself and his government. If he succeeds, he will have bought time, but that is probably all. Behind him, hovering in the wings, is the 1922 committee. If the adverse word is spoken there, he will eventually be dethroned, dependent on their judgment as to whether he is an asset or liability to his party.

I would gamble that Macmillan, a man gifted with courage and resolution, will remain in office for the present, and, probably, for some months to come, unless to the already intolerable dereliction of one Cabinet associate, another is added.

It is impossible to foretell whether such will be the case. But the ubiquitous Keeler may supply the final element of an "upright statement's doom." It is commonly thought here that if another Cabinet member, in addition to Profumo, was the probable recipient of her favors, the government as presently constituted could not survive.

The reticences of British law are such that gossip, even when well-founded, does not spill over into public print, except when substantiated through legal processes. It is rumored that ever ready Miss Keeler, whose memoirs are being purveyed each Sunday in news of the world, did not deny her person to a second lusty minister, whom she serviced during a nocturnal automobile excursion in Richmond Park. If such be true, or if, despite denial, the public believes it, the PM could scarcely survive this unkindest cut.

Moreover, the incidents in which she and Ward were involved, are everywhere speculated about. One prominent Englishman is said to have converted a large holding into cash, prepared for a precipitate move to foreign parts. The general impression in London newspaper circles is that there is a lot of sludge under the already exposed scum.

Meanwhile, Miss Keeler is being tempted with non-amatory offers to which she gives every indication of complacently yielding. Five thousand pounds a week has been proposed for appearance in a nightclub, and she formed a company to deal with her film and other contracts. Rarely has a body promised such lucrative returns.

Until Dr. Ward, pimp, painter, bone cracker extraordinary, gives his dreaded testimony, the scenario will not be completed. When it is, it may reflect the squalid aspects of a few British public men, and not the excellent fundamental qualities of the great majority.

Bruce

416. Memorandum of Conversation

Washington, November 26, 1963.

SUBJECT

General Discussion

PARTICIPANTS

US	United Kingdom
President Johnson[1]	Sir Alec Douglas-Home, Prime
Under Secretary Ball	Minister
Assistant Secretary Tyler	Sir David Ormsby Gore,
	Ambassador

After a brief discussion of the events of the last few days, the President said that the United States and the United Kingdom had many problems which must be faced in common. He was looking forward to having the same cordial and intimate relationship with UK as President Kennedy had. The Prime Minister echoed these sentiments with great emphasis. He asked the President if he would let him know when he would have time for a more extensive meeting in order to discuss world problems together. He said he would like to be able to tell the press today that he feels sure that the United States intends to keep up the same close and friendly relationship which had existed up to now. The President agreed to his doing so.

The President said that there was a good deal of Congressional and budget business that he must attend to first, and that when this had been taken care of, he would be glad to see when it would be possible to have a meeting. The Prime Minister said that he might perhaps say to the press that a meeting would be held next year, and the President said that he could say "some time early in the New Year." The Prime Minister said that Chancellor Erhard was coming to London in the middle of January. There might be a possibility of having a meeting either before or after that date. Mr. Ball said that we would have to take a look at the calendar.

The Prime Minister asked whether the President thought that we were going to have much trouble with the French. The President gave an account of his conversation with President de Gaulle on the previous evening.[2] He said that it had been surprisingly warm, but there had not been much substance. He had found de Gaulle very affable. The Prime

---

Source: Department of State, Central Files, Pol UK-US. Secret. Drafted by Tyler and approved in the White House on December 2. A memorandum of the President's conversation with the Prime Minister on Indonesia is ibid.

[1] President Kennedy was assassinated November 22 in Dallas, Texas.

[2] See Document 276.

Minister observed that de Gaulle certainly was very friendly in manner, but that this did not necessarily reflect a change in his views or intentions. Mr. Ball said that Foreign Minister Couve de Murville had told him on the previous day that he did not expect anything of very great importance to come up in the NATO Ministerial meeting in Paris in December.[3] The Prime Minister said that he was worried about the French position on strategic problems. He thought that the French might now block outright any further progress to harmonize the views of the Alliance on strategy. The curious thing was, he said, that de Gaulle had told him only about eighteen months ago all about the concept of forward strategy, which should be supported with mobile divisions. And now, he had switched to an entirely different concept of the "absolute trip wire," under which if one single Russian crossed the frontier, we would all find ourselves in nuclear war.

The Prime Minister said he assumed that the United States Government continued to attach great importance to the German question. The President agreed and Mr. Ball added that he felt that Chancellor Erhard was creating a good impression in his first weeks of office. Foreign Minister Butler in London had told him that he had also been favorably impressed by Erhard. The Prime Minister said that he thought Erhard was much more flexible than Adenauer and that he had a certain element of laziness in his makeup, so that he was much less arbitrary.

The Prime Minister referred to the message he had received from Khrushchev on Berlin four or five days ago, in which Khrushchev suggested the possibility of an additional parallel declaration on Berlin by the Soviet Government. He said that the language which the Soviet Government had proposed was not really much good, but he thought the idea was worth looking at carefully to see if it might lead to further progress. The Prime Minister said that a copy of Khrushchev's message to him had been sent to Bonn to be given to the Germans, and that he would tell Chancellor Erhard about it at lunch today. The Prime Minister went on to say that he felt it was most important that contact between President Johnson and Chairman Khrushchev should be maintained. He said he thought it was also very important to keep in close touch with Chancellor Erhard. Ambassador Ormsby Gore also said that, in spite of the difficulties involved, it was most important to continue to work at keeping the dialogue with the Russians going.

The President said he hoped there was no feeling, or conclusion in Europe that there would be a change in the approach of the United States to international problems. He said that he had embraced President Kennedy's approach. The United States was not coveting any territory, nor seeking any aggrandizement. The United States was seeking to

---

[3] No record of the conversation has been found.

find a common ground for the peaceful solution of problems. He said we must lead from strength, but at the same time make some progress. He had been encouraged by the conclusion of the Test Ban Treaty,[4] and by the fact that it had found support both in Congress and from the American people. He had also been encouraged by the prospects of the sale of wheat, to the Soviet Union. All this showed, he said, that President Kennedy's leadership had some effect in the country at large. He did not want to reverse this trend. The major problem of our time is: Can we live together? In order to find this out, we should keep our contacts with the Soviet Union and try to meet them more than half way.

The Prime Minister said he was much gratified by the President's words. He said that the principal difficulty before us was "this wretched business of Berlin." He said this was an awful thing to have been left with. The commitment of the West to protect and defend Berlin must be firm, but he wished that the necessity for it had not arisen. The President said that perhaps there was some increased flexibility in the new German leadership which would enable us to make some progress. This had not been possible when Adenauer was Chancellor. The Prime Minister agreed, and said he thought it would be easier to discuss the German problem with Erhard.

---

[4] For text of the Nuclear Test Ban Treaty, signed August 5, 1963, at Moscow, see 14 UST 1313.

---

417. Message From President Johnson to Prime Minister Home

Washington, December 24, 1963.

DEAR MR. PRIME MINISTER: Thank you very much for your note of December 20[1] about the understandings which have existed among our predecessors on the use of nuclear weapons. In a general way the understandings seem reasonable to me, but I would like to take advantage of your suggestion that we might settle this matter definitely when we

---

Source: Johnson Library, National Security File, Aides Files, Bundy. Top Secret. Sent by private channel.

[1] Not printed; in it Home referred to President Kennedy's letter of February 6, 1961 (see footnote 2, Document 379), and asked President Johnson whether the US-UK understanding still remained in force. (Department of State, Presidential Correspondence: Lot 66 D 204)

meet. I am taking particular care with all matters affecting decisions on nuclear weapons, as I am sure you are too, and it will be a help to me not to make any mere formal decision on this point until February. Meanwhile, of course, it is clear (1) that no U.S. nuclear weapons will be used from British territory without your consent, and (2) that we should consult if possible before either of us uses them anywhere.

Sincerely,

Lyndon B. Johnson[2]

---

[2] Printed from a copy that bears this typed signature.

Canada

418. Memorandum of Conversation

Washington, February 20, 1961, 12:05 p.m.

SUBJECT

Visit of Canadian Prime Minister Diefenbaker

PARTICIPANTS

The President
The Honorable Dean Rusk, Secretary of State
The Honorable Livingston T. Merchant, Ambassador-designate to Canada

Prime Minister Diefenbaker
The Honorable A. D. P. Heeney, Ambassador of Canada
The Honorable Howard C. Green, Secretary of State for External Affairs

The meeting began about 12:05 in the President's office and ran until a few minutes after one when the participants moved to luncheon in the family dining room. During luncheon the conversation was general and lasted until about 2:45 when the Prime Minister and his party departed the White House.

After an opening exchange of greetings the Prime Minister inquired of the President concerning his view on the situation in the Congo. The President asked Mr. Rusk (who had just come from a telephone conversation with Ambassador Stevenson in New York) if he would describe the present situation. Mr. Rusk did so at some length, pointing out the extremely damaging effect on progress toward a consensus at the United Nations which had been done by the just reported murder of seven more political enemies of Kasavubu. The Secretary went on to say that there were really two situations, the one in New York at the United Nations where feelings ran high and the other on the ground in the Congo. These two were not always in focus. Indeed in New York there was an excess of nationalism and in the Congo the ab-

Source: Kennedy Library, National Security Files, Canada. Secret. Drafted by Merchant. Approved in S on March 3. In the statement to the House of Commons on February 2 Diefenbaker expressed his hope of paying an unofficial visit to Washington before the Commonwealth Prime Ministers meeting in London in March. The idea was supported by the Department of State (Merchant memorandum to Rusk, February 3; Department of State, Central Files, 033.4211/2–361), and the meeting arranged for February 20. For another account of the conversation, see John G. Diefenbaker, *One Canada, The Years of Achievement, 1957–1962,* pp. 167–169 and 177–180. For text of the communiqué issued at the end of the meeting, see *American Foreign Policy: Current Documents, 1961,* pp. 442–443.

sence of sufficient Congolese nationalism made it extremely difficult to find the foundation for a broadly based, effective government. There was considerable further discussion of the situation and the prospects, with the President and Mr. Rusk making clear what United States objectives were both with respect to the Congo and support for the United Nations and its Secretariat. Mr. Diefenbaker and Mr. Green seemed extremely interested in the discussion and in complete sympathy with United States purposes. In response to a question from the Prime Minister, the President confirmed that we would support a demand that Belgian military personnel, whom he described as freebooters and soldiers of fortune, be removed but were anxious to insure that under some arrangement covered by the United Nations the several thousand Belgian civilian technicians and advisers be retained.

The Prime Minister spoke of the coming meeting in London of the Commonwealth Prime Ministers and the problem created by the necessity of the Union of South Africa seeking readmission to the Commonwealth now that it had determined to become a republic. He said that this question of its readmission would cause great difficulty with the colored members of the Commonwealth and that it placed him in a very difficult position. He indicated his view that the Commonwealth could only prosper if its members pursued enlightened racial policies. The President acknowledged the problem posed and smilingly said that in this case it was fortunate for us that the United States was not a member of the Commonwealth.

The Prime Minister then raised the question of Laos, noting that the United States apparently preferred the establishment of a neutral nations commission rather than the recall of the ICC. The President and Mr. Rusk explained the pursuit of a U.S. policy to achieve a genuinely independent neutral Laos which would not be pro-Western to a degree to disturb its Communist neighbors. Mr. Green expressed some skepticism as to whether our proposal would be acceptable to the Soviets. Mr. Rusk replied that he felt there was at least a chance of this if we were able to convince the Communists of the absence of any desire on the part of the West to dominate Laos or build military bases there or otherwise militarily align it with the free world. Mr. Green noted that Canada had not been enthusiastic over the restoration of the ICC but was willing to do its duty. He also remarked that he understood the Indians have been considerably put out by our neutral nations commission.

The Prime Minister then raised the question of Communist China by inquiring of the President whether the United States had undergone any change of views with respect to Communist China and its recognition or admission to the United Nations.

The President replied that any feeling that it might be possible to move in a new direction with respect to Communist China had been checked by the virulence of the Chinese Communist propaganda attacks on the new Administration. He mentioned his earlier expressed belief that it was desirable to associate Peking with the nuclear test negotiations, as well as the possibility earlier considered of the opening of some trade and the reciprocal admission of journalists, as possible moves which might have reduced tension. Any such hopes, however, had been dashed by the hardening line developed by Peking against the United States in the past month.

The Prime Minister expressed himself as unable to understand the basis for this attitude by the Chinese Communists.

The President went on to cite Chou-En-lai's interview with Edgar Snow[1] as reflecting the absence of any interest on the part of Peking in a two-China solution. It was difficult to see any solution acceptable to us to which the Chinese Communists would be amenable. We will proceed next month with resumed talks in Warsaw with the Chinese Communists, but their belligerence so far would seem to indicate no desire on their part to reach an accommodation. Under the circumstances it was hard indeed to see how one could contemplate bringing them into the United Nations, and certainly the United States had no intention of abandoning Formosa.

The Prime Minister commented that he fully appreciated that, were the United States to sacrifice Formosa, the position of the free world throughout all of Asia would be destroyed. The President agreed heartily. The Prime Minister inquired whether the President saw any alternative courses of policy. The President repeated that, whereas we were anxious to ease tensions, it was difficult to see how this was possible at present.

The Secretary of State mentioned that not only in words but in actions were the Chinese Communists taking a hard line. He referred to the fact that only Snow had received a Chinese visa out of thirty correspondents who had U.S. passports validated for travel to China. He also referred to the harsh terms in which Peking repulsed the Quakers' offer of food for China.

The Prime Minister mentioned the experience of the *Globe and Mail* whose editor had traveled several years ago to China and thereafter had become an enthusiast for recognition of Peking. Parenthetically the Prime Minister said that he considered it had been a mistake by Canada not to have recognized the Chinese Communist regime ten years ago when such action would have been a simple juridical act. Today, however, it could not be done without it being construed as a formal act giv-

---

[1] For a transcript of Snow's interview with Chou En-lai, see *Look* magazine, January 31, 1961.

ing political approval to the Chinese Communist regime. He went on to say that the *Globe and Mail* had opened an office in Peking but six months later their representatives had been thrown out and the office closed down.

The Prime Minister then said that he did not intend to talk trade today but he did wish to make one point. This was that Canada's policy is to trade with all Communist countries in goods other than those which had strategic importance. In the case of Cuba, however, Canada was going further then this criterion by forbidding transshipment through Canada of goods originating in the United States. He added that Canada was not expanding trade with Cuba and cited figures of the last few years to demonstrate this. He noted that U.S. trade with Cuba, which is confined to food and medicines, even currently is running several times the volume of Canadian exports to Cuba.

The Prime Minister then noted his desire to invite the President to Ottawa to address a joint session of Parliament. He said that if the President spoke along the lines of his address in New Brunswick several years ago[2] it would do untold good. He went on to say that Canada reads quantities of news about the United States and welcomes the President every week via TV into its living rooms but that Canadian news gets less treatment in the United States than that from a "banana republic." He went on to refer to alleged anti-Americanism in Canada. He said there was no such widespread sentiment but that it was perfectly true when Canada disagreed with the United States on policy it would not follow the United States' lead. He cited the press handling of Canadian trade relations with Cuba as harmful to our relations, mentioning in this connection that Canada's situation had been different in that, unlike the United States, it had its properties and investments seized. In continuing his discussion of Canadian policy on trade with Communist countries, the Prime Minister noted the recent sale of a substantial quantity of wheat to Communist China.

On this subject the Prime Minister said that a very serious difficulty had come to his attention three days ago. Imperial Oil had been asked to supply bunker oil for Canadian ships which will carry Canadian wheat to Communist China. The Prime Minister said that Imperial Oil's parent company, Standard Oil of New Jersey, had gone to the Foreign Assets Control section of the United States Treasury Department in this connection and received a very cold reaction.

The President interrupted to say that he had had some talk about this case a day or so ago and that the initial decision had been to author-

---

[2] A copy of the address at the convocation of the University of New Brunswick on October 8, 1957, is in the Kennedy Library, Pre-Presidential Papers, Box 898.

ize Imperial Oil to sell the bunker oil only if the Canadian Government asked the United States Government to do this. The President added that he had told Secretary of the Treasury Dillon that we should do this only if the Canadian Government made the request and there was no other source of supply available to provide the oil.

The Prime Minister rejoined "this is politically an inflammatory issue." It has not yet been in the press but if it does it will create great antagonism toward the United States. It will affect the position of and attitudes toward all the United States-owned subsidiaries in Canada. He greatly hoped that the President's initial decision would be reconsidered.

The President said that this issue is sensitive also from our point of view. There is deep feeling in the United States about trading with or otherwise strengthening the Communist regime in China, particularly in light of their present truculence. He inquired if there were not other Canadian companies not United States-owned who could sell the oil.

The Prime Minister said that this problem ran deeper than this. Imperial Oil is a Canadian corporation incorporated in Canada and doing business in Canada. He recalled the unhappy incident three or four years ago when Ford of Canada was prohibited from supplying trucks to Communist China. This was finally worked out but it was important that this sort of issue not arise again. Canadians could not understand the United States Government dictating the actions of a Canadian corporation.

The President again reminded the Prime Minister of the sensitivity in the United States on Chinese Communist belligerence and threatening talk.

The Prime Minister asked how we would like it if Canada dictated the actions of an American corporation which happened to be owned by the Canadians. He went on to say that it would be impossible for him formally to ask the United States Government to allow Imperial Oil to supply the bunker oil.

Ambassador Heeney noted that the United States directors of Imperial Oil in the absence of action by the United States Government would be exposed to sanctions for selling the oil for this purpose.

The President said there was a need to take a hard look at the broad question of U.S. control of companies operating in Canada. He inquired again as to whether there was not some other company which could sell the oil. The Prime Minister said that it would be obtained elsewhere but that word inevitably would get out that Imperial Oil had been prevented from accepting a lucrative business contract by the exercise on the part of the United States Government of extra-territorial control. He said that Canada has welcomed the tremendous United States investments in Canada but this does create a source of great friction. He pointed out there is equity and not debt ownership; that the United States owns 75 per cent of Canadian oil; 56 per cent of Canadian manufacturing; and 50 per cent of Canada's mineral resources. The case in point concerns Canadian oil and a Canadian company.

The President acknowledged that all of these elements had not been brought out when he had first considered the problem and that the matter should be re-examined.

The Prime Minister noted this discussion as a tribute to the informal and friendly character of relations between our two countries. We must live together in friendship and cooperation. Neither of us can survive without the other.

The President closed the discussion on this point by saying he would check on this matter of the bunker oil during lunchtime with a view to straightening it out before the Prime Minister's departure. (Before leaving for lunch the President called in Mr. Dutton, explained the matter to him, and asked him to ascertain the position from the Treasury Department and others concerned immediately, reporting to him the result by the end of lunch.)

The Prime Minister then referred briefly to certain Canadian legislation which has its origin in Canada's currently unfavorable balance of trade. He pointed out that Canada's situation was greatly different from that of Germany, for example. He said that certain of these actions might be mistakenly construed as anti-American in that they are in a sense restrictive but that they had no such motivation. The Prime Minister went on to discuss at some length the character of Canadian trade and trade relations, mentioning the problem of its textile industry due to Japanese and Hong Kong competition. The President noted that we were similarly concerned with respect to textiles. The Prime Minister closed this aspect of the discussion by saying that within their GATT obligations Canada will be forced to take some restrictive actions in defense of its difficult economic position.

The Prime Minister then raised the question of joint defense of North America. He expressed himself as very pleased by the consideration now being given by the United States Defense Department to the sharing of production with Canada on F–104G's. He was very appreciative of this. He pointed out the imbalance between Canadian defense purchases in the United States and United States purchases in Canada. He said that the Government of Canada desires to cooperate in every way in joint defense of this continent. They are under attack from the Liberals on this issue, and he added that, if we can strengthen Canada's economy in the defense production field, it will uphold and support the Canadian Government in the pursuit of a forthright policy of joint defense. The Prime Minister referred to his speech at Port Arthur last night and his discarding of any notion that Canada should confine its contribution to joint defense merely to detecting and identifying enemy planes and operating the warning lines. This would put Canada in a subservient role and his government would not permit the acceptance of a policy of laying on the United States a task which should be done jointly.

The President expressed his appreciation for this attitude and then inquired whether Canada had recently been losing gold. There was a brief discussion of invisibles and the relative stability of Canada's reserves.

The group then moved on to lunch.

At the luncheon table the Prime Minister raised the question of a visit by the President to Canada. He said it would give all Canadians great pleasure and that he hoped the President would find it possible to come to Canada some time in June. The Prime Minister was anxious to have him address a joint session of Parliament which would be in session presumably until the end of June. The President said that he was very anxious to visit Canada and that they could work out later a mutually acceptable date. The President then agreed to the Prime Minister's query as to whether he could announce this fact to the House of Commons this evening when he makes his report on his visit to Washington. (Subsequently, it was agreed between the Prime Minister and the President, with Mr. Salinger present, that the Prime Minister would state in effect that he has issued an invitation to the President to speak before Parliament and that the President is anxious to visit Canada at a mutually convenient date to be fixed later. Mr. Salinger, if asked, would then confirm the Prime Minister's statement.)

The Prime Minister then said that he wished to inform the President of the Canadian Government's attitude with respect to nuclear weapons in Canada. The Canadian Government will not decide at the present time whether or not Canadian forces should be equipped with nuclear weapons. Efforts in the disarmament field are still in progress. If and when the Canadian Government reaches this decision, there must be provision for joint control and joint custody. The President inquired as to whether or not the arrangements we have in this regard with the British Government would satisfy the Prime Minister. The Prime Minister said that he thought something along these lines would do so. The Prime Minister indicated that the expenditure of atomic weapons in or from Canada must require a joint political decision.

The Prime Minister went on to say that with respect to the storage of nuclear weapons [less than 1 line of source text not declassified] as requested by the United States Government they must be subject to joint control. The Prime Minister then said that he was prepared to move ahead with negotiations to complete the text of the agreement or agreements which would cover all these arrangements but that these agreements would not be signed or go into effect until the Canadian Government had reached the decision to provide its own forces with a nuclear capability. The President expressed his pleasure at this willingness to move ahead in this field and inquired how the preliminary negotiations have been conducted. Ambassador Heeney pointed out that he had been negotiating on them with the United States Government and that the matter had also been substantively discussed at the Joint Cabinet Committee on Defense meeting at the Seigniory Club last summer.[3]

In concluding this discussion the Prime Minister expressed the view that all our defense arrangements, including both joint defense production sharing and nuclear storage problems, should be settled at the same time.

The Prime Minister then asked the President for his views on an early meeting of heads of government at NATO, indicating that certain major questions could only be settled at this level. The President noted that there had been some discussion of turning the spring Foreign Ministers' meeting of NATO to be held at Oslo into a heads of government meeting but that Norway had indicated it lacked the necessary facilities. The President indicated some skepticism of holding a heads of government meeting unless important decisions had already been worked out by advance negotiation. The Prime Minister expressed general agreement on this point and commented disparagingly on the limited results obtained at the heads of government meeting in Paris in December, 1957.[4] The matter was left with no specific understanding or agreement.

The President then asked Mr. Green his views with respect to disarmament noting that his interest and knowledge in this field were well known. Mr. Green recapitulated the history of disarmament negotiations in recent months and outlined Canadian views as they had been expressed from time to time. The President inquired as to what sectors of disarmament seemed to Mr. Green most promising for conclusion of an agreement. The Secretary of State for External Affairs indicated that he felt there were certain points such as limitation of conventional forces where the Russians and ourselves were quite close together. He was hopeful that a package of such nearly agreed points might be made up and negotiated, thereby providing a basis for further progress in future. There was some further general discussion of the subject with no conclusions reached. The Canadians, however, seemed to note with satisfaction the President's deep interest in the subject and the description he

---

[3] Regarding the third meeting of the Joint Cabinet Committee on Defense, July 12–13, 1960, see *Foreign Relations,* 1958–1960, vol. VII, Part 1, pp. 807–808.

[4] For documentation on the December 1957 Heads of Government meeting at Paris, see ibid., 1955–1957, vol. IV, pp. 218 ff.

gave of the steps he was taking to insure a more thorough and intensive examination of the problem and to obtain high caliber individuals to head the study and the negotiations. He said of necessity the first concentration in the past month had been on the nuclear test field and that he doubted we would have our general disarmament views correlated until some time in summer.

Mr. Rusk then inquired whether it might not be possible to make limited progress on regional arms limitation agreements. For example, he was considering the possibilities of seeking an agreement for all of Africa under which both potential suppliers of arms outside the continent and the African nations themselves would agree to strict limitations on armaments thereby insuring the devotion of their resources to economic development.

There was some general interest expressed in this.

The President then said that he was interested in the possibility of the future development in Africa of an association comparable to the OAS in Latin America. He noted the extent to which the United States had committed its prestige in the Congo by its support of the United Nations and said that the last thing he would like to see would be hatred of the United States becoming the unifying force for all of Africa. The Prime Minister remarked on the rivalries that exist between various African leaders, mentioning Nasser's and Nkrumah's personal ambitions as well as the competition for influence between Nigeria and Ghana.

The Prime Minister then noted that it had been agreed that the Joint United States-Canadian Committee on Trade and Economic Affairs would meet in Washington on March 13.[5] He noted the value the Canadians attached to these meetings. He also raised the question of a food bank for NATO which he suggested several years ago and spoke of the recent United States initiative for a Food for Peace drive. He referred to Canada's interest in the disposal of wheat abroad and expressed satisfaction with the consultation which goes on between our two governments and our attention to provision for normal commercial marketing.

The President then inquired of the Prime Minister as to his estimate of the prospects for an economic recovery in Canada. This launched a protracted discussion of the economic situation and measures for its improvement on both sides of the border. The Prime Minister referred ruefully to the divergent advice he receives from economists. He also mentioned that Canada had already placed in effect measures equivalent to six of the eight proposed by the President in his recent message

---

[5] Documentation on the sixth meeting of the Joint United States-Canadian Committee on Trade and Economic Affairs, March 13–14, is in Department of State, Conference Files: Lot 65 D 366, CF 1814. For text of the communiqué issued at the end of the meeting, see *American Foreign Policy: Current Documents, 1961*, pp. 443–446.

on this subject to Congress.[6] There was agreement between the President and the Prime Minister that high unemployment in a prosperous economy is probably the most baffling and difficult domestic problem faced by either country.

The President then inquired as to the outlook for general elections in Canada, and this led to a prolonged discussion between the President and the Prime Minister on politics in general, during the course of which the Prime Minister referred to the formation of a new party in Canada designed to combine the farmer, labor, and socialist intellectuals. He mentioned in this connection the problem created by Canadian labor unions which are controlled by headquarters in the United States and said that the pending requirement for disclosures by the Canadian unions might have a considerable political effect.

The lunch then broke up and there was a brief further discussion of the Imperial Oil problem based on a memorandum handed the President by Mr. Dutton (of which Secretary Rusk retained a copy).[7] The President told the Prime Minister that, if the Canadian Government will ask Imperial Oil to supply the bunker oil, he, the President, will make sure that no action is taken by the United States to frustrate the transaction and that the American directors in the company will be protected against sanctions. The Prime Minister indicated some doubt as to the propriety of the Canadian Government making such a request of a Canadian corporation. He said that he would wish to think this over and that, having done so, he would telephone Ambassador Heeney.

(At the airport Ambassador Heeney told Mr. Merchant that he would follow up this matter with the United States Treasury Department.)

The President then accompanied the Prime Minister to the executive offices and they made their farewells.

---

[6] For text of the special message to Congress, "A Program for Economic Recovery and Growth," February 2, 1961, see *Public Papers of the Presidents of the United States: John F. Kennedy, 1961*, pp. 41–53.

[7] Not further identified.

419. Memorandum of Conversation

Washington, March 8, 1961.

SUBJECT

Call on the President prior to departure for post

PARTICIPANTS

The President
Livingston T. Merchant, Ambassador-Designate to Canada

The President saw me this morning for about fifteen minutes to pay my farewell respects. At the outset I told him I thought Prime Minister Diefenbaker's visit had been a great success and that the Canadians were extremely happy as a result.

The President said that he liked the Prime Minister and gained the impression that on any really important issue he would be stoutly on our side. I agreed fully and commented that, despite its large majority and its three years in office, the Diefenbaker government never seemed fully to have gained self-confidence, and hence it had been exposed to attacks from the opposition on ground originally occupied by the Conservative Party.

The President inquired whether the problem of oil bunkering which the Prime Minister raised with him had been successfully solved. I told him that a formula had been worked out in the Department with the Treasury Department which should now be on Secretary Rusk's desk. I said that the formula would appear to meet the Canadian problem. The President expressed pleasure and hope that this difficulty would be promptly disposed of.

The President then inquired how we were coming on military arrangements with the Canadians and what the real basis of our difficulties were. I said that I understood talks had already been resumed with the Defense Department representatives on the problems relating to nuclear storage in Canada. This was one area of difficulty. Other related ones were the question of nuclear armaments for the RCAF and participation in NATO stockpile arrangements for the Canadian brigade in Germany. I said fundamentally the Canadians were concerned over appearing to be too closely tied, and hence subordinated to the United States in continental defense arrangements. This they felt presented to them domestic political difficulties. They would prefer if our general de-

Source: Department of State, Central Files, 611.42/3–861. Confidential. Drafted by Merchant and approved in M on March 8. Merchant presented his credentials on March 15.

fense arrangements could be under NATO rather than a bilateral umbrella.

We then briefly discussed the range of economic problems with Canada, on which the President is well informed.

Finally, the question came up as to the projected visit of the President to Canada in June to address a joint session of Parliament. He indicated clearly that he would like to restrict the period of his visit to the minimum necessary to achieve the desired effect. In answer to his questions, I told him that the customary period for an official visit would be approximately three days and three nights, entailing being guest of honor at a dinner at Government House the first evening, and returning the dinner at the Embassy the following evening. The President asked that I bear in mind his desire to keep the period short and expressed the hope that it would be acceptable to the Canadians for him to come up one afternoon, attend the Governor General's dinner, give in return an official luncheon at the Residence for the Governor General the following day, address Parliament that same afternoon, and return late that same afternoon or early evening to Washington.

I said that undoubtedly the question of timing and the character of the visit would be one of the first things the Prime Minister would raise with me and that I would be guided by the President's desires. He indicated some flexibility, and as to a date said that under his present schedule he could do it almost any time in June.

In taking my leave I mentioned to the President that Mr. Diefenbaker placed great store on a personal relationship and I hoped that the President would bear in mind that whenever an issue of importance arose where we needed Canadian support, the most effective means of gaining it would be a personal note from him to the Prime Minister. The President indicated interest and asked me to recommend to him the transmission of a personal message at any time when I thought it might be useful.

420. **Telegram From Secretary of State Rusk to the Department of State**

Geneva, May 14, 1961, 2 p.m.

Secto 113. Eyes only for the President and Acting Secretary. Ottawa for Ambassador only. Believe it would be important for President to have frank talk with Prime Minister during Canadian visit about neutralist tendencies Canadian policy especially as presented by Minister External Affairs Green. Following examples are recent items:

1. At NATO meeting Green indicated Canada felt itself positioned between two nuclear giants and felt special interest in reducing tensions between. He thus seemed to join the long parade of those who have wished to provide a bridge, meaning continuous concessions on our part to an insatiable power determined to pursue its world revolution by every available means.

2. Recent *Washington Post* story came from conversations Green had on airplane with reporters during flight Oslo to Geneva.[1] I had explained to him Cuban rebuff of all earlier efforts to find negotiated settlement, that offer of mediation distorted problem into bilateral US-Cuban affair and that we were consulting members OAS about next steps and would be in touch with Canada. When I discussed *Washington Post* story with him in Geneva, he replied lamely that what he intended was to say that if he were asked to mediate he would be glad to do so.

3. US, UK and France were startled to have Green decline to join us here in Geneva in consultation about conference problems on ground that he did not think it appropriate to attend "Western caucus" since Canada is a member of the ICC. Last evening I challenged him on this concept, had him confirm that Poles are hand in glove with Communists and asked him whether that meant the ICC now contained one Communist and two neutrals. His reply attached far more importance to good relations with India than with Western world on such issues. For example, when Indian Chairman ICC Hanoi refused to go into question Soviet airlift going through Hanoi, Green thought Indian point was sound, that ICC Hanoi could not know where such flights were going in the absence of an ICC Laos. Further, Canadian members of ICC have given us minimum information about such matters.

Source: Department of State, Central Files, 751J.00/5–1461. Secret. Repeated to Ottawa. According to another copy, this telegram was drafted by Rusk who was in Geneva to attend the conference on Laos. (Ibid., Rusk Files: Lot 72 D 193, Chron)

[1] *Washington Post*, May 12, 1961.

4. Green's attitude this conference one of relative indifference to far-reaching stakes which free world has in Laotian situation and in general is more like that of neutrals than Western countries.

I would not suggest that President personify discussion by involving Green by name but rather press Prime Minister on general attitude Canada on questions directly affecting free world. Green is obviously bemused by great peace-making role which Canada (obviously usefully) plays in such situations as Suez, Congo and other affairs on which they have been asked to participate. Be it said, Green's point of view seems to be supported by considerable amount of Canadian public opinion. Suggest Merchant brief President this situation prior conversation Prime Minister.

Rusk

421. Memorandum of Conversation

US/MC/1   Ottawa, May 17, 1961, 10 a.m.

SUBJECT

    Conversation between President Kennedy and Prime Minister
    Diefenbaker—Cuba and Latin America

PARTICIPANTS

    The President of the United States
    John Diefenbaker, Prime Minister of Canada
    Livingston T. Merchant, U.S. Ambassador to Canada
    Arnold E.P. Heeney, Canadian Ambassador to the U.S.
    Robert B. Bryce, Clerk to the Privy Council and Secretary to the Cabinet

Source: Department of State, Conference Files: Lot 65 D 366, CF 1884. Top Secret; Eyes Only. Drafted by White and approved by the White House on May 23. The meeting was held in the Prime Minister's office. See also Documents 422–425. Memoranda of conversation on Southeast Asia, China, the Common Market, civil defense, the Congo, Nasser, West New Guinea, space, the President's meeting with Khrushchev, disarmament, and recruitment for a Cuban expeditionary force are in Department of State, Conference Files: Lot 65 D 366, CF 1884. During his visit, May 16–18, the President addressed Parliament and together with the Prime Minister issued a joint communiqué. For text of the address to Parliament, see Department of State *Bulletin*, June 5, 1961, pp. 839–843; for text of the communiqué, see ibid., p. 843. For Diefenbaker's account of the visit, see *One Canada, The Years of Achievement, 1957–1962*, pp. 169–171 and 182–184.

Henry Basil Robinson, Special Assistant to the Prime Minister
Walt W. Rostow, Deputy Special Assistant to the President
Ivan B. White, Deputy Assistance Secretary for European Affairs

After an exchange of pleasantries, the Prime Minister said that unless the President desired to take up immediate specific problems, he thought it would be valuable if Mr. Kennedy could give him a review of world conditions as he saw them.

The President replied that Cuba and the Western Hemisphere constituted one of the foremost problems. The recent Cuban episode raised the question whether it is possible to conduct covert operations in an open society. The United States had placed limitations on the use of its own planes and this had impeded operations. The dilemma posed had been whether the 1300 well-trained Cubans in Guatemala, who had been there some time, would either have to be broken up as a group or permitted to return to the homeland. The operation had begun well but the air control by Cuban planes had been disastrous and the invasion group had run out of ammunition.

As far as the future of Cuba was concerned, the United States had been trying to persuade as many countries as possible to face up to the true character of the regime and to take collective action, but a number of them were reluctant to do so. Mexico, as an example, is almost neutral and when the Prime Minister inquired as to how Mr. Kennedy explained the situation in Mexico, the President replied that it was due to the influence of President Cardenas and the leftward pull exercised by his faction in the National Revolutionary Party. Likewise, Brazil was a problem. President Quadros feels that he cannot afford politically to be anti-Castro in foreign policy at the same time he is pursuing a deflationary policy at home. The President added that he was perturbed about the situation in Latin America and hoped that Canada would consider greater participation in Inter-American affairs and organizations.

The Prime Minister referred to press reports of an alleged statement by External Affairs Minister Green that Canada was willing to mediate between Cuba and the United States. He said that this statement was not made and he, the Prime Minister, wanted nothing to do with mediation. The President replied that the United States did not want it; that the problem was one of for the entire hemisphere. Mr. Diefenbaker commented that he thought the Canadians were farther away today from membership in the Organization of American States than they had been previously. The Prime Minister added that he believed Canada could exercise more influence outside than in the organization. If in, Canada would be in the position of either disagreeing with the United States or being called a puppet of the United States. The President commented smilingly that he assumed in most cases of disagreement Canada would be right. The President added while the OAS had not lived up to expectations he thought it important that it be rebuilt into a more effective organization. The Cuban regime had predicted that within six months five countries in Latin America would adopt Castroism. The situation in Venezuela was shaky and Bolivia was on the razor's edge. When the Prime Minister inquired as to whether there was any indication that Cuba was receiving nuclear arms from the Soviet Union, the President replied that there was no evidence of this except that they had planes which would carry nuclear weapons. The President added that the United States did not plan intervention in Cuba unless there was a flow of interventionist activities from Cuba to other countries in the hemisphere. One other possibility of military intervention in Cuba existed in its use as a countermeasure to measures which the Soviet Union might adopt in the case of Berlin. The President would want to talk with the Prime Minister about any plans for military intervention before such actually took place.

422. Memorandum of Conversation

US/MC/2   Ottawa, May 17, 1961, 10 a.m.

SUBJECT

Canada, the OAS and IA-ECOSOC

PARTICIPANTS

[Here follows the same list as in Document 421.]

After the discussion on Cuba, the President again took up the question of Canada's participation in Inter-American organizations and requested the Prime Minister to consider this matter carefully. Latin America was vulnerable and very weak socially. When the Prime Minister reverted to the earlier discussion regarding Mexico, the President recalled that Jose Figueres, former President of Costa Rica, had told him that when he had sent five students to Mexico, four of them had become Communists. The Prime Minister then outlined Canada's trade policy towards Cuba, remarking that Canada's current Cuban trade volume

Source: Department of State, Conference Files: Lot 65 D 366, CF 1884. Confidential. Drafted by White and approved by the White House on May 23. See Documents 421 and 423–425.

was smaller than that of the United States. Generally there was no objection by Canada to dealing in non-strategic goods with Communist countries.

The trade with Cuba was entirely in normal goods and precautions had been taken by the Canadian Government that there would be no bootlegging of shipments originating in the United States. The President commented that the only important import into the United States from Cuba currently was in tobacco needed by the Tampa cigar trade and that our exports were at an annual rate of only $9 million, virtually all in food and medicines. Consideration had been given to a trade embargo which would require the imposition of Foreign Assets Control regulations. He, the President, did not want to take this step and would not do so until Cubans had taken some new provocative measures. The Prime Minister at this point expressed his appreciation for the way in which the United States had handled the problem of oil bunkering in the case of ships carrying grain to Soviet China. The Canadian public did not know that this had been discussed with the United States and it was most important to keep it confidential.

The President reiterated his request that Canada reconsider membership in the Organization of American States and expressed the hope that Canada would find it possible to send an observer to the Inter-American Economic and Social Council meeting which was being convened in Montevideo in July. This conference would attempt to make plans for operation Pan America and for the Alliance for Progress and would consider common markets, commodity problems and economic planning. When the Prime Minister inquired as to what the President had in mind on the economic side, Mr. Kennedy replied that $500 million was now being appropriated for the Social and Economic Development Program in Latin America; furthermore the Administration would soon submit a $4 billion request for foreign aid funds needed globally. Generally it was anticipated that a strenuous fight would be required to obtain adequate appropriations for this purpose. The public generally was unenthusiastic about appropriations of this type, but it was most important that they be obtained.

423. Memorandum of Conversation

US/MC/3   Ottawa, May 17, 1961, 10 a.m.

SUBJECT

    NATO and Nuclear Weapons

PARTICIPANTS

    [Here follows the same list as in Document 421.]

The Prime Minister said that he was greatly worried abut the future of NATO. When fear recedes, the cement which holds the alliance together loosens. The Prime Minister referred to the possibility of a heads of government meeting and inquired of the President as to his views of the NATO situation. He, the Prime Minister, had become convinced that NATO could not survive without fundamental changes in economic relationships.

The President said that there should be an increase in conventional forces although he was uncertain as to the degree. The United States was resolved to keep its divisions in Europe and was considering sending a STRAAC division to Europe at some future time. With reference to nuclear weapons, the French were interested in obtaining assistance in developing an independent capability and he, the President, had discussed this with Prime Minister Macmillan. It was the United States opinion that we should not help the French in this matter. The Prime Minister commented that the Canadian position has been there should be no expansion in the number of countries producing nuclear weapons. In Canada there had been an upsurge of feeling against nuclear weapons generally; this movement was not limited to Communists and Leftwingers, but also included professors and many others. His mail was running very heavy in letters against nuclear weapons, including a very high percentage from mothers and wives.

The Prime Minister then turned to the specific question of storage of nuclear weapons on Canadian soil. He said that at some time in the future this might be possible under some form of joint control. It was, however, politically impossible today. It just could not be done at this time. In fact, he doubted whether he could carry his own Cabinet with him on this issue. Mr. Diefenbaker said, however, that he was going to make an effort to change public opinion on this question this summer and fall. He attributed the attitude of the Canadian public in part to the

Source: Department of State, Conference Files: Lot 65 D 366, CF 1884. Secret. Drafted by White and approved by the White House on May 23. See also Documents 421, 422, 424, and 425.

sacrifices which had been made in two World Wars and remarked that it appeared that even the United States had a problem, citing the recent petition of a group of Harvard professors who had taken a position against nuclear armament. The President in reply discounted the importance of this particular group, pointing out that they were the same individuals who had regarded the Chinese Communists as "agrarian reformers." The President said that American public opinion generally was more militant than the policies being followed by the United States Government. With this the Prime Minister agreed.

After a brief reference to the situation in Iran concerning which the President said that he regarded the new Prime Minister as representing the last chance to stabilize the situation in that country, the conversation turned again to the world situation. The President said that he was sending a message to Congress next week requesting additional funds for space developments, conventional forces and civil defense.[1] When the Prime Minister commented that a recent civil defense exercise in Canada had indicated a need for strengthening in this field, Mr. Bryce said that the exercise had revealed several weaknesses; namely, the operations were very slow, communications were poor, and the public did not feel vitally concerned. The President commented that in the United States civil defense was likewise in a weak posture.

When the Prime Minister inquired as to the attitude of France towards NATO, the President replied that the most difficult problem for the United States had been the continuation of testing by the French but this was now out of the way. De Gaulle's refusal to support integration of NATO forces in Europe was not good but it was something the United States could live with.

---

[1] For text of this special message, see *Public Papers of the Presidents of the United States: John F. Kennedy, 1961*, pp. 396–406.

424. Memorandum of Conversation

US/MC/4   Ottawa, May 17, 1961, 10 a.m.

SUBJECT

NATO and Berlin

PARTICIPANTS

[Here follows the same list as in Document 421.]

The President stated he had offered five Polaris submarines to NATO. Norstad wanted roaming Minutemen, which we did not regard as a satisfactory solution. We are prepared to add to the five Polaris submarines in time. We would expect the NATO nations to work out control principles and procedures, which we would accept. We wish to reassure NATO nations that nuclear weapons would be used either in case of nuclear attack on NATO or if NATO forces were being overwhelmed. The question of a command procedure is difficult; but we hope the whole exercise will persuade Western Europe that we are committed to defend that area with nuclear force.

The Prime Minister asked about Berlin.

The President said that Mr. Acheson is working over the contingency plans for Berlin. In Laos we learned that military plans had been drafted without taking into account whether they are politically viable in the international community. In the discussions with Khrushchev he hoped to make the American position clear on Berlin. A Soviet treaty with East Germany itself would not be a cause for alarm; but it is possible East Germany might harass traffic to Berlin. Our response would be a military probe which would give us time to decide what then to do.

The Prime Minister stated that he would like to be informed of the Berlin contingency plan, in which Canada has a direct interest.

The President said the contingency plan is now being reviewed by Mr. Acheson; the question was whether a political basis for the military plan could be negotiated. Also, the question of whether the probe in the existing plan is too small. Perhaps a divisional probe would be better. The British position on Berlin was somewhat ambiguous; the French, more precise. The President stated he would undertake to keep the Canadians informed as contingency planning developed. In a general sense, the tide is not now running in our direction in some parts of the world; and we simply could not accept a setback on Berlin.

Source: Department of State, Conference Files: Lot 65 D 366, CF 1884. Secret; Limit Distribution. Drafted by White and approved by the White House on May 23. See also Documents 421–423 and 425.

The Prime Minister wholeheartedly concurred. He stated if we accept a setback on Berlin, then neutralist sentiment throughout the world would grow and NATO would be proved a weak reed. The President asked Ambassador Merchant for his views on the probe.

Ambassador Merchant said deGaulle's commitment was precise: force in Europe must be met with force. But deGaulle's divisions were mainly in Algeria. Military planning thus far had been hypothetical. There had been no political decisions made in advance. We must go into this matter more deeply with the British. There must be greater precision about what will be done under particular circumstances. We could live with the East Germans stamping the transit documents to Berlin. What we have most to fear are salami tactics leading to strangulation of Berlin. A total reexamination of the military and political planning on Berlin would be helpful. The President stated that our reaction to pressure on Berlin might be indirect. It might take the form of action versus Cuba, or possibly of supplying Berlin by air.

---

425. Memorandum of Conversation

US/MC/5   Ottawa, May 17, 1961, 10 a.m.

SUBJECT

   Triangular Aircraft Arrangement

PARTICIPANTS

   [Here follows the same list as in Document 421.]

Following a brief discussion of the question of nuclear weapons for Canadian forces, the Prime Minister raised the matter of the triangular aircraft arrangement which Ambassador Merchant had discussed with him on May 11.[1] [17 lines of source text not declassified]

At the President's request, Ambassador Merchant reviewed the essential elements in the triangular proposal. He pointed out that in order

---

Source: Department of State, Conference Files: Lot 65 D 366, CF 1884. Secret; Limit Distribution. Drafted by White and approved by the White House on May 23. See also Documents 421–424.

[1] No other record of this meeting has been found.

to be in a position to defend offshore procurement in Canada of $200 million worth of F104G's in the face of a depressed aircraft industry in the United States and a balance of payments problem, it was essential to be able to demonstrate that the air defenses of both our countries were being improved by the transfer of the F101B's to the RCAF, where they would be deployed northward on Canadian bases. The Ambassador said that the United States' considered military judgment was that to make the transfer of these fighters currently in the USAF inventory and currently equipped with nuclear-tipped rockets would result in a degradation rather than an improvement of our air defense if they were armed with conventional rockets.

[*1 paragraph (2-1/2 lines of source text) not declassified*]

[*9 lines of source text not declassified*] The Prime Minister said that there was very widespread public opinion against all nuclear weapons. He referred to his mail, which was heavy on this point, and to various organizations, including a women's committee which was strongly agitating on the point. [*4 lines of source text not declassified*]

[*4 lines of source text not declassified*] The Prime Minister said that he intended to speak across Canada this summer and fall on this issue and thought he could gain public support for the acceptance of nuclear weapons on Canadian soil as part of Canada's defenses.

The Prime Minister went on to say that he hoped that the aircraft arrangements could proceed without awaiting a governmental decision on the matter of nuclear weapons for Canada.

The President again expressed perplexity at the fact that the difficulties were so great for Canada in taking this step.

The matter was left that the President would consider the points raised by the Prime Minister.

426. Telegram From the Department of State to the Embassy in Canada

Washington, August 3, 1961, 6:01 p.m.

98. Eyes only for Ambassador. Please deliver following Presidential message to Prime Minister Diefenbaker of Canada. Advise date time delivery. Signed original being pouched.

"August 3, 1961

Dear Mr. Prime Minister:

I need not tell you how preoccupied I am with the Soviet challenge to our position in West Berlin.

I believe that the posture of our military forces is an essential element in preventing any miscalculation on Khrushchev's part of our will. The members of NATO must convincingly demonstrate their seriousness by improving substantially the collective strength of the alliance.

The defense of this continent and the protection of our strategic forces are vital elements in the defensive power of the alliance. The intimacy of our mutual air defense arrangements in North America testifies to the understanding of this fact on both sides of our border.

There is, however, an aspect of our continental defense which, for reasons which we both understand, is imperfect. This is the lack of orderly arrangements for insuring that the RCAF as well as the USAF should be possessed of nuclear weapons to respond to any attack across the Pole.

I recall during our talk in Washington last February your statement to me that you were prepared to proceed with the negotiation of necessary agreements looking toward the presence on Canadian soil of nuclear weapons at such time as the Canadian Government should reach a decision in this regard. Then in May in Ottawa when we were discussing the aircraft agreement you explained to me how matters then stood and of your thoughts and plans in this regard.

It seems to me that it would now only be prudent to renew with vigor our efforts to conclude negotiations on the language of the necessary agreements so that they may be complete and ready to hand if your Cabinet later makes the authorizing decision. Unless we do so we will have failed to take a necessary preliminary and possibly time-consuming step. By taking this step now we would in effect advance toward the strengthening of our common air defense.

Source: Department of State, Central Files, 700.5611/8–361. Secret; Priority; Verbatim Text. On July 30, Rusk had sent a memorandum to the President stating that Merchant recommended the reopening of negotiations with Canada on the language of an agreement to put nuclear weapons on Canadian soil. Attached to the memorandum was the draft of a slightly longer message to the Prime Minister. (Ibid., 700.5611/7–3061)

I recognize that this is not an easy matter for you, but I do believe that we cannot achieve a successful negotiating position on Germany and Berlin until we have taken every reasonable step to strengthen our military security. We can talk when it is clear that we are attending to our arms.

I look forward to hearing your thoughts on this problem, and I hope we will be able to make progress on it together.[1]

With best personal wishes,

Sincerely,

John F. Kennedy"

Rusk

---

[1] On August 11 Diefenbaker replied, stating that he would take the necessary steps within the Canadian Government to initiate the discussions. (Message transmitted in telegram 138 from Ottawa, August 15; ibid., 700.5611/8–1561)

---

427. Telegram From the Embassy in Canada to the Department of State

Ottawa, November 27, 1961, 2 p.m.

519. Please inform the President that during the course of long rambling talk with Prime Minister Diefenbaker November 27, I raised the subject of arrangements for storage of nuclear weapons in Canada. I told him of the interest the President expressed to me regarding this paralyzed problem on November 10.[1] The Prime Minister told me in strict confidence that this matter would again be discussed by cabinet during coming week, and that he hoped to have an answer for the President in 10 days or 2 weeks. He intimated, but did not explicitly state that the response would be affirmative in the sense of at least enabling a renewal of negotiations on the text of an agreement. Diefenbaker said that the

---

Source: Department of State, Central Files, 711.5611/11–2761. Secret; Limited Distribution.

[1] A memorandum of Merchant's conversation with the President on November 10 is in the Kennedy Library, National Security Files, Canada.

cabinet had been on verge of decision on the matter last September, but that press stories emanating from the White House sources to the effect that the President had sent a personal message on this subject to the Prime Minister had made it impossible for the Canadian cabinet to appear to be acting under pressure from Washington.

The continuing conflict within the cabinet between Green and Harkness on the issue of nuclear weapons on Canadian soil coupled with the Prime Minister's sensitivity to what he considers public opinion in Canada, make it improbable, in my opinion, that the cabinet will be prepared to go further at this time than the resumption of negotiations on an agreement, which if successfully concluded would be initialed but not brought into force immediately thereafter.

The Prime Minister referred glancingly to the troublesome spate of resolutions on nuclear arms in the UNGA. I told him we were reassured by Canada's switch of position to vote negatively in the GA last week on the Ethiopian resolution.

Merchant

---

428. Telegram From the Department of State to Embassy in Germany

Washington, January 15, 1962, 10:02 p.m.

1933. Brussels and Luxembourg pass USEC, Paris pass USRO. As January 12 and 13 meeting Joint US-Canada Cabinet Committee[1] largely concerned Common Market implications may be some speculation on what decisions if any reached. May be some effort to see in Communiqué and news stories change basic U.S. policies.

Purpose regular annual meeting was to exchange views on two important interrelated subjects: (1) prospective U.K. adherence Common Market and (2) new U.S. trade program. In view sensitivity of Canadians and their current sense of frustration we felt U.S.-Canadian relations required ministerial confrontation.

Source: Department of State, Central Files, 611.42/1–1562. Confidential. Drafted and approved by Schaetzel and cleared with Burdett, E, and the Department of the Treasury. Also sent to Brussels, London, Luxembourg, and Paris, and repeated to Ottawa, Bern, Canberra, The Hague, Rome, Stockholm, Vienna, and Wellington.

[1] The U.S. record of this meeting and briefing papers for it are ibid., Conference Files: Lot 65 D 533, CF 2028. For text of the communiqué issued at the end of the meeting, see *American Foreign Policy: Current Documents, 1962*, pp. 531–532.

Meeting itself held in friendly atmosphere. Canadian Ministers obviously preoccupied in jockeying for domestic political position in anticipation early Canadian elections. General Canadian position still basically reserved to hostile about U.K. adherence Common Market although position more moderate than previously; suspicions about European integration in general mixed with worry about possible adverse impact Canadian exports; emphasis on value Commonwealth system and essentiality preferences to its preservation. While Canadians expressed keen interest in outline of President's trade program, unprepared state public support of it arguing to so so would amount interference U.S. governmental processes.

As Communiqué's principal impact in Canada, U.S. Delegation did not press for statement which fully expressed U.S. views. Nor did U.S. Delegation want to highlight our differences with them in Communiqué. We did not insist, for instance, on reiterating in Communiqué U.S. support European integration movement and virtues we see U.K. adherence. Nor did we insist on restatement long-term U.S. opposition to preferences and particularly to extension Commonwealth preferences into Common Market. Canadians nonetheless made clearly aware during meetings U.S. views. Canadians, however, did press their hope U.S. would refrain from public utterances against preferences while U.K. negotiated with Six as a means of improving U.K. negotiating position. U.S. said could give no commitment to Canadians on this point.

Should questions be raised about whether U.S. positions have shifted, particularly on basic value to free world of Common Market or more tolerant U.S. view re preferences, missions may draw on foregoing while adhering to established policy lines.

Rusk

429. **Telegram From the Embassy in Canada to the Department of State**

Ottawa, February 26, 1962, 11 a.m.

807. Eyes only Secretary from Merchant. As you know greatest single outstanding problem between US and Canada is Canadian failure

Source: Department of State, Central Files, 700.5611/2–2662. Secret.

face up to question nuclear warheads. Problem falls in three general categories: 1) Canadian acquisition warheads for Canadian NATO troops in Europe (Honest John rocket for ground troops; air to ground rockets for Canadian air division which converting to NATO strike role); 2) Warheads for Bomarc ground to air missile and tips for air to air missiles for RCAF 101B squadrons in Canada under NORAD command; 3) Storage on Canadian soil of warheads for USAF and USN use.

Diefenbaker Government continues procrastinate with strong elements in Cabinet, particularly Foreign Minister Green, opposed to dirtying Canadian hands and reputation with nuclear weapons under any circumstances.

President discussed matter privately with Diefenbaker during visit here May 1961. President's letter to Diefenbaker August 3 (Deptel 98)[1] discussed matter in some detail and argued we should proceed with negotiation bilateral control agreements in order be ready move promptly when GOC takes basic decisions. Prime Minister agreed in his reply of August 11 (Embtel 138).[2]

As reported Embtel 386 October 7[3] apparent progress this problem received setback from leak to press confirming existence of correspondence between President and Prime Minister. On November 27 however (Embtel 519)[4] once again looked as though Prime Minister on point authorizing resumption negotiations.

Since then question has been stalled on dead center despite fact Canadian Armed Forces have now taken delivery substantial quantities expensive military hardware which next to useless without nuclear tips.

I do not share apparent Canadian Government assessment that acquisition nuclear weapons constitutes issue on which it would encounter overwhelming opposition. It is nevertheless a fact that Diefenbaker Government virtually paralyzed on this question and appears determined not face issue until after next general elections, which still unscheduled. (Whether it or some other government would then squarely and willingly face issue is also open to question.)

Under these circumstances I believe we should not let matter lie comfortably at rest and I therefore propose that you recommend to the President he send private personal communication to Diefenbaker along following lines.

Verbatim text.

"Dear Mr. Prime Minister:

---

[1] Document 426.
[2] See footnote 1, Document 426.
[3] Not printed. (Department of State, Central Files, 320/10–761)
[4] Document 427.

You will recall that in our exchange of letters of last August regarding our joint commitment for the defense of the North American Continent we discussed the need for proceeding as rapidly as possible with certain pending negotiations. You indicated at that time that you would be sending me a further message about the matter.

I have been conscious that you have faced difficult problems and that a premature remark to the press here in Washington must have added a complicating factor for you at the time, which I regret. I would not, however, want you to think that my silence since then means I am any less interested in the problem nor any less persuaded of the urgency and importance of our going ahead as planned. I was encouraged by your conversation with Ambassador Merchant in late November, when you thought you might have further word before long.

I would hope that we might proceed promptly along the lines we discussed last May, and I should be grateful to have your views.

With best personal wishes,

Sincerely,"

End verbatim text.

Merchant

---

430. Telegram From the Embassy in Canada to the Department of State

Ottawa, February 27, 1962, 1 p.m.

823. Embassy telegram 814.[1] Prime Minister Diefenbaker's remarks on nuclear weapons reported reference telegram are nothing short of dismaying since they represent irresponsible treatment of subject of vital importance to both Canada and US. They probably stem from com-

---

Source: Department of State, Central Files, 742.5611/2–2762. Confidential; Priority.

[1] Telegram 814, February 27, reported an exchange in the House of Commons among Pearson, Diefenbaker, and Martin on Canadian policy on nuclear weapons. For the full text, see *House of Commons Debates, Official Report, 1962,* vol. II, pp. 1250–1251. For Rusk's reaction to this exchange, see Department of State *Bulletin,* March 19, 1962, pp. 457–458. In telegram 819, February 27, Merchant suggested that in view of this exchange, any action on the proposed letter to Diefenbaker (see Document 429) should be suspended. (Department of State, Central Files, 700.5611/2–2762)

pound of ignorance of complex subject, profound reluctance face up to disagreeable subject, unfortunate propensity point to US as immovable stumbling block, and heat of moment in lively parliamentary exchange with Pearson for whom he feels positive personal dislike.

Inconsistencies in Diefenbaker position which so obvious to US are unfortunately somewhat less so to most Canadian observers. Nevertheless prospect is that liberal opposition, despite its own less than forthright stand on nuclear weapons, will not let matter lie and will seek daily to probe this soft spot in Government's defense policy.

Press reaction limited thus far. (Embassy replying with "no comment" to press inquiries. Would appreciate Department's guidance.)

Whatever else may eventually result fact is that at moment Diefenbaker is farther than ever from position we would like see his government take on nuclear weapons.

Merchant

---

431. Telegram From the Embassy in Canada to the Department of State

Ottawa, March 8, 1962, 5 p.m.

873. In accordance with Prime Minister's March 5 request[1] I call on him in few days to discuss information in Paul Martin's hands I saw Diefenbaker at length this morning. Contrary to his state in our original telephone call he was relaxed completely. I told him Washington was as shocked as he and I at alleged revelation content confidential talk between the President and himself and said that investigation was underway, with view to corrective action, to indentify US officer alleged to have talked in Detroit. I said that fracture security and indiscipline

---

Source: Department of State, Central Files, 742.5611/3–862. Secret; Limit Distribution; Priority.

[1] In telegram 855, March 5, Merchant reported that Diefenbaker had called him on March 5 to say that Martin intended to question him about a Canadian undertaking made during President Kennedy's visit in May 1961 to receive nuclear arms. The Prime Minister added that he wanted to talk to Merchant about this in the next day or so. (Ibid., 742.5611/3–562)

could not be condoned but reminded him of circumstances in which he had informed the President of his intention re nuclear arms. I recalled that agreement by Canada to their acceptance had been element in original package proposed last spring which included placement by US of $150 million aircraft purchase in Canada. On basis his statement that this at the moment politically impossible, President in May had eliminated it as component of package. But I said it was obvious that in order to obtain necessary funds for so domestically unpopular a contract limited number congressional and military leaders had to be informed in strict confidence of Prime Minister's personal attitude and plans. Diefenbaker said he understood this entirely and that only subject his complaint was violation by others of such confidence. He repeatedly expressed admiration for the President and he is fully recovered from original agitation.

Question along lines foreshadowed has not yet been asked in House by Martin or their opposition leaders. Prime Minister rather expects it is being held for general debate on defense estimates now scheduled for next week. This is likely to be occasion for full-scale discussion entire nuclear questions. Answer he plans to give in House if asked by Martin to confirm information allegedly given by US officer in Detroit and US legislator in Bermuda is along lines "diplomatic usage unfortunately prevents him from commenting on any private conversations but failure to do should not be interpreted one way or the other."

Incidentally, March 5 memo of record[2] re Martin's intention to ask question refers to "high ranking US General" and not "high ranking US Army officer" as he had first told me on phone. Prime Minister also made clear that pipeline which periodically leaks to Martin according to his suspicions runs from Canadian civil servants and not any US source.

Our discussion then turned to other matters being reported separately.[3]

Merchant

---

[2] Not found.

[3] Telegram 871, March 8, reported briefly on negotiations for nuclear agreements, stating that Diefenbaker expected to begin them once the debate on defense estimates in the House of Commons was completed. (Department of State, Central Files, 742.5611/3–862)

432. Memorandum of Conversation

Washington, April 17, 1962, 11 a.m.

SUBJECT

Canadian Ambassador's Farewell Call

PARTICIPANTS

The President
Ambassador Heeney, Canadian Ambassador
Mr. William R. Tyler, Acting Assistant Secretary

The Ambassador expressed his regret at leaving Washington, and commended his successor, Mr. Charles Ritchie, to the President.[1]

The President said he was sorry the Ambassador was leaving, and asked when elections were going to be held. The Ambassador said he thought the announcement of elections in June would be made within a day or two. He said things were "getting pretty rough" in Canada with sharp exchanges between Pearson and Diefenbaker. According to the polls, Diefenbaker was strong in the prairie provinces (because of the wheat sales to Communist China) and in the maritime provinces. Quebec was running strongly Liberal, and Ontario was evenly balanced. Polls indicated there were 29% undecided votes. The President observed that in reality, the percentage of those who did not decide which way they would vote until the last minute did not exceed 3% or 4%, but a much larger number than this didn't commit themselves openly.

The President inquired what Canada thought she was getting in return for the wheat sales. Ambassador Heeney said that these were made on a hard cash basis, and that they tended to create some degree of dependence of Communist China on the West. The President commented that, while these wheat sales might be of help to the Chinese regime in the midst of its difficulties, he didn't think that the West derived any benefits from them.

The President said he noted with appreciation the remarks of Prime Minister Diefenbaker on nuclear testing a few days ago. Ambassador Heeney said that the Prime Minister had made further remarks along the same lines yesterday.

The President said that Khrushchev's message of April 10 to Prime Minister Macmillan had been pretty harsh, and had not provided many

---

Source: Kennedy Library, National Security Files, Canada. Secret; Limit Distribution. Drafted and initialed by Tyler.

[1] For Ritchie's account of his presentation of credentials on May 6, see *Storm Signals*, p. 6.

grounds for encouragement on the nuclear test issue. Ambassador Heeney agreed, and asked the President whether he thought that the Soviets really want to conduct further tests themselves. The President said he thought this might be the case, and that we would have to see after the next round of tests whether there was a chance of making a successful approach with the aim of achieving an effective and mutually acceptable nuclear atmospheric test ban.

The President said he hoped that after the Canadian elections, another visit might be arranged, and that there would be some forward movement, for example, in the nuclear field, which was of great importance to the defense of Canada as well as the United States.

The President said he hoped that there might be some increase in Canada's aid effort, which seemed low in terms of Canada's resources. Ambassador Heeney said that the figures on which we had based our estimate of Canada's contribution were "phony" in the sense that they went back much too far, and thus unduly minimized their share of the aid effort. He said that the figure of 1/5 of 1%, which had been used last year, was inaccurate and much too low. He added that he had other figures which he would be glad to make available to the President, which presented the real state of affairs. (It was agreed that Ambassador Heeney would send these figures to Mr. Tyler, who would send them on to the President through Mr. Bundy.)

The President said he would like to take up the problem of British Guiana with the Canadian Government on the next go around. He said he wished that Canada could have seen its way to join the OAS, as this would have been very helpful to our efforts. Ambassador Heeney said he thought Canadian public opinion would have welcomed this, but the people who were thinking of their elections had not been of this opinion.

In conclusion, there was some reference to the Nobel prize winners' dinner with the President on April 29, with the presence of Lester Pearson. Ambassador Heeney commented that this would be taking place while the electoral campaign was in full swing, and observed that Pearson would be the only Nobel peace prize winner who would be present. The President smilingly said that a lot of people seem to be out to win the Nobel peace prize these days.

433. **Letter From the Ambassador to Canada (Merchant) to Acting Secretary of State Ball**

Ottawa, May 5, 1962.

DEAR GEORGE: I am sending this letter to you by the hand of Rolfe Kingsley of the Embassy staff in the belief that you will want to discuss its contents with the President at the earliest possible opportunity.

Its subject is my talk with Prime Minister Diefenbaker late yesterday afternoon in which he gave vent to a most disturbed and disturbing attitude with respect to the President's forty minute conversation with Mike Pearson during the latter's visit to Washington to attend the White House Dinner for the Nobel Prize winners of this hemisphere.[1] Realizing that the Prime Minister would be in Ottawa only for a brief interlude in his campaign, I had asked for a fifteen minute appointment to pay my farewell call on him. The time was set for four yesterday afternoon at his official residence. In confirming the appointment, Basil Robinson, his confidential assistant, forewarned me that Mr. Diefenbaker was in an extremely agitated frame of mind over the political capital which Pearson had made out of his talk with the President earlier in the week.

My call on Mr. Diefenbaker lasted nearly two hours, and not fifteen minutes. After saying nice things about my two tours of duty as Ambassador, he launched into what can be only described as a tirade. I describe our conversation below in summary and not seriatim, since I interrupted him a number of times and the exchanges, while personally friendly, became heated.

The gist of what the Prime Minister said was this. He could only interpret the President's devoting so much time to a personal talk with Pearson, which the latter had described to the press as covering a wide range of subjects including disarmament, NATO, and the Common Market, as an intervention by the President in the Canadian election. He was satisfied that, if not Pearson himself, then his campaign lieutenants would present this to the Canadian electorate as the President turning for advice on international affairs to a single Canadian who was the Leader of the Opposition and running for Prime Minister against the present government. The Prime Minister asserted that the night before in a speech in Toronto Walter Gordon (running on the Liberal ticket and generally regarded as likely to be Minister of Finance in a Liberal Cabinet) had stated in effect that the Liberals were more competent than the

---

Source: Department of State, Central Files, 611.42/5–562. Secret.

[1] For Pearson's account of the conversation with Kennedy on April 29, see *Mike, The Memoirs of The Right Honourable Lester B. Pearson*, vol. 3 (Toronto, 1975), pp. 63–64.

Conservatives to manage Canada because the President had turned to Mr. Pearson a few days before for advice on the international situation.

The Prime Minister said that he fully expected this line to be increasingly used throughout the country by the Liberals in their campaign. He said that during the afternoon he had had phone calls to this effect from supporters from the Maritimes to British Columbia. The Prime Minister then went on to say that Canada-United States relations would now be the dominant issue in the campaign. He said the campaigning would be more bitter than it was in 1911 and he referred to Champ Clark's statement during the course of that campaign which it took the Canadians until 1917 to recover from. (According to my recollection, Champ Clark who was the Speaker of The House of Representatives, said publicly something along the line that it was inevitable that the United States should annex Canada. The basic issue of the campaign was the question of a reciprocal trade agreement with the United States and the outcome of the campaign was won and lost on the slogan of the Conservatives, "No truck or trade with the Yankees.")

Mr. Diefenbaker then said that he was shocked by your recent speech or statement[2] to the effect that the United States wanted to get rid of Commonwealth preferences and that, hence, he concluded that we thought we could achieve this by supporting Pearson who was prepared to accept without argument Britain's unconditional entrance into the European Common Market.

The Prime Minister then said that he had no choice except to meet head-on the expected Liberal line that Pearson was better able to manage Canadian relations with the United States. He thought he would probably be forced into this by the middle of or end of next week. He said he was opening the Conservative campaign in London, Ontario, this evening and he would not then raise this issue himself. In countering the Liberal line, he said he would publicly produce a document which he has had locked up in his private safe since a few days after the President's visit to Ottawa last May. This document he says is the original of a memorandum on White House stationery, addressed to the President from Walt Rostow and initialled by the latter, which is headed "Objectives of the President's Visit to Ottawa." The Prime Minister says that the memorandum starts:

"1. The Canadians must be pushed into joining the OAS.
2. The Canadians must be pushed into something else . . .
3. The Canadians must be pushed in another direction . . ."[3]

---

[2] Not further identified.

[3] For the full text of this memorandum, May 16, 1961, and Diefenbaker's brief account of the meeting with Merchant, see *One Canada, The Years of Achievement, 1957–1962*, p. 183.

The Prime Minister said that the document came into his possession a few days after the President left, through External Affairs, under circumstances with which he was not familiar, but his understanding was that it had been given by someone to External Affairs. The Prime Minister said that this authoritative statement of the intention of the United States to "push" Canada would be used by him to demonstrate that he, himself, was the only leader capable of preventing United States domination of Canada.

The Prime Minister said that he was talking to me privately and on a basis of personal trust and frankness which had characterized our personal relationship and which did not even exist, as far as he was concerned, in his relations with the British. He said, however, he had told Macmillan most of this story, and that he had also once been warned by a prominent Conservative Party member in Britain that the United States would support Pearson in Canadian politics because through the latter's attitude toward the Common Market the United States could secure the commercial benefits of the wiping out of Commonwealth preferences.

During the course of his tirade the Prime Minister also made a glancing reference to Stew Udall's alleged intervention into Canadian domestic affairs in connection with the Columbia River Treaty.[4] He also said that he was causing an investigation to be made to ascertain whether some Liberal supporter of Pearson in the Canadian Foreign Service now attached to the Canadian Embassy in Washington had taken the initative of arranging for Pearson's private interview with the President. He concluded by saying that the incident would "blow our relations sky high."

As you can imagine, I was not silent throughout this extraordinary disquisition. I should note that the Prime Minister was physically tired from a return early that morning from an exhausting and frustrating whistle-stop campaign in Newfoundland, and uneasy over his self-confessed inability to put together a speech for his keynote address at London tonight, which he said, must set the tone for his entire campaign. He was excited to a degree disturbing in a leader of an important country, and closer to hysteria than I have seen him, except on one other possible occasion. Nevertheless, he interjected from time to time expressions of confidence on the outcome of the election and was willing to hear me out on my interjections and my closing summation. His wife, Olive, however, I felt was hovering over him when I arrived and obviously doing the same when I chatted with the two of them for ten min-

---

[4] Presumably a reference to the statement described in The New York Times, December 1, 1961, p. 19.

utes before departure. The conversation I described above, however, was conducted with no one else in attendance.

The points I made were that, first, it was entirely understandable that Mike Pearson should attend a White House dinner given by the President and Mrs. Kennedy for all the living Nobel Prize winners of North and South America. (The Prime Minister agreed on this and said that he regarded it as understandable when he learned of the invitation.) I said, moreover, that I could not see any basis for criticizing the President in taking advantage of the visit to Washington of a prominent Canadian public figure to discuss with him international affairs. It was childish to assume that this constituted any effort or intent to intervene in Canadian domestic politics. Moreover, I said that I could give him my personal word that there was no favoritism on the part of the President or the Administration for the Liberal party in Canada as against the present Government. I said the President's respect for him was great, and our relations were good. There were, as would always be the case, problems between us.

Secondly, I urged him in strongest terms to discard any thought of revealing publicly the document which he said he had in his possession. I said that I had never seen or heard of it and that it was not conceivable to me that if such a memorandum were genuine, it could have been transmitted officially or unofficially to anyone in the Canadian Government. If it was what the Prime Minister described it to be, then it reflected the advice to the President of a member of his personal staff who at the time had no Constitutional or administrative responsibility for advising the President on foreign affairs. I said that if it were genuine and as described, the Prime Minister, might criticize the phraseology or the use of the word "push" (which word the Prime Minister had repeatedly and bitterly underlined in his discourse) but that there must be many informal, confidential recommendations to him from his personal advisors for his dealings with other Governments which used phraseology which would be objectionable to a foreign government. The document, therefore, I said, had no official status and was not intended for Canadian eyes. Moreover, I said that were he to reveal it publicly there would be a serious backlash, if not in Canada, then certainly in the United States. People would ask how the Prime Minister had come into possession of such a privileged internal document addressed to the President of the United States, and why it had not been immediately returned, without comment or publicity.

Finally, I said that the Prime Minister bore a heavy responsibility as an ally of the United States and as a member of the Free World coalition. Domestic elections could be divisive in any country. I thought he should give sober historic thought before he responded as he said he intended to the capitalization by his political rival on an incident which was innocent and certainly not intended as intervention.

I then went back at the Prime Minister on Fulton's attack on Udall's press statement some months ago, which the Prime Minister had cited as an earlier intervention in Canadian politics. I told him that it was the United States and not Canada which had the right to be infuriated in this matter and I set him straight on the facts. On this point the Prime Minister quickly backed down and repudiated Fulton's actions at the time.

There was, as you will understand, give and take and repetition in the protracted argument. At its conclusion I felt I had made an impression on the Prime Minister, but I left with no sense of assurance that I had dissuaded him from his originally stated intent to use the Rostow memorandum in the campaign. I have seen the Prime Minister on several earlier occasions heated and excited only to find that two or three days later the storm had passed. On this occasion, however, his only assurance as I left, was that he would not raise this issue tonight, and in fact, he said half jokingly (after learning that I was not leaving until next week) that he would not bring it up until I had left Canada, since, he said, it would be up to another American Ambassador to pick up the pieces and he didn't want to spoil my last few days in Ottawa.

As is apparent, we have a problem. I think the chances are three or four to one that, having blown his top to me, the Prime Minister will not do as he has threatened, but will, in fact, act responsibly. It is necessary, however, that we take out any available insurance against the worst.

Given Canadian sensibilities and apprehensions of American influence, it is in our interest neither to intervene in Canadian domestic elections nor to give the appearance of doing so. Were we to intervene and be successful, our candidate would be labeled as a running dog of the United States and inhibited from acting along lines agreeable to us. Were we to intervene unsuccessfully, the winner would hate us. Pearson has successfully given the impression of being so knowledgeable that the United States has sought his advice. This the Prime Minister believes has built up his rival's prestige and, hence, electoral appeal. The problem is not now to show overt support for Diefenbaker, but to redress the balance to give the impression of United States Government neutrality in the election.

What is required, it seems to me, is for the President promptly to arrange to see Diefenbaker within the next few weeks on some matter which could be publicly stated and which would seem both plausible and natural. If some place other than Washington were the location for the meeting it would contribute to this appearance. Possibly the President's schedule for travel in the next two or three weeks would permit him to state publicly that he had invited Mr. Diefenbaker to meet him for a few hours at a time and place not disrupting to the Prime Minister's

own engagements. Informality would be a useful stage prop. As for subject matter, I would suggest disarmament or as another alternative
North American problems arising from possible British entrance into
the Common Market. I think before any publicity from the White
House, either a phone call or a letter from the President to Mr. Diefenbaker making the suggestion would be the best procedure. Thereafter, if
a meeting were successfully arranged, it could be announced together
with a general statement of its purpose. If a meeting could not be arranged, I think by agreement with the Prime Minister the fact could become public that the President had taken the initiative in seeking one.

Needless to say I am distressed to bring this problem to your and
the President's attention. Its implications are so serious, however, as, in
my judgment, to require the President's consideration and prompt effort to forestall what could be a very damaging development in relations
between Canada and the United States.

Sincerely,

Livie

---

434. Telegram From the Department of State to the Embassy in Canada

Washington, May 8, 1962, 8:52 p.m.

1081. For Ambassador from Acting Secretary. Very appreciative
your letter May 5.[1] Questions you raise have received most serious consideration highest levels. Basis this consideration request that you now
pursue following course of action with regard this matter.

1. You should go back to Prime Minister and, with reference to
conversation May 4, indicate your own personal reluctance report to
Washington anything which could be construed as a threat to publish
private communication directed to President US by one of his staff officers. Such publication would cast grave shadow over public attitudes
between our two countries and make difficult future relations between
President and Prime Minister. Indicate your view that even suggestion
possibility such publication would have bad effect in Washington and
that President would be troubled about relations with a Government

---

Source: Department of State, Central Files, 611.42/5–862. Secret; Eyes Only; No Distribution. Drafted by Springsteen (U) and approved by Ball. The instruction in this telegram is a close paraphrase of a memorandum from Bundy to Ball, May 8. (Kennedy Library, National Security Files, Canada)

[1] Document 433.

which would consider using his personal papers for a political purpose. As friend of PM's and of Canada you have therefore held off reporting to Washington pending further talks with him.

2. Should PM not respond satisfactorily you should add that if document published it would be impossible for you or any friend of Canada to explain this action to USG. Both Canadian and US Governments have complete record Ottawa discussions between President and Prime Minister and we all know that no improper pressure of any sort exerted. Record clearly indicates that Canadian response President's speeches in Ottawa as well as reaction those who took part in private talks was that of greatest enthusiasm.

3. Re Pearson visit. You should indicate this was an entirely informal meeting arranged at Pearson's request through personal friend of both men. You have checked with Washington and find that meeting lasted only 20 minutes—from 7:30 to 7:50—during period when President had small private reception in his apartment before going down to dinner. Intent was for a private and off-the-record meeting. Its existence became known only when newsmen saw Pearson arrive early.

4. You should also indicate that it would be most unusual for President refuse receive former Foreign Minister and opposition leader of friendly country. President has had many such meetings in past including recent lunch which he gave for Gaitskell and recent meeting with Erler which lasted longer than meeting with Pearson.

5. You may wish remind PM that invitations to Nobel Prize dinner were issued before elections called. To recall invitation because of political campaign would have indeed been an act of intervention.

6. You should show real sympathy with Diefenbaker on strains characteristic of political campaigns. You might indicate this happens in US and that you have heard President himself express his feelings of resentment about situation in 1960 campaign when it appeared that certain foreign leaders were making statements favorable to Mr. Nixon. You should also indicate the fact the no one in authority in US Government, least of all the President, has said or done anything that could be construed as interference in any way in Canadian election.

FYI. President has no intention or desire to seek meeting near future with PM. We also cabling separately for your information Rostow memo[2] which quite innocent, and should strengthen your position. End FYI.

Ball

---

[2] Transmitted in telegram 1080 to Ottawa, May 8. (Department of State, Central Files, 611.42/5–862)

435. Telegram From the Embassy in Canada to the Department of State

Ottawa, May 13, 1962, midnight.

1164. For Secretary and Under Secretary. From Ambassador. Reference: Department telegrams 1080 and 1081;[1] Embassy telegram 1157.[2] I saw Prime Minister at his residence evening May 12 immediately after his return to Ottawa.

I opened by saying I had delayed my departure by reason my grave and growing concern over our talk on May 4. I said I had not reported to the President his stated intent to reveal in present campaign his possession of confidential document of the President presenting advice of member his personal staff. I said I had only reported to the Department his belief Pearson intended capitalize in campaign on private conversation with the President on Nobel Prize occasion which I said had been informal twenty-minute chat in advance of formal dinner. Then I said I had independently obtained copy Walt Rostow's memo which I found unexceptionable and concerning four subjects which had been frequently discussed and regarding which I had thought PM's personal attitude favorable. Verb "push" I said corresponded to British "press" or Canadian phrase "seek to persuade".

PM did not interrupt as I went on to say that I had not reported his threat to use existence or contents memo because consequences of his so doing would be catastrophic. PM interjected "they would so be in Canada". I said I was not talking of Canada but of reaction in the US. I said if he did this the result in the US would be of incalculable harm with public opinion, in the government and in his personal relations and that consequently I had delayed my departure to urge once more that he abandon any such thought.

Mr. Diefenbaker having heard me out said that he had given matter further consideration and in light of what I had said to him on May 4 he had no present intention of using or in any way referring to memo in question. He said if he changed his mind he would personally telephone me in Washington before doing so but he was now decided to discard any such thought. He then said only three other men know of memo, cabinet members Green, Fleming and Churchill. (All are cool steady men.)

Source: Department of State, Central Files, 611.42/5–1362. Secret; Priority; Eyes Only; No Distribution.

[1] Document 434 and footnote 2 thereto.

[2] Telegram 1157, May 11, reported that Merchant planned to see Diefenbaker on May 13. (Department of State, Central Files, 611.42/5–1162)

I replied that I was relieved for the sake of both countries at this decision. He went off at this point on an emotional sidetrack on the US "trying to push" Canada around but calmed down when I asked what in his talks with the President or any other dialogue gave any grounds for suspecting such an intent.

Then the PM described his prairie campaign tour with gusto (it apparently went well) and bemoaned time on hustings and travel still ahead. He came back to Pearson White House visit and said he expected latter to emphasize it heavily though he admitted that he had not yet done so. Winding up, he reiterated his decision not to inject "push" issue. He did refer to article in *Toronto Telegram* (which Embassy will secure) entitled "Ouch" and based he said on Scripps-Howard pieces critical of his government and expressing view administration desired to see conservatives in Canada defeated.

Notwithstanding fact PM nervous and in my judgment on verge of exhaustion, I believe storm has passed and that chances are now minimal that he will embark on all-out anti-American line using reference memo in process. At end conversation we both lowered our voices and with complimentary close he bade me warm good night.

I have of course kept Armstrong fully informed this entire episode so he can carry on as well as I could should need for further interchange arise.

Merchant

---

436. **Telegram From the Embassy in Canada to the Department of State**

Ottawa, June 18, 1962, 5 p.m.

1309. Department please pass copy this telegram to Secretary Goldberg.[1] Reference: Embtel 1259 and Department telegram 1183.[2] Se-

---

Source: Department of State, Central Files, 911.7342/6–1862. Confidential; Priority. Repeated to Toronto and Montreal.

[1] Secretary of Labor Authur J. Goldberg.

[2] Telegram 1259, June 6, reported that Ritchie had been instructed to request an investigation by U.S. authorities of incidents against Canadian ships in the Great Lakes. (Ibid., 911.7342/6-662) Telegram 1183, June 7, summarized the discussion with the Canadian Ambassador on June 6 and stressed that the United States was "quite prepared to comply with Canadian request." (Ibid., 811.062/6-662) A memorandum of the conversation with Ritchie on June 6 is ibid.

rious harm is being done to US-Canadian relations by interference of AFL–CIO and some of its affiliates in disputes between unions in Canada, especially after such disputes settled in accordance Canadian procedures.

Dispute which is causing most trouble presently is that between Seafarers International Union and Canadian Maritime Union over representation of men employed on ships of upper lakes and island shipping companies. SIU-instigated harassment of these ships in US and Canada has thus far cost companies about $500,000 resulted in beatings of both CMU and company representatives, involved courts and quasi-judicial labor relations bodies of US and Canada as well as other government agencies, and no end to the struggle is in sight, even though violence may be curbed. This dispute, issue of which is settled in Canada under Canadian law, would long since have been over were it not for continual interference of US unions and AFL–CIO in US.

Understand that ship *Howard L. Shaw* has been immobilized in Chicago for over two weeks by refusal of International Longshoremen to handle her despite court injunction against SIU picketing.

Efforts of Canadian Labour Congress in direct discussions with AFL–CIO to settle matter including meeting of liasion committee in Washington June 4–5 have ended in failure. On June 5 according to CLC official Meany responded to request for guidance from Duluth Labor Council with telegram saying "No new policy necessary. SIU is affiliate of AFL–CIO and CMU is not." This is tantamount to saying that Canadians do not have right to choose union to represent them unless it is affiliate of AFL–CIO.

Discussions of liasion committee equally unfruitful on other issues including recent decision by AFL–CIO to use its dispute machinery to settle jurisdictional dispute in Canadian paper mill.

There is feeling in CLC and on part of upper lakes management that retaliatory action against SIU-organized American ships only course available in view inability to persuade AFL–CIO or to obtain effective relief through NLRB and US courts. Some Canadian Government officials inclined to agree. Liberal leader Pearson reported to have expressed his shock and disgust at SIU-inspired violence. Feelings are rising and resentment increasing against AFL–CIO and international unions in general. Meetings this week of union members working on St. Lawrence Seaway and at Orr Docks Seven Islands and other points expected to order boycott of SIU-organized American ships effective immediately.

I believe these considerations should be brought promptly to George Meany's serious attention and he should be urged strongly by high administration spokesman to place AFL–CIO in position of scrupulous neutrality with regard to unsettled Canadian disputes and of respect for Canadian settlements and decisions when they are reached. Representation on upper lakes and island shipping vessels is decided, and American unions should abide by decision.

Representation of Newfoundland loggers is also decided, and CLC will be compelled to recognize that fact. Where representation in Canada not yet decided, Canadians must make decisions. Naturally all such decisions are subject to change and international unions have right to try to alter situations to their advantage. However, they should confine their efforts to what is lawful and permissible with Canada and not try to impose solutions from US. Any other course will only exacerbate relations between two countries and cause restriction of international unionism in Canada.

Armstrong

---

437.   **Telegram From the Embassy in Canada to the Department of State**

Ottawa, June 28, 1962, 2 p.m.

1364. At suggestion of Rasminsky, Governor of Bank of Canada, I called on him today and had a general discussion, primarily of economic matters. Rasminsky said he had wanted to talk with me to express in most sincere and heartfelt terms the profound gratitude and appreciation he entertains for the USG and particularly for officials in the Treasury, Federal Reserve and EXIM Bank for their excellent response last week to the problems faced by the Bank of Canada and Canadian Government. He went on to say he believes the financial measures have afforded a reasonable breathing space which should enable the Canadian Government to take necessary action to rectify the structure of its trade and payments. He noted that Canadians [have] been running a current account deficit of about $1,500 million with the US which is the main element in its imbalance of payments. He said it

Source: Department of State, Central Files, 842.00/6–2862. Secret; Priority; Limit Distribution.

had been wrong for Canada to assume that the net inflow of capital investment, which has for years balanced Canada's payments, would continue indefinitely. He feels strongly that Canada must have in sight a means of resolving the problem of trade imbalance which would not be so dependent on an unpredictable flow of capital.

Rasminsky believes that the essential internal measures required to rectify Canada's position as a potential recipient of investment include major tax reform, which would make the personal and corporation income tax less onerous at the middle levels. He said that unfortunately the kind of tax reform required would look like soaking the poor. He was apprehensive over what the politicians may do to the financial and trade program announced over the weekend. He implied unhappiness with the rather grudging support given by Pearson to the government's measures thus far.

Rasminsky noted that it had been a very bitter pill for Diefenbaker to have to accept financial support from other countries, and he emphasized the great sensitivity of Diefenbaker in this regard. He said he realized that there would be a tendency on the part of the USG, now that election is over, to expect action on a number of pending questions. He recognized this as quite reasonable and understandable, but he warned that any attempt to imply that the US expected such action as a "payoff" for the support given last week, might well be counter-productive. I said I thought it unlikely that the US would talk in such terms, since our own payments system and our own balance of payments problems were closely related to the Canadian situation, and that it obviously was not in our self interest to have the Canadian financial position deteriorate. Rasminsky said that he had been very anxious that Canada not be the Kreditanstalt of 1962, and he understood how the US felt about the matter. He added that it was unfortunate that an improvement in Canada's balance of payments almost inevitably resulted in an adverse development in the US balance of payments.

Rasminsky informed me that the Government of Canada is planning a $250 million bond issue to be floated in New York in the near future. When this is completed, I understand $250 million worth of the EXIM Bank line of credit will be allowed to lapse.

Rasminsky was reasonably optimistic about the success of present measures, but felt that the import surcharge program contained so many inconsistencies that it would be subjected to heavy attack. These inconsistencies arise because the action had to be taken without asking for any legislation.

Armstrong

438.   Letter From the Under Secretary of State (Ball) to Secretary of the Treasury Dillon

Washington, July 5, 1962.

DEAR DOUGLAS: I have the uncomfortable feeling that the Diefenbaker Government is being less than straightforward with us, and I think we must be careful not to let the Administration be put in an indefensible position.

What the Canadians Said to the United States

On the basis of my notes at the time we discussed the Canadian proposal on June 22 and 23,[1] it appears that the Canadian Government represented the situation to you as follows:

1. The import surcharges were to be "temporary." Temporary meant that it would take three to four months to enact legislation which would enable them to substitute internal taxes for import surcharges as a means of providing the necessary $200 million increment to the federal revenue.

2. These surcharges were designed primarily to produce additional revenue for the budget. They were the only available means whereby this additional revenue could be obtained through executive action. It was anticipated that the surcharges would have only a "slight" balance of payments effect in terms of the reduction of imports from the United States, since they were to be imposed primarily on luxury items and items that Canada needed but could not produce domestically.

3. The Canadian Government would discuss with its major trading partners in the GATT the details as to the application of these duties to specific commodities. This would give us an opportunity to protest the application of high duties to sensitive items.

What the Canadians Have Said to Others

The following Canadian statements in connection with the announcement of their financial scheme seem to me inconsistent with the above representations:

1. In his broadcast to the Canadian people on June 26 Prime Minister Diefenbaker said: "These surcharges I ask you to support in the national interest until the foreign exchange problem has been solved by an increase of exports *or by producing in Canada at competitive prices more of*

Source: Department of State, Central Files, 611.42/7–562. Official Use Only. Drafted by Ball. Copies were sent to Kaysen, E, and EUR.
[1] No other record of these meetings has been found.

the commodities that we are now importing." This statement makes no reference to any intention to substitute internal taxes for import surcharges. By suggesting that the surcharges would be continued until Canada is able to produce "more of the commodities that we are now importing", it clearly contemplates that imports would be supplanted by domestic production.

That this is, in fact, what the Canadian Government has in mind is borne out by Prime Minister Diefenbaker's further statement: *"What is saved on imports will help to balance the foreign exchange situation."* This sounds like pure protectionism to me.

2. The Order of Council, issued after the announcement of the financial plan, applied the 10 percent import surcharge to a wide range of consumers goods, including everything from automobiles to television sets, *"for which it is possible for consumers to defer some of their purchases or for which additional Canadian production is available."* This group covers about $650 million of annual imports at current levels.

The Order applies the 5 percent surcharge to another group of less essential imports for which either *"surplus capacity exists in Canada"* or *"alternative or substitutable Canadian products are available."* This 5 percent duty covers about $2.3 million of annual imports at current levels.

This language again contemplates that the surcharges will operate to restrict imports. Again this sounds like pure protectionism.

3. The Canadian Government has notified the GATT Secretariat of the import surcharges. In its message of notification the Government made no specific reference to revenue needs or fiscal objectives. It referred instead to a lack of machinery to administer a system of import licensing and expressed the belief that surcharges would have a less restrictive effect on trade than quantitative import restrictions. The concluding part of the notification used the terminology of Article XII of GATT, which provides for the direct control of imports through quantitative import restrictions.

The Problem for the United States

My immediate concern is with the effect of the Canadian action on the trade bill—which, as you know, still faces the Senate hurdle. Already we are beginning to hear from American producers who fear that they will be hurt by higher Canadian import duties. We have also heard from American producers who are seeking similar protection to that accorded Canadian industry by these surcharges. I think it essential that we demonstrate that we intend to take a firm line with the Canadians.

For that reason I strongly oppose our agreeing to a GATT session that ends in October. We can, of course, make it clear that we will be prepared to discuss the Canadian Government's legislative plans at that time, and, if it needs two or three more months to pass internal tax legislation as a substitute for the import surcharges, we might be willing to agree to an extension of the waiver until the end of the year.

But if we were to agree to a waiver until next July, as the Canadians are asking, we would almost certainly have to demand compensation or be prepared to take retaliatory measures. Otherwise we could never justify our position before the Congress during the trade bill discussions.

I understand that the Canadians are asserting that we will shake confidence in the Government if we do not agree to a waiver beyond October. If they were sincere in their representations as to the temporary character of the import surcharges, I cannot believe that there should any impairment of confidence.

I am seeing the Canadian Ambassador at 6:00 p.m. on Friday[2] and plan to take this line with him unless you feel it essential to have further discussions.

Proposed Canadian Loan in the New York Market

Bill Armstrong's telegram from Ottawa on June 28[3] mentioned that the Canadians plan to float a loan of $250 million in the New York market in order to refinance obligations for which the Export-Import Bank line of credit is designed to provide only interim assistance. We do not have the details on this in the State Department, but I have the impression that certain of these obligations are to European creditors. If this is correct wouldn't it be appropriate for our two Departments to suggest to the Canadians that they seek funds in Europe to cover the European part of their refinancing problem?

You made a brilliant argument in Rome[4] that we should try to discourage flotations in the New York market by foreign governments and public authorities. In view of the magnitude of the help we gave the Canadian Government to meet their financial crisis, I think we are in a strong position to insist that they tap the European capital market for this money.

Our General Attitude Toward the Canadian Program

In approaching the present Canadian request for a year's waiver of GATT requirements I feel we must bear in mind what the *Economist* this week refers to as the "beggar-my-neighbor" character of the Canadian program. Granted that we had to run a fast rescue operation in view of the urgency of the crisis, I think it would be a great mistake for us to let the Canadians get away, for any length of time, with such a cheap and

---

[2] July 6; no record of this meeting has been found.

[3] Document 437.

[4] For text of Dillon's speech to the Conference of the American Bankers' Association at Rome, May 18, see RIIA, *Documents on International Affairs, 1962*, pp. 536–545.

easy solution as increased import restrictions. This is a very dangerous precedent. It is in direct violation of GATT. In my judgment it is unworthy of an economically advanced country. Obviously Prime Minister Diefenbaker finds it agreeable to provide increased protection for Canadian industry, but I see no reason why we should let him do this at our expense.

I'd like to talk with you about all these matters after you have had a chance to read this.

Yours ever,

George W. Ball[5]

---

[5] Printed from a copy that bears this typed signature.

---

439. Telegram From the Embassy in Canada to the Department of State

Ottawa, July 17, 1962, 4 p.m.

75. In accordance with External Affairs Minister Green's suggestion, I called on him this morning to say goodbye and to discuss Canadian-American relations. Green was most cordial throughout the 40-minute conversation. His tone was serious and thoughtful. He expressed the most profound gratitude for US financial assistance and for the understanding attitude shown by Secretary Dillon and Under Secretary Ball in dealing with Canada's balance of payments problems. He was gratified that the GATT waiver problem had been resolved. He asked me for my views on Canadian-American problems. I responded by saying I thought the Columbia River treaty[1] was a major issue, and

---

Source: Department of State, Central Files, 611.42/7–1762. Confidential. Repeated to Vancouver.

[1] Reference is to the agreement on the cooperative development of the water resources of the Columbia River Basin, signed at Washington, January 17, 1961, and entered into force September 16, 1964; TIAS 5638 (15 UST 1555).

that many people in the US Government were extremely anxious to know of the prospects for ratification.

Mr. Green agreed that the Columbia River treaty was indeed a problem. He said that the Liberals and the NDP both wanted re-negotiation. He asked me what the US reaction to re-negotiation would be. I said I thought anything apart from minor adjustments would be extremely difficult if not impossible, and that even minor adjustments would present problems. Green said that the chief accusation against the government was that the deal had resulted in a "sellout" of Canadian interests. He said he was himself convinced that it was a fair and reasonable treaty, and that no "sellout" of Canadian interests had occurred. Nevertheless, the charge made it difficult to proceed with ratification, especially given the parliamentary situation. I asked him whether the government had as yet made a deal with Bennett,[2] and he said no. He was unable to forecast whether any deal with Bennett seemed feasible in the period before Parliament assembles in September. He dwelt at some length on the sale of downstream benefits implying that the US would like to see the Bennett proposal adopted. I assured him we were quite neutral on whether downstream benefits were sold or not. He said one of the criticisms from the Liberals and NDP was that no price was quoted in the treaty for the sale of power; he wondered whether a price could be quoted. I told him the price depended on the amount of power offered and the term for which it might be available.

Green said that the government proposes to put the treaty before commons in September, where it will be subjected to the committee process during which General McNaughton will have extensive opportunity present his views. Liberals and NDP will join chorus, but Green feels Liberals unlikely wreck chances ratification and therefore treaty may conceivably be ratified. I got impression that government intends put treaty before Commons regardless whether deal had been made with Bennett.

I asked Green what attitude on part of US would be most helpful in advancing ratification of treaty, and he replied that it would be best for US to keep as quiet as possible, as we have been doing. I asked him whether he thought we should indicate that re-negotiation was out of question, if this were the case, and he said such statement might strengthen hands of those who say Canada was out-negotiated. I urged that Canadian Government keep USG confidentially informed of its plans with respect to ratification so that US actions and statements might be helpful rather then unwittingly harmful. Green implied he thought this good idea but made no categorical promises.

---

[2] W.A.C. Bennett, Premier of British Columbia.

I told Green I thought other major question which made relations difficult was in field of defense. (Separate telegram will cover this part of conversation.)[3]

Green said he felt that relations between Canadian and American peoples, businesses, professional institutions, labor groups and governments were essentially very good, and that there only two or three topics about which we disagreed. I told him I thought this true numerically, but that both Columbia River and defense loomed large in thoughts of those in USG who dealt with Canadian affairs. I said I thought improvement in relations would depend in substantial measure on some changes in Columbia situation and in connection with defense. He did not disagree, but said that it was important to maintain public posture to effect that relations were good. I said that this was desirable but should be accompanied by candor in diplomatic discussions of unresolved problems and be some evidence of progress.

Green closed conversation by saying he was sure that Canada had more troubles than anybody and it needed American help. I told him I was sure we were prepared to be helpful, but that we had problems too.

Armstrong

---

[3] Telegram 78, July 16, reported that Green had stated that the Canadian Government had given no thought to the nuclear weapons issue since the election on June 18 and noted that any initiative on the question should come from Ottawa. (Department of State, Central Files, 611.42/7–1762)

---

440. Editorial Note

During a visit to Ottawa August 24–25, Secretary of State Rusk met once with Prime Minister Diefenbaker and twice with Minister for External Affairs Green. Memoranda of his conversations with the Prime Minister at 11 a.m. on August 24 concerning, Berlin, Cuba, and disarmament are in Department of State, Conference Files: Lot 65 D 533, CF 2146. Memoranda of his conversations with Green at 10:15 a.m. and 2:20 p.m. on August 24 concerning subjects that might arise in the United Nations General Assembly, U.S.-Canadian defense sharing, the Middle East, the Congo, NATO, Laos, and West New Guinea are ibid.

441. Memorandum From Livingston T. Merchant to Secretary of State Rusk and the Under Secretary of State (Ball)

Washington, undated.

On December 3 I lunched alone with the Canadian Minister in the Embassy here, Mr. Basil Robinson, on his invitation. He is an old friend and had frequently been of great value to me in Ottawa in his capacity of Confidential Assistant to Prime Minister Diefenbaker. After discursive conversation, he mentioned that Ambassador Ritchie had seen the Prime Minister in Ottawa a week earlier and said the Prime Minister is seriously concerned over the future implications of the absence of genuine consultation and the limited advance notice of the President's decision on Cuba announced October 22. He added that this was understandable from the viewpoint of domestic politics for the leader of any country. He then questioned me in detail concerning the PM's attitude and reaction when I saw him in Ottawa the afternoon of October 22.[1] I replied that, even allowing for the fact that he was harried from the debate on the floor of the House which he had just left, I had felt that he was at the outset somewhat brusque in manner and openly skeptical in attitude concerning the missile menace until the full intelligence briefing had been given him. I said I had not been permitted by him to make the orderly presentation I had planned and that the early minutes of our talk were a bit difficult. However, by the close of the session his whole attitude swung around to sympathetic understanding and I had thought a willingness to give public support to the President. I added, that the PM's first statement that same evening in the House and Mr. Green's later TV interview had surprised and disappointed me.

Mr. Robinson said these first reactions had pained and dismayed everyone in the Embassy. He then said the PM's later stance had been helpful and I agreed. Mr. Robinson then repeated that the PM had been placed in a difficult position by public recognition that there had in fact been no advance consultation—even my arrival in Ottawa a few fours earlier would have helped. I pointed out this would have meant I could not have carried the full text of the President's speech[2] and I also reminded him that the phrase to which the PM strongly objected had not

---

Source: Department of State, Central Files, 611.42/12–1062. Confidential; Limited Distribution.

[1] A memorandum of Merchant's conversation with Diefenbaker at 5 p.m. on October 22, in which he briefed the Prime Minister on the developing Cuban missile crisis, is ibid., 611.3722/10–2262. For Diefenbaker's account of the briefing and his subsequent statement in the House of Commons, see *One Canada: The Tumultuous Years, 1962–1967*, Chapter IV.

[2] For text of the President's speech on October 22, see *Public Papers of the Presidents of the United States: John F. Kennedy, 1962*, pp. 806–809.

been in the speech as actually delivered. Mr. Robinson said the PM had taken comfort in this. He then repeated one could feel sorry for the PM.

I replied that I personally didn't feel a tenth as sorry for the PM as I had for Harold Macmillan who had had comparably short advance notice. I said I didn't think Canada had earned, by its actions and by certain non-actions, the right to the extreme intimacy of relations which had existed in years past. I also pointed out the dilemma of achieving surprise by secrecy and at the same time consulting well in advance all our friends and allies.

Mr. Robinson said he could understand this. Certain things were beginning to move encouragingly in the nuclear area and elsewhere. Then he said "if only we could do something about that piece of paper." I reacted in no way to this cryptic reference being unsure of his knowledge of a particular incident going back to May 1961.

Beyond friendliness, I am certain there was a purpose behind this lunch. I believe it was to pass on through an additional channel word of the PM's worry and sense of grievance over the Cuban matter. There *may* also have been intended a veiled suggestion that we take some action now regarding a "piece of paper". Whether or not he is already privy to the facts, Mr. Robinson might be a useful channel to make clear the necessity of something being done about it if matters are to improve.

Our conversation then passed on to other aspects of the Canadian scene and we parted on our usual informal, friendly terms.

Livingston T. Merchant[3]

---

[3] Printed from a copy that bears this typed signature.

---

442. **Telegram From the Embassy in Canada to the Department of State**

Ottawa, December 17, 1962, 6 p.m.

797. This morning I paid my initial call on Prime Minister Diefenbaker.[1] The conversation lasted about half an hour. Although vigorous

---

Source: Department of State, Central Files, 611.42/12–1762. Secret; Limit Distribution.

[1] Butterworth presented his credentials on December 11.

in speech and gesture, he struck me as being unwell and exhibited evident signs of palsy or perhaps Parkinson's disease. After the usual but briefest of pleasantries he immediately queried me regarding the Nassau meetings, but I refused to be drawn, explaining that I had left Washington for New York before detailed arrangements were formulated. He left the subject with great reluctance for the Common Market and UK entry.

I thought it was wise to meet directness with equal directness and thus replied frankly to a series of forthright questions he put to me. Although he found the purport of the answers unpalatable, the conversation proceeded amicably enough on an even tone. After pointing out that the US was not a party to the negotiations and the opinions I expressed were personal, my replies in brief indicated that the UK must have known the probable terms for entry and these would not be much better or much worse than could have been anticipated. His theory that De Gaulle would place some arbitrary roadblock in the path had not thus far been supported by evidence and the French elections would not result in a change of direction of French policy but merely a reinforcement of the French position which on many issues was shared by the other 5. The common external tariff was the most important tangible factor binding the Six and they were conscious of this fact which would entail that the UK would have to pay the entrance fee (except for transitional arrangements, et cetera) and the annual dues to be a full member of the club.

Diefenbaker dissertated at length about British statements and assurances and implied that our dislike of preferences was the source of the difficulty that Canada and the Commonwealth now faced. I refrained from discussing our attitude toward preferences, but concentrated on quoting chapter and verse, indicating that the initiative had not been ours or EEC, but solely the UK's. I should judge that Diefenbaker has been made hopeful in the past month that the British negotiations might well not succeed and when, in reply to further direct questions, I told him I thought they would, and pressed further, that the Macmillan Government had nailed its political sail to that mast, he was evidently disappointed. I did not get the sense he knew very much about what he was talking.

He did not bring up the subject of nuclear weapons. When I left he volunteered that he would always be glad to see me and I should not hesitate to come to him.

Butterworth

443. Memorandum From the Assistant Secretary of State for European Affairs (Tyler) to the Under Secretary of State (Ball)

Washington, January 29, 1963.

SUBJECT

Proposed Press Statement on United States-Canadian Negotiations Regarding Nuclear Weapons

Last Friday, January 25, Prime Minister Diefenbaker made a long rambling statement (Tab A) in a Canadian House of Commons debate on foreign policy. In it he revealed that Canada had been negotiating with the United States for arrangements to provide nuclear weapons for Canadian forces "if and when" needed. These negotiations had been classified top secret, at the request of the Canadian Government, and we had no advance warning of the Prime Minister's remarks.[1]

In his remarks, Diefenbaker beclouded the whole issue of nuclear weapons for Canadian forces with misleading references to Nassau, to NATO, to multilateral nuclear forces, to NORAD, and to "not enlarging the nuclear family". His purpose was to stop if possible, and at least to slow down, the momentum towards a clarification of Canadian defense policy which began as a popular movement after the Cuban crisis, and which reached a high point in Liberal leader Pearson's speech earlier this month, in which he unequivocally called for Canada to adopt nuclear weapons for its forces, as a fulfillment of its existing NATO and NORAD commitments, and for a full review of those commitments.

The Embassy in Ottawa believes that prompt action should be taken by us to clarify the record and to sweep away the confusion which Diefenbaker's statement can cause in Canadian minds. Ambassador Butterworth sent a vigorous cable on January 27 (Tab B), suggesting a note to the Canadian Embassy which would be released to the public simultaneously. The Political Counselor of the Embassy in Ottawa came to Washington at the Ambassador's initiative, and our proposal, which modifies the Ambassador's suggestion, has his approval.

Source: Department of State, Central Files, 742.5611/1–2963. Secret. Drafted by Armstrong; concurred in by Johnson, Kitchen, G/PM, P, and the Department of Defense; and initialed by Tyler.

[1] Tabs A, B, and D were not attached to the source text. Telegrams 945 and 948 from Ottawa, January 26 (Tab A), transmitted summary and verbatim accounts of Diefenbaker's statement. (Ibid., 742.13/1–2663) For the full text of this statement, see *House of Commons Debates, Official Records, 1962,* vol. III, pp. 3125–3128. In telegram 949 from Ottawa, January 27 (Tab B), Butterworth stated that Diefenbaker's remarks could not go unanswered and suggested that the United States transmit an unclassified note to the Canadian Embassy that would subsequently be released to the press and would set the record straight on the negotiations with Canada on nuclear weapons. Tab C is not printed. For text of Tab D as released, see Document 444.

What we propose is a public statement by the Department, issued anonymously, which in a factual and logical way will clarify our position. The material it contains will be useful to those who oppose Diefenbaker, but the tone is designed not to irritate the Diefenbaker government, or to tempt it to engage in a polemical exchange with us, which a note might well spark.

If you approve this statement and its issuance, we plan to put it out quickly, simultaneously calling in the Canadian Minister and giving him a copy. The interview can be used to make points mentioned by Ambassador Butterworth, but not included in the public statement.

In proposing this statement, we are mindful of the risk. There is no assurance of an early election in Canada, and a Liberal victory in the next election is by no means certain. We have to live with the Diefenbaker government, and there are many matters in the field of defense, in particular, where we urgently need Canadian cooperation. Some of these are more important to us militarily than the provision of nuclear weapons for Canadian forces. Nevertheless, on balance we feel that the statement we propose should be issued, and we think it will inspire respect. Mr. Diefenbaker will or will not decide to use an anti-American line, almost regardless of what we do, and the statement should not push him into any new actions injurious to us. The statement carefully leaves open the matter of negotiations, which have in fact deadlocked because Canada has thus far not accepted any arrangements for warheads for BOMARCs and F–101B's which appear practical to us. There is some reason to think the Canadian position might change, but not much.

On January 28, Defence Minister Harkness issued a public statement (Tab C) which appeared more encouraging, commenting on what the Prime Minister had said on January 25. In the House of Commons debate afterwards, the Prime Minister did not confirm that Harkness' statement represented his views. This particular encounter seems to make it all the more necessary that we go on the record with a statement. Our proposal, which has the concurrence of the Defense Department, is attached at Tab D.

Recommendation[2]

That you authorize us to issue the proposed statement, and to speak to the Canadian Embassy along the lines of Ambassador Butterworth's telegram of January 27, to cover points not included in the statement.[3]

---

[2] Approved by Ball.

[3] On February 4 Secretary of State Rusk testified before the Subcommittee on Canadian Affairs of the Senate Foreign Relations Committee concerning the reasons that led the Department of State to express its dissatisfaction with Canada on continental defense by a press release rather than through normal diplomatic channels. For text of his testimony and related questions on continental defense and nuclear weapons for Canada, see *Executive Sessions of the Senate Foreign Relations Committee*, vol. XV, pp. 125 ff.

444. Department of State Press Release No. 59

Washington, January 30, 1963.

UNITED STATES AND CANADIAN NEGOTIATIONS REGARDING NUCLEAR WEAPONS

The Department has received a number of inquiries concerning the disclosure during a recent debate in the Canadian House of Commons regarding negotiations over the past two or three months between the United States and Canadian Governments relating to nuclear weapons for Canadian armed forces.

In 1958 the Canadian Government decided to adopt the BOMARC–B weapons systems. Accordingly two BOMARC–B squadrons were deployed to Canada where they would serve the double purpose of protecting Montreal and Toronto as well as the U.S. deterrent force. The BOMARC–B was not designed to carry any conventional warhead. The matter of making available a nuclear warhead for it and for other nuclear-capable weapons systems acquired by Canada has been the subject of inconclusive discussions between the two governments. The installation of the batteries in Canada without nuclear warheads was completed in 1962.

In addition to BOMARC–B, a similar problem exists with respect to the modern supersonic jet interceptor with which the RCAF has been provided. Without nuclear air defense warheads, they operate at far less then their full potential effectiveness.

Shortly after the Cuban crisis in October 1962, the Canadian Government proposed confidential discussions concerning circumstances under which there might be provision of nuclear weapons for Canadian armed forces in Canada and Europe. These discussions have been exploratory in nature; the Canadian Government has not as yet proposed any arrangement sufficiently practical to contribute effectively to North American defense.

The discussions between the two governments have also involved possible arrangements for the provision of nuclear weapons for Canadian NATO forces in Europe, similar to the arrangements which the United States has made with many of our other NATO allies.

During the debate in the House of Commons various references were made to recent discussions at Nassau. The agreements made at Nassau have been fully published. They raise no question of the appro-

Source: Department of State, Central Files, 742.5611/1–3063. Also printed in *American Foreign Policy: Current Documents, 1963*, p. 369.

priateness of nuclear weapons for Canadian forces in fulfilling their NATO or NORAD obligations.

Reference was also made in the debate to the need of NATO for increased conventional forces. A flexible and balanced defense requires increased conventional forces, but conventional forces are not an alternative to effective NATO or NORAD defense arrangements using nuclear-capable weapons systems. NORAD is designed to defend the North American continent against air attack. The Soviet bomber fleet will remain at least throughout this decade a significant element in the Soviet strike force. An effective continental defense against this common threat is necessary.

The provision of nuclear weapons to Canadian forces would not involve an expansion of independent nuclear capability, or an increase in the "nuclear club". As in the case of other allies custody of U.S. nuclear weapons would remain with the U.S. Joint control fully consistent with national sovereignty can be worked out to cover the use of such weapons by Canadian forces.

---

445. Telegram From the Embassy in Canada to the Department of State

Ottawa, February 3, 1963, 3 p.m.

990. Paris for USRO. Embtel 987.[1] Following is interim Embassy appraisal where we stand in readjustment US-Canadian relations now that initial shock Department's January 30 press release wearing off and Canadians beginning take stock realities facing them.

In view our patient tolerance of unrealistic Canadian view of external world past half dozen years, witness GOC foot dragging in vital matter continental defense and pretentious posturing in various international arenas, our sudden dose of cold water naturally produced immediate cry of shock and outrage. Traditional psychopathic accusations of unwarranted US interference in domestic Canadian affairs, while vehement, are subsiding quickly and both public and political leadership find hard realities, as set forth in Department release, are staring them in face and cannot be ignored.

Source: Department of State, Central Files, Def 12 Can. Secret; Niact. Repeated to Paris.

[1] Telegram 987, February 2, transmitted a summary of Canadian reaction to the U.S. press release. (Ibid.)

Preponderance of evidence available—news media, editorial comment, private citizens expression of views—indicate shift of public attention from US statement to clear recognition Diefenbaker indecisiveness, with frequent and widespread reaffirmation of identity of US and Canadian interests and explicit acknowledgment that Canada has somehow gone astray. Department will recall this was basic aim of exercise (Embtel 949)[2]—i.e., to bring Canadian thinking back to state of relevance to hard realities of world situation. Defense policy, particularly nuclear weapons issue, was key element this psychological problem, and its resolution will have profound bearing on Canadian attitude toward other less important foreign policy questions.

For past four or five years we have—doubtless correctly—tolerated essentially neurotic Canadian view of world and of Canadian role. We have done so in hope Canadians themselves would make gradual natural adjustment to more realistic understanding. For long period there were good grounds for hope this shift would occur relatively painlessly and without our help.

Inconclusive outcome last June's general elections, GOC fumbling and indecision during Cuban crisis, continued GOC evasiveness on vital defense matters suggested reappraisal necessary. However we had been encouraged recent weeks that liberal opposition beginning to crystallize and were beginning at long last to press government to focus on major questions. GOC performance in Commons January 24 and 25 nevertheless clearly showed Prime Minister Diefenbaker determined carry on in dream world as long as possible, and continue to postpone acquisition nuclear warheads for Canadian forces to carry their share of defense of continent, at same time refusing us permission stockpile for our own use, not to mention failure arm 104 G's of Canadian air division in NATO.

In effect we have now forced issue and outcome depends on basic common sense of Canadian electorate. Our faith in their good judgment is based on our reading that public has been way ahead of political leadership of all parties. Moreover Embassy had benefit recent grass roots assessment, in form reports from all eleven Consulates during January 24–25 principal officers conference, which independently reached same conclusion with greater emphasis on importance attached by public to Canada honoring its commitments. Public reaction to current developments (Embtel 987 and Tousi 34[3]) supports this assessment. In short we think Canadian public is with us, even though some liberal politicians have been afraid we have handed Diefenbaker an issue he can use

---

[2] Telegram 949, January 27, summarized Diefenbaker's statement on defense on January 26. (Ibid., 742.13/1–2763)

[3] Not found.

against them and US. We think Canadians will no longer accept irresponsible nonsense which political leaders all parties, but particularly progressive-conservatives under Diefenbaker, have got away with for several years.

If our appraisal is sound and if trend continues, we face transitional period uncertainty, probably until general elections return a new government with an absolute majority and thus a clear mandate. Whether government will be brought down on early no-confidence motion or whether Diefenbaker will seek take initiative by calling snap election is not yet clear but it has become exceedingly doubtful present Parliamentary situation can long continue and in any case an election before summer was regarded as virtually certain. Diefenbaker now faces probable no-confidence defeat on defense policy by Tuesday evening. Under these circumstances he may decide dissolve Parliament and seek justify as necessary consequence US "intrusion". In any event Diefenbaker can be counted on to mount his campaign on anti-US platform and had earlier last month launched "made in Canada" slogan at National Party Convention. However, we are persuaded such a campaign would not have the success some observers predict. Not only is this not 1911, when "no trade or truck with the Yankees" was slogan which won an election, but it is not even 1957, when Diefenbaker first came to power on wave of anti-US jingoism. World has changed and Canadian people know it. Polls show strong Canadian majority support for acquisition nuclear warheads and for close cooperation with us. Cuban crisis last October evoked widespread evidence public unhappiness with Foreign Minister Green's moralizing and Diefenbaker's flexible inaction. Our own observations coincide with those of all eleven consulates to point where we are convinced anti-Americanism could not now effect a Canadian Government.

We should not be unduly disturbed at steam of resentment which first blew off upon publication of Department's release. Diefenbaker's reaction was expected. He is undependable, unscrupulous political animal at bay and we are ones who boxed him in. Pearson and other party leaders could not permit him pose as sole spokesman for Canadian nationalism; hence they had to protect their flanks and join chorus of protest at our "intrusion". Let us also face fact that we are forcing Pearson to go faster and further than he desires in the direction we favor. What is significant is celerity with which this issue is being recognized as false and attention returning to facts in Department's statement, which remain unrebutted. If this assessment is not premature then we are entering new phase in US-Canadian relations. It may not be so superficially euphorious but we should be able establish more realistic basis for our relationship. We look forward to clearer Canadian appraisal of what our proximity means to them and greater Canadian realization of their need to cultivate good relations with us. Correspondingly, we think we will wish take more coolly appraising look at concessions we offer in return for their readiness to accommodate themselves to us. Of course we benefit from undefended border and from having friendly neighbor to north but we do not want to buy same asset time and again as is now the case. We have reached point where our relations must be based on something more solid than accommodation to neurotic Canadian view of us and world. We should be less the accoucheur of Canada's illusions.

As this appraisal indicates, we see grounds for optimism that over the long run this exercise will prove to have been highly beneficial and will substantially advance our interests. We have introduced element of realism which no government, whether progressive-conservative or liberal, will be able ignore.

One thing which could bring it all to naught would be backing away from our present stand. I recommend therefore that Department and all other agencies concerned continue stand politely but firmly behind January 30 release and that nothing be said or done to indicate any doubt whatsoever that time for hard decisions has come. On maintenance of this stance depends framework of our future relations with Canada.

Butterworth

---

446. Memorandum From the President's Special Assistant for National Security Affairs (Bundy) to Secretary of State Rusk and Secretary of Defense McNamara

Washington, April 1, 1963.

SUBJECT

Canadian Election Campaign

During this climactic week of the Canadian election campaign it is likely that intensified efforts will be made to implicate the United States in one way or another, especially by accusing us of trying to influence

---

Source: Kennedy Library, National Security Files, Canada. Secret. No drafting information appears on the source text. Copies were sent to the Chairman of the Joint Chiefs of Staff and to the Director of USIA.

the outcome. The President wishes to avoid any appearance of interference, even by responding to what may appear to be untruthful, distorted, or unethical statements or actions.

Will you, therefore, please insure that no one in your Departments, in Washington or the field, says anything publicly about Canada until after the election without first clearing with the White House. This applies to all contacts with the press regardless of the degree of non-attribution.

McGeorge Bundy

---

447. Telegram From the Embassy in Canada to the Department of State

Ottawa, April 15, 1963, 6 p.m.

1327. Of course I accept the decision contained in the Department's telegram 1033 of April 12 regarding the forged letter,[1] although I think it is mistaken. However, what concerns me more is lest this be an indication that the Department is reverting to its old ways of treating Canada like a problem child for whom there was always at the ready a cheek for the turning.

The Department had the temerity to act (in substance though not in form) on the recommendations contained in my telegram 949 of January 27,[2] with the beneficial results predicted in my telegram 990 of February 3,[3] [4 lines of source text not declassified]. In the process, a somewhat more mature Canada has emerged from the electoral crucible and a measure of its neuroses has been exorcised.

I do hope that in future we will deal with Canada with considered care and courtesy but in a more normal, matter-of-fact manner, and with due regard to the importance of obtaining quids for quos.

Butterworth

Source: Department of State, Central Files, Pol Can-US. Confidential; Limited Distribution.

[1] In telegram 1317 from Ottawa, April 11, Butterworth had repeated a recommendation that the United States pursue the matter of a forged letter from him to Pearson that had appeared during the election campaign. (Ibid.) In telegram 1033 to Ottawa, April 12, Butterworth was informed that while Washington appreciated the reasons for investigating the letter, it believed it was better to let the matter rest and accent the positive factors in relations with Canada. (Ibid.)

[2] See footnote 2, Document 445.

[3] Document 445.

448. National Security Action Memorandum No. 234

Washington, April 18, 1963.

MEMORANDUM FOR

The Secretary of State
The Secretary of Defense
The Secretary of the Treasury
The Secretary of Commerce
The Secretary of the Interior
The Attorney General
The Director of Central Intelligence
The Chairman, Atomic Energy Commission
Special Representative for Trade Negotiations

The advent of a new government in Canada has naturally stirred nearly all branches of the government to new hope that progress can be made in effective negotiations with this most important neighbor on all sorts of problems. It is the President's wish that these negotiations should be most carefully coordinated under his personal direction through the Department of State. It is therefore requested that any department or agency which intends to pursue important discussions or negotiations with the new Canadian Government should discuss its plans with the Office[1] of European Affairs of the Department of State so that, in the event that further coordination is needed, it may be appropriately arranged.

McGeorge Bundy

Source: Department of State, NSAMs: Lot 72 D 316. Confidential. No drafting information appears on the source text.

[1] At this point on the source text the words "(sic) Bureau" are written.

---

449. Telegram From Hyannis Port to the Department of State

Hyannis Port, May 11, 1963.

HYWH02–63. From Tyler. Following uncleared summary conversation, Friday, May 10. President and Prime Minister met Friday after-

---

Source: Kennedy Library, National Security Files, Canada. Secret; Operational Immediate; Limit Distribution. Individual memoranda of the subjects discussed are in the Department of State, Conference Files: Lot 66 D 110, CF 2238. For two other accounts of this meeting and the one on May 11, see Lester B. Pearson, *Mike, The Memoirs of The Right Honourable Lester B. Pearson*, vol. 3, pp. 100–102 and 111–113, and Charles Ritchie, *Storm Signals*, pp. 48–49.

noon from 2:30 to 5 o'clock. Also present Ambassadors Ritchie and Butterworth, Tyler, Ed Ritchie and Basil Robinson. President showed Prime Minister Khrushchev's reply to joint US-UK démarche on test ban.[1] Prime Minister commented reply obviously not very encouraging. He found it hard to make up his own mind in view of complexity of scientific factors. Said Macmillan more optimistic on means of detection than US Govt. Prime Minister noted that first part Khrushchev's message very negative, but later appeared almost to be contradicting himself and not excluding possibility further discussions. Prime Minister said he hoped US would continue plugging away at test ban question even if outlook poor so as to reassure public opinion that every effort being made. Stressed sensitivity Canadian opinion to nuclear issue. Added that nevertheless Canadian Govt does not expect US Govt to accept anything which would prejudice its own security. President reaffirmed desire to get some solution this field and said that sentiment within administration ahead of Congress in this respect.

Conversation then turned to US-Canadian nuclear relations. Prime Minister affirmed his govt's intention to fulfill commitments previously entered into by Canada. Said that note had been drafted in Ottawa which would be sent to President after Prime Minister's return. He was hopeful that US Govt reply to this note would constitute agreement between governments. Considered that changes which Canadian Govt proposing were largely matter of wording for domestic political reasons, but felt confident substance would be acceptable to US Govt. Said that he would not be able to table text of any agreement because there would be secret clauses. Prime Minister said Canadian note would cover stockpiling for US, and equipment, including CF–104's, Voodoos, Bomarcs and Honest Johns. Said that Canadian Govt would go ahead on this basis "and stand or fall by it."

PM said he wished commitments had not been made in first place but this was water over the dam. He said he found greater difficulty with regard to stockpile for strategic weapons. President commented that latter was of lower priority. PM, in answer to President's question re communiqué, said we should say that we have agreed to initiate negotiations at once which will permit Canadian Govt to move ahead, consistent with parliamentary procedures.

PM stressed desirability US Govt informing Canadian Govt ahead of time if any change is contemplated in military field. Canadian Govt had been embarrassed by testimony of Secretary of Defense re Bomarcs.[2] President commented testimony had been checked from se-

---

[1] For text, see vol. VI, Document 95.

[2] On February 13 McNamara testified that the Bomarc missile would be useful in drawing Soviet missile fire away from other targets. The statement was released on March 29.

curity standpoint but not in terms of political implications. President suggested we might say that question of Bomarcs should be reviewed, and that if it were at any time decided to move to newer weapons, situation would be looked at again. PM stressed importance of Canadian air contribution in Europe which was second in importance only to that of United States.

The President and the PM then reviewed the established and institutional channels of communication between US and Canada such as the PJDB and Parliamentarians Committee and agreed that the work of these bilateral committees should be harmonized and brought into common focus. PM said his govt would be setting up Defense Committee in Canadian Parliament, and that he wanted increase consultation. He would like Foreign Minister Martin and Defense Minister Hellyer to go to Washington for talks. PM commented on one problem in Canadian public opinion: when US Govt moves US air squadrons to Canada, people ask why this should happen while Canadian squadrons are overseas in Europe. Also pointed out it costs much more to maintain military units in Europe than to raise them locally.

On defense production sharing, PM said present agreement[3] working out very well, since Canada has favorable balance which important in light of Canada's adverse trade balance of over $1 billion. President at this point drew on text of message received from Secretary of Defense[4] and said we planned to go ahead as we now are. President said we should have conversations in this field. PM said he had been disturbed by possibility cancellation Caribou aircraft. President and PM agreed that Canadian Minister Defense Production should come to Washington for talks to discuss this and other matters relating to production sharing. President commented that Canadian balance of trade adverse but balance of payments was relatively much better. PM said that over 10-year period Canada had contributed equivalent of $6 billion to US balance of payments. President said that the West has more or less been living on the US balance of payments deficit for 10 years. It was agreed that no decision should be made on Caribou aircraft without consultation.

The President then gave the PM a rundown on Nassau and the MLF. He told PM that he had sent letter to Macmillan asking him to come in on MLF.[5] Emphasized political significance of MLF in relation to European unity and to German role in Europe. PM said he had at first had doubts about military value MLF but was fully sympathetic to idea

---

[3] For text of the Defense Production Sharing Agreement, signed at Ottawa, June 12, 1961, see 12 UST 723.

[4] Not found.

[5] See Document 195.

of its political role in relation to Germany. Said did not think it desirable for Canada to participate in MLF since there was much for Canada to do on this side of the Atlantic. On the other hand, PM was very sympathetic to IANF.

Expressed some worry that differences between UK and France might result in flare-up at NATO meeting. Hoped matter would not be pushed to point of open row with French. President said he hoped Canada would give its support to MLF and PM agreed and said he would "make good noises." President said we would send PM briefing paper on where we stand with regard to MLF. Said he felt a better case for MLF could be made than had been done hitherto. PM commented there was some worry about the large part which Germans would play in MLF and President said it was better to have Germans in on that basis than to have them stay out.

With regard to trade matters, PM said that talks with Governor Herter in Ottawa[6] had been very good and that Canadian Govt was always delighted to have people like him and Ambassador Merchant come to see them. He agreed that new approach was required in GATT and felt that linear tariff cut desirable. Stressed need for equivalent concessions in US-Canadian trade. Also stated that if there is to be failure at Geneva it won't be Canadians' fault. Paid tribute to imaginative concept embodied in TEA. Pointed out Canada has some difficulties with 50 percent cut because this does not help some of their trade problems. Ruefully admitted that enunciation of principle in opposition was wonderful, but application in practice sometimes difficult.

There was some discussion of Canadian oil exports. PM said northwest Canada must develop its economy on basis of oil exports and base metals. President mentioned that present agreement runs only for a few more months. PM hoped that conditions would provide for gradual increase Canadian oil exports, in view of Canada's balance of payments problem. President referred to increase in District Five. Ritchie commented Canada considered District Five was free in any case, and that Districts One through Four were the important ones. President said he would be glad to have this matter discussed with Canadians by Feldman so that we could arrive at a joint prognosis for next two years. PM pointed out that from viewpoint security there was definite advantage to United States to have supply available on same continent. Also said that US owns over 60 percent Canadian oil so might as well take exports from Canada. Ambassador Butterworth pointed out that as far as security factor was concerned, US Govt had long recognized this,

---

[6] Documentation on Herter's visit to Ottawa, April 26–27, 1963, to discuss GATT and the Trade Expansion Act is in Department of State, Central Files, Pol 7 US/Herter.

which was why we had allowed considerable expansion to take place in Canadian oil exports which had vitiated the other purposes of our quota control of imports.

With regard to US-Canadian trade balance, PM stressed heavy Canadian payments imbalance of $1,200,000,000. Canada does not want to discourage import of capital which has been most helpful to her economic development but fact remained that more than half Canadian industry owned by United States. Canada was going to take steps which would not penalize US investments, but would encourage Canadians to buy in, so as to have real sense participation. Said that US management Canadian properties getting more and more enlightened. PM said his govt going to set up Canadian development corporation with private as well as public capital.

President referred to great lakes labor union problem, and PM stressed his concern. Said SIU playing harmful role, specifically in person Hal Banks. President said he had talked with George Meany, and pointed out difficulties for US Govt to do anything. It was agreed between President and PM that Secretary of Labor and George Meany would meet at some unspecified time in near future with Canadian Minister of Labor and Canadian Labor Union leader Jodoin.

Referring to Latin America, PM said the new govt would continue the interest of previous govt in developing relations with Latin America. Said that "perhaps if we were invited to join OAS, and if circumstances very propitious, we might accept." Recalled that during campaign, he had said that Liberals would give "sympathetic consideration" to possibility joining OAS. Said problem was that Canada already belongs to good many clubs and sometimes felt it was doing enough in terms of its resources. He said he personally would like to see Canada moving in direction greater involvement Western Hemisphere affairs. Canadian public opinion was divided on this point. He though Canada had certain assets in Latin America and was well regarded there. He wanted to wait until Canada obtained more specific conditions of admission and would have to weigh matter. For example, Canada would not want to have to play a role opposed to former British colonies. Cuba was discussed briefly. PM stressed US action last October very well received in Canada, and that he had been cheered during campaign when he referred to it. He felt United States was doing right thing: to continue to exert economic pressure on Cuba without provocation. President referred to possibility that Soviet Union might be willing to pay economic price required to make Cuban economy prosperous which would be adverse development. President said he attached great importance to warding off possibility of new Communist country being established in Western Hemisphere, especially on continent. PM said Canada intended to continue its diplomatic representation in Cuba but would be careful to avoid any statements implying approval of Cuban regime. PM said he had unfavorable impressions from his visits in Brazil and Mexico. He considered first "very rocky" while in the second he had found even non-Communist youth very excited about what is going on in Cuba.

President raised question of Canadian contributions to aid to LDC's and commented that Canada seemed to have done relatively much better under Marshall Plan when its contribution was approximately 10 percent of that of United States. PM countered by pointing to Canadian adverse balance of payments. President asked whether Canada could do more in the India consortium. PM pleaded "financial mess" Canada found herself in but said Canada "would try to do better though she is undeveloped country." Said that burden US was carrying was inseparable from power which we exerted in world affairs: "US calls the tune so let them pay the piper."

President and PM met subsequently at PM's house for drinks with US and Canadian press and held informal briefing with PM doing most of talking.

Conversations resuming 10 a.m. Saturday. General atmosphere talks excellent with Pearson giving repeated evidence his determination create and sustain cordial and frank relationship between two countries whose destiny closely linked by history as well as geography, while maintaining Canadian identity and defending Canadian interests.[7]

---

[7] On May 11 the President and the Prime Minister discussed the Columbia River project, air transport, the territorial sea, Canadian lumber and cheese, Laos, Jordan, and the Congo. Memoranda of these conversations are in Department of State, Conference Files: Lot 66 D 110, CF 2238. For text of the joint communiqué issued at the conclusion of the meeting, see *American Foreign Policy: Current Documents, 1963*, pp. 371–374.

---

450. Memorandum of Conversation

US/MC/6   Ottawa, May 23, 1963.

PARTICIPANTS

    Prime Minister of Canada Lester Pearson
    Secretary of State Dean Rusk
    Secretary of Defense Robert S. McNamara
    Ambassador W. Walton Butterworth

Source: Department of State, Secretary's Memoranda of Conversation: Lot 65 D 330. Confidential. Drafted by Butterworth and approved in S on May 26. Rusk and McNamara were in Ottawa for the NATO Ministerial Meeting May 22–24.

SUBJECT

  Canadian Internal, Trade and Defense Affairs

At the invitation of the Prime Minister, the Secretary and Mrs. Rusk, Secretary McNamara, and Ambassador and Mrs. Butterworth, met with the Prime Minister and Mrs. Pearson at their residence following the dinner given at the Chateau Laurier on the evening of May 22. The Secretary's call on the Prime Minister on the morning of May 21[1] was cut somewhat short due to the opening of the Parliamentary Session, and the Prime Minister obviously wished to continue the conversation, although he had no particular purposes to achieve. Accordingly, while the conversation of last evening was intimately friendly and interesting, no spot information about any specific topic emerged.

Perhaps the most noteworthy assertions of Pearson related to the British Commonwealth and the "crisis" with respect to French Canada.

As regards the former, Pearson frankly stated that the British Empire and Commonwealth, as it had previously existed, was in rapid dissolution by the emergence of colonial entities into independent states and that this advent of African Commonwealth states doomed the Commonwealth system. He expressed the hope, but by no means confidently, that some special relationship could continue to be maintained between Canada, New Zealand, Australia and the United Kingdom, and perhaps India. By implication he also sold the continuation of empire preferences short.

He said that the gravity of the crisis about French Canada could not be underestimated and he indicated that this would be the most difficult and dangerous issue with which his administration would have to deal. He obviously believes that the Confederation is at stake and described the extent of the ambitions of Quebec as so encompassing the functions of the central government as to constitute a state within a state, the latter to have left only such powers as control of tariffs, foreign affairs, etc.

This led to a discussion of economic policy. The Prime Minister indicated that just after the war he had favored the adoption of a free trade area with the United States but this had come to nothing because the government would not face the repercussions during the six to nine years of painful adjustment which secondary industries in Canada would have to make. He expressed himself as having had confidence then and again now in Canada's inherent ability to stand on its own feet and compete effectively with United States industry, but he was obviously still uncertain as to how the painful transition could be made. He

---

[1] A memorandum of this conversation, US/MC/9, is ibid., Conference Files: Lot 66 D 110, CF 2263. Memoranda of Rusk's conversation with Martin on May 21 covering the international situation, Laos, and a nuclear test ban, are ibid.

made reference to the Canada Development Corporation and indicated it would assist Canadians in financing industrial development and in obtaining a greater ownership share in existing enterprises, but he was by no means clear how this was to be brought about or whether legal coercion was involved. The question of Canadian municipalities borrowing for non-productive purposes also was mentioned, the avoidance of which having evidently been the subject of Cabinet deliberation, no doubt in connection with the new Municipal Development and Loan Board. The Prime Minister also referred to the wheat farmers' vote in the United States and expressed some concern about the effect on prices and whether the wheat agreements price of $1.75 could, in fact, be maintained.

In referring to the recent defense debate and vote of confidence by a mere 11 votes, the Prime Minister indicated he had instituted discussions with the French, since the bases of some of the Canadian squadrons were in France and, therefore, presented a problem of storage of nuclear weapons. He pointed out that due to the attitude the Diefenbaker government had taken in refusing to store weapons in Canada on the theory that war heads could be picked up at the last moment in the United States, he could not and would not attempt to solve the problem of the Canadian squadrons in France by any such means. He also indicated that he had been unperturbed about the possible outcome of the debate, stating that if the Opposition had forced an election, his party would have been returned not with 129 seats, but 200-odd seats.

The Secretary of Defense took the opportunity Pearson offered him briefly to explain the plans for the Multilateral Force, but the Prime Minister showed no more enthusiasm for it than he had during the discussion at Hyannis Port.

There was also some discussion about the United Nations and the voting problem created by the enlarged membership and the Prime Minister was very interested in the explanation which the Secretary gave to him showing that weighted voting would offer no panacea.

WW Butterworth

451. Telegram From the Department of State to the Embassy in
Canada

Washington, June 28, 1963, 7:53 p.m.

1357. Assistant Secretary Johnson and BNA called in Canadian
Chargé (accompanied by Schwarzmann, Hudon, Taylor) June 28 and
made points summarized briefly below in representation re Canadian
budget. Memcon follows.[1]

US views had not been previously presented pending study and
waning of internal political difficulties for GOC. However, discriminatory features of budget had come as real surprise. While Pearson had
indicated at Hyannis Port some consideration would be given problem
of investment we had no impression any measures contemplated so directly affecting US investment.

Reasons for US concern include (1) principle of national treatment
which we observe with most advanced nations highly important and we
presumed Canada would think it also important especially in context
US-Canadian relations; (2) budget clearly discriminatory; (3) many US
subsidiaries will be placed in most unfair position since prospect is for
insufficient Canadian buyers to enable subsidiaries to qualify especially
with relatively short deadline; (4) precedent and encouragement
furnished for other but less developed countries to promote measures
discriminatory against US and foreign investment generally; (5) unfortunate to erect new barriers between Canada & US in area where none
previously extant.

Dept extremely unhappy re these budget proposals and hopes
GOC in course forthcoming detailed consideration in Committee of
House will take our points into full account in considering question of
approval. While we recognize Canadian anxiety over foreign investment we hope there will be full recognition of advantages to Canada
such investment and consideration other less objectionable ways of
accomplishing general goal.

Chargé expressed appreciation for US understanding in not making immediate formal representations. He thought no Canadian party
could ignore political difficulties associated with foreign investment be-

---

Source: Department of State, Central Files, Fn 15 Can. Confidential; Priority. Drafted
by Carlson, cleared with Armstrong, and approved by Johnson.

[1] Not found. On June 20 the Department of State had told the Canadian Chargé that
the United States was reserving its judgment on the new Canadian budget. On the following day the Chargé informed the Department of State that the parliamentary situation on
the budget was very precarious and that Pearson had instructed him formally to convey
his preference that the United States not make representations about it. (Telegram 1333,
June 21; ibid., Pol Can-US)

cause of its preponderance and despite its advantages. He did not think there was any inconsistency between Pearson's remarks at Hyannis Port[2] and budget but perhaps slight difference of interpretation of remarks. He would report our views promptly to Ottawa.

Ball

---

[2] See Document 449.

---

452. Memorandum of Conversation

Washington, July 19, 1963.

SUBJECT

Canadian Reaction to Proposed U.S. Balance of Payments Measures

PARTICIPANTS

Charles S.A. Ritchie, Canadian Ambassador
E.R. Rettie, Counselor, Canadian Embassy

The Secretary
The Under Secretary
Delmar R. Carlson, Officer in Charge Canadian Affairs

Ambassador Ritchie called at his request on an urgent basis to discuss our proposed measures to ameliorate the balance of payments problem. The Ambassador said that the news of these measures had caused the Canadian stock markets to plunge. The Secretary asked whether the news of the proposals should legitimately have a drastic effect since the essential development was to equalize the borrowing rate. The Ambassador said there had been insufficient time to assess the impact but he thought the measures would bear most heavily on Canada.

Source: Department of State, Secretary's Memoranda of Conversation: Lot 65 D 330. Confidential. Drafted and initialed by Carlson and approved in S on July 25. For another report of Canadian representations to the United States on the interest equalization tax, see the account by Louis Rasminsky, Governor of the Bank of Canada, of his conversation with Secretary of the Treasury Dillon in Peter Stursberg, *Lester Pearson and the American Dilemma*, pp. 189–192. For text of the joint U.S.-Canadian statement released following these talks, see Department of State *Bulletin*, August 12, 1963, p. 256.

The purpose of his call, however, related to the Canadian Government's concern over charges of the Conservative Opposition, together with the conclusions being drawn by some of the public and press in Canada that the measures were retaliation for the recent Canadian budget measures.

The Under Secretary informed the Ambassador that earlier in the afternoon the Department had given a statement to the press refuting any suggestion of retaliation or discrimination. In addition, Under Secretary of the Treasury Roosa had held a background briefing for Canadian press correspondents to provide a full explanation.[1]

The Under Secretary explained that the purpose of the measures was to slow down foreign utilization of the U.S. money markets but not to stop such use. He pointed out that the measures were part of a large package aimed at reducing the deficit in our balance of payments. This deficit had been caused to a considerable extent in the last few years and months by an increasing amount of purchasing of foreign issues by United States nationals. The United States had decided not to employ capital controls but to use a much less restrictive device of equalizing the cost of money through an interest equalization tax. While investment in Canada might be more heavily affected than investment in other countries, this fact was due to the circumstance that the greatest recent increase in capital outflow due to foreign issues was related to investment in Canada. The Under Secretary offered categoric assurance that there was no element of retaliation or discrimination in the development of these measures. Rather they were the consequence of the need to meet an urgent situation.

The Under Secretary also observed that the United States had shown much restraint in reacting to the Canadian budget measures although they would act to exacerbate our balance of payments problem by promoting a tendency to shift from equity investment in Canada to debt investment. In addition, United States assistance to the Canadian Government during the 1962 balance of payments crisis was mentioned. The Under Secretary noted that the United States had taken a number of measures affecting U.S. citizens, e.g., reduction of tourist duty exemptions, and could not simply let the money market go its own way. Finally, he pointed out that if serious defects should come to light, there would be opportunity to correct them during the legislative process.

Ambassador Ritchie expressed his appreciation for the information he had received but reiterated his fears of the effects on the Canadian economy.

---

[1] Neither the statement nor the briefing has been identified further.

453. Memorandum of Conversation

Washington, September 9, 1963, 12:45 p.m.

SUBJECT

Great Lakes Labor Dispute

PARTICIPANTS

Charles S. A. Ritchie, Canadian Ambassador
H. Basil Robinson, Minister, Canadian Embassy
Patrick Conroy, Labor Attaché, Canadian Embassy
John R. Sharpe, First Secretary, Canadian Embassy

The Secretary
Under Secretary W. Averell Harriman
George P. Delaney, Special Assistant to the Secretary and Coordinator of
 International Labor
Abram Chayes, Legal Adviser
William C. Burdett, Deputy Assistant Secretary, EUR
Andreas F. Lowenfeld, Assistant Legal Adviser for Economic Affairs, L/E
Willis C. Armstrong, Director, BNA

The Ambassador expressed appreciation for the opportunity to see the Secretary on short notice. He said that Prime Minister Pearson had called him last night to indicate that public opinion in Canada had risen markedly to condemn the violence against the Canadian ship in Chicago, which occurred on Saturday, September 7.[1] He said that the pressure on the government had become so intense that thought had to be given to the possibility of a special session of Parliament, although the Prime Minister was very reluctant. He said there was no new element in the situation since the discussion of External Affairs Minister Martin with the Secretary on September 7,[2] but there was continued anxiety over Canadian lives and property. The Ambassador went on to say that he and his government greatly appreciated the attention being given to the matter by the FBI. If the United States Government could be shown to the Canadian public to be taking effective action for around-the-clock

---

Source: Department of State, Secretary's Memoranda of Conversation: Lot 65 D 330. Limited Official Use. Drafted by Armstrong and approved in S on September 12. The meeting was held in the Secretary's office.

[1] See the attachment to Document 455.

[2] A brief memorandum of Rusk's conversation with Martin on the labor dispute as well as memoranda of their conversations on relations with Soviet bloc countries and the forthcoming U.S. Economic Committee Meeting are in Department of State, Secretary's Memoranda of Conversation: Lot 65 D 330. For text of the communiqué of the eighth meeting of the Joint U.S.-Canadian Committee on Trade and Economic Affairs, Washington, September 21, see *American Foreign Policy: Current Documents, 1963*, pp. 375–377. A 42-page record of the committee's meeting is in Department of State, Conference Files: Lot 66 D 110, CF 2311.

protection of the lives and property of Canadians in United States ports, he felt that there would be a good deal less pressure for a special session of Parliament.

The Secretary inquired what had happened to Canadian personnel on board the ship, and the response was that they were only caretakers on board but some of these had been beaten when they went ashore. Until the last couple of weeks, according to Mr. Chayes, there had been only a moderate amount of violence. The Ambassador responded by saying that Mr. Martin had observed this morning that he had heard that violence might be repeated during the next week. Mr. Chayes said that as a factual matter, there would be a hearing next Monday on the contempt charges before the United Sates District Court of the Northern District of Illinois. The position of the longshoremen is that they have told their members there is no strike against the *Howard Shaw*, but that the members individually fear harm, and therefore do not report for work. It is conceivable, said Mr. Chayes, that violence might just happen during the coming week, so as to provide a basis for this claim.

The Secretary inquired what the Canadian Ambassador meant by around-the-clock protection. He said that we could not very well provide a policeman for each sailor in town, and it was assumed that the sailors might not wish this much protection while in port. He said we of course would do everything we could with local and State authorities to assure normal police protection and to frustrate acts of violence. The Ambassador said that he appreciated the problems of jurisdictional distinction between Federal and State authorities, and he realized that these distinctions were not always clear to the people in Canada. The fact that the Canadian radio had reported that the FBI was taking a hand is in fact helpful, since it gives the impression to the Canadian public that Federal authorities are in the act, and this is most reassuring. He asked Mr. Robinson and Mr. Conroy to comment. Mr. Robinson noted that the problem was not confined to Chicago, but existed in other ports. Mr. Conroy said that protection includes the concept of reason. He said it was the obligation of personnel from the ship not to roam all over town and invite attack. Mr. Sharpe commented that ships in Upper Lakes Shipping do go in and out of Marquette, Toledo, Superior, and Cleveland, but not without difficulty. He also spoke of the fact that there had been bombing of railroad tracks on dock property in Toledo.

The Secretary asked how we could phrase a description of the effort we are making. Mr. Chayes said we have to say that we will do our best. Local authorities have to work with local ground rules, and we have to talk to the local people. Chicago is the most important place. The FBI, or for that matter the Federal Government, does not have custodial functions, but simply investigates and brings charges if warranted. The only Federal resources available for guarding property are troops. In connection with the injunction being sought in the Federal Court, it might be worthwhile to look into the question of a Deputy United States Marshal, but basically the best way is to jack up the local police. They do have the resources and this is more useful than Federal intervention.

Ambassador Ritchie spoke of the symbolic importance of Federal intervention, and the Secretary noted the presence already of the FBI. Mr. Chayes observed that the FBI has specialists in labor union and bombing matters, and they already have their special task force at work on this subject.

The meeting ended with assurances that the matter will be followed vigorously on the United States side.

(*Note:* Following the meeting Mr. Chayes, the Canadian Minister, and Mr. Armstrong agreed that the Department's press spokesman would at noon acknowledge the fact of the Ambassador's representations, and say that the United States was actively looking into what could be done to give improved police protection to Canadian ships and personnel.)

---

454. Memorandum of Conversation

Washington, November 25, 1963.

SUBJECT

Meeting of the President and Canadian Prime Minister Pearson

PARTICIPANTS

Prime Minister Pearson
External Affairs Minister Paul Martin
Ambassador C. S. A. Ritchie

The President[1]
The Secretary
Wharton D. Hubbard, Canadian Desk Officer, BNA

Canadian Prime Minister Pearson, accompanied by External Affairs Minister Martin and Ambassador Ritchie, called on the President and the Secretary at 7:45 p.m., November 25, 1963, at the Secretary's office.

Source: Department of State, Central Files, Pol 15–1 Can. Secret; Noforn. Drafted by Hubbard, approved in S on November 26 and by the White House on December 2.

[1] Lyndon B. Johnson became President following the November 22 assassination of President Kennedy in Dallas, Texas.

The President, in greeting the Prime Minister, thanked the latter for coming to have a brief talk and remarked that U.S. and Canadian problems and interests had a great deal in common. The President assured the Prime Minister that he wished to maintain close and harmonious relations with Canada and that, as a matter of fact, he wanted to visit Canada so as to show his interest in that country and to get to know it better.

The Prime Minister, for his part, made it clear that the Canadian Government wished to cooperate to the greatest extent possible with the President and his administration. The Canadian Government could be counted on to understand the many problems facing the United States Government. The two governments must work in harmony and they could not do without each other. The Prime Minister believed it only candid to point out, however, that quite a few bilateral problems did exist and gave the Great Lakes labor dispute as an example. He had telephoned President Kennedy, as one practicing politician to another, about this matter and had explained the domestic, Canadian political implications. The Prime Minister had indicated he hoped President Kennedy could offer his help in the matter. According to the Prime Minister, President Kennedy said he understood the problem but also pointed out that this dispute presented political problems for him, too. The Canadian Prime Minister gave this as an example of a bilateral problem where a President and a Prime Minister both understood the practical considerations of each other's position. The Prime Minister believed he had had a very good relationship with President Kennedy in these matters.

The President agreed that such a relationship was essential to the proper conduct of business by the two countries and said he wished very much to carry on in the same spirit.

(There then followed a few minutes interval while the press photographed the President and Prime Minister, after which the Secretary, Minister Martin, and Ambassador Ritchie, who had been conversing in another corner of the room, joined the President and the Prime Minister.)

The Prime Minister mentioned that he was arranging for a "hot line" (presumably Ottawa/Washington). A discussion of the "hot line" between Washington and Moscow ensued. (However, the Prime Minister did not elaborate on why he had raised the subject.)

The conversation then turned to a possible visit to Canada by the President. The Prime Minister suggested that perhaps it would be best if he came first to Washington to talk to the President and that the latter could then visit Canada later at the President's convenience. At this juncture, the Prime Minister remarked that President Kennedy had been scheduled in the near future to receive an honorary degree from his (the Prime Minister's) alma mater, the University of Toronto. It was agreed that the Prime Minister would have a talk with the President in Washington first, after the President had had "a few weeks" time to organize his work, and that the Canadian Prime Minister would then invite the President to Canada.

The President said he could see no reason why problems between Canada and the United States could not be resolved and that he believed that relations between the two countries were on a fundamentally sound basis. The Prime Minister generally agreed but insisted that there were more bilateral problems than was generally supposed. Likewise, he pointed out that Canadian sensitivities were not always understood. However, the Prime Minister said the Canadian Government would be straightforward with the U.S. Government and would support it on the big issues.

The Prime Minister then noted that he would be holding a Canadian federal-provincial conference in Ottawa, beginning the next day, November 26, 1963, and that it was of the utmost importance to him. In a somewhat jocular mood, he said he might be calling on the President for help in regard to it. In the same vein, the President said he was available for any kind of help at any time.

As the meeting came to an end, the Secretary turned to External Affairs Minister Martin and said he hoped to be able to arrange a side meeting with him at Paris over the weekend before the NATO Ministerial Meeting. Mr. Martin agreed, saying he would be leaving Ottawa for Paris the previous Friday evening. The Prime Minister, at the mention of Paris, said this reminded him that he, too, would be visiting Paris soon, in early January, to visit President DeGaulle.

The meeting was terminated at 8:00 p.m.

---

455. Memorandum From Secretary of State Rusk to President Johnson

Washington, December 12, 1963.

SUBJECT

U.S.-Canadian Problems

In accordance with my promise at the Cabinet meeting yesterday, I am attaching a memorandum briefly describing the principal current problems between the United States and Canada.

Source: Department of State, Central Files, Pol Can-US. Secret. Drafted by Ball.

Over the past few years, our relations with Canada have grown increasingly sticky. The Canadians have maneuvered themselves into an impossible dilemma. Their economic prosperity depends on the continual inflow of U.S. capital. This necessarily brings with it control of their enterprises by U.S. management. They could undoubtedly improve their standard of living if they accepted the full consequences of this situation and permitted a gradual integration of the Canadian market with our own. But because they are so conscious of the overwhelming size and power of the United States, they tend to pursue highly nationalistic policies—fearing that otherwise Canada would become, if not the 51st State, at least a neighbor heavily dependent on the U.S. Colossus.

The result is that, no matter which party may be in power, every Canadian Government feels compelled to try to reduce the economic control that necessarily accompanies reliance on U.S. capital. The Diefenbaker Government pushed such measures too far and precipitated a balance-of-payments crisis that required us to mount a costly rescue operation. When Diefenbaker later attempted to renege on his defense commitments to the United States, his Government was voted out of office.

The Pearson Government is, in spirit, friendly to us and, in principle, much more sympathetic with U.S. objectives. But it, too, has felt compelled to take a series of measures that have kept our relations on the edge of tension—measures that can, if carried too far, result in serious economic and political problems between our two countries.

In late October, President Kennedy established a Subcommittee of the National Security Council, under the Chairmanship of George Ball, to try to bring together the problems each of our Departments was having with the Canadian Government, and to explore broad lines of policy that could result in improved relations. Up to this point, the Subcommittee has gathered information from each of the Departments. Its proposals should be ready in time to be considered when you meet with Prime Minister Pearson in January.

Dean Rusk[1]

---

[1] Printed from a copy that bears this stamped signature.

[Attachment]

ROUND-UP OF U.S.-CANADIAN PROBLEMS

Petroleum

Imports of petroleum and products from Canada are excluded from the U.S. licensed import quota program. Since 1962, imports from Canada are calculated within the total permissible imports into the United States, and any increase in imports from Canada would therefore be at the expense of imports from some other source. The Canadian Government has voluntarily limited expansion of exports during 1963 but has indicated that they will be unable to do so in 1964 without formal controls. Imposition of formal controls would be regarded in Canada as making a mockery of the national security rationale for the program under which the overland exemption has been justified.

Canadian Softwood Lumber Exports

Increasing imports of softwood lumber from Canada since the end of 1961 have brought considerable pressure from Pacific Northwest lumber communities for some restriction of imports. The Tariff Commission reviewed the problem under the terms of the Trade Expansion Act of 1962 and in its report in February this year ruled that increasing imports due to tariff concessions were not the cause of injury to the domestic industry. After failing to achieve quotas or increased tariffs under the existing legislation, the industry has sought to have Congress pass various bills which would require that imports of lumber and logs be marked as to origin or otherwise impose restrictive measures. The Administration is on record as opposing these bills which are inconsistent with U.S. trade policy. A House-Senate conference committee approved the measure December 11 and the Canadian Ambassador has requested an appointment with Mr. Ball to register his government's concern.

Passamaquoddy Tidal Project

Secretary Udall reported to the President July 1 on the results of a re-study of the proposed Passamaquoddy Tidal Project and development of the Upper Saint John River, which found the project economically feasible. The Department is proceeding with necessary discussions at an early date with the Canadians so that legislation may be introduced into Congress early next year. Thus far, there has been no indication of strong interest in the project from the Canadian Government although the Provincial Government of New Brunswick has been more enthusiastic. Technical discussions were held with the Canadian Government December 4–5, 1963, but no negotiations have been scheduled.

Wheat Pricing Policies

Disagreement between Agriculture and the Canadian Wheat Board over pricing policies has been aired in the press in recent months in both countries. The Department of Agriculture has argued that market conditions are good for an increase in the international price which would benefit the U.S. balance of payments and reduce the cost of the wheat subsidy program. As the two largest sellers of wheat in the world market, Canada and the United States have an important effect on prices. The Canadians believe that a large increase in price would be undesirable since it would not only encourage future uneconomic production but would also antagonize regular customers who might be lost in future years. Compounding Agriculture's unhappiness is a belief that the Canadians had failed to keep a commitment to consult closely on price policies. The matter has subsided somewhat but close consultation has not been resumed.

Differences regarding wheat policies are a continuing item in U.S.-Canadian relations which can continue to be controlled by use of the consultative mechanism.

U.S. Interest Equalization Tax

This proposed legislation would raise by 1% the effective rate of interest paid on borrowings by foreigners in United States markets and is designed to reduce but not eliminate such borrowing in order to alleviate the U.S. balance of payments problem. There was an immediate and severe reaction in Canadian stock and money markets reflecting a fear that Canadian borrowing in the U.S. would dry up and result in serious balance of payments and internal economic problems for Canada. The Administration subsequently proposed an exemption from the tax for new Canadian issues, announcement of which relieved the situation. While the measure is pending in Congress, foreign borrowing in the U.S. has come to virtually a standstill. Canadian officials have indicated a belief that a total exemption for Canada would be needed if it were to avoid another balance of payments crisis.

Gordon Budget Measures on Taxation of Foreign Investment

The 1963 Canadian budget proposed discriminatory tax treatment on firms which are more than 75% owned by a foreign owner (person or corporation). Considerable opposition was expressed in Canada on the grounds of practicability which resulted in later administrative modifications. Some criticism has also been made of the effect which the measures might have on investor confidence and, in turn, on the economy of Canada. The discriminatory taxation of dividends paid to non-residents would raise taxation from 15% to 20% for non-qualifying firms, effective January 1, 1965.

The U.S. rate would automatically go to 30% unless the double tax treaty between the U.S. and Canada were renegotiated. The Canadian measure became law December 5, 1963.

Automobile Export Incentive Scheme

The Canadian Government introduced effective November 1 new measures which would provide for a refund on duties paid on automobiles and parts imported into Canada to any firm which by itself or through independent parts manufacturers increased the exports of automobiles and parts. A potential $200 million of dutiable imports into Canada annually are involved.

The Canadian measure aims at increasing Canada's share in production of and trade in automobiles, particularly vis-à-vis the United States where the products are similar and parts are virtually interchangeable for similar models. The scheme is somewhat objectionable because of the artificiality of the measures and their interference in normal business decisions. However, they aim at more economic production and an intended effective removal of Canadian tariffs which average 20% and contribute to the high cost of cars in Canada. The Canadian Government hopes that this will lead to lower costs, lower prices, expanding markets and benefit therefore to industry on both sides of the border. The applicability of U.S. countervailing duties has been considered by Treasury. The recent decision of Studebaker to close its U.S. plant but continue production in Canada appears to be a result of other economic factors. However, the Canadian scheme has been mentioned as a contributing factor.

Great Lakes Labor Dispute

The Seafarers International Union of North America (SIU) was expelled from the Canadian Labour Congress in 1960 for corrupt and antidemocratic practice. The CLC organized the Canadian Maritime Union (CMU) and SIU, which controlled by far the largest number of Canadian seamen, reacted by instituting harassment, picketing and boycotting within Canada of ships manned by CMU. The Canadian Government successfully enjoined this SIU action in Canada. Harassment of CMU ships then took place in 1962 and 1963 in U.S. ports—where injunction was only partially successful.

The report of a Royal Commission (Justice Norris) sustained the charges leveled by CLC against Banks and recommended a Canadian Government trusteeship over the five Canadian maritime unions with power to remove any union officials it deemed necessary.

Secretary Wirtz with the support of the State Department and Minister of Labor MacEachen attempted unsuccessfully this year to arrange a joint trusteeship by the AFL–CIO and CLC. The Canadian Govern-

ment passed a bill providing for a government trusteeship. At the urging of the trustees, the SIU of Canada continued to work the ships, but
sporadic picketing and boycotting of Canadian vessels has occurred in
U.S. ports. Thus far, however, this harassment has been limited to half a
dozen vessels, but the situation remains potentially dangerous.

Defense Matters

Essentially, U.S.-Canadian defense problems are susceptible of orderly resolution through existing channels. A major problem in
U.S.-Canada defense relations was resolved by the recent nuclear weapons agreements.[2]

The Canadian Government has underway a complete reappraisal
of defense policy. The goal is to attain a more "coherent" defense posture and reduce defense costs. We can live with the present level of Canadian defense spending as long as Canada's defense policies are
symmetrical with our own. We have reason to believe that this requirement will be met. However, it is important that Canadian leaders and
public continue to be made aware of the vital need for nuclear weapons
in the defense of North America and in NATO.

Canada is greatly interested in the Defense Production Sharing Program. Secretary McNamara and Canadian Minister of Defence Production Drury last June reaffirmed the Program at the highest practical level
in balance (thus removing it from the balance of payments). The program essentially is in balance. The present problem relates to the Caribou airplane, which has been the principal Canadian produced item and
the visible symbol of the Program in Canadian eyes. The U.S. is ending
its purchases of the present model, but hopes to continue participating
in research and development of a promising second model. The latter,
however, depends on Congressional approval for reprogramming
funds.

Law of the Sea

Canada has announced its intention to proclaim in May 1964 a
12-mile exclusive fisheries zone measured from straight baselines which
would close off from the high seas certain important areas of its coastal
waters. In an effort to deter any action which would create undesirable
precedential repercussions affecting our defense and commercial interests, we have offered to recognize the 12-mile zone provided it is

---

[2] The first agreement, on warheads for U.S. forces in Canada, was executed by an
exchange of notes on August 16; the second agreement, on warheads for Canadian forces
in Canada and in Europe, was executed by an exchange of notes on September 28 and 30.
Both agreements were terminated on March 9, 1987. Documentation on the negotiation of
the agreements is in Department of State, Central Files, Def 12–2 Can.

measured from valid baselines and our traditional fishing rights are undisturbed. Further, we have agreed to acquiesce in the Canadian claim to Hudson Bay. Baselines acceptable to us being not too different from those drawn by Canada, we now propose to offer a joint examination of the fisheries problem before the third negotiating meeting in January in the hope of reaching further accommodation without jeopardy to our vital worldwide interests. Deputy Under Secretary Johnson is in charge of these negotiations.

Columbia River Treaty

The treaty providing for development of the Columbia River was signed in January 1961 and ratified by the Senate shortly thereafter. Canadian ratification has been held up by a change in policy of the British Columbia Government which now wishes to sell to U.S. consumers the power benefits it would receive under the treaty rather than use the power itself as originally envisaged. Negotiators reached agreement ad referendum December 11, 1963 on a draft Exchange of Notes which would clarify the terms of the treaty.[3] If the U.S. Government approves the negotiators' recommendations vis-à-vis the sale of the power, it is highly probable the notes can be exchanged before the end of the year and ratifications exchanged by late spring. U.S. negotiators will be meeting next week with Secretary Udall and White House staff to formulate a U.S. Government position.

Civil Aviation

Canada has long wished to renegotiate its bilateral air agreement with the U.S. to obtain deeper penetration routes into the U.S. instead of essentially transborder operations now permitted. Ambassador Galbraith did a study for the White House in the early fall of 1963 and negotiations have been proposed on the basis of the report. The Canadian Government has agreed and negotiations are expected to begin in early 1964.

---

[3] For text of the Columbia River Treaty, signed January 17, 1961, with attached exchange of notes, which entered into effect on September 19, 1964, see 15 UST 1555.

Index

ISBN 0-16-041810-0

9 780160 418105

90000

DATE DUE

GAYLORD   #3522PI   Printed in USA